D0032650

Canada

THIS EDITION WRITTEN AND RESEARCHED BY

Karla Zimmerman,

Celeste Brash, John Lee, Sarah Richards, Brendan Sainsbury, Caroline Sieg,

Andy Symington, Ryan Ver Berkmoes, Benedict Walker

PLAN YOUR TRIP

ABORIGINAL CULTURES
P845

YOHO NATIONAL PARK
P749

ON THE ROAD

Contents

WILDLIFE P856

THOMAS KOKTA / GETTY IMAGES ©

Contents

UNDERSTAND

SURVIVAL GUIDE

SPECIAL FEATURES

Welcome to Canada

Canada is more than its hulking-mountain, craggy-coast good looks: it also cooks extraordinary meals, rocks cool culture and unfurls wild, moose-spotting road trips.

The Great Outdoors

The globe's second-biggest country has an endless variety of landscapes. Sky-high mountains, glinting glaciers, spectral rainforests and remote beaches are all here, spread across six times zones. It's the backdrop for plenty of *ah*-inspiring moments – and for a big provincial menagerie. That's big as in polar bears, grizzly bears, whales and, everyone's favorite, moose.

The terrain also makes for a fantastic playground. Whether it's snowboarding Whistler's mountains, surfing Nova Scotia's swells or kayaking the white-frothed South Nahanni River in the Northwest Territories, adventures abound. There are gentler options, too, like strolling Vancouver's Stanley Park or swimming off Prince Edward Island's pink-sand beaches.

Captivating Cultures

Sip a *café au lait* and tear into a flaky croissant at a sidewalk bistro in Montréal; head to an Asian night market and slurp noodles in Vancouver; join a wild-fiddling Celtic party on Cape Breton Island; kayak between rainforest-cloaked aboriginal villages on Haida Gwaii: Canada is incredibly diverse across its breadth and within its cities. You'll hear it in the music, see it in the arts and taste it in the cuisine.

Foodie Fare

Canada is a local food smorgasbord. If you grazed from west to east across the country, you'd fill your plate like this: wild salmon and velvety scallops in British Columbia, poutine (golden fries topped with gravy and cheese curds) in Québec, and lobster with a dab of melted butter in the Maritime provinces. Tastemakers may not tout Canadian food the way they do, say, Italian or French fare, so let's just call the distinctive seafood, piquant cheeses, and fresh, seasonal fruits and veggies our little secret. Ditto for the bold reds and crisp whites produced from the country's vine-striped valleys.

Artistic Flair

The arts are an integral part of Canada's cultural landscape, from the International Fringe Theater Festival (the world's second-largest) in Edmonton to mega museums such as Ottawa's National Gallery. Montreal's Jazz Festival and Toronto's star-studded Film Festival draw global crowds. And did you know Ontario's Stratford Festival is the continent's largest classical repertory theater? Even places you might not automatically think of – say St John's or Woody Point – put on renowned shindigs (an avant-garde 'sound symposium' and a big-name writers festival respectively).

Why I Love Canada

by Karla Zimmerman, Author

I'm always blown away by Canada's vastness, its enormous open landscapes. You can drive for hours in many areas and see almost no one. I love that Canada's wildlife spotting is for real – moose, bears, whales – you *will* see them if you go looking. I love that the nation's most popular restaurant – Tim Hortons – is a doughnut shop named after a hockey player. And I'm just going to come out and admit it: the more I'm in Canada, the more I appreciate rock band Rush.

For more about our authors, see page 912

Above: Moraine Lake, Banff National Park (p600)

Canada

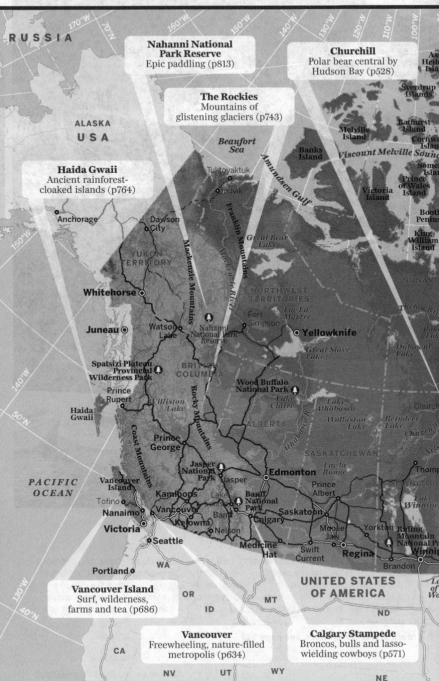

RUSSIA

ALASKA
USA

Beaufort
Sea

Amundsen Gulf

Banks
Island

Axel
Heib
Isla

Sverdrup
Islands

Melville
Island

Bathurst
Island

Cornwa
Island

Viscount Melville Sound

Somer
Island

Prince
of Wales
Island

Booth
Penins

King
William
Island

Tuktoyaktuk

Inuvik

Anchorage

Dawson
City

YUKON
TERRITORY

Mackenzie Mountains

Franklin Mountains

Mackenzie River

Great Bear
Lake

NORTHWEST
TERRITORIES

NUNAVU

Whitehorse

Juneau

Watson
Lake

Nahanni
National Park
Reserve

Fort
Simpson

Yellowknife

Lac La
Martre

Thelon Rive

Bake
Lake

Great Slave
Lake

Dubawnt
Lake

Spatsizi Plateau
Provincial
Wilderness Park

BRI
COLUMBIA

Prince
Rupert

Williston
Lake

Rocky Mountains

Wood Buffalo
National Park

Lake
Claire

Lake
Athabasca

Wollaston
Lake

Reindeer
Lake

Churchi

Churchil

Haida
Gwaii

Coast Mountains

Prince
George

Athabasca R.

ALBERTA

SASKATCHEWAN

Nels

PACIFIC
OCEAN

Vancouver
Island

Tofino

Nanaimo

Victoria

Jasper
National
Park

Jasper

Lake
Louise

Kamloops

Vancouver

Kelowna

Banff
National
Park

Banff

Nelson

Edmonton

Lac la
Ronge

Prince
Albert

Saskatoon

Calgary

Moose
Jaw

Thomp

MANITOBA

Lake
Winnipeg

Yorkton

Riding
Mountain
National Pa

Seattle

Medicine
Hat

Swift
Current

Regina

Winnip

Brandon

La
of t
Woo

Portland

WA

OR

ID

MT

UNITED STATES
OF AMERICA

ND

CA

NV

UT

WY

NE

Baffin Island
The Inuit's forlorn,
brutal landscape (p824)

Québec City
Stroll the atmospheric
Old Town (p271)

Bay of Fundy
Extreme tides and
whales (p407)

Cabot Trail
Coastal scenery and
Celtic culture (p376)

Montréal
Feel the beat at Jazz Fest
(p229)

Ottawa
Explore the capital's
grand museums (p208)

Toronto
Canada's multicultural
megacity (p67)

Niagara Falls
North America's most
voluminous cascade (p122)

ELEVATION

3000m
2500m
2000m
1500m
1000m
600m
300m
100m
0

GREENLAND
DENMARK
ICELAND

Ellesmere Island
Nares Strait
Devon Island
Baffin Island
Davis Strait
Gulf of Boothia
Prince Charles Island
Nettilling Lake
Melville Peninsula
Foxe Basin
Amadjuak Lake
Iqaluit
Southampton Island
Hudson Strait
Coats Island
Hudson Bay
ATLANTIC OCEAN
Labrador Sea
Labrador
NEWFOUNDLAND & LABRADOR
Smallwood Reservoir
George River
Churchill R.
Northern Peninsula
St John's
Corner Brook
Newfoundland
Belcher Islands
Lac Bienville
Lac Caniapiscau
Caniapiscau R.
Mélèze R.
Outardes R.
Reservoir Manicouagan
Anticosti Island
Îles de la Madeleine
Cape Breton Highlands National Park
Severn River
Winisk R.
James Bay
Reservoir Robert Bourassa
Lac Mistassini
QUÉBEC
Tadoussac
Port aux Basques
PEI
Charlottetown
Moosonee
ONTARIO
Rivière-du-Loup
Reservoir Gouin
Québec City
NEW BRUNSWICK
Fredericton
Moncton
Amherst
Saint John
Halifax
NOVA SCOTIA
Thunder Bay
Lake Nipigon
Lake Superior
Sudbury
North Bay
OTTAWA
Montréal
St Stephen
ME
Yarmouth
ATLANTIC OCEAN
MN
Sault Ste Marie
Georgian Bay
Lake Huron
Kingston
VT
NH
Boston
WI
Lake Michigan
Toronto
Lake Ontario
MA
Minneapolis
MI
Stratford
London
Niagara Falls
NY
CT
RI
Detroit
Lake Erie
PA
IA
Chicago
New York

20°W
60°N
30°W
40°W
50°N
60°W
40°N

Canada's
Top 25

Haida Gwaii (BC)

1 Once known as the Queen Charlotte Islands, this dagger-shaped archipelago (p764) 80km off British Columbia's coast is a magical trip for those who make it. Colossal spruce and cedars cloak the wild, rain-sodden landscape. Bald eagles and bears inhabit the ancient forest, while sea lions and orcas patrol the waters. But the islands' real soul is the resurgent Haida people, best known for their war canoe and totem pole carvings. See the lot at Gwaii Haanas National Park Reserve, which combines lost Haida villages, burial caves and hot springs with some of the continent's best kayaking.

The Rockies (BC/Alberta)

2 The sawtooth of white-topped mountains straddling the BC/Alberta border inspires both awe and action. Four national parks – Banff, Yoho, Kootenay and Jasper – offer opportunities for hiking, kayaking and skiing. The train (p46) provides another popular way to experience the grandeur: luminous lakes, jumbles of wildflowers and glistening glaciers glide by as the steel cars chug up mountain passes and down river valleys en route to points east o west. Right: Elk, Jasper National Park, Alberta

Nahanni National Park Reserve (Northwest Territories)

3 Gorgeous hot springs, haunted gorges and gorging grizzlies fill this remote park (p813) near the Yukon border, and you'll have to fly in to reach them. Only about 1000 visitors per year make the trek, half of them paddlers trying to conquer the South Nahanni River. Untamed and spectacular, it churns 500km through the Mackenzie Mountains. Thirty-story waterfalls, towering canyons and legends of giants and lost gold round out the journey north.

Vancouver (BC)

4 Vancouver (p634) always lands atop the 'best places to live' lists, and who's to argue? Sea-to-sky beauty surrounds the laid-back, cocktail-lovin' metropolis. With skiable mountains on the outskirts, 11 beaches fringing the core and Stanley Park's thick rainforest just blocks from downtown's glass skyscrapers, it's a harmonic convergence of city and nature. It also mixes Hollywood chic (many movies are filmed here) with a freewheeling counterculture (a popular nude beach and the Marijuana Party political headquarters) and buzzing multicultural communities. Below: Science World (p642)

BRIAN SYTNYK / GETTY IMAGES ©

Niagara Falls (Ontario)

5 Crowded? Cheesy? Well, yes. Niagara (p122) is short, too – it barely cracks the top 500 worldwide for height. But c'mon, when those great muscular bands of water arc over the precipice like liquid glass, roaring into the void below, and when you sail toward it in a mist-shrouded little boat, Niagara Falls impresses big time. In terms of sheer volume, nowhere in North America beats its thundering cascade, with more than one million bathtubs of water plummeting over the edge every second.

Cabot Trail (Nova Scotia)

6 The 300km Cabot Trail (p50) winds and climbs over coastal mountains, with heart-stopping sea views at every turn, breaching whales just offshore, moose nibbling roadside and plenty of trails to stop and hike. Be sure to tote your dancing shoes – Celtic and Acadian communities dot the area, and their foot-stompin', crazy-fiddlin' music vibrates through local pubs.

7

Driving the Trans-Canada Highway

7 Canada's main vein (p37) stretches 7800km from St John's, Newfoundland to Victoria, BC and takes in the country's greatest hits along the way. Gros Morne National Park, Cape Breton Island, Québec City, Banff National Park and Yoho National Park are part of the path, as are major cities including Montréal, Ottawa, Calgary and Vancouver. It takes most road-trippers a good month to drive coast to coast, so what are you waiting for? Fuel up, cue the tunes, and put the pedal to the metal.
Above: Banff National Park, Alberta

Old Québec City (Québec)

8 Québec's capital (p271) is more than 400 years old, and its stone walls, glinting-spired cathedrals and jazz-soaked corner cafes suffuse it with atmosphere, romance, melancholy, eccentricity and intrigue on par with any European city. The best way to soak it up is to walk the Old Town's labyrinth of lanes and get lost amid the street performers and cozy inns, stopping every so often for a *café au lait*, flaky pastry or heaped plate of poutine (fries smothered in cheese curds and gravy) to refuel.

Montréal Jazz Festival (Québec)

9 Where else can you join more than two million calm, respectful music lovers (no slam dancing or drunken slobs) and watch the best jazz-influenced musicians in the world, choosing from 500 shows, many of which are free? Only in Montréal, Canada's second-largest city and its cultural heart. BB King, Prince and Astor Piazzolla are among those who've plugged in at the 11-day Montréal Jazz Festival (p246) in late June. You might want to join them after your free drumming lesson and street-side jam session. The good times roll 24/7.

Northern Lights

10 Canada has a lot of middle-of-nowhere places, from the Saskatchewan prairie to the Labrador coast to its Arctic villages. They may not seem like much during the day, but at night the show begins. Drapes of green, yellow, aqua, violet and other polychromatic hues – aka the aurora borealis – light up the sky. The shapes flicker and dance, casting a spell across the heavens. Below: Aurora borealis, Wapusk National Park, Manitoba

Manitoulin Island (Ontario)

11 The largest freshwater island in the world and floating right smack in Lake Huron's midst, Manitoulin (p170) is a slowpoke place of beaches and summery cottages. Jagged expanses of white quartzite and granite outcroppings edge the shoreline and lead to shimmering vistas. First Nations culture pervades, and the island's eight communities collaborate to offer local foods (wild rice, corn soup) and eco-adventures (canoeing, horseback riding, hiking). Powwows add drumming, dancing and stories to the mix. Right: Powwow, Manitoulin Island

10

RICK RUDNICKI / GETTY IMAGES ©

BARRETT & MACKAY / GETTY IMAGES ©

The Prairies (Saskatchewan, Manitoba, Alberta)

12 Solitude reigns in Canada's middle ground. Driving through the flatlands of Manitoba, Saskatchewan and Alberta turns up wheat, swaying wheat and then more wheat, punctuated by the occasional grain elevator rising up in relief. Big skies mean big storms that drop like an anvil, visible on the horizon for kilometers. Far-flung towns for respite include arty Winnipeg (p512), boozy Moose Jaw (p541) and Mountie-filled Regina (p535), sprinkled between with Ukrainian and Scandinavian villages. Top right: Grain elevator, Saskatchewan

Bay of Fundy

13 This ain't your average bay, though lighthouses, fishing villages and other maritime scenery surround it. The unique geography of Fundy (p407) results in the most extreme tides in the world. And they stir up serious whale food. Fin whales, humpbacks, endangered North Atlantic right whales and blue whales swim in to feast, making whale watching here extraordinary. Tidal bore rafting, where outfitters harness the blasting force of Fundy's waters, is another unique activity. Above: Humpback whale, Bay of Fundy

Charlevoix (Québec)

14 A pastoral strip of rolling hills northeast of Québec City, the Charlevoix (p291) region harvests much of the province's food. Gastronomes road-trip out, knowing that the produce from the farms and orchards that flash by will end up as part of their next meal in true farm-to-table fashion. Village inns and alehouses serve the distinct, locally made produce: think a tomato aperitif with foie gras or pear ice wine served with fresh sheep cheese. Artsy towns such as Baie St-Paul and La Malbaie make good bases for exploration.

Calgary Stampede (Alberta)

15 You can always find a few cowboys kicking up dust in booming, oil-rich Calgary. But when you look down and everyone is wearing pointy-toe boots, it must be mid-July, time for the Stampede (p576). Bucking broncos, raging bulls and lasso-wielding guys in Stetsons converge for the 'Greatest Outdoor Show on Earth,' which highlights western rodeo events and chuckwagon racing. A huge midway of rides and games makes the event a family affair.

14

15

ROBERT CHIASSON / GETTY IMAGES ©

Drumheller (Alberta)

16 Dinosaur lovers get weak-kneed in dust-blown Drumheller (p612), where paleontological civic pride runs high thanks to the Royal Tyrrell Museum, one of the planet's preeminent fossil collections. The World's Largest Dinosaur is here, too – a big, scary, fiberglass T-rex where you can climb up and peer out its mouth. Beyond the dino-hoopla, the area offers classic badlands scenery and eerie, mushroom-like rock columns called hoodoos. Scenic driving loops take you past the good stuff. Top: Royal Tyrrell Museum of Palaeontology

Viking Trail (Newfoundland)

17 The Viking Trail (p488), aka Rte 430, connects Newfoundland's two World Heritage sites on the Northern Peninsula. Gros Morne National Park, with its fjordlike lakes and geological oddities, rests at its base, while the sublime, 1000-year-old Viking settlement at L'Anse aux Meadows – Leif Eriksson's pad – stares out from the peninsula's tip. The road is an attraction in its own right, holding close to the sea as it heads resolutely north past Port au Choix' ancient burial grounds and the ferry jump-off to big bad Labrador. Above: L'Anse aux Meadows

Green Gables (Prince Edward Island)

18 How did the tiny town of Cavendish (p451) become one of PEI's biggest moneymakers? It's a long story – a whole book actually, about a red-pigtailed orphan named Anne. Lucy Maud Montgomery wrote *Anne of Green Gables* in 1908, drawing inspiration from her cousins' bucolic farmhouse. Today fans descend to see the gentle, creek-crossed woods and other settings. Bonus for visitors: the surrounding area bursts with fresh-plucked oysters, mussels and lobsters to crack into.

Toronto (Ontario)

19 A hyperactive stew of cultures and neighborhoods, Toronto (p67) strikes you with sheer urban awe. Will you have dinner in Chinatown or Greektown? Five-star fusion or a peameal bacon sandwich? Designer shoes from Bloor-Yorkville are accessorized with tattoos in Queen West. Mod-art galleries, theater par excellence, rockin' band rooms and hockey mania add to the megalopolis. It is far and away Canada's largest city, as well as its most diverse – about half of its residents were born in another country.

20

Churchill (Manitoba)

20 The first polar bear you see up close takes your breath away. Immediately forgotten are the two bum-numbing days on the train that took you beyond the tree zone onto the tundra, to the very edge of Hudson Bay. Churchill (p528) is the lone outpost here, and it happens to be smack in the bears' migration path. From late September to early November, tundra buggies head out in search of the razor-clawed beasts, sometimes getting you close enough to lock eyes. Summer lets you swim with beluga whales. Left: Polar bears, Churchill

Hockey

21 Hockey (p852) is Canada's national passion, and if you're visiting between October and April taking in a game is mandatory (as is giving a shout-out to the nation's 2010 Olympic gold medal-winning team). Vancouver, Edmonton, Calgary, Toronto, Ottawa, Winnipeg and Montréal all have NHL teams who skate hard and lose the odd tooth. Minor pro teams and junior hockey clubs fill many more arenas with rabid fans. And if you're still looking for a fight, pond hockey brings out the sticks in communities across the land.

Baffin Island (Nunavut)

22 The forlorn, brutal landscape of the Inuit, Baffin (p824) is home to cloud-scraping mountains and a third of Nunavut's population. The island's crown jewel is Auyuittuq National Park – whose name means 'the land that never melts' – and indeed glaciers, fjords and vertiginous cliffs fill the eastern expanse. The park is a siren call to hard-core hikers and climbers and more than a few polar bears. Baffin is also a center for Inuit art; studios for high-quality carving, printmaking and weaving pop up in many wee towns.

Vancouver Island (BC)

23 C'mon, can a place really 'have it all'? Yes, if it's Vancouver Island (p686). Picture-postcard Victoria is the island's heart, beating with bohemian shops, wood-floored coffee bars and a tea-soaked English past. Brooding Pacific Rim National Park Reserve sports the West Coast Trail, where a wind-bashed ocean meets a mist-shrouded wilderness, and surfers line up for Tofino's waves. Then there's the Cowichan Valley, studded with welcoming little farms and boutique wineries, prime for wandering foodies.

Fall Foliage

24 Canada blazes come autumn, which should come as no surprise in a country that's half-covered by forest. Québec's Laurentian Mountains (p259) flame especially bright from all the sugar maple trees (which also sauce the nation's pancakes). Cape Breton, Nova Scotia flares up so pretty they hold a festival to honor the foliage – it's called Celtic Colours (p375), and it's in mid-October. New Brunswick's Fundy Coast and Ontario's Muskoka Lakes area pull in leaf peepers, too. Top right: Radar Hill, near Tofino, British Columbia

Rideau Canal (Ontario)

25 This 175-year-old, 200km-long canal/river/lake system (p213) connects Ottawa and Kingston via 47 locks. It's at its finest in wintry Ottawa, when it becomes the world's longest skating rink. People swoosh by on the 7km of groomed ice, pausing for hot chocolate and scrumptious slabs of fried dough called beavertails. February's Winterlude festival kicks it up a notch when townsfolk build a massive village of ice. Once it thaws, the canal becomes a boater's paradise.

Need to Know

For more information, see Survival Guide (p867)

Currency
Canadian dollars ($)

Languages
English and French

Visas
Generally not required for stays of up to 180 days; some nationalities require a temporary resident visa.

Money
ATMs widely available. Credit cards accepted in most hotels and restaurants.

Mobile Phones
Local SIM cards can be used in European and Australian phones. Other phones must be set to roaming.

Time
Atlantic Standard Time (GMT/UTC minus four hours)
Central Standard Time (GMT/UTC minus six hours)
Pacific Standard Time (GMT/UTC minus eight hours)

When to Go?

Dry climate
Warm to hot summers, mild winters
Mild to hot summers, cold winters
Polar climate

Churchill
GO Sep–Nov

Banff
GO Jul–Sep

Vancouver
GO Jun–Aug

Montréal
GO Jun–Aug

Halifax
GO Jul–Sep

High Season
(Jun–Aug)

➡ Sunshine and warm weather prevail; far northern regions briefly thaw

➡ Accommodation prices peak (30% up on average)

➡ December through March is equally busy and expensive in ski resort towns

Shoulder
(May, Sep & Oct)

➡ Crowds and prices drop off

➡ Temperatures are cool but comfortable

➡ Attractions keep shorter hours

➡ Fall foliage areas (ie Cape Breton, Québec) remain busy

Low Season
(Nov–Apr)

➡ Places outside the big cities and ski resorts close

➡ Darkness and cold take over

➡ April and November are particularly good for bargains

Useful Websites

Canadian Tourism Commission (www.canada.travel) Official tourism site.

Environment Canada Weather (www.weather.gc.ca) Forecasts for any town.

Lonely Planet (www.lonelyplanet.com/canada) Destination information, hotel bookings, traveler forum and more.

Government of Canada (www.gc.ca) National and regional information.

Parks Canada (www.pc.gc.ca) Lowdown on national parks.

Canadian Broadcasting Corporation (www.cbc.ca) National and provincial news.

Important Numbers

Country code	1
International access code	011
Emergency	911
Directory assistance	411

Exchange Rates

Australia	A$1	C$0.93
Europe	€1	C$1.38
Japan	¥100	C$1.05
New Zealand	NZ$1	C$0.81
UK	UK£1	C$1.59
USA	US$1	C$1.04

For current exchange rates see www.xe.com.

Daily Costs

Budget:
Less than $100

➡ Dorm bed: $25-40

➡ Campsite: $25-35

➡ Self-catered meals from markets/supermarkets: $8-12

Midrange:
$100–250

➡ B&B or room in a midrange hotel: $80-180 ($100-250 in major cities)

➡ Meal in a good restaurant: from $20 plus drinks

➡ Rental car: $35-65 per day

➡ Attraction admissions: $5-20

Top end:
More than $250

➡ Four-star hotel room: from $180 (from $250 in major cities)

➡ Three-course meal in a top restaurant: from $50 plus drinks

➡ Skiing day-pass: $50-80

Opening Hours

Opening hours vary throughout the year. We've provided high-season opening hours; hours will generally decrease in the shoulder and low seasons.

Banks 10am-5pm Monday to Friday; some open 9am-noon Saturday

Restaurants breakfast 8-11am, lunch 11:30am-2:30pm Monday to Friday, dinner 5-9:30pm daily; some open for brunch 8am to 1pm Saturday and Sunday

Bars 5pm-2am daily.

Shops 10am-6pm Monday to Saturday, noon-5pm Sunday; some open to 8pm or 9pm Thursday and/or Friday

Supermarkets 9am-8pm; some open 24 hours

Arriving in Canada

Toronto Pearson Airport Express buses ($28) run downtown every 20 to 30 minutes from 6am to midnight; taxis cost around $60 (45 minutes).

Montréal Trudeau Airport Public buses ($9) run downtown every 10 to 12 minutes from 8:30am to 8pm, every 30 to 60 minutes at other times. Taxis cost a flat $40 (30 to 60 minutes).

Vancouver International Airport Trains ($7.50 to $9) run downtown every 6 to 20 minutes; taxis cost around $40 (30 minutes).

Land Border Crossings The Canadian Border Services Agency (www.cbsa-asfc.gc.ca/bwt-taf/menu-eng.html) posts wait times (usually 30 minutes).

Getting Around

Car An extensive highway system links most towns. The Trans-Canada Hwy stretches from Newfoundland to Vancouver Island. Away from the population centers, distances can be deceivingly long and travel times slow due to single-lane highways. All major rental-car companies are readily available.

Train Outside the Toronto–Montréal corridor, train travel is mostly for scenic journeys.

Ferry Public ferry systems operate extensively in British Columbia, Québec and the Maritime provinces.

For much more on **getting around**, see p880

What's New

Legacy Trail, Alberta

The paved trail between Banff and Canmore parallels Hwy 1 and is ideal for people who want to undertake safe, easy cycling through splendid mountain scenery. (p594)

Rendez-Vous de la Baie, Nova Scotia

This cultural center has an art gallery, musical performances, a museum, and information on activities and gastronomy in the Acadian region of Nova Scotia's southwest coast. (p356)

Parkbus, Ontario

You no longer need to rent a car in Toronto to reach Algonquin and Killarney parks, or Tobermory on the Bruce Peninsula. Parkbus now offers a low-cost transportation alternative. (p884)

Robert Bateman Centre, British Columbia

Victoria's new Robert Bateman Centre showcases the work – and campaigning environmentalism – of Canada's leading nature painter. Dozens of photo-realistic artworks capture animals and landscapes in BC and beyond. (p687)

Rio Tinto Planetarium, Québec

Making stars look sexy, Montréal's $48-million planetarium marries art and science with a theatrical light-and-sound show that makes good use of brand-new, state-of-the-art equipment. (p241)

Fogo Island Inn, Newfoundland

Part of a sustainable tourism plan to preserve Fogo's heritage, this uberluxe, 29-room inn is an architectural wonder clasping the edge of the world on the remote island. (p487)

Grand Pré National Historic Site, Nova Scotia

The site of the 1755 Acadian deportation became a Unesco World Heritage site in 2012. The first new development: a viewing area above the plains. (p363)

Yellowknife Bay Floating B&B, Northwest Territories

Join the houseboaters on Great Slave Lake by staying in this floating B&B: utter relaxation just a short paddle from the center of town. (p803)

Stewart-Cassiar Highway, British Columbia

Now paved for its full 874km, this scenic route is a great way to see the north. You can cover it easily in a day (but don't miss a detour to Stewart). (p770)

Ripley's Aquarium Canada, Ontario

Fearsome sharks, graceful stingrays and good ol' Canadian largemouth bass are among the creatures swimming in this aquarium next to the CN Tower in Toronto. (p72)

For more recommendations and reviews, see lonelyplanet.com/

If You Like...

Adrenaline Activities

Whistler If you want to ski or snowboard Canada's best, Whistler (p675) reigns supreme. Ziplining and mountain biking take over in summer.

Tofino Little Tofino (p709) packs big adventure with its Pacific coast surfing, kayaking, hiking and storm-watching.

Banff In the heart of the Rockies, Banff (p584) has it all: skiing, snowboarding, hiking, rafting, horseback riding, mountain biking – phew.

Laurentians The mountain villages speckling the landscape outside Montréal let you ski, luge and rock climb (p259).

Marble Mountain Skiing and snow-kiting in winter, caving and kayaking in summer, and ziplining year-round in western Newfoundland (p496).

Wine & Spirits

Wine Festivals Galore Sip and spit at wine events (p866) across the country – from British Columbia (BC) to Nova Scotia.

Niagara Wine Tours International Cycle backroads from winery to winery on guided trips tailored to all fitness levels (p133).

Taste Trail Take a self-guided driving tour through rural Prince Edward County's farms and vineyards (p197).

Myriad View Distillery Visit Canada's only legal moonshine producer and put hair on your chest with its mouth-burning, 75% alcohol elixir (p443).

Merridale Estate Cidery Sip the six apple ciders or brandy this distiller stirs up in Vancouver Island's verdant Cowichan Valley (p701).

Historical Sites

L'Anse aux Meadows Poke around Viking vestiges that Leif Eriksson and friends left behind in Newfoundland (p493) around AD 1000.

Québec City History is palpable throughout the walled city (p271) where the French put down stakes in 1608.

Louisbourg Munch soldiers' rations and bribe guards at Nova Scotia's recreated 1744 fortress (p385).

Batoche See the moody prairie site where Métis leader Louis Riel clashed with the Canadian army over land rights in 1885 (p552).

Klondike Sites The rush was on after prospectors struck gold in the Yukon in 1896; preserved structures in Dawson City (p791) tell the tale.

Live Music

Montréal The city hosts Canada's most prolific indie rock scene, known for its bo-ho, underground clubs (p229).

North by Northeast Nearly 1000 bands spill off stages throughout Toronto for a rockin' week in June (p93).

Evolve Festival The hills around Antigonish, Nova Scotia host this summer fest (p374), a sort of young, funky, jam-band Woodstock.

Horseshoe Tavern Toronto's legendary venue (p113) is the place for emerging acts to cut their teeth. Buzz bands take the stage most nights.

IF YOU LIKE...SURFING

Lawrencetown Beach in Nova Scotia gets exceptional wrapping waves. Learn to ride them at a surf school (p344).

George Street This St John's street (p468) is chock-full of musical pubs – supposedly more per square kilometer than anywhere in North America.

Red Shoe Pub World-renowned Celtic fiddlers scorch the strings on Cape Breton Island (p376).

Lighthouses

Peggy's Cove This lighthouse (p345) near Halifax is absolutely picture perfect – which is why it's one of the most photographed of all time.

Point Amour Atlantic Canada's tallest lighthouse (p504) pays off with killer views over Labrador's black-rock landscape and iceberg-strewn sea.

Cape Enrage The 150-year-old cliff-top tower (p420) presides over the highest, meanest tides in the world (hence the name) .

Lighthouse Park Point Atkinson Lighthouse (p670) gets a whole park named after it in West Vancouver.

Swallowtail Set on New Brunswick's Grand Manan Island, this lighthouse (p410) looms atop a moss-covered cliff with seals swimming below.

Roads Less Traveled

Route 132, Québec Rocky shores, glinting silver churches and wooded hills from Ste-Flavie to Forillon National Park (p302).

Highway 17 along Lake Superior, Ontario Fjordlike passages, hidden beaches and primeval forests coated in mist on the lake's northern shore (p178).

Old River Road (Route 102), New Brunswick Farmhouses, hay barns and wildflowers

(Top) Gaspé Peninsula (p307), Québec
(Bottom) Peggy's Cove lighthouse (p345), Nova Scotia

alongside an island-filled river (p399).

Route 199, Québec Wee coastal road passing sand dunes and fishing villages on the Îles de la Madeleine (p321).

Highway 37A to Stewart, BC Vintage toasters and converted school-bus restaurants along with the requisite glaciers (p771).

Route 470, southwest Newfoundland Rippled coastal ride past windswept terrain and fishing hamlets (p501).

Wildlife-Watching

Churchill Polar bears rule the tundra at Hudson Bay's edge (p529), while beluga whales chatter in the river.

Digby Neck Endangered North Atlantic right whales, blue whales, humpbacks and seals swim offshore from Nova Scotia (p357).

Gros Morne They say there are six moose per square kilometer in Newfoundland's premier park (p488), plus caribou and black bear.

Khutzeymateen Grizzly Bear Sanctuary Guess what creature lives here? The refuge, near Prince Rupert, BC (p761), is home to more than 50 big guys.

Wood Buffalo National Park Shaggy bison and packs of huge wolves play out nature's deadly dance (p629).

Icefields Parkway The scenic road (p588) in the Rockies pretty much guarantees bear and elk sightings.

Algonquin Provincial Park Moose and loons provide quintessential Canadian viewing; howling wolves provide the soundtrack (p190).

Victoria Resident pods of killer whales ride the local waves (p686).

Art

National Gallery of Canada The Ottawa museum (p209) holds the world's largest collection of Canadian and Inuit art among its trove.

Art Gallery of Ontario This big Toronto institution (p79) boasts rare Québecois religious statuary, First Nations carvings and works by the famed Group of Seven.

UBC Museum of Anthropology Vancouver's top collection centers on soaring, beautifully carved totem poles (p645).

Sunshine Coast Gallery Crawl Artisans' studios stud the BC coast (p683). A purple flag fluttering over a property means the artist is in.

Cape Dorset This small, wintry town (p827) in Nunavut is the epicenter of Inuit art. See soapstone carvers in action at local studios and co-ops.

Seafood

Digby Foodies from around the globe salivate over the giant, butter-soft scallops from this Nova Scotia town (p358).

St Ann's Lobster Supper Don a bib and crack into a crustacean in this quintessential Prince Edward Island church basement (p450).

Malpeque Head to the tiny PEI town where the namesake oysters come from, famed for their moist, briny taste (p453).

Coast It's where Vancouver's movers and shakers sate their salmon and oyster cravings (p653).

Red Fish Blue Fish This takeout shack (p693) on Victoria's waterfront serves sustainably caught seafood in dishes such as wild salmon sandwiches and oyster tacos.

Markets

Kensington Market It's a blast rummaging through the vintage shops of this bohemian Toronto neighborhood (p83).

Summer Night Market Taste-trip through steaming Malaysian, Korean, Japanese and Chinese food stalls at this huge bazaar (p672) in Richmond, near Vancouver.

Marché Jean Talon Farmers from the surrounding countryside bring their fruits, veggies, cheeses and sausages to Montréal's lively marketplace (p251).

St Lawrence Market Butchers, bakers and pasta makers fill Toronto's awesome 1845 market hall (p73). Art and antiques make appearances, too

Salt Spring Island Saturday Market Gobble island-grown fruit and piquant cheeses while perusing local arts and crafts on a day trip from Vancouver (p719).

Halifax Seaport Farmer's Market With 250 vendors, this

IF YOU LIKE...WRECK DIVING

The east coast of Canada teems with 4500 sunken ships. The Empress near Rimouski (p306), Québec, is a famous one .

Polar bear, Hudson Bay, Manitoba

market (p342) is a prime spot to people-watch and buy organic produce, wine and seafood.

Beaches

Basin Head Beach Many PEI locals rate this sweeping stretch of sand (p444) as their favorite; the grains 'sing' when you walk on them.

Sauble Beach The warm, clear waters are why this shore near Southampton, Ontario (p148) was voted Canada's best freshwater beach.

Eastern Shore Beaches Several white-sand beaches with lifeguards, boardwalks, swimming and even surfing brush the coast near Halifax (p344).

Greenwich Follow the boardwalk over marshlands and dramatic dunes onto PEI's most unspoiled, pink-sand beach (p445).

Long Beach Located near Tofino, it takes a pounding from the Pacific's waves, but that's why surfers and beach bums flock here (p707).

English Bay Beach This sandy curve in downtown Vancouver bustles with buskers, sunbathers and volleyballers (p640).

Starry Nights

Moose Factory There are no roads to this speck on the

Ontario map (p187), just a small Cree settlement and ecolodge.

Torngat Mountains National Park Labrador's raw, chilly tip (p507) is about as isolated as you can get, with no towns for hundreds of kilometers.

Yellowknife The Northwest Territories' far-flung, kitted-out capital (p800) lets you see the lights while dogsledding.

Churchill Visit Manitoba's little piece of Hudson Bay (p528) around October and you'll have northern lights with a side of polar bears.

Whitehorse The Yukon's arty main town is another up-there spot with outfitters who'll take you out under the night sky (p775).

Month by Month

January

Ski season is in full swing, and many mountains receive their peak snowfall. Toward the end of the month, cities begin their winter carnivals to break the shackles of cold, dark days.

Ice Wine Festivals

British Columbia's Okanagan Valley (www.thewinefestivals.com) and Ontario's Niagara Peninsula (www.niagarawinefestival.com) celebrate their ice wines with good-time festivals. The distinctive, sweet libations go down the hatch amid chestnut roasts, cocktail competitions and cozy alpine-lodge ambience.

February

Yes it's cold, as in 'coldest temperature ever recorded' cold (that'd be Snag, Yukon on February 3, 1947 a −62.8°C). But that doesn't stop folks from being outdoors. February is a party month, filled with all kinds of wintry events.

Chinese New Year

Dragons dance, firecrackers burst and food sizzles in the country's Chinatowns. Vancouver (www.vancouverchinatown.com) hosts the biggest celebration, but Toronto, Calgary, Ottawa and Montréal also have festivities. The lunar calendar determines the date.

Québec City's Winter Carnival

Revelers watch ice-sculpture competitions, hurtle down snow slides, go ice fishing and cheer on their favorite paddlers in an insane canoe race on the half-frozen, ice-floe-ridden St Lawrence River. It's the world's biggest winter fest (www.carnaval.qc.ca).

Winterlude in Ottawa

Another snowy bash, this one along the Rideau Canal, where skaters glide by on the 7km of groomed ice. When they're not sipping hot chocolate and eating beavertails (fried, sugared dough), the townsfolk build a massive village entirely of ice (www.canadascapital.gc.ca/winterlude).

Yukon Quest

This legendary 1600km dog-sled race (www.yukonquest.com) goes from Whitehorse to Fairbanks, Alaska, through February darkness and -50°C temperatures. It's the ultimate test of musher and husky. Record time: 10 days, 2 hours, 37 minutes.

World Pond Hockey Tournament

Small Plaster Rock, New Brunswick plows 20 rinks on Roulston Lake, rings them with straw-bale seating for 8000-odd spectators and invites 120 four-person teams to hit the puck. Teams travel from as far as the UK, Egypt and the Cayman Islands (www.worldpondhockey.com).

Northern Manitoba Trappers' Festival

The Pas puts on a weekend of frosty anarchy featuring dogsled races, snowmobiling, ice sculptures, torchlight parades and trapping games (www.trappers-festival.com). Bundle up: the daily mean temperature is -16.1°C.

March

Snow lessens and temperatures moderate from the brunt of winter. Ski resorts still do brisk business, especially mid-month when kids typically have a week-long school break.

 Sugar Shacks

Québec produces three quarters of the world's maple syrup and March is prime time when the trees get tapped. Head out to local sugar shacks, scoop up some snow, put it on a plate and have steaming syrup from a piping cauldron poured onto it.

Regina Powwow

Students at First Nations University of Canada initiated this Saskatchewan powwow (www.fnuniv.ca/pow-wow) 30-plus years ago to celebrate spring and give thanks for the land's rebirth. Dancers arrive from around North America, and traditional crafts and foods abound.

Vancouver Wine Festival

Vancouver uncorks 1700 wines from 200 vintners at the Vancouver International Wine Festival (www.van-winefest.ca), a rite of spring for oenophiles. You're drinking for art's sake, since the event raises funds for the city's contemporary theater company.

April

Apart from the far north, winter's chill fades and spring sprouts (though the weather can waver, so be prepared for anything). It's a good time for bargains since ski season is winding down but the summer influx hasn't yet begun.

☆ Stratford Theater Festival

Canada's Stratford, a few hours outside Toronto, nearly outdoes England's Stratford-upon-Avon. The Stratford Festival (www.stratfordfestival.ca) plays a monster season from April to November. Four theaters stage contemporary drama, music, operas and, of course, works by Shakespeare. Productions are first-rate and feature well-known actors.

World Ski & Snowboard Festival

Ski bums converge on Whistler for 10 days of adrenaline events, outdoor rock and hip hop concerts, film screenings, dog parades and a whole lotta carousing (www.wssf.com). Heed the motto: Party in April. Sleep in May.

☆ Hot Docs

Want to learn more about Ontario's Hwy 7? Millionaires who live in Mumbai's slums? Belly dancers working in Cairo? Toronto hosts North America's largest documentary film festival (www.hotdocs.ca), which screens 170-plus docos from around the globe.

May

May is a fine time for shoulder-season bargains and wildflower vistas. The weather is warm by day, though nippy at night. Victoria Day at month's end marks the official start of summer.

Tiptoe Through the Tulips

After a long winter, Ottawa bursts with color – more than three million tulips of 200 types blanket the city for the Canadian Tulip Festival (www.tulipfestival.ca). Festivities include parades, regattas, car rallies, dances, concerts and fireworks.

Chocolate Festival

Plays about chocolate, painting with chocolate, jewelry making with chocolate – are you sensing a theme? Québec's Fête du Chocolat de Bromont (www.feteduchocolat.ca) is all about the sweet stuff. The best part: eating the chocolate. Bromont lies 75km east of Montréal.

June

Take advantage of long, warm days to hike, paddle and soak up the great outdoors (but bring repellent for black flies). Attractions don't get mega-busy until later in the month, when school lets out for the summer.

☆ Luminato

For 10 days in early June, big-name musicians, dancers, artists, writers, actors and filmmakers descend on Toronto for a celebration of creativity that reflects the city's diversity (www.luminatofestival.com). Many performances are free.

☆ North by Northeast

Around 1000 emerging indie bands spill off the stages in Toronto's coolest clubs. You might catch the rock stars of tomorrow. Film screenings and comedy shows add to the mix. Over its 20-year history, NXNE (www.nxne.com) has become a must on the music-industry calendar.

☆ Montréal Jazz Festival

Two million music lovers descend on Montréal in late June, when the heart of downtown explodes with jazz and blues for 11 straight days (www.montrealjazzfest.com). Most concerts are outdoors and free, and the party goes on round the clock.

🎊 Pride Toronto

Toronto's most flamboyant event (www.pridetoronto.com) celebrates all kinds of sexuality, climaxing with an out-of-the-closet Dyke March and the outrageous Pride Parade. Pride's G-spot is in the Church-Wellesley Village; most events are free.

🎊 Elvis Festival

If you're in Penticton, British Columbia in late June and you keep seeing Elvis, rest assured it's not because you've swilled too much of the local Okanagan Valley wine. The town hosts Elvis Fest (www.pentictonelvisfestival.com) with dozens of impersonators and open-mike sing-alongs.

(Top) Ice skaters on the Rideau Canal, Ottawa, Ontario
(Bottom) Gay Pride parade, Toronto, Ontario

☆ Saskatchewan Jazz Festival

Come show your soul patch at this jazzy 10-day festival (www.saskjazz.com) at venues throughout Saskatoon. Blues, funk, pop and world music are also on the agenda. Herbie Hancock and Ziggy Marley are among the acts that have trekked to the prairie.

July

This is prime time for visiting most provinces, with the weather at its warmest, a bounty of fresh produce and seafood filling plates, and festivals rockin' the nights away. Crowds are thick.

☆ Country Music in Cavendish

Some of the biggest names in country music come to Prince Edward Island for the Cavendish Beach Festival (www.cavendishbeach-music.com). They croon beachside while campers get their party on. This is one of the largest outdoor music festivals in North America and the island swells with people.

☆ Montréal Comedy Festival

Everyone gets giddy for two weeks at the Just for Laughs Festival (www.hahaha.com), which features hundreds of comedy shows, including free ones in the Quartier Latin. The biggest names in the biz yuck it up for this one.

☆ Calgary Stampede

Raging bulls, chuckwagon racing and bad-ass, boot-wearing cowboys unite for the 'Greatest Outdoor Show on Earth.' A midway of rides and games makes it a family affair well beyond the usual rodeo event, attracting 1.1 million yee-hawin' fans (www.calgarystampede.com).

☆ Winnipeg Fringe Festival

North America's second-largest fringe fest (www.winnipegfringe.com) stages creative, raw and oddball works from a global line-up of performers. Comedy, drama, music, cabaret and even musical memoirs are on tap over 12 days.

◉ Arctic Art

The Great Northern Arts Festival (www.gnaf.org) in Inuvik, Northwest Territories, draws scores of carvers, painters and other creators from across the circumpolar world. It's an ideal place to buy arctic art, watch it being made, or participate in workshops.

August

The sunny days and shindigs continue. Visitors throng most provinces, and prices reflect it. It can get downright hot and humid away from the coasts.

☆ Festival Acadian

Acadians tune their fiddles and unleash their Franco-Canadian spirit for the Festival Acadien (www.festivalacadien.ca) in Caraquet, New Brunswick. It's the biggest event on the Acadian calendar, with singers, musicians and dancers letting loose for two weeks in early August.

☆ Newfoundland Rowing Regatta

The streets are empty, the stores are closed and everyone migrates to the shores of Quidi Vidi Lake for the Royal St John's Regatta (www.stjohnsregatta.org). The rowing race began in 1825 and is now the continent's oldest continuously held sporting event.

☆ Edmonton Fringe Festival

You thought Winnipeg's fringe fest was something? Edmonton's is even bigger. That's right: it's North America's largest fringe bash, staging some 1600 performances of wild, uncensored shows over 11 days in mid-August. Acts are democratically chosen by lottery (www.fringe-theatreadventures.ca).

◉ Canadian National Exhibition

Akin to a state fair in the USA, 'The Ex' (www.theex.com) features more than 700 exhibitors, agricultural shows, lumberjack competitions, outdoor concerts and carnivalia at Toronto's Exhibition Place. The 18-day event runs through Labour Day and ends with a bang-up fireworks display.

September

Labour Day in early September heralds the end of summer, after which crowds (and prices) diminish. But the weather is still decent in most places, making it an excellent time to visit. Plus moose mating season begins!

🍴 Prince Edward Island Fall Flavours

This island-wide kitchen party merges toe-tapping traditional music with incredible seafood at events over the course of three weeks (www.fallflavours. ca). In Charlottetown, don't miss the oyster-shucking championships or the chowder challenge.

☆ Toronto International Film Festival

Toronto's prestigious 10-day celebration (www.tiff.net) is a major cinematic event. Films of all lengths and styles are screened in September, as celebs shimmy between gala events and the Bell Lightbox building. Buy tickets well in advance.

🍴 Newfoundland Coastal Cookout

The wee town of Elliston in eastern Newfoundland gathers many of Canada's best chefs and has them cook at stations set up along a gorgeous 5km coastal trail. Foodies flock in to eat and hike and eat some more (www.roots-rantsandroars.ca).

☆ Canadian Deep Roots Festival

Tune in to Mi'kmaw, Acadian, African–Nova Scotian and other unique music – all with local roots – in the fun university town of Wolfville, Nova Scotia (www.deeprootsmusic.ca).

Workshops are available with some of the performers, so you can learn to drum, strum or fiddle.

October

With fall foliage flaming bright and the weather dawning cool but comfortable, October welcomes lots of visitors. Grab a stick, because hockey season gets underway.

🎵 Celtic Colours

With foot-stompin' music amid riotous foliage, this roving festival in Cape Breton attracts top musicians from Scotland, Spain and other countries with Celtic connections (www.celtic-colours.com). Community suppers, step-dancing classes and tin whistle lessons round out the cultural celebration.

🍷 Oktoberfest in Ontario

Willkommen to this nine-day beery Bavarian bash in Kitchener, supposedly the largest Oktoberfest outside of Germany (www.oktoberfest.ca). The sauerkraut, oompah bands, lederhosen and *biergartens* bring 500,000 people to clink steins under the tents.

November

After the fall-color events and early in the ski season, this is an offbeat time to visit. It's cold, but just a tease as to what's

coming over the next three months.

☆ Canadian Finals Rodeo

If you missed the Calgary Stampede, here's your other chance to see top cowboys test their skills with bucking broncos, steer wrestling and lasso throwdowns (www.canadianfinalsrodeo.com). Held in Edmonton mid-month.

December

Get out the parka. Winter begins in earnest as snow falls, temperatures drop and ski resorts ramp up for the masses. 'Tis the holiday season, too. Resorts get especially busy over the last few weeks of the month.

🎿 Mountain Time

Powder hounds hit the slopes from east to west. Whistler in BC, Mont-Tremblant in Québec and the Canadian Rockies around Banff, Alberta, pull the biggest crowds, but there's downhill action going on in every province (snowboarding and cross-country skiing, too).

🎵 Niagara Festival of Lights

The family friendly Winter Festival of Lights (www.wfol.com) gets everyone in the holiday spirit with three million twinkling bulbs and 125 animated displays brightening the town and the waterfall itself. Ice-skate on the 'rink at the brink' of the cascade.

Itineraries

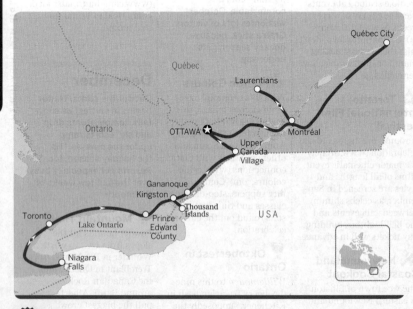

2 WEEKS The Central Corridor

This 1450km route from Toronto to Québec City encompasses Canada's largest cities, mightiest waterfalls and prettiest islands.

Spend two days in the multicultural mecca of **Toronto** (p67), and wallow in the wealth of architecture, art museums, restaurants and nightclubs. Spend day three at **Niagara Falls** (p122), then begin your eastward haul. The Loyalist Parkway (Hwy 33) rambles shoreside in winery-laden **Prince Edward County** (p196) and pulls into colonial **Kingston** (p199). From there, the misty, mansion-covered **Thousand Islands** (p204) dot the St Lawrence River; **Gananoque** (p204) makes a good break for a day in their midst. Make a half-day stop at **Upper Canada Village** (p207), a re-created 1860s town, before heading to **Ottawa** (p208) for a couple of days to get your culture fix at the national museums. Save room for your next stop, **Montréal** (p229), where the French *joie de vivre* seduces via Euro-cool clubs and foodie-beloved cafes. Had your fill? Swing over to the **Laurentians** (p259) to spend a day or two and hike, cycle or ski yourself back into shape. Finish in **Québec City** (p271) – the charismatic old town, walled and dramatically poised on a bluff, will leave an impression long after you return home.

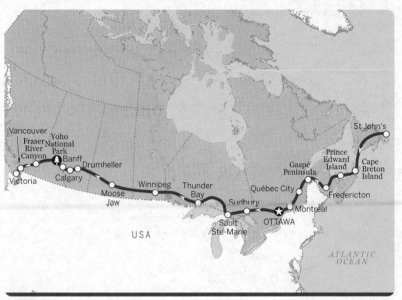

Trans-Canada Highway

The world's longest highway – a 7800km belt of asphalt cinched around Canada's girth – is technically a patchwork of provincial roads. Scenic stretches alternate with mundane ones; many of the best sights require a detour off the highway.

The road begins in **St John's** (p460), Newfoundland, Canada's oldest city and a heck-of-a-pub-filled good time. It rolls all the way through the province until it hits the sea, at which point you must ferry over to North Sydney, Nova Scotia, where the road resumes on **Cape Breton Island** (p375). Continue to New Brunswick – or take the longer route to **Prince Edward Island** (p431) – then follow the St John River via **Fredericton** (p393) to Québec. The **Gaspé Peninsula** (p307) entices as a pastoral side-trip east. Otherwise, the highway follows the St Lawrence River to romantic **Québec City** (p271).

Carry on the urban theme in **Montréal** (p229) before plunging into Ontario near museum-fortified **Ottawa** (p208). From there, follow in fur traders' footsteps to **Sudbury** (p174) and **Sault Ste-Marie** (p176), the gateway to the Algoma wilderness that inspired the Group of Seven painters. Savor the superb stretch of road skirting Lake Superior to **Thunder Bay** (p182). And voila, there goes week two.

Next the highway enters the prairie flatlands of Manitoba, where **Winnipeg** (p512) provides an enlivening patch of cafes and culture. The road dawdles under Saskatchewan's big skies until reaching bad-ass **Moose Jaw** (p541), where Al Capone used to hide his bootlegged booze. In Alberta, dinosaur junkies can detour to **Drumheller** (p612). And put on your cowboy boots before arriving in **Calgary** (p571), a former cow town that's become one of Canada's fastest-growing cities. So passes week three...

You're in the Rockies now. They offer a dramatic change of scenery as the highway meanders through **Banff** (p584) before entering British Columbia at **Yoho National Park** (p749) and reaching its highest point (1643m) at Kicking Horse Pass. The mountains eventually give way to river country. The most memorable section leads through the **Fraser River Canyon** (p725) from where it's only a quick jaunt to multicultural **Vancouver** (p634) and the ferry to **Victoria** (p686). Snap a picture at the Mile 0 sign. You made it!

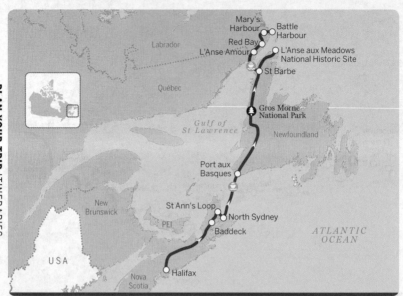

Wild Eastern Excursion

2 WEEKS

Wild, windswept and whale-riddled, this 1700km route through Nova Scotia, Newfoundland, Labrador and Québec unfurls sea-and-cliff vistas, Viking vestiges and much more.

Start in **Halifax** (p332) and spend a few days enjoying the beer, farmers markets and cosmopolitan life. Then hit the road to Celtic-tinged Cape Breton Island for two days. It's about a five-hour drive and a connecting causeway means there's no ferry involved. You won't have time to traverse Cape Breton in depth, but you can certainly get a feel for its beauty in pastoral **Baddeck** (p382) and along the art-studio-dotted **St Ann's Loop** (p381). Industrial **North Sydney** (p383) is nearby for the ferry to Newfoundland.

It's a six-hour sail over the Cabot Strait to **Port aux Basques** (p499). The ferry goes daily, but be sure to book in advance. Spend a day in the sleepy town, then steer for **Gros Morne National Park** (p488), about four hours north on the Trans-Canada Hwy. This World Heritage site is rich with mountain hikes, sea-kayak tours, fjord-like lakes and weird rock formations. After soaking it up for three days, continue on the Viking Trail to its awe-inspiring endpoint: **L'Anse aux Meadows** (p493). This was North America's first settlement, where Leif Eriksson and his Viking pals homesteaded 1000 years ago. Poke around for a day before backtracking about two hours to **St Barbe** (p493), where the ferry for Labrador departs. Reservations are wise for the daily, two-hour crossing.

And then you're in the Big Land. (Actually, the ferry lands in Québec, but more on that province later.) Turn your wheels northeast and head for **L'Anse Amour** (p504), intriguing for its tall lighthouse and shipwreck-strewn hiking trail. Further along is **Red Bay** (p506), Canada's newest World Heritage site, which preserves a massive, 16th-century whaling port. To really get away from it all, drive 90km onward to Mary's Harbour and spend the night on the offshore island that holds **Battle Harbour** (p506), a restored village. After a few days in Labrador, it's time to head back. Before getting on the ferry, detour for a few hours down Rte 138 in Québec. It makes a beautiful drive past waterfalls and lookouts to see the crashing surf. Afterward, you'll need a couple of (long) days to retrace your path to Halifax.

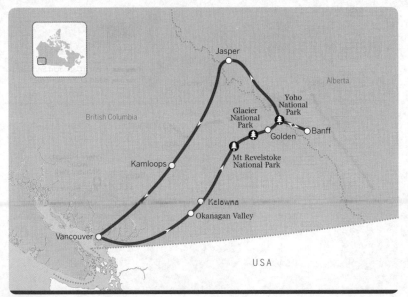

The Rockies

2 WEEKS

Prepare to feast on a smorgasbord of scenic delights on this 2000km trek, which loops through British Columbia and Alberta.

Start with a couple of days in mountain-meets-the-sea **Vancouver** (p634), where you'll be spoiled by urban hiking, biking and other activities, plus western Canada's best cuisine scene. Make the wine pilgrimage east through rolling hills to the lake-studded **Okanagan Valley** (p727), famous for its fruit orchards, crisp whites and bold reds. **Kelowna** (p736) makes a good sipping base in the area.

Next it's time to get high in BC's Rocky Mountains. A trio of national parks pops up in quick succession, each providing plenty of 'ah'-inspiring vistas. **Mt Revelstoke** (p747) has a cool scenic drive and hikes. **Glacier** (p748) has 430 of its namesake ice sheets. And **Yoho** (p749) is home to looming peaks and crashing waterfalls. **Golden** (p748) is a convenient base.

Cross the border into Alberta, and park it in **Banff** (p590). You won't be able to stop the cliches from flying forth: grand! majestic! awe-inspiring! Allot plenty of time – at least three days – for hiking, paddling, gawking at glaciers and spotting grizzly bears (best done from a distance). Sapphire-blue Lake Louise is a must, surrounded by alpine-style teahouses that let you fuel your hikes with scones, beer and hot chocolate.

From Banff, the Icefields Pkwy (Hwy 93) parallels the Continental Divide for 230km to **Jasper** (p604). Try to keep your eyes at least partially on the road as you drive by the humungous Columbia Icefield and its numerous fanning glaciers. Foaming waterfalls, dramatic mountains and the sudden dart of a bear (or was that a moose?) are also part of the journey. Jasper itself is bigger and less crowded than Banff, and offers superb hiking, horseback riding, rock climbing, mountain biking and rafting.

It's a shame to have to leave, but we must return to Vancouver. The Yellowhead Hwy (Hwy 5) plows south to **Kamloops** (p725), a handy spot to spend the night before motoring back to the City of Glass.

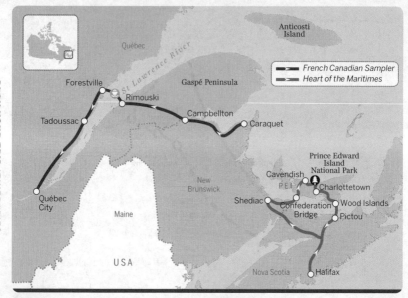

 ## French Canadian Sampler

Get a taste of Gallic Canada on this 700km jaunt through New Brunswick and Québec.

Start in **Caraquet** (p429) and immerse in Acadian culture at the historic sites and via local foods such as *pets de soeur* ('nun's farts' in English – try one to see if you can figure out why). If you visit in August, the fiddle-fueled Festival Acadien takes over the town.

Ramble east through **Campbellton** (p430) and cross into Québec. **Rimouski** (p306), on the St Lawrence River, is your target. Explore its intriguing museums and delicious cafes, and day-trip east up the Gaspé Peninsula on Rte 132, where fluttering Acadian flags, tidy farming hamlets and rocky shores flash by.

From Rimouski, a ferry crosses the river to Forestville, from where you can head south to welcoming **Tadoussac** (p297). It's all about whale-watching in this boho little town; zodiacs motor out to see the blue whales that patrol the area.

Finish your trip in atmospheric **Québec City** (p271). Check in at a cozy inn, wander the Old Town's labyrinth of lanes and stop often to sip in the corner cafes.

 ## Heart of the Maritimes

This 650km loop lassos the core of the Maritime provinces (Nova Scotia, New Brunswick and Prince Edward Island).

Eat and drink your way through **Halifax** (p332), then make a break northwest for New Brunswick. Festive **Shediac** (p425) is home to the world's biggest lobster sculpture and – no surprise – the local cooked version is a highlight.

Barrel over the 12.9km **Confederation Bridge** (p435) that links New Brunswick to PEI and begin the pilgrimage to Anne's Land. Anne, of course, is the fictional red-headed orphan of Green Gables fame, and **Cavendish** (p451) is the wildly developed town that pays homage to her.

Continue the red theme by exploring the red sandstone bluffs at **Prince Edward Island National Park** (p446). Stop in PEI's compact, colonial capital **Charlottetown** (p435) before taking the ferry from **Wood Islands** (p442) back to **Pictou** (p372) in Nova Scotia. You can stroll Pictou's boardwalk and, if you're lucky, the town might be hosting its First Nations Powwow. Its about two hours from here back to Halifax.

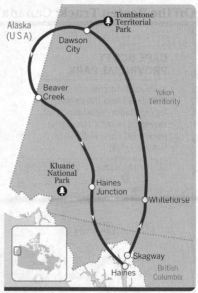

1 WEEK — Bite of British Columbia

You don't have to drive far to experience a range of landscapes in southern BC. Ocean, mountains, forests, islands – all present and accounted for in roughly 550km.

Begin in **Vancouver** (p634) and take a couple of days to check out the indie shops, foodie fare, and forested seawall vistas of Stanley Park. On day three, drive to the **Tsawwassen ferry terminal** (p665) for the dreamy boat trip to Swartz Bay on Vancouver Island. Zip over to **Victoria** (p686), spending an overnight exploring the picture-perfect capital and its historic buildings. On day four, drive north up the island on Hwy 1, stopping off at **Chemainus** (p701), a former logging settlement that's reinvented itself as an art town. Continue north for a late lunch and an overnight in **Nanaimo** (p702), then, next morning, catch the ferry back to the mainland's Horseshoe Bay terminal in **West Vancouver** (p669).

From here, the Sea to Sky Hwy (Hwy 99) runs cliffside through formidable mountains to **Whistler** (p675). The resort town has heaps of adrenaline activities and fun, ski-bum bars to occupy your final few days. It's 130km back to Vancouver.

1 WEEK — Klondike Highway & Around

Heed the call of the wild, and set your wheels for this epic roadway. Know it'll be a lot of driving for one week (approximately 30 hours), but the road *is* the main attraction for the trip.

Start in **Skagway** (p786), Alaska, as the Klondike Hwy does, then leave the cruise ships behind and enter the rugged land Jack London wrote so much about. Follow the road to lively **Whitehorse** (p775), with its groovy arts and organic bakeries, then continue north to offbeat **Dawson City** (p789). Linger a few days and check out the gold rush historic sites, take a mine tour and blow a kiss to the dancing girls. Day-trip to **Tombstone Territorial Park** (p796) for its wide, steep grandeur.

Next, follow the Top of the World Hwy (Hwy 9) across mountain tops to the Alaskan border, and connect down through the US and onto the Alaska Hwy in the Yukon at **Beaver Creek** (p784). The road between here and well-stocked **Haines Junction** (p782) is sublime, paralleling Kluane National Forest and the St Elias Mountains. The gawk-worthy Haines Hwy rolls in to **Haines** (p785), Alaska, where your journey ends.

Off the Beaten Track: Canada

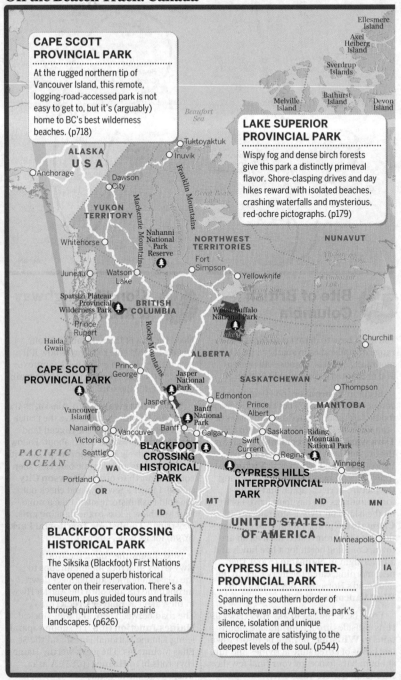

CAPE SCOTT PROVINCIAL PARK

At the rugged northern tip of Vancouver Island, this remote, logging-road-accessed park is not easy to get to, but it's (arguably) home to BC's best wilderness beaches. (p718)

LAKE SUPERIOR PROVINCIAL PARK

Wispy fog and dense birch forests give this park a distinctly primeval flavor. Shore-clasping drives and day hikes reward with isolated beaches, crashing waterfalls and mysterious, red-ochre pictographs. (p179)

BLACKFOOT CROSSING HISTORICAL PARK

The Siksika (Blackfoot) First Nations have opened a superb historical center on their reservation. There's a museum, plus guided tours and trails through quintessential prairie landscapes. (p626)

CYPRESS HILLS INTER-PROVINCIAL PARK

Spanning the southern border of Saskatchewan and Alberta, the park's silence, isolation and unique microclimate are satisfying to the deepest levels of the soul. (p544)

0 —— 1,000 km
0 —— 500 miles

PANGNIRTUNG

This artistic Baffin Island Inuit community is the gorgeous launching pad to the soaring cliffs and utterly spellbinding magnificence of Auyuittuq National Park. (p825)

TORNGAT MOUNTAINS NATIONAL PARK

You'll have to fly or boat in to Labrador's chilly tip, home to polar bears and some of the highest peaks east of the Rockies. Local Inuit guides lead the way for otherworldly hiking and flightseeing. (p507)

GASPÉ PENINSULA

This is the windswept, rocky spot where Jacques Cartier landed in 1534, surrounded by steep limestone cliffs, pebble beaches, whales, seals and the ever-crashing sea. (p307)

CHIPUTNETICOOK LAKES

Disappear into the wilderness in this 180km chain of untouched lakes hugging the border with the US state of Maine. Canoeists, in particular, will find their bliss in the forest-cloaked waterways. (p402)

TAYLOR HEAD PROVINCIAL PARK

This beachy park on Nova Scotia's undeveloped eastern shore juts out into the Atlantic, offering trails of wildflowers and beach grass and plenty of perfect sheltered coves for kayaking. (p388)

GREENLAND
DENMARK

ICELAND

Baffin
Island

Auyuittuq
National
Park

PANGNIRTUNG

Melville
Peninsula

Foxe
Basin

Davis Strait

ATLANTIC
OCEAN

Iqaluit

Southampton
Island

Hudson Strait

Labrador
Sea

Coats
Island

Hudson
Bay

Labrador

NEWFOUNDLAND
& LABRADOR

Belcher
Islands

Northern
Peninsula

St John's

James
Bay

QUÉBEC

Corner
Brook

Newfoundland

Anticosti
Island

Port aux
Basques

GASPÉ
PENINSULA

Moosonee

NEW
BRUNSWICK

PEI
Charlottetown

ONTARIO

CHIPUTNETICOOK
LAKES

Fredericton

TAYLOR HEAD
PROVINCIAL PARK

Thunder
Bay

LAKE SUPERIOR
PROVINCIAL PARK

Québec
City

Halifax

NOVA
SCOTIA

Lake
Superior

OTTAWA

Montréal

ME

Yarmouth

Sault
Ste Marie

North
Bay

Lake
Huron

Toronto

Lake
Ontario

VT
NH

Boston

WI

MI

NY

MA

Lake
Michigan

Niagara Falls

CT RI

PA

New
York

Cabot Trail (p376), Nova Sco

Plan Your Trip
Scenic Drives & Train Trips

Canada – blessed with a huge expanse of wild landscapes, with motorways unfurling right through the good parts – is made for road-tripping. Spiky mountains, ocean vistas, moose and Tim Hortons doughnut shops flash by. Even if you have just one day, you can take a gobsmacking journey. With more time you can really roll....

BEST EXPERIENCES

➡ Dance at a traditional ceilidh on the Cabot Trail

➡ Visit a misty, gothic castle on the Thousand Islands Parkway

➡ Hike and bike on the Sea to Sky Hwy

➡ See whales from shore on the Cabot Trail

➡ Gape at dazzling mountain views on the Rockies Rail Route

MAJOR SIGHTS

➡ Jasper National Park (Rockies Rail Route)

➡ The Chief (Sea to Sky Hwy)

➡ Thousand Islands National Park (Thousand Islands Parkway)

➡ Cape Breton Highlands National Park (Cabot Trail)

KEY STARTING POINTS

➡ Vancouver or Whistler, British Columbia (Sea to Sky Hwy)

➡ Gananoque or Brockville, Ontario (Thousand Islands Parkway)

➡ Chéticamp or Baddeck, Nova Scotia (Cabot Trail)

➡ Jasper, Alberta or Prince Rupert, British Columbia (Rockies Rail Route)

Sea to Sky Highway

Otherwise known as Hwy 99, this cliffside roadway offers a heart-leaping, humbling drive from Vancouver's ocean to Whistler's peaks. It begins at sea level, clasping the shore of Howe Sound, before twisting into the Coast Mountains and climbing through old-growth rainforests. You'll rise 670m (2200ft) during the 130km route, with plenty of opportunities for scenic vistas, waterfall gaping and outdoor activities along the way.

Highlights

In West Vancouver, not long after you cross the Lion's Gate Bridge, drop by Lighthouse Park to see the picture-perfect namesake structure along with shimmering sea views. Next you'll pass Horseshoe Bay, where ferries glide in and out for the 20-minute ride to Bowen Island – a rustically charming retreat populated by writers and artists.

Back on Hwy 99, about 30km north is the kid-friendly Britannia Mine Museum. Descend into the former copper pit for an underground train tour, followed by gold panning. About 6km onward you'll hear the rushing waters of Shannon Falls Provincial Park. Pull into the parking lot and stroll the 10-minute trail to British Columbia's third-highest waterfall, which gushes 335m down the rock face.

Continuing your drive, you'll soon see a sheer, 652m-high granite rock face looming ahead. It's called the 'Chief' and it's the highlight of Stawamus Chief Provincial Park. Climbers go ga-ga over it. The town just beyond is Squamish, a haven for mountain bikers, hikers, kiteboarders and microbrew aficionados. It's a great spot to hang out for a day.

Nearby Brackendale attracts thousands of salmon-hungry eagles in winter. Hikers will want to pit stop at Garibaldi Provincial Park. Pull over at any of the designated trailheads to meander past scenic alpine meadows and breathtaking mountain views.

Back on the road, you'll be in Whistler before you know it. Canada's favorite ski resort combines a gabled, Christmas card village with some jaw-dropping dual-mountain terrain. Skiers and snowboarders will be in their glory in winter, while summer is almost as busy with mountain bikers and hikers.

When to Go

This is a beautiful, well-maintained drive any time of year.

Time & Mileage

It's 130km from Vancouver to Whistler on the Sea to Sky Hwy. You can drive it in under two hours. But why hurry? It works best when stretched into a two- or three-day jaunt.

Western Road & Rail

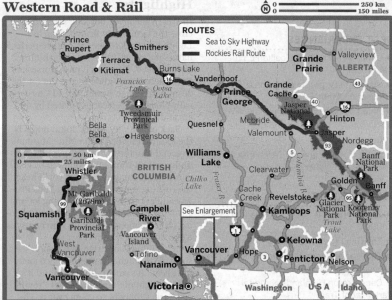

ADVANCE PLANNING

➜ Join an automobile club (p884) that provides 24-hour emergency roadside assistance and discounts on lodging and attractions.

➜ Some international clubs have reciprocal agreements with Canadian automobile associations, so check first and bring your member card from home.

➜ International travelers might want to review Canada's road rules and common road hazards (p886).

➜ Make sure your vehicle has a spare tire, tool kit (eg jack, jumper cables, ice scraper, tire pressure gauge) and emergency equipment (eg flashers).

➜ Bring good maps, especially if you're touring off-road or away from highways. Don't rely on a GPS unit – it can malfunction, and in remote areas it may not even work.

➜ Always carry your driver's license and proof of insurance (p884).

Resources

Tourism BC (www.hellobc.com/driving-routes/31/sea-to-sky-highway-route.aspx) Driving directions for the route and stop-off points along the way.

Mountain FM Radio (107.1) Provides handy traffic and road-condition updates en route.

Drive BC (www.drivebc.ca) Driving conditions and alerts.

Rockies Rail Route

Rail buffs consider the Jasper to Prince Rupert train a must-do journey. It traverses epic Canadian scenery, from the cloud-wrapped peaks and glacial streams in Alberta's Rockies to the hauntingly beautiful Pacific coast of British Columbia. In between a whole lot of pine, spruce and hemlock trees whiz by, as do rustic settlements, rivers and sawmills. But then – did you see it? A black bear loping trackside. And totem poles that mark an ancient aboriginal village veiled by trees. And

Train passing through Jasper National Park, Alberta

unbelievably turquoise lakes glistening in the valleys...

Highlights

The train – a retro silver bullet from the 1950s – chugs during daylight hours only, so you see the landscape in all its glory. (You spend the night in Prince George, a long-standing lumber town at roughly the halfway point.)

The route traces an old aboriginal trading path. It climbs over the Yellowhead Pass at 1130m and follows the Skeena River to the ocean. You can't help but relax, what with the train's gentle swaying and storybook images flashing by: bridges, canyons, tunnels, snowy mountains.

The trip starts and ends with a scenic bang. Jasper National Park has the white-dipped peaks and glistening glaciers you see on postcards, while Prince Rupert is a misty, unspoiled town with an intriguing aboriginal heritage. Both are hot spots for adventure seekers.

When to Go

Mid-June to late September is peak period, when 'touring class' tickets (which include tour guides, meals and access to the train carriage with a panoramic dome) are available. The rest of the year only 'economy class' seats are available.

Time & Mileage

The train runs year-round, departing three times a week on Wednesday, Friday and Sunday. The 1160km trip between Jasper and Prince Rupert, including an overnight stay in Prince George, takes 33 hours.

Resources

Via Rail (www.viarail.ca) Prices and specifics on train routes.

Prince George Tourism (www.tourismpg.com) Lodging listings for your overnight stay.

Prince Rupert Tourism (www.visitprincerupert.com) For help planning onward adventures.

GUENTHER SCHWERMER / GETTY IMAGES ©

Boldt Castle, St Lawrence River

Thousand Islands Parkway

The Thousand Islands Parkway rolls along a pastoral strip by the St Lawrence River, where a fog-cloaked constellation of 1800 islands floats between Kingston and Brockville, Ontario. The road offers dreamy vistas and dainty Victorian towns, where you can pull over to spend the night at an inn or take a boat ride through the isles, many of which hold rambling old mansions and castles. It's a mist-kissed trip into a slower, gentler era.

Highlights

Even though the islands start around Kingston – a pretty, historical town with loads of museums on everything from shipbuilding to penitentiaries – the scenic drive doesn't really pick up until the town of Gananoque, some 33km east along Hwy 401. That's where the parkway dips south of the highway and rolls into gorgeous territory.

Gananoque is the area's star for ambience, filled with quaint inns and mani-

cured gardens. It's also the jump-off point for boat cruises through the islands, especially to Boldt Castle, a turreted, gothic palace by the gent who was the original proprietor of New York City's famous Waldorf Astoria Hotel. It's technically in the USA, so bring your passport.

Ivylea is 22km onward, where soaring bridges link Ontario to New York State over several islands. Halfway across there's an observation deck with killer views (mists permitting). If boat tours aren't your thing, you can keep driving over the bridges and reach Boldt Castle by car.

Back on the parkway, the road continues to snake along the river, with furry green islands dotting the water beside it. In 18km you'll come to Mallorytown, the home base for Thousand Islands National Park. Twenty rugged, pine-laden islands are protected, home to lumbering turtles and peregrine falcons. It's a sublime area for backcountry camping and kayaking.

The parkway moseys on, hugging the river for a few more kilometers before rejoining Hwy 401 for the final approach into Brockville. This is another atmospheric town, with opulent 19th-century manors and vintage-looking streets where you can imagine the clip-clop sounds of carriage horses that used to ring through the area.

When to Go

June through September is peak season when the weather is most pleasant. May and October are good shoulder-season times. Many boat companies and activity outfitters close between November and April.

Time & Mileage

The parkway runs for 35km between Gananoque to just north of Mallorytown. The islands themselves stretch from Kingston to Brockville (about 90km). With boat trips or detours into the USA, you'll need a full day, and it's well worthwhile to spend the night along the way.

Resources

1000 Islands Gananoque Visitor Services Centre (www.1000islandsgananoque.com) Activity, restaurant and lodging info.

RON ERWIN / GETTY IMAGES ©

Above: Bridge
connecting Canada
and the US, Thousand
Islands Seaway

Right: Rowing on the St
Lawrence River

Eastern Excursions

Cabot Trail

The Cabot Trail rings Cape Breton Island, Nova Scotia's lush tip. Driving it is a singular, brake-smoking journey. The road twists and climbs over coastal mountains, and around every bend something awesome reveals itself: ocean views, dramatic cliffs, breaching whales just offshore or moose snacking by the roadside. Celtic and Acadian communities dot the area, and their crazy-fiddlin' music vibrates through local pubs. Their unique foods get heaped on local plates, too, so loosen the belt for a full cultural immersion.

Highlights

Most road trippers start at Chéticamp, a deeply Acadian fishing community known for its crafty hooked rugs and lively music. It's also the gateway into Cape Breton Highlands National Park, where moose and bald eagle sightings are common. To stretch your legs, the park's hiking trails zigzag to spectacular, edge-of-cliff sea vistas. And how about some Acadian stewed chicken and potato pancakes with molasses? Chéticamp's eateries are prime for sampling.

Next along the roadway you'll reach Pleasant Bay, known for its whale-watching tours and its Tibetan Buddhist monastery, where the monks give tours. Continuing onward, Meat Cove is a good place to look for whales from shore. Park by the town's trailhead, walk out a short distance, spend an hour gazing at the ocean, and you're almost guaranteed to see a pod of frolicking pilot whales.

Little fishing towns, world-famous golf courses, lighthouses and divine seafood houses pop up as you keep heading around the Cabot Trail. The area around St Ann's is a center for Celtic arts. Baddeck is the unofficial end of the road, a beautiful spot to wind down and take in a traditional ceilidh (gathering for fiddling and dancing) in the town parish hall.

When to Go

July and August are peak season, with the nicest weather. September and October are good months to go, especially the latter for the Celtic Colours festival. Many places close from November through May.

Cape Breton, Nova Scotia

TOP 10 ROAD TRIP ALBUMS

These Canadian artists – some old, some new, spanning genres and provinces – will provide the proper soundtrack for your trip. Load up the iPod, hit shuffle and 'keep the car running,' as the first group on our list sings.

➡ Arcade Fire *Neon Bible*
➡ Tragically Hip *Fully Completely*
➡ Neil Young *Massey Hall 1971*
➡ The New Pornographers *Mass Romantic*
➡ Rush *Moving Pictures*
➡ Great Big Sea *Road Rage*
➡ Feist *The Reminder*
➡ Bachman-Turner Overdrive *Bachman-Turner Overdrive II*
➡ Stompin' Tom Connors *Ballad of Stompin' Tom*
➡ Jill Barber *Chansons*

Time & Mileage

The Cabot Trail winds for 300km around Cape Breton Island's northeastern tip. The highlights lie on the coastal portion between Chéticamp and Baddeck. You can do the drive in a day, but that's pushing it, as the road is narrow, hilly and slow-going most of the way.

Resources

Cabot Trail Working Association (www.cabot-trail.travel) Lists accommodations, restaurants and events for towns along the way and has a useful interactive map.

Tourism Nova Scotia (www.novascotia.com) Look under 'Regions' for listings info.

Plan Your Trip

Travel with Children

Deciding where to go with your kids in Canada can be a daunting decision. Mountains, prairies, beaches, ice fields and easy-going cities are strewn across six time zones. Yet between sure-bet wildlife sightings, meeting real-life cowboys, hands-on learning about pirate history, roaming the plains for dinosaur fossils and ice skating on mountain lakes, it's impossible to make a bad choice. Add the fact that Canada caters to kids better than nearly any other country in the world and you may find yourself (as many do) bringing the kids back year after year.

Best Regions for Kids

Vancouver

Sandwiched between sea and mountains, build a sandcastle one day and go snowboarding the next while enjoying the comforts of the city.

Canadian Rockies

Hike, ski, camp or snowshoe while looking out for moose, bear, elk and whistling marmot.

Montréal

Historic streets, year-round ice skating, an inner-city beach and the Biôdome full of critters will make you understand the meaning of *joie de vivre*.

Maritime Provinces

Climb a lighthouse, sail on a pirate ship, whale watch and beach hop in summer; watch the trees turn red, orange and gold in fall.

Toronto

Chase through parks in summer, ice-skate in winter and don't forget to visit Niagara Falls!

Canada for Kids

As if seeing moose, eagles and whales or running around in the snow, on the beach or in the woods all day wasn't fun enough, everywhere you turn, those crafty Canadians have cooked up some hands-on learning experience, living history lesson or child-oriented theater.

Museums & Monuments

Most large Canadian cities have science museums that specialize in hands-on activities while, at historic sites strewn across the country, costumed thespians get you right into the period and often have demonstrations of everything from blacksmithing to cooking. At some of these places there are also puppet or theatrical performances for children and other events such as hayrides. Teens usually enjoy these sites as well since they are often large and diverse enough for self-exploration and touch on subjects they've studied at school.

Outdoor Activities

Canada is all about open spaces, fresh air, rivers, lakes and mountains, snow, sand and wildlife.

➡ Most Canadian cities are endowed with parks and promenades set up for even the tiniest **cyclists**, but finding a child-sized bike rental can be hit or miss. For a cycling-oriented holiday try the mostly flat Confederation Trail that traverses bucolic Prince Edward Island or the traffic-free Kettle Valley Trail (KVR; British Columbia) that's one of the least strenuous stretches of the Trans Canada Trail.

➡ The Canadian National Park system contains easy strolls as well as longer **hiking trails** that teens might enjoy. **Horseback riding** is widely on offer and can be especially fun in cowboy country around Calgary.

➡ Most lake areas offer **canoe** rentals perfect for leisurely family outings, while seafront regions are packed with **kayak** outfits. For a bigger adrenaline rush for older kids, try **white-water rafting** or **'playboating'** spots, particularly on the Ottawa River in Beechburg.

➡ There are plenty of **fishing** lodges, but you'd be surprised at how lucky you can get just casting into any lake or river. Likewise, try **clamming** (PEI and BC are tops) – ask locals where to go and bring a shovel and a bucket.

➡ On the coasts and the Bay of Fundy, **whale watching** can be thrilling, but be prepared with seasickness pills, extra snacks, sunscreen and warm clothes.

➡ The tiny summer waves on the east and west coast are an excellent way to start learning **surfing**; rent a board or wetsuit or take a class.

➡ Heading out **skiing** or **snowboarding** is an obvious family choice. Children under six often ski for free, ages six to 12 usually pay around 12% to 50% of the adult price and ages 12 to 18 pay a little more than 33% to 75% of the adult price. Then, of course, there's also **ice skating**, **sledding** and **snowshoeing**.

Eating Out

Everywhere you turn in Canada you'll find fast food and fried fare. If you're health conscious, a hurdle will be finding more wholesome options; in small towns your only choice might be to self-cater. Fortunately there are plenty of cabin and family suite–style options that allow you to cook for yourself, and some B&Bs will also let you cook. In cities, every restaurant option is available from vegan to steakhouses.

Easy-to-find Canadian foods your kids will love if you let them include poutine (French fries topped with brown gravy and cheese), fish and chips, Montréal-style bagels (wood-fired, dense and slightly sweet), pancakes or French toast with maple syrup, bear-claw doughnuts, butter tarts, and Nanaimo bars (crumb crust topped with custard and then melted chocolate). You may all gain a few kilos on this trip!

Most Canadian restaurants offer booster seats and child friendly servers as soon as you steer your progeny through the door. However, families with even the most well-behaved children may not feel comfortable at fine-dining establishments.

Children's Highlights

History Lessons

➡ **Dinosaurs** Royal Tyrrell Museum of Palaeontology, Drumheller (Alberta)

➡ **First Nation** Haida Gwaii (British Columbia), Head-Smashed-in Buffalo Jump World Heritage site (Alberta), Aboriginal Experiences (Ottawa), Wanuskewin Heritage Park (Saskatchewan)

➡ **European Colonization** L'Anse aux Meadows (Newfoundland), Louisbourg National Historic Site (Nova Scotia), Fort William Historical Park (Ontario)

Winter Wonderlands

➡ **Winter Carnivals** Québec City Winter Carnival, Cavalcade of Lights (Toronto), Vancouver Festival of Lights

➡ **Ice skating** Rideau Canal (Ottawa), Lake Louise (Alberta), Harbourfront Centre (Toronto), Lac des Castors (Montréal)

➡ **Skiing, Snowboarding & Sledding** Whistler-Blackcomb (British Columbia), Norquay (Banff), Mont-Ste-Anne (Québec)

➡ **Dog-sledding** Yellowknife (Northwest Territories), Iqaluit (Nunavut)

Wet & Wild

➡ **Beaches** Prince Edward Island and British Columbia

➡ **Surfing** Lawrencetown Beach (Nova Scotia), Vancouver Island (British Columbia)

➡ **Kayaking** Johnstone Strait (Vancouver Island), Georgian Bay (Ontario),

➡ **Canoeing** Algonquin National Park (Ontario), Bowron Lakes (British Columbia), Kejimkujik National Park (Nova Scotia)

➡ **Fishing** Lunenburg, Nova Scotia (lobster), Point Prim, Prince Edward Island (clams), Northern Saskatchewan (freshwater fish), Maritime Provinces (deep-sea fish)

Urban Adventures

➡ **Calgary's Cowboys & Cowgirls** Calgary Stampede, Heritage Park Historical Village, horse rides at family ranches

➡ **Vancouver's Outside Action** Capilano Suspension Bridge, Stanley Park

➡ **Ottawa's Museum Mission** Canada Agricultural Museum, Museum of Nature, Science & Technology Museum, Museum of Civilization

➡ **Toronto's Heights & Depths** CN Tower to the subterranean corridors connecting downtown

➡ **Montréal's Culture Infusion** Old Montréal, Little Italy

➡ **Halifax's Pirates & the Titanic** Maritime Museum of the Atlantic, *Titanic* graveyards

Theme Park Delights

➡ **Canada's Wonderland** (p88) Amusement and water park, Toronto

➡ **Galaxy Land** (www.galaxyland.com; West Edmonton Mall; day pass adult/child from $37/31; ⊙11am-9pm Mon-Sat, to 6pm Sun) World's largest indoor amusement park, Edmonton

➡ **La Ronde** (p242) Amusement park, Montréal

➡ **Calaway Park** (p580) Amusement park and campground, Calgary

➡ **Playland** (www.pne.ca/playland; Hastings Park; day pass adult/child $33/24; ⊙10am-6pm, variable by date, MayI–late Sep) Oldest amusement park in Canada, Vancouver

➡ **Avonlea** (p451) *Anne of Green Gables*–themed park, Prince Edward Island

---

EXTRAS BY AGE

Babies & Toddlers

➡ Kids' car seats: car-hire companies rent them for high rates; in Canada babies need a rear-facing infant safety seat, while children under 18kg (40lb) must be in a forward-facing seat.

➡ A front or back sling for baby and toddler if you're planning on hiking and a stroller for city jaunts (nearly everywhere is stroller-accessible).

➡ Sandcastle or snowman-making tools.

Six to 12 years

➡ Kids' car seats: children between 18kg (40lb) and 36kg (80lb) should have a booster seat. Seatbelts can be used as soon as a child is either 36kg, 145cm (4ft 9in) tall or eight years old.

➡ Binoculars for young explorers to zoom in on wildlife.

➡ Field guides about Canada's flora and fauna.

➡ A camera to inject newfound fun into 'boring' grown-up sights and walks.

➡ Kite (for beaches).

Teens

➡ Canada-related iPhone or Android apps.

➡ Canada-related novels (find a list of Young Adult Canadian Book Award winners at www.cla.ca).

➡ French-Canadian phrasebook.

CHRIS CHEADLE / GETTY IMAGES ©

Above: Roller coaster, La Ronde amusement park, Montréal, Québec

Right: Dinosaur replica at the Royal Tyrrell Museum of Palaeontology, Drumheller, Alberta

Planning

Traveling around Canada with the tots can be child's play. Lonely Planet's *Travel with Children* offers a wealth of tips and tricks. The website **Travel For Kids** (www. travelforkids.com) is another good, general resource.

When to Go

Festivals fill Canadian calendars year-round and most are very family-oriented. Summer is the most festival-heavy time, with lots of outdoor-oriented get-togethers from jazz festivals to rodeos. Fall is a lovely time to visit Canada if you can arrange it around your children's school schedule. At this time the trees are changing colors, daytime temperatures are still manageably warm and most of the crowds have gone.

The best time for fresh snow and snow sports is January to April. Santa Claus parades usually kick off the holiday season in November and early December. Around the same time or just after, come the festivals of light where you can expect fireworks, parades and Christmas tree lightings.

Accommodations

Hotels and motels commonly have rooms with two double beds. Even those that don't have enough beds may bring in rollaways or cots, usually for a small extra charge. Some properties offer 'kids stay free' promotions, while others (particularly B&Bs) may not accept children. Ask when booking.

Another good option are 'cabins,' which are usually rented out by the week and come with kitchens, any number of bedrooms, and other perks such as barbecues. You can find full listings with each province's visitors guides online and in print (order them for free at each province's tourism website).

Camping is huge in Canada and many campgrounds also offer rustic cabins (bring your own bedding) that sometimes have kitchens, fire pits or barbecues. Some grounds offer exotic options such as teepees or yurts, while others have swimming pools, minigolf or might be on a lake. Bring twice the bug spray.

What to Pack

Canada is very family oriented so anything you forget can probably be purchased in-country. Breastfeeding in public is legal and tolerated, although most women are discreet about it. Most facilities can accommodate a child's needs; public toilets usually have diaper-changing tables.

What you will need is layered clothing for everyone, as it can get spontaneously cool even during the summer months. Sunscreen is a must – you'd be surprised how much you can burn on the greyest of days – as are rain gear and bug spray. It's also a good idea to bring activities for lengthy car rides since getting anywhere in Canada can involve very long distances.

Regions at a Glance

You can't go wrong in Canada. Each region has eye-popping landscapes and a slew of activities to match. Ontario, Québec and British Columbia (BC) – the most populated provinces – are the ones with the most going on. In addition to outdoor action, they hold Canada's largest cities – Toronto, Montréal and Vancouver – with multicultural museums, sophisticated eateries and wee-hours nightlife. Alberta booms in the Rockies with parks and oil-rich towns. Manitoba and Saskatchewan in the Plains hold big wildlife and arty surprises. The salty Atlantic provinces are tops for seafood munching and whale watching. And the far north is the place to lose the crowds (and roads) and get well off the beaten path.

Ontario

Cuisine
Parks
Culture

Farms & Vineyards

At a geological and climactic nexus, Ontario is ripe with agriculture and viticulture. The province's wines are internationally recognized – well-matched to the delicious farm-to-table fare.

Fresh Air

If you're looking for a simple stroll, a multiday backpacking trip or some time on the water, Ontario supplies anything from green city spaces to massive provincial parks. This is the place to bring your binoculars and break in your hiking boots.

Museums

From tiny sports-memorabilia shrines to world-class collections of ancient artifacts and geological remnants, Ontario is a museum mecca.

p62

Québec

Culture
Winter Sports
Architecture

Joie de Vivre

Imagine: sipping a *café au lait* and eating a flaky croissant on a sidewalk terrace while the murmurs of a foreign language waft through the air. It's easy to be swept away by the Québecois zest for life when fine wines and foods are so accessible.

Snow

The Laurentians' jagged peaks offer skiing and snowboarding opportunities, but it's the French panache of Mont-Tremblant that draws the international crowds.

Historic Style

Nowhere are the vestiges of Canada's colonial past more apparent than in the cobbled streets and grandiose facades of Old Montréal, and within the ancient city walls of Québec City's Old Town.

p225

Nova Scotia

Culture
Activities
History

Cultural Mix

Tartan shops, native French speaking villages and First Nation communities are all within kilometers of each other, rendering the province one big cultural melting pot.

Coves, Cliffs & Tides

Coastal coves rich in flora and fauna beg you to go paddling. Cape Breton Island's vertiginous cliffs and the Fundy Coast with its megahigh tides are also gorgeous areas for adventure and wildlife.

Time Warp

Nova Scotians don't just preserve their historical vestiges, they get into period costume and re-enact old-time activities from lace making to blacksmithing, recreating the scene as it might have been hundreds of years ago.

p328

New Brunswick

Activities
Fishing
Wildlife

You in a Canoe

From the tranquil Chiputneticook Lakes to the quicksilver Tobique River, New Brunswick is absolutely tops for canoeing, surely the most Canadian of activities. You can even meet artisans who still make canoes.

Tie Your Flies

New Brunswick's famed rivers are the kind anglers dream of – where they flycast into the current and within minutes reel in a fat silvery salmon or speckled trout.

Puffin Lovin'

Whether you're a hardcore birdwatcher or you just want to glimpse a moose, New Brunswick's got plenty of animal action to go around. Your best bet: observing rare Atlantic puffin on desolate Machias Seal Island.

p390

Prince Edward Island

Culture
Cuisine
Beaches

All About Anne

Personified by LM Montgomery's redheaded star of the *Anne of Green Gables* series, PEI is as pretty as it's portrayed in the books. Red sands mimic Anne's hair, while white picket fences paint the real-life backdrop.

Lobsters & Spuds

The province vies with Idaho as potato capital of the Americas. Seek out town halls serving supersized suppers of the island's famous lobster – alongside PEI spud salad!

Pink & White Sands

PEI showcases sienna beach flats topped by red-and-white lighthouses, cream-colored dunes and stretches of white sand that 'sing' when you walk on them.

p431

Newfoundland & Labrador

Seascapes
Culture
History

Great Big Sea

'There's one!' someone shouts, and sure enough, a big, barnacled humpback steams through the water, backdropped by a vista of hulking icebergs. Whether you're hiking alongshore or out in a boat, Newfoundland's sea delivers.

Strange Brew

The brogue is vaguely Irish and the slang indecipherable. Plates arrive with cod tongues, bakeapple jam and figgy duff. This place is so offbeat it even has its own time zone: a *half* hour ahead of the mainland.

Viking Vestiges

Feel the Vikings' edge-of-the-world isolation at L'Anse aux Meadows, Leif Eriksson's 1000-year-old settlement set on a bare, forlorn sweep of land.

p457

Manitoba

Wildlife
Open Spaces
Culture

White Bears & White Whales

Polar bears prowling on the ice: that's what sub-arctic Churchill is all about. The hemisphere's biggest predators turn up by the hundreds in the fall. Out on the water in summer, expect to see scores of shockingly white beluga whales.

Muskeg & Wheat

Drive through the south and you'll be mesmerized by kilometer after kilometer of wheat, punctuated by giant grain elevators. In the sub-arctic north, a year-round evergreen swath grows in the rich muskeg – think marshy soil from eons of plants.

Oh Winnipeg!

This surprising oasis of great dining, fun nightlife and hip culture rises up from the prairies around it.

p510

Saskatchewan

Wildlife
History
Culture

Moose & Critters

Although remote, the web of backroads that stretch across this huge province are not empty. Saskatchewan is alive with Canada's iconic critters, especially moose, which love roadside salt pools.

Revolution Rocks

In 1885 Louis Riel fought the law and, while the law won, he and a band of followers almost beat the army at Batoche, an Aboriginal town that declared independence after the national government broke treaties.

The Good Twins

Regina and Saskatoon both offer plenty to do after dark. Inventive restaurants using the province's produce combine with pubs serving regional microbrews.

p532

Alberta

Activities
Winter Sports
Festivals

Banff & Jasper

Two parks, hundreds of miles of trails, and acres of easily accessible wilderness. If you're ever going to fulfill your latent hiking ambitions, these protected areas are the places to do it.

Cross-country Skiing

While Alberta's downhill resorts heave with skiers, the backcountry is so quiet you can almost hear the snowflakes fall. There's nothing like breaking trail in Jasper's roadless Tonquin Valley on a pair of cross-country skis.

Fringe Festival

Edinburgh invented it, but Edmonton has taken the concept of 'alternative theater' and given it a Canadian twist. At the International Fringe Festival, cutting-edge performers offer comedy, satire and weirdness.

p554

British Columbia

Landscapes
Cuisine
Wildlife

Breathtaking Scenery

From jaw-dropping mountains and multifjorded coastlines to dense old-growth forest and lush islands, BC is an idyll for landscape-lovers.

Dining Delights

From North America's best Asian dining scene in Vancouver to a cornucopia of regional seafood and produce, local flavors are a foodie focus here – accompanied, of course, by a BC wine or microbrewery beer.

Wildlife Wonderland

The Inside Passage is alive. Hop a ferry along the coast and stay glued to the deck for orca, whale, seal and birdlife sightings. Ashore, the entire cast of animal characters is here, especially huge grizzlies in the north.

p630

Yukon Territory

Wildlife
Parks
History

Bears, Oh My!

The Alaska Hwy cuts across the lower Yukon on its twisting journey to its namesake state. But stop to admire the wildlife and you may not bother reaching your destination. Keep your eyes peeled for bear, moose, bison, wolf and elk.

Unimaginable Beauty

Kluane National Park is a Unesco-recognized wilderness of glaciers cleaving through granite peaks. You won't just feel small here, you'll feel minute.

Gold!

The Klondike gold rush of 1898 still shapes the Yukon with its spirited sense of adventure. Paddle your way to Dawson City, a time capsule town that's as lively now as then.

p772

Northwest Territories

Northern Lights
Activities
Winter Sports

Aurora Borealis

Fantastically remote and light-pollution-free, NWT is prime for seeing the green-draped flickerings. Outfitters take you far into the night, with heated viewing areas to fend off the chill.

Nahanni National Park

Nahanni National Park is a Unesco World Heritage site that offers some of the most spectacular river kayaking in Canada. With no road access, it is a true back-of-beyond adventure.

Dog-sledding

With zero ski resorts, the Northwest Territories specialize in more esoteric winter activities such as dog-sledding. This traditional form of arctic transportation is a thrilling way to travel.

p797

Nunavut

Wildlife
Culture
Parks

Arctic Animals

Yes, animals live up here, it's just that they're not easy to spot. Hook up with a professional arctic outfitter for rare viewings of polar bear, caribou, walrus, narwhals and beluga whales.

Aboriginal Art

Shopping is the last thing on most Nunavut travelers' minds, but genuine Inuit art is one of the region's biggest draws. Unlikely souvenir outlets can be found in Cape Dorset, Pangnirtung and Iqaluit.

Untamed Wilderness

With annual visitation numbers that rarely hit three figures, Nunavut's four national parks guarantee an extreme wilderness experience. Sky-high costs are tempered by the moon-like emptiness of the incredible terrain.

p818

On the Road

Ontario

Includes ➡

Best Places to Eat

➡ Lee (p103)

➡ Allen's (p109)

➡ ND Sushi (p104)

➡ Beckta Dining & Wine (p219)

➡ Buoys (p172)

Best Places to Stay

➡ Trump Toronto (p95)

➡ Drake Hotel (p99)

➡ Taboo Resort (p159)

➡ Three Houses (p145)

➡ Planet Travelers Hostel (p99)

Why Go?

The breathtaking four-seasonal palette of Ontario's vast wilderness, endless forests and abundant wildlife awaits. Almost 40% of Canada's population lives here for good reason: Ontario is larger than France and Spain combined. Over 250,000 lakes contain a third of the planet's fresh water.

Most Ontarians call behemoth Toronto or Ottawa, the nation's cosmopolitan capital, home. Foodies, fashionistas and funsters converge on Toronto's vibrant multicultural neighborhoods. Both cities have hopping arts and entertainment scenes, kept current by the neighborly influences of New York and Montréal.

Whether you want to reconvene with nature or lose yourself in the excitement of the most multiculturally diverse and socially cohesive region on earth, you've come to the right place. Let Ontario surprise you with the striking beauty of her scenery and welcome you with the warmth of her people.

When to Go
Toronto

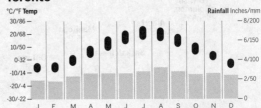

May–Jul Celebrate spring, marveling at moose, trilliums and loons in Ontario's parks.

Jul–Sep Join the frenzy of Toronto's festival mania or savor summer in cottage country.

Sep–Nov Unleash your inner artist as the maple leaves turn provincewide.

Don't Miss

The **Niagara Peninsula** (p122) is *the* day trip out of Toronto's hustle and bustle, but stay a few days if you can. Once you've experienced the awe-inspiring power of the world-famous falls and maxed out on gaudy tourist attractions, head up the road to the photogenic township of **Niagara-on-the-Lake** (p132) and its many wineries, galleries, boutiques and bistros. There's no shortage of delicious rooms in which to lay your weary head.

Consider scooting east to **Prince Edward County** (p196), Ontario's emerging culinary destination, where vineyards and organic farms dot the landscape. Here you'll also find **Sandbanks Provincial Park** (p197), with some of Lake Ontario's best swimming beaches.

Hungry for more? For a quaint riverside romp within an hour and a half of Toronto, try the neighboring historical villages of **Elora** and **Fergus** (p141). Get your Puck on at the **Stratford** (p143) Shakespeare Festival. If you really want to get away, head north to **Thunder Bay** (p182) and the wild shores of **Lake Superior** (p178), or the magnificent scenery of the **Bruce Peninsula** (p167) flanked to the west by the sandy beaches and warmer waters of **Lake Huron** (p146), and to the east by the stunning **Georgian Bay** (p162).

WHAT TO EXPECT

Ontario is Canada's breadbasket, cheese plate and salad bowl, and its plethora of breweries and wineries will exercise your drinking arm and whet your appetite for some seriously good food. When you're ready to burn off all those calories, why not hit a stretch of the many thousands of kilometers of scenic cycling trails? Of course, you may need to be adaptable and have a sense of humor in the face of temperamental weather, whatever the season. And remember, wildlife abounds – bring your binoculars to spot birds and beavers, moose, otter and deer.

For indoorsy days, almost every significant town sports a museum – Ottawa's and Toronto's are some of the world's best. Make sure you pack your patience – Toronto transit and traffic frequently grinds to a halt. You've got lots of ground to cover, so allow yourself time to explore and prepare to be surprised!

Ontario's Top Parks

➡ Algonquin Provincial Park (p190)

➡ Lake Superior Provincial Park (p179)

➡ Killarney Provincial Park (p174)

➡ Bruce Peninsula National Park (p169)

➡ Pukaskwa National Park (p181)

➡ Quetico Provincial Park (p185)

PLANNING

Ontario is alive with activity during the long days of the short summer, when there's always a festival or something fun going on. Be sure to book your accommodations in advance.

Ontario weather can change rapidly. If you're camping, or planning outdoor pursuits, pack for variations in temperature and remember the bug spray.

Fast Facts

➡ Population: 13,505,900

➡ Area: 1,076,395 sq km

➡ Capital: Toronto

➡ Quirky fact: the longest street in the world, Yonge St, begins in Toronto and runs 1896km to the border of Ontario and Minnesota.

Divine Wine...

Ontario's wines improve with every vintage. Delve into the lovely vineyards of Niagara-on-the-Lake and Prince Edward County.

Resources

➡ Ontario Travel Information Centre (www.ontariotravel.net) Has offices throughout the province.

➡ Toronto Tourism (www.seetorontonow.com) Run by the Toronto Convention and Visitors Association.

➡ Ottawa Tourism (www.ottawatourism.ca) Ottawa's official tourist site.

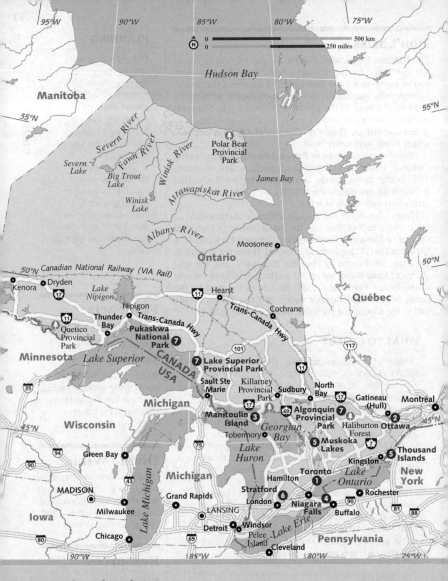

Ontario Highlights

1 Find out what fashionistas and foodies adore about the vibrant neighborhoods of **Toronto** (p67).

2 Get cultured in the capital, **Ottawa** (p208), with its French flavors, world-class museums and bustling market.

3 Explore the Bruce Peninsula then catch the ferry from Tobermory to **Manitoulin Island** (p170), ancient home of the Great Spirit.

4 Marvel at the awesome **Niagara Falls** (p170) from aboard the *Maid of the Mist*.

5 Drool over cottage-cum-mansions as you cruise the **Thousand Islands** (p204) and **Muskoka Lakes** (p158).

6 Wine, dine and head back in time in **Stratford** (p143) with its festival celebrating Shakespeare and the arts.

7 Get off the grid in Ontario's northern parks: **Algonquin Provincial Park** (p190), **Pukaskwa National Park** (p181) and **Lake Superior Provincial Park** (p179).

History

When Europeans first stumbled through the snow into Ontario, several Aboriginal nations already called the region home. The Algonquin and Huron tribes had long occupied the southern portion of the province, but by the time European colonization took hold in the early 18th century, the Iroquois Confederacy (aka the Five Nations) held sway in the lands south of Georgian Bay and east to Québec. The Ojibwe occupied the lands north of the Great Lakes and west to Cree territory on the prairies (today's Alberta and Saskatchewan).

The first Europeans on the scene were 17th-century French fur traders, who established basic forts to facilitate trade links with the Mississippi River. With the arrival of the British Loyalists around 1775, large-scale settlement began. After the War of 1812, British immigrants arrived in larger numbers, and by the end of the 19th century Ontario's farms, industries and cities were rapidly developing. In the aftermath of both world wars, immigration from Europe boomed – Toronto has since evolved into one of the world's most multicultural cities.

An industrial and manufacturing powerhouse, Ontario is home to around 40% of Canada's population. Despite boom times in Alberta, Ontario remains the first choice of immigrants from across the globe, with solid employment prospects and Toronto's well-established immigrant support services proving a powerful draw.

Local Culture

There's something for everyone in Toronto. Torontonians love their city and seem somewhat blinded to its flaws: bitter winters, expensive housing, congested roads and inadequate public transit. They smile through gritted teeth as if it were their duty to defend the city against criticism. Toronto's ethnocultural makeup is so diverse that it defies attempts to define or resist it: people just get along. You'll find all walks of life and all colors, flavors and traditions of the world represented here.

Outside cosmopolitan Toronto and Ottawa, rural Ontario is generally homogenous and unassuming, although communities have French, Belgian, German, Chinese and First Nations roots and influences and there's a strong immigrant labor force. Farmers are practical, no-fuss folks who work hard, value things for their functionality and don't get too involved with life beyond the farm. Most Ontarians are mild-mannered folk who enjoy a good to high standard of living, but don't feel the need to boast about it.

More than any other province, Ontario is hockey-mad: this is the home of Wayne 'The Great One' Gretzky, though less violent winter sports like curling still have a following. One thing is universal – when the weather is fine, city and country folk all head for the sunshine and the water, where they commune with nature and their families: food, wine, good friends, healthy conversation and debate are all valued here.

Land & Climate

Ontario is big. Its longest north–south span is 1730km and 1568km separate east from west. The two main highways are the Trans-Canada from Ottawa to just past Kenora, and the 401 which runs from the Ontario–Québec border, southwest to Windsor and the US border with Detroit. Unlike Canada's rugged west, the landscape is largely flat, with some mountainous regions and more lakes than you could skim stones across in a year: four of the five Great Lakes have shoreline in Ontario. Fifty percent of Ontario's (around 500,000 sq km) is part of the boreal forest (aka 'Amazon of the North') which transverses Canada. It's one of the world's largest storehouses of carbon, begins around the 50th parallel, between Lake Superior and Hudson Bay, and extends across the province in an east–west band up to 1000km wide.

In southern Ontario, cold air from the north collides with warm air from the Great Lakes, causing plenty of rain, humid summers and milder winters. The entire province gets blanketed with heavy snowfalls, but towns in the snowbelt, such as Parry Sound, Barrie and London (from Georgian Bay to Lake Huron) are generally hardest hit. Lake Ontario often spares downtown Toronto from the brunt of the snowfall, but winter storms have been known to shut down the city. January averages around -4°C on the Niagara Peninsula and -18°C in the north.

As summer draws closer, southwestern Ontario and the Niagara Peninsula get increasingly hot and sticky. It can feel oppressively humid in Toronto, where pollution can be stifling. Summer storms are common along the Niagara Escarpment and conditions sometimes produce tornadoes. July averages around 23°C here and 15°C in the north. Late spring and early fall are the best times to visit, when temperatures are mild, days long and sunny and nature puts on its finest displays.

Parks & Wildlife

Ontario contains six of Canada's national parks: in the south, Georgian Bay Islands National Park, Bruce Peninsula National Park, Fathom Five National Marine Park and Point Pelee National Park, the southernmost point of the Canadian mainland. In the north are Pukaskwa National Park and St Lawrence Islands National Park. There are more than 330 provincial parks here, many offering hiking and camping facilities. Campsites for up to six people cost between $14 and $42 per night (plus $11.50 booking fee). They range from basic sites without showers or electricity to well-located powered plots with showers. Make reservations with **Ontario Parks** (888-668-7275; www.ontarioparks.com).

Fauna is abundant in the province. Deer, black bears, chipmunks, raccoons, beavers, skunks, turtles and all manner of birdlife can be seen. The moose, Ontario's charismatic megafauna, has largely disappeared from the south, but you're likely to spot one of these hairy roadside individuals as you head north: they come out in spring to eat the leftover winter salt from the road, and are often seen on the roadside .

ONTARIO ITINERARIES

Four Days

Get yourself oriented to **Toronto** (p67) with a visit to **Yonge & Dundas Square** (p75), then scoot down to scan the scene from atop the **CN Tower** (p70). When you've got your bearings, head out to explore the sights, sounds and smells of Toronto's neighborhoods, starting with **Queen Street West** (p82) and **Kensington Market** (p83). On another day, focus on King St: the **Entertainment District** (p75) and over to **St Lawrence Market** (p73) and the **Distillery District** (p73). You'll barely scratch the surface of what's on offer.

Take a tour with Chariots of Fire (p90) for the most comfortable and affordable way to cram the best of **Niagara Falls** (p122) and **Niagara-on-the-Lake** (p132) into just one day. Or rent a car, take yourself and stay a night. Head west to the pretty riverside villages of **Elora and Fergus** (p141), step back in time to the Mennonite community of **St Jacobs** (p140) and onward to arty-foodie **Stratford** (p143) for the night, catching a play at the festival before hotfooting it back to Toronto.

Two Weeks

In the warmer months, Ontario does road trips well. You could simplify and combine both loops below, but you'll be covering a lot of ground.

Nature Loop: Head north to explore the beauty of the **Muskoka Lakes** (p158), dip in to the West Gate of **Algonquin Provincial Park** (p190) for a few days kayaking and moose-spotting, then back out and scoot up to regroup in **North Bay** (p188) or **Sudbury** (p174). Avid campers could head down to **Killarney Provincial Park** (p174), while those who prefer creature comforts with their isolation will delight in **Manitoulin Island** (p170). If you're feeling adventurous, scoot through **Sault Ste-Marie** (p176) and onward to **Lake Superior Provincial Park** (p179), but you'll have to backtrack to catch the Chi-Cheemaun ferry down to magical **Tobermory** (p168), the magnificent **Bruce Peninsula** (p167) and back to Toronto, via **Collingwood** (p165).

Culture Loop: Start with an extended version of the four-day trip above, then set your sights east, stopping first to sample the rustic charm of a **Prince Edward County** (p196) B&B and the region's fine food and wine. Stop by **Sandbanks Provincial Park** (p197) for a swim, then spend a night or two in historic **Kingston** (p199). Journey on to **Gananoque** (p204) for a cruise around the delightful **Thousand Islands** (p204), then continue through **Brockville** (p205) and **Morrisburg** (p207), before arriving in **Ottawa** (p208), the nation's proud capital. When you're done, head back the way you came, stopping at all the spots you missed.

ℹ Getting There & Around

AIR

Most Canadian airlines and major international carriers arrive at Toronto's **Lester B Pearson International Airport** (YYZ; ☑866-207-1690, Terminal 3 416-776-5100, Terminals 1 & 2 416-247-7678; www.gtaa.com). From here, **Air Canada** (www.aircanada.com) and **WestJet** (www.westjet.com) operate extensive services within the province and beyond. From the downtown **Billy Bishop Toronto City Airport** (YTZ; ☑416-203-6942; www.torontoport.com/airport.aspx), **Porter** (☑888-619-8622; www.flyporter.com) services Northern Ontario as well as Ottawa, Montréal, Chicago, New York, Boston, Washington and more. **First Air** (☑800-267-1247; www.firstair.ca) and **Canadian North** (☑800-661-1505; www.canadiannorth.com) connect Toronto and Ottawa with Iqaluit in Nunavut.

BUS

As a general rule **Greyhound Canada** (www.greyhound.ca) covers southwestern Ontario and Ottawa, from Toronto. **Ontario Northland** (www.ontarionorthland.ca) takes care of Northern Ontario and **Megabus** (☑866-488-4452; www.megabus.com) offers dirt-cheap services between Toronto along the eastern corridor to Montréal as well as Niagara Falls and across the border to Buffalo, NY. Booking tickets at least seven days in advance can sometimes halve the fare. If one carrier doesn't service the route you need, check the others. Parkbus (p884) offers limited seasonal departures to Ontario's best national and provincial parks.

CAR & MOTORCYCLE

Outside Toronto, Ontario's roads are in good shape and offer pleasant driving (once you're off Hwy 401). Car rental is practically essential if you want to enjoy the province, but not for exploring Toronto – driving and parking downtown is painful enough for residents who know their way around. Pick up your rental on the day you're leaving Toronto and use the Toronto Tranist Commission (TTC) while you're in the city: there are no shortage of car-rental companies. When driving in Ontario, you can turn right on a red light after first having made a full stop. It's illegal to text or talk on a mobile device while driving.

TRAIN

VIA Rail (☑888-842-7245; www.viarail.ca) trains service the busy Ontario–Québec corridor, from Windsor in the southwest, all the way to Montréal ($162, 11½ hours, three daily). VIA Rail also operates Trans-Canada services which stop in Northern Ontario en route to Manitoba and beyond. Trains have free wi-fi on board.

GO Train (www.gotransit.com) is Toronto's irregularly scheduled commuter train, sometimes servicing Hamilton, Niagara Falls and Barrie.

TORONTO

POP 5.2 MILLION

Welcome to Toronto, the most multiculturally diverse city *on the planet:* over 140 languages are spoken. The flavors, aromas, sights and sounds of almost every nation converge peacefully in the streets of Toronto's many neighborhoods: microcosms of culture thriving in a somewhat hazy 'bigger picture' that proud locals defend regardless. You're likely to feel accepted here: it's estimated that over half of Toronto's residents were born outside Canada, and despite its complex makeup, Torontonians generally get along. Reports of intolerance and race-related violence are uncommon; no doubt a factor in Toronto winning the bid to host the Pan-Am Games in 2015 (July 10–26). The third-largest international multisport games comes with a $1.5 billion price tag and is expected to draw 250,000 visitors to town.

When the weather is fine, Toronto is a blast: a vibrant, big-time city abuzz with activity: some of the world's finest restaurants, happening bars, clubs and eclectic festivals are found here. At the height of summer, humid downtown neighborhoods become an endless convergence of patios bursting at the seams: alfresco is the way to drink and dine. Locals lap up every last drop of sunshine, beer or martini while they can.

Winter in Toronto, however, can be a real drag. Things get messy on the web of unacceptably congested highways. An archaic public transit system groans under the weight of a growing population and struggles to adequately serve the ever-widening boundaries of the urban explosion. At the time of writing, when the large-scale construction of infrastructure to support Toronto's insatiable expansion should have long since begun, only a vague vision for the future of public transportation was apparent and but a handful of long-overdue essential projects had begun (see p71).

Come with patience, an open mind and during the delightfully temperate and colorful spring or fall, and you're bound to have a great time. Whatever you're looking for, you're almost certain to be able to find it – eventually – in Toronto.

History

In the 17th century present-day Toronto was Seneca aboriginal land. Frenchman Étienne Brûlé was the first European here in 1615, but unwelcoming locals impeded French invasion until 1720 when the French established a fur-trading post in what's now the west end. In 1793 the British took over and John Simcoe, lieutenant governor of the new Upper Canada, moved the capital from Niagara-on-the-Lake and founded the town of York. On April 27, 1813, during the War of 1812, American forces looted and razed York, but were only able to hold sway for six days before Canadian troops hounded them back to Washington.

Toronto was born in 1834, when Mayor William Lyon Mackenzie renamed the town from an aboriginal name meaning 'gathering place.' The Victorian city, controlled by conservative politicians, became known as 'Toronto the Good.' Religious restraints and strong anti-vice laws were such that on Sundays it was illegal to hire a horse, the curtains of department-store windows were drawn (window-shopping was sinful!) and film screenings prohibited.

In 1904, Toronto had a great fire, burning about 5 hectares of the inner city and leveling 122 buildings. Amazingly, no one was killed, and by the 1920s Bay St was booming, in part due to gold, silver and uranium discoveries in northern Ontario.

Prior to WWII, 80% of the population was Anglo-Celtic. After the war, then Prime Minister Lester B Pearson introduced the world's first points-based immigration system. Since then, Toronto has welcomed millions of skilled immigrants and refugees from all corners of the globe. The figure is now closer to 50%. In 1998 five sprawling Toronto suburbs – York, East York, North York, Etobicoke and Scarborough – fused to become the Greater Toronto Area (GTA). As the fifth-largest city in North America, contemporary Toronto is booming – a million miles from its beginnings as 'Muddy York,' Ontario's second-choice town.

☉ Sights

Downtown Toronto is an easy-to-navigate grid, bounded by a hodgepodge of bohemian, ethnic and historic neighborhoods. Yonge St, the world's longest, dissects the city: any downtown street with an East or West designation refers to its position relative to Yonge. Unlike New York, there is no distinction between the directions of avenues and streets: Spadina Ave runs north–south, but Danforth Ave runs east–west. There's also a street called Avenue Rd. Go figure!

Most tourist sights hug the Harbourfront, Entertainment and Financial Districts at the southern end of downtown. The CN Tower, Rogers Centre stadium, Harbourfront Centre, Union Station and Theatre District are all here. South of the lakeshore, locals retreat to the Toronto Islands for solace and the hands-down best views of Toronto's gargantuan skyline – well worth the half-day round trip. Back on the mainland, east and west of Yonge and west of the Don Valley Parkway, the former Old York area is home to some of Toronto's oldest and most well-preserved neighborhoods. That said, you're not likely to be seduced by Toronto's beauty, so we recommend you get a taste of its charm and character: you'll find both a little further afield. There are too many neighborhoods to list here, so we've selected those of most appeal. Be sure to read the opening paragraph for each section first, to get the lowdown on that 'hood. Many argue that West is best: The Annex, Kensington Market and Queen West are all here.

The East has a completely different feel: as full of flavor, but a little more grounded. Leslieville, everybody-loves-to-eat Greektown (aka the Danforth) and The Beaches, slightly San Franciscan in their sensibilities, are the main draws.

We suggest using the TTC (Toronto Transit Commission) to get around – driving in Toronto is an art that many locals have not yet mastered, the cost of parking is extortionate and roads congested. Avoid the morning and evening rush hours when subways and streetcars are packed and services frequently late.

☉ Harbourfront

At the foot of Yonge and York Sts on Lake Ontario is the redeveloped Harbourfront area. Once a run-down district of warehouses,

Greater Toronto Area (GTA)

0°

5 km
2.5 miles

Lester B
Pearson
International
Airport

Macdonald - Cartier Pwy

Mimico Creek

Etobicoke Creek

Dundas St E

409
401
427

Eglinton Ave W

Burnhamthorpe Rd

Rathburn Rd

Islington Ave

Islington
Golf
Club

Bloor St

Kipling Ave

Queensway East

Gardiner Expwy

Lake Shore Blvd W

Brownsline

Toronto
Golf
Club

St George's
Golf &
Country
Club

Royal York Rd

Scarlett Rd

Weston Golf
& Country
Club

Weston Rd

Jane St

Black Creek Dr

Keele St

Dundas St W

Mimico Creek

Bloor St W

The Queensway

Humber Bay

Humber River

Humber Marshes Park

High Park

Dundas St W

Canada's
Wonderland
(15km)

400
401

Allen Expwy

Downsview
Airport

401

Wilson Ave

Bathurst St

Eglinton Ave W

St Clair Ave W

Davenport Rd

Dundas St W

Queen St W

Lake Ontario

See West
Toronto
Map (p84)

Casa
Loma

Avenue Rd

Yonge St

Mt Pleasant Rd

Mount
Pleasant
Cemetery

See Downtown
Toronto
North Map (p74)

Bay St

See Downtown
Toronto South
Map (p78)

Lawrence Ave W

David Dunlap
Observatory (13km);
Toronto Centre for
the Arts (15km)

Eglinton Ave W

Sunnybrook
Park

Don Mills Rd

Don Valley Pkwy

Lawrence Ave E

Edwards
Gardens

Charles Saurial
Conservation
Reserve

Todmorden
Mills

O'Connor Dr

Gerrard St E

Queen St E

Riverdale
Farm

Distillery
District

Toronto
City Centre
Airport

Toronto
Islands

Woodbine Ave

St Clair Ave E

Danforth Ave

Ivan Forrest
Gardens

Kew
Beach

Kew Gardens

Woodbine
Beach Park

Balmy
Beach

Tommy
Thompson
Park

Warden Ave

Eglinton Ave E

Lawrence Ave E

Ellesmere Rd

Cathedral
Bluffs Park
(1km)

Pine Hills
Cemetery

Danforth Rd

Kingston Rd

401

factories and docklands, the area now teems with folk milling about the restaurants, theaters, galleries, artists' workshops, stores, condominiums and parklands along Queens Quay. Ferries for the Toronto Islands dock here.

★ CN Tower   NOTABLE BUILDING

(La Tour CN; Map p78; ☑416-868-6937; www.cn-tower.ca; 301 Front St W; Tower Experience adult/child $32/24, Skypod +$12, Edgewalk $175; ⊙9am-10pm Sun-Thu, to 11pm Fri & Sat; ⑤Union) Toronto's iconic CN Tower, a marvel of 1970s engineering, looks like a giant concrete hypodermic needle. Its function as a communications tower takes a backseat to relieving tourists of as much cash possible: riding those glass elevators up the highest freestanding structure in the world (553m) is one of those things in life you just *have* to do. If not, you're bound to catch a glimpse of the tower at night, when the entire structure puts on a brilliant free light show year-round. Try the intersection of McCaul St and Queen St W, due north of the tower, for best vantage.

On a clear day, the views from the top are astounding; if it's hazy (often) you won't see a thing. Queues for the elevator can be up to two hours long in each direction. Buying tickets online saves 15%. There's an obligatory revolving restaurant (called 360°): it's expensive, but the elevator price is waived for diners. Cashed-up daredevils (13 years plus) can now opt for the EdgeWalk, a 20-minute outdoor walk around the unbounded perimeter of the main pod (356m). Not for the fainthearted.

Harbourfront Centre   LANDMARK

(Map p78; ☑416-973-4000; www.harbourfront-centre.com; York Quay, 235 Queens Quay W; ⊙box office 1-6pm Tue-Sat, to 8pm show nights; ☐509, 510) The 4-hectare not-for-profit Harbourfront Centre exists to educate and entertain Toronto's diverse community, through a kaleidoscope of performamces and events held in its numerous stages and halls. Many are kid-focused, some are free. There's also a lakeside ice-skating rink where you can slice up the winter ice. Don't miss the free galleries,

TORONTO IN...

Two Days

Quick weekend? Take an elevator ride up the CN Tower – as high as Torontonians get without wings or drugs. Lunch at **St Lawrence Market** (p102), then head up to **Bloor-Yorkville** (p80) to window shop. Once inspired, max out your style-to-value ratio in **Kensington Market** (p83) followed by a thrifty dinner of dumplings in **Chinatown** (p103). Start early on day two and check out the amazing **Royal Ontario Museum** (p80), intriguing **Casa Loma** (p81) or the **Art Gallery of Ontario** (p79) – then take a long lunch in **Baldwin Village** (p103). Afterwards, ride the ferry to the **Toronto Islands** (p86) and bike until the sun sets. Back on the mainland, relax with a pint at the **Mill Street Brewery** (p110) in the atmospheric **Distillery District** (p73).

Four Days

Begin with a loop on a double-decker sightseeing tour (p90) to get your bearings, then explore **The Annex** (p81) and have dinner in **Little Italy** (p99). On day two, take our neighborhood **Walking Tour** (p91), or head east for brunch in **Leslieville** (p109) to up your energy for **The Beaches** (p85). Pick a **patio** (p111) for dinner and drinks before catching a show or hitting the dance floor in the **Entertainment District** (p75) or **Church-Wellesley Village** (p80).

Devote a whole day or two to explore the boutiques, bars and eateries along **Queen West, Trinity Bellwoods** and **West Queen West** (p82). Head to **High Park** (p87) for a picnic, or if you're more about hot-dogs-and-beer, catch some baseball at the **Rogers Centre** (p116), hockey at the **Air Canada Centre** (p117), or all three for half the price at **Wayne Gretzky's** (p110).

One Week

Go beyond the downtown core: explore **Scarborough Bluffs** (p88), the **Sharon Temple** (p89) or the **McMichael Canadian Art Collection** (p88). Take a day trip to **Niagara Falls** (p122) and **Niagara-on-the-Lake** (p132).

WHAT'S IN A MAYOR?

In 2013 a scandal made headlines around the world when Toronto's democratically elected mayor, Rob Ford, admitted smoking crack. A video, allegedly showing him in the act, brought on the confession. The ensuing global media circus did nothing for the beleaguered mayor, nor the city's reputation within and outside Canada. The latest revelations gave Mr Ford's opponents further reason to call for his resignation adding to their dissatisfaction over 'suburban politics' and a lack of, shall we say, charisma. At the time of writing, despite being stripped of most of his powers, Mr Ford has resisted all calls to step down.

What does all this mean for the people of Toronto? Opinions are mixed, but there's a general sense of mayoral malaise and embarrassment surrounding these events. Since coming to power in 2010, in an effort to cut the city's expenditure by $3 billion, Mr Ford removed a revenue-generating car tax, reversed a number of recently installed bike lanes, slashed the formerly well-established Transit City plan for the future of public transportation, privatized city garbage services and made substantial cuts to city beautification projects and park maintenance. The result has been happier suburban drivers, but dirtier downtown neighborhoods passively seething with frustrated commuters.

Mr Ford remains a polarizing figure, whose support from the the sizable 'Ford Nation' camp of constituents from outer-lying suburbs has not waned. The next time Torontonians go to the polls, they'll likely be paying much more attention to the democratic process. A resilient Mr Ford promises he'll be there in the race.

including the **Photo Passage** and the functioning **Craft Studio**.

Delicately strung along the western harborfront, the **Toronto Music Garden** was designed in collaboration with cellist Yo-Yo Ma. It expresses 'Bach's Suite No 1 for Unaccompanied Cello' through landscape, with an arc-shaped grove of conifers, a swirling path through a wildflower meadow and a grass-stepped amphitheater where free concerts are held.

Canada Square (Map p78) and **Ontario Square** (Map p78), two vast new public spaces, opened in June 2013. At the time of writing, construction works continued to improve access to the site and provide additional parking. Check the homepage for the latest details.

Power Plant Gallery GALLERY
(Map p78; ☑416-973-4949; www.thepowerplant. org; ☉10am-6pm Tue, Wed & Sun, to 8pm Thu-Sat) FREE Easily recognized by its painted smokestack, the Power Plant gallery is at the Harbourfront Centre and is just that – a former power plant transformed into Toronto's premier gallery of contemporary Canadian art. Best of all, it's free and exhibitions change regularly.

Steam Whistle Brewing BREWERY
(Map p78; www.steamwhistle.ca; 255 Bremner Blvd; 45min tour $10; ☉noon-6pm Mon-Thu, 11am-6pm Fri & Sat, to 5pm Sun; ⑤Union, ☐509, 510) ✐ 'Do

one thing really really well' is the motto of Steam Whistle Brewing, a microbrewery that makes only a crisp European-style pilsner. Bubbling away in a 1929 train depot, Steam Whistle continually works on being environmentally friendly, in part by using renewable energy, steam heating, all-natural (and often local) ingredients, and using supercool ginger ale bottles that can be reused up to 40 times. Tours depart half-hourly from 1pm to 5pm and include tastings.

Rogers Centre STADIUM
(Map p78; ☑416-341-2770; www.rogerscentre. com; 1 Blue Jays Way; 1hr tour adult/child $16/10; ⑤Union) Technically awe-inspiring, the Rogers Centre sports stadium opened in 1989 with the world's first fully retractable dome roof and seating for up to 55,000 people. Tours include a brain-scrambling video-wall screening footage of past sporting glories, concerts and events, a sprint through a box suite, a locker-room detour (sans athletes) and a memorabilia museum. A budget seat at a Blue Jays baseball or Argonauts football game is the cheapest way to see the center.

Fort York National Historic Site HISTORIC SITE
(☑416-392-6907; www.fortyork.ca; 250 Fort York Blvd; adult/child $9/4.25; ☉10am-5pm; ☐509, 511) Established by the British in 1793 to defend the then town of York, Fort York was almost entirely destroyed during the War of 1812 when a small band of Ojibwe warriors

and British troops were unable to defeat their US attackers. A handful of the original log, stone and brick buildings have been restored. The fort is open year-round; check the homepage for special events and tour details. From May to September, men decked out in 19th-century British military uniforms carry out marches and drills, firing musket volleys into the sky.

Spadina Quay Wetlands   PARK
(Map p78; ☑416-392-1111; www.toronto.ca/harbourfront/spadina_quay_wet.htm; 479 Queens Quay W; ⊙dawn-dusk; ᵫ509, 510) A former lakeside parking lot has been transformed into the 2800-sq-meter Spadina Quay Wetlands, a thriving, sustainable ecosystem full of frogs, birds, fish and butterflies. When lakeside fishers noticed that northern pike were spawning here each spring, the city took it upon itself to create this new habitat. Complete with flowering heath plants, poplar trees and a birdhouse, it's a little gem leading the way in Harbourfront redevelopment.

Ripley's Aquarium of Canada   AQUARIUM
(Map p78; ☑416-360-7831; www.ripleysaquariumof canada.com; 288 Bremner Blvd; adult/child $30/20; ⊙9am-9pm daily, to 6pm Sun-Thu Jan-Jun) Ripley's Aquarium of Canada is earmarked to be Toronto's hottest new attraction for young and old. Expect over 15,000 aquatic animals, 5.7 million litres of water in the combined tanks, as well as sleepovers, touch tanks and educational dive presentations.

Exhibition Place   LANDMARK
(☑416-263-3600; www.explace.on.ca; off Lake Shore Blvd W, btwn Strachan Ave & Dufferin St; ᵫ509, 511) Every August, historic Exhibition Place is revived for its original purpose, the Canadian National Exhibition, when millions of visitors flood the midway for carnival rides, lumberjack competitions and more good, honest, homegrown fun than a Sunday-school picnic. The beaux-arts *Victory* statue over Princes' Gate has stood proud since Canada's 60th birthday in 1927. Other events held at Exhibition Place include the Honda Indy Toronto in July and a slew of spectator sports and indie design shows. At other times the grounds are often spookily bereft of visitors.

⊙ Financial District

Union Station is Canada's busiest transport hub, serving 250,000 passengers daily. Currently under extensive revitalization until its estimated completion in 2016, the station,

subway area and surrounding streetscape are a mess. We hope to have better things to say by next edition. The area just north of the station on King and Adelaide and west to Bay St equates to Toronto's 'Wall St' – the nicest of the skyscrapers are here, where the 'Bay St Boys' do their darndest to convince themselves this is actually New York.

Hockey Hall of Fame   MUSEUM
(Map p78; ☑416-360-7765; www.hhof.com; Brookfield Pl, 30 Yonge St; adult/child $17.50/11; ⊙9:30am-6pm; ⓢUnion) Inside an ornate rococo gray stone Bank of Montréal building (c 1885), the Hockey Hall of Fame is a Canadian institution. Even those unfamiliar with the superfast ultraviolent sport are likely to be impressed by this, the largest collection of hockey memorabilia in the world. Check out the collection of *Texas Chainsaw Massacre*–esque goalkeeping masks or go head to head with the great Wayne Gretzky, virtual-reality style.

Cloud Gardens Conservatory   GARDENS
(Map p74; ☑416-392-7288; 14 Temperance St; ⊙10am-2:30pm Mon-Fri; ⓢQueen) ᴳᴿᴱᴱ An unexpected sanctuary with its own waterfall, the steamy Cloud Gardens Conservatory is crowded with enormous jungle leaves, vines and palms. Information plaques answer the question 'What Are Rainforests?.' It's a great place to warm up during winter, but avoid the area after dark – the adjacent park attracts some shady characters.

TD Gallery of Inuit Art   MUSEUM
(Map p78; ☑416-982-8473; www.td.com/inuitart/gallery/inuit-gallery; ground fl & mezzanine, TD Centre, 79 Wellington St W; ⊙8am-6pm Mon-Fri, 10am-4pm Sat & Sun; ⓢSt Andrew) ᴳᴿᴱᴱ A quiet pause in the bustle of the Financial District, the Toronto Dominion Gallery of Inuit Art provides an exceptional insight into Inuit culture. Inside the Toronto-Dominion Centre, a succession of glass cases displays otter, bear, eagles and carved Inuit figures in day-to-day scenes.

Design Exchange   MUSEUM
(DX; Map p78; ☑416-363-6121; www.dx.org; 234 Bay St; adult/child $10/8, special exhibition prices vary; ⊙10am-6pm Sun-Wed, to 9pm Thu-Sat) The original Toronto Stock Exchange now houses eye-catching industrial-design exhibits. The permanent collection includes more than 1000 Canadian pieces that span six decades. The 30-minute tours ($15) should be booked in advance.

TORONTO FOR CHILDREN

Toronto is a kid-friendly city: there's plenty of things to see and do when traveling with little ones in tow.

The Harbourfront Centre (p70) produces ongoing events through HarbourKIDS. The Canadian National Exhibition (p93) also has events in August.

Inquisitive minds will love the CN Tower (p70), Ontario Science Centre (p88), Royal Ontario Museum (p80) and LEGOLAND Discovery Centre (p88).

Arty and creative kids might enjoy the clay classes at the Gardiner Museum of Ceramic Art (p81), or they might like to drop in for storytime at the **Toronto Public Library – Lillian H Smith Branch** (Map p74; ☑ 416-393-7746; www.torontopubliclibrary. ca; 239 College St; ☉ 9am-8:30pm Mon-Thu, to 6pm Fri, to 5pm Sat, 1:30-5pm Sun; ☒ 506, 510) or catch a show at the **Lorraine Kimsa Theatre for Young People** (Map p78; ☑ 416-862-2222; www.lktyp.ca, 165 Front St E; ☉ box office 9am-5pm; ☒ 503, 504).

The environmental custodians and animal doctors of the next generation will want you to take them to Ripley's Aquarium, Riverdale Farm (p83), High Park (p87), Spadina Quay Wetlands and Tommy Thompson Park (p83).

If they've got ants in their pants, they won't have after a trip to Canada's Wonderland (p88) or, for a way tamer version, the Centreville Amusement Park (p86). Teenagers will also enjoy the Eaton Centre (p117) and Kensington Market (p83).

Roomier digs for families that shouldn't break the bank are at the Eaton Chelsea (p97), with its massive waterslide; Courtyard Toronto Downtown (p98); the Grand Hotel and Suites (p97); and Cambridge Suites (p97).

A handy online resource for parents is www.helpwevegotkids.com, which lists everything child-related in Toronto, including babysitters and day-care options.

◎ Old York

Historically speaking, the old town of York comprises just 10 square blocks. But today the neighborhood extends east of Yonge St all the way to the Don River, and from Queen St south to the waterfront esplanade. The ghosts of Toronto's past are around every corner.

★ Distillery District   LANDMARK

(Map p69; ☑ 416-364-1177; www.thedistillerydistrict.com; 9 Trinity St; ☉ 10am-7pm Mon-Wed, to 8pm Thu-Sat, 11am-5pm Sun; ☒ 503, 504) Centered around the 1832 Gooderham and Worts distillery – once the British Empire's largest – the 5-hectare Distillery District is one of Toronto's best downtown attractions. Its Victorian industrial warehouses have been converted into soaring galleries, artists studios, design boutiques, cafes and eateries. The Young Centre for Performing Arts and the Mill Street Brewery are also here.

On weekends, newlyweds pose before a backdrop of redbrick and cobblestone, young families walk their dogs, and savvy hipsters shop for art beneath charmingly decrepit gables and gantries. In summer expect live jazz, activities, exhibitions and foodie events.

★ St Lawrence Market   MARKET

(Map p78; ☑ 416-392-7129; www.stlawrencemarket.com; 92-95 Front St E; ☉ 8am-6pm Tue-Thu, to 7pm Fri, 5am-5pm Sat; ☒ 503, 504) Old York's sensational St Lawrence Market has been a neighborhood meeting place for over two centuries. The restored, high-trussed 1845 **South Market** houses more than 50 specialty food stalls: cheese vendors, fishmongers, butchers, bakers and pasta makers. Inside the old council chambers upstairs, the **Market Gallery** (Map p78; ☑ 416-392-0572; www.toronto.ca/culture/the_market_gallery; ☉ 10am-4pm Tue-Fri, 9am-4pm Sat) FREE has rotating displays of paintings, photographs, documents and historical relics.

On the opposite side of Front St, the **North Market** hosts a Saturday farmers market and a fantastic Sunday antique market – get in early for the best stuff. In 2010 the winners of a design competition to transform the North Market building were announced, but there's no sign of construction yet. A few steps further north, the glorious St Lawrence Hall (1849) is topped by a mansard roof and a copper-clad clock tower that can be seen for blocks.

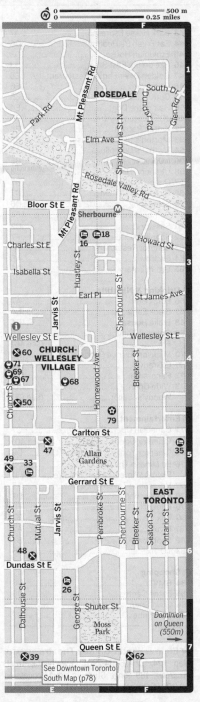

◉ Entertainment District & King Street West

West of the Financial District, on King St, between University and Spadina Aves, Toronto's Entertainment District is home to theaters and performance halls, pre-show bars and the acclaimed Toronto International Film Festival Bell Lightbox Theatre. The whole area as far west as Spadina is nightclub central. East on King, toward the Distillery District, you'll find high-end furniture and design stores, good for window-shopping, and some fine historic architecture.

★ 401 Richmond   GALLERY

(Map p74; www.401richmond.net; 401 Richmond St W; ⊙9am-7pm Mon-Fri, to 6pm Sat; 🚋510) FREE Inside an early-20th-century lithographer's warehouse, restored in 1994, this 18,500-sq-m New York–style artist collective hums with the creative vibes of 130 diverse contemporary galleries showcasing works in almost any artistic medium you can think of. Grab a snack and a latte at the ground-floor cafe and enjoy it on the expansive roof garden: a little-known oasis in the summer.

Canadian Broadcasting Centre   MUSEUM

(CBC; Map p78; 🕿416-205-5574; www.cbc.ca/museum; 250 Front St W; ⊙9am-5pm Mon-Fri; ⓈUnion, 🚋504) FREE Toronto's enormous Canadian Broadcasting Centre is the headquarters for English-language radio and TV across Canada. You can peek at the radio newsrooms anytime or attend a concert in the world-class Glenn Gould Studio. Be sure to check out the **CBC Museum** with its fantastic collection of antique microphones and broadcasting memorabilia. Next door, the **Graham Spry Theatre** screens ever-changing CBC programming. Best of all, it's free!

◉ Downtown Yonge

Heading north on Yonge St, Yonge & Dundas Sq, Toronto's homage to New York's Times Square, is regarded as the center of the downtown core. It's an oddly positioned public space that neither looks good nor really delivers. There's usually something going on here, but it's as frequently about commercial exploits as community-building. Across the street, the landmark Eaton Centre mall, which sprawls between Dundas and Queen Sts, is the primary draw along with some historic theaters and Ryerson University. The mixed-bag continues

Downtown Toronto North

north on Yonge, skirting past the colorful Church and Wellesley gay village, into chichi Yorkville at the intersection with Bloor St.

★ **Elgin & Winter Garden Theatre** THEATER
(Map p74; ☎416-314-2901; www.heritagetrust.
on.ca/ewg; 189 Yonge St; tours adult/concession
$12/10; ⑤Queen) A restored masterpiece,

the Elgin & Winter Garden Theatre is the world's last operating double-decker theater. Celebrating its centennial in 2013, the Winter Garden was built as the flagship for a vaudeville chain that never really took off, while the downstairs Elgin was converted into a movie house in the 1920s. Fascinating tours run Thursdays at 5pm and Saturdays at 11am.

Saved from demolition in 1981, the theaters received a $29-million-facelift: bread dough was used to uncover original rose-garden frescoes, the Belgian company that made the original carpet was contacted for fresh rugs, and the floral Winter Garden ceiling was replaced, leaf by painstaking leaf.

City Hall
HISTORIC BUILDING

(Map p74; ☎416-392-2489, 311; www.toronto.ca; 100 Queen St W; ⊗8:30am-4:30pm Mon-Fri; Ⓢ Queen) **FREE** Much-maligned City Hall was Toronto's bold leap of faith into architectural modernity. Its twin clamshell towers, central 'flying saucer,' ramps and mosaics were completed in 1965 to Finnish architect Viljo Revell's award-winning design. An irritable Frank Lloyd Wright called it a 'headmarker for a grave'; in a macabre twist, Revell died before construction was finished. Collect a self-guided tour pamphlet at the info desk.

Out front is **Nathan Phillips Square**, a meeting place for skaters, demonstrators and office workers on their lunch breaks. Extensively redeveloped in 2013, the new green roof is at last impressive! In summer look for the Fresh Wednesdays farmers market, free concerts and special events. The fountain pool becomes a fun-filled ice-skating rink in winter.

Old City Hall
HISTORIC BUILDING

(Map p74; ☎416-327-5614; www.toronto.ca/old_city-hall; 60 Queen St W; ⊗8:30am-4:30pm Mon-Fri) **FREE** Across Bay St is the 1899 definitive work of Toronto architect EJ Lennox. Now housing legal courtrooms, the hall has an off-center bell tower, interesting murals and grimacing gargoyles.

Church of the Holy Trinity
CHURCH

(Map p74; ☎416-598-4521; www.holytrinitytoronto.org; 10 Trinity Sq; ⊗11am-3pm Mon-Fri, 10am-2pm Sat, 8am-4pm Sun, services 12:15pm Wed, 10:30am & 2pm Sun; Ⓢ Dundas) Tucked away behind the west side of the gargantuan Eaton Centre is the oasislike Trinity Sq, named after the welcoming Anglican Church of the Holy Trinity. When it opened in 1847, it was the first church in Toronto not to charge parishioners for pews. Today it's a cross between a house

of worship, a small concert venue and a community drop-in center – everything a downtown church should be!

Of particular note, the labyrinth outside the church is of similar design to the one found in Chartres cathedral in France. Of ancient origins, a labyrinth is a constrained unicursal pattern with a single winding pathway to its central rosette, regarded as a place for prayer and reflection. Its length is deceptive – it takes about 20 minutes to walk in and back out, in silence – a kind of ambulatory meditation in the middle of the hustle and bustle of the city.

Textile Museum of Canada
MUSEUM

(Map p74; ☎416-599-5321; www.textilemuseum.ca; 55 Centre Ave; adult/concession $15/6, admission free 5-8pm Wed; ⊗11am-5pm Thu-Tue, to 8pm Wed, tours 2pm Sun; Ⓢ St Patrick) Obscurely located at the bottom of a condo tower, this museum has exhibits drawing on a permanent collection of 10,000 items from Latin America, Africa, Europe, Southeast Asia and India, as well as contemporary Canada. Workshops teach batik making, weaving, knitting and all manner of needle-stuff.

◉ Chinatown & Baldwin Village

Toronto's grotty Chinatown occupies a chunk of downtown from University Ave to Spadina Ave between College and Queen Sts; a vermilion twin dragon gate marks the

Downtown Toronto South

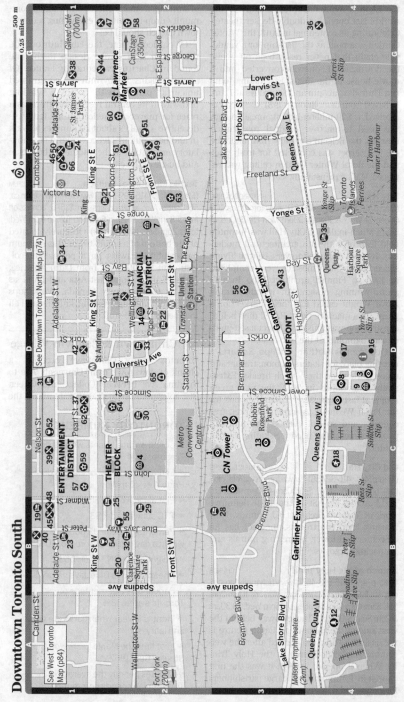

500 m
0.25 miles

See West Toronto
Map (p84)

ENTERTAINMENT
DISTRICT

THEATER
BLOCK

See Downtown Toronto North Map (p74)

FINANCIAL
DISTRICT

Metro
Convention
Centre

CN Tower

Bobbie
Rosenfeld
Park

HARBOURFRONT

St Lawrence
Market

Lower
Jarvis St

Harbour
Square
Park

Toronto
Islands
Ferries

Toronto
Inner Harbour

Downtown Toronto South

epicenter. Between Beverley and McCaul Sts, on Baldwin St, leafy Baldwin Village is a pretty strip of cheap eats and good vibes tucked away from the madding crowds. The village has Jewish roots, but today's bohemian air stems from counterculture US exiles who decamped here during the Vietnam War.

Art Gallery of Ontario GALLERY
(AGO; Map p74; ☑877-225-4246, 416-979-6648; www.ago.net; 317 Dundas St W; adult/concession $19.50/11, admission free 6-8:30pm Wed; ☉10am-5:30pm Tue & Thu-Sun, to 8:30pm Wed; ☐505) The AGO houses art collections both excellent and extensive (bring your stamina). Renovations of the facade, designed by the great Frank Gehry and completed in 2008, fail to impress at street level: perhaps because of a drab downtown location. Fortunately, everything changes once you step inside. Highlights of the permanent collection include rare Québecois religious statuary, First Nations and Inuit carvings, stunningly presented works by Canadian greats the Group of Seven (p172), the Henry Moore

ONTARIO TORONTO

sculpture pavilion and a restored Georgian house, The Grange.

There's a surcharge for special exhibits but visits to the permanent collection on Wednesday evenings are free. Half-hour mini-tours leave from Walker Court daily at 11:30am and 2:30pm and on Wednesday evenings at 7 pm.

⊙ Church-Wellesley Village

North of Yonge & Dundas Sq along Yonge St, toward College St and Bloor St, you'll find Ryerson University and a smattering of cheap eats, sex shops and strip clubs, straight and gay. Toronto's gay village, known as 'Church & Wellesley' or 'the Village,' starts on the corner of Church and College and is centered a few blocks north on the intersection of Church and Wellesley Sts. Every summer, around the Canada Day long weekend, over a million shiny happy people descend on the streets for Toronto's massive Pride Parade and Festival, a celebration of sexuality, diversity and freedom.

Former Maple Leaf Gardens LANDMARK
(Mattamy Athletic Centre and Loblaws; Map p74; ☑ 416-598-5966; www.mattamyathleticcentre. ca; 50-60 Carlton St; ⑤ College) This hallowed hockey arena was built in an astounding five months during the Great Depression, and was home to the Toronto Maple Leafs for over 50 years until they relocated to the Air Canada Centre in 1999. In its heyday, Elvis, Sinatra and the Beatles all belted out tunes here.

After a monumental redevelopment project, the facility is now home to Ryerson University's Athletic Centre and the must-see flagship megastore of the Loblaw's grocery chain, with its killer Patisserie and Wall of Cheese.

⊙ Bloor-Yorkville

Once Toronto's version of New York's Greenwich Village or San Francisco's Haight-Ashbury, this formerly counter-cultural leopard has changed its spots to become the downtown home of Toronto's rich, famous, glam and fabulous. Yorkville's main drag is the stretch of Bloor St W to Avenue Rd, otherwise known as the Mink Mile: where to go if high-end brand label shopping is your thing. The Holt Renfrew department store is here, along with Gucci, Prada, D&G and Louis Vuitton. There are some lovely boutiques and cafes in the streets north of Bloor to Davenport Rd and east of Avenue Rd. Hollywood celebrities are frequently spotted in Yorkville bars when TIFF is in town.

★Royal Ontario Museum MUSEUM
(ROM; Map p74; ☑ 416-586-8000; www.rom.on.ca; 100 Queen's Park; adult/child $15/12, special exhibit surcharges apply; ⊙10am-5:30pm Sat-Thu, to 8:30pm Fri; ⑤ Museum) Celebrating its centennial in 2014, the multidisciplinary ROM is Canada's biggest natural-history museum and one of the largest museums in North America. You'll either love or loathe the synergy between the original heritage buildings at the main entrance on Bloor St and the 2007 addition of 'the Crystal,' which appears to pierce the original structure and juts out into the street like a massive shard.

Inside, the permanent collection features over six million specimens and artifacts, divided between two main galleries: the Natural History Galleries (all on the 2nd floor) and the World Culture Galleries (on floors 1, 3 and 4). The Chinese temple sculptures, Gallery of Korean Art and costumes and textile collections are some of the best in the world. Kids rush to the dinosaur rooms, Egyptian mummies and Jamaican bat-cave replica. The cedar crest poles carved by First Nations tribes in British Columbia are wonderful. Each year, the ROM hosts a variety of big temporary exhibits from around the world. The on-site Institute of Contemporary Culture explores current issues through art, architecture, lectures and moving image. There are free museum tours daily. Keep an eye out for the Friday Night Live programs in spring and fall when the museum opens its doors, stocks its bars and calls in the DJs for a makeshift disco. Check the website for updates about ROM's centennial celebrations.

Bata Shoe Museum MUSEUM
(Map p74; ☑ 416-979-7799; www.batashoemuseum.ca; 327 Bloor St W; adult/child $14/5, admission free 5-8pm Thu; ⊙10am-5pm Tue, Wed, Fri & Sat, to 8pm Thu, noon-5pm Sun; ⑤ St George) It's important in life to be well shod, a stance the Bata Shoe Museum takes seriously. Impressively designed by architect Raymond Moriyama to resemble a stylized shoebox, the museum displays 10,000 'pedi-artifacts' from around the globe. Peruse 19th-century French chestnut-crushing clogs, Canadian aboriginal polar boots or famous modern pairs worn by Elton John, Indira Gandhi

and Pablo Picasso. Come along for something truly different!

Gardiner Museum of Ceramic Art MUSEUM
(Map p74; ☑416-586-8080; www.gardinermuseum.on.ca; 111 Queen's Park; adult/child $12/free, 4-9pm Fri half-price, 4-9pm 3rd Fri of month Fri free; ☉10am-6pm Mon-Thu, to 9pm Fri, to 5pm Sat & Sun; ⓢMuseum) Opposite the Royal Ontario Museum, the Gardiner Museum of Ceramic Art was founded by philanthropists. Spread over three floors, collections cover several millennia; various rooms focus on 17th- and 18th-century English tavern ware, Italian Renaissance majolica, ancient American earthenware and blue-and-white Chinese porcelain. There are free guided tours daily at 2pm.

University of Toronto & The Annex

Founded in 1827, the prestigious University of Toronto (U of T) is Canada's largest, with close to 80,000 students and 18,000 employees. Feel free to stroll through the central St George campus to admire its collection of stately Victorian and Romanesque buildings. West and north of U of T lies The Annex, Toronto's largest downtown residential neighborhood, favored by students and academics. The number of pubs, organic grocery stores, world eats and spiritual venues comes as no surprise. Some of Toronto's most satisfying architecture is here.

★**Casa Loma** HISTORIC BUILDING
(Map p69; ☑416-923-1171; www.casaloma.org; 1 Austin Tce; adult/child $18/10; ☉9:30am 5pm, last entry 4pm; ⓠ127, stop Davenport & Spadina, ⓢDupont) Toronto's only castle may have never housed royalty, but it certainly has grandeur, lording over The Annex on a cliff that was once the shoreline of the glacial Lake Iroquois, from which Lake Ontario derived. Climb the 27m **Baldwin Steps** up the slope from Spadina Ave, north of Davenport Rd.

The 98-room mansion – an architectural orgasm of castellations, chimneys, flagpoles, turrets and Rapunzel balconies – was built between 1911 and 1914 for Sir Henry Pellat,

GAY & LESBIAN TORONTO

To say Toronto is GLBT-friendly is an understatement. That it embraces diversity more fully than most other centers of its size, is closer to the mark. In 2003 Toronto became the first city in North America to legalize same-sex marriage. Just over a year later, an Ontario Court also recognized the first legal same-sex divorce, as if to remind us that marriage can be hard work, whatever your orientation!

Toronto's LGBT (yup, the acronym swings both ways!) Pride Festival is one of the largest in the world. On Parade day, the streets around Church and Wellesley swell with over a million happy homosexuals and their friends and families. If Pride is your bag, be sure to book accommodations well in advance as beds fill fast...literally. At other times of the year, the Church St strip of the Village draws everyone from biker bears and lipstick lesbians to its modest smattering of sunny patios, pubs, cafes and restaurants for much promenading and people-watching. After dark it's all about the dancing: whether cabaret or drag, thumping top-40 and R&B or queer alterna-punk, late-night revelers spill on to the streets, especially on weekends.

Other gay-friendly neighborhoods include The Annex, Kensington, Queen West and Cabbagetown. Gay nightlife venues are abundant and although men's bars and clubs vastly outnumber lesbian venues, Toronto is also home to drag kings, women-only bathhouse nights and lesbian reading series.

Toronto is a great place to be gay or to explore your sexuality. Look for the *Xtra!* weekly free press – you'll find it everywhere in the Village. There are also plenty of fantastic free community resources and support groups available:

519 Community Centre (Church St Community Centre; Map p74; ☑416-392-6874; www.the519.org; 519 Church St; ☉9am-10pm Mon-Sat, 10am-5pm Sun; ⓢWellesley)

Canadian Lesbian & Gay Archives (Map p74; ☑416-777-2755; www.clga.ca; 34 Isabella St; ☉7:30-10pm Tue-Thu, 11am-2pm Fri; ⓢWellesley)

Hassle-Free Clinic (p118)

Queer West (www.queerwest.org)

a wealthy financier who made bags of cash from his contract to provide Toronto with electricity. He later lost everything in land speculation, the resultant foreclosure forcing Hank and his wife to downsize. A variety of themed guided tours are available. If you're in Toronto around Christmas, a visit is a must. Check the website for details.

★ Spadina Museum   MUSEUM
(📞 416-392-6910; www.toronto.ca/culture/spadina; 285 Spadina Rd; tours adult/child $8/5, grounds admission free; ☺ noon-4pm Tue-Sun; S Dupont) Atop the Baldwin Steps, this gracious home and its Victorian-Edwardian gardens were built in 1866 as a country estate for financier James Austin and his family. Donated to the city in 1978, it became a museum in 1984 and was recently painstakingly transformed to evoke the heady age of the roaring 1920s and '30s: highly recommended.

Provincial Legislature   HISTORIC BUILDING
(Map p74; www.ontla.on.ca; Queen's Park; ☺ tours every hour 9:30am-5:30pm Mon-Fri; S Queen's Park) FREE The seat of Ontario's Provincial Legislature resides in a fabulously ornate 1893 sandstone building, north of College St in Queen's Park. For some homegrown entertainment, head for the visitors gallery when the adversarial legislative assembly is in session (Monday, Tuesday and Thursday March to June and September to December). Viewing is free, but security regulations are in full force. Free 30-minute tours depart from the information desk.

Wychwood Park   PARK
(cnr Davenport Rd & Bathurst St; S Dupont) Formerly a gated artists colony, Wychwood Park, established in the late 19th century, showcases some of Toronto's most beautiful and fascinating heritage architecture. It's a great place for a stroll. Note that Wychwood is an actual residential community where people go about their daily lives: please be respectful.

Native Canadian
Centre of Toronto   CULTURAL BUILDING
(Map p84; 📞 416-964-9087; www.ncct.on.ca; 16 Spadina Rd; ☺ 9am-8pm Mon-Thu, to 6pm Fri, 10am-4pm Sat; S Spadina) This community center hosts Thursday-night drum socials, seasonal powwows and elders' cultural events that promote harmony and conversation between tribal members and non–First Nations peoples. You can also sign up for workshops and craft classes, such as beading and dancing.

◉ Queen West & Trinity Bellwoods

Although Queen West isn't home to any significant attractions, a trip to Toronto's best-known 'hood is a must. Any self-respecting 20-to-40-something with an interest in popular culture will want to make this hip strip their first port of call.

To do Queen St justice, make a day of it: start at the corner of Yonge St and head west, although nothing really happens until the Osgoode subway station at the intersection of Queen St W and University Ave. The Queen West district begins here and continues for about 1.5km to Bathurst St. The first few blocks over to Spadina are a wonderful mix of mainstream retailers, bars and an eclectic bunch of boutiques, but it's really from Spadina to Bathurst where the wild things are. Infinitely more grungy, here you'll find all manner of cheap and delicious eats slotted between fabric, furniture, art and music stores. There's plenty of cafes and bars in which to glean inspiration and lose track of time.

West of Bathurst, past Trinity Bellwoods Park, for about 2km over to Dufferin St, is known as West Queen West. The first bit between Bathurst and happening Ossington Ave, south of Bloor, all the way down to Queen, is one of our favorite strips for food, drink and people-watching. This is the Trinity Bellwoods neighborhood – *the* place to live if you're a hipster, designhead, scenester or nonmainstream gay. (Yes, Toronto's neighbornoods can be this transparent...) The proliferation of excellent food and beverage joints on and around Ossington arose when high rents pushed many businesses further west. What emerged is a revitalised strip of Queen St, infinitely more trendy than the original.

Streetcars run the length of Queen St W, before it becomes the Queensway: nice to know if your feet get tired or you're loaded up with too many bags after a hard day hipsterising your wardrobe – it's a long walk back downtown.

Museum of Contemporary
Canadian Art   MUSEUM
(MOCCA; Map p84; 📞 416-395-0067; www.mocca. ca; 952 Queen St W; admission by donation; ☺ 11am-6pm Tue-Sun; 🚋 501) At Queen and Ossington,

in the heart of West Queen West's design and arts precinct, MOCCA's mandate is to exhibit innovative works by Canadian and international artists that address themes of contemporary relevance. The permanent collection is not presently on display, but temporary exhibits – promoting emerging artists from Nova Scotia to British Columbia and beyond – are changed every six to eight weeks.

◉ East End

The area east of Parliament St to the Don River was settled by Irish immigrants fleeing the potato famine of 1841. Because the area's sandy soil proved cabbage-conducive, it became known as Cabbagetown. Predominantly residential and officially designated a Heritage Conservation District, it has one of the largest concentrations of domestic Victorian architecture in North America, making for a pleasant stroll. It's nice to walk across Riverdale Park, north on Broadview Ave, then east on Danforth Ave where you'll find yourself in Greektown/The Danforth. Further east on Gerrard St E you'll come to Little India. Both are heavenly haunts for the food-focused. Dropping south to Queen St E, discover Leslieville. Favored by armies of young cashed-up moms, it's Toronto's antithesis to Queen W: chichi, sanitised and a lovely spot for a fancy brunch. Since 2005, when the *New York Times* pronounced the then up-and-coming Leslieville as Toronto's

'it' neighborhood, real estate prices and interest in the area have soared.

Tommy Thompson Park   PARK
(Map p69; ☏ 416-661-6600; www.tommythompsonpark.ca; Leslie St, off Lake Shore Blvd E; ⊘9am-6pm Sat & Sun; ☒83 Jones S, ☒501) A 5km-long artificial peninsula between the Harbourfront and The Beaches, Tommy Thompson Park reaches further into Lake Ontario than the Toronto Islands. This 'accidental wilderness' – constructed from Outer Harbour dredgings and fill from downtown building sites – has become a phenomenal wildlife success. It's one of the world's largest nesting places for ring-billed gulls, and is a haven for terns, black-crowned night herons, turtles, owls, foxes and even coyotes.

Open to the public on weekends and holidays; cars and pets are prohibited. Summer schedules offer interpretive programs and guided walks, usually with an ecological theme. At the end of the park there's a lighthouse and great city views. To get here, take any streetcar along Queen St E to Leslie St, then walk 800m south to the gates, or follow the Martin Goodman Trail.

★ Riverdale Farm   MUSEUM
(Map p69; ☏ 416-392-6794; www.toronto.ca/parks/featured-parks/riverdale-farm; 201 Winchester St; ⊘9am-5pm; ☒506) FREE On the former site of the Riverdale Zoo, where from 1888 to 1974 prairie wolves howled at night and spooked the Cabbagetown kids, Riverdale

---

KENSINGTON MARKET & LITTLE ITALY

Tattered around the edges, elegantly wasted Kensington Market is multicultural Toronto at its most authentic. It's not a constrained market as much as a working residential neighborhood. Eating here is a cheap and cheery trip around the flavors and aromas of the world. Shopping too is a blast, with the biggest and best proliferation of vintage and secondhand clothing, books and bric-a-brac in the city. You'll find dreadlocked urban hippies, tattooed punks, potheads and dealers, bikers, goths, musos, artists and anarchists, generally behaving well and getting along fine. Hooch and Hendrix tinge the air. On weekends, it can feel like a small festival, especially on Pedestrian Sundays, when bi-peds rule. It's more chilled on weekdays, when that extra personal space makes it easier to browse.

To get here, take the College streetcar to Spadina Ave or Augusta Ave and follow the activity. Augusta Ave between College and Dundas is the main strip, but the little stretch of Nassau St between Augusta and Bellevue has some wonderful cafes and can be a welcome oasis from the crowds.

Further along College St, Little Italy is what you expect – a tasty slice of the homeland. There's a long-established strip of outdoor cafes, bars and stylish restaurants that frequently change hands – affluent clientele are notoriously fickle. The further west you go on College, the more traditional things become, with aromatic bakeries, sidewalk gelaterias and rootsy ristoranti.

West Toronto

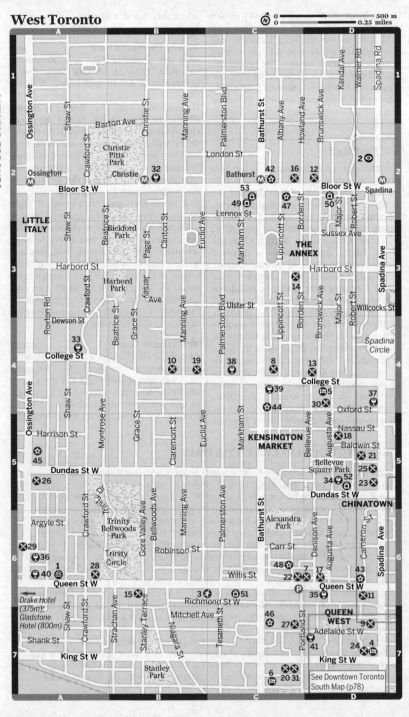

N
0   500 m
0   0.25 miles

LITTLE ITALY

THE ANNEX

KENSINGTON MARKET

CHINATOWN

QUEEN WEST

Drake Hotel (375m); Gladstone Hotel (800m)

See Downtown Toronto South Map (p78)

West Toronto

Farm is a rural oasis in the downtown. Now a working-farm museum, it has two barns, a summer wading pool and pens of feathered and furry friends. Kids follow the farmer around as he does his daily chores, including milking the cows at 10:30am. There's a farmers market on Tuesdays (3pm to 7pm May to October).

◉ The Beaches

To residents, The Beaches has become a wealthy, professional neighborhood by the lake. To everyone else, it means the neighborhood, the beaches themselves and the parklands along Lake Ontario. Of all the beaches, **Kew Beach** (Map p69; ☎416-392-8186; www.toronto.ca/parks/beaches/beaches; ☉dawn-dusk; 🚌501) is the most popular; its boardwalk runs east to **Balmy Beach** and west to **Woodbine Beach**.

Adjacent **Kew Gardens** (Map p69) has rest rooms, snack bars, a skating rink, lawn bowls and tennis courts; at the western end there's an Olympic-sized public swimming pool. For cyclists and in-line skaters, the **Martin Goodman Trail** leads past Ashbridge's Bay Park. Off Queen St E, the sunken **Ivan Forrest Gardens** leads to Glen Stewart Ravine, a wilder patch of green running north to Kingston Rd.

RC Harris Filtration Plant   LANDMARK
(☎416-392-2934; www.toronto.ca; 2701 Queen St E; 🚌501) Commanding heavenly views of the lakefront on a priceless slab of real estate, the elegantly proportioned RC Harris Filtration Plant is an art-deco masterpiece that has appeared in countless movies and TV shows. Originally disparagingly dubbed the 'Palace of Purification,' due to hefty construction costs during the Great Depression, the fully operational plant is rarely open to

OFFBEAT TORONTO

→ **Cineforum** (Map p84; ☑ 416-603-6643; www.cineforum.ca; 463 Bathurst St; over/under 24yr $20/10; ⊙ screenings 7pm & 9pm Sat-Thu; ☒ 506, 511) Eccentric Toronto character Reg Hartt wraps posters around telephone poles advertising his 20-seat home cinema playing avant-garde films. Come prepared for idiosyncratic lectures like 'What I Learned from LSD,' sometimes delivered during the film. Expect the unexpected.

→ **Theatre Passe Muraille** (Theater Beyond Walls; Map p84; ☑ 416-504-7529; www. passemuraille.on.ca; 16 Ryerson Ave; tickets $20-35, previews $16; ⊙ shows 7:30pm Tue-Sat, matinees 2pm Sat; ☒ 501) Since the 1960s, this alternative theater in the old Nasmith's Bakery & Stables has focused on radical plays with contemporary Canadian themes. Saturday matinees are 'Pay What You Can.'

→ **Beguiling** (Map p84; ☑ 416-533-9168; www.beguilingbooksandart.com; 601 Markham St; ⊙ 11am-7pm Mon-Thu & Sat, to 9pm Wed & Fri, noon-6pm Sun; ⑤ Bathurst) Need a comic-book fix? This is the kind of crowded, mixed-up joint that Robert Crumb would drop by; in fact, he once did. Be mesmerized by original 'zines, indie comics, pop-culture books, limited-edition artworks and posters.

→ **New Tribe** (Map p74; ☑ 416-977-2786; www.newtribe.ca; 2nd fl, 232 Queen St W; minimum for tattooing $80; ⊙ 11am-8pm Mon-Thu, to 10pm Fri & Sat, noon-6pm Sun; ☒ 501) Body art in Toronto is *almost* mainstream: you'd run out of body parts before running out of tattoo and piercing shops. This one, in the heart of Queen St W, is one of our favorites.

→ **Come as You Are** (Map p84; ☑ 416-504-7934; www.comeasyouare.com; 493 Queen St W; ⊙ 11am-7pm Mon-Wed, to 8pm Thu & Sat, to 9pm Fri, noon-5pm Sat; ☒ 501) Catering to all genders and orientations, Canada's pioneering co-op sex shop sells it all. Sign up for a workshop on erotic photography or Bondage 101!

the public, but makes a great photographic subject.

◉ Toronto Islands

Once upon a time there were no Toronto Islands, just an immense sandbar stretching 9km into the lake. On April 13, 1858, a hurricane blasted through the sandbar and created the gap now known as the Eastern Channel. Toronto's jewel-like islands were born – nearly two-dozen isles covering 240 hectares and home to close-knit, 800-strong communities on **Algonquin Island** and **Ward's Island**. The islands are only accessible by ferry (15 minutes, adult/child $7/3.50). To get to the ferry docks from Union Station, take the 509 Harbourfront or the 510 Spadina streetcar south to the Bay and Queens Quay stop.

Centreville Amusement Park AMUSEMENT PARK (☑ 416-203-0405; www.centreisland.ca; all-day ride pass adult/child/family $37/25.95/111.80, grounds admission free; ⊙ 10:30am-8pm May-Sep; ☒ Centre Island) From Centre Island ferry terminal, wander past the information booth to quaint Centreville's antique carousel, goofy golf course, miniature train and sky gondola. **Far Enough Farm** zoo presents kids with plenty

of opportunities to cuddle something furry and step in something sticky. There's no admission fee to the park, but you need to purchase a pass to use the rides.

South over Centreville bridge is a hedge maze and ticket booths for Toronto Islands tram tours. Further south are changing rooms, snack bars, bicycle rentals and a pier striking out into the lake. To the east is a boathouse where you can rent canoes, kayaks or paddleboats to explore the islands' lagoons.

Hanlan's Point PARK (☒ Hanlan's Point) At the west end of Centre Island by the Toronto City Centre Airport is Hanlan's Point, named after world-champion sculler 'Ned' Hanlan (1855–1904), a member of the first family to permanently settle here. Babe Ruth hit his first professional home run here in 1914 while playing minor-league baseball – the ball drowned in Lake Ontario, the ultimate souvenir lost forever!

Beyond the free tennis courts and a fragile ecosystem of low-lying dunes sustaining rare species, the not-so-rare nekkid humanus roams free on the gray sand of Hanlan's Point Beach. Popular with gay men, the beach's 'clothing optional' status was legalized in 1999.

Ward's Island   ISLAND
(⛴ Ward's Island) At the western end of Ward's Island is an 18-hole **Frisbee Golf Course** (www.discgolfontario.com; ⊙ dawn-dusk) `FREE`. An old-fashioned boardwalk runs the length of the south shore of the island, passing the back gate of the year-round Rectory Cafe with its delightful lakeside patio.

◉ Greater Toronto Area (GTA)

Further afield, in outlying areas of the GTA, where Toronto's neighborhoods start to become suburbs and begin to look the same, are a number of worthy attractions. The downside is they can be frustrating to get to by public transport and even with a car. We've listed some of the best spots below in order of their proximity to downtown, the higher up the list being the closest and easiest to get to.

★ High Park   PARK
(Map p69; www.toronto.ca/parks/featured-parks/high-park; 1873 Bloor St W; ⊙ dawn-dusk; Ⓢ High Park, 🚌 501, 506, 508) Toronto's favorite and best-known park is a wonderful place to unfurl a picnic blanket, swim, play tennis, bike around, skate on the **Grenadier Pond** in the winter, or in the spring meander through the groves of cherry blossoms donated to the park by the Japanese ambassador in 1959. There's also a theatrical stage, a small children's zoo and Colborne Lodge, built in 1836

by the Howard family, who donated much of High Park to the city in 1873.

To get here, bus 30B picks up at High Park subway station, then loops through the park on weekends and holidays from mid-June to early September. Otherwise it's a 200m walk to the north gates. The 506 High Park streetcar drops off on the east side of the park. If you exit the park by Colborne Lodge at the south gates, walk to Lake Shore Blvd W and catch any eastbound streetcar to downtown.

Evergreen Brick Works   PARK
(☑ 416-596-7670; http://ebw.evergreen.ca; 550 Bayview Ave; ⊙ 9am-5pm Mon-Fri, 8am-4pm Sat, 10am-4pm Sun; 🚌 28A, Ⓢ Broadview) ✔ `FREE` Famed for the wonderful transformation of its originally deteriorating heritage buildings into a prime location for all things geotourism, this dynamic Leadership in Energy & Environmental Design–certified community environmental center and park hosts interactive workshops and community festivals around the themes of ecology, technology and the environment. There's a garden market and lots of nature trails. Check the website to see what's going on. Take the free shuttle bus from Broadview subway station.

Todmorden Mills   HISTORIC SITE
(Map p69; ☑ 416-396-2819; www.toronto.ca/todmorden; 67 Pottery Rd; adult/child $5.30/2.40, gallery admission free; ⊙ 10am-4:30pm Mon-Fri, noon-5pm Sat & Sun Apr-Dec) In an idyllic setting by the Don River, Todmorden Mills is

ONTARIO TORONTO

LAKE ONTARIO

Unlike nearby Chicago, a city of similar size, population and lake frontage, Toronto has neglected its waterfront. Where Chicago has 29km of contiguous loved-by-locals lakefront trails, parks and beaches, Toronto has the toxic Gardiner Expressway, Lake Shore Boulevard and a wall of waterfront condos obscuring the lake from general view. Lakeshore access has only opened up in recent decades and projects are ever so slowly trying to revitalize the shoreline. Updates can be found at www.toronto.ca/waterfront, and info on Toronto's section of a much bigger lakeshore trail project at www.waterfront-trail.org.

Chemicals, sewage and fertilizer runoff have traditionally fouled the waters of Lake Ontario, although the situation is improving. Many locals now seem content to swim in Toronto's eight Blue-Flag sanctioned beaches: www.toronto.ca/parks/beaches. For most citizens though, Lake Ontario is simply a big, gray, cold thing that stops the Americans from driving up Yonge St.

Lake Ontario is the 14th-largest lake in the world and the smallest and most easterly of the five Great Lakes: 311km long, 85km wide and 244m deep. The name 'Ontario' derives from *Skanadario*, an Iroquois word meaning 'sparkling water.' The name rings true and despite what lurks beneath, it still sparkles. Visit the Toronto Islands or Tommy Thompson Park to see the lake for what it really is – stoic, powerful and very beautiful. Be sure to tell the locals all about it.

a late-18th-century gristmill-turned-sawmill, then brewery and distillery, then paper mill. Historical relics are on display inside. Enthusiastic guides show visitors around old millers' houses and the petite Don train station. To get here, take the subway to Broadview station then board any bus. Alight at Mortimer/Pottery Road (Dairy Queen), turn left and walk down Pottery Rd.

The renovated **Papermill Theatre and Gallery** showcases local and emerging artists. Nature paths start near the bridge and wind back to the secluded **Todmorden Mills Wildflower Preserve** (www.hopscotch. ca/tmwp), 9 hectares of wildflowers growing on former industrial wasteland, complete with boardwalks and viewing platforms.

Ontario Science Centre   MUSEUM

(⎘416-696-1000;   www.ontariosciencecentre. ca; 770 Don Mills Rd; Science Centre adult/child $22/13, Omnimax $13/9, combined ticket $28/19; ⏲10am-4pm Mon-Fri, to 7pm Sat & Sun; ☐34 from Eglinton TTC, ☐25 from Pape TTC) Climb a rock wall, journey to the center of a human heart, catch a criminal with DNA fingerprinting and race an Olympic bobsled at the excellent, interactive Ontario Science Centre. Over 800 high-tech exhibits and live demonstrations wow the kids (and the adults feigning interest at the back). There's also the giant domed Omnimax cinema. Check the website for family events, including theme-night sleepovers.

Scarborough Bluffs   PARK

(⎘416-392-1111;   www.toronto.ca/waterfront/ tour/scarborough_bluffs.htm;   Scarborough; ⏲dawn-dusk; ☐12, ⓢVictoria Park) Atop this 14km stretch of glacial lakeshore cliffs, enjoy stunning views across Lake Ontario. Erosion has created cathedral spire formations, exposing evidence of five different glacial periods. Without wheels, getting to the bluffs can be a drag. Take the subway to Victoria Park, then bus 12 along Kingston Rd to Cathedral Bluffs Dr, east of the St Clair Ave E intersection.

If you're driving, from Kingston Rd (Hwy 2), turn south at Cathedral Bluffs Dr to reach the highest section of the bluffs (65m), **Cathedral Bluffs Park**. You can also access the shore at Galloway Rd further east. About 6km further east, you'll come to **Guildwood Park**, one of Toronto's most fascinating, filled with architectural relics and sculptures collected from the 1950s to '70s by the forward-thinking Rosa and Spencer Clark.

David Dunlap Observatory   OBSERVATORY

(off Map p69; ⎘905-883-0174; www.theddo.ca; 123 Hillsview Dr, Richmond Hill; adult/child $10/2; ⏲8:30pm Sat Jun-Oct, also 8:30pm Fri Jul & Aug; ☐91, ⓢFinch) North of the Toronto city limits, the David Dunlap Observatory houses Canada's largest optical telescope (the reflector measures 1.9m). On Saturday evenings, the observatory presents introductory talks on modern astronomy, followed by some interplanetary voyeurism. Check that weather conditions are favorable and book ahead for limited tickets.

Take the subway north to Finch station then transfer to the 91 Bayview bus (operated by York Region Transit) and request a stop at Hillsview Dr, from where it's a 1km walk to the observatory. Otherwise, drive north on Bayview Ave past 16th Ave to Hillsview Dr, turn left onto Hillsview Dr then head 1km further west until you see the white dome on your left.

LEGOLAND Discovery
Centre   AMUSEMENT PARK

(⎘1-855-356-2150; www.legolanddiscoverycentre. ca/toronto; 1 Bass Pro Mills Dr, Vaughan; adult/child $22/18; ⏲10am-9pm Mon-Sat, 11am-7pm Sun; ⓢYorkdale) Loved by kids and former kids alike, one of Toronto's newest attractions delights with its collection of hands-on, educational Lego-centric attractions including an earthquake table, 4D cinema and Lego factory. It's in the sprawling Vaughan Mills shopping center; take the subway to Yorkdale station and transfer onto the 360 YRT Maple Express bus to Vaughan Mills.

Canada's Wonderland   AMUSEMENT PARK

(Map p69; ⎘905-832-8131; www.canadaswonderland.com; 9580 Jane St, Vaughan; day pass adult/child $59/35; ⏲10am-10pm Jun-Aug, Sat & Sun only May & Sep; ⓢYork Mills) Amusement park lovers will want to trek to this, Canada's largest, featuring over 60 rides, including the mammoth Leviathan, with a peak height of 93m! There's also an exploding volcano, 20-hectare Splash Works water park and white-water canyon. Queues can be lengthy; most rides operate rain or shine and tickets are cheaper online. From York Mills subway, catch the 60 GO Bus (additional fee).

McMichael Canadian Art
Collection   GALLERY

(⎘888-213-1121, 905-893-1121; www.mcmichael. com; 10365 Islington Ave, Kleinburg; adult/child $15/free; ⏲10am-5pm) Handcrafted wooden buildings (which include painter Tom

Thomson's cabin, moved from its original location) are set amid 40 hectares of conservation trails contain works by Canada's best-known landscape painters, the Group of Seven, as well as First Nations, Inuit and other acclaimed Canadian artists. It's a 34km, 45-minute drive from Toronto: be sure to use a GPS. Parking is $5.

Sharon Temple   HISTORIC BUILDING
(☑905-478-2389; www.sharontemple.ca; 18974 Leslie St, East Gwillimbury; adult/child $5/free; ☉10am-4:30pm Thu-Sun) A national historic site and one of the oldest museums in Canada, this quaint and fascinating temple was built in 1832 by a Quaker sect called the Children of the Peace, to a unique architectural style. Lovingly restored in 2011, the simple museum tells the story of its founders and makes a wonderful day trip out of Toronto. It's about 55km north of downtown.

🏃 Activities

They're often mummified in winter layers, but Torontonians still like to keep fit. Outdoor activities abound: folks bike, blade and run along the lakeshore and hike up the city's ravines. Ice skating and hockey are winter faves.

Cycling & In-Line Skating

For cyclists and in-line skaters, the **Martin Goodman Trail**, a paved recreational trail from The Beaches through Harbourfront to the Humber River in the west, is the place to go. Head for the lake and you'll find it. On the way you can connect to the Don Valley mountain-bike trails at Cherry St. On the **Toronto Islands**, the south-shore boardwalk and the interconnecting paved paths are car-free. For a longer trek, the Martin Goodman Trail is part of the **Lake Ontario Waterfront Trail** (www.waterfronttrail.org), stretching 450km from way east of Toronto to Niagara-on-the-Lake.

If you choose to explore Toronto by bike, stick to marked cycling trails when possible. Although many locals bike to work, the downtown is fraught with perils: aggressive drivers, iPod-blinded pedestrians and streetcars. Cyclists do get hit by car doors, and rider accidents from connecting with streetcar tracks aren't uncommon. It's not a legal requirement to wear a helmet in Ontario.

Essential information for cyclists can be found at www.toronto.ca/cycling/map. Folks with smartphones should go to www.ridethecity.com for real-time route planning.

★BIXI   CYCLING
(☑1-877-412-2494; www.toronto.bixi.com; subscription per 24hr $5, usage 1st 30min free then $1.50 for next 30min, $4 for next 30min, $8 per additional 30min) Launched in 2011, BIXI is a subscription-based automated bike-sharing project. Look for the BIXI stations dotted around the city or check the homepage for specific locations – there are many. Collect from one station and return to the same or any other, but the longer you have your bike, the more it costs. A credit card is required.

The trick is to break your journeys down to half-hour blocks and to consider BIXI an alternative means of public transportation. It helps if you're good with directions. A $250 security deposit is frozen on your credit card at time of collection.

Community Bicycle Network   CYCLING
(Map p84; ☑416-504-2918; www.communitybicyclenetwork.org; 761 Queen St W; rental 1st day/weekend/week $25/35/65; ☉noon-6pm Tue-Fri, 10am-6pm Sat; ⛟501) Celebrating 20 years of championing for sustainable transportation, CBN offers rentals, repairs, workshops and events from a convenient Queen St W location.

Europe Bound Outfitters   CYCLING
(Map p78; ☑416-601-1990; www.europebound.com/store; 47 Front St E; ☉10am-7pm Mon-Fri, to 6pm Sat, 11am-5pm Sun; ⛟503) Mountain bikes and tandems with helmets from $30 per day.

Toronto Bicycling Network   CYCLING
(TBN; www.tbn.on.ca) This recreational cycling club welcomes nonmembers to organized rides for a $5 fee.

Toronto Islands Bicycle Rental   CYCLING
(☑416-203-0009; www.torontoislandbicyclerental.com; Centre Island; per hour bicycles/tandems $8/15, 2-/4-seat quadricycles $17/30; ☉10:30am-6pm May-Sep; ⛴Centre Island) One of the best ways to explore Centre Island is by bicycle. Rent bikes here, beside Outlook Pier.

Wheel Excitement   CYCLING, IN-LINE SKATING
(Map p78; ☑416-260-9000; www.wheelexcitement.ca; 249 Queens Quay W; bicycles & in-line skates per hour/day $15/35; ☉10am-6pm; ⛟509, 510) Close to the ferries for Toronto Islands; day rentals here are cheaper than hiring on Centre Island and give you the freedom to explore further afield.

Hiking

Feel like stretching your legs? Delve into Toronto's city parks, nature reserves or ravines.

Alternatively, hook up with a group such as **Hike Ontario** (☎800-894-7249, 905-277-4453; www.hikeontario.com) or **Toronto Bruce Trail Club** (☎416-763-9061; www.torontobrucetrail-club.org) for hardy day hikes.

Ice Skating

Locals love to skate. When the weather is freezing and the snow falling lightly, downtown Toronto's outdoor ice rinks come alive. The best-known rinks are at Nathan Phillips Square outside City Hall and at the Harbourfront Centre. These artificial rinks are open daily (weather permitting) from 10am to 10pm mid-November to March. Admission is free; skate rental costs adult/child $10/5. **Toronto Parks & Recreation** (☎416-397-2628; www.toronto.ca/parks) has info on other rinks around town, including those at Kew Gardens near Kew Beach and Trinity Bellwoods Park in West Toronto. If it's been *really* cold, you can skate on Grenadier Pond in High Park. Beginners might prefer the lesser-known Ryerson Rink, tucked away just north of Yonge & Dundas Sq at 25 Gould St – in summer the rink is a water feature.

Swimming

Torontonians generally avoid swimming in Lake Ontario, despite the presence of a dozen city beaches tended by lifeguards from July to August, eight of which are Blue Flag certified. Before taking the plunge, check with the **Beach Water Quality Hotline** (☎416-392-7161; www.city.toronto.on.ca/beach), as water quality deteriorates after heavy rain and the presence of E coli bacteria is a potential risk.

From June to September, the City of Toronto operates over 50 outdoor swimming pools, generally open from dawn to dusk. The complete list is found at: www.toronto.ca/parks/prd/facilities/outdoor-pools.

☞ Tours

Boat

Between May and September cruise operators sail from the Harbourfront beside Queens Quay Terminal or York Quay Centre. Reservations are recommended for brunch and dinner cruises. Keep in mind that ferries to the Toronto Islands offer similar views for half the price.

Great Lakes Schooner Company BOAT TOUR
(Map p78; ☎416-203-2322; www.tallshipcruisestoronto.com; Suite 111, 249 Queens Quay W; 90min cruise adult/child $21.95/11.95; ☉ Jun-Aug; ⛴509, 510) The dashing black three-master *Kajama*, a 1930 German trading schooner, sails from the foot of Lower Simcoe St, but there's usually a ticket kiosk beside Queens Quay Terminal. Reservations can be made online.

Mariposa Cruises BOAT TOUR
(Map p78; ☎416-203-0178, 866-627-7672; www.mariposacruises.com; Queens Quay Terminal, 207 Queens Quay W; 1hr tour adult/child $20/13; ☉May-Sep; ⛴509, 510) Narrated harbor and two-hour buffet lunch tours (adult/child $49/25). Sunday brunch and dinner-and-dance cruises, too.

Bus

Toronto isn't exactly London, Paris or Rome, where it's easy to ooh and ahh at endless historical marvels from the comfort of a coach. If traveling on a budget, you might find better value in a TTC day pass, exploring for yourself.

★City Sightseeing Toronto BUS TOUR
(☎416-410-0536; www.citysightseeingtoronto.com; adult/child $35/20) Hop-on, hop-off sightseeing tours on an open-top double-decker London bus, around a 24-stop city loop. The route takes in most major sights with commentary and includes a free (seasonal) Lake Ontario cruise. Tickets are valid for 72 hours: good value if you plan to use the bus over three days and a great way to get oriented.

★Chariots of Fire BUS TOUR
(☎1-905-877-0855; www.chariots-of-fire.com; 33 Yonge St; day tours $60) Low-cost day tours from Toronto to Niagara Falls including a *Maid of the Mist* boat ride and free time at Niagara-on-the-Lake. These guys are highly organized and comfortably present the best of the Falls, from Toronto, for those who only have a day to experience it all. Highly recommended.

ROMBus BUS TOUR
(Map p74; ☎416-586-5797; www.rom.on.ca/en/activities-programs/walks-travel-bus-events/bus; 100 Queen's Park; full-day tours $110-140; ⛎Museum) Toronto's Royal Ontario Museum organizes irregular special-events tours with educated, informative guides around historical, cultural and architectural themes. Full-day tours although pricey can be worth the expense if the subject matter falls in your sphere of interest.

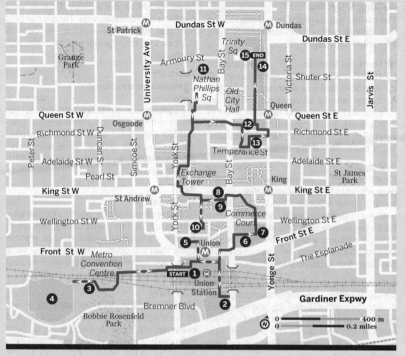

🏃 City Walk
Subterranean Toronto Blues

START UNION STATION
END TRINITY SQ
LENGTH ONE DAY

When it's just too cold to be outside, duck into Toronto's underground PATH system, a 28km (and growing) labyrinth of subterranean corridors connecting downtown sights, skyscrapers and shops. You'll be surprised at how much is interconnected. Allow yourself a full day if you want to try to do all of the following.

From ❶ **Union Station** (p120), you can head to the ❷ **Air Canada Centre** (p117) or follow the tubular SkyWalk over the railroad tracks to the ❸ **CN Tower** (p70), next to the ❹ **Rogers Centre** (p71).

Cross beneath Front St and up the staircase into ❺ **Fairmont Royal York** (p95). From here, follow the color-coded arrows to ❻ **Brookfield Place** and the ❼ **Hockey Hall of Fame** (p72). Wander through Commerce Court to the ❽ **TD Centre**. Beyond the digital stock-market displays, go left and emerge at the ❾ **Design Exchange** (p72).

From back beneath TD Centre follow signs for the TD Waterhouse Tower to the ❿ **Toronto Dominion Gallery of Inuit Art** (p72).

Next, head toward the Standard Life Centre, the Exchange Tower and then the Richmond-Adelaide complex. You will pass the Sheraton Centre to reach ⓫ **City Hall** (p77) and Nathan Phillips Sq.

From City Hall you can head back underground and follow the signs for ⓬ **The Bay** (Canada's oldest department store) and shop till you drop; or pass The Bay, diverting right and up some stairs to Temperance St and the ⓭ **Cloud Gardens Conservatory** (p72).

The PATH continues to the ⓮ **Eaton Centre** (p117) whose large atrium plazas bring the feeling of outside in. From here, it's easy to reach Trinity Sq in the shadows of the ⓯ **Church of the Holy Trinity** (p77), or pick up the subway at Dundas station for your onward journey.

Walking & Cycling

The easiest way to experience Toronto is on foot, though cycling tours allow you to cover a bit more territory.

★ Heritage Toronto
WALKING TOUR

(☑ 416-338-3886; www.heritagetoronto.org; 3F, 157 King St E; donations encouraged; ⊙ Apr-Oct) A diverse offering of fascinating historical, cultural and nature walks and bike and bus (TTC) tours led by museum experts and neighborhood historical society members. Tours generally last one to three hours.

ROMWalks
WALKING TOUR

(☑ 416-586-8097; www.rom.on.ca/en/activities-programs/walks-travel-bus-events/walks; per person $10; ⊙ Wed & Sun May-Sep) Well informed volunteers from the Royal Ontario Museum lead one- to two-hour historical and architectural walking tours, including some of the city's lesser-known but most interesting buildings and neighborhoods.

A Taste of the World
WALKING TOUR

(☑ 416-923-6813; www.torontowalksbikes.com; 2-3½hr tours $25-45) Quirky, well-qualified guides lead offbeat walking and cycling tours of Toronto's nooks and crannies, usually with a foodie focus. Reservations are recommended.

✦ Festivals & Events

What Toronto lacks in visual appeal it makes up for in activity: there's always fun and excitement to be had in this vibrant city and the Toronto festival scene is no exception. In the long balmy days and nights of the short summer (June to August) there's so much on that it's hard to choose what to do. At times, when events overlap, it's best just to get out there and leave it to fate.

January

Winterlicious
FOOD

(www.toronto.ca/special_events/winterlicious) For two weeks in January, a staggering array of restaurants lure residents out of their living rooms for a prix-fixe extravaganza of lunches and dinners, showcasing Toronto's culinary diversity. If you're visiting in winter, we strongly recommend taking advantage of these fantastic cheap eats at every possible opportunity!

Next Stage Festival
THEATER

(www.fringetoronto.com/next-stage-festival) From the people behind the Toronto Fringe Festival, Next Stage showcases the work of 10 fringe artists at the Factory Theatre, as a platform for future success. There's a heated beer tent where audiences can mingle with the cast and crew before and after the performances.

February

Canadian International Auto Show
MOTOR SHOW

(www.autoshow.ca) Revheads from around the world converge on the Metro Toronto Convention Centre for all things cutting edge about cars, with a little bit of automotive history thrown in. The show is in its 40th year in 2014.

April

Hot Docs
FILM

(Canadian International Documentary Festival; www.hotdocs.ca) In late April, North America's largest documentary film festival screens more than 100 docos from around the globe from its home at the revamped-in-2012 Bloor Hot Docs Cinema.

420 Rally
CULTURE

(420rally.ca/420toronto/) On April 20, lovers of weed emerge from their basements and converge on Yonge & Dundas Sq in their thousands for this public pro-legalisation smokeout in the middle of Canada's largest city.

May

InsideOut
FILM

(Toronto LGBT Film Festival; www.insideout.ca) Approaching its 25th anniversary, the Toronto LGBT Film Festival showcases a huge range of gay-themed/interest films from around the world, with some screenings at the fantastic TIFF Bell Lightbox.

Doors Open Toronto
CULTURE

(www.toronto.ca/doorsopen) Over 500 public and private buildings of architectural and historical significance creak open their doors for you to sneak a peek at what's hot and what's not in other peoples' digs.

June

Luminato
CULTURE

(www.luminatofestival.com) Luminato seeks to bring a broad selection of the world's most accomplished musicians, dancers, artists, writers, actors and filmmakers to venues across Toronto in a celebration of creativity that reflects the city's diversity. Many performances are free. Past performers include Aretha Franklin, Joni Mitchell, KD Lang and Rufus Wainwright.

North by Northeast PERFORMING ARTS
(NXNE; www.nxne.com) Musos can safely write off the entire week in order to sample the plethora of indie bands (around 1000), films, shows and booze to be had in all of Toronto's coolest venues. A variety of wristbands tailored to your tastes are exceptional value. The festival's 20th anniversary in 2014 promises to be a big one indeed.

Pride Toronto GAY PRIDE
(www.pridetoronto.com) In late June, Toronto's most flamboyant event celebrates the diversity of human sexuality, with a week of community events, workshops and gatherings, mostly free. The exploration climaxes with an out-of-the-closet Dyke March and Pride Parade when the streets of Church and Wellesley village, Pride's G-spot, throb with the beat of over one million revelers. In 2014, Toronto Pride will merge with the world's biggest international LGBT event, WorldPride, for the first time in North America.

National Aboriginal Day CULTURE
(www.aboriginalaffairs.gov.on.ca/english/events/national_aboriginal_day) Canada's heritage of First Nations, Inuit and Métis cultures is celebrated on the summer solstice (June 21), with events leading up to it the week before.

Toronto Jazz Festival JAZZ
(www.tojazz.com) In late June/early July, jazz, blues and world beats blaze in the city's streets, nightclubs and concert halls, with musical workshops, film screenings and harbor cruises.

July
Summerlicious FOOD
(www.toronto.ca/special_events/summerlicious) Be sure to book your tables in advance for this culinary extravaganza held at almost 200 restaurants, bars and cafes across the city. Great-value prix-fixe menus in three price categories mean there's something to suit everyone's tastes and budget.

Toronto Fringe Festival CULTURE
(www.fringetoronto.com) Celebrating 25 years in the spotlight, in 2014, Toronto's largest theater and performance festival hosts dozens of plays on as many stages over two weeks in early July. Ranging from utterly offbeat to seriously emotive and including a program of kids' plays, the festival's aim is to make theater accessible to the community.

Open Roof Festival FILM
(www.openrooffestival.com) An enthusiastic bunch of film and music lovers put together a season of rooftop/outdoor film screenings and bands from hip urban locations. Check the website for venue info.

Honda Indy Toronto CAR RACE
(www.hondaindyoronto.com) Drivers from the international circuit compete in front of massive crowds, reaching speeds of up to 300km/h along Lake Shore Blvd and causing locals to flee the city for the sake of their continued ability to hear.

Beaches International Jazz Festival MUSIC
(www.beachesjazz.com) FREE Held in late July, this free three-day jazz fest (which celebrated its 25th anniversary in 2013) plays to stages at Woodbine Gardens, Kew Gardens and along the Beaches Boardwalk. The highlight is the two-day Streetfest where a 2km stretch of Queen St E is closed to traffic and opened to the sounds of more than 50 Canadian bands and thousands of pedestrian admirers.

August
Caribana CARNIVAL
(www.caribana.com) North America's largest Caribbean festival, from late July into early August. The carnival parade, featuring florid and almost-not-there costumes, takes five hours to gyrate past.

Canadian National Exhibition AGRICULTURAL
(CNE; www.theex.com) Dating from 1879, 'The Ex' features over 700 exhibitors, agricultural shows, lumberjack competitions and outdoor concerts at Exhibition Place. The air show and Labour Day fireworks take the cake.

Scotiabank Buskerfest MUSIC
(www.torontobuskerfest.com) For three days in late August, a ragtag troupe of Canadian and international buskers descends upon downtown Yonge St in support of Epilepsy Toronto: expect sword-swallowers, jugglers and musicians of unpredictable merit.

SummerWorks Theatre Festival THEATER
(www.summerworks.ca) Ten days of predominantly New Canadian plays in the largest juried theater festival in Canada.

September
Toronto International Film Festival FILM
(TIFF; torontointernationalfilmfestival.ca) The jewel in Toronto's international social and cultural crown has become one of the world's

largest and most prestigious celebrations of the cinematic art. Some come for the films, many screened in the stunning and state-of-the-art Bell Lightbox Cinema. Others come hoping to catch a glimpse of the celebrity circus as it pulls into town. Buy tickets and book your accommodation well in advance, and expect to pay a premium for rooms if you happen to be in Toronto over festival dates.

October

Nuit Blanche
CULTURE
(www.scotiabanknuitblanche.ca) One night. Over 130 overnight urban art experiences, all over town. Contrived 'chance encounters,' interactive dance pieces and an all-night street market are part of the fun.

International Festival of Authors
LITERATURE
(www.readings.org) For 11 days in mid-October, this festival corrals acclaimed authors from Canada and beyond to the Harbourfront Centre for readings, discussions, lectures, awards and book signings. There are kid-friendly events too.

November

Royal Agricultural Winter Fair
AGRICULTURAL
(www.royalfair.org) Since 1922, the largest indoor agricultural and equstrian fair in the world has been warming up audiences at Exhibition Place for 10 days in November.

Santa Claus Parade
CHRISTMAS
(www.thesantaclausparade.ca) A Toronto tradition since 1905, the annual Santa Claus Parade features exactly that: a bunch of old guys dressed as Santa stopping downtown traffic for hours and exciting children way too early before Christmas. The date varies each year.

December

Toronto Christmas Market
CHRISTMAS
(www.torontochristmasmarket.com) The Distillery District is at its festive best over the first two weeks in December for this European-style Christmas Market, showcasing hundreds of local handcrafted products.

🛏 Sleeping

Toronto has no shortage of accommodations, but it can get expensive, especially in summer when rooms sell quickly at up to double their regular rates. Plan ahead and you'll be able to find something to suit your style and budget. It's essential to book in advance for stays from mid-May to late September. Remember, 13% harmonized sales tax (HST) is almost always applied on top of the quoted rate. Avoid visiting in March if possible: the weather can be lousy and the enormous annual PDAC mining convention secures the majority of downtown beds.

Since 2011, a number of long-overdue luxury hotels have opened their doors, creating a surplus of fancy, expensive beds. There hasn't been similar investment in the midrange category: rooms of this ilk can feel drab and out of date for what you pay.

Unlike the rest of Ontario where budget beds are in short supply, Toronto has some great hostels. Trust us when we advise you to book in advance: the best digs fill quickly in summer. Plenty of B&Bs can be found through the following agencies.

Bed & Breakfast Homes of Toronto
ACCOMMODATIONS SERVICE
(☏416-363-6362; www.bbcanada.com/associations/toronto2) Anything from modest family homes to deluxe suites.

ROLL OUT THE RED CARPET: TIFF

Since its inception in 1976, the Toronto International Film Festival (TIFF) has grown to be the crowning jewel of the Toronto festival scene and a key player in the world film circuit. Attracting over 400,000 eager cinephiles to the red-carpet celebrity frenzy of its 10-day run, the festival has become an important forum for showcasing new films.

In 1990 the festival expanded operations to include the year-round TIFF Cinematheque program, showcasing works from around the world. Two decades later, the Bell Lightbox (p116), with its five stunning cinemas, funky restaurants and bar, opened its doors as the permanent home for the festival and organisation.

If you're in town for TIFF, be sure to book ahead: tickets for screenings and events sell fast, while already elevated room rates go through the roof closer to showtime. Celebrities and paparazzi are in town and Torontonians come from far and wide to embrace the Hollywood spirit: catch a glimpse if you can!

Downtown Toronto Association of Bed and Breakfast

Guest Houses ACCOMMODATIONS SERVICE
(☑647-654-2959; www.bnbinfo.com) Rooms in various neighborhoods, mostly in renovated Victorian houses.

Toronto Bed & Breakfast Reservation Service ACCOMMODATIONS SERVICE
(☑877-922-6522, 705-738-9449; www.toronto-bandb.com) The oldest agency in town with a dozen central listings.

🛏 Harbourfront

Renaissance Toronto HOTEL $$
(Map p78; ☑800-237-1512, 416-341-7100; www.renaissancetoronto.com; 1 Blue Jays Way; d/ste from $199/289; ⊖❄️🛜🔁; ⑤Union) Seventy suites here overlook the Rogers Centre playing field – be prepared for floodlights and hollering sports fans! If you'd rather use your room for sleeping, the restaurant and bar also overlook the field.

Westin Harbour Castle HOTEL $$
(Map p78; ☑416-869-1600; www.westinharbourcastletoronto.com; 1 Harbour Sq; d from $239; 🔁; 🖬509, 510) If this were a hamburger, it'd be with 'the works' – restaurants, shops, gym, conference center, pool, disabled-access suites etc. Staff are surprisingly chipper for such a big hotel. Maybe the lobby keeps them amused, with enough marble to rival any Hollywood mansion. Tasty lake views.

🛏 Financial District

Hotel Victoria BOUTIQUE HOTEL $$
(Map p78; ☑800-363-8228, 416-363-1666; www.hotelvictoria-toronto.com; 56 Yonge St; d from $159; ⊖❄️🛜; ⑤King) The early-20th-century Hotel Victoria retains a charming period lobby. Guest rooms are on the smaller side but have been simply and sylishly refurbished and have free wi-fi. Bathrooms have great tubs but ladies might be disappointed by the lack of vanity space.

Strathcona Hotel HOTEL $$
(Map p78; ☑800-268-8304, 416-363-3321; www.thestrathconahotel.com; 60 York St; d from $125; ⊖❄️🛜; ⑤Union) This downtown hotel features compact, renovated rooms with decent bathrooms. The downstairs pub and cafe are convenient. Despite the lack of on-site parking, its proximity to Union Station is ideal, although some will find the long-term construction projects there an annoyance.

One King West HOTEL $$
(Map p78; ☑416-548-8100; www.onekingwest.com; 1 King St W; d from $209; ⊖🛜🔁; ⑤King) One of our favorite buildings in the Toronto skyline, the sleek One King West tower soars above the historic former head office for the Toronto Dominion bank with an effortless synergy. Studio and one-bedroom apartments are large, stylish and in a prime downtown location with subway and streetcars at your door.

Fairmont Royal York HOTEL $$$
(Map p78; ☑866-440-5489, 416-368-2511; www.fairmont.com/royalyork; 100 Front St W; d from $179; ❄️🛜🔁; ⑤Union) Since 1929 the eminent Royal York (a former grand dame of the Canadian Pacifc Railway and Toronto icon) has accommodated everyone from Tina Turner to Henry Kissinger, and it shows. Fortunately, the 1300-plus guest rooms are undergoing significant renovation, which will take some time. Consider coming for high tea in the Library Bar and a chance to visit the lesser-known rooftop herb garden and bee apiary.

Until completion, snap up a deal on older rooms, or pay a premium for the new luxury product. Note also that long-term construction projects in and around Union Station (opposite the hotel) are less than convenient.

★ Trump Toronto HOTEL $$$
(Map p78; ☑416-306-5800; www.trumphotelcollection.com/toronto/; 325 Bay St; d from $425; ⊖❄️🛜🔁; ⑤King) Words to describe Trump Toronto's oversized, modern guest rooms: sumptuous, decadent, bold, indulgent. High ceilings and full-length windows add to the feel of space and luxury. Opened in 2012, the Trump name is synonymous with status, big business and success, and this hotel is no exception. Expect only the most attentive service and finest Clefs d'Or concierges. If money is no obstacle, welcome home.

🛏 Old York

Hostelling International Toronto HOSTEL $
(Map p78; ☑877-848-8737, 416-971-4440; www.hostellingtoronto.com; 76 Church St; dm member/nonmember from $22/26, d member/nonmember from $89/109; ⊖🛜; 🖬504) This award-winning hostel doesn't look much from the outside, but gets votes for its rooftop deck and friendly staff. Most dorms have their own bathrooms, and deluxe rooms offer good-value private accommodations,

including breakfast. The on-site Cavern Bar & Bistro has themed game nights to help you make friends.

Cosmopolitan
BOUTIQUE HOTEL **$$**

(Map p78; ☑416-350-2000; www.cosmotoronto. com; 8 Colborne St; ste from $209; ⊖✿🗑; Ⓢ King) This compact hotel is sleek and quiet, with only five rooms per floor. Entry-level Zen suites are on the small side. Lotus and Tranquility suites are significantly larger, have kitchens and some have lake views. All have balconies. Both the treatment spa and funky downstairs wine bar, Eight (with its $1 per ounce Friday-night special) add to the appeal.

🏨 Entertainment District & King Street West

★ Clarence Park
HOSTEL **$**

(Map p78; ☑647-498-7070; www.theclarencepark. com; 7 Clarence Sq; dm $27, d $70-85; 🗑) In a prime and picturesque downtown location, this budget gem has cozy clean dorms and private rooms, some overlooking the leafy square: all have en suite bathrooms. There's free wi-fi, a fabulous new communal kitchen and huge rooftop deck with BBQ for those lazy summer afternoons in the city.

Canadiana Guesthouse & Backpackers
HOSTEL **$**

(Map p78; ☑877-215-1225, 416-598-9090; www. canadianalodging.com; 42 Widmer St; dm $27-34, s/d from $68/80; ⊖✿@🗑; 🅿504) On a quiet side street midway between two happening strips of Queen W and King W, location is not Canadiana's only plus. Pancake breakfasts, a movie room, barbecue nights, gas cooking and decent private rooms all add to the appeal. Occupying a Victorian terrace row, the place feels more intimate than its 200 beds would suggest.

★ Residence Inn Toronto Downtown
HOTEL **$$**

(Map p78; ☑416-581-1800; www.marriott.com; 255 Wellington St W; ste incl breakfast from $209; ⊖✿🗑✿; 🅿504, 508) Perfect for longer stays or traveling with kids, this modern business/tourist hotel is in a prime location and has a variety of comfortable, functional room types, up to two-bedroom suites. All have fully equipped kitchens, pleasant decor and lots of light. The full breakfast buffet makes for excellent value.

★ Thompson Toronto
HOTEL **$$$**

(Map p84; ☑416-640-7778; www.thompsonhotels. com/toronto; 550 Wellington St W; d from $229; ✿🗑✿; 🅿504, 508) We love Thompson Toronto – it's just so LA. Funky, sharp rooms will be favored by those with a penchant for design; the rooftop bar, patio and pool are easily Toronto's finest; and the two on-site dining options, Thompson Diner and Scarpetta, independently deserve mention. Combine all this with a brilliant location and exceptional service and you've got something that's worth splurging on, but don't bring grandma (check the website to see what the fuss is about).

Hilton Garden Inn Toronto Downtown
HOTEL **$$**

(Map p78; ☑416-593-9200; www.hiltongardeninn. com; 92 Peter St; d from $169; ⊖✿🗑✿; 🅿501) Not to be confused with its sister property on Jarvis St, this Garden Inn is a great mid-range option, well located in the heart of the Entertainment District, near Queen St W – perfect for nocturnal explorations. It can get noisy on Friday and Saturday nights. Otherwise, the lobby and spacious rooms are of a high standard and staff are generally accustomed to the vagaries of a predominantly corporate weekday clientele.

Soho Metropolitan Hotel
BOUTIQUE HOTEL **$$$**

(Map p78; ☑416-599-8800; www.soho.metropolitan.com; 318 Wellington St W; d from $260; ✿🗑✿; 🅿510) Luxury and style await in Soho Met's 92 guest rooms and suites, featuring beautiful maple woodwork, private dressing rooms, floor-to-ceiling opening windows and Italian linens. Exquisite marble bathrooms feature a deep soaker tub, separate shower and everybody-loves Molton Brown amenities. Repeat guests don't flinch at the rates.

Hôtel Le Germain
BOUTIQUE HOTEL **$$$**

(Map p78; ☑866-345-9501, 416-345-9500; www. germaintoronto.com; 30 Mercer St; d/ste from $250/$545; ✿🗑🗑; 🅿504) Hip and harmonious, Le Germain resides in a quiet Entertainment District side street. Clean lines, soothing spaces and Zen-inspired materials deliver the promised 'ocean of well-being.' Aveda bath amenities, in-room Bose stereos and a rooftop terrace are bonuses. Parking costs $35.

Ritz Carlton
HOTEL **$$$**

(Map p78; ☑416-585-2100; www.ritzcarlton.com/ toronto; 181 Wellington St W; d from $445; ✿🗑✿;

S St Andrew) Opened in 2011, as the first of Toronto's new batch of shiny five-star hotels, the Ritz Carlton name is loaded with connotations, but there's something about the modernity of the property that just doesn't fit with the the old-world Ritz styling emulated in the guest rooms. Of course, expect exceptional service, a wealth of comforts and five-star 'tude. There are better options for the price.

Downtown Yonge

Baldwin Village Inn
B&B $
(Map p74; 416-591-5359; www.baldwininn.com; 9 Baldwin St; d incl breakfast with shared bathroom $90-110; ❄✳🌐; 🚇505, 506) Technically in the pretty enclave of Baldwin Village, just a few blocks from the Art Gallery of Ontario, this yellow-painted B&B faces a leafy street filled with cheap eateries and cafes. The front courtyard is perfect for lounging about and watching the people.

★ Cambridge Suites
HOTEL $$
(Map p74; 416-368-1990; www.cambridgesuitestoronto.com; 15 Richmond St E; ste from $175; ❄✳🌐📺; S Queen) 🏊 An excellent midrange choice, this all-suite hotel has spacious, good-looking rooms with separate living and kitchen facilities. Cityscape suites are on upper floors, are more luxuriously appointed and include continental breakfast in the restaurant. Three impressive penthouses are available.

Les Amis Bed & Breakfast
B&B $$
(Map p74; 416-928-0635; www.bbtoronto.com; 31 Granby St; s/d with shared bathroom incl breakfast from $85/115; ❄✳🌐; S College) Run by a multilingual Parisian couple, this cheery B&B offers full, gourmet vegetarian breakfasts. Colorful rooms are adorned with the owners' art and the leafy back deck is a great spot to chill out. It's a short walk from the Eaton Centre. Parking costs $10.

Eaton Chelsea
HOTEL $$
(Map p74; 416-595-1975; http://chelsea.eatonhotels.com; 33 Gerrard St W; d/ste from $139/239; ❄✳🌐; S College) Formerly the Delta Chelsea, now part of the Langham Hospitality Group, Toronto's largest (almost 1600 rooms!) and arguably best-value hotel caters to everyone, but is especially popular with families who appreciate the apartment-style suites and indoor waterslide. Many rooms have balconies.

Pantages
BOUTIQUE HOTEL $$
(Map p74; 888-897-1401; www.pantageshotel.com; 200 Victoria St; ste from $179; ✳@; S Dundas, Queen) A good choice for longer stays, each of the 89 rooms in this all-suite hotel, the closest to Yonge & Dundas Sq, Massey Hall and the Eaton Centre, have full bathrooms, kitchen and laundry facilities. It's in a residential building: once in the main doors, turn left for the hotel lobby.

Grand Hotel & Suites
HOTEL $$
(Map p74; 416-863-9000; www.grandhoteltoronto.com; 225 Jarvis St; d/ste incl breakfast from $199/249; ❄✳🌐📺; S Dundas, 🚇505) A somewhat grotty and slightly seedy location is the bane of this otherwise solid performer's existence, although all that will change in the next few years as nearby condo projects reach completion. A variety of room types up to two-bedroom suites all have free wi-fi, kitchenettes and marble bathrooms. Breakfast is a hearty buffet. The indoor pool and two rooftop hot tubs are also worth a splash.

Shangri-La Hotel
HOTEL $$$
(Map p78; 647-788-8888; www.shangri-la.com/toronto; 188 University Ave; d from $355; ❄✳@🌐📺; S St Andrew, Osgoode) Five-star Shangri-la's spanking-new, elegant guest rooms strive to synthesize Asian simplicity with Western indulgence and are among Toronto's largest. Each has separate bath, shower and toilet room, opening floor-to-ceiling-windows, Nespresso machines, iPod docks and L'Occitane and Bvlgari bathroom amenities. The University Ave location is fantastic.

Church-Wellesley Village

Neill-Wycik College Hotel
HOSTEL $
(Map p74; 416-977-2320; www.torontobackpackershotel.com/; 96 Gerrard St E; s/tw/d/tr with shared bathroom $53/75/90/100; ❄🌐; S College) Pronounced 'Why-zik,' this budget travelers' favorite operates from early May to late August when the students are out. Private bedrooms with telephones are inside apartment-style suites that share a kitchen/lounge and bathroom. There are laundry facilities, lockers, TV lounges, a student-run cafeteria and incredible sundeck views.

Victoria's Mansion Inn & Guesthouse
INN $
(Map p74; 416-921-4625; www.victoriasmansion.com; 68 Gloucester St; s/d/studio from $69/99/139; ✳🌐; S Wellesley) Festooned with

international flags, gay-friendly Victoria's Mansion accommodates travelers in a renovated 1880s redbrick heritage building with a lovely garden out front. All rooms have fridge, microwave and private bathrooms, making the smaller singles good downtown value.

Holiday Inn Toronto
Downtown Centre
HOTEL **$$**

(Map p74; ☑416-977-6655; www.holidayinn.com; 30 Carlton St; d from $120; ❄️🛜⚡; ⓢCollege) Funky renovated bedrooms and a great location, steps from College subway station and a variety of inexpensive shopping, dining and entertainment options, make this hulking Holiday Inn a good choice for most budgets. That said, there's really no view to speak of and standard rooms are quite compact.

Courtyard Toronto Downtown
HOTEL **$$**

(Map p74; ☑416-924-0611, 800-874-5075; www.marriott.com; 475 Yonge St; d from $116; ❄️🛜⚡; ⓢCollege) The closest major hotel to the Village is also a good stock-standard choice for a midrange hotel, with a walk-to-everything location, gym, hot tub and pool. All rooms are of a decent size, have free ultra-high-speed wi-fi and some have balconies. Great rates can be found online, in advance.

🛏 Bloor-Yorkville

Holiday Inn Toronto
Bloor-Yorkville
HOTEL **$$**

(Map p74; ☑888-2654329, 416-968-0010; www.holiday-inn.com/torontomidtown; 280 Bloor St W; d from $164; ❄️🛜; ⓢSt George) The familiar green banners outside this high-rise, brick monolith do little to improve its aesthetics. Inside, generic guest rooms have comfy queen- or king-sized beds and plenty of room. Price and location are everything: the subway is at your feet, and the Univeristy of Toronto, Royal Ontario Museum and Bloor St shopping are minutes away.

Comfort Hotel
HOTEL **$$**

(Map p74; ☑800-424-6423, 416-924-1222; www.choicehotels.ca/cn228; 15 Charles St E; d from $169; ❄️🛜; ⓢBloor-Yonge) It's generic and by no means fancy, but this basic tourist hotel is near some excellent cafes and is a hop, skip and jump from the Bloor St strip, where you'll pay three times the price for a room. The check-in of 1pm is another plus.

★ Four Seasons
LUXURY HOTEL **$$$**

(Map p74; ☑416-964-0411; www.fourseasons.com/toronto; 60 Yorkville Ave; d from $455; ⓢBay) One of Toronto's most senior and well-respected high-end hotels has moved to a brand-new building in an even better location. It's all about luxury, relaxation and enjoyment: crisp, clean, light-filled guest rooms with stunning views exude comfort, granite bathrooms are to-die-for and the exquisite lobby is one of the most beautiful we've seen.

If the rates don't shock, you won't flinch picking up the tab at Michelin-starred Café Boulud and should happily submit to body pampering and soul elevation at 'spa': it's up there with heaven.

★ Hazelton
BOUTIQUE HOTEL **$$$**

(Map p74; ☑416-963-6300; www.thehazletonhotel.com; 118 Yorkville Ave; d from $450; ❄️🛜⚡🐾) With a bunch of competitors in the luxury hotel class opening their doors in recent years, it's becoming harder for the Hazleton to uphold its self-professed reputation as Toronto's most exclusive hotel: but try it will, and you'll only benefit from its efforts. Sophisticated, dramatic and sexy, this hotel is small enough (62 rooms, 15 suites) to make you feel like the someone special that we all know you are.

Design afficionados will be spoiled for things to appreciate here. When it comes to dining, Toronto culinary master Mark McEwan's 'ONE' restaurant might further decimate your wallet, but is destined to delight your tastebuds.

Windsor Arms
BOUTIQUE HOTEL **$$$**

(Map p74; ☑416-971-9666; www.windsorarmshotel.com; 18 St Thomas St; ste incl breakfast from $356; ⊖❄️🛜⚡🐾; ⓢBay) The Windsor Arms is an exquisite piece of Toronto history – stay the night or drop in for afternoon tea. It's a 1927 neo-Gothic mansion boasting a grand entryway, stained-glass windows, polished service and its own coat of arms. Luxurious, oversized suites have separate tub and shower, Molton Brown amenities, Nespresso maker, butler service, buffet breakfast and wi-fi. Creatives will love that each comes with its own musical instrument!

🛏 University of Toronto & The Annex

Havinn
B&B **$**

(Map p74; ☑888-922-5220, 416-922-5220; www.havinn.com; 118 Spadina Rd; s/d with shared bathroom incl breakfast $59/74; ⊖❄️@; ⓢDupont) Located on busy Spadina Rd, this small guesthouse has six basic rooms with shared bathrooms and a communal kitchen. The price is right: cheaper than most B&Bs and more private than a hostel.

Global Guesthouse INN $
(Map p74; ☑ 416-923-4004; www.globalguest-house.com; 9 Spadina Rd; s/d $76/86, with shared bathroom $66/76; ❁❂⊛; ⑤ Spadina) Built in 1889, this old-fashioned redbrick Victorian has beautiful carved gables and sits just north of Bloor St, right on Spadina station. The hostel has 10 gaudy rooms, cable TV, hippie wall hangings, wooden floors and murals and fills up quickly.

Annex Quest House INN $$
(Map p74; ☑ 416-922-1934; www.annexquesthouse.com; 83 Spadina Rd; d from $95; ❁❂⊛; ⑤ Spadina) Engaging the principles of *vastu,* an Indian architectural science promoting tranquility through natural materials and asymmetrical layouts (similar to feng shui), this glorified backpackers has quaint, simple rooms. Wooden floors, patterned bedspreads and crafted copper bowls highlight the spaces.

Madison Manor BOUTIQUE HOTEL $$
(Map p74; ☑ 416-922-5579; www.madisonmanor-boutiquehotel.com; 20 Madison Ave; d incl breakfast $99-189; ❁❂; ⑤ Spadina) A refurbished Victorian home near the University of Toronto. Rooms have private bathrooms and are furnished in a traditional style; a few have a fireplace or balcony. Note that the Manor is sandwiched between a frat house and the Madison Avenue Pub: readers have complained of noise on weekends.

🛏 Kensington Market & Little Italy

★Planet Travelers Hostel HOSTEL $
(Map p84; ☑ 416-599-6789; www.theplanettraveler.com; 357 College St; dm/d/tr $30/75/90; ❁❂⊛; 🚌506) 🛈 The Planet has moved up the street to a bigger and better location and continues to delight our readers and its guests with an awesome rooftop patio bar, great rates and commitment to being clean and green: it's arguably one of Canada's most environmentally friendly accommodations. With 94 dorm beds, 10 private rooms and shiny, slick communal areas, you'll have everything you need to make friends and enjoy hostel life.

🛏 Queen West & Trinity Bellwoods

Global Village Backpackers HOSTEL $
(Map p84; ☑ 888-844-7875, 416-703-8540; www.globalbackpackers.com; 460 King St W; dm $26-29, d from $72; ❁⊛; 🚌504, 511) This kaleidoscopically colored independent hostel was once the Spadina Hotel, where Jack Nicholson, the Rolling Stones and Leonard Cohen lay their heads. It likely hasn't been updated since those glory days, and despite its increasing grubbiness, remains popular. It does have a great location and outdoor party-patio, but look elsewhere if cleanliness is a priority.

★Drake Hotel BOUTIQUE HOTEL $$
(☑ 416-531-5042; www.thedrakehotel.ca; 1150 Queen St W; d/ste from $169/319; ❁❂⊛; 🚌501) While other hotels have rooms, the Drake has 'crash pads, dens, salons' and a rockin' little suite, beckoning bohemians, artists and indie musicians with a little cash to burn. The crash pads are tiny yet ineffably stylish and functional. In fact, all the rooms are on the small side, but are impeccably furnished with a sense of fun and good design. The attached bar and band room is one of Toronto's finest venues for live music, and in summer the Sky Yard rooftop patio goes off to DJ beats and icy buckets of Coronas.

★Gladstone Hotel BOUTIQUE HOTEL $$
(☑ 416-531-4635; www.gladstonehotel.com; 1214 Queen St W; d/ste from $199/375; ❁❂⊛; 🚌501) The 37 artist-designed rooms at this trendsetting hotel could have leapt straight from a Taschen design book. Pick a room theme from the awesome website, then when you arrive, take the hand-cranked birdcage elevator to your arty boudoir on the 3rd and 4th floors. Locally produced bathroom products and a green roof showcase the Gladstone's eco commitment. Downstairs, the Melody Bar band room and Café are integral to the Toronto indie scene, while the 2nd floor is dedicated to studio space and exhibitions for renting artists.

Bonnevue Manor B&B $$
(☑ 416-536-1455; www.bonnevuemanor.com; 33 Beaty Ave; d incl breakfast from $99; ❁❂@; 🚌501, 504, 508) Tucked away on a side street between the furthest extents of Queen St W and King St W, this cozy place occupies a restored 1890s redbrick mansion with divine handcrafted architectural details. Six guest

ONTARIO TORONTO

rooms exhibit warm-colored interiors; all have bathrooms. Enjoy your cooked breakfast out on the grapevine-covered deck.

East End & The Beaches

★ Only Backpackers Inn   HOSTEL $
(www.theonlycafe.com/inn/accomodations; 972 Danforth Ave; dm $23-25; ❋🐾@; ⓢDonlands) We love everything about the Only! Inspired by owner James' globetrotting adventures, it's everything you want a hostel to be: clean, intimate, convenient (subway to door) and in a perfect spot on The Danforth. There's free wi-fi, waffles for brekky and two private patios. Downstairs in the annexed licensed cafe where it all started, there's a large patio with 24 gourmet brews on tap.

Au Petit Paris   B&B $
(Map p74; ✎416-928-1348; www.bbtoronto.com/aupetitparis; 3 Selby St; d $85-129; ⊖❋🐾; ⓢSherbourne) Hardwood floors blend with modern decor inside this exquisite bay-and-gable Cabbagetown Victorian. The pick of the four en suite rooms are the skylit Nomad's Suite and the Artist's Suite, with garden views and extra-large bathtubs. At time of writing breakfast was no longer provided.

Toronto Townhouse B&B   B&B $$
(Map p74; ✎877-500-0466, 416-323-8898; www.torontotownhouse.com; 213 Carlton St; d incl breakfast $129-179; ⊖❋🐾; 🚗506) The six quaint rooms inside this 140-year-old heritage row house, just east of Church & Wellesley Village, are beautifully restored. A few come with private balconies and en suite bathrooms; breakfast includes homemade granola, baked goodies, pancakes and omelettes.

1871 Historic House B&B   B&B $$
(Map p74; ✎416-923-6950; www.1871bnb.com; 65 Huntley St; s/d with shared bathroom incl breakfast from $95/105; ⊖❋🐾; ⓢSherbourne) What other property can claim both Ernest Hemingway and John Lennon have walked the halls? In this historic Cabbagetown Victorian home, which displays its art and antiques in sunny common areas, all rooms are without a bathroom, but the coach-house suite has its own hot tub.

Jare's Place   B&B $$
(✎416-778-1940; www.jaresplace.ca; 87 Empire Ave; s/d incl tax & breakfast $96/125; ❋🐾; 🚗501) Colorful, clean, cozy (only three rooms) and convenient, young entrepreneur Jare's place is in a great spot, minutes from both the downtown (heading west) and trendy Leslieville district. There's free wi-fi and breakfasts to remember. Those not traditionally accustomed to staying in B&Bs might well reconsider after first visiting Jare's place in cyberspace.

Accommodating the Soul   B&B $$
(✎866-686-0619, 416-686-0619; www.accommodatingthesoul.com; 114 Waverley Rd; d incl breakfast $125-145; ⊖❋🐾; 🚗501) An early-20th-century home in The Beaches, boasting antiques and fabulous gardens, just a short walk from the lake. One room has an en suite, the other two share a bathroom.

Toronto Islands

Smiley's B&B   B&B $$
(✎416-203-8599; www.erelda.ca; 4 Dacotah Ave, Algonquin Island; r with shared bathroom $100, apt per night/week $250/1400; ⊖❋🐾; 🚢Ward's Island) Sleep the night away in 'Belvedere' – a sunny B&B room – and dine with the hosts, or hole-up in the studio apartment with its own kitchen and bathroom. Either way, on the car-free islands, relaxation is sure to come easy.

✖ Eating

Nowhere is Toronto's multiculturalism more potent and thrilling than on the plates of its restaurants. Eating here is a delight – you'll find everything from Korean walnut cakes to sweat-inducing Thai curries, New York steaks and good ol' Canuck pancakes with peameal bacon and maple syrup. Fusion food is the future: traditional Western recipes invaded with handfuls of zingy Eastern ingredients and cooked with pan-Asian flare. British influences also linger – fizzy lunchtime pints and formal afternoon high teas are much-loved traditions.

Executive diners file into classy restaurants in the Financial District and Old York, while eclectic, affordable eateries fill Baldwin Village, Kensington Market, Queen West and the Yonge St strip. More ethnically consistent are Little Italy, Greektown (The Danforth), Little India and Chinatown. Ponder your profoundest cravings, identify your neighborhood of choice, then dive right in!

✖ Harbourfront

Against the Grain Urban Tavern   PUB $$
(Map p78; ✎647-344-1562; http://corusquay.aturbantavern.ca; 25 Dockside Dr; mains $14-26;

⊘11am-11pm Sun-Thu, to 1am Fri & Sat; 🚌509)
The best feature of this glorified pub is its
enormous lakefront patio (seasonal) with
some of the best views of the Toronto Harbourfront. Come with a friend to enjoy the
sunshine and a martini, share a plate of pork
belly or spicy lobster tacos, or get messy
with the signature pulled pork sandwich.
Mondays have $5 pints and half-price share
plates from 3pm to 7pm.

Harbour Sixty Steakhouse STEAKHOUSE $$$
(Map p78; ☑416-777-2111; www.harboursixty.com;
60 Harbour St; mains $32-130; ⊘11:30am-late
Mon-Fri, 5pm-late Sat & Sun; 🚌509, 510) Inside
the Gothically isolated 1917 Toronto Har-
bour Commission building, this opulent ba-
roque dining room glows with brass lamps
and plush booths. Indulge yourself in an
eminent variety of enormous steaks, salmon
or seasonal Florida stone-crab claws and
broiled Caribbean lobster tail. Side dishes
are big enough for two. Prepare to burn a
significant hole in your wallet. Reservations
essential.

✗ Financial District

★**Richmond Station** INTERNATIONAL $$
(Map p74; ☑647-748-1444; www.richmondstation.
ca; 1 Richmond St W; mains $20-29; ⊘11:30am-
10:30pm Mon-Fri, 5:30-10:30pm Sat; Ⓢ Queen)
Reservations are strongly advised at this
busy and uncomplicated restaurant, brainchild of celebrity *Top Chef Canada* season-
two winner, Carl Heinrich. Dishes are 'in-
gredient focused and technique driven.'
We loved the chunky lobster cocktail and
buttery mushroom fettuccine. The eclectic
menu is simple but gratifying, priced right
and complemented by a well-paired wine
list and daily chalkboard specials. Highly
recommended.

Terroni ITALIAN $$
(Map p78; ☑416-203-3093; 57 Adelaide St E;
mains $8-18; ⊘9am-10pm Mon-Wed, to 11pm
Thu-Sat; Ⓢ King) The Adelaide St branch of
this popular Italian eatery (there are two
others, and one in LA) occupies a former
courthouse with high vaulted ceilings and
labyrinthine dining areas. It's open, funky
and, despite the size, generally packed.
A DJ spins beats while the punters eat.
Reasonably priced wood-fired pizzas, rich
pastas and fresh panini would make the
Godfather proud. Modifications to dishes
are a no-no.

OLD-SCHOOL DINERS

In a city where franchised everything is
inescapable, where neighborhoods are
in a constant state of flux and restau-
rants come and go, it's refreshing to
know that some things never change.
We've sniffed out some of Toronto's
most classic diners, greasy spoons
and cheap eats to transport you back
the golden age of vinyl and laminate
booths, elbow grease and good ole'
fashioned home cookin': cheap, oh-so
tasty and not-so good for the waistline.
Aren't you on vacation, anyway?

➡ Patrician Grill (p102)

➡ Avenue Open Kitchen (p102)

➡ Golden Diner (p105)

➡ Gale's Snack Bar (p109)

➡ Senator Restaurant (p104)

For a shiny new take on the classic
theme, perfect for late-night people-
watching and open 24/7, hit Thompson
Diner (p103).

Nami JAPANESE $$
(Map p78; ☑416-362-7373; www.namirestaurant.
ca; 55 Adelaide St E; lunch sets from $13.95, din-
ner mains from $19.95, sukiyaki per person $33;
⊘11:45am-2:30pm Mon-Fri, 5:30-10:30pm Sat;
Ⓢ King) The name means 'wave' (as in tsu-
nami) – the neon wave on the outside of
the building is unmissable and cool. Bustling about the black lacquered interior are
kimono-clad hostesses and intense sushi
chefs, who make only small concessions to
North American palates. *Robatayaki* grill-
ing is a specialty, so is this *the* place to try
homestyle sukiyaki hotpot.

Earl's MODERN AMERICAN $$
(Map p78; ☑416-916-0227; www.earls.ca; Suite
100, 150 King St W; mains $13-33; ⊘11:30am-late;
Ⓢ St Andrew) The Financial District branch
of this upscale restaurant chain can be hit
and miss: it's all about the timing. From
5pm in the warmer months, the beautiful
streetside patio fills with suits and singles
looking for spouses. If you time it wrong,
you won't get a table. Reservations aren't
accepted. Come for cocktails and upscale
versions of North American favorites.

VEGETARIAN HAVENS

....

Meat-free restaurants in food-obsessed Toronto run the gamut from gourmet to passe. We like the following:

➡ Govinda's (p106)

➡ Grasslands (p108)

➡ Sadie's Diner (p107)

➡ Urban Herbivore (p107)

Bymark
FUSION $$$

(Map p78; 416-777-1144; www.bymark.mcewangroup.ca; TD Centre, 66 Wellington St W; mains $27-90; 11:30am-3pm Mon-Fri & 5pm-midnight Mon-Sat; St Andrew) Toronto culinary powerhouse Mark McEwan brings his sophisticated menu of continentally hewn cuisine to this hip, bi-level downtowner. His creative kitchen crew whips seasonal regional ingredients (wild truffles, quail, soft-shell crab) into sensational combinations, each with suggested wine or beer pairings. It's on street level.

Old York

St Lawrence Market
MARKET $

(Map p78; 416-392-7120; www.stlawrencemarket.com; South Market, 92 Front St E; items $2-10; 8am-6pm Tue-Thu, to 7pm Fri, 5am-5pm Sat; 503, 504) Buskers and classical trios provide an acoustic backdrop at the city's beloved market, offering a mouthwatering range of quality produce, baked goods and imported foodstuffs. The **Carousel Bakery** is famed for its peameal bacon sandwiches (chunky back bacon cured in cornmeal served on a fresh bun) and **St Urbain** for its authentic Montréal-style bagels. The farmers market livens up the North Market from 5am every Saturday.

Patrician Grill
DINER $

(Map p78; 416-366-4841; 219 King St E; meals $3.75-10.95; 8am-4pm Mon-Sat) Built in the 1950s, the Patrician has been run by the same family since 1967 and looks the part. Photographers will have a field day with the neon outside and the original decor inside. Burgers, BLTs, bacon and eggs (cooked to perfection) and home fries are the order of the day. Friday lunchtime meatloaf is a local instituition and sells out before you can say, 'Please sir, I want some more'!

Bombay Palace
INDIAN $

(Map p78; 416-368-8048; www.bombaypalacetoronto.com; 71 Jarvis St; lunch buffet $12.99; 11:30am-2pm & 5-9:30pm) This welcoming Indian restaurant occupies the front half of a quirky old house. It has a fine-dining atmosphere, polite, old-fashioned service and authentic, well-presented dishes. The à la carte dinner menu is a little pricey, but you can't go past the daily lunch and Sunday dinner buffets for excellent value.

Sultan's Tent & Café Maroc
MIDDLE EASTERN $$

(Map p78; 416-961-0601; www.thesultanstent.com; 49 Front St E; mains $17-39; noon-3pm Mon-Fri & 5-10:30pm Mon-Sat; 503, 504) Dark and atmospheric, replete with stained-glass lanterns, candles and fringed cushions, the Sultan's Tent serves traditional Moroccan cuisine. We liked the couscous royale ($24) and for dessert the *keskesu* (sweet couscous, cinnamon, almonds, raisins and orange-blossom water). Belly dancers may or may not help you digest.

Hiro Sushi
SUSHI $$$

(Map p78; 416-304-0550; www.hirosushi.ca; 171 King St E; lunch specials from $12, dinner $35-70; noon-2:30pm Tue-Sat & 5:30-10:30pm Sat; 503, 504) If sushi is your thing, good-humored Hiro is your man. This authentic Japanese *sushi-ya* prefers to operate on the traditional principle of *omakase:* leave it to the chef. If you do, a tantalizing journey awaits. However, Hiro understands the particular sensibilities of Western diners and offers a limited à la carte menu which varies according to the availability of produce and his mood.

Entertainment District & King Street West

Wvrst
EUROPEAN $

(Map p84; 416-703-7775; www.wvrst.com; 609 King St W; sausage from $6; 11:30am-late; 504, 508) Like sausage? If Wvrsts phenomenal success is any indication, then Toronto's hipsters do too. With more bangers and snags than you can poke a stick at, do yourself a favor and get some pork on your fork. Will you have the duck fat or dirty fries with that?

Avenue Open Kitchen
DINER $

(Map p84; 416-504-7131; 7 Camden St; sandwiches from $3, burgers from $4.50; 7am-5pm Mon-Fri; 504) This cozy little joint off Spadina Ave feels like it's been here forever, but it's spotlessly clean and great value. Go on, have a BLT with cheese and a side of fries and gravy for your lunch: we dare you. Breakfasts and burgers are truly old school and easy on the wallet. There's always a daily special.

Burger Brats BURGERS $
(Map p78; ☑ 647-352-4786; www.burgerbrats.ca; 254 Adelaide St W; burgers from $5.50; ⊙ 11am-9pm Mon-Thu, to 4am Fri & Sat) Home of 'the Great Canadian Hangover,' a burger with an obscene amount of meat, peameal bacon, an egg, mushrooms and the standard garnish thrown in for good measure ($15). Not feeling it? Keep the calories down around 1500 with the Classic and those awesome hand-cut fries. Don't forget the gravy! Mmmmm.

Burrito Banditos MEXICAN $
(Map p78; 120 Peter St; burritos from $5.75; ⊙ 11:30am-11pm Mon-Thu, to 4am Fri & Sat, noon-9pm Sun; ⓖ 501, 502) Club-hounds who haven't got lucky pile into this basement booth to assuage their disappointment with a hefty injection of chili, sour cream and salsa. There's not enough room in here for both you and your burrito – grab one to go.

Ravi Soups INTERNATIONAL $
(Map p78; ☑ 647-435-8365; www.ravisoup.com; 322 Adelaide St W; soups $8.99; ⊙ 11am-10pm Mon-Fri, to 6pm Sat; ⓖ 504, 508) This one is pretty simple: a small menu of six soups (think corn chowder with blue crab and porcini mushroom wild rice bisque) and four wraps (curried beef with roasted yams) that are done to perfection – all are delicious. There's a small eating area with a sharing table which is usually jam-packed.

Thompson Diner DINER $$
(Map p84; ☑ 416-601-3533; www.thompsondiner.com; 550 Wellington St W; breakfast from $10, mains from $11.75; ⊙ 24hr; ⓖ 504, 511) The casual dining option at the sexy Thompson hotel is open 24 hours (breakfast served 5am to 11am). Whatever time of day, there's likely good people-watching to be had: this is nightclub territory, remember. Comfort food is a sure thing, and the decor a classy modern twist on the classic diner theme. Will it be peameal eggs Benedict or buttermilk fried chicken with cheddar mash for breakfast?

Khao San Road THAI $$
(Map p78; ☑ 647-352-5773; www.khaosanroad.ca; 326 Adelaide St W; mains $13-16; ⊙ 11:30am-2:30pm & 5-10pm Mon-Sat; ☑; ⓖ 504, 508) Folks

line around the block for what's billed as Toronto's best Thai restaurant. Reservations aren't accepted. Granted, if you're a fan of the genre, it can be worth the wait. Once inside, everything functions like a machine: orders are turned around fast and the food is awesome. There's a vegan menu too.

Patria SPANISH $$
(Map p84; ☑ 416-367-0505; www.patriatoronto.com; 480 King St W; small plates $6-16; ⊙ 11am-2:30pm Sun-Fri & 5:30pm-close daily, tapas 2:30-5:30pm Sun & Mon; ⓖ 504, 508) Everything works beautifully in this expansive, stylish and modern restaurant specializing in Spanish tapas and cuisine. Reservations are highly recommended: it's usually packed. Knowledgeable servers help navigate the mouthwatering menu of cheeses, meats and seafood. Tapas are meant to be shared: order plenty and don't bother coming alone. Sunday brunch is a delightful deviation from the usual suspects.

Big Daddy's Bourbon St Bistro SEAFOOD $$
(Map p78; ☑ 416-599-5200; www.bigdaddys.ca; 212 King St W; mains $12-35; ⊙ 11:30am-late; ⓢ St Andrews) In the heart of the theater strip, Big Daddy's is the perfect spot for a pre-show dinner or drink. Straight from the heart of Louisiana y'all, the menu is seafood-centric with a Cajun bent. There are cheesy seafood fondues, scallops, calamari and crab cakes as well as a prix-fixe three-course option. Burp.

★**Lee** ASIAN $$$
(Map p84; ☑ 416-504-7867; www.susur.com/lee; 601 King St W; plates $7-35; ⊙ 5:30-10:30pm Mon-Wed, to 11:30pm Thu-Sat; ⓖ 504, 508) Truly a feast for the senses, dinner at acclaimed *cuisinier* Susur Lee's self-titled flagship restaurant is an experience best shared. Slick servers assist in navigating the artisan selection of East-meets-West Asian delights: you really want to get the pairings right. It's impossible to adequately convey the wonderful dance of flavors, textures and aromas one experiences in the signature Singaporean slaw, with... how many?? ingredients!

✕ Chinatown & Baldwin Village

Phở Hu'ng VIETNAMESE $
(Map p84; ☑ 416-593-4274; 350 Spadina Ave; mains $6-13; ⊙ 10am-10pm; ⓖ 510) Clipped service and infernally busy tables are the price you pay for Phở Hu'ng's awesome Vietnamese soups. A few dishes may be a touch

too authentic for some (pork intestines and blood) but the coffee is spot-on.

Mother's Dumplings
CHINESE $

(Map p74; ☑ 416-217-2008; www.mothersdumplings.com; 421 Spadina Ave; dumplings 12 pieces from $6.39; ⊘ 11:30am-10pm; 🚃 506, 510) The cleanest and best located of Chinatown's dumpling houses (it's actually closer to Kensington Market) prepares plump and juicy dumplings to authentic recipes passed on down generations. However you like them, steamed or pan-fried, pork, chicken, beef, shrimp or vegetarian, these dumplings will fill your tum and delight your wallet.

Kinton Ramen
NOODLES $

(Map p74; ☑ 647-748-8900; www.kintonramen.com; 51 Baldwin St; noodles from $9.50; ⊘ 11:30am-10:30pm; 🚃 505, 506) Ramen noodles are practically a religion in Japan and they're becoming increasingly popular in Toronto. The cool brains behind this clever outfit leapt upon the bandwagon with their own distinct flavor: caramelized pork. There's even a version with cheese, if you can imagine. This place oozes atmosphere – it's lively, noisy, steamy and beery. Join in the fun.

★ND Sushi
JAPANESE $$

(Map p74; ☑ 416-551-6362; www.ndsushiandgrill.com; 3 Baldwin St; mains $15-22; ⊘ 11:30am-3pm Mon-Fri & 5-10pm Mon-Sat; 🚃 505, 506) From its pole position at the beginning of Baldwin St, this unassuming *shokudō* prepares favorite Japanese treats like *gyoza*, tempura and mouthwatering sashimi with authenticity. Its specialty is sushi, including a variety of not-so-traditional Western *maki* rolls: the spicy rainbow roll is divine. You could pay a whole lot more for Japanese food of this caliber.

Cafe la Gaffe
CAFE $$

(Map p74; ☑ 416-596-2397; www.cafelagaffe.com; 24 Baldwin St; mains $7-25; ⊘ noon-11pm Mon-Fri, 11am-11pm Sat & Sun; 🚃 505, 506) Stripy cotton tablecloths and fresh-cut flowers adorn the tables in this little cafe. There's a street patio and a leafy garden patio where you can dine on market salads, a filet mignon sandwich or the hand-tossed pizzas. A small-print wine list offers an extensive selection.

Swatow
CHINESE $$

(Map p74; 309 Spadina Ave; mains $8-14; ⊘ 11am-2am; 🚃 505, 510) Catering to a late-night crowd, the menu here covers cuisine from Swatow (a city now known as Shantou, on

the coast of China's Guangdong province). Nicknamed 'red cooking' for its potent splashings of fermented rice wine, the house noodles are fiery. Cash only; be prepared to queue.

✖ Downtown Yonge

Urban Eatery
CAFETERIA $

(Map p74; 1 Dundas St W; ⊘ 10am-9pm Mon-Sat, to 7pm Sun; Ⓢ Dundas) More than just a food court, the Urban Eatery opened in the basement level of the gargantuan Eaton Centre in 2011, with 24 outlets from fast food to seated dining. If you're at a pinch for something to eat and tired of walking, you're bound to find something here; in fact, you'll be spoiled for choice. In winter it's an underground haven connected to the PATH and subway system, too.

Good View
CHINESE $

(Map p74; ☑ 416-861-0888; www.goodviewrestaurant.ca; 134 Dundas St E; items from $8; ⊘ 11:30am-late Mon-Sat; Ⓢ Dundas) Delicious Cantonese cuisine is prepared fresh at this glorified Chinese takeout not far from Yonge & Dundas Sq. Lunch and dinner specials are great value to take back to your hotel, but the real delight is in eating in with a few friends and choosing a variety of dishes from the à la carte menu.

Salad King
THAI $

(Map p74; ☑ 416-593-0333; www.saladking.com; 340 Yonge St; mains $5.50-9.75; ⊘ 11am-10pm Mon-Fri, noon-11pm Sat, to 9pm Sun; Ⓢ Dundas) An institution among students of neighboring Ryerson University, colorful and somewhat misleadingly named Salad King dispenses large bowls of rich Thai curries, noodle soups, rice and, yes, salads, for under $10. Long stainless-steel sharing tables and cozy booths are usually full of hungry patrons. You can specify your desired level of spice on a scale of 1-20!

Senator Restaurant
DINER $$

(Map p74; ☑ 416-364-7517; www.thesenator.com; 249 Victoria St; mains $8.45-17.95; ⊘ 8am-2:30pm Mon-Sun & 5-9pm Tue-Sat; Ⓢ Dundas) Art deco buffs will delight in the Senator's curved glass windows, fluted aluminum counterface and original booths. Meals are refreshingly simple and home-style: we love the fish and chips, meatloaf and macaroni. Say no more?

Eat Fresh Be Healthy
INTERNATIONAL $$

(Map p74; ☑ 647-258-8808; www.eatfreshbe-healthy.com; 185 Dundas St W; lunch from $10.49, dinner from $13.49; ⊙ 11:30am-9pm Mon-Fri, 3-9pm Sat; ⌨ 505) Truly a case of 'don't judge a book by its cover,' the exterior of this wonderful restaurant on a rather drab strip of Dundas St is easy to pass by. Don't. Inside, a variety of hearty, healthy, home-style meals await, from fresh filled sandwiches and lean pastas for lunch to braised lamb and mustard-glazed pork chops for dinner. The prix-fixe lunch and dinner specials are excellent value.

JOEY Eaton Centre
MODERN AMERICAN $$$

(Map p74; ☑ 647-352-5639; www.joeyrestaurants.com/eaton-centre; 1 Dundas St W; mains $13-30; ⊙ 11am-1am Sun-Wed, to 2am Thu-Sat; ⑤ Dundas) The downtown Toronto branch of this upscale casual (if the cap fits...) grill and lounge bar has decor to impress and a menu to match with a center-of-town location atop Dundas Station at the Eaton Centre. Favorite items include the Baja fish tacos, crispy chicken sandwich and lobster grilled cheese. Variations can be made for gluten-free and vegetarian diners.

🗺 Church-Wellesley Village

Golden Diner Family Restaurant
DINER $

(Map p74; ☑ 416-977-9898; 105 Carlton St; breakfast from $2.50; ⊙ 6.30am-10pm; ⑤ College) This good old-fashioned basement-level Greek diner has some natty booths and one of the best-value all-day breakfasts in the city. The $6.95 breakfast special includes three eggs, a handful of crispy bacon or peameal bacon, a mound of home fries and a bottomless cup of coffee. Pancakes are $2.50! It's not the best breakfast in town, but it will fill you up and save you some coin, so there's more to spend on dinner.

Ethiopian House
AFRICAN $

(Map p74; ☑ 416-923-5438; www.ethiopianhouse.com; 4 Irwin Ave; mains $11-17; ⊙ noon-11pm; ☑; ⑤ Wellesley) You won't find cutlery at this culturally authentic dining experience: slather chunks of *sherro wot* (seasoned chickpeas) and *gored-gored* (spiced beef) onto wonderful moist *injera* (bread) and eat with your hands, then try the after-dinner coffee ceremony: it's widely regarded that coffee originated in the then Ethiopian kingdom of Kaffa. Numerous vegetarian dishes are available.

★ Hair of the Dog
PUB $$

(Map p74; ☑ 416-964-2708; www.hairofdogpub.com; 425 Church St; share plates from $8, mains from $13; ⊙ 11:30am-late Mon-Fri, 10:30am-late Sat & Sun; ⑤ College) At its best in the warmer months when two levels of shaded patios spring to life with a mixed gay/straight crowd, this chilled puppy is delightfully less mainstream than its Village neighbors a few blocks north. Equally listable as a 'Drinking' venue, the pub's food stands on its own: sharing plates and salads are great. Show me a nonvegetarian who can resist the butter chicken grilled cheese, and I'll buy you a pint of Sapporo.

Fire on the East Side
FUSION $$

(Map p74; ☑ 416-960-3473; www.fireontheeastside.ca; 6 Gloucester St; mains $10-25; ⊙ 11:30am-10:30pm Mon-Fri, 10am-10:30pm Sat & Sun; ⑤ Wellesley) Best for brunch, with a feisty selection of 'East Side Bennies' and morning after cocktails, this neighborhood fave also serves dinner from 4pm with a modest selection of well-prepared modern American and European dishes. It was once known for its haywire variations on Caribbean and Cajun themes, but after some kitchen changes only the buttermilk biscuits and fried chicken have echoes of the deep South.

Guu
JAPANESE $$

(Map p74; ☑ 416-977-0999; www.guu-izakaya.com/toronto; 398 Church St; ⊙ 11:30am-2pm & 5-11:30pm Mon-Fri, 4:30-11:30pm Sat & Sun; ⑤ College) Hip young Japanese use the street-word *'guu'* for 'good' or 'cool.' This so-named reproduction of a Japanese *izakaya* is always packed, loud and lively. Come with friends for beer, sake and a selection of mouthwatering small plates like spicy *negitoro* (fatty tuna), deep-fried brie with mango and berry sauce, and banana tempura with coconut ice cream! You'll likely have to queue to get in unless you make a reservation online. Hint, hint.

Sambucas on Church
ITALIAN $$

(Map p74; ☑ 416-966-3241; www.sambucas.ca/home; 489 Church St; mains $9.95-21.95; ⊙ 10:30am-10:30pm; ⑤ Wellesley) Great for weekday lunches, weekend brunches and dinner anytime, Sambucas' Italian menu has some North American twists. Pastas are hearty, risottos creamy and the chicken dishes noteworthy. We really dig the calamari. If you're lucky, try for the window table to watch the Villagers walk by.

Bloor-Yorkville

Okonomi House
JAPANESE $

(Map p74; 23 Charles St W; mains $6-12; ⊙11:30am-10pm Mon-Sat, noon-8pm Sun; ⑤Bloor-Yonge) Okonomi House is one of the only places in Toronto (and perhaps North America) dishing up authentic *okonomiyaki* – savory Japanese cabbage pancakes filled with meat, seafood or vegetables. A must for Japanophiles.

7 West Café
CAFE $$

(Map p74; ☑416-928-9041; www.7westcafe.com; 7 Charles St W; mains $10.95-17.95; ⊙24hr; ⑤Bloor-Yonge) Three floors of moody lighting, textured jade paint, framed nudes, wooden church pews and jaunty ceiling angels set the scene for a dazzling selection of pizzas, pastas and sandwiches, and 24-hour breakfasts. Make like a vampire sipping blood-red wine (by the glass or bottle) as the moon dapples shadows across the street. Cool.

Bloor Street Diner
INTERNATIONAL $$

(Map p74; ☑416-928-3105; www.bloorstreetdiner.com; Manulife Centre, 55 Bloor St W; mains $10.50-26, brunch $25.95; ⊙noon-1am; ⑤Bloor-Yonge) Deceptively named, the swanky Bloor Street Diner has been a Toronto favorite for over 30 years, loved for its Parisian-style patio, distinguished wine list and impressive Sunday brunch buffet with chocolate fountain. Hit the cafe section in the mall out front for speedy takeout sandwiches.

Carens Wine and Cheese Bar
FUSION $$

(Map p74; ☑416-962-5158; www.carenswineandcheese.com; 158 Cumberland St; lunch $14-24, dinner $16-35; ⊙11:30am-10pm; ⑤St George) The staff of this delightful, rustic bi-level restaurant will happily recommend wine pairings for their amazing selection of world cheeses. Bright pashminas drape over chairs in case you get a chill on the intimate and stylish back patio, and Thai lanterns hang from the trees. Weekend brunches are delightful, and the spicy baked mac 'n cheese ($16) is ah-mah-zing – add lobster for an extra $12.

Morton's the Steakhouse
STEAK $$$

(Map p74; ☑416-925-0648; www.mortons.com/toronto; 4 Avenue Rd; mains from $28; ⊙5:30-11pm; ⑤Bay) If you like steak and don't find what you get here absolutely to your liking, we'd be extremely surprised if they didn't rectify the situation quick smart. These people are serious about steak: your server will bring a trolley of shrinkwrapped cuts to your table, so you can see just what you're getting. Expect to drop a couple of hundred here on a dinner for two with wine, then slip into a food coma.

Sassafraz
FUSION $$$

(Map p74; ☑416-964-2222; www.sassafraz.ca; 100 Cumberland St; mains $21-39; ⊙11:30am-2am Tue-Sat, to midnight Sun & Mon; ⑤Bay) Popular with visiting celebrities and the nouveau riche, Sassafraz's style epitomizes Yorkville. Jazz combos serenade weekend brunchers; sassy receptionists distribute clientele between the sun-drenched patio and leafy indoor courtyard. The food? Predictably good. Dress: to impress.

University of Toronto & The Annex

Govinda's
VEGETARIAN $

(☑888-218-1040; www.govindas.ca; 243 Avenue Rd; by donation; ⊙noon-3pm & 6-8pm Mon-Sat; ☑; ⑤Rosedale) The Hare Krishna movement has been feeding poor travelers around the globe for decades. Toronto is no exception. Politely decline any offers of religious conversion, make a small donation and enjoy tasty, karma-free vegetarian fare that is on the whole good for body and soul. It's a little out of the way, on the very northern fringe of the Annex.

Chabichau
FRENCH $

(Map p84; ☑647-430-4942; www.chabichou.ca; 196 Borden St; ⊙10am-7pm Mon-Fri, 9am-7pm Sat & Sun; ⊟510) This French *traiteur* has a mouthwatering selection of fine cheeses and pâté (try the duck and pistachio), filled sandwiches on freshly baked bread and daily specials such as pork-apple stew: simple, hearty, awesome. The small cafe is a delight, but the booty on offer cries 'put me in your picnic basket'!

★ Country Style
HUNGARIAN $$

(Map p84; ☑416-536-5966; 450 Bloor St W; schnitzels from $18; ⊙11am-10pm; ⑤Bathurst) This delightful Hungarian diner with its red-and-white checkered tablecloths and friendly family staff hasn't changed a bit in at least a generation. The variety of enormous breaded schnitzels, cooked to crunchy perfection, are the best in town, and the cucumber salad is a treat. We hope they don't change a single thing for as long as they possibly can. Note that menu prices include tax.

By the Way MIDDLE EASTERN $$
(Map p84; ☑416-967-4295; www.bythewaycafe.com; 400 Bloor St W; mains $9-17; ☺9am-9pm Sun-Wed, to 10pm Thu-Sat; ☒; ⑤Bathurst, Spadina) An Annex fixture, this cheerful corner bistro has a fusion menu that leans toward Middle Eastern. Although there's plenty of meat on the menu, vegetarians won't go hungry. There's an extensive and well-selected wine list.

✖ Kensington Market & Little Italy

Aunties & Uncles CAFE $
(Map p84; ☑416-324-1375; www.auntiesanduncles.ca; 74 Lippincott St; mains $2-8.75; ☺9am-3pm; ☐510) There's usually a line on the sidewalk outside the picket fence of this always-bustling brunch/lunch joint with a simple menu of cheap and cheery homemade favorites. Plop yourself down in one of the mismatched chairs and dig into dishes like grilled brie with pear chutney and walnuts on challah, banana oatmeal pancakes, or grilled Canadian cheddar.

Jumbo Empanadas CHILEAN $
(Map p84; ☑416-977-0056; www.jumboempanadas.com; 245 Augusta Ave; items from $4.50; ☺9am-8pm Mon-Sat, 11am-6pm Sun; ☐510) They're not kidding – chunky Chilean empanadas (toasted delights stuffed with beef, chicken, cheese or vegetables) and savory corn pie with beef, olives and eggs always sell out early. A mini empanada will only set you back $1.50. Bread and salsas are also homemade.

Nguyen Huong SANDWICHES $
(Map p84; ☑416-599-4625; www.nguyenhuong.ca; 322 Spadina Ave; sandwiches from $5; ☺8:30am-8:30pm; ☐510) Cheap and delicious filled Vietnamese sandwiches are the name of the day at the original precursor to Toronto's *banh-mi* phenomenon.

Urban Herbivore VEGETARIAN $
(Map p84; ☑416-927-1231; www.herbivore.to; 64 Oxford St; mains $4-10; ☺8am-8pm; ☒; ☐510) This humble wholefoods joint specializes in vegetarian meals *sans* additives and preservatives, including salads, rice bowls, chunky soups and specialty vegan gluten-free baked goodies. There's also a branch at the Eaton Centre's Urban Eatery (p104).

Kalendar CAFE $$
(Map p84; ☑416-923-4138; www.kalendar.com; 546 College St; mains $11-25; ☺11:30am-late Mon-Fri, from 10:30am Sat & Sun; ☐510) Kalendar feels like France in Little Italy, with dark wood, tiled floors and a dainty sidewalk patio. The menu funks things up with different types of scrolls (crepe-style roti topped with all sorts of veggies and sauces) and nannettes – naan topped with yummies such as pesto, artichoke hearts and Asiago cheese. There's a long list of cocktails to help you wash it all down.

Bar Italia ITALIAN $$
(Map p84; ☑416-535-3621; www.bar-italia.ca; 582 College St; mains $14-27; ☺11am-late Mon-Fri, from 10am Sat & Sun; ☐506) Locals love Bar Italia, a place to see and be seen (especially from a vantage point on the coveted front patio). Grab a sandwich or al dente pasta, with a lemon gelato and a rich coffee afterward – and while away the entire afternoon or evening.

Caplansky's Deli DINER $$
(Map p84; ☑416-500-3852; www.caplanskys.com; 356 College St; mains $7-18; ☺11am-10pm Mon-Fri, from 9am Sat & Sun; ☐510) All-day breakfasts and Montréal-style hot smoked-meat deli sandwiches are the claim to fame of this authentic Jewish deli, also serving rich meaty dinners and daily specials. The friendly folks won't make you feel like chopped liver, though you're more than welcome to order some if you wish ($7).

✖ Queen West & Trinity Bellwoods

New York Subway FAST FOOD $
(Map p84; ☑416-703-4496; www.newyork-subsburritos.com; 520 Queen St W; 'burritos' from $3.49; ☺11:30am-midnight Mon-Fri, to 10pm Sat) It's hard to describe the weird burrito creations that late-night punters have been flocking here to consume for years, but they're awesome. The joint ain't fancy, but these things are cheap, delicious and filling. Mushroom lovers should stick to their instincts and will be rewarded.

Sadie's Diner DINER $
(Map p84; www.sadiesdiner.com; 504 Adelaide St W; mains $9-13; ☺7:30am-10pm Mon-Fri, 9am-10pm Sat & Sun; ☒; ☐504, 511) This quaint diner and juice bar specializes in all-day breakfasts and healthy-ish comfort foods and is vegan-friendly and celiac-conscious.

★ Queen Mother Café   FUSION $$

(Map p74; 416-598-4719; www.queenmothercafe. com; 208 Queen St W; mains $9-23; 11:30am-1am Mon-Sat, to midnight Sun; Osgoode) A Queen St institution, the Queen Mother is beloved for its cozy, dark wooden booths and excellent pan-Asian menu. Canadian comfort food is also on offer – try the Queen Mum burger. Check out the display of old stuff they found in the walls the last time they renovated. The patio is hidden and one of the best in town.

Burger's Priest   BURGERS $$

(Map p84; 647-748-8108; www.theburgerspriest. com; 463 Queen St W; burgers from $5.49; noon-9:30pm Mon-Sat) There's a lot of hype surrounding the Priest – some say the burgers are the best in town. They're good and simple: fresh ground beef, soft bun, griddled to perfection. We recommend 'the Priest' (of course), topped with a breaded deep-fried portobello mushroom, but check out the secret menu online, if you're brave. For dessert, don't shy from the Vatican on ice: an ice-cream sandwiched between two grilled cheese sandwiches (that's right). It's an experience.

5th Element   INDIAN $$

(Map p84; 416-504-3213; www.5thelementt.com; 506 Queen St W; lunch sets from $6.95; 11:30am-10pm Mon-Fri, 5-10pm Sat & Sun) This pleasant Indian restaurant has all the usual suspects and presents them consistently well. We're including it for the excellent-value lunch specials: choose one dish off the menu (prices vary for vegetarian, meat, seafood) with naan and rice.

Chippy's   FISH & CHIPS $$

(Map p84; 416-866-7474; www.chippys.ca; 893 Queen St W; fish from $8.50, chips from $3.99; 11:30am-9pm; 501) For a city as food-diverse as Toronto, there's a definite lack of good fish and chipperys. Chippy's is an exception: the fish is as fresh as you get in the big smoke, the chips are cut daily from Ontario and Prince Edward Island potatoes and the batter has two bottles of Guinness added to every batch. Sit in Trinity Bellwoods park, opposite, to enjoy your catch.

Grasslands   VEGETARIAN $$

(Map p84; 416-504-5127; www.grasslands.to; 478 Queen St W; dishes $9-19; 5:30-10pm Wed-Sun; ; 501) Grasslands was born in 2013 as a fresh revamp of former zenith of vegetarian and vegan dining in Toronto, Fressen. Keeping the same team and premises, Grasslands' superior service and sumptuous brick-and-wood dining room tempts even hardy carnivores. A stylish seasonally adjusted organic menu traverses world cuisines. Dishes are marked as wheat free, nut free, gluten free and Buddhist friendly.

Swan   CAFE $$

(Map p84; 416-532-0452; 892 Queen St W; mains $18-23; noon-10pm Mon-Fri, from 10am Sat & Sun; 501) This art-deco diner features a small and deceptively simple menu, with items like smoked oyster with pancetta and egg scrambles, club sandwiches, and mussels that rest iced in a vintage Coca-Cola cooler. The coffee is divine, and it's a great place to sit at the counter and read the paper on a rainy Sunday – if you can get a table.

Pizzeria Libretto   ITALIAN $$

(Map p84; 416-532-8000; http://ossington.pizzerialibretto.com; 221 Ossington Ave; mains $10-17; noon-11pm; 505) A bit north of Queen West in Portugal Village, Pizza Libretto crafts what is arguably the best pizza in town. The secret?

BEST COFFEE SHOPS?

Too early for beer? Sidestep the coffee chains for some *real* barista action:

➡ **Rooster Coffee House** (416-995-1530; www.roostercoffeehouse.com; 479 Broadview Ave; 7am-7pm; 504, 505) Opposite Riverdale Park.

➡ **Te Aro** (416-465-2006; www.pilotcoffeeroasters.com; 983 Queen St E; 7am-6pm Mon-Fri, from 8am Sat & Sun; 501, 502, 503) Leslieville.

➡ **Dark Horse Espresso** (Map p74; 416-979-1200; www.darkhorseespresso.com; 215 Spadina Ave; 7am-7pm Mon-Fri, from 8am Sat & Sun; 510) Fashion District/Chinatown.

➡ **B Espresso Bar** (Map p74; 416-866-2111; bespressobar.com; 111 Queen St E; 7:30am-5pm Mon-Fri; 501) Financial District/Corktown.

➡ **Moonbean Coffee Company** (Map p84; 416-595-0327; www.moonbeamcoffee.com; 30 St Andrews St; 7am-9pm; 510) Kensington Market.

➡ **Jet Fuel** (416-968-9982; www.jetfuelcoffee.com; 519 Parliament St; 7am-8pm; 506) Cabbagetown.

➡ **Remarkable Bean** (416-690-2420; 2242 Queen St E; 7am-10pm; 501) The Beaches.

A wood-fired oven built by a third-generation pizza-oven builder with stones shipped from Italy. Besides certified Neapolitan pizza and other Naples staples, the menu also includes a prix-fixe lunch (salad, pizza and gelato for $15) and an all-Italian wine list. Make sure you reserve your table for weekends.

Julie's Cuban   LATIN AMERICAN **$$**
(☎416-532-7397; www.juliescuban.com; 202 Dovercourt Rd; tapas from $4.25, mains $9-20; ⊘5:30-10pm Tue-Sun; ⌂501) This West Queen West neighborhood joint serves traditional Cuban dishes like *ropa vieja* (shredded beef in spicy tomato sauce with ripe plantains, white rice and black beans). The restaurant was once a corner store, and every effort has been made to retain the vibe.

★Union   FUSION **$$$**
(Map p84; ☎416-850-0093; www.union72.ca; 72 Ossington Ave; mains $18-34; ⊘6-10pm Mon & Tue, noon-3pm & 6-11pm Wed-Sun; ⌂501) This dandy little hipster kitchen serves a delicious fusion of French- and Italian- inspired dishes which it touts as 'simple done right,' although the menu feels more convoluted than simple. Fortunately, the food, decor and service are masterfully executed: steak, chicken, ribs and fish are staples. There's a delightful little patio out back.

✕ East End & The Beaches

★Gilead Café   CAFE **$**
(☎647-288-0680; www.jamiekennedy.ca/intro-gc.php; 4 Gilead Pl; mains $9-18; ⊘8am-3pm Mon-Sat, from 10am Sun; ⌂503, 504) Counter service meets haute Canadian cuisine in this Jamie Kennedy kitchen. The menu, featuring items like gourmet poutine, Canadian artisan cheese plates and cider mayo, is written on the chalkboard daily. Ingredients are sourced from Ontario farms; if you're watching your mileage, the Gilead is a great choice for the 100-mile diet.

Schnitzel Queen   EUROPEAN **$**
(Map p74; ☎416-363-9176; 237 Queen St E; schnitzels $7-10; ⊘11am-7pm Mon-Fri) This poky German takeout specializes in golden delicious breaded schnitzel sandwiches that make great picnic fodder. These mammoth creations are excellent value and usually good for two meals – the schnitzel is literally double the size of the bun. Purists should try for one of the few bar stools and stay in for the authentic dinner plates with mushroom sauce,

potato salad and sauerkraut ($9.99). Not open weekends.

Gale's Snack Bar   DINER **$**
(539 Eastern Ave; meals from $3.25; ⊘10am-6pm Mon-Fri, noon-5pm Sat; ⌂501, 502, 503) Off the gentrified Leslieville strip, on a working-class corner with high-vehicular traffic, you'll find this gritty hole-in-the-wall. If you can get past the fact that it hasn't been updated in decades, you'll discover some of Toronto's cheapest, greasy-spoon eats. Great value and tasty too.

Siddhartha   INDIAN **$$**
(☎416-465-4095; www.thesiddhartha.com; 1450 Gerrard St E; mains $9-18; ⊘11:30am-10pm; ⌂506) In a neighborhood stuffed with excellent South Asian food, Siddhartha is a consistent favorite. Although it's popular for its all-you-can-eat lunch and dinner buffets, don't be afraid to order off the menu. The naan is perfect, the curries are classic and the samosas are massive. Cool your burning tongue with a Kingfisher.

Pan on the Danforth   GREEK **$$**
(☎416-466-8158; www.panonthedanforth.com; 516 Danforth Ave; mezes $8-24, mains $17-59; ⊘noon-11pm Sun-Thu, to midnight Fri & Sat; ⓢChester) As Greek as Greektown, colorful, casual Pan serves unpretentious fare with traditional Greek flavors, like calamari, moussaka, Santorini chicken stuffed with spinach and feta, with new potatoes and seared veggies. Finish with a sticky chocolate baklava.

★Allen's   PUB **$$$**
(☎416-463-3086; www.allens.to/allens; 143 Danforth Ave; mains $12-36; ⊘11:30am-2am; ⓢBroadview, ⌂504, 505) Featuring one of the city's nicest patio dining areas (in warmer months), Allen's is more than just a pub, although it is a great place to come for lovers of Irish music and dance. The menu changes with the seasons. Expect hearty but sophisticated Irish fare: cuts of hormone- and additive-free beef (including one of Toronto's best burgers), lamb and veal, ale-battered halibut and Yukon gold fries, and spicy, creamy curries.

Gio Rana's Really Really Nice Restaurant   ITALIAN **$$$**
(☎416-469-5225; www.gioranas.com; 1220 Queen St E; mains $25-35; ⊘6pm-late Tue-Sat; ⌂501, 502, 503) There's no signage at this quirky, fun joint – just a massive Italianate nose on the exterior of an otherwise nondescript 1950s bank building. Locals come here for the

atmosphere, good humor (the website will give you a sense of what's in store) and old-fashioned Italian comfort food: enormous meatballs, hot sausage risotto, veal and 'sexy duck.'

 Toronto Islands

Rectory Café
CAFE **$$**

(☑ 416-203-2152; http://therectorycafe.com; 102 Lakeshore Ave, Ward's Island; mains $13-21; ⊘ 11am-9pm Sun-Thu, to 10pm Fri & Sat; ⛴ Ward's Island) Propped up next to the boardwalk, this cozy gallery-cafe serves light meals, cups of tea and weekend brunch with views of Tommy Thompson Park. Reservations recommended for brunch and dinner; quick snacks and drinks are more casual. Try to nab a seat on the lakeside patio if the sun is shining.

Drinking & Nightlife

Bars & Pubs

The Toronto pub and bar scene embraces everything from sticky-carpet beer holes, cookie-cutter franchised 'Brit' pubs and Yankee-style sports bars to slick martini bars, rooftop patios, sky-high wine rooms and an effervescent smattering of gay and lesbian hangouts. Thirsty work! Strict bylaws prohibit smoking indoors in public spaces, although some outdoor patios are permissive. Taps start flowing around midday and last call hovers between 1am and 2am.

Mill Street Brewery
BREWERY

(☑ 416-681-0338; www.millstreetbrewery.com; 55 Mill St, Bldg 63, Distillery District; ⊘ 11:30am-midnight; ⛴ 503, 504) With 13 specialty beers brewed on-site in the atmospheric Distillery District, these guys are a leading light in local microbrewing. Order a sample platter so you can taste all the award-winning brews, including the Tankhouse Pale Ale, Stock Ale and Organic Lager. On a sunny afternoon, the courtyard is the place to be. Typical brewery fare is served, with beer-friendly pairings like burgers, sandwiches and wraps.

Panorama
BAR

(Map p74; ☑ 416-967-0000; www.panoramalounge.com; 51st fl, Manulife Centre, 55 Bloor St W; ⊘ 5pm-late; ⛿ Bay) Swanky and priced to match, the city's highest licensed patio has arguably Toronto's best views outside the CN Tower. It's in the Manulife Centre building and unlike the tower, there's no admission fee, though you'll be scoffed at if you don't drop some cash on a martini or a meal.

C'est What
PUB

(Map p78; ☑ 416-867-9499; www.cestwhat.com; 67 Front St E; ⊘ 11:30am-1am; ⛴ 503, 504) Over 30 whiskeys and six dozen Canadian microbrews (mostly from Ontario) are on hand at this underground pub. An in-house brewmaster tightly edits the all-natural, preservative-free beers on tap, and there's good bar food that makes the most of fresh produce from St Lawrence Market next door.

Gladstone Hotel
BAR

(☑ 416-531-4635; www.gladstonehotel.com; 1214 Queen St W; ⊘ 8am-10pm; ⛴ 501) This historic hotel revels in Toronto's avant-garde arts scene. The Art Bar and Gladstone Ballroom sustain offbeat DJs, poetry slams, jazz, book readings, alt-country and blues, while the Melody bar hosts karaoke and other musical ventures. Cover varies, usually $10 or less.

Black Bull
PUB

(Map p74; ☑ 416-593-2766; www.blackbulltavern.ca; 298 Queen St W; ⊘ noon-1am; ⛴ 501; ⛶) The Black Bull may have Toronto's most desired patio in that it seems to catch more sunlight than anywhere else, and has a prime drinking spot for when you need a rest from Queen St shopping. Line up behind the others to wait for a table, and don't give it up until the sun goes down. Free wi-fi is a nice touch.

Wayne Gretzky's
PUB

(Map p78; ☑ 416-348-0099; www.gretzkys.com; 99 Blue Jays Way; ⊘ 11:30am-late Mon-Fri, 10am-late Sat & Sun; ⛴ 503, 504) Once part owned by Canada's favorite hockey legend but now just sharing his name, Gretzky's is a sports bar, restaurant and awesome rooftop patio serving fairly innocuous modern American food. Sports fans come to view the hockey memorabilia, but it's otherwise a good downtown spot for a beer.

Sweaty Betty's
BAR

(Map p84; ☑ 416-535-6861; 13 Ossington Ave; ⊘ 5pm-2:30am Mon-Thu, 3.30pm-2:30am Fri-Sun; ⛴ 501) In a city of infused vodkas and creative cocktails, Betty's refuses to mix anything with more than three ingredients. This no-nonsense approach pares a night out at the bar to the essentials: having a good time and chatting people up. The tiny place is packed with hipsters on the weekends, and the liv-

PICK OF THE PATIOS

With such short summers, vitamin-D starved locals beeline for Toronto's patio bars and restaurants at the first available opportunity. Be prepared for stiff competition for the best tables...or just any table really! Here are some of our favorites:

➡ Hair of the Dog (p105)
➡ Earl's (p101)
➡ Rectory Café (p110)
➡ Panorama (p110)
➡ Java House (p111)
➡ Allen's (p109)
➡ Drake Hotel (p111)
➡ Against the Grain (p100)

ing room-ish setup kinda makes it feel like a college house party.

Blake House — PUB
(Map p74; ☑ 416-975-1867; www.theblakehouse.ca; 449 Jarvis St; ☺11am-2am) Just east of the Village, this historic 1891 mansion is a good all-round performer. Nicely renovated in dark tones, it's wonderfully cozy and inviting in winter, and has a great patio out front in the summer months. There's cold beer, great food and friendly servers. It's popular, but not crowded.

Red Room — PUB
(Map p84; ☑ 416-929-9964; 444 Spadina Ave; ☺11am-late; ☒506, 510) The Red Room rules. Part pub, part diner, part funky lounge – this arty Kensington Market room is the place to drag your hungover bones for a recuperative pint of microbrew, an all-day breakfast and an earful of Brit pop. Sink into a booth and forget your misdemeanors.

Handlebar — BAR
(Map p84; ☑ 647-748-7433; 159 Augusta Ave; ☺6pm-late Mon-Fri, from 3pm Sat & Sun) A jolly little spot paying homage to the bicycle and its lovers, this newcomer to the Toronto bar scene comes from owners with a fine pedigree. In a great spot south of Kensington Market, there's some wonderful retro styling and a nice mix of shiny happy punters.

Madison Avenue Pub — PUB
(Map p74; 14-18 Madison Ave; ☺11am-2am; ☒Spadina) Comprising three Victorian hous-

es in The Annex, the Madison draws a late-20s U of T crowd. Think billiards, darts, a sports bar, polished brass, antique-y lamps lighting the curtained upper floors, *five* patios and lots of hormones colliding between the boys and the girls.

Java House — BAR
(Map p84; ☑ 416-504-3025; 537 Queen St W; ☺9am-1am; ☒510) In the grungy heart of Queen W you'll find this haven for seriously well-priced drinks and eats with a huge side patio that is mostly packed in the summer months.

Wide Open — BAR
(Map p74; ☑ 416-727-5411; www.wideopenbar.ca; 139a Spadina Ave; ☺5pm-2am; ☒510) If you blink you'll miss this grotty little nondescript hole-in-the-wall, but if you do find it, you'll also have tracked down some of Toronto's cheapest booze: half-price and $10 pitchers on Mondays, and happy hour Thursday when *all drinks* are $2.50 (5pm to 8pm). There's a drink special every day.

Crocodile Rock — PUB
(Map p78; ☑ 416-599-9751; www.crocrock.ca; 240 Adelaide St W; ☺4pm-2am Wed-Fri, 7pm-2am Sat, 9pm-2am Sun) Like a thorny island in the middle of clubland and entertainment central, Crocodile Rock caters to a slightly older crowd, particularly since the recent renovation to its excellent rooftop patio. Expect out-of-towners, after-work suits for $3 specials and anyone who remembers the '80s and still likes to party.

Smokeless Joe — BAR
(Map p84; ☑ 416-966-5050; 488 College St; ☺5pm-1am Tue-Thu, noon-1am Fri-Mon; ☒506) Formerly a basement bar in clubland, Smokeless Joe has moved to a new home in Little Italy but retains its cozy 'everybody knows your name' feel. With more than 200 beers available, you're spoiled for choice.

Underground Garage — BAR
(Map p78; ☑ 416-688-8787; www.undergroundgarage.ca; 365 King St W; ☺10pm-2:30am; ☒504, 510) Trying valiantly to keep it real in the otherwise skin-deep Entertainment District, this urban rock bar is down a steep staircase lined with Led Zeppelin, Willie Nelson and John Lennon posters. Wailing guitars, cold beer and good times – just as it should be.

Drake Hotel — BAR
(☑416-531-5042; www.thedrakehotel.ca; 1150 Queen St W; ☺8am-11pm; ☒501) The Drake is

part hotel, part pub, part live-music venue, part nightclub: with a bunch of different areas to enjoy, including lounge, patio, the wonderful rooftop Sky Yard and a basement underground.

Sneaky Dee's
BAR

(Map p84; ☑ 416-603-3090; www.sneaky-dees. com; 431 College St; ⊙ 11am-3am Mon-Fri, 9am-3am Sat & Sun; ☒ 506, 511) Spangled with graffiti on the prominent Bathurst/College St corner, Sneaky Dee's downstairs bar is true grunge with battered booths and years of history: fill up on Tex-Mex (half-price fajitas on Tuesdays!) while downing cheapish beer. The upstairs band room is a darkened breeding ground for new local rock n roll although Saturdays go off to '60s to '80s 'Shake-a-tail' club nights.

Clinton's
BAR

(Map p84; www.clintons.ca; 693 Bloor St; ⊙ 4pm-2am Mon-Fri, 11am-2am Sat & Sun; ⑤ Christie) Weekly themed DJ nights, live music and comedy are all part of the line-up at iconic Clinton's, attracting a fun, arty crowd. There's a pub at the front serving decent food and a wicked dance hall at back: the 'Girl & Boy '90s Dance Party' on Fridays is kickass.

Ossington
BAR

(Map p84; ☑ 416-850-0161; www.theossington. com; 61 Ossington Ave; ⊙ 6pm-2am) With a moody candlelit front bar and cavernous backroom hosting Friday and Saturday DJ nights, local fave the Ossington is a great mix of 20-to-30-somethings who still have a little life left in them and choose to stray from the mainstream mania.

Clubs

'Clubland' convenes around Richmond St W and Adelaide St W at John St. After dark, nondescript doorways creak open, thick-necked bouncers cordon off sidewalks and queues of scantily clad girls and awkward guys in their Sunday best begin to form. The air hangs heavy with hormones and excitement but a few hours later, things get messy: drunk girls stagger, guys swing apocalyptic fists and hot-dog cart owners struggle to maintain order among the condiments. Many clubs now offer/require 'bottle service,' where you pay through-the-nose prices to reserve a bottle of liquor and a table for your group. This also helps you skip queues. Most clubs open around 9pm or 10pm (but

don't get swinging until later) and close around 4am.

Not your idea of a good time? Head to neighborhoods like Little Italy, Church and Wellesley, Queen West and The Annex for more intimate haunts and wider scope. Cover charges range from $5 to $15. Bars with band rooms or mini-clubs out back open early and don't close until 2am or 3am.

Guvernment
CLUB

(Map p78; www.theguvernment.com; 132 Queens Quay E; ⊙ 10pm-late Tue-Sat; ☒ 6, 75) For diversity, nothing beats the gargantuan Guv. DJs play hip-hop, R&B, progressive house and tribal music to satisfy all appetites. Rooftop skyline views are as impressive as the Arabian fantasy lounge and art-deco bar. Koolhaus is the midsize live venue.

Mod Club
CLUB

(Map p84; www.themodclub.com; 722 College St; ⊙ 8pm-midnight Mon-Thu, 6pm-3am Fri & Sat; ☒ 506) Celebrating all things UK, this excellent Little Italy club plays electronic, indie and Brit pop, with occasional live acts like Paul Weller, The Killers and Muse taking the stage. Up-to-the-nanosecond lighting gives way to candlelit chill-out rooms.

Uniun
CLUB

(Map p84; ☑ 416-603-9300; www.uniun.com; 473 Adelaide St W; ⊙ 10pm-3am Fri-Sun; ☒ 504, 508) The entrance to this ultra-schmick, ultra-cool, bottle-service nightclub – Toronto's newest – is off Portland St. Don't even try to get in unless you look and feel a million bucks and have the cash to back it up. There's an insane LED-lighting system encased in the walls and ceilings, room enough for 1500 and style to burn.

Gay & Lesbian Venues
O'Grady's
PUB

(Map p74; ☑ 416-323-2822; www.ogradyschurch. ca; 517 Church St; ⊙ 11am-2am; ⑤ Wellesley) The Village's largest patio fills up quick as soon as the sun comes out, but in the colder months there's nothing particularly noteworthy about this fairly standard gay-friendly Irish pub.

Woody's/Sailor
BAR

(Map p74; ☑ 416-972-0887; www.woodystoronto. com; 465-7 Church St; ⊙ noon-2am; ⑤ Wellesley) Toronto's most well-known gay bar is a sprawling complex with a grab-bag of tricks, from drag shows, 'best ass' contests, billiards tables and nightly DJs. Sailor is a slick bar off to one side.

Black Eagle
BAR

(Map p74; ☑ 416-413-1219; www.blackeagletoronto. com; 457 Church St; ⊙ 2pm-late; ⑤ Wellesley) The men-only Eagle lures leather-men, uniform fetishists and their admirers. The year-round rooftop patio is the perfect place to meet a Daddy: Sunday afternoon barbecues draw a strong crowd. There's a cruising area upstairs and a newly renovated dance area downstairs. While not for the fainthearted, the folks and staff are generally as friendly as they come.

Crews & Tangos
BAR

(Map p74; ☑ 416-972-1662; www.crewsandtangos. com; 508 Church St; ⊙ 5pm-2am; ⑤ Wellesley) A sprawling bar by day (with an excellent rear patio) and a crowded nightclub by night, featuring live drag and cabaret shows and DJs out back. Boys who like boys, girls who like girls, girlish boys and boyish girls and all their friends tend to make up the lively crowd in this welcoming space.

Fly
CLUB

(Map p74; ☑ 416-410-5426; www.flynightclub.com; 8 Gloucester St; ⊙ 10pm-4am Fri & Sat; ⑤ Wellesley) This fun multi-level club, just outside the Village, off Yonge St, spins hard-house, tribal and trance and is frequently home to the butch and beary Pitbull parties (www. pitbullevents.com). Music from the club is piped next door into Fire on the East Side (p105), so you can enjoy a lounge scene before hitting the dance floor.

El Convento Rico
CLUB

(Map p84; ☑ 416-588-7800; www.elconventorico. com; 750 College St; cover $8-10; ⊙ 10pm-3am Thu, 8pm-3am Fri & Sat; ☐ 506) With a friendly mixed crowd, this LGBT dance bar has free salsa lessons on Friday at 10pm as well as nightly drag shows.

☆ Entertainment

As you might have guessed, there's always something going on here, from jazz to art-house cinema, offbeat theater, opera, punk-rock, hip-hop and hockey. In summer free outdoor festivals and concerts are the norm but Toronto's dance and live-music scene keeps grooving year-round. Gay life is also rich and fulfilling, with plenty of clubs, groups, bar nights and activities for the community.

For the latest club, alt-culture and live-music listings, look for Toronto's free street press in venues, by subway entrances or online: *Now* (www.nowmagazine.com), *The Grid* (www.thegridto.com), and *Xtra!* (www. xtra.ca) for LGBT readers.

In an effort to promote arts and culture, many venues and events operate a 'Pay What You Can' (PWYC) policy: admission is free or by donation; give what you think is reasonable. Otherwise, **Ticketmaster** (☑ 1-855-985-5000; www.ticketmaster.ca) sells tickets for major concerts, sporting matches and events. **TO Tix** (Map p74; www.totix.ca; Yonge & Dundas Sq, 5 Dundas St E; ⊙ noon-6:30pm Tue-Sat) sells half-price and discount same-day 'rush' tickets and **TicketKing** (☑ 800-461-3333, 416-872-1212; www.mirvish.com/ticketking) covers shows at Royal Alexandria, Princess of Wales, Ed Mirvish and Panasonic Theatres.

Live Music

Dust off your Iggy Pop T-shirt, don your Docs and hit the pit. Alt-rock, metal, ska, punk and funk – Toronto has a thriving live-music scene. Bebop, smoky swamp blues and acoustic balladry provide some alternatives. Expect to pay anywhere from nothing to a few dollars on weeknights; up to $20 for weekend acts. Megatours play the Rogers Centre, the Air Canada Centre and the Molson Canadian Amphitheatre (Map p78).

★ Horseshoe Tavern
LIVE MUSIC

(Map p74; ☑ 416-598-4753; www.horseshoetavern. com; 370 Queen St W; ⊙ noon-2am; ☐ 501, 510) Well past its 65th birthday, the legendary Horseshoe still plays a crucial role in the development of local indie rock. Not so local, The Police played here on their first North American tour – Sting did an encore in his underwear and Bran Van 3000 made their long awaited comeback. This place just oozes a history of good times and classic performances. Come for a beer and check it out.

Massey Hall
CONCERT VENUE

(Map p74; ☑ 416-872-4255; www.masseyhall.com; 178 Victoria St; ⊙ box office from noon on show days; ⑤ Queen) Few venues have hosted as diverse a range of performances as Massey Hall, with its over 120 years in the business. Extensive back-of-house renovations are slated to bring the 2500-seat space into the next generation, while retaining its period charm.

Opera House
CONCERT VENUE

(☑ 416-466-0313; www.theoperahousetoronto.com; 735 Queen St E; ☐ 501, 502, 503) The old Opera House is an early 1900s vaudeville hall. Over the years, rockers like The Black Crowes, Rage Against The Machine, Eminem, A Perfect Circle and Beck have all strutted out beneath the proscenium arch, as well as a number of dance parties and performances.

Sound Academy
CONCERT VENUE

(☑ www.sound-academy.com; 11 Polson St; ☐ 72, 72A) This Harbourside venue can hold around 3000 for rock concerts and live shows. Past acts include Guns & Roses, The Killers and Fallout Boy.

Phoenix
CONCERT VENUE

(Map p74; ☑ 416-323-1251; www.libertygroup.com; 410 Sherbourne St; ☐ 506) The 1000-capacity Phoenix has occupied the former Harmonie Club, a grand ol' room that now sees the harmonious rock of bands like the Tragically Hip.

Sony Centre for the
Performing Arts
CONCERT VENUE

(Map p78; ☑ 416-872-7669; www.sonycentre.ca; 1 Front St E; ☉ box office 10am-5:30pm Mon-Fri, to 1pm Sat; ⑤ Union) With an entry awning protruding over Front St like a hummingbird beak, this place is hard to miss. Phone or book online for shows as diverse as the Soweto Gospel Choir, Pet Shop Boys and Russell Brand.

Rivoli
LIVE MUSIC

(Map p74; ☑ 416-596-1908; www.rivoli.ca; 334 Queen St W; ☉ 11:30am-1am; ☐ 501) Songbird Feist got her start here. Nightly live music (rock, indie and solo singer-songwriters), weekly stand-up comedy and monthly hip-hop nights are all part of the line-up. There's an awesome pool hall upstairs and great food.

Lee's Palace
LIVE MUSIC

(Map p84; ☑ 416-532-1598; www.leespalace.com; 529 Bloor St W; ☉ 9am-2:30am; ⑤ Bathurst) Legendary Lee's Palace has set the stage over the years for Dinosaur Jr, Smashing Pumpkins and Queens of the Stone Age. Kurt Cobain started an infamous bottle-throwing incident when Nirvana played here in 1990. You can't miss it – look for the primary-colored mural that seems to scream out the front.

Dakota Tavern
LIVE MUSIC

(Map p84; ☑ 416-850-4579; www.thedakotatavern.com; 249 Ossington Ave; ☉ 6pm-2am Mon-Fri, 11am-2am Sat & Sun; ☐ 63, ☐ 501) This basement tavern rocks with wooden-barrel stools and a small stage where you can catch some twang. You'll hear mostly country, blues and some rock. Saturday and Sunday bluegrass brunches ($15; 11am to 3pm) are a *big* hit – they're tasty, filling and fun, but you'll have to queue to get in.

Reservoir Lounge
BLUES, JAZZ

(Map p78; ☑ 416-955-0887; www.reservoirlounge.com; 52 Wellington St E; ☉ 7:30pm-2am Tue-Sat; ☐ 503, 504) Swing dancers, jazz singers and blues crooners call this cool candlelit basement lounge home, and it has hosted its fair share of musical greats over the years. Where else can you enjoy a Grey Goose martini while dipping strawberries into chocolate fondue during the show?

Cameron House
JAZZ

(Map p84; ☑ 416-703-0811; www.thecameron.com; 408 Queen St W; ☉ 4pm-late; ☐ 501, 510) Singer-songwriters, soul, jazz and country performers grace the stage; artists, musos, dreamers and slackers crowd both front and back rooms.

Rex
BLUES, JAZZ

(Map p74; ☑ 416-598-2475; www.therex.ca; 194 Queen St W; ☉ 9am-2am; ☐ 501) The Rex has risen from its pugilistic, blue-collared past to become an outstanding jazz and blues venue. Over a dozen different Dixieland, experimental and other local and international acts knock over the joint each week. Cheap drinks; affordable cover.

Dominion on Queen
JAZZ

(☑ 416-368-6893; www.dominiononqueen.com; 500 Queen St E; ☉ 11am-1am Mon-Sat, to 11pm Sun; ☐ 501, 502, 503) This jazzy pub has earned a rep for sassy vocalists, trios and sextets through to full-blown swing bands. Music starts nightly around 9pm. Beers have a crafty edge, and there's plenty of *vin rouge* to soothe your big-city heartbreak.

Canadian Opera Company
OPERA

(Map p74; ☑ 416-363-8231, 800-250-4653; www.coc.ca; Four Seasons Centre for the Performing Arts, 145 Queen St W; ☉ box office 11am-7pm Mon-Sat, to 3pm Sun; ⑤ Osgoode) Canada's national opera company has been warbling its pipes for over 50 years. Tickets sell out fast; the Richard Bradshaw Amphitheatre (in the fabulous Four Seasons Centre) holds free concerts from September through June, usually at noon. Check the website for specific days.

Toronto Symphony Orchestra
CLASSICAL MUSIC

(TSO; Map p78; ☑ 416-593-4828; www.tso.ca; Roy Thomson Hall, 60 Simcoe St; ☉ box office 10am-6pm Mon-Fri, noon-5pm Sat; ⑤ St Andrew) A range of classics, Cole Porter–era pops and new music from around the world are presented by the TSO at Roy Thomson Hall, Massey Hall and the Toronto Centre for the Arts. Consult the website for the answers to such questions as 'What if I need to cough?' and 'Should I clap yet?'.

Harbourfront Centre
CLASSICAL MUSIC

(☑ 416-973-4000; www.harbourfrontcentre.com; York Quay Centre, 235 Queens Quay W; tickets $10-40; ☉ box office 1-6pm Tue-Sat; ⋒ 509, 510) The vibrant Harbourfront Centre puts on a variety of world-class musical performances throughout the year, including Sunday family shows and free outdoor summer concerts in the Toronto Music Garden and on the Concert Stage.

Glenn Gould Studio
CLASSICAL MUSIC

(Map p78; ☑ 416-205-5555; www.cbc.ca/glenngould; Canadian Broadcasting Centre, 250 Front St W; tickets $15-40; ☉ box office 2-6:30pm Mon-Fri, to 8pm Sat; ⑤ Union, ⋒ 504) Glenn Gould Studio's acoustics do the namesake famous pianist honor. Purchase advance tickets for evening concerts of classical and contemporary music by soloists, chamber groups, choirs and orchestras between September and June. Young international artists are often featured.

Toronto Centre for the Arts
CLASSICAL MUSIC

(off Map p69; ☑ 416-733-9388; www.tocentre.com; 5040 Yonge St; ☉ box office 11am-6pm Mon, to 8pm Tue-Sat, noon-4pm Sun; ⑤ North York Centre) Way north on Yonge St, the 1000-seat George Weston Recital Hall is home to the **Toronto Philharmonia** (www.torontophil.on.ca). The 1700-seat Main Stage Theatre and intimate Studio Theatre also host ballet and theater.

Theater

Long winter months indoors are conducive to the creation and performance of theatrical works. This, and Toronto's relative proximity to Broadway and cosmopolitan Montréal, help sustain the city's reputation as a theater maker's playground. Broadway and off-Broadway musicals and plays pack theaters around the Theatre Block in the Entertainment District, and Yonge & Dundas Sq, but there are numerous smaller venues and vibrant young production companies around Harbourfront, in the Distillery District and Queen West. Check the free street press for listings. Tickets for major productions are sold through TicketKing. For last-minute discounted tickets, go to TO Tix or ask about 'rush' tickets at box offices.

CanStage
THEATER

(Canadian Stage Company; ☑ 416 368 3110; www.canstage.com; 26 Berkeley St; ☉ box office 10am-6pm Mon-Sat, to 8pm show days; ⋒ 503, 504) Contemporary CanStage produces top-rated Canadian and international plays by the likes of David Mamet and Tony Kushner from its own Berkeley Street Theatre, and the wonderfully accessible (pay-what-you-can) midsummer productions of 'Shakespeare in the Park,' under the stars in High Park: bring a blanket and show up early.

Elgin & Winter Garden Theatre
THEATER

(Map p74; ☑ 416-314-2901; www.heritagetrust.on.ca/ewg; 189 Yonge St; ⑤ Queen) The restored double-decker Elgin & Winter Garden Theatre stages high-profile productions in an amazing setting.

Ed Mirvish Theatre
THEATER

(Map p74; ☑ 800-461-3333, 416-872-1212; www.mirvish.com; 244 Victoria St; ⑤ Dundas) Formerly the Canon, the Ed Mirvish Theatre was renamed in 2011 in honor of the late Ed Mirvish, Toronto's well-loved businessman, philanthropist and patron of the arts. One of four Mirvish theaters, the 1920s-era vaudeville hall is a hot ticket for musical extravaganzas.

Royal Alexandra Theatre
THEATER

(Map p78; ☑ 800-461-3333, 416-872-1212; www.mirvish.com; 260 King St W; ⋒ 504) The 'Royal Alex,' as she is sometimes affectionately known, is one of the more impressive theaters in the city and home to splashy Broadway musicals.

Princess of Wales Theatre
THEATER

(Map p78; ☑ 800-461-3333, 416-872-1212; www.mirvish.com; 300 King St W; ⋒ 504) The POW is a 2000-seat playhouse showing big-ticket items such as *Miss Saigon* and *Rock of Ages*.

Young Centre for Performing Arts
THEATER

(☑ 416-866-8666; www.youngcentre.ca; 55 Mill St, Bldg 49; ⋒ 503, 504) The $14 million Young Centre houses four separate performance spaces, utilized by theatrical tenants including **Soul Pepper** (www.soulpepper.ca) and **George Brown Theatre Co** (www.george-brown.ca/theatre). There's an on-site bookshop and bar too.

Factory Theatre   THEATER

(Map p84; ☑ 416-504-9971; www.factorytheatre.ca; 125 Bathurst St; ⓢ 511) This innovative theater company – 'Home of the Canadian Playwright' – has been busy for 35 years. Sunday matinees are 'Pay What You Can.'

Cinemas

Torontonians love going to the movies: we think it might have something to do with the weather. Tickets cost around $14 for adults. Tuesday is discount day: expect to pay around half that.

★ Bell Lightbox   CINEMA

(Map p78; www.tiff.net; cnr 350 King St W; ⓢ 504) Home of Toronto International Film Festival (TIFF; p94), this resplendent cinema complex was completed in 2010 and is the hub of all the action when the festival is in town. Throughout the year, it's used primarily for TIFF Cinematheque, screening world cinema, independent films and directorial retrospectives and other special events. Try to see a film here if you can.

Bloor Hot Docs Cinema   CINEMA

(Map p84; ☑ 416-637-3123; www.bloorcinema.com; 506 Bloor St W; ⓢ Bathurst) This art-deco theater with a two-tiered balcony screens a wonderfully varied schedule of new releases, art-house flicks, shorts, documentaries and vintage films and is home to the mind-expanding Hot Docs Canadian International Documentary Festival.

Cineplex Yonge & Dundas   CINEMA

(Map p74; ☑ 416-977-9262; www.cineplex.com; 10 Dundas St E; ⓢ Dundas, ⓢ 505) At the heart of Yonge & Dundas Sq, this enormous cinema complex has 24 huge screens with fabulous stadium seating, IMAX, a food court and direct subway access to the building, perfect for those super-cheap Tuesdays or freezing winter Sundays.

Scotiabank Theatre   CINEMA

(Map p74; ☑ 416-368-5600; www.cineplex.com; 259 Richmond St W; ⓢ Osgoode) Managed by Cineplex, this fun gargantuan multiplex in the heart of Queen West features the latest technology, including IMAX 3D. Buy tickets downstairs then take the gigantic escalator

upstairs where you can buy pizza, poutine and popcorn for the show.

Cineplex Odeon Varsity   CINEMA

(Map p74; ☑ 416-961-6304; www.cineplex.com; Manulife Centre, 55 Bloor St W; ⊘ noon-midnight; ⓢ Bloor-Yonge) This state-of-the-art multiplex has VIP theaters and smaller screens.

Rainbow Cinemas   CINEMA

(Map p78; ☑ 416-491-9731; www.rainbowcinemas.ca; 80 Front St E; ⓢ 503, 504) Plays first-run movies at second-run prices, right in Market Sq. Tuesdays are $5.

Polson Pier Drive-In Theatre   CINEMA

(☑ 416-465-4653; www.polsonpier.com; 11 Polson St; ⊘ from 8:30pm Fri-Sun Apr-Oct) Drive-in isn't dead – even downtown! First-run blockbusters and special features start around dusk, down by the lake. Summer only.

Sports

Many Torontonians weep with joy at the very mention of their beloved sporting teams: professional baseball (the Blue Jays) and football (the Argonauts) through the summer; ice hockey (the Maple Leafs), basketball (the Raptors) and lacrosse (Toronto Rock) through the winter. **Ticketmaster** (www.ticketmaster.ca) sells advance tickets, as do the box offices at the Air Canada Centre and Rogers Centre. Ticket scalping is illegal, but that doesn't seem to stop anybody.

Toronto Blue Jays   SPECTATOR SPORT

(☑ 416-341-1234; bluejays.com; ⊘ Apr-Sep) Toronto's Major League Baseball team plays at the **Rogers Centre** (Map p78; ☑ 416-341-2770; www.rogerscentre.com; 1 Blue Jays Way; ⓢ Union). Buy tickets through Ticketmaster or at the Rogers Centre box office near Gate 9. The cheapest seats are way up above the field. Instead, try for seats along the lower level baselines where you have a better chance of catching a flyball (or wearing one in the side of the head). The Jays haven't won the World Series since 1993, but who knows, this could be their year.

Toronto Argonauts   SPECTATOR SPORT

(☑ 416-341-2746; www.argonauts.ca; ⊘ Jun-Oct) The Toronto Argonauts crack their Canadian Football League (CFL) helmets at the Rogers Centre. The Argonauts have won the Grey Cup a record 16 times, most recently in 2012. Bring a jacket – the open-roof Rogers Centre cools off at night. Tickets through Ticketmaster or the Rogers Centre.

Toronto Maple Leafs
SPECTATOR SPORT

(📞 416-815-5982; www.mapleleafs.com; ☉ Oct-Apr) The 13-time Stanley Cup–winning Toronto Maple Leafs slap the puck around the **Air Canada Centre** (ACC; Map p78; 📞 416-815-5500; www.theaircanadacentre.com; 40 Bay St; 🚇 Union) in the National Hockey League (NHL). Every game sells out, but a limited number of same-day tickets go on sale through Ticketmaster at 10am and at the Air Canada Centre ticket window from 5pm. You can also buy tickets via the website from season ticket-holders who aren't attending – expect to pay around $80 and up.

Toronto Raptors
SPECTATOR SPORT

(📞 416-815-5500; www.nba.com/raptors; ☉ regular season Oct-Apr) During hockey season, the Toronto Raptors also play at the Air Canada Centre. The 'Raps' have been around since 1995, but haven't yet caused much of a flap.

Toronto Rock
SPECTATOR SPORT

(📞 416-596-3075; www.torontorock.com; ☉ regular season Jan-Apr) Lacrosse may not immediately spring to mind when someone mentions Canadian sports, but Toronto's team is red hot, having won the championship six times. Games at the Air Canada Centre; tickets through Ticketmaster.

🛍 Shopping

Shopping in Toronto is a big deal. When it's -20°C outside, you have to fill the gap between brunch and the movies with *something*, right? People like to update their wardrobes and redecorate their homes, or just walk zombie-like around warm sprawling malls like the **Eaton Centre** (Map p74; 📞 416-598-8560; www.torontoeatoncentre.com; 220 Yonge St; ☉ 10am-9pm Mon-Fri, to 7pm Sat, 11am-6pm Sun; 🚇 Queen, Dundas). This habit continues through to summer, overflowing into the streets of neighborhoods like boho-central **Kensington Market** and the full length of **Queen Street West**, with its smatterings of almost anything fashion, art and design you could imagine.

The Annex features a dwindling hodge-podge of art shops, bookstores and second-hand music, especially along Harbord St and on Markham St (aka Mirvish Village). **Bloor-Yorkville**, formerly 'Free Love' central in the 1960s, is now Toronto's most exclusive shopping district where nothing is free and snobby sales clerks aren't uncommon.

Downtown, underground **PATH** (www.toronto.ca/path) shops are bargain basements for discount clothing, goods and services. Canadian and international design stores line **King Street East** between Jarvis and Parliament Sts, in a trendy area known as the **Design Strip**, priced accordingly. Close-by, the boutiques, galleries and craft studios of the burgeoning **Distillery District** are a major draw. Cheap retailers in **Downtown Yonge**, near Ryerson University, target students and the **Church-Wellesley Village** is festooned with all manner of gay-themed boutiques.

Typical retail shopping hours are 10am to 6pm Monday to Saturday and noon to 5pm Sunday, but this varies according to season, neighborhood and the amount of foot traffic. Phone ahead before setting out, or just pick a neighborhood, wing it and see what you find: that's half the fun.

There are far too many great stores to list here, so we've chosen a handful to get you started. Tourism Toronto also has some good ideas on its searchable database at www.seetorontonow.com/shopping/.

Bay of Spirits Gallery
SOUVENIRS

(Map p78; 📞 416-971-5190; www.bayofspirits.com; 156 Front St W; ☉ 10am-6pm Mon-Sat; 🚇 Union) The works of Norval Morrisseau – the first indigenous artist to have a solo exhibit at the National Gallery of Canada – are proudly on display in this atmospheric space, which carries aboriginal art from across Canada. Look for the Pacific West Coast totem poles (from miniature to over 4m tall), Inuit carvings and Inukshuk figurines.

Guild Shop
SOUVENIRS

(Map p74; 📞 416-921-1721; www.theguildshop.ca; 118 Cumberland St; ☉ 10am-6pm Mon-Wed & Sat, to 7pm Thu & Fri, noon-5pm Sun; 🚇 Bay) The **Ontario Crafts Council** (www.craft.on.ca) has been promoting artisans for over 70 years. Ceramics, jewelry, glassworks, prints and carvings make up most of the displays, but you could also catch a special exhibition of Pangnirtung weaving or Cape Dorset graphics. Staff are knowledgeable about First Nations art.

Courage My Love
CLOTHING

(Map p84; 📞 416-979-1992; 14 Kensington Ave; ☉ 11:30am-6pm Mon-Sat, 1-6pm Sun; 🚌 505, 510) Vintage clothing stores have been around Kensington Market for decades, but Courage My Love amazes fashion mavens with its secondhand slip dresses, retro pants and white dress-shirts in a cornucopia of styles.

ONTARIO TORONTO

The beads, buttons, leather goods and silver jewelry are hand-picked.

Open Air Books & Maps
BOOKS

(Map p78; ☎ 416-363-0719; www.openairbooks-andmaps.com; 25 Toronto St; ⏱10am-5:30pm Mon-Sat; Ⓢ King) A rather ramshackle basement full of travel guides and maps plus books on nature, camping, history and outdoor activities.

BMV
BOOKS

(Map p74; Dundas Sq, 10 Edward St; ⏱10am-11pm Mon-Sat, noon-8pm Sun; Ⓢ Dundas) The biggest (and most loved) secondhand bookstore in Toronto, with a second outlet on **Bloor St** (Map p84; 471 Bloor St W; ⏱11am-10pm Mon-Wed, to midnight Thu-Sat, noon-10pm Sun; Ⓢ Spadina).

Honest Ed's
DEPARTMENT STORE

(Map p84; ☎ 416-537-1574; www.honesteds.sites.toronto.com; 581 Bloor St W; ⏱10am-9pm Mon-Fri, 11am-6pm Sat & Sun; Ⓢ Bathurst) The legendary late Ed Mirvish's Toronto institution is a delightful old-fashioned bargain bazaar. Come to photograph the flashy iconic sign.

ℹ Information

DANGERS & ANNOYANCES

By North American standards, Toronto is a safe city in which to live and visit, but don't be complacent. It's not a brilliant idea for women to walk alone after dark around Parliament and Jarvis Sts at the intersections with Carlton, Dundas St E and Queen St E, particularly around Allan Gardens and George St – and probably not a good idea during the day, either. The Entertainment District can get messy with drunken fools after midnight.

Many social service agencies have shut their doors in recent years, creating a tide of homeless, often mentally ill people on the streets – a real problem for Toronto. Most are more likely to be assaulted themselves, than to do so to you. Spare a thought for what their lives must be like in winter as you contemplate the 700-plus names of those who have perished on Toronto's streets since 1985, at the Toronto Homeless Memorial. It's outside the Church of the Holy Trinity.

EMERGENCY

Police (☎ nonemergency 416-808-2222, emergency only 911; www.torontopolice.on.ca)

SOS Femmes (☎ 416-487-4794; www.sos-femmes.com) French-language crisis line for women.

Toronto Rape Crisis Centre (☎ 416-597-8808; www.sexualassaultsupport.ca/toronto)

INTERNET ACCESS

Toronto's cheapest internet cafes congregate along the Yonge St strip; Bloor St W in The Annex and Koreatown; and Chinatown's Spadina Ave. Rates start around $2 per hour. Wi-fi is becoming increasingly available at restaurants and coffee shops: check out www.wirelesstoronto.ca for a list of free hot spots in the city.

FedEx Office Queen St & Dundas Sq(☎ 416-979-8447; 505 University Ave, Queen St & Dundas Sq; ⏱24hr; Ⓢ St Patrick); The Annex (☎ 416-928-0110; 459 Bloor St W; ⏱24hr; Ⓢ Spadina)

Net Plaza (267 College St; ⏱8am-2am Sun-Fri, 24hr Fri & Sat; 🚌510)

MEDIA

Globe & Mail (www.theglobeandmail.com) Elder statesman of the national daily newspapers.

Grid (www.thegridto.com)

Metro (www.metronews.ca) Free daily rag with bite-sized news, sports and entertainment (often left on subway seats).

NOW (www.nowtoronto.com) Alternative weekly (good for events and concerts) free every Thursday.

Toronto Life (www.torontolife.com) Upscale monthly mag: lifestyle, dining, arts and entertainment.

Toronto Star (www.thestar.com) Canada's largest newspaper; a comprehensive left-leaning daily.

Toronto Sun (www.torontosun.com) Sensational tabloid with predictably good sports coverage.

Where Toronto (www.where.ca/toronto) The most informative of the free glossy tourist magazines.

Xtra! (www.xtra.ca) Free weekly gay and lesbian street press.

MEDICAL SERVICES

Dental Emergency Clinic (☎ 416-485-7172; 1650 Yonge St; ⏱8am-midnight; Ⓢ St Clair)

Hassle-Free Clinic (☎ 416-922-0566; www.hasslefreeclinic.org; 2nd fl, 66 Gerrard St E; ⏱women 10am-3pm Mon, Wed & Fri, 4-8pm Tue & Thu, men 4-8pm Mon & Wed, 10am-3pm Tue & Thu, 4-7pm Fri, 10am-2pm Sat; Ⓢ College) Provides anonymous, free walk-in STD/HIV testing and reproductive health services.

Hospital for Sick Children (☎ 416-813-1500; www.sickkids.ca; 555 University, emergency 170 Gerrard St W; ⏱24hr; Ⓢ Queens Park)

Mount Sinai Hospital (☎ 416-596-4200, emergency 416-586-5054; www.mountsinai.on.ca; 600 University Ave; ⏱24hr; Ⓢ Queens Park)

St Michael's Hospital (☎ 416-360-4000; www.stmichaelshospital.com; 30 Bond St; ⏱24hr;

Queen, Dundas) The emergency unit of this major teaching and research hospital is in the heart of downtown on the corner of Victoria and Shuter Sts.

Toronto General Hospital (416-340-3111, emergency 416-340-3111; www.uhn.ca; 190 Elizabeth St; 24hr; Queens Park)

Women's College Hospital (416-323-6400; www.womenscollegehospital.ca; 76 Grenville St; 24hr; College) Nonemergency women's and family health.

MONEY

It's easy to get money from overseas credit cards or debit cards with the Cirrus or Plus symbols from ATMs which are on practically every street corner and in many convenience stores. **American Express** (905-474-0870, 800-869-3016; www.americanexpress.com/canada) branches function as travel agencies and don't handle financial transactions. Instead, tackle the banks or try **Money Mart** (416-920-4146; www.moneymart.ca; 617 Yonge St; 24hr; Wellesley).

POST

Toronto no longer has a main post office. There are a number of outlets in Shopper's Drug Mart stores around town. The most central full service post offices are below.

Adelaide Street Post Office (Map p78; 800-267-1177; www.canadapost.ca; 31 Adelaide St E; 8am-5:30pm Mon-Fri; Queen)

Atrium on Bay Post Office (Map p74; 800-267-1177; www.canadapost.ca; 595 Bay St; 9am-6pm Mon-Fri; Dundas)

TOURIST INFORMATION

Ontario Travel Information Centre (Map p74; 416-314-5899; www.ontariotravel.net; 20 Dundas St W; 10am-6pm Mon-Sat, noon-5pm Sun; Dundas) This large branch opposite the Eaton Centre on Dundas St has knowledgeable, multilingual staff and overflowing racks of brochures that cover every nook and cranny of Ontario...almost. This is an easy and sensible first port of call when you get to town.

Tourism Toronto (Map p78; 800-499-2514, 416-203-2500; www.seetorontonow.com; 207 Queens Quay W; 8:30am-6pm Mon-Fri; Union) Contact one of the telephone agents; after hours use the automated touch-tone information menu.

❶ Getting There & Away

AIR

Most Canadian airlines and international carriers arrive at Canada's busiest airport, Lester B Pearson International Airport (Map p69), 27km northwest of downtown Toronto; it's a giant and attracts one of the highest airport taxes in the world. Don't worry, you'll have unknowingly paid that in the price of your ticket. Terminal assignments vary; be sure to check with your airline which one you'll be coming in to or leaving from.

Air Canada and WestJet compete heavily in the domestic market, and match one-way fares between Toronto and Ottawa (from $99), Montréal (from $99), Calgary (from $219), Edmonton (from $239), Vancouver (from $249) and Victoria (from $304). Don't expect to see these kind

PORTER: FLYING RE(DE)FINED

Porter's meteoric rise to becoming the beloved darling of gridlocked downtowners began when it opened the doors of its Billy Bishop Toronto City Airport terminal in 2010. Since then, accessibility, low fares, great service and a rapidly expanding network of destinations within Canada and the US have ensured its continued success. Far-flung cities like Sault Ste-Marie and Thunder Bay benefit from an influx of domestic tourists, and residents of Toronto's inner neighborhoods now pop over to New York, Boston, Chicago and Washington for the weekend.

It is incomparably smaller than Toronto's gargantuan Lester B Pearson airport; and access by a free ferry shuttle makes air travel in and out of Toronto easy. Operating a quiet fleet of Bombardier turbo-prop aircraft, manufactured here in Canada, Porter is in the process of negotiations between the local council and residents to commence service of a new CS100 whisper-quiet jet aircraft, which would enable the airline to expand its operations. Porter flies right past a bunch of waterfront condos, so not everyone is on board. Yet.

Construction of a pedestrian tunnel to the airport is under way and a free shuttle bus links Union Station to the ferry terminal for the Island airport (as it is also known). When planning your itinerary, be sure to keep your eyes on www.flyporter.com: seat sales are frequent and offer excellent value. With construction of a rail link to Pearson International airport also under way (at last!), there's sure to be competition in the skies for years to come.

of prices all the time: domestic air travel within Canada is comparatively expensive.

Billy Bishop Toronto City Airport (Map p69), on a small island just off the lakeshore, is the proud home of Porter airlines (p119), with competitive fares to a wide range of destinations within eastern Canada and the USA. Air Canada also has services to Montréal from here (p67).

BUS

Long-distance buses operate from the art deco **Metro Toronto Coach Terminal** (Map p74; ☑ 416-393-4636; 610 Bay St; Ⓢ Dundas).

Greyhound Canada has numerous routes from Toronto. Megabus has a smaller, and cheaper, selection of destinations. Advance tickets offer significant savings.

Union Station downtown serves as the bus and train depot for **GO Transit** (Map p78; www.gotransit.com), the commuter service of the GTA.

Parkbus (www.parkbus.ca) offers limited seasonal departures to the Bruce Peninsula, Algonquin and Killarney Provincial Parks and plans to expand its range and frequency of service: check the website for latest details.

CAR & MOTORCYCLE

Toronto is wrapped in a mesh of multi-lane highways, frequently crippled by congestion. The Gardiner Expwy runs west along the lakeshore into Queen Elizabeth Way (QEW) to Niagara Falls. At the city's western border Hwy 427 runs north to the airport. Hwy 401 is the main east–west arterial and is regularly jammed. On the eastern side of the city, the Don Valley Pkwy connects Hwy 401 to the Gardiner Expwy. Hwys 400 and 404 run north from Toronto. A GPS is strongly recommended.

All major car-rental agencies have desks at Pearson airport and offices downtown and throughout the city. Book in advance for best rates. Cars sell out on busy summer weekends.

Smaller independent agencies offer lower rates, but may have fewer (and older) cars. **Wheels 4 Rent** (☑ 416-585-7782; www.wheel-

s4rent.ca; 77 Nassau St; ☑ 510) rents compact cars from around $35 per day excluding taxes.

For long-distance trips, try **Auto Drive-Away Co** (☑ 800-561-2658, 416-225-7754; www.torontodriveaway.com; 5803 Yonge St; ☑ 97), a private vehicle relocation service for Canadian and US destinations.

TRAIN

Grand **Union Station** (☑ 416-869-3000; www.viarail.com; 140 Bay St) downtown is Toronto's main rail hub, with currency-exchange booths and Traveller's Aid Society help desks. VIA Rail plies the heavily trafficked Windsor–Montréal corridor and beyond. The station is under renovation until 2016.

Amtrak trains link Toronto's Union Station with Buffalo ($50, four hours, one daily) and New York City ($120, 13 hours, one daily).

GO Transit trains and buses also use the station.

ⓘ Getting Around

TO/FROM THE AIRPORT

Airport Express (☑ 800-387-6787; www.torontoairportexpress.com) operates an express bus (adult/child one-way $28/free) connecting Pearson International with the Metro Toronto Coach Terminal and a few downtown hotels. Buses depart every 20 to 30 minutes from 6am to midnight. Services are frequently late: allow 1½ hours for the journey.

The cheapest (and at times, quickest) way to get to the airport is on the TTC ($3) but it's a pain with heavy luggage: many stairs. Catch the subway to Kipling station (you may need to change lines at Bloor/Yonge) then connect with the 192 Airport Rocket Express bus. From the airport, the bus departs Terminals 1, 2 and 3 every 20 minutes from 5:30am to 2am. Allow *at least* an hour for the journey.

Taxis from Pearson to the city take anywhere from 40 to 70 minutes, depending on traffic. The Greater Toronto Airports Authority (GTAA) regulates fares by drop-off zone: it's $60 to

GREYHOUND BUS INFORMATION

DESTINATION	COST	DURATION	FREQUENCY
Hamilton	$9	2hr	4 daily
London	$36	2½-3½hr	12 daily
Montréal	$56	8-10hr	frequent
Niagara Falls	$18	1½-2hr	5 daily
Ottawa	$64	5½hr	8 daily
Sault Ste-Marie	$110	10-11hr	2 daily
Sudbury	$75	5hr	5 daily
Thunder Bay	$190	20hr	2 daily

WHAT'S UP WITH THE TTC ?

Seriously. It's the question on everyone's lips, usually a few times a week. Love it or hate it, you have to use it and tens of thousands of people do, every day. Operated by the Toronto Transit Commission and known by locals as the TTC, Toronto's antiquated subway, streetcar and bus system is adequate, at best. At worst, it seriously underdelivers services to a city continuing to expand more rapidly than infrastructure can be built to keep up. On a good day, you'll get to where you need to in the expected time frame. On a bad day – usually in midsummer or the throes of winter – you might wish you had just stayed put.

Service delays and overcrowding are the most common complaints. Streetcars are clunky, packed to the hilt and move at a snail's pace during the long rush hours, twice a day. Be sure to have the exact change as you board or ye shall not pass. Subway trains are better, with some fancy new rolling stock on the rails, but equally subject to delays. Of course, it's very Canadian to make like a sardine or wait patiently in line and *never* complain: especially at staffed ticket booths where you'll often see your train whizz past as you wait in line to get through. Attempts to automate ticketing haven't taken off.

Improvements are happening in dribs and drabs, but alas, we don't see much respite for ragged Torontonians any time soon. A bunch of new streetcars, trains and tracks are on the way, and civic action groups are lobbying like crazy. Check out www.your32.com.

For the official word on what's being done, see: www.bigmove.ca.

downtown. Don't pay more and remember to tip. Airport limos often match the rate and have nicer cars and drivers.

At the time of writing a long overdue rail link from Pearson Airport to Union station called the Union Pearson Express had commenced, slated for completion in 2015. It's estimated that travel times will be slashed to just 25 minutes. For details, stay tuned to www.bigmove.ca.

BOAT

From April to September, **Toronto Islands Ferries** (Map p78; ☎ 416-392-8193; www.city. toronto.on.ca/parks/island/ferry.htm; adult/child/concession $6/2.50/3.50) runs ferries every 15 to 30 minutes from 8am to 11pm. The journey (to either Ward's Island or Hanlan's Point) only takes 15 minutes, but queues can be long on weekends and holidays. From October to March, ferries run on a reduced schedule. The Toronto Islands Ferry Terminal is at the foot of Bay St, off Queens Quay.

CAR & MOTORCYCLE

Parking in Toronto is expensive, usually $3 to $4 per half-hour. Private lots offer reduced rate parking before 7am and after 6pm. Traffic is horrendous amid ongoing construction. We don't recommend driving downtown. If you do, you must stop for streetcars – behind the rear doors, when the streetcar is collecting or ejecting passengers – and for pedestrians at crosswalks when signals are flashing. Look out for cyclists in your blindspots.

Hwy 407 (www.407etr.com) running east–west from Markham to Mississauga is an electronic toll road. It can be a wonderful alternative to the congested 401. Cameras record your license plate and the time and distance traveled. Expect a bill in the mail (Canada, US or Zanzibar, they'll find you).

PUBLIC TRANSPORTATION

Rides anywhere on the Toronto Transit Corporation (TTC) network of trains, streetcars

VIA RAIL TRAIN INFORMATION

DESTINATION	COST	DURATION	FREQUENCY
Kingston	$73	2½hr	frequent
London	$56	2hr	7 daily
Montréal	$110	5¼hr	9 daily
Niagara Falls	$24	2hr	seasonal, infrequent
Ottawa	$99	4½hr	7 daily
Sudbury Junction	$79	7hr	1 daily
Vancouver	from $590	83hr	3 weekly

and buses cost adult/child $3/0.75. Seven tokens cost $18.55: a little cheaper. Day passes ($10.75) are good value if you plan on making three rides and are excellent value on weekends, when up to two adults and two children can use one pass. Purchase them at TTC stations and some convenience stores.

You can transfer from one form of TTC transit to another using your paper streetcar/bus ticket or by collecting a transfer ticket from automated dispensers near subway exits. You must be joining a connecting service. Exact change is required for streetcars and buses.

Subway lines operate regular service from around 6am (9am Sunday) until 1:30am daily. The two main lines are crosstown Bloor–Danforth line, and the U-shaped Yonge–University–Spadina line. Stations are generally very safe and have Designated Waiting Areas (DWAs) monitored by security cameras.

Streetcars are notoriusly slow during rush hours, stopping frequently. The main routes run east–west along St Clair Ave and College, Dundas, Queen and King Sts. North–south streetcars grind along Bathurst St and Spadina Ave. TTC buses generally serve suburban areas. For more far-flung travel, the TTC system connects with GO Transit's network to surrounding areas like Richmond Hill, Brampton and Hamilton.

TAXI

Metered fares start at $4, plus $1.60 per kilometer, depending on traffic.

Crown Taxi (☑416-240-0000; www.crowntaxi.com)

Diamond Taxicab (☑416-366-6868; www.diamondtaxi.ca)

Royal Taxi (☑416-777-9222; www.royaltaxi.ca)

NIAGARA PENINSULA

Jutting east from Hamilton and forming a natural divide between Lake Erie and Lake Ontario, the Niagara Peninsula is a legitimate tourist hot spot. Though many only see the falls and Clifton Hill on a day tour from Toronto, there is lots to explore here. Consider a several-day visit to fully experience the delights of the peninsula.

Water flows from Lake Erie, 100m higher than Lake Ontario, via two avenues: stepping down steadily through the locks along the Welland Canal, or surging over Niagara Falls in a reckless, swollen torrent. A steep limestone escarpment jags along the spine of the peninsula, generating a unique microclimate. Humid and often frost-free, this is prime terrain for viticulture: a fact not lost

on the award-winning wineries of Niagara-on-the-Lake.

Niagara Falls
POP 83,000

An unstoppable flow of rushing water surges over the arcing fault in the riverbed with thunderous force. Great plumes of icy mist rise for hundreds of meters as the waters collide, like an ethereal veil concealing the vast rift behind the torrent. Thousands of onlookers delight in the spectacle every day, drawn by the force of the current and the hypnotic mist.

Niagara is not the tallest of waterfalls (it ranks a lowly 50th) but in terms of sheer volume, there's nothing like it – more than a million bathtubs of water plummet downward every *second*. By day or night, regardless of season, the falls never fail to awe: 12 million visitors annually can't be wrong. Even in winter, when the flow is partially hidden and the edges freeze solid, the watery extravaganza is undiminished. Very occasionally the falls stop altogether. This first happened on Easter Sunday morning in 1848, when ice completely jammed the flow.

Otherwise, Niagara might not be what you expect: the town feels like a tacky outdated amusement park. It has been a saucy honeymoon destination ever since Napoléon's brother brought his bride here – tags like 'For newlyweds and nearly deads' and 'Viagra Falls' are apt. A crass morass of casinos, sleazy motels, tourist traps and strip joints line Clifton Hill and Lundy's Lane – a Little Las Vegas! Love it or loathe it, there's nowhere quite like it.

The old downtown area, where you'll find the bus and train stations, focuses along Queen St, and despite many attempts to bring life back into tired and shuttered buildings, there's not a lot going on. Check the enthusiastic www.niagarafallsdowntown.com to see what's happening.

◎ Sights & Activities

Parking access for sights and activities around the falls and Clifton Hill is expensive and limited.

◉ The Falls & Around

Niagara Falls forms a natural rift between Ontario and New York State. On the US side, **Bridal Veil Falls** (aka the American Falls) crash onto mammoth fallen rocks. On the Canadian side, the grander, more powerful **Horseshoe Falls** plunge into the cloudy **Maid of the Mist Pool**. The prime falls-watching spot is **Table Rock**, poised just meters from the drop – arrive early to beat the crowds.

Tickets for the four falls attractions listed below can be purchased separately, but the online 30% discounted **Niagara Falls Adventure Pass** (www.niagaraparks.com) is better value. It includes admission to Maid of the Mist, the Journey Behind the Falls, White Water Walk, Niagara's Fury and two days transportation on the WEGO bus system. Passes are also available from the Niagara Parks Commission at Table Rock Information Centre and most attractions.

★**Maid of the Mist**   BOATING
(☏905-358-5781; www.maidofthemist.com; 5920 River Rd; adult/child $19.75/12.65; ⊘9am-7:45pm Jun-Aug, to 4:45pm Apr, May, Sep & Oct) This brave little boat has been plowing head-long into the falls' misty veil since 1846. It's loud and wet and heaps of fun. Everyone heads for the boat's upper deck, but views from either end of the lower deck are just as good. Departures are every 15 minutes, weather permitting.

White Water Walk   WALKING
(☏905-374-1221; 4330 Niagara Pkwy; adult/child $10.95/7; ⊘9am-7:30pm) At the northern

end of town, next to Whirlpool Bridge, the White Water Walk is another way to get up close and personal, this time via an elevator down to a 325m boardwalk suspended above the rampaging torrents, just downstream from the falls.

Whirlpool Aero Car   GONDOLA
(☏905-354-5711; 3850 Niagara Pkwy; adult/child $13.50/8.50; ⊘9am-8pm Mar-Nov) Dangling above the Niagara River, 4.5km north of Horseshoe Falls, the Whirlpool Aero Car was designed by Spanish engineer Leonardo Torres Quevedo and has been operating since 1916 (but don't worry – it's still in good shape). The gondola travels 550m between two outcrops above a deadly whirlpool created by the falls – count the logs and tires spinning in the eddies below. No wheelchair access.

Niagara's Fury   SIMULATOR
(☏905-358-3268; 6650 Niagara Pkwy; adult/child $13.50/8.80; ⊘every 30min 10:30am-4pm) On the upper level of Table Rock, the falls' latest Universal Studios–style attraction takes visitors into an interactive 360-degree cinema-simulation of how the falls were created. Expect lots of high-tech tricks to suspend disbelief, including plenty of water, snow and a rapid drop in temperature.

Floral Showhouse   GARDENS
(☏905-354-1721; www.niagaraparks.com; 7145 Niagara Pkwy; ⊘9:30am-8pm) **FREE** Around

ONTARIO NIAGARA FALLS

WELLAND CANAL AREA

Built between 1914 and 1932, the historic Welland Canal, running from Lake Erie into Lake Ontario, functions as a shipping bypass around Niagara Falls. It's part of the St Lawrence Seaway, allowing shipping between the industrial heart of North America and the Atlantic Ocean, with eight locks along the 42km-long canal overcoming the difference of about 100m in the lakes' water levels.

Before it shifted east to Port Weller, the original Welland Canal opened into Lake Ontario at Lakeside Park in **Port Dalhousie**. This rustic harbor area is a blend of old and new, with a reconstructed wooden lock and an 1835 lighthouse alongside bars, restaurants and ice-cream parlors. Hikers and cyclists can stretch out along the 45km **Merritt Trail** (www.canadatrails.ca/tct/on/merritt.html), an established track along the Welland Canal from Port Dalhousie to Port Colborne.

For a more up-to-date look at the canal, the **Welland Canals Centre** (☏905-984-8880; www.stcatharineslock3museum.ca; 1932 Welland Canals Pkwy; ⊘9am-5pm) **FREE** at Lock 3 has a viewing platform close enough to almost touch the building-sized ships as they wait for water levels to rise or fall. You can check the ships' schedules on the website and plan your visit accordingly.

Port Colborne, where Lake Erie empties into the canal, contains the 420m Lock 8 – one of the longest in the world. Check it out at **Lock 8 Park** (Mellanby St; ⊘24hr), south of Main St. The quiet, good-looking town has a canal-side boardwalk and shops and restaurants along West St, good for an afternoon stroll or evening meal.

Niagara Falls

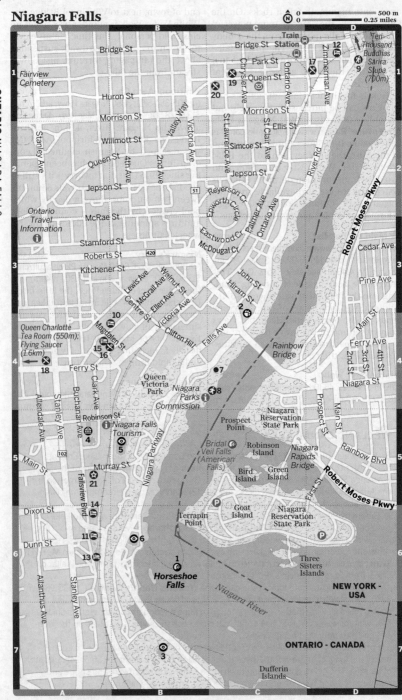

0 — 500 m
0 — 0.25 miles

Fairview Cemetery

Bridge St
Huron St
Morrison St
Willmott St
Queen St
Jepson St
McRae St

Ontario Travel Information

Stamford St
Roberts St
Kitchener St

Stanley Ave
4th Ave
2nd Ave
Valley Way
Victoria Ave

Queen Charlotte Tea Room (550m); Flying Saucer (1.6km)

Magdalen St
Ferry St
Clark Ave

Queen Victoria Park

Niagara Parks Commission

Robinson St
Niagara Falls Tourism

Murray St

Dixon St
Dunn St

Stanley Ave
Buchanan Ave
Allendale Ave
Main St
Fallsview Blvd

Niagara Parkway

Horseshoe Falls

Bridge St
Train Station
Park St
Queen St
Chrysler Ave
St Lawrence Ave

Morrison St
St Clair Ave
Simcoe St
Jepson St

Reyerson Ct
Epworth Circle
Eastwood Cr
McDougal Ct

Palmer Ave
Ontario Ave

Zimmerman Ave
Ten Thousand Buddhas Sarira Stupa (700m)

River Rd

Robert Moses Pkwy

Cedar Ave
Pine Ave

Lewis Ave
McGrail Ave
Walnut St
Centre St
Ellen Ave
Victoria Ave
Clifton Hill

John St
Hiram St
Falls Ave

Rainbow Bridge

Main St
4th St
3rd St
2nd St
Ferry Ave
Niagara St

Prospect Point

Niagara Reservation State Park

Bridal Veil Falls (American Falls)

Robinson Island

Bird Island
Green Island

Niagara Rapids Bridge

Prospect St
Rainbow Blvd

Robert Moses Pkwy

Terrapin Point

Goat Island

Niagara Reservation State Park

1st St

Three Sisters Islands

NEW YORK - USA

Niagara River

ONTARIO - CANADA

Dufferin Islands

Niagara Falls

1km south of Horseshoe Falls, the showhouse offers year-round floral displays and some warm respite on a chilly day. Opposite, lodged on rocks in the rapids, the **Old Scow** is a rusty steel barge that's been waiting to be washed over the falls since 1918 – a teetering symbol of Western imperialism, perhaps?

◉ Clifton Hill

Clifton Hill is a street name, but refers to a broader area near the Falls occupied by a sensory bombardment of artificial enticements. You name it – House of Frankenstein, Madame Tussaud's Wax Museum, Castle Dracula – they're all here. In most cases, paying the admission will leave you feeling like a sucker.

IMAX Theatre &
Daredevil Gallery   MUSEUM

(☑ 905-358-3611;   http://imaxniagara.com; 6170 Fallsview Blvd; Daredevil Gallery adult/child $8/6.50, movie prices vary; ☺9am-9pm) The most engaging thing around here is the Daredevil Gallery attached to IMAX Niagara (which screens blockbusters and films about the falls; combo tickets are available). Scratch your head in amazement at the battered collection of barrels and padded bubbles in which people have ridden over the falls (not all of them successfully). There's also a history of falls 'funambulism' (tightrope walking) here.

Bird Kingdom   ZOO

(☑ 905-356-8888, 866-994-0090; www.birdkingdom.ca; 5651 River Rd; adult/child $17/12; ☺9am-6:30pm) The jungly Bird Kingdom claims to be the world's largest indoor aviary, with 400 species of free-flying tropical birds from around the globe. You can also buddy-up with a boa constrictor in the Reptile Encounter Zone.

Ten Thousand Buddhas
Sarira Stupa   TEMPLE

(☑ 905-371-2678; 4303 River Rd; ☺9am-5pm, main temple Sat & Sun only) If the tourist bustle is messing with your yang, find some tranquility at this out-of-context Buddhist temple. The modern building of Western construction is ultra-tacky. Visitors are welcome to wander the complex and view the various sculptures, bells and artworks.

Skylon Tower   VIEWPOINT

(☑ 905-356-2651; www.skylon.com; 5200 Robinson St; adult/child $13/8; ☺8am-10pm) The Skylon Tower is an ugly 158m spire with yellow elevators crawling like bugs up the exterior. The views from the indoor and outdoor observation decks are eye-poppers. There's also a revolving restaurant.

◉ Around Niagara Falls

The slow-roaming, leafy Niagara Pkwy meanders for 56km along the Niagara River, from Niagara-on-the-Lake past the falls all the way to Fort Erie. Along the way you'll find parks, picnic areas and viewpoints. The idyllic 3m-wide **Niagara River Recreation**

Trail (www.niagaraparks.com/nature/rectrailarea.php) for cycling, jogging or walking runs parallel to the parkway. The trail can easily be divided into four chunks, each of which takes around two hours to pedal. In season, fresh-fruit stands selling cold cherry cider adorn the side of the trail. Download a map online, or pick one up at a visitors center.

Niagara Glen Nature Reserve   PARK

(☑905-371-0254; www.niagaraparks.com; Niagara Pkwy; ⊙dawn-dusk) About 8km north of the falls is this exceptional reserve, where you can get a sense of what the area was like pre-Europeans. There are 4km of walking trails winding down into a gorge, past huge boulders, cold caves, wildflowers and woods. The Niagara Parks Commission offers **guided nature walks** daily during the summer season for a nominal fee. Bring something to drink – the water in the Niagara River is far from clean.

Botanical Gardens and Butterfly Conservatory   GARDENS

(☑905-356-8119; www.niagaraparks.com; 2565 Niagara Pkwy; Butterfly Conservatory adult/child $12.95/8.25, gardens free; ⊙10am-4pm Mon-Fri, to 5pm Sat & Sun) Entry to the 40 hectares of Botanical Gardens is free, but you'll need to pay to enter the Butterfly Conservatory, with its more than 50 species of butterflies (some as big as birds) flitting around 130 species of flowers and plants. This is also a breeding facility where you can see young butterflies being released.

Queenston Heights Park   HISTORIC SITE

(☑905-262-6759; www.niagaraparks.com; 14184 Niagara Pkwy, Queenston; ⊙dawn-dusk) **FREE** In Queenston village, a snoozy historic throwback north of the falls near the Lewiston Bridge to the US, is Queenston Heights Park, a national historic site. Here,

the commanding **Brock Monument** honors Major General Sir Isaac Brock, 'Savior of Upper Canada.' Self-guided walking tours of the hillside recount the 1812 Battle of Queenston Heights and include a walk to the top for a magnificent view.

Mackenzie Printery & Newspaper Museum   MUSEUM

(☑905-262-5676; www.mackenzieprintery.org; 1 Queenston St, Queenston; adult/child $5/3.75; ⊙10am-5pm May-Sep) This ivy-covered museum was where the esteemed William Lyon Mackenzie once edited the hell-raising *Colonial Advocate*. Enthusiastic young staff conduct tours every half-hour.

Bruce Trail   WALKING

(www.brucetrail.org) The southern extent of the Bruce Trail, which extends 800km to Tobermory on Georgian Bay, is at Queenston Heights Park. There are numerous access points in the Niagara area.

⚐ Tours

Journey Behind the Falls   WALKING TOUR

(☑905-354-1551; 6650 Niagara Pkwy; adult/child Apr-Dec $15.95/10.95, Dec-Apr $11.25/6.95; ⊙9am-10pm) From Table Rock Information Centre you can don a very unsexy plastic poncho and traverse rock-cut tunnels halfway down the cliff – as close as you can get to the falls without getting in a barrel. It's open year-round, but be prepared to queue.

Double Deck Tours   BUS TOUR

(☑905-374-7423; www.doubledecktours.com; cnr River Rd & Clifton Hill; tours adult/child from $79/49; ⊙11am Apr-Oct) Offers a deluxe four-hour tour on a red double-decker bus. The price includes admission to the Whirlpool Aero Car, Journey Behind the Falls *and* the Maid of the Mist.

THE BRUCE TRAIL

For 800km the Bruce Trail winds along the top of the Niagara Escarpment, from the Niagara Peninsula to the Bruce Peninsula. This wide, well-maintained path is excellent for hiking during summer months, while those armed with cross-country skis take it through its winter paces. Opened in 1967, it's the oldest hiking trail in Canada and the longest in Ontario. The trail winds through public and private land, as well as roadways. Wander past wineries, farmlands and forests and marvel at Georgian Bay's shimmering azure from the escarpment's white cliffs. Day hikes along the trail are an appealing way to spend a sunny afternoon. A multitude of campgrounds en route have budget accommodations for those on longer trips, and trail towns offer B&Bs galore. Get prepared at www.brucetrail.org.

DAREDEVILS

Surprisingly, more than a few people who have gone over Niagara Falls have actually lived to tell the tale. The first successful leap was in 1901, by a 63-year-old schoolteacher named Annie Taylor, who did it in a skirt, no less. This promoted a rash of barrel stunters that continued into the 1920s, including Bobby Leach, who survived the drop but met his untimely death after slipping on an orange peel and developing gangrene!

In 1984 Karl Soucek revived the tradition in a bright red barrel. He made it, only to die six months later in another barrel stunt in Houston. Also during the 1980s, two locals successfully took the plunge lying head to head in the same barrel.

A US citizen who tried to jet ski over the falls in 1995 might have made it – if his rocket-propelled parachute had opened. Another American, Kirk Jones, survived the trip over the falls unaided in 2003. After being charged by Canadian police with illegally performing a stunt, he joined the circus.

Only one accidental falls-faller has survived – a seven-year-old Tennessee boy who fell out of a boat upstream in 1960 and survived the drop without even breaking a bone.

Take the virtual plunge at IMAX Niagara, and check out the over-the-falls barrels folks have used at the Daredevil Gallery.

Niagara Helicopters   HELICOPTER TOUR
(☑ 905-357-5672; www.niagarahelicopters.com; 3731 Victoria Ave; 10min flights adult/child $137/85; ⊙ 9am-sunset, weather permitting) A fantastic falls encounter, but pricey and not the most environmentally sensitive option.

✪✫ Festivals & Events

Winter Festival of Lights   LIGHT SHOW
(☑ 905-374-1616, 800-563-2557; www.wfol.com) A season of events from late November to mid-January, including more than 125 animated displays and three million tree and ground lights, the undisputed highlight of which is an over-the-top nocturnal light display along a 36km route. There are also concerts, fun runs and a cheerleading championship.

🛏 Sleeping

There are more beds than heads in Niagara Falls, but the town is sometimes completely booked up. Prices spike sharply in summer, on weekends and during holidays. Check B&B availability online at www.bbniagara-falls.com. Cheap motels line Lundy's Lane.

★ ACBB Hostel Niagara   HOSTEL $
(☑ 905-359-4815; www.hostelniagara.ca; 5741 Mc-Grail Ave; dm/d incl breakfast from $29/38; ⊜ 🛜) With comfortable, spacious dorms, kitchens on every floor and balconies galore, freshly renovated ACBB continues to be a notch above the rest. Owner Patrick is passionate about Niagara and hosteling, and always has time to make suggestions or draw you a map. His breakfasts are legendary.

Hostelling International Niagara Falls   HOSTEL $
(☑ 888-749-0058, 905-357-0770; www.hostelling-niagara.com; 4549 Cataract Ave; dm/d incl linen from $28/79; ⊜ @ 🛜) Quietly adrift in the old town, this homey, multicolored hostel sleeps around 90 people. The facilities, including a sizable kitchen, pool table, lockers and cool basement lounge, are in good shape; staff are friendly and ecofocused. It's close to the train and bus stations, and you can rent bicycles for $15 per day.

Niagara Parkway Court   MOTEL $
(☑ 905-295-3331; www.niagaraparkwaycourt.com; 3708 Main St; d from $59; ❉ 🛜) Recently renovated rooms in a variety of styles, free wi-fi and transport to the falls from its pleasant spot, just outside town, combined with excellent customer service make this motel a great choice for low-cost accommodations.

Oakes Hotel   HOTEL $$
(☑ 877-843-6253, 905-356-4514; www.oakeshotel.com; 6546 Fallsview Blvd; d $99-159; ⊜ ❉ 🛜 ▨) A jaunty silver spire next to the Fallsview Casino, the Oakes has front-row-center views of the great cascades. Not all rooms have falls views; try for a terrace room if you can – you'll likely pay extra. Some rooms have Jacuzzis and fireplaces. If you're on a budget, ask about the cheaper drive-up motel rooms, from $69.

Sterling Inn & Spa   BOUTIQUE HOTEL $$
(☑ 289-292-0000; www.sterlingniagara.com; 5195 Magdalen St; r from $125) The stylish rooms of this affordable boutique hotel (with either

a Jacuzzi or steam shower) beckon you to relax and unwind with someone special, even if that is yourself. Quality furnishings, amenities and breakfast-in-bed baskets are the kind of touches to expect. The on-site AG Restaurant is fancy and delicious and there's a full-service treatment spa. Perfect for couples. Note that it is a low-rise property a little distance from the falls: no views.

Embassy Suites   HOTEL $$

(✆800-420-6980; www.embassysuitesniagara.com/; 6700 Fallsview Blvd; ste incl breakfast from $145) This mammoth all-suite hotel has a great position that makes you feel like you're almost on top of the Canadian falls. For that reason, its generic rooms get a lot of use. That said, they're spacious and a variety of suite types are available: most have great views. A welcome drink is also included.

Marriott Niagara Falls   HOTEL $$

(✆888-501-8916; www.niagarafallsmarriott.com; 6740 Fallsview Blvd; r from $149) This sprawling giant is so close that you could almost touch the falls. A variety of room types are available, but we love the two-level loft suites with Jacuzzi, fireplace and awesome views from the floor-to-ceiling windows.

✖ Eating

The old downtown section is seeing a lot of new restaurants crop up and is worth exploring. Fast food is abundant in the touristy strip, but the best eats can be found a little further afield. For cuisine a cut above, you're better off heading up the road to Niagara-on-the-Lake.

Edwin's   FUSION $

(✆289-990-7305; www.edwinsrestaurant.com; 4616 Erie Ave; mains $2.50-6.50; ⊙11:30am-11pm) Born in Jamaica and trained in England, the illustrious Edwin blends Caribbean and Mediterranean cuisine at this little spot near the train station. Jerk chicken, fried plantains, curried goat and salmon salad are all on offer, as is a weekend breakfast buffet ($6.99).

Flying Saucer   FAST FOOD $

(✆905-356-4453; www.flyingsaucerrestaurant.com; 6768 Lundy's Lane; mains $8-27; ⊙6am-10pm) For extraterrestrial fast food, you can't go past this iconic diner on the Lundy's Lane motel strip. Famous $1.99 early-bird breakfasts are served from 6am to 10am (eggs, fries and toast) with the purchase of a beverage. Heftier meals in the way of steaks, sea-

food, fajitas, burgers and hot dogs are also onboard. Takeout is in the saucer to the left.

Queen Charlotte Tea Room   BRITISH $

(✆905-371-1350; www.queencharlottetearoom.com; 5689 Main St; light meals $7-14; ⊙9am-7pm Tue-Fri, from 10am Sat & Sun) Expats craving a decent or even fancy cuppa, cucumber sandwiches, steak and kidney, or fish and chips with mushy peas should head straight to this quaint establishment on Main St near the intersection with Lundy's Lane for a spot of tiffin!

Taps on Queen
Brewhouse & Grill   INTERNATIONAL $$

(www.tapsbeer.com; 4680 Queen St; mains $9-14; ⊙noon-10pm Mon, Tue & Sun, to midnight Wed-Sat) Does a mix of stuff, from shepherd's pie to ancient grains curry (quinoa, couscous, adzuki beans, mung beans and veggies). All dishes are, naturally, best when paired with one of the brewery's tasty beers.

Paris Crepes Cafe   FRENCH $$

(✆289-296-4218; www.pariscrepescafe.com; 4613 Queen St; mains $12-30; ⊙10am-10pm Mon-Fri, from 9am Sat & Sun) In the revitalized area of Queen St you'll find this quaint creperie, a very long way from the streets of Paris: you can't miss the dark red building. Sweet and savory crepe sensations are served among other continental delights from the wonderfully authentic Parisian menu.

Napoli Ristorante Pizzeria   ITALIAN $$

(✆905-356-3345; www.napoliristorante.com; 5545 Ferry St; mains $14-30; ⊙4-11pm) Head to Napoli for the best Italian in town, hands down. Delicious pizza, rich pasta, creamy risotto and veal parmigiana all feature on the familiar menu.

AG   CANADIAN $$$

(✆289-292-0005; www.agcuisine.com; 5195 Magdalen St; mains $18-36; ⊙5:30-9:30pm Tue-Sun) Fine dining isn't something you find easily at the Falls, which makes this fine restaurant at the Sterling Inn & Spa so refreshing. Service, decor, presentation and especially the quality of the food all rate highly. Has a seasonal menu featuring dishes like fennel pollen pickerel, roasted venison loin and crispy skinned trout, sourced locally.

☆ Entertainment

Niagara Fallsview Casino   CASINO

(✆905-371-7569; www.fallsviewcasinoresort.com; 6380 Fallsview Blvd; ⊙24hr) This casino never closes. The building itself is worth a look – an amazing complex of commerce and crapshoots, with a fantastical fountain in the lobby. Corny old-timers like Kenny Rogers and Donny Osmond are regularly wheeled out to perform.

❶ Information

Accessible Niagara (www.accessibleniagara.com) Advice for the mobility-impaired.

Greater Niagara General Hospital (☑905-378-4647; www.niagarahealth.on.ca; 5546 Portage Rd; ⏰24hr) Emergency room.

Info Niagara (www.infoniagara.com) Privately run website with helpful links.

Niagara Falls Public Library (☑905-356-8080; www.nflibrary.ca; 4848 Victoria Ave; ⏰9am-9pm Mon-Thu, to 5:30pm Fri & Sat; @ 🛜) Free internet and wi-fi internet access.

Niagara Falls Tourism (☑905-356-6061, 800-563-2557; www.niagarafallstourism.com; 5400 Robinson St; ⏰8am-5pm Mon-Fri, 10am-4pm Sat & Sun) Everything you need to know about Niagara, served with a smile.

Niagara Parks Commission (☑877-642-7275, 905-371-0254; www.niagaraparks.com; ⏰9am-11pm Jun-Aug) The falls' governing body, with information desks at Maid of the Mist Plaza and Table Rock Information Centre.

Ontario Travel Information (☑905-358-3221; www.ontariotravel.net; 5355 Stanley Ave; ⏰8am-8pm) On the western outskirts of town; free tourist booklets containing maps and discount coupons.

Post office (www.canadapost.ca; 4500 Queen St; ⏰8am-5pm Mon-Fri)

❶ Getting There & Away

BUS

The **Niagara Transportation Centre** (☑800-461-7661, 905-357-2133; 4555 Erie Ave) is in the old part of town. Greyhound Canada buses depart for Toronto ($18, 1½ to two hours, seven daily) and Buffalo, New York ($10.30, one to 1½ hours, six daily). GO Transit also operates services from Toronto (via Burlington) by combination of rail/bus and, in recent years, direct rail services on weekends (June to September). Check with www.gotransit.com.

Niagara Airbus (☑800-268-8111, 905-374-8111; www.niagaraairbus.com) operates a door-to-door shared shuttle service between Niagara Falls and Toronto Pearson airport (one way/return $87/137, 1½ hours) or Buffalo International airport, NY ($89/146, 1½ hours).

TRAIN

Rail services from **Niagara Falls Train Station** (☑888-842-7245; www.viarail.ca; 4267 Bridge

FORT ERIE

East of Port Colborne and south of Niagara Falls is the town of Fort Erie, where the Niagara River leaks out of Lake Erie. Across from Buffalo, New York, it's connected to the US by the Peace Bridge. The main drawcard here is the historic, star-shaped **Fort Erie** (☑905-871-0540; www.oldforterie.com; 350 Lakeshore Rd; adult/child $12.25/7.95; ⏰10am-5pm May-Nov), a key player in the War of 1812, and 'Canada's bloodiest battlefield.' Also known as the Old Stone Fort, it was first built in 1764. The US seized it in 1814 before retreating. Inside there's a museum and immaculate, uniformed soldiers performing authentic military drills. Take the worthwhile guided tour (every 30 minutes), included in the admission.

St) to Toronto were suspended in recent years, with the exception of a weekend summer service operated by GO Transit. You can, however, get to New York City ($87, 11½ hours, once daily).

❶ Getting Around

BICYCLE

The Niagara region is perfect for biking. The excellent **Zoom Leisure Bicycle Rentals** (☑866-811-6993; www.zoomleisure.com; 431 Mississauga St, Niagara-on-the-Lake) also has offices in Niagara Falls and on the Niagara Parkway, and will deliver to anywhere in the Niagara region. Excellent bike tours are also available.

CAR & MOTORCYCLE

Driving and parking around the center is an expensive headache. Park way out and walk, or follow the parking district signs and stash the car for the day (around $6 per 30 minutes, or $15 per day). The huge Rapidsview parking lot (also the WEGO depot) is 3km south of the falls off River Rd.

PUBLIC TRANSPORTATION

Cranking up and down the steep 50m slope between the falls and Fallsview Blvd is a quaint **Incline Railway** (www.niagaraparks.com; 6635 Niagara Pkwy; one way/day pass $2.50/$6).

Formerly the seasonal Niagara Parks People Mover, **WEGO** (www.niagaraparks.com/wego; day pass adult/child $7/4) is an economical and efficient year-round transit system, geared for tourists. There are three lines: red, green and blue; between them, they've got all the major sights and accommodations covered. For areas further afield, locals use **Niagara Transit** (☎ 905-356-7521; www.niagarafalls.ca/living/transit/bus-routes.aspx; one-way adult/child $2.50/2.25, day pass $6), but most have their own cars.

WALKING

Put on your sneakers and get t'steppin' – walking is the way to go! You'll only need wheels to visit outlying sights along the Niagara Pkwy or if you're staying on Lundy's Lane.

Niagara Peninsula Wine Country

The Niagara Peninsula adheres to the 43rd parallel: a similar latitude to northern California and further south than Bordeaux, France. A primo vino location, the mineral-rich soils and moderate microclimate are the perfect recipe for viticulture success. A visit to the area makes an indulgent day trip or lazy weekend, with haughty old vineyards

and brash newcomers competing for your attention.

Touring the vineyards by car is the best way to go. There are two main areas to focus on: west of St Catharines around Vineland, and north of the Queen Elizabeth Way (QEW) around Niagara-on-the-Lake. Regional tourist offices stock wine-route maps and brochures, which are also available at winery tasting rooms. For more info, check out www.winesofontario.ca.

Tours

Crush on Niagara   WINERY TOUR
(☎ 866-408-9463, 905-562-3373; www.crushtours.com; tours $85-120) Small-group morning and afternoon van tours departing from various pickup points in the Niagara region.

Grape Escape Wine Tours   WINERY TOUR
(☎ 866-935-4445; www.tourniagarawineries.com; tours $44-135) A range of wine-flavored regional tours, by bike, van or SUV. Tours in-

---

WINERY DRIVING TOUR

The following drive weaves through the best Niagara wineries. Apart from tastings, most offer tours and dining; check the respective websites for more info. Parking is free at all vineyards.

Coming from Toronto, take Queen Elizabeth Way (QEW) exit 78 at Fifty Rd into Winona and **Puddicombe Estate Farms & Winery** (☎ 905-643-1015; www.puddicombefarms.com; 1468 Hwy 8, Winona; tastings $0.50; ☽ 9am-5pm Mon-Fri, 10am-4pm Sat & Sun), a rustic farm specializing in fruit wines (try the peach and the iced apple). Light lunches available.

Off QEW exit 74 is **Kittling Ridge Winery** (☎ 905-945-9225; www.kittlingridge.com; 297 South Service Rd, Grimsby; tastings free; ☽ 10am-6pm Mon-Sat, 11am-5pm Sun, free tours 2pm Tue-Sat year-round & 11am Sun Jun-Aug). It looks like a factory, but friendly staff and award-winning ice-wines and late-harvest wines will win you over.

Continue southeast on Main St W to King St; photogenic **Peninsula Ridge Estates Winery** (☎ 905-563-0900; http://peninsularidge.com; 5600 King St W, Beamsville; tours $5; ☽ 10am-5pm, tours 11:30am Jun-Nov) is unmissable on a hilltop. The lofty timber tasting room, restaurant and hilltop setting are magic.

Turn right at Cherry Ave, about 10km further down the road, go up the hill, then turn left onto Moyer Rd for the stone buildings of **Vineland Estates Winery** (☎ 905-562-7088, 888-846-3526; www.vineland.com; 3620 Moyer Rd, Vineland; tastings $3, tours $6; ☽ 10am-6pm), the elder statesman of Niagara viticulture. Almost all the wines here are excellent. The restaurant and accommodations are fabulous too.

Backtrack up to King St, to the intersection of King and Cherry where you'll find beloved hockey star's winery, **Wayne Gretzky Estate** (www.gretzkyestateswines.com; 3751 King St, Vineland; ☽ 10am-8pm Mon-Sat, 11am-5pm Sun).

Follow King Rd east, turn right onto Victoria Ave, then left onto 7th Ave for friendly **Flat Rock Cellars** (☎ 905-562-8994; www.flatrockcellars.com; 2727 7th Ave, Jordan; tastings $1-2, tours $10-25; ☽ 10am-5pm Mon-Sat, from 11am Sun). The hexagonal architecture and lake views here are almost as good as the wine.

Wander back toward the lake to 4th Ave and cheery **Creekside Estate Winery** (☎ 905-562-0035, 877-262-9463; www.creeksidewine.com; 2170 4th Ave, Jordan Station; tastings free if purchasing, tours free; ☽ 10am-6pm), where you can tour the crush pad and underground cellars (book online).

clude some kind of meal (cheese platters on cheaper tours through to full gourmet dinners). There's free hotel pickup/drop-off.

Niagara Airbus
WINERY TOUR

(☑ 800-268-8111, 905-374-8111; www.niagaraair-bus.com; tours from Niagara Falls $49-129, from Toronto $129-190) Stops at well-known wineries; some itineraries include vineyard tours, lunch and shopping in Niagara-on-the-Lake.

⚒ Festivals & Events

Niagara Wine Festivals
WINF

(☑ 905-688-0212; www.niagarawinefestival.com) There are three wine-related festivals throughout the year: Niagara New Vintage Festival, celebrating Niagara's new-season vino and regional cuisine in late June; the main event, Niagara Wine Festival, a week-long event in mid-September celebrating the region's finest picks off the vine; and Niagara Icewine Festival, a 10-day winter festival held throughout the Niagara region dur-ing mid-January and showcasing Ontario's stickiest, sweetest ice wines.

🛏 Sleeping & Eating

Bonnybank
B&B $$

(☑ 888-889-8296, 905-562-3746; www.bonnybank.ca; RR 1, Vineland Station; r incl breakfast $105-135; ⊜❋🛜) A stately Tudor-meets-Grimsby-sandstone house in an owl-filled wilderness setting. It's a little off the beaten track.

Squirrel House Gardens
B&B $$$

(☑ 905-685-1608; www.squirrelhouseniagara.ca; 1819 5th St, St Catharines; ste incl breakfast $180; ⊜@⚍) Stay in a massive suite in the old barn, built in 1850 as part of this country estate. Lovingly decorated, the room opens onto a massive garden and features brick and colored cement floors, original wood beams, and French doors that open onto a deck. The grounds have a swimming pool, patio and fire pit. The delightful, arty owners are welcoming and friendly, and take as

---

From 7th Ave, scoot back onto the QEW and truck east into the Niagara-on-the-Lake region. Take exit 38 and head north onto Four Mile Creek Rd, which will take you to **Trius Winery at Hillebrand** (☑ 800-582-8412; www.hillebrand.com; 1249 Niagara Stone Rd, Niagara-on-the-Lake; tastings $5-10; ⏱ 10am-9pm). Mass-market wines are the name of the game here, but hourly introductory tours and tasting-bar presentations are great for newcomers to the wine scene.

Further north, superiority emanates from elite **Konzelmann Estate Winery** (☑ 905-935-2866; www.konzelmann.ca; 1096 Lakeshore Rd, Niagara-on-the-Lake; tours May-Sep $5; ⏱ 10am-6pm), one of the oldest wineries in the region and the only one to take full advantage of the lakeside microclimate. Late-harvest vidal and ice wines are superb.

Next on the right is **Strewn** (☑ 905-468-1229; www.strewnwinery.com; 1339 Lakeshore Rd, Niagara-on-the-Lake; tours free; ⏱ 10am-6pm, tours 1:30pm), producing medal-winning vintages and home to a classy restaurant and **Wine Country Cooking School** (☑ 905-468-8304; www.winecountrycooking.com; 1339 Lakeshore Rd, Niagara-on-the-Lake), where one-day, weekend and week-long classes are a gastronomic delight.

Closer to Niagara-on-the-Lake, **Sunnybrook Farm Estate Winery** (☑ 905-468-1122; www.sunnybrookfarmwinery.com; 1425 Lakeshore Rd, Niagara-on-the-Lake; tastings $1-3; ⏱ 10am-6pm) specializes in unique Niagara fruit and berry wines, and brews a mean 'hard' cider. It's only a little place, so tour buses usually don't stop here.

★ **Stratus** (☑ 905-468-1806; www.stratuswines.com; 2059 Niagara Stone Rd, Niagara-on-the-Lake; ⏱ 11am-5pm) , south of Niagara-on-the-Lake, was the first building in Canada to earn Leadership in Energy & Environmental Design (LEED) certification. The design addresses complex recycling, organic, energy-efficiency and indigenous concerns.

Heading south down the Niagara Pkwy, **Reif Estate Winery** (☑ 905-468-7738; www.reifwinery.com; 15608 Niagara Pkwy, Niagara-on-the-Lake; tours $5-20; ⏱ 9am-6pm), pronounced 'Rife,' is a well-established winery. Ice wines are what you're here for.

Complete your tour (if you're still standing) at **Inniskillin** (☑ 888-466-4754; www.inniskillin.com; 1499 Line 3, cnr Niagara Pkwy, Niagara-on-the-Lake; tastings $1-20, tours $5-15; ⏱ 9am-6pm, tours hourly May-Oct), master of the ice-wine craft.

good care of you as they do their impressive country garden.

Peach Country Farm Market
MARKET $

(905-562-5602; 4490 Victoria Ave, Vineland Station; items from $2; 9am-8pm Jun-Aug, to 6pm Sep & Oct) An open-fronted barn selling fresh fruit, jams, ice cream and fruit pies, all grown, picked and baked on-site by fourth-generation farmers – a roadside gem!

Pie Plate
BAKERY $

(905-468-9743; www.thepieplate.com; 41516 Niagara Stone Rd, Virgil; sandwiches $7-11; 10am-6pm Tue-Sun) Simple but delicious lunches (we devoured the pear and brie sandwich) at reasonable prices. It wouldn't be an Ontario bakery without butter tarts, but there are also thin-crust pizzas, meat pies, salads and a few beers on tap. A great place to fill up your belly while touring the wine country.

Peninsula Ridge
FUSION $$$

(905-563-0900; 5600 King St W, Beamsville; mains $24-34; noon-2:30pm & 5-9pm Wed-Sat, 11:30-2:30pm Sun) Sit outside, upstairs or down in this high-Victorian 1885 manor, serving haute cuisine paired with local wines...of course.

ℹ Getting There & Away

The 100km drive from Toronto to the central peninsula takes around 1½ hours – take Hwy 403 then the QEW east from Hamilton toward Niagara Falls. The official Wine Route is signposted off the QEW, on rural highways and along backcountry roads.

Niagara-on-the-Lake

One of the best-preserved 19th-century towns in North America, affluent N-o-t-L is an undeniably gorgeous place, with tree-lined streets, lush parks and impeccably restored houses. Originally a neutral First Nations village, the town was founded by Loyalists from New York State after the American Revolution and later became the first capital of the colony of Upper Canada. Today, tour-bus stampedes overrun the streets, puffing Cuban cigars and dampening the charm; the town fountain is full of coins but there are no homeless people here to plunder it. Is this a *real* town, or just gingerbread? Is there a soul beneath the surface? Yes, after 5pm.

◉ Sights

Lovely Queen St teems with shops of the ye olde variety selling antiques, Brit-style souvenirs and homemade fudge.

Fort George
HISTORIC SITE

(905-468-6614; www.pc.gc.ca/fortgeorge; 51 Queens Pde; adult/child $11.70/5.80; 10am-5pm May-Oct, Sat & Sun only Apr & Nov) On the town's southeastern fringe, restored Fort George dates from 1797. The fort saw some bloody battles during the War of 1812, changing hands between the British and US forces a couple of times. Within the spiked battlements are officers' quarters, a working kitchen, a powder magazine and storage

---

ICE, ICE BABY

Niagara's regional wineries burst onto the scene at Vinexpo 1991 in Bordeaux, France. In a blind taste test, judges awarded a coveted gold medal to an Ontario ice wine – international attendees' jaws hit the floor! These specialty vintages, with their arduous harvesting and sweet, multidimensional palate, continue to lure aficionados to the Niagara Peninsula.

To make ice wine, a certain percentage of grapes are left on the vines after the regular harvest is over. If birds, storms and mildew don't get to them, the grapes grow ever-more sugary and concentrated. Winemakers wait patiently until December or January when three days of consistent, low temperature (-8°C) freeze the grapes entirely.

In the predawn darkness (so the sun doesn't melt the ice and dilute the grape juice), the grapes are carefully harvested by hand, then pressed and aged in barrels for up to a year. After decanting, the smooth ice vintages taste intensely of apples, or even more exotic fruit, and pack a serious alcoholic punch.

Why are ice wines so expensive? It takes 10 times the usual number of grapes to make just one bottle. This, combined with labor-intensive production and the high risk of crop failure, often drives the price above $50 per 375mL bottle. Late-harvest wines picked earlier in the year may be less costly (and less sweet), but just as full-flavored and aromatic.

houses. Ghost tours, skills demonstrations, retro tank displays and battle re-enactments occur throughout the summer. Parking costs $6, but this is reimbursed with your ticket.

Niagara Historical Society Museum
MUSEUM

(☑905-468-3912; www.niagarahistorical.museum; 43 Castlereagh St; adult/child $5/1; ◔10am-5pm) The Niagara Historical Society Museum, south of Simcoe Park, has a vast collection relating to the town's past, ranging from First Nations artifacts to Loyalist and War of 1812 collectibles (including the prized hat of Major General Sir Isaac Brock).

Lincoln & Welland Regimental Museum
MUSEUM

(☑905-468-0888; www.lwmuseum.ca; cnr King & John Sts; adult/child $3/2; ◔10am-4pm Wed-Sun) The Lincoln & Welland Regimental Museum has wonderfully aged displays of Canadian military regalia.

☞ Tours

Jetboat Niagara
BOAT TOUR

(☑905-468-4800, 888-438-4444; www.whirlpooljet.com; 61 Melville St; 45min tours adult/child $61/51; ◔Apr-Oct) A wet and wild ride, full of fishtails and splashy stops – bring a change of clothes (and maybe underwear). Reservations required.

Niagara Wine Tours International
FOOD TOUR

(☑800-680-7006, 905-468-1300; www.niagaraworldwinetours.com; 92 Picton St; tours $65-165) Bicycle and gourmet lunch and dinner tours around local wineries, including tastings.

🛏 Sleeping

Although there are over 300 B&Bs in town, accommodations are expensive and often booked out. When the Shaw Festival is running, lodging is even tighter. Plan ahead.

★Historic Davy House B&B Inn
B&B $$

(☑888-314-9046; www.davyhouse.com; 230 Davy St; d incl breakfast $155-204; ☎) This reasonably priced Historically Designated home built in 1842 has been beautifully restored to maintain its colonial charm and is meticulously maintained by expert hosts who've been in the hospitality biz for over 30 years. Guests are invited to enjoy the lush, landscaped grounds and rustic guest parlor. It's an excellent choice for comfortable, restful and authentic accommodations in this B&B-saturated area.

Britaly B&B
B&B $$

(☑905-468-8778; www.britaly.com; 57 The Promenade; r incl breakfast $120-140; ✳☎) This simple three-room B&B (choose from the English, Italian or Canadiana rooms) is extremely popular for its reasonable rates and wonderful hosts who maintain their lovely home and gardens to the highest standard.

White Oaks Resort & Spa
HOTEL $$

(☑800-263-5766; www.whiteoaksresort.com; 234 Taylor Rd SS4; d from $159) This sprawling 220-room resort just off the QEW, 15km from Niagara-on-the-Lake, offers well-appointed rooms and resort-style service and facilities: there's a full-service spa and on-site restaurant. A variety of stay packages are available online. Rates can be cheaper than downtown accommodations.

Charles Inn
HOTEL $$$

(☑905-468-4588; www.niagarasfinest.com/properties/charlesinn; 209 Queen St; d incl breakfast from $185) We love this romantic little inn (c1832) by the golf course. Rooms of varying sizes are sumptuously decorated to a diverse range of styles. Check the website to see which you like best: each is wonderfully comfortable – there's even a pillow menu.

Moffat
INN $$$

(☑905-468-4116; www.moffattinn.com; 60 Picton St; d from $189; ◗✳☎) Green trim and flower boxes lend an Irish pub feel to the outside of the Moffat, which bills itself as 'cottage chic.' Twenty-four rooms are tastefully decorated, and you'll probably find the word *charming* pop out of your mouth more than once while visiting.

Prince of Wales Hotel
HOTEL $$$

(☑888-669-5566, 905-468-3246; www.vintagehotels.com; 6 Picton St; d/ste from $289/$429; ◗✳@☎⛱) Prince of N-o-t-L, an elegant Victorian hotel, was knocked into shape around 1864 and retains much of its period primp: vaulted ceilings, timber-inlay floors, red-waistcoated bellhops. Frills and floral prints seem angled toward the elderly and honeymooners, but it's the perfect spot for anyone looking to splash out. Also on-site are a spa, afternoon tea and the excellent Escabeche restaurant. Parking costs $10. It's on the corner of King St.

✖ Eating

A few blocks from Queen St, Queen's Royal Park is a sweet spot for a picnic beside the water. Check out www.niagaraonthelake.com

A SHAW THING

In 1962, lawyer and passionate dramatist Brian Doherty led a group of residents in eight performances of George Bernard Shaw's *Candida* and 'Don Juan in Hell' from *Man and Superman*. Doherty's passionate first season blossomed into today's much-esteemed **Shaw Festival** (☏800-511-7429, 905-468-2172; www.shawfest.com; 10 Queens Pde, Niagara-on-the-Lake; ⊙box office 10am-8pm). Plays run from April through October, infusing a variety of works from Victorian drama to contemporary plays, musicals and classics from Wilde, Woolf and Coward. Specialized seminars are held throughout the season, plus informal 'Lunchtime Conversations' on selected Saturdays.

Actors tread the boards in three theaters around town – the Festival, Royal George and Court House theaters. Rush seats go on sale at 9am on performance days (except for Saturdays). Students, under-30s and seniors receive discounts at some matinees; weekday matinees are the cheapest. Check the website for what's on when.

for updates on the Fabulicious food festival held in March.

1875 Restaurant
CANADIAN $$
(☏905-468-3424; www.notlgolf.com/restaurant-home; 143 Front St; mains $10-27; ⊙8am-10pm) The restaurant in North America's oldest golf course was one of N-o-t-L's best-kept secrets, until now: its prime waterfront patio is incomparable, the vibe casual (for N-o-t-L) and service, friendly. The menu is refreshingly familiar: we love the crab cakes and fish and chips. Come for brunch, lunch, dinner or a drink and be pleasantly surprised.

Irish Harp Pub
PUB $$
(☏905-468-4443; www.theirishharppub.com; 245 King St; mains $12-20; ⊙noon-11pm Mon-Thu, 11am-11pm Fri-Sun) Loved by locals throughout the Niagara region for its hearty pub meals (think Irish hot pot and steak & guinness pie), although some just come for the Irish 'craic' (fun and conversation) and of course, beer! There's Guinness on tap and Irish Harp lager, brewed locally from a traditional recipe. All told, plenty to wet your whistle and fill your tum.

Epicurean
CAFE $$
(☏905-468-3408; www.epicurean.ca; 84 Queen St; mains $11-29; ⊙9am-9pm Wed-Sat, to 5:30pm Sun-Tue) By day this fare-thee-well cafeteria dishes up fresh, tasty sandwiches, salads, pies and quiches. The ambience ramps up at night with a bistro menu offering the likes of crispy-skin chicken with steamed rice, scallions and shiitake mushrooms in Thai coconut curry. The streetside patio is always full.

Fans Court
CHINESE $$
(☏905-468-4511; 135 Queen St; lunch mains $7-10, dinner $15-20; ⊙noon-9pm Tue-Sun) A menu graced with Cantonese, Szechuan and pan-Asian dishes distinguishes this place from its neighbors in this most Anglo of towns. The best part about Fans, however, is not the mango pork (though that's delish), but the wonderful flowered courtyard.

★REST/Stone Road Grille
MODERN CANADIAN $$$
(☏905-468-3474; www.stoneroadgrille.com; 238 Mary St; $16-34; ⊙5-9pm Tue-Sun) Don't be fooled by the rather drab strip-mall location: you've found one of the best restaurants in town. Menus vary with what's in season, but expect only the freshest of ingredients. Modern takes on classic themes include scallop risotto and slow-roasted pork loin. Locals love the gourmet 'Rest: to go-go' takeout: isn't it a great day for a picnic?

Escabeche
FUSION $$$
(☏905-468-3246, 888-669-5566; www.vintagehotels.com; 6 Picton St; mains $25-48; ⊙7am-9pm) The fine-dining room at the opulent Prince of Wales Hotel takes its food seriously. The contemporary menu offers taste inventions like a tart of locally cured prosciutto, cacciatore sausage, tomato and mascarpone, followed by roast lamb with fine mustard, fingerling potatoes and baby amber turnips in ice-wine-braised shank jus. Leave room for dessert (you've been warned).

ℹ Information

Chamber of Commerce Visitors Information Centre (☏905-468-1950; www.niagaraonthelake.com; 26 Queen St; ⊙10am-7:30pm) A brochure-filled info center; staff can book accommodations for a $5 fee. Pick up the *Niagara-on-the-Lake Official Visitors' Guide* for maps and a self-guided walking tour.

❶ Getting There & Around

There are no direct buses between Toronto and Niagara-on-the-Lake, so head for St Catharines or Niagara Falls then transfer.

5-0 Taxi (☑ 800-667-0256, 905-358-3232; www.5-0taxi.com) shunts folks between Niagara Falls and Niagara-on-the-Lake. Call for pickup locations and times. A regular one-way taxi between the two towns costs around $45.

Cycling is an ace way to explore the area. Rent a bike from (or have one delivered to you by) the reader-recommended **Zoom Leisure Bicycle Rentals** (☑ 866-811-6993, 905-468-2366; www.zoomleisure.com; 2017 Niagara Stone Rd; rental per half-day/day/2 days $20/30/50; ⊙ 9am-5pm). Free delivery.

SOUTHWESTERN ONTARIO

Arcing around Lake Ontario is a heavily populated industrialized zone encompassing a number of the GTA's 'satellite' cities. Highway 403 will get you to Hamilton and Brantford, but most will take the 401 for Guelph, Kitchener-Waterloo and beyond: it's an impenetrable concrete artery linking Toronto to the US border at Windsor, and the Québec border to the east. The stretch through Toronto is regarded as one of the busiest and widest freeways in the world. Those who venture off it can uncover a heritage of aboriginal and colonial settlement, well-preserved architechture, tree-lined boulevards, healthy rivers and verdant pastures. Don't be discouraged by the feeling that Toronto never ends – press on to the delightful villages of Elora, Fergus and the unique Mennonite settlement of St Jacobs and you will be rewarded.

Guelph, Waterloo and London are thriving university centers, each with their own appeal – first appearances can be deceptive; dig deeper than what lies immediately beyond the highway. Get off the 401 at Kitchener for Stratford (-upon-Avon), birthplace of the 'Beebs' and yet a remarkably cultured country town, and home to the penultimate festival of Shakespearean theater outside the *other* Stratford-upon-Avon.

From here, you can head northwest until the farmlands dissolve into the sandy shores of Lake Huron, or drop down to London and get back on the 401, following the dead-flat fields of gold – wheat, corn and everything-growing regions where you'll cheer for even

the most modest of hills – until you reach the north shore of Lake Erie and quirky Pelee Island, Canada's southernmost point. The end of the road is in Windsor at the Detroit/USA border: both were once automotive giants, now they wrestle with the winds of change.

Hamilton & Brantford
COMBINED POP 774,250

En route to the Niagara Peninsula, blue-collar Hamilton – center of Canada's iron and steel industries – isn't famed for tourism, although cleanup efforts and downtown revitalization have improved things for visitors. If you can see past the smokestacks on approach and ignore the vague whiff of sulfur in the air, there are some interesting sights, a handful of decent eateries and some sweeping views.

Brantford, 40km southwest of Hamilton on Hwy 403, has plenty of niche tourism sites. Southeast of town, the Six Nations territory has been a First Nations' center for centuries. Captain Joseph Thayendanegea Brant led the Six Nations people here from upper New York State in 1784 and established a village that long served the district's First Nations tribes.

◉ Sights

Dundurn Castle MUSEUM
(☑ 905-546-2872; 610 York Blvd, Hamilton; adult/child $11.25/5.75; ⊙ 11am-4pm) Delightful and unexpected, this column-fronted, 36-room mansion once belonged to Sir Allan Napier McNab, Canadian prime minister from 1854 to 1856. It sits on a cliff overlooking the harbor amid lovely chestnut-studded grounds and is furnished in mid-19th-century style. Castle admission includes entry into the Hamilton Military Museum.

Royal Botanical Gardens GARDENS
(☑ 1-800-694-4769; www.rbg.ca; 680 Plains Rd W, Burlington; adult/child incl shuttle-bus rides $12.50/7.50; ⊙ 10am-5pm) Canada's largest and most spectacular botanic gardens comprise over a thousand hectares of trees, flowers and plants, including numerous rare species. There's also a rock garden, an aboretum and a wildlife sanctuary with trails traversing wetlands and wooded ravines. From June to October, thousands of delicate jewels bloom in the Centennial Rose Garden,

Southwestern Ontario

and in spring over 125,000 flowering bulbs awaken in an explosion of color.

African Lion Safari
ZOO
(☎800-461-9453; www.lionsafari.com; 1386 Cooper Rd, Hamilton; adult/child $32.95/25.95; ⏱10am-5:30pm May-Oct) Get up close and personal with lions, giraffes, zebras, monkeys and other wild beasts from the comfort of your own car in this cageless, open-air game reserve. There's also a tour bus ($5 per person) for meek visitors. Immensely popular with families, the park is about 25km northwest of Hamilton, off Hwy 8.

Woodland Cultural Centre
CULTURAL BUILDING
(☎519-759-2650; www.woodland-centre.on.ca; 184 Mohawk St, Brantford; adult/child $5/3; ⏱9am-4pm Mon-Fri, 10am-5pm Sat & Sun) The Woodland Cultural Centre functions as an indigenous performance space, cultural museum and gallery. Exhibits follow a timeline from prehistoric Iroquoian and Algonquian exhibits through to contemporary indigenous art. The attached shop stocks basketry and jewelry, plus books, ceramics and paintings. Check the website for updates.

Bell Homestead National Historic Site
HISTORIC SITE
(☎519-756-6220; www.bellhomestead.ca; 94 Tutela Heights Rd, Brantford; adult/child $6.25/free; ⏱9:30am-4:30pm Tue-Sun) You might have known that Alexander Graham Bell, on July 26, 1w874, shaped our futures by inventing the telephone. Did you know it happened in Brantford? Bell's first North American home has been lovingly restored to original condition. There's a cafe here, too.

Her Majesty's Chapel of the Mohawks
CHURCH
(☎519-756-0240; www.mohawkchapel.ca; 291 Mohawk St, Brantford; admission by donation; ⏱10am-5pm daily Jul & Aug, Wed-Sun May, Jun, Sep & Oct) Captain Brant's tomb is on the grounds of the tiny but exquisite Her Majesty's Chapel of the Mohawks, best visited on sunny afternoons when light streams through the gorgeous stained-glass windows. On the site of the original village, it's the oldest Protestant church in Ontario (1785) and the world's only Royal Indian Chapel. To get here, follow the signs off Colborne St E.

Six Nations of the Grand River Territory
FIRST NATIONS TERRITORY
(www.sixnations.ca) Southeast of Brantford is Six Nations of the Grand River Territory – the

six nations being Mohawk, Oneida, Ononda-ga, Cayuga, Seneca and Tuscarora – and the village of **Ohsweken**, a well-known Aboriginal community. Established in the late 18th century, the territory gives visitors a glimpse of traditional and contemporary First Nations culture.

🛏 Sleeping & Eating

Rutherford House
B&B $$

(☑ 905-525-2422; 293 Park St S, Hamilton; s/d incl breakfast $120/130; ❄ ✱) A short walk from downtown, the Rutherford is a lovingly restored redbrick Victorian. Its two period furnished guest rooms feature downy beds and extravagant wallpaper.

C Hotel by Carmen's
HOTEL $$

(☑ 905-381-9898; www.bestwestern.com; 1530 Stone Church Rd E, Hamilton; s & d from $140; ✱ 🛜 ✱) You may be surprised that a hotel of this caliber is both a Best Western and in Hamilton. New in July 2011, the handsome building pays an impressive tribute to art deco; its rooms and suites are both spacious and elegant. With an indoor pool and all the comforts of home, you'll be more impressed by the price.

Black Forest Inn
GERMAN $$

(☑ 905-528-3538; www.blackforestinn.ca; 255 King St E, Hamilton; mains $9.90-29.90; ⊙ 11:30am-9pm Tue-Sun) This downtown institution has been satisfying meat lovers and beer drinkers since 1967. If you're a fan of schnitzel, goulash, wurst or German beer, you've found yourself a reason to visit Hamilton. The prices are great, so it's usually packed. In summer, the patio becomes a *biergarten* – perfect !

ℹ Information

Brantford Visitors & Tourism Centre (☑ 800-265-6299, 519-751-1771; www.discoverbrantford.com; 399 Wayne Gretzky Pkwy, Brantford; ⊙ 9am-8pm Mon-Fri, to 9pm Sat, to 5pm Sun) Just north of Hwy 403, the sparkling tourism center is optimistic about Brantford's future, with plenty of brochures and helpful staff.

Six Nations Tourism (☑ 866-393-3001; www.sntourism.com; 2498 Chiefswood Rd; ⊙ 9am-4:30pm Mon-Fri, 10am-3pm Sat & Sun) At the corner of Hwy 54 find this visitors center, with information on local sites, attractions and events in Six Nations.

Tourism Hamilton (☑ 1-800-263-8590; www.tourismhamilton.com; 28 James St N, Hamilton; ⊙ 10am-4pm Mon-Fri, to 3pm Sat & Sun) This downtown tourist office is keen to assist with all things Hamilton and surrounds, or just visit its impressive and up-to-date website.

ℹ Getting There & Away

If you're in a squeeze finding a cheap flight out of Toronto, see if Westjet also flies to your destination from **John C Munro Hamilton International Airport** (YHM; ☑ 905-679-1999; www.flyhi.ca; 9300 Airport Rd, Mt Hope), 10km south of town – airport taxes are cheaper here.

GO Transit operates a combination of regular scheduled bus and train services between Hamilton and Toronto ($10.45, one to two hours) from the Hamilton **GO Centre** (www.gotransit.com; 36 Hunter St E; ⊙ 5am-11pm Mon-Fri, from 6:15am Sat & Sun). Trains operate only during rush hour and on certain weekends in summer.

Greyhound Canada and Megabus also make stops in Hamilton. Greyhound Canada connects Toronto ($28, one to two hours, five daily), London ($26.40, 1½ hours, four daily) and (via Hamilton) Niagara Falls ($35, four hours, two to three daily) to the **Brantford Transit Terminal** (☑ 519-756-5011; 64 Darling St).

VIA rail operates trains to Toronto ($40, one hour, five daily) and London ($36, one hour, five daily) from the **train station** (☑ 519-752-0867; www.viarail.ca; 5 Wadsworth St).

Guelph

POP 121,700

Founded in 1827 by a Scottish novelist who planned the town's footprint in a European style, Guelph is best known for its popular university and... beer! Sleeman Breweries and two microbreweries call Guelph home. Strong manufacturing and education sectors contribute to Guelph's low unemployment rate, which fuels a vibrant youth scene: funky cafes, great food, rocking pubs and hip boutiques await. With a wealth of local history, a fantastic museum and lovely Victorian archtitecture, Guelph is worth a visit.

◎ Sights & Activities

★ Guelph Civic Museum
MUSEUM

(☑ 519-836-1221; www.guelph.ca/museum; 6 Dublin St S; adult/child $4/free; ⊙ 1-5pm) Extensively transformed in 2012, in what was originally an 1854 sandstone convent, this attractive LEED-certified museum offers exhibitions, programs and events digging up the history of the city (named after the British royal family's ancestors, the Guelphs). The 'Growing Up in Guelph' kids' exhibition makes a happy distraction.

Church of Our Lady Immaculate
CHURCH

(☎519-824-3951; www.churchofourlady.com; 28 Norfolk St; admission by donation; ⊙7am-dusk) Lording over downtown Guelph is the dominant stone-faced bulk of the Church of Our Lady Immaculate. It's hard to move around town without catching a glimpse of Our Lady's twin towers and elegantly proportioned rose window, which have been awing parishioners since 1888.

University of Guelph Arboretum
GARDENS

(☎519-824-4120; www.uoguelph.ca/arboretum; College Ave E; ⊙8:30am-4:30pm Mon-Fri; 🖈) 🎔FREE Modeled after the Arnold Arboretum of Harvard University, this stunning microcosm of flora and fauna has 8.2km of paths traversing 165 hectares of thoughtfully cultivated land. The variety of species represented here boggles the mind, and best of all, it's free!

Macdonald Stewart Art Centre
GALLERY

(☎519-837-0010; www.msac.ca; 358 Gordon St; suggested donation $3; ⊙noon-5pm Tue-Sun) Over 7000 works belong to the collection exhibited here in the Raymond Moriyama–designed galleries, specializing in Inuit and Canadian art. The **Donald Forster Sculpture Park** is the largest at a public gallery in Canada and offers 1 hectare to explore: gravity-defying cubes, beached boats and cell phones spiked onto agricultural sickles.

Speed River Canoe & Kayak Rentals
KAYAKING

(116 Gordon St; kayak/canoe rental per hr Tue-Fri $10/12, Sat & Sun $12/15; ⊙10am-dusk Tue-Sun Jun-Aug) Get on the water then tackle the ice-cream store next door. This is also the starting point of a self-guided eco-heritage walk along the banks of the Speed and Eramosa Rivers, a 6km circuit with interpretive signs.

★☆ Festivals & Events

Hillside Festival
PERFORMING ARTS

(☎519-763-6396; www.hillsidefestival.ca) Having celebrated its 30th anniversary in 2013, Hillside continues to delight with an eclectic mix of furry and fuzzy, hippy and huggy performers from seasoned pros to the up-and-coming artists of tomorrow. Feel the love and jump on board for one short weekend in July. Consult the website for this year's lineup and details.

🛏 Sleeping

The **Guelph Area Bed & Breakfast Association** (www.gabba.ca) has a crop of quality B&Bs on its books. If motels are more your style, there are a couple on Woodlawn Rd W, just north of town. The University of Guelph lets rooms during the summer months.

Comfort Inn
MOTEL $

(☎519-763-1900; www.choicehotels.ca; 480 Silvercreek Pkwy; d from $90) Tastefully renovated in 2012, this spotlessly maintained motel about 5km north of the town center offers great-value rooms including a light breakfast.

Norfolk Guest House
B&B $$

(☎519-767-1095; www.norfolkguesthouse.ca; 102 Eramosa Rd; r incl breakfast $139-269; 🕸🐾) A central location and sumptuously furnished themed bedrooms, most with en suite Jacuzzi, make the Norfolk – a delightfully restored Victorian home – the logical choice for luxury B&B accommodations in downtown Guelph.

Delta Guelph Hotel & Conference Centre
HOTEL $$

(☎519-780-3700; www.deltahotels.com; 50 Stone Rd W; d/ste from $125/$175) Conveniently located near the University of Guelph, 3km from downtown, this modern, tastefully furnished property has spacious standard rooms with dark woods and comfy beds. A variety of well-priced suites, some with fireplaces, kitchenettes and downy sofas, complete the package.

🍴 Eating & Drinking

★ Joint Cafe
CAFE $

(☎519-265-8508; www.thejointcafe.com; 43 Cork St E; mains $6-18; ⊙9am-3pm Mon-Wed & Sun, 9am-4pm & 5-10pm Thu-Sat; 🐾🖉) The Joint is a great all-rounder. Come for brunch or coffee, dinner or drinks and you're bound to find something on the diverse and original menu that tickles your fancy – there's a definite emphasis on healthy comfort food and plenty of options for vegetarians.

Cornerstone
CAFE $

(☎519-827-0145; 1 Wyndham St N; mains $6-10; ⊙8am-midnight Mon-Fri, from 9am Sat & Sun; 🖉) Thick stone walls plus scuffed wood floors equal serious comfy-ness at this well-loved vegetarian cafe. Go for coffee in the morning and return for a pint and some live music in the evening. If you're looking for a sandwich, consider the Taste of Downtown: avocado, brie, red peppers and garlic aioli ($8).

Bookshelf
CAFE $$

(☑ 519-821-3311; www.bookshelf.ca; 41 Québec St; mains $12-15; ⊗ e-Bar 5pm-late, bookstore 9am-9pm) Forty years young, Bookshelf is the pacemaker of Guelph's cultural heartbeat: part bookstore, cinema, cafe and music venue. Swing by to read the paper, catch an art-house flick or have a bite in the e-bar/Greenroom. Featuring regular salsa nights, poetry slams and flashback Fridays, there's something for everyone.

Bollywood Bistro
INDIAN $$

(☑ 519-821-3999; www.thebollywoodbistro.com; 51 Cork St E; mains $12-17; ⊗ 11:30am-2pm Mon-Fri & 5:30-8:30pm daily; ☑) Guelph's favorite Indian restaurant isn't the cheapest, but uses a traditional tandoor oven to create well-known dishes with a contemporary twist, with influences from Nepal, Delhi and Bombay. The creamy butter chicken ($17) is one of the best we've had.

Artisanale
FRENCH $$$

(☑ 519-821-3359; www.artisanale.ca; 214 Woolwich St; mains $23-28; ⊗ 11:30am-2:30pm & 5-9pm Tue-Sat) With an emphasis on fresh, seasonal local produce, this French country kitchen has a wonderfully simple lunch menu and is popular for its prix-fixe $25 dinners, although they're not so fixed with irresistable hors d'oevres and sides ($3 to $5) and a number of the more tempting mains attracting a $5 surcharge.

★ Woolwich Arrow
PUB

(☑ 519.836.2875; www.woolwicharrow.ca; 176 Woolwich St; ⊗ 11:30am-late) The 'Wooly,' as it's affectionately known, stands on its own two feet as a microbrewery but also ranks highly for delicious gourmet eat-with-beer munchies like longhorn beef chili poutine (small $7) and Lake Erie pickerel tacos ($14).

Manhattan's
BAR

(☑ 519-767-2440; www.manhattans.ca; 951 Gordon St; ⊗ 11am-late Mon-Fri, from 4pm Sat & Sun; ☏) The pizza here is hot and fresh like the smooth, smooth jazz: there's live music most nights. Check the website for details. Free wi-fi. No cover charge.

ⓘ Information

Guelph Tourism Services (☑ 800-334-4519; www.visitguelphwellington.ca; 1 Carden St; ⊗ 9am-4:30pm Mon-Sat) In the new city hall,

friendly staff are local experts. Ask them about self-guided walking tours.

ⓘ Getting There & Away

The **Guelph Bus Station** (☑ 519-824-0771; www.greyhound.ca; cnr MacDonnell & Carden Sts) has buses to Toronto ($22, 1¼ hours, 12 daily) and London ($26, 2¼ hours, three daily).

VIA rail operates trains to Toronto ($24, 1½ hours, twice daily) and London ($36, two hours, two daily). GO Transit operates commuter trains to Toronto ($13, 1½ hours, twice daily). Both depart from the **Guelph Train Station** (☑ 888-842-7245; www.viarail.ca; cnr Wyndham & Carden Sts; ⊗ 6am-1pm & 4pm-midnight Mon-Fri, 9am-2pm & 4pm-midnight Sat & Sun).

Kitchener-Waterloo
POP 280,000

The adjacent cities of Kitchener (formely called Berlin, due to its Germanic origins) and Waterloo, like Siamese twins, are as different as they are connected. 'Downtown' Kitchener lacks appeal and although prettier 'uptown' Waterloo has some nice sandstone architecture, two universities and the largest community museum in Ontario, neither city is particularly exciting. The best time to visit is festival time, when the twins come to life – Oktoberfest here is the second largest outside Munich, Germany! Otherwise, just pass through on your way to Elora and Fergus, St Jacobs or Stratford.

⊙ Sights & Activities

Waterloo Region Museum
MUSEUM

(www.waterlooregionmuseum.com; 10 Huron Rd, Kitchener; adult/child $10/5; ⊗ 9:30am-5pm Mon-Fri, 11am-5pm Sat & Sun) Waterloo's newest attraction is this primary-colored local-history museum set on 24 hectares. Its the gateway to the **Doon Heritage Crossroads**, a re-created pioneer settlement where costumed volunteers do their best to help you time-travel.

Joseph Schneider Haus
HISTORIC SITE

(☑ 519-742-7752; www.region.waterloo.on.ca; 466 Queen St S, Kitchener; adult/child $2.25/1.25; ⊗ 10am-5pm Mon-Sat, from 1pm Sun Jul-Aug, 10am-5pm Wed-Sat, from 1pm Sun Sep-Jun) A national historic site, Joseph Schneider Haus was one of the first homes built in the area, and has been restored to full 19th-century splendor. Originally built for a prosperous Pennsylvanian Mennonite, the architecture is amazing, as are demonstrations of day-today 1800s chores and skills (everything from beadwork to making corn-husk dolls). When we visited, a two-story washhouse was under construction.

Waterloo Central Railway   STEAM RAILWAY
(📞519-885-2297; www.waterloocentralrailway.com; 10 Father David Bauer Dr; from $10; ☺Apr-Dec) This lovingly restored steam train shuttles between Waterloo and St Jacobs on Tuesdays, Thursdays and Saturdays in the warmer months: check the homepage for schedule details.

✨ Festivals & Events

Uptown Waterloo Jazz Festival   JAZZ
(www.uptownwaterloojazz.ca) Big-time jazz, small-town environment: mid-July.

Oktoberfest   BEER
(📞519-570-4267, 888-294-4267; www.oktoberfest.ca) *Willkommen* to this nine-day beery Bavarian bash – the biggest of its kind in North America and possibly the largest outside of Germany. It's K-W's favorite event, bringing in about 500,000 people each year from early to mid-October – sauerkraut, oompah bands, *lederhosen* and *biergartens* galore. Book accommodations well in advance.

🛏 Sleeping & Eating

Bingemans Camping Resort   CAMPGROUND $
(📞519-744-1002, 800-565-4631; www.bingemans.com; 425 Bingemans Centre Dr, Kitchener; campsites/RV sites $35/45, cabins from $65, reservations $8; ☒) South of Hwy 401, Bingemans is a combined water park and campground with enough pools, ponds and waterslides to warrant 'Great Lake' status. The cabins are nothing spectacular, but sleep four. A wide range of camping and waterpark packages are available; check online.

Walper Terrace Hotel   HOTEL $$
(📞519-745-4321, 800-265-8749; www.walper.com; 1 King St W, Kitchener; r/ste from $89/$159; ☺❄🕸) There's a rich sense of history at the Walper, a classy downtown dame looking good for her age – the hotel was built in 1893 and renovated in 2011. All rooms have high ceilings and period features, flatscreen TVs and free wi-fi, but standard rooms are a tad cozy. Suites are more spacious.

Crowne Plaza Kitchener-Waterloo   HOTEL $$
(📞519-744-4144; www.crowneplaza.com; 105 King St E, Kitchener; d from $144; ❄🕸☒) Formerly the Delta, Crowne Plaza extensively renovated this property, which re-opened in late

---

THE MENNONITES OF ST JACOBS & ELMIRA

The Mennonite story harks back to a 16th-century Swiss Protestant sect who moved around Europe due to religious disagreements. They ended up in the rural setting of what is now Pennsylvania, USA where they were promised religious freedom and prosperity. Cheaper land and their unwillingness to fight under the American flag lured many Mennonites to southern Ontario in the late 19th century, where they remain today, upholding the same basic values of family, humility, simplicity, modesty and pacifism.

For a detailed history and information see www.mhsc.ca, or take a day trip to the quaint villages of St Jacobs, about 20 minutes' drive from Kitchener, and Elmira, 8km further north. Here, black buggies rattle past, the scent of cattle fills the air, and bonnets, braces and buttons are de rigueur.

The quintessential **country market** (📞519-747-1830; www.stjacobs.com; cnr King & Weber Sts, St Jacobs; ☺7am-3:30pm Thu & Sat, also 8am-3pm Tue Jun-Aug), 3km south of St Jacobs, has an earthy soul. Folks come from miles for the farm-fresh produce, smoked meats, cheese, baked treats, arts and crafts. Pop in to the **visitors center** (📞519-664-3518; www.stjacobs.com; 1406 King St, St Jacobs; ☺9am-5pm Mon-Sat) to see the Mennonite Story, an insightful exhibition on the Mennonites' history, culture and agricultural achievements. One of these is the production of maple syrup: learn about it at the **Maple Syrup Museum & Quilt Gallery** (📞519-664-1232; www.stjacobs.com; 1441 King St N, St Jacobs; ☺10am-6pm Mon-Sat, noon-5:30pm Sun) FREE or sample the liquid gold at the **Maple Syrup Festival** (www.elmiramaplesyrup.com) in early April. Round out the day with a traditional lunch at **Benjamin's Restaurant** (📞519-664-3731; www.stjacobs.com/country-inns; 1430 King St N, St Jacobs; meals $10-30; ☺11:30am-9pm; 🕸), grab a fresh fruit pie and some scones for the road from the **Stone Crock Bakery** (📞519-664-2286; 1402 King St N, St Jacobs; items $2-8; ☺7am-3pm Mon & Tue, to 8pm Wed-Sat, 11am-8pm Sun) and be on your way.

2013. With a futuristic new lobby and 201 sparkling, modern guest rooms, these are the best digs for miles.

Princess Cafe
CAFE $

(🗷 519-886-0227; www.princesscafe.ca; 46 King St N, Waterloo; panini $6.50; ⊙ 11:30am-10pm Sun-Thu, to 3:30am Fri & Sat) This quaint cafe next door to the cinema serves up coffee, toasted panini and other snacky delights. If you're a night owl, stop in for 'Cheeses Murphy': the ultimate post-drinking grilled cheese (midnight to 3:30am Friday and Saturday).

Concordia Club
GERMAN $$

(429 Ottawa St S, Kitchener; lunch mains $7-12, dinner $12-20; ⊙ 11:30am-11pm Mon-Sat, to 2pm Sun) Polish up your German verbs and fill up on schnitzel at Concordia, a Teutonic fave that's been around for decades. Dark wood, low ceilings, white linen and loud conversation complement the menu. There's red-hot polka action on Friday and Saturday nights, and a summer *biergarten*.

❶ Information

KW Tourism (🗷 519-745-3536; www.explore-waterlooregion.com; 200 King St W, Kitchener; ⊙ 8:30am-5pm Mon-Fri) Inside city hall.

Waterloo Visitors Centre (🗷 519-885-2297; www.explorewaterlooregion.com; 10 David Bower Dr, Waterloo; ⊙ 9am-4pm Mon-Sat Apr-Dec) Friendly staff! At the terminus of the Waterloo Central Railway.

❶ Getting There & Away

From **Waterloo International Airport** (YFK; 🗷 519-648-2256; www.waterlooairport.ca; 4881 Fountain St N, Breslau), 7km east of town, there are flights to Calgary, Detroit and Chicago.

Greyhound Canada operates from the **Charles Street Transit Terminal** (🗷 800-661-8747; www.greyhound.ca; 15 Charles St W, Kitchener), a five-minute walk from downtown. Buses run to Toronto ($28, 1½ to two hours, hourly) and London ($25, 1½ to two hours, three daily).

Kitchener Train Station (🗷 888-842-7245; www.viarail.ca; cnr Victoria & Weber Sts, Kitchener) is an easy walk north of downtown. VIA rail operates trains to Toronto ($28, two hours, twice daily) and London ($35, 1½ hours, twice daily). GO Transit operates commuter trains to Toronto ($15.55, two hours, twice daily).

Elora & Fergus

No longer one of Ontario's best-kept secrets, the delightful Wellington County river-side towns of Elora and Fergus, straddling the banks of the twisty Grand River, await your visit. Both have done a magnificent job preserving their heritage facades and streetscapes. Enticing Elora with its gorge and swimming hole is a wonderful place to escape the summer heat, while neighboring Fergus evokes nostalgia for a lost age and a distant northern kingdom... along with the desire to sample all of its cozy pubs.

⊙ Sights

Wellington County Museum
MUSEUM

(🗷 519-846-0916; www.wcm.on.ca; Rte 18, Elora; by donation; ⊙ 9:30am-4:30pm Mon-Fri, noon-4pm Sat & Sun) Midway between Fergus and Elora, an austere, red-roofed former 'Poor House' provided refuge for the aged and homeless for almost a century before becoming the Wellington County Museum in 1957. Historical and local modern-art exhibits extend through 12 galleries, displaying an obvious pride in local history and current culture. The centerpiece is the new 'If These Walls Could Speak' exhibit, which examines the lives of those who lived or worked there.

Elora Gorge Conservation Area
PARK

(www.grandriver.ca; Rte 21, Elora; adult/child $5.75/2.75, tubing rentals $15; ⊙ late Apr–mid-Oct) About 2km south of Elora is the photo-worthy Elora Gorge Conservation Area, a plunging limestone canyon through which the Grand River seethes. Easy walks extend to cliff views, caves and the Cascade waterfalls – a sheet of white water spilling over a stepped cliff. For a free gorge view, head to the end of James St, off Metcalfe St in Elora. Tubing is a lazy way to spend a warm afternoon at the gorge. You can also camp here.

Elora Quarry Conservation Area
PARK

(www.grandriver.ca; Rte 18, Elora; adult/child $5.75/2.75; ⊙ dawn-dusk Jun-Aug) A short walk east of Elora are the possibly bottomless waters and 12m limestone cliffs of the Elora Quarry Conservation Area – a superb swimming hole. Hormone-fueled teens plummet from great heights, despite signs suggesting they don't.

⛬ Tours

Elora Culinary Walking Tours
WALKING TOUR

(🗷 226-384-7000; www.eloraculinarywalkingtour.com; per person $15; ⊙ 2pm Sat May-Sep) Sample some of Elora's culinary treats on this two-hour guided tour. Rain or shine, meet in front of the Village Olive Grove (8 Mill St W).

✲✲ Festivals & Events

Elora Festival
MUSIC

(www.elorafestival.com) A classical, jazz, folk and arts festival held from mid-July to mid-August, with concerts at the quarry and around town. Singers and musos from around the country crowd the schedule of Elora's premier event.

Fergus Scottish Festival & Highland Games
CULTURE

(www.fergusscottishfestival.com) If it's not Scottish, it doesn't count: tugs-of-war, caber tossing, bagpipes, Celtic dancing, kilts, haggis and Scotch nosing (aka tasting). Hoots! Held over two days in mid-August.

🛏 Sleeping

There are many B&Bs in the area. If you don't have any luck with the below, try **Fergus Elora Bed & Breakfast Association** (www.ferguselorahosts.com).

Elora Gorge Conservation Area Campground
CAMPGROUND $

(☎519-846-9742, 866-668-2267; www.grandriver. ca; Rte 18, Elora; campsites $32.50-40, reservations $13) More than 550 campsites in six distinct, riverside zones. They're overflowing during summer, especially on holiday weekends.

★ Stonehurst B&B
B&B $$

(☎519-843-8800; www.stonehurstbb.com; 265 St David St S, Fergus; s/d incl breakfast $113/130) This gorgeous country home, belonging to one of the wealthiest families in the area from 1853 to 1933, had a brief stint as a nursing home and newspaper office before adopting its best-suited fate as a B&B in 2001. Four comfortable rooms each have en suite bathrooms. Your welcoming hosts maintain the house, its common areas and gardens magnificently. Great value.

Bredalbane
INN $$

(☎519-843-4770; www.breadalbaneinn.com; 487 St Andrew St W, Fergus; r $90-225) Rooms at this compact inn are classically furnished without being tacky. Some have canopy beds and most have Jacuzzis. It has an annexed pub and bistro and a prime main street location, so you won't need to venture far for entertainment, though it can sometimes get noisy.

Drew House
INN $$

(☎519-846-2226; www.drewhouse.com; 120 Mill St E, Elora; r incl breakfast from $125; ❁❋) Drew House unites the old world with the new. On spacious grounds, the inn has both reno- vated stable suites (with private bathrooms) or guest rooms (with shared bathrooms) in the main house. Meter-thick stone walls whisper history as you drift into dreams, before waking to a breakfast of fresh fruit, hot coffee, and bacon and eggs cooked how you love them.

🍴 Eating & Drinking

Gorge Country Kitchen
DINER $

(☎519-846-2636; 23 Wellington Rd 7, Elora; meals $8-22; ⏱7am-8:30pm) The Gorge is usually hopping for its family-friendly country-style cheap eats, especially the hearty breakfasts. There are daily specials.

Mill St Bakery & Bistro
CAFE $$

(☎519-384-2277; www.millstreetbakerybistro.com; 15 Mill St E, Elora; mains $11-24; ⏱9am-7pm Mon-Sat, from 10am Sun) This busy breakfast-and-lunch joint has a fantastic river-view patio and serves sandwiches, your favorite comfort foods and a limited dinner menu.

Brewhouse
PUB $$

(☎519-843-8871; www.fergusbrewhouse.com; 170 St David St S, Fergus; mains $10-22; ⏱11:30am-1am Mon-Sat, to 1pm Sun) Wave to the fly-fishers on the Grand River from the shady Brewhouse patio as you weigh up the benefits of cheddar and ale soup, bangers and mash, or curried chicken enchilada. It sports a cozy bar, European beers on tap and live music to boot.

Cork
EUROPEAN $$$

(☎519-846-8880; www.eloracork.com; 146 Metcalfe St, Elora; mains $24-34; ⏱11:30am-9pm) Run by a mother and daughter team, Cork is a casual fine-dining restaurant turning heads in Wellington County for its excellent service, delicious food and sunny patio. From the grilled beet and goat cheese salad to the saffron lobster risotto, we think you'll be pleased with your investment.

Goofie Newfie
PUB

(☎519-843-4483; www.goofienewfie.ca; 105 Queen St W, Fergus; ⏱11:30am-late) Good food, cold booze, live entertainment and happy patrons make the Goofie Newfie the jolly place it is.

Shepherd's Pub
PUB

(8 Mill St W, Elora; mains $9-13; ⏱noon-10pm) Pubby mains and cold pints of Guinness by the river. All-day breakfast fry-ups, beer-battered fish and chips, and hearty beef pies will revive you if you spent too long here the night before.

ℹ Information

Elora Welcome Centre (📞 519-846-2563, 877-242-6353; www.elora.info; 9 Mill St E, Elora; ⊙ 9am-5pm Mon-Fri, 10am-6pm Sat, to 5pm Sun) The friendly staff at the Elora Welcome Centre by the bridge are a font of knowledge for all things Wellington County.

ℹ Getting There & Away

Greyhound Canada stops on Bridge St in Fergus and at the **Little Katy Variety Store** (185 Geddes St, Elora; ⊙ 9am-7pm) in Elora, heading to/from Toronto ($25, two hours, one to two daily).

Stratford

Stratford is a success story, a wonderful country town that refuses to surrender to the depopulization syndrome plaguing rural centers worldwide. As the story goes, in 1952, upon hearing the announcement that the Canadian National Railways (the region's largest employer) was closing the doors of its Stratford facility, a young journalist by the name of Tom Patterson approached his council for a loan. His plan was to find and bring back a troupe of actors to capitalise on the town's namesake: the birthplace of Shakespeare. It worked. In 1953 the first performance of what has grown to become the Stratford Festival (the largest of its kind) was born, creating a whole new industry which continues to support the town today.

Charming, cultured and classy, with a bunch of *other* festivals to boot, Stratford packs more punch than cities twice its size: there are plenty of great places to eat and stay. Whatever the season, you'll enjoy the nature, arts and architecture and the proud locals will make you feel welcome.

SWANS ON PARADE

Stratford's beloved swans don't paddle around the Avon all winter; instead, they are kept warm in winter pens. Come early April, the release of the birds to their summer home on the river is a Stratford celebration. The swans waddle down the street in parade formation, backed by bagpipe players marching in kilts. Check www.welcometostratford.com for exact dates and more information.

⊙ Sights

Avon River   RIVER
Stratford's swan-filled Avon River (what else were they going to call it?) flows slowly past the town, with plenty of riverbank lawns on which to chill out. Just west of Stratford Tourism on the riverbank, the **Shakespearean Gardens** occupy the site of an old wool mill. Parterre gardens, manicured box hedges, herbs, roses and a bronze bust of Bill – pick up a brochure at Stratford Tourism. Further along the river is **Queen's Park**, with paths leading from the Festival Theatre along the river past Orr Dam and an 1885 stone bridge to a formal **English flower garden**.

Stratford-Perth Museum   MUSEUM
(📞 519-393-5311; www.stratfordperthmuseum.ca; 4275 Huron Rd; suggested donation $5; ⊙ 10am-4pm Tue-Sat, from noon Sun & Mon) The diverse and significant Stratford-Perth Museum collection includes artifacts and memorabilia from the early 1800s to the present day. Its mission is to celebrate and remember the community stories of Stratford and Perth County.

Gallery Stratford   GALLERY
(📞 519-271-5271; www.gallerystratford.on.ca; 54 Romeo St; adult/child $5/free; ⊙ 10am-5pm Tue-Sun) In a wonderful renovated yellow-brick pump house (c 1880), Gallery Stratford exhibits innovative contemporary art with a Canadian emphasis. Regular art studios, movie nights and family days are held. It's very kid friendly.

🗗 Tours

★ **Downloadable Guides**   WALKING TOUR
(www.visitstratford.ca/toursandguides.php) These genius folk out here are one step ahead of the rest! Download a wide range of audio podcasts and PDF guides of themed walking, driving and cycling tours through the streets of Stratford and surrounding region. Themes include food, wine, gardens, antiques and even... Justin Beiber!

Boat Tours   CRUISE
(📞 519-271-7739; www.avonboatrentals.ca; 30 York St; tours from adult/child $7/3, rentals from $15; ⊙ 9am-dusk May-Oct) Take in the parks, swans, riverbanks and grand gardens on Avon River. Tours depart below Stratford Tourism by the river. Canoes, kayaks and paddleboats are available.

THE STRATFORD FESTIVAL

Sir Alec Guinness played Richard III on opening night of the much-lauded **Stratford Festival** (📞800-567-1600, 519-273-1600; www.stratfordfestival.ca), which began humbly in a tent at Queen's Park. The festival, with over 60 seasons under its belt, has achieved international acclaim. Aside from the plays, there's a peripheral schedule of interesting programs: post-performance discussions, backstage tours, lectures, concerts and readings. Some are free.

Far from its tented origins, four theaters stage contemporary and period dramas, opera and, of course, works by the Bard, over a monster season lasting April to November. Main-stage productions occur at the 1800-seat Festival Theatre and 1000-seat Avon Theatre. The Tom Patterson and Studio Theatres are more intimate. Actors from around the world prize festival residencies.

Tickets go on sale to the general public in early January. By showtime nearly every performance is sold out: book ahead! Spring previews and fall end-of-season shows are often discounted by 30%, with 50%-off 'rush' tickets, two hours before showtime.

🎉 Festivals & Events

Savour Stratford Festival   FOOD
(📞519-271-7500; www.visitstratford.ca/culinaryfestival) Beer, wine and food tastings, workshops, farm tours and special dinners all highlight Perth County's abundance in mid-September. Prices vary with the event.

Stratford Garlic Festival   FOOD
(www.stratfordgarlicfestival.com) Held in mid-September. Bring your breath mints.

Stratford Garden Festival   GARDEN
(www.stratfordgardenfestival.com; admission $9) A four-day horticultural extravaganza held in early March, featuring flora from around the world, guest speakers and presentations.

Stratford Summer Music   MUSIC
(www.stratfordsummermusic.ca; tickets $10-40) Four weeks of classical, cabaret and theatrical music from mid-July to mid-August, with acclaimed musicians from around Canada tuning up and letting loose.

🛏 Sleeping

There's a plethora of accommodations in Stratford but savvy locals know how to make a buck: room rates can go through the roof. Check out www.stratfordaccommodations.com.

Stratford General
Hospital Residence   HOSTEL $
(SGH Residence; 📞519-271-5084; www.sgh.stratford.on.ca/residence; 130 Youngs St; s/d $59/69; ⊛☒) These renovated nurses' quarters are the closest thing you'll find to a youth hostel in town: 360 rooms with shared bathrooms, kitchens and a heated pool. Cheap, clean and comfy, but not party central.

Forest Motel and
Woodland Retreat   MOTEL $$
(📞519-271-4573; www.forestmotel.on.ca; 2941 Forest Rd RR 4; d $99-205) Friendly hosts welcome you to this wonderful woody lakeside gem that's secluded, but only 10 minutes from town and close to highway amenities. Comfy renovated rooms emphasize Conrad's carpentry skills. You'll feel more like you've stepped into a country cottage than a motel. All rooms have microwave, fridge and homely touches.

Parlour Historic Inn & Suites   HOTEL $$
(📞519-271-2772; www.bestwestern.com; 101 Wellington St; d from $139) This handsome hotel occupies a heritage building in the center of town, but has been fully refitted to a high standard – most rooms are spacious and light filled. There's a pub downstairs with a lovely patio but it doesn't get too rowdy or noisy.

Festival Inn   MOTEL $$
(📞519-273-1150; www.festivalinnstratford.com; 1144 Ontario St; d $99-189) This sprawling four-wing motel complex has more than 160 pleasantly renovated rooms and suites in a variety of styles, offering good value during the festival period. On the highway near a bunch of amenities, it's a few minutes' drive to the festival and downtown attractions.

Swan Motel
MOTEL $$
(519-271-6376; www.swanmotel.on.ca; 960 Downie St S; r $105-130; ❄❋🖥🏊) A fabulously maintained 1960s roadside motel 3km south of town, the Swan has spotless rooms with costume sketches and original artwork on the walls. The parklike grounds feature hammered-steel sculptures, fountains and a pool. The motel is closed from late October to early May.

Acrylic Dreams
B&B $$
(519-271-7874; www.acrylicdreams.com; 66 Bay St; r incl breakfast $135-160, ❄❋🖥) Owned by a husband-and-wife team, this renovated 1879 B&B has polished wooden floorboards and spa amenities. Besides being artists (there are more than a few acrylic master-pieces on the walls) the owners also practice chair massage, reflexology and can accommodate all diets.

Lofts at 99
BOUTIQUE HOTEL $$
(800-361-5322, 519-271-1121; www.bentleysannex.com; 99 Ontario St; r $99-299; ❄❋🖥) This modern, dark-wood furnished inn houses commodious bi-level suites and lofts. Skylights, kitchenettes and period furnishings are standard, the receptionists are friendly and the cafe downstairs is always pumping.

Mercer Hall Inn
BOUTIQUE HOTEL $$
(888-816-4011, 519-271-1888; www.mercerhallinn.com; 108 Ontario St; d $90-200; ❄❋🖥) Downtown Mercer Hall Inn has more class than most: uniquely artistic rooms feature handcrafted furniture, kitchenettes and electric fireplaces. Some have Jacuzzis.

★Three Houses Bed & Breakfast
B&B $$$
(519-272-0722; www.thethreehouses.com; 100 Brunswick St; ste incl breakfast $195-495; ❄❋🖥🏊) Two Edwardian townhouses, a garden carriage house and an 1870s Italianate house make up this meticulous, *almost* over-the-top 18-room inn. No detail has been spared in decorating these light-filled spaces – even the luggage racks match the quirky individual room designs. A saltwater pool and secret oasis garden add relaxing touches.

🍴 Eating

A local chef's school and surrounding farmland make Stratford a gourmand's delight. Reservations are recommended during festival time.

Boomer's Gourmet Fries
FAST FOOD $
(519-275-3147; www.boomersgourmetfries.com; 26 Erie St; items $3-15; 11:30am-7pm Tue-Sun) Crazy, weird, killer, delicious, amazing, irresistable, to die for, what the? All of these words have been used to describe the fries, poutines, burgers and fried creations that come out of this kooky and friendly little joint. Jump on the bandwagon, it's rockin'. You know you want to.

York Street Kitchen
SANDWICHES $
(519-273-7041; www.yorkstreetkitchen.com; 24 Erie St; mains $6-16; 8am-8pm) This cozy kitchen serves up show-stopper sandwiches on homemade bread, brie fritters, salads, quiches and desserts. Try the 'Mennonite' sandwich: sausage, cheddar, corn relish, tomato, honey mustard, mayo and lettuce.

Let Them Eat Cake
CAFE $
(519-508-2253; www.letthemeatcake.ca; 23 Albert St; mains $6-20; 7am-8pm) This Stratford institution serves all-day breakfasts, fresh-baked scones and muffins, tasty sandwiches, salads, burgers and has a limited dinner menu.

Raja
INDIAN $$
(519-271-3271; www.rajaindiancuisine.ca; 10 George St W; mains $12-22; 11:30am-2:30pm & 5-9pm; 🚗) Challenging Stratford's demure Anglo tastes with funky lashings of chili and spice, Raja plates up super curries, soups, salads, breads, vegetarian and tandoori dishes and serves them on white linen. Staff are dapper and unfailingly polite.

Down the Street Bar & Restaurant
INTERNATIONAL $$
(519-273-5886; www.downthestreet.ca; 30 Ontario St; dinner $19-29; 5:30pm-2am Tue-Sun) Darkly atmospheric, with gorgeous gilt mirrors and old neons stirring memories of Parisian cafes, this delicious bar/restaurant offers pre-theater dining, microbrews and wines by the glass. The menu is multicultural (thin-crust pizzas, goat cheese enchiladas) and after 10pm the bar steps up as one of Stratford's more kickin' nocturnal haunts.

Mercer Hall
EUROPEAN $$
(519-271-9202; www.mercerhall.com; 104 Ontario St; lunch $6-16, dinner $10-28; 11:30am-9pm Sun-Wed, to midnight Thu-Sat) This stylish artisanal eatery features a fantastic brunch menu and seasonal dinner delights such as beef brisket, aged bison and a delicious lentil and vegetable curry.

Bijou

FRENCH $$$

(☑519-273-5000; www.bijourestaurant.com; 105 Erie St; lunch $8-18, dinner $46-52; ⊘11.30am-1pm Fri & Sat & 5-9pm Tue-Sat) Classy and delightful, this French joint has a different set menu written on the chalkboard each evening. The locally sourced meals might include quail, heirloom tomato salad or Lake Huron whitefish ceviche. Creaky wooden floorboards and children's artwork on the walls add a personal touch.

ℹ Information

Stratford Public Library (☑519-271-0220; www.stratford.library.on.ca; 19 St Andrew St; ⊘1-9pm Mon, 10am-9pm Tue-Thu, 10am-5pm Fri & Sat; @) Free internet access.

Stratford Tourism (☑519-271-5140, 800-561-7926; www.visitstratford.ca; www.welcome-tostratford.com;) Downtown (47 Downie St; ⊘8:30am-6pm Mon-Fri); Riverside (30 York St; ⊘10am-6pm Tue-Sun Jun-Sep) Staff can help with accommodations and all things 'Festival.' The websites are an excellent information source, with loads of tour options. The downtown location has one of Justin Beiber's signed guitars (an endless source of fascination for giggling teen fans from around the world). There's even a self-guided Justin Beiber tour, where you can see where the tween star went on his first date, if you really have absolutely nothing better to do.

ℹ Getting There & Away

The **Stratford Direct** (www.stratfordfestival.ca) is a shuttle service between Toronto and Stratford's four theaters during Festival season (performance days only, May-Oct) for only $20 round-trip. Buses pick up and drop off passengers at Simcoe St, south of Front St, beside the Intercontinental Toronto. You must purchase your ticket by 11pm the day before you travel. There are no stops between Toronto and Stratford, but there's wi-fi and a washroom onboard. Departure times vary; check the homepage for details and booking.

The **Stratford Airporter** (☑1-888-549-8602, 519-273-0057; www.stratfordairporter.com; from $69pp) runs daily shuttles to Pearson International Airport. It's cheaper if you're traveling with someone.

VIA Rail runs from **Stratford Train Station** (☑888-842-7245; www.viarail.ca; 101 Shakespeare St) to Toronto ($37, two hours, twice daily) and London ($20, one hour, twice daily).

Lake Huron Shoreline

Lake Huron has some of the cleanest waters of the Great Lakes and is wide enough that the sun sets on the waterline of its western shore: expect wonderful sunsets. If you've been lingering around Toronto and Lake Ontario, Lake Huron's 'blueness' will be both surprising and refreshing, as will its whitish sandy beaches. Hwy 21 hugs the underpopulated shoreline, in parts. When it doesn't, you're separated from the water only by pine forests and lakefront mansions.

Grand Bend

For most of the year, Grand Bend is a sleepy, shuttered town on the southeastern shore of Lake Huron, but from late May to late October the town heaves to life with sun-hungry university students from nearby London, Kitchener and Windsor. It's hard to imagine the transformation: the handful of year-round residents' peaceful lives interrupted by a mini Florida-style Spring Break on their doorsteps.

From a vantage point on the broad, sandy shoreline of the main beach, you can see how the town got its name: the coastline arcs dramatically from this point until it becomes almost a straight line, headed north. In early spring it's quite a surreal experience to stand on the sandy shore in the sunshine and gaze out at the frozen, snow-covered lake, its edges whipped by the wind into frozen waves.

🛏 Sleeping & Eating

Bars and cheap eats line Main St W as it approaches the beach: there are some great patios for a cold beer... or two.

Pinery Provincial Park

CAMPGROUND $

(☑info 519-243-2220, reservations 888-668-7275; www.pinerypark.on.ca; RR2. Grand Bend; rates vary) South of Grand Bend is popular, picturesque Pinery Provincial Park with 10km of wide sandy beaches and lots of trails winding through wooded sections and sand dunes (bike/kayak rental per day $45/40). There are hundreds of campsites and a number of yurts to choose from. Be sure to book in advance through Parks Ontario's snazzy website: www.reservations.ontarioparks.com, as spots fill fast.

Bonnie Doone Manor on the Beach
INN $$

(☑ 519-238-2236; www.bonniedoone.ca; 16 Government Rd; d $90-325; ✳ @ ✿) We love this ramshackle holiday motel – the only one on the beach – lovingly updated and maintained by the same family for over 50 years. Rooms are a retro time warp with bright, colorful accents. Many face the water for unimaginably beautiful sunsets. There's also a quaint private cottage. It's right on the beach and a hop, skip and jump from Main St.

Schoolhouse Restaurant
INTERNATIONAL $$

(☑ 519-238-5515; www.grandbendschoolhouse.ca; 1981 Crescent St; mains $14-26; ☺ 9am-9pm Mon-Fri, from 8am Sat & Sun) There's something for everyone at this foodie-friendly restaurant occupying, you guessed it, the former Grand Bend Public School. From tender roast chicken to succulent steak, ribs, lake-fresh seafood and a variety of delicious local salads, you'll be delighted to find this alternative to Main St's touristy offerings.

Sunset House
INTERNATIONAL $$

(☑ 519-238-2622; www.sunsethouse.ca; 85 Main St W; mains $11-24; ☺ 11am-11:30pm) This place scored Grand Bend's prime beachfront spot. It's a lovely place to linger over dinner and drinks as the sun dips over the horizon. Choose from sizzling fajitas, seafood, burgers and salads or just go a few rounds of appys with your liquid refreshments.

🍸 Drinking & Nightlife

Riverbend Bar & Grill
BAR

(☑ 519-238-6919; 26 Ontario St S; ☺ 1-10pm) Open year-round, Riverbend's regulars return for huge portions of succulent hot chicken wings, karaoke nights and cold beer on the patio. Sounds tough, eh!

❶ Getting There & Away

There's no public transportation to Grand Bend. Renting a car from London is a great way to explore the Huron Coast and to avoid the daunting experience of driving in/out of Toronto. Both **Avis** (☑ 800-230-4898; www.avis.ca) and **Enterprise** (☑ 800-261-7331; www.enterprise-rentacar.ca) have locations on Horton St, near London Train Station (p153).

Goderich

Previously awarded the title of Canada's prettiest town, charming Goderich's most recent and tragic claim to fame was for the EF-3 tornado which tore through it at 4:03pm on August 21, 2011. It was a Sunday and the crowded market square had just emptied. The twister formed over Lake Huron and followed a direct path across the town's distinctive octagonal town square, City Hall and beyond. Of the 97 century-old trees in the square, only three remained; hundreds of buildings were damaged or destroyed, scores injured and one life lost.

A few years on, the town continues to work to regain its former title. Most of the restoration and reconstruction work is now complete. The friendly staff at **Tourism Goderich** (☑ 519-524-6600; www.goderich.ca; 91 Hamilton St; ☺ 9am-5pm) will be delighted to provide you with a self-guided Heritage Walking Tours brochure and field any questions you have about the town, tornado or otherwise.

◉ Sights & Activities

Huron County Museum
MUSEUM

(☑ 519-524-2686; www.huroncounty.ca/museum; 110 North St; adult/child $5/3.50; ☺ 10am-4:30pm Mon-Fri, 1-4:30pm Sat Jan-Apr, 10am-4:30pm Mon-Sat, from 1pm Sun May-Dec) Walk the wooden floorboards at Huron County Museum for an informed look at local history, industry and transportation. Displays include everything from antique furniture and china to an old steam engine and a tank.

Huron Historic Gaol
MUSEUM

(☑ 519-524-6971; www.huroncounty.ca/museum; 181 Victoria St N; adult/child $5/3.50; ☺ 10am-4:30pm Mon-Sat, from 1pm Sun May-Sep, 10am-4:30pm Sat, 1-4pm Sun-Fri Sep-Nov) Follow a creepy, prison-gray corridor into the Huron Historic Gaol, an octagonal fortress that served as the courthouse and jail for almost 130 years (and was the site of Canada's last public hanging in 1869).

Boardwalks
WALKING

Goderich has three sandy Lake Huron beaches, linked by kilometers of boardwalks. Don't miss a dusk stroll for swoon-worthy sunsets.

✵ Festivals & Events

Blyth Festival
THEATER

(www.blythfestival.com) The nearby village of Blyth has the kind of main street that Bruce Springsteen likes to sing about, and is home to the esteemed summer Blyth Festival. From June to August, primarily Canadian plays get an airing, from outdoor

ONTARIO LAKE HURON SHORELINE

pioneer performances to indoor gut-busting comedies.

Celtic Roots Festival   CULTURE
(www.celticfestival.ca) The town fills up early August for this, one of the largest celebrations of Celtic history and culture in North America.

⬛ Sleeping & Eating

Maple Leaf Motel   MOTEL $
(☑ 519-524-2302; www.themapleleafmotel.com; 54 Victoria St N; d from $79; ❈ ❆ ❡) This central 11-room motel with quaint country decor is lovingly maintained to a high standard.

Colborne B&B   B&B $$
(☑ 519-524-7400; www.colbornebandb.com; 72 Colborne St; d incl breakfast $90-120; ❈ ❡) Formerly the manse for the Presbyterian Church, this handsome three-story property has four bright, smartly furnished guest bedrooms, each with en suite: two have whirlpools. Delicious gourmet breakfasts, served in the dining room, are a great way to start your day. Excellent value.

Benmiller Inn & Spa   INN $$$
(☑ 800-265-1711; www.benmiller.ca; 81175 Benmiller Line; from d $149-289; ❈ ❡ ❆) Just outside Goderich, riverside Benmiller is somewhere to treat yourself with a little old-fashioned luxury and country hospitality. There's a fantastic indoor swimming pool with river views, full-service Aveda treatment spa, the 'Ivey' fine dining restaurant and 57 charming rooms.

Culbert's Bakery   BAKERY $
(☑ 519-524-7941; 49 West St; items from $2; ⊙ 8am-5:30pm Mon-Sat) Folks come from far and wide for this old-school bakery serving delicious and decadent cream puffs, muffins, tarts and fresh-from-the-oven loaves. The early bird catches the early calories.

West Street Willy's   DINER $
(☑ 519-524-7777; 42 West St; items $8-18; ⊙ 7am-9pm Tue-Sat, to 8pm Sun) Hearty breakfasts and homestyle faves await you at Willy's: perogies, pizza, meatloaf, burgers are all on the menu.

Thyme on 21   INTERNATIONAL $$$
(☑ 519-524-4171; www.thymeon21.com; 80 Hamilton St; mains $19-34; ⊙ 11:30am-2pm Tue-Fri & 5-9pm Tue-Sun) Goderich's only casual fine-dining establishment does a good job upholding its fine reputation. Global influences are present in the mouthwatering menu, with mains including lobster, veal, pad thai and souffle.

❶ Getting There & Away

Aboutown Northlink (☑ 888-666-5466; www.aboutown.com/northlink) operates a limited service to/from London (adult/child $27/13.50) on Fridays and Sundays year-round. It connects with a Greyhound service to/from Toronto.

Southampton & Port Elgin

Southampton has happily sequestered itself from the beaten path of rowdy summer holidays. The quaint colony's sandy beach feels almost undiscovered at times, and a stroll down the main streets reveals mom-and-pop shops and the piecemeal architecture of Queen Anne–styled homes.

To the south, neighboring Port Elgin is the year-round home to the bulk of shopping, dining and nightlife options for the region. It also has some of the better, more accessible (free parking) and lesser known beaches on this strip of Lake Huron.

About 20km north of Southampton, **Sauble Beach** has a delicious wide strip of white sand and warm, clear waters, but its huge popularity with holidaymakers and revelers and the high cost of car parking take some of the magic away. In winter it's a ghost town.

◉ Sights & Activities

Chantry Island   ISLAND
Chantry Island, just 2km off the shoreline, is home to a lonely lighthouse and a sanctuary for migratory birds. The only way to reach the island is with **Chantry Island Tours** (☑ 866-797-5862, 519-797-5862; www.chantryisland.com; per person $30; ⊙ Jun-Sep). Informative outings are led by the Marine Heritage Society and provide fascinating insights into the region's nautical history as well as a chance to climb the blinking lighthouse. Book in advance as only nine people can be accommodated per tour.

Bruce County Museum   MUSEUM
(☑ 519-797-2080, 866-318-8889; www.brucemuseum.ca; 33 Victoria St N, Southampton; adult/child $8/4; ⊙ 10am-5pm Mon-Sat, from 1pm Sun) This museum has an extensive collection of artifacts relating to shipwrecks in the region. There are also rotating summer exhibits for kids.

Rail Trail
CYCLING

Cyclists will enjoy this 25km stretch of abandoned railway, which starts at the corner of Albert and Adelaide Sts and ends in the small town of Paisley.

Thorncrest Outfitters
KAYAKING

(🗹 519-797-1608; www.thorncrestoutfitters.com; 193 High St, Southampton; canoe rental from $35) The Saugeen River, which flows into Lake Huron at Southampton, is one of the best-established routes for canoeing and kayaking in southern Ontario. Thorncrest Outfitters runs an extensive program of short self-guided and organized trips aimed at inexperienced paddlers.

🛏 Sleeping & Eating

Aunt Mabel's Inn
MOTEL $

(🗹 866-868-2880; www.auntmabels.com; 5084 Hwy 21 S, Port Elgin; d from $65) These spotless, compact rooms have flatscreen TVs, fridge and microwave and comfy beds. Some have soaker tubs. It's a few minutes' drive from some of the coast's best swimming beaches. Better still, Aunt Mabel's kitchen whips up the best home cookin' for miles, from 6am.

Chantry Breezes
B&B $$

(🗹 866-242-6879, 519-797-1818; www.chantry-breezes.com; 107 High St, Southampton; r incl breakfast $120-160; 🌐🛜) This old Queen Anne manor, tucked gently behind gnarled evergreens, features seven rooms spread out among endearingly cluttered antiques and a private garden cottage. Made-to-order breakfasts are delightful to enjoy on the porch.

Southampton Inn
INN $$

(🗹 888-214-3816, 519-797-5915; www.thesouth-amptoninn.com; 118 High St, Southampton; r/ste $135/$155; 🌐❄🛜) If the beachy blend of sand and wind isn't a good enough exfoliant, head downstairs for a full spa treatment. The upper level is dedicated to sprawling accommodations; each suite has a private sunny sitting room.

Armen's
FUSION $

(224 High St, Southampton; mains $5-12; ⊙9am-4pm daily & 5-8pm Wed-Sat) Forget the local greasy spoons and say hi to chatty Armen as he prepares a tasty sandwich from the ever-changing menu. A rotating dinner menu in June, July and August highlights global cuisine; one night it's Canadian, another it's Moroccan. It keeps your taste buds on their toes. Sneak upstairs and enjoy your fresh eats on the sunny rooftop deck.

Elk and Finch
CAFE $

(www.elkandfinch.com; 54 Albert St, Southampton; mains $8-24; ⊙8am-8pm Sun-Thu, to 9pm Fri & Sat) This 'coffee pub' serves more than caffeinated and alcoholic beverages: sandwiches, salads and thin-crust pizzas will fill you up. Sip your trendy brew in the wobbly house or park yourself at a table on the grassy lawn.

❶ Information

The small **Southampton Chamber of Commerce** (🗹 888-757-2215, 519-797- 2215; 201 High St, Southampton; ⊙10am-4pm Mon-Sat, from noon Sun) can be found in the town hall – the large brick building with a clock tower. The **Saugeen Shores Chamber Office** (🗹 800-387-3456, 519-832-2332; 559 Goderich St, Port Elgin; ⊙ 9am-5pm Mon-Fri, 10am-4pm Sat, noon-4pm Sun), 8km down the shoreline in Port Elgin, offers a wider array of information about the region. Check in with **Sauble Beach Tourism** (🗹 Jul-Aug 519-422-1262, Sep-Jun 519-422-2457; www.saublebeach. com; 672 Main St, Sauble Beach; ⊙9am-5pm) for the lowdown on party town.

❶ Getting There & Away

Passengers arriving at Lester B Pearson International Airport in Toronto can take the **Grey Bruce Airbus** (🗹 800-361-0393; www.grey-bruceairbus.com), which connects to Southampton and Port Elgin ($74, three hours, four daily). From Toronto Union bus terminal, **Can-ar** (🗹 800-387-7097; www.can-arcoach.com) operates a bus service to Port Elgin ($35 to $44, 4¾ hours, one daily), arriving at Ralph's Hi-way Shoppette in the center of town.

London

POP 366,000

Ontario's third-most populous city (after the GTA and Ottawa), midway between Toronto and Detroit, is London, aka the 'forest city.' It bears little resemblance to its namesake, short of its substantial collection of fine Victorian homes, River Thames and a plethora of leafy parks and gardens. Aside from a smattering of beautiful art-deco buildings, London's downtown core is predictably turn-of-the-millennium, if not a little bit 1970s. You might notice some sketchy characters walking along Dundas St toward Adelaide St, but you'll also notice plenty of police cars keeping the peace.

London is home to the University of Western Ontario in the city's north, favored by wealthy Toronto families as *the* spot to send their kids. The student population ensures a young, upbeat vibe: during the end of summer before term begins, London's 'Richmond Row' becomes 'party central.'

The close-to-downtown neighborhoods of Wortley Village and Woodfield have echoes of the great architect Frank Lloyd Wright's hometown of Oak Park in Illinois (USA), although there is no connection between the two or his architectural style: it's more about the quiet leafy streets, the era of construction and those rustic front porches. There's plenty of accommodations in town, some good student-priced eateries and a handful of interesting tourist attractions: it's a great place to visit in the warmer months (it gets heavy snows in the winter) and a wonderful place to live. As Toronto continues to expand, we predict eyes will be more focused on London in years to come.

⊙ Sights

Museum London   MUSEUM
(☑519-661-0333; www.museumlondon.ca; 421 Ridout St N; admission by donation; ⊙11am-5pm Fri-Wed, to 9pm Thu) Focusing on the visual arts and how they fit together with history, London's vibrant museum has 5000-plus works of art and 25,000-plus artifacts. Free tours run on Sundays at 2pm.

Eldon House   HISTORIC BUILDING
(☑519-661-5169; www.eldonhouse.ca; 481 Ridout St N; adult/child $7/5; ⊙2-4pm Tue-Sun) Built in 1834, London's oldest surviving house remains virtually unchanged since the last century. Inside you'll find heirlooms and treasures belonging to the Harris family, a fascinating bunch, while outside you can enjoy the beautiful 19th-century garden.

Museum of Ontario Archaeology   MUSEUM
(☑519-473-1360; www.uwo.ca/museum; 1600 Attawandaron Rd; adult/child $4/2; ⊙10am-4:30pm) An educational and research facility affiliated with the University of Western Ontario, the Museum of Ontario Archaeology displays materials and artifacts spanning 11,000 years of aboriginal history in Ontario. Next door is the Lawson site, an active excavation of a 500-year-old pre-contact Neutral Iroquoian village.

Ska-Nah-Doht
Village & Museum   HISTORIC SITE
(☑519-264-2420; www.lowerthames-conservation.on.ca/Ska-Nah-Doht; Longwoods Rd Conservation Area; adult/child $3/free; ⊙9am-4:30pm) This museum, 32km west of London, re-creates a 1000-year-old Iroquois longhouse community. Village structures are encircled by a maze; the museum contains artifacts thousands of years old and recounts the area's history.

Fanshawe Pioneer Village   HISTORIC SITE
(☑519-457-1296; www.fanshawepioneervillage.ca; 1424 Clarke Rd; adult/child $7/free; ⊙10am-4:30pm Tue-Sun May-Oct) Explore London's history at the 30-building Fanshawe Pioneer Village on the eastern edge of town. Costumed blacksmiths, farmers and craftspeople carry out their duties in 19th-century pioneer-village style. At the adjoining **Fanshawe Conservation Area** you can swim, walk and camp.

Royal Canadian
Regiment Museum   MUSEUM
(☑519-660-5275; www.theroyalcanadianregiment.ca/thercrmuseum; 750 Elizabeth St; adult/child

$5/3; ⊙10am-4pm Tue-Fri, from noon Sat & Sun) Inside the austere Wolseley Hall, the Royal Canadian Regiment Museum focuses on the oldest infantry regiment in Canada, with displays covering the North-West Rebellion of 1885 through both world wars to the Korean War.

✯ Festivals & Events

London Fringe Festival
CULTURE
(www.londonfringe.ca) Eleven days of theater, spoken word, film and visual arts around downtown, mid-June.

Sunfest
MUSIC
(www.sunfest.on.ca) Canada's premier world-music festival, held in July.

London Pride
LGBT
(www.pridelondon.ca) London is big enough and gay enough to celebrate its very own pride festival, in July.

Londonlicious
FOOD
(www.londonlicious.ca) A London homage to Toronto's hit Summerlicious festival brings cheap fancy eats to the peeps. It's held from July to August.

Rock the Park
MUSIC
(www.rockthepark.ca) Rock the Park turned 10 in 2013. For a weekend in July, riverside Harris Park swells with longhaireds and rockers for the likes of Whitesnake, Platinum Blonde and the Tragically Hip.

🛏 Sleeping

There's a bombardment of cheap chain motels on the Wellington Rd approach from Hwy 401, but stay downtown if you can.

Fanshawe Conservation Area Campground
CAMPGROUND $
(☑866-668-2267, 519-451-2800; www.thamesriver.on.ca; 1424 Clarke Rd; campsites $25-29, reservations $9; ⊙May-Oct; 🐾) Convenient camping within the city limits, across from Fanshawe Pioneer Village.

Woodfield Bed & Breakfast
B&B $
(☑519-675-9632; www.woodfieldbb.com; 499 Dufferin Ave; s $80, d $90-120) In the heart of historic Woodfield, one of London's most attractive neighborhoods, you'll find this gorgeous new B&B in a sprawling Victorian mansion. An alternative to London's generic tourist hotels, it's a great way to experience what this picturesque city has to offer.

Holiday Inn Express & Suites
HOTEL $$
(☑519-661-0233; www.holidayinn.com; 374 Dundas St; d incl breakfast from $109; ⊜❉🐾🛜) Centrally located, with some great restaurants nearby, this recently refurbished property has bright rooms with comfy beds and good showers. Rooms have a fridge, microwave, large TV, and there's free internet.

Delta Armouries
HOTEL $$
(☑519-679-6111; www.deltahotels.com; 325 Dundas St; d from $119; ⊜❉🛜) The Armouries wing of London's premier hotel was originally a historic military training facility. Its period features remain to be enjoyed, though most rooms are in the tower wing. Expect comfortable, neutrally furnished accommodations, a central location and reasonable rates.

Metro
BOUTIQUE HOTEL $$
(☑519-518-9000; www.hotelmetro.ca; 32 Covent Market Pl; d from $129) Rooms in this funky boutique hotel in the heart of downtown have exposed-brick walls, rainfall showers, deep soaker tubs and plenty of interesting design elements to keep you entertained.

StationPark All Suite Hotel
HOTEL $$
(☑800-561-4574; www.stationparkinn.ca; 242 Pall Mall St; ste from $139; 🛜) This all-suite hotel has oversized bedrooms with separate living rooms. Granted, they could do with a makeover, but the service is excellent and the location near Richmond Row and Victoria Park can't be beat.

✕ Eating

★ Covent Garden
MARKET $
(☑519-439-3921; www.coventmarket.com; 130 King St; items from $2; ⊙8am-6pm Mon-Sat, 11am-4pm Sun) This humongous, barn-shaped market will whet and satisfy any appetite. There's a permanent collection of delis, bakeries, chocolate shops, fresh produce stalls and world-cuisine eateries, plus seasonal vendors and a sunny, busker-fueled buzz on the patio.

Early Bird
DINER $
(☑519-439-6483; 355 Talbot St; items $5-20; ⊙11am-3pm Mon, to late Tue-Sun) Delicious Early Bird delivers its own take on from-scratch, home-style cooking. When we say unique, how about the Fat Elvis: smoked bacon, *panko*-crumbed fried bananas, peanut butter and local honey sandwiched between French toast. Don't knock it till you've tried it.

Morrissey House

PUB $

(☎ 519-204-9220; www.themorrisseyhouse.com; 359-361 Dundas St; mains $9-16; ⊗11am-late; ☉) This centrally located 'grub-pub' offers classy, well-prepared menus and a relaxed vibe inside its Victorian manor rooms, or on the large sunny patio out front. Free wifi and great tunes are a bonus. Come for a meal, a few pints or both: everyone else is.

★ Budapest

EUROPEAN $$

(☎ 519-439-3431; 348 Dundas St; mains $11-25; ⊗11am-9pm Mon-Sat, 4-9pm Sun) If you've been in business for over 50 years, you've got to be doing something right. We love the authenticity of owner Marika's humble establishment. Over the years, she's perfected her schnitzels, chicken paprikash and pierogies. Yum! Lunch specials are excellent value.

Zen Gardens

VEGETARIAN $$

(☎ 519-433-6688; www.zen-garden.ca; 344 Dundas St; combination boxes $10.50; ⊗11:30am-9pm Mon-Sat, 5-9pm Sun) This Asian vegetarian restaurant downtown will impress vegetarians and their most hardened carnivorous mates alike. Combinations, served in Japanese *bentō* boxes, offer the best value.

Bertoldi's Trattoria

ITALIAN $$

(☎ 519-438-4343; www.bertoldis.ca; 650 Richmond St; mains $12-29; ⊗11am-11pm Mon-Fri, 4-11pm Sat & Sun) On Richmond Row, casual yet classy Bertoldi's does authentic Italian and has special regional menus and a substantial vino list. There's a nice patio in the warmer months.

Thaifoon

THAI $$

(☎ 519-850-1222; www.thaifoonrestaurant.com; 120 Dundas St; mains $10-21; ⊗11:30am-2:30pm Mon-Fri & 5-9pm daily) Classing Dundas St up a bit is Thaifoon. A calm, composed atmosphere and babbling water features provide relief from the mean streets, while chili-laden curries, stir-fries, soups and salads provide a kick in the pants.

☗ Drinking & Entertainment

The vibrant student population ensures plenty of youthful, boozy entertainment; check out the local rag *Scene* (www.scene-magazine.com) for listings.

Honest Lawyer

PUB

(☎ 519-433-4913; www.honestlawyer.ca; 228 Dundas St; ⊗11am-late) Is there such a thing as an honest lawyer? Maybe not, but it's a sure-fire conversation starter at this long, narrow

beer room where an upbeat crowd is usually knocking back a few. Student specials, wing nights, big-screen sports and live music on the weekends.

Barneys/CEEPS

PUB

(671 Richmond St; ⊗11am-2am) Don't ask about the name – we don't get it either. Hands down London's largest and most hopping patio as well as bands and DJs, pool tables, shuffleboard, and local beers on tap. The original Richmond Row institution.

Up on Carling

CLUB

(www.uponcarling.ca; 153 Carling St; ⊗9pm-late Thu-Sat) A stylish, martini-soaked affair, spinning Latin, R&B, funk house and soul. Dress code enforced.

Call the Office

LIVE MUSIC

(☎ 519-432-4433; www.calltheoffice.com; 216 York St; ⊗5pm-late) A grungy dive bar with cheap drinks and alt-rock live bands, sometimes pulling names like the Jon Spencer Blues Explosion.

London Music Club

LIVE MUSIC

(☎ 519-640-6996; www.londonmusicclub.com; 470 Colborne St; ⊗7pm-late Wed-Sat) Touring blues and folk acts fall over themselves to play here, a rockin' room out the back of a cream-brick suburban house. Electric blues jam on Thursday nights; acoustic open mic on Fridays.

❶ Information

London Public Library (www.londonpublicli-brary.ca; 251 Dundas St; ⊗9am-9pm Mon-Thu, to 6pm Fri, to 5pm Sat, 1-5pm Sun; ☉) A fabulous modern setting with a cafe, reading garden, and free internet and wi-fi.

Post Office (☎ 800-267-1177; www.cana-dapost.ca; 515 Richmond St at Dufferin St; ⊗9am-5pm Mon-Fri)

Tourism London (☎ 800-265-2602, 519-661-5000; www.londontourism.ca) Downtown (267 Dundas St; ⊗8:30am-4:30pm Mon-Fri, 10am-5pm Sat); Wellington Road (696 Wellington Rd S; ⊗8:30am-8pm) The downtown office shares a building with the Canadian Medical Hall of Fame and its interesting/gory displays of brains, hearts and bones.

❶ Getting There & Around

London International Airport (YXU; www.lon-donairport.on.ca; 1750 Crumlin Rd) is a regional base for Air Canada, WestJet and Delta with flights to Toronto, Detroit, and limited Canadian and US destinations.

Greyhound Canada rolls out of **London Bus Station** (☑ 800-661-8747; www.greyhound.ca; 101 York St; ☺ 6:30am-9pm) to Toronto ($36, 2½ hours, 12 daily) and Windsor ($36, 2½ hours, five daily).

London Train Station (☑ 519-672-5722; www.viarail.ca; cnr York & Clarence Sts; ☺ 5am-9:30pm Mon-Fri, from 6:30am Sat & Sun) has trains to Toronto ($56, two hours, seven daily) and Windsor ($46, two hours, four daily).

London Transit (www.ltconline.ca; 150 Dundas St; ☺ 7:30am-7pm Mon-Fri, 8:30am-6pm Sat) has extensive bus services around town ($2.75 a ride).

Windsor

POP 209,000

At the end of the highway on the southwestern tip of Ontario (across the river from Detroit, USA) this once-booming center for trade and manufacturing has seen better days. Recent approval to commence work on the New International Trade Crossing, a bridge that will increase the volume of trade and speed of passage over the border, may change all that.

For the moment, Windsor's empty facades bear the scars of decline. The upside? Cheap real estate, adjacency to the US and proximity to Lake Erie slowly lure cityslickers looking for a change of pace.

◎ Sights

Visitors will enjoy walking along the Riverwalk, a multi-use path that extends from under the Ambassador Bridge for 5km along the riverfront. The historic Walkerville neighborhood is worth a look.

Dieppe Gardens GARDENS
(cnr Ouellette St & Riverside Dr) These beautiful gardens, on land once used by Detroit–Windsor ferries before the 1929 bridge and 1930 tunnel put them out of business, offer the best views of the smoke-and-mirrors Detroit skyline.

Art Gallery of Windsor GALLERY
(AGW; ☑ 519-977-0013; www.agw.ca; 401 Riverside Dr W; ☺ 11am-5pm Wed-Sun) FREE The jaunty glass-and-concrete prow of the AGW has an awesome permanent collection focused on contemporary Canadian sculpture and painting. Best of all, it's now free!

Canadian Club
Brands Centre DISTILLERY
(☑ 519-973-9503; www.canadianclubwhisky.com; 2072 Riverside Dr E; adult/child $8/2; ☺ Thu-Sat Jan-Apr, Wed-Sun May-Dec) Canadian Club has been sluicing here (formerly known as the Walkerville Distillery) since 1858. One-hour tours (noon, 2pm and 4pm) explore the history of the ornate Italiante building, the distilling process and offer a taste.

Walls Underground
Railroad Museum MUSEUM
(☑ 519-727-6555; www.undergroundrailroadmuseum.org; 855 Puce Rd, Maidstone; admission $5; ☺ 10am-4pm May-Oct) Some 20km east of Windsor, the 1846 log cabin built by John Freeman Walls, a fugitive slave from North Carolina, is the focal point of this site, which functioned as a safe terminal for others searching for freedom. Walls' descendants still run the museum.

★ Festivals & Events

Bluesfest International MUSIC
(www.thebluesfest.com) Featuring the likes of Los Lobos and Steve Earle. Held mid-July.

UNCLE TOM'S CABIN

About 100km northeast of Windsor, before Chatham, is the **Uncle Tom's Cabin Historic Site** (☑ 519-683-2978; www.uncletomscabin.org; 29251 Uncle Tom's Rd, Dresden; adult/child/concession/family $6.25/4.50/5.25/20; ◷ 10am-4pm Mon-Sat, from noon Sun May-Oct). Uncle Tom was the fictional protagonist and namesake of the book written by Harriet Beecher Stowe in 1852, based on real-life hero Reverend Josiah Henson. The 5-hectare site displays articles relating to the story and the Underground Railroad, as well as a theater, gallery and interpretive center. To get here, take exit 101 off Hwy 401 and follow the signs.

🛏 Sleeping & Eating

There are plenty of beds in Windsor. Chain hotels and local motels dominate Huron Church Rd, leading off the Ambassador Bridge.

Oullette Ave (Thai, Indian and coffee shops) and Chatham St (bars and grills) lend foodie focus to the downtown area. The Italian district on Erie St E has a happening vibe.

University Place Accommodations   HOTEL $
(☑ 866-618-1112, 519-254-1112; www.windsorexecutivestay.com; 3140 Peter St; r with shared bathroom from $39; ❄ ❀ ☎ ❋) Though not affiliated with the university, this long- and short-term residence offers clean rooms with shared facilities including laundry. Rooms with en suites and bike rentals are available.

Kirk's B&B   B&B $$
(☑ 888-271-2624, 519-255-9346; www.kirksbandb.com; 406 Moy Ave; s/d from $75/89; ◷ ❀ ☎) One block from the river, Kirk's is a three-story, old-fashioned brick affair, with a lush garden. Warm, tidy rooms have comfortable beds.

Holiday Inn Windsor Downtown   HOTEL $$
(☑ 519-256-4656; www.holidayinn.com; 430 Ouellette Ave; d from $119; ❄ ☎ ❋) This generic Holiday Inn is looking a little dated, but has a great downtown position, comfy beds and spacious rooms. There's a full service restaurant on-site, inground swimming pool and plenty of parking.

Squirrel's Cage   CAFE $
(☑ 519-252-2243; www.facebook.com/TheSquirrel-Cage; 1 Maiden Lane W; items $2-14; ◷ 8:30am-8pm Mon-Wed, to late Thu-Sat, 10am-3pm Sat & Sun) Former city slickers love their new life in Windsor and bring a taste of cosmopolitan Toronto to town in this stylish, upbeat licensed cafe. Expect coffees, soups, delicious filled panini, healthy salads daily and weekend brunches.

Spago Trattoria e Pizzeria   ITALIAN $$
(☑ 519-252-2233; www.spagos.ca; 690 Erie St E; mains $10-22; ◷ 11:30am-10pm Mon-Sat, 1-9pm Sun) Windsor has a reputation for its Italian, and Spago's fits the bill. If you're not in the mood for delicious pasta, staff also deliver outstanding wood-fired pizzas, seafood, salad and scaloppine. Mmm...amma mia!

Cook's Shop   ITALIAN $$
(☑ 519-254-3377; http://cooksshoprestaurant.wordpress.com; 683 Ouellette Ave; mains $15-24; ◷ from 5pm Tue-Sun) This reasonably priced fine-dining establishment has been operating for over 30 years from its century-old premises. Specializing in seafood, pasta, lamb and beef; reservations are strongly advised.

🍷 Drinking & Entertainment

Manchester   PUB
(☑ 519-977-8020; www.themanchester.ca; 546 Ouellette Ave; ◷ 11:30am-late) Friendly staff, hearty British pub fare and a convenient downtown location make the Manchester a sensible choice for a casual relaxed meal and a couple of pints. There's plenty of North American munchies on the menu too.

Caesar's Windsor   CASINO
(☑ 800-991-7777; www.caesarswindsor.com; 377 Riverside Dr E; ◷ 24hr) This provincially owned casino (affiliated with the Caesar's Las Vegas family) gives Windsor an economic boost, although crowds have declined with tighter border security and a strong Canadian dollar. Minimum age 19 years. The annexed hotel has the best rooms in town.

ℹ Information

Ontario Travel Information Centre (☑ 519-973-1338; www.ontariotravel.net; 110 Park St E; ◷ 8:30am-8pm) Well stocked with brochures and helpful staff.

Tourism Windsor Essex (☑ 800-265-3633, 519-255-6530; www.visitwindsoressex.com; Suite 103, 333 Riverside Dr; ◷ 8:30am-4:30pm

Mon-Fri) Information on Windsor and the area; best accessed from Pitt St.

❶ Getting There & Away

Detroit–Windsor is a major international border crossing, via either the famously expansive Ambassador Bridge (toll $4.75/US$4), or the Detroit–Windsor Tunnel (toll $4.50-4.75/US$4-4.50) connecting the two downtowns.

The **Windsor Bus Station** (📞 519-254-7577; www.greyhound.ca; 300 Chatham St W; ⏰7am-9pm) runs buses to Toronto ($54, five hours, five daily) via London ($36, two hours five daily) US-bound trips to Chicago ($105, nine hours, three daily) transfer from Greyhound Canada to Greyhound in Detroit. Cheaper fares are available online, in advance. Also here is **Transit Windsor** (📞 519-944-4111; www.citywindsor. ca), running buses to Detroit ($4, 30 minutes, every 30 minutes) – bring your passport.

Windsor Train Station (📞 888-842-7245; www.viarail.ca; cnr Walker & Wyandotte Sts; ⏰5:15am-11:30pm), 3km east of downtown, has trains to Toronto ($76, four hours, four daily) via London ($46, two hours).

Lake Erie Shoreline

From the Welland Canal near Niagara to the Detroit River at Windsor, the Lake Erie shoreline is a scenic, thinly populated strip of sandy beaches, small towns and peaceful parks. Many Ontarians have cottages here. Recent environmental efforts are such that you can swm in Lake Erie (the shallowest and warmest of the Great Lakes), but do check with the locals before you go in. If you really want to get *away*, try quirky Pelee Island, Canada's southernmost point. There's next to no public transport along the shoreline: the following listings assume you're driving between towns.

Amherstburg

War of 1812 and Underground Railroad buffs will find some enthralling diversions in historic Amherstburg, a small town south of Windsor, where the Detroit River flows into Lake Erie – although much more happened here in the past than has of late.

◉ Sights

**Fort Malden National
Historic Site**   HISTORIC SITE
(📞 519-736-5416; www.pc.gc.ca; 100 Laird Ave; adult/child $4/2; ⏰10am-5pm May-Oct) This British fort was built on earthwork embank-

ments along the river in 1840. Beginning with the arrival of the fur traders, the area saw a lot of friction between the French, First Nations and English and, later, the Americans. Here, during the War of 1812, General Brock (together with his ally, Shawnee Chief Tecumseh) conspired to take Detroit.

Park House Museum   MUSEUM
(📞 519-736-2511; www.parkhousemuseum.com; 214 Dalhousie St; adult/child $3/1; ⏰10am-5pm) The oldest house in town, and the only one not *from* town. It was built on the other side of the river, ferried across in 1799, and is now furnished in 1850s style.

**North American Black Historical
Museum**   MUSEUM
(📞 519-736-5433, 800-713-6336; www.black-historicalmuseum.com; 277 King St; adult/child $5.50/4.50; ⏰10am-5pm Tue-Fri, from 1pm Sat & Sun) The Nazrey African Methodist Episcopal Church here, a national historic site, was built by former slaves and played a role in the Underground Railroad.

✦✦ Festivals & Events

Shores of Erie   WINE
(www.soewinefestival.com) Wine and entertainment are the name of the game during this late-summer/early-fall festival. Book accommodations well in advance.

🛏 Sleeping & Eating

Pier 41   B&B $$
(📞 519-737-9187; www.pier41bb.com; 41 Mickle Dr; r $100) Sleep and wake to the gentle lapping of the waves at the shoreline from these two private suites in the friendly owner's former family home.

Artisan Grill   MODERN CANADIAN $
(📞 519-713-9009; www.artisangrill.ca; 269 Dalhousie St; meals $8-25; ⏰11am-10pm Tue-Sun) It's nice to know that a small town like Amherstburg has decent casual fine dining as found here in the Artisan Grill: wraps, sandwiches, salads and steaks – even lobster – make the cut.

Lord Amherst Public House   PUB $
(📞 519-713-9165; www.lordamherst.ca; 273 Dalhousie St; mains $10-16; ⏰11:30am-late Mon-Sun) Fancy, delicious pub meals and top-shelf beers make this quaint historic watering hole a lovely diversion from your heritage adventures.

❶ Information

Amherstburg Visitors Information Centre

(☑ 519-736-8320; www.amherstburg.ca; cnr Sandwich & William Sts; ☺late May-Oct) This new facility can point you in the right direction for your historical research.

Leamington & Pelee Island

Lakeside Leamington is the 'Tomato Capital of Ontario,' though most people come here just to get the ferry to Pelee Island. Southeast of town, Point Pelee National Park (the southernmost point of mainland Canada) is a pit stop for thousands of migratory birds during spring and fall.

Canada's southernmost outpost, Pelee Island is a surprising, sleepy oasis in the middle of Lake Erie. In 1788 the Ojibwe and Ottawa Nations leased it to Thomas McKee, though it remained undeveloped until William McCormick bought it in 1823. By 1900 Pelee had 800 residents, four churches and four schools. These days there are just 275 residents and not much else. Life revolves around a very relaxed and humble form of tourism. The island is as green as green can be and surrounded by sandy beaches and shallow water; come to get away from it all without leaving the province. Access is by a bumpy grassroots car ferry from April to December. At other times, you'll need a plane. Remember folks, it's an island: many of the roads are unpaved and services and amenities are limited, including internet.

◉ Sights

Point Pelee National Park   PARK

(☑ 866-787-3533, 519-322-2365; www.pc.gc.ca; Point Pelee Dr, Leamington; adult/child $8/4; ☺dawn-dusk) About 13km southeast of Leamington, this well-loved national park features nature trails, a marsh boardwalk, forests and lovely sandy beaches within the park. The fall migration of monarch butterflies is a spectacle of swirling black and orange.

Pelee Island Heritage Centre   MUSEUM

(☑ 519-724-2291; www.peleeislandmuseum.ca; 1073 West Shore Rd, Pelee Island; adult/child $3/2; ☺10am-5pm May-Oct) Near West Dock, the small Pelee Island Heritage Centre has one of the best natural history collections in Ontario. Engrossing displays cover indigenous to 20th-century history, geology, wildlife, industry, sailing and shipwrecks.

Fish Point Nature Reserve   PARK

(www.ontarioparks.com; 1750 McCormick Rd, Pelee Island; ☺dawn-dusk) Fish Point Nature Reserve is a long sandy spit – absolutely the southernmost point of Canada. A 3.2km return forest walkway leads to the point, one of the island's best swimming spots. It's a birdwatcher's Eden with black-crowned night herons and a multitude of shorebirds.

Pelee Island Winery Wine Pavilion   WINERY

(☑ 800-597-3533; www.peleeisland.com; 20 East-West Rd, Pelee Island; special tours adult/child $5/free; ☺10am-6pm Mon-Sat, 11am-5pm Sun May-Oct) Enjoy the fruits of island life at the Pelee Island Winery Wine Pavilion. Regular tours are free at noon, 2pm and 4pm most days; special wine-and-cheese and wine-and-chocolate tours can be scheduled by calling. Check the website for details of its outlet on the mainland.

❏ Tours

Explore Pelee   BIKE TOUR

(☑ 519-724-2285; www.explorepelee.com; tours from $40) Explore Pelee tours will take you from the oldest home through to the canals, pump houses, lighthouse and island graveyard. Wine-tasting combos are available.

⌶ Sleeping & Eating

All accommodations on Pelee Island are seasonal, matching the ferry's operational dates.

Stonehill Bed & Breakfast   B&B $

(☑ 519-724-2193; www.stonehillbandb.com; 911 West Shore Rd, Pelee Island; s/d with shared bathroom $70/85; ☺) Built in 1875 with limestone from the quarry in back, this old farmhouse has waterfront views, a parklike setting and friendly hosts. Cozy bedrooms have patchwork quilts.

Anchor & Wheel Inn   MOTEL, CAMPGROUND $$

(☑ 519-724-2195; www.anchorwheelinn.com; 11 West Shore Rd; unpowered/powered campsites $20/35, d $85-115, cottage from $150; ☺✳) The effervescent Anchor & Wheel in the northwest corner of Pelee has a range of beds from grassy campsites through to air-conditioned guest rooms with Jacuzzis and a dockside cottage.

Wandering Pheasant Inn   INN $$

(☑ 519-724-2270; www.thewanderingpheasantinn.com; 1060 E West Rd, Pelee Island; d incl breakfast $115-175) The most southern inn in Canada occupies 1 hectare on the island's eastern shore. With no streetlights in sight, it's easy to watch the magical fireflies. There are 15 simple rooms and a hot tub. No kids.

Conorlee's Bakery & Delicatessen BAKERY $
([icon] 519-724-2321; rickolte.wix.com/bakery; 5 Northshore Dr; sandwiches $5-7; [icon] 7:30am-3pm) Conorlee's bakes fresh breads, cakes, pizzas and pies, brews espresso and sells local honey. Grab a sandwich and eat it on the beach.

 Drinking & Nightlife

Scudder Beach Bar & Grill BAR
([icon] 519-724-2902; www.scudderbeach.com; 325 North Shore Rd; mains $8-16; [icon] noon-10pm May-Sep) This woody bar room serves wraps and sandwiches plus gallons of cold beer; there might be a live band on a Saturday night.

 Information

For information on Leamington, go to www.tourismleamington.com or look for the Big Tomato on Talbot St.

All there is to know about Pelee Island can be found at www.pelee.org. Book ferries and accommodations in advance. There's an ATM at Scudder Beach Bar & Grill but it can run out of money on busy weekends! Bring cash.

Getting There & Around

From Leamington (and sometimes Kingsville), **Ontario Ferries** ([icon] 519-326-2154; www.ontarioferries.com; adult/child/concession $7.50/3.75/6.25, car/bicycle/motorcycle $16.50/3.75/8.25; [icon] Apr–mid-Dec) services the island. Schedules depend on the day and season; reservations essential. The trip takes 1½ hours each way. Ferries also connect Pelee with Sandusky, Ohio. In winter, forget it.

Bicycles can be rented at **Comfortech Bicycle Rentals** ([icon] 519-724-2828; www.comfortechbikerental.com; West Shore Rd, Pelee Island; per hr/day $8/20; [icon] May-Oct) near the West Dock.

Port Stanley

A working fishing village in a nook of Kettle Creek, **Port Stanley** (www.portstanley.net) has a pretty downtown and an agreeable, unpretentious atmosphere: the kind of place where people talk to you in the streets.

Rail buffs and the young at heart will enjoy **Port Stanley Terminal Rail** ([icon] 877-244-4478; www.pstr.on.ca; 309 Bridge St; adult/child $15/9), a 14km section of the historic London–Port Stanley railroad. The schedule varies: check the website for details.

SMOKE GETS IN YOUR EYES

The flat, sandy soils of northern Norfolk County between Port Stanley and Port Dover provide ideal growing conditions. What used to be a strictly tobacco-growing area now also supports hemp and ginseng fields. For a sniff of old 'baccy, take Hwy 3 inland to the **Delhi Tobacco Museum & Heritage Centre** ([icon] 519-582-0278; www.delhimuseum.ca; 200 Talbot Rd, Delhi; admission by donation; [icon] 10am-4:30pm Mon-Fri, 1-4pm Sat & Sun Jun-Aug), a wooden-crate, leaf-filled multicultural museum with displays on the local history of tobacco production.

The **Port Stanley Festival Theatre** ([icon] 519-782-4353; www.portstanleytheatre.ca; 302 Bridge St) keeps locals and visitors amused over its summer season.

If the pace endears you, consider staying at the **Inn on the Harbour** ([icon] 519-782-7623; www.innontheharbour.ca; 202 Main St; d $129-239; [icons]) where you can watch fishing boats come and go from this upmarket, maritime-hewn inn.

Port Dover & Around

Port Dover is a summer-centric beach town with a sandy, laid-back vibe. Sunburned midlifers, bikini-clad teens and ice-cream-dripping kids patrol the main drag on summer vacation. **Port Dover Visitors Centre** ([icon] 519-583-1314; www.portdover.ca; 19 Market St W, Port Dover; [icon] 10am-5pm) can help with accommodations and loan bicycles for free. The **Port Dover Harbour Museum** ([icon] 519-583-2660; www.portdovermuseum.ca; 44 Harbour St, Port Dover; admission by donation; [icon] 11am-6pm) is a reconstructed fishing shack focusing on the Lake Erie fishing industry and the exploits of local sea-dog Captain Alexander McNeilledge ('Wear no specks, use no tobacco, take a wee dram as necessary'). The most central beds in town are at the white-walled **Erie Beach Hotel** ([icon] 519-583-1391; www.eriebeachhotel.com; 19 Walker St, Port Dover; d $90-110; [icons]). Kitschy rooms overlook impossibly perfect lawns, while the pubby dining rooms obsess over perch and shrimp (mains $10 to $20).

If you head southwest along the coast you'll first come to the excellent **Turkey**

Point Provincial Park (☑519-426-3239; www.ontarioparks.com; 194 Turkey Point Rd, Turkey Point; unpowered/powered campsites $28/33, admission per car $11; ☺May-Oct). Here, forests teem with bird nerds and nature lovers. Around 30km further southwest, **Long Point Provincial Park** (☑519-586-2133; www.ontarioparks.com; 350 Erie Blvd, Port Rowan; unpowered/powered campsites $28/33, admission per car $11; ☺May-Oct) occupies a sandy spit jagging into the lake, great for swimming.

MUSKOKA LAKES

The city of Barrie marks the end of Toronto's suburban sprawl and the gateway to the Muskoka Lakes region. Although pleasant, lakeside Barrie can feel like just another Toronto suburb at times. It's worth stopping at the large **Ontario Travel Information Centre** (☑800-668-2746, 705-725-7280; 21 Maple View Dr; ☺8am-8pm) along Hwy 400 as you approach the lakes to arm yourself with maps and brochures.

The Muskoka Lakes (or just Muskoka) is a broader name for the region comprising Lakes Muskoka, Rosseau and Joseph, among many smaller others. Originally rich in lumber production and shipbuilding, the area is now at the heart of 'cottage country': a popular place for families to enjoy the water and, for many, to retire. Schedule a few days to explore the beauty and serenity of this forested, watery region, particularly delightful in the fall. Ontario's most extravagant cottages are here, many in the fabulous 'Millionaires' Row' on Lake Muskoka.

There's limited public transportation in the region, which is best explored by car: www.discovermuskoka.ca/suggested-driving-tours. Note that Friday northbound traffic (from Toronto) and southbound Sunday traffic on Hwy 400 can be a nightmare from May to October.

Orillia

Orillia proudly sits at the northern end of Lake Simcoe, which pours into Lake Couchiching. Neither are technically part of the Muskoka Lakes, but are major stops along the Trent-Severn Waterway. Triangular sails and grumbling motorboats clutter the harbor, while drivers turn off Hwy 11 for a stroll down time-warped Mississauga St, Orillia's main drag.

⊙ Sights & Activities

Leacock Museum   MUSEUM
(☑705-329-1908; www.leacockmuseum.com; 50 Museum Dr; adult/child $5/2; ☺9am-5pm Mon-Sat) In 1928, Canadian humorist Stephen Leacock built a lavish waterfront house that has since become the Leacock Museum. In July the museum hosts the **Leacock Summer Festival**, a well-regarded literary festival.

Coldwater Canadiana Heritage Museum   MUSEUM
(☑705-955-1930; www.coldwatermuseum.com; 1474 Woodrow Rd, Coldwater; admission by donation; ☺10am-4pm Mon-Sat, from 1pm Sun late May-Oct) West of Orillia on Hwy 12 before it connects with Hwy 400, you'll find this charming riverside folk museum with its sweet collection of colonial buildings tracing the history of village life from 1830 to 1950.

Island Princess   CRUISE
(☑705-325-2628; www.orilliacruises.com; ☺Jun-Oct) Orillia offers a variety of sightseeing cruises on the *Island Princess,* though Penetanguishene and Parry Sound have more picturesque cruising options. There are up to four cruises daily here in July and August. Lunch and dinner cruises require advance booking: check the website for cruise types, schedules and fares.

🛏 Sleeping & Eating

Cranberry House   B&B $
(☑866-876-5885, 705-326-6871; www.orillia.org/cranberryhouse; 25 Dalton Cres S; r from $95) This B&B sits on a quiet street that feels a lot like the set for the TV show *The Wonder Years.* Every house seems tidy and welcoming, and Cranberry House is no exception. Rooms have en suite bathrooms.

Stone Gate Inn   HOTEL $$
(☑705-329-2535, 877-674-5542; www.stonegateinn.com; 437 Laclie St; r incl breakfast from $132; ❄️🛜🏊) It's the extra perks that set this modern inn apart from the rest: a swimming pool, full business center, hors d'oeuvres over the weekend and bathrobes in the rooms.

Webers Hamburgers   BURGERS $
(☑705-325-3696; www.webers.com; Hwy 11; hamburgers $4.79; ☺10:30am-late) Just 12km north of Orillia on Hwy 11, this legendary charcoal barbecued burger joint lures passers-by with cheap eats and a shmancy sky bridge to nab commuters on the other side. Endless lines of lip-lickers form salivating over greasy treats.

Mariposa Market
MARKET **$**
(🖋 705-325-8885; www.mariposamarket.ca; 109 Mississauga St E; items from $2; ⊗ 8am-5pm) This half-bakery, half-knickknack shack is a feast for the eyes and the tastebuds. Try the assortment of savory pastries for a light lunch, grab a dessert then shop for souvenirs.

☆ Entertainment

Casino Rama
CASINO
(🖋 705-329-3325; www.casinorama.com; 5899 Rama Rd; ⊗ 24hr) Glitzy Casino Rama is also a main stage on the touring entertainment circuit. A courtesy shuttle links many accommodations to the frenzy.

Orillia Opera House
PERFORMING ARTS
(🖋 705-326-8011; www.orilliaoperahouse.ca; 20 Mississauga St W) The turreted Orillia Opera House hosts a variety of productions including the likes of *Cats* and *Oklahoma!*

❶ Getting There & Away
Greyhound Canada provides services between Orillia and Toronto ($31.25, 2½ hours, four daily). **Ontario Northland** (www.ontarionorthland. ca) also offers passenger services ($27.75, two hours, four daily).

Gravenhurst
While nearby Bracebridge is favored among visitors, Gravenhurst is coming into its own. Check out Muskoka Wharf, a post-millennial waterfont development including shops, restaurants, condos, a farmers bazaar and a museum.

◉ Sights

Muskoka Boat & Heritage Centre
MUSEUM
(🖋 705-687-2115; www.realmuskoka.com; 275 Steamboat Bay Rd; adult/child $7/2; ⊗ 10am-4pm Tue-Sat) This museum tells the region's rich history of steamships and hoteliers with displays of over 20 wooden vessels. Also here, you'll find two ships: the *Segwun*, the oldest operating steamship in North America, and the *Wenonah II*, a new cruiser with an old-school design. In a past life, the *Segwun* was a mail ship serving secluded Muskoka enclaves. A variety of cruises are available; check the website for details.

Bethune Memorial House
HISTORIC BUILDING
(🖋 705-687-4261; www.pc.gc.ca/bethune; 297 John St N; adult/child $3.90/1.90; ⊗ 10am-4pm Tue-Sat Jun-Oct) This small museum honors Canadian doctor Norman Bethune who spent much of his life in China as a surgeon and educator. Bethune set up the world's first mobile blood-transfusion clinic while in Spain during the Spanish Revolution.

☞ Tours

Muskoka Autumn Studio Tour
ART TOUR
(www.muskokaautumnstudiotour.com) For over 35 years, each September, local artists open their studio doors to the public.

✦ Festivals & Events

Music on the Barge
MUSIC
(www.musiconthebarge.webs.com; Gull Lake Park; admission by donation) In summer, thousands flock to hear big-band numbers, jazz or country. Concerts start at 7:30pm each Sunday from late June to late August.

🛏 Sleeping & Eating

Residence Inn Muskoka Wharf
HOTEL **$$**
(🖋 705-687-6600; www.marriott.com; 285 Steamship Bay Rd; d/ste incl breakfast from $125/$155; ❄🛜🏊) If you want to be by the water, it's hard to get closer than this hulking new property in the Muskoka Wharf complex, offering large, freshly decorated studios and suites with full kitchens, separate living and sleeping areas and generous bathrooms. Some have balconies and lake views. Rates spike in peak periods.

★ Taboo Resort
RESORT **$$$**
(🖋 705-687-2233; www.tabooresort.com; 1209 Muskoka Beach Rd; d from $199; ❄🛜🏊) Finally, a boutique Ontario property with international appeal. Occupying a stunning lake frontage on a compact peninsula, Taboo's hotel rooms and suites have clean, minimalist lines, gray and maple woods and slick bathrooms with Molton Brown amenities. Tri-level chalets are perfect if you're bringing the kids: they'll disappear into kids' clubs so you can enjoy a cocktail by the pool, a round of golf or the fabulous cuisine.

Blue Willow Tea Shop
TEAHOUSE **$**
(🖋 705-687-2597; www.bluewillowteashop.ca; 900 Bay St; high tea $23, meals $8-24; ⊗ 10am-4pm Mon-Wed, to 8pm Thu-Sat, noon-4pm Sun) This lovely waterfront tearoom serves high tea daily from 2pm. There's a limited dinner menu with British staples like bangers and mash and fish and chips.

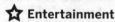

Pizza Station
PIZZERIA $

(🖉705-687-3111; 415 Bethune Dr N; small pizzas from $6; ☺noon-3pm & 6-11pm) Locals swear by this nondescript pizza joint for its steaming-hot cheesy goodness with just the right amount of toppings and a crispy crunchy crust. Take out and eat by the water.

☆ Entertainment

Gravenhurst Opera House
THEATER

(🖉705-687-5550; www.gravenhurstoperahouse. com; 295 Muskoka Rd S) This charming heritage building presents a summer season of professional theater.

❶ Information

Gravenhurst Chamber of Commerce (🖉705-687-4432; www.gravenhurstchamber.com; 685 Muskoka Rd N; ☺8:30am-5pm Mon-Fri, 9am-noon Sat) Located on the edge of town. Additional information can be found at www. gravenhurst.ca.

❶ Getting There & Away

Ontario Northland (www.ontarionorthland.ca) runs buses between Toronto and Gravenhurst ($36.45, three hours, four to five daily) on the North Bay route, which pull in to the Gravenhurst Train Station. Since late 2012, trains no longer serve the region.

Bracebridge

Woodsy Bracebridge sits on the 45th parallel, halfway between the North Pole and the equator! This enchanting town reveals its natural charms throughout the year, with towering evergreens, gushing waterfalls and brilliant maples.

◉ Sights

Waterfalls
WATERFALL

Near the visitors center you'll find the best known of Bracebridge's 22 waterfalls, Bracebridge Falls. Other favorites include Muskoka South Falls (33m), about 6km south of town, Wilson's Falls and High Falls, both to the north.

Muskoka Brewery
BREWERY

(🖉705-646-1266; www.muskokabrewery.com; 13 Taylor Rd; ☺11am-5pm Mon-Sat, to 4pm Sun) Muskoka Brewery bottles some delicious flavors including a cream ale and a couple of lagers. In summer, free taste-testing tours depart 12:30pm to 3:30pm on the half-hour Thursday to Saturday.

☞ Tours

Lady Muskoka
BOAT TOUR

(🖉705-646-2628, 800-263-5239; www.lady-muskoka.com; cruises adult/child from $29/14; ☺May-Oct) Muskoka's largest cruise ship takes in the beauty of Lake Muskoka, including jaw-dropping 'Millionaires Row' where the other half relax. A variety of sailings including brunch cruises are available. Check the website for schedules and fares.

⬛ Sleeping & Eating

Wellington Motel
MOTEL $$

(🖉705-645-2238; www.wellingtonmotel.com; 265 Wellington St; r $80-120, ste $140; ✳) This tidy, centrally located redbrick motel is retro but clean. Rooms have fridge, microwave and huge bathrooms. Suites come with full kitchens.

Inn at the Falls
HOTEL $$

(🖉877-645-9212, 705-645-2245; www.innatthefalls.net; 1 Dominion St; d $109-205; ✳🐾) Iron lanterns, antique candelabras, portraits and picket fences uphold the 1870s vibe of this local landmark, with its grand main building and six cottages. It's a popular wedding spot. Suites have charming decor and gargantuan beds that feel like boats. The on-site gourmet pub has a stunning patio surrounded by tiered gardens overlooking the bay.

Old Station
PUB $$

(🖉705-645-9776; www.oldstation.ca; 88 Manitoba St; mains $12-35; ☺11am-10pm) On summer evenings this is the most happening place in town. The patio overlooks the main drag – perfect for post-kayak recovery sessions. Dig into a pulled-pork sandwich and wash it back with a pint of Muskoka ale from the brewery just over the road.

Riverwalk
MEDITERRANEAN $$$

(🖉705-646-0711; www.riverwalkrestaurant.ca; 1 Manitoba St; lunch mains $12-18, dinner $28-37; ☺11:30am-2:30pm & 5:30-7:30pm Tue-Sat) Tear your eyes away from the view to focus on the menu, if you can. You'll need to choose between pork, chicken, duck, veal, beef, lamb or seafood. Reservations recommended.

❶ Information

Bracebridge Visitors Centre (🖉705-645-8121, 866-645-8121; 1 Manitoba St; ☺9am-5pm Mon-Fri, from 10am Sat, noon-4pm Sun Jun-Aug) Open year round.

ℹ Getting There & Away

Ontario Northland (www.ontarionorthland. ca) buses connect Bracebridge with Toronto ($39.30, three hours, four to five daily) on the North Bay route.

Rosseau & Port Carling

You'll pass through sleepy Rosseau on a Discover Muskoka self-driving tour: www. discovermuskoka.ca/suggested-driving-tours. It's a quaint little village with a small beach, a historic library, a few antique shops and one or two cafes. It's your closest village if you choose to stay in Muskoka's newest 'buzz' resort, the **Rosseau** (JW Marriott Resort & Spa; ✆705-765-1900; www.therosseau. com; 1050 Paignton House Rd, Minett; d/ste from $199/249): ideal for couples with kids and/or money, it's the kind of place where Mom and Dad can swim by the pool while the youngsters ramble on guided nature walks. Dining is limited to the resort's expensive offerings. Suites have kitchens, but cost a small fortune. In short, it's huge, handsome and has it all, but isn't for everyone.

North of Bracebridge along Rte 118, in wealthy Port Carling, is a fantastic **mural** of an old ship. A closer glance reveals that the mural is actually a mosaic of vintage photographs: truly remarkable. Muskoka's majestic beauty serves as an inspiring backdrop for many other artists in the region. Contact the **Arts Council of Muskoka** (www.artscouncilofmuskoka.com) for more information.

Huntsville

Pretty Huntsville, Muskoka's largest town, set among twisting lakes and furry pines, is the gateway to Algonquin Provincial Park in eastern Ontario. Base yourself here for day trips to the park, around Muskoka, or before setting off on an Algonquin adventure, although you'll have to have your own wheels. At time of writing, there was no longer scheduled public transport between Huntsville and the park.

◉ Sights

Muskoka Heritage Place MUSEUM
(✆705-789-7576; www.muskokaheritageplace. org; 88 Brunel Rd; adult/child $16/11; ⊙May-Oct) Come here for a historic perspective of the region, which includes an authentic pioneer village, several informative museums and

a working steam train from 1902 (departs several times per day; rides included in admission).

✯ Festivals & Events

Festival of the Arts ARTS
(www.huntsvillefestival.on.ca) Music, films and general celebrations of the arts held year-round.

🛏 Sleeping

Huntsville Inn MOTEL $
(✆866-222-8525; www.hunstvilleinn.com; 19 King William St; d from $50; ✻ 🔊) In a prime location by the bridge, fully refurbished rooms with flatscreen TVs and free wi-fi offer excellent value.

Au Petit Dormeur INN $$
(✆705-789-2552; www.aupetitdormeur.com; 22 Main St W; d $80-100; ✻ 🔊) Set in a beautiful colonial home, rooms are stylish – there's even a fitness facility. Breakfast can be taken on the balcony overlooking the nearby lake.

Hidden Valley Resort RESORT $$
(✆705-789-2301; www.hvmuskoka.com; 1755 Valley Rd; d from $115; ✻) Most of the well-proportioned, recently refurbished rooms in this '90s style resort have a balcony with a wonderful vista of the lake and expansive well-tended grounds. There's a restaurant with a fabulous patio, outdoor and indoor pools and even a small ski-hill nearby. It's 8km north of Huntsville.

Sunset Inn Motel MOTEL $$
(✆866-874-5360, 705-789-4414; www.sunsetinnmotel.com; 69 Main St W; d incl breakfast from $115; ✻ 🔊) In a nice hillside spot near the train station, this quality lakeside motel provides breakfast in a sunny common room.

🍴 Eating & Drinking

★ That Little Place by the Lights ITALIAN $
(✆705-789-2536; www.thatlittleplacebythelights. ca; 76 Main St E; meals $6-14; ⊙11am-8pm Mon-Sat) A local favorite, this little place by the lights is loved for its old-school pizzas, pastas and gelati. Excellent value.

Louis' II DINER $
(✆705-789-5704; 24 Main St E; items $6-18; ⊙8am-8pm) This pleasant family diner is great for cheap breakfasts and cheery lunches like old-school BLTs, burgers and souvlaki. Daily specials.

Bo's Authentic Thai
THAI $$

(📞705-789-8038; www.bothai.ca; 79 Main St E; mains $10-19; ⊙11am-9pm; 🖋) As the name suggests, authentic Thai dishes (although only with English names on the menu) are presented with flair in this new joint by the water. Vegetarian options are available.

Mill on Main
MODERN CANADIAN $$

(📞705-788-5150; www.themillonmain.ca; 50 Main St E; mains $12-26; ⊙11am-10pm) Try the famous cheese balls – you won't regret it. With a lovely covered patio glimpsing the water and some classy original twists on old favorites, the Mill is a good spot for a casual meal or a few drinks. There's sometimes live music on weekends.

On the Docks
PUB

(📞705-789-7910; www.onthedockspub.com; 90 Main St E; items $6-14; ⊙11:30am-1am) Swing by for tasty wraps, appys and sandwiches on the fantastic multi-level water-view patio.

Cottage Bar and Grill
BAR

(📞705-789-6842; www.huntsvillecottage.com; 7 John St; ⊙11am-10pm) The sprawling waterfront patio gets packed in the summer, but you can't beat the location for a beer and a burger in the sunshine. There's live local music, most nights.

ℹ Information

Chamber of Commerce (📞705-789-1751; www.huntsville.ca; 8 West St N; ⊙9am-5pm Mon-Fri, 10am-3pm Sat) Loaded with local info.

ℹ Getting There & Away

Ontario Northland (www.ontarionorthland.ca) buses from Toronto ($39.30, three hours, four to five daily) continue to North Bay.

GEORGIAN BAY

A vast realm of blues and greens, Georgian Bay is a land of infinite dreaming. Summer breezes blow gently along sandy shores. Maples ignite in the fall and thick pines quiver at winter's frosty kiss. These ethereal landscapes inspired Canada's best-known painters and today the bay remains home to scores of thriving artistic communities.

We begin our journey on its eastern shore in Parry Sound, at the northern fringe of Muskoka, then trace the shoreline south to Midland, with its spectacular murals, and to pretty Penetanguishine. In the bay's southern arc sits Wasaga Beach, the longest freshwater beach in the world: a summer sizzler. Neighboring Collingwood and Blue Mountain are home to the province's most popular downhill and cross-country skiing in the winter.

Heading north on its western shore from Owen Sound, the magnificent Bruce Peninsula is famed for its jagged limestone outcrops, shimmering cliffs and craggy beaches. At the Bruce's tip, tiny Tobermory offers some of Ontario's most spectacular scenery and a relaxed alternative vibe, but be prepared to share it. A pleasant sail on the Chi-Cheemaun ferry brings you to the beauty of sparsely populated Manitoulin Island, believed by many First Nations to be the home of the Great Spirit. Linger here for a few days if you can.

Parry Sound

Formerly a busy shipping port, little Parry Sound is gently tucked behind hundreds of tiny islands in Georgian Bay. The atmosphere is laid-back and serene, despite the giant set of railroad tracks soaring through the sky near the docks.

⊙ Sights & Activities

Bobby Orr Hall of Fame
MUSEUM

(📞877-746-4466; www.bobbyorrhalloffame.com; 2 Bay St; adult/child $9/6; ⊙10am-5pm Tue-Sat, from 11am Sun) For the uninitiated, local legend and hockey hero Bobby Orr forever changed the role of defensemen with his huge modern shrine, fans can pretend to be a sports announcer or strap on goalie gear and confront an automated puck-firing machine.

White Squall
KAYAKING

(📞705-342-5324; www.whitesquall.com; 53 Carling Bay Rd, Nobel; rentals from $30, day tours from $120; ⊙9am-5:30pm Apr-Oct) Explore the area's waterways with rental kayaks and guided tours: friendly staff offer a range of programs. Check the website for details. HQ is about 15km northwest of Parry Sound near Nobel, en route to Killbear Provincial Park.

Island Queen
CRUISE

(📞800-506-2628; www.island-queen.com; 9 Bay St; 2hr cruise adult/child $28/14, 3hr cruise $38/19; ⊙Jun-Oct) Cruise through the nearby 30,000 islands (yes, that's right!) on the

Georgian Bay

good ship *Island Queen*. A variety of sailings are available.

MV Chippewa III   CRUISE
(☑888-283-5870, 705-746-6064; www.spiritofthe-sound.ca; Seguin River Parkette, Bay St; ☺Jun-Oct) Lunch and dinner cruises are among the variety of options aboard this tiny green tugboat. Check the website for fares and schedules.

⭐ Festivals & Events

Festival of the Sound   MUSIC
(www.festivalofthesound.ca) Parry Sound hosts a nationally renowned festival of classical music from mid-July to mid-August. Ticket prices vary.

🛏 Sleeping & Eating

Area B&Bs can be found on www.parry-soundbb.com.

Bayside Inn   B&B $$
(☑866-833-8864, 705-746-7720; www.psbaysideinn.com; 10 Gibson St; r $93-143; ✿❊@) Built in the 1880s as a luxurious private residence, this refurbished estate is full of pleasant surprises: a twisting staircase behind the fireplace and 12 beautiful bedrooms with memory-foam mattresses. All have en suite

bathrooms and are decorated in soothing colors.

Mad Hatter Café   CAFE $
(35 Seguin St; items $6-12; ☺7am-4pm Mon-Fri, from 8:30am Sat, 10am-3pm Sun) Bustling and cheerful, this place has excellent coffee and baked goods to have you grinning like the Cheshire cat.

Wellington's   PUB $$
(105 James St; mains $9-20; ☺11am-11pm) Wellington's is the 'light beer' of pubs – it looks like a bar, but it's healthier for you. The menu has some calorie-conscious options like pecan chicken.

ℹ Information

Georgian Bay Country Visitors Centre
(☑705-746-1287; www.gbcountry.com; 70 Church St; ☺9am-5pm Mon-Fri) At the former train station.

ℹ Getting There & Away

Ontario Northland (www.ontarionorthland.ca) buses connect Parry Sound with Toronto ($52.40, 3½ hours, three daily) on the Sudbury route.

THE BUZZ ON BLACK FLIES

From the spring thaw until there's been at least three weeks of hot summer weather, anywhere north of Toronto is subject to minor plagues of black flies, mosquitoes, deer flies and horseflies. Unlike the pesky mosquito with their pointy stingers, black flies are small and voracious: they actually have teeth that gnaw away at your skin, leaving raised bumps (often scores of them) and frequently causing streaks of blood to suddenly appear on your precious skin. Sounds like a horror film, right? They're generally not as bad as it sounds, but can be. Hardened locals swear by eating leeks for breakfast, lunch and tea, or taking lots of vitamin B to dissuade the bloodthirsty critters, but we find an electrified tennis racquet called 'the Executioner' works just as well. Whatever you do, remember the insect repellent when you're heading north.

Midland & Penetanguishine

The native Huron-Ouendat people first settled the region and developed a confederacy to encourage cooperation among neighboring Aboriginal tribes. This alliance attracted French explorers and Jesuit missionaries eager to save their souls. Much of Midland's fascinating history focuses on the bloody altercations between the Huron and the Christian stalwarts. Midland is also known for the over 30 vibrant murals which have transformed downtown into an outdoor art/history lesson.

Less than 6km up the road, Penetanguishine (pen-uh-tang-wa-sheen) is a small town with a big name that makes a great base for exploring the 30,000 islands that are sprinkled around Georgian Bay. Together, they make a fine day trip or easy weekend away from Toronto.

Sights & Activities

Martyrs' Shrine MONUMENT
(www.martyrs-shrine.com; Hwy 12, Midland; adult/child $4/free; ◎8:30am-9pm May-Oct) This monument to six Jesuit missionaries who met their gruesome demise at the hands of the Huron features a large lawn strewn with crosses and the imposing cathedral-esque Shrine church. Each year, thousands make a pilgrimage here to pay homage to martyred St Jean de Brébeuf.

Ste-Marie among the Hurons HISTORIC SITE
(☎705-526-7838; www.saintemarieamongthe-hurons.on.ca; Hwy 12, Midland; adult/child $10/9; ◎10am-5pm Apr-Oct) Costumed staff members dote on visitors to this reconstruction of the 17th-century Jesuit mission, offering stories about hardship and torture with a cheerful smile.

Huronia Museum & Huron-Ouendat Village MUSEUM
(☎705-526-2844; www.huroniamuseum.com; 549 Little Lake Park Rd, Midland; adult/child $10/6; ◎9am-5pm) The Huronia Museum & Huron-Ouendat Village is a replica of a 500-year-old Huron-Ouendat settlement. The musuem houses a collection of almost a million pieces – not all are on display!

Discovery Harbour MUSEUM
(☎705-549-8064; www.discoveryharbour.on.ca; 93 Jury Dr, Penetanguishine; adult/concession $7.25/6.25; ◎May-Sep) Recommended guided tours of this reconstructed British garrison lead visitors through two replica vessels and recount the fort's history.

Awenda Provincial Park PARK
(☎705-549-2231; Awenda Park Rd; day use per vehicle $12-20, campsites $16-46; ◎May-Oct) About 15km from Penetanguishine, this picturesque park boasts four sandy swimming beaches, 30km of easy walking trails and over 200 species of bird.

MS Georgian Queen CRUISE
(☎800-363-7447, 705-549-7795; www.georgian-baycruises.com; ◎May-Oct) A variety of cruises depart the Penetanguishine town dock; check the website for latest schedules and fares.

Tours

30,000 Island Tours BOAT TOUR
(☎705-549-3388, 888-833-2628; www.mid-landtours.com; 177 King St, Midland; adult/child $27/14; ◎May-Oct) *Miss Midland* isn't a regional beauty pageant, but the name of a vessel: cruise on her daily at 2pm from Midland dock. Lunch and dinner cruises operate July to August.

📖 Sleeping & Eating

Silver Star
MOTEL $

(☎705-526-6571; www.silverstarmotel.ca; 748 Yonge St, Midland; d from $60; ❋🛜) Cheap, cheery, clean and central! Recently renovated rooms have flatscreen TVs and free wi-fi. Best value in town.

Comfort Inn
MOTEL $

(☎705-526-2090; www.comfortinnmidland.com; 980 King St, Midland; d from $79; ❋🛜❅) Drive-up units, good rates and friendly staff win points for this dated but well-maintained motel in a leafy spot about 3km from downtown.

★ Little Lake Inn
B&B $$

(☎888-297-6130; www.littlelakeinn.com; 669 Yonge St, Midland; r $124-175; ❋@🛜) Each room at this modern B&B offers a flat-screen TV, DVD player and whirlpool. Its friendly, welcoming hosts are attentive but not intrusive. The green room has a separate entrance and private outdoor sitting area. True to its name, Midland's 'Little Lake' is out back.

Georgian Terrace
B&B $$

(☎705-549-2440, 888-549-2440; www.georgianterrace.ca; 14 Water St, Penetanguishene; r incl breakfast $150-175; ❇❋🛜) Dramatic pillars front this beautifully restored and updated heritage home. Rooms are elegant without being frilly, have en suite bathroom, wi-fi and flatscreen TVs.

Ciboulette et cie
DELI $

(☎705-245-0410; www.cibouletteetcie.ca; 248 King St, Midland; items from $6; ⊙8am-6pm Mon-Sat, 10am-4pm Sun) This gourmet deli/cafe is stocked to the hilt with fine foods, cold meats, cheeses, freshly made soups and sauces. The cafe serves great coffees and light meals, and there's a range of products to go: perfect for a lakeside picnic.

★ Captain Ken's Diner
FISH & CHIPS $$

(☎705-549-8691; www.captainkensdiner.com; 70 Main St, Penetanguishene; mains $10-25; ⊙7am-9pm) Come say hello to Ken as he fries your lightly battered fresh lake pickerel to perfection. He got a part-time job here at 14 when it was a pool hall, bought the joint at 17 and over decades turned it into the smoothly operating fish, chips and sports-bar success story it is today. The food is as good as the story.

Explorer's Cafe
INTERNATIONAL $$

(☎705-527-9199; www.theexplorerscafe.com; 345 King St, Midland; mains $14-30; ⊙11:30am-10pm) This quirky restaurant remains a favorite: its walls are lined with booty from around the world. While meals are just as international (Singapore noodles, Argentine steak and maple chipotle salmon), only local produce is used in their creation.

Cellarman's Ale House
PUB $$

(☎705-526-8223; 337 King St, Midland; mains $8-25; ⊙11:30am late) This cozy pub has an intimate location, tucked away off King St. Hearty British fare keeps the locals strong during drafty winters: try a scotch egg with your steak and mushroom pie. Mmm.

☆ Entertainment

King's Wharf Theatre
THEATER

(☎888-449-4463; www.kingswharftheatre.com; 93 Jury Dr, Penetanguishine; ⊙May-Sep) Hosts small-town productions of big-name musicals from its wonderful wooden lakeside theater.

ℹ Information

Southern Georgian Bay Chamber of Commerce (☎705-526-7884; www.southern-georgianbay.on.ca; 208 King St, Midland; ⊙9am-5pm Mon-Fri) Produces the *Southern Georgian Bay Visitor Guidebook*: download it from the website.

Tourist office (☎705-549-2232; 2 Main St, Penetanguishine; ⊙9am-5pm May-Oct) You can't miss this seasonal office on the docks.

ℹ Getting There & Around

There are no direct buses from Toronto to the area. Greyhound Canada buses connect Barrie with Midland and Penetanguishine ($17.50, one hour, two daily). **Central Taxi** (☎705-526-2626; www.centraltaximidland.ca) can take you between Midland and Penetanguishene if you don't have wheels.

Collingwood & Blue Mountain

Pretty lakeside Collingwood and neighboring Blue Mountain, a handsome ski resort and summer playground, have become a year-round mecca for those who enjoy activity with their scenery. The area is called Blue Mountains, the resort is called Blue Mountain. If healthy outdoorsy

WASAGA: WORLD'S LONGEST FRESHWATER BEACH

It's true, the 14km stretch of sand at **Wasaga Beach Provincial Park** (☏705-429-2516; day use per vehicle $15; ☉May-Oct) is the longest *freshwater* beach in the world. It's also the closest beach town to Toronto, drawing mega-crowds in summer: things can get rowdy and camping is prohibited. In winter pristine sand dunes transform into snowy hills, perfect for cross-country skiing. There are plenty of beds in town, but most are basic and expensive. Hit www.wasaga.com for the full listing. Greyhound operates services from Toronto to Wasaga Beach ($39, 2½ hours, twice daily).

pursuits aren't your thang, why not sink your teeth into the Apple Pie Trail (www.applepietrail.ca), then slip into a blissful food coma.

🏃 Activities

★ Blue Mountain
SKIING
(☏705-445-0231; www.bluemountain.ca; 108 Jozo Weider Blvd, Blue Mountains; day & night lift ticket adult/concession $72/55; ☉9am-10pm) Hands down the best skiing and snowboarding in Ontario, from the folks who brought you Whistler and Mont-Tremblant: freestyle terrain, half-pipes, jump-on jump-off rails, 16 lifts and over 35 runs from beginner to double black diamond. The Blue Mountain Snow School offers a variety of lessons for all experience levels. Courses including day lift pass, rentals and instruction start at $79. In summer activities abound, including mountain biking, sailing, climbing, hiking and windsurfing.

Free Spirit Tours
ADVENTURE SPORTS
(☏519-599-2268, 705-444-3622; www.freespirittours.com; 236720 Grey Rd 13, Heathcote; activities from $45) Escape the crowds and enjoy a sensational day rock climbing, caving or kayaking (summer) or take a stab at snowshoeing in the winter. Check the website for details.

Scanidnave Spa
SPA
(☏705-443-8484; www.scandinave.com/en/blue-mountain; 152 Grey Rd 21, Blue Mountains; baths $48; ☉10am-9pm) Indulge yourself silly whatever the season in this fine Scandinavian-style treatment spa featuring hot baths, cold baths, waterfalls, snow-rolling (winter only) and saunas. It's $10 cheaper on Wednesdays. Book in advance.

🎭 Festivals & Events

Elvis Festival
PERFORMING ARTS
(www.collingwoodelvisfestival.com) Since 1995, every July, Collingwood becomes a sea of Elvises in this, one of the largest competitions for Elvis impersonators in the world.

Wakestock
SPORTS
(www.wakestock.com) In August, young wakeboarders descend on Collingwood with their expensive toys for this loud festival of action sports and music.

🛏 Sleeping & Eating

Rates can spike dramatically in this year-round destination. Retiree-friendly Collingwood has plenty of decent dining options around Hurontario St, and Hwy 26 is lined with fast-food chains.

Theme-park-esque Blue Mountain Village has some satisfying though unspectacular selections.

Mariner Motor Hotel
MOTEL $
(☏705-445-3330; 305 Hume St, Collingwood; d from $89; 🐾) Who would have thought a piece of the great architect Frank Lloyd Wright's legacy would end up as a roadside motel in Collingwood. Basic, retro and even a little awkward, we just love the authenticity of this place.

Blue Mountain Inn
HOTEL $$
(☏877-445-0231, 705-445-0231; www.bluemountain.ca; 110 Jozo Weider Blvd; r $89-499; ❋@☈) Accommodations range from standard guest rooms to upscale mosaic three-bedroom suites, all of which have seen a facelift in recent years. Check the website for the wide variety of options: rates can vary dramatically.

Days Inn & Suites
MOTEL $$
(☏705-444-1880; www.daysinncollingwood.com; 15 Cambridge St, Collingwood; d from $109) Midway between Collingwood and Blue Mountain, this 76-room chain motel is well maintained by professional staff. Neutrally furnished rooms have microwaves. There's a guest laundry on-site. Fireplace and jacuzzi suites are available.

★ Westin Trillium House
RESORT $$$

([☎705-443-8080; www.westinbluemountain. com; 220 Gord Canning Dr, Blue Mountains; d/ste from $189/239) Couple-friendly, pet-friendly and family friendly, this Westin upholds its brand's reputation for excellence in service. A wide range of guest rooms and suites are all luxuriously furnished and most overlook the Blue Mountain Village, pond or outdoor pools. Experiment with your dates for the best rates and packages.

Grandma Lambe's
MARKET $

(Hwy 26; ⊗8am-6pm Sat-Thu, to 7pm Fri) You won't regret the 35km trek to Grandma Lambe's (west on Hwy 26 between Thornbury and Meaford). The store is a delicious jumble of maple-syrup vintages, butter tarts, bushels of vegetables and tables piled high with pies, buns and jellies.

Café Chartreuse
CAFE $$

([☎705-444-0099; www.cafechartreuse.com; 70 Hurontario St, Collingwood; meals $8-18; ⊗8am-5pm Wed-Mon) Pancakes with warm maple butter, sandwiches on fresh-baked bread: these French-trained chefs have got it right. Stay and sample the ever-changing menu, or take a spinach spanakopita or savory tart to go.

Tremont Cafe
EUROPEAN $$$

([☎705-293-6000; www.thetremontcafe.com; 80 Simcoe St, Collingwood; mains $16-36; ⊗11am-3pm & 5:30-9:30pm Wed-Mon) Come for a mouthwatering weekend brunch or classic dinner at this delightful fine-dining cafe in the historic Tremont building. Will you have the duck confit or Atlantic salmon after your lamb lollipops? Dinner menus change regularly.

ℹ Information

Georgian Triangle Tourism Association
([☎705-445-7722; www.visitsouthgeorgianbay. ca; 45 St Paul St, Collingwood; ⊗9am-5pm) Pop in to get inspired about this wonderful region.

ℹ Getting There & Around

Greyhound Canada has limited services from Toronto to Collingwood ($42, three hours, two daily) continuing to Owen Sound ($24, 1½ hours, two daily).From December to April, **AUC Tours** ([☎416-741-5200; www.auctours.com) operates a shuttle from Toronto to Blue Mountain. Refer to the website for rates and online bookings.

Ace Cabs ([☎705-445-0300, 705-445-3300) can drive you between Collingwood and Blue Mountain ($20, 15 minutes).

Bruce Peninsula

The Bruce is a 100km limestone outcrop of craggy shorelines and green woodlands at the northern end of the Niagara Escarpment. The fingerlike protrusion separates the cooler crystal waters of Georgian Bay from warmer Lake Huron. Owen Sound is the largest regional center, while delightful Tobermory is the reward at the tip of the peninsula. Visit www.explorethebruce.com for the latest.

Owen Sound

Owen Sound has a sordid past as a port rife with booze and prostitution. Things got so out of hand that alcohol was banned here for over 60 years – hard to believe, today. By the time the embargo was lifted in 1972, the town had transformed into a thriving artists' colony and remains so today: check out the **Owen Sound Artist's Co-op** (www.osartists-co-op.com; 279 10th St E; ⊗9:30am-5:30pm Mon-Sat, noon-4pm Sun) when you're in town.

⊙ Sights

Tom Thomson Art Gallery
MUSEUM

([☎519-376-1932; www.tomthomson.org; 840 1st Ave W; adult/child $5/3; ⊗11am-5pm Mon-Fri, noon-5pm Sat & Sun) This gallery displays the work of Tom Thomson, granddaddy of modern Canadian landscape painting. His intimate and smoldering portrayal of nature is said to have inspired the formation of the Group of Seven painters. Thomson grew up near Owen Sound and many of his works were composed in nearby thickets of fall leaves.

Grey Roots Museum & Archives
MUSEUM

([☎519-376-3690; www.greyroots.com; 102599 Grey Rd 18, RR 4; adult/child $8/4; ⊗10am-5pm) This interesting museum highlights the region's rich pioneering history through displays about early settlers and local heroes. Interactive presentations focus on natural resources, climate and topography. Past exhibits have explored themes as diverse as Albertan dinosaurs and the history of the toilet.

Billy Bishop Heritage Museum
MUSEUM

([☎519-371-3333; www.billybishop.org; 948 3rd Ave W; adult/child $5/2; ⊗11am-5pm Tue-Fri, noon-5pm Sat & Sun) Hometown hero William Avery ('Billy') Bishop, Canada's notorious flying ace in WWI, is honored here at his childhood home, now the Billy Bishop Heritage Museum, celebrating Canada's aviation history.

Waterfalls   WATERFALL
There are eight scenic waterfalls in the area, four of which are close to downtown. Go to www.visitgrey.ca for a downloadable waterfall tour.

Owen Sound Farmers Market   MARKET
(114 8th St E; ⊙7am-12:30pm Sat) This co-op of vendors is one of the oldest in Ontario. Expect the freshest produce, as well as maple syrup, soaps and baked goods.

🎇 Festivals & Events

Summerfolk Music Festival   MUSIC
(www.summerfolk.org) This epic three-day folk fest in mid-August draws world-class performers and artisans from far and wide.

🛌 Sleeping & Eating

For a list of area B&Bs, go to www.bbgreybruce.com.

Diamond Motor Inn   MOTEL $$
(☑519-371-2011; www.diamondmotorinn.com; 713 9th Ave E; r $60-89; ⊠) A pleasant, no-frills choice, this small motel contains bright rooms with wooden paneling and kitchenettes.

Highland Manor   B&B $$
(☑519-372-2699; www.highlandmanor.ca; 867 4th Ave A W; d $120-170; ❄🐾) This magnificent Victorian mansion (c 1872) has been elegantly furnished by attentive hosts. Decadent, spacious suites all have their own bathrooms. Many have original fireplaces. Enjoy a glass of wine on the wraparound deck, or curl up by the fireplace with a Lonely Planet guidebook. Highly recommended.

Rocky Racoon Café   FUSION $$
(☑519-376-2232; 941 2nd Ave E; mains $15-23; ⊙11am-11pm Mon-Sat; 🍴) These organic advocates serve up wild boar and Tibetan dumplings, with vegan and vegetarian options. You'll find plenty of south Asian flavors, especially delicious curries.

Shorty's Bar & Grill   CANADIAN $$
(☑519-376-0044; www.shortysonline.com; 967 3rd Ave E; mains $12-32; ⊙11:30am-late Mon-Sat) Locals love Shorty's and so do we. Appetizers like escargot, crab cakes and calamari fail to disappoint seafood lovers, while mains range from burgers and steaks to chicken and seafood. And of course, there's plenty of cold beer and good conversation to boot.

ℹ Information

Owen Sound Visitors Information Centre
(☑519-371-9833, 888-675-5555; www.owensound.ca; 1155 1st Ave W; ⊙9am-5pm Mon-Fri) Ask the friendly locals about the Bruce Peninsula's hidden gems.

ℹ Getting There & Away

Greyhound Canada runs bus services to Toronto ($42, 4¼ hours, twice daily) and Barrie ($34, 2½ hours, twice daily).

First Student (☑519-376-5712) operate a limited bus schedule to Tobermory on Friday, Saturday and Sunday from July to early September ($32, 1½ hours, one daily).

Owen Sound to Tobermory

The 100km stretch of highway from Owen Sound to Tobermory is monotonous at best. Consider taking a side road or two to get a taste of the scenery that makes the Bruce so special.

From Owen Sound, follow Grey County Rd 1 which winds along the scenic shoreline of staggering pines between Owen Sound and the quaint village of **Wiarton**. Stop here to say hello to **Wiarton Willy**, Canada's version of Punxsutawney Phil, then continue on Hwy 6 to the sleepy and picturesque bay at **Lion's Head**, a great place to stop for lunch.

Heading further north on Hwy 6 for about 25km, you'll reach Dyer's Bay Rd. Turn right and maintain your heading for another 10km to the little village of **Dyer's Bay**, reminiscent of Cape Cod with its pretty clapboard houses and shoreline scenery. From here you must decide if you'll plow on the further 11km to remote **Cabot Head Lighthouse** (admission by donation; ⊙May-Oct), promising stunning views from the keeper's perch. It's wild and wonderful, but the windy unpaved road is slow going and there's only one way in and out...back to Hwy 6 and north to Tobermory.

Tobermory

You've made it to the tip of the Bruce Peninsula: quite the trek from Toronto! Tiny Tobermory is a hippy, nature-lover's paradise boasting some of Ontario's most stunning scenery and sunsets. The village centers on the harbor area known as Little Tub, which is bustling during ferry season (May to late October) and all but deserted in winter.

Some of the best wreck-diving in North America exists in these brilliant blue waters. Meander through 22 separate wrecks, some dating back to the 1800s, but note that the water is usually about 1 degree short of an ice bath. All divers must register in person at the Parks Canada Visitors Centre (p170).

❂ Sights & Activities

Fathom Five National Marine Park PARK
(☑ 519-596-2233; www.pc.gc.ca/fathomfive; adult/child $6/3) Established to protect the numerous shipwrecks and islands around Tobermory, this was the first park of its kind in Canada. Aside from the wrecks, the park is known for much loved Flowerpot Island with its top-heavy 'flowerpot' formations, eroded by waves.

Bruce Peninsula National Park OUTDOORS
(☑ 519-596-2233; www.pc.gc.ca/brucepeninsula; day use per vehicle $11.70; ☺ May-Oct) Much of the area just south of Tobermory is protected by this national park, flaunting some of Ontario's finest assets: the Niagara Escarpment, 1000-year-old cedars, rare orchids and crystal-clear, limestone-refracted waters. Be sure to check in with the visitors center. Must-see locations include **Little Cove**, the **Grotto** and **Singing Sands**, on the other side of Hwy 6. The park remains stoic despite the recent spike in interest: be prepared to share the magic with tourist busloads during the short summer season.

Bruce Anchor Cruises CRUISE
(☑ 800-591-4254, 519-596-2555; www.bruceanchorcruises.com; 7468 Hwy 6; adult/child from $37/28; ☺ May-Oct) Glass-bottom boat tours over the tops of rusty, barnacled shipwrecks and onward to Flowerpot Island depart from this private dock at the very end of Hwy 6, also a brilliant spot to catch the sunset. Some sailings include shipwrecks, others go to Flowerpot direct: check online. Pay the surcharge to explore the island like Robinson Crusoe.

Thorncrest Outfitters KAYAKING
(☑ 888-345-2925, 519-596-8908; www.thorncrestoutfitters.com; Hwy 6; rentals from $35, day courses from $100) Choose from a variety of kayaking trips geared more toward intermediate paddlers. Independent paddlers can rent just about anything from this friendly outfitter.

Diver's Den DIVING
(☑ 519-596-2363; www.diversden.ca; 3 Bay St S) These guys can hook you up with gear rentals, certification courses (open-water certification from $545) and walk-on dives from $40.

🛏 Sleeping & Eating

In summer it's absolutely essential to book accommodations in advance. There are so few restaurants in Tobermory that if you stay here for any length of time, you'll try them all!

Cyprus Lake Campground CAMPING $
(☑ 519-596-2263; www.pc.gc.ca; Cyprus Lake Rd; sites from $23.50, yurts from $120) Sites at the most central and substantial campground within the Bruce Peninsula National Park must be reserved through Parks Canada in advance (recommended) or at the visitors center. You can even glam it up in a yurt! Backcountry sites are available.

JAGGED EDGES

The Niagara Escarpment, a 725km-long land formation that creates Niagara Falls, is a designated Unesco World Biosphere Reserve. Sweeping from eastern Wisconsin and along the shore of northern Lake Michigan, down through Lake Huron and across Manitoulin Island, slicing through Ontario and then curving under Lake Ontario and ending in New York State, the escarpment is a long spine of brush-covered stone. A combination of what was originally lime bed and ancient sea floor, the dolomitic limestone that makes up the land formation is more resistant than the land around it, which has eroded and left the bulge of limestone slithering around the Great Lakes: look for the cliffs near Hamilton, Milton, Lion's Head and Tobermory.

Great waterfalls are just one result of the escarpment. Together with Lake Ontario, the geological formation has created a microclimate perfect for viticulture. The soil (a combination of limestone and clay) and the warmth created by Lake Ontario generate growing conditions very similar to those of France's Burgundy region.

Peacock Villa
MOTEL $

(☑ 519-596-2242; www.peacockvilla.com; 31 Legion St; d from $45; 🐾) Six simple but pleasantly furnished motel rooms and four cozy cabins in a peaceful, woodsy setting a hop, skip and jump from downtown, offer excellent value. Friendly owner Karen is a wealth of information about the town and surrounds.

Big Tub Harbour Resort
MOTEL $

(☑ 519-596-2219; www.bigtubresort.ca; 236 Big Tub Rd; d from $60; 🐾) On the other side of Big Tub Harbour, a short drive or decent walk from the town and Little Tub, this quiet motel has spacious, woody rooms and manicured gardens with a wonderful outlook. Both the isolation and on-site Bootlegger's Cove Pub are wonderful. Water-sport rentals keep you occupied.

Innisfree
B&B $$

(☑ 519-596-8190; www.tobermoryaccommodations.com; 46 Bay St; r $89-154; ⊙ May-Oct; 🐾🐾) Whether it's the scent of fresh blueberry muffins, or the stunning harbor views from the sunroom and large deck, guests will adore this charming country home.

Blue Bay Motel
MOTEL $$

(☑ 519-596-2392; www.bluebay-motel.com; 32 Bay St; d from $95; 🐾❄🐾) Many of this centrally located motel's 16 bright and spacious guest rooms overlook Little Tub Harbour. Fresh and funky, each room is different: choose from double-double, queen and king beds. Some have fireplaces, soaker tubs and LCD TVs. Peek and choose on the website.

Bootlegger's Cove
PUB $$

(☑ 519-596-2219; 236 Big Tub Rd; items $7-25; ⊙ noon-8pm) Good service, tasty food and a stunning patio overlooking Big Tub Harbour make this joint the local secret we couldn't keep to ourselves. The fun menu includes wraps, quesadillas, pizzas and s'mores.

Craigie's
FAST FOOD $$

(☑ 519-596-2867; 4 Bay St; fish & chips $10.50; ⊙ 7am-7pm May-Oct) This white sea shanty has been serving fish and chips in Tobermory since 1932. Greasy breakfast specials are *the* way to start the day before an early-morning ferry or hike into the wilderness.

🍷 Drinking & Nightlife

Crows Nest Pub
PUB

(☑ 519-596-2575; www.crowsnestpub.ca; 5 Bay St; ⊙ 11am-late Apr-Oct) The only pub in Little Tub, recently renovated Crows Nest has an elevated outdoor patio overlooking the town. Wraps, burgers and pizzas feature on the pub-style menu which includes plenty of beers on tap.

ℹ Information

Parks Canada Visitors Centre (☑ 519-596-2233; www.pc.gc.ca/fathomfive; Alexander St; ⊙ 8am-8pm May-Oct) Has a fantastic interpretive center, exhibits, a movie theater, several hiking trails and a 20m viewing platform (112 steps). To get here by foot, follow the beaver signs from the Bruce Trail Monument opposite the LCBO. It's a 10-minute walk.

Tobermory Chamber of Commerce (☑ 519-596-2452; www.tobermory.org; Hwy 6; ⊙ 9am-9pm) As you pull into town (from the south) it's to your right: drop in for latest updates.

ℹ Getting There & Around

First Student (☑ 519-376-5712) operates a limited bus schedule from Owen Sound to Tobermory on Friday, Saturday and Sunday from July to early September ($32, 1½ hours, one daily). From Toronto, **Parkbus** (www.parkbus.ca) offers a limited schedule of express services ($58, five hours) with a number of downtown collection points. Check schedules and make bookings online.

Tobermory is not the end of the line: take the Chi-Cheemaun ferry from the Bruce Peninsula across the mouth of Georgian Bay to Manitoulin Island. Operated by **Ontario Ferries** (☑ 800-265-3163; www.ontarioferries.com; adult/child/car $17/9/37; ⊙ May-late Oct), the boat connects Tobermory with South Baymouth (two hours). There are four daily crossings from late June to early September, and two daily crossings during the rest of the season, with an additional voyage on Friday evenings. Reservations are highly recommended.

When in Tobermory, the **National Park Shuttle Bus** (☑ 519-596-2999; www.tobermoryparkbus.com; adult/senior/child $4.50/2.50/3.50) can take you between Little Tub, the Bruce Peninsula National Park Visitors Centre and Head of Trails.

Manitoulin Island

Manitoulin (meaning 'Spirit Island' in the Ojibwe language) is a magical and remote place. There's a real sense of being 'away' up here. Jagged expanses of white quartzite and granite outcrops lead to breathtaking vistas and hidden runes, but you'll need patience to find them: Manitoulin is the largest freshwater island in the world and its small communities, with names like Mindemoya, Sheguiandah and Wikwemikong, are many kilometers apart. Haweaters (people born on Manitoulin) will spot you a mile away as you fumble over six-syllable words. But don't let these syllabic setbacks deter you from visiting – a few days on Manitoulin is food for the soul.

There are two ways on and off the island: South Baymouth is the port of call of the Chi-Cheemaun vehicular ferry, from Tobermory. From here, Hwy 6 continues north for 65km to Little Current and the swinging bridge that reconnects it to the mainland. It meets the Trans Canada Hwy at Espanola, 50km further up the road.

◉ Sights & Activities

Manitoulin isn't laden with historical sights as much as natural beauty. Take some time to drive around the island and explore its enclaves.

Church of the Immaculate Conception   CHURCH
(M'Chigeeng) This church in the round represents a tepee, a fire pit and the circle of life and welcomes aboriginal traditions and Catholic beliefs. Colorful paintings by local artists depict the Stations of the Cross, while magnificent carvings represent both Christ and the Great Spirit Kitche Manitou.

Ojibwe Cultural Foundation   MUSEUM
(☑705-377-4902; www.ojibweculture.ca; Hwys 540 & 551, M'Chigeeng; adult/child $7.50/free; ☺9am-6pm Mon-Fri, 10am-4pm Sat, noon-4pm Sun) You're free to explore on your own, but guided tours of this insightful museum are highly recommended. Rotating exhibits reflect a rich history of legends and skilled craftwork.

Bridal Veil Falls   WATERFALL
(Kagawong) Just off Hwy 540 before Kagawong, there's a lovely picnic area at the top of this pretty waterfall. Walking trails lead down to the base where you can take a dip before continuing into the old town.

★ Great Spirit Circle Trail   CULTURAL TOUR
(☑877-710-3211; www.circletrail.com; 5905 Hwy 540; activities & tours from $30) The eight local First Nation communities have collaborated to form this consortium, offering a wide variety of fun activities and cross-cultural day and overnight tours throughout the year: a wonderful way to get a sense of Manitoulin and its people.

Cup & Saucer Trail   HIKING
From its origin near the junction of Hwy 540 and Bidwell Rd (18km southwest of Little Current) this 12km trail, with its 2km of dramatic 70m cliffs, leads to the highest point on the island (351m) with breathtaking views of the crinkled shoreline along the North Channel.

✿ Festivals & Events

Wikwemikong Powwow   CULTURE
(☑705-859-2385; www.wikwemikongheritage.org; adult/child $10/2) The unceded First Nation of Wikwemikong (locals say 'Wiki') hosts a huge powwow on the first weekend in August. Expect vibrant and colorful displays of dancing, drumming and traditional games.

De-ba-jeh-mu-jig Theatre Group   THEATER
(www.debaj.ca) Canada's foremost Aboriginal troupe, whose name appropriately means 'storytellers,' performs moving pieces of original work transcending various mediums. Check the website for the full story.

⌯ Sleeping & Eating

Accommodations on the island are limited; many people have cottages here. Check out www.manitoulintourism.com for additional listings.

Auberge Inn   HOSTEL $
(☑877-977-4392, 705-377-4392; www.aubergeinn.ca; 71 McNevin St, Providence Bay; dm/d incl breakfast $39/90; ☜) Ethusiastic Auberge Inn is a hostel-plus. With one bunk room and one private room, the place isn't large but it's comfortable and sociable with warm colors and custom cedar bunks. It's a short stroll to the beach.

My Friends Inn   MOTEL $
(☑705-859-3115; www.myfriendsinn.com; 151 Queen St, Manitowaning; d from $85; ❋☜☜) First-time hotelier and former nurse Maureen Friend retired to Manitoulin with her husband to be closer to their daughter: they're doing a wonderful job. Rooms in this Friendly little motel outside the pretty village of Manitowaning in central Manitoulin are smart and homely. Highly recommended.

Southbay Gallery & Guesthouse   B&B $$
(☑877-656-8324; www.southbayguesthouse.com; 15 Given Rd, South Baymouth; d incl breakfast $89-150; ☺May-Sep; ❋☜❋) A one-minute walk from the ferry docks you'll find this delightful melange of colorful guest rooms and summery cottages: friendly owner Brenda's

breakfasts are overflowing. Check out the gallery of handcrafted works by talented local artisans.

Queen's Inn
B&B $$

(☏ 416-450-4866, 705-282-0665; www.thequeensinn.ca; 19 Water St, Gore Bay; s/d from $95/105; ⊘ May-Dec) Like a pillared temple to remote elegance, this stately B&B peers over the silent cove of Gore Bay. Grab a book from the antique hutch library and idly thumb through while relaxing on the white verandah among potted lilacs.

★ Buoys
SEAFOOD $

(☏ 705-282-2869; www.buoyseatery.com; 1 Purvis Dr, Gore Bay; items $8-18; ⊘ noon-8pm) We love everything about this little joint by the Gore Bay beach and marina: the vibe, the location, the food: sourced from local providers and prepared fresh. The seasoned whitefish melts in your mouth, but if you're not feeling fishy, pizza, pasta and burgers are likely to please. When you're done, linger with a beer on the sunny patio and feel a million miles from home.

Garden Shed
CAFE $

(10th Side Rd, Tehkummah; mains $3-10; ⊘ 9am-2pm) The Garden Shed takes rustic charm to a new level by placing you right inside a working greenhouse. Nibble among flats of greens, or sip your coffee in the light and airy shed. Breakfast from $2.99!

Lake Huron Fish and Chips
FISH & CHIPS $

(☏ 705-377-4500; 20 McNevin St, Providence Bay; ⊘ noon-8pm) You're going to crave it at some point surrounded by all this water, and this is the place to go: golden fried fresh lake fish and crispy crunchy fries.

Garden's Gate
CAFE $$

(☏ 705-859-2088; www.manitoulin-island.com/gardensgate; Hwy 542, Tehkummah; items $5-19; ⊘ noon-8pm) Seriously good homestyle food can be found here, near the junction of Hwys 6 and 542. Rose, the owner, makes everything from scratch; she's always inventing desserts, which are regularly featured in the local newspaper.

ℹ Information

Manitoulin Tourism Association (☏ 705-368-3021; www.manitoulintourism.com; Hwy 6, Little Current; ⊘ 8am-8pm May-Oct) Pamphlets and maps of the island can be found in the South Baymouth ferry terminal, as well as onboard the Chi-Cheemaun. If you're coming from the other side, drop in here to get your bearings.

ℹ Getting There & Around

The Chi-Cheemaun ferry operated by **Ontario Ferries** (p170) runs from Tobermory to South Baymouth (two hours, two to four daily). Reservations are recommended.

A thin swinging bridge links the island to the mainland in the north along Hwy 6. In summer, the bridge closes for the first 15 minutes every hour to allow shipping traffic through the channel.

There is no land-based public transportation to or around Manitoulin.

NORTHERN ONTARIO

'Big' is a theme in Northern Ontario. The area is so big that it could fit six Englands and still have room for a Scotland or two. Big industry has made its home here: most of the world's silver and nickel ore comes from massive local mines, and vast forests

---

THE MAGNIFICENT SEVEN

Fired by an almost adolescent enthusiasm, the Group of Seven (aka the Algonquin School) were an all-male troupe of Canadian painters. They rampaged through the wilds of northern Ontario from 1920 to 1933, capturing the rugged Canadian wilderness through all its seasons, their joyful energy expressed in vibrant, light-filled canvases: mountains, lakes, forests and towns.

In 1917, before the group officially formed, their fellow painter and friend Tom Thomson drowned, just as he was producing his most prolific works. Other members – Jackson, Lismer, MacDonald, Johnston, Varley and Carmichael – considered him their leading light. Thomson's deep connection to the land is evident from his works hanging in Toronto's AGO (p79) and Ottawa's National Gallery (p209). His rustic cabin has been moved onto the grounds of the McMichael Canadian Art Collection (p88). Each has magnificent examples of the Group of Seven's profound talents.

Northern Ontario

Québec

Ontario

Manitoba

Minnesota

Wisconsin

Michigan

CANADA
USA

James Bay
Moose Factory
Moosonee
Abitibi River
Missinaibi River
Albany River
Ottokwin River
Trout Lake
Red Lake
Lac Seul
Pickle Lake
Sioux Lookout
Kenora
Dryden
Sioux Narrows
Lake of the Woods
Fort Frances
Rainy Lake
Voyageurs National Park
Quetico Provincial Park
Atikokan
Ignace
Upsala
Graham
Armstrong
Shabaqua Corners
Kakabeka Falls
Thunder Bay
Ouimet Canyon Provincial Park
Nipigon
Lake Nipigon
Wabakimi Provincial Park
Beardmore
Geraldton
Longlac
Long Lake
Rossport
Terrace Bay
Sleeping Giant Provincial Park
Isle Royale
Isle Royale National Park
Lake Superior
Marathon
White River
Neys Provincial Park
Pukaskwa National Park
Wawa
Lake Superior Provincial Park
Agawa Canyon
Goulais
Sault Ste Marie
St Joseph Island
Lake Huron
Duluth
St Paul
Minneapolis
Lake Michigan
Michigan
Chapleau Crown Game Reserve
Chapleau
Hearst
Kapuskasing
Moonbear
Missinaibi Provincial Park
Eagle's Earth
Cochrane
Timmins
Matheson
Gogama
Lady Evelyn Smoothwater Provincial Park
Mississagi Provincial Park
Elliot Lake
Serpent River
Manitoulin Island
South Baymouth
Tobermory
Espanola
Killarney Provincial Park
Sudbury
Wanapitei Lake
Georgian Bay
Rouyn-Noranda
Kirkland Lake
Lake Abitibi
Cobalt
Temagami
Finlayson Point Provincial Park
North Bay
Lake Nipissing
Samuel de Champlain Provincial Park
Algonquin Provincial Park
Barrie (85km)
Abitibi River
Ontario Northland Railway
Canadian National Railway (VIA Rail)
Algoma (Central) Railway
Missinaibi River

200 km
100 miles

have made the region a key producer of timber. Even the mosquitoes are big. Really big. Bring your bug spray! What's not so big is the region's population – only Sudbury and Thunder Bay have over 100,000 citizens, with little growth to speak of.

Two main highways (Hwys 17 and 11) weave an intersecting course accross the province. The Trans-Canada Hwy (Hwy 17) unveils the provincial pièce de résistance, the northern crest over Lake Superior. Driving between Sault Ste-Marie and Thunder Bay offers some of the country's most dramatic scenery: misty fjordlike passages hide isolated beaches among dense thickets of pine, cedar and birch. Remote Hwy 11 stretches deep into the north before linking back up to Hwy 17. This far-flung area offers access to isolated James Bay. From Cochrane, a whistle-stop train shuttles passengers to Moose Factory, an aboriginal reservation and former trading hub of the legendary Hudson's Bay Company.

If wilderness isn't your thing, move on. Otherwise, bear witness to a stunning, silent expanse where ancient aboriginal canoe routes ignite under the ethereal evening lightshow of the aurora borealis.

Killarney Provincial Park

Killarney Provincial Park (☑705-287-2900; Hwy 637; day use per vehicle $13, campsites $29.75-42.25, backcountry camping $11) is considered one of the finest kayaking destinations in the world. The Group of Seven artists had a cabin near the park's Hwy 6 entrance and were instrumental in its establishment; Killarney's 100km **La Cloche Silhouette Trail** is named after Franklin Carmichael's legendary painting. This rugged trek for experienced hikers twists through a mountainous realm of sapphire lakes, thirsty birches, luscious pine forests and shimmering quartzite cliffs. A network of shorter, less challenging hikes also offers glimpses of the majestic terrain, including the **Cranberry Bog Trail** (a 4km loop) and the **Granite Ridge Trail** (a 2km loop).

Most people access the park from the Hwy 637 turnoff along Hwy 69, which terminates in the tiny village of **Killarney**. The popular **George Lake** access point features an information center and limited campsites: none are powered. Contact **Ontario Parks** (www.ontarioparks.com) for advance reservations.

Stock up with supplies at **Grundy Lake Supply Post** (☑705-383-2251; www.grundy-lakesupplypost.com; cnr Hwys 69 & 522; ⊙8am-9pm May-Oct), 40km south of the Killarney turnoff on Hwy 69. Once at the park, **Killarney Kanoes** (☑888-461-4446, 705-287-2197; www.killarneykanoes.com; canoe rental per day $24-39; ⊙7am-7pm May-Oct) provides canoe and kayak rentals from **Bell Lake** and **George Lake**, but can deliver to **Carlyle Lake** and **Johnny Lake** on request. Advance reservations are strongly recommended. **Killarney Outfitters** (☑705-287-2828; www.killarneyoutfitters.com; 1076 Hwy 637, Killarney; canoe & kayak rental per day $26-37, activities from $35) offers a similar service and a variety of guided adventures, including hiking, paddling and photography workshops, organized through its property, **Killarney Mountain Lodge** (☑800-461-1117; www.killarney.com; 3 Commissioner St, Killarney; d per person incl meals $135-210; ⊙May-Oct). It's a sprawling holiday lodge with a bunch of facilities, woody lodge rooms and cabins – a great alternative for noncampers.

Parkbus has limited seasonal services to the park ($61, 5½ hours) from Toronto; otherwise, you'll need wheels.

Sudbury

POP 160,000

Sudbury gets props for making something out of nothing. In the 1880s it was but a desolate lumber camp called Ste-Anne-des-Pins. Then, when the Canadian Pacific Railway plowed through in 1883, the discovery of a motherlode of nickel-copper ore transformed the dreary region into the biggest nickel producer worldwide. By 1920, industrial toxicity and acid rain had killed the trees and fouled the soil, leaving Sudbury a barren place of blackened boulders. It's easy to understand why NASA used Sudbury's terrain to test moon-landing equipment.

Today, the story is a lot greener: locals have planted more than 12 million trees since 1980, although heavy industry and mining still rule. Sudbury has a university, two fantastic science museums, some cool haunts and chilled locals, but there's little reason to visit unless you're passing through.

Sudbury no longer has a visitors information center. Try www.sudburytourism.ca.

⊙ Sights

If you're planning to tackle Science North and Dynamic Earth, save money with the 'Dynamic Duo' discount coupon (adult/child $48/40).

★ Science North   MUSEUM
(☑705-523-4629; www.sciencenorth.ca; 100 Ramsey Lake Rd; adult/child $20/18; ⊙9am-6pm) After passing through a tunnel dug deep within the 2.5-billion-year-old Canadian Shield, work your way down through the spiral of exciting hands-on activities in this fantastic museum. Wander through a living butterfly garden, stargaze in the digital planetarium or fly away on a bush plane simulator. Visiting exhibits and IMAX films change regularly.

Dynamic Earth   MUSEUM
(☑705-522-3701; www.dynamicearth.ca; 122 Big Nickel Rd; adult/child $32/28; ⊙9am-6pm) Dynamic Earth's main attraction is the underground tour with simulated dynamite blast. Visitors stand to learn lots about geology and our planet from thought-provoking interactive exhibits. Be sure to take a happy snap in front of the 9m-high Big Nickel, made entirely of stainless steel.

Copper Cliff Museum   HISTORIC BUILDING
(☑ext 2460, 705-674-3141; 26 Balsam St, Copper Cliff; ⊙10am-4pm Tue-Sun Jun-Aug) FREE This pioneer log cabin 6km west of downtown is filled with relics from an era when settlers first arrived to survey the land, oddly juxtaposed with the unmissable nearby smoke-spewing shaft, affectionately known as the 'Superstack.'

🛏 Sleeping & Eating

Holiday Inn   HOTEL $$
(☑705-522-3000; www.holidayinn.com; 1696 Regent St; d from $119; ✽ 🛜 ⊛) Outside, this Holiday Inn looks frozen in 1972. Inside is what you'd expect: refurbished, generic rooms of a good size. There's an indoor pool.

Radisson Sudbury   HOTEL $$
(☑705-675-1123; www.radisson.com; 85 St Anne Rd; d from $139; ✽ 🛜 ⊛) Centrally located and recently refurbished, Radisson's rooms aren't anything to write home about, but there's something about this hotel that's just that little bit a cut above the rest.

Auberge du Village   B&B $$
(☑705-675-7732; www.aubergesudbury.com; 104 Durham St; ste $165; ✽ 🛜) Lofted above

a quaint *boulangerie*, these two spacious suites transport guests away from the steel jungle of factories to a quiet hamlet in Provence with soft pastels and overflowing wine.

Deluxe Hamburgers   FAST FOOD $
(1737 Regent St; mains $4-9; ⊙8am-10pm) McDonald's has the golden arches; Deluxe has the golden arch. So maybe the concept isn't original, but this blast from the past is a local institution.

Pasta e Vino   ITALIAN $$
(☑705-674-3050; 118 Paris St; pasta from $12; ⊙5-9pm Mon-Sat) So it's not the best Italian restaurant in the world, but there's a lovely vibe about this quaint pasta joint in a little house on the edge of downtown. Something in the air: it's the kind of place you'd go on a date if you lived here.

★ Respect is Burning   ITALIAN $$$
(www.ribsupperclub.com; Durham St; lunch mains $8-12, dinner $14-29; ⊙5-9pm; 🛜) This self-proclaimed supper club's focus is on rustic Tuscan cuisine but chefs aren't shy about getting experimental. The ever-shifting menu promises bursting flavors with every bite. Weekend evenings feature delectable sample platters and late-night drinks.

🍷 Drinking & Entertainment

Laughing Buddha   BAR
(☑705-673-2112; www.laughingbuddhasudbury. com; 194 Elgin St; ⊙11am-2am) Sudbury's prime hangout for hipsters and slackers pulls off snobby sandwiches (like the 'Brie LT') while maintaining an uberchill vibe. In summer, slip out to the crimson-brick courtyard and enjoy your casual lunch or one of the 100-plus types of beer.

SRO CLUB
(☑705-670-1361; www.sronightclub.com; 94 Durham St; ☺8pm-2am Mon-Sat, from 5pm Fri) Grab a martini from the swirling stainless-steel bar: the drinks are so large you can swim in them. Weekends are standing room only, so strap on the dance shoes and prepare to get down.

Zig's BAR
(☑705-586-9447; www.zigsbar.com; 54 Elgin St; ☺8pm-2am Tue-Sat) You're guaranteed to turn a head in this fun subterranean gay bar where everyone knows everyone.

Towne House Tavern LIVE MUSIC
(☑705-674-6883; www.thetownehouse.com; 206 Elgin St; ☺11am-2am) You won't find any cover band here – this beloved institution is all about Canadian indie from punk to gospel. It's grungy and right along the train tracks. Naturally.

❶ Getting There & Around

Sudbury airport is about 25km northeast of downtown. Air Canada, Bearskin Airlines and Porter operate services to Toronto, Ottawa, Sault Ste-Marie and Thunder Bay. Several car-rental options are available at the airport, including **Enterprise** (☑800-736-8222; www. enterpriserentacar.ca) and **National** (☑705-387-4747; www.nationalcar.ca).

Ontario Northland (www.ontarionorthland. ca) connects Sudbury to Toronto ($74, 5¾ hours, three daily). Greyhound connects Sudbury to Toronto ($75, five hours, three daily), Thunder Bay ($201, 14 hours, twice daily) and Ottawa ($75, 7½ hours, three daily).

Sudbury Train Station (☑800-361-1235; cnr Minto & Elgin Sts) services a small network of remote towns including White River and Chapleau.

City buses roam the downtown region from the **transit center** (☑705-675-3333; cnr Notre Dame Ave & Elm St). One-way fares are $2.80.

Sault Ste-Marie
POP 75,000

'The Soo,' as it's commonly known, quietly governs the narrow rapids between Lakes Huron and Superior. Perched along the last 'steps' of the St Lawrence Seaway, this sleepy city is the unofficial gateway to the far-flung regions of northwestern Ontario. Originally known as Baawitigong ('Place of the rapids'), it was a traditional gathering place for the Ojibwe and remains a strong First Nations' area today. French fur traders changed the name to Sault Ste-Marie (soo-saynt muhree) or 'St Mary's Falls,' but don't expect to see any today: they've been tamed into a series of gargantuan locks.

Let's face it, Sault Ste-Marie is not the prettiest town. In many parts, it's dreary. Downtown feels like a ghost town and can be sketchy after dark. Despite appearances, the Soo may be the friendliest place in Ontari-oo (sic) and it's a logical overnight on Trans-Canada itineraries. There's a US border crossing here too.

◉ Sights & Activities

Canadian Bushplane Heritage Centre MUSEUM
(☑705-945-6242; www.bushplane.com; 50 Pim St; adult/child/student $12/3/7; ☺9am-6pm) A visit to the Soo's most dynamic and kid-friendly museum is a great way to get a sense of how Northern Ontario works: bush planes are crucial to remote communities that are not

---

MISSISSAGI PROVINCIAL PARK

The tree-lined jaunt between Sudbury and Sault Ste-Marie offers little more than forest views out the car window. **Elliot Lake**, the largest community in the area, is popular with retirees on a tight budget. This little town made headlines in 2012 after a concrete section of a mall's roof catastrophically collapsed without warning. The slab fell three floors, taking the lives of two women: it took rescue teams four days to find the deceased. At time of writing, the inquiry continues into how this could happen in a mall inspected by city and provincial officials.

Mississagi Provincial Park (☑705-865-2021, 705-848-2806; Hwy 639; day use per vehicle $13, backcountry sites $9.50, campsites $27-34; ☺May-Sep), 25km north of the lake, is a secluded expanse of hemlock forests, sandy beaches, trembling aspens and chirping birds. A hike around **Flack Lake** reveals ripple rock – a geological feature formed by a billion years of wave action. It's quiet and undeveloped: none of the campsites have electricity and the limited facilities on **Semiwite Lake** (the gatehouse and toilets) are solar-powered. Reserve your spot with **Ontario Parks** (www.ontarioparks.com) .

ALGOMA CENTRAL RAILWAY

Constructed in 1899 to facilitate the transport of raw materials to Sault Ste-Marie's industrial plants, the **Algoma Central Railway** (ACR; ☑ 705-946-7300; www.agawacanyontourtrain.com; round-trip from adult/child $88/41) is a 475km stretch of railroad from Sault Ste-Marie, due north to Hearst. Nowadays, from mid-June to mid-October, it ferries passengers through unspoiled wilderness along the pristine lakes and jagged granite of the Canadian Shield. The best time to ride is from late September to early October as the train twists its way through jaw-dropping blazing autumn foliage for as far as the eye can see.

Two options are available. The **Agawa Canyon Tour Train** ($88/41 adult/child) departs at 8am and returns at 6pm, with a two-hour layover in the lush Agawa Canyon, 185km north of Sault Ste-Marie. The **Tour of the Line** ($233/145 adult/child) is a whistle-stop train that goes all the way to sleepy Hearst, where you must overnight if you're returning to Sault Ste-Marie. Surcharges apply during peak fall departures.

Extended wilderness adventures are available in conjunction with the many retreats dotted along the railway, known as the **Lodges along the Line**. How about snowmobiling through 4000km of groomed winter trails, or spending a weekend fishing for plump trout? Check the webiste for schedules, packages and to make reservations.

accessible by road. Stroll among retired aircraft to see how tiny these flyers really are. A flight simulator takes passengers on a spirited ride along sapphire lakes and towering pines.

Sault Ste-Marie Museum
MUSEUM
(☑ 705-759-7278; www.saultmuseum.com; 690 Queen St E; adult/concession $6/4; ☺ 9am-5pm Tue-Sat) Constructed in the old post office, an important historical tribute to the early 1900s, this three-story museum details the town's history through several perspectives. The Skylight Gallery is a must-see for industrial-history buffs; an interactive timeline from prehistory to the 1960s incorporates the local historical society's unique collection of preserved fossils and relics.

Sault Ste-Marie Canal National Historic Site
HISTORIC SITE
(☑ 705-941-6262; 1 Canal Dr) **FREE** Stroll through the quiet islands on the Canadian side of the waterway; the majority of freighter traffic occurs further afield in the American locks – the older Canadian locks, built in 1895, are used for recreational vessels only. The **Attikamek walking trail** is a short, self-guided hike around South St Mary's Island. The meandering path winds through wooded knolls, encircles the trenchlike locks and dips under the International Bridge, allowing visitors to grasp the interesting juxtaposition of nature and industry.

Fort St Joseph National Historic Site
HISTORIC SITE
(☑ 705-246-2664; www.pc.gc.ca/fortstjoseph; Hwy 548; adult/child $3.90/1.90; ☺ 9:30am-5pm Jun-Oct) St Joseph Island, a quiet expanse of woodland about 50km east of Sault Ste-Marie, is between Canada and the USA in the northwest corner of Lake Huron. It's linked by bridge off Hwy 17. Here, the Fort St Joseph National Historic Site was once the most remote outpost of the British landhold in North America. The preserved ruins of the 200-year-old fort are an archaeologist's dream.

Treetop Adventures
ADVENTURE ACTIVITIES
(☑ 705-649-5455; www.treetopadventures.ca; 6 Post Office Rd, Goulais River; admission from $30) This woodsy adventure park offers a variety of heart-pounding activities such as ropewalking high above the tree line and ziplining, Tarzan-style. It's open daily year-round by reservation; phone ahead.

🛏 Sleeping & Eating

While the bulk of motels are found along Great Northern Rd, with all the conveniences of one giant strip mall, there are several options scattered downtown, where there's some scenic interest in the waterfront and the majority of attractions, but few amenities after 8pm.

Sleep Inn
MOTEL $
(☑ 705-253-7533; www.sleepinnssmarie.ca; 727 Bay St; d incl breakfast from $79; ❀ ❷) This

tourist motel in a nice spot by the water has pleasantly refurbished rooms with comfy beds and good showers.

Holiday Inn Express MOTEL **$$**
(☑705-759-8200; www.holidayinn.com; 320 Bay St; d incl breakfast from $109; ❄☎) Conveniently located opposite the Station Mall, this completely rebranded and refurbished motel has large, new rooms with dark woods and plenty of light.

Water Tower Inn HOTEL **$$**
(☑800-461-0800; www.watertowerinn.com; 360 Great Northern Rd; d from $119; ❄@☎≋) The Water Tower continues to stand out from the rest with its plethora of pools, bar/ restaurant and treatment spa. A variety of room types including family rooms and suites are available.

Muio's DINER **$**
(☑705-254-7105; www.muios.com; 685 Queen St E; mains $8-24; ☺7am-8pm Sun-Thu, to 9pm Fri & Sat) Like a shrine to the era of roller discos and drive-in movie theaters, Muio's continues to bask in its own anachronistic glory. The joint is famed for its breakfasts and broasted (half broiled, half roasted) chicken-on-a-bun smothered in rich gravy. OMG.

★ Arturo Ristorante ITALIAN **$$**
(☑705-253-0002; www.arturo.ca; 515 Queen St E; mains $12-28; ☺5-10pm Tue-Sat) A shimmering jewel in a dismal downtown strip, Arturo is the kind of place you remember once your vacation has ended. It's atmospheric but unpretentious with soft lighting, starched white tablecloths and antiques aplenty. The meals are equally as presentable: Italian mains like veal marsala and chicken piccata are tender and succulent as they should be, sauces rich and wines appropriately paired.

Panna Bar & Grill MEDITERRANEAN **$$**
(☑705-949-8484; 472 Queen St E; lunch mains $8-16, dinner $14-28; ☺11.30am-10pm Mon-Sat) Stylish Panna puts its own spin on traditional Mediterranean fare: appetizers like calamari and garlic shrimp feature alongside tempura vegetables. Choose from a variery of seafood and pasta dishes as well as burgers and steaks juicy enough to turn any starving carnivore's frown upside down.

🍷 Drinking & Entertainment

If cheap beer is what you're after, follow the bar-hoppers across the International Bridge to Michigan for half-priced hooch. Most visitors won't.

Docks BAR
(☑705-256-6868; www.docksriverfrontgrill.ca; 89 Foster Dr; ☺11am-late) Great views, cold booze, pool, live bands and tasty bar-eats all help make Docks your safest bet for a good time in the Soo.

LopLops LIVE MUSIC
(☑705-945-0754; www.loplops.com; 651 Queen St E; ☺5pm-late Thu-Sat) Grab a glass of vino from the glittering steel bar and enjoy an evening amid strumming guitars and the restless murmurs of tortured artists. Unleash your inner diva on an open-mic night or just come to contemplate the art. Where the cool kids hang.

❶ Information

Ontario Travel Information Centre (☑705-945-6941; www.ontariotravel.net; 261 Queen St W; ☺8am-6pm) Sells fishing permits and snowmobiling licenses.

❶ Getting There & Around

Sault Ste-Marie Airport (YAM; ☑705-779-3031; www.saultairport.com; 475 Airport Rd) is about 20km from downtown. Air Canada and Porter have scheduled services to Toronto. Bearskin Airlines services locations in Ontario and Manitoba including Ottawa, Winnipeg, Thunder Bay and Sudbury. Airport car-rental providers include **Avis** (☑800-230-4898; www. avis.ca) and **National** (☑877-222-9058; www. nationalcar.ca).

Greyhound (☑800-661-8747; www.grey-hound.ca) runs buses to Sudbury ($56, 4½ hours, twice daily) and Thunder Bay ($125, 10 hours, twice daily) from the downtown **bus station** (☑705-949-4711; 73 Brock St). For $2.50 a ride, try the network of city buses.

From here, you can also get the **International Bridge Bus** (☑906-632-6882; one-way $2; ☺7am-7pm Mon-Fri, 9am-5pm Sat) over to sister Sault Ste-Marie in Michigan. Buses depart the Canada side every hour on the half-hour, and every hour on the hour from the US side. You must have your passport.

Lake Superior Shoreline

Superior in size and beauty, Lake Superior covers a surface area of 82,100 sq km: it's the largest freshwater lake on the planet, with its own ecosystem and microclimate. Much of its dazzling Canadian shoreline is hugged by the Trans-Canada Hwy (at this point Hwy

17) with the section of road between Sault Ste-Marie and Wawa regarded by many as the most picturesque of the highway's 8030km span. A 90km stretch of the highway passes directly through Lake Superior Provincial Park.

This section covers the journey west from Sault Ste-Marie, before reaching the park. The Great Lake freezes over for many months at a time and most of the following locations are seasonal (May to October). Keep an eye out for scraggly moose as you drive the highway, especially at dusk or dawn.

◉ Sights & Activities

Harmony Beach   BEACH
(Hwy 17) Heading west from Sault Ste-Marie on Hwy 17 for about 40km, look for a left-hand turn to a poorly signposted 'Harmony Beach Road,' to reach this popular summer swimming spot.

Chippewa Falls   WATERFALL
These powerful waterfalls, 52km west of Sault Ste-Marie on the side of Hwy 17, are at their best in spring when the volume of melting snow turns their otherwise steady flow into a thunderous roar.

Pancake Bay Provincial Park   PARK
(☑705-882-2209, 888-668-7275; www.ontarioparks.com/park/pancakebay; Hwy 17; day use $9.50) It's been a long drive, but you've made it to one of Canada's finest stretches of white sandy beach, and if you time it right, you might have it all to yourself. In summer that won't be the case. Be sure to reserve one of the 325 campsites (from $27.50) in advance through Parks Canada, or just stop by for a swim.

Caribou Expeditions   KAYAKING
(☑800-970-6662; www.caribou-expeditions.com; 1021 Goulais Mission Rd, Goulais Bay; courses from $75, tours from $135) Join the team of experienced nature lovers (based about 34km north of the Soo, on the quiet waters of Goulais Bay) for a variety of kayaking expeditions along the northern crest of Lake Superior. Canoe and kayak rentals are also available.

🛏 Sleeping

★ Voyageur's Lodge and Cookhouse   MOTEL $
(☑705-882-2504; www.voyageurslodge.com; Hwy 17, Batchawana Bay; d $79-109, ste from $139; 🛜) On the highway opposite Batchawana

Bay's 4km of sandy beach, you'll find this roadside motel and diner. Clean and cozy woodsy rooms are perfect for a beach break. Two housekeeping suites have a full kitchen. Open year-round, the cookhouse does regular fish fries, mammoth burgers and the best tastin' gravy for miles. You can rent canoes and buy booze on-site too!

Salzburgerhof Resort   RESORT $
(☑705-882-2323; www.salzburgerhofresort.com; Corbeil Point Rd, Batchawana Bay; d from $85; 🛜) Family owned for over 40 years, this little piece of Austria looks right at home on the shores of Lake Superior. In fall the surrounding trees are truly breathtaking. Rooms are predictably woodsy, European and a little bit retro, but that all just adds to the charm. There's a private beach and Austrian restaurant on-site. Take Hwy 563 west off Hwy 17 at Batchawana Bay.

Twilight Resort   CAMPGROUND $
(☑705-882-2183; www.facebook.com/TwilightResort; Hwy 17, Montreal River Harbour; cabins from $70; ☺May-Oct) This wonderfully isolated spot, just before the entrance to Lake Superior Provincial Park, was once a camp for Mennonite war objectors sent to work on the Trans-Canada Hwy. Today, it's a no-frills, back-in-time holiday spot with a few fisher's cabins and plenty of campsites, all facing due west for jaw-dropping sunsets over Superior.

Lake Superior Provincial Park

Lake Superior Provincial Park (☑705-856-2284, 705-882-2026; www.lakesuperiorpark.ca; Hwy 17; day use per vehicle $13, backcountry sites $9.50, campsites $27.25-32.75) protects 1600 sq km of misty fjordlike passages, thick evergreen forest and tranquil sandy coves that feel like they've never known the touch of humankind. The best bits of the park require some level of hiking or canoeing to access, but if you're not so inclined or have limited time, there are numerous picture-perfect vistas just off the highway which goes straight through the park. Sights and facilities generally open from May to October.

Your first stop should be the **Agawa Bay Visitors Centre**, 9km in from the park's southern boundary. The interactive museum and park experts will advise you well. There's a smaller information area at **Red**

CHAPLEAU

About 140km inland from Wawa, Little Chapleau (*chap*-loh) is the gateway to the world's largest Crown game preserve, with nearly 1 million hectares of land: hunting is strictly prohibited. For information, check out www.chapleau.ca, or stop by the **Centennial Museum & Information Centre** (705-864-1122; 94 Monk St; 9am-4pm May-Aug). Critters you might encounter include bald eagles, beavers, lynx, black bears, moose and more.

The Missinaibi River tumbles down from James Bay flowing deep within Chapleau's preserve to **Missinaibi Provincial Park** (705-864-3114, 705-234-2222; day use per vehicle $10, campsites $32-39; May-Sep). Several outfitters operate at various points along the river, including **Missinaibi Headwaters Outfitters** (800-590-7836; www.missinaibi.com; Racine Lake), based in the preserve.

Rock Lake, 53km further north, if you're coming from the other direction.

Katherine Cove picnic area is a must for panoramas of misty sand-strewn shores. Budding anthropologists will appreciate the **Agawa Rock Pictographs**: red-ocher images up to 400 years old. A rugged 500m trail leads you to a rock ledge where, if the lake is calm, the mysterious pictographs can be seen.

Avid hikers will delight in the park's 11 exceptional trails. The signature hike is the 65km **Coastal Trail**, a steep, challenging route along craggy cliffs and pebble beaches (allow five to seven days). There are five road access points for those who wish to do a smaller section. The **Nokomis Trail** (5km) loops around iconic **Old Woman Bay**, so named because it is said you can see the face of an old woman in the cliffs. Depending on the weather, wispy beardlike fog and shivering Arctic trees exude a distinctly primeval flavor. The diverse **Orphan Lake Trail** (8km) just north of Katherine Cove is a tasting plate of the park's ethereal features: isolated cobble beaches, majestic waterfalls, elevated lookouts and dense maple forests.

There's a burgeoning paddling culture here. Eight charted inland routes range from the mild 16km **Fenton-Treeby Loop** (with 11 short portages) to challenging routes accessible only via the Algoma Central Railway (p177), which departs from Sault Ste-Marie. Naturally Superior Adventures (see below) and Caribou Expeditions (p179) run extensive paddling programs in and around the park.

There are three campgrounds close to the highway: Crescent Lake (no flushing toilets), Agawa Bay and Rabbit Blanket Lake. Bookings through Ontario Parks (www.ontarioparks.com) are essential.

Wawa

In the middle of nowhere, enduring winters straight out of a Siberian nightmare, little Wawa is a tough bird. Literally. *Wawa* is the Ojibwe word meaning 'wild goose.' This resilient 1720s fur-trading post was so named because of the millions of geese that would rest by Lake Wawa during their seasonal migration. It's also the idea behind the shabby, 8.5m-tall gander that's been unapologetically luring travelers off the highway into town since the 1960s. And rightly so: Wawa is an obligatory Trans-Canada stop for many drivers and that's likely why you'll visit. There's a glut of motels here from spick and span to cheap and nasty.

Sights & Activities

Wawa Goose MONUMENT
(26 Mission Rd) A trip through Wawa would be incomplete without getting up close and personal with the Wawa Goose in front of the visitors information center, before it flies the coop: engineers say the goose is cooked and needs costly repairs. There are two other big geese in town: see if you can find them.

Naturally Superior Adventures KAYAKING
(800-203-9092, 705-856-2939; www.naturallysuperior.com; RR1 Lake Superior; courses/ day trips from $50/$95) Based 8km southwest of Wawa, the robust gang at Naturally Superior delight in guiding folks eager to get acquainted with Lake Superior by water. Trips and courses range from day affairs to weekend and week-long expeditions, including beach camping. Equipment rental is also available. Other workshops, from photography to yoga and guide-certification courses, are also offered.

🛏 Sleeping & Eating

Parkway Motel
MOTEL **$**

(☑705-856-7020; www.parkwaymotel.com; Hwy 17; r $69-99; ❋@🐾) Refurbished rooms feature LCD TVs with DVD players and complimentary movies as well as microwaves and decent bathrooms. There's a hot tub out back. It's 5km south of Wawa along the highway.

Rock Island Lodge
LODGE **$$**

(☑800-203-9092; www.rockislandlodge.ca; RR1 Lake Superior; d incl breakfast $98-109; ⊙May-Oct; 🐾) Naturally Superior Adventures' lodge sits along Lake Superior between a craggy expanse of stone and smooth, sandy beach. The four basic rooms are spotless, comfortable, have en suites and offer views of the evening sun as it gently melts into the lake. There's wi-fi but no TV.

Columbia Restaurant
DINER **$**

(☑705-856-1300; 71 Broadway Ave; items from $6; ⊙7am-8pm) There's nothing fancy about this greasy-spoon diner, but it does do the best breakfasts and pizzas in town – not that there's a lot of competition.

Kinniwabi Pines
INTERNATIONAL **$$**

(☑705-856-7226; 56 Hwy 17; mains $12-26; ⊙noon-3pm & 6-10pm) What would you expect to find lurking behind the facade of a highway motel in remote Northern Ontario? Food from Trinidad, mon! Add some spice to your trip and try the baked pork or the stewed catfish. European and Chinese dishes are also available for those who don't care to dare their palate.

ℹ Information

Visitors Information Centre (☑705-856-2244, 800-367-9292; 26 Mission Rd; ⊙8am-8pm Jun-Aug) Drop in for info on the town and nearby Lake Superior Provincial Park and Pukaskwa National Park.

ℹ Getting There & Away

Greyhound Canada buses connect Wawa with Sault Ste-Marie (three hours, three daily) and Thunder Bay (6½ hours, three daily).

Pukaskwa National Park

At **Pukaskwa** (☑807-229-0801, ext 242; www.parkscanada.gc.ca/pukaskwa; Hwy 627; day use adult/child $5.80/2.90, backcountry sites $9.80, campsites $15-29), bear hugs are taken literally. Open May through October, the park offers many of the same topographical features

as Lake Superior Provincial Park and has an intact predator-prey ecosystem, including a small herd of elusive caribou. There are only 4km of roads in the entire park.

Pukaskwa's front country is based around the only general-use campground at **Hattie Cove**, near the park's entrance. Check in the **visitors center** (☑807-229-0801; ⊙9am-4pm Jul-Aug) when you arrive: guided hikes and activities depart here most evenings around 7pm.

Three short trails begin at **Hattie Cove**, offering glimpses of the pristine setting. The popular **Southern Headland Trail** (2.2km) is a rocky, spear-shaped route that offers elevated photo-ops of the shoreline and craggy Canadian Shield. Look for the curious stunted trees, so formed by harsh winds blowing off the lake. The **Halfway Lake Trail** (2.6km) loops around a small lake: informative signs offer a scientific perspective on the inner workings of the ecosystem. The **Beach Trail** (1.5km) winds along Horseshoe Bay and Lake Superior revealing sweeping vistas of crashing waves and undulating sand dunes.

Pukaskwa's stunning backcountry is not for the fainthearted: 1878 sq km of remote, untouched wilderness defines isolation. The **Coastal Hiking Trail** (60km) is the main artery for hikers, dipping along the vast shoreline. For a taste of the backcountry, many fit hikers opt to traverse the first 7.6km of this trail, culminating at the 30m-long, 25m-high **White Water Suspension Bridge**. The trek is damp, arduous, and there's only one way in and out (15km total).

Paddlers choose from three incredible routes, including the acclaimed **White River Canoe Route** (72km), which links Hattie Cove to **White Lake Provincial Park**. Do not attempt any of these hiking or water voyages without proper preparation. If you need a water taxi, **McCuaig Marine Services** (☑807-229-0193; mccuaigk@onlink.net) pick up and drop off anywhere along the coast, though fickle weather can delay pickup service. If you're not a skilled independent hiker, Naturally Superior Adventures and Caribou Expeditions (p179) both offer a variety of guided excursions through Pukaskwa's backcountry.

Marathon to Nipigon

The winding path over the northern crest of Lake Superior is a pleasant jaunt with several places that make a good excuse to stretch your legs. Rocky **Neys Provincial Park** (☑807-229-1624; www.ontarioparks.com/park/neys; day use per vehicle $9.50), just west of Marathon, has craggy beaches, furry caribou, and long, lingering sunsets.

Drop by the town of **Terrace Bay** and catch a boat to the **Slate Islands**, home to the largest herd of woodland caribou in the world.

Consider spending the night in little **Rossport**, tucked between the grumbling railroad and one of Lake Superior's only natural harbors. The **Rossport Inn** (☑807-824-3213; 6 Bowman St; cabins $65-95; ☺mid-May–mid-Oct) has pleased passers-through since 1884, but its last generation of kind owners recently retired. It still rents its idyllic cabins from May to October: call in advance.

Sleeping Giant Provincial Park

The jagged Sleeping Giant Peninsula takes the shape of a large reclining man: it's been considered a sacred realm for millennia. The **Sleeping Giant Provincial Park** (☑807-977-2526; Hwy 587; day use per vehicle $9.50, campsites $32-42) lies at the southern tip of the craggy mass, offering unforgettable views of Lake Superior.

The park is rugged enough to offer backcountry camping, yet compact enough for a fulfilling day trip from Thunder Bay, 45km away. Contact **Ontario Parks** (www.ontarioparks.com) for reservations. The three-day **Kabeyun Trail** follows the dramatic west coast of the peninsula. Hope to meet white-tailed deer, moose and porcupines.

At the tip of the peninsula, where the sealed road deteriorates into a path of dirt and pebbles, you'll find the remote community of **Silver Islet**. In the mid-1880s the town exploded with the world's richest silver mine; now it lies abandoned.

Thunder Bay

POP 102,300

Thunder Bay is about as comfortably isolated as you can get – it's 692km west of Sault Ste-Marie and 703km east of Winnipeg (Manitoba). If you're arriving by road, it's a welcome and obligatory return to civilization: no matter how beautiful *those* forests and *that* shoreline, it starts to blur together after a while. With a smattering of decent historical attractions, pervading natural beauty and a handful of creative restaurants and bars, you might be pleasantly surprised that Thunder Bay hums along strong, in defiance and celebration of its long, dark winters. Maybe it has something to do with the fact that 10% of the population are of Finnish descent.

The Ojibwe have inhabited the region continuously for thousands of years. Europeans arrived in the 1600s, but it wasn't until 1803 that the British erected Fort William as the trading hub for the lucrative North West Company (beaver-pelt central). Shortly after, the rival settlement of Port Arthur was born 5km up the road and became a center for mining and shipping prairie grain: these granaries are the gargantuan industrial structures you see along the lakeshore. It

---

WINNIE THE WHO?

The little logging town of **White River** (www.whiteriver.ca) lays claim to being the home of the original Winnie the Pooh.

As the story goes, back in 1914 a trapper returned to White River with an orphaned black-bear cub. A veterinarian soldier named Harry Colebourn was on a rail layover in White River when he came across the trapper and fell in love with the cub, purchasing her for $20. He named her 'Winnipeg.' She boarded the Québec-bound troop train with Harry, en route to his native Britain.

When Harry was called to serve in France, he left Winnie in the care of the London Zoo, where she became an instant hit. One of the many hearts she won over belonged to a young Christopher Robin Milne, son of AA Milne. A frequent visitor to the zoo, young Christopher's pet name for the little bear was 'Winnie-the-Pooh.' In his 1926 first edition, Mr Milne noted that his stories were about Winnie, the bear from the London Zoo, his son, Christopher, and Christopher's stuffed animals.

Eventually, Disney purchased Milne's tales of Winnie-the-Pooh and Christopher Robin, and… the rest is history. A monument to both bears, actual and fictional, stands in the park in White River, by the visitors center.

was only in the late 1960s that Fort William and Port Arthur became one, choosing the evocative moniker 'Thunder Bay' from the aboriginal name for the region, Animikie, meaning 'thunder.'

If you're passing through, consider staying two nights to get a sense of the place. Otherwise, if you're looking for something different, why not watch for a seat sale and fly in from Toronto for the weekend.

⊙ Sights

The city itself is sprawling and doesn't have a tonne of things for visitors to do, but there's a definite sense of urban revival downtown and some lovely residential streets to explore: photographers will have fun here. You'll need a car to make the most out of the historical and natural wonders dotted around a 40km radius.

★ Fort William Historical Park   MUSEUM
(☑ 807-473-2344; www.fwhp.ca; 1350 King Rd; adult/child $12/9; ⊙ 10am-5pm May-Oct) French voyageurs, Scottish gentlemen and Ojibwe scuttle about while re-enacting life in the early 1800s at this historical park. From 1803 to 1821, Fort William was the headquarters of the North West Company. Eventually the business was absorbed by the Hudson's Bay Company and the region's importance as a trading center declined. Today, the large heritage center offers 42 historic buildings stuffed with entertaining and antiquated props like muskets, pelts and birch-bark canoes.

David Thompson Astronomical Observatory   OBSERVATORY
(☑ 807-473-2344; www.fwhp.ca; 1350 King Rd; adult/child $10/8; ⊙ Thu-Sat, times vary) You too can take a peek at the stars through the largest telescope in Canada on a star walk at this fantastic, accessible observatory. Check the website for latest conditions.

Terry Fox Lookout and Memorial   MONUMENT
This memorial honors Terry Fox, a young cancer sufferer and amputee who began a trans-Canada walk on April 12, 1980 to raise money for cancer research. After traveling 5373km from St John's, Newfoundland, he arrived in Thunder Bay as his condition deteriorated. He never left. Today's memorial is erected close to where Terry ended his great 'Marathon of Hope.'

Kakabeka Falls Provincial Park   PARK
(☑ 807-473-9231; www.ontarioparks.com/park/ kakabekafalls; Hwy 11-17; day use per vehicle $9.50) About 25km west of Thunder Bay, just off Hwy 11-17, you'll find the spectacular 40m-high Kakabeka Falls, the source of many local legends. The moody chute is most powerful in early spring during the thaw, or after heavy rains. There are a number of campsites ($32 to $42) and a small village before the park.

Amethyst Mine Panorama   HISTORIC SITE
(☑ 807-622-6908; www.amethystmine.com; East Loon Rd; admission $8; ⊙ 10am-5pm May-Oct) Visit the mine, 40km east of Thunder Bay, and dig for your very own purple chunk of amethyst, Ontario's official gemstone. While pulling into the parking lot, you may notice that the gravel has a faint indigo hue, a testament to the fact that the area is truly overflowing with these semiprecious pieces.

Thunder Bay Museum   MUSEUM
(☑ 807-623-0801; www.thunderbaymuseum.com; 425 Donald St E; adult/child $3/1.50; ⊙ 11am-5pm) This century-old museum is engaging for adults and children alike. Displays about Ojibwe culture, fur trading, military history and recent developments incorporate well-presented artifacts to offer visitors a glimpse of the region's 10,000 years of human history.

Thunder Bay Art Gallery   GALLERY
(☑ 807-577-6427; www.theag.ca; 1080 Keewatin St, Confederation College; adult/student $3/1.50; ⊙ noon-8pm Tue-Thu, to 5pm Fri-Sun) Thunder Bay's premier gallery offers an eclectic assortment of contemporary art, including Aboriginal artists. The use of natural imagery, haunting masks and scorching primary colors will leave lasting impressions on visitors. It's free on Wednesdays.

Mt Mackay   MOUNTAIN
Mt Mackay rises 350m over Thunder Bay, offering sweeping views of the region's patchwork of rugged pines and swollen rock formations. The lookout is part of the **Fort William First Nation** (☑ 807-622-3093; www.fwfn.com; Mission Rd; per vehicle $5; ⊙ 9am-10pm May-Sep), and reveals its most majestic moments in the evening when the valley is but a sea of blinking lights. A walking trail leads from the viewing area to the top of the mountain. Watch your step while climbing – the shale rock can cause tumbles.

OUIMET CANYON PROVINCIAL PARK

Ouimet Canyon (☑807-977-2526; admission by $2 donation; ☺May-Oct), just 80km east of Thunder Bay, is a treacherous crevasse scoured out by ice and wind during the last Ice Age. A microclimate supporting a small collection of rare arctic-alpine plants has formed at the bottom, 150m below. A 1km loop hugs the jagged bluffs offering views that will make your knees tremble. Camping is prohibited. The canyon is 12km from the highway turnoff.

Nearby, **Eagle Canyon Adventures'** (☑807-857-1475; www.eaglecanyonadventures.ca; 275 Valley Rd, Dorion; entry $18, zip line $55, campsites $30; ☺9am-9pm Apr-Nov) 183m-long bridge over the deep canyon floor is the longest suspension footbridge in Canada. It also claims the country's longest zip line, to satisfy almost-insatiable adventurers.

Activities

Kangas
SAUNA

(☑807-344-6761; www.kangassauna.com; 379 Oliver Rd; sauna hire from $14; ☺7:30am-9pm Mon-Fri, 8am-11pm Sat & Sun) Friday night at Kangas is a well-established social event. The saunas are private and can be hired for up to five hours, so go it alone, or grab a 'conference room' for you and your 'associates.' There's also a hot tub, fantastic dining area, tanning booths and a hair salon!

Chippewa Park
SWIMMING

(www.chippewapark.ca; City Rd) This waterfront park is a great place to swim, frolic or picnic on a sunny day.

Loch Lomond Ski Area
SKIING

(☑807-475-7787; www.lochlomond.ca; 1800 Loch Lomond Rd; full-day lift tickets from $38; ☺Dec-Apr) With 14 runs, equally distributed between beginner, intermediate and advanced, this is a great hill to learn on and a wonderful place to ski with kids.

Sleeping

Thunder Bay has plenty of beds: most of the big motel chains are represented around the intersection of Hwys 11-17 and 61.

Thunder Bay International Hostel
HOSTEL $

(☑807-983-2042; www.thunderbayhostel.com; 1594 Lakeshore Dr; campsites $13, dm $20; @ 🖀) Colorful bric-a-brac, including antlers and a baby grand piano, lies splayed across the shrubby lawn as though Alice in Wonderland were having a garage sale. Charismatic owner Lloyd champions the backpacking lifestyle; he's a kindhearted, well-traveled soul who cares about his guests. The hostel is 25km east of town.

Strathcona Motel
MOTEL $

(☑807-683-8136; www.strathconamotel.ca; 545 Hodder Ave; d from $50; 🖀) We love this tiny motel that's been in the family since Ken was a kid. Units with separate bedrooms are a veritable time warp, but spotlessly clean and atmospheric. It's a few kilometers east of downtown in a lovely neighborhood.

McVicar Manor
INN $$

(☑807-344-9300; www.bbcanada.com/3918.html; 146 Court St N, Port Arthur; s/d from $105/120; 🖀) This sumptuous Victorian home has been proudly perched on its large lot for over one hundred years. Ask the owners what the local unionists did to the manor in the 1960s (it involves a bomb), but don't let that scare you off – McVicar takes comfort and quality a step beyond most other B&Bs.

Days Inn & Suites
MOTEL $$

(☑807-622-3297; www.daysinn.com; 645 Sibley Dr; d incl breakfast from $119; 🖀 🖵 🛁) This family-friendly motel is as central to everything as you can get in spread-out Thunder Bay. Kids love the indoor pool. Rooms are clean, spacious and neutrally decorated.

Nor'Wester
MOTEL $$

(☑807-473-9123; www.bestwestern.com; 2080 Hwy 61; d from $119) It doesn't seem to matter that this fantastic motel is about 15km from downtown – if you can say Thunder Bay has such a thing. The setting is lovely, the staff are excellent, rooms are clean and comfortable and there's a fantastic selection of suites. There's a huge indoor pool and hot tub for those wintry nights. Highly recommended.

Eating

Growing Season Juice Collective
JUICE BAR $

(☑807-344-6869; 210 Algoma St S; items $4-12; ☺11am-7pm Mon-Sat) Healthy blended juice is the name of the game here, but there are also scrumptious dishes to accompany your smoothie. Wash down your carrot sticks with a shot of organic wheatgrass.

THUNDER BAY TO MANITOBA

Decisions, decisions: if you're driving further west, you have two choices. Neither are particularly inspiring: the northern route is faster, but the southern route has some impressive diversions.

Traffic and highway vistas thin out after **Kakabeka Falls**. Then, at **Shabaqua Corners**, the highway forks: the northern route along Hwy 17 plows straight toward Winnipeg, while the southern route (Hwy 11 and Hwy 71) takes two extra hours as it ambles through more scenic landscapes . Both routes shuttle you through prime fishing country.

Signs mark the beginning of a new time zone (you save an hour going west).

Northern Route

Ignace and **Dryden** have plenty of motels and basic restaurants. If you're passing through at the beginning of July, check out the annual **Dryden Moose Fest** (www.moosefest.ca).

The biggest and best place to pause is **Kenora** (www.visitkenora.ca), the unofficial capital of the striking **Lake of the Woods** region and tourism hub for local summer cottages and fishing trips. Accommodations are plentiful: the usual army of franchise motels lines the highway.

Canadian Native Cultural Tours (☑807-468-9124; www.mskenora.com; adult/child $27/14) offers scenic cultural cruises aboard the MS *Kenora*. The **Lake of the Woods Museum** (☑807-467-2105; www.lakeofthewoodsmuseum.ca; 300 Main St S, Kenora; adult/child $3/2; ☺10am-5pm) features the aboriginal and industrial history of the area, with a particular focus on the last century of rapid change.

Greyhound Canada connects Kenora with Thunder Bay ($95, six hours, twice daily) and Winnipeg ($40, 2½ hours, twice daily).

Southern Route

The longer route has some spectacular distractions. **Atikokan** is the first major stop after the highways diverge. This crusty mining town has several motel and lodge options, making it a good base for a day trip to the stunning and secluded **Quetico Provincial Park** (☑807-597-4602; www.ontarioparks.com/parks/quetico; Hwy 11; day use per vehicle $9.50, campsites per person campground $14-43, backcountry $11-19). The endless waterlogged preserve has one small campground, and over 1500km of canoe routes stretching into unexplored backcountry. **Canoe Canada Outfitters** (☑807-597-6418; www.canoecanada.com; 300 O'Brien St, Atikokan; tours from $240) provides both self-guided and guided adventures through this dramatic wilderness.

Further west, **Fort Frances** sits right on the American border. The **Fort Frances Museum** (☑807-274-7891; www.fort-frances.com/museum; 259 Scott St, Fort Frances; adult/child $3.75/2.75; ☺10am-5pm) is worth a look, offering a historical introduction to the area. **Kay-Nah-Chi-Wah-Nung** (☑807-483-1163; Shaw Rd, Emo; admission $10; ☺10am-6pm Wed-Sat Jun-Sep), 50km west of Fort Frances, is a sacred Ojibwe site containing the largest ancient ceremonial burial grounds in Canada.

Travelers who wish to continue along the Trans-Canada Hwy must follow Hwy 71 north after passing tiny **Emo**, since Hwy 11 veers south across the border: do not pass without your passport.

Before linking back up with Hwy 17, consider making two more scenic pit stops, at **Nestor Falls** and **Sioux Narrows**, serene resort towns offering a glut of rentable cottages and houseboats.

Sweet Pea　　　　　　VEGETARIAN **$**
(☑807-344-8543; www.sweetpeashomecatering.com; 252 Algoma St S; items from $6; ☺11:30am-3pm & 4:30-7:30pm Tue-Fri) Fresh, earthy, organic, healthy and sustainable: all are words one can use to describe the fantastic made-with-love cooking of this delightful little catering joint/cafe.

Hoito Restaurant BREAKFAST $

(📞 345 6323; www.hoito.ca; 314 Bay St; mains from $8; ⏱8am-8pm) You'll think you've stumbled into a staff cafeteria in Finland – in fact, that's how the Hoito started, over one hundred years ago, providing affordable meals to Finnish bush workers. This Thunder Bay institution serves breakfast until 7:30pm with lunch from 10:45am. It's famed for its flattened pancakes served around the clock.

Giorg ITALIAN $$

(📞 807-623-8052; www.giorgristorante.com; 114 Syndicate Ave N; mains $14-28; ⏱noon-3pm & 6-10pm) The exterior is a throwback to a time when good taste and architecture weren't especially synonymous (the 1970s), but the charming Italian restaurant inside ranks as one of Thunder Bay's best, with scrumptious pastas served by poised waiters.

Tokyo House ASIAN $$

(📞 807-622-1169; www.tokyohouse.ca; 231 Arthur St; buffet from $15; ⏱noon-10pm) There's nothing authentically Japanese about this shiny all-you-can-eat restaurant, but this is Thunder Bay and we're grateful Asian food is represented this far north at all! Most of your favorite Japanese dishes are here with a ton of sushi options, all prepared to order.

Bistro One INTERNATIONAL $$$

(📞 622 2478; www.bistroone.ca; 555 Dunlop St; ⏱5-10pm Tue-Sat) A diamond in the rough hidden among clunky uninspired neighbors, Bistro One sizzles with an innovative, ever-changing menu, sleek decor and a legendary wine list.

Caribou Restaurant & Wine Bar FUSION $$$

(📞 807-628-8588; www.caribourestaurant.com; 727 Hewitson St; mains $16-39; ⏱11:30am-2pm Thu & Fri & 5-9pm daily) Between the confusing haze of wide-set freeways and boxy megamarts lies one of Thunder Bay's best dining options. The facade positively reeks of franchise banality; however, the inside is filled with lovely touches like white-clothed tables and designer stemware.

Prospector Steakhouse STEAKHOUSE $$$

(📞 807-345-5833; www.prospectorsteakhouse.com; 27 Cumberland St S; mains $20-40; ⏱5-9pm) Appetites beware: you're about to be obliterated. Hefty carnivorous portions are dished out amid ranchlike curios. The infamous prime rib will give your arteries a workout.

🍸 Drinking & Nightlife

★Sovereign Room BAR

(📞 807-343-9277; www.sovereignroom.com; 220 Red River Rd; ⏱4pm-late Tue, Wed, Sat & Sun, from 11am Thu & Fri) From the chandelier behind the bar to the ornate olive wallpaper, dark woody booths and upward curling staircase by the storefront window, the Sovereign Room stands on its own as a great spot for a beer. There's live music here too. Better still, the regularly updated menu is both surprising and delightful. Some come just for the food, others the beer, many for both. The vibe goes from mellow as a cello to seriously happening.

Foundry PUB

(📞 807-285-3188; www.thefoundrypub.com; 242 Red River Rd; ⏱4pm-late Tue, Wed, Sat & Sun, from 11am Thu & Fri) New kid on the block, The Foundry is making waves in the Bay: with 24 beers on tap, live music most weekends and dinner nightly within a smart two-level venue.

Madhouse Tavern Grill BAR

(📞 807-344-6600; 295 Bay St; ⏱11:30am-11pm) A great place to relax and take a load off among warm, friendly chatter and cold beer. The dangling portraits of famous writers and artists have a swirling style similar to Dalí.

ℹ️ Information

Both information centers have wireless internet connections, as do the city's four central libraries.

Pagoda Information Center (📞807-684-3670; cnr Red River Rd & Water St; ⏱9am-5pm Tue-Sat Jun-Aug; 📶) This is the most central source of visitor information and the oldest tourist-information bureau in Canada!

Tourism Thunder Bay (📞800-667-8386; www.tourismthunderbay.com; 1000 Hwy 11-17; ⏱9am-5pm; 📶) Located 6km east of town at the Terry Fox Lookout and Memorial.

ℹ️ Getting There & Away

Thunder Bay Airport (YQT; www.tbairport.on.ca) is served by Air Canada, WestJet, Porter, Delta, Wasaya and Bearskin airlines. The airport is about 3km southwest of the city, at the junction of West Arthur St and Hwy 61. Flight connections include Sudbury, Sault Ste-Marie, Ottawa, Toronto, Winnipeg and Minneapolis.

Greyhound buses run to and from Sault Ste-Marie ($126, nine hours, twice daily) and Winnipeg ($127, nine hours, twice daily). The

Greyhound **bus depot** (☏ 807-345-2194; 815 Fort William Rd) lies between the two downtown areas near the Intercity Mall.

❶ Getting Around

Car-rental chains are well represented at the airport.

Thunder Bay Transit (☏ 807-684-3744; www. thunderbay.ca) has the city covered. Buses have two main hubs: the **Thunder Bay South Terminal** (cnr May & Donald Sts) and the **Thunder Bay North Terminal** (cnr Water & Camelot Sts), though at the time of writing a central bus station was in the works as part of a transit Master Plan. One-way trips cost $2.65.

Cochrane to Moosonee & Moose Factory

Time has not been kind to little Cochrane, whose raison d'être is the *Polar Bear Express* – the whistle-stop train shuttling passengers north to the remote recesses of James Bay. Cochrane doesn't pretend to be a dainty tourist destination and, in a way, that honesty is refreshing. Evidence of harsh, long winters is conspicuous in this wind-swept town, but despite the inhospitable winters, the largely Francophone population is warm and accommodating.

Moosonee and Moose Factory sit near the tundra line, and are as far north as most people ever get in eastern Canada. Expeditions further north will undoubtedly involve floatplanes, canoes, snowmobiles, dogsleds or snowshoes. The railway reached Moosonee in 1932, about 30 years after it was established by Révillon Frères (known today as Revlon) as a trading post. A quick boat trip links Moosonee to the island of Moose Factory, which is not an industrial site that churns out large hairy beasts, but a small Cree settlement and the historic site of the Hudson's Bay Company trading hub founded in 1672.

While you ponder a lengthy journey to this ultraremote locale, consider the following: when fur trading peaked 300 years ago, the main access to Ontario's interior was *from* the north via the Hudson and James Bays. It's hard to fathom.

◉ Sights & Activities

Most visitors come just for the day and miss out on what the secluded area has to offer. Moosonee and Moose Factory could not be more different. Moosonee has a banal industrial vibe, while Moose Factory is a spirited reservation of friendly people and scores of smoke huts. The best way to experience the region is through a tour with the local Moose Cree.

Polar Bear Habitat & Heritage Village ZOO
(☏ 800-354-9948, 705-272-2327; www.polar-bearhabitat.ca; 1 Drury Park Rd, Cochrane; adult/child $16/10; ⊙ 9am-5pm) Despite all the polar bear talk, there are no wild polar bears in the region. This center is dedicated to the conservation, care and well-being of polar bears: Ganuk is presently its only beary resident. Visitors can interact with him at daily 'meet the bear' sessions, or swim with him in a pool divided by a thick sheet of glass (swim session $5).

Cree Cultural Interpretive Centre MUSEUM
(www.moosecree.com/tourism/ccic; ⊙ Jul & Aug) Located in Moose Factory, this center features indoor and outdoor exhibits of artifacts, including bone tools, traditional toys, reusable diapers and dwellings from the precontact era. You'll learn about *pashtamowin,* or 'what goes around, comes around' – the Cree's version of karma, if you will. It is best to explore the center with the aid of a guide, as they can relay fascinating details and personal anecdotes about the interesting displays.

Polar Bear Express TRAIN TRIP
(☏ 800-268-9281; www.ontarionorthland.ca; round-trip adult/child $104.90/52.40; ⊙ Sun-Fri) This whistle-stop train is the only way to reach the remote communities of Moosonee and Moose Factory. It departs Cochrane in the morning, arriving in the afternoon, before turning around. The assortment of passengers is a sight in itself: locals, trappers, biologists, geologists, tourists, anglers and paddlers. It's a five-hour trip each way, so if you return the same day you'll only have time for a short visit. From September to June, the train is commonly known as the Little Bear.

Moose Cree Outdoor Discoveries & Adventures OUTDOORS
(☏ 705-658-4619; www.creeadventures.com) Run by the Moose Cree First Nation, this outfit offers customized trips incorporating cultural activities (storytelling and traditional foods) with canoeing in summer and snowshoeing in winter. In tailoring your adventure, friendly staff will ask you: 'what do you want to experience?' and 'what are you not

looking for?' Prices vary depending on the number in your party, season and how long you want to visit. These trips offer a unique opportunity to experience Cree life as it is today.

🛏 Sleeping

Reserve accommodations before you arrive. There are a couple of lodging options in Moosonee, though we strongly suggest staying on the island of Moose Factory.

Station Inn
MOTEL $

(✆ 705-272-3500; www.ontarionorthland.ca; 200 Railway St, Cochrane; d from $95; ❀ @ 🛜) Go one better than staying near the train station by staying on top of it! You'll meet lots of fellow travelers here and you won't be late for your train.

Cree Village Ecolodge
INN $$

(✆ 888-273-3929, 705-658-6400; www.creevillage. com; 61 Hospital Dr, Moose Factory; r from $160) 🌿 The Cree Village Ecolodge is the first lodge owned and operated by Aboriginals in the northern hemisphere. This fascinating place was designed and furnished to reflect traditional Cree values. The environmentally conscious design extends to the organic wool and cotton used in the carpets, blankets and bed linen, organic soaps in every room, and some composting toilets. All meals are available.

Washow Lodge
LODGE $$

(✆ 705-658-4619; www.washow.ca; Hannah Bay; contact for quote) A stay at the Washow Lodge, 65km east of Moosonee, is to be welcomed into the family of Moose Cree and experiencea way of life that has remained largely unchanged by technology, with the exception of the snowmobile. Hope for a glimpse of the northern lights, black bears and beluga whales, and expect a unique cultural experience communing with nature from the comfort of this isolated new facility.

❶ Getting There & Around

Ontario Northland runs buses from **Cochrane Train Station** (✆ 705-272-4228) to North Bay ($75, 6¾ hours, twice daily) and Sudbury ($74, six hours, one daily).

Moosonee and Moose Factory are not accessible by car and can only be reached by the Polar Bear Express (p187). From Moosonee, water taxis shuttle passengers the 3km over to Moose Factory ($12, 15 minutes). In winter the river becomes an ice bridge stable enough for cars

and trucks. Van taxis from Moosonee station to the docks cost $6 per person.

Temagami

While god-fearing Egyptians were commissioning wondrous pyramids, this region of majestic old-growth pines and hushed lakes was a thriving network of trading routes. Evidence of these ancient trails exists today as hidden archaeological sites strewn throughout the region's provincial parks. For information about the group of preserves around Temagami, visit **Finlayson Point Provincial Park** (✆ 705-569-3205; www.ontarioparks. com/park/finlaysonpoint; Hwy 11; day use per vehicle $9.50; ⊗ May-Sep), 2km south of town on Hwy 11. Temagami's **Welcome Centre** (✆ 800-661-7609; www.temagamiinformation.com; 7 Lakeshore Rd; ⊗ 9am-4:30pm Mon-Fri) also offers information about the area and has displays about the region's history.

Check out **Obabika River Park**, or the vast **Lady Evelyn Smoothwater Provincial Park**, which has Ontario's highest point, **Ishpatina Ridge** (693m). There are no facilities, and campsites can only be reached by canoe. The easily accessible **White Bear Forest** has a soaring fire tower at Caribou Mountain offering a bird's-eye view of the stocky trunks below.

For something different, why not embark on an exhilarating and educational adventure, dogsledding through snow-drenched forests and frozen lakes. You're in good hands with **Wolf Within Adventures** (✆ 705-840-9002; www.wolfwithin.ca). In summer canoe trips through Temagami's rugged wilderness are also available.

Affable owners Doug and Marg have been running **Northland Paradise Lodge** (✆ 705-569-3791; www.northland-paradise.com; 51 Stevens Rd; s/d/ste $55/85/150), their friendly lakeside lodge, since 1986. The comfortable motel-style rooms, with full kitchen facilities, make the perfect base for any type of adventure in Temagami. Ontario Northland connects Temagami with North Bay by bus ($20, 1¼ hours, two daily).

North Bay

POP 54,000

North Bay bills itself as 'just north enough to be perfect,' which begs the question: perfect for what? It's just north enough to make visiting Torontonians feel like adventurers, and the lakeshore is lovely, but other parts of town have seen better days. That said, there's plenty of decent accommodations and some great food to be enjoyed by the water.

Ontario's two major highways (11 and 17) converge just outside of town, making North Bay a logical layover for Trans-Canada tourists. The highways don't link up again until after Thunder Bay, 1100km away.

◉ Sights & Activities

Dionne Quints Museum   MUSEUM
(☎705 472 8400; www.northbaychamber.com/tourism/museum; 1375 Seymour St N; adult/child $3.75/2.25; ⊙10am-4pm May-Oct) This museum, dedicated to five little girls, the Dionne Quints, identical quintuplets who briefly turned the city into the most visited Ontario destination after Niagara Falls. Born during the Great Depression, they were exploited as a tourist attraction by the provincial government: they even starred in four Hollywood films. The museum contains a fascinating collection of artifacts from their early years.

Lake Nipissing Waterfront   PARK
(adult/child $21/12) A walk along the scenic Lake Nipissing shoreline reveals several enjoyable activities including antique carousel rides.

Chief Commanda II   CRUISE
(☎866-660-6686, 705-494-8167; www.chiefcommanda.com; King's Landing, Memorial Dr; ⊙May-Sep) This jolly passenger liner cruises through the Manitou Islands (adult/child $22/12), along the French River ($38/20) and down to Callander Bay at sunset ($28/14). Three-hour 'Blues Cruises' are a big hit and meals are available on many departures: book in advance.

🛏 Sleeping

North Bay's downtown lacks appeal, but the strip of motels along Lakeshore Dr, from when the highway used to come through town, is pleasant enough.

★ Sunset Inn   MOTEL $
(☎705-472-8370; www.sunsetinn.ca; 641 Lakeshore Dr; d/ste from $89/169; ❉@🖧) We love this spotless waterfront option with its own private beach in a secluded cove off Lake Nipissing. Friendly hosts continue to update the variety of room types which include a number of luxurious suites with twin Jacuzzis and large flatscreen TVs, and two-bedroom family suites with full kitchens.

There's an adorable romantic cabin for two in front of the beach.

Comfort Inn   MOTEL $
(☎705-494-9444; www.lakeshore.comfortnorthbay.com; 676 Lakeshore Dr; d incl breakfast from $79; 🖧) Opposite the waterfront, this early-1990s motel has been well looked after. Drive-up ground-floor rooms are convenient and the leafy outlook is pleasant.

Gray's Log House   INN $
(☎705-495-2389; www.graysloghouse.com; 5270 Hwy 63, Trout Lake; r $90, cabin $50) Escape the downtown bustle and retreat to this lovely log cabin near Trout Lake (5.7km after Average Joe's). Evenings can be spent chatting with the affable owner over homemade desserts, or you can snuggle up with a handmade quilt and watch the snow fall in winter. There's a rustic camping cabin out back, full of charm.

🍴 Eating & Drinking

Burger World   BURGERS $
(☎705-497-9755; www.burgerworld.ca; 1308 Algonquin Ave; burgers from $4; ⊙7am-8pm) Punters line up for the juicy burgers and crispy fries at this local institution and you'd be well advised to join the club. Dine in or head down to the waterfront for an impromptu picnic.

Dave's Green Papaya   ASIAN $$
(☎705-476-8883; www.davesgreenpapaya.com; 652 Fraser St; mains $10-18; ⊙11am-2pm Tue-Fri & 4-9pm Tue-Sun) An eclectic pan-Asian selection of mouthwatering meals, including dishes from China, Korea, Thailand and Japan, are presented with flavor and flair at this hopping downtown eatery. The price is right.

Kabuki House   JAPANESE $$$
(☎705-495-0999; www.kabukihouse.com; 349 Main St W; lunch mains $9-19, dinner $20-34; ⊙11:30am-2pm Mon-Fri & 5-10:30pm daily) It's so nice to find authentic Japanese cuisine this far north. Dinner here might put a dent in your wallet, but Kabuki House is guaranteed to please lovers of sushi, sashimi and teppanyaki. *Omakase* (chef special) and set menus are highly recommended.

White Owl Bistro   CANADIAN $$$
(☎705-472-2662; www.thewhiteowlbistro.ca; 639 Lakeshore Dr; mains $21-39; ⊙11am-9pm Mon-Sat) Dinners at this lovely little bistro, built in 1934, are a little pricey, so we recommend you enjoy a better-value lunch or weekend

brunch on the beautiful lakefront patio instead.

Average Joe's   BAR

(☑705-474-1982; www.averagejoes.net; 3501 Trout Lake Rd; ☉11am-11pm) Average Joe's is anything but average. Arriving by land, water, or frozen lake in the winter, enjoy tasty fare from the broad menu (mains $8-29) while staring out over the serene Trout Lake. The bar keeps the gregarious locals around until 1am or 2am.

❶ Information

North Bay Chamber of Commerce (☑705-472-8480; www.northbaychamber.com; 1357 Seymour St; ☉9am-7pm) Near the junction of Hwys 11 & 17, 5km south of downtown, beside the Quints museum.

❶ Getting There & Away

Ontario Northland buses connect Toronto and North Bay ($73, 5½ hours, four to five daily). Greyhound connects North Bay with Sudbury ($29, 1¾ hours, three daily) and Ottawa ($75, 5¼ hours, three daily). The terminus for all services is the **North Bay Train Station** (☑705-495-4200; 100 Station Rd), which no longer serves passenger rail services.

EASTERN ONTARIO

Eastern Ontario encompasses the countryside east of Toronto as far as the Québec border. Not too far past the suburban sprawl of Oshawa, the GTA's easternmost extent, the fertile pastures of Prince Edward County support a rich farming tradition. Travelers journeying between Montréal and Toronto along Hwy 401, the nation's busiest corridor, should allow a few days to enjoy this scenic, historic and culinary realm.

For a dose of colonial history, eastern Ontario is tops. Stately Kingston was the first capital of modern-day Canada: the picturesque city offers a wealth of museums and attractions. Continuing east, the smaller towns of Gananoque, Brockville and Prescott have a genteel Victorian vibe with their abundance of stately inns and estates. Tiny Merrickville, a former Loyalist stronghold, has changed little since the American Revolution. These horse-and-buggy townships straddle the stunning Thousand Islands region, a foggy archipelago of lonely isles along the deep St Lawrence Seaway.

Eastern Ontario's natural beauty extends far into the province's sparsely populated interior, which overflows with scenic parks, preserves and private cottage retreats. Internationally acclaimed Algonquin Provincial Park is the area's flagship domain, offering unparalleled hiking, canoeing and wildlife-spotting through twisting sapphire lakes and towering jack pines. Similar topography extends to the Kawarthas and Land O' Lakes, once inhabited by ancient Aboriginal tribes.

Surprisingly, there is still no major highway running directly between Toronto and Ottawa. The speediest option is to take Hwy 401 from Toronto to Prescott, then scoot up north on Hwy 416 to the capital. The rural, two-lane Hwy 7 is a pleasant but slower alternative.

Algonquin Provincial Park

Established in 1893, Ontario's oldest and largest park is a sight for sore eyes, with 7800 sq km of thick pine forests, jagged cliffs, trickling crystal streams, mossy bogs and thousands (thousands!) of lakes. An easily accessible outdoor gem, this rugged expanse is a must-see for canoeists and hikers.

Hwy 60 intersects a small portion of the park near its southern edge. Each kilometer of highway within the park is tagged, starting at the West Gate (known as 'km 0') and terminating at the East Gate (known as 'km 56'). Outfitters and accommodations use

---

CRYING WOLF

Algonquin Provincial Park is very active in wolf research, and public 'howls' are an incredible way to experience the presence of these furry beasts. Wolves will readily respond to human imitations of their howling, so the park's staff conducts communal howling sessions on the occasional August evening. These events are highly organized: you could be one of 2000 people standing in the darkness waiting for the chilling wails. Wolf howls are announced only on the days they are actually held. They often take place on Thursdays, but check the bulletin boards, park website or phone the visitors center (☑613-637-2828) to be sure.

Eastern Ontario

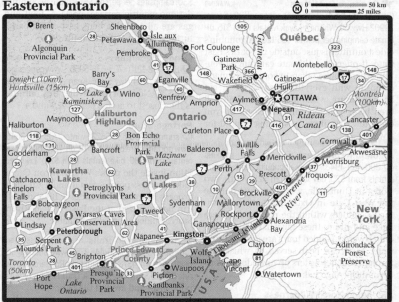

these markers when giving directions: 'turn north off Hwy 60 at km 15.4 to reach Arowhon Pines lodge.' Numerous campgrounds and hiking trails are accessible from this well-trodden corridor. The vast, wooded interior of Algonquin is only accessible via 2000km of charted canoe routes and intense hiking trails.

Aside from the main gates, Algonquin Park has 29 access points located around the periphery of the park and along Hwy 60, for access to the park's backcountry.

The two large Muskoka towns of Bracebridge and Huntsville are within an hour's drive of the West Gate. Other small townships include Whitney, Maynooth and Bancroft, south of the East Gate, and Mattawa, north of the park on Hwy 17.

The official website for the Friends of Algonquin Park is www.algonquinpark.on.ca.

Sights

Algonquin is famous for its wildlife-watching and scenic lookouts. During spring, you're almost certain to see moose along Hwy 60, as they escape the pesky black flies to lick the leftover salt from winter de-icing. Other creatures you may encounter include deer, beaver, otter, mink and many bird species.

There's no limit to the breathtaking natural scenic beauty on offer.

Algonquin Art Centre
GALLERY
(705-633-5555; www.algonquinartcentre.com; km 20 on Hwy 60; ⊙10am-5pm Jun-Oct) FREE Exhibits display an array of wilderness-themed art through several media including paintings, carvings and sculpture.

Algonquin Logging Museum
MUSEUM
(613-637-2828; km 54.5 on Hwy 60; ⊙9am-5pm Jul-Oct) FREE This excellent museum has extensive exhibits and interpretation of the park's logging heritage. The displays are spread along a 1.5km trail that remains open even when the reception area, bookstore and theater are closed.

Activities

Algonquin is a great place to give canoeing or kayaking a whirl. Outfitters offer many opportunities for novice paddlers as well as advanced wilderness adventures for the experienced outdoors person. Self-guided paddling trips are a popular option. A quota system governs the number of tourists on each canoe route, so plan ahead. Canoe Lake and Opeongo Lake are popular starting points for beginners, although the launching docks are frequently crowded.

★ **Opeongo Outfitters** KAYAKING
(☏800-790-1864; www.opeongooutfitters.com; 29902 Hwy 60, Whitney; kayak rentals from $16, ultimate camping per person $85-120) Algonquin's oldest outfitter is just outside the park's East Gate. It offers the ultimate camping adventure where you're taken to your ready-made campsite with everything you need to get back to nature, without the hassle. Staff will even bring you food and check up on you every few days if you're sticking around for a while.

Algonquin Outfitters KAYAKING
(☏800-469-4948; www.algonquinoutfitters.com; rentals from $20, day tours from $25) With two stores in Huntsville, a location just outside the West Gate in Oxtongue Lake and two further outlets within the park at Opeongo Lake and Brent, these guys have got Algonquin covered. Guided tours are available and water taxis can be reserved to whisk you through rougher waters up to wilder regions beyond Opeongo Lake.

Algonquin North Wilderness Outfitters KAYAKING
(☏877-544-3544; www.algonquinnorth.com; Hwy 17 & Hwy 630, Mattawa; kayaks from $25) This outfitter is north of the park at the junction of Hwy 17 and Hwy 630 in Mattawa, from where a gravel road takes you to the Brain Lake access point for secluded backcountry explorations.

Algonquin Portage KAYAKING
(☏613-735-1795; www.algonquinportage.com; 1352 Barron Canyon Rd, Pembroke; canoes from $22, dm $30, campsites per person $5) Rustic accommodations, shuttle service, portage, food and gas are all available here, east of the park's furthest eastern extent, on Rte 28.

Canoe Algonquin KAYAKING
(☏800-818-1210, 705-636-5956; www.canoealgonquin.com; 1914 Hwy 518 E, Kearney; kayak rentals from $20) North of Huntsville; this outfitter is the closest to access points 2, 3 and 4.

Portage Store KAYAKING
(☏summer 705-633-5622, winter 705-789-3645; www.portagestore.com; km 14 on Hwy 60; canoe rentals from $30, bike rentals from $25) Located 14km inside the park's West Gate on Canoe Lake at access point 5, you'll find a gift shop, grocery store and outfitters. Bike rentals can be organized at the Lake of Two Rivers Store. Guided tours also available.

South Algonquin Trails HORSE RIDING
(☏800-758-4801, 705-448-1751; www.southalgonquintrails.com; 4378 Elephant Lake Rd, Harcourt; 1hr ride $60) Scenic horseback trail riding is very popular in and around the park.

 Tours

A seemingly endless range of tours are available to all types of adventurers. Guided trips range from day hikes to customized remote adventures that last as long as your stamina allows.

Northern Edge Algonquin KAYAKING
(☏888-383-8320; www.algonquincanada.com; 100 Ottawa Ave, South River) Features paddling

---

TOP FIVE HIKES IN ALGONQUIN PROVINCIAL PARK

Whether you're visiting for a day or a month, sampling some of the over 140km of hiking trails, including many shorter jaunts accessible from Hwy 60, is a must! Hikes depart from various mileposts (actually kilometer-posts) along Hwy 60 between the West Gate (km 0) and the East Gate (km 56).

Mizzy Lake (moderate 11km loop) – An excellent chance to see some diverse wildlife: all known species within the park have been witnessed here at some point in time (at km 15).

Track & Tower (moderate 7.7km loop) – A serene lakeside trail and an unusual elevated lookout point along an abandoned railway (at km 25).

Booth's Rock (difficult 5km loop) – Follow an abandoned railway for breathtaking views of the sweeping lakes and forests (follow the road from km 40).

Centennial Ridges (difficult 10km loop) – The best panoramas in the park, bar none (follow the road from km 37).

Lookout Trail (difficult 1km loop) – The busiest hike in Algonquin, but for good reason: a spectacular view of untouched nature awaits (at km 40).

trips, women's weekends, and tailored programs in winter.

Voyageur Quest KAYAKING
(☎800-794-9660, 416-486-3605; www.voyageurquest.com; Round Lake, South River) Has lodge rentals in addition to popular paddling trips.

🛏 Sleeping & Eating

Algonquin is a nature preserve, which means that most noncamping accommodations are outside the park boundaries. Consider basing yourself in Huntsville or Bracebridge (43km and 73km from the West Gate, respectively) or Whitney, just outside the East Gate, if you plan on day-tripping to the park.

There are nine car-accessible developed campgrounds within the park (some with yurts) that can be reached from Hwy 60, as well as backcountry camping, accessible only by hiking or canoeing. Three additional sites (Achray, Brent and Kiosk) are accessible via minor roads further north. You must contact the centralized reservation service for **Ontario Parks** (www.ontarioparks.com) for all reservations. Fees vary by site.

There are three upscale lodges in the park's interior; each has restaurants. Otherwise, you'll need to bring your own munchies and supplies.

🛏 West Gate

Wolf Den HOSTEL $
(☎866-271-9336, 705-635-9336; www.wolfdenbunkhouse.com; 4568 Hwy 60, Oxtongue Lake; dm/s from $25/45) ⬮ If you're in the backpacking spirit, this hostel has an awesome buzz. Guests stay in shiny log cabins and bunkhouses scattered around the grounds or the large central lodge with huge kitchen and stunning 2nd-floor lounge.

Dwight Village Motel MOTEL $
(☎705-635-2400; www.dwightvillagemotel.com; 2801 Hwy 60; r $79-149) You'll notice this excellent motel from the highway: spotless rooms offer all the creature comforts and the friendly owners assure a comfortable stay. It's 25km west of the park, just east of the village of Dwight. There's a lovely outdoor picnic area with fire pits and plenty of room for kids to play.

Riverside Motel MOTEL $
(☎705-635-9021; www.riversidemoteldwight.com; Hwy 60, Dwight; r from $95; ❄☎) ⬮ Few roadside motels can claim a 4-hectare plot with

its own waterfall and swimming hole. You can hear the river from the rooms, some of which come with kitchenettes and Jacuzzi tubs. Flower gardens and walking trails round out the offerings.

🛏 Park Interior

The only permanent resorts within the park are the following upscale lodges, which operate between mid-May and mid-October. Each option includes breakfast, lunch and dinner in the pricing scheme. Dining rooms are open to nonguests as well.

Arowhon Pines LODGE $$$
(☎866-633-5661; www.arowhonpines.ca; turnoff at km 15.4 on Hwy 60; r per person from $198, private cabins per person from $328) If you've ever wondered what it might be like to go to adult summer camp, Arowhon Pines is the answer. The largest and most luxurious of Algonquin's all-inclusive lodges has canoes, kayaks, tennis courts, hiking and gourmet fine dining (BYOW – Bring Your Own Wine). It's wonderfully, blissfully secluded, well north of Hwy 60.

Killarney Lodge LODGE $$$
(☎866-473-5551; www.killarneylodge.com; turnoff at km 33.2 on Hwy 60; cabins per person from $219) Take a trip back in time to an age where rustic lakeside cabins were synonymous with family vacations. Killarney is an idyllic place for a paddle on the lake or to relax on your private deck with a few glasses of red (BYO). The delightful dining room functions like a well-oiled machine, serving three hearty and delicious meals per day. Only the ocassional distant rumble of trucks along Hwy 60 interrupts the blissful silence.

Bartlett Lodge LODGE $$$
(☎866-614-5355; www.bartlettlodge.com; turnoff at km 23.3 on Hwy 60; d per person from $195) ⬮ One especially interesting cabin sets this place apart: 'Sunrise' runs completely on solar power, but a variety of studio rooms, cabins and two flashpacking tents are available. Bartlett Lodge is accessed by boat (provided for you) from a point 23km inside the West Gate.

🛏 East Gate

★ **Arlington Hostel & Pub** HOSTEL $
(☎613-338-2080; www.thearlington.ca; Hwy 62, Maynooth; HI members dm/d $20/52, nonmembers dm/d $25/58 taxes incl; ☉pub 3-10pm

Thu-Sun) There's something about this towering century-old monster that makes you just want to disappear into it. If Jack Kerouac were alive and came to Canada, well, you could just see him hanging out on the porch. In tiny Maynooth, the Arlington is a great place for artists, writers and lonely wanderers who want to disappear into their craft for a while: there's nothing here but a rocking pub downstairs.

Algonquin East Gate Motel   MOTEL $

(☑613-637-2652; www.algonquineastgatemotel. com; Hwy 60, Whitney; d from $60) This cozy little motel just outside the park's East Gate has spotless retro rooms, a funky dining room and friendly, helpful staff. There's even a private housekeeping cottage out back.

Magnificent Hill   HOSTEL $

(☑705-448-9453; www.magnificenthill.ca; 1258 Magnificent Rd, Highland Grove; dm from $25) ⊘ Set on a 40-hectare organic farm, this rustic lodge is a winner. One dorm room above a woodshop sleeps a handful, while a separate 'Zen room' offers a chill-out space. Workstay/WWOOFing (Willing Workers on Organic Farms) programs are available, or you can just enjoy the chickens, baby goats, and miles and miles of quiet. It's near the park's southern boundary.

Couples Resort   RESORT $$$

(☑866-202-1179; www.couplesresort.ca; 139 Galeairy Lake Rd, Whitney; r from $236) Don't let the name fool you into thinking this is some kind of a swinger's den, although you are correct in that it caters specifically for couples. All accommodations benefit from a lovely position on Galeairy Lake, just outside the park border. Entry level rooms are comfortable and modern, but the real appeal lies in the decadent, private (and a little gaudy) lakeview 'chateaus' with outdoor hot tubs, indoor Jacuzzis, fireplaces and every conceivable amenity for eliciting romance. Rates are competitive during low season.

❶ Information

Algonquin Provincial Park is accessible year-round. Drivers can pass through the park along Hwy 60; you must pay the day-use fee to stop and look around ($16 per vehicle). The Hwy 60 corridor has limited cell-phone coverage for several kilometers on each side of the park, as well as a couple of payphones.

Algonquin Visitors Centre (☑613-637-2828; www.algonquinpark.on.ca; km 43 on Hwy 60; ⊙9am-9pm; ☎) This world-class visitors center is worth a stop in its own right. Displays and dioramas illustrate the park's wildlife, history and geology. The center also has a bookstore, cafeteria, wi-fi and a lookout with spectacular views.

Information Centres (☑613-637-2828; www. algonquinpark.on.ca) West Gate (⊙8am-8pm May-Sep); East Gate (⊙8am-7pm) Small info centers at either end of the park along Hwy 60 at km 0 and km 56.

❶ Getting There & Away

The closest form of public transportation to Algonquin Park is the Greyhound bus connecting Toronto to Maynooth ($55, five hours), 44km from the East Gate.

Parkbus (www.parkbus.ca) offers limited (but increasing) express departures from Toronto and at the time of writing was trialing a service from Ottawa. Check the website for the latest schedules.

Haliburton Highlands

This rugged expanse of needleleaf trees feels like a southern extension of Algonquin Provincial Park. Over 240 sq km of the densely forested region is part of the **Haliburton Forest** (☑705-754-2198; www.haliburtonforest. com; 1095 Redkenn Rd, Haliburton). This privately owned woodland, 30km north of Haliburton town, can be accessed through its main office on Kenneisis Lake. A variety of activities are available: the recommended 'Walk in the Clouds' four-hour guided hike ($95) takes you on a pulse-quickening adventure along suspended planks (20m above the ground) through the treetops while providing a bird's-eye view of the woods below. A visit to the Wolf Centre is included; visitors can glimpse a pack of wolves from a safe distance as they meander through their 6-hectare enclosure. Thick pillows of snow in the winter encourage a thriving snowmobiling culture, and dogsledding ($175 for a half-day tour) is a popular attraction as well.

The small town of **Bancroft** (www.bancroftontario.com) is particularly well known for its mineral-rich soils and the **Rockhound Gemboree** (www.rockhoundgemboree.com), Canada's largest gem festival, held in early August. During the yearly event, geologists lead tours around nearby abandoned mines to scout out stones. These 'rockhounding' adventures are usually quite successful: examples of over 80% of the minerals found in Canada are regularly dug up in the area.

COTTAGE COUNTRY

Much of Ontario, from the shores of Lake Erie to Muskoka, the Kawarthas, Haliburton and the Thousand Islands, is cottage country. Thousands of lakes are dotted with rocky islands and forested shorelines offering dazzling sunsets. It won't be long after you arrive in Toronto before you're introduced to the slow pace and hospitality of someone's cottage, for that's what Ontario summers are all about – communing with friends, family and nature over cold beer, fine wine and good food.

Torontonians flock to the lakes as soon as the weather gets warm. Ramshackle fisher's huts are prised open at the first available moment after the spring thaw, while sprawling winterised waterfront mansions awake from their slumber: flowerpots are replanted, freezers restocked and families begin their weekly pilgrimage from the city.

The common denominator of the cottage phenomenon is the sense of pride in one's place and the desire to be in the great outdoors. Canoes, kayaks, ski-boats and Sea-Doos all come out and the lazy days and wild nights begin, until winter, when the lakes freeze over, the snowmobiles appear and they do it all again.

Peterborough & the Kawarthas

Peterborough, in the heart of the wooded Kawarthas, is the best place to start your visit through this sacred aboriginal land. The handsome **Peterborough & the Kawarthas Visitors Centre** (☑705-742-2201, 800-461-6424; www.thekawarthas.ca; 1400 Crawford Dr; ☺9am-5pm Mon-Fri, 10am-4pm Sat & Sun May-Oct) should be your first stop: helpful staff will point you in the right direction toward cultural attractions or scenic nature preserves. It's a green university town with a bustling community surrounded by thousands of private cottages dotted around the area's many lakes. Stoney Lake, one of the largest, has some of the most lavish and beautiful private homes in the area.

If you feel like hanging around, consider staying a night in pretty **Lakefield**, 14km north of town at the bottom of Stoney Lake. Nearby **Lake Edge Cottages** (☑705-652-9080; www.lakeedge.com; 45 Lake Edge Rd, Lakefield; cottages from $240; ☎☒☼) has rustic, well-appointed lakefront cottages with decks on a secluded woody property. There's a wonderful swimming pool and private hot tubs appear as if by magic in the winter. A further 22km northwest, on Country Road 23, the **Whetung Ojibwa Gallery** (☑705-657-3661; www.whetung.com; Curve Lake Indian Reserve; ☺9am-6pm) FREE has an extensive collection of aboriginal crafts from around the country, including the valued works of noted artist Norval Morrisseau.

Back in Peterborough, you'll find plenty of dining and shopping options and a quaint city center. Abandoned railroads and the impressive hydraulic lift lock are relics of a bygone era. The **Canadian Canoe Museum** (☑866-342-2663; www.canoemuseum.ca; 910 Monaghan Rd, Peterborough; adult/child $10.50/8.25; ☺10am-5pm Mon-Sat, from noon Sun) is a must-see. Although the outside looks like a warehouse, the refurbished dimly lit interior contains a phenomenal collection of over 200 canoes and kayaks. Walk around amid the calming sound of a trickling waterfall as you learn about the surprising and lengthy history of aquatic navigation in the region. If you're not inspired to pick up a paddle when you're done, how about ice cream from the Peterborough branch of much-loved **Kawartha Dairy** (☑705-745-6437; www.kawarthadairy.com; 815 High St, Peterborough)?

Northeast from Peterborough on Warsaw Road, the **Warsaw Caves Conservation Area** (☑877-816-7604; www.warsawcaves.com; admission per vehicle $10; ☺May-Oct) offers hiking, swimming, camping and spelunking in eroded limestone tunnels. Continuing north for another 30km will bring you to **Petroglyphs Provincial Park** (☑705-877-2552; www.ontarioparks.com/park/petroglyphs; 2249 Northey's Bay Rd, Woodview; admission $9.50; ☺10am-5pm May-Oct), with one of the best collections of prehistoric rock carvings in the country. Rediscovered in 1954, this important spiritual site is home to over 900 icons carved into the park's limestone ridges (although only a small percentage are discernible). Visitors will be pleased to find that the site is generally quite empty and has an earthy spiritual vibe. Camping is not permitted.

Land O' Lakes

South of the Haliburton Highlands and east of the Kawarthas, the majestic Land O' Lakes region (www.travellandolakes.com) links the vast inland expanse of yawning lakes and bulky evergreens to the temperate pastures of the St Lawrence Seaway. Half of the region belongs to the Thousand Islands–Frontenac Arch reserve – Canada's 12th biosphere, appointed by Unesco in 2002.

The region's crown jewel is the serene **Bon Echo Provincial Park** (☑888-668-7275, 613-336-2228; www.ontarioparks.com/park/bonecho; Hwy 41; day use per car $9.50, campsites from $14; ☺May-Oct), one of eastern Ontario's largest preserves, 80km due north of **Napanee**. Its untainted beauty lures artists and adventurers alike. The park's highlight is a 1.5km sheer rock face known as **Mazinaw Rock**, jutting sharply out from the depths of Mazinaw Lake for 100m. The rock features the largest visible collection of aboriginal pictographs in Canada, best observed by canoe. For camping reservations and information, contact **Ontario Parks** (www.ontarioparks.com).

BRIGHTON & PRESQU'ILE PROVINCIAL PARK

Pop off Hwy 401 at exit 509 to find quiet Brighton and the curious L-shaped **Presqu'ile Provincial Park** (☑613-475-4324; www.ontarioparks.com/park/presquile; 328 Presqu'ile Pkwy, Brighton; day use per car $9.50, campsites from $14), which juts out onto Lake Ontario. Relax on the beach among migrating birds, or try the **Jobes Wood Trail**, a 1km circular path that's just rural enough to glimpse the diverse woodlands and wildlife. The **Friends of Presqu'ile** (www.friendsofpresquile.on.ca) provides all there is to know about local flora and fauna. Camping reservations (May to October) must be made through **Ontario Parks** (www.ontarioparks.com). Drop by the Brighton District Chamber of Commerce **visitors center** (☑877-475-2775, 613-475-2775; www.brighton.ca; 74 Main St; ☺9am-4pm Mon-Fri) for more information about the town and region of Northumberland.

Frontenac Provincial Park (☑613-376-3489; www.ontarioparks.com/park/frontenac; 1090 Salmon Lake Rd, Sydenham; day use per car $9.50, campsites from $14) straddles both the lowlands of southern Ontario and the rugged Canadian Shield as a unique menagerie of wild plants and animals. The entrance and the information center are at **Otter Lake**, off Rte 19 north of Sydenham. From here, hikers and paddlers venture deep within the park, using the 160km of trails to spot beaver, black bear, coyote and osprey. **Frontenac Outfitters** (☑800-250-3174, 613-376-6220; www.frontenac-outfitters.com; 6674 Bedford Rd, Sydenham; rentals from $25; ☺9am-5pm Wed-Mon Apr-Oct) offers canoe rentals near the entrance to the park. The **Friends of Frontenac** (www.frontenacpark.ca) website is particularly handy.

Prince Edward County

Photographers will delight in the sweeping expanses of dappled branches, undulating pastoral hills, rugged bluffs and windswept shorelines of Prince Edward County. Golden fields yield bountiful harvests in this region rich in farm-to-table cuisine, peppered with providors of the finest foods, inviting B&Bs and up-and-coming wineries. Along the shores of Lake Ontario, Sandbanks Provincial Park's sandy beaches summon old-school holidaymakers to revel in the long hot days, summer storms and balmy nights around the campfire. In winter it's a different story entirely.

Wineries sprawl throughout the terrain, but the food scene is equally intoxicating: cheesemakers, bakers and restaurateurs who source only local produce all make for a sumptuous visit. Prince Edward County has the same soil composition as France's Burgundy, a mix of clay and soft calcitic limestone. Recent techniques to manage cooler winter climates have seen an influx of winemakers and growing recognition for the region's wines. Check out the **Ontario Culinary Tourism** (www.ontarioculinary.com) website for ideas around the food and wine theme.

The **Loyalist Parkway** (Hwy 33) unfurls for 94km from Trenton, along Lake Ontario, to Kingston, retracing the steps of the British Loyalists who settled here after fleeing the American Revolution. There's a brief interruption to the road at Glenora, beneath the mystical Lake on the Mountain, where a free car ferry whisks you across to Adolphustown.

Small-but-active **Picton** is the unofficial capital of the isthmus.

◉ Sights & Activities

If you're looking for culture and museums, you'll get your fill in Kingston and Ottawa. Savor Prince Edward County for its beauty, architecture and cuisine. Points of interest are scattered around a broad area. We suggest you hit the Loyalist Parkway, stopping (frequently) when something tickles your fancy.

Sandbanks Provincial Park PARK
(☑613-393-3319; www.ontarioparks.com/park/sandbanks; Country Rd 12; day use per car $9.50) Offering some of the best sandy swimming beaches in Ontario, popular Sandbanks Provincial Park is divided into two sections: **the Outlet**, an irresistible strip of white sandy beach, and **Sandbanks**, with its undulating dunes, some over three stories high. The less frequented, undeveloped section at the end of the beach is unlike anywhere else in Ontario.

Lake on the Mountain Provincial Park PARK
(☑613-393-3319; www.ontarioparks.com/park/lakeonthemountain; RR1, Picton) Lake on the Mountain, near Glenora, is somewhat of a mystery: 60m *above* adjacent Lake Ontario, it has a constant flow of clean, fresh water. Scientists are yet to confirm its source. The Mohawks offered gifts to its spirits, and settlers thought it was bottomless. There's a delightful picnic ground with wonderful views of the Bay of Quinte on Lake Ontario.

Bloomfield Bicycle CYCLING
(☑613-393-1060; www.bloomfieldbicycle.ca; 225 Bloomfield Main St, Bloomfield; half-day rentals from $25; ◎10am-6pm Apr-Oct) In little Bloomfield, just past the turnoff for Sandbanks, you can rent bicycles and gear to explore the surrounding countryside. In June visitors can ride around picking luscious strawberries from the vine at numerous farms. Check out the website for a printable PDF cycling map of the area. Tours are available.

☞ Tours

★ **Taste Trail** FOOD TOUR
(www.tastetrail.ca) The Taste Trail is a great way to explore the wines and food producers of the county. Download a printable PDF of the self-guided tour, through restaurants, farms and wineries, from the website. It's a gourmet adventure for the taste buds.

Arts Trail ARTS TOUR
(www.artstrail.ca) The Arts Trail is a self-guided tour leading to 28 studios and galleries across the county. Ceramics, glassworks, photography, jewelry and painting are some of the mediums you'll encounter. You can download a PDF map from the website.

Waupoos Winery WINERY TOUR
(☑613-476-8338; www.waupooswinery.com; Country Rd 8; tour $5, tasting $1; ◎10:30am-6pm May-Oct) White-gabled Waupoos Winery, with its patio among the vines and scenic lake vistas, offers tours and tastings. If the wine tickles your taste buds, why not stop for lunch?

🛏 Sleeping

Prince Edward County has a wide range of upscale B&Bs, boutique hotels and inns scattered among its three largest towns: Picton, Bloomfield and Wellington. The Picton Chamber of Commerce and Tourism office maintains a detailed list.

Sandbanks Provincial Park CAMPGROUND $
(☑888-668-7275, 519-826-5290; www.ontarioparks.com/park/sandbanks; campsites from $14; ◎Apr-Oct) Summer camping at Sandbanks is scenic and stress-free, but sites along the sandy dunes get booked months in advance. There are some first-come, first-served options as well, and two rentable cottages, each requiring a two-night minimum stay. Both chalets feature several bedrooms, a working fireplace, satellite TV and a full kitchen. Bookings must be made through Ontario Parks. Rates for sites vary.

Red Barns HOSTEL $
(☑613-476-6808; www.theredbarns.com; 167 White Chapel Rd, Picton; dm/d from $60/90; ❀🖥) It's difficult to classify Red Barns: part hostel,

---

TRENT-SEVERN WATERWAY

This scenic **waterway** (www.trentsevern.com; ◎May-Oct) cuts diagonally across eastern Ontario, following the lakes and rivers of Lake Simcoe County and the forested Kawarthas. The scenic hydro-highway starts on Lake Huron and passes 45 locks before emptying out near Prince Edward County on Lake Ontario. A hundred years ago, this 386km-long aboriginal canoe route bustled with commercial vessels. Today, it's purely recreational.

part B&B, part art school, this 10-hectare retreat has it all. Artists rent studio space (there's a glass-blowing studio and a woodshop) or participate in workshops; you'll likely be sharing with some of them. B&B rooms are in the farmhouse, while dorms share a common room in an outbuilding.

Lake on the Mountain Resort
INN **$$**

(✆613-476-1321; www.lakeonthemountain. com; 268 County Rd 7; cottages/r/ste from $90/$140/$250; ⊙May-Nov) Comprising eight homey cottages and the 'House across the Road,' a beautiful Victorian with tastefully restored rooms and stunning views, this quaint country resort is the kind of secret you'll want to keep but just can't help sharing. Check the website for a taste of what's on offer, including what's cooking at the equally noteworthy restaurant.

Drake Devonshire Inn
BOUTIQUE HOTEL **$$**

(www.drakedevonshire.ca; 24 Wharf St, Wellington; d from $149) From the folks behind Toronto's legendary Drake Hotel comes the Drake Devonshire, a lakeside foundry being converted into a delicious 11-room boutique hotel, hovering on Lake Ontario. Scheduled to open in 2014, the Devonshire Inn and dining room are set to take the county by storm. Be a trendsetter and get in before everyone else does.

Newsroom Suites
HOTEL **$$**

(✆613-399-5182; www.newsroomsuites.ca; 269 Main St, Wellington; d from $155) Upstairs from the working offices of the *Wellington Times* you'll find these two delightful and spacious private suites, furnished to a high standard of comfort and privacy.

Claramount Inn & Spa
INN **$$**

(✆613-476-2709; www.claramountinn.com; 97 Bridge St, Picton; d from $175) It's easy to be impressed by this opulent yellow mansion, now a luxurious spa retreat and fine-dining restaurant. Individually themed rooms are of generally grand proportions and include such features as Georgian period furniture, canopy beds, exotic fabrics, fireplaces and decadent bathrooms with separate soaker tubs and showers.

✗ Eating & Drinking

Fifth Town Artisan Cheese
DAIRY **$**

(✆613-476-5755; www.fifthtown ca; 4309 County Rd 8, Picton; ice creams $4, cheeses $7-18; ⊙10am-5pm) ✐ Pop into this funky, solar-powered dairy for a scoop of lavender honey goat cheese ice cream, taste the spread of goat and sheep cheeses, and then leave with a sack full of them. You can enjoy your snack on the grounds, which has an eating pavilion and a cheese lover's herb garden, or take it back to your accommodation and pair it with a PEC chardonnay.

County Cider Company
CAFE **$**

(✆613-476-1022; www.countycider.com; 657 Bongards Crossroad, Waupoos; mains $10-18; ⊙11am-4pm May-Oct) Served on a hilltop patio surrounded by a vineyard and overlooking the lake, lunch consists of pizzas, burgers, salads and wraps made from local ingredients, accompanied, of course, by a range of sparkling ciders.

The Inn
INTERNATIONAL **$$**

(✆613-476-1321; www.lakeonthemountain.com; 268 County Rd 7; mains $8-29; ⊙11am-9pm) At the Lake on the Mountain Resort, this charming restaurant and its beautiful leafy patio overlooks the Bay of Quinte, 60m below. Meals are prepared using only the finest local ingredients. Highly recommended.

Blūmen Garden Bistro
FUSION **$$$**

(✆613-476-6841; www.blumengardenbistro.com; 647 Hwy 49, Picton; lunch $12-18, dinner $21-32; ⊙11:30am-2pm & 5-10pm Wed-Mon) Haute cuisine without the pretense equals 'honest food,' say the owners. With a relaxed, comfortable ambience, the bistro, true to its name, features a lovely garden where stepping stones lead to private, candlelit tables surrounded by fragrant flowers. Reservations are recommended.

East and Main
MODERN CANADIAN **$$$**

(✆613-399-5420; www.eastandmain.ca; 270 Main St, Wellington; mains $19-29; ⊙noon-2:30pm & 5:30-9pm Wed-Sun) The meals at this fine bistro taste as good as they look: farm-fresh meats, vegetables and lake-fresh seafood form the basis of this 'secret treasure of epicurean delight,' which pairs local wines beautifully to the chef's creations.

Acoustic Grill
BAR

(✆613-476-2887; www.theacousticgrill.com; 172 Main St, Picton; mains $8-14; ⊙11:30am-late Mon-Sat, from 3pm Sun) Acoustic folk, roots and blues acts can all be heard at this thigh-slappin' good time bar and grill. The beer is cold, the delicious bar menu is refreshingly down to earth for this foodie county, but still made fresh from local ingredients and the music is live. We highly rate the burgers.

☆ Entertainment

Regent Theatre THEATER
(☑613-476-8416; www.theregenttheatre.org; 224 Main St, Picton) Continually restored and updated, the funky Regent Theatre hosts a diverse series of plays, concerts and readings. A new projector has expanded its repetoire to include some fantastic art-house and cult cinema.

ℹ Information

Chamber of Tourism & Commerce (☑800 640-4717, 613-476-2421; www.pecchamber. com; 116 Main St, Picton; ⊙9am-5pm Mon-Sat, 10am-4pm Sun) Offers touring brochures and cycling maps, and will help with booking B&Bs and bike rentals.

Kingston

POP 115,000

Modern-day Canada's first capital, albeit for a short time (three years), Kingston was stripped of the title when Queen Victoria worried that it was too close to the American border and could not be properly defended. Today, the pretty city finds itself strategically placed as the perfect pit stop between Montréal or Ottawa and Toronto.

Often called the 'Limestone City,' Kingston is stocked with clunky halls of hand-cut stone and prim Victorian mansions. A noticeable lack of modern architectural eyesores helps to maintain the historical charm. A slew of interesting museums, historical sites and the Royal Military College keeps culture alive, while a pretty waterfront location, plenty of established trees and vibrant, colorful gardens add to the visual appeal.

Founded in 1841, at the same time the town was proclaimed capital, Queen's University adds a dash of hot-blooded youthfulness to the mix. An assortment of great dining options, some with student-friendly prices, and a crankin' nightlife round out the package. If you have the time, and history is your thing, stay a night or two on your way to the capital.

◎ Sights & Activities

Conveniently, most sites are found around the central, historic downtown.

Fort Henry National Historic Site HISTORIC SITE
(☑613-542-7388; www.forthenry.com; Fort Henry Dr; adult/child $15/12; ⊙9:30am-5pm) This re-

stored British fortification, dating from 1832, dominates the town from its hilltop perch. The postcard-perfect structure is brought to life by colorfully uniformed guards trained in military drills, artillery exercises and the fife-and-drum music of the 1860s. The soldiers put on displays throughout the day; don't miss the 3pm Garrison Parade. Admission includes a guided tour of the fort's campus. Special events are held throughout the year.

City Hall NOTABLE BUILDING
(261 Ontario St; ⊙9am-4pm Mon-Fri) The grandiose City Hall is one of the country's finest classical buildings and a relic from the time when Kingston was capital. Friendly red-vested volunteers conduct free tours on request, revealing colorful stained glass, dozens of portraits, dusty jail cells and an ornate council chamber.

Open-Air Market MARKET
(www.kingstonpublicmarket.ca; King St; ⊙Apr-Nov) On Tuesday, Thursday, Saturday and Sunday, the oldest continuous market in Canada takes place in the square behind City Hall.

Marine Museum of the Great Lakes MUSEUM
(☑613-542-2261; www.marmuseum.ca; 55 Ontario St; adult/child $8.50/5.50; ⊙10am-4pm Mar-Nov) Kingston was an important shipbuilding center. This museum sits on the site of the old shipyard, offering a detailed history of the fascinating vessels built at the yard.

Pump House Steam Museum MUSEUM
(☑613-542-2261; www.steammuseum.ca; 23 Ontario St; adult/child $5/2; ⊙10am-4pm Tue-Sun May-Sep) The one-of-a-kind, completely

OFFBEAT KINGSTON

Canadian bureaucrats call the nation's jail system the 'correctional service.' The **Penitentiary Museum** (☑613-530-3122; www.penitentiarymuseum.ca; 555 King St W; admission by donation; ⊙9am-4pm Mon-Fri, from 10am Sat & Sun May-Oct) is the best way to get a taste of that kind of service, without stealing a car. The museum, across from the actual penitentiary (which closed late in 2013, after over 175 years), has a fascinating collection of weapons and tools confiscated from inmates during attempted escapes.

Kingston

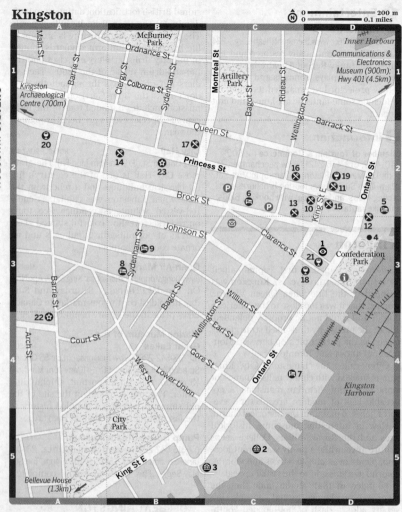

restored, steam-run pump house was first used in 1849. Today the warehouse features all things steam-related, including two full-model train sets as well as the recently restored steamboat *Phoebe*.

Bellevue House   MUSEUM

(☎613-545-8666; 35 Centre St; adult/child $4/2; ⊙10am-5pm Thu-Mon Apr-Oct) This national historic site was once home to Sir John A Macdonald, Canada's first prime minister and a notorious alcoholic. Perhaps the architect also enjoyed a drop, as the Italianate mansion is wholly asymmetrical, a pompous

use of bright color abounds and balconies twist off in various directions. There are also plenty of antiques and a sun-drenched garden, adding further kooky charm and intrigue.

Military Communications & Electronics Museum   MUSEUM

(☎613-541-5395; www.c-and-e-museum.org; Hwy 2 E; admission by donation; ⊙8am-4pm Mon-Fri, 11am-5pm Sat & Sun May-Sep) Despite the driest of names, this is a comprehensive and well-designed museum on the military base, offering chronological displays on commu-

Kingston

nications technology and sundry military gadgets.

Kingston Archaeological Centre MUSEUM
(☑ 613-542-3483; www.carf.info/archaeological-centre; 611 Princess St; ⊙ 9:30am-4pm Mon-Fri) FREE If you've been traveling along the boring stretch of Hwy 401, you probably spotted the sedimentary rock outcrops – the only interesting thing on the road. Swing by the archaeological center to learn more about the craggy formations, and while you're there check out the archaeological record detailing the 8000-year-old human history of the area.

Wolfe Island Car Ferry FERRY
(☑ 613-548-7227; www.wolfeisland.com) FREE The largest island in the Thousand Islands chain, Wolfe Island is actually bigger than Kingston. Getting there on the free Wolf Island car ferry is half the fun: the 25-minute trip affords views of the city, fort and islands. The island is cycle-friendly, with four routes marked with colored signs. Download a map at www.wolfeisland.com. The Kingston Tourism visitors center can advise you on the best way to explore the terrain.

⛱ Tours

Kingston Trolley Tours TOUR
(☑ 613-549-5544; www.1000islandscruises.ca; adult/child $18.50/9.25; ⊙ Apr-Oct) A trackless mini-train departs regularly from the tourist office for hour-long tours with cheery historical commentary. From May to September

there's a six-stop hop-on, hop-off loop bus (adult/child $22.50/11.25).

Haunted Walk WALKING TOUR
(☑ 613-549-6366; www.hauntedwalk.com; adult/child $14/8) Tours featuring stories of hangings and grave robbers leave from 200 Ontario St, in front of the Prince George Hotel. Tour content and times vary: check the website for details.

Kingston 1000 Island Cruises BOAT TOUR
(☑ 613-549-5544; www.1000islandcruises.on.ca; 1 Brock St; cruises from $25; ⊙ May-Oct) A variety of scenic cruises depart from the *Island Queen* dock, on Ontario St at the foot of Brock St. Lunch and dinner cruises are available. Check the website for the latest rates and sailing times.

☆ Festivals & Events

Visit www.kingstoncanada.com for a complete list of events throughout the year.

Kingston Buskers Rendezvous MUSIC
(www.kingstonbuskers.com) Four days of tomfoolery in July.

Limestone City Blues Festival MUSIC
(www.kingstonblues.com) All-star musicians gather for a four-day jam session in August.

🛏 Sleeping

Accommodations in Kingston are top heavy, with a larger confluence of pricier stays than budget options. Motels are strung along Princess St and along Hwy 2 on each side of town. The knowledgeable staff at the tourism office in Confederation Park can help track down additional options, including on Wolfe Island. B&B buffs should check out www.historicinnskingston.com for extra ritzy digs.

Queen's Inn
BOUTIQUE HOTEL **$$**

(☑613-546-0429, 866-689-9177; www.queensinn.ca; 125 Brock St; r $99-159; ❀❄🅿) Constructed in 1839, the Queen's Inn is one of the oldest hotels in the country. The outside has a stately limestone facade and some rooms have stone walls, dormer windows and leafy views. A downstairs pub and the downtown location make this place a worthy option.

Fireside Inn
MOTEL **$$**

(☑613-549-2211; www.bestwesternkingston.ca; 1217 Princess St; d from $139; ❄🅿≋) The best thing about this uptown motel are the gaudy but fun fantasy suites, reminiscent of an American-sized Japanese love hotel. Standard rooms have been recently refurbished and have pillowtop mattresses. There's an outdoor heated pool.

Rosemount Inn
B&B **$$**

(☑888-871-8844, 613-531-8844; www.rosemount-inn.com; 46 Sydenham St; r $139-299; ❀❄🅿) Enjoy a decadent stay at this former dry-goods merchant's home. Built in 1850, the massive stone building features arched doorways and intricate flooring. A small spa offers wine baths and chocolate face masks, and the full breakfast (prepared by two chefs) includes gourmet chocolate.

Holiday Inn Kingston Waterfront
HOTEL **$$**

(☑613-549-8400; www.hikingstonwaterfront.com; 2 Princess St; d from $169; ❄🅿≋💧) You can't beat the location of this waterfront hotel. Its spacious rooms have balconies and some have microwaves. There's an indoor and an outdoor pool.

Residence Inn by Marriott Kingston Water's Edge
HOTEL **$$**

(☑613-544-4888; www.marriottresidenceinnkingston.com; 7 Earl St; d from $179; ❄🅿≋) Kingston's largest rooms can be found in this hulking new hotel in a prime spot on the water, near the university. It's a few minutes' walk from downtown.

Secret Garden
B&B **$$**

(☑877-723-1888, 613-531-9884; www.the-secret-garden.com; 73 Sydenham St; r incl breakfast $145-189; ❀❄🅿) Whether you recline in the stately salons with dripping chandeliers

overhead, or retreat upstairs to your canopied bed, don't forget to say hello to tiny Mork and Mindy, the resident dogs.

🍴 Eating

Praise be to Queen's University for sparking the proliferation of tasty options at student-friendly prices.

★ Pan Chancho
BAKERY **$**

(☑613-544-7790; www.panchancho.com; 44 Princess St; items $6-16; ⊙7am-6pm) This phenomenal bakery and cafe fuses unlikely ingredients into palate-pleasing light and savory lunches. For breakfast, delight in amazing maple sausages, spicy chutney and perfect eggs. Try the fennel and cream-cheese spread on anything from your table's freshly baked bread basket.

Mlt Dwn
FAST FOOD **$**

(☑613-766-1881; www.mltdwn.com; 292 Princess St; sandwiches from $4.50; ⊙10am-10pm Mon-Thu, to 3am Fri & Sat, 11am-9pm Sun) We predict that this original Kingstonian fast-food joint is going to go global. You won't be able to resist the calorific goodness oozing from just about every conceivable twist on the humble grilled cheese sandwich...especially if it's late and you're stumbling back from the pub. Cheesetastic.

Wok Inn
ASIAN **$**

(☑613-549-5369; 30 Montréal St; dishes from $6.95; ⊙11:30am-2:30pm & 4:30-9pm Tue-Sat) Cambodian, Vietnamese and Thai delights feature in this plain Jane downtown eatery favored for takeout by starving university students.

Sleepless Goat
VEGETARIAN **$**

(☑613-545-9646; www.thegoat.ca; 91 Princess St; meals $7-11; ⊙7am-9pm Mon-Fri, 8am-10pm Sat & Sun; 🖉) With a name that sounds like an Alanis Morissette lyric, it's no surprise that this low-key joint attracts gaggles of artists and angsty intellectual types. A self-proclaimed co-op, the restaurant is run by a clan of savvy cooks who churn out the tastiest vegetarian options in town.

Coffee & Company
CAFE **$**

(☑613-547-9211; 53 Princess St; ⊙7am-6pm Sun-Wed, to 9pm Thu-Sat; 🖉) Get your daily dose of barista-brewed organic free-trade coffee here with your daily dose of free wi-fi. Why not have a Godiva chocolate with that?

Curry Original
INDIAN $$

(☑ 613-531-9376; www.curryoriginal.ca; 253A Ontario St; mains $11-19; ⊙11:30am-2pm Tue-Sat & 5-9pm Tue-Sun) Kingston's finest Indian cuisine can be found at this smart outfit with an excellent waterfront patio. All your favorites are well represented here.

Chez Piggy
FUSION $$$

(☑ 613-549-7673; www.chezpiggy.com; 68-R Princess St; mains $16-35; ⊙11am-midnight) Hidden in a flowery stone courtyard, the city's best-known restaurant has earned its reputation with an innovative menu, charming ambience and memorable weekend brunches. Mains include marinated ostrich loin and seared sea scallops. Reservations are strongly recommended on weekends.

Le Chien Noir
FRENCH $$$

(☑ 613-549-5635; www.lechiennoir.com; 69 Brock St; mains $17-36; ⊙11:30am-9pm) It's a tad pricey but locals love this little taste of Paris with a hint of Québec in downtown Kingston: consider the gourmet poutine. Mains include lobster, duck and the obligatory steak frites.

▼ Drinking & Entertainment

Kingston Brewing Company
PUB

(☑ 613-542-4978; www.kingstonbrewing.ca; 34 Clarence St; mains $8-18; ⊙11am-2am) Chow down on tasty tavern munchies amid flickering Christmas lights and kitschy beer-themed paraphernalia, or make a meal of it and grab a patio table outside. Try the Dragon's Breath and White Tail Cream Ales, both so popular they're brewed and bottled off-site.

Red House
PUB

(☑ 613-767-2558; www.redhousekingston.com; 369 King St E; ⊙11:30am-2am) The new ranch-raunchy pub has a killer selection of beers on tap and a fantastic bar menu ranging from comfort food to seriously smart dining (in a casual pub setting). We love that there are roasted herbed potatoes cooked in duck fat as a side dish.

Tir nan Og
PUB

(☑ 416-544-7474; 200 Ontario St; ⊙11am-late) Set inside one of the oldest and most charming buildings along the waterfront, this Irish oasis serves up live music and overflowing pints, as well as a full menu.

Stages
CLUB

(☑ 613-547-5553; www.stages.ca; 390 Princess St; ⊙10pm-3am Fri & Sat) This is where young Kingston folk get their groove on and dance till they drop.

Grad Club
LIVE MUSIC

(☑ 613-546-3427; http://queensgradclub.wordpress.com; 162 Barrie St; ⊙10:30am-close Mon-Fri) Housed in an imposing Victorian mansion, this Queen's campus mainstay is one of the hottest venues for live music. It's open on weekends for special events.

Grand Theatre
THEATER

(☑ 613-530-2050; www.kingstongrand.ca; 218 Princess St) Once an opera house, then a movie theater, and now the city's premier venue for theater, the symphony, concerts and comedy. The Grand has undergone extensive renovations since 1967, including a massive overhaul in 2008.

ℹ Information

Hotel Dieu Hospital (☑ 613-544-3310; www.hoteldieu.com; 166 Brock St; ⊙emergency room 8am-10pm) Yes, it's a hospital: centrally located.

Kingston Tourism (☑ 888-855-4555, 613-548-4415; www.kingstoncanada.com; 209 Ontario St; ⊙9am-5pm) This useful information center has intelligent, friendly staff, well versed in the city's history. It's across from City Hall.

Post office (☑ 800-267-1177; www.canadapost.ca; 120 Clarence St; ⊙8am-5:30pm Mon-Fri)

ℹ Getting There & Away

The **Kingston Coach Terminal** (☑ 613-547-4916; 1175 John Counter Blvd) is 1km south of Hwy 401, just west of Division St. Megabus offers regular services to Toronto ($20, three hours, 14 daily) and Montréal ($31, three hours, 14 daily).

If you're arriving by car on Hwy 401, exits 611, 613, 615, 617, 619 and 623 will lead you downtown. For car rental, try **Enterprise** (☑ 613-389-8969; 2244 Princess St), which offers complimentary pickup and drop-off.

Kingston station (☑ 888-842-7245; www.viarail.ca; 1800 John Counter Blvd) is about 400m east of where Princess St and John Counter Blvd meet. Trains run to Montréal ($70, 2½ hours, nine daily), Ottawa ($57, two hours, six daily) and Toronto ($73, 2½ hours, 11 daily).

ℹ Getting Around

For information on getting around by bus, call **Kingston Transit** (☑ 613-546-0000). To get to town from the bus terminal, there is a city bus stop across the street; buses depart 15 minutes before and after the hour. From the train station, bus 1 stops on the corner of Princess St and John Counter Blvd, just a short walk from the bus station. Frequency is decreased on Sundays.

Cyclists will be happy to note that the Kingston area is generally flat, and both Hwys 2 and 5 have paved shoulders. Rentals are available at **Ahoy Rentals** (☑ 613-539-3202; www.ahoyrentals.com; 23 Ontario St; bike rental per day $25).

Gananoque

Little Gananoque (gan-an-*awk*-way) is the perfect place to rest your eyes after a long day of squinting at the furry green islands on the misty St Lawrence. The dainty Victorian town, deep in the heart of the Thousand Islands region, teems with cruise-hungry tourists during summer and early fall. In spring and late fall, it's quiet as a mouse.

◉ Sights & Activities

★ Boldt Castle
CASTLE

(☑ 315-482-9724; www.boldtcastle.com; 1 Tennis Island Rd, Alexandria Bay, NY, USA; adult/child $10/6; ☺ 10am-5pm) Technically in the USA, though only 36km from Gananoque, so you'll need your passport to visit this lavish turn-of-the-century island castle in the middle of the St Lawrence. It was built by George C Boldt, original proprietor of New York's famous Waldorf Astoria Hotel. As they say, if you haven't seen Boldt Castle, you haven't seen Boldt Castle. The castle is accesible by road, off the Thousand Islands Pkwy: it's linked by

bridge. Many Thousand Island cruise tours also stop here.

Skydeck
VIEWPOINT

(☑ 613-659-2335; www.1000islandsskydeck.com; Hill Island; adult/child $10/6; ☺ 9am-dusk Apr-Oct) In Ivylea, 22km from Gananoque, a series of soaring bridges link Ontario to New York State over several islands. Halfway across, you'll find the Skydeck, a 125m-high observation tower offering some fantastic views of the archipelago from three different balconies.

Gananoque Boat Line
CRUISE

(☑ 888-717-4837; www.ganboatline.com; 6 Water St; tour prices vary; ☺ May-Oct) Several trip options including a stopover at Boldt Castle make this a popular choice for cruising the Thousand Islands. The castle is technically in the USA, so be sure you have your passport if you are planning to visit. A variety of sailings are available; check the website for details.

1000 Islands Kayaking
KAYAKING

(☑ 613-329-6265; www.1000islandskayaking.com; 110 Kate St; rentals from $35, tours from $85) If you're feeling energetic, paddling is a great way to tour the islands. Choose from a multitude of packages including courses, excellent half-day and overnight trips.

⛏ Sleeping & Eating

Gananoque sports an abundance of memorable accommodations including several upmarket and architecturally eye-catching inns. Otherwise, virtually every motel chain is represented along King St E near Hwy 401.

THOUSAND ISLANDS

The 'Thousand Islands' are a constellation of over 1800 rugged islands dotting the St Lawrence River from Kingston to Brockville. The lush archipelago offers loose tufts of fog, showers of trillium petals, quaking tide pools and opulent 19th-century summer mansions, the turrets of which pierce the prevailing mist.

The narrow, slow-paced **Thousand Islands Parkway** dips south of Hwy 401 between Gananoque and Elizabethtown, running along the river for 35km before rejoining the highway. The scenic journey winds along the pastoral strip of shoreline offering picture-perfect vistas and dreamy picnic areas. The **Bikeway** bicycle path extends the full length of the parkway.

In Mallorytown, the **Thousand Islands National Park** (☑ 613-923-5261; www.pc.gc.ca/pn-np/on/lawren/index.aspx; 2 County Rd 5, Mallorytown) preserves a gentle green archipelago, consisting of over 20 islands scattered between Kingston and Brockville. A walking trail and interpretive center allow visitors to learn more about the lush terrain and resident wildlife. Over a dozen of the freckle-sized islands support backcountry camping (between mid-May and early September) and they are accessible only by boat (BYO boat).

Misty Isles Lodge LODGE $

(☑ 613-382-4232; www.mistyisles.ca; 25 River Rd, Lansdowne; r from $85) Located about 4km east of Gananoque on the Thousand Islands Pkwy, you'll find this laid-back beachfront property boasting comfortable units with wicker furnishings. A variety of adventure outfitting is offered as well, including kayak rentals (from $25 per hour), guided tours (from $39) and camping packages on some of the river's shrubby islands.

★ **Victoria Rose Inn** INN $$

(☑ 888-246-2893, 613-382-3368; www.victoria-roseinn.com; 279 King St W; d incl breakfast from $165; ☻❋🐾) A monument to Victorian splendor, this former mayoral residence has been refurbished to its original elegance. A glassed-in porch overlooks manicured terraced gardens. Guest rooms are spacious, comfortable and elegantly furnished in a neutral, classic style. Personal touches such as champagne and flowers can be ordered in advance. Lovely.

Gananoque Inn INN $$

(☑ 888-565-3101; www.gananoqueinn.com; 550 Stone St S; r $179-395) Signature green shutters denote this stately inn at the junction of the Gananoque River and the St Lawrence Seaway: the former carriage-works first opened its doors in 1896 and has retained much of its charm. Discounted rooms and day-spa pamper packages are frequently offered online.

Houseboat Holidays HOUSEBOAT $$$

(☑ 613-382-2842; www.houseboatholidays.ca; RR3, Gananoque; weekend/midweek/weekly rates from $525/725/950) The only thing better than staying near the seaway is staying *on* the seaway! This experienced outfit just 3km east of Gananoque will set you up with your very own floating hotel and provides a brief instructional course for nautical newbies.

Maple Leaf Restaurant EUROPEAN $$

(Czech Schnitzel House; ☑ 613-382-7666; www.mapleleafrestaurant.ca; 65 King St E; mains $9-20; ☺11am-9:30pm Tue-Sat, from 10am Sun) As Canadian an old-school family diner as the Maple Leaf can be, the name belies the real European gems found inside: golden breaded schnitzel, goulash, borscht and beer. There's a little patio out back, in summer.

Stonewater Pub & Irish Eatery PUB $$

(☑ 613-382-2116; www.stonewaterbb.com; 490 Stone St; mains $12-16; ☺8am-late May-Oct) This homely little pub by the waterfront serves up delicious hearty fare: the Irish meatloaf and drunken shepherd are both must-tries for self-respecting carnivores. There's a bunch of creative salads and veggie options too. The vibe inside is straight out of Moby Dick: delightful in the colder months.

Ivy Restaurant MODERN CANADIAN $$$

(☑ 613-659-2486; www.ivylea.ca; 61 Shipman's Lane, Lansdowne; mains $14-34; ☺noon-3pm & 5-9pm Wed-Sat, 10:30am-2pm Sun) The beautifully refurbished restaurant belonging to the opulent Ivy Lea Marina and Club is open to the public. It's in a charming waterfront spot about 15 minutes' drive from Gananoque. Casual patio lunches and Sunday brunches are the more affordable way to enjoy the stunning environment but evening fine dining is available. Otherwise, just stop by for a look and a lick: there's an incredible ice-cream booth out front.

☆ **Entertainment**

Thousand Islands Playhouse THEATER

(☑ 866-382-7020, 613-382-7020; www.1000islandsplayhouse.com; 185 South St) This delightful waterfront theater has presented a quality lineup of mainly light summer plays and musicals since 1983.

OLG Casino CASINO

(☑ 613-382-6800; www.olg.ca; 380 Hwy 2; ☺9am-4am Mon-Wed, 24hr Thu-Sun) This small but almost always open casino – often filled with senior citizens – can be a sad indictment of modern society, but the staff are friendly and for many punters, it's just good, clean fun.

ⓘ **Information**

Visitor Services Centre (☑ 800-561-1595, 613-382-3250; www.1000islandsgananoque.com; 10 King St E; ☺10am-7pm Mon-Fri, to 8pm Sat, to 5pm Sun) The delightful staff at this immaculate visitors center are a font of information for all things Thousand Islands and beyond.

ⓘ **Getting There & Away**

There's no public transport into Gananoque. It's a short detour off Hwy 401 about 35km east of Kingston.

Brockville & Prescott

Attractive Brockville marks the eastern edge of the Thousand Islands region. The 'City of the Thousand Islands,' as it's known, has a cache of extravagant estates. Rows of Gothic spires twisting skyward make it easy to imagine that the clip-clop of carriage horses once rang through the streets. It's also the end of the Unesco World Heritage Rideau Canal.

Neighboring Prescott, 20km up the road, could be Brockville's younger brother: it's smaller, scrappier and hasn't quite developed into a full-fledged city of its own. The 19th-century town is home to the International Bridge to Ogdensburg, New York State.

⊙ Sights

Brockville Museum
MUSEUM

(☑ 613-342-4397; www.brockvillemuseum.com; 5 Henry St, Brockville; adult/child $4.50/2.50; ⊙10am-5pm Mon-Fri, 1-5pm Sat & Sun) Take a look at the area's history here, where you'll find displays on Brockville's railroad past, its hat-making industry and other community tidbits. The museum encompasses the Isaac Beecher house, a historic landmark and example of a typical New England home built before American independence.

Fulford Place
MUSEUM

(☑ 613-498-3003; www.heritagetrust.on.ca/Fulford-Place; 287 King St E, Brockville; adult/child $5/ ⊙11am-4pm Tue-Sun) **FREE** This stunning 35-room Edwardian mansion from the 1900s

---

was once the home of George Taylor Fulford, the producer of the 'Pink Pill for Pale People.' Why not stop by for a cup of tea on the veranda? Admission includes a guided tour.

Brockville Arts Centre
CULTURAL BUILDING

(☑ 877-342-7122, 613-342-7122; www.brockvilleartscentre.com; 235 King St W, Brockville; ⊙ box office 10am-5pm Mon-Fri, to 3pm Sat) Built in 1858 as Brockville's Town Hall, what is now the arts centre has survived one fire and several incarnations. Today, it doubles as a theater and art gallery, where local artists get billing alongside biggish names.

Fort Wellington National Historic Site
HISTORIC BUILDING

(☑ 613-925-2896; 370 Vankoughnet St, Prescott; adult/child $4/2; ⊙10am-5pm May-Sep) The original fort was built during the War of 1812 and was used again as a strategic locale in 1838 when an American invasion seemed imminent. Some original fortifications remain, as does a blockhouse and officers' quarters. Renovations and improvements are ongoing.

⚐ Tours

1000 Islands Cruises
BOAT TOUR

(☑ 800-353-3157, 613-345-7333; www.1000islandscruises.com; 30 Block House Island Pkwy, Brockville; ⊙May-Oct) Offers sightseeing tours of the Thousand Islands on two vessels: a traditional sightseeing cruiser and the high speed *Wildcat*. Check the website for details, schedules and rates.

⏿ Sleeping

Nearby Prescott has some of the most original accommodations options along the St Lawrence, though Brockville has plenty to satisfy.

Dewar's Inn
INN $

(☑ 877-433-9277, 613-925-3228; www.dewarsinn.com; 1649 County Rd 2, Prescott; r $68-91, cottages $87-107; ☀▣) Constructed from the bricks of an old distillery, this jumble of quaint seaside cottages and units are tastefully furnished and spotlessly clean. Scuba dives in the backyard revealed sunken bottles of old brew. No pets or children.

Green Door
B&B $$

(☑ 613-341-9325; www.greendoorbb.com; 61 Buell St, Brockville; d from $115; ☀▣) This old brick tabernacle has found a new calling as a B&B. Crisp sunlight dances through the ample common space during the day. Spend your

---

> ### FRONTENAC ARCH BIOSPHERE RESERVE
>
> One of only 15 Unesco-designated reserves in Canada, Frontenac Arch encompasses a small portion of the Canadian Shield that extends down through Ontario. What was once a range of towering mountains has been weathered down to rolling hills and rugged cliffs: still dramatic after driving through flatlands. Archaeological finds in the area indicate that it was once part of a human migration route; knives from the Yellowknife region as well as shells from the Caribbean have been found in the area.
>
> The 2700-sq-km reserve has ample recreation opportunities from biking and hiking to canoeing and diving. It's easily accessed from Hwy 401, between Gananoque and Brockville. The excellent www.frontenacarchbiosphere.ca will guide you to various entry points.

evenings by the piano or snuggled up in an antique bed.

Ship's Anchor Inn
B&B $$

(☑ 613-925-3573; www.shipsanchorinn.com; 495 King St W, Prescott; d from $109; ⊖☒) Once the beachside abode of a crusty sea captain, this 175-year-old hand-hewn stone manor is packed to the rafters with sea-shanty relics of bygone days: schools of taxidermic fish, anchors aplenty and models of wooden frigates. Hearty breakfasts, fit for a sailor, will keep you chugging along until dinnertime.

✕ Eating

Buell Street Bistro
INTERNATIONAL $$

(☑ 613-345-2623; www.buellstreetbistro.com; 27 Buell St, Brockville; mains $12-31; ⊙11am-10pm Mon-Fri, 5-10pm Sat & Sun) Three levels and a delectable patio break the space up at this locals' favorite. Seafood and pasta dishes mingle with Thai and Indian flavors: there's enough variety to please the fussiest of palates, including a full gluten-free menu.

Mill
ITALIAN $$

(☑ 613-345-7098; www.themillrestaurant.ca; 123 Water St W, Brockville; mains $9-26; ⊙11:30am-2pm & 5-9pm Mon-Fri, 4-9pm Sat) There's a wonderful, romantic ambience to this quaint Italian restaurant located in a restored 1852 mill. Pasta, seafood and veal feature on the menu: we recommend the *scallopine al marsala*. Dishes are, refreshingly, reasonably priced.

Georgian Dragon Ale House
PUB

(☑ 613-865-8224; 72 King St W, Brockville; meals $9-24; ⊙11:30am-late) This British alehouse on the main drag has a good selection of beers on tap and tasty British pub faves like butter chicken and fish and chips.

ℹ Information

Brockville District Tourism (☑ 613-342-4357; www.brockvilletourism.com; 10 Market St, Brockville; ⊙9am-5pm Mon-Fri) Open year-round and provides ample information about attractions all along the seaway.

ℹ Getting There & Away

VIA Rail trains leave Brockville's **train station** (www.viarail.ca; 141 Perth St) for Toronto ($80, three hours, six daily) and Ottawa ($31, 1¼ hours, five daily). **Megabus** (☑ 866-488-4452; www.megabus.com) runs daily buses from Toronto (from $21, four hours, three daily) and Montréal ($46, 2½ hours, three daily).

Merrickville

Tiny Merrickville can thank the Canadian Railroad for never laying tracks through town. Had the wee burg become a stop on the line, it would have swapped its stone structures for industrial eyesores. Fortunately, today, visits can still be a step back in time to when the area was a Loyalist stronghold ready to defend the Crown against the rebellious Americans. Merrickville was such a desirable locale that Colonel By, the master planner of the Rideau Canal, built his summer home here, and Benedict Arnold was given a tract in town as a reward for betraying the Americans.

History buffs will enjoy exploring the **Blockhouse** (☑ 613-269-2229; cnr Main & St Lawrence Sts; ⊙May-Oct) FREE and boutique-browsers will love the numerous artisan workshops. Pause for a meal at **Gad's Hill** (☑ 613-269-2976; www.dickens-restaurant.com; 118 St Lawrence St; mains $9-26; ⊙11am-9pm), where menus are tucked inside leather-bound tomes, encouraging the pronounced Dickensian motif. Catch a dinner show while you're there; *A Christmas Carol* is an annual event.

Morrisburg

Little Morrisburg is known far and wide for its quality historic site, **Upper Canada Village** (☑ 613-543-4328; www.uppercanadavillage.com; 13740 County Rd 2; adult/child $15/12; ⊙10am-5pm May-Oct). Costume-clad interpreters animate this re-created town by emulating life in the 1860s. Plan to spend three or four hours at the village in order to explore the over 40 buildings. Wander through Cook's Tavern, the Blacksmith's Shop, Asselstine's Woollen Factory, the Schoolhouse, the Gazette Printing Office and the many other dwellings to learn about the intricacies of colonial life.

Hwy 2 along the river is slower but more scenic than Hwy 401. The **Upper Canada Migratory Bird Sanctuary** (☑ 613-537-2024; www.uppercanadabirdsanctuary.com; 5591 County Rd 2, Ingleside; ⊙May-Oct) FREE offers 8km of self-guided trails that meander through wooded thickets and lush wetlands. Over 200 bird species can be glimpsed. Inquire at the park office about the dozen camping options.

Ottawa

POP 933,500

Descriptions of Ottawa read like an appealing dating profile: dynamic, gregarious, bilingual, likes kids and long walks on the river. In person, the attractive capital fits the bill.

Canada's gargantuan Gothic Parliament buildings regally anchor the downtown core, an inspiring jumble of pulsing districts at the confluence of three rivers. In the distance, the rolling Gatineau hills tenderly hug the cloudless valley. Ottawa has a wonderful conglomeration of world-class museums, from the smooth, undulating walls of the Museum of Civilization to the haunting arches of the Museum of Nature; all are architecturally inspiring homes to a variety of intriguing collections.

Ottawa's cultural diversity is reflected in its culinary prowess. A compact footprint makes finding great food simple: there's a plethora of excellent dining options catering to most tastes and budgets. Look forward to a dynamic mix of flavors and aromas from around the globe, prepared using fresh, local ingredients.

The capital is truly a year-round destination. Parks, gardens and wide, open public spaces pay an accesible homage to all four seasons – don't dismiss a winter visit because of the bracing cold. Locals celebrate the city's seemingly longest season with a bunch of outdoor pursuits. Many skate to work or school on the frozen Rideau Canal, the largest skating rink in the world. Visitors from far and wide come to delight in the Winterlude festival with its sprawling village made entirely of ice. Once everything melts, auspicious tulips cheer the downtown as spring clicks to summer. Vibrant autumn leaves round out the year, lining the streets with a blaze of eye-popping reds and yellows.

Whether it's for the stunning museums or mouthwatering eats, the rainbow of seasons or outdoor retreats, we think you'll be smitten with Ottawa.

History

Like many colonial capitals, Ottawa's birth was not an organic one. The site was chosen by Queen Victoria as a geographic compromise between Montréal and Toronto, and poof – the city was born. Canadians were initially baffled by her decision; Ottawa was far away from the main colonial strongholds. Many thought the region to be a desolate snowfield, when in fact the Ottawa area was long inhabited by Algonquin, who named the rolling river Kichissippi (Great River).

For almost a century, Ottawa functioned as a quiet capital. Then, after WWII, Paris city planner Jacques Greber was tasked with giving Ottawa an urban facelift. The master

---

OTTAWA IN...

One Day

If you're only here for a day, there's no time to waste! Get yourself to **Parliament Hill** (p209) for happy snaps with the Peace Tower and a quick tour of the lavish, Harry Potter–esque interior. Next, be seduced by the shimmering glass spires of the **National Art Gallery of Canada** (p209), with its carefully curated collection of Canadian and world art and the restored remains of a lovely wooden chapel. Pause for lunch at the **ByWard Market** (p222) where you'll uncover scores of vendors hawking fresh farm produce and over 1000 kinds of cheese! Sample a beavertail at the **Rideau Canal** (p213): in winter it becomes the largest ice-skating rink in the world (7.8km).

Three Days

After completing the one-day itinerary, gravitate toward the awe-inducing architecture, skyline views and fascinating exhibits of the **Canadian Museum of Civilization** (p209). Ogle at taxidermic megafauna at the **Canadian Museum of Nature** (p211) before heading for an inspired hike or swim in picturesque **Gatineau Park** (p224). Make sure you're back in town in time for tea: honor your cravings – the city will satisfy. After a lazy brunch and morning stroll around **Confederation Park**, head to the quirky, Cold War marvel of the **Diefenbunker** (p213) and the pretty landscapes outside town. After another delicious dinner, round out your final day with a show at the **National Arts Centre** (p222) or rock out with some live music in the ByWard Market area's many venues.

planner created a distinctive European feel, transforming the city into the stunning cityscape of ample common and recreational spaces we see today.

◎ Sights

Most of Ottawa's numerous world-class museums are within walking distance of each other. Many are closed on Mondays in the winter and several will let you in for free if you arrive less than an hour before closing time, smiling politely: although you won't have much time to appreciate the extensive collections. A number of museums offer free general admissions on Thursday evenings. If you plan to visit both the Musem of Civilization and the War Museum, discounted tickets are available: inquire at either museum.

★**Canadian Museum of Civilization**   MUSEUM
(Map p210; ☑819-776-7000; www.civilization.ca; 100 Laurier St, Gatineau; adult/child $13/8; ◎9am-6pm Fri-Wed, to 8pm Thu) Allow plenty of time to experience this high-tech, must-see museum across the river, in Hull, Québec. Documenting the history of Canada through a range of spectacular exhibits, it's an objective recounting of the nation's timeline from the perspectives of its Aboriginal peoples, its colonial beginnings and the rich multicultural diversity of Canada today. Entry includes admission to the **Children's Museum**, based around a theme of 'the Great Adventure': over 30 permanent and visiting exhibits allow kids an opportunity to travel the world.

Outside, there are stunning views of Parliament Hill, across the river. The building's striking stone exterior has been sculpted into smooth ripples, like an undulating wave, to honor the aboriginal belief that evil dwells in angled nooks. A variety of visiting hands-on exhibitions, events and IMAX films maintain year-round appeal.

★**Canadian War Museum**   MUSEUM
(Map p210; ☑800-555-5621; www.warmuseum.ca; 1 Vimy Pl; adult/child $13/8; ◎9:30am-6pm Fri-Wed, to 8pm Thu) Fascinating displays twist through the labyrinthine interior of this sculpturelike, modern museum, tracing Canada's military history with the nation's most comprehensive collection of war-related artifacts. Many of the touching and thought-provoking exhibits are larger than life, including a replica of a WWI trench. Take a look at the facade in the evening, if you can: flickering lights pulse on

---

---

and off spelling 'Lest We Forget' and 'CWM' in both English and French morse code.

Parliament Hill   HISTORIC BUILDING
(Map p216; ☑613-996-0896; www.parl.gc.ca/Visitors; 111 Wellington St; ◎9am-5pm) Vast, yawning archways, copper-topped turrets and Gothic-revival gargoyles dominate the facade of the stunning lime and sandstone Parliament buildings. The main building, known as the Centre Block, supports the iconic Peace Tower, the highest structure in the city. Completed in 1865, Canada's nexus of political activity welcomes visitors year-round. You can download informative PDFs of self-guided walking tours from www.canadascapital.gc.ca, but we recommended the free 45-minute guided tours. From May to September a limited number of tickets are distributed from the Hill Centre, across the street. In other months, head to the main visitor entrance beneath the Peace Tower.

Question Time in the House of Commons occurs every afternoon and at 11am on Fridays, when parliament is in session. Visitors are welcomed to watch the antics on a first-come, first-served basis. Expect security checks. At 10am daily in summer, see the colorful changing of the guard on the front lawns, and at night enjoy the free bilingual sound-and-light show on Parliament Hill.

National Gallery of Canada   MUSEUM
(Map p216; ☑800-319-2787, 613-990-1985; www.gallery.ca; 380 Sussex Dr; adult/child $12/6; 5-8pm Thu free; ◎10am-5pm Fri-Wed, to 8pm Thu) The National Gallery is a work of art in itself: its striking ensemble of pink granite and glass spires echo the ornate copper-topped towers of nearby Parliament. Inside, vaulted

Ottawa

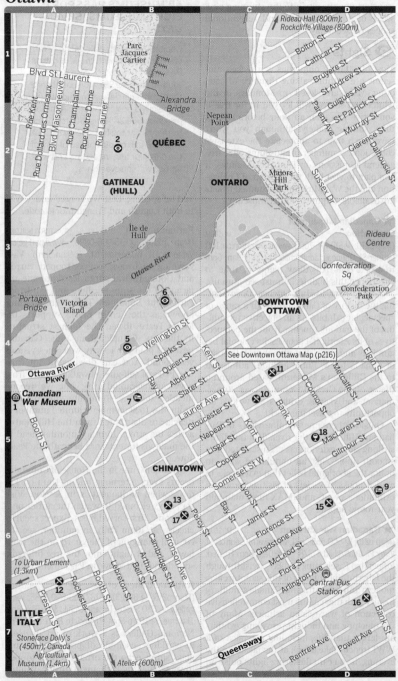

Rideau Hall (800m);
Rockcliffe Village (800m)

Bolton St
Cathcart St
Bruyere St
St Andrew St
Guigues Ave
St Patrick St
Parent Ave
Murray St
Clarence St
Dalhousie St

Blvd St Laurent

Rue Kent
Rue Dollard des Ormeaux
Blvd Maisonneuve
Rue Champlain
Rue Notre Dame
Rue Laurier

Parc Jacques Cartier

Alexandra Bridge

Nepean Point

QUÉBEC

2

GATINEAU (HULL)

ONTARIO

Majors Hill Park

Sussex Dr

Île de Hull

Ottawa River

Rideau Centre

Confederation Sq

Portage Bridge

Victoria Island

DOWNTOWN OTTAWA

Confederation Park

6

Ottawa River Pkwy

5

Wellington St

Sparks St

Queen St

Kent St

Elgin St

See Downtown Ottawa Map (p216)

Canadian War Museum

1

Booth St

7

Bay St

Albert St

Slater St

11

Laurier Ave W

Gloucester St

10

Nepean St

Kent St

O'Connor St

Metcalfe St

Lisgar St

Bank St

18

MacLaren St

Cooper St

Gilmour St

CHINATOWN

Somerset St W

Lyon St

Bay St

James St

9

13

Percy St

15

17

Florence St

Gladstone Ave

Cambridge St N

Bronson Ave

Arthur St

Bell St

McLeod St

Flora St

To Urban Element (1.3km)

Lebreton St

Arlington Ave

Central Bus Station

12

Rochester St

Booth St

Preston St

16

Bank St

LITTLE ITALY

Stoneface Dolly's (450m); Canada Agricultural Museum (1.4km)

Atelier (600m)

Queensway

Renfrew Ave

Powell Ave

Ottawa

galleries exhibit predominantly Canadian art, classic and contemporary, including an impressive collection of Inuit works. It's the largest such collection in the world, although additional galleries of European and American treasures include several recognizable names and masterpieces. Chronological displays guide visitors through an annotated retelling of the nation's history.

Deep within the gallery's interior you'll find two smooth courtyards and the remarkable **Rideau Street Convent Chapel**. Built in 1888, this stunning wooden chapel was saved from demolition and restored piece by piece within the main building – quite extraordinary.

Canadian Museum of Nature   MUSEUM
(Map p210; ☏ 613-566-4700; www.nature.ca; 240 McLeod St; adult/child $12/10, 5-8pm Thu freee; ☉9am-6pm Sat-Wed, to 8pm Thu & Fri; ☐ route 5, 6, 14, stop McLeod St) Sparkling after a massive renovation, this vast museum pokes its

Gothic head just above the skyline, south of downtown. It houses an impressive collection of fossils, the full skeleton of a blue whale and an excellent stock of dinosaurs from Alberta. Everyone loves the realistic mammal and bird dioramas depicting Canadian wildlife. The taxidermic creatures are so lifelike, you'll be glad they're behind a sheet of glass.

Ottawa Locks   HISTORIC BUILDING
(Map p216) The series of steep, steplike locks, between the Château Laurier and Parliament Hill, marks the north end of the 200km Rideau Canal which flows all the way down to Kingston. Colonel By, the canal's visionary engineer, set up headquarters here in 1826.

Bytown Museum   MUSEUM
(Map p216; ☑ 613-234-4570; www.bytownmuseum. com; 1 Canal Lane; adult/child $6.50/3; ☉ 10am-5pm) Take the stairs alongside the Ottawa locks on Wellington St to find the Bytown Museum, sitting at the last lock before the artificial canal plunges into the waters of the Ottawa River. This well-curated collection of artifacts and documents about Ottawa's colonial past is displayed in the city's oldest stone building.

Canada Science & Technology Museum   MUSEUM
(☑ 613-991-3044; www.sciencetech.technomuses.ca; 1867 St Laurent Blvd; adult/child $12/8; ☉ 9:30am-5pm) Ambient squeaks and boinks fill the air of this hands-on museum as contented visitors gingerly turn knobs and push buttons, exploring the physical laws governing things like optical illusions and time. A walk through the 'Crazy Kitchen' is a blast: the lopsided galley makes you stumble from start to finish. There are trains out back to enlighten you on the science of coal and steam propulsion and a large display of space technology. Popular with adults and kids alike, it's informative and fun!

Canada Aviation and Space Museum   MUSEUM
(☑ 613-993-2010; www.aviation.technomuses.ca; 11 Aviation Pkwy; adult/child $13/8; ☉ 9am-5pm; ☑ 129) With nearly 120 aircraft housed in this mammoth steel hangar about 5km northeast of downtown, you could be forgiven for thinking you were at the airport. Wander through the warehouse, try the flight simulator and get up close and personal with colorful planes ranging from the Silver

Dart of 1909 to the first turbo-powered Viscount passenger jet.

Royal Canadian Mint   NOTABLE BUILDING
(Map p216; ☑ 613-993-8990; www.mint.ca; 320 Sussex Dr; guided tours adult/child $6/3; ☉ 10am-5pm) Although Canada's circulation-coin mint is in Winnipeg, the royal mint holds its own by striking special pieces. The imposing stone building, which looks a bit like the Tower of London, has been Canada's major gold refiner since 1908. Weekday tours of the coin-making process are highly recommended: visitors can glimpse the transformation as sheets of metal are spun into loads of coins. This doesn't happen on weekends, so the tour price is discounted.

Notre Dame Cathedral-Basilica   CHURCH
(Map p216; 385 Sussex Dr; ☉ 7am-6pm) Built in 1841, this shimmering tin-topped house of worship is the oldest church in all of Ottawa and the seat of the city's Catholic archbishop. At the entrance, pick up the small pamphlet outlining the church's many idiosyncratic features, including elaborate wooden carvings and the dazzling indigo ceiling peppered with gleaming stars.

Supreme Court of Canada   NOTABLE BUILDING
(Map p210; ☑ 613-995-5361; www.scc-csc.gc.ca; 301 Wellington St; ☉ 9am-5pm) FREE This intimidating structure strikes an intriguing architectural balance with a modern concrete shell and a traditional copper roof. Visitors can stroll around the scenic grounds, vaulted lobby and dark oak-paneled courtroom. In summer law students from the University of Ottawa conduct friendly and insightful tours, which depart every 30 minutes. During the rest of the year, tours must be booked in advance.

Library & National Archives of Canada   NOTABLE BUILDING
(Map p210; ☑ 613-996-5115; www.collectionscanada.gc.ca; 395 Wellington St; ☉ 8:30am-11pm) FREE The mandate of this monstrous concrete institution is to collect and preserve the documentation of Canada. Behind the tiny checkered windows lies a vast anthology of records, including paintings, maps, photographs, diaries, letters, posters and 60,000 cartoons and caricatures collected over the past two centuries. Rotating exhibits are displayed on the ground floor.

Laurier House National Historic Site
HISTORIC SITE

(Map p210; ✆613-992-8142; 335 Laurier Ave; adult/child $4/2; ◷9am-5pm) This copper-roofed Victorian home built in 1878 was the residence of two notable prime ministers: Wilfrid Laurier and the eccentric Mackenzie King. The home is elegantly furnished, displaying treasured mementos and possessions from both politicos. Don't miss the study on the top floor.

Rideau Hall
NOTABLE BUILDING

(Off map p210; ✆613-993-8200; www.gg.ca; 1 Sussex Dr; ◷9am-5pm) FREE Home of the governor-general, Rideau Hall was built in the early 20th century. There are free 45-minute walking tours of the fancy residence, with poignant anecdotes about the various goings-on over the years. Otherwise, the grounds are free to be enjoyed at your leisure. At the main gate, the small changing of the guard ceremony happens on the hour throughout the day from the end of June until the end of August.

Walk east along Sussex/Princess Dr to take a glance at **Rockcliffe Village** (off map p210), Ottawa's swankiest neighborhood and home to prominent Canadians and most foreign diplomats.

RCMP Musical Ride Centre
HISTORIC SITE

(✆613-998-8199; 1 Sandridge Rd; ◷9am-4pm) FREE While the name sounds like Disney's newest attraction starring chipper red-vested policemen, the musical ride center is actually the stage where the Mounties perfect their pageant. The public are welcome to watch the dress rehearsals and equestrian displays, though it mostly appeals to equestrian enthusiasts. It's about 7km northeast of Centretown. Call for schedules.

Diefenbunker
HISTORIC BUILDING

(✆613-839-0007; www.diefenbunker.ca; 3911 Carp Rd, Carp; adult/child $14/8; ◷10am-6pm) During the Cold War, paranoid government officials commissioned this gargantuan four-floored secret underground shelter, designed to house over 300 'important persons' for 30 days during a nuclear attack. Admission includes an optional one-hour tour, the highlights of which include the prime minister's suite, the CBC radio studio and the Bank of Canada vault. It's about 40km west of town, in the village of Carp.

RIDEAU CANAL

On June 28, 2007, the Rideau Canal became Canada's 14th location to be named a Unesco national historic site. This 175-year-old, 200km-long system connects Kingston with Ottawa through 47 locks, climbing 84m from Ottawa over the Canadian Shield before dropping 49m into Lake Ontario.

After the War of 1812, there was a fear of future skirmishes with the Americans. The Duke of Wellington decided to link Ottawa and Kingston in order to have a reliable communications and supply route between the two military centers. Construction was a brutal affair, involving as many as 4000 men battling malaria and the Canadian Shield, some of the world's hardest rock. Despite their blood, sweat and tears, the canal never saw military service, although it later proved useful for shipping goods.

Today, it's a nautical paradise, lined with charming parks, lakes and towns to enjoy.

Saunders Farm
PARK

(✆613-838-5440; www.saundersfarm.com; 7893 Bleeks Rd, Munster; admission $16.50; ◷Jun-Sep) About 40 minutes' drive southwest of Ottawa, this fun family farm is chock-full of hedge mazes and has a water park, pedal carts, hay rides and picnic areas for you to enjoy.

🏃 Activities

Residents of this city of long, harsh winters love to be outside, whatever the season.

The **Rideau Canal**, Ottawa's most famous outdoor attraction, doubles as the largest **ice-skating rink** in the world. The 7.8km of groomed ice is roughly the size of 90 Olympic-sized hockey rinks. Rest stops and changing stations are sprinkled throughout, but, more importantly, take note of the wooden kiosks dispensing scrumptious slabs of fried dough called beavertails. The three **skate and sled rental stations** are located at the steps of the National Arts Centre, Dow's Lake and 5th Ave.

Several nearby **skiing** resorts offer a variety of alpine and cross-country trails. In the **Gatineau Hills**, about 20km from downtown, over 50 groomed slopes are available.

OTTAWA FOR CHILDREN

Nope, the **Canada Agricultural Museum** (Map p210; ✆ 613-991-3044; www.agriculture. technomuses.ca/; 930 Carling Ave at Prince of Wales Dr; adult/child $10/7; ☺ 9am-5pm Mar-Oct) isn't about the history of the pitchfork – it's a fascinating experimental farm. This government-owned property includes over 500 hectares of gardens and ranches. Kids will love the livestock as they hoot and snort around the barn. Affable farmhands will let the tots help out during feeding time. Guided tours lead visitors to an observatory, a tropical greenhouse and an arboretum. The rolling farmland is the perfect place for a scenic summer picnic, and in winter the grounds become a prime tobogganing locale. Just as farmlike, but without the animals, the mazes at Saunders Farm (p213) will keep the kids going in circles for ages, so you can put your feet up! Otherwise, most of Ottawa's museums have been designed with families in mind; several have entire wings devoted to child's play, like the Canadian Museum of Nature (p211), the Canada Science & Technology Museum (p212) and the Canadian Museum of Civilization (p209). Family-friendly accommodations include the Albert at Bay Suite Hotel (p215), Les Suites (p218) and Courtyard Ottawa East (p215).

Camp Fortune (✆ 819-827-1717; www.campfortune.com; 300 Chemin Dunlop, Chelsea) is a year-round adventure spot with ski runs that turn into a paradise for mountain bikers in the summer. If that's not enough, there's also plenty of ziplining to be had. Popular ski resort **Mont Cascades** (✆ 819-827-0301; www.montcascades.ca; 448 Mont Cascades Rd, Cantley) also flips its tricks in the summer, operating an expansive water park. **Mount Pakenham** (✆ 613-624-5290; www.mountpakenham.com; 577 Ski Hill Rd, Pakenham), 60km west of Ottawa, is a strictly winter affair. Cross-country skiers will love the trails in Gatineau Park (p224).

Hot-air ballooning has long been a popular leisure activity in the capital region. **Sundance Balloons** (✆ 613-247-8277; www.sundanceballoons.com; per person from $250) offers sunrise and sunset trips departing from several locations in the Ottawa valley.

☞ Tours

The Capital Information Kiosk (p223) offers several handy brochures for self-guided walking tours.

Ottawa Walking Tours　　　WALKING TOUR
(✆ 613-799-1774; www.ottawawalkingtours.com; tours $15) These informative and fun tours with professional guides depart in front of the Capital Infocentre. Cash only.

Haunted Walk　　　WALKING TOUR
(Map p216; ✆ 613-232-0344; www.hauntedwalk. com; 73 Clarence St; walks $14-17) Has several ghoulish walking tours including visits to the old county jail. A new 'Naughty Ottawa'

pub crawl is also available for those who want to get their beer on.

Lady Dive Amphibious　　　BUS TOUR
(Map p216; ✆ 613-223-6211; www.ladydive.com; cnr Sparks & Elgin Sts; tours from $31; ☺ May-Oct) This half-bus half-boat drives around Ottawa's favorite sights and then plunges into the Ottawa River. Free hotel pickup is available.

Paul's Boat Lines　　　BOAT TOUR
(Map p216; ✆ 613-255-6781; www.paulsboatcruises.com; Ottawa Locks or Rideau Canal Dock; cruises from adult/child $20/12; ☺ May-Oct) Scenic cruises offer picture-perfect moments.

Gray Line　　　BUS TOUR
(Map p216; ✆ 613-562-9090; www.grayline.ca; cnr Sparks & Elgin Sts) Tours depart from the cornerside ticket kiosk. A variety of tours including a hop-on, hop-off service is available. Check the website for schedules and pricing.

☆彡 Festivals & Events

The nation's capital is abuzz year-round with over 60 annual festivals and events. Here are our picks.

Winterlude　　　WINTER
(✆ 613-239-5000; www.canadascapital.gc.ca/winterlude) Three consecutive weekends in February celebrate Ottawa's winter, centering on the frozen Dows Lake and the canal. Awe-inspiring ice sculptures abound.

Canadian Tulip Festival　　　FLOWER
(✆ 613-567-5757; www.tulipfestival.ca) In May, after the winter thaw, Ottawa explodes with

color as beds of over 200 species of tulip come to life. Over 100,000 bulbs were gifted to the city in 1945 by the Dutch royal family in gratitude for Canada sheltering their princess and her daughters during the war. Festivities include parades, regattas, car rallies, dances, concerts and fireworks.

Ottawa Bluesfest
MUSIC

(✓ 613-241-2633; www.ottawabluesfest.ca) The world's second-biggest blues festival after Chicago's brings in the big names for memorable concerts in late June.

Canada Day
CULTURE

(✓ 613-239-5000; www.canadascapital.gc.ca/canadaday) The best place in Canada to celebrate the nation's birthday on July 1. Noteworthy fireworks crackle and boom above the Parliament buildings.

HOPE Volleyball Summerfest
SPORTS

(✓ 613-237-1433; www.hopehelps.com) A giant volleyball tournament in mid-July to raise money for local charities.

SuperEX
AGRICULTURAL

(✓ 613-237-2222; www.ottawasuperex.com) This enormous carnival has been running for over 120 years, but had been temporarily canceled at time of writing. We hope it gets back on its feet again.

Capital Pride
CULTURE

(✓ 613-421-5387; www.capitalpride.com) A week's worth of rainbows culminating in a rowdy parade in mid-August.

🛏 Sleeping

Ottawa has an impressive array of accommodations available in all price ranges, with plenty of great choices in the downtown core. Reservations are recommended during summer and over festival dates, especially Winterlude.

Locals call downtown 'Centretown.' To its east, the Sandy Hill district with its cache of stately heritage homes and international embassies has a number of pleasant B&Bs, boutique hotels and, closer to ByWard Market, hostels. All are within a healthy walking distance from downtown.

🛏 Centretown

Hostelling International (HI) Ottawa Jail
HOSTEL $

(Map p216; ✓ 613-235-2595; www.hihostels.ca/ottawa; 75 Nicholas St; members dm/s $29/54,

nonmembers dm/s $34/59; @ 🖥) This quirky hostel in the former Ottawa Jail, considered to be one of the most haunted buildings in town, isn't for everyone, especially those who've served time or are scared of their own shadow. Others will love its originality. Guests can sleep in the stone penitentiary's old wrought-iron cell block. Check out the on-site gallows where numerous criminals were hanged for their wretched crimes.

Lord Elgin Hotel
HOTEL $$

(Map p216; ✓ 613-235-3333; www.lordelginhotel.ca; 100 Elgin St; d from $169; ❄ 🖥 ≋) In one of Ottawa's finest locations, the stately Lord Elgin was built in 1941 in a similar, but less grandiose style to the Fairmont Royal York in Toronto. Its large, bright rooms are comfortably furnished and were recently refurbished with large flatscreen TVs. Many feature wonderful views over Confederation Park. Check online for frequent special rates at this landmark property.

Albert at Bay Suite Hotel
HOTEL $$

(Map p210; ✓ 1-800-267-6644; www.albertatbay.com; 435 Albert St; ste from $159; ❄ 🖥) This all-suite hotel offers excellent value for traveling families and those who prefer the comforts of home. Oversized multiroom one- and two- bedroom suites, Ottawa's largest, all have full kitchens and plush, comfortable furnishings, though we're not sure how all that white will stay looking sharp. Many rooms have balconies. It's a little far west of the downtown action, but still offers excellent value.

Courtyard Ottawa East
HOTEL $$

(✓ 613-741-9862; www.marriott.com; 200 Coventry Rd; d from $119; ≋) The closest hotel to Ottawa's not-so-central VIA rail station is also a great choice if you're driving: free parking. One of Ottawa's newest hotels, it has spacious, functional rooms with trendy furnishings. There's a rooftop pool and on-site bar/restaurant. Consider elsewhere if you need to be very downtown, or if you're traveling in winter without a vehicle.

Victoria Park Suites
HOTEL $$

(Map p210; ✓ 800-465-7275; www.victoriapark.com; 377 O'Connor St; d incl breakfast from $139) A delightful position in a leafy downtown backstreet, bright, airy rooms with kitchenettes and plush, comfortable beds make this property an excellent choice for travelers with a limited budget. Deluxe continental breakfast, on-site gym and a fantastic

Downtown Ottawa

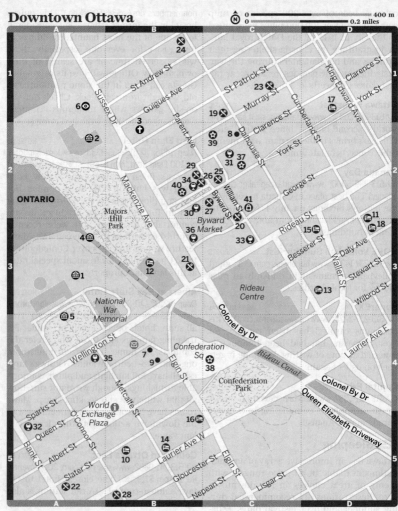

rooftop courtyard with great views are all bonuses.

Hotel Indigo
HOTEL $$

(Map p216; ☎613-216-2903; www.ottawadown-townhotel.com; 123 Metcalfe St; d from $139; ❄@☎) A prime downtown location helps score points for this trying-to-be boutique hotel that doesn't quite pull it off. Quirks include an atrium lobby, floor-to-ceiling murals in each room, plasma TVs, and customer information written in haiku form, but rooms are a little small and dark. It's a good bet if the price is right.

Arc
BOUTIQUE HOTEL $$

(Map p216; ☎613-238-2888; www.arcthehotel.com; 140 Slater St; d from $129; ❄@☎) Arc is a savvy boutique hotel with 112 minimal-yet-elegant rooms in a great location; call it low-key, muted and restfully hip. This mellow adult atmosphere continues through the quiet bar and trendy restaurant.

Fairmont Château Laurier
HOTEL $$$

(Map p216; ☎866-540-4410, 613-241-1414; www.fairmont.com/laurier; 1 Rideau St; d from $269; ❄@☎⛱) ☕ The city's best-known hotel by the Ottawa Locks is a landmark in its own right. Rooms are predictably large and fea-

Downtown Ottawa

ture original antique furnishings. Feel free to walk the opulent marble hallways, admire the art and recline on the overstuffed chaises as though you were the toast of the town.

Byward Market & Sandy Hill

Ottawa Backpackers Inn　　　　HOSTEL $
(Map p216; ☎613-241-3402; www.ottawahostel. com; 203 York St; dm/s $27/65, apt from $150; @ 🛜) This laid-back hostel lives in a converted 19th-century house boasting fresh-faced bathrooms, sun-drenched dorms, and handy power outlets at every bed.

Barefoot Hostel　　　　　　　HOSTEL $
(Map p216; ☎613-237-0335; www.barefoothostel. com; 455 Cumberland St; dm $38; ✳@🛜) Thick duvets, generous bursts of air-conditioning, excellent bathrooms and common areas and a quaint patio make this 'boutique hostel' a clear winner.

Australis Guest House　　　　　B&B $
(☎613-235-8461; www.australisguesthouse.com; 89 Goulburn Ave; s/d from $75/115; 🛜) ✦ This eco-friendly guesthouse in hilly Sandy Hill

offers 100% cotton sheets, reusable cloth napkins, all-natural cleaning products and loos with a low-flush option.

Avalon　　　　　　　　　　　　B&B $
(Map p210; ☎613-789-3443; www.avalonbedand-breakfast.com; 539 Besserer St; d $85-125; 🛜) A refreshing departure from the usual antique-laden B&Bs, Avalon, on a lovely street near the canal, has a tasteful blend of modern furnishings. Enormous healthy breakfasts are the norm. Each of the four stylish rooms has en suite bathroom.

★**Swiss Hotel**　　　　　BOUTIQUE HOTEL $$
(Map p216; ☎613-237-0335; www.swisshotel.ca; 89 Daly Ave; r incl breakfast from $128; ✳@🛜) Reduced rates are available for extended stays, making this beautiful boutique hotel a wonderful place to call your Ottawa home. The old stone guesthouse has 22 stylish rooms, all a little different but each with iPads, free wi-fi and plush bedding. The optional Swiss buffet breakfast features delicious imported coffees, muesli, cheese and much, much more.

Benner's B&B
B&B $$

(Map p210; ☎613-789-8320; www.bennersbnb.com; 541 Besserer St; d $95-130; ☎) Well-appointed and spacious, this 100-year-old house stands out as a comfortable option in Sandy Hill District, a 15-minute walk to downtown. The King loft room is a great deal.

McGee's Inn
INN $$

(Map p210; ☎613-262-4337; www.mcgeesinn.com; 185 Daly Ave; d incl breakfast $119-198; @☎) This vast Victorian mansion has all the period trappings, from floral prints and embroidered chair caning to plush button-eyed teddy bears and varnished sewing machines: there's so much atmosphere in here. A variety of private suites are available – we love the John McGee room. Enjoy the full breakfast in the dining room amid chirps from antique cuckoo clocks. This is an excellent choice for those who love history and charm.

Les Suites
HOTEL $$

(Map p216; ☎866-682-0879; www.les-suites.com; 130 Besserer St; ste from $151; ✳☎☎☎) Spacious suites in this downtown hotel at the edge of the Byward Market district feature one or two bedrooms, full kitchens and in-suite laundries. Staff have a reputation for their excellent customer service. Some suites have been refurbished more recently than others; clarify before you book.

✕ Eating

Ottawa's smorgasbord of gastronomic goodness rivals that of Toronto and Montréal, but is more accessible: you'll never have to travel too far for great dining options catering to all tastes and budgets. Bounteous **ByWard Market** (www.byward-market.com) boasts 150 options squished into one condensed epicurean district. When it's warm, diners spill out onto the streets as patio seats fill fast.

Follow Bank St south to the colorful Glebe neighborhood for a surplus of less touristy pubs, restaurants and cafes between First St and Fifth St or take an evening stroll down Preston St, aka 'Corso Italia,' for a little slice

---

SAVOR OTTAWA

Check out www.savourottawa.ca for details about the burgeoning local initiative that strives to match regional restaurants with the area's farmers.

---

of the homeland. Ottawa's lively Chinatown, spread along Somerset St W near Bronson Ave, is also a great spot to visit and there's a tasty smattering of Vietnamese flavors west of Booth St.

✕ Centretown & Chinatown

Eggspectation
BRUNCH $

(Map p210; ☎613-569-6505; www.eggspectation.ca; 171 Bank St; meals $8-23; ⊙7am-5pm Sat-Tue, to 9pm Wed-Fri) The downtown location of this breakfast (and more) franchise is so handy and the menu so *egg-citing* that we couldn't resist sharing. It's cheap, cheery and full of sunshine. Literally. Bright open windows give you plenty of personal space to navigate through your hangover, but you might want to keep the shades on.

Hung Sum
CHINESE $

(Map p210; ☎613-238-8828; 870 Somerset St; dishes $2-9; ⊙11am-8pm Mon-Sun) Traditional Cantonese dim sum is served all day in this wonderfully plain and nontraditional little restaurant. All dishes are prepared and served fresh, unlike the pick-from-the-trolley joints you might be familiar with. Best eaten with friends, this is one of the tastiest, best-value and fun-to-eat meals you'll find in Ottawa.

★ Town
MODERN CANADIAN $$

(Map p210; ☎613-695-8696; www.townlovesyou.ca; 296 Elgin St; mains $13-34; ⊙11:30am-2pm Wed-Fri & 5-10pm Tue-Sun) Town loves you and we love Town. Slick, smart and ineffably cool, this joint is always packed: arty-farty hipsters bump elbows with wealthy coiffured housewives. Anyone around who knows about food knows the food here is good: real good. Town's clever young owners have pulled together the right mix of style, location, marketing and an exceptionally executed menu that everyone is talking about.

Brasserie Métropolitain
FRENCH $$

(Map p216; ☎613-562-1160; www.metropolitainbrasserie.com; 700 Sussex Dr; mains $11-38; ⊙8am-midnight) This trendy hot spot puts a modern spin on the typical brasserie with a swirling zinc countertop, flamboyant fixtures and the subtle oompah-pah from a distant accordion: you'll feel like you're dining on the set of *Moulin Rouge*. 'Hill Hour' (4pm to 7pm on weekdays) buzzes with the spirited chatter of hot-blooded pollys as they down cheap drinks and plats du jour.

The Works   BURGERS $$

(Map p210; ✆613-235-0406; www.worksburger.
com; 580 Bank St; burgers from $9.50; ⊘11am-
10pm Sun-Wed, to midnight Thu-Sat) It's hard to
believe that in one short decade this clever
burger joint has flourished into a success-
ful franchise. Brand your patty how you like
it with over 60 quirky toppings, from fried
eggs to brie cheese and peanut butter.

Tosca   ITALIAN $$

(Map p216; ✆613-565-3933; www.tosca-ristorante.
ca, 144 O'Connor St; mains $16 36; ⊘11:30am late
Mon-Fri, 4-10pm Sat & Sun) In the heart of the
downtown core, this upscale but accessible
Italian *ristorante* offers delicious, authentic
food, an extensive wine list and excellent
service. The evening atmosphere is candlelit
and serene, perfect for romancing or long
conversations with old friends.

C'est Japon à Suisha   JAPANESE $$

(Map p216; ✆613-236-9602; www.japaninottawa.
com; 208 Slater St; sushi & sashimi from $6, mains
$18-35; ⊘11:30am-2pm Tue-Fri & 5pm-9:30pm Tue-
Sat) While strong in other culinary branches,
Ottawa lacks a ton of good Japanese restau-
rants. This is the exception: mouthwatering
authentic dishes are delivered in a tradition-
ally styled setting with sushi boats and pri-
vate *washitsu* Japanese rooms. A wide va-
riety of combinations and sets are available
from an extensive menu.

Shanghai   CHINESE $$

(Map p210; ✆613-233-4001; www.shanghaiottawa.
com; 651 Somerset St W; items $8-17; ⊘11:30am-
2pm Tue-Fri & 4:30-10pm Tue-Sun; ⊘) This
restaurant is widely known as the first establishment in Ottawa's Chinatown, and is now
run by the artistic children of the original
owners. The food is great – modern Chinese
cuisine with lots of vegetarian options – but
the real draw is the trendy decor, rotating
art exhibits and fabulous weekend events
(think 'Disco Bingo' and karaoke) hosted by
the local diva tranny goddess China-Doll.

ZenKitchen   VEGAN $$

(Map p210; ✆613-233-6404; www.zenkitchen.ca;
634 Somerset St W; mains $18-21; ⊘11:30am-2pm
Thu & Fri, 10am-2pm Sat & Sun & 5-10pm daily;
⊘) ⊘ The dining concept here works on
the premise that vegan food can be visually
appealing, delicious and healthy. Only the
freshest local ingredients are used in the
preparation of a menu that seeks to bring
out the rich flavors of individual ingredients
like tomatoes, mangoes, peaches and limes.

An award-winning Ontario wine list softens
the palate. Highly recommended for the veg-
curious out there.

★Beckta Dining & Wine   FUSION $$$

(Map p210; ✆613-238-7063; www.beckta.com; 226
Nepean St; mains $28-39; ⊘5:30-10pm) ⊘ Book
in advance for the hottest table in town, if
not one of the hottest in the country. Beckta
offers an upmarket dining experience with
an original spin on regional cuisine. The inspired five-course tasting menu ($85) is the
collective brainchild of chef and sommelier
and a great way to experience the bigger picture at work here. Serious foodies won't fail
to get a table.

Whalesbone Oyster House   SEAFOOD $$$

(Map p210; ✆613-231-8569; www.thewhalesbone.
com; 430 Bank St; mains $24-35; ⊘11:30am-2pm
Mon-Fri & 5-10pm daily) ⊘ If the local chefs
are purchasing their fish from Whalesbone's
wholesale wing (or should we say 'fin'), then
there's really no doubt that it's the best place
in town for seafood. The on-site restaurant
offers up a short list of fresh faves like lob-
ster, halibut and scallops ceviche on small
plates.

🗡 Byward Market & Sandy Hill

Boulangerie Moulin de Provence   BAKERY $

(Map p216; ✆613-241-9152; www.moulindepro-
vence.com; 55 ByWard Market Sq; items from $2;
⊘7am-10pm) Still riding on the buzz left by
a visit from President Obama, this wonder-
ful bakery is packed to the hilt with sugary
and savoury goodness. The 'Obama Cookies'
are a big hit, but we recommend the flaky
croissants, which have often held the title of
the city's best.

Boulanger Français   BAKERY $

(Map p216; ✆613-789-7941; www.bennysbistro.ca/
bakery; 119 Murray St; pastries from $2; ⊘7am-
5:30pm) The smell of freshly baked *pain au
chocolat* will destroy even the smallest of
diets. Pastries are prepared using tried-and-
true recipes from France.

Zak's Diner   DINER $

(Map p216; ✆613-241-2401; www.zaksdiner.
com; 14 ByWard Market Sq; mains $8-15; ⊘24hr)
Shoo-bop along to the '50s music that sup-
plements the *Grease*-like atmosphere. The
kitschy diner is at its best in the middle of
the night when the joint fills up for post-
party munchies. The club sandwich is a big

hit, as are the breakfast items. Wraps are also on offer, so it's not a total time warp.

Market Square
MARKET $

(Map p216; ☑ 613-562-3325; www.bywardmarket.com; 55 ByWard Market Sq, cnr William & George Sts; ☺ 7am-8pm) Anchoring the market district, this sturdy brick building is the perfect place to stop when hunger strikes. Aside from the fresh produce and cheese, there's an array of international takeaway joints offering falafel, spicy curries, flaky pastries, sushi (the list goes on). Look for the stand selling beavertails, Ottawa's signature sizzling flat-dough dish.

I Deal Coffee
CAFE $

(Map p216; ☑ 613-562-1775; www.idealcoffees.com; 176 Dalhousie St; ☺ 7am-7pm Mon-Fri, 9am-6pm Sat & Sun) Ideal indeed; handcrafted blends are produced and roasted on-site. The decor is thin – it's all about rich, flavorful cups of joe.

Planet Coffee
CAFE $

(Map p216; ☑ 613-789-6261; 24 York St; ☺ 7:30am-10pm Mon-Sat, 9am-7pm Sun) Skip Starbucks and grab a latte around the corner in the quiet courtyard. Sweetened ice coffees are a big hit.

★ Fraser Cafe
CAFE $$

(☑ 613-749-1444; www.frasercafe.ca; 7 Springfield Rd; brunch items $9-15, mains $12-29; ☺ 11:30am-2pm Tue-Fri, 10am-2pm Sat & Sun & 5:30-10pm Tue-Sun) It's worth taking a little trek over to this smart cafe/restaurant across the canal, just east of Sandy Hill, especially if you're in the mood for brunch (weekends only). Healthy, tasty, creative meals are prepared from the freshest ingredients. The atmosphere is lively and casual and the service, despite the bustle, is excellent. Reservations are recommended.

Chez Lucien
FRENCH $$

(Map p216; ☑ 613-241-3533; 137 Murray St; mains $6-16; ☺ 11am-2am) Exposed burgundy brick, classics playing on the free jukebox, shucking down butter-soaked escargot, all makes wonderful sense at Chez Lucien, one of Ottawa's favorite places to kick back in style.

Lapointe
SEAFOOD $$

(Map p216; ☑ 613-241-6221; www.lapointefish.ca; 55 York St; mains $10-29; ☺ 11:30am-9:30pm) This fish market has served the community since 1867. The basement restaurant lacks ambience but offers a versatile array of fishy dishes from sashimi to chowder and old-school fish and chips.

LUXE Bistro & Steakhouse
STEAKHOUSE $$$

(Map p216; ☑ 613-241-8805; www.luxebistro.com; 47 York St; mains $12-37; ☺ 11:30am-1am) If you like your steak a little French with a twist of New York, this smart ByWard Market bistro is bound to appeal. The decor is slick and the new outdoor patio is a hit in the warmer months. Dress smart.

Le Cordon Bleu Bistro @ Signatures
FRENCH $$$

(Map p210; ☑ 613-236-2499; www.bistroatsignatures.com; 453 Laurier Ave E; mains $26-35; ☺ 11:30am-1:30pm Wed-Fri & 5:30-9:30pm Wed-Sat) Housed in a Tudor-style castle, this restaurant belongs to the prestigious Le Cordon Bleu culinary school. Well-seasoned instructors prepare nightly à la carte dinners. Weekday *table d'hôte* lunches ($26) crafted by graduating students offer the best value, though can be hit-and-miss. The lengthy wine list looks more like an encyclopedia.

✕ Further Afield

White Horse Restaurant
DINER $

(☑ 613-746-7767; 294 Tremblay Rd; ☺ 5am-7pm Mon-Fri, 7am-4pm Sat & Sun) This wonderful little greasy spoon is the closest place to get a meal near Ottawa station and boasts good old-fashioned home cooking and the cheapest breakfast in town.

Petit Bills
CANADIAN $$$

(☑ 613-729-2500; www.petitbillsbistro.com; 1293 Wellington St W; mains $22-33; ☺ 11:30am-9pm Mon-Sat, 4:30-9pm Sun) It's worth the cab fare to get to this charming family-run bistro in Ottawa's Fisher Park neighborhood. We think the secret-recipe east coast seafood chowder is one of the best we've had.

Urban Element
FUSION $$$

(Map p210; ☑ 613-722-0885; www.theurbanelement.ca; 424 Parkdale Ave; courses from $90; ☺ 9am-5pm, meals by appointment) ✦ Housed in a vacant brick firehouse, this gustatory option wins on concept alone. Think *Iron Chef* meets Martha Stewart. Make a reservation at this kitchen-cum-classroom and cook your own three-star gourmet meal, with the help of a skilled cook, of course. The team of instructors includes a regular crew of chefs and several visiting professionals who work at the finest restaurants around town.

Atelier FUSION $$$

(Map p210; ☑ 613-321-3537; www.atelierrestaurant.ca; 540 Rochester St; menu $110; ☺5-10pm) ✐
The brainchild of celebrated chef and molecular gastronomy enthusiast Marc Lépine, Atelier is a white-walled laboratory dedicated to tickling the taste buds. There's no oven or stove – just Bunsen burners, liquid nitrogen and hot plates to create the unique 12-course tasting menu. Each dish is a mini science experiment that toys with texture, taste and temperature, and pushes the limit of 'normal' cuisine (think taco ice cream). This isn't fusion, it's fission.

Wellington Gastropub STEAKHOUSE $$$

(☑ 613-729-1315; www.thewellingtongastropub.com; 1325 Wellington St W; mains $19-27; ☺11:30am-2pm Mon-Fri & 5:30-9:30pm Mon-Sat) Although 'gastropub' might sound like some sort of British indigestion, the Wellington is luring foodies to the west end with its savvy selection of hearty mains and funky waiters. The rotating menu is best paired with a pint of crafted microbrew.

Le Baccara FRENCH $$$

(☑ 819-772-6210; Blvd du Casino; dinner mains $30-50; ☺5:30-11pm Wed-Sun) How do you say 'shmancy' in French? The answer is 'Baccara.' This world-class dining experience in the Casino du Lac Leamy, across the river in Hull, features an open-concept dining room where patrons can watch the master chefs prepare their meal. Tours are available of the cavernous wine cellar, which contains over 13,000 bottles of wine! All customers must be at least 18 years of age.

🍸 Drinking & Nightlife

From cheap-and-crusty beery dives to cheery local pubs and plush, see-and-be-seen lounges, Ottawa has it all. Most bars start up around 9pm, and when they shut down (usually 2am) people scurry over to Hull to continue the party.

Highlander Pub PUB

(Map p216; ☑ 613-562-5678; www.thehighlanderpub.com; 115 Rideau St; ☺11am-1am) Kilted servers, 17 taps and 200 single malt scotches all add to the wonderful Scottish appeal of this ByWard Market area pub. The food is good too!

Parliament Pub PUB

(Map p216; ☑ 613-563-0636; www.parliamentpub.com; 101 Sparks St; ☺noon-2am Mon-Sat, to 9pm Sun) There's no better place to down a quiet beer while contemplating the history of this fine city than from this summer patio directly opposite Parliament Hill.

Château Lafayette PUB

(Map p216; ☑ 613-241-4747; www.thelaff.ca; 42 York St; ☺11am-2am) Many would argue that 'the Laff' puts the 'crap' in crapulence, but this run-down relic does a good job of capturing ByWard's laid-back attitude.

Manx BAR

(Map p210; ☑ 613-231-2070; 370 Elgin St; ☺11:30am-2am Mon-Fri, 9:30am-2am Sat & Sun) A homey velvet sea awaits you at this basement pub-style hangout. Most people come for the great selection of Canadian microbrews (including the beloved Creemore) served on copper-top tables.

Stoneface Dolly's BAR

(Map p210; ☑ 613-564-2222; www.stonefacedollys.com; 416 Preston St; ☺8:30am-2:30pm & 5-9pm) Named for the owner's mother, who perfected the art of a stone-cold poker bluff, this popular joint is a great place to grab a pint of Beau's or Hobgoblin – there's food throughout the day, too.

Clock Tower Brew Pub BAR

(Map p216; ☑ 613-241-8783; www.clocktower.ca; 89 Clarence St; ☺11am-2am) Enjoy homemade brews like Raspberry Wheat and Fenian Red amid exposed brick and ByWard bustle. There are three additional locations around town.

Social BAR

(Map p216; ☑ 613-789-7355; www.social.ca; 537 Sussex Dr; ☺noon-midnight) A chic, flowing lounge with slick DJ beats, overstuffed furniture and oversized drinks appeals to a trendy crowd. The cocktails are so large, there should be a lifeguard on duty.

Gay & Lesbian Venues

Ottawa has a happening small-town gay scene, but it's less happening than neighbor Montréal, two hours up the road. Check out *Xtra* (www.xtra.ca) for details.

Centretown Pub PUB

(Map p210; ☑ 613-594-0233; http://centretownpub.blogspot.ca; 340 Somerset St W; ☺2pm-2am) This handsome little neighborhood pub has friendly staff, pool out the back and a small rear patio. On weekends, the upper and lower levels open up revealing multiple dance floors which can quickly become standing (or dancing) room only.

ONTARIO OTTAWA

Lookout Bar
BAR

(Map p216; ☑613-789-1624; www.thelookoutbar. com; 41 York St; ☺2pm-2am Mon-Sat, to 9pm Sun) This popular joint in the ByWard Market caters to a wide range of patrons, especially lesbians.

Edge
CLUB

(Map p216; ☑613-237-2284; www.clubedgeottawa.com; 212 Sparks St; ☺10pm-3am Fri & Sat) A younger gay crowd grinds to Top 40 and house in this bumping and grinding nightspot.

☆ Entertainment

Ottawa has a variety of publications (print and web-based) that offer the latest scoop on the various goings-on around town. *Express* (www.ottawaxpress.ca) is the city's free entertainment weekly, also found around town in cafes, bars and bookshops. Try www.ottawaentertainment.ca for additional info and check out Thursday's *Ottawa Citizen* for complete club and entertainment listings.

Nightlife venues generally cluster in three zones: the ByWard Market, along Bank St in the Glebe neighborhood, and down Elgin St about halfway between the Queensway and Parliament Hill.

Casino du Lac Leamy
CASINO

(☑819-772-2100; 1 Blvd du Casino; ☺11am-3am) Across the river in Hull, Québec, Ottawa's little slice of Vegas is this posh gambling hall with docking facilities and a helipad – just in case you were thinking about bringing your helicopter. The sizable casino complex is complete with a towering hotel, dinner theater, glitzy shows, a high-class restaurant and a felt sea of gambling tables. Take the third exit after the Macdonald-Cartier Bridge from Ottawa, and don't forget to dress up.

Live Music

Zaphod Beeblebrox
LIVE MUSIC

(Map p216; ☑613-562-1010; www.zaphods.ca; 27 York St; ☺5pm-1am) 'Zaphod Beeblebrox' means 'kick-ass live-music venue' in an otherwise undecipherable alien tongue. Grab a Gargleblaster cocktail, and let the trippy beats take you on a ride to the edge of the universe. Well, maybe.

Fat Tuesday's
LIVE MUSIC

(Map p216; ☑613-241-6810; www.fattuesdays.ca; 62 York St; ☺11:30am-1am) Ottawa's little slice of New Orleans is known around town for its dueling pianos on Friday and Saturday nights. Palm readings and happy-hour discounts lure the locals on the other days of the week.

Rainbow Bistro
LIVE MUSIC

(Map p216; ☑613-241-5123; www.therainbow.ca; 76 Murray St; ☺4pm-midnight) An oldie but a goodie: the best place in town to catch live blues.

Irene's Pub
LIVE MUSIC

(Map p210; ☑613-230-4474; www.irenespub.ca; 885 Bank St; ☺11:30am-midnight) This friendly and funky lil' pub offers live Celtic, folk or blues, and a great selection of imported beers.

Theater

National Arts Centre
THEATER

(NAC; Map p216; ☑613-755-1111; www.nac-cna.ca; 53 Elgin St) The capital's premier performing-arts complex delivers opera, drama, and performances from the symphony orchestra. The modish complex stretches along the canal in Confederation Sq.

Cinemas

Mayfair Theatre
CINEMA

(Map p210; ☑613-730-3403; www.mayfairtheatre. ca; 1074 Bank St) Check out this art-house cinema which hasn't changed much since the early '30s.

Bytowne Cinema
CINEMA

(Map p210; ☑613-789-3456; www.bytowne.ca; 325 Rideau St) Ottawa's indie heart has been screening independent and international movies for over 60 years.

Sports

Ottawa is a hard-core hockey town. It's worth getting tickets to a game even if you're not into hockey: the ballistic fans put on a show of their own. The NHL's Senators play at the **ScotiaBank Place** (☑613-599-0100; www.senators.com; Palladium Dr, Kanata) in the city's west end.

Those on a budget can catch the Ottawa 67s, a minor-league hockey team, at the **Civic Center** (Map p210; ☑613-232-6767; www. ottawa67s.com; 1015 Bank St).

🛍 Shopping

The **ByWard Market** (Map p216; ☑613-562-3325; www.byward-market.com), at the corner of George St and ByWard St, is the best place in town for one-stop shopping. Vendors cluster around the old maroon-brick market building, erected in the 1840s. Outdoor merchants operate booths from 6am to 6pm year-round (although the winter weather drastically reduces the number of businesses). In summer more than 175 stalls fill the streets, selling fresh produce from local farms, flowers, seafood, cheese, baked goods and kitschy souvenirs. Dalhousie St, a block east of the market, has been rising in popularity with a smattering of hipster boutiques and fashion houses.

The Glebe, a colorful neighborhood just south of the Queensway, bustles with quirky antique shops and charismatic cafes. Most of the action crowds along Bank St.

Information

The Ottawa Tourism website (www.ottawatourism.ca) offers a comprehensive glance at the nation's capital and can assist with planning itineraries and booking accommodations. Several banks and currency-exchange outlets cluster along the Sparks St mall.

Accu-Rate Foreign Exchange (613-238-8454; 1st fl, World Exchange Plaza, 111 Albert St) Accommodates currency exchange, traveler's checks and EFTs.

Capital Information Kiosk (Map p216; 800-465-1867, 613-239-5000; www.canadascapital.gc.ca; World Exchange Plaza, 111 Albert St; 9am-6pm;) The hub of information for all things Ottawa.

Market Cleaners (613-241-6222; 286 Dalhousie St; 7am-9pm Mon-Fri, from 8am Sat & Sun) A laundromat and internet cafe all rolled into one.

Ottawa Hospital (613-722-7000; www.ottawahospital.on.ca; 501 Smyth Rd; 24hr) Southeast of downtown in Alta Vista; has an emergency room.

Post office (Map p216; 800-267-1177; www.canadapost.ca; 59 Sparks St; 8am-5:30pm Mon-Fri)

Getting There & Away

AIR

The state-of-the-art **Ottawa MacDonald-Cartier International Airport** (YOW; 613-248-2000; www.ottawa-airport.ca; 1000 Airport Rd) is 15km south of the city and is, perhaps surprisingly, very small. Main airlines serving the city include Air Canada, WestJet, Porter American Airlines, British Airways, Northwest Airlines, KLM and US Airways. Almost all international flights require a transfer before arriving in the capital.

BUS

The **central bus station** (Map p210; 613-238-5900; 265 Catherine St) is 20 blocks south of the Parliament, near Kent St. Several companies operate bus services from the station, the largest being Greyhound Canada with services to Toronto ($64, five hours, eight daily).

CAR & MOTORCYCLE

Major car-rental chains are represented at the airport and offer several locations around town, especially along Laurier and Catherine Sts.

TRAIN

The **VIA Rail Station** (Map p210; 888-842-7245; 200 Tremblay Rd) is 7km southeast of downtown, near the Riverside Dr exit of Hwy 417. VIA Rail operates trains to Toronto ($99, 4¼ hours, seven daily) and Montréal ($50, 1¾ hours, seven daily).

Getting Around

TO/FROM THE AIRPORT

The cheapest way to get to the airport is by city bus. Take bus 97 from the corner of Slater and Albert Sts, west of Bronson Ave (make sure you are heading in the 'South Keys & Airport' direction). The ride takes 30 minutes.

Ottawa Shuttle Service (613-680-3313; www.ottawashuttleservice.com; from $25; 10am-10pm) offers private and shared shuttles from most major hotels.

Blue Line Taxis (613-238-1111; www.bluelinetaxi.com) and **Capital Taxi** (613-744-3333; www.capitaltaxi.com) offer cab service to and from the airport; the fare is $20 to $30. If you're having a hard time snagging a cab, there's always a cluster on Metcalfe St between Sparks and Queen Sts.

BICYCLE

The friendly staff at **Rent-A-Bike** (613-241-4140; www.rentabike.ca; East Arch Plaza Bridge, 2 Rideau St; rentals from $9/hr; Apr-Oct) will set you up with a bike and can offer tips about scenic trails.

CAR & MOTORCYCLE

There is free parking in World Exchange Plaza on weekends, and it's always the best place to park when visiting the downtown tourist office. Hourly metered parking can be found throughout downtown. During winter, overnight on-street parking is prohibited. Call the **City of Ottawa** (613-580-2400) for additional parking queries.

PUBLIC TRANSPORTATION

Ottawa and Hull/Gatineau operate separate bus systems. A transfer is valid from one system to the other, but may require an extra payment.

OC Transpo (613-741-6440, 613-741-4390; www.octranspo.com) operates buses and a light-rail system known as the O-train. An extension of the light rail system is being built and

BONNECHERE CAVES

The **Bonnechere Caves** (☎613-628-2283; www.bonnecherecaves.com; Fourth Chute Rd; tours adult/child $16/12; ⊙10am-4:30pm May-Oct), about 130km west of Ottawa, are one of the finest examples of a solution cave (a cave dissolved out of solid rock by acidic waters) in the world. Formed 500 million years ago from the floor of a tropical sea, the dank passages feature a haunting collection of prehistoric fossils including a well-defined octopus. Learn about speleology from the humorous tour, which details the site's quirky history. Nimble guests will enjoy squeezing through a few extra-narrow, damp passages.

is scheduled to open in 2018. Until then public transportation can be tedious: services are at times infrequent and excessively crowded. Bus tickets cost $1.50 and most rides require a minimum two tickets. A book of six passes can be purchased at most convenience stores. Be sure to grab a transfer pass from the driver when boarding the bus; they are valid for 90 minutes.

Around Ottawa

Across the river, after Hull, Québec, the Ottawa Valley becomes the Outaouais (pronounced as though you were saying 'Ottawa' with a French-Canadian accent). This large, mostly rural region extends from the Ottawa River north past Maniwaki, west past Fort Coulonge, and east to Montebello.

Gatineau Park

Gatineau Park is a deservedly popular 36,000-hectare area of woods and lakes in the Gatineau Hills of Québec. The **visitors center** (☎819-827-2020; 33 Scott Rd; ⊙9am-5pm) is 12km from Ottawa's Parliament Hill, off Hwy 5.

In summer this green expanse of cedar and maple offers 150km of hiking trails and over 90km of cycling paths. Winters are just as crowded with dozens of alpine skiing hills. Lac Lapêche, Lac Meech and Lac Philippe have beaches for swimming (including Lac Meech's nude gay beach), which lure the land-locked locals for a refreshing dip (watch out for the occasional leech!).

Also in the park is the **Mackenzie King Estate** (☎800-465-1867; admission per car $10; ⊙11am-5pm May-Oct), the summer estate of William Lyon Mackenzie King, Canada's prime minister in the 1920s, late 1930s and early 1940s. A capable speaker, quirky King was known for his gregarious nature; he even talked to his dead dog and deceased mother. His home, Moorside, is now a museum with a pleasant tearoom.

Fall Rhapsody (☎800-465-1867; www.canadascapital.gc.ca/gatineau) gives leaf-peepers a chance to glimpse the blazing fall foliage before the powdery snow blankets the gnarled trunks. Regular activities include organized walks, art exhibits and brunches with live music.

Wakefield

Charming and scenic, historic Wakefield is an amiable mix of heritage buildings, cafes and tourist-oriented shops. Northwest of Gatineau Park, there are several outfitters that use a turbulent section of the Ottawa River for rafting adventures.

Esprit Rafting (☎800-596-7238; www.whitewater.ca) 🏊, which is further out in the Outaouais, just off Hwy 148 in Davidson, near Fort Coulonge, uses small, bouncy self-bailing rafts. The one-day rafting trip is a favorite, while many people opt for multi-day trips, which go as far as Algonquin. For those who want to stay a little longer, the rustic **Auberge Esprit hostel**, run by the folks at Esprit Rafting, includes breakfast and use of canoes and kayaks. Campsites are also available. Try **Wilderness Tours** (☎888-723-8669; www.wildernesstours.com; 33 Scott Rd, Old Chelsea) or **OWL Rafting** (☎800-461-7238; www.owl-mkc.ca; 40 Owl Lane, Foresters Falls, Old Chelsea) for a mix of wild and mild trips. Both companies offer meals, camping and pricey cabin accommodations.

Québec

Best Places to Eat

➡ L'Express (p250)
➡ Le Lapin Sauté (p283)
➡ Manoir Hovey (p268)
➡ Vices Versa (p295)
➡ sEb (p262)

Best Places to Stay

➡ Auberge Saint-Antoine (p282)
➡ Hôtel Gault (p247)
➡ Maison Historique James Thompson (p280)
➡ Hôtel Le Germain (p247)

Why Go?

Once an outpost of Catholic conservatism, an isolated island of *francophonie* languishing in a sea of anglo culture, Québec has finally come into its own and has crafted a rich, spirited culture independent of its European motherland. The people of Québec are vibrant and inviting and the province is strewn with colorful Victorian facades, lush rolling hills and romantic bistros.

Montréal and Québec City are bustling metropolises with a perfect mixture of sophistication and playfulness, and history-soaked preserved quarters tucked away around town. The rustic allurements of old Québec are scattered among the Eastern Townships, and produce from bucolic Charlevoix graces the tables of the region's stellar restaurants. The Laurentians abound with ski resorts and peaks, while the jagged coasts of the unblemished Gaspé Peninsula and the cliffs soaring high above the Saguenay River are equally as breathtaking.

When to Go
Montréal

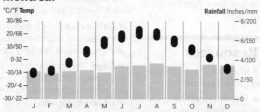

Dec & Jan Head to Mont-Tremblant – one of North America's best ski hills.

Feb Bundle up and join in the frigid festivities in Québec City's fete of the year, Carnaval.

Jul Montréal's summer-long party gets under way with the Festival International de Jazz.

QUÉBEC

QUÉBEC À PIED

If you're visiting either Montréal or Québec City, consider leaving the car at home. Unlike other North American cities, Québec's metropolises are European in design – easily navigated on foot, with bustling sidewalks lined with outdoor cafes.

Fast Facts

➡ Population: 7,870,000

➡ Area: 1,540,687 sq km

➡ Capital: Québec City

➡ Quirky fact: the Château Frontenac in Québec City is the most photographed hotel in the world

Québec Creations

➡ Birthplace of: Trivial Pursuit, AM radio, Ski-Doo snowmobile, Plexiglas

➡ Home of: Leonard Cohen, Norm MacDonald, William Shatner, Jacques Villeneuve, Rufus Wainwright

➡ Kitschiest souvenir: cow-shaped maple syrup lollipops

Resources

➡ Montréal Lifestyle: www. cultmontreal.com

➡ Tourism Montréal: www. tourisme-montreal.org

➡ Tourism Québec: www. bonjourquebec.com

➡ Tourism Québec City: www.quebecregion.com

Local Culture

Quebecers are passionate folks; just bring up the subject of separatism if you're keen to test the theory. Life here is sipped slowly, like the strong, rich coffee, which is often accompanied by a *chocolatine* (chocolate croissant) and engaging conversation with friends or family.

The Québecois drink more alcohol than the average Canadian, and predominantly liberal views contribute to a laid-back atmosphere that feeds an effervescent nightlife in Montréal and Québec City. On weekend evenings, city streets are often packed with pedestrians well into the early hours of the morning.

QUÉBEC ITINERARIES

One Day

Start with brunch in Montréal at **L'Express** and work the calories off on a hike up **Parc du Mont Royal**. Descend through **Mile End** or the **Plateau Mont-Royal**, where you'll be spoiled for choice for dinner and drinks.

Three Days

Limit your time savoring **Montréal's** chilled-out vibe to one day, and then drive through the Laurentians to **Mont-Tremblant**. Leave a day to stroll within **Québec City's** walls in the **Old Upper Town**, before searching for the ultimate table d'hôte in the **Old Lower Town**.

Seven Days

Follow the three-day itinerary, then ramble through **Charlevoix** en route to the **Saguenay River** for two days. Stop for lunch in **Baie St-Paul** or **La Malbaie**. Spend the last two nights in welcoming **Tadoussac**, whale-watching or cruising the fjord.

Québec's Comfort Foods

➡ **Poutine** French fries, gravy and squeaky cheese curds – what's not to like?

➡ **Café au lait** Dark French-roast coffee served with steamed milk, usually in a bowl-shaped mug. A perfect accompaniment to a flaky, buttery croissant.

➡ **Bagel** The quintessential Montréal bagel is smaller, denser and sweeter than its New York counterpart. The secret is that it's hand-rolled and boiled in honey water before being baked in a wood-fired oven.

➡ **Maple syrup** Hit a sugar shack in February or March and try this staple slathered over sausages or drizzled on pancakes.

➡ **Tourtière** This hearty meat pie makes an appearance at Christmas time; at other times of the year it's called *pâté à la viande*.

Québec Highlights

1 Drink up the dynamic nightlife in happening **Montréal** (p229).

2 Savor the unparalleled culture, history and charm of walled **Québec City** (p271).

3 Get sprayed by whales in the Saguenay River fjord at **Tadoussac** (p297).

4 Soak up the artsy vibe and sample local delicacies in **Baie St-Paul** (p291).

5 Hike the stunning peaks above the tree line in **Parc de la Gaspésie** (p310).

6 Swoosh the slopes at action-packed ski resorts such as **Mont-Tremblant** (p261).

7 Get back to nature in spectacular **Parc du Bic** (p306).

8 Sea kayak amid the remote, sculpted islands of the **Mingan Archipelago National Park** (p320).

History

Québec has had a tumultuous history and, by Canadian standards, a very long and complicated one.

At the time of European exploration, the entire region was fully settled and controlled by various Aboriginal groups, all of whom are resident today, including the Mohawks along the St Lawrence River, the Cree above them, the Innu still further north and east, and the Inuit in the remote far north. Relations between the Europeans and aboriginal groups were tense at times but generally amicable, and the two groups forged a relationship based on commerce (specifically the fur trade), not politics.

French explorer Jacques Cartier landed in what is now Québec City and Montréal in 1535. Samuel de Champlain, also of France, first heard and recorded the word 'kebec' (an Algonquin word meaning 'where the river narrows') when he founded a settlement at Québec City some 70 years later, in 1608.

Throughout the rest of the 17th century the French and English skirmished over control of Canada, but by 1759 the English, with a final battle victory on the Plains of Abraham at Québec City, assumed a leadership role in the new colony of Canada. From that point onward, French political influence in the New World waned.

When thousands of British Loyalists fled the American Revolution in the 1770s, the new colony divided into Upper (today's Ontario) and Lower (now Québec) Canada; almost all the French settled in the latter region. Power struggles between the two groups continued through the 1800s, with Lower Canada joining the Canadian confederation as Québec in 1867.

The 20th century saw Québec change from a rural, agricultural society to an urban, industrialized one, but one that continued to be educationally and culturally based upon the Catholic Church, which wielded immense power and still does (about 90% of the population today is Roman Catholic).

The tumultuous 1960s brought the so-called 'Quiet Revolution,' during which time all aspects of francophone society were scrutinized and overhauled. Political systems were reorganized, massive secularization and unionization took place, and a welfare state was created. Intellectuals and extremists alike debated the prospect of independence from Canada, as Québecois began to assert their sense of nationhood.

Formed in 1968, the pro-independence Parti Québécois came to power in 1976, headed by the charismatic René Lévesque. Since then, two referendums have returned 'No' votes on the question of separating from Canada. In the new century, the notion of an independent Québec is less attractive to a younger generation with more global concerns.

Land & Climate

Québec is quite simply stunning, from the mountainous Laurentians to the jagged, windswept coastlines of the Gaspé Peninsula. Charlevoix is flat and agricultural with checkerboard farms. The landscape of the Far North is littered with untamed forests and parkland that give way to arctic tundra at the province's northern corners.

In terms of temperature, the province is saddled with extremes. Montréal and Québec City can go from 40°C to -40°C in six months, and May could see a dump of snow. Generally, the summers are comfortably warm, although high humidity can make Montréal pretty steamy. Winters are very snowy, but usually bright, sunny and dry.

Parks

The province's protected areas are a highlight of any trip to Québec. In addition to preserving regions of remarkable beauty, they offer a host of invigorating activities, including canoeing, kayaking, rafting, hiking, cycling and camping in the wild. Forillon National Park and Saguenay, Bic, Mont-Tremblant and Gaspésie Provincial Parks are especially recommended.

Parks Canada (☑ 888-773-8888; www.pc.gc. ca) administers three national parks and 30 national historic sites in Québec. The historic sites, such as forts and lighthouses, are mostly day-use areas and reveal fascinating bits of history.

The **Société des Établissements de Plein Air du Québec** (Sépaq; ☑ 418-890-6527, 800-665-6527; www.sepaq.com) oversees Québec's 25 provincial parks and 15 wildlife reserves. Confusingly, they refer to their parks as 'national.' The parks, which range from beaches and bird sanctuaries to rugged gorges, provide some outstanding camping, wildlife-viewing, eco-adventure and other outdoor recreation.

Réserve fauniques (wildlife reserves) conserve and protect the environment but also make these spaces publicly accessible. Hunters and fishers use the reserves (permits required), but more and more visitors are discovering them as less crowded alternatives to national and provincial parks.

ℹ Getting There & Around

Québec is easily accessible by air, bus, car and train. It shares borders with the US states of New York, Vermont, New Hampshire and Maine.

AIR

Québec's main airport is in Montréal, although Québec City is also busy. Carriers serving the province include Air Canada, Air Canada Express, Air France, Porter Airlines and bargain airlines Air Transat and WestJet. Traveling to the Far North are First Air, Air Inuit and Air Creebec. Air Canada Express covers the North Shore and Îles de la Madeleine from Québec City and Montréal.

BOAT

There are numerous ferry services across the St Lawrence River, as well as to islands in the Gulf, such as the Îles de la Madeleine, and along the remote Lower North Shore toward Labrador.

BUS

Maritime Bus connects the province with Atlantic Canada, and Greyhound Canada and Megabus link Québec City and Montréal with Ontario. From the US, Greyhound operates five daily bus services between Montréal and New York City. The province is particularly well served by bus lines.

Autobus Maheux (www.autobusmaheux.qc.ca) Covers the northwest regions.

Autobus Viens (☑877-348-5599)

Galland (☑514-333-9555; www.galland-bus.com)

Greyhound Canada (☑800-661-8747; www.greyhound.ca)

Intercar (www.intercar.qc.ca)

Limocar (☑866-692-8899; www.limocar.ca)

Maritime Bus (www.maritimebus.com)

Megabus (☑866-488-4452; www.ca.megabus.com)

Orléans Express (☑514-395-4032; www.orleansexpress.com)

CAR & MOTORCYCLE

Continental US highways link directly with their Canadian counterparts at numerous border crossings. These roads connect to the Trans-Canada Hwy (Hwy 40 within Québec), which runs directly through Montréal and Québec City.

Highways throughout the province are good. In the far eastern and northern sections, however, slow, winding, even nonpaved sections are typical, and services may be few. For road

conditions – a serious factor in winter – call ☑877-393-2363. Note that turning right at red lights is not permitted anywhere on the island of Montréal or in Québec City.

The ride-share agency **Allô Stop** (www.allostop.com) offers an inexpensive way to travel within Québec by linking up drivers and paying passengers headed in the same direction. Passengers pay $7 for a one-year membership, plus a portion of the ride cost to the agency; the rest goes to the driver. New to the scene is another ride-share agency, the Québec City–based **Kangaride** (☑855-526-4274; www.kangaride.com), which is rapidly expanding across Canada and the US (which translates to more rides and cheaper seats). It charges $7.50 for a yearly membership and $5 per ride (on top of what the driver charges); reservations are online only.

TRAIN

VIA Rail (☑888-842-7245; www.viarail.ca) has fast and frequent services along the Québec City–Windsor corridor, via Montréal, and services the South Shore and Gaspésie. From the US, **Amtrak** (☑800-872-7245; www.amtrak.com) trains run once daily between Montréal and New York City.

MONTRÉAL

POP 3.4 MILLION

Historically, Montréal – the only de facto bilingual city on the continent – has been torn right in half, the 'Main' (Blvd St-Laurent) being the dividing line between the east-end Francophones and the west-side Anglos. Today French pockets dot both sides of the map, a new wave of English-speaking Canadians have taken residence in some formerly French enclaves and thanks to constant waves of immigration, it's not uncommon for Montréalers to speak not one, or two, but three languages in their daily life. With the new generation concerned more with global issues (namely the environment), language battles have become so passé.

One thing not up for debate is what makes Montréal so irresistible. It's a secret

REGIONAL DRIVING DISTANCES

Montréal to Québec City: 250km
Montréal to Mont-Tremblant: 145km
Montréal to Toronto: 540km
Québec City to Tadoussac: 215km

blend of French-inspired joie de vivre and cosmopolitan dynamism that has come together to foster a flourishing arts scene, an indie rock explosion, a medley of world-renowned boutique hotels, the Plateau's extraordinary cache of swank eateries and a cool Parisian vibe that pervades every *terrasse* (patio) in the Quartier Latin. It's easy to imagine you've been transported to a distant locale, where hedonism is the national mandate. Only the stunning vista of a stereotypical North American skyline from Parc du Mont Royal's Kondiaronk Lookout will ground you.

History

In May 1642, a small fleet of boats sailed up the St Lawrence River. The few dozen missionaries aboard had survived a cold winter crossing the fierce Atlantic Ocean from their native France. Finally they had reached the spot their fellow countryman, explorer Jacques Cartier, had stumbled across over

a century earlier. Led by Paul Chomedey de Maisonneuve, the pioneers went ashore and began building a small settlement they called Ville-Marie, the birthplace of Montréal.

Ville-Marie soon blossomed into a major fur-trading center and exploration base, despite fierce resistance from the local Iroquois. Skirmishes continued until the signing of a peace treaty in 1701. The city remained French until the 1763 Treaty of Paris, which saw France cede Canada to Great Britain. In 1775, American revolutionaries briefly occupied the city, but left after failing to convince the Québecois to join forces with them against the British.

Despite surrendering its pole position in the fur trade to Hudson Bay in the 1820s, Montréal boomed throughout the 19th century. Industrialization got seriously under way after the construction of the railway and the Canal de Lachine, which in turn attracted masses of immigrants.

Montréal

MONTRÉAL IN...

One Day

Start your day in **Mile End**, partaking in a local ritual – a long and leisurely brunch. Hike up **Mont Royal** (p236), stopping to catch your breath and snap the cityscape from the **Kondiaronk Lookout** before ending up in the **Plateau Mont-Royal** (p238) for dinner and evening entertainment.

Two Days

Follow the one-day itinerary, and on day two begin by exploring the cobblestone alleys of **Old Montréal**. Get a dose of history at **Musée d'Archéologie et d'Histoire de Pointe-à-Callière** (p234) or soak up some culture at **Musée des Beaux-Arts** (p234). Head to **Little Italy** (p239) for dinner, then sample the club scene in **The Village** (p253).

Four Days

Start day three at the **Olympic Park** (p239). If the weather is behaving, follow up a visit to the **Biodôme** (p241) with a trip up the **Tour de Montréal** (p241). Or head straight to the **Jardin Botanique** (p239) for a more fragrant affair.
On the last day, hit the **Marché Atwater** (p253) for picnic supplies, then rent bicycles for a cruise along the **Canal de Lachine** (p244) or take a jet boat ride on the **Lachine Rapids** (p245).
After dinner at a big shot such as **Toqué!** (p249) or **L'Express** (p250), head to the glitzy **Casino de Montréal** (p242) to blow the last of your holiday money.

After WWI the city sashayed through a period as 'Sin City' as hordes of Americans seeking fun flooded across the border to escape Prohibition. By the time mayor Jean Drapeau took the reins, Montréal was ripe for an extreme makeover. During his long tenure (1954–57 and 1960–86), the city gained the métro system, many of downtown's high-rise offices, the underground city and the Place des Arts. Drapeau also twice managed to firmly train the world's spotlight on Montréal: in 1967 for the World Expo and in 1976 for the Olympic Games.

Montréal has been enjoying a consistently positive growth rate for the past two decades, faring extremely well during the global economic recession thanks to a boom in the high-tech sector.

☉ Sights

First on most itineraries is Old Montréal, where the heart of the city's history and grandeur can be chased through a labyrinth of winding lanes. Waterfront attractions in the Old Port have benefited immensely from recent rejuvenation, and across the water the attractions and trails of Parc Jean-Drapeau make a great summer escape from the urban jungle. Downtown encompasses stellar museums and universities, while the bohemian Mile End and Plateau Mont-Royal districts are perfect for meandering. The Village and Quartier Latin jolt awake at nighttime. Just outside the city, the Olympic Park and Lachine hold the greatest sightseeing appeal. From the panorama at Mont Royal it's possible to take it all in at once.

☉ Old Montréal

The oldest section of the city is a warren of crooked cobblestone lanes flanked by colonial and Victorian stone houses filled with intimate restaurants, galleries and boutiques. A stroll around here will delight romantics and architecture fans, especially at night when the most beautiful facades are illuminated. And the waterfront is never far away.

Old Montréal is anchored by lively Place Jacques Cartier and dignified Place d'Armes, which are linked by busy Rue Notre-Dame. The southern end of Place Jacques Cartier gives way to Rue St-Paul, the district's prettiest and oldest street.

★ Basilique Notre-Dame   CHURCH
(Map p232; www.basiliquenddm.org; 110 Rue Notre-Dame Ouest; adult/child $5/4, sound-and-light show $10/5; ☉8am-4:30pm Mon-Sat, 12:30-4pm Sun) Montréal's famous landmark, Notre-Dame Basilica, is a visually pleasing if slightly gaudy symphony of carved wood, paintings, gilded sculptures and stained-glass windows.

Old Montréal

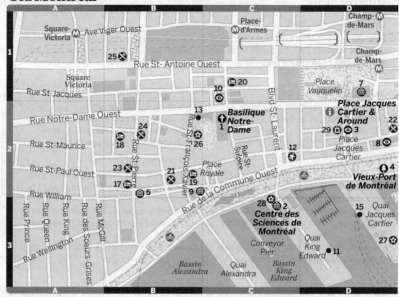

Built in 1829 on the site of an older and smaller church, it also sports a famous Casavant organ and the Gros Bourdon, said to be the biggest bell in North America. The interior looks especially impressive during an otherwise overly melodramatic **sound-and-light show**, staged from Tuesday to Saturday night.

The basilica made headlines in 1994 when singer Céline Dion was married under its soaring midnight-blue ceiling, and again in 2000 when Jimmy Carter and Fidel Castro shared pall-bearing honors at the state funeral of former Canadian Prime Minister Pierre Trudeau.

A popular place for regular Montréalers to tie the knot is the much smaller **Chapelle du Sacré Coeur** (Sacred Heart Chapel) behind the main altar. Rebuilt in a hotchpotch of historic and contemporary styles after a 1978 fire, its most eye-catching element is the floor-to-ceiling bronze altarpiece.

Place d'Armes
HISTORIC SITE

(Map p232) The twin-towered Notre-Dame Basilica lords over this dignified square, where the early settlers once battled it out with the local Iroquois. A statue of Maisonneuve stands in the middle of the square, which is surrounded by some of Old Montréal's finest historic buildings. In fact, the **Old Seminary**, next to the basilica, is the city's oldest, built by Sulpician missionaries in 1685 and still occupied today.

Behind the temple-like curtain of columns in the northwest corner lurks the Bank of Montreal. It harbors the head office of Canada's oldest bank, founded in 1817. The opulent marble interior is worth a gander, and there's a small money museum as well.

Looming on the square's east side is the red sandstone New York Life Building (1888), which was the city's first skyscraper. Today it is dwarfed by the art deco Aldred Building (1937), which was intended to emulate the Empire State Building until the Great Crash of 1929 put an end to such lofty ambitions.

Centre d'Histoire de Montréal
MUSEUM

(Map p232; 335 Place d'Youville; adult/child $6/4; ☉10am-5pm Tue-Sun) This small museum puts a human spin on city history in an engaging multimedia exhibit. You can listen to the tales of real people while sitting in a period kitchen or travel back in time while watching archival footage from the 1940s or '60s. For sweeping views, head to the rooftop.

★ Place Jacques Cartier & Around
HISTORIC SITE

(Map p232) Gently sloped Place Jacques Cartier in the heart of Old Montréal is a beehive of activity, especially in summer, when it's filled with flowers, street musicians, vendors and visitors. The cafes and restaurants lining it are neither cheap nor good, but they do offer front-row seats for the action.

At the square's north end stands the **Colonne Nelson** (Nelson's Column), a monument erected by the British to the general who defeated the French and Spanish fleet at Trafalgar. Nelson faces a small statue of Admiral Vauquelin across the street, put there as a riposte by the French.

The petite palace across the street is the **Château Ramezay**, built in 1705 as the residence of Montréal governor Claude de Ramezay. During the American Revolution, Benjamin Franklin stayed here, fruitlessly attempting to convince the Canadians to join the cause. Now a museum of early Québec history, its web of rooms brims with an eclectic assortment of furniture, art and objects. The mahogany-paneled Salle de Nantes is a feast for the eyes, and there's a pretty garden as well.

There is a tourist office in the northwest corner.

Hôtel de Ville
HISTORIC BUILDING

(City Hall; Map p232; 275 Rue Notre-Dame Est; ☉ 8:30am–5pm, tours Jul & Aug) **FREE** Far from being a humdrum administrative center, this handsome city hall (built between 1872 and 1878) is actually steeped in local lore. Most famously, it's where French leader Charles de Gaulle took to the balcony in 1967 and yelled to the crowds outside '*Vive le Québec libre!*' ('Long live a free Québec!'). Those four words fueled the fires of Québecois separatism and strained relations with Ottawa for years.

Peer into the Great Hall of Honor for some scenes of rural Québec and busts of Jacques Viger, the first French-speaking mayor (1833–36), and Peter McGill, the first English-speaking mayor (1840–42).

Marché Bonsecours
MARKET

(Bonsecours Market; Map p232; 350 Rue St-Paul Est; ☉ 10am–9pm late-Jun–Aug, to 6pm Sep-Mar) The silvery dome standing sentinel over Old Montréal like a glamorous lighthouse belongs to Bonsecours Market. After a stint as city hall, the neoclassical structure served as the city's main market hall until supermarkets drove it out of business in the 1960s. These days, the flower and vegetable stands have been replaced with fancy boutiques selling arts, crafts and clothing produced in Québec. This is not a bad place to pick up some quality souvenirs.

★ Vieux-Port de Montréal
PARK

(Map p232) Montréal's old port has morphed into a park and fun zone paralleling the mighty St Lawrence River for 2.5km and punctuated by four grand quais. Locals and visitors alike come here for strolling, cycling and in-line skating. Cruise boats, ferries, jet boats and speedboats all depart for tours from various docks. In winter, you can cut a fine figure on an outdoor ice-skating rink.

Historical relics include the striking white Clock Tower at the northern end of Quai Jacques Cartier. Built in 1922 to honor sailors who died in WWI, it affords commanding views of the river and city.

★ Centre des Sciences de Montréal
MUSEUM

(Montréal Science Centre; Map p232; www.montreal-sciencecentre.com; King Edward Pier; adult/child $14.50/8.50, with IMAX 3-D movie $21.50/14; ☉ 9am–5pm) In this sleek, glass-covered science center housing virtual and interactive games, there are plenty of buttons to push,

Old Montréal

knobs to pull and games to play as you make your way through the high-tech exhibition halls. The permanent exhibit – Mission Gaia – seeks solutions to environmental or social disasters, while idTV allows you to write your own news story with a virtual editor and report it live.

The center also has an IMAX cinema showing nature and science films.

Musée d'Archéologie et d'Histoire
Pointe-à-Callière   MUSEUM

(Museum of Archaeology & History; Map p232; www.pacmuseum.qc.ca; 350 Place Royale; adult/child $20/7; ⊗10am-5pm Mon-Fri, 11am-5pm Sat & Sun) Housed in a striking contemporary building, this excellent museum sits near the original landing spot of the early settlers and provides a good overview of the city's beginnings. Make time for the multimedia show before plunging underground into a maze of excavated foundations, an ancient sewerage system and vestiges of the first European cemetery. Artifacts and interactive stations help bring the past to life. The **lookout tower** and restaurant can be visited free of charge.

⊙ Downtown

Montréal's modern downtown has a North American look, with wide thoroughfares chopping a forest of skyscrapers into a grid pattern. At street level you'll find some of the city's most beautiful churches, striking buildings, museums, green spaces and major shopping areas. You'll find that an almost Latin spirit pervades the cafes, restaurants and bars, especially along Rue Crescent.

★ Musée des Beaux-Arts de
Montréal   MUSEUM

(Museum of Fine Arts; Map p236; www.mbam.qc.ca; 1380 Rue Sherbrooke Ouest; special exhibitions $20, 5-9pm Wed half-price; ⊗11am-5pm Thu-Tue, to 9pm Wed (special exhibition only)) FREE A must for art lovers, the Museum of Fine Arts has amassed several millennia worth of paintings, sculpture, decorative arts, furniture, prints, drawings and photographs. European heavyweights include Rembrandt, Picasso and Monet, but the museum really shines when it comes to Canadian art. Highlights include works by Jean-Baptiste Roy-Audy and Paul Kane, landscapes by the Group of Seven, abstractions by Jean-Paul Riopelle and a fair amount of Inuit and aboriginal artifacts.

Exhibits are spread across the classical, marble-clad Michal and Renata Hornstein Pavilion and the crisp, contemporary Jean-Noël Desmarais Pavilion across the street.

There are lots of fancy decorative knickknacks, including Japanese incense boxes and Victorian chests. The temporary exhibits are often exceptional.

Chinatown
NEIGHBORHOOD

Although this neighborhood, perfectly packed into a few easily navigable streets, has no sites per se, it's a nice area for lunch or for shopping for quirky knickknacks. The main thoroughfare, Rue de la Gauchetière, between Blvd St-Laurent and Rue Jeanne Mance, is enlivened with Taiwanese bubble-tea parlors, Hong Kong–style bakeries and Vietnamese soup restaurants. The public square, **Place Sun-Yat-Sen** (Map p240; cnr Rue de la Gauchetière & Rue Clark; Ⓜ Place-d'Armes), attracts crowds of elderly Chinese and the occasional group of Falun Gong demonstrators.

Centre Canadien d'Architecture
MUSEUM

(Canadian Centre for Architecture; Map p236; www.cca.qc.ca; 1920 Rue Baile; adult/child $10/free, 5:30-9pm Thu admission free; ⏱ 11am-6pm Wed & Fri-Sun, to 9pm Thu) Architecture buffs should make a beeline to the Canadian Centre for Architecture. It combines a museum and a research institution in one sleek, innovative complex that seamlessly integrates with the historic **Shaughnessy House**.

The center's galleries contain prints, drawings, models and photos of remarkable buildings, both local and international. There's also a sculpture garden with a dozen or so works scattered about a terrace overlooking southern Montréal. It's especially impressive when illuminated at night.

Free English-language **tours** run at 2pm throughout the year, with an additional tour at 5:30pm on Thursdays.

Once the home of a wealthy businessman, the gray limestone Shaughnessy House encapsulates 19th-century high-class living. The ritziest room is a lounge with intricate woodwork and a grand fireplace.

Musée McCord
MUSEUM

(McCord Museum of Canadian History; Map p236; www.mccord-museum.qc.ca; 690 Rue Sherbrooke Ouest; adult/student $14/8, special exhibitions extra $5; ⏱ 10am-6pm Tue-Fri, to 5pm Sat & Sun) Beaded headdresses, fine china, elegant gowns, letters, photographs and toys are among the more than 1.2 million objects forming the collection of the well-regarded McCord Museum of Canadian History. Changing and permanent exhibitions tell the history of the people who settled here from abroad, zeroing in on the unique challenges they faced, from icy winters to cultural clashes.

The museum is especially renowned for its **Notman Photographic Archives**, which offer an unparalleled visual record of Canada's evolution since 1840.

Twenty-minute thematic tours highlight the museum's offerings; tours are bilingual and free. Ask about specific times and days.

★ McGill University
UNIVERSITY

(Map p236; www.mcgill.ca; 845 Rue Sherbrooke Ouest) This university counts two Canadian prime ministers, six Nobel laureates and William Shatner among its alumni. These days some 30,000 students try to uphold the university's grand reputation, which is especially stellar in medicine and engineering.

It was founded in 1821 with money and land donated by James McGill, a Scottish-born fur trader. The leafy campus with its Victorian edifices is a pretty place for a quiet stroll or a picnic.

The university's **Musée Redpath** (Map p236; ⏱ 9am-5pm Mon-Fri, 11am-5pm Sun) FREE is one of the oldest museums in Canada, and it shows. Nevertheless, it has some interesting natural history exhibits, including a life-size dinosaur skeleton and Egyptian mummies.

★ Musée d'Art Contemporain
MUSEUM

(Map p240; www.macm.org; 185 Rue Ste-Catherine Ouest; adult/child $12/free, 5-9pm Wed admission free; ⏱ 11am-6pm Tue & Thu-Sun, to 9pm Wed) Canada's first major showcase of contemporary art, this museum offers an excellent survey of Canadian, and in particular Québecois, creativity. All the local legends, including Jean-Paul Riopelle, Paul-Émile Borduas and Geneviève Cadieux, are well represented. There are great temporary shows, too. Free English-language **tours** run at 6:30pm Wednesday and at 1pm Sunday.

---

❶ MONTRÉAL MUSEUM PASS

Custom-made for culture buffs, this handy **pass** (www.museesmontreal.org; $80) is valid for three consecutive days and gets you admission to 38 museums, plus unlimited use of the bus and métro system. It's available at tourist offices, major hotels and participating museums. Note that most museums are closed on Monday.

Downtown Montréal

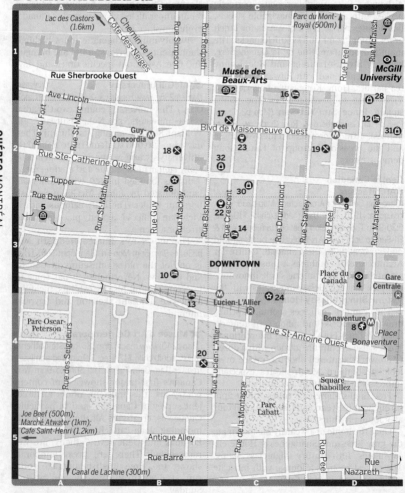

◉ Parc du Mont Royal Area

Mont Royal can be entered via the steps at the top of Rue Peel. Buses 80 and 129 make their way from the Place des Arts métro station to the Georges Étienne Cartier monument. Bus 11 from the Mont Royal métro stop traverses the park.

Parc du Mont Royal PARK
(Map p230; www.lemontroyal.qc.ca) This 'mountain,' the work of New York Central Park designer Frederick Law Olmsted, is a sprawling, leafy playground that's perfect for cycling, jogging, horseback riding, picnicking and, in winter, cross-country skiing and tobogganing. In fine weather, enjoy panoramic views from the **Kondiaronk Lookout** near **Chalet du Mont-Royal**, a grand old stone villa that hosts big-band concerts in summer, or from the **Observatoire de l'Est**, a favorite rendezvous for lovebirds. It takes about 30 minutes to walk between the two.

En route you'll spot the landmark 40m-high **Cross of Montréal** (1924; it's illuminated at night). It's there to commemorate city founder Maisonneuve, who single-handedly carried a wooden cross up the mountain in

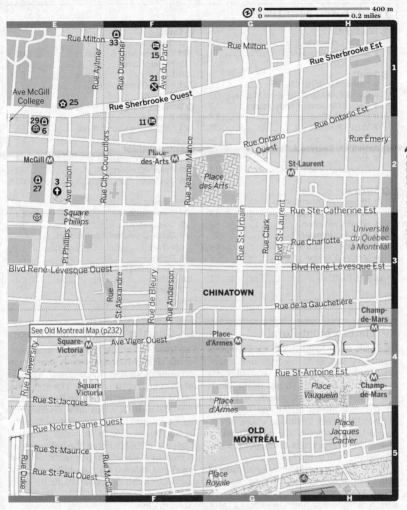

1643 to give thanks to God for sparing his fledgling village from flooding.

Lac des Castors
LAKE

(Map p230) Known to Anglophones as Beaver Lake, this is where locals come to rent paddleboats in summer and ice skates and sleds in winter. North of here are two vast cemeteries. The Catholic **Cimetière de Notre-Dame-des-Neiges** holds the remains of mayors, artists, clerics and *Titanic* victims. Further north, the Protestant **Cimetière Mont-Royal** is smaller and more noted for its bird-watching than celebrity tombs.

Georges Étienne Cartier Monument
STATUE

On the park's northeastern edge, on Ave du Parc, this statue draws hundreds of revelers every Sunday for impromptu drumming and dancing in what has been dubbed 'Tam Tam Sundays' – it's nothing less than an institution. If the noise doesn't lead you all the way there, just follow your nose toward whiffs of 'wacky tabaccy.' This is also a good spot to pick up some unusual handicrafts sold by local artisans.

Downtown Montréal

◉ Top Sights
1 McGill University D1
2 Musée des Beaux-Arts............................C1

◉ Sights
3 Cathédrale Christ Church......................E2
4 Cathédrale Marie-Reine-du-Monde D3
5 Centre Canadien d'Architecture........... A3
6 Musée McCord..E2
7 Musée Redpath D1

◉ Activities, Courses & Tours
8 Atrium D4
9 Gray Line/Coach Canada D3

◉ Sleeping
10 HI Montréal International Youth
    Hostel B3
11 Hilton Garden Inn....................................F2
12 Hôtel Le Germain D2
13 Les Bons Matins......................................B4
14 Montréal Y Hotel C3
15 Parc Suites... F1
16 Ritz-Carlton C1

◉ Eating
17 Boustan C2
18 Café Myriade B2
19 Ferreira Café D2
20 Nora Grey B4
21 Pikolo Espresso Bar F1

◉ Drinking & Nightlife
22 Brutopia..C3
23 Sir Winston Churchill Pub C2

◉ Entertainment
24 Montréal Canadiens...............................C4
25 Pollack Concert Hall...............................E1
26 Upstairs B2

◉ Shopping
27 Centre Eaton..E2
28 Cheap Thrills D1
29 Guilde Canadienne des Métiers
    d'Art E2
30 Ogilvy C2
31 Paragraphe Bookstore D2
32 Parasuco..C2
33 Word...F1

◉ Plateau Mont-Royal

East of Parc du Mont Royal, the Plateau is Montréal's youngest, liveliest and artiest neighborhood. Originally a working-class district, it changed its stripes in the 1960s and '70s, when writers, singers and other creative folk moved in. Among them was playwright Michel Tremblay, whose unvarnished look at some of the neighborhood's more colorful characters firmly put the Plateau on the path to hipdom.

These days, many Montréalers dream of living here if only house prices would stop rising. As you stroll through its side streets, admiring the signature streetscapes with their winding staircases, ornate wrought-iron balconies and pointy Victorian roofs, you'll begin to understand why.

The Plateau is bordered roughly by Blvd St-Joseph to the north and Rue Sherbrooke to the south, Mont Royal to the west and Ave de Lorimier to the east. The main drags are Blvd St-Laurent ('The Main'), Rue St-Denis and Ave du Mont-Royal, all lined with sidewalk cafes, restaurants, clubs and boutiques. Rue Prince Arthur, Montréal's quintessential hippie hangout in the 1960s, and Rue Duluth are alive with BYOW eateries.

◉ Quartier Latin & The Village

The Quartier Latin is Montréal's most boisterous neighborhood, a slightly grungy entertainment district made glitzy with an infusion of French panache. The area blossomed with the arrival of the Université de Montréal in 1893, which drew several prestigious cultural institutions and the wealthy French bourgeoisie in its wake. Although it fell out of fashion after the university relocated to a larger campus north of Mont Royal and suffered from an influx of crime and neglect, things began looking up again when the Université de Québec was established in 1969.

A hotbed of activity, especially during the International Jazz Festival, FrancoFolies and Just for Laughs, the quarter bubbles 24 hours a day in its densely packed rows of bars, trendy bistros, music clubs and record shops. The Quartier Latin fits nicely within the borders of Rue Sanguinet, Rue Sherbrooke, Rue St-Hubert and Blvd René-Lévesque. Old Montréal is just south of here, best reached via Rue St-Denis.

Over the past decade or so, Montréal's gay community has breathed new life into The Village, a once poverty-stricken corner of the east end. Today, gay-friendly doesn't even begin to describe the neighborhood. People of all persuasions wander Rue Ste-Catherine and savor the joie de vivre in its cafes, bistros and discerning eateries. The nightlife is renowned for its energy, but during the day the streets bustle with workers from the big media firms nearby. Summer is the most frenetic time, as hundreds of thousands of international visitors gather to celebrate Divers/Cité, a major annual gay pride parade.

The spine of the (Gay) Village is Rue Ste-Catherine Est, and its side streets are Rue St-Hubert in the west and Ave de Lorimier in the east.

⊙ Little Italy & Mile End

The zest and flavor of the old country find their way into the lively Little Italy district, north of the Plateau, where the espresso seems stiffer, the pasta sauce thicker and the chefs plumper. Italian football games seem to be broadcast straight onto Blvd St-Laurent, where the green-white-red flag is proudly displayed. Soak up the atmosphere on a stroll, and don't miss the Marché Jean Talon (p251), which always hums with activity.

Dubbed the 'new Plateau' by the exodus of students and artists seeking a more affordable, less polished hangout, the Mile End district has all the coolness of its predecessor as well as two phenomenal bagel shops, upscale dining along Ave Laurier and tons of increasingly trendy hangouts at its epicenter: Rue St-Viateur and Blvd St-Laurent. The flavor here is multicultural – Hasidic Jews live side by side with immigrants from all over Europe – visible in the authentic Greek restaurants along Ave du Parc and Rue St-Urbain's neo-Byzantine Polish church, **Église St-Michel** (☏514-277-3300; www.swmichalmontreal.com; 5580 Rue St-Urbain; ⊙9am-10am Mon-Fri, 9:30am-12:30pm Sun; Ⓜ Rosemont).

Many of celebrated Canadian novelist Mordecai Richler's novels are set in the Mile End, including *The Apprenticeship of Duddy Kravitz*.

⊙ Olympic Park & Around

Montréal hosted the 1976 Olympic summer games, which brought a host of attractions, including a beautiful botanical garden, to the area east of central Montréal, accessible from Rue Sherbrooke.

Jardin Botanique & Insectarium   GARDEN
(www.espacepourlavie.ca; 4101 Rue Sherbrooke Est; adult/child $29.50/15; ⊙9am-6pm; Ⓜ Pie-IX) Opened in 1931, Montréal's Botanical Garden is the world's third largest after those in London and Berlin. Approximately 22,000 species of plants grow in 30 outdoor gardens here, including the tranquil **Japanese Garden**, a symphony of stone and water sprinkled with rhododendrons, water lilies and bonsai trees. Other highlights include the **First Nations Garden**, the **Chinese Garden**, the **Rose Garden**, as well as the **Insectarium** with its intriguing collection of creepy crawlies, most of them dead and mounted, but there are also living species, including tarantulas, bees and scorpions. Not to be missed is the **Butterfly House**.

OTHER CHURCHES WORTH EXPLORING

➜ The gigantic, domed **Oratoire St-Joseph** (Map p230; St-Joseph's Oratory; ☏514-733-8211; www.saint-joseph.org; 3800 Chemin Queen Mary; ⊙6am-9:30pm; Ⓜ Côte-des-Neiges), in the Côte-des-Neiges neighborhood, was built by a devoted monk named Brother André who had a knack for healing people. Crutches left by the cured still fill a chapel illuminated by thousands of votives. Three free English tours take place per day.

➜ In 1987 the Anglican **Cathédrale Christ Church** (Christ Church Cathedral; Map p236; 635 Rue Ste-Catherine Ouest; ⊙7am-6pm), a beautiful neo-Gothic confection, was temporarily supported by concrete stilts while a shopping mall was carved out directly underneath it.

➜ The **Chapelle Notre-Dame-de-Bonsecours** (Map p232; ☏514-282-8670; 400 Rue St-Paul Est; ⊙10am-6pm Tue-Sun May-Jan) occupied a special spot in the heart of seafarers who came here to pray for safe passage. Small ship models left here by grateful survivors still dangle from its ceiling.

➜ The **Cathédrale Marie-Reine-du-Monde** (Map p236; ☏514-866-1661) was modeled after St Peter's Basilica in Rome.

The Plateau, Quartier Latin & The Village

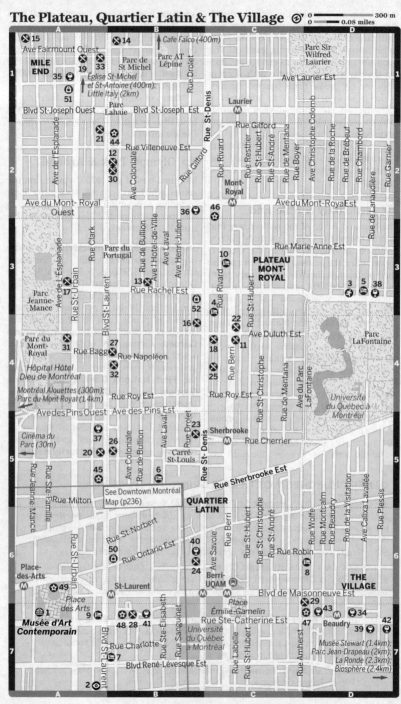

0 — 300 m
0 — 0.08 miles

15
14
↑ Cafe Falco (400m)
Ave Fairmount Ouest
Parc de
St Michel
Parc AT
Lépine
Parc Sir
Wilfred
Laurier

MILE
END
19
33
35
51
↑ Église St-Michel
et St-Antoine (400m);
Little Italy (2km)

Ave Laurier Est

Blvd St-Joseph Ouest
Parc
Lahaie
Blvd St-Joseph Est

Laurier
Rue Gilford

21
44
Rue Villeneuve Est

12
30
Ave Coloniale

Mont-
Royal

Ave du Mont- Royal
Ouest

36
46

Ave du Mont-Royal Est

PLATEAU
MONT-
ROYAL

Rue Marie-Anne Est

13
Rue Rachel Est

Parc du
Portugal

10

3
5
38

Parc
Jeanne-
Mance

17

52
16
4

22

Ave Duluth Est

Parc
LaFontaine

Parc du
Mont-
Royal
31
27
Rue Bagg
Rue Napoléon
32
18
11
25

Hôpital Hôtel
Dieu de Montréal

Montréal Alouettes (300m);
Parc du Mont Royal (1.4km)

Rue Roy Est
Rue Roy Est

Université
du Québec à
Montréal

Ave des Pins Ouest
Ave des Pins Est

Cinéma du
Parc (30m)
37
26
23
Sherbrooke

20
Carré
St-Louis
Rue Cherrier

45

6

See Downtown Montréal
Map (p236)

Rue Sherbrooke Est

Rue Milton

QUARTIER
LATIN

Rue St-Norbert

50
Rue Ontario Est
40

Place-
des-Arts

24

Rue Robin

8

THE
VILLAGE

49
St-Laurent

Berri-
UQAM

Blvd de Maisonneuve Est

1
Place
des Arts
9

29
43
34

Musée d'Art
Contemporain
48 28 41

Place
Émilie-Gamelin
Rue Ste-Catherine Est
47
Beaudry
39
42

7
Université
du Québec
à Montréal
Rue Charlotte

Blvd René-Lévesque Est

2

Musée Stewart (1.4km);
Parc Jean-Drapeau (2km);
La Ronde (2.3km);
Biosphère (2.4km)

The Plateau, Quartier Latin & The Village

The best way to get around this huge place is by the hop-on, hop-off trolley that makes its rounds every 30 minutes or so (late June to September only). Free guided tours leave at 10:30am and 1:30pm daily (except Monday from November to May) from the reception center. All facilities are wheelchair-accessible.

Biodôme MUSEUM
(www.espacepourlavie.ca; 4777 Ave Pierre de Coubertin; adult/child $18.75/9.50; ⊙9am-6pm; ⓜViau) The Biodôme beautifully recreates four ecosystems teeming with plant and animal life. In the hot and humid Tropical Forest, the anacondas, caimans and two-toed sloths draw the biggest crowds. From there it's off to the more temperate Laurentian woodlands, with trees that change color in fall just like in the real world. A giant aquarium and a rocky cliff are at the heart of the Gulf of St Lawrence section, although

the penguins of the Sub-Antarctic habitat steal the show.

A free shuttle runs between the Biodôme and the Jardin Botanique from late June to September.

Rio Tinto Planetarium PLANETARIUM
(www.espacepourlavie.ca; 4801 Ave Pierre de Coubertin; adult/child $18.75/9.50; ⊙9:30am-10:30pm) This $48-million extravaganza, which opened its doors in April 2013 to much fanfare, has two theaters. The first is traditional and appeals to star-gazing purists, with educational shows that teach viewers about stars and the solar system. The other, more glitzy theater is more Hollywood blockbuster, with bean bag chairs and an awesome sound-and-light show.

Tour de Montréal TOWER
(www.parcolympique.qc.ca; 4141 Ave Pierre de Coubertin; adult/child $22.50/7.50; ⊙1-10pm Mon, 9am-10pm Tue-Sun) On a nice day, it's

well worth boarding the bi-level funicular zooming up the Tour de Montréal, the world's largest inclined structure (190m at a 45-degree angle), for 360-degree views of the city, river and surrounding countryside from the glassed-in observation deck.

Down below is the Centre Sportif (p245) and the centerpiece of the sprawling Olympic Park, the multipurpose Stade Olympique, which seats up to 80,000 and today hosts sporting events, concerts and trade shows.

◉ Parc Jean-Drapeau

Occupying the site of the hugely successful 1967 World's Fair, **Parc Jean-Drapeau** (Map p230; www.parcjeandrapeau.com) consists of two islands surrounded by the St Lawrence: Île Ste-Hélène and Île Notre-Dame. Although nature is the park's main appeal, it's also home to a Vegas-size casino, a Formula One racetrack and an old fort museum. In summer an **information kiosk** (☎514-872-4537; ⊙10am-6pm) opens near the Jean-Drapeau métro stop.

Drivers should take Pont (Bridge) Jacques Cartier for Île Ste-Hélène and Pont de la Concorde for Île Notre-Dame. **Ferries** (Quai Jacques Cartier; adult/child $7.50/free; ⊙mid-May–mid-Sep) shuttle pedestrians and bicycles to the park from the Old Port. Cyclists and in-line skaters can access the park by following the signs for Cité du Havre, then for Île Notre-Dame from the Canal Lachine bike path.

Buses 777 (Casino) and 767/769 (La Ronde) run between the islands.

Île Ste-Hélène   ISLAND

(Map p230) Walkways meander around this island, past gardens and among the old pavilions from the World's Fair. One of them, the American pavilion in the spherical Bucky Fuller dome, has become the **Biosphère** (www.biosphere.ec.gc.ca; adult/child $12/free; ⊙10am-5pm daily Jun-Sep, Wed-Sun Oct-May). Using hands-on displays, this center explains the Great Lakes–St Lawrence River ecosystem, which makes up 20% of the planet's fresh water reserves; demonstrates sustainable living; and provides tours of a self-sufficient, solar-powered home. There's a great view of the river from the Visions Hall.

La Ronde   AMUSEMENT PARK

(www.laronde.com; adult/child $49/43; ⊙hours vary) The northern tip of Île Ste-Hélène is occupied by La Ronde, Québec's largest amusement park. There's a battery of bone-shaking thrill rides, including Le Splash, which will leave you soaked, Le Monstre, the world's highest wooden roller coaster, and Le Vampire, a suspended coaster with five gut-wrenching loops. For a more peaceful experience, there's a Ferris wheel and a gentle minirail that offers views of the river and city.

Concerts and shows are held throughout the summer, and fireworks explode overhead on weekend evenings (when the park stays open later).

Musée Stewart   MUSEUM

(www.stewart-museum.org; adult/child $13/10; ⊙11am-5pm Wed-Sun) Inside a former British garrison (where troops were stationed in the 19th century), this museum displays relics from Canada's past as well as a multimedia model of Old Montréal. Demonstrations are given outside by actors in period costume, and there's a military parade every day in summer. It's a 15-minute walk from métro Jean-Drapeau station on Île Ste-Hélène.

Île Notre-Dame   ISLAND

(Map p230) Created from 15 million tons of earth and rock excavated when the métro was built, Île Notre-Dame hosts the Grand Prix du Canada Formula One race each year on **Circuit Gilles Villeneuve** – a smoothly paved track open for cyclists and in-line skaters from mid-April to mid-November. The island's beach, **Plage des Îles**, draws thousands on hot summer days. Nearby, the **Bassin Olympique**, the former Olympic rowing basin, hosts the popular Dragon Boat Race & Festival in late July.

Casino de Montréal   CASINO

(1 Ave du Casino; ⊙24hr) Throughout the year, Île Notre-Dame's main draw is the huge, spaceship-like Casino de Montréal in the former French pavilion from the World's Fair. You can challenge Lady Luck at 3000 slot machines and 115 gaming tables. Alcohol is not allowed on the floor and you must be 18 to enter. Bridges link the pavilion to the **Jardin des Floralies**, a lovely rose garden.

Habitat 67   NOTABLE BUILDING

Between Old Montréal and Île Ste-Hélène lies Cité du Havre, a narrow land-filled jetty built to protect the harbor from currents and ice. Here, for the 1967 World's Fair, Moshe Safdie designed Habitat 67, an experimental housing complex. It's a hotchpotch of reinforced

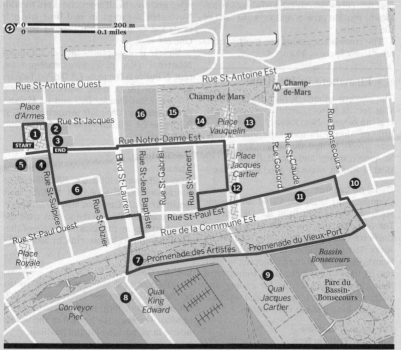

City Walk
Architectural Montréal

START PLACE D'ARMES
END PLACE D'ARMES
LENGTH 1.5 KM; TWO HOURS

Start at ❶ **Place d'Armes** (p232), where the Iroquois battled against early settlers, who were led by Maisonneuve. You'll find him in bronze at the square's center with his back to the city's first skyscraper, the ❷ **New York Life Building**, and the fantastic art-deco ❸ **Aldred Building**.

The neo-Gothic ❹ **Basilique Notre-Dame** (p231) steals the show for its outlandishly ornate interior and celebrity appeal: Céline Dion was married here in 1994. To the west of the church lies the ❺ **Old Seminary**, the city's oldest building.

Take Rue St-Sulpice and duck down ❻ **Rue Le Royer**, where the city's first condo lofts overlook the walkway. Zigzag down to the Old Port, accessible via ❼ **Promenade des Artistes**, with its views of the Victorian facades of Rue de la Commune. Play in the ❽ **Centre des Sciences de Montréal**

(p233), or get a ferry to Parc Jean-Drapeau from the ❾ **Quai Jacques Cartier**.

At Rue Bonsecours, go to the corner of Rue St-Paul, where the city's oldest stone church, ❿ **Chapelle Notre-Dame-de-Bonsecours** (p239) stands, and ⓫ **Marché Bonsecours** (p233), the former market hall turned boutique bastion sprawls west.

Peek into the artsy stalls dotting the small streets of Rue St-Amable, then end up in ⓬ **Place Jacques Cartier** (p233). At the northern end of the street, just beyond Colonne Nelson, the breathtaking ⓭ **Hôtel de Ville** (p233) is where French President Charles de Gaulle announced '*Vive le Québec libre!*' to cheering crowds in 1967.

Return to Rue Notre-Dame and go west past ⓮ **Vieux Palais de Justice** (Old Courthouse) and the neoclassical ⓯ **Cour d'Appel du Québec** (Québec Appellate Court) adjacent, which contrasts with the modern ⓰ **Palais de Justice** across the street. End back in Place d'Armes.

concrete cubes cleverly stacked at bizarre angles to provide privacy and views to each of the 150 units.

The condos are among the most sought-after living space in Montréal.

👁 Elsewhere in Montréal

The western suburb of Lachine is worth a visit for its history, architecture and general ambience. Not touristy, it reveals a little of Montréal's roots and culture. The side streets behind the impressive College St-Anne nunnery and City Hall, both along Blvd St-Joseph, make for good wandering.

Canal de Lachine CANAL
Completed in 1825, the Canal de Lachine stretches for 14.5km from the Old Port to Lac St-Louis and was built to circumvent the fierce Lachine Rapids of the St Lawrence River. The construction of the St Lawrence Seaway led to its closing to shipping in 1970, but its banks have since been transformed into a park that's terrific for cycling and walking. Since 2002, pleasure and sightseeing boats have plied its calm waters.

Fur Trade at Lachine
National Historic Site HISTORIC SITE
(www.pc.gc.ca; 1255 Blvd St-Joseph; adult/child $3.90/1.90; ☉10am-5pm Apr-Sep; 🚍195, Ⓜ Angrignon) In an old stone house on the waterfront, the exhibit here tells the story of the fur trade in Canada. Lachine became the hub of Montréal's fur-trading operations because the rapids made further river navigation impossible before the canal was built.

Nearby, a **visitors center** (500 Rue des Iroquois; ☉10am-5pm Mon-Fri, to 6pm weekends late Jun–early Oct) runs guided tours and presents historical exhibits about the canal – including watching how the locks work.

🏃 Activities

Cycling & In-line Skating
Montréal is a cyclist's haven with more than 500km of bicycle and skating paths. **Bixi** (http://montreal.bixi.com; refundable security deposit $250, basic fees per 24hr/month $7/31, usage fees per 30/60/90min free/$1.75/3.50; ☉24hr Apr-Nov) is a self-service, solar-powered bicycle rental system with more than 300 stations downtown.

One popular route parallels the Canal de Lachine for 14.5km, starting in Old Montréal. The smooth **Circuit Gilles Villeneuve** on Île Notre-Dame is another cool track. It's open and free to all from mid-April to mid-November – except in mid-June when it hosts the Grand Prix du Canada Formula One car race.

Bicycle rental options include **Ça Roule Montréal** (Map p232; www.caroulemontreal.com; 27 Rue de la Commune Est, Old Port; bicycles per hr/24hr $8/35, in-line skates 1st/additional hr $9/4; ☉9am-8pm Apr-Oct) and **La Maison des Cyclistes** (Map p240; www.velo.qc.ca; 1251 Rue Rachel Est; ☉8:30am-6pm Mon-Fri, from 9am Sat & Sun).

Ice-Skating
Atrium SKATING
(Map p236; www.le1000.com; 1000 Rue de la Gauchetière Ouest; adult/child $7.50/5, skate rentals $7; ☉11:30am-6pm Mon-Fri, 12:30-9pm Sat, to 6pm Sun) Take to the ice any time the mood strikes at this gigantic, state-of-the-art glass-domed indoor rink in Montréal's tallest tower.

Lac des Castors SKATING
(Parc du Mont Royal; admission free, skate rentals per 2hr $8.50; ☉9am-9pm Sun-Thu, to 10pm Fri & Sat, weather permitting) An excellent place for outdoor skating – it's nestled in the woods near a large parking lot and pavilion.

Patinoire du Bassin Bonsecours SKATING
(Map p232; Parc du Bassin Bonsecours, Old Port; adult/child $6/4, skate rentals $8; ☉10am-9pm Mon-Wed, to 10pm Thu-Sat Dec-Mar) One of Montréal's most popular outdoor skating rinks.

Swimming
Plage des Îles BEACH
(Île Notre-Dame; adult/child $8/4; ☉10am-7pm Jun-Aug) On hot summer days, this artificial sandy beach can be a cool place to go for a swim.

Centre Sportif POOL
(4141 Ave Pierre de Coubertin; adult/child $7.25/5.50; ☉6:30am-9pm Mon-Fri, 9am-4:30pm Sat & Sun) The best place to do laps is at Olympic Park's Centre Sportif, a huge indoor complex with six swimming pools, diving towers and a 20m-deep scuba pool.

👉 Tours

Gray Line/Coach Canada BUS TOUR
(Map p236; 🕿514-934-1222; www.grayline.com; adult/child $49/32, Deluxe Montréal tours $89/64; ☉9am & 1pm daily, Deluxe Montréal 10am Tue & Thu) This well-known tour operator runs three-hour Greater Montréal tours

that provide a basic overview of Old Montréal, the Olympic Park, St Joseph's Oratoire and the downtown area. The six-hour tour **Deluxe Montréal** includes admission to the Tour de Montréal, Biodôme and Jardin Botanique. Tours depart from outside the Centre Infotouriste (p257).

Lachine Rapids Tours
BOAT TOUR

(Map p232; ☑514-284-9607; www.jetboating-montreal.com; jet-boat tour adult/child $67/47; ☉10am-6pm Jun-Sep) Prepare to get wet on jet-boat tours of the Lachine Rapids, bouncy half-hour jaunts around Parc des Îles leaving from Quai Jacques Cartier five times a day.

Le Bateau Mouche
BOAT TOUR

(Map p232; ☑514-849-9952; www.bateau-mouche.ca; 1hr tours adult/child $24/12; ☉11am, 2:30pm & 4pm May-Oct) Leaving from Quai Jacques Cartier, hour-long cruises aboard climate-controlled, glass-roofed boats explore the Old Port and Parc Jean-Drapeau. A 90-minute version ($28/15) departs at 12:30pm. You can also have breakfast, including crepes, omelets, and fancy pastries, aboard the 'sunrise' cruise at 11am on Sundays (adult/child $50/40).

Guidatour
WALKING TOUR

(Map p232; ☑514-844-4021; www.guidatour. qc.ca; tours $12.50-21; ☉May-Oct) Guidatour's bilingual guides spice up historical tours of Downtown (9:30am and 10:45am), East Old Montréal (11am and 12:30pm) and West Old Montréal (1:30pm and 3pm) with colorful tales and anecdotes. Tours depart from the Basilique Notre-Dame (p231) for Old Montréal, and from the Centre Infotouriste (p257) for Downtown.

AML Cruises
BOAT TOUR

(Map p232; ☑514-842-9300; www.croisieresaml. com; adult/child $29/16; ☉11:30am & 2pm May-Oct) AML runs 90-minute tours taking in the Old Port and Île Ste-Hélène. Tours depart from Quai King Edward.

⚔ Festivals & Events

In the peak summer season (June to August), Montréalers live festival to festival as big portions of the downtown district come alive with free outdoor concerts and street performances. For big ones, such as the Festival International de Jazz and Just For Laughs, expect closed roads in festival areas.

Fête des Neiges
WINTER

(www.parcjeandrapeau.com; ☉late Jan–early Feb) Fun in the snow over three consecutive weekends in Parc Jean-Drapeau.

Highlights Festival
MUSIC, FOOD

(www.montrealenlumiere.com; ☉late Feb) A collection of festivals showcasing local cuisine, music and fine arts, culminating in an 'all-nighter' party and communal breakfast with a frying pan that can hold a 10,000-egg omelet.

Grand Prix du Canada
CAR RACING

(www.circuitgillesvilleneuve.ca; Circuit Gilles-Villeneuve, Île Notre-Dame; tickets $42-557; ☉Jun; ⓜJean-Drapeau) The world's best drivers

QUÉBEC MONTRÉAL

MONTRÉAL FOR CHILDREN

Children adore Montréal. The Olympic Park area is the ultimate kid-friendly zone: the Biodôme (p241), home to porcupines, penguins and other local and exotic critters, is a sure winner, and the creepy crawlies at the Insectarium (p239) are sure to provide plenty of gasps and tickles.

Budding scientists will have a field day at the Centre des Sciences de Montréal (p233), which has dozens of interactive stations and video games, and space travelers can catch a show at the Rio Tinto Planetarium (p241). Many museums have special kid-oriented workshops and guided tours.

On hot summer days, a few hours spent at the Plage des Îles, the big beach on Île Notre-Dame, will go a long way toward keeping tempers cool. On nearby Île Ste-Hélène awaits La Ronde (p242) amusement park, where the stomach-churning roller coasters and other diversions are especially thrilling for teens.

There's ice skating all year long at the grand Atrium, which offers special kids' sessions on Sundays until 11:30am. In winter, you can take a spin on the frozen Lac des Castors in Parc du Mont Royal or on the popular Patinoire du Bassin Bonsecours outdoor rink in Old Montréal.

Many hotels can provide referrals to reliable, qualified babysitting services.

descend on Circuit Gilles Villeneuve on Île Notre-Dame for North America's biggest Formula One event.

Les FrancoFolies CULTURE
(www.francofolies.com; late Jun) This annual international showcase of French-language music and theater spotlights today's biggest stars and those on the rise; held over 10 days.

Festival International de Jazz JAZZ
(www.montrealjazzfest.com; late Jun–early Jul) For 11 days the heart of downtown explodes in jazz and blues during 650 concerts, most of them outdoors and free.

Just for Laughs Festival COMEDY
(www.hahaha.com; Jul) Everyone gets giddy for two weeks at this international comedy festival that puts on hundreds of shows, including free ones in the Quartier Latin.

L'International Des Feux Loto Québec FIREWORKS
(http://internationaldesfeuxloto-quebec.com/en/; mid-Jun–late Aug) This international fireworks competition features the world's best pyrotechnics in 10 30-minute shows held at La Ronde each Friday or Saturday night during the competition.

🛏 Sleeping

Hotels fill up fast in the summer, when warm weather and festivals galore bring hordes of tourists to Montréal, making reservations essential. Old Montréal is great if you like being close to the waterfront, although accommodations here – mostly in the form of *auberges* (inns) and a brand-new crop of ultradeluxe boutique hotels – do not come cheap unless you're visiting during the offseason. Prices are lower in the vibrant Plateau and Village neighborhoods – veritable B&B bastions that put you in the thick of the city's best nightlife. Most of the bigger hotels are west of here in downtown, close to the major museums and abundant shopping.

The agencies **BBCanada** (www.bbcanada.com/quebec) and **BedandBreakfast.com** (www.bedandbreakfast.com/montreal-quebec.html), and the **Centre Infotouriste** (www.bonjourquebec.com), can help to book accommodations.

🛏 Old Montréal

Alternative Backpackers HOSTEL $
(Map p232; 514-282-8069; www.auberge-alternative.qc.ca; 358 Rue St-Pierre; dm incl tax $22-25, r $75-85; @ 🛜) The owners of this hip hostel went for a chic grunge style in an 1875 building with original art, colorful walls and sunny interiors. You'll find fair-trade coffee and organic breakfasts ($5) here instead of televisions. This is the city's best option for the financially challenged.

Le Petit Hôtel BOUTIQUE HOTEL $$
(Map p232; 514-940-0360, 877-530-0360; www.petithotelmontreal.com; 168 Rue St-Paul Ouest; r $169-299; ❄ @ 🛜) This 'small hotel' is indeed tiny, with only 24 small, medium, large and extra-large rooms, but it's *très* chic, with hardwood floors, colorful furniture and plenty of modern electronic gadgets.

Bonaparte INN $$
(Map p232; 514-844-1448; www.bonaparte.com; 447 Rue St-François-Xavier; r $189-240, ste $355; ❄ 🛜) This elegant property exudes refined, classic European ambience, with wooden floors, Louis-Philippe furniture, French windows – some with views of the Basilique Notre-Dame – and exposed stone walls. After a satisfying three-course breakfast head up to the rooftop patio for snap-worthy views.

Le Place d'Armes HOTEL $$
(Map p232; 888-450-1887, 514-842-1887; www.hotelplacedarmes.com; 55 Rue St-Jacques; r from $209, ste from $289; ❄ 🛜) Contemporary rooms in this ornate 19th-century property, many of which overlook the stunning Place d'Armes and Basilique Notre-Dame, carry the refreshing scents of the hotel's spa and hammam.

★ Hôtel Gault BOUTIQUE HOTEL $$$
(Map p232; 514-904-1616, 866-904-1616; www.hotelgault.com; 449 Rue Ste-Hélène; r $220-750; ❄ @ 🛜) A design aficionado's haven, the Hôtel Gault features a soothing minimalist palette with polished concrete floors and steel accents, original 19th-century cast-iron columns and the occasional splash of warm blondwood. Custom-built beds, decadent linens, iPod docks, flatscreen TVs and heated bathroom floors add warmth and comfort to each of the 30 serenely stark loft-style rooms.

Downtown

HI Montréal International Youth Hostel
HOSTEL $

(Map p236; ☑866-843-3317, 514-843-3317; www.hostellingmontreal.com; 1030 Rue Mackay; dm members/nonmembers from $21/$26, r member/nonmember $80/$90; ✳@ ☎) Large, central and well organized, this hostel has dorms sleeping four to 10 people, plus several private rooms; all rooms have air-conditioning and bathrooms. The big kitchen, cafe and common areas often buzz with activity, especially in summer, when reservations are a must.

Montréal Y Hotel
HOTEL $

(Map p236; ☑514-866-9942; www.ydesfemmes-mtl.org; 1355 Blvd René-Lévesque Ouest; s/d from $60/70; ✳@ ☎) This nonprofit hotel offers spacious, appealing rooms to both men and women, in a refreshingly noninstitutional setting. All guests have access to communal kitchens and laundry machines; the shared bathrooms are spotless.

L'Abri du Voyageur
HOTEL $

(Map p240; ☑866-302-2922, 514-849-2922; www.abri-voyageur.ca; 9 Rue Ste-Catherine Ouest; r with shared bathroom from $65, studio with bathroom $125; ✳☎) Grandiose with high ceilings, bare-brick walls and wooden floorboards, this popular hotel (which also has apartment rentals) in Montréal's seedy, but safe, 'red-light district' offers great value.

Hotel Zero 1
HOTEL $$

(Map p240; ☑514-871-9696; www.zero1-mtl.com; 1 Blvd René-Lévesque Est; r from $139; ✳☎) This mixed condo/hotel development on the edge of Chinatown and near all the major summertime festivals is the closest Montréal comes to embracing the no-frills capsule-hotel idea. Minimalist rooms, with sleek black-and-white decor, are teeny tiny, but they don't scrimp on style.

Les Bons Matins
B&B $$

(Map p236; ☑514-931-9167, 800-588-5280; www.bonsmatins.com; 1401 Ave Argyle; r $99-119, ste $149-169; ✳☎) Charming and seductive, with exposed bricks and vibrant colors splashed across bedsheets and wall hangings, this classy establishment fills a series of adjoining turn-of-the-century step-ups. Breakfasts couldn't get better, with gourmet quiche, homemade waffles and Italian-style espresso. Parking is $12 per night.

Hilton Garden Inn
HOTEL $$

(Map p236; ☑877-840-0010; www.hiltongarden-montreal.com; 380 Rue Sherbrooke Ouest; r $152-229; ✳@ ☎) This incarnation of this popular hotel chain's budget series has garnered quite a reputation for its spacious rooms, friendly staff and excellent location. The airy rooftop swimming pool and exercise room are big pluses for families, and the free internet access and in-room fridges, microwaves and coffeemakers only sweeten the deal.

★Hôtel Le Germain
HOTEL $$$

(Map p236; ☑514-849-2050, 877-333-2050; www.germainmontreal.com; 2050 Rue Mansfield; r from $229; ☎) An air of calm and sophistication greets you at this unassuming hotel just a stone's throw from the McGill University campus. Rooms are sexy, with crisp white linens, dark, seductive Québec-crafted furniture, and see-through showers (with blinds for shy bathers). The free continental breakfast is a classy affair.

Later in the day, the same restaurant is where superstar chef Laurie Raphaël presents his edgy local food creations to discerning lunch and dinner crowds.

Ritz-Carlton
LUXURY HOTEL $$$

(Map p236; ☑514-985-0464, 800-363-0366; www.ritzmontreal.com; 1228 Rue Sherbrooke Ouest; r from $445; ✳@ ☎✳✳) Exuding style and sophistication, this original landmark of the 'Golden Mile' – Montréal's strip of upscale boutiques, cafes and restaurants – reopened its doors in 2012 just in time for its centennial anniversary, after a four-year, $200-million refurb that doubled the size of the guest rooms and added a glitzy rooftop swimming pool.

Rooms blend 19th-century charm (like marble fireplaces) with 21st-century convenience (like motion-detecting lights, towel warmers and heated floors). Star chef Daniel Boulud dazzles in the on-site restaurant, the city's newest see-and-be-seen hotspot.

Plateau Mont-Royal

Parc Suites
HOTEL $$

(Map p236; ☑800-949-8630, 514-985-5656; www.parcsuites.com; 3463 Ave du Parc; ste $149-219; ☎) Totally revamped in 2006, these eight modern one-bedroom suites have all the creature comforts – air conditioning, two flatscreen TVs, wi-fi and free long-distance calls within North America. Kitchens are spacious and well-equipped, and thanks to the hotel's

QUÉBEC MONTRÉAL

location in the heart of the student ghetto, there's a 24-hour grocery store, a 24-hour coffee shop and repertoire theater next door.

Gingerbread Manor B&B
B&B $$

(Map p240; ☎514-597-2804; www.gingerbread-manor.com; 3445 Ave Laval; r without/with bathroom from $89/119; ☎) Warm hosts Ephraim and Yves have taken this beautifully restored Victorian manor, replete with original crown moldings and ceiling pendants, and added tasteful classic decor and modern comforts. Breakfasts are unforgettable: don't be surprised to find quiche made with local organic vegetables one day and white-chocolate-and-orange French toast the next.

Auberge de la Fontaine
INN $$

(Map p240; ☎514-597-0166, 800-597-0597; www.aubergedelafontaine.com; 1301 Rue Rachel Est; r $122-179, ste $159-225; ❀☎) Located on the edge of the massive Parc LaFontaine, this charming, turreted inn is sophisticated yet relaxed. Breakfast is a generous spread and you're free to raid the fridge for snacks and dessert all day long. Room 21 is the nicest, with a dual whirlpool tub and park-facing terrace.

Anne Ma Soeur Anne
HOTEL $$

(Map p240; ☎514-281-3187; www.annema-soeuranne.com; 4119 Rue St-Denis; s $72-170, d $97-180; ❀☎) Buttery croissants delivered to your door and a fresh pot of coffee brewed in your own small kitchen is the way mornings get started in this hotel. Smallish rooms feature clever beds that fold up to reveal a full dining table, but the real draw here is the central Plateau location.

Shézelles
B&B $$

(Map p240; ☎514-849-8694; www.shezelles.com; 4272 Rue Berri; s $80-90, d $95-105, studios $135-150; ☎) A red door and bright yellow staircase hint at the color and flair awaiting you inside this humble abode of warm and welcoming hosts Lucie and Lyne. The giant basement studio sleeps up to six and comes with whirlpool, balcony, full kitchen and separate entrance.

🛏 Quartier Latin & The Village

La Loggia Art & Breakfast
B&B $$

(Map p240; ☎866-520-2493, 514-524-2493; www.laloggia.ca; 1637 Rue Amherst; r without/with bathroom from $105/145; ❀☎) Although plain-looking from the exterior, the inside of this 19th-century townhouse in the Gay Village

is anything but average. The artwork of co-host, Joel, brings the five modern guest rooms alive; a sprawling breakfast buffet prepared by his partner, Rob, is served in a leafy sculpture garden behind the house.

🍴 Eating

Food is serious business in Montréal, and refined palates demand high standards: there is zero tolerance for limp lettuce or an uninspired sauce. The city's top chefs have one foot in the traditions of the Old World and another in the innovative atmosphere of North America's gastronomic culture, resulting in a sort of *nouvelle cuisine Québecois*. Thanks to the competition and proliferation of choice in Montréal – over 5000 restaurants at last count – diners get a bang for their buck.

Downtown and especially the Plateau are a foodie's heaven. More than any other street, Blvd St-Laurent epitomizes the city's gastronomic wealth – from boisterous soup parlors in Chinatown to Schwartz's smoked meat emporium to funky Plateau trendsetters. Still further north looms Mile End, the birthplace of the famous Montréal bagel, and Little Italy, with its comfortable trattoria and not-to-be-missed Marché Jean-Talon.

🍴 Old Montréal

Olive + Gourmando
CAFE $

(Map p232; www.oliveetgourmando.com; 351 Rue St-Paul Ouest; mains $5-10; ⊙8am-6pm Tue-Sat; 🖉) Push and shove (if necessary) through thick lunchtime crowds in this little corner cafe for a little bit of heaven, as manifested in hot panini and sultry soups made with fresh, often organic produce. Leave room for the infamous chocolate brownies, infused with rich coffee.

Titanic
SANDWICHES $

(Map p232; 445 Rue St-Pierre; mains $9.50-15.50; ⊙8am-4:30pm Mon-Fri) Friendly staff here know a thing or two about delicious sandwiches and can make mouth-watering masterpieces with a baguette, a mountain of brie or pâté and sprigs of fresh herbs.

L'Usine de Spaghetti Parisienne
ITALIAN $

(Map p232; 273 Rue St-Paul Est; mains $9-12; ⊙11am-11pm Mon-Fri, from 5pm Sat) Brimming with tourists and hearty piles of pasta, this family-friendly Italian restaurant is a good-value alternative to the tourist traps lining Place Jacques Cartier.

Gandhi
INDIAN $$

(Map p232; www.restaurantgandhi.com; 230 Rue St-Paul Ouest; mains $15-20; ☺noon-2pm Mon-Fri & 5:30-10:30pm daily) Curries are like culinary poetry at this elegant Indian restaurant, which also does a mean tandoori duck and butter chicken. Portions are ample, fragrant and steamy, and the service is impeccable.

Toqué!
FRENCH $$$

(Map p232; ☎514-499-2084; www.restaurant-toque.com; 900 Place Jean-Paul-Riopelle; tasting menus $110; ☺11:30am-2pm Tue-Thu, 5.30-10:30pm Tue-Sat) Toqué! is consistently touted as Montréal's top restaurant, with a long list of accolades that add credence to this claim. Chef Normand Laprise's seven-course tasting menu brings fresh Québec produce to the table in a symphony of taste ingenuity and flawless presentation. Reservations essential.

✗ Downtown

Boustan
LEBANESE $

(Map p236; 2020 Rue Crescent; mains $5-10; ☺11am-4am; Ⓜ Guy-Concordia) This little Lebanese joint scores high in popularity on the city's shawarma circuit. Its late hours make it a favorite with night owls in need of sustenance between bars.

Ferreira Café
PORTUGUESE $$$

(Map p236; ☎514-848-0988; www.ferreiracafe. com; 1446 Rue Peel; mains $26-45; ☺noon-3pm Mon-Fri & 5:30-11pm Mon-Wed & Sun, to midnight Thu-Sat) Munch complimentary olives while perusing the menu at this beautiful Portuguese restaurant. The chef, Marino Tavares, gives sardines, sea bass and snapper the gourmet treatment. There's also a superb port selection. Reservations essential.

Nora Grey
ITALIAN $$$

(Map p236; ☎514-419-6672; www.noragray.com; 1391 Rue St-Jacques; mains $20-40; ☺5:30-11:30pm Tue-Sat) Retro-chic decor (black-and-white photos, leather banquettes and marble floors) sets the scene for this new hipster hangout that surprises with its array of creative takes on Italian-ish elements, like deer tartare with arugula and Parmesan, pork chops with cauliflower couscous and chickpea-basil stew.

---

❶ DO YOU HAVE A RESERVATION?

No-show reservations are a real bone of contention in Montréal. New technology employed at some of the hottest spots ensures that patrons confirm their reservations by 5pm, and many restaurateurs are considering a new penalty system. Some blame concierges for securing several time slots to please picky guests, but locals certainly do their fair share of blowing off reservations. So ignore the old adage, 'When in Rome...' and keep your reservation. Or at least call!

✗ Plateau Mont-Royal

Ong Ca Can
VIETNAMESE $

(Map p240; 79 Rue Ste-Catherine Est; mains $8-13; ☺11:30am-2pm & 6pm-late Tue-Sun) Despite its crisp white linens and intricate artwork, this bustling Vietnamese restaurant only looks pricey. The lemongrass rolls and anything involving beef get especially high marks from loyal patrons.

Fairmount Bagel
BAKERY $

(Map p240; 74 Ave Fairmount Ouest; bagels $0.50-$1.50, sandwiches $3.50-7; ☺24hr; Ⓜ Place des Arts, then bus 80) The original Montréal bagel baker still churns them out 24/7, from the classic onion to the newfangled muesli, sun-dried tomato and pesto variations.

Wilensky's Light Lunch
SANDWICHES $

(Map p240; 34 Ave Fairmount Ouest; sandwiches $2.50-5; ☺9am-4pm Mon-Fri, 10am-4pm Sat; Ⓜ Place des Arts, then bus 80) Generations of meat-lovers have flocked to Moe Wilensky's corner joint to order 'The Special' – a pressed bologna and salami sandwich. It has even been immortalized in Mordecai Richler's novel *The Apprenticeship of Duddy Kravitz*. Wash it down with a cherry cola from the fountain.

Schwartz's
SANDWICHES $

(Map p240; www.schwartzsdeli.com; 3895 Blvd St-Laurent; sandwiches $6-17; ☺8am-12:30am Sun-Thu, to 1:30am Fri, to 2:30am Sat) Don't be deterred by the line that inevitably forms outside this legendary smoked-meat parlor. Join the eclectic clientele – from students to celebrities – at the communal tables, and don't forget to order the pickles, fries and coleslaw.

Juliette et Chocolat
CAFE $

(Map p240; www.julietteetchocolat.com; 3600 Blvd St-Laurent; mains $8-12; ⊙11am-11pm Sun-Thu, to midnight Fri & Sat; 🖉) The menu at this bright and boisterous restaurant is stocked with a decent selection of savory buckwheat crepes, but true chocoholics won't be able to resist dressing their side salads with a tangy co-coa vinaigrette. Dessert is essential: the salty caramel brownies and lavender truffles are smart choices.

Café Sardine
CAFE $

(Map p240; 🖉514-802-8899; 9 Ave Fairmount Est; mains $2-15; ⊙8am-5pm & 6:30pm-1am) A rarity in Montréal, this hipster coffee shop special-izes in homemade donuts to go and crea-tive sandwiches at lunchtime. Dinner goes upscale with tapas while still retaining the casual Mile End vibe for which Sardine has become famous. The funky cocktails draw in a trendy after-hours crowd.

Santropol
SANDWICHES $

(Map p240; www.santropol.com; 3990 Rue St-Urbain; mains $7-11; ⊙10:30am-10:30pm Mon-Wed, from 7:30am Thu-Sun; 🖉) Creative sweet and savory sandwiches piled high with fresh fruits and vegetables are the main draw here. Earthy soups and soy lattes are big hits with locals, too.

★L'Express
FRENCH $$

(Map p240; 🖉514-845-5333; 3927 Rue St-Denis; mains $15-29; ⊙8am-2am Mon-Fri, from 10am Sat & Sun) This place is so fantastically French, you half expect to see the Eiffel Tower out the window, especially after guzzling too much of the excellent wine. The food's clas-sic Parisian bistro – think *steak frites,* bouil-labaisse, tarragon chicken – and so is the attitude. Reservations essential.

La Sala Rosa
SPANISH $$

(Map p240; 4848 Blvd St-Laurent; mains $12-15; ⊙5-11pm Tue-Thu & Sun, to midnight Fri & Sat; 🖉) Wash down flavorful tapas and every shade of paella with a pitcher of sangria in this unique restaurant, which shares a floor with the Spanish Social Club. Thursdays see free flamenco dance performances.

Crudessence
VEGAN $$

(Map p240; www.crudessence.com; 105 Rue Rachel Ouest; mains $11-17; ⊙11am-10pm; 🖉) The raw, vegan, organic *and* mostly gluten-free fare here is guaranteed to pique your interest, if not satisfy your hunger. Start the day with a bowl of chia, granola and almond milk, or wait for lunch to experience unbaked lasagna with macadamia nut ricotta and olive-crust pizza with 'crumesan' (Brazil nut parmesan).

The busy all-organic juice bar churns out wheatgrass, smoothies and power shakes to flocks of locals.

Chu Chai
VEGETARIAN, THAI $$

(Map p240; 4088 Rue St-Denis; mains $14-22; ⊙noon-10pm; 🖉) In Montréal's first vegetar-ian upscale eatery, zippy Thai-inspired stir-fries and coconut soups feature the flavours of fragrant Kaffir lime, lemongrass and sweet basil. The fake duck could fool even the most discerning carnivore.

Robin des Bois
FUSION $$

(Map p240; www.robindesbois.ca; 4653 Blvd St-Laurent; mains $14-20; ⊙11:30am-10pm Mon-Fri, 5-10pm Sat) 🖉 Montréal's own Robin Hood, restaurateur Judy Servay, donates all profits and tips from this St-Laurent hot spot to lo-cal charities. Ever-changing dishes scribbled on the chalkboard could include a succulent venison steak or *mujadarrah* with organic local vegetables, delivered with a smile by volunteer staff.

Eduardo
ITALIAN $$

(Map p240; 404 Ave Duluth Est; mains $10-15; ⊙11am-11pm Mon-Fri, from 3pm Sat & Sun) Hop-ping any night of the week, this cozy little bistro dishes up Italian favorites such as simple, yet bang-on, rich and gooey stuffed cannelloni and *spaghetti napoletana,* all in a dimly lit, warm atmosphere. BYOW.

Aux Vivres
VEGAN $$

(Map p240; 4631 Blvd St-Laurent; mains $10-14; ⊙11am-11pm Tue-Fri, from 10am Sat & Sun; 🖉) The chefs here make vegan cuisine accessi-ble to all with winning combinations such as the 'CLT' – a BLT with smoked coconut to replace the bacon – and creative rice bowls topped with fresh vegetables and zippy sauces.

Le Jardin de Panos
MEDITERRANEAN $$

(Map p240; www.lejardindepanos.com; 521 Ave Du-luth Est; mains $15-22; ⊙noon-midnight) Sample a stellar selection of tastes and textures in the mixed appetizer platter on the flower-filled back courtyard of this delightful Greek eatery.

Au Pied de Cochon FRENCH $$$
(Map p240; ☑ 514-281-1114; www.restaurantaupied-decochon.ca; 536 Ave Duluth Est; mains $26-43; ⊙ 5pm-midnight Wed-Sun) French-trained chef Martin Picard quickly captured the hearts and tummies of Montréal gourmets with his avant-garde interpretations of classic country fare. No animal is safe from his kitchen. Reservations recommended.

Moishe's STEAKHOUSE $$$
(Map p240; ☑ 514-845-3509; 3961 Blvd St-Laurent; mains $24-38; ⊙ 5:30-11pm) Moishe's feels a bit like a social club, although guests from all backgrounds come to consume its legendary grilled meats and seafood. Closely set tables and old-fashioned wood paneling set the backdrop to the feasting. Skip the appetizers and launch straight into a gargantuan rib steak served with tasty fries or a Monte Carlo potato. Reservations essential.

Maestro SVP SEAFOOD $$$
(Map p240; www.maestrosvp.com; 3615 Blvd St-Laurent; mains $14-40; ⊙ 4-10pm Sun-Wed, to 11pm Thu-Sat) A changing palette of 60 varieties of oysters is the specialty at this trendy bistro where tables are lit by a halo of halogen. If you're not into slimy mollusks, try the fried scallops, grilled shrimp or any of the pasta dishes.

✗ Quartier Latin & The Village

Les 3 Brasseurs ALSATIAN $$
(Map p240; www.les3brasseurs.ca; 1658 Rue St-Denis; mains $11-14; ⊙ 11:30am-midnight) If you'd like to cap a day of sightseeing with belly-filling fare and a few pints of handcrafted beer, stop by this convivial brewpub, with stylized warehouse looks and a rooftop terrace. The house specialty is *flammekeuche*, a French spin on pizza.

Le Nil Bleu ETHIOPIAN $$
(Map p240; ☑ 514-285-4628; 3706 Rue St-Denis; mains $19-28; ⊙ 11:30am-11:30pm; ✔) The presentation of the food here is as intriguing as the taste: imagine dollops of fragrant, spiced stews decorating the surface of *injera*, a sourdough flatbread. The soft trickle of the fountain in the background makes this Ethiopian dining experience even more mystical. Reservations recommended.

✗ Little Italy & Mile End

La Croissanterie Figaro CAFE $
(www.lacroissanteriefigaro.com; 5200 Rue Hutchison; mains $8-11; ⊙ 7am-1am; Ⓜ Place des Arts, then bus 80) Locals at this lovely cafe, self-dubbed *un petit coin perdu de Paris* (a little lost corner of Paris), keep the sidewalk patio packed solid, with a marbled, classy interior fielding the spillover. Attractive, black-clad servers deliver steamy bowls of café au lait; the casual table d'hôte menu appears around 4pm. It's just off Ave Fairmount, about seven blocks west of Blvd St-Laurent.

Marché Jean-Talon MARKET $
(7075 Ave Casgrain; ⊙ 7am-6pm Mon-Wed & Sat, to 8pm Thu & Fri, to 5pm Sun; Ⓜ Jean-Talon) The gem of Little Italy, this kaleidoscopic market is perfect for assembling a gourmet picnic or for partaking in a little afternoon grazing. A great stop is **Marché des Saveurs**, devoted entirely to Québec specialties such as wine and cider, fresh cheeses, smoked meats and preserves. The market sprawls south of Rue Jean-Talon between Blvd St-Laurent and Rue St-Denis.

Le Petit Alep MIDDLE EASTERN $
(☑ 514-270-9361; 191 Rue Jean-Talon Est; mains $5-12; ⊙ 11am-11pm Tue-Sat; ✔ ; Ⓜ De Castelnau) The complex flavors of Syrian-Armenian cuisine draw diners from all over Montréal. A big menu includes hummus, salads and *muhammara* (spread made of walnuts, garlic, breadcrumbs, pomegranate syrup and cumin), plus beef kebabs smothered in tahini, spices and nuts. Big brother, Alep, is the slightly swish dining room next door.

La Maison du Bagel BAKERY $
(263 Rue St-Viateur Ouest; bagels $0.50-$1.50, sandwiches $4-8; ⊙ 24hr; Ⓜ Place des Arts, then bus 80) Also known as St-Viateur bagel shop, this place has one of the grandest (and most justified) reputations for bagel artistry, strictly adhering to the classic Montreal style: small, dense, a tad sweet and baked in a wood-fired oven. It's north of Ave Fairmount and west of Blvd St-Laurent.

Pastaga QUÉBECOIS $$
(☑ 438-381-6389; www.pastaga.ca; 6389 Blvd St-Laurent; small dishes $13-16; ⊙ 11:30am-2pm Fri, 10am-2pm Sat & Sun & 5-10pm daily) Creative small dishes are great for sharing at this laid-back, yet up-to-the-minute trend-setting restaurant whose name is a play on 'pastis.'

MONTRÉAL'S THIRD WAVE

Like most North American cities, Montréal has been swept away by the so-called 'Third Wave' of cafes that have pushed coffee-drinkers away from the mass-produced, accessible-to-all coffee brands such as Folgers (first wave) to chains like Starbucks that focus on regional production and Italian espresso drinks (second wave), and toward a generation of artisanal, highly specialized coffee producers that practice direct-sourcing from single farms and in-house roasting.

Essentially the journey from bean to cup is a narrative, one that is just as important to the connoisseur as the taste of the coffee itself. Like the variety of grape to a wine-maker, baristas and roasters at Third Wave establishments care about the flavor (the aromatics, tones, depth), the bean varietal, and the farm from which the bean was sourced, with 'single-origin' being most desirable. To fuel a long day of wandering and sightseeing and experience haute cafe culture at its finest, consider one of the following:

Cafe Falco (off Map p240; www.cafefalco.ca; 5605 Ave de Gaspé; ⊙11am-5pm Mon, 9am-5pm Tue-Thu, to 4pm Fri; M Beaubien)

Café Névé (Map p240; www.cafeneve.com; 151 Rue Rachel Est; ⊙8am-9pm Mon-Fri, 9am-9pm Sat & Sun)

Cafe Saint-Henri (off Map p236; www.sainthenri.ca; 3632 Rue Notre-Dame Ouest; ⊙7:30am-8pm Mon-Fri, 8:30am-8pm Sat & Sun; M Lionel-Groulx)

Caffè in Gamba (Map p240; www.cafeingamba.com; 5263 Ave du Parc; ⊙7:30am-10pm Mon-Fri, 8:30am-10pm Sat & Sun)

Café Myriade (Map p236; www.cafemyriade.com; 1432 Rue Mackay; ⊙8am-7pm Mon-Fri, 9am-7pm Sat & Sun)

Pikolo Espresso Bar (Map p236; www.pikoloespresso.com; 3418B Ave du Parc; ⊙7am-7pm Mon-Fri, 9am-7pm Sat & Sun)

Pourquoi Pas Espresso Bar (Map p240; 1447 Rue Amherst; ⊙7:30am-7pm Mon-Fri, 9am-5pm Sat & Sun; M Beaudry)

There are three dining areas: choose a spot at the front window, sink into a massive banquette in the middle, or perch at a table in the kitchen, in the middle of the action.

Lucca   ITALIAN $$$
(☎514-278-6502; 12 Rue Dante; mains $18-36; ⊙noon-2:30pm Mon-Fri & 6-10pm Mon-Sat; M De Castelnau) This hot little Italian number is on the speed dial of many Montréal foodies. The menu, put together daily from market-fresh ingredients and written on a chalkboard, ranges from classics to adventurous culinary spins. It's *la dolce vita*, Québec style. Rue Dante is just off Blvd St-Laurent, south of Rue Jean-Talon. Reservations recommended.

✕ Elsewhere in Montréal

Marché Atwater   MARKET $
(138 Ave Atwater; ⊙7am-6pm Mon-Wed, to 7pm Thu, to 8pm Fri, to 5pm Sat & Sun; ⊘; M Atwater) This superb market brims with vendors selling mostly local and regional products, from perfectly matured cheeses to crusty breads, exquisite ice wines and tangy tapenades. It's

all housed in a 1933 brick hall just west of downtown, at the intersection of Ave Atwater and Rue Ste-Catherine Ouest.

Maison Indian Curry   INDIAN $
(996 Rue Jean-Talon Ouest; mains $8; ⊙11am-10pm; ⊘; M Acadie) In the up-and-coming Parc-Extension neighborhood, redubbed 'Little India' by locals, the cheap and hearty dishes (of both the northern and southern varieties) at this little hole-in-the-wall are outstanding. The lunchtime *thali* platter ($5), with three curries, rice and bread, is a steal.

Joe Beef   QUÉBECOIS $$$
(☎514-935-6504; www.joebeef.ca; 2491 Rue Notre-Dame Ouest; mains $22-35; ⊙6pm-late Tue-Sat; M Lionel-Groulx) In the heart of the Little Burgundy neighborhood, Joe Beef is the current darling of food critics for its unfussy, market-fresh fare. The rustic, country-kitsch setting is a great spot to linger over fresh oysters, tender Wagyu beef, fresh fish and a changing selection of hearty Québecois dishes – all

served with a dollop of good humor and a welcome lack of pretension.

Drinking & Nightlife

The best drinking areas are along the stylish strips of the Plateau – Blvd St-Laurent, Rue St-Denis and Ave du Mont-Royal – and along the noisy cafe-terrace-lined Rue Crescent downtown. The bars along Rue Ste-Catherine in The Village are slightly gay-focused, but frequented by all types.

The city's club scene is vibrant and exuberant, with much of the action unfolding along Blvd St-Laurent, Rue Ste-Catherine Est (in The Village) and, in the western part of town, Rue Crescent.

Montréal Clubs (www.montreal-clubs.com) has its finger on the pulse of Montréal's latest nightlife hot spots.

Le Ste-Elisabeth PUB
(Map p240; www.ste-elisabeth.com; 1412 Rue Ste-Elisabeth; ⊘4pm-3am Mon-Fri, from 6pm Sat & Sun) Microbrews, imported Euro beers and quality Scotch sing their sweet siren song to the low-key crowd at this popular pub. It's a pretty place with a lovely garden overlooked by an upstairs terrace.

Brutopia BREWERY
(Map p236; www.brutopia.net; 1219 Rue Crescent; ⊘3pm-3am Sat-Thu, noon-3am Fri) Boisterous and brick-lined Brutopia brews its own beer, including its outstanding India Pale Ale, in sparkling copper vats right behind the bar. A friendly young crowd invades nightly, not least for the live bands.

Le Saint Sulpice PUB
(Map p240; www.lesaintsulpice.ca; 1680 Rue St-Denis; ⊘1pm-3am) On a hot summer night, a cool place to be is the huge beer garden of this always bustling hangout. There's great people-watching potential here, as well as in the cafe, which has three terraces and a disco. Did we mention the place was huge?

Baldwin Barmacie BAR
(Map p240; www.baldwinbarmacie.com; 115 Ave Laurier Ouest; ⊘5pm-3am Mon-Sat, 7pm-3am Sun) This hip bar, with retro paisley orange textiles and bubble-shaped light fixtures, attracts a young crowd for its ambient and trip-hop music. The eclectic drinks menu includes martinis, wine and gin/vodka cocktails.

Bily Kun BAR
(Map p240; www.bilykun.com; 354 Ave du Mont-Royal Est; ⊘3pm-3am) One of the pioneers of 'tavern chic,' Bily Kun is a favorite local hangout for a chilled DJ-spun evening. First-time visitors usually gawk at the ostrich heads that overlook the bar but soon settle into the music groove of DJs and occasional bands.

Gogo Lounge BAR
(Map p240; 3682 Blvd St-Laurent; ⊘3pm-3am) This groovy outpost, decorated in a psychedelic Austin Powers sort of way, is famous for its huge martini selection. All drinks are listed on old vinyl records. Dress nicely.

Lab BAR
(Map p240; 1351 Rue Rachel Est; ⊘5pm-3am) Although this creative cocktail bar has a dark and secluded front door, it can be heard from blocks away. If you're feeling adventurous, try the Jerky Lab Jack – whisky with beef jerky and BBQ bitters – or a more subtle drink flavored with basil, raspberry or ginger. They might even light it on fire!

Sir Winston Churchill Pub PUB
(Map p236; www.winniesbar.com; 1455 Rue Crescent; ⊘11:30am-3am) This quintessential Crescent St watering hole was founded in 1967 by Johnny Vale, a one-time comrade of Che Guevara. The late local author Mordecai Richler used to knock back cold ones in the bar upstairs. Things get clamorous between 5pm and 8pm, when it's two-for-one happy hour.

Whisky Café LOUNGE
(www.whiskycafe.com; 5800 Blvd St-Laurent; ⊘5pm-1am Mon-Wed, to 3am Thu-Sat, 7pm-1am Sun; MPlace des Arts, then bus 80) The last of a dying breed of bars in Montréal, this classy lounge offers over 150 Scotch whiskeys and an impressive selection of Cuban cigars.

☆ Entertainment

Music lovers can easily get their fill from the extensive menu of jazz and classical to pop and new age to world beats. And fans of performing arts have plenty of theater and dance troupes of international renown from which to choose. Quiet and laid back by day, Montréal sports fans have a secret rowdy side that bursts into life in the bleachers.

Tickets for major concerts, shows, festivals and sporting events are available from the box offices of individual venues or from **Admission** (☑514-790-1245, 800-361-4595;

www.admission.com) or **Ticketmaster** (☑ 514-790-1111; www.ticketmaster.ca).

Cinemas

Multiplex theaters showing Hollywood blockbusters abound, but plenty of art and indie houses survive as well. Look up what's showing where at www.cinema-montreal.com, with reviews and details of discount admissions.

Popular independent theaters include **Cinéma du Parc** (☑ 514-281-1900; www.cinemaduparc.com; 3575 Ave du Parc; Ⓜ Place des Arts, then bus 80) and **Ex-Centris Cinema** (Map p240; ☑ 514-847-2206; www.cinemaexcentris.com; 3530 Blvd St-Laurent).

IMAX CINEMA
(Map p232; ☑ 877-496-4724, 514-496-4724; www.montrealsciencecentre.com; King Edward Pier; adult/child $11.50/8.50; ☑ 10am-11:30pm) Part of the Centre des Sciences de Montréal, this is a great place to take the kids. Discounted tickets with museum admission and for double features are available.

Live Music

Casa del Popolo LIVE MUSIC
(Map p240; www.casadelpopolo.com; 4873 Blvd St-Laurent; ☑ noon-late) Low-key and funky, this cafe-bar/art gallery/performance venue usually has several live music and spoken-word events scheduled in three locations. The cafe serves fair-trade coffee and vegetarian fare.

L'Esco LIVE MUSIC
(Map p240; ☑ 514-842-7244; 4467 Rue St-Denis; ☑ 6pm-1am) This smoky and intimate Plateau club serves up wicked jazz or indie rock from some of Montréal's up-and-coming artists.

Metropolis LIVE MUSIC
(Map p240; ☑ 514-844-3500; www.montrealmetropolis.ca; 59 Rue Ste-Catherine Est) Of its many faces (a skating rink, a porn movie theater and disco, among others), rock venue suits this 2300-person-capacity concert hall best. The stage was graced by the likes of Radiohead, David Bowie and Coldplay earlier in their careers.

Upstairs JAZZ
(Map p236; ☑ 514-931-6808; www.upstairsjazz.com; 1254 Rue Mackay; ☑ 11:30am-1am Mon-Fri, 5pm-1am Sat, 6:30pm-1am Sun) Some mighty fine talent, both home-grown and imported, has tickled the ivories of the baby grand in this intimate jazz joint. Shows start at 10pm. Nice terrace and respectable dinner menu.

Foufounes Electriques LIVE MUSIC
(Map p240; 87 Rue Ste-Catherine Est; ☑ 3pm-3am) The graffiti-covered walls and industrial charm should tip you off that 'Electric Buttocks' isn't exactly a mainstream kinda place. Punk, hardcore and grunge often rule the night at this two-decades-old alternative bastion. There's cheap beer and a nice terrace.

Opéra de Montréal OPERA
(Map p240; ☑ 514-985-2222; www.operademontreal.com; Place des Arts) The Montréal Opera has delighted fans of Mozart, Wagner and Bizet for almost three decades. Productions are in the original language with subtitles.

Orchestre Symphonique de Montréal CLASSICAL MUSIC
(Map p240; ☑ 514-842-9951; www.osm.ca; Maison Symphonique, Place des Arts) One of Canada's most accomplished orchestras, the OSM has been helmed by such famous conductors as Otto Klemperer, Zubin Mehta and Charles Dutoit.

McGill Chamber Orchestra CLASSICAL MUSIC
(☑ 514-487-5190; www.ocm-mco.org) Founded in 1939, this fine chamber ensemble is one of Canada's oldest. Concert series are held in various venues, including the **Pollack Concert Hall** (Map p236; 555 Rue Sherbrooke Ouest), the Maison Symphonique, and Bourgie Hall at the Musée des Beaux-Arts (p234).

Theater & Dance

Centaur Theatre THEATER
(Map p232; ☑ 514-288-3161; www.centaurtheatre.com; 453 Rue St-François-Xavier) Based in the beautiful Old Stock Exchange in Old Montréal, the Centaur ranks among the country's leading theater companies. Its repertoire ranges from Shakespeare classics to experimental fare by local English-language playwrights.

Cirque du Soleil THEATER
(Map p232; www.cirquedusoleil.com) For the past two decades, this phenomenally successful troupe has redefined what circuses are all about. Headquartered in Montréal, it usually inaugurates new shows in the city every year or two. Check with the tourist office.

Mado Cabaret CABARET
(Map p240; www.mado.qc.ca; 1115 Rue Ste-Catherine Est; tickets $5-15) Outrageous drag shows and stand-up comedy; Tuesday nights are the most rollicking.

GAY & LESBIAN MONTRÉAL

Montréal is one of Canada's gayest cities, with the rainbow flag flying especially proudly in The Village along Rue St-Catherine between Rue St-Hubert and Rue Dorion. Dozens of high-energy bars, cafes, restaurants, saunas and clubs flank this strip, turning it pretty much into a 24/7 fun zone. The authoritative guide to the gay and lesbian scene is **Fugues** (www.fugues.com), a free monthly mag found throughout The Village.

The big event on The Village calendar is the **Divers/Cité Festival** (☑514-285-4011; www.diverscite.org), Montréal's version of Pride Week, usually held in late July. It draws as many as one million people. Almost as much of a pull is the **Black & Blue Festival** (☑514-875-7026; www.bbcm.org) in October, with major dance parties, cultural and art shows and a mega-party in the Olympic Stadium.

Bars and clubs worth checking out:

Sky Pub & Club (Map p240; ☑514-529-6969; 1474 Rue Ste-Catherine Est) Huge place with rooftop terrace complete with Jacuzzi and pool.

Aigle Noir (Map p240; ☑514-529-0040; 1315 Rue Ste-Catherine Est) For the leather-and-fetish crowd.

Le Drugstore (Map p240; ☑514-524-1960; 1360 Rue Ste-Catherine Est) Fun-seekers of every persuasion will be satisfied on at least one of the six multithemed floors.

The Unity (Map p240; ☑514-523-2777; 1171 Rue Ste-Catherine Est) Sexy dance club humming with shirtless techno ravers, muscle queens and mellow straights.

Mado Cabaret (see below) Attracting drag fans from far and wide, Mado hosts live shows from Tuesday to Sunday.

QUÉBEC MONTRÉAL

Les Ballets Jazz de Montréal DANCE
(☑514-982-6771; www.bjmdanse.ca) This modern dance troupe has earned a sterling reputation for its classically trained dancers and experimental forms. Performances take place at various venues around town.

Les Grands Ballets Canadiens DANCE
(Map p240; ☑514-849-0269; www.grandsballets.qc.ca; Place des Arts) Québec's leading ballet troupe stages shows almost monthly. They range from classical to modern programs and are both innovative yet accessible to general audiences.

Sports

Hockey and Catholicism are regarded as national religions in Québec, but football also attracts a fair number of worshippers.

Montréal Canadiens HOCKEY
(Map p236; ☑514-932-2582; www.canadiens.com; Bell Centre, 1200 Rue de la Gauchetière Ouest; tickets $29-260) Bell Centre is home base for this National Hockey League team and 24-time Stanley Cup winners (the last time in 1993). Although they have struggled in recent years, Montréalers still have a soft spot for the 'Habs' and games routinely sell out. After the first drop of the puck you might be able to snag a half-price ticket from the

scalpers lurking by the entrance. Bring binoculars for the rafter seats.

Montréal Alouettes FOOTBALL
(☑514-871-2255; www.montrealalouettes.com; Molson Stadium, Ave des Pins Ouest; tickets $20-120; Ⓜ Square Victoria) This once-defunct Canadian Football League team is the unlikely hottie of the city's sports scene, especially since winning the league's Grey Cup trophy in 2009 and 2010. They have sold out every game since 1999, so order tickets early. Free shuttle buses from Square Victoria metro station (with a stop at McGill metro station) start two hours before each game.

Shopping

Just spending time in this stylish city, where personal appearance tops many Montréalers' priority lists, may prompt a spending spree. Hard-core shoppers will inevitably end up on Rue Ste-Catherine Ouest, which is chock-a-block with department, chain and one-of-a-kind stores, plus multilevel malls. And that's just at street level. Head underground and you'll have hundreds more retailers displaying everything from turquoise to tank tops.

For shopping at a more leisurely pace, head to the Plateau. Blvd St-Laurent, Rue St-Denis and Ave du Mont-Royal are famous for their unique boutiques hawking trendy must-haves. On Rue St-Paul in Old Montréal, the focus is on tourist-oriented trinket shops with some very respectable art galleries thrown into the mix. Antiques aficionados can easily spend a day scouring the shops along Rue Notre-Dame Ouest, between Ave Atwater and Rue Guy, known as Antique Alley.

Ogilvy
CLOTHING

(Map p236; www.ogilvycanada.com; 1307 Rue Ste-Catherine Ouest; ⊙10am-6pm Mon-Wed, to 9pm Thu & Fri, 9am-5pm Sat, noon-5pm Sun) Dripping with tradition, this Victorian-era department store stocks all the top international labels. Be sure to visit the historic concert hall on the 5th floor. Since 1927, a kilt-clad bagpiper has roamed the store daily at noon.

Galerie Le Chariot
ART

(Map p232; 446 Place Jacques Cartier; ⊙10am-6pm) This three-level gallery specializes in museum-quality Inuit art, primarily soapstone sculptures. Each piece has been authenticated by the Canadian government.

Guilde Canadienne des Métiers d'Art
ART

(Map p236; www.canadianguildofcrafts.com; 1460 Rue Sherbrooke Ouest; ⊙10am-6pm Tue-Fri, to 5pm Sat) This gallery-like space showcases only the finest in Canadian arts and crafts from all over the nation.

Centre Eaton
MALL

(Map p236; Rue St-Catherine, btwn Ave McGill College & Rue University; ⊙10am-9pm Mon-Fri, 10am-7pm Sat, 11am-5pm Sun) This five-story retailing palace on the main shopping drag is home to 175-plus stores and restaurants, and six movie screens. The tax-refund service **Global Refund Canada** is on the 4th floor. The **Promenade de la Cathédrale** is an underground passage of the complex that runs beneath the Cathédrale Christ Church.

Parasuco
CLOTHING

(Map p236; www.parasuco.com; 1414 Rue Crescent; ⊙9:30am-9pm Mon-Fri, to 6pm Sat, 11am-6pm Sun) Made right here in Montréal, Parasuco has become one of Canada's hottest labels for jeans and casual wear. Its high-energy flagship store stocks all the latest styles.

Eva B
CLOTHING

(Map p240; www.eva-b.ca; 2015 Blvd St-Laurent; ⊙11am-9pm Mon-Sat, noon-7pm Sun) The '60s, '70s and '80s are alive and well at this groovy retro boutique. Stock up on styles guaran-

teed to make you a standout at any party. Costume rentals, too.

Les Touilleurs
HOMEWARES

(Map p240; www.lestouilleurs.com; 152 Ave Laurier Ouest; ⊙10am-6pm Mon-Wed, to 9pm Thu & Fri, 11am-5pm Sat & Sun) Kitchenware has never looked so sexy. Almost as impressive as the vast collection of ultra-high-quality, brand-name toasters and cake tins is the minimalist interior design.

Cheap Thrills
MUSIC

(Map p236; www.cheapthrills.ca; 2044 Rue Metcalfe; ⊙11am-6pm Mon-Wed & Sat, to 9pm Thu & Fri, noon-5pm Sun) It's easy to lose track of time as you browse through this big selection of used books and music (CDs and some vinyl), both mainstream and offbeat, sold at bargain prices.

Paragraphe Bookstore
BOOKS

(Map p236; www.paragraphbooks.com; 2220 Ave McGill College; ⊙8am-9pm) This pleasant shop near McGill University stocks books in English covering general subjects.

Word
BOOKS

(Map p236; www.wordbookstore.ca; 469 Rue Milton; ⊙10am-6pm Mon-Wed, to 9pm Thu & Fri, 11am-6pm Sat) Long-standing student hangout with used academic books and modern literature. North of Rue Sherbrooke Ouest and east of Rue University.

Ulysses
BOOKS

(Map p240; 4176 Rue St-Denis; ⊙10am-6pm Mon-Wed, Sat & Sun, to 9pm Thu & Fri) Travel books and maps.

ℹ Information

EMERGENCY
Montréal Police Station (☑emergencies 911, non-emergencies 514-280-2222)

MEDIA
The *Montréal Gazette* is the main English-language daily newspaper with solid coverage of national affairs, politics and arts. The Saturday edition has useful what's-on listings, although the online alternative magazines, *Cult* (www.cultmontreal.com) and *Hour Community* (www.hour.ca) are better sources.

MEDICAL SERVICES
CLSC (☑514-934-0354; 1801 Blvd de Maisonneuve Ouest; ⊙8am-8pm Mon-Fri, to 4pm Sat & Sun) Walk-in community health center for minor ailments; costs $105 (cash only) per visit, not including tests.

Pharmaprix Pharmacy (www.pharmaprix.ca) Mont-Royal (5122 Chemin de la Côte-des-Neiges; ⊘24hr; Ⓜ Côte-des-Neiges); Downtown (1500 Rue Ste-Catherine Ouest; ⊘8am-midnight; Ⓜ Guy-Concordia) Check the website for additional branches.

Royal Victoria Hospital (☎514-934-1934; 687 Ave des Pins Ouest; ⊘24hr) McGill University–affiliated, with an emergency room; the best option for English-speaking patients.

MONEY

You'll find currency-exchange counters at the airport, the train station, the main tourist office, the casino (open 24 hours) and throughout the central city, especially along Rue Ste-Catherine.

Calforex (1230 Rue Peel; ⊘8:30am-9pm Mon-Sat, 10am-6pm Sun) Currency exchange.

National Bank of Canada (www.nbc.ca) Plateau Mont-Royal (4506 Rue St-Denis); Quartier Latin (801 Rue Ste-Catherine Est) Check the website for additional branches.

POST

Main Post Office (Map p236; 677 Rue Ste-Catherine Ouest; ⊘7am-7pm Mon-Fri, 10am-5pm Sat, 11am-5pm Sun) The largest branch.

Station Place d'Armes (157 Rue St-Antoine; ⊘8:30am-5:30pm Mon-Fri) Have poste restante mail sent to this station, 157 Rue St-Antoine, Montréal, Québec H2Y 1L0.

TOURIST INFORMATION

Montréal and Québec province maintain a central phone service for tourist information (☎514-873-2015, 877-266-5687).

Centre Infotouriste (Map p236; www.bonjourquebec.com; 1255 Rue Peel; ⊘8:30am-7pm) Information about Montréal and all of Québec. Free hotel, tour and car reservations, plus currency exchange.

Montréal Tourist Office (Map p232; www.tourism-montreal.org; 174 Rue Notre-Dame Est; ⊘10am-7pm Apr-Oct) Just off bustling Place Jacques Cartier, this little office is always humming and staff are extremely helpful.

TRAVEL AGENCIES

Voyages Campus (www.travelcuts.com; 407 Blvd de Maisonneuve Est; ⊘9am-6pm Mon-Wed, to 7pm Thu & Fri, 11am-5pm Sat) Known as Travel Cuts outside Québec, this agency specializes in adventure travel and student fares.

USEFUL WEBSITES

City of Montréal (www.ville.montreal.qc.ca) The official city website.

Tourisme Montréal (☎877-266-5687; www.tourisme-montreal.org) Official website of the Montréal tourist office, with reams of information and a user-friendly hotel search engine with good deals.

> ### ⓘ WI-FI ACCESS
>
> **Île Sans Fil** (ilesansfil.org) offers free wi-fi access to anyone who registers. There are hot spots in Juliette et Chocolat (p250), Titanic (p249) and Santropol (p250), as well as at Le Saint Sulpice (p253), Marché Jean-Talon (p251) and a few clubs in The Village such as The Unity (p255) and Le Drugstore (p255).

ⓘ Getting There & Away

AIR

Both domestic and international airlines land at **Pierre Elliott Trudeau International Airport** (YUL; ☎800-465-1213, 514-394-7377; www.admtl.com), formerly known as Dorval Airport, about 20km west of downtown. Facilities include lockers, a left-luggage office, ATMs and a currency exchange desk.

BUS

Buses to the airports and to Canadian and US destinations depart from the **Station Centrale de l'Autobus** (Central Bus Station; Map p240; ☎514-842-2281; 505 Blvd de Maisonneuve Est).

Greyhound (www.greyhound.ca) runs daily services to New York City ($84, eight hours, 10 daily) and regular and express buses to Ottawa ($29, 2¼ hours, 21 daily), while **Orléans Express** (www.orleansexpress.com) serves Québec City ($57, 3¼ hours, 24 daily) as well as the Mauricie and Gaspésie regions.

Megabus (www.ca.megabus.com) offers the best deal and the shortest trip to Toronto ($32 to $45, 5¾ hours, eight daily). **Galland** (www.galland-bus.com) goes to the Laurentian resorts, and **Limocar** (www.limocar.ca) cuts through the Eastern Townships en route to Sherbrooke.

Montréal is also a stop on the eastern Canada circuit run by Moose Travel Network (p887).

CAR & MOTORCYCLE

All the major international car-rental companies have branches at the airport, main train station and elsewhere around town. **Auto Plateau** (☎514-281-5000; www.autoplateau. com; 3585 Rue Berri; Ⓜ Sherbrooke) is a reputable local company.

The ride-share agency **Allô Stop** (☎514-985-3032; www.allostopmontreal.com; 4317 Rue St-Denis; Ⓜ Mont-Royal) has an office in the Plateau. **Kangaride** (p229) is another ride-share agency with a greater selection but an online presence only. A sample fare with either company is $13 to Québec City.

TRAIN

Montréal's **Gare Centrale** (Central Train Station; 895 Rue de la Gauchetière Ouest) is the local hub for **VIA Rail** (p229). The overnight service between Montréal and Halifax ($165, 21½ hours) is a treat aboard modern and comfortable cars. There are six trains daily to Toronto ($135, 4½ hours) on immaculate trains fitted with wi-fi connection and a beverage service.

Amtrak (p229) runs one train daily to/from New York City (US$65, 11 hours).

ⓘ Getting Around

TO/FROM THE AIRPORT

STM, the city's public transportation system, runs two bus lines from Montréal Trudeau to downtown. Rte 747 (one-way $9 in exact change, one hour) is the express service to downtown, with stops at Lionel-Groulx métro station, the central train station and Berri-UQAM métro station. The service runs every 12 minutes from 8:30am to 8pm, every half-hour from 5:30am to 8:30am and from 8pm to 1am, and hourly between 2am and 5am.

You can also make the trip on bus 204 Est, from Gare Dorval (Dorval Train Station) to the Lionel-Groulx métro station. A shuttle bus runs between the airport and Gare Dorval. Buses operate every 30 minutes from 6am to midnight; the entire journey takes about an hour and costs $3 (in exact change).

Drivers heading into town should take Autoroute 13 Sud, which merges with Autoroute 20 Est; this in turn takes you into the heart of downtown, along the main Autoroute Ville-Marie (the 720). The trip takes between 20 minutes and an hour depending on traffic.

A taxi to/from Trudeau airport costs a flat rate of $40.

CAR & MOTORCYCLE

Though Montréal is fairly easy to navigate, public transportation is preferable to driving a car while you're just getting around town. If you choose to drive, you'll find metered street parking (with meters set back from the curb) and public garages throughout the central area, especially underneath big hotels and shopping complexes. Expect to pay $12 to $20 per day.

Note that turning right at red lights is illegal on the island of Montréal.

PUBLIC TRANSPORTATION

Montréal has a modern and convenient bus and métro system run by **STM** (www.stm.info). The métro is the city's subway system and runs quickly and quietly on rubber tires. It operates until at least 12:30am. Some buses provide service all night.

One ticket can get you anywhere in the city. If you're switching between buses, or between bus and métro, get a free transfer slip, called a *correspondence*, from the driver; on the métro take one from the machines just past the turnstiles. Transfers are valid for 90 minutes only for travel in one direction.

Tickets cost $3 but are cheaper in packages of 10 ($24.50). There are also 'Tourist Cards' for $9/18 for one/three days (also valid for the express Rte 747 to the airport) and weekly cards for $23.75 (valid starting on Monday and expiring Sunday).

Note that bus drivers don't give change.

TAXI

Flag fall is $3.45, then it's $1.70 per kilometer. You can flag down a cab on the street or order one by phone. Try **Taxi Diamond** (☏ 514-273-6331) or **Taxi Co-Op** (☏ 514-636-6666).

THE LAURENTIANS

The Laurentians, or Les Laurentides in French, are perhaps the best-kept secret of Montréal day-trippers and are just an hour's drive from the city. Here you'll find yourself amid gentle rolling mountains, crystal blue lakes and meandering rivers peppered with towns and villages too cute for words. A visit to this natural paradise is like putting your feet up after a long day.

Although sometimes criticized for being over-commercialized, Mont-Tremblant offers outstanding skiing, rivaled only by Whistler in the whole of Canada. Speckling the Laurentians are many more lower-profile resort villages, whose miniature town centers deliver an air of the Alps, with breezy patios and exclusive, independent designer-clothing shops.

Expect higher prices and heavy crowds during high season, which includes the summer months and Christmas holidays. Check ahead for opening hours in the winter months.

Nearly all towns in the Laurentians can be accessed via Hwy 15, the Autoroute des Laurentides. Old Rte 117, running parallel to it, is slow but considerably more scenic.

ℹ️ Information

Association Touristique des Laurentides
(Laurentian Tourist Association; ☎ 450-436-8532, reservation service 450-436-3507; www.laurentides.com; ⏰ 9am-5pm) Regional tourist office; can answer questions on the phone, make room bookings and mail out information. It operates a free room reservation service, which specializes in lodgings along Le P'tit Train du Nord trail.

La Maison du Tourisme des Laurentides (La Porte du Nord, exit 51 off Hwy 15; ⏰ 8:30am-8pm) Information office maintained by the Association Touristique des Laurentides, with helpful staff and lots of maps and brochures, including the excellent *Official Tourist Guide*.

ℹ️ Getting There & Around

Galland runs buses from Montréal's Central Bus Station to the Laurentians three times daily. Towns serviced include St-Jérôme ($18, 1¼ hours), St-Sauveur ($22, 1½ hours), Val-David ($25, two hours) and Mont-Tremblant ($32, three hours).

From mid-May to mid-October, **Autobus du P'tit Train du Nord** (www.autobuslepetittraindunord.com) runs two buses daily between St-Jérôme and Mont Laurier (tickets $25 to $65), stopping as needed. Bicycles are transported at no charge.

Drivers coming from Montréal should follow either Hwy 15 or the slower Rte 117.

St-Jérôme

Some 43km north of Montréal, St-Jérôme is the official gateway to the Laurentians. Despite its administrative and industrial demeanor, it's worth a stop for the stunning stained-glass windows and Venetian chandeliers of its castle-like, Roman-Byzantine-style **cathedral** (355 Place du Curé-Labelle; ⏰ 8:30am-4:30pm Mon-Fri, to noon Sat & Sun) FREE and nearby **La Musée D'Art Contemporain des Laurentians** (www.museelaurentides.ca; 101 Place du Curé-Labelle; admission $4; ⏰ noon-5pm Tue-Sun), which often presents superb exhibitions featuring regional artists.

St-Jérôme is also the southern terminus of the **Parc Linéaire du P'tit Train du Nord** (www.laurentians.com/parclineaire), a trail system built on top of old railway tracks and snaking 230km north to Mont Laurier, passing streams, rivers, rapids, lakes and great mountain scenery. In summer it's open to bicycles and in-line skates, and you'll find rest stops, information booths, restaurants,

B&Bs and bike rental and repair shops along the way. Snow season lures cross-country skiers to the section between St-Jérôme and Val-David, while snowmobile aficionados rule between Val-David and Mont Laurier.

St-Sauveur-des-Monts

St-Sauveur-des-Monts (or St-Sauveur, for short) is the busiest village in the Laurentians and is often deluged with day-trippers thanks to its proximity to Montréal (60km). A pretty church anchors Rue Principale, the attractive main street, and is flanked by restaurants, cafes and boutiques.

🏃 Activities

St-Sauveur Valley Resort   SNOW SPORTS
(www.mssi.ca) With about 100 runs for all levels of expertise crisscrossing the area's five major ski hills, the downhill skiing is excellent in this region. The biggest hill, **Mont St-Sauveur** (www.montsaintsauveur.com; admission per day $40-54) is famous for its night skiing, with many slopes open until 11pm. In summer, it's transformed into the **Parc Aquatique** (Water Park; www.parcaquatique.com; 350 Rue St-Denis; adult/child per day $34/18, half-day $28/15; ⏰ 10am-7pm Jun-Sep). Kids of all ages love getting wet in the wave pool, plunging down slides (some accessible by chairlift) or being pummeled on rafting rides.

Thrill-seekers might also enjoy Le Dragon, a double zipline, and Viking, a scenic, dry 1.5-km-long toboggan ride through rugged mountain terrain. Cross-country skiers flock to the over 150km of interconnecting trails at Morin Heights.

🎭 Festivals & Events

Festival des Arts   PERFORMING ARTS
(www.fass.ca) For eight days starting in late July, St-Sauveur's Festival des Arts brings dozens of international dance troupes to town. Many performances are free.

🛏️ Sleeping & Eating

Auberge Sous L'Edredon   B&B $$
(☎ 450-227-3131; www.aubergesousledredon.com; 777 Rue Principale; r $119-199; ❄️🐾🛜🐾) This Victorian inn, about 2km from the village center and close to a little lake, is overflowing with character. Some of the delightfully decorated rooms have fireplaces and Jacuzzis.

Le Petit Clocher
B&B $$$

(450-227-7576; www.lepetitclocher.com; 216 Rue de l'Église; s $175-215, d $185-235; ✳🁢) A gorgeous inn occupying a converted monastery on a little hillside above town, Le Petit Clocher has seven rooms decorated in French Country style, many of which have extraordinary views.

La Brûlerie des Monts
CAFE $

(www.bruleriedesmonts.com; 197 Rue Principale; mains $5-10; 🕖7am-9pm) *The* place in town for breakfast and sandwiches, with a great terrace. Coffee beans are roasted on site.

Chez Bernard
DELI $

(www.chezbernard.com; 407 Rue Principale; dishes $6-15; 🕙10am-6pm Mon-Thu, to 8pm Fri, 9am-6pm Sat, 10am-5pm Sun) Superb deli with local specialties, some of which are homemade, plus full meals perfect for picnics.

Orange & Pamplemousse
MEDITERRANEAN $$

(www.orangepamplemousse.com; 120 Rue Principale; mains $12-32; 🕗8am-3pm daily & 5-9pm Wed-Sun) Tranquil, with the soft sounds of a Japanese bamboo water fountain, this restaurant is a great place to devour complex pasta dishes and extraordinary grilled fish. The breakfasts are also divine.

Le Rio
BARBECUE $$

(www.riorestaurant.ca; 352 Rue Principale; mains $11-30, meals from $26; 🕔5-10pm) It's a bit strange to imagine ordering a barbecue dinner in the mountains of rural Québec, but this classy diner gets rave reviews from American tourists and locals alike. Don't leave without at least a taste of the succulent, fall-off-the-bone baby back ribs.

ℹ Information

Banque Nationale (6 Rue de la Gare)

Café Saint-Sau (Galerie des Monts mall, Block I-2, 75 Rue de la Gare; internet per 15/30min $3/5; 🕗8am-5pm)

Pays d'en Haut Tourist Office (450-229-3729; www.lespaysdenhaut.com; 1490 Rue St-Joseph, Ste-Adèle) Guided tours and information about accommodations.

Val-David

Val-David is a pint-size village with an almost lyrical quality and a gorgeous setting along the Rivière du Nord and at the foot of the mountains. Its charms have made it a magnet for artists, whose studios and galleries line the main street, Rue de l'Église.

🏃 Activities

The great outdoors is one of Val-David's main attractions. **Roc & Ride** (819-322-7978; www.rocnride.com; 2444 Rue de l'Église) rents cross-country skis, snowshoes, skates. There's a juice/espresso bar on site in the summer months. **Aventure Nouveau Continent** (819-322-7336; www.aventurenouveau-continent.com; 2301 Rue de l'Église) rents bicycles, kayaks and canoes, and offers cycle-canoe packages and guided tours on the Rivière du Nord.

Rock climbing is to Val-David what skiing is to other Laurentian villages, with more than 500 routes – from easy walls to challenging cliffs. The mountain-climbing school **École Escalade** (819-323-6987; www.ecole-escalade.com; 2374 Rue Bastien; courses from $100; 🕙Apr-Oct) offers full-day and multi-day courses for beginning and experienced rock hounds.

🎉 Festivals & Events

From mid-July to mid-August, the **1001 Pots Festival** (www.1001pots.com; admission $2), a huge ceramic exhibit and sale with workshops, brings around 100,000 people to town. It's the brainchild of Japanese-Canadian artist Kinya Ishikawa, whose utilitarian yet stylish pieces are displayed year-round at his **Atelier du Potier** (2435 Rue de l'Église; 🕙10am-5pm Tue-Sun).

🛌 Sleeping & Eating

La Maison de Bavière
B&B $$

(819-322-3528; www.maisondebaviere.com; 1470 Chemin de la Rivière; r $100-160; @🁢) Fall asleep to the sound of Rivière du Nord outside the window at this inn, where hand-painted Bavarian stencils and wooden beams give it a European ski-chalet feel. Everything is geared toward a day of outdoors pursuits, from its location on the P'tit Train du Nord trail to the energizing full gourmet breakfasts served each morning.

You can even raid a well-stocked fridge at the end of an activity-filled day and then take your spoils out to the sprawling, pristine grounds overlooking the river. The restaurants and shops of Val-David are a short walk away.

La Vagabonde
BAKERY $

(www.boulangerielavagabonde.com; 1262 Chemin de la Rivière; light meals $3-9; 🕗8am-6pm Wed-Sun) This popular cafe and bakery serves delicious handcrafted organic breads and pastries and fair-trade coffees and teas.

Le Grand Pa MEDITERRANEAN **$$$**
(www.legrandpa.com; 2481 Rue de l'Église; mains $22-32; ⊙ 11:30am-2pm & 5-10pm) This convivial restaurant attracts a winning mix of locals and visitors nibbling on creative grilled meat and fish dishes or wood-fired pizzas. A chansonnier serenades diners on Friday and Saturday nights. Big terrace.

❶ Information

Tourist Information Office (www.valdavid. com; 2525 Rue de l'Église)

Ville de Mont-Tremblant

The Mont-Tremblant area is the crown jewel of the Laurentians, lorded over by the 960m-high eponymous mountain and dotted with pristine lakes and traversed by rivers. It's a hugely popular four-season playground, drawing ski bums from late October to mid-April, and hikers, bikers, golfers, water sports fans and other outdoor enthusiasts the rest of the year.

The area of Ville de Mont-Tremblant is divided into three sections: **Station Tremblant**, the ski hill and pedestrianized tourist resort at the foot of the mountain; **Mont-Tremblant Village**, a sweet and tiny cluster of homes and businesses about 4km southwest of here; and **St-Jovite**, the main town and commercial center off Rte 117, about 12km south of the mountain.

◎ Sights & Activities

Station Tremblant (www.tremblant.com; half-/ full-day lift tickets $57/76), founded in 1938, is among the top-ranked international ski resorts in eastern North America according to *Ski* magazine and legions of loyal fans. The mountain has a vertical drop of 645m and is laced with 95 trails and three snow parks served by 14 lifts, including an express gondola. Ski rentals start at $32 per day.

A summer attraction is the **Skyline Luge** (1/3/5 rides $11/20/26), which snakes down the mountain for 1.4km; daredevils can reach speeds up to 50km/h. The nearby **Activity Centre** (☑ 891-681-4848; www.tremblant-activities.com; ⊙ 9am-6pm) can arrange for a wide variety of outdoor pursuits, from fishing to canoeing to horseback riding; inquire here also for more information about the Scandinavian-style spa, dune buggy trails,

zip lines, rock climbing, paintball, and helicopter tours.

The southern mountain base spills over into a sparkling **pedestrian tourist village**, with big hotels, shops, restaurants and an amusement park atmosphere. The cookie-cutter architecture doesn't quite exude the rustic European charm its planners sought to emulate, but this seems of little concern to the 2.5 million annual visitors milling along its cobbled lanes year after year.

✪✪ Festivals & Events

Festival International du Blues MUSIC
(www.tremblantblues.com) For 10 days every early July, the resort is abuzz with music during the country's biggest blues festival.

Ironman SPORT
(www.ironman.com) Late August sees the annual Ironman North American Championship, which includes a 3.8km swim in Lac Tremblant, a 180km bike ride through surrounding forests and mountains, and a 42.2km run that follows the P'tit Train du Nord trail and ends in the pedestrian village. A shorter, less grueling Ironman 70.3 competition takes place here in late June.

⊨ Sleeping

HI Mont-Tremblant Hostel HOSTEL **$**
(☑ 819-425-6008; www.hostellingtremblant.com; 2213 Chemin du Village, Mont-Tremblant Village; dm/s/d $29/66/74; @ 🛜) This attractive hostel right next to Lac Moore (free canoe rentals) has a big kitchen and large party room with bar, pool table and fireplace. The clean and spacious rooms often fill to capacity, especially in the ski season.

Homewood Suites HOTEL **$$**
(☑ 819-681-0808; www.homewoodsuites.com; 3035 Chemin de la Chapelle; ste from $139; ✳ @ 🛜 ⊠) In the middle of the pedestrian village, in the heart of all the action in both summer and winter (the ski gondola is 500m from the door), this homey chain has great-value suites with stunning mountain views, spiffy decor and basic hot breakfasts. There's a 24-hour convenience store on site.

Auberge Le Lupin B&B **$$**
(☑ 877-425-5474, 819-425-5474; www.lelupin.com; 127 Rue Pinoteau, Mont-Tremblant Village; r $108-157; @ 🛜) This 1940s log house offers snug digs just 1km away from the ski station, with private beach access to the sparkling Lac

Tremblant. The tasty breakfasts whipped up by host Pierre in his homey rustic kitchen are a perfect start to the day.

Hotel Quintessence BOUTIQUE HOTEL $$$
(☑866-425-3400; www.hotelquintessence.com; 3004 Chemin de la Chapelle, Mont-Tremblant Village; ste from $280; ✳@☏☎) This luxurious estate fuses Old World splendor with North American nature. From calming wood fireplaces and private balconies overlooking Lac Tremblant to heated marble floors and plunge baths, suites at this small, exclusive resort are definitely splurge-worthy.

✗ Eating

Microbrasserie La Diable PUB $$
(www.microladiable.com; Station Tremblant; mains $12-27; ☉11:30am-2am) After a day of tearing down the mountain, the hearty sausages, burgers and pastas served at this lively tavern at Station Tremblant fill the belly nicely, as do the tasty home brews.

Coco Pazzo ITALIAN $$
(www.coco-pazzo.com; Station Tremblant; mains $14-33; ☉noon-3pm & 5-9pm) Modern Italian with a twist is on offer at this upscale eatery, which overlooks the stage at Place des Lauriers.

★sEb MODERN CANADIAN $$$
(☑819-429-6991; www.seblartisanculinaire.com; 444 Rue St-Georges, St-Jovite; mains $27-36, meals from $45; ☉6-11pm Wed-Sun) 🍃 Escape the mediocre and get a taste of what local culinary artisans can create with seasonal, sustainable local ingredients. A flexible, eager-to-please kitchen, an unforgettable menu, and a never-ending wine list enhance the jovial atmosphere here that can be best described as alpine chalet meets globetrotter (think African masks) meets Hollywood chic (Michael Douglas is a regular). Reservations essential.

ℹ Information

Au Grain de Café (Homewood Suites, Station Tremblant; per 10min $2; ☉7:30am-11pm) Internet access.

Banque Nationale (Le Kandahar Hotel, Station Tremblant; ☉10am-5pm)

Centre Médical de St-Jovite (☑819-425-2728; 992 Rue de St-Jovite, St-Jovite; ☉8am-8pm Mon-Thu, to 5pm Fri, 8:30am-12:30pm Sat & Sun) Medical clinic.

Mont-Tremblant Tourism (☑819-425-3300; www.tourismemonttremblant.com) St-Jovite (☑800-322-2932; 8 Chemin de Brébeuf);

Mont-Tremblant Village (☑877-425-2434; 5080 Montée Ryan, cnr Rte 327); Station Tremblant (☑800-322-2932; Place des Voyageurs).

ℹ Getting Around

A shuttle bus ($3) connects Station Tremblant, Mont-Tremblant Village and St-Jovite from 6am to 8pm Sunday to Thursday and 6am to 11pm on Friday and Saturday.

Parc du Mont-Tremblant

Nature puts on a terrific show in **Parc du Mont-Tremblant** (☑819-688-2281, reservations 800-665-6527; www.sepaq.com; Chemin du Lac Supérieur; adult/child $6.50/3) the province's biggest and oldest park – it opened in 1895. Covering 1510 sq km of gorgeous Laurentian lakes, rivers, hills and woods, the park has rare vegetation (including silver maple and red oak), hiking and biking trails, and canoe routes. It is home to fox, deer, moose and wolves, and is a habitat for more than 206 bird species, including a huge blue heron colony.

The park is divided into three sectors. The most developed area is the **Diable sector**, home to beautiful Lac Monroe. The main entrance is 28km northeast of Station Tremblant. The year-round service center, which also has equipment rentals, is another 11km from the entrance.

Diable's incredible trails range from an easy 20-minute stroll past waterfalls to daylong hikes that take in stunning views of majestic valleys. You can also take your bike out on some trails or rent canoes to travel down the serpentine Rivière du Diable. The gentle section between Lac Chat and La Vache Noire is perfect for families.

A popular half-day guided tour, **Via Ferrata** (June to August, $39 to $65), scales the rock face of La Vache Noire to take in a stunning vista of Rivière du Diable with the Laurentians behind. No rock-climbing experience is needed as guides cover the basics and supply the equipment. Reservations can be made through the park.

Further east, the **Pimbina sector** is a 10-minute drive from St-Donat. Here you'll find an **information center** (☉mid-May–mid-Oct & mid-Dec–Mar), canoe and kayak rentals and campgrounds with some amenities. Activities include swimming at Lac Provost and hiking and biking trails nearby. A highlight is the **Carcan Trail**, a 14.4km route to the top of the park's second-highest peak (883m), passing waterfalls and lush scenery on the way.

Further east is the **L'Assomption sector**, accessible via the town of St-Côme. It is the most untamed part of the park, with more trails, secluded cottages and remote camping options. In winter, you can't access this sector by car, as snow covers the roads.

The wilder interior and eastern sections are accessible by dirt roads, some of which are old logging routes. The off-the-beaten-track areas abound in wildlife. With some effort, it's possible to have whole lakes to yourself, except for the wolves whose howls you hear at night.

By late August, nights start getting cold and a couple of months later a blanket of snow adds a magic touch. That's when cross-country skiing and snowshoeing are popular activities in the Diable and Pimbina sectors.

Some of the park's many **campgrounds** (campsites $22-42) come with amenities, but most are basic. Reservations are recommended in busy periods. Some of the nicest spots can only be reached by canoe. There's also lodging in four-person **yurts** (per night $134) on Lac Provost (Pimbina) and Lac des Cyprès (L'Assomption), and cozy two- to eight-person **cabins** ($116-234) on the shores of Lac Chat (Diable), Lac Monroe (Diable) and Lac Provost (Pimbina).

MONTRÉAL TO QUÉBEC CITY

There's so much charm packed into the idyllic stretch of pastoral patchwork between Québec's two metropolises that it's bursting at the borders. Kick back and stay awhile to enjoy the picture-postcard scenery of the Eastern Townships and take in the unique bilingual atmosphere that constant American tourist traffic to this area has fostered. Alternatively, the Mauricie region – from Trois-Rivières north to Lac St-Jean and following the flow of the mighty Rivière St-Maurice – has been known to enchant unsuspecting visitors in search of wild, unadulterated natural beauty.

The Trans-Canada Hwy (Hwy 20) cuts a straight path to Québec City from Montréal. The Eastern Townships are nestled between here and the Vermont border, mainly along Hwy 10; Mauricie falls to the north of Hwy 20 along Hwy 40.

Eastern Townships

Lush rolling hills, crystal-clear blue lakes and checkerboard farms fill the Eastern Townships, or the 'Cantons-des-l'Est' as it's known by French-speaking inhabitants. The region begins 80km southeast of Montréal, south of Hwy 20, and finds itself squished in between the labyrinth of minor highways that stretch all the way to the Vermont and New Hampshire borders. New Englanders will feel right at home; covered bridges and round barns dot the bumpy landscape, which is sculpted by the tail end of the US Appalachian mountain range.

A visit during spring is rewarding, as it's the season for 'sugaring off' – the tapping, boiling and preparation of maple syrup. Summer brings fishing and swimming in the numerous lakes; in fall the foliage puts on a show of kaleidoscopic colors, to be toasted with freshly brewed apple cider, which is served in local pubs. The district is also home to a fast-growing wine region that produces some respectable whites and an excellent ice wine – a dessert wine made from frozen grapes. Cycling is extremely popular in the warmer months, with nearly 500km of trails taking in sumptuous landscapes. Winter means excellent downhill skiing at the three main ski hills: Bromont, Mont Orford and Sutton.

Originally the territory of the Abenaki people, the townships were settled in the aftermath of the 1776 American Revolution by New England Loyalists seeking to remain under the British crown. They were joined by successive waves of immigrants from Ireland and Scotland as well as French Canadians, who today make up the vast majority of residents.

ⓘ Information

Eastern Townships Tourism Association (www.cantonsdelest.com; Hwy 10 exit 68) At the turnoff for Granby/Bromont. There's another one at exit 115, the turnoff for Memphrémagog.

ⓘ Getting There & Away

BUS

Limocar operates bus services between Montréal's Station Centrale de l'Autobus and Magog ($44, 1½ hours) and Sherbrooke ($40, 2½ hours) up to 15 times daily. Two of these buses also stop in Granby ($25, one to 1½ hours), while Bromont is served twice daily ($28, 2¼ hours).

Orléans Express goes to Trois-Rivières ($35, two hours, eight daily) in the Mauricie region.

Autobus Viens operates three daily bus services between Montréal's central bus station and the townships of Sutton ($18, two hours) and Lac Brome ($19, 2¼ hours).

CAR

Coming from Montréal, Hwy 10 will take you straight to the Eastern Townships to just east of Sherbrooke, where it continues as Rte 112. Coming from Québec City via Hwy 20, the fastest route is via Hwy 55, which you pick up near Drummondville.

The ride-share organization **Allô Stop** (☏888-985-3032; allostop.com; 1221 Rue King Ouest) has a branch in Sherbrooke, or you can reserve online with **Kangaride** (p229). Trips usually cost $10 to $15, plus agency fees, from Sherbrooke to Montréal and/or Québec City.

Bromont

This town revolves around **Ski Bromont** (www.skibromont.com; 150 Rue Champlain; full/half day $55/47), a year-round resort on the slopes of 533m-high Mt Brome. In summer its 100km of marked trails, including 15 thrilling downhill routes, have made it a Mecca for mountain-bike aficionados (Bromont has hosted world championships). In winter, skiers and snowboarders take over the 104 trails, including 50 trails open for night skiing.

On weekends from April to October, Bromont's other major attraction is its giant **flea market** (16 Rue Lafontaine; ⊙9am-5pm Sat & Sun; FREE), just off Hwy 10, with more than 1000 vendors attracting thrifty treasure-hunters from near and far.

Limocar buses stop at Dépanneur Shefford, 624 Rue Shefford.

Montréal to Québec City & Around

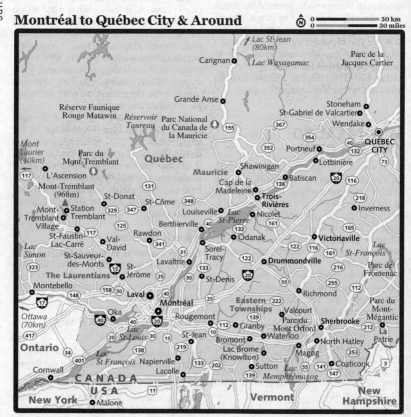

Lac Brome (Knowlton)

Lac Brome is the name of seven amalgamated towns orbiting the eponymous lake, with Knowlton on the southern shore being the largest and most attractive. Although there is evidence of early habitation by Abenaki peoples, the area was first formally settled by Loyalists in 1802 and the town still retains an upmarket British flair and numerous 19th-century buildings. A stroll around its cute downtown, which teems with quality boutiques, art galleries, cafes and restaurants, is a fun way to spend an hour or two. Pick up a free walking tour pamphlet from the Auberge Knowlton, which has been in business since 1849 – making it the oldest continuously operating inn in the Eastern Townships.

For more local history, drop in to the **Musée Historique du Comté de Brome** (130 Rue Lakeside; adult/child \$5/2.50; ⊙10am-4:30pm Mon-Sat, 11am-4:30pm Sun May-Sep), where exhibits include a recreated general store and courthouse (Sunday only) and, incongruously, a WWI Fokker D-VII plane.

Auberge Knowlton (☑450-242-6886; www.aubergeknowlton.ca; 286 Chemin Knowlton; d incl breakfast \$142; 🛜), in a landmark Victorian building, has been in business since 1849 but has come a long way since the stagecoach days. Antique-style furniture meets modern amenities in the country-themed, spacious rooms. Breakfast is à la carte.

Le Relais (286 Chemin Knowlton; lunch mains \$9-20, dinner mains \$14-25), at Auberge Knowlton, is a great place to try the juicy Brome duck paired with a glass of local wine. In summer, the tables on the upstairs terrace are much in demand. Guests of Auberge Knowlton get a 10% discount here.

Lac Brome is famous for its ducks, which have been bred here since 1912 on a special diet that includes soy and vitamins. Pick up pâté and other products at the **Brome Lake Duck Farm** (www.canardsdulacbrome.com; 40 Chemin Centre; ⊙8am-5pm Mon-Fri, 9:30am-5pm Sat & Sun). There's a second branch in Montréal.

There is a **tourist office** (255C Chemin Knowlton; ⊙Jun-Aug) at exit 68 on Hwy 10.

To get to Lac Brome from Hwy 10, take Rte 243 south. Autobus Viens stops at Dépanneur Rouge, 483 Rue Knowlton.

KIDS LOVE GRANBY

You'll score big with your kids if you take them to the **Granby Zoo** (☑450-372-9113; www.zoodegranby.com; 525 Rue St-Hubert; adult/child \$35/23; ⊙10am-5pm daily Jun, to 7pm Jul & Aug, 10am-5pm Sat & Sun Sep & Oct). The tigers, kangaroos, elephants and some 170 other species of finned, feathered and furry friends rarely fail to enthrall the little ones. Tickets include admission to the **Parc Aquatique Amazoo**, a small water park with a churning wave pool and rides. Take exit 68 off Hwy 10.

Sutton

Sutton is a little Loyalist town with a pretty main street where you can shop to your heart's content or let your hair down during après-ski partying in the many bars.

Sutton is surrounded by the Sutton Mountains, a string of velvety, round hills whose highest peak (Sommet Rond) rises to 968m. Not surprisingly, this makes Sutton a major winter sports hub, with much of the action centered on **Mont Sutton** (www.montsutton.com; 671 Chemin Maple; day tickets adult/child \$64/36; ⊙9am-4pm). There are 60 trails for plunging down the mountain; the longest run is 2.85km.

In summer, Sutton is prime hiking territory, especially in the conservation area **Parc d'Environnement Naturel de Sutton** (☑450-538-4085; www.parcsutton.com; adult/child \$5/3; ⊙Jun-Oct), where 80km of trails have been carved through the thickly forested mountains. Backpackers can unfold their tents at three primitive campgrounds (the one at Lac Spruce is the nicest).

Inside a perfectly restored heritage building, **Le Pleasant Hôtel & Café** (☑888-538-6188, 450-538-6188; www.lepleasant.com; 1 Rue Pleasant; r \$150-250; @) is a luxurious inn and a great place for a weekend escape or romantic interlude. Some of the sleek and modern rooms have views of Mont Sutton, and the breakfasts are memorable. The restaurant serves Mediterranean-influenced dinners (mains \$18 to \$26).

There is a small **tourist office** (www.sutton.ca; 11b Rue Principale Sud; ⊙9am-5pm).

Sutton is 18km south of Knowlton via Rtes 104 and 215. Autobus Viens stops at the Esso gas station, 28 Rue Principale.

LOCAL KNOWLEDGE

MAPLE SYRUP & THE SUGAR SHACK

Maple syrup is Canada's most famous export, with three-quarters of the world's total output hailing from Québec. It was Aboriginal tribes who taught Europeans how to make the sweet nectar, and by the 19th century cultivating the sap and transforming it into syrup had quickly become a local tradition.

Every summer, starches accumulate in sugar maple trees, which are native to North America. When the mercury dips below zero, they turn into sucrose. To tap the sugar inside the tree, inventive types have come up with a system that sucks out the sap through a series of tubes, which snake through the maple grove to machines that cook the juice into syrup. The different grades are based on how long the syrup is cooked and to what temperature (taffy, for example, is cooked to 26°C above boiling point).

Sugar shacks became part of the Québecois experience in the early 20th century and remain the best places to experience the maple tradition. The 'taffy pull' is the most fun: steaming syrup from a piping cauldron is poured onto some snow on a plate. The syrup hardens as it hits the snow and can then be twisted onto a Popsicle stick. Eat and repeat!

Sugar shacks are only open for a month or so, in February and March. Tourist information offices can offer recommendations.

Valcourt

Valcourt would be a mere blip on the radar were it not for local resident Joseph Armand Bombardier, the father of the Ski-Doo (snowmobile), whose invention is a great source of pride to Canadians. At the **Musée J Armand Bombardier** (www.bombardiermuseum.com; 1001 Ave J-A Bombardier; adult/child $7/ free; ⊙ 10am-5pm daily May-Aug, Tue-Sun Sep-Apr), you can see early models of his Ski-Doo (and amusing historic clips of how they looked in action), the original workshop, and a collection of contemporary and vintage snowmobiles. Tours of the plant, which also churns out ATVs and Sea-Doos, are offered as well (for an additional $12/5).

To get to Valcourt, take exit 90 off Hwy 10, then follow Rte 243. There are no buses.

Magog

Magog occupies a prime spot on the north shore of Lac Memphrémagog, a banana-shape lake that stretches south for 44km, all the way across the US border. It's the biggest township, with a pretty main street and plenty of decent restaurants and hotels.

◉ Sights & Activities

There's a **beach** in Magog, but in summer carving out space for your towel can be a tall order. The rest of the shore is largely in private hands, so the lake is best explored from the water. **Club de Voile** (☑ 819-847-3181; www.voilememphremagog.com; Plage des Cantons) is among several outfitters renting kayaks, sailboats and windsurfing equipment, while **Croisières Escapades Memphrémagog** (☑ 819-843-7000; www.escapadesmemphremagog.com; adult $37-72, child $15-62; ⊙ May-Oct) offers 1¾-hour, 2½-hour and seven-hour narrated cruises (most with meals included). Watch for Memphré, the feisty yet elusive creature that lives, Nessie-style, at the bottom of the lake.

About 12km south of Magog, on the western lakeshore, is the **Abbaye St-Benoît-du-Lac** (☑ 819-843-4080; www.st-benoit-du-lac.com; admission free; ⊙ church 5am-8:30pm, gift shop 9am-6pm Mon-Sat), home to about 50 Benedictine monks. The complex is a striking blend of traditional and modern architecture, including a hallway awash in colorful tiles and a lofty church with exposed structural beams and brick walls. If you can, visit at 7:30am, 11am or 5pm, when the monks practice Gregorian chanting. Music CDs, cheeses and apple cider are among the products for sale in the gift shop.

🛌 Sleeping & Eating

À L'Ancestrale B&B　　　　　　　B&B $$
(☑ 819-847-5555; www.ancestrale.com; 200 Rue Abbott; r incl breakfast $88-160; @ 🛜) Wake up to a five-course gourmet breakfast at this intimate retreat, whose four rooms are dressed in a romantic, countrified way and outfitted with refrigerators and coffee makers. It's central but on a quiet street.

Ô Bois Dormant
B&B $$

(☑ 888-843-0450, 819-843-0450; www.oboisdormant.qc.ca; 205 Rue Abbott; r incl breakfast $95-145; ✹ @ ☎ ⊠) Although only a short walk from the main street, the rambling back lawn at this towering Victorian feels like a secluded resort. Rooms are cozy and bright.

Fondissimo
FRENCH $$

(☑ 819-843-8999; www.fondissimo.ca; 276 Rue Principale Est; mains $22-25; ⊘ 5-11pm) With a name like Fondissimo, it's not hard to guess the specialty of this hip restaurant in an old renovated factory – there are eight varieties of Swiss fondue alone. Chinese fondue – meat, veggies and seafood, and a piping hot vat of oil in which to cook it yourself – is also a popular choice.

Bistro Lady of the Lake
MEDITERRANEAN $$$

(www.bistrolady.com; 125 Plage des Cantons; mains $21-35; ⊘ 4-10pm Thu-Sun) This popular eatery, its success enhanced by its great lakeside setting, serves Mediterranean with a twist. Dishes get daring, with interesting combinations such as dill, almonds and fresh trout, and the wine list is decent.

❶ Information

CLSC Health Clinic (☑ 819-843-2572; 50 Rue St-Patrice Est)

La Petite Place (108 Place du Commerce; per hr $6; ⊘ 8:30am-5pm Mon-Fri, to 2pm Sat) Internet access; tucked into the basement, in the back of the parking lot.

Tourist Office (www.tourisme-memphremagog.com; 2911 Rue Milletta; ⊘ 9am-5pm, to 7pm late-Jun–Aug) Off Rte 115.

❶ Getting There & Away

Limocar buses stop at 768 Rue Sherbrooke.

Parc du Mont Orford

Parc du Mont Orford (3321 Chemin du Parc; adult/child $6.50/3), home to snapping turtles and countless bird species, is fairly compact and often gets busy. Fitness fanatics can hike the park's two mountains, **Mont Chauve** (600m) and **Mont Orford** (853m), while water babies have three lakes in which to play. The biggest is Lac Stukely, which has a beach, camping and boat rentals.

Winter activities include snowshoeing and cross-country skiing in the park, as well as downhill skiing at the **Station de Ski Mont-Orford** (www.orford.com; lift tickets adult/child $57/35; ⊘ 9am-4pm). It has a vertical drop of 589m and 62 slopes, mostly for be-

ginners and intermediate skiers, plus a snow park with a half pipe and other fun features.

Just outside the park boundaries, the **Centre d'Arts Orford** (Orford Arts Center; www.arts-orford.org; 3165 Chemin du Parc; tickets free-$52) hosts the **Festival Orford**, a prestigious series of 40 to 50 classical concerts, held from late June to mid-August.

The woodsy grounds are home to the **Auberge du Centre d'Arts Orford** (☑ 819-843-3981; 3165 Chemin du Parc; r incl breakfast $68-78), offering basic but modern and comfortable rooms.

The park is about a 10-minute drive north of Magog.

North Hatley

North Hatley wins top honors as the cutest of all the cute Eastern Townships. It occupies an enchanting spot at the northern tip of the crystal-clear (and monsterless) Lac Massawippi, about 17km east of Magog.

Wealthy Americans have always loved it here: they started building their stately vacation homes as early as 1880. A Yankee influence still makes itself felt (there are as many cow paintings and scented candles here as anywhere in New England!), and there's even a 'Main St' (well, technically 'Rue Main'). Many of the fancy homes have been converted into B&Bs, inns or gourmet restaurants, including the ultradeluxe Manoir Hovey.

A great way to explore the delightful terrain surrounding North Hatley is on horseback with **Randonées Jacques Robidas** (www.equitationjacquesrobidas.com; 32 Chemin McFarland; riding from $67, overnight packages from $135). There are two newish chalets on site for multiday packages.

★**Manoir Hovey** (☑ 819-842-2421; www.manoirhovey.com; 575 Chemin Hovey; r incl breakfast & 3-course dinner per person $95-325; ✹ @ ☎ ⊠) is the area's premier resort, with a dining room that emphasizes refined Québecois fare prepared from fresh local ingredients (a tasting menu is $70 for nonguests). Lucky overnight guests can run wild in the expansive gardens, which are lined with beautiful wildflowers and overlook the lake, or take refuge in sumptuous bedrooms hidden within the massive country house. There's a heated pool, an ice rink (in winter), tennis courts and a jovial pub on site, and a whole slew of outdoor activities, such as windsurfing, kayaking, golfing and fishing, can be arranged.

Pilsen (www.pilsen.ca; 55 Rue Main; mains $12-27; ⊙11:30am-3am) is the liveliest restaurant in town, famous for its salmon, both grilled and smoked, and upmarket pub fare, like grilled flank steak. There's a nice riverside terrace and another facing the lake.

There is a small information center, free internet access and great coffee at **Café North Hatley** (90 Rue Main; ⊙9am-5pm; 🛜).

North Hatley is east of Magog along Rte 108. Coming from Sherbrooke, take Rte 243 to Rte 108. There is no bus service.

Sherbrooke

This bustling city is perfect for refueling on modern conveniences before returning to the Eastern Townships. The historic center sits at the confluence of two rivers and is bisected by Rue Wellington and Rue King, the main commercial arteries. Stick to this area, 'Vieux Sherbrooke,' where the smattering of decent restaurants and cafes stands defiant against the blight of overdevelopment in other parts of the city. Sherbrooke lies along Hwy 10, about 25km northeast of Magog.

⊙ Sights

Bishop's University   HISTORIC BUILDING
(Rue du Collège; ⊙chapel 8:30am-5pm) `FREE`
If you're interested in scholarly pursuits, head 5km south (or catch bus 2 or 11) to Lennoxville to see the Anglican Bishop's University, founded in 1843 and modeled after Oxford and Cambridge in England. The campus's architectural highlight is **St Mark's Chapel**, richly decorated with carved pews and stained-glass windows.

La Société d'Histoire de Sherbrooke   MUSEUM
(☑819-821-5406; 275 Rue Dufferin; adult/child $6/2; ⊙9am-5pm Tue-Fri, 10am-5pm Sat & Sun) This center offers an engaging introduction to the town's history and rents out MP3 players for self-guided city tours on foot or by car ($10).

Cathédrale St-Michel   CATHEDRAL
(130 Rue de la Cathédrale; ⊙9am-noon & 2-4pm) Quietly overlooking the action from its hilltop perch is the Cathédrale St-Michel, a monumental granite edifice.

Musée des Beaux-Arts   MUSEUM
(www.mbas.qc.ca; 241 Rue Dufferin; adult/student $10/7; ⊙noon-5pm) This museum has a good

permanent collection featuring works by regional artists; it also stages temporary exhibitions.

Lac des Nations   LAKE
South of all the sights, Rivière Magog flows into the pretty Lac des Nations, which is surrounded by a scenic paved trail perfect for walking, in-line skating and cycling (rentals available).

❶ Information

Banque Nationale (3075 Blvd Portland; ⊙10am-3pm Mon & Tue, to 5pm Wed, to 8pm Thu, to 4pm Fri)

Brûlerie de Café (180 Rue Wellington Nord; ⊙7:30am-11pm Mon-Fri, 9am-11pm Sat & Sun) Free internet access.

Hospital Hôtel-Dieu (☑819-346-1110; 580 Rue Bowen Sud; ⊙24hr)

Tourist Office (www.tourismesherbrooke. com; 785 Rue King Ouest; ⊙9am-6pm Mon-Fri, 10am-5pm Sat & Sun)

ZAP Sherbrooke (www.zapsherbrooke.org) For a list of free wi-fi zones in Sherbrooke.

❶ Getting There & Away

The Limocar bus terminal is at 80 Rue du Depôt.

Parc du Mont-Mégantic

At the heart of a scenic and delightfully un-crowded area, the **Parc du Mont-Mégantic** (189 Rte du Parc; adult/child $6.50/3; ⊙9am-11pm daily Jun-Aug, to 5pm Sat & Sun Sep-May) holds mega-size appeal for wilderness fans and stargazers. Encounters with moose, white-tailed deer, coyote and other wildlife are pretty much guaranteed as you roam the trails of this park.

The park's **AstroLab** (☑800-665-6527, 819-888-2941; www.astrolab-parc-national-mont-meg-antic.org; adult/child $19/9.50, summit tour adult/child $22.25/12; ⊙noon-11pm daily Jul & Aug, noon-5pm & 8-11pm Sat, noon-5pm Sun May, Jun, Sep & Oct) is an astronomy research center that explains space through interactive exhibits and a multimedia show. A highlight is a tour of the observatory at the summit. Reservations are required.

The park is approximately 60km east of Sherbrooke along Rtes 108 and 212. There is no bus service.

Mauricie

Mauricie is one of Québec's lesser-known regions, despite being in a strategic spot halfway between Montréal and Québec City. Stretching 300km from Trois-Rivières north to Lac St-Jean, it follows the flow of the mighty Rivière St-Maurice, which for centuries has been the backbone of the area's industrial heritage. Logs were being driven down the river to the pulp and paper mills until as recently as 1996. Centuries earlier, the region had given birth to the country's iron industry, the original forge is now a national historic site. Industry still dominates the lower region, but things get considerably more scenic after the river reaches the Parc National du Canada de la Mauricie.

Trois-Rivières

Founded in 1634, Trois-Rivières is North America's second-oldest city north of Mexico, but you'd never know it: a roaring fire that swept through in 1908 left little of the city's historic looks. Still, the city center, right on the north shore of the St Lawrence River, is not without charms and some bona fide tourist attractions.

The name, by the way, is a misnomer as there are only two, not three, streams here. There are, however, three branches of the St Maurice River at its mouth, where islands split its flow into three channels.

⊙ Sights

Rue Notre Dame and Rue des Forges, the main arteries in Trois-Rivières' compact downtown, are lined with cafes and bars. A riverfront promenade leads to the oldest section of town along Rue des Ursulines.

En Prison   MUSEUM
(In Prison; ☑819-372-0406; www.enprison.com; 200 Rue Laviolette; adult/child \$12/7; ☺10am-6pm) Ex-cons bring the harsh realities of the lockup vividly to life during 90-minute tours that include a stop at dank underground cells known as 'the pit.' English tours run between 11am and 3:15pm from late June to the end of August – and by reservation the rest of the year. The prison exhibit is connected to adjacent **Musée Québécois de Culture Populaire** (☑819-372-0406; www.culturepop. qc.ca; adult/child \$12/7, incl En Prison \$19/10.50; ☺10am-6pm), with its renowned regional

folk art collection and changing exhibitions, which often have a quirky pop-culture bent.

Musée des Ursulines   MUSEUM
(www.museedesursulines.com; 734 Rue des Ursulines; adult/child \$4/free; ☺10am-5pm Tue-Sun) For a slice of the town's religious history, stop at this former hospital founded by Ursuline nuns in 1639. It forms a pretty backdrop for the fine collection of textiles, ceramics, books and prints related to religion that are on display. Beautiful frescoes adorn the chapel.

Cathédrale de l'Assomption   CATHEDRAL
(☑819-374-2409; 362 Rue Bonaventure; ☺9-11:30am & 1:30-5:30pm) Church fans should make a beeline to this colossal cathedral, a soaring neo-Gothic confection with exquisite sculpture and 125 intricate Florentine stained-glass windows by Guido Nincheri.

Sanctuaire Notre-Dame-du-Cap   CHURCH
(626 Rue Notre Dame; ☺8:30am-8pm) In nearby Cap de la Madeleine (take bus 2), about 4km northeast of the center, the grand Sanctuaire Notre-Dame-du-Cap looks like a spaceship sitting on a launch pad. Up to 1660 worshippers can congregate underneath the dome while being serenaded by a giant Casavant organ. A Marian shrine with a miracle-performing statue draws believers all year round.

Les Forges-du-St-Maurice   MUSEUM
(www.pc.gc.ca; 10000 Blvd des Forges; adult/child \$4/2; ☺10am-5pm) About 7km northwest of the center (take bus 4), Les Forges-du-St-Maurice is a national historic site preserving the 18th-century birthplace of the Canadian iron industry. Costumed guides take you around the grounds and into the blast furnace, while a sound-and-light show reveals the daily operations of Canada's first ironworks.

🛏 Sleeping & Eating

Le Gîte Loiselle   B&B \$\$
(☑819-375-2121; www.giteloiselle.com; 836 Rue des Ursulines; r \$79-115; ❋@☎) Local artwork, magnificent woodwork, tasteful antiques, and warm hosts Lisette and Mario greet you at this Victorian redbrick. Basic rooms with private toilets and a shared shower put you right in the center of the historic quarter and one block from the river. Breakfast is an ample and varied kick-start to the day.

Café Morgane
CAFE $

(100 Rue des Forges; dishes $3-7; ⊙8am-9pm; 🛜)
On most afternoons, this is the busiest spot in Trois-Rivières. Espresso, herbal teas and decadent sweets infuse the airy space with delightful smells. There's a free wi-fi connection here.

Restaurant Le Grill
STEAKHOUSE $$

(350 Rue des Forges; mains $13-32; ⊙11:30am-10pm Mon-Fri, 5-11pm Sat & Sun) Locals flock to this trendy steakhouse on the main strip in droves for the filet mignon and happening night scene. The streetside patio puts you right in the middle of all the action.

❶ Information

Hôpital St-Joseph (☑819-697-3333; 731 Rue Ste-Julie)
Main Post Office (cnr Rue des Casernes & Rue des Ursulines)
Tourist Office (www.tourismetroisrivieres.com; 1457 Rue Notre Dame; ⊙9am-7pm)

❶ Getting There & Away

Trois-Rivières lies about 150km northeast of Montréal and 130km southwest of Québec City and is easily accessible via Hwys 40 and 20 or Rtes 138 and 132.

The **bus station** (☑819-374-2944; 275 Rue St-Georges) is behind the Hôtel Delta. Orléans Express runs to Montréal ($34, 2½ hours, eight daily) and Québec City ($34, 2½ hours, five daily).

Shawinigan

There would be little reason to stop in Shawinigan were it not for the unique **Cité de l'Énergie** (City of Energy; www.citedelenergie.com; 1000 Ave Melville; adult/child $18/11, tours $12; ⊙10am-6pm daily Jun-Aug, to 5pm Tue-Sun Sep). Built around a 1901 hydroelectric power station and the country's oldest aluminum smelter, the 'City of Energy' celebrates the region's industrial legacy with lots of different exhibits and experiences. Learn about turbines, electrochemistry, aluminum and pulp and papermaking in a multimedia show and exhibits. Race along a 'walk-through comic book' with scientists as they try to save the environment by switching to non-polluting hydrogen. There are river and trolleybus cruises, a 115m-high observation tower and the nightly **multimedia show** (adult/child $55/25; ⊙Jul & Aug) featuring musicians, dancers and acrobats. Throughout the summer, the National Gallery of Canada moves into the aluminum smelter with different world-class temporary exhibitions. Most labeling is in English and French, but the tours are in French only. Last admissions are 2½ hours before closing.

Shawinigan is about 40km north of Trois-Rivières via Hwy 55. Orléans Express runs two buses daily from Trois-Rivières ($15, 50 minutes).

Parc National du Canada de la Mauricie

Moose foraging by an idyllic lake, the plaintive cry of a loon gliding across the water, bear cubs romping beneath a potpourri of birch, poplar, maple and other trees waiting to put on a spectacular show of color in the fall – these are scenes you might possibly stumble across while visiting **La Mauricie National Park** (☑888-773-8888, 819-538-3232; www.pc.gc.ca/mauricie; adult/child $7.80/3.90). What may well be Québec's best-run and best-organized park is also among its most frequented. The arresting beauty of the nature here, whether seen from a canoe or a walking trail, is everyone's eye candy, but particularly suits those who don't want to feel completely disconnected from 'civilization.'

The park covers 550 sq km, straddling northern evergreen forests and the more southerly hardwoods of the St Lawrence River Valley. The low, rounded Laurentian Mountains, which are among the world's oldest, are part of the Canadian Shield, which covers much of the province. Between these hills lie innumerable small lakes and valleys. The Canadian government created the park in 1970 to protect some of the forest that the paper industry was steadily chewing up and spitting out. At one point, two sawmills were operating in the park's current territory. But that's all in the past now.

The main entrance is at St-Jean-des-Piles (Hwy 55, exit 226), but there's another at St-Mathieu (Hwy 55, exit 217). Both are well indicated and double as **information centers** (⊙7am-9:30pm May-Oct). They are connected by the 63km-long Rte Promenade, which runs through the park. Both centers are closed from late October until early May.

🏃 Activities

The numerous **walking trails**, which can take anywhere from half an hour to five days to complete, offer glimpses of the indigenous flora and fauna, brooks and waterfalls (the **Chutes Waber** in the park's western sector are particularly worth the hike), as well as panoramic views onto delicate valleys, lakes and streams.

The longest trail, **Le Sentier Laurentien**, stretches over 75km of rugged wilderness in the park's northern reaches. Backcountry campsites are spaced out every 7km to 10km. No more than 40 people are allowed on the trail at any time, making reservations essential. There's a fee of $46 and you must arrange for your own transport to cover the 30km from the trail's end back to Rte Promenade. Topographic maps are for sale at the park.

The park is excellent for **canoeing**. Five canoe routes, ranging in length from 14km to 84km, can accommodate everyone from beginners to experts. Canoe and kayak rentals ($14/40 per hour/day) are available at three sites, the most popular being **Lac Wapizagonke**, which has sandy beaches, steep rocky cliffs and waterfalls. One popular day trip has you canoeing from the Wapizagonke campground to the west end of the lake, followed by a 7.5km loop hike to the Chutes Waber and back by canoe.

The most popular winter activity is **cross-country skiing** (adult/child $9.80/4.90), with some 85km of groomed trails.

🛏 Sleeping & Eating

Camping at designated sites costs $25.50 without electricity and $29 with it; camping in the wild during canoe trips costs $15 without firewood, or $25 with firewood.

You can also sleep in four- to 10-person dorms in one of two **outdoor lodges** (☑819-537-4555; www.info-nature.ca; per person $29-35). They are 3.5km from the nearest parking lots, so you must come in by foot, bike, canoe or ski.

Ideal for families, couples, and groups (up to five people), part-cabin, part-tent **oTEN-Tiks** (☑519-826-5391; cabins $120) put you in a good spot in the Rivière-à-la-Pêche section in the east end of the park. Each one has a wood stove and dishes; you bring the linens, food, and drinks.

There are no restaurants in the park, so the best thing is to stock up on supplies in Trois-Rivières or Shawinigan before heading north.

QUÉBEC CITY

POP 167,000

Québec, North America's only walled city north of Mexico City, is the kind of place that crops up in trivia questions. Over the centuries, the lanes and squares of the Old Town – a World Heritage site – have seen the continent's first parish church, first museum, first stone church, first Anglican cathedral, first girls' school, first business district and first French-language university. Most of these institutions remain in some form. The historical superlatives are inescapable: flick through the *Québec Chronicle-Telegraph* and you're reading North America's oldest newspaper; if you have to visit L'Hôtel-Dieu de Québec, console yourself with the thought that it's the continent's oldest hospital.

Once past Le Château Frontenac, the most photographed hotel in the world, you'll find yourself torn between the various neighborhoods' diverse charms. In Old Upper Town, the historical hub, many excellent museums and restaurants hide among the tacky fleur-de-lis T-shirt stores. Old Lower Town, at the base of the steep cliffs, is a labyrinth, where it's a pleasure to get lost among street performers and cozy inns before emerging on the north shore of the St Lawrence. Leaving the walled town near the star-shaped Citadelle, hip St-Jean-Baptiste is one of the less historical but still interesting areas, and the epicenter of a vibrant nightlife.

History

A Huron village, 'Stadacona' – the *kanata* (settlement) referred to in Canada's name – stood on the site of Québec City when French explorer Jacques Cartier landed in 1535, on his second voyage to the New World. He returned in 1541 to establish a permanent post, but the plan failed, setting back France's colonial ambitions for 50 years. Explorer Samuel de Champlain finally founded the city for the French in 1608, calling it Kebec, from the Algonquian word meaning 'the river narrows here.' It was the first North American city to be founded as a permanent settlement, rather than a trading post.

The English successfully attacked in 1629, but Québec was returned to the French under a treaty three years later and became the center of New France. Repeated English attacks followed. In 1759, General Wolfe led the British to victory over Montcalm on the Plains of Abraham. One of North America's most famous battles, it virtually ended the long-running conflict between Britain and France. In 1763, the Treaty of Paris gave

Canada to Britain. In 1775, the American revolutionaries tried to capture Québec but were promptly pushed back. In 1864, meetings were held here that led to the formation of Canada in 1867. Québec became the provincial capital.

In the 19th century, the city lost its status and importance to Montréal. When the Great Depression burst Montréal's bubble in 1929, Québec regained some stature as a government center. Some business-savvy locals launched the now-famous Winter Carnival in the 1950s to incite a tourism boom. Obviously, it's still working.

In 2001, the city was the site of the Summit of the Americas, which exploded into mass demonstrations against globalization. In 2008, the city marked the 400th anniversary of Québec's founding.

 Sights

Part of the city sits atop the cliffs of Cap Diamant (Cape Diamond), and part lies below. Québec City is thus divided into Haute Ville (Upper Town) and Basse Ville (Lower Town), each with old and new sections. The Citadelle, a fort and landmark, stands proudly on the highest point of Cap Diamant. Together, the historic upper and lower areas form the appealing Vieux Québec (Old Town), which spreads over a 10-sq-km area within the stone walls.

The two main streets heading southwest from Old Upper Town are Blvd René-Lévesque and, to the south, Grande Allée, which eventually becomes Blvd Wilfrid Laurier. If you're driving to Old Upper Town, arrange parking through your hotel, or find a spot outside the walls to avoid steep prices.

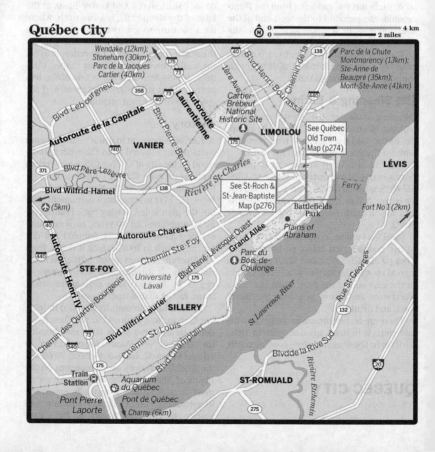

Québec City

Old Upper Town

Fortifications of Québec HISTORIC SITE
(www.pc.gc.ca/eng/lhn-nhs/qc/fortifications; Rue d'Auteuil, near Rue St-Louis; guided walks adult/child $10/5; ⊘10am-6pm May-Oct, guided walks 10am & 2pm; ⊠3, 11) The largely restored old wall is a national historic site. You can walk the 4.6km circuit on top of it all around the Old Upper Town, with much of the city's history within easy view. At the old powder magazine beside Porte St-Louis, the **interpretive center** (Map p274; 100 Rue St-Louis; adult/child $4/2, walking tours adult/child $10/5; ⊘10am-6pm May-Oct) examines the city's defenses through displays, models and a short film. The center's enthusiastic guides run 90-minute **walking tours** from here and the Kiosk Frontenac.

Beside Porte St-Jean, another national historic site, the Parc d'Artillerie, housed French military headquarters, a British garrison and a munitions factory. The interpretive center includes an early-19th-century scale model of Québec City and a children's history lesson. In the summer there are costumed guides and musket-firing demonstrations.

The complex also includes a 19th-century officers' mess, a former powder magazine and **Les Dames de Soie** (Map p276; 2 Rue d'Auteuil; ⊘11am-5pm Mon-Sat) FREE. This *économusée* has a sizable doll population, including folk figures wearing costumes from different regions of Québec, a doll hospital and doll-making courses.

★**La Citadelle** FORT
(Map p274; ☎418-694-2815; www.lacitadelle.qc.ca; Côte de la Citadelle, Fort; adult/child $10/5.50; ⊘9am-5pm) The Citadelle is the base of Canada's Royal 22s (known in bastardized French as the Van Doos, from the French for 22, vingt-deux). Founded in WWI, the regiment earned three Victoria Crosses in that conflict and in WWII.

The changing of the guard ceremony takes place at 10am each day in the summer months. The beating of the retreat, which features soldiers banging on their drums at shift's end, happens at 7pm on Friday, Saturday and Sunday during July and August.

The dominating Citadelle is North America's largest fort, covering 2.3 sq km. Begun by the French in 1750 and completed by the British in 1850, it served as part of the defense system against an American invasion that never came.

QUÉBEC CITY'S TOP SIGHTS

➡ **Le Château Frontenac** (see below) The world's most photographed hotel.

➡ **Battlefields Park** (p278) Where England and France clashed.

➡ **Place Royale** (p276) The cradle of Nouvelle-France.

➡ **Fortifications** Almost 5km of walkable walls.

➡ **Lévis ferry** (p286) City and cliff views.

Admission to the site is by one-hour guided tour, which takes in the regimental museum, numerous historical sites and a cannon called Rachel. Tours depart regularly during the summer; from late October to early April, there's only one tour a day, at 1:30pm. A separate tour of the **Governor General's Residence** (⊘11am-4pm daily Jul & Aug, 10am-4pm Sat & Sun May, Jun, Sep & Oct) FREE is also available.

It's a small bit of Canadiana right in the heart of Québec.

Latin Quarter

Wedged into the northeast corner of the Old Upper Town, this area is classic Québec City, with dewy-eyed tourists drifting along narrow streets toward Le Château Frontenac.

★**Le Château Frontenac** HISTORIC BUILDING
(Map p274; 1 Rue des Carrières) Said to be the world's most photographed hotel, Le Château Frontenac was built in 1893 by the Canadian Pacific Railway (CPR) as part of its chain of luxury hotels. During WWII, Prime Minister MacKenzie King, Winston Churchill and Franklin Roosevelt planned D-Day here. Facing the hotel along Rue Mont-Carmel is **Jardin des Gouverneurs**, with a monument to both Wolfe and Montcalm.

Musée de l'Amérique Française MUSEUM
(Museum of French America; Map p274; ☎418-692-2843; www.mcq.org; 2 Côte de la Fabrique; adult/child $8/2; ⊘9:30am-5pm) Purported to be the country's oldest museum, this is the place to learn about North America's Francophone diaspora, including the Québecois in the surrounding city, the '*petits* Canadas' (waves of French-speaking immigrants that headed south in the late 19th century) in New England and the Métis in western Canada and the American Mid-

Québec Old Town

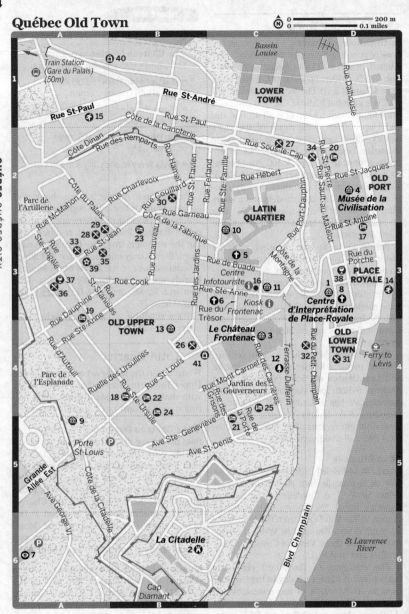

0 — **200 m**
0 — **0.1 miles**

Train Station
(Gare du Palais)
(50m)

Bassin Louise

LOWER TOWN

Rue St-André

Rue St-Paul

Rue St-Paul

Côte de la Canoterie

Côte Dinan

Rue des Remparts

Rue Sous-le-Cap

Côte du Palais

Rue Charlevoix

Rue Hamel

Rue St-Flavien

Rue Ferland

Rue Ste-Famille

Rue Hébert

Rue St-Pierre

Rue Sault-au-Matelot

Rue St-Jacques

OLD PORT

Parc de l'Artillerie

Rue McMahon

Rue Couillard

Rue Garneau

Musée de la Civilisation

Rue St-Antoine

Rue Ste-Angèle

Rue St-Jean

Côte de la Fabrique

LATIN QUARTIER

Côte de la Montagne

Rue du Porche

PLACE ROYALE

Rue Chauveau

Rue de Buade

Centre Infotouriste

Rue Cook

Rue des Jardins

Rue Ste-Anne

Centre d'Interprétation de Place-Royale

Rue Dauphine

Rue St-Stanislas

Rue Ste-Anne

OLD UPPER TOWN

Rue du Trésor

Kiosk Frontenac

Rue d'Auteuil

Le Château Frontenac

Terrasse Dufferin

Rue du Petit-Champlain

OLD LOWER TOWN

Ferry to Lévis

Parc de l'Esplanade

Ruelle des Ursulines

Rue St-Louis

Rue Ste-Ursule

Rue Mont Carmel

Jardins des Gouverneurs

Rue des Grisons

Rue des Carrières

Porte St-Louis

Ave Ste-Geneviève

Rue de la Porte

Ave St-Denis

Grande Allée Est

Ave George VI

Côte de la Citadelle

Blvd Champlain

St Lawrence River

La Citadelle

Cap Diamant

---

west. As well as artifacts relating to French settlement in the New World, there are interactive changing displays. The museum occupies part of a 17th-century seminary, built by Monseigneur de Laval under the order of Louis XIV.

Basilica Notre-Dame-de-Québec CHURCH
(Map p274; ☑418-694-0665; 16 Rue de Buade; ⊘8:30am-6pm) This cathedral towers above the site of a chapel erected by Samuel de Champlain in 1633. It became one of the continent's first cathedrals in 1674, follow-

Québec Old Town

ing the appointment of the first bishop of Québec, Monseigneur de Laval, whose tomb is inside. Ever bigger replacements were constructed over the centuries, with the last being completed in 1925. The grandiose interior recreates the spirit of the 17th century.

Ursuline Convent & Museum   MUSEUM
(Map p274; www.museedesursulines.com; 12 Rue Donnacona; museum adult/child $8/free, chapel admission free; ⊗museum 10am-5pm Tue-Sun, chapel 10-11:30am Tue-Sat & 1-4:30pm Tue-Sun Apr-Oct) Founded in 1639, this convent is the oldest girls' school on the continent. The museum recounts the generally forgotten story of the Ursuline sisters, the first order of nuns to come to North America. They were cloistered until 1965; there are some 50 nuns today, with an average age of 78. One room houses intricate gold and silver embroidery. At the same address, the lovely **chapel** dates to 1902 but retains some interiors from 1723.

Cathedral of the Holy Trinity   CHURCH
(Map p274; ☑418-692-2193; 31 Rue des Jardins; ⊗10am-5pm) Built in 1804, the elegantly handsome Cathedral of the Holy Trinity, modeled on London's St Martin-in-the-Fields, was the first Anglican cathedral built outside the British Isles. The 47m-high bell tower competes with Basilica Notre-Dame for attention.

Musée du Fort   MUSEUM
(Map p274; ☑418-692-2175; www.museedufort. com; 10 Rue Ste-Anne; adult/child $8/free; ⊗English shows hourly 10am-5pm) It's a little hokey and overpriced, but this diorama provides an enjoyable, easy-to-grasp audio-visual survey of Québec City's battles and history. It has a 1200-sq-meter model of the city in 1750.

Terrasse Dufferin   PARK
(Map p274) Outside Le Château Frontenac along the riverfront, 425m-long Terrasse Dufferin is marvelous for a stroll, with dramatic views over the river, perched as it is

St-Roch & St-Jean-Baptiste

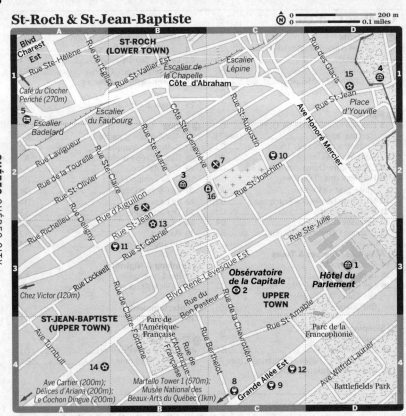

60m high on a cliff. It's peppered with quality street performers vying for attention.

Old Lower Town

From Upper Town, you can reach this must-see area in several ways. Walk down Côte de la Canoterie from Rue des Remparts to the Old Port, or edge down the charming and steep Côte de la Montagne. About halfway down on the right, a shortcut, the Break-Neck Stairs (Escalier Casse-Cou) leads down to Rue du Petit-Champlain. You can also take the **funicular** ($2 one-way) from Terrasse Dufferin.

Teeming **Rue du Petit-Champlain** is said to be, along with Rue Sous-le-Cap, the narrowest street in North America, and is the center of the continent's oldest business district. Look out for the murals decorating the 17th- and 18th-century buildings, which, along with numerous plaques, statues and

street performers, give this quarter its distinct, history-meets-holiday feel.

Place Royale, Old Lower Town's central, principal square, has had an eventful 402 years. When Samuel de Champlain founded Québec City, he settled this bit of shoreline first. In 1690 cannons placed here held off the attacks of the English naval commander Phips and his men. Today the name 'Place Royale' generally refers to the district.

Built around the old harbor, north of Place Royale, the **Vieux Port** (Old Port) is being redeveloped as a multipurpose waterfront area.

★ Musée de la Civilisation   MUSEUM
(Museum of Civilization; Map p274; ☎ 418-643-2158; www.mcq.org; 85 Rue Dalhousie; adult/child $15/5, admission free Tue Nov-May & 10am-noon Sat Jan & Feb; ☺ 9:30am-6:30pm) This museum offers a dozen exhibitions in its airy halls, including permanent shows on the culture of Québec's 11 Aboriginal peoples, and tells

St-Roch & St-Jean-Baptiste

the province's story from the French settlers to today's distinct society. Quirky displays, videos and interactive features bring the weighty subjects to life. The striking building incorporates some pre-existing structures; it shares an early-18th-century wall with Auberge Saint-Antoine.

Église Notre-Dame-des-Victoires CHURCH
(Our Lady of Victories Church; Map p274; ☑418-692-1650; 32 Rue Sous-le-Fort; ⊙9:30am-8:30pm Jul & Aug, to 5pm May & Jun) Our Lady of Victories Church is the oldest stone church in North America, built in 1688 and devastated by cannon fire in 1759. It stands on the spot where de Champlain set up his 'Habitation,' a small stockade. Inside are copies of works by Rubens and van Dyck. Hanging from the ceiling is a good-luck charm in the shape of a ship: a replica of the *Brézé*, in which the Carignan-Salières regiment sailed to New France in 1664 to fight the Iroquois.

The gold hearts above the altar date to 1855, when Mother Marcelle Mallet hung a heart there after taking a vow.

★ Centre d'Interprétation de Place-Royale MUSEUM
(Map p274; ☑418-646-3167; 27 Rue Notre-Dame; adult/child $7/2; ⊙9:30am-5pm) This interpretive center touts the area as the cradle of French history in North America with a series of good participatory displays. While here, pick up a brochure on Place Royale's 27 vaulted cellars (ancient stone basements), five of which can be visited for free, including the one right here, complete with costumed barrel-maker.

◉ Outside the Walls

Most visitors venture through Porte St-Louis to take a peek at Québec City's most significant attraction outside the walls: Battlefields Park, site of the famous Plains of Abraham. Unfortunately, most then scuttle back to the safety of that fairy-tale land inside the walls. Some of the sights here are certainly more interesting than taking yet another snap of the Château – notably Hôtel du Parlement and Obsérvatoire de la Capitale. The St-Jean-Baptiste and St-Roch areas, which offer a taste of everyday Québec, are a depressurization chamber after the onslaught of historical tourism in the Old Town.

★ Hôtel du Parlement HISTORIC BUILDING
(Parliament Building; Map p276; ☑418-643-7239; cnr Ave Honoré Mercier & Grande Allée Est; ⊙9am-4:30pm) FREE Just across from Porte St-Louis is the Parliament Building. The Second Empire structure, dating from 1886, houses the Provincial Legislature, known as the Assemblée Nationale. Its facade is decorated with 22 bronze statues of significant historical Québecois figures, made by much-loved Québecois sculptor Louis-Philippe Hébert. Admission (at door three) is by half-hour tour, available in French, English and Spanish.

★ Obsérvatoire de la Capitale NOTABLE BUILDING
(Capital Observatory; Map p276; ☑888-497-4322, 418-644-9841; 1037 Rue de la Chevrotière; adult/child $10/free; ⊙10am-5pm) The Capital Observatory offers great views from 221m up on the 31st floor over St-Jean-Baptiste's red and green roofs and across the city to the

TOP FIVE FREEBIES

➡ **Les Dames de Soie** (p273) Visit the doll hospital.

➡ **Musée de la Civilisation** (p276) Free on Tuesday and Saturday morning for part of the year.

➡ **Fou-Bar** (p285) Tuesday-night jazz.

➡ **Marché du Vieux-Port** (p285) Sample local farm fare.

➡ **Choco-Musée Érico** (opposite page) Anyone for chocolate?

Laurentians. Bone up on local history by reading the information panels.

Battlefields Park HISTORIC SITE

(Map p272) Though it looks like any urban North American park, this was once a bloody battleground where the course of Canadian history was determined. The part closest to the cliff is known as the **Plains of Abraham**, where the British finally defeated the French in 1759.

Within the park are diverse sites. The reception center at the **Discovery Pavilion** (Map p274; ☎ 418-648-4071; 835 Ave Wilfrid-Laurier; ☺ 8:30am-5:30pm) is a good place to start. It contains a tourist office and the **Canada Odyssey** (Map p274; adult/child $14/4; ☺ 10am-5pm), a 45-minute multimedia spectacle. After covering life before and after the battle, the odyssey concludes with an exhibition on the lot of the soldiers who fought in the battle and on the park itself, used in the 18th and 19th centuries for executions, pistol duels and prostitution. Admission includes a bus tour and entry to **Martello Tower 1** (☎ 418-648-4071; adult/child $14/4; ☺ 9:30am-5:30pm). One of four circular defense structures built by the British in the early 19th century, Martello Tower 1 was never used. Admission includes a bus tour and entry to the Canada Odyssey.

Musée National des Beaux-Arts du Québec MUSEUM

(☎ 866-220-2150, 418-643-2150; www.mnba.qc.ca; Battlefields Park; adult/child $18/free; ☺ 10am-6pm Thu-Tue, to 9pm Wed) Visit this sprawling museum in Battlefields Park to see the province's most important collections of Québécois art and Inuit sculptures, as well as international work. One gallery narrates the clash between academia and modern-

ism in Québec's salons between 1860 and 1945; another looks at artistic responses to the British government's Durham Report (1839), which dismissed French Canadians as having 'no history and no culture.' The holdings include the largest collection of works by Jean-Paul Riopelle, the most internationally renowned Québécois artist of the modern era.

St-Jean-Baptiste NEIGHBORHOOD

Strolling along **Rue St-Jean** is a great way to feel the pulse of this bohemian area. The first thing that strikes you, once you've recovered from crossing busy Ave Honoré Mercier, is the area's down-to-earth attitude. Good restaurants, hip bars and interesting shops, some catering to a gay clientele, line the thoroughfare as far as Rue Racine.

To the southwest, the colorful **Ave Cartier** has exploded in recent years with hip eateries, cafes and boutiques.

From Rue St-Jean, take any side street and walk downhill (northwest) to the narrow residential streets, such as Rue d'Aiguillon, Rue Richelieu and Rue St-Olivier. The miniature, scrunched-together houses here, some with very nice entrances, are typical of Québec City's residential landscape. The fanciful, protruding windows are known as oriels.

The Ave Cartier district is most buzzing on hot days, when the dozen or so patios open up for business. The epicenter of this little restaurant district is the intersection of Ave Cartier and Blvd René-Lévesque Ouest.

St-Roch NEIGHBORHOOD

Walking down Côte Ste-Geneviève in St-Jean-Baptiste, you will come to a steep staircase, the Escalier de la Chapelle, which takes you down to St-Roch. Cyclists can access Côte d'Abraham from Côte Ste-Geneviève.

Traditionally a working-class district for factory and naval workers, St-Roch has been slowly gentrifying. On the main artery, **Rue St-Joseph**, spiffy new restaurants and bars have sprung up among the junk shops and secondhand clothes stores. Art galleries are also found here and on **Rue St-Vallier Est**.

Cartier-Brébeuf National Historic Site MUSEUM

(Map p272; 175 Rue de l'Espinay; special events adult/child $5/3; ☺ 9am-noon Apr-Jun, 9am-noon & 1-4pm Jul & Aug) **FREE** On the St Charles River, northwest of the walled section of the city, this national historic site marks the spot where Iroquois people helped Cartier and his soldiers stave off scurvy and keep warm through the winter of 1535. The center features a full-scale replica of Cartier's ship, a reproduction of an aboriginal longhouse, and exhibits about Jesuitism, introduced to Canada in 1625 by Jean de Brébeuf.

Parc du Bois-de-Coulonge   PARK

(Map p272; ☑ 800-442-0773, 418-528-0773; 1215 Grande Allée Ouest) Not far west of the Plains of Abraham lie the colorful gardens of this park, a paean to the plant world and a welcome respite from downtown. Adorned with extensive horticultural displays, the woodland was the residence of the Canadian and Québecois political elite from 1854 to 1966.

Activities

Cyclo Services   CYCLING

(Map p274; ☑ 418-692-4052, 877-692-4050; www. cycloservices.net; 289 Rue St-Paul; bicycles per 2hr/24hr $15/35; ☺8:30am-8pm) This shop rents bikes and organizes excellent cycle tours of the city and outskirts, available in English. It has good cycling maps covering the vicinity.

Roc Gyms   ROCK CLIMBING

(www.rocgyms.com; 2350 Ave du Colisée; ☺9am-10pm Mon-Sat, to 6pm Sun) Offers indoor climbing and excursions to the canyons and crevices around Québec City. On Monday or Wednesday evenings (7pm) or Saturday

morning (10am), you can join a three-hour intro climbing course for $47.

Tours

Guided walking tours can pack a lot of specialized knowledge into a short time. For example, on one tour a cannonball wedged into a tree beside the sidewalk on Rue St-Louis is pointed out by a guide as strollers pass blindly by.

Boat Tours   CRUISE

Operators **Croisières AML** (Map p274; ☑ 866-856-6668; www.croisieresaml.com; Quai Chouinard) and **Groupe Dufour Croisières** (☑ 418-692-0222; www.dufour.ca) cruise downriver to Montmorency Falls and Île d'Orléans from near Place Royale. A little further north, next to the Bassin Louise gate, **Croisières le Coudrier** (☑ 418-692-0107, 888-600-5554; www. croisierescoudrier.qc.ca; Pier 19, 180 Rue Dalhousie, Vieux Port; adult/child tours $73.50/31.50) operates tours to Grosse Île. For city views, you can't beat the cheap ferry (p286) to Lévis.

Les Services Historiques
Six Associés   WALKING TOUR

(☑ 418-692-3033; www.sixassocies.com; 1½-hr walking tours $17) Costumed guides lead excellent walking circuits, such as the ever-popular 'Lust and Drunkenness,' which creaks open the rusty door on the history of alcohol and prostitution in the city. Other

---

QUÉBEC CITY FOR CHILDREN

Certainly, this town is about history, architecture and food. While much of the old city, including accommodations and restaurants, is geared toward adults, there are good things to do with younger ones in the central core, while around the edges are sights fully designed for kids' enjoyment.

In the historic area, walking the Fortifications (p273 suits all ages. La Citadelle ceremonies (p273), with uniformed soldiers, are winners too. Terrasse Dufferin (p276), with its river views and buskers, always delights children. Place d'Armes and Place Royale are also good for street performers. When the little ones have tired of climbing over cannons, there's always the cheap ferry to Lévis (p286), boat cruises or a horse-drawn calèche (p280).

Choco-Musée Érico (Map p276; www.chocomusee.com; 634 Rue St-Jean; ☺10:30am-6pm Mon-Wed & Sat, to 9pm Thu & Fri, 11am-6pm Sun, extended hours in summer) FREE is a museum and store devoted to all things chocolaty. Get a history lesson, see the kitchen, sample a chunk and try to resist the shop.

Aquarium du Québec (Map p272; ☑ 418-659-5264, 866-659-5264; 1675 Ave des Hôtels; adult/child $17/8.50; ☺10am-5pm Jun-Aug, to 4pm Sep-May) has walrus, seals, polar bears and thousands of smaller species.

Children enjoy the 'bee safari' and adults enjoy the mead at **Musée de l'Abeille** (☑ 418-824-4411; www.musee-abeille.com; 8862 Blvd St-Anne; ☺9am-5pm May, Jun & Sep, to 6pm Jul & Aug, 11am-5pm Oct) FREE, a beekeeping économusée 30km northeast of the city on Hwy 138.

tours, offered in English and French, focus on epidemics and crimes. A cheery bunch, they are. Reservations must be made in advance, by phone, email or via an online form.

Calèches
TOUR

(40-min rides $90) Departing from Place d'Armes, horse-drawn carriage rides (for up to four people) take in the Old Upper Town and Battlefields Park, with some commentary from the driver.

Les Tours Voir Québec
WALKING TOUR

(Map p274; ☑ 866-694-2001, 418-694-2001; www.toursvoirquebec.com; 12 Rue Ste-Anne; 2hr tours from $23) These tours explore the significant areas across the Old Town, as well as less obvious aspects, such as religious communities and interior courtyards. They also do food tours that take you to markets, restaurants, and stores across Old Town for snacks and drinks.

Old Québec Tours
BUS TOUR

(Map p274; ☑ 800-267-8687, 418-644-0460; www.toursvieuxquebec.com) This outfitter offers double-decker bus tours and a 4½-hour trip to Île d'Orléans, Montmorency Falls and Ste-Anne-de-Beaupré ($50), among others. They'll pick you up at your hotel.

Les Promenades Fantômes
WALKING TOUR

(Map p274; www.promenadesfantomes.com; 12 Rue Ste-Anne; adult/child $18.50/15.75; ⊙ 8pm May-Oct) Take a nocturnal trip by the light of a swinging lantern and learn about bygone Québec City's shadowy side.

✯ Festivals & Events

Carnaval
WINTER

(www.carnaval.qc.ca; ⊙ Feb) This famous annual event is unique to Québec City. It bills itself as the biggest winter carnival in the world, with parades, ice sculptures, a snow slide, boat races, dances, music and lots of drinking. Activities take place all over town; the iconic slide is on the Terrasse Dufferin behind the Château. Plan ahead as accommodations fill up fast.

Fête Nationale
CULTURAL

(Festival of John the Baptist; ⊙ 24 Jun) On this night, Québec City parties hard. Originally a holiday honoring John the Baptist, this day has evolved into a quasi-political event celebrating Québec's distinct culture and nationalistic leanings. Major festivities on the Plains of Abraham start around 8pm.

Festival d'Été
SUMMER

(www.infofestival.com; ⊙ early Jul) The Summer Festival features some 500 free shows, concerts, drama and dance performances, and 900,000 spectators wandering the streets. Most squares and parks in the Old Town host daily events; a good area to check out is Place d'Youville.

Les Grands Feux Loto-Québec
FIREWORKS

(www.lesgrandsfeux.com) Major fireworks displays on the river between Québec City and Lévis.

Fêtes de la Nouvelle-France
CULTURE

(www.nouvellefrance.qc.ca) Periodic reenactments of the last days of the French regime are conducted at various locations.

🛏 Sleeping

There are many, many places to stay in Québec City, and the competition keeps prices reasonable. The best options are the small, European-style hotels scattered around the Old Town. They offer character, convenience and a bit of romance. The larger downtown hotels tend to be expensive.

As you'd expect in such a popular city, the top choices are often full. Look for a room before 2pm or reserve ahead. Midsummer and the winter Carnaval are especially busy times. Most rooms have been upgraded to include private bathrooms, unless otherwise noted here. Prices drop markedly in the low season.

🛏 Old Upper Town

HI Auberge Internationale de Québec
HOSTEL $

(Map p274; ☑ 418-694-0775; www.aubergeinternationaledequebec.com; 19 Rue Ste-Ursule; dm incl breakfast $28-34, r with/without bathroom $109/75; 🕸@🛜) It's dauntingly large, but it's the best hostel in town, with friendly staff who organize all sorts of tours and pub crawls. In the basement, backpackers flock to the bar in the evening while rock music blares (or line up for the buffet breakfast). Despite school groups tearing along the institutional corridors, you can usually get a decent night's sleep.

★ Maison Historique James Thompson
B&B $$

(Map p274; ☑ 418-694-9042; www.bedandbreakfastquebec.com; 47 Rue Ste-Ursule; r $75-135) History buffs will get a real kick out of staying in the 18th-century former residence of

ONE HECK OF AN IGLOO

North America's first ice hotel may be a good example of wacky 'novelty architecture,' but every winter, guests pay serious sums of money to sleep in its frosty chambers. Located half an hour's drive from central Québec City, the **Hôtel de Glace** (r from $259) first opened its cool, blue doors in 2001, following similar Scandinavian establishments.

Yes, almost everything is made of ice (hot tubs and fireplaces are two understandable exceptions). This architectural feat strikes you, like an ice mallet, as soon as you step into the entrance hall: tall, sculpted columns of ice support a ceiling where a crystal chandelier hangs, and carved sculptures, tables and chairs line the endless corridors. Your bed will also be made of ice, but you can stay cozy and warm thanks to thick Arctic sleeping bags laid on lush deer pelts.

The 3000-sq-meter structure's public areas include exhibition rooms, a chapel, a sugar shack, a slide and an ice bar with DJ. The hotel melts in the spring and has to be rebuilt every winter, a job that takes five weeks, 12,000 tons of snow and 400 tons of ice.

The ice hotel offers several packages, starting at $600 per double, including a welcome vodka, dinner and breakfast. If you're not staying, simply take the tour (adult/child $17.50/8.75). To get to the hotel, take Rte 73 North and get off at Exit 154 toward Rue de la Faune.

James Thompson, a veteran of the Battle of the Plains of Abraham. Spacious rooms are bright, with host Guitta's cheerful artwork; and it's easy to while away an afternoon chatting with host Greg, who has a wealth of knowledge on all things Québec and historical.

Next to the front door of this beautifully restored house, you can see the original 'murder hole,' an opening through which a weapon could be inserted in the case of a surprise attack.

La Marquise de Bassano   INN $$

(Map p274; ☑ 418-692-0316, 877-692-0316; www.marquisedebassano.com; 15 Rue des Grisons; r $109-185; ⊚) Rooms sporting canopy beds, claw-foot tubs or a rooftop deck are part of the allure of this serene Victorian house, run by young, gregarious owners. The sweet scent of fresh-baked croissants for breakfast will have you up before the alarm clock.

Chez Hubert   B&B $$

(Map p274; ☑ 418-692-0958; www.chezhubert.com; 66 Rue Ste-Ursule; s incl breakfast $60-85, d $80-120; @ 🛜) This dependable choice is in a Victorian townhouse with chandeliers, stained-glass windows and oriental rugs. One of the three tasteful rooms has a view of the Château.

Manoir sur le Cap   INN $$

(Map p274; ☑ 418-694-1987, 866-694-1987; www.manoir-sur-le-cap.com; 9 Ave Ste-Geneviève; r $85-240; ❄🛜) Some rooms in this house by the boardwalk overlook the Jardin des Gou-

verneurs, the Château or the river. They're modern, but many have attractive stone or brick walls; a few have king-size beds.

Le Clos Saint-Louis   INN $$$

(Map p274; ☑ 800-461-1311, 418-694-1311; www.clossaintlouis.com; 69 Rue St-Louis; r incl breakfast $199-299; ❄🛜) It's hard to tell which trait is more evident here: the obvious care that the owners devote to the place or the natural 1844 Victorian charm. The 18 spacious, lavishly decorated rooms each have a whirlpool tub in a beautifully tiled bathroom. The suites are like Victorian apartments, apart from the TV in the mini drawing room.

Fairmont Le Château Frontenac   HOTEL $$$

(Map p274; ☑ 418-692-3861, 800-257-7544; www.fairmont.com/frontenac; 1 Rue des Carrières; r from $360; ❄🛜) More than just a hotel, more than just a landmark, the 618-room Château is the enduring symbol of Québec City. Scenes of films such as *Catch Me If You Can*, starring Leonardo DiCaprio, and Alfred Hitchcock's *I Confess* have been shot here. Previous guests include Queen Elizabeth II, President Jacques Chirac, Charlie Chaplin and Grace Kelly.

L'Hôtel du Vieux-Québec   INN $$$

(Map p274; ☑ 418-692-1850, 800-361-7787; www.hvq.com; 1190 Rue St-Jean; r incl breakfast from $218; ❄@🛜) ✐ Snacks like fruit and cookies are always on hand at this cozy inn near City Hall. Chic and modern rooms have exposed brick and espresso machines, and a breakfast basket containing pastries, yogurt, cheese and fruit awaits each morning outside your door. The hotel is carbon-neutral.

🛏 Old Lower Town

★ Auberge Saint-Antoine BOUTIQUE HOTEL $$$
(Map p274; ✆ 418-692-2211; www.saint-antoine.com; 8 Rue St-Antoine; r $199-999; ❊ @ ⌘) History and modernity are ecstatically married in this hotel, where understated contemporary luxuries enhance one of the city's most significant archaeological sites. A daily tour takes in the 700 artifacts on display, discovered when the heated underground car park was installed. The restaurant is housed in a 19th-century warehouse overlooking the St Lawrence.

In the original, 250-year-old part of the complex, the rooms and historical suites are stacked with antique furniture and personality. If you prefer to be drinking in outstanding views of the Château Frontenac rather than sleeping inside it, then this hotel fits the bill.

Hôtel Le Germain-Dominion BOUTIQUE HOTEL $$$
(Map p274; ✆ 418-692-2224, 888-833-5253; www.germaindominion.com; 126 Rue St-Pierre; r $189-315; ❊ @ ⌘) This winner by local luxury chain, Groupe Germain, tucked away in a cozy spot in the heart of the Lower Town, hits high notes with fresh, modern decor, a never-ending list of amenities and flawless customer service.

🛏 Outside the Walls

Prices are drastically lower and rooms bigger outside the walls, and for drivers, parking suddenly becomes a less complicated affair. All of the lodgings listed are within a 15-minute drive or walk from the Old Town.

Camping Municipal de Beauport CAMPGROUND $
(✆ 418-641-6112, 877-641-6113; www.camping-beauport.qc.ca; 95 Rue de la Sérénité; campsites & RV sites from $34; ⊙ Jun–early Sep) This excellent campground near Montmorency Falls is green, peaceful and just a 15-minute drive from the Old Town. To get there, take Hwy 40 toward Montmorency, get off at exit 321 and turn north.

Auberge Le Vincent INN $$
(Map p276; ✆ 418-523-5000; www.aubergelevincent.com; 295 Rue St-Vallier Est; r incl breakfast

$149-279; @ ⌘) Style-conscious budget travelers love the rainwater showers, exposed brick walls and windows (with quadruple glazing) overlooking the downtown St-Roch district in the affordable rooms at this inn. The outstanding staff provide excellent advice, and the gourmet hot breakfasts have Italian-style coffee. It's a short walk to the Old Town.

ALT Québec HOTEL $$
(✆ 800-463-5253, 418-658-1224; www.quebec.althotels.ca; 1200 Ave Germain-des-Prés; r $144-184; @ ⌘) For drivers who prioritize convenience and want to leave the sometimes overwhelmingly touristy walled city behind at the end of the day, this hotel just off Blvd Wilfrid Laurier (7km from the Old Town) is a rare gem. Boutique-hotel service, slick, modern decor and free parking are just a few of the pluses.

Auberge JA Moisan B&B $$
(Map p276; ✆ 418-529-9764; www.jamoisan.com; 699 Rue St-Jean; s $120-150, d $130-160; ❊ ⌘) Tucked away above the oldest supermarket in North America, the old-fashioned yet unstuffy rooms of this charming 18th-century home look out over the restaurants and bars of the funky St-Jean-Baptiste district. After a filling breakfast (with chocolates for dessert) cooked by hosts Clément and Nathalie, it's an easy walk to the Old Town.

✕ Eating

Restaurants are abundant and the quality is generally high in Québec City. Central places pack in the crowds by serving an odd mix of highbrow and lowbrow cuisine. Many of these places are reasonable value and have unbeatable locations, but the less obvious choices usually provide superior dining experiences. For the best bargains, get the table d'hôte, especially at lunch.

✕ Old Upper Town

Paillard BAKERY $
(Map p274; ✆ 418-692-1221; www.paillard.ca; 1097 Rue St-Jean; mains $7-15; ⊙ 7am-10pm) This light, modern New York–style cafe with long wooden tables is perfect for a quick breakfast or coffee break.

Casse Crêpe Breton CREPERIE $
(Map p274; ✆ 418-692-0438; cassecrepebreton.com; 1136 Rue St-Jean; crepes $4.50-8.75, mains

$10; ☺7am-9:30pm; ✈) Small and unassuming, this find dishes up hot, fresh crepes of every kind. Some diners like to sit at the counter and watch the chef at work.

Chez Ashton   FAST FOOD $
(Map p274; ✆418-692-3055; 54 Côte du Palais; mains $5-10; ☺11am-11:30pm Sun-Wed, to 4am Thu-Sat) This snack bar is one of the establishments that claims to have invented poutine. It's popular throughout the day and night for all varieties of poutine, burgers and subs.

Chez Temporel   CAFE $$
(Map p274; ✆418-694-1813; 25 Rue Couillard; mains $11-17; ☺7am-1:30am Sun-Thu, to 2:30am Fri & Sat) For a sandwich or leisurely breakfast of a perfect café au lait and fresh croissants, you can't beat this Parisian-style hideaway. Later in the day, it's the province of solitary book readers and wistful music.

Un Thé au Sahara   AFRICAN $$
(Map p274; 7 Rue Ste-Ursule; mains $14-22; ☺11:30am-2:30pm Thu & Fri, 5pm-late daily) Bring your own wine or hit the mint tea at this basic but popular Moroccan restaurant. All the classics are available: tabbouleh, hummus, couscous, brochettes and *tagine keffa* (veal croquettes in tomato sauce).

Le Patriarche   FUSION $$$
(Map p274; ✆418-692-5488; www.lepatriarche. com; 17 Rue St-Stanislas; mains $42-50; ☺5:30-10pm) The nouvelle cuisine at this top-class restaurant is complemented by the contemporary art on the 180-year-old stone walls. On the menu (which is stocked almost entirely with local products), starters include foie gras and buffalo tartare; mains range from New Brunswick salmon fillet to Appalachian deer and Québec lamb.

Aux Anciens Canadiens   QUÉBECOIS $$$
(Map p274; ✆418-692-1627; www.auxanciensca-nadiens.qc.ca; 34 Rue St-Louis; mains $20-89; ☺noon-9pm) Occupying the historic 1676 Jacquet house, this 40-year-old restaurant's name comes from the novel by Philippe Aubert de Gaspé, who lived here during his stint as sheriff of Québec. The menu preserves classic Québecois specialties and country dishes, such as 'trapper's treat' (Lac St-Jean meat pie with pheasant and buffalo).

It's well worth negotiating the hordes for the $20 lunchtime special, which includes a beer or wine.

✗ Old Lower Town

Rue St-Paul and Rue du Petit-Champlain are lined with restaurants and their outdoor tables.

Buffet de l'Antiquaire   QUÉBECOIS $
(Map p274; ✆418-692-2661; 95 Rue St-Paul; mains $8; ☺6am-10:30pm) This is one of the most authentic spots in town, with local characters enjoying the soundtrack of waiters wheezing orders above the clatter of pots and pans. The Québec home-cooking on offer includes filling meat and fish dishes, and there's Boréale on tap.

★Le Lapin Sauté   FRENCH $$
(Map p274; ✆418-692-5325; www.lapinsaute.com; 52 Rue du Petit-Champlain; mains $15-30; ☺11am-10pm Mon-Fri, 9am-10pm Sat & Sun) If you only splash out once in Québec City, do it at this cozy restaurant specializing in country cooking. Naturally, *le lapin* (rabbit) is available, in lasagna and sausages, among other things, but so are duck, salmon and chicken, and there's maple syrup crème brûlée for dessert. In good weather you can sit on the flowery patio, overlooking tiny Félix Leclerc park.

Le Cochon Dingue   FRENCH $$
(Map p274; ✆418-692-2013; www.cochondingue. com; 46 Blvd Champlain; mains $10-28; ☺8am-11pm) Since 1979, this Gallic gem among touristy eateries has delighted diners with its attentive service and outside seating. A French feel pervades its checkered tablecloths and its dishes, which range from *croque monsieur* to *steak frites*. There's a second **branch** (46 Blvd René-Lévesque Ouest) with the same menu, in the Ave Cartier district.

L'Échaudé   FRENCH $$$
(Map p274; ✆418-692-1299; 73 Rue Sault-au-Matelot; mains $19-32; ☺11:30am-2:30pm & 6pm-late Mon-Fri, 10am-2:30pm & 6pm-late Sat & Sun) This 25-year-old bistro is a favorite with locals, although they're increasingly being outnumbered by tourists lured by its hype. There is a pleasing atmosphere, with waiters bustling between full tables, and meat lovers will enjoy dishes such as duck confit, stuffed guinea fowl and the popular steak tartare ($23).

✗ Outside the Walls

Beyond the walls, there are three main eating districts. Rue St-Jean, away from the tourist haunts, has inexpensive eateries,

POUTINE, BIEN SÛR

Like all fast food, Québec's beloved poutine is perfect if you have a *gueule de bois* (hangover) after a night on the Boréale Blonde. In the calorie-packing culinary Frankenstein, the province's exemplary fries (fresh-cut, never frozen or served limp and greasy) are sprinkled with cheese curds and smothered in gravy. The dish was devised in the early 1980s and spread across Québec like a grease fire.

Poutine is a staple of the oft-seen roadside diners, *cantines* or *casse croûtes*, where you can sample embellished versions such as Italienne – with spaghetti. The eateries generally have their own top-secret recipe; for example, Cantine d'Amour in Matane has its Poutine d'Amour. As a general guide, these house specialties include mincemeat and green peppers. Chez Ashton in Québec City is a good place to take the poutine challenge.

many with a BYOW policy. Bistros line Ave Cartier between Grande Allée Ouest and Blvd René-Lévesque Ouest, attracting a local clientele. Lastly, in the artsy St-Roch district, a smattering of bistros and cafes featuring trendy nouveau cuisine have appeared in recent years.

Le Billig
CREPERIE $

(Map p276; 526 Rue St-Jean; crepes $3.50-16; ⊘11am-2pm & 5-9pm Tue-Fri, 11am-9:30pm Sat, to 3pm Sun) A Breton bistro specializing in crepes, featuring winning combinations like duck confit and onion marmalade, and buckwheat inventions such as the Roscoff, which crams in ham, asparagus, Swiss cheese, apple and béchamel sauce.

Délices d'Ariana
AFGHAN $

(102 Blvd René-Lévesque Ouest; mains $7-14; ⊘11:30am-2pm Mon-Fri & 5-10pm daily; 🖉) Frequented almost exclusively by locals in the know, this turreted restaurant is one of the best-kept secrets in Québec City. The exotic menu includes sumac-scented kebabs and traditional central Asian curries such as *borani bodenjan* (stewed eggplant in tomato sauce with homemade yogurt), which accompanies the *qabli pulao* (cardamom-flavored rice with lentils, fruit and nuts) perfectly.

Café du Clocher Penché
FRENCH $$

(☎418-640-0597; 203 Rue St-Joseph Est; mains $20-26; ⊘11:30am-2pm & 5-10pm Tue-Fri, 9am-2pm & 5-10pm Sat, 9am-2pm Sun) This light and airy bistro has a simple, understated design that mimics the unpretentious menu. It's *the* happening spot in the St-Roch district to pair modern French cuisine with a glass of wine, which you can choose from a vast array of high-quality European vintages.

Chez Victor
BURGERS $$

(☎418-529-7702; 145 Rue St-Jean; mains $10-15; ⊘11:30am-9:30pm Sun-Wed, to 10pm Thu-Sat; 🖉) Burgers are done to perfection – stacked high with all the fixings and paired with a mountain of crispy fries – at this bustling resto. Choose from over 20 burgers that feature black Angus beef, deer, duck, pork, salmon, chicken, tofu or vegetarian patties.

Le Hobbit
PUB $$

(Map p276; ☎418-647-2677; 700 Rue St-Jean; mains from $13; ⊘8am-10pm) This popular St-Jean-Baptiste meeting point has outside seating, a casual atmosphere and good-value lunch and dinner specials. The delicious *steak frites* ($20) is among the best deals in town. Various fresh pasta dishes and salads round out the menu.

🍷 Drinking & Nightlife

L'Oncle Antoine
PUB

(Map p274; ☎418-694-9176; 29 Rue St-Pierre; ⊘11am-late) In the Old Port area, in the stone cellar of one of the city's oldest surviving houses (dating from 1754), this tavern has several beers on tap *(en fût)* plus Québec microbrews (the coffee-tinted stout is particularly reviving).

Bar Ste-Angèle
BAR

(Map p274; 26 Rue Ste-Angèle; ⊘8pm-late) A low-lit, intimate hideaway, where the genial staff will help you navigate the list of cocktail pitchers and local and European bottled beers.

L'Inox
PUB

(Map p276; 655 Grande Allée Est; ⊘noon-3am) The city's first brewpub is along the tourist-heavy Grande Allée strip of restaurants and is a must-visit for beer connoisseurs.

Le Sacrilège
BAR

(Map p276; ☎418-649-1985; 447 Rue St-Jean) The pumping heart of St-Jean-Baptiste, this indie-soundtracked hangout has a conservatory and a sculpture-filled walled garden.

Chez Maurice
CLUB

(Map p276; ☑ 418-647-2000; 575 Grande Allée Est; ☺9pm-3am) This Babylonian nightspot in a Victorian mansion has a nightclub, cigar lounge, 'ultralounge' bar and the VooDoo Grill restaurant. The disco, open Wednesday to Sunday, offers Latino, happy house and live pop-music nights.

Chez Dagobert
CLUB

(Map p276; ☑ 418-522-2645; 600 Grande Allée Est; ☺9.30pm-3am Wed-Sun) With a huge mirror ball spinning above its terrace that overlooks Grande Allée Est, Dagobert competes with Chez Maurice opposite for the attention of local clubbers. Inside, multifloors play everything from rock to dance.

Le Drague
GAY & LESBIAN

(Map p276; ☑ 418-649-7212; 815 Rue St-Augustin; ☺10am-3am) The city's gay and lesbian scene is small, but this popular institution is its star player: a multifaceted bar with various 'zones.' The drag shows on Thursday, Friday and Sunday nights are among the city's most raucous and hilarious nights out, whatever your sexual inclination. From Thursday to Saturday nights, there are two packed floors of dancing ($4 entry).

☆ Entertainment

Though Québec City is small, it's active after dark. The entertainment paper *Voir* (www.voir.ca), published each Thursday, has listings in French. Rue St-Jean, and to a lesser degree Grande Allée and Ave Cartier, are the happening streets. Rue St-Jean attracts a young, bohemian crowd; Grande Allée Est is the stamping ground of the '*m'as-tu vu?*' (literally 'did you see me?'; show-off) set.

Fou-Bar
LIVE MUSIC

(Map p276; ☑ 418-522-1987; 525 Rue St-Jean; ☺3pm-3am) Laid-back and with an eclectic mix of bands, this is one of the town's classics for live music. The jazz on Tuesdays from 9pm is a winner.

Grand Théâtre de Québec
THEATER

(Map p276; ☑ 418-643-8131; 269 Blvd René-Lévesque Est) The city's main performing arts center presents classical concerts, dance and theater, all usually of top quality. The Opéra de Québec often performs here.

Les Yeux Bleus
LIVE MUSIC

(Map p274; 1117 Rue St-Jean) The city's best *boîte a chanson* (informal singer/songwriter club), this is the place to catch newcomers, the occasional big-name francophone concert and Québecois classics.

Le Capitole
THEATER

(Map p276; www.lecapitole.com; 972 Rue St-Jean) A small spot to catch performing arts, this theater-restaurant offers cabaret and musical revues.

🔒 Shopping

Claustrophobically narrow, and thick with gawkers, **Rue du Trécor**, by the Château, is nonetheless worth a wander for the easel-touting artists and their finished products.

A smattering of medieval shops can be found along **Rue St-Jean**, stocking bodices for the maiden, capes for the knight, axe pens, gargoyle candlesticks and other essential archaic paraphernalia.

In the Old Lower Town, **Rue St-Paul** has a dozen shops piled with antiques, curiosities and old Québecois relics.

Marché du Vieux-Port
FOOD

(Map p274; ☑ 418-692-2517; 160 Quai St André; ☺9am-6pm Mon-Fri, to 5pm Sat & Sun) Further along, at the waterfront, is this farmers market, where you can stock up on fish, *fromage* (cheese), flowers, foie gras, iced cider and garden gnomes. It's open until 5pm daily, but peaks on summer Saturday mornings, when local farmers flock here and stalls are set up outside the building.

JA Moisan Épicier
FOOD

(Map p276; ☑ 418-522-0685; www.jamoisan.com; 699 Rue St-Jean; ☺8:30am-6pm Mon-Sat, 10am-7pm Sun) Established in 1871, this is considered the oldest grocery store in North America. An old-fashioned atmosphere lingers between the herbal teas, scented toiletries, jars of coffee beans and other goodies.

Musée d'Art Inuit
ART

(Map p274; 35 Rue St-Louis; ☺9:30am-5:30pm) A stunning gallery selling soapstone, serpentine and basalt Inuit sculptures from northern Québec. Prices range from $45 to several thousand dollars.

ℹ️ Information

Centre Infotouriste (Map p274; ☑ 418-649-2608, 877-266-5687; www.bonjourquebec.com; 12 Rue Ste-Anne; ☺8:30am-7:30pm) This busy provincial tourist office also handles city inquiries. Tour operators have counters here.

Info Santé (Health Info; ☑ 418-648-2626; ☺24hr) For consultations with nurses.

Kiosk Frontenac (Map p274; ⊙9:30am-5:30pm Jun-Oct) A tourist information booth on Terrasse Dufferin facing Le Château Frontenac; makes reservations for city activities and is the starting point for some tours.

L'Hôtel-Dieu de Québec (☑418-525-4444; 11 Côte du Palais; ⊙24hr) A centrally located hospital with emergency services.

ⓘ Getting There & Away

AIR

Jean Lesage airport (www.aeroportdequebec. com) is west of town off Hwy 40, near where north–south Hwy 73 intersects it.

Air Canada flies to Montréal, Toronto, Ottawa, Gaspé, the Îles de la Madeleine and Sept Îles, as well as to Chicago and Washington. There are also United and Delta flights to US destinations including Chicago, Washington and New York.

BOAT

The **ferry** (Map p274; ☑877-787-7483; www. traversiers.com; car & driver/adult/child one-way $7.75/3.25/2.25) between Québec City and Lévis (10 minutes, frequent between 6am and 2am) provides great views of the river, Le Château Frontenac and the Québec City skyline. The terminal is at Place Royale.

BUS

The **bus station** (Map p274; ☑418-525-3000; 320 Rue Abraham-Martin) is beside the main train station, Gare du Palais. Buses run to Montréal ($56, three to four hours, hourly).

Intercar (www.intercar.qc.ca) serves Charlevoix ($36, two hours), Saguenay ($86, 2½ hours) and the North Shore, stopping in major towns as far as Havre St-Pierre ($112, 12 hours).

Orléans Express (www.orleansexpress.com) buses cover the south shore including Rimouski ($65, 4½ hours), and do a circuit of the Gaspé Peninsula, including Gaspé ($119, 12 hours); for Edmundston, New Brunswick, take one of the regular services to Rivière du Loup ($51, three hours) and pick up **Maritime Bus** (www.maritimebus.com) there ($25).

US-bound coaches go via Montréal.

CAR & MOTORCYCLE

Allô Stop (www.allostop.com; 665 Rue St-Jean) and **Kangaride** (p229) get drivers and passengers together for cheap rides to other parts of Québec. A lift to Montréal costs around $14.

Kangouroute (☑888-768-8388, 418-683-9000; www.kangouroute.net; 6345 Blvd Wilfrid Hamel) is a local car- and truck-rental agency.

Avis (☑418-523-1075; 1100 Blvd René-Lévesque), **Budget** (☑418-692-3660; 29 Côte du Palais), **Enterprise** (☑418-523-6661; 690 Blvd René-Lévesque) and **Hertz** (☑418-694-1224; 44 Côte du Palais) have central offices, though it may be worth making the trek to **Budget** (☑418-872-9885; 7115 Blvd Wilfrid Hamel) in Ste-Foy for a good deal. **Discount** (☑800-263-2355, 418-522-3598; 240 3e Rue), also in Ste-Foy, offers pickups and drop-offs.

Avis (☑418-872-2861), **Budget** (☑418-872-8413), **Enterprise** (☑418-861-8820), **Discount** (☑418-877-1717) and **Hertz** (☑418-871-1571) have desks at the airport.

TRAIN

Québec City has three train stations. In the Lower Town, the renovated and gorgeous **Gare du Palais**, off Rue St-Paul, complete with bar and cafe, is central and convenient. Daily **VIA Rail** (p229) trains go to Montréal (from $60, three hours) and destinations further west. Bus 800 from Place d'Youville runs to the station.

The **Ste-Foy station** (Map p272; 3255 Chemin de la Gare), southwest of downtown, is used by the same trains and is simply more convenient for residents who live in that area.

The third station is across the river in the town of **Charny**, east of Hwy 73. Trains here mainly serve eastern destinations, such as Gaspé ($92, 14 hours), and the Maritimes, but some also go to Montréal (from $60, three hours). Overnight trains go to Moncton, New Brunswick (from $118, 12½ hours) every second day. Shuttle buses connect to Gare du Palais station before and after trains come in to Charny (bus fare is included in price of VIA Rail ticket).

ⓘ Getting Around

TO/FROM THE AIRPORT

A **Taxi Co-op** (☑418-525-5191) cab between the tourist area and the airport is $34.25. Tour companies Old Québec Tours (p280) and **Dupont Tours** (☑418-649-9226) sometimes run cheaper shuttle buses (by reservation, $22).

BICYCLE

Many bike paths run through and around the city, covered by the *Plan du Réseau Cyclable* and more-detailed *Parcours Cyclables* available at any tourist information center or bicycle-rental shop.

Cyclo Services (p279) rents bikes, tandems and electric bikes. You'll need to leave identification there.

CAR & MOTORCYCLE

In Old Town, driving isn't really worth the trouble. You can walk just about everywhere, the streets are narrow and crowded, and parking is limited. But if you're stuck driving, the tourist offices have a handy map of city-operated parking lots that don't gouge too much. The public lot beside Discovery Pavilion is affordable and close to the Old Town. Better still are the lots in

St-Roch, including a few off Rue St-Vallier Est, which charge about half the price of those in Upper Town. Parking there means a 10-minute hike uphill, but you can buy yourself a treat with the money you save.

If you venture outside the walls and into Greater Quebec City and beyond, a car is very useful.

Motorcycles are not permitted within the walls of the Old Town.

PUBLIC TRANSPORTATION

A ride on the city **bus system** (☑ 418-627-2511) costs $2.75, with transfer privileges, or $7.25 for a day pass. Buses go out as far as Ste-Anne de Béaupré on the North Shore. The tourist offices can supply route maps and information.

Many buses serving the Old Town area stop in at Place d'Youville, just outside the wall on Rue St-Jean. Bus 800 goes to Gare du Palais, the central long-distance bus and train station.

AROUND QUÉBEC CITY

As tempting as it may be to wander Old Québec for days, the larger Québec region is well worth exploring. Other than Lévis, the sights here are all on the north side of the river: Wendake, St-Gabriel de Valcartier, Stoneham and Parc de la Jacques Cartier to the north of Québec City, and the rest to the northeast. The south side of the river also possesses some excellent places to visit.

Lévis

On the 1km ferry crossing to the town of Lévis, the best views are undoubtedly on the Québec side of the vessel. The Citadelle, the Château Frontenac and the seminary dominate the clifftop cityscape. Once you disembark, riverside Lévis is a relaxing escape from the intensity of Québec City's Old Town.

Tourisme Lévis (☑ 418-838-6026; ☉ May-Oct), at the ferry landing, has maps and an Old Lévis package ($9), which includes return ferry and a 30-minute guided bus shuttle to several points of interest.

Near the ferry landing, the **Terrasse de Lévis**, a lookout point inaugurated in 1939 by King George VI and (the then future) Queen Elizabeth II, offers excellent vistas of Québec and beyond from the top of the hill on Rue William-Tremblay.

Between 1865 and 1872, the British built three forts on the south shore to protect Québec. One, known as **Fort No 1** (41 Chemin

du Gouvernement; adult/child $3.90/1.90; ☉ 10am-5pm Jul & Aug), has been restored and operates as a national historic site with guided tours. It's on the east side of Lévis, just off Rte 132/Blvd de la Rive Sud.

Bikes, tandems and rollerblades can be rented at the ferry terminal (rates are lower than those in Québec City).

In Old Lévis, the main shops and restaurants are on Ave Bégin. For more views of Québec, head south on the riverside path through Parc de l'Anse-Tibbits.

Wendake

In Huron-Ouendat, the number eight is a letter, pronounced 'oua' (like the 'wh' in 'what'), which explains the curious name of the reconstructed Huron village **On-hoüa Chetek8e** (☑ 418-842-4308; www.huron-wendat.qc.ca; 575 Rue Stanislas Kosca; adult/child $12.75/7.75; ☉ 9am-5pm). It's in small Wendake, about 15km northwest of the city via Hwy 73 (exit 154).

Entry to the village is by a 45-minute tour. You can also have lunch in the log cabin, tucking into venison, caribou, and mint tea, though this is one of the more theme park–like aspects of the experience.

The tour includes a longhouse, a sweat lodge, a smoker (a wigwam for smoking meat) and a shaman's hut, where you learn how dream-catchers work and how shamans exorcised sick people using bear skulls. It's the world's only Huron village, and the surrounding reserve is a relatively dynamic Aboriginal community. In 1960, it became the first reserve with its own bank; today, it provides employment for other tribes.

Entertainment such as dances ($7), canoe rides ($31.25), jewelry making ($6.50) or a workshop on animal skins ($6.25) can make it a full day. The tax-free shop sells Huron crafts and souvenirs.

Bus 72 runs half-hourly from Québec ($3, 30 minutes).

St-Gabriel de Valcartier

Announced by the 'pirate's den' slide overshadowing the packed car park, **Village Vacances** (1860 Blvd Valcartier; adult/child $31/24, evening $34/27; ☉ 10am-7pm Jun-Sep) is a water city that looms above the village like Jabba the Hutt next to Princess Leia. With 11 sections, each with slides, water games and heated pools, it's heaven on earth for children. Rafting, carting, diving displays and a campground are also on offer. It's 13km northwest of Wendake, accessible via Rte 371.

Stoneham

Leaving Québec City's suburbs, Rte 371 winds along Rivière Jacques Cartier and through the hills. At Stoneham, the **Station Touristique** (☑800-463-6888, 418-848-2415; www.ski-stoneham.com; 600 Chemin du Hibou) offers an array of activities in a friendly resort atmosphere with lodgings and a restaurant. Stoneham is one of the province's main ski centers, switching to hiking, climbing, geocaching and kayaking in summer.

Parc de la Jacques Cartier

This 600-sq-km **wilderness park** (☑800-665-6527, 418-848-3169; adult/child $6.50/3), just off Rte 175 about 40km from Québec, is ideal for a quick escape. Travel less than an hour from the city, and you can be hiking or biking along trails, or canoeing along Rivière Jacques Cartier. L'Epéron (5.5km) is a steamy forest walk with lookouts giving views down the valley, while Les Loups (10km) and Du Hibou (13km) are two tough, rewarding trails.

Some 10km from the southernmost 'Valley Sector' entrance to the park, the information center provides services such as showers. It hires out camping equipment, canoes and bikes, and organizes activities (in French) from caving to survivalist training. Yurts and family-size tents ($99 to $247) and campgrounds ($28 to $35) are scattered throughout the park. In winter, there's cross-country skiing with shelter huts along some routes.

A little further east is the 7861-sq-km **Réserve Faunique des Laurentides** (Rte 175), wilder and less organized but popular for fishing.

Aventures Nord-Bec (☑418-848-3732; 4 Chemin des Anémones; camping $28, treehouse $130, 2-person/4-person yurt $110/130), off Rte 175, 2km north of the Valley Sector entrance to the park, has riverside camping, yurts, a few treehouses and a restaurant. Their main business during winter is dog-sledding, as the huskies hanging at the door suggest.

Intercar's Québec City–Alma bus ($78, 2½ hours, two to three times daily) can drop you at one of the four entrances, all of which are on Rte 175.

Île d'Orléans

Before Jacques Cartier named Île d'Orléans in the Duke of Orleans' honor, it was known as L'Île de Bacchus for its wild vines. Four centuries later, Québecois troubadour Félix Leclerc, who died here in 1988, likened the island to France's famous Chartres cathedral.

Today, there are no signs of Dionysian orgies on sleepy Île d'Orléans, which is 15km northeast of Québec City, but there is plenty to attract day-trippers and those lucky visitors with more time to spare. The island, still primarily a pastoral farming region with gentle landscapes and views across to both shores of the St Lawrence, has emerged as the epicenter of Québec's agritourism movement. Foodies from all around flock to the local *économusées* (workshops) to watch culinary artisans at work, and then hit the island's stellar restaurants to sample hearty, regionally sourced dishes.

One road (60km) circles it, with two more running north–south. Their edges are dotted with strawberry fields, orchards, cider producers, windmills and arts and crafts workshops and galleries. Some of the villages contain houses that are up to 300 years old, and there are wooden or stone cottages in the Normandy style.

At the island's more developed southwestern end, where the bridge crosses from the north shore, it feels at times like a floating suburb of Québec. The city soon becomes a distant memory as you head northeast.

⊙ Sights & Activities

Le Vignoble Isle de Bacchus　　　　WINERY
(1071 Chemin Royal, St-Pierre; ⊙10am-6pm daily May-Dec, Sat & Sun Jan-Apr) A tour and tasting here should be on your agenda, and there's a *gîte* (B&B) if you can't drag yourself away from the red, white and rosé.

La Forge à Pique-Assaut　　　　GALLERY
(www.forge-pique-assaut.com; 2200 Chemin Royal, St-Laurent; ⊙9am-5pm daily Jun-Oct, Mon-Fri Oct-Jun) Artisan blacksmith Guy makes star railings and decorative objects at this *économusée*. There's a store attached.

Croisières le Coudrier　　　　CRUISES
(☑418-692-0107; www.croisierescoudrier.qc.ca; 1515 Chemin Royal, St-Laurent; adult/child $73.50/31.50; ⊙May-Oct) Boat tours from St-Laurent, in the southwest corner of the island, to Grosse Île.

ÉcoloCyclo
CYCLING

(www.ecolocyclo.net; 517 Chemin Royal, St-Laurent; ⊙10am-6pm daily Jun-Sep) Hires out tradition-al bikes (per hour/day $16/38) in addition to electric bikes (per hour/day $30/63) and tandems (per hour/day $27/72). It's near the bridge, around the corner from the tourist office.

📩 Sleeping & Eating

If you refuse to leave, the island is blessed with memorable places to sleep and eat, and it's an easy commute to Québec City by car. The website www.gitesiledorleans.com includes information about 16 B&Bs on the island.

Camping Orléans
CAMPGROUND $

(☑418-829-2953; www.campingorleans.com; 357 Chemin Royal, St-François; campsites $43-54; ⊙May-Oct; 🐾⚏) This leafy site is at the wa-ter's edge at the far end of the island from the bridge. It's the only campsite left in the greater Québec City area. There's a swim-ming pool and pub on site.

Dans les Bras de Morphée
B&B $$

(☑418-829-3792; www.danslesbrasdemorphee. com; 225 Chemin Royal, St-Jean; r $128-168; ✸@🛜) 🍴 A locavore's dream, this stone mansion sits amidst unspoiled gardens, streams and farms from which owners Marc and Louise source the ingredients for break-fast. It's no run-of-the-mill breakfast, either: Marc, a professional chef, constructs beau-tiful and tasty gourmet three-course affairs worthy of the front cover of *Bon Appétit*.

Views of the mighty St Lawrence are spectacular from three out of four of the bedrooms; the fourth overlooks the sprawl-ing countryside.

Au Toit Bleu
B&B $$

(☑418-829-1078; 3879 Chemin Royal, Ste-Famille; r $87-120) Next to Le Mitan microbrewery, this eclectic B&B uses the decor gathered on the owner's travels to beautiful effect, with African, Indian, Indonesian and Japanese rooms. Choose between a shared bathroom or your own freestanding tub, then ponder the big questions in a hammock overlooking the river.

La Maison du Vignoble
B&B $$

(☑418-828-9562; 1071 Chemin Royal, St-Pierre; r $70-110) A 300-year-old farmhouse at the winery has Montmorency Falls at the back-yard, vineyards at the front. Life's tough.

La Boulange
BAKERY $

(☑819-829-3162; 2001 Chemin Royal, St-Jean; light meals $5-10) A memorable bakery with a small irresistible store, La Boulange is the perfect spot for a light lunch of sandwiches or pizza, or to gather picnic supplies. Devour to-die-for croissants while taking in views of the St Lawrence and an 18th-century parish church next door.

Le Moulin de St Laurent
MEDITERRANEAN $$

(www.moulinstlaurent.qc.ca; 754 Chemin Royal, St-Laurent; mains $18-35, meals $34-51, chalets from $120; ⊙11:30am-2:30pm & 5:30-8:30pm May-Oct) You'd be hard-pressed to find a more agree-able place to dine than the terrace at the back of this early-19th-century flour mill, with tables inches from a waterfall. The well-prepared, diverse menu is continental with regional flourishes, such as trout and veal. Chalets are also available.

Resto-Pub l'O2 Île
PUB $$

(1025 Rte Prévost, St-Pierre; mains $8-24; ⊙8am-10pm) The island's hottest hangout, this pub attracts locals for its long menu of decent grilled meats, pizzas, inventive poutines and pastas.

🛍 Shopping

Domaine Steinbach
FOOD

(www.domainesteinbach.com; 2205 Chemin Royal, St-Pierre; ⊙10am-7pm May-Oct) This store stocks 50 farm products, including six ci-ders made using apples from the organic or-chard, one with maple syrup. If the generous tasting tickles your taste buds, tuck into a cheese or duck platter ($14.25) on the ter-race overlooking the river.

Cassis Monna & Filles
FOOD

(721 Chemin Royale, St-Pierre; ⊙10am-6pm May-Nov) Learn all you ever wanted to know about *cassis* (black currant), also known as *gadelle noire* in Québécois, and pick up some treats to go, including jam (currant-onion is a popular pick), vinaigrette, mus-tard, wine and liquor. The on-site restaurant pairs the star of the show with light lunches like warm goat cheese salad or duck confit.

Chocolaterie de l'Île d'Orléans
FOOD

(www.chocolaterieorleans.com; 150 Chemin du Bout-de-Île, Ste-Pétronille; ⊙9:30am-5pm) Using cocoa beans from Belgium, the chocolatiers at this 200-year-old house churn out tasty concoctions, including almond bark and fla-vored truffles. There's a cute little ice-cream parlor in the summer months.

ⓘ Information

It's worth spending $1 on a brochure at the helpful **tourist office** (☑ 866-941-9411, 418-828-9411; www.iledorleans.com; 490 Côte du Pont; ⊙ 8:30am-7:30pm), which you'll see soon after you cross the bridge.

Parc de la Chute Montmorency

This waterfall is 30m higher than Niagara Falls and as much of a tourist trap, if not as impressive. It's perfectly visible from the main road and can be visited for free. During winter, snowboarders make the most of the *pain de sucre* (sugar loaf) next to the plunge pool, formed by ice and snow blanketing a huge rock. The cascade was harnessed to power sawmills and cotton factories, as detailed in an exhibition in the clifftop Manoir Montmorency.

From May to November the **park** (☑ 418-663-3330; 2490 Ave Royale) charges $9.50 for parking, at both the foot and the top of the falls. From the visitors center, off Rte 138 at the base of the falls, you can take the **cable car** (one-way adult/child $9/4.50) to the top or climb the 487 steps. The suspended footbridge right above the waterfall provides the best views.

The park is 13km northeast of Québec City. To enter for free, either park your car at the church parking lot in neighboring Beauport, then walk 1km to the falls, or catch bus 800 at Place d'Youville in Québec and transfer at the Beauport terminal, taking bus 50 to the top of the falls or bus 53 to the bottom. You can also cycle here from Québec.

Ste-Anne de Beaupré

Approaching Ste-Anne de Beaupré along Rte 138, the twin steeples of the 1920s **basilica** (www.ssadb.qc.ca; 10018 Ave Royale; ⊙ 8:30am-4:30pm) FREE tower above the motels and *dépanneurs* (convenience stores). It's one of the few remaining megaattractions related not to nature or artificial diversions, but to faith. Since the mid-1600s, the village has been an important Christian site; the annual late-July pilgrimage draws thousands of visitors, who crowd every open space.

Before you even enter the basilica, it becomes apparent that this is going to be a case study in the human ability to mix the sacred and the profane. During the summer, visitors line up at the Blessings Bureau to have a priest bless the Jesus keychain they've just bought. Inside the building, the crutches piled up against the pillars are ex-voto offerings, left behind over decades by believers who no longer needed them after praying to the saint. There is impressive tilework, stained glass and glittering ceiling mosaics depicting the life of Saint Anne. Unfortunately, the next things that strike you are the signs and screens blaring 'silence' and asking pilgrims not to deface the stonework, and the security cameras and earpiece-wearing heavies. However, the basilica is grand enough and the religious theme park of a village surreal enough to justify a stop here.

Nearby is the **Cyclorama of Jerusalem** (☑ 418-827-3101; www.cyclorama.com; 8 Rue Régina; adult/child $9/6; ⊙ 9am-6pm May-Oct), which is not an IMAX cinema, but a wraparound, 110m painting of Jerusalem on the day Jesus was crucified.

Facing the basilica is the chapel-like **Auberge de la Basilique** (☑ 418-827-4475; 5 Rue du Sanctuaire; dm/s/d $24/49/67; ⊙ May-Oct), which has a self-service restaurant.

PLUMobile (☑ 866-824-1433, 418-827-8484) buses (one-way $3.75, three daily Monday to Friday) run between Place d'Youville and Gare du Palais in Québec City and the basilica. The comfortable buses have free wi-fi.

Mont-Ste-Anne

Some 6km northeast of Beaupré on Rte 138, the **Mont-Ste-Anne** (www.mont-sainte-anne.com; 2000 Boul du Beaupré; day passes adult/child $73/39) ski resort has the highest vertical for night skiing in Canada and one of the longest ski seasons. There are 67 trails and 14 lifts, including the new detachable quad chair, with breathtaking views of the St Lawrence and Québec City.

In the summer time, a popular activity is hiking to the 74m-high **Jean Larose Waterfalls** (206 Rte 138; adult/child $11.50/5.50; ⊙ 9am-5:30pm May-Oct) in a deep chasm. You can walk around and across them via a series of steps, ledges and bridges. Though busy, this is a pleasant spot – it's less developed and more dramatic than other waterfall tourist attractions. **Canyoning-Québec**

(☎888-827-4579; adult/child $96/45; ◷9am & 2pm May-Oct) offers half-day rappelling classes.

Cap Tourmente National Wildlife Area

This **bird sanctuary** (570 Chemin du Cap Tourmente; adult/child $6/free; ◷8:30am-5pm) is home to 700 species, including the flocks of snow geese that migrate to its wetlands in spring and autumn. It's beyond the villages of St Joachim and Cap Tourmente, signposted along Rte 138 from Ste-Anne de Beaupré.

CHARLEVOIX

For 200 years, this pastoral strip of rolling hills has been a summer retreat for the wealthy and privileged. Unesco has classified the entire area a World Biosphere Reserve, which has resulted in worthwhile restrictions on the types of permitted developments, as well as a palpable sense of pride among residents. There's also a lot to be proud of in the lovely local towns such as Baie St-Paul, with its *ateliers* (artists studios), galleries and boutiques lining its few streets.

Charlevoix is also known as a center for the culinary arts. The Route des Saveurs (Route of Flavors) takes in 16 farms and eateries, including the home of Éboulmontaise lamb and one of Québec's best restaurants. Local menus generally read like inventories of Charlevoix produce.

The area totals 6000 sq km yet is home to just 30,000 people. Glacier-carved crevices, cliffs and jagged rock faces overlook a unique geographical feature: the immense valley formed by a prehistoric meteor. A space rock weighing 15 billion tons, with a diameter of about 2km, smashed into the earth here some 350 million years ago, leaving a crater measuring 56km in diameter. The point of impact was the present-day Mont des Éboulements, halfway between Baie St-Paul and La Malbaie, some 10km inland.

A driving route to consider taking is the 'River Drive' (Rte 362) one way, through Baie St-Paul, Ste-Irénée and La Malbaie. On the way back you can ride the ear-popping hills of the 'Mountain Drive' (Rte 138) inland and stop in at Parc des Hautes Gorges de la Rivière Malbaie for a hike en route.

Le Massif

Outside of Petite Rivière St Francois is **Le Massif** (www.lemassif.com; 1350 Rue Principale), perhaps the best little-known ski center in the country. It offers the highest vertical drop (770m) and most snow (600cm) east of the Rockies and has fabulous views over the St Lawrence. The chalet at the top of the hill houses **Mer & Monts Restaurant** (☎877-536-2774, 418-632-5276; meals from $20; ◷11:30am-2pm Wed-Sun Dec-Mar), which serves up a three-course table d'hôte highlighting regional cuisine, not heat-lamp burgers.

Baie St-Paul

The clowning, juggling troupe Cirque du Soleil started out in Baie St-Paul, but most of the entertainment here is of a gentler nature. The small town has some 30 galleries and studios, along with historic houses converted into superb restaurants and *gîtes*. With its prosperous, holiday atmosphere and its location among wood-covered hills at the meeting of the St Lawrence and Gouffre Rivers, Baie St-Paul is one of the North Shore's most appealing towns.

◉ Sights & Activities

Musée d'Art Contemporain   MUSEUM
(www.macbsp.com; 23 Rue Ambroise-Fafard; adult/child $7/free; ◷10am-5pm Tue-Sun) Across the main drag, this architecturally attention-grabbing gallery houses contemporary art by local artists and some photographic exhibits on loan from the National Gallery of Canada. The museum also organizes an international contemporary art symposium in August.

Carrefour Culturel Paul Médéric   GALLERY
(4 Rue Ambroise-Fafard; ◷10am-5pm daily Jun-Oct, 1:30-5pm Thu & Fri, 10am-5pm Sat & Sun Nov-May) FREE This gallery is named after a local priest and writer who founded a youth movement here. Stay for a while as it's possible to watch local artisans working in their studios.

Randonnées Nature-Charlevoix   OUTDOORS
(randonneesnature.com; 11-1 Rue Ambroise-Fafard; adult/child $35.50/15; ◷1:30pm Jul & Aug) Non-profit organization Randonnées Nature-Charlevoix runs two-hour tours of the meteor crater. It's based at Boutique Le Cratère, where you can learn about the

Charlevoix, Saguenay & South Shore

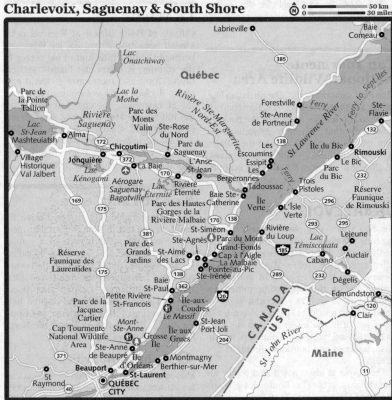

world's largest inhabited crater by looking at the 3D map and talking to guide François.

Air du Large
WATER SPORTS

(☎418-435-2066; www.airdularge.com; 210 Rue Ste-Anne; ⊙8am-5pm) This outfit offers kayaking, sailing, climbing, canyoning, biking and paragliding lessons and rentals. Guided tours are also available.

🛏 Sleeping & Eating

La Balcon Vert
CAMPGROUND $

(☎418-435-5587; www.balconvert.com; 22 Côte du Balcon Vert; campsite/dm/d $23/23/52; ⊙May-Sep) With its nightly bonfires, this hilltop hideaway is an involving place to stay, though guests should be prepared to rough it. A campground, private and shared cabins, a games room with table tennis, and a bar-restaurant nestle among the trees. The site is east of town, signposted off Rte 362.

Auberge La Muse
INN $$

(☎800-841-6839, 418-435-6839; www.lamuse. com; 39 Rue St-Jean-Baptiste; r $79-179; ❋) This cheerful yellow mansion is right in the center of the bustling village. Breakfast is outstanding, but dinner can be hit-or-miss so consider one of the many pubs and bistros within walking distance. Tip: rooms 12, 14, and 15 are the biggest, and room 1 tends to get noisy as it's next to the front door.

Nature et Pinceaux
B&B $$

(☎418-435-2366; www.natureetpinceaux.qc.ca; 33 Rue Nordet; r $95-125; ⊙Apr-Nov) Atop the mountain peeking out over the river below, the spacious rooms at this charming B&B have views that are surpassed only by the phenomenal three-course breakfasts cooked by host Mariette. The house is east of town, signposted off Rte 362.

Café des Artistes
CAFE $

(25 Rue St-Jean-Baptiste; lunches from $6.50; ☉9:30am-midnight) For excellent coffee and a light but zippy lunch, head to this pizzeria on the main strip.

Le Mouton Noir
FRENCH $$$

(☑418-240-3030; 43 Rue Ste-Anne; set meals $33-39; ☉5-10pm Wed-Sun) Since 1978, the rustic-looking Black Sheep has been home to fine French cuisine. Fish – including walleye, the freshwater queen – is on offer when available, as are buffalo, caribou and steak, all enlivened by a deft touch that incorporates wild mushrooms and local produce. The outdoor terrace overlooks the Gouffre River. Reservations advised.

L'Orange Bistro
FRENCH $$$

(www.orangebistro.com; 29 Ambroise-Fafard; set meals $26-37; ☉11am-9pm) This central, colorful restaurant's terrace overlooks the main road into town, but it's easy to forget the cars when the food's this good. Local produce on offer includes organic chicken, spare ribs, veal, venison and mussels, while fresh herbs and organic vegetables edge the menu closer to perfection.

Le Saint Pub
PUB $$$

(www.saint-pub.com; 2 Rue Racine; set meals $20-30; ☉11am-2am) Ale lovers will foam at the mouth in this former brewery, where the dinner menu begins with beers and continues via beer-based sauces, dressings and marinades. For $6 you can sample four regional brews including the local malt.

❶ Information

Charlevoix Tourist Office (www.tourisme-charlevoix.com; 444 Blvd Mgr-de-Laval; ☉9am-7pm) On Rte 138 just west of town.
Town Tourist Office (☑418-240-3218; 6 Rue St-Jean-Baptiste; ☉9am-7pm)

❶ Getting There & Away

The **bus station** (☑418-435-6569; 2 Chemin de l'Équerre) is at La Grignotte restaurant, about a 20-minute walk from downtown. Intercar buses go to Québec City thrice daily ($26, 1¼ hours), with a fourth service on Thursday and Friday and only two services on Sunday between November and April.

Parc des Grands Jardins

This **provincial park** (☑418-439-1227, reservations 800-665-6527; www.sepaq.com/pq/grj; adult/child $6.50/3; campsites/cottages from

$22/25, cabins per 2 people $101) covers 310 sq km, much of it taiga. Excellent hiking and rugged topography are the lure at this gem. The hills frame well over 100 small lakes. Caribou may be spotted. The half-day trek up **Mont du Lac-des-Cygnes** (Swan Lake Mountain) is an exceptional short hike. One of the longest and most difficult continuous trails east of the Rockies, **La Traversée** stretches 100km from the park, snaking down the great valleys in the Parc des Hautes Gorges de la Rivière Malbaie and winding up in the Parc du Mont Grand-Fonds. An intermediate-level hiker needs about seven days for the full trek. You can rent canoes, kayaks and bikes, and stay at primitive campsites, rustic, pioneer-style cottages, or larger cabins. Bring all necessary supplies.

Information is available from the **Thomas-Fortin Service Center** (☉1-10pm Mon, Wed & Fri, to 8pm Tue, Thu, Sat & Sun Jul-Aug), at the main entrance, and **Mont du Lac-des-Cygnes visitors kiosk** (☉9am-4pm).

To get to the park, take Rte 381 north from Baie St-Paul; it's 30km to the visitors kiosk and 46km to the main entrance.

Île-aux-Coudres

Quiet and rural, Île-aux-Coudres feels remarkably remote. The hills of the north shore are never far from view, but this is nonetheless a place to forget the rest of the world.

◎ Sights & Activities

Musée Maritime
MUSEUM

(305 Rue de l'Église; adult/child $5/free; ☉9am-5pm May-Oct) Before or after boarding the ferry in St-Joseph-de-la-Rive, drop into Musée Maritime. It details the schooner-building history of a region where it was common to see 20 different types of commercial boat on the St Lawrence. Visitors can climb aboard some beauties in the shipyard. There's also a display on the area's famous meteorite crater.

Musée les Voitures d'Eau
MUSEUM

(1922 Chemin des Coudriers; adult/child $4/2; ☉10am-5pm daily Jun-Sep) The antique-shop-like Musée les Voitures d'Eau tells the island's nautical history through boat engines, buoys, anchors, plodding voiceovers and cheery explanations of the perils of the St Lawrence. There are also boats you can climb on.

Les Moulins   MUSEUM
(36 Chemin du Moulin; adult/child $8.50/4.50; ◷10am-5:30pm May-Oct) *Économusée* Les Moulins has two restored 19th-century mills and exhibits showing how wheat and buckwheat were once ground using grindstones.

Centre Vélo-Coudres   BICYCLE RENTAL
(☑418-438-2118; 2926 Chemin des Coudriers; bicycles per hour $4; ◷ 9am-8:30pm Jul & Aug, to 5pm May, Jun & Sep) You can use the (free) climbing wall here, or rent bikes and bike equipment such as helmets and child carriers. They offer a free shuttle service from the ferry terminal if you call ahead.

🛏 Sleeping & Eating

For a range of dining options, head for Chemin des Coudriers for everything from *casse-croûtes* (fast-food spots) to casual bistros to hotel dining rooms featuring regional cuisine. Also along this street are a number of places to stay, including campgrounds, B&Bs and motels.

Le Long Détour   B&B $$
(☑418-438-1154; 3101 Chemin des Coudriers; r $95-105; 🔊) You have two choices at this tastefully decorated B&B – the 'autumn' room or the 'spring' room. Both have DVD players and king-size beds. Hosts Michelle and Louis aim to please, with extravagant breakfasts that include dessert. You can also arrange to have lunch and dinner (July and August only) here, too.

ℹ Information

Tourist Office (www.tourismeisleauxcoudres. com; 1024 Chemin des Coudriers; ◷9am-5pm Jul-Oct) Near the crossroads just beyond the port. You can pick up a set of three CDs here for a self-guided driving tour of the island.

ℹ Getting There & Away

Free **ferries** (☑877-787-7483) (15 minutes) depart St-Joseph-de-la-Rive, on the north shore of the island, for the mainland on the half hour from May to October, less frequently the rest of the year.

Ste-Irénée

With its cafes overlooking one of the area's best beaches, Ste-Irénée is an inviting stop between Baie St-Paul and La Malbaie. Between June and August, the **Domaine Forget** (www.domaineforget.com) festival of classical music, jazz and dance attracts performers from around the world. **Katabatik** (☑418-665-2332; 180 Rte 362; half-day/2-day tour $57/360) offers sea-kayaking tours.

In a grand house built for an industrialist, **Hôtel Le Rustique** (☑418-452-8250; www. charlevoix.qc.ca/lerustique; 285 Rue Principale; s/d from $75/85) is one of Charlevoix' friendliest and most alluring B&Bs. With their pale colors and photos from owner Diane's travels, the rooms have the feel of an artist's seaside cottage. Three self-contained apartments are also available. The restaurant serves mouth-watering Charlevoix chow (mains $17 to $27), such as chicken breast with local Migneron cheese.

La Malbaie

Now encompassing five previously separate villages, La Malbaie was one of Canada's first holiday resorts. From the late 19th century, steamers run by the Richelieu and Ontario Navigation Company and Canada Steamship Lines docked here.

Arriving from the south on Rte 362 or the west on Rte 138, the first village you come to is **Pointe-au-Pic**. The village was a holiday destination for the wealthy at the beginning of the 20th century, drawing the elite from as far away as New York. One of its famous residents was former US president William Howard Taft, who had a summer home built here. Some of these large, impressive 'cottages' along Chemin des Falaises have been converted into comfortable inns.

Ste-Agnès lies to the northwest, away from the St Lawrence. Adjoining Pointe-au-Pic is **La Malbaie**, which begins to the west of the Malbaie River and continues to the other side. North of La Malbaie is **Rivière Malbaie**, while **Cap à l'Aigle** and **St-Fidèle** are east on Rte 138.

◉ Sights & Activities

Manoir Richelieu   HISTORIC BUILDING
The gray country cousin of Québec City's Château Frontenac, this mega-hotel is also owned by the Fairmont chain. Nonetheless, the sprawling, copper-roofed castle-like structure, which was built in 1928, attests to the area's longtime prosperity. Wander the clifftop gardens, have a drink on the terrace and drop by the gallery displaying local art. Outside, coachloads of hopefuls stream into the much-advertised **Casino de Charlevoix** (Point au Pic; ◷10am-late).

Maison du Bootlegger   HISTORIC BUILDING
(☑418-439-3711; www.maisondubootlegger.com; 110 Rang du Ruisseau-des-Frênes, Ste-Agnès; adult/child $10/5, meal, tour & entertainment from $40; ☻10am-6pm Jun-Sep) This unexpected hostelry in a conventional-looking 19th-century farmhouse was surreptitiously modified by an American bootlegger during the Prohibition period. Tours reveal the marvel of secret doorways and hidden chambers intended to deter the morality squad. From 6pm, it turns into a party restaurant where meat feasts are accompanied by Al Capone beer in boot-shaped glasses and lots of boisterous entertainment.

Musée de Charlevoix   MUSEUM
(www.museedecharlevoix.qc.ca; 10 Chemin du Havre, Pointe-au-Pic; adult/child $7/free; ☻9am-5pm) Part art gallery, part museum, this waterfront museum portrays the life and times of Charlevoix through a variety of media.

Les Jardins du Cap à l'Aigle   GARDEN
(www.villagedeslilas.com; 625 Rue St-Raphael; adult/child $6/free; ☻9am-5pm Jun-Oct) In Cap à l'Aigle, a little village 2km east of La Malbaie, are these gardens, where 800 types of lilac range up the hill between a waterfall, a footbridge and artists selling their daubs.

Katabatik   KAYAKING
(☑418-665-2332; www.katabatik.ca; Cap à l'Aigle marina; half-day tours adult/child $57/45, full-day tours $107/80) Offers sea-kayak expeditions lasting from half a day to five days.

🍴 Sleeping & Eating

Gîtes line the approach to Manoir Richelieu. There's an enticing strip of moderately priced B&Bs on Rue du Quai at the water's edge in Pointe-au-Pic. Down-to-earth La Malbaie is less tourist-trampled, offering services, eating options and stores, and some good accommodations.

Camping des Chutes Fraser   CAMPGROUND $
(☑418-665-2151; www.campingchutesfraser.com; 500 Chemin de la Vallée, La Malbaie; tent & RV sites from $29, cottages from $95; ☻camping May-Oct, cottages year-round) This campground with a waterfall, toward Mont Grand-Fonds park, is idyllic.

Auberge des Eaux Vives   B&B $$
(☑418-665-4808; www.aubergedeseauxvives.com; 39 Rue de la Grève, Cap à l'Aigle; r $145-165) Sylvain and Johanne are the perfect hosts at this three-room B&B with breakfasts to write home about – think smoothies and a four-course extravaganza on a sunny terrace overlooking the St Lawrence. The decor is modern and chic, and there's a guest-only nook with a Nespresso machine, a full kitchen, two fireplaces, and killer views.

Auberge des 3 Canards   INN $$
(☑418-665-3761; www.auberge3canards.com; 115 Côte Bellevue, Pointe-au-Pic; r from $110; ❄🅿🐾) With its 49 rooms sporting flat-screen TVs, vintage photos of the steamers, local art and balconies overlooking the tennis court (with the St Lawrence behind), this 50-year-old institution is more special than it looks from Rte 138. The staff are attentive and the restaurant features impeccably presented regional cuisine (set meal $64).

Manoir Richelieu   HOTEL $$$
(☑418-665-3703, 866-540-4464; www.fairmont.com/richelieu; 181 Rue Richelieu, Pointe-au-Pic; r $189-529; ❄🅿🐾) With its overwhelming size, dark, winding hallways, old-fashioned decor and location – perched on a cliff beating off the howling winds from the St Lawrence below – you may feel like you've been cast in a British murder mystery. But that's the allure of this creaky old castle – that and the four restaurants, spa, casino, golf course and pool.

There's a never-ending list of kids' amenities, including a gym, indoor and outdoor swimming pools, a movie theater and nightly treasure hunts.

Pains d'Exclamation   BAKERY $
(398 Rue St-Étienne, La Malbaie; sandwiches $6-8; ☻7am-5:30pm Tue-Sat) This bakery makes a good lunchtime stop, mainly for the grilled sandwich with Brie-like local cheese, le Fleurmier, with apples and walnuts.

★ Vices Versa   QUÉBECOIS $$$
(☑418-665-6869; 216 Rue St-Étienne, La Malbaie; set meals $65; ☻6-9:30pm Tue-Sun) The name comes from the split personality menu, on which owner-chefs Danielle and Eric have each created a column of choices. The menu is underpinned by local produce (Éboulmontaise lamb, calf's sweetbreads with Grand-Fonds oyster mushrooms, Cornish stew with Charlevoix beer), but the tangy, peppery sauces keep you guessing exactly which ingredient it is that tastes so good. Reservations essential.

QUÉBEC LA MALBAIE

Restaurant Bistro le Patriarche
QUÉBECOIS **$$$**

(☑418-665-9692; 30 Rue du Quai, Pointe-au-Pic; set meals $36-56; ⊙5-9pm Tue-Sun) This elegant, 10-table bistro in a house that dates to 1860 is quickly making a name for itself. Chef Michel churns out interestingly presented, impeccably executed French cuisine that often makes good use of the region's best ingredients. Reservations essential.

ⓘ Information

Regional Tourist Office (☑418-665-4454, 800-667-2276; www.tourisme-charlevoix. com; 495 Boul de Comporté, Pointe-au-Pic; ⊙8:30am-4:30pm)

Parc des Hautes Gorges de la Rivière Malbaie

Work off all that Charlevoix produce with an invigorating hike in this 233-sq-km **provincial park** (☑reservations 800-665-6527; adult/child $6.50/3; ⊙7am-9pm May-Oct), which has several unique features, including the highest rock faces east of the Rockies. Sheer rock plummets (by as much as 800m) to the calm Rivière Malbaie, creating one of Québec's loveliest river valleys.

There are trails of all levels, from ambles around the Barrage des Érables (Maple Dam) to vigorous hikes ascending from maple grove to permafrost.

A highlight is the **boat cruise** (adult/child $34/26; ⊙Jun-Sep) up the river, squeezed between mountains. The river can also be seen from a canoe or kayak, which are available for hire, as are bikes. Boat tickets are available at the visitors center at the park entrance, and rentals 7km further on at the dam.

Many people make it a day trip from La Malbaie, but there are basic **campsites** ($22-35) available. Canoes can be used to reach the three riverside campgrounds. Bring all required supplies.

The park is about 45km northwest of La Malbaie. To reach it from La Malbaie, head northwest on Rte 138 toward Baie St-Paul, then take the turn for St-Aimé des Lacs and keep going for 30km.

St Siméon

Parc d'Aventure Les Palissades (1000 Rte 170; adult/child $4.40/3.50; ⊙9am-5pm), 12km north of St Siméon on Rte 170, is an adventure sports center. There are 15km of trails with lookouts to admire the unusual geological formations, and access to the **Trans Canada Trail (TCT)**. The main attraction, however, is the rock climbing, with 150-plus routes, a suspension bridge, rappelling and two via ferrata cliff walks (from $43.50) with safety cables (no experience required). There's also a zip line ($15). Accommodations range from camping and dorms to chalets; there's also a lakeside spa and sauna.

A **ferry** (adult/child/car $20/13.50/42.40; ⊙Mar-early Jan) connects St Siméon with Rivière du Loup. During the summer, there are three or four daily departures. No reservations are taken; arrive at least 90 minutes before departure in summer. A motion-sickness pill may be welcome on the sometimes rough, 65-minute crossing.

Baie Ste-Catherine

It's overshadowed by nearby Tadoussac, but Baie Ste-Catherine is an attractive spot, its line of multicolored roofs punctuated by glinting barns and patches of grass. Most of the activities offered in Tadoussac can also be arranged from here.

Up the hill from the ferry landing, **Pointe Noire Observation Center** (Rte 138; adult/child $5.80/2.90; ⊙10am-5pm daily Jun-Aug, Fri-Sun Sep & Oct), a whale-study post at the confluence of the Saguenay and St Lawrence Rivers, features an exhibit, a slide show and films, plus an observation deck with a telescope. From the boardwalk, you can often spy belugas in the Saguenay very close to shore, especially when the tide is coming in.

Three of the four cruise companies operating out of Tadoussac pick up from Baie Ste-Catherine pier en route to spotting whales on the St Lawrence or exploring the Saguenay fjord. **Groupe Dufour** (☑418-692-0222, 800-463-5250), **AML** (☑800-563-4643) and **Croisières 2001** (☑800-694-5489) all have booths around the pier.

Friendly and professional **Azimut Aventure** (☑418-237-4477, 888-843-1100; 185 Rte 138) tends to attract a clientele who is serious about sea kayaking. The excursions last hours to days, including a memorable two-day trip to L'Anse St-Jean ($325 including food), and you can rent kayaks ($35 per day).

If it's busy in Tadoussac, there are some decent B&Bs here along Rte 138.

At the southern end of town, the free 10-minute **ferry** to Tadoussac runs across the Saguenay River. The 24-hour service departs every 20 minutes from 7am to 9pm from late April to October; at other times, it leaves every 40 minutes to one hour.

SAGUENAY

Some fans of the Rivière Saguenay fjord, where a dramatic, towering canyon ploughs northwest from the St Lawrence, rank it as the province's most beautiful area. The 100km river, fed by Lac St-Jean, stretches from north of Chicoutimi to the village of Tadoussac. From its dark waters rise majestic cliffs up to 500m high. Formed during the last Ice Age, the fjord is the most southerly one in the northern hemisphere. As deep as 270m in some places, the riverbed rises to a depth of only 20m at the fjord's mouth at Tadoussac. This makes the relatively warm, fresh waters of the Saguenay jet out atop the frigid, salt waters of the St Lawrence, leading to massive volumes of krill, which in turn attract the visitor highlight of the region: whales. They and the entire waterway now enjoy protected status.

There are two main areas of the Saguenay region. The first hugs the Rivière Saguenay and consists of park and tiny, scenic villages along both sides. The second is the partially urban, industrialized section with midsize Chicoutimi as its pivot.

Tadoussac

For many visitors to Québec, Tadoussac is the one place in the province they visit outside Montréal and Québec City. What consistently draws the hordes to this small spot is the whales. Not only do Zodiacs zip out in search of the behemoths, but smaller whales such as belugas and minkes can be glimpsed from the shore.

Added to that are activities such as sea kayaking, 'surfbiking,' exploring the fjord by boat or on foot, or simply wandering the dunes and headlands. Some of Tadoussac's vibrancy departs with the whales between November and May, but it remains a historic, bohemian town where the locals invariably have time for a chat.

History

Tadoussac became the first fur-trading post in European North America in 1600, eight years before the founding of Québec City. The word *tatouskak* in the Innu-aimun (Montagnais) language means breast, and refers to the two, rounded hills by the fjord and bay. When the Hudson's Bay Company closed its doors, Tadoussac was briefly abandoned, only to be revived as a resort with the building of Hotel Tadoussac in 1864, and as an important cog in the pulp and paper wheel.

◉ Sights

Centre d'Interprétation des Mammifères Marins   MUSEUM
(CIMM; 108 Rue de la Cale Sèche; adult/child $12/ free; ☉9am-8pm May-Oct) The CIMM gives excellent background information on local sea creatures through multimedia exhibits. There are also pretty gardens.

Poste de Traite Chauvin   HISTORIC SITE
(157 Rue du Bord de l'Eau; adult/child $4/2.50; ☉9am-7pm Jun-Oct) This replica of the continent's first fur-trading post offers some history on the first transactions between Aboriginals and Europeans.

Petite Chapelle   HISTORIC SITE
(Rue du Bord de l'Eau; adult/child $3/1; ☉9am-8pm Jun-Sep) Built in 1747 by the Jesuits, Petite Chapelle is one of North America's oldest wooden churches. Also known as the Indian Chapel, it contains a small exhibition on missionary life.

☆ Activities

Whale-Watching
From May to November, tourists flock to Tadoussac. The whale-watching is phenomenal, particularly between August and October, when blue whales are spotted. All over town, tickets are available for boat tours, from 12-person Zodiacs to the 600-person *Grand Fleuve*; check out the options carefully. Wait for a calm day, when the view won't be marred by waves and a rocking boat, and go out in the early morning or evening, when the whales are livelier and there are fewer vessels around. Zodiac passengers are given waterproofs; whatever trip you do, take lots of warm clothes.

Otis Excursions (www.otisexcursions.com; 431 Rue du Bateau-Passeur; 2hr Zodiac trips $64, 3hr boat trips $74) is a local company that has been running for 35 years. Its Zodiacs get closest to the waves and offer the most exciting, if roughest, rides. Young children aren't permitted, however.

The Zodiac operated by **Croisières AML** (www.croisieresaml.com; 177 Rue des Pionniers; 2hr

QUÉBEC TADOUSSAC

Zodiac trips $64, 3hr boat trips $74) is twice the size of the others.

For the adventurous, sea-kayaking supremo **Mer et Monde** (www.mer-et-monde.qc.ca; 148 Rue du Bord de l'Eau; 3hr trips from $52) offers whale-watching expeditions and excursions up the fjord. Similar **Azimut Aventure** (www.azimutaventure.com) has a booth on the beach during the summer.

Hiking

There are four 1km paths in and around Tadoussac, marked on the map given out by the tourist office. The trails around the peninsulas **Pointe de l'Islet**, by the quay, and, at the other end of the beach, **Pointe Rouge** are the best for spying whales from the shore.

Parc du Saguenay borders the fjord on both sides of the river. The provincial park has over 100km of splendid hiking trails, views down the fjord from atop 350m-plus cliffs, plus trailside refuges where you can spend the night. There are three refuges on the 43km trail from Tadoussac to Baie Ste-Marguerite, open May to October. To book a hut, contact Parc du Saguenay; its local office is at **Maison des Dunes** (418-235-4238; 750 Chemin du Moulin à Baude; 10am-5pm Sat & Sun Jun–Aug, 1:30-5:30pm Fri-Sun Sep & Oct). You pay park fees (adult/child $6.50/3) here, and there's also an exhibit explaining why what everyone calls 'dunes' in the area are actually marine terraces – formed by waves, not wind, as dunes are. It's a 7km walk along the shore from town, and there are 1km trails leading through the dunes to lookout points.

Overlapping with Parc du Saguenay, and extending to the Saguenay, Charlevoix and North Shore regions, with various entry points, **Parc Marin du Saguenay–St-Laurent** (http://parcmarin.qc.ca; 197 Rue des Pionniers) was the first conservation project in Québec to be jointly administered by the federal and provincial governments. This park covers and protects 1138 sq km of the two rivers and their coastlines, from Gros Cap à l'Aigle to Les Escoumins and up the Saguenay as far as Cap à l'Est, near Ste-Fulgence.

✦✦ Festivals & Events

Festival de la Chanson   MUSIC
(Song Festival; 418-235-2002; www.chansontadoussac.com; Jun) Tadoussac's busy summer season begins with a vengeance at the 25-year-old Festival de la Chanson, a celebration of Francophone, mostly Québecois, music and a serious party. Stages spring up

all over town and accommodations fill up for the long weekend.

🛏 Sleeping

Domaine des Dunes   CAMPGROUND $
(418-235-4843; www.domainedesdunes.com; 585 Chemin du Moulin à Baude; tent & RV sites $32, trailer or motorhome sites $45, chalet from $156;) The smaller and leafier of Tadoussac's two campgrounds, 3km from town. Self-catering chalets are also available.

Auberge la Sainte Paix   INN $
(418-235-4803; www.aubergelasaintepaix.com; 102 Rue Saguenay; r $98-133) Cheery host Marie is a ray of sunshine in the morning, as are her plentiful, fresh breakfasts. She's happy to help out with tour-planning and sightseeing, and can make good local recommendations. There are only seven rooms, so book well in advance.

Hôtel Tadoussac   HOTEL $$
(800-561-0718, 418-235-4421; www.hoteltadoussac.com; 165 Rue du Bord de l'Eau; r from $155;) This 149-room, red-and-white landmark has extensive gardens, a pool overlooking the port, and vintage photos of steamers and the hotel looking considerably smaller in 1870. Somewhat dated bedrooms have plush carpets, ceiling fans and river views.

Maison Clauphi   MOTEL, B&B $$
(418-235-4303; www.clauphi.com; 188 Rue des Pionniers; B&B/motel rooms $99/139; May-Oct) The accommodations range from motel and B&B rooms to studios and suites in this building built in 1932 by the owner's parents. Bikes and waterborne 'surfbikes' can be rented.

🍴 Eating

Restaurant Le Bateau   QUÉBECOIS $$
(246 Rue des Forgerons; lunch/dinner buffet $12.50/18; 11am-2:30pm & 5-9:30pm May-Oct) A great view comes with the buffet of traditional Québec workers' fare at this friendly restaurant. Fill up on Lac St-Jean meat pie, followed by blueberry, sugar or vinegar pie.

Café Bohème   CAFE $$
(239 Rue des Pionniers; set meals $15-20; 8am-10pm May-Oct) The village's hangout of choice is a prime place for a breakfast of fruit and yogurt or a panino, or just to sip fair-trade coffee among the local intellectuals. Later in the day, choose between dishes such as duck confit salad and fresh pasta of the day.

Chantmartin   FAST FOOD $$
(412 Rue du Bateau Passeur; set meals $15-25; ⊘5:30am-10pm) Despite its truck-stop-like appearance and attached line of generic motel rooms, Chantmartin is a good, rapid stop for everything from poutine and pizza to crab, prawns and roast chicken.

Chez Mathilde   FUSION $$$
(227 Rue des Pionniers; set meals from $25; ⊘11am-9:30pm Jun-Oct) The stellar chef at this cute little house utilizes plenty of local produce in his creative, though limited, menu. The innovative dishes, cooked to perfection, are served up alongside a view of the port from an airy patio.

La Galouine   FUSION $$$
(251 Rue des Pionniers; set meals $22-38; ⊘8am-10pm) Entered by a fairy-light-covered balcony above an organic market, this is a whole-food cafe taken up a notch. Dishes such as seafood casserole are satisfyingly earthy, though the prices are a little steep.

❶ Information
Café Bohème (239 Rue des Pionniers; ⊘8am-10pm May-Oct; ☎) Free wi-fi and internet access.
Tourist Information Office (☎418-235-4744, 866-235-4744; www.tadoussac.com; 197 Rue des Pionniers; ⊘8am-9pm) In the middle of town, with very patient staff that can help with accommodations.

❶ Getting There & Away
The 24-hour, 10-minute ferry from Baie Ste-Catherine in Charlevoix is free. The terminal is at the end of Rue du Bateau Passeur.

Tadoussac is off Rte 138. Intercar buses connect Tadoussac with Montréal ($108, eight hours) and Québec City ($55, four hours) twice a day and run as far northeast as Sept Îles. The bus stop is opposite Camping Tadoussac at the Petro-Canada garage.

Les Bergeronnes
The slow pace of the North Shore begins in Les Bergeronnes, which is pleasingly deserted. With a handful of attractions and an excellent campground, it's worth leaving Tadoussac for.

Archéo Topo (498 Rue de la Mer; adult/child $6/3; ⊘8am-8pm Jul & Aug, 9am-5pm Jun & Sep) is a research and exhibition center dedicated to archaeological findings along the

North Shore. Outside, trails lead down to the beach.

A few kilometers northeast of Les Bergeronnes, signposted from Rte 138, the **Cap de Bon Désir Interpretation Centre** (13 Chemin du Cap de Bon Désir; adult/child $7.80/3.90; ⊘9am-6pm Jun-Oct) has captivating marine life exhibits and scheduled activities, but the real attraction is the natural stone terrace for whale-watching.

Eight kilometers further northeast, the **Marine Environment Discovery Centre** (41 Rue des Pilotes; adult/child $7.80/3.90; ⊘9am-6pm daily Jun-Aug, Fri-Sun Sep) has sophisticated facilities such as a video link with naturalist-divers foraging on the estuary floor.

Outside of Les Escoumins, 12km northeast of Les Bergeronnes on Rte 138, is Essipit, an Innu community. The **Essipit Centre** (☎888-868-6666, 418-233-2266; 46 Rue de la Réserve; ⊘7am-11pm) sells local crafts and makes reservations for a campground and chalets. The center offers whale-watching cruises at slightly lower prices than in Tadoussac (Zodiac tours from $50). Blue whales are more likely to be seen in this area.

At **Camping Paradis Marin** (☎418-232-6237; 4 Chemin Émile Boulianne; campsites from $13; ⊘May-Oct), off Rte 138 northeast of Les Bergeronnes, you can hear whales breathing from your tent (or wigwam) and rent kayaks ($9 per day).

L'Anse-St-Jean
Heading west up the Saguenay is a fine drive on either side of the fjord. There are more good stops on the south side and there's more access to the river, but the north shore is memorable for its rugged topography and little lakes strung along the roadside.

First stop on the south side is L'Anse-St-Jean, a little village with a lot going on in its *ateliers*. There's also trails at the Parc du Saguenay, water-based activities and **Mont Édouard**, Saguenay's highest summit. There are marvelous fjord views at **L'Anse de Tabatière**.

❰ Activities
Croisière Personnalisée
Saguenay   WHALE-WATCHING
(☎418-272-2739; 15 Rue du Quai; cruises $40-70; ⊘Jul-Sep) One of several cruise operators, this offers one- to four-hour cruises in a

seven-person motorboat, taking in the fjord and beluga whales.

Fjord en Kayak
KAYAKING

(☑ 418-272-3024; www.fjord-en-kayak.ca; 359 Rue St-Jean-Baptiste; 3hr tours $58) Offers great excursions lasting from two hours to five days.

Centre Équestre des Plateaux
HORSEBACK RIDING

(Equestrian Center; ☑ 418-272-3231; 34 Chemin des Plateaux; per hr $30) Has horses, ponies and even a horse-drawn sleigh for winter fun. It's signposted up the hill from Rue St-Jean-Baptiste.

🛏 Sleeping & Eating

L'Auberge du Boutdumonde
INN $

(☑ 418-272-9979; www.boutdumonde.ca; 40 Chemin des Plateaux; dm/shared yurt/r $25/35/50; 🛜) 🎣 It does indeed feel like it's at the end of the world, secluded on a steep hill (even by car it's a challenge). The former eco-commune has been renovated by the new owners: five 20-somethings who grew up here. Yoga classes, a cultural center, a lake, a herbal garden and forest are on the doorstep. As breakfast is not served, be sure to stock up on groceries before arriving. Cash only.

Auberge des Cévennes
INN $$

(☑ 418-272-3180, 877-272-3180; www.auberge-des-cevennes.qc.ca; 294 Rue St-Jean-Baptiste; r $75-105) You can hear the river gurgling across the street at this lovely inn, with a restaurant (set meal $30) overlooking the covered bridge.

Chalets du Fjord
INN $$

(☑ 800-561-8060, 418-272-3430; www.chalets-sur-le-fjord.com; 354 Rue St-Jean-Baptiste; studios/condos/chalets from $85/119/140, mains $28; 🍽) Accommodations ranging from studios to condos to hillside cabins of varying sizes and amenities. It overlooks the marina and has its own quality restaurant.

Bistro de L'Anse
PUB $$

(319 Rue St-Jean-Baptiste; mains $14-22; ⊙3pm-1am Thu-Sat, 5pm-midnight Sun-Wed) This is a local hub where you can catch live music on Saturday nights and tuck into sandwiches, salad and pasta on the veranda.

❶ Getting There & Away

Transport Adapté du Fjord (opposite page) runs a minibus to Chicoutimi ($22, 5½ hours). Reserve ahead and the bus will pick you up.

Rivière Éternité

This town is rather lacking in anything other than unlikely collections of religious art, but it is one of the main access points for both the Parc Marin du Saguenay–St-Laurent and Parc du Saguenay. Contact the Rivière Éternité-based **park information office** (☑ 800-665-6527, 418-272-1556; 91 Rue Notre Dame; ⊙8:30am-9pm May-Oct) about trips, trails, sea kayaking, sailing, Zodiac outings and numerous guided activities.

A four-hour-return hike, including a brutally long staircase, leads to an 8m-tall statue of the **Virgin Mary**. She stands on one of the fjord's highest cliffs, protecting the sailors and boats below. Charles Robitaille erected it in 1881, having narrowly escaped death the previous winter when his horse crashed through the ice on the river. Vowing to honor the Virgin Mary for saving his life, he commissioned the 3200kg statue, which took over a week to cart and assemble.

Back in town, the **church** has a renowned collection of 250 Christmas manger vignettes. Nearby, over the wooden bridge off Rte 170, the **Halte des Artistes** is a free, drive-through park containing sculptures in little mangers.

Chicoutimi

This regional center is a pleasant place to take care of chores before returning to the Saguenay wilds. The site of a 1676 fur-trading post, it was founded as late as 1842, and became a world pulp and paper capital in the early 20th century. It looks rather industrial from the approach roads, but downtown buzzes with students from the town's university and Cégep (pre-university college).

◉ Sights

La Pulperie
MUSEUM

(www.pulperie.com; 300 Rue Dubuc; adult/child $14.50/6.50; ⊙9am-6pm daily Jun-Aug, 10am-4pm Wed-Sun Sep-May) This was once the world's biggest pulp mill. A guided tour and exhibitions explain the mill's history and its pivotal role in the development of a town that increased its population from 708 in 1899 to 4255 in 1929. The site also features the **House of Arthur Villeneuve**, now a museum. The barber-artist painted the entire building inside and out like a series of canvases in his bright, naive folk style.

Musée de la Petite
Maison Blanche   MUSEUM
(Little White House; 441 Rue Gédéon; adult/child $5/2.60; ⊗9am-9pm daily Jun-Aug, to 6pm Sat & Sun Sep-Oct) In the area known as 'the Basin' is this spindly museum. Built in 1900, the house withstood water with a force equivalent to Niagara Falls in a 1996 flood that caused $16 billion of damage to Chicoutimi.

🛏 Sleeping & Eating

Auberge Racine   B&B $$
(☑418-543-1919; 334 Rue Racine Est; s/d from $89/99; ☎) In this 19th-century house, the delightful rooms have original details and are named after some of the first owner's three wives and 12 children.

Artis Resto Lounge   ITALIAN $$
(416 Rue Racine Est; mains $12-25; ⊗4pm-late Mon-Fri, 8am-3am Sat & Sun) With a popular terrace, Artis serves typical Italian fare but is more interesting than the pubs nearby.

❶ Information

Tourist Office (☑418-698-3157, 800-463-6565; 295 Rue Racine Est; ⊗8:30am-4:30pm Mon-Thu, to 8pm Fri, 10am-4pm Sat & Sun) The helpful staff here also speak good English.

❶ Getting There & Away

Intercar (☑418-543-1403; 55 Rue Racine Est) buses connect (four times daily) to Québec City ($86, 2½ hours), Montréal ($117, six hours) and Tadoussac ($122, 6½ hours).

Transport Adapté du Fjord (☑418-272-1397) runs a minibus down the Saguenay to L'Anse St-Jean ($22, 5½ hours) on Monday, Tuesday, Thursday and Friday (leaving Chicoutimi at 1:30pm).

Lac St-Jean

Motorists crossing the nondescript flats between Chicoutimi and Lac St-Jean may wonder if the area is popular among Québecois for quasi-political reasons alone. The region touts itself as the heartland of Québec nationalism. However, upon reaching the lake, there is a subtle beauty in this open area, where the meeting of sky and water is interrupted only by pale wooden houses and shining church spires. The area also claims to be the province's blueberry and *tourtière* (meat pie) capital; look out for chocolate-covered blueberries.

◉ Sights & Activities

Village Historique Val Jalbert   HISTORIC SITE
(95 Rue St-Georges; adult/child $23/11.50; ⊗9am-6pm Jun-Sep) The Val Jalbert Historic Village is a ghost town that was inhabited from 1901 until a few years after the pulp mill closed in 1927. There's a trolleybus with running commentary from one of the zealous, costume-wearing guides, and a pleasant restaurant in the old mill by the dramatic waterfall. The peaceful spot also has a campground and cabins.

Musée Amérindien de
Mashteuiatsh   MUSEUM
(www.museeilnu.ca; 1787 Rue Amishk, Mashteuiatsh; adult/child $10/6; ⊗9am-6pm) North of Roberval on the lakeshore, one of the province's best-organized aboriginal villages is home to this museum, featuring good exhibits on the area's Pekuakamiulnuatsh group.

Véloroute des Bleuets   CYCLING
The 272km of cycling trails around the lake combine to form the **Blueberry Bike Trail**, and nearly every town along the way has facilities to make the trip easier: rental and repair shops, B&Bs that cater to cyclists and rest areas. For maps, suggested itineraries and a list of helpful stops, visit the **Maison du Vélo** (Bicycle Tourism Information Center; ☑418-668-4541; www.veloroute-bleuets.qc.ca; 1692 Ave du Pont Nord; ⊗8:30am-noon & 1-4:30pm) in Alma.

🛏 Sleeping

Auberge Île du Repos   CAMPGROUND, HOSTEL
(☑418-347-5649; 105 Rte Île du Repos; campsites/dm/r from $21/31/64) Taking up an entire little island off Péribonka and Parc de la Pointe Taillon, Auberge Île du Repos is a resort featuring dorms, kitchen facilities, private chalet rooms, camping, a cafe-bar, a beach, croquet and volleyball. With the closest Intercar terminal in Dolbeau-Mistassini, some 25km northwest, it can be a little ghostly despite its cheery pink facade.

Ste-Rose du Nord

On the Saguenay River's less-frequented north side, Ste-Rose du Nord is a member of the Association of the Most Beautiful Villages of Québec. Wander beneath the purple cliffs to the quay with the fjord beyond and it's easy to see why.

Above the village on Rue de la Montagne, there are short walks through the trees to viewing points.

Signposted off Rte 172 between Ste-Fulgence and Ste-Anne du Rose, **Pourvoirie du Cap au Leste** (☑ 418-675-2000; www.capauleste.com; 551 Chemin du Cap à l'Est; s $77-142, d $104-192, meals $30) is worth the bumpy 7km on a side road for its dramatic views over a large stretch of the fjord. The frugal but charming cabins have wood burners and balconies, and the restaurant serves superb regional cuisine; nonguests should reserve. Hiking, canoeing, kayaking, climbing and mountain biking can be organized.

You can pitch your tent on a hill at **Camping Descente des Femmes** (☑ 418-675-2581; 154 Rue de la Montagne; campsites $20-28; ☉ Jun-Sep) and wake up to a view over the village and onto the fjord. The showers and toilets are in a converted grange, and the owner's a hoot.

SOUTH SHORE

It's tempting to rush through the South Shore, which includes the Chaudière-Apalaches and Bas St-Laurent regions, en route to the Gaspé Peninsula. However, the area has a wonderfully eclectic mix of attractions, from haunting Grosse Île to refined Rivière du Loup. Other stops include a major woodcarving center, an island once used as a smugglers' stash, and museums devoted to a *Titanic*-like tragedy, Basque whalers and squeezeboxes.

Added to this are the spectacular views across the island-dotted St Lawrence to the undulating North Shore. Hwy 20 is fastest, but Rte 132 is more scenic and goes through the heart of numerous riverside villages.

Grosse Île

The first stop outside Québec City's urban sprawl is one of the region's most interesting. Grosse Île served as the major quarantine station for immigrants arriving from Europe from 1832 to 1937. A tour of the **Grosse Île National Historic Site** (☑ 888-773-8888, 418-234-8441; ☉ daily Jul & Aug, Wed-Sun May, Jun, Sep & Oct) sheds light on this little-known aspect of North American history, through visits to the disinfecting chambers, the original hospital and immigrants' living quarters, and the memorial cemetery, which holds the remains of 7500 people. Knowledgeable guides explain the tragic histories lived out on the island. A 14.5m Celtic cross, the tallest in the world, commemorates the 76,000 Irish immigrants wiped out by a typhus epidemic in 1847.

It is also possible to visit the 21-island Île aux Grues archipelago. For all trips, wear warm clothing and comfortable shoes.

Berthier-sur-Mer marina, 55km northeast of Québec City on Rte 132 (also accessible via Hwy 20), is the closest departure point for the boat tours to Grosse Île. Times and prices are determined by the boat tour operators.

Croisières Lachance (☑ 855-268-9090, 418-692-1752; www.croisiereslachance.com; 110 Rue de la Marina, Berthier sur Mer; adult/child tours $54/30) offers two daily tours: a narrated return cruise and a Parks Canada–guided walk.

Croisières le Coudrier (p279) operates full-day tours from Québec City and Île d'Orléans on the north shore.

Montmagny

The main reason to stop beneath the green copper steeple in Montmagny, the first town of any size east of Lévis, is to go to **Île aux Grues**. This 10km-long island, part of an otherwise uninhabited 21-island archipelago, has one of North America's largest unspoiled wetlands. Birders flock to the area in spring and autumn to spot migratory birds including snow geese. The island has a couple of **walking trails**. Free **ferries** (☉ Apr-Dec; two to four daily) leave from Montmagny marina for the 25-minute crossing. Other commercial excursions to the archipelago are also possible.

In Montmagny is the **Centre des Migrations** (Migration Educational Center; 53 Ave du Bassin Nord; ☉ 10am-5pm Jun-Sep) FREE, an interpretive center with exhibits on migration, feathered and human, to Grosse Île and the South Shore.

The **Musée de l'Accordéon** (Accordion Museum; www.accordeonmontmagny.com; 301 Blvd Taché Est; adult/child $8/2; ☉ 10am-4pm daily Jul & Aug, Mon-Fri Sep-Jun), North America's only one, gives an insight into this giant of the Gallic music scene. Squeezeboxes date back to 1820, and incorporate materials such as ivory and mother-of-pearl. In late August, the four-day **Carrefour** features performances by squeezebox aficionados from around the globe.

St-Jean Port Joli

St-Jean became known as a center of craftsmanship in the 1930s, a reputation it works hard to keep. Riverside Parc des Trois Berets, named after the three beret-wearing brothers who launched the town as a woodcarving capital, is the venue for an international **sculpture festival** in June.

There are scores of *ateliers*, boutiques and roadside pieces of art, covered by a free map available from the seasonal **tourist office** (☑ 418-598-3747; Rte 132; ⊙ 9am-5pm).

Musée des Anciens Canadiens (332 Rte 132 Ouest; adult/child $7.50/3; ⊙ 8:30am-9pm May-Oct) has over 250 wood-carved figures from René Lévesque to Harry Potter, providing a good introduction to the work of the beret-clad Bourgaults and other local notables.

Philippe-Aubert de Gaspé, author of *Les Anciens Canadiens*, is buried in the 18th-century **church**.

🛏 Sleeping & Eating

Camping de la Demi Lieue   CAMPGROUND $
(☑ 418-598-6108, 800-463-9558; 598 Rte 132; campsites from $28.50; ⊙ May-Sep; @ ⚐) Huge but well equipped and closer to town than the other campgrounds.

La Maison de l'Ermitage   B&B $$
(☑ 418-598-7553, 877-598-7553; www.maisonermitage.com; 56 Rue de l'Ermitage; r incl breakfast with/without bathroom from $95/80) This eye-catching house with red-and-white towers hides artfully decorated rooms inside. The friendly alpacas in the backyard are popular with kids.

Gîte La Mer Veille   B&B $$
(☑ 418-598-3112; www.gite-lamerveille.com; 261 Rue Lionel Groulx; s/d incl breakfast from $72/92; ⚐) In a leafy garden near the quay, this family-run hotel is one of the only ones not overlooking Rte 132.

Pizzeria Porto Bellissimo   ITALIAN $
(318 Rue de l'Église; mains $5-14; ⊙ 9am-10pm Sun-Wed, to 11pm Thu-Sat; ✐) For homemade pizzas, sandwiches and decadent desserts in a bright and cheery atmosphere, this cafe in the center of town is a smart choice.

La Boustifaille   QUÉBECOIS $$
(547 Rte 132 Est/Ave de Gaspé Est; set meals $16-26; ⊙ 8am-8pm May-Oct) Renowned for huge portions of local classics such as pork ragout, *tourtière* (meat pie) and cheese quiche, and its adjacent theater.

❶ Getting There & Away

Orléans Express buses to/from Québec City ($28, 2½ hours, two daily) stop in the center of town at Épicerie Régent Pelletier, 10 Rte 132.

Rivière du Loup

Its curious name (the Wolf River) either refers to seals (sea wolves), an Amerindian tribe or a 17th-century French ship, but one thing is certain: Rivière du Loup is a town of some distinction. Its key position on the fur and postal routes between the Maritimes and the St Lawrence made it the main town in eastern Québec during the 19th century. Formerly an English-speaking town, it was planned according to the British model, with open spaces in front of grand buildings such as the Gothic silver-roofed St Patrice. Having declined in the early 20th century, it's booming again, with one of the province's highest birthrates, as well as an influx of urban runaways and graduates returning to their beautiful birthplace.

◉ Sights

Parc des Chutes   PARK
Short trails make the most of the small but seductive Parc des Chutes, a few minutes' walk from downtown at the end of Rue Frontenac. If you get lost, just follow the sounds of the cars and the 30m waterfalls that power a small hydroelectric power station.

Parc de la Croix   PARK
A short drive into the hilly part of town leads to tiny Parc de la Croix, where an illuminated cross guards a stunning view across town and the river. To get there from downtown, take Rue Lafontaine south to the underpass leading to Rue Témiscouata. Make a left on Chemin des Raymond, then turn left at Rue Alexandre, right at Rue Bernier and left at Rue Ste-Claire.

Musée du Bas St-Laurent   MUSEUM
(300 Rue St-Pierre; adult/student $5/3; ⊙ 9am-6pm daily Jul & Aug, 1-5pm Wed-Sun Sep-Jun) The lively Musée du Bas St-Laurent has a collection of contemporary Québec art, but the main event is the 200,000 vintage photos of the local area, used in thematic, interactive exhibits that explore life on the St Lawrence.

Fraser Manor
NOTABLE BUILDING

(www.manoirfraser.com; 32 Rue Fraser; adult/child $6/2; ⏱ 9:30am-5pm Jul-Sep) Rivière du Loup was called Fraserville in the 19th century, named after the powerful Scottish dynasty that inhabited the grand Fraser Manor. Today the Manor gives an insight into life in the upper echelons of the developing colony.

🏃 Activities

La Société Duvetnor
CRUISE

(☎ 418-867-1660; www.duvetnor.com; 200 Rue Hayward) Offshore, a series of protected islands sport bird sanctuaries and provide habitat for other wildlife. The nonprofit group La Société Duvetnor offers bird-watching and nature excursions to the islands. Sighting belugas is common. There are 45km of trails on the largest island, l'Île aux Lièvres, and accommodations, including a campground. Prices start at $25 for a 1½-hour cruise to Pot au l'Eau de Vie (the brandy pot), named for its use as a bootlegging way station during the Prohibition era.

Croisières AML
CRUISE

(☎ 418-867-3361, 800-563-4643; 200 Rue Hayward; 3½hr tours $69; ⏱ Jun–Aug) For whale-watching there's Croisières AML. If you're crossing the river to Tadoussac, save your trip for there.

Rivière du Loup/St-Siméon Ferry
CRUISE

(www.traverserdl.com; adult/child round-trip $16.80/11.10) You can take a return trip on the St-Siméon ferry without disembarking (three hours). Beluga whales are commonly spotted.

Petit Témis Interprovincial Linear Park
CYCLING, WALKING

The Petit Témis Interprovincial Linear Park is a scenic bike and walking trail, mainly flat, which runs along an old train track for 135km to Edmundston, New Brunswick. The tourist office has maps, and **Hobby Cycles** (278 Rue Lafontaine; rental per day from $30) rents bikes.

🛌 Sleeping

Rue Fraser is a good place to look for motels. There are campgrounds and B&Bs near the marina – convenient if you're catching an early morning ferry.

Auberge Internationale
HOSTEL $

(☎ 418-862-7566; www.aubergerdl.ca; 46 Blvd de l'Hôtel de Ville; dm/r incl breakfast from $23/52; @ 🛜) This excellent, central HI hostel in an old house has small dorms with attached bathrooms. The long-term staff create a placid, welcoming atmosphere.

L'Innocent
INN $

(☎ 418-862-1937, 418-714-2098; 460 Rue Lafontaine; r with shared bathroom $35) This paint-splashed cafe has four simple, tiny double rooms.

Auberge la Sabline
B&B $$

(☎ 800-470-4890, 418-867-4890; 343 Fraser Ouest; r $85-105; @ 🛜) In a quiet, residential neighborhood, this grand Victorian with many original features has four elegant rooms. Breakfast is a decadent affair, with smoothies and over-the-top pastries, in addition to crepes, eggs, and waffles.

Au Vieux Fanal
MOTEL $$

(☎ 418-862-5255; www.motelauvieuxfanal.com; 170 Rue Fraser; r $60-120; ⏱ May-Nov; ❄ 🏊) One of the best motels on the strip is this multi-colored place with great views of the river and a heated swimming pool.

🍴 Eating

Chez Antoine
FRENCH $$

(433 Rue Lafontaine; lunch/dinner mains from $16/20; ⏱ 11am-2pm Mon-Fri & 5-9pm daily) Long considered the best in town, Chez Antoine maintains its tradition. Specialties include Atlantic salmon, duBreton pork tenderloin, and filet mignon, all served in an old white house with a classy dining room enrobed in wood paneling.

L'Innocent
CAFE $$

(460 Rue Lafontaine; mains $10-15; ⏱ 9am-9pm Wed-Sat, to 2pm Sun) The hippest cafe around serves great-value daily specials to a ska soundtrack. It's the best place in town to meet locals; and if you're in a hurry, they serve coffee to go.

L'Estaminet
PUB $$

(299 Rue Lafontaine; mains $10-20; ⏱ 7am-midnight Mon-Fri, from 8am Sat & Sun) Feast on hearty pub grub and specials, including house-specialty mussels with fries, in this 'bistro du monde' with 150 types of beer.

L'Intercolonial
FUSION $$

(407 Rue Lafontaine; mains $10-20; ⏱ 11am-9pm Mon & Tue, to 10pm Wed-Fri, 4-10pm Sat) The name refers to the train that once stopped in Rivière du Loup, but it's also a good description of a menu featuring European dishes, Asian flavors and creations that could only come from the Québecois imagination, such as salmon with pear cream.

ℹ Information

Tourist Office (☑ 418-862-1981; www.touris-meriviereduloup.ca; 189 Blvd de l'Hôtel de Ville; ☺ 8:30am-8pm) Has internet access and a free Old Town walking map.

ℹ Getting There & Away

A ferry (see opposite page) runs between Rivière du Loup marina and St Siméon.

Hwy 20 (exit 503), Rte 132 and Hwy 85 lead directly into Rivière du Loup.

Orléans Express buses to Québec City ($42, 2¼ to four hours, five daily) and Rimouski ($33, 1½ hours, four daily) stop at the **bus station** (317 Blvd de l'Hôtel de Ville). Transfer at Rimouski for New Brunswick.

Rivière du Loup is linked by **VIA Rail** (☑ 418-867-1525, 888-842-7245; 615 Rue Lafontaine) every second day to Charny, Québec City ($40, two hours) and Halifax ($142, 15 hours), and three times a week to Percé ($97, 11 hours). The station is only open when the trains arrive, in the middle of the night.

Île Verte

For some respite from the road, which thins to one lane after Rivière du Loup but is busy as far as Rimouski, take the 15-minute ferry crossing to Île Verte.

Summer cottages have only recently begun creeping onto the 11km-long island, which has a permanent population of 45. It's popular for birding, cycling, whale-watching and, in the winter, ice-fishing.

In the last 10 years, the island has gained some culinary celebrity for *l'agneau de pré-salé* (saltwater lamb). This comes from sheep that graze on the flats during low tide. The animals have more muscle and less fat than other sheep, and their meat is more tender and flavorful. The specialty can be tried on the island at the 'saltwater lamb ambassador,' **La Maison d'Agathe** (set meals from $31; ☺ Jul & Aug).

The river's oldest **lighthouse** (1809) contains a museum, and you can stay in the adjacent cottages, **Les Maisons du Phare** (☑ 418-898-2730; s/d incl breakfast $70/90; ☺ May-Oct). There's also a campground.

Ferries (☑ 418-898-2843; one-way $5.25) shunt between the island and mainland according to tides.

Consider leaving the car on the mainland and renting a bike (reservations recommended) from **Location de Bicyclettes Entre Deux Marées** (☑ 418-860-7425, 418-898-2199; 4404 Chemin de l'Île).

Trois Pistoles

On the northern outskirts of Trois Pistoles, a village memorable only for the business names that seem to all refer to its Basque heritage, rises the blue-and-red **Parc de l'Aventure Basque en Amérique** (66 Ave du Parc; adult/student $7/4; ☺ 10am-6pm). Inside, an exhibition tells the story of the Basque whalers who were the first Europeans after the Vikings to navigate the St Lawrence, predating Jacques Cartier. The exhibits are in French only, but an English booklet is available. In July, the museum hosts the **International Basque Festival**, with music, a small parade and games.

Outside is Canada's only **pelota court**, or *fronton,* where the Basque sport, one of the world's oldest bat-and-ball games, is played. *Pelote* aficionados travel from as far afield as Montréal to use the court; *palas* (bats), *pelotes* (balls) and the court can be rented for $5 per hour.

Inquire at the Parc de l'Aventure Basque en Amérique about guided excursions to **Île-aux-Basques** (☑ 418-851-1202; adult/child $2/free; ☺ Jun-Aug), 5km offshore, with its 16th-century Basque ovens, 2km of trails and bird refuge. Admission is by tour only. **Kayak des Îles** (☑ 418-851-4637; 60 Ave du Parc; 3hr/6hr tours $45/90) runs sea-kayaking expeditions.

Camping & Motel des Flots Bleus Sur Mer (☑ 418-851-3583; Rte 132; tent & RV sites $25, r $60; ☺ May–mid-Oct; ☎), 5km west of town, is a small, quiet campground with a neighboring bare-bones motel.

On a hill above the church near hiking rails and waterfalls, **La Rose des Vents** (☑ 888-593-4926, 418-851-4926; 80 2ème Rang Ouest; s/d incl breakfast $70/80; @☎), a lovely old place with a modified roofline, has a breakfast room with huge windows gazing at the North Shore.

Parc du Bic

This 33-sq-km park, half covered by water, is one of the smaller parks in Québec and among the most beautiful. A striking sight even from Rte 132, its rotund headlands that shelter bays and islands have provided sanctuary for Aboriginal peoples dating back 9000 years; it has also harbored colonial vessels and a multitude of flora and fauna. There are 700 types of plants, thousands of marine birds, seals (between July and

October), deer and one of North America's highest-density porcupine populations.

The **park** (☎418-736-5035; 3382 Rte 132; adult/child $6.50/3; ⊙Jun-Oct & Dec-Mar) has an excellent interpretation center. The activities on offer, most of which can be organized by the helpful staff, include excellent hiking, mountain biking, sea kayaking, guided walks and drives, wildlife observation by day and night, snowshoeing and Nordic skiing. The two-hour-return trail to **Champlain Peak** (346m) rewards with views across to Îlet au Flacon; the park runs a shuttle there.

The park has three campgrounds, igloos, a hut and even a luxurious yurt. Avoid the noisy campground by Rte 132.

Rimouski

A fairly large, oil-distribution town, Rimouski has a prosperous air and some of the area's best cafes and museums. The student population gives it some atmosphere, making it a reasonable place to do chores or wait for a ferry.

Sights & Activities

Musée de la Mer MUSEUM
(www.shmp.qc.ca; 1034 Rue du Phare; adult/child $14.75/8.75; ⊙9am-6pm Jun-Sep) Seven kilometers east of town, this museum narrates the *Empress of Ireland* tragedy, the worst disaster in maritime history after the *Titanic*. In the 14 minutes it took for the ship to disappear into the St Lawrence after colliding with a Norwegian collier, 1012 people lost their lives. The disaster was all but forgotten with the outbreak of WWI two months later.

You can also join a free tour of **Pointe au Père Lighthouse** (adult/child $4/3) next door, the highest in eastern Canada.

The former keeper's cottage has displays on navigating the river and diving to the Empress, 45m down.

The wreck itself is considered one of the world's premier scuba diving sites. However, this is a dangerous dive; several inexperienced divers have died. Currents, visibility and water temperature are serious challenges.

Musée Régional de Rimouski GALLERY
(35 Rue St-Germain Ouest; adult/child $5.50/4; ⊙9:30am-6pm Jun-Aug, noon-5pm Wed & Fri-Sun, to 8pm Thu Sep-May) In a renovated stone church, this gallery has contemporary art exhibitions and regular events including film nights.

Le Canyon des Portes de l'Enfer HIKING
(Chemin Duchénier; adult/child $10/5; ⊙May-Oct) For hiking, mountain biking and a view of a canyon and waterfalls from the province's highest suspended bridge (62m), head to Le Canyon des Portes de l'Enfer, near St Narcisse de Rimouski, 30km south of town along Rte 232.

Sleeping & Eating

Accommodations can be found on the waterfront and around Ave de la Cathédrale.

Hôtel Rimouski HOTEL $$
(☎800-463-0755, 418-725-5000; www.hotelrimouski.com; 225 Blvd René-Lepage Est; r from $99; ❄@🛜≋) With a genteel elegance and a slightly faded regal demeanor, this grande dame of Rimouski has neat rooms, most with views of the boardwalk and water across the street. It's big with business travelers, for the on-site convention center, and families, for the superfast, superfun waterslide and indoor pool.

Auberge de l'Évêché INN $$
(☎866-623-5411, 418-723-5411; 37 Rue de l'Évêché Ouest; r incl breakfast $80-114; 🛜) Above a *chocolaterie* opposite the town hall, the eight rooms here have TVs and are attractively decorated with vintage photos.

La Brûlerie d'Ici CAFE $
(91 Rue St Germain Ouest; sandwiches $6; ⊙8am-11pm; 🛜) A hip hangout offering Guatemalan and Ethiopian coffees, bites from bagels to banana bread, wi-fi and live music during the summer.

Le Crêpe Chignon CAFE $$
(www.crepechignon.com; 140 Ave de la Cathédrale; set meals $18-19.50; ⊙7-11am Mon-Fri, 8am-2pm Sat & Sun) This bright light on the Rimouski dining scene serves delicious savory and dessert crepes. The only drawback is there's often a wait for a table.

Central Café CAFE $$
(31 Rue de l'Évêché Ouest; mains $12-16; ⊙11am-10pm Mon-Sat, 4-10pm Sun) Set in a two-story house built in 1947, this is where locals go to pig out on burgers, pasta, pizza and smoked-meat sandwiches.

Information

Tourist Office (☎418-723-2322; www.tourisme-rimouski.org; 50 Rue St-Germain Ouest; ⊙8:30am-7:30pm Jun-Aug, 9am-4:30pm Mon-Fri Sep-May) On Place des Veterans, at the intersection of Rue St-Germain and Ave de la Cathédrale, is the busy but helpful tourist office.

ℹ Getting There & Away

BOAT

A **ferry** (☑ 800-973-2725, 418-725-2725; ☺ May–early Oct) links Rimouski with Forestville on the North Shore (one-way adult/child/car $23/15/43, 1¾ hours, two to four daily). Reservations are accepted.

The **Relais Nordik** (☑ 800-463-0680, 418-723-8787; www.relaisnordik.com; 17 Ave Lebrun; ☺ early Apr–mid-Jan) takes passengers on its weekly cargo ship to Sept Îles, Île d'Anticosti, Havre St-Pierre, Natashquan and the Lower North Shore. It departs Rimouski marina on Tuesday morning and gets to Blanc Sablon by Friday evening. Return fares start at $525 for the full journey and range up to $1147 for a deluxe cabin containing a porthole, toilet and shower. Meals (breakfast/lunch/dinner $7/15/20) are available on board. Cars can be taken, although it's extremely costly (fares are calculated according to the weight of the vehicle) and a bicycle is more convenient at the brief stopovers. Reservations are best made months in advance.

BUS

Orléans Express buses leave from the **bus station** (90 Rue Léonidas) to Québec City ($63, four hours, five daily), Rivière du Loup ($34, 1½ hours, six daily) and Gaspé ($78, seven hours, five daily).

CAR

Ride-share agencies **Allô Stop** (☑ 418-723-5248; www.allostop.com; 307 Rue St-Germain Est) and **Kangaride** (p229) hook up drivers and passengers for locations including Québec City (from $15) and Montréal (around $30 to $35).

TRAIN

For VIA Rail services, the **train station** (57 Rue de l'Évêché Est) is only open when trains pull in, which is usually after midnight. Every second day, trains travel to/from Montréal ($120, eight hours).

GASPÉ PENINSULA

The isolated promontory, known locally as 'La Gaspésie,' has remnants of a colorful colonial past, which can be seen on a coastline that bulges into the gulf, overlooking rusting shipwrecks and migratory whales. Like the whales, Normans, Bretons, Basques, Portuguese and Channel Islanders were attracted by the rich fishing grounds. English, Scottish and Irish fugitives from upheavals such as the Great Famine and American independence settled on the south shore, leaving isolated anglophone communities. Flags that were erected by the descendents of Acadian settlers flutter above Rte 132.

Between the small communities' colorful farm buildings and silver spires, the landscape is also striking. There's the famous pierced rock in Percé, of course, and there are endless beaches overshadowed by glacier-patterned cliffs. The mountainous, forested hinterlands, home to the breathtaking Parc de la Gaspésie, are crossed by few routes, among them the Matapédia Valley drive, the International Appalachian Trail and Rte 198, one of the province's quietest roads.

The tourist season runs from about June to mid-September. Outside those times, things seriously wind down and, from November to mid-May, the main activity you'll see will be the waves crashing against the rocks.

Ste-Flavie

The gateway to Gaspé is also one of the peninsula's most touristy towns. Nonetheless, it's a relaxing place to pause before tackling the rocky landscape that soon rises above Rte 132.

The 19th-century windmill **Vieux Moulin** (141 Rte de la Mer; museum admission $2.50; ☺ 8am-9pm) FREE offers tastings of Shakespeare's favorite tipple, mead, and has a small museum containing colonial and prehistoric aboriginal artifacts.

The star of the town's art trail is the **Centre d'Art Marcel Gagnon** (www.centredart.net; 564 Rte de la Mer; ☺ 7:30am-10pm) FREE. Outside, the extraordinary sculpture *Le Grand Rassemblement* (*The Great Gathering*) has more than 100 stone figures filing out of the St Lawrence. Unfortunately, the gallery, displaying work by Gagnon and his son, feels a little too commercial, with all manner of *Gathering* souvenirs for sale.

Upstairs, the **auberge** (☑ 866-775-2829, 418-775-2829; r incl breakfast $95-135) has understatedly artistic rooms with private bathrooms. The **restaurant** (mains $13-25; ☺ 7:30am-8:30pm) serves pizza, pasta and a plethora of seafood with a great view.

Also overlooking the St Lawrence, **Capitaine Homard** (180 Rte de la Mer; mains $15-35; ☺ 11am-11pm May-Aug) has been the local 'kilometer 0' since 1968. It serves exquisite

Gaspé Peninsula

seafood beneath a Davy Jones' Locker–like ceiling, and offers internet access, camping and chalets.

On Rte 132, the large **Tourisme Gaspésie** (☏800-463-0323, 418-775-2223; 357 Rte de la Mer; ⏰8am-8pm) office is Gaspé's main tourist office. If you're here in the off-season, pick up the pamphlet listing winter facilities.

Grand Métis

One of Gaspé's most revered attractions, the **Jardins de Métis** (www.refordgardens.com; 200 Rte 132; adult/child $18/free; ⏰8:30am-8pm Jul & Aug, to 6pm Jun & Sep) comprises more than 90 hectares of immaculately tended gardens boasting 3000 varieties of plants. Begun in 1910, the gardens are also known as the Reford Gardens – after Elsie Reford, who inherited the land from her uncle, Lord Mount Stephen, the founder of the Canadian Pacific Railway whose 37-room villa is now a museum. The International Garden Festival blooms here from late June to September. The villa and cafe serve lunch and English teas.

About 10km east of Grand Métis are the beach towns of **Métis Beach** and **Métis sur Mer**. With big lawns and British names on their street signs and mailboxes, they resemble American towns. Traditionally a retreat for the Anglophone bourgeoisie, the area has a predominantly native-English-speaking population.

Matane

Matane is a commercial fishing port famous for its shrimp. While it's hardly the peninsula's prettiest town, it is popular for salmon fishing and for sampling local hauls in the markets and restaurants.

🏃 Activities

Observation Center   FISHING
(260 Ave St Jerôme; adult/child $3/free; ⏰7:30am-9:30pm Jun-Sep) Salmon weighing up to 19kg swim up the Rivière Matane to spawn in June. The observation center at the dam is worth a visit before or after dinner. It sells permits to fish the 100km river starting right in town.

Absolu Écoaventure   HIKING
(☏418-562-7885; www.ecoaventure.com) This outfitter organizes advanced and beginners' hikes on part of the International Appalachian Trail, which cuts through the wild, rugged Réserve Faunique de Matane. Reserve by phone or email.

🛏 Sleeping & Eating

Camping Rivière
CAMPGROUND $

(✉418-562-3414; 150 Rte Louis Félix Dionne; tent & RV sites from $22) Southwest of downtown, this campground has 124 secluded, private sites among the trees. From town, head south toward Amqui, on Rue Henri Dunant.

Hôtel Motel Belle Plage
HOTEL $$

(✉888-244-2323, 418-562-2323; www.hotelbelle-plage.com; 1310 Rue Matane sur Mer; r $69-182; 🐾) You can order smoked salmon and white wine to your room and dine on the balcony. Pretty swish for a motel! It's close to the ferry terminal and away from the noise of Rte 132.

La Seigneurie
INN $$

(✉418-562-0021, 877-783-4466; 621 Ave St-Jérôme; r $99-159) This friendly B&B occupies a grand property dating from 1919 with attic rooms, a grand piano and a freestanding bath in the 'lovers' room.'

Le Rafiot
SEAFOOD $$

(1415 Ave du Phare Ouest; mains $15-23, meals from $23; ⊙11am-2pm Mon-Fri & 5-9pm daily) At this casual bistro with maritime-themed decor, seafood duos and upscale 'terres et mers' (surf and turf) platters abound.

🛍 Shopping

Poissonnerie Boréalis
FOOD

(985 Rte 132; ⊙8am-9pm) A good choice for fish, fresh or smoked.

ℹ Information

The **tourist office** (✉418-562-1065; www.touris-mematane.com; 968 Ave du Phare Ouest; ⊙9am-9pm Jul & Aug, to 6pm Jun & Sep) is based in a lighthouse alongside a maritime museum.

ℹ Getting There & Away

A **ferry** (✉418-562-2500, 877-562-6560) service runs between Matane, Baie Comeau and Godbout (adult/child/car $17.50/11.50/42, four to six daily). The ferry terminal is off Rte 132, about 2km west of the town center.

Buses (✉418-562-4085; 521 Rte 132) arrive at and depart from the Irving gas station, 1.5km east of the town center. Orléans Express buses go to Gaspé ($41, five hours, two daily) and Rimouski ($28.50, 1½ hours, three daily).

Cap Chat

Cap Chat is a typical Gaspé village...apart from those 133 windmills beating above the white houses. This is Canada's largest wind farm and the world's most economical, producing 100 megawatts of electricity. Covering a 100km area, the dreamlike structures perch on hilltops above the start of the St Lawrence gulf. Dominating the gang is the world's largest vertical-axis windmill, which, alas, is no longer used.

If you'd like to take a one-hour tour, including the biggest windmill, contact **Éole Cap-Chat** (www.eolecapchat.com; tours $10; ⊙9:30am-5:30pm Jul-Oct). Look for the signs on Rte 132 just west of Cap Chat. English-language tours are available.

Off Rte 132 east of the bridge at Cap Chat, **Camping au Bord de la Mer** (✉418-809-3675; 173 Rue Notre Dame Est; campsites $13-20, RV sites $28) is a simple campground offering river views.

Ste-Anne-des-Monts

A regional service center at the turnoff for Parc de la Gaspésie, Ste-Anne-des-Monts is the place to stock up, refuel and get a sea fix before heading inland to the wilderness. It's also a pretty spot, with an idyllic waterfront and cute downtown.

If you have kids in tow, the **Exploramer** (www.exploramer.qc.ca; 1 Rue du Quai; adult/child $13.50/8.25; ⊙9am-5pm Jun-Oct) complex, which focuses on the marine life of the St Lawrence, is a great place for a pit stop. There's an aquarium with tactile exhibits – in case you've ever wanted to touch a sea cucumber – and also a maritime museum, sea excursions and a peek into the process of sea harvesting. Little little ones might prefer the nautically themed playground outside.

Off Rte 132 east of town, the funky HI member **Auberge Festive Sea Shack** (✉866-963-2999, 418-763-2999; www.aubergefestive.com; 292 Boul Perron Est; campsites $15, dm member/nonmember $26/30, cabins from $74; @🐾) is a highlight on the 'party hostel' circuit. Bands play at the beach bar and water-lovers take out kayaks or gaze at the St Lawrence from the outdoor Jacuzzi.

For a less energetic stay, the **Auberge Château Lamontagne** (✉418-763-7666, 888-783-2663; www.chateaulamontagne.com; 170 1ere Ave Est; r $95-120), perched on a hill overlooking the St Lawrence, is a colorful inn. Its seven modern rooms have polished oak floors and subtle, refined decor.

La Seigneurie des Monts (✉800-903-0206, 418-763-5308; bonjourgaspesie.com; 21 1-ère Ave Est; r $134-184), built in 1864, exudes a vintage atmosphere with its creaky floorboards, 'his and hers' dressing gowns, antiquarian books and chaise longue.

The **tourist bureau** (☑418-763-0044; 96 Boul Ste-Anne Ouest; ☉9am-8pm Jul & Aug, 10am-6pm Jun & Sep) is on Rte 132, next to the Orléans Express bus stop.

Parc de la Gaspésie

From Ste-Anne-des-Monts, Rte 299 runs south to this outstanding, rugged **park** (☑800-665-6527, 418-763-7494; www.sepaq.com/pq/gas/en; adult/child $6.50/3), 802 sq km of spectacular scenery dotted with lakes and two of Québec's most beautiful mountain ranges, the Chic Choc and McGerrigle, which together include 25 of the province's 40 highest summits. Some of Québec's most scenic camping spots are here, as well as 140km of hiking tracks, including one of the best sections of the International Appalachian Trail. What's more, the only herd of caribou south of the St Lawrence River lives in the park. If you're lucky, you'll see the animals in the distance, but stay on the paths to protect them and the fragile vegetation.

Activities

Québec's second-highest peak, **Mont Jacques Cartier** (1268m), is also its highest accessible summit. Hiking the mountain takes about 3½ hours return, passing through alpine scenery with fantastic views and a good chance of spying woodland caribou.

Other fabulous walks include the strenuous trek to the top of **Mont Albert** (1151m) and the lesser-known, exhilarating half-day return trip up **Mont Xalibu** (1140m), with alpine scenery, mountain lakes and a waterfall on the way. **Mont Ernest Laforce** is good for moose, which also often feed at **Lac Paul** in the morning and evening.

Sleeping & Eating

Ste-Anne-des-Monts makes a convenient base for the park.

Park Campgrounds CAMPGROUND $
(tent & RV sites $28.50, tents/cabins from $99/101) The park has four campgrounds. The busiest serviced grounds are near the Interpretation Center; try for a spot at the quietest – Lac Cascapédia. Two- to eight-person cabins and permanent tents are also available.

Gîte du Mont Albert INN $$
(☑418-763-2288, 866-727-2427; r from $149; ☉Jan-Oct; ❋@❂❄) This is a large, comfortable lodge next to the Interpretation Center for those who like their nature spliced with luxury. Facilities include a pool, sauna and first-class restaurant (set meals from $35) with mountain views through the floor-to-ceiling windows.

❶ Information

Interpretation Center (☉8am-10pm mid-May–mid-Oct, 8:30am-4:30pm late Dec–mid-Apr) At the park's Interpretation Center, the staff are extraordinarily helpful in planning a schedule to match your time and budget. They also rent hiking equipment.

❶ Getting There & Around

A bus (round-trip adult/child $6.25/4.75) runs from the Ste-Anne-des-Monts tourist information center to the Interpretation Center. It leaves at 8am daily from late June to the end of September, returning at 5pm.

The daily service (round-trip adult/child $15.40/11.50) between the Interpretation Center and Mont Jacques Cartier trailhead leaves the Center at 9am and returns from the trailhead at 4pm. Five daily shuttles go between Mont Jacques Cartier campground and the trailhead (round-trip adult/child $6.25/4.75).

Driving to Mont St-Pierre from the Interpretation Center, taking Rte 299 and the coastal Rte 132 is faster, safer and more scenic than the tree-lined track through the park.

Réserve Faunique des Chic Chocs

This reserve surrounds and bleeds into Parc de la Gaspésie. Mainly a site for hunting and fishing, it also attracts geological expeditions. Agates are common and you can go gem-collecting at **Mont Lyall Mine** (adult/child $9/6; ☉9am-5pm Jun-Sep).

To reach the main entrance, go south on Rte 299 from Parc de la Gaspésie, 12km past the Gîte du Mont Albert, then east for 1.5km on the Rte du Lac Ste-Anne toward Murdochville.

Mont St-Pierre

The scenery on the Gaspé Peninsula becomes ever more spectacular east of Ste-Anne-des-Monts. The North Shore, across the St Lawrence, disappears from view, and the road winds around rocky cliffs, every curve unveiling a stretch of mountains cascading to the sea.

Appearing after a dramatic bend in the road, Mont St-Pierre takes its name from a 418m mountain with a cliff that's one of the continent's best spots for **hang gliding** and **paragliding**. At the end of July, the 10-day hang-gliding festival **Fête du Vol Libre** fills the sky with hundreds of sails. Near the eastern end of town and south of Camping Municipal, rough roads climb Mont St-Pierre, where there are takeoff stations and excellent views. If you're not hoofing it up the mountain, which takes an hour, you must have an ATV.

Beneath the scree slopes of Mont St-Pierre, **Camping Municipal** (☑ 418-797-2250; 103 Rte 2; campsites/RV sites $22/35; ☺ Jun-Sep; ☒) is well equipped, with laundry facilities, a pool and a tennis court.

Parc de la Gaspésie and Réserve Faunique des Chic Chocs can be reached via Rte 2, which turns to gravel a few kilometers south of town. Take a map and watch out for logging trucks. If you're heading to the Interpretation Center, take the main roads.

East of Mont St-Pierre

The landscape in this area is majestic, with towering cliffs, pebbly beaches, telegraph poles protruding from mounds of scree and the occasional hang-glider overhead.

Next to the **lighthouse** (entry $2.50) at **Ste-Madeleine de la Rivière Madeleine** is a cafe with internet access, a fishing center and a **museum** (entry with lighthouse $6) about the local paper mill that employed over 1200 workers at its peak in 1921.

As the road dips in and out of towering green valleys around **Grande Vallée**, there are more waves in the strata-lined cliff faces than in the calm bays on the other side of the road.

Petite Vallée is a quaint waterfront village, particularly around the blue-and-white **Théâtre de Vieille Forge** (☑ 418-393-2222; 4 Rue de la Longue-Pointe), the venue for much of the **Festival en Chanson** (☺ late Jun–early Jul). This has become one of Québec's most important folk-song festivals, but has retained an intimate feel. Kids and even the local butcher participate impromptu on stage.

Miniscule **St Yvon** is noteworthy for having been hit by a wayward torpedo in WWII.

At **Cap-des-Rosiers**, the gateway to Forillon, the village's history of Irish, French and Channel Island settlers is described in the epitaphs in the clifftop **Cimetière des Ancêtres**. The **lighthouse** is the highest in Canada.

Parc National du Canada Forillon

Covering Gaspé's northeastern-most tip, this small **park** (www.pc.gc.ca/forillon; adult/child $7.80/3.90; ☺ reception 10am-5pm Jun-Oct) feels like a fitting place to end a journey along the top of the peninsula. Its rugged sea cliffs attract seabirds, including great blue herons, and whales and seals make frequent appearances offshore. Inland are rolling, forest-covered hills, where you might come across moose, deer, fox and, increasingly, black bears.

There are two main entrances with visitors centers where you can pick up maps: one at L'Anse au Griffon, east of Petite Rivière au Renard on Rte 132, and another on the south side of the park at Penouille.

◎ Sights & Activities

The north coast consists of steep limestone cliffs, some as high as 200m, and long pebble beaches, best seen at **Cap Bon Ami**. Keep a lookout through the telescope there for whales and seals. In the **North Sector**, south of Cap-des-Rosiers, you'll find a great picnic area with a small, rocky beach.

The south coast features more beaches, some sandy, with small coves. **Penouille Beach** is said to have the warmest waters. The rare maritime ringlet butterfly flourishes in the salt marshes here, and the end of the curving peninsula is a prime sunset-watching spot.

The trails that meander through the park range from easy, 30-minute loops to a rigorous 18km trek that takes 6½ hours one-way. The gentle hike east to **Cap Gaspé** provides seashore views. The International Appalachian Trail ends in the park, where the Appalachians plunge into the sea.

Parks Canada organizes activities (at least one a day in English), including a whale-watching cruise, sea kayaking, fishing, scuba diving and horseback riding.

CANADIAN APPALACHIAN

The 1034km Canadian segment of the 4574km International Appalachian Trail (IAT) was added to the American portion in 2001 and, though still not well known, it forced the 'International' prefix. Crossing the peaks and valleys of the Appalachian Mountains, one of the world's oldest chains, North America's longest continuous hiking trail stretches from Mt Springer, Georgia, USA, to Forillon National Park at the tip of the Gaspé Peninsula.

The Canadian section begins on the Maine/New Brunswick border, crosses New Brunswick, including the province's highest peak, Mt Carleton, and enters Québec at Matapédia. The 644km Québec part of the trail winds up the Matapédia Valley to Amqui, where it swings northeast for the highlight of this section, Parc de la Gaspésie and the surrounding reserves. It then descends from the mountains to Mont St-Pierre and follows the coast for 248km to its final destination, Cap Gaspé.

The trail is clearly marked and well maintained, apart from in the Matapédia Valley, and there are shelters and campgrounds along the way. Some portions should only be attempted by experienced hikers, and everyone should seek advice about matters such as black bears. More information and maps are available at tourist offices and park information offices in locations such as Matapédia, by calling ☑ 418-562-7885 and by visiting www.sia-iat.com.

🛏 Sleeping

Auberge Internationale
Forillon   HOSTEL $

(☑418-892-5153; www.aubergeforillon.com; 2095 Blvd Grande Grève, Cap-aux-Os; dm/r $30/60; ⊙May-Nov; ☎) This hostel makes a great base for explorers, with friendly staff who dole out walking advice. The restaurant offers overpriced, average grub. The building could feel institutional when full, but the view across the bay is the ultimate redeeming feature. A *dépanneur* (convenience store) and bike and kayak rental are nearby.

Forillon Campgrounds   CAMPGROUND $

(☑877-737-3783, 418-368-5505; www.pccamping. ca; campsites/RV sites $25.50/29.40, tents $70-100; ⊙Jun-Sep) The park contains 367 campsites in three campgrounds, and it often fills to capacity. Petit-Gaspé is the most popular ground, as it is protected from sea breezes and has hot showers. Cap Bon Désir is the smallest, with 41 tent-only sites. Permanent basic tents with beds called 'oTENTiks' can be found in and near Petit-Gaspé.

❶ Getting There & Around

Transportation is limited. Orléans Express buses between Rimouski and Gaspé stop in the park daily during the summer, at locations including Cap-des-Rosiers and Cap-aux-Os. A drawback is that this still leaves a walk along Rte 132 to the hiking trails and campgrounds, though the bus driver may drop passengers within the park.

Gaspé

The most scenic aspect of the peninsula's nominal capital is its view of Forillon. However, it has two interesting attractions and is a better place than touristy Percé to adjust to civilization after a few days in the park.

This was where Jacques Cartier first landed in July 1534. After meeting the Iroquois of the region, he boldly planted a wooden cross and claimed the land for the king of France.

◉ Sights

Musée de la Gaspésie   MUSEUM

(80 Blvd Gaspé; adult/child $10/5; ⊙9am-5pm) Here you can get to grips with the peninsula's history, evoking its maritime heritage through artifacts such as a 17th-century hourglass. Most involving is the exhibition on Jacques Cartier, the former ship's boy who persuaded the French navy to back his 'voyage to that kingdom of the New World.' Outside, a bronze **monument** commemorates Cartier's landing.

Site d'Interpretation de la
Culture Micmac de Gespeg   MUSEUM

(783 Blvd Pointe-Navarre; adult/student $8/6; ⊙9am-5pm Jun-Sep) Northwest of town, next to the **Notre Dame des Douleurs** church, a Catholic pilgrimage site, is this center, which explains the culture and history of the local Mi'kmaq group through an exhibition, English- and French-language tours (10am, 11am, 2pm and 3:30pm) and workshops.

📖 Sleeping & Eating

Motel Adams   MOTEL $$
(☑418-368-2244, 800-463-4242; www.moteladams.com; 20 Rue Adams; r $88-119; ✴🔊) Central, with 96 large units and a bar and restaurant. The vibe is no-frills, but the owner is friendly and knowledgeable.

Motel Plante   MOTEL $$
(☑418-368-2254, 888-368-2254; 137 Rue Jacques-Cartier; ste $85-150; ✴@🔊) Atop a small hill overlooking downtown Gaspé with basic suites and studios with kitchens.

Hôtel des Commandants   HOTEL $$
(☑800-462-3355, 418-368-3355; www.hoteldescommandants.com; 178 Rue de la Reine; r from $130) For sleek, modern luxuries (like coffee makers and industrial-chic decor), this large, business-friendly hotel complex is your best bet.

Café des Artistes   CAFE $
(101 Rue de la Reine; sandwiches $8-12; ⊙7am-10pm) There's world music on the stereo, a list of teas and coffees as long as Gaspé and grub ranging from croissants to pizza.

Bistro Bar Brise-Bise   PUB $$
(135 Rue de la Reine; mains from $15; ⊙11am-10pm) Devour pizzas, burgers and mussels while enjoying nightly entertainment.

ℹ Getting There & Away

Daily Air Canada flights link the small **airport** (☑418-368-2104) 6.5km south of town with Îles de la Madeleine and Montréal via Québec City.

Orléans Express buses stop at Motel Adams.

Percé

Gaspé's charms seem to lurk deep in its national parks rather than in its towns, but then there's Percé and its famous Rocher Percé (Pierced Rock). One of Canada's best-known landmarks, the rock rears out of the sea near North America's largest migratory bird refuge, Île Bonaventure. Both sit in a patch of gulf that, from 1784, attracted schools of European cod fishers. Having stained a lobster bib, you can work off the fishy pounds with a hike in the hills, part of the Appalachians, that shelter the peninsula's most appealing town.

◉ Sights & Activities

Access to the **Parc National** (4 Rue du Quai; adult/child $6.50/3; ⊙9am-5pm Jun-Oct) campus, overlooking the rock, includes the reception, some of the surrounding waters, Île Bonaventure and an interpretation center covering local history, birdlife, flora, fauna and geology.

Rocher Percé   LANDMARK
This 88m-high, 475m-long chunk of multihued limestone has inspired descriptive entries in travel journals dating back to Samuel de Champlain's captain's log of 1603. The town's landmark attraction is only accessible from the mainland by cruise or boat. Île Bonaventure cruises always include a journey around the rock with commentary on its history and folklore.

Signs warning of falling rocks should be taken seriously: each year, some 150,000 tons of rock debris detach from the big rock. There used to be two holes in it, but one arch collapsed in 1845; in 2003, 100,000kg of debris fell at once.

Île Bonaventure   ISLAND
Meeting the more than 100,000 gannets on green Île Bonaventure is an active antidote to gorging on Percé's tempting fish platters. Head toward the dock in Percé and you'll come across the tour operators' booths and touts selling tickets for cruises to the island. All of the boats circle Rocher Percé, get up close to the gannets on the side of the island, and then pull into the dock on Île Bonaventure's west side. You can disembark here and go for a hike, or stay on board for the return journey to Percé. If you choose to linger, note that you'll have to pay a national park entrance fee upon disembarkation.

Club Nautique de Percé   WATER SPORTS
(199 Rte 132) Club Nautique de Percé offers kayak and scuba-diving tours and rentals. Transportation to a dive sight and equipment rental costs $95 for one dive and $155 for two.

Hiking   HIKING
Above town are some great hikes around southern Gaspé's most rugged, hilly area. Hike up the 3km path to **Mont Ste-Anne** (340m), beginning above the church, to enjoy the view and detour to **La Grotte** (The Cave). Another 3km trail leads to the **Great Crevasse**, a deep crevice in the mountain. The tourist office gives out a useful map.

🚶 Tours

Les Traversiers de l'Île
BOAT

(☑418-782-5526; Rue du Quai; ☺Jun-Sep) One of three cruise companies, it offers a lobster fishing excursion and tours (adult/child $25/8) of Île Bonaventure, where you have the option of disembarking and walking the island's trails.

La Revasse
JEEP

(☑418-782-2102; 16 Rue St-Michel; ☺Jun-Sep) Runs 2½-hour jeep tours of scenic spots such as Mont Ste-Anne, La Grotte and Le Pic d'Aurore ($28), saving you the hike.

🛏 Sleeping

Le Macareux
MOTEL $

(☑418-782-2414, 866-602-2414; cnr Rte 132 & Rte des Failles; s/d with shared bathroom from $35/70; ☺May-Oct; 🐾) Behind a breezy seaside exterior, the sparkling rooms with TVs and shared bathrooms are good value. Downstairs, the souvenir shop offers a 15% discount on boat tours.

Au Pic de l'Aurore
CHALET $$

(☑418-782-2151, 866-882-2151; www.percechalet. com; 1 Rte 132 Ouest; r $69-174, chalets $69-207; ☺May-Oct; ❄@🐾🐾) Perched high on a cliff overlooking Percé, the sprawling grounds of the 'Peak of Dawn' offer something for everyone: chalets with or without kitchenettes, classy motel rooms and even a whole four-bedroom house to rent (from $925 per week). Interiors have a cozy log-cabin feel with pine furniture, and there's free wi-fi and a bar with outstanding views. Free pickup from train station.

Gîte au Presbytère
B&B $$

(☑418-782-5557, 866-782-5557; www.perce-gite. com; 47 Rue de l'Église; s/d incl breakfast $82/119; ☺May-Oct; @🐾) With a well-tended garden by the massive church, this sizable, bright old rectory with gleaming hardwood floors is one of the best options. The friendly and gracious host, Michel, is a wealth of local knowledge.

Hôtel La Normandie
HOTEL $$$

(☑418-782-2112, 800-463-0820; www.normandie perce.com; 221 Rte 132 Ouest; r $129-249; ☺May-Oct; @🐾) The classiest spot in town, the retreatlike Normandie has serious amenities: the beach, room balconies, a dining room for seafood and expansive lawns with panoramic views of the rock.

🍴 Eating

Percé has budget eateries, but if you're hankering to splash out and sample some seafood, this is the place to do it. Along the main strip, Rte 132, are a string of casual cafes that offer pretty much the same menu of pizzas, seafood, salads and burgers.

Boulangerie Le Fournand
CAFE $

(194 Rte 132; snacks $2-10; ☺7:30am-8pm Mon-Sat, to 7pm Sun May-Oct) For picnic breads, decent Italian coffee and mouth-watering French pastries and quiche, try this colorful bakery.

Café Champêtre
CAFE $

(164 Rte 132 Ouest; mains $6-15; ☺11am-10pm Jun-Oct) The tourist-trappy Café Champêtre caters to families with its wide patio with a small playground and ice-cream parlor next door.

GANNET GATHERING

Of the hundreds of feathered species found in Québec, none is closer to the hearts of Québecois than the northern gannet (fou de bassan). Île Bonaventure is home to 104,000 of them, one of the world's largest colonies and certainly the most accessible. But it's not their sheer numbers or the squawking din that makes seeing them memorable. Adult gannets are strikingly beautiful, with blazing white plumage and, at the base of a handsome gray-blue bill, piercing blue eyes surrounded by a black patch. During mating season, their heads turn pale yellow, as if glowing from within.

Mature gannets have a wingspan of about 2m, which is evident in their graceful flight, which sometimes seems to not require a single flap. Seeing them return to their life-long mates, evidently without a moment's confusion despite the mob, and indulge in a little friendly caressing is both touching and amusing.

And then there's the birds' dive-bomb approach to hunting. They strike from a distance of about 20m, plunging straight down, sending spray all over the place and, more often than not, resurfacing from as deep as 5m with a mouthful of fish.

Visiting them on the island, where you can get close without disturbing them, is a highlight of any already engaging Île Bonaventure cruise.

La Maison du Pêcheur SEAFOOD $$
(☑418-782-5331; 155 Place du Quai; pizzas $13-23, set meals $18-40; ☺11am-2:30pm & 5-10pm Jun-Oct; 🛜) In a former fishers' shack that became a commune in the 1960s (graffiti remains on the ceiling), this award-winning restaurant serves seafood, including lobster, and 15 types of pizza (even octopus!) baked in a maplewood-heated stove. There's web access downstairs in bistro-cafe L'Atlantique. Reservations strongly recommended.

Café Couleurs CAFE $$
(1004 Rte 132 Est; set meals $8-20; ☺9am-5pm Jun-Sep) In a quiet and retreatlike house in idyllic Barachois, about a 20-minute drive from town, you can get good food all day and decent coffee. There's also a small art gallery and appealing gift shop. Start the day with Belgian waffles and a mountain of fruit on the patio, and soak up views of the ocean, mountains, and Rocher Percé.

Resto du Village CAFE $$
(162 Rte 132; set meals $20; ☺8am-9:30pm) This casual, long-running cafe has a boisterous patio right on the road and decent food.

ℹ Information

Tourist Office (☑418-782-5448, 855-782-5448; 142 Rte 132; ☺8am-9pm Jul & Aug, to 5pm Jun, Sep & Oct) In the middle of town.

ℹ Getting There & Away

Orléans Express buses stop at the tourist office en route to Gaspé (one-way $7, 55 minutes, two daily), where you can transfer to Forillon National Park, and west to Rimouski (one-way $84, eight hours, two daily).

New Carlisle

One of the main English towns, Loyalist-founded New Carlisle has New Brunswick–style clapboard houses and Protestant, Anglican and Presbyterian churches on grid-arranged streets. Incongruously, René Lévesque grew up here, on 16 Rue Mount Sorel.

The Palladian **Hamilton Manor** (☑418-752-6498; www.manoirhamilton.com; 115 Rue Gérard Lévesque; tours $5, r incl breakfast $80; ☺May-Dec; @) was built in 1852 by the town's first mayor. It's a wonderful portrait of colonial life – from the picture of Queen Victoria to the bread oven to the maids' attic quarters – and the guest rooms are decked out in 19th-century decor and haven't changed much since. From Wednesday to Sunday between June and September, afternoon tea is served in porcelain cups and saucers. The *petit théâtre* screens classic films in the living room.

Bonaventure

Founded by Acadians in 1791, Bonaventure is a nondescript, spread-out town, but it's worth a stop to learn about the Acadians' 'Great Upheaval' or to drift up the Rivière Bonaventure, one of Québec's cleanest.

The small **Musée Acadien** (95 Ave Port-Royal; adult/child $9.25/6.25; ☺9am-5pm) houses artistic interpretations of the Acadian plight, with bilingual explanations. It hosts popular outdoor Acadian music concerts on Wednesday evenings during the summer.

Northeast of town, the almost 500,000-year-old **Grotte de St Elzéar** (☑877-524-7688, 418-534-3905; 136 Chemin Principal; adult/child $39.50/29.50; ☺four tours daily 8am-3pm Jul & Aug) is one of Québec's oldest caves. You descend into the cool depths (bring warm clothes) and view the stalactites, stalagmites and moon milk (a mysterious, semiliquid deposit found in caves). Book English tours in advance. To get there, follow the signs after Cime Aventure.

The young, dynamic **Cime Aventure** (☑800-790-2463, 418-534-2333; www.cimeaventure.com; 200 Athanase-Arsenault; campsites/chalets/ecolodges from $25/269/159) leads canoe/kayak trips lasting from 9km, or half a day ($37), to seven days ($1354), with food and equipment, mostly on the scenic, tranquil Rivière Bonaventure. It also runs one of the province's best campgrounds, with 8- or 12-person chalets, eco-lodges reached by treetop walkways and a rustic resto-bar. To get there from Rte 132, take Ave Gran Pré, which turns into Chemin de la Rivière. Cime Aventure is signposted to the left of Chemin de la Rivière, just after you cross Rivière Bonaventure.

Overlooking the marina, the boatshedlike **Café Acadien** (☑418-534-4276; 168 Rue Beaubassin; mains $11-25, s/d incl breakfast $70/80; ☺7:30am-9:30pm) is great for breakfast crepes and salmon, bacon and eggs. Bagels and Acadian, Cajun, and Italian food are also on the menu. There are some rooms upstairs.

The **tourist office** (☑418-534-4014; Rte 132; ☺9am-7pm Jul & Aug, to 4pm Jun & Sep) has free wi-fi and computer access.

New Richmond

The **British Heritage Village** (351 Blvd Perron Ouest; adult/child $8/5; ⊘10am-5pm Jul & Aug), in English-speaking New Richmond, shows what the village would have looked like in the late 1700s, recreating a Loyalist settlement of the time. You can take a carriage ride around buildings, including a military museum, forge, school and general store.

Carleton-sur-Mer

One of the best spots on the Baie-des-Chaleurs, Carleton-sur-Mer is much loved by Gaspésien day-trippers for its sandbars, bird-watching and walking in 550m-plus mountains.

From the quay, boats depart for fishing or sightseeing excursions. At the **bird observation tower** on the Banc de Carleton, beyond the marina, you can see herons, terns, plovers and other shore birds along the sandbar. Walking paths and Rue de la Montagne climb to the blue metal-roofed oratory on top of **Mont St-Joseph** (tours $6; ⊘9am-7pm Jun-Aug, to 5pm Sep & Oct) (555m), which provides fine views over the bay to New Brunswick. You can also find stunning mosaics, stained-glass windows, and art-deco marble finishes inside, plus an art gallery.

🛏 Sleeping & Eating

Camping de Carleton   CAMPGROUND $
(☎418-364-3992; 319 Ave du Phare; campsites/RV sites $18/41; ⊘Jun-Sep) This campground occupies a spit of land between the Baie-des-Chaleurs and the calm inner bay, with access to miles of beach, which you can camp on.

Manoir Belle Plage   HOTEL $$
(☎800-463-0780, 418-364-3388; www.manoir belleplage.com; 474 Blvd Perron; r from $106; ❋@🅿) Modern rooms with luxurious linens await in this cheery hotel on the highway. There's an upscale restaurant on site serving local specialties and a tasteful, whimsical nautical theme throughout the hotel – think strategically placed driftwood and marine poetry.

Brûlerie du Quai   CAFE $
(200 Rte du Quai; coffees from $2; ⊘8am-6pm) Locals flock to this lively roastery, store and coffee shop for out-of-this-world espresso drinks. There's a small patio overlooking the quai area, and you're welcome to bring

lunch or picnic supplies – the excellent nearby bakery **La Mie Véritable** (578 Blvd Perron) can help with that.

Le Marin d'Eau Douce   SEAFOOD $$
(215 Rte du Quai; mains from $16, meals $32-37; ⊘5-9:30pm Mon-Sat) An inviting dockside eatery right on the water that serves fresh seafood and other specialties using local ingredients. It has an upscale feel and friendly staff.

ℹ Information

Tourist Office (☎418-364-3544; 629 Blvd Perron; ⊘8am-8pm Jun-Sep) There's a tourist office in the Hôtel de Ville.

ℹ Getting There & Away

Orléans Express buses stop at 561 Blvd Perron; get tickets here inside Restaurant Le Héron. Buses go to Rimouski ($56, three to four hours, three times daily) and Gaspé ($37, four hours, twice daily).

The **VIA Rail station** (Rue de la Gare) is 1km from the center of town, back against the mountains.

Parc de Miguasha

The small peninsula 7km south of Rte 132, near Nouvelle, was the second place in Québec to be named a Unesco World Heritage site. It's the world's premier fossil site for illustrating the Devonian period, or the 'age of fish,' when sea creatures started evolving into tetrapods, which could walk on land. In the museum, fossils show fish with bones in their fins that are similar to the bones that humans have in their arms and legs.

Inquire at the **information center** (☎418-794-2475; 231 Rte Miguasha Ouest; adult/child $10.50/5.25, additional park admission adult/child $6.50/3; ⊘9am-5pm) about guided walks through the museum and along the fossil-filled cliffs. Do not collect your own fossils!

Pointe à la Garde

Among the trees in otherwise nondescript Pointe à la Garde is an extraordinary wooden chateau with red metal roofs topping its emerald green towers: **Château Bahia** (☎418-788-2048; www.chateaubahia.com; 152 Blvd Perron; dm $25, s/d from $33/66; ⊘May-Oct; @). Basic rooms and dorms with private and shared bathrooms are split between the castle's towers and an annex. Candlelit banquets ($15) take place in the great hall, and room rates include a wild-berry pancake breakfast.

Pointe à La Croix/Listuguj

A few kilometers west of Pointe a La Croix/Listuguj, the **Battle of the Restigouche National Historic Site** (Rte 132; adult/child $3.90/1.90; ☺9am-5pm Jun-Sep) details the 1760 naval battle in the nearby Restigouche River estuary, which finished off France's New World ambitions. The interpretive center with simulated ship explains the battle's significance to the British and displays salvaged articles and even parts of a sunken French frigate.

Matapédia Valley

While you're driving through the Matapédia Valley, you'll get a taste of the terrain that challenges walkers on the International Appalachian Trail. The trees covering the hillsides only stop for rivers, cliffs and lines of huge pylons charging through the wilderness. If it's raining, the mist-swathed forests look like the highlands of a Southeast Asian country. The Rivière Matapédia, famous for its salmon fishing, attracted former US presidents Nixon and Carter.

Matapédia

Matapédia is squaring up to Causapscal as a center for outdoor pursuits, but, thankfully, it has a long way to go before it resembles a tourist town. A gateway for the International Appalachian Trail, it has a **reception center** (www.sia-iat.com; Rte 132; ☺Jun-Oct), which doubles as the local tourist office. A free map, available here, covers trails on the hilltop plateau to the west, such as a 10km walk via St Alexis to the **Horizon du Reve lookout**.

Nature-Aventure (☎418-865-3554; ☺mid-May–Sep) leads rugged paddles of varying difficulty along local rivers, including the Matapédia ('the accessible') and the Restigouche ('the magnificent'). Packages include two-hour tours ($45), and excursions lasting one/two/three/four/five days ($90/250/340/460/580). It also rents canoes, wet suits and camping gear.

Causapscal

As its monolithic statue of 'the king of our rivers' suggests, Causapscal is crazy about **salmon**. The largest salmon caught here weighed over 16kg. Other outdoor activities on the town's doorstep include **hiking**, with trails meandering through the surrounding hills. The town itself has a beautiful stone **church** and many old **houses** with typical Québecois silver roofs, though odors from nearby sawmills sometimes spoil the picturesque scene.

Rivière Matapédia is the healthiest river for salmon; 13kg beauties are regularly netted there at the beginning of the season. There are covered bridges south of town and, in the center, a pedestrian-only suspension bridge across the Matapédia. Anglers go there to cast their lines where the Matapédia and Causapscal meet.

Check out the **Matamajaw Historic Site** (www.sitehistoriquematamajaw.com; 53 Rue St-Jacques; admission $8; ☺9:30am-5:30pm Jun-Sep) to see how the chaps in the fishing club used to relax in wood-paneled luxury after a hard day on the river. On the other side of Rte 132 is a salmon pool.

Appealingly old-fashioned **Auberge La Coulée Douce** (☎888-756-5270, 418-756-5720; www.lacouleedouce.com; 21 Rue Boudreau; r/chalet from $89/149) is perfect for fishers, and for those who simply want to sit in the comfortable dining room listening to ripping fishing yarns.

There is a **tourist office** (53 Rue St-Jacques; ☺8am-8pm Jul & Aug) and, for (expensive) fishing permits, an office of **CGRMP** (1 Rue St-Jacques Nord; ☺Jun-Sep).

Twice daily Orléans Express buses to Gaspé ($45, seven hours) and Rimouski ($34, two hours) stop at 560 Rue St-Jacques Nord.

NORTH SHORE

The Côte Nord (North Shore) comprises two regions: Manicouagan (stretching to Godbout) and Duplessis (east to the Labrador border). Statistics here are as overwhelming as the distances you have to drive to cross the areas. The two regions encompass an awesome 328,693 sq km (the size of New Zealand, Belgium and Switzerland combined). In this vast expanse live just over 100,000 hardy souls, mostly on the 1250km of coastline, making the area's population density just 0.3 persons per square kilometer.

Traveling north from Tadoussac, the landscape becomes a blur of rich wildlife, windswept beaches, stunning vistas of the ever-present St Lawrence River, and trees that gradually decrease in size until they completely vanish by Havre St-Pierre. There's just one way in and out – Rte 138 – evoking an eerie sense of isolation.

Baie Comeau

This unattractive city owes its existence to Robert McCormick, former owner of the *Chicago Tribune*, who in 1936 decided to build a colossal pulp and paper factory here. This enterprise necessitated harnessing the hydroelectric power of the Manicouagan and Outardes Rivers, which in turn begat other hydro-dependent industries such as aluminum processing.

Baie Comeau is at the beginning of Rte 389, which runs north past the **Manicouagan Reservoir**, the fifth-largest meteorite crater in the world, to Labrador City and Wabush. Along the way is a fascinating landscape of lake-filled barrens, tundra and, about 120km north of the hydroelectric complex Manic Cinq, the **Groulx Mountains**, where the peaks reach as high as 1000m.

A year-round **ferry** (✆877-562-6560; 14 Rte Maritime; per adult/child/car $17.50/11.50/42) makes the 2½-hour journey to Matane four times daily, providing the easternmost link to the south shore. It's essential to make a reservation for vehicles; it's advised to reserve at least a day ahead for foot passengers.

Godbout

The principal activity in this sleepy village is the arrival of the ferry. The **Musée Amérindien et Inuit** (134 Rue Pascal Comeau; adult/child $5/2; ⊙9am-10pm Jul-Sep) owns a nice collection of Inuit and aboriginal sculptures. If you feel like **swimming**, hit the beach below the museum.

Lovingly maintained and cheerfully decorated, **Gîte LaRichardière** (✆418-568-7446; www.gitelarichardiere.com; 109 Rue St-Régis; s/d $80/85) is your best bet in Godbout. The convivial owner speaks English and cooks a mean breakfast.

The **tourist information office** (✆418-568-7462; 115 Rue Pascal Comeau; ⊙7am-7pm Jul-Sep) is at the ferry terminal.

The **ferry** (117 Rue Pascal Comeau) links Godbout with Matane.

Pointe-des-Monts

This marks the point where the coast veers north and the St Lawrence graduates from river to gulf. The 1830 **lighthouse** here, one of Québec's oldest, has lorded over dozens of shipwrecks, despite its function. Sitting on a picturesque spit of land, it has been converted into a **museum** (1830 Chemin du Vieux Phare Casier; adult/child $6/free; ⊙9am-5pm Jun-Sep) explaining the lives of the keepers and their families.

Next to the lighthouse is **Le Gîte du Phare de Pointe-des-Monts** (✆866-369-4083, 418-939-2332; 1937 Chemin du Vieux Phare Casier; chalets per day/week from $78/500; ⊙May-Oct), which also has packages on offer including fishing and birding. The on-site restaurant serves first-rate local specialties (set meals $26 to $35); reservations are advised for nonguests.

Baie Trinité

If you've developed a morbid interest in the St Lawrence's history of shipwrecks, stop at **Centre National des Naufrages** (National Shipwrecks Center; www.centrenaufrages.ca; 27 Rte 138; adult/child $8/6; ⊙9am-6pm Jun-Sep), 34km northeast of Godbout on Rte 138.

Sept Îles

The last town of any size along the North Shore and one of Canada's busiest ports, Sept Îles is a quietly attractive place with alphabetically ordered streets. Exploring its excellent museums and archipelago is the perfect cure for the fatigue of long-distance driving.

⊙ Sights

Musée Régional de la Côte Nord   MUSEUM (www.mrcn.qc.ca; 500 Blvd Laure; adult/child $5/free; ⊙9am-5pm daily Jul & Aug, 10am-12pm & 1-5pm Tue-Fri, 1-5pm Sat & Sun Sep-Jun) This museum is a must-visit. It tells the history of the North Shore and its 8000 years of human habitation through a mix of gadgets and artifacts such as 17th-century maps.

Musée Shaputuan
MUSEUM

(290 Blvd des Montagnais; adult/child $5/free; ☉8am-4:30pm Mon-Fri, 1-4pm Sat & Sun Jul & Aug, Mon-Fri Sep-Jun) This is the North Shore's best museum on aboriginal culture. The atmospheric circular exhibition hall, divided into four sections symbolizing the seasons, follows the Innu (Montagnais) people as they hunt caribou or navigate the treacherous spring rivers. Photography, traditional clothes, sculptures and mythological tales are incorporated.

Le Vieux Poste
HISTORIC SITE

(Blvd des Montagnais; adult/student $12/10; ☉10am-5pm Jul & Aug) Seventeenth-century fur-trading post Le Vieux Poste has been reconstructed as a series of buildings showing the lifestyles of the hunters who called the forest home.

Île Grande Basque
ISLAND

The largest island of the small archipelago off Sept Îles is a pretty spot to spend a day, walking on the 12km of trails or picnicking on the coast. During the summer, **Croisière Petit Pingouin** (☎418-968-9558) and **Les Croisières du Capitaine** (☎418-968-2173) run regular 10-minute ferry crossings between the island and Sept Îles port (adult/child $25/15), as well as archipelago cruises. Tickets are available at the port, Parc du Vieux Quai. Camping is possible with a permit, available from the cruise companies and the tourist office. Nearby Île du Corossol is a bird refuge.

🛏 Sleeping & Eating

You'll find several motels along Rte 138 (Blvd Laure).

Le Tangon
HOSTEL $

(☎418-962-8180; www.aubergeletangon.net; 555 Rue Cartier; campsites/dm $10/22, s with shared bathroom $26-30, d $44-48; @☎) The wooden balcony here is an uplifting sight after miles of Rte 138. Inside, this HI hostel has friendly faces in reception, power showers, small dorms and a homey lounge and kitchen.

Hôtel le Voyageur
HOTEL $$

(☎418-962-2228; www.hotellevoyageur.com; 1415 Blvd Laure; r $89-219; ❄☎) Snazzy rooms with modern furniture betray the kitschy retro sign out front. The jaw-dropping views and decent breakfast are added bonuses.

RIDING THE TSHIUETIN RAILS

Aboriginal-owned **Tshiuetin Rail Transportation** (Map p227; ☎866-962-0988, 418-962-5530; www.tshiuetin.net; 1005 Blvd Laure, Sept Îles) operates a twice-weekly service between Sept Îles and Schefferville, 568km north, one of the province's most remote spots, though once a thriving mining town. The scenery en route is phenomenal. Cutting through forests, the tracks pass over gorges, dip inside valleys, curve around waterfalls and rapids, slice through a section of mountain and jut along stretches of lakes, rivers and hills as far as the eye can see. The train crosses a 900m-long bridge, 50m over Rivière Moisie and past the 60m-high Tonkas Falls. You can stop in the wilderness to camp and fish, then catch the next service back.

Pub St Marc
PUB $$

(588 Ave Brochu; set meals $20-29; ☉11:30am-1pm & 4pm-3am) With an outdoor patio with heat lamps, this mellow bar serves a dozen draft beers, pasta and salads.

Les Terrasses du Capitaine
SEAFOOD $$$

(295 Ave Arnaud; set meals from $25; ☉11am-2pm Mon-Fri, 4:30-9pm daily) Behind the fish market, this is the best place in town to taste local catches.

ℹ Information

The main **tourist office** (☎888-880-1238, 418-962-1238; 1401 Blvd Laure Ouest; ☉7:30am-9pm daily May-Sep, Mon-Fri Oct-Apr) is on the highway west of town. A smaller, seasonal office is at the port.

ℹ Getting There & Away

Sept Îles airport is 8km east of town; a taxi will cost about $10 to the center of town. **Air Labrador** (☎800-563-3042; www.airlabrador.com) serves the Lower North Shore, Labrador, Newfoundland, Québec City and Montréal.

The **Relais Nordik** (☎800-463-0680, 418-968-4707; www.relaisnordik.com) ferry travels to Île d'Anticosti and along the Lower North Shore (from Rimouski).

Intercar (☎418-962-2126; 126 Rue Mgr Blanche) runs a daily bus to/from Baie Comeau ($46, four hours) and, Monday to Friday, another to/from Havre St-Pierre ($44, 2¾ hours).

Mingan

Beyond Sept Îles, the landscape becomes primeval and sparse, with stretches of muskeg as far as the eye can see. Mingan is a former fishing and trading post, populated partly by a dynamic Innu community that calls the village Ekuanitshit. The small Catholic church **Église Montagnaise** (15 Rue Nashipetimit; ⊙8am-7pm) `FREE` contains a striking mix of Catholicism and aboriginal culture: a tepee form enshrines the crucifix, the pulpit is made of antlers, and tasseled cloth covers the altar, showing hunting scenes.

Mingan Archipelago National Park

By far the region's main attraction, this **park** (adult/child $5.80/2.90; ⊙ Jun-Sep) is a protected string of 40 main offshore islands stretching more than 85km from Longue Pointe de Mingan to 40km east of Havre St-Pierre. The islands' distinguishing characteristics are the odd, erosion-shaped stratified limestone formations along the shores. They're dubbed 'flowerpots' for the lichen and small vegetation that grow on top. Perched there might be the goofy puffin (*macareux moine* in French), a striking cross between a parrot and penguin and one of some 200 bird species here.

The **Reception & Interpretation Centre** (☑418-949-2126; Longue Pointe de Mingan; ⊙8am-6:30pm Jun-Aug) has a lot of information. In the same building is the nonprofit **Cetacean Interpretation Centre** (adult/child $8.50/4), built by the researchers at **Mingan Island Cetacean Study** (MICS). It gives as much of an insight into the science of studying whales as it does the mysterious mammals themselves. For a unique view of the whales in their natural habitat, join a MICS scientist on a **field-research day trip** (☑418-949-2845; www.rorqual.com; $115 per person incl equipment; ⊙Jun-Oct). You can register at the Reception & Interpretation Centre; boats depart the Mingan dock at 7:30am daily (weather permitting).

Half-a-dozen **tour** companies operate out of Havre St-Pierre and Longue Pointe de Mingan. In general, the smaller the boat, the better the experience. Trips last between three and five hours and cost $38 to $60.

Camping (sites from $15.70, plus $5.80 registration fee) is allowed on some of the islands, but you must register at the Reception & Interpretation Centre or the Havre St-Pierre tourist information office.

Havre St-Pierre

This fishing town is worth a stop on the way northeast, mainly because it has the last garage for 124km.

Auberge Boréale (☑418-538-3912; www.aubergeboreale.com; 1288 Rue Boréale; r $55) has nine cool, blue-and-white rooms and a pretty sea view. The 2nd-floor **Gîte Chez Françoise** (☑418-538-3778; gitechezfrancoise.qc.ca; 1122 Rue Boréale; s/d from $58/62; @ ⊛) has four artistically decorated rooms. Both offer **bike rental**.

The **tourist information office** (☑418-538-3285; 1010 Promenade des Anciens; ⊙9am-9pm mid-Jun–mid-Sep) is also a hub for Mingan Archipelago tours.

The Intercar bus stops at **Variétés Jomphe** (843 Rue de l'Escale).

Île d'Anticosti

This 7943-sq-km island has only recently begun to unfold its beauty to a growing number of visitors. A French chocolate maker named Henri Menier (his empire became Nestlé) bought the island in 1895 to turn it into his own private hunting ground. With its thriving white-tailed deer and salmon populations, it has long been popular with hunters and fishers. Now wildlife reserves are attracting nature-lovers to the heavily wooded, cliff-edged island with waterfalls, canyons, caves and rivers.

In Port Menier, the closest thing to a village on the island, there is a **tourist office** (☑418-535-0250; 7 Chemin des Forestiers; ⊙ Jun-Aug) and a few restaurants and B&Bs; accommodations should be arranged with the tourist office before arrival. From here, the island's lone road ventures to the interior.

Though it's possible to reach and tour the island yourself, it requires much planning. Most visitors go with a small-group tour; **Sépaq** (☑800-463-0863; www.sepaq.com) offers two- and seven-day packages with flights. They also offer shorter, half-day trips, if you arrive on the island on your own. The Havre St-Pierre tourist office has more information.

Relais Nordik provides the only regular transportation. For more information see p307.

Natashquan

Natashquan is still getting used to its connection to the rest of the province. Rte 138 reached the village in 1996, and it had been paved only since 1999. Romantics are drawn here for the experience of reaching the end of the road at Pointe Parent, 7km further on, and for Natashquan's peaceful, windswept beauty.

The **tourist information office** (☑ 866-726-3054, 418-726-3060; 32 Chemin d'en Haut; ☺ 10am-noon & 1-4pm Jul-Sep) doubles as an interpretive center.

Natashquan is the birthplace of the great Québecois singer-songwriter Gilles Vigneault. An exhibition in the **Vieille École** (Old School; 24 Chemin d'en Haut; adult/child $5/2; ☺ 10am-4pm Jul-Sep) looks at the local characters who inspired his songs.

Les Galets is a cluster of white huts with bright red roofs, huddled together on a windblown peninsula. Fishers used to salt and dry their catch here, an important communal activity. Aside from enjoying the surrounding beaches, you can hike inland trails through isolated, peaceful woods full of waterfalls and lookouts; the tourist office has a free map.

ÎLES DE LA MADELEINE

Everything about the Magdalen Islands, a stringy archipelago that resembles a Mandelbrot set on maps, is head-turning. The islands are 105km north of Prince Edward Island, and the six largest are connected by the 200km-long, classically named Rte 199. Between the islands' 350km of beach are iron-rich, red cliffs, molded by wind and sea into anthropomorphic forms and caves just crying out to be explored by kayak. As you circle above the crescent beaches on one of the tiny airplanes that fly here, the Magdalens look like desert islands; in fact, 13,000 lucky blighters live here, and that figure quadruples in the summer.

A great way to meet the islanders is at *boîtes à chansons*. The archipelago has a vibrant nightlife, and on Cap aux Meules you can normally catch wistful Acadian songs

being strummed on summer evenings. During the day, if you're not busy in rock pools or trying to keep your bike upright on a blustery sand spit, other forms of creativity can be enjoyed in the seafood restaurants, *économusées* and boutiques. The islands are teeming with artists, often encountered looking for inspiration in a *pot-en-pot* (a local specialty, with mixed fish, seafood and sauce baked in a pie crust) or a Pas Perdus (one of three beers brewed on Cap aux Meules).

The islands fall in the Atlantic Time Zone, one hour ahead of mainland Québec.

❶ Getting There & Around

The airport is on the northwest corner of Île du Havre aux Maisons. **Air Canada Express** (☑ 888-247-2262; www.aircanada.com) offers daily flights from Montréal, Québec City and Gaspé; **Pascan** (☑ 450-443-0500, 888-313-8777; www.pascan.com) flies from the two cities and Bonaventure.

The cheapest and most common arrival method is by ferry from Souris, Prince Edward Island, to Île du Cap aux Meules. **CTMA Ferries** (☑ 418-986-3278, 888-986-3278; www.ctma.ca; adult/child/bicycle/car $48.75/24.50/11.75/91) makes the five-hour cruise year-round. Ferries depart daily from July to early September; every day but Monday in May, June and September; and from October to April, two or three times a week. In midsummer, reservations are strongly recommended. There are discounts between mid-September and mid-June.

Between June and October, CTMA also operates a two-day cruise from Montréal via Québec City, Tadoussac and Chandler (one-way/return from $435/1000). It's a great way of seeing the St Lawrence River, and you could always take your car ($287) and return by road.

There is no public transportation. **Le Pédalier** (☑ 418-986-2965; 545 Chemin Principale; rental 1hr/4hr/1 week $6/18/85), in Cap aux Meules, rents bicycles. Hertz and local companies have airport car-rental outlets; book as far ahead as possible.

Île du Cap aux Meules

With more than half the archipelago's population and its only Tim Hortons, the islands' commercial center is disappointingly developed compared with its neighbors. Nonetheless, it's still 100% Madelinot and, with its amenities, accommodations and lively nightlife, it makes an ideal base.

👁 Sights & Activities

On the west side of the island, you can see the red cliffs in their glory. Their patterns of erosion can be glimpsed from the clifftop path between La Belle Anse and Fatima. Southwest, the lighthouse at **Cap du Phare** (Cap Hérissé) is a popular place to watch sunsets, and a cluster of bright boutiques and cafes overlooks a shipwreck at **Anse de l'Étang du Nord**. In the middle of the island, signposted on Chemin de l'Église near the junction with Rte 199, **Butte du Vent** offers views along the sandbanks running north and south.

À l'Abri de la Tempête
BREWERY

(☎ 418-986-5005; 286 Chemin Coulombe; tours $6.50; ☺ tours 11am-7pm May-Oct) Finish the day at this microbrewery on the beach.

Aerosport Carrefour d'Aventures
KAYAKING

(☎ 418-986-6677; www.aerosport.ca; 1390 Chemin Lavernière) Young, enthusiastic thrill-seekers run this company, which offers kayak expeditions and cave visits. When the wind is right, you'll have an unforgettable experience if you opt for the power-kite-buggy ride. They also offer a three-hour guided tour of the cliffs at Gros-Cap, Belle-Anse, and L'Étang du Nord ($44, three tours a day July to mid-September).

Vert et Mer
KAYAKING

(☎ 418-986-3555; www.vertetmer.com; 84 Chemin des Vigneau) This eco-outfit offers guided walks and sea-kayaking excursions. You can choose from half-day, full-day or overnight trips as far away as Île Brion, an uninhabited ecological preserve at the northern end of the Magdalen archipelago, where yurt lodgings are provided.

👉 Tours

MA Poirier
BUS TOUR

(☎ 418-986-4467; 1027 Chemin du Grand-Ruisseau; tours from $99) Runs seven-hour guided bus tours of the main sights throughout the islands.

🛏 Sleeping & Eating

Camping Le Barachois
CAMPGROUND $

(☎ 418-986-4447; 87 Chemin du Rivage; campsites/RV sites $23/30; ☺ May-Sep) This 153-site campground, surrounded by trees, lake and sea, has great sunsets.

Parc de Gros-Cap
HOSTEL, CAMPGROUND $

(☎ 418-986-4505, 800-986-4505; www.parcde-groscap.ca; 74 Chemin du Camping; campsites/RV sites $22/31, dm/r from $29/58; ☺ Jun-Sep; @ 🖥) Situated on the Gros Cap peninsula overlooking a bay dotted with fishers in waders, this could be the HI network's most tranquil retreat. It has a family atmosphere and is a good place to organize activities such as sea kayaking. Rates are lower for HI members.

For longer stays, there's a 'workers' hostel' ($24/140/350 per night/week/month): a house with 10 small rooms (each with two single beds) and shared facilities (kitchen, bathrooms, living room and laundry).

Pas Perdus
INN $$

(Not Lost; ☎ 418-986-5151; 169 Chemin Principale; s/d $45/90, mains $12-20; ☺ 11am-8pm) Munching on a shark burger on the terrasse at Pas Perdus, or in the red interior among curvy mirrors, is a sure way to feel the islands' bohemian pulse. You can actually get a decent night's sleep in the bright bedrooms above the restaurant now the musical entertainment has shifted next door.

This venue hosts live acts most summer nights; on Monday, a free jam session (10pm); and on Friday (11pm) local DJs. Everyone drops by to surf the internet or sip a Pas Perdus from the nearby microbrewery.

Pas Perdus is on the east side of the island, just west of the tourist office.

La Factrie
SEAFOOD $$

(521 Chemin du Gros Cap; mains $15-30; ☺ 8am-7pm Mon-Sat, 1-6pm Sun May-Sep) Top-notch seafood in a cafeteria above a lobster-processing plant: only in Îles de la Madeleine! Try lobster in salad, boiled, thermidore, sandwich or crepe form.

Café la Côte
CAFE $$

(499 Chemin Boisville Ouest; mains $9-20; ☺ 11am-10pm Jun-Sep) Near the fishers statue in L'Etang du Nord, this beach-hut-like place is perfect for breakfast or a quick lunch of seafood or pasta. The adjoining *boîte à chansons* puts on outdoor Acadian music shows on summer evenings.

ℹ Information

The **main tourist office** (☎ 877-624-4437, 418-986-2245; www.tourismeilesdelamadeleine.com; 128 Chemin Principale; ☺ 8am-8pm Jul & Aug, 9am-8pm Jun & Sep, 9am-5pm Oct-May), near the ferry terminal, is a helpful source of information about all the islands.

Île du Havre Aubert

Heading south from Cap aux Meules to the archipelago's largest island, Rte 199 glides between dunes backed by the blue Atlantic and Baie-du-Havre-aux-Basques, popular with kite surfers.

The liveliest area of **Havre Aubert** town is La Grave, where the rustic charm of a fishing community remains in the old houses, small craft shops and restaurants. Beyond, walk along the **Sandy Hook** to feel like you're at the end of the world (except during the sandcastle contest in late August).

The excellent **Musée de la Mer** (1023 Rte 199; adult/child $8/5; ☉10am-6pm) covers Madelinot history from Jacques Cartier's impressions of walruses onwards.

At **Le Site d'Autrefois** (3106 Chemin de la Montagne; adult/child $10/4; ☉9am-5pm Jun-Aug, 10am-4pm Sep), flamboyant fisher Claude preserves Madelinot traditions through storytelling, singing and a model village.

On rainy days, the 'petting pool' in the small **aquarium** (982 Chemin de la Grave; adult/child $8/5; ☉10am-6pm Jun-Sep) is a popular stop.

Chez Denis à François (☑418-937-2371; www.aubergechezdenis.ca; 404 Chemin d'en Haut; r incl breakfast $85-145) was built using lumber salvaged from a shipwreck. The spacious, Victorian-style rooms have ceiling fans, fridges, sofas and private bathrooms.

Café de la Grave (969 Rte 199; mains $9-15; ☉9am-3am late-Apr–Oct) is more than a local institution – it's one of the islands' vital organs. *Pot-en-pot*, *croque monsieur*, soups and cakes meet an appreciative crowd in the former general store.

Économusée **Artisans du Sable** (907 Rte 199; ☉10am-9pm) sells chessboards, candlesticks and other souvenirs…all made of sand.

Île du Havre aux Maisons

The home of the airport is one of the most populated islands but certainly doesn't feel it. The area to the east of Rte 199 is probably the most scenic, and is best seen from Chemin des Buttes, which winds between green hills and picture-perfect cottages. A short climb from the car park on Chemin des Échoueries near Cap Alright, the crosstopped **Butte Ronde** has wonderful views of the lumpy coastline.

🛏 Sleeping & Eating

Domaine du Vieux Couvent   HOTEL $$$
(☑418-969-2233; www.domaineduvieuxcouvent. com; 292 Rte 199; r incl breakfast $150-275; ☉Mar-Dec, restaurant 5-9pm May-Dec; ☎) Smack-dab in the middle of the archipelago, the Domaine has the swankiest digs in Îles de la Madeleine. Every room overlooks the ocean through a wall of windows. The very popular restaurant is a must-visit for adventurous foodies, who can sample local dishes made with seafood, veal, boar, wild fruits and cheeses from the islands (set meals from $27).

La Butte Ronde   B&B $$
(☑866-969-2047, 418-969-2047; www.labutteronde.com; 70 Chemin des Buttes; r incl breakfast $120-165) With ticking clocks, classical music, beautiful rooms decorated with photos of Tuareg nomads, and a sea-facing conservatory, this grand home in a former schoolhouse has a calming, library-like air.

Grosse Île

This island is home to most of the archipelago's English-speaking minority, their Newfoundlandlike accents telling of their Celtic roots. The Anglophone community has an uneasy relationship with its Francophone neighbors and you'll hear comments such as, 'We want our English signs back.'

At the end of a windswept sandbank, the island's **salt mine** (☑418-985-2318; 53 Chemin Principal; adult/child $6/5; ☉10am-6pm Mon-Fri & noon-6pm Sat Jun-Sep) excavates at a depth of 300m below sea level.

Built in 1925, **Trinity Church** at Pointe de la Grosse Île reflects island life. The stained-glass windows of this Anglican church depict Jesus clad in a woolen jumper and boots, saying, 'Come with me and I will make you fishers of men.'

Between Pointe de la Grosse Île and Old Harry, the 684-hectare East Point bird reserve has the archipelago's most impressive beach, **Plage de la Grande Échouerie**. The 10km sweep of pale sand extends northeast from Pointe Old Harry; there are car parks there and en route to Old Harry from East Cape.

The **Veteran's Museum & Memorial Park** (787 Chemin Principale; ☉8am-4pm Mon-Fri) FREE in Old Harry is housed in a former schoolhouse built in 1921. Honoring island citizens who lost their lives in WWII, this museum displays relics including 19th-century sailors' tombstones from Île Brion, 16km north. Brion is now an ecological reserve with 140 species of birds and much interesting vegetation.

Seacow Rd in Old Harry leads to the site where walrus were landed and slaughtered for their oil. Nearby, **St Peter's by the Sea**, built in 1916 using wood from shipwrecks, is bounded by graves of Clarkes and Clarks. The surname evolved as it was misspelt on formal documents.

Île de la Grande Entrée

Even by Madelinot standards, Grand Entry is a remote outpost, its 650 residents' homes seemingly outnumbered by the masts at the fishing port.

La Salicorne (☑ 888-537-4537, 418-985-2833; www.salicorne.ca; 377 Rte 199; campsites/RV sites $19/24) is a hive of activity, offering sea kayaking, windsurfing, caving, nature walks, archipelago tours, seafood tasting, fishers' storytelling and even mud baths. It has a campground and a ho-hum cafeteria (mains $13 to $25); the bedrooms are for tour packages only.

On site, the **Seal Interpretation Center** (adult/child $7.50/4; ⊙10am-6pm Jun-Sep) delves into the world of seals and particularly the controversial act of seal clubbing.

The center overlooks **Île Bordeau**, which has a hiking trail and is reached via Chemin du Bassin Ouest, near the end of Rte 199.

Délices de la Mer (907 Chemin Principal; set meals $15-30; ⊙11am-8pm Jun-Sep), formerly the office of the local fishing cooperative, serves affordable seafood such as lobster-garnished bread and chips.

FAR NORTH

This area truly represents the final frontier of Québec, where the province runs barren and eventually disappears into the depths of the Arctic Ocean. Here in the great Far North, remote villages, a strong Aboriginal presence and stunning geography entice those wanting to drop right off the tourist radar. The earth brims with valuable resources, such as silver, gold and copper, caribou run free and the waters teem with fish.

The North is an immense region, the most northerly sections of which are dotted with tiny Inuit and First Nations settlements accessible only by bush plane. The developed areas largely owe their existence to massive industrial operations – mining, forestry and hydroelectricity. While accessing the really far North (the Inuit communities in Nunavik) requires expensive flights, other areas of the Abitibi-Témiscamingue and James Bay regions can easily, with time, be reached by car and bus, and will provide a taste of Canada's true North.

Abitibi-Témiscamingue

The people barely outnumber the lakes in the over 65,140 sq km here. But despite the shortage of humans, this sparsely populated area occupies a special place in the Québecois imagination. The last area to be settled and developed on a major scale, it stands as a symbol of dreams and hardships.

The traditional land of the Algonquins, Abitibi-Témiscamingue is an amalgamation of two distinct areas, each named after different tribes. Témiscamingue, accessible via Northern Ontario or Rte 117 west from Val d'Or, sees few tourists. It's more diversified in its vegetation and landscape, with valleys and the grand Lac Témiscamingue. Most of Abitibi's slightly more visited terrain is flat, which makes the stunning valleys and cliffs of Parc d'Aiguebelle all the more striking.

Abitibi-Témiscamingue was colonized following the usual pattern of resource exploitation. Before the 19th century, the only Europeans in the area were hunters and fur traders. Then forestry and copper mining brought more development. In the 1920s gold fever struck, and thousands flooded the region in search of their fortune. Boomtowns bloomed around deposits.

Today, this vast region of Québec retains an exotic air, partially due to its remoteness. Generally, visitors are seeking solitude in its parks or are en route to still more epic northern destinations.

Réserve Faunique la Vérendrye

Relatively accessible, this immense **park** (☑ 800-665-6527, 819-736-7431; www.sepaq.com; Hwy 117; adult/child $6.50/3, campsites $19-46, chalets from $121; ⊙May-Sep) is best as a canoeing destination. Very satisfying circuit routes of varying lengths have been mapped, and there are stunning campgrounds and chalets sprinkled around the lakes' edges.

Even in a heat wave in midsummer, you may well have entire lakes virtually to yourself. And you don't need to be an expert or an athlete to enjoy the peace in this park.

The park is accessed at four points, all on Hwy 117. Coming from the Laurentians, **Le Domaine Registration Centre** (☑819-435-2541; 1 117 Road, Montcerf-Lytton), 58km past the village of Grand Remous, has information, canoe rentals and services such as laundry, phones, a store, a restaurant and a playground.

During the 180km drive across the reserve from the south end to Val d'Or, there are no villages – make sure your tank is full.

Val d'Or

Born in 1933 around the Sigma gold mine, Val d'Or today looks like a mining boomtown of yesterday, with wide avenues and a main street (Ave 3-ième) that one can easily imagine was frenzied in gold-rush days. That main street retains its traditional rough edge. The Sigma mine still operates, though it's no longer the city's economic engine.

La Cité de l'Or (☑819-825-1274; www.citedelor.com; 90 Ave Perreault; adult/child $25.25/12.25; ☺tours 8:30am-5:30pm Jul & Aug, by appointment Sep-Jun) offers guided excursions 91m underground to show what gold mining's all about. On the same site is the **Village Minier de Bourlamaque** (audioguide tours adult/child $7/3), a restored mining village with 80 log houses. Call to reserve tours in advance, and don't forget to bring warm clothes if you're going underground.

If you're staying the night, the newest kid on the block, **Quality Inn & Suites** (☑819-874-8800; www.qualityinn.com; 1111 Rue de L'Escale; r from $100), has modern amenities and friendly service. Recently refurbished **Motel Prélude** (☑877-825-0096, 819-825-0090; www.motelprelude.ca; 1159 Ave 3-ième; r from $90) is about as central as you can get in Val d'Or.

The **tourist office** (☑819-824-9646; 1070 3-ième Ave Est; ☺9am-5pm) is on Hwy 117 at the eastern end of town.

Air Creebec flies into Val d'Or from Montréal ($600, 1¼ hours). **Autobus Maheux** (www.autobusmaheux.qc.ca) buses go to Montréal ($102, seven hours, three times daily), Matagami ($63, 3½ hours, daily except Saturday) and Chibougamau via Senneterre ($87, six hours, daily).

Parc d'Aiguebelle

As the Abitibi landscape can be a tad on the dull side, the stunning scenery in this **provincial park** (☑819-637-7322; 1737 Rang Hudson; adult/child $6.50/3) comes as a doubly pleasant surprise. Suddenly there are magnificent canyons and gorges, massive rocky cliffs with fascinating geological formations and excellent, rugged hiking trails (some 60km worth) flanked by trees 200 years old.

The small park (only 268 sq km) has two entrances – via Mont Brun (well marked on Hwy 117 west of Val d'Or; this is the closest to the suspended bridge) and Taschereau (south from Rte 111 between La Sarre and Amos). There are lovely **campgrounds** (sites from $26.75) near both, as well as canoe and kayak rentals.

James Bay

This area truly represents Québec's hinterland, where a seemingly endless forest of boreal spruces sprout from the earth. On many evenings, the northern lights dye the sky a kaleidoscope of pinks and blues, which eventually give way to blazing orange sunsets. Only 30,000 people live here, in the world's largest administrative municipality (350,000 sq km), which is roughly the size of Germany. Almost half of them are Cree living on eight reserves separated by hundreds of kilometers.

The near mythic Rte de la Baie James ends at Radisson, a small village 1400km north of Montréal and 800km north of Amos. A 100km extension branches westward to Chisasibi, a Cree reserve near James Bay. This area is defined by the immense James Bay hydroelectric project, a series of hydroelectric stations that produces half of Québec's energy resources. Many visitors make the trek just to get a glimpse of these.

While temperatures sporadically attain 30°C (86°F) in July or August, it is essential to bring warm clothes for the evenings. The usual July daytime temperature is around 17°C (63°F). In winter – which can come as early as October – the temperatures are often below -15°C (5°F) and can reach -40°C (-40°F).

Most people access the region via Abitibi. Rte 109 runs 183km north to Matagami, the last town before Rte 109 becomes the Rte de la Baie James and continues 620km to Radisson.

Matagami

For a dreary town in the middle of nowhere, this place sure feels busy. Since 1963, when the town was founded, it has been the site of a copper and zinc mine. It is also Québec's most northerly forestry center. Both of these industries are still going strong here, and shift workers are always coming and going. Plus, almost everyone driving through on Rte 109 on the way to Radisson stops here for the night.

Hôtel Matagami (✆877-739-2501, 819-739-2501; www.hotelmatagami.com; 99 Blvd Matagami; r from $105; ⊘restaurant 5am-10pm; ✳@☎) is considered the top place in town. It's decent enough and always seems to be crowded – mainly because of the restaurant.

Motel Le Caribou (✆866-739-4550, 819-739-4550; 108 Blvd Matagami; r from $70; ✳ @ ☎) is in need of refreshing, but is fine for a night. The on-site bar is popular with locals.

Every day but Saturday, the Autobus Maheux bus travels to/from Val d'Or ($63, 3½ hours) stopping at Hôtel Matagami.

Route de la Baie James

This road, an extension of Rte 109 to the James Bay hydroelectric projects, is paved, wide and in good shape.

At Kilometer 6, a **tourist office** (✆819-739-4473) operates 24 hours a day throughout the year. It's recommended that you stop; for safety reasons, everyone traveling north should register themselves here. It's also worth going inside since you can pick up several booklets and pamphlets that detail the geological and geographical features along the way and contain information about forest fires. There are bilingual information panels all along the road and emergency telephones at Kilometers 135, 201, 247, 301, 444 and 504.

At Kilometer 38, you'll reach the route's only **campground** (✆819-739-8383; campsites/RV sites $22/26; ⊘mid-Jun–early Sep).

Everyone needs to stop at Kilometer 381, the so-called Relais Routier, the only gas station and service stop on the road. It's open 24 hours a day. There's a cafeteria and a no-frills **motel** (✆819-638-8502; r $120) with 24 rooms.

Radisson

Named after explorer Pierre-Esprit Radisson, this village was set up in 1973 to house the workers on the James Bay hydroelectric project. It looks and feels larger than its population of 350 would suggest – partly because it was built to accommodate fluctuating numbers of workers (who work for eight days, then fly home for six) and partly because some families have decided to settle permanently here and create a real village.

The scenery around Radisson is spectacular, with views of the majestic Rivière La Grande from the built-up area around the larger-than-life LG2 hydroelectric power station (also called Robert Bourassa station), just outside town.

Everyone who makes it here takes a free, guided tour of the power station (get details at the tourist office). The main offices of **Hydro Québec** are in the Pierre Radisson Complex. After an introduction to hydroelectricity, you'll be taken inside and outside the massive LG2. This, together with LG2A, the world's largest underground power station (as tall as a 15-story building but buried 140m deep in the bedrock), produces 25% of the province's energy and ranks among the top handful in size globally.

There are several functional motels. **Camping Radisson** (✆819-638-8687; 198 Rue Jolliet; campsites & RV sites $35; ⊘mid-Jun–early Sep) is on a hill behind the tourist office.

The **tourist office** (✆819-638-8687; 98 Rue Jolliet; ⊘8am-8pm Jun-Oct) is at the village's entrance. At other times, contact the **town hall** (✆819-638-7777; 101 Place Gérard Poirier).

Chisasibi

Near the point where Rivière La Grande meets James Bay, 100km west of Radisson, Chisasibi is a Cree village well worth visiting. The surrounding environment, windswept taiga doused by the arctic breezes from James Bay, is haunting.

The town as it looks now has existed only since 1981. Before this, the residents lived on the island of Fort George, 10km from town, where the Hudson's Bay Company had set up a fur-trading post in 1837. A vestige of the old-fashioned way of life survives in the many tepees seen in backyards, mainly used for smoking fish.

The **Mandow Agency** (✆819-855-3373; mandow@chisasibi.ca) offers guided excursions of varying lengths to Fort George, where most of the original structures, including churches, schools and cemeteries remain. Traditional meals can be ordered. They also arrange fishing trips, canoe trips, cultural exchanges and winter activities. Email them with your desire and they may well be able to set it up.

Motel Chisasibi (☑819-855-2838; s/d $97/122) offers the only commercial accommodations.

Nunavik

The desolate expanse of Québec's northern limits, Nunavik is a tad smaller than France, yet fewer than 10,000 people live here in 14 villages. Hundreds of kilometers of tundra separate them from one another, with no roads to join them. Almost 90% of the population is Inuit; the remainder includes Cree, Naskapis and white Québecois. This surreal territory stretches from the 55th to the 62nd parallel, bordered by Hudson Bay to the west, the Hudson Strait to the north and Ungava Bay and the Labrador border to the east.

Socially, the villages hold great interest. The adaptability of the Inuit locals has helped them make a radical transition in their lifestyles in a relatively short period of time. The villages range in population from 195 (Aupaluk) to 2375 (Kuujjuaq). Half the population is under 18, as you might guess by the sheer number of little ones running around. After Inuktitut, the most widely spoken language here is English. More youngsters are learning French than their parents did, but elders rarely speak anything other than Inuktitut.

Because Nunavik can only be accessed by plane, few casual tourists make the trip. Yet those willing to make their own local contacts can travel independently. Be prepared for high prices for goods and services. On average, food prices are close to double what they are in Québec City.

Land & Climate

There is great geographic diversity here. Even the tundra has many rich shades of beauty, and the region is far from a desolate plain of snow and ice. In the southwest, beaches and sand dunes stretch as far as the eye can see. In the northeast, the formidable Torngat Mountains extend in a series of bare, rocky peaks and untamed valleys 300km along the border of Labrador. The province's highest peak, **Mont d'Iberville** (1652m), is here.

There are also three meteorite-formed craters in Nunavik (of the 144 known on earth). The largest – indeed one of the largest on earth – is called **Pingualuit**, a 1.4-million-year-old cavity with a diameter of 3.4km and a depth of 433m (the height of a 145-story building) in parts. The lake that's formed inside the crater contains water considered among the purest in the world. In terms of transparency, it's second only to Japan's Lake Masyuko. Pingualuit lies 88km southwest of Kangiqsujuaq.

Floating above this unusual terrain are the magical **northern lights** (aurora borealis), which can be seen an average of 243 nights each year.

ℹ Getting There & Around

First Air (☑800-267-1247; www.firstair. ca) provides service between Montréal and Kuujjuaq (one-way $680 to $1000, 2¼ hours, daily). **Air Inuit** (☑800-361-2965; www. airinuit.com) flies the same route (at similar prices) as well as from Montréal to Puvirnituq (one-way $1200 to $1400, 3½ hours, daily). From there, flights go to other villages such as Whapmagoostui-Kuujjuarapik (one-way $500, two hours, daily).

With **Air Creebec** (☑800-567-6567; www. aircreebec.ca), you can go directly from Montréal to Whapmagoostui-Kuujjuarapik ($1000 one-way, six hours, daily) and Chisasibi ($975 one-way, five hours, daily).

QUÉBEC NUNAVIK

Nova Scotia

Includes ➡

Best Places to Eat

Best Places to Stay

Why Go?

If provinces were mother Canada's children, Nova Scotia would be the cute kid who charms the world with her lupine-studded fields, gingerbread-like houses, picture-perfect lighthouses and lightly lapping waves on sandy shores. But then you put her in a hockey rink or perhaps a fishing boat in a strong gale and another side comes out. Good looks aside, this near island and her residents are tough, resourceful and bad ass; most enjoy a drink, a song, a dance and a new face to share it with. If it's nature you're seeking, it's easy to discover empty coastal beach trails and wilderness paths through mixed forest to vistas with briny breezes. For something more cosmopolitan, head to Halifax for world-class dining and a rocking music scene.

When to Go
Halifax

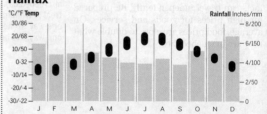

| **Jun–Aug** Wild-flowers carpet the country while whales come close to feed. | **Sep & Oct** Trees aflame with golds and reds provide a backdrop to fall music festivals. | **Aug–Nov** Put on a thick wetsuit, hood and booties to surf icy hurricane swells. |

History

From time immemorial, the Mi'kmaq First Nation lived throughout present-day Nova Scotia. When the French established the first European settlement at Port Royal (today's Annapolis Royal) in 1605, Grand Chief Membertou offered them hospitality and became a frequent guest of Samuel de Champlain.

That close relationship with the French led to considerable suspicions by the British after they gained control of Nova Scotia, and rewards were offered for Mi'kmaw scalps. Starting in 1755, most French-speaking Acadians were deported to Louisiana (where they became Cajuns) and elsewhere for refusing to swear allegiance to the British Crown.

Nova Scotia was repopulated by some 35,000 United Empire Loyalists retreating from the American Revolution, including a small number of African slaves owned by Loyalists and also freed black Loyalists. New England planters settled other communities and, starting in 1773, waves of Highland Scots arrived in northern Nova Scotia and Cape Breton Island.

Most Nova Scotians trace their ancestry to the British Isles, as a look at the lengthy 'Mac' and 'Mc' sections of the phone book easily confirms. Acadians who managed to return from Louisiana after 1764 found their lands in the Annapolis Valley occupied. They settled instead along the French Shore between Yarmouth and Digby and, on Cape Breton Island, around Chéticamp and on Isle Madame. Today Acadians make up some 18% of the population, though not as many actually speak French. African Nova Scotians make up about 4% of the population. There are approximately 20,000 Mi'kmaq in 18 different communities concentrated around Truro and Bras d'Or Lake on Cape Breton Island.

Local Culture

With nearly 8000km of coastline, Nova Scotia has a culture that revolves around the sea. Historically, it has been a hard-working region of coal mines and fisheries. The current culture is still very blue collar but, with the decline of the primary industries, many young Nova Scotians are forced to leave their province in search of work.

Perhaps because of the long winters and hard-working days, an enormous number of Nova Scotians play music. Family get-togethers, particularly Acadian and Scottish, consist of strumming, fiddling, foot-tapping and dancing.

NOVA SCOTIA FAST FACTS

➡ Population: 921,727

➡ Area: 55,491 sq km

➡ Capital: Halifax

➡ Quirky fact: Has the only tidal power plant in the western hemisphere

---

🛈 Getting There & Away

AIR

Most flights go to/from Halifax, but there's also an international airport in Sydney on Cape Breton Island. Airlines include **Air Canada** (www.aircanada.com), **Westjet** (www.westjet.com), **United** (www.united.ca), **Delta** (www.delta.com) and **Iceland Air** (www.icelandair.ca). There are multiple flights daily between Halifax and cities such as Toronto, Montréal, Ottawa, Saint John, Moncton and Boston (Massachusetts). In summer and fall there are direct flights to London and Iceland.

BUS

Maritime Bus (p884) provides a bus service through the Maritimes and connects with **Orleans Express** (www.orleansexpress.com) buses from Québec. From Halifax, destinations include Charlottetown ($58.25, 5½ hours, two daily) and Moncton ($49, four hours, three daily).

Contactable through Maritime Bus, several shuttles service the rest of the province.

BOAT
New Brunswick

Bay Ferries (☑ 888-249-7245; www.bayferries.com; adult/child/car/bicycle $43/28/81/10) has a three-hour trip from Saint John in New Brunswick to Digby. Off-season discounts and various packages are available.

Newfoundland

Marine Atlantic (☑ 800-341-7981; www.marine-atlantic.ca) operates ferries year-round to Port aux Basques in Newfoundland from North Sydney (adult/child/car $42/20/109). Daytime crossings take between five and six hours, and overnight crossings take about seven hours. Cabins and reclining chairs cost extra.

In summer, you can opt for a 14-hour ferry ride (adult/child/car $112/54/225) to Argentia on Newfoundland's east coast. Reservations are required for either trip.

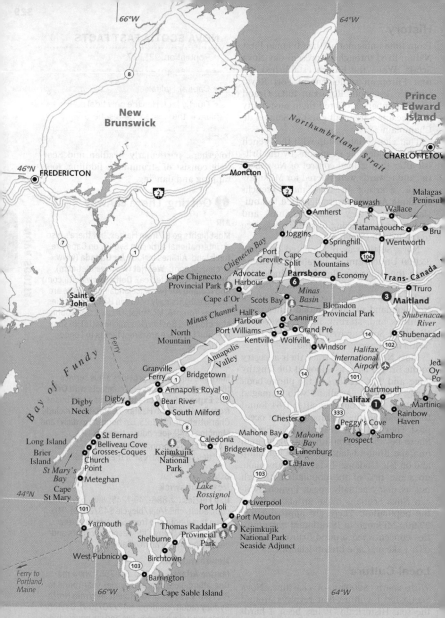

Nova Scotia Highlights

1 People-watch along the waterfront and take in an unforgettable meal in **Halifax** (p332).

2 Sample French soldiers' rations or a general's feast

c1744 at **Louisbourg National Historic Site** (p385).

3 Crash through the waves of the tidal bore at **Maitland** (p365).

4 Experience the misty peace of kayaking through the deserted islands and protected coves around **Tangier** (p389).

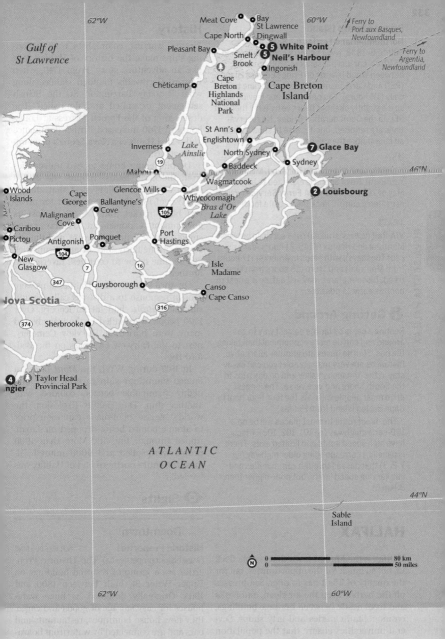

Meat Cove
Bay St Lawrence
Cape North · **Dingwall**
Pleasant Bay · ⑤ **White Point**
⑤ **Neil's Harbour**
Smelt Brook
Ingonish

Gulf of St Lawrence

Chéticamp

Cape Breton Highlands National Park

Cape Breton Island

St Ann's
Englishtown
Inverness · *Lake Ainslie* · **North Sydney**
⑲
Mabou · **Baddeck** · **Sydney**
46°N
Wagmatcook
Glencoe Mills
Whycocomagh · ⑦ **Glace Bay**
⑩ **Wood Islands**
Cape George
Ballantyne's Cove
Bras d'Or Lake
Malignant Cove
⑩ **Louisbourg**
Caribou
Pictou
Antigonish
⑩⑩
Pomquet
Port Hastings
New Glasgow
⑦
⑯
Isle Madame
⑩⑦
Guysborough
Canso
Cape Canso
Nova Scotia
⑯⑥
Sherbrooke

④ **Taylor Head Provincial Park**
ngier

ATLANTIC OCEAN

44°N

Sable Island

Ⓝ 0 ——————— 80 km
    0 ——————— 50 miles

62°W   60°W

⑤ Eat hot chowder after looking for eagles and whales from **White Point** to **Neil's Harbour** (p381).

⑥ Search the sand flats exposed by extreme Fundy tides for semiprecious stones around **Parrsboro** (p368).

⑦ Voyage under the ocean floor to the coal mines of **Glace Bay** (p385) while listening to the yarns of a retired miner.

Prince Edward Island

Northumberland Ferries (☎ 888-249-7245, 902-566-3838; www.peiferry.com; adult/child $17/free, car incl passengers $68) cruises between Wood Islands on Prince Edward Island (PEI) and Caribou, near Pictou, up to nine times daily (1¼ hours). You only pay when leaving PEI, so it's slightly cheaper to arrive by ferry then exit PEI via the Confederation Bridge. No reservations are required, but it's wise to show up half an hour before the sailing.

USA

A nightly service between Portland, Maine and Yarmouth, Nova Scotia is expected to begin in May of 2014 with **NS-USA Ferry Service** (www.nsusaferry.com). Check the website for details.

TRAIN

VIA Rail (www.viarail.ca) runs services between Montréal and Halifax ($145, 21 hours, daily except Tuesdays), with stops in Amherst (17 hours from Montréal) and Truro (18 hours from Montréal). Discount fares may sell out, so it's best to book as early as possible.

ⓘ Getting Around

Renting a car is by far the easiest way to get around and can be more economical than taking the bus. Shuttle buses are another alternative. Distances are very manageable; you can easily stay in the Annapolis Valley and do day trips to the South Shore and vice versa. The longest drive most people will do is the four-hour haul to Cape Breton Island from Halifax.

The direct route to most places will be on a 100-series highway (eg 101, 102, 103), which have high speed limits and limited exits. There is usually a corresponding older highway (eg 1, 2, 3) that passes through communities and has varying speed limits, but none higher than 80km/h.

HALIFAX

POP 390,096

Halifax is the kind of town that people flock to, not so much for the opportunities, but for the quality of life it has to offer. Sea breezes off the harbor keep the air clean, and parks and trees nestle between heritage buildings, cosmopolitan eateries and arty shops. Several universities ensure that the population is young and the bars and nightclubs full. Stroll the historic waterfront, catch some live music and enjoy the best of what the Maritimes have to offer. In summer, never-ending festivals ignite the party ambience that much more.

History

Pirates, warring colonialists and exploding ships make the history of Halifax read like an adventure story. From 1749, when Edward Cornwallis founded Halifax along what is today Barrington St, the British settlement expanded and flourished. The destruction of the French fortress at Louisbourg in 1760 increased British dominance and sealed Halifax as Nova Scotia's most important city.

Despite being home to two universities from the early 1800s, Halifax was still a rough and ready sailors' nest that, during the War of 1812, became a center for privateer black-market trade. As piracy lost its government endorsement, Halifax sailed smoothly into a mercantile era, and the city streets, particularly Market and Brunswick Sts, became home to countless taverns and brothels.

On April 14, 1912, three Halifax ships were sent in response to a distress call: the 'unsinkable' *Titanic* had hit an iceberg. Over 1500 people were killed in the tragedy and many were buried at Fairview Cemetery, next to the Fairview Overpass on the Bedford Hwy.

In 1917 during WWI, the *Mont Blanc,* a French munitions ship carrying TNT and highly flammable benzol, collided with another ship. The 'Halifax Explosion,' the world's biggest man-made explosion prior to atomic bombs being dropped on Japan, ripped through the city. More than 1900 people were killed and 9000 injured. Almost the entire northern end of Halifax was leveled.

◉ Sights

◉ Downtown

Historic Properties   NOTABLE BUILDING
(www.historicproperties.ca) The Historic Properties are a group of restored buildings on Upper Water St, built between 1800 and 1905. Originally designed as huge warehouses for easy storage of goods and cargo, they now house boutiques, restaurants and bars and are connected by waterfront boardwalks. Artisans, merchants and buskers do business around the buildings in the summer. The 1814 **Privateers Warehouse** is the area's oldest stone building. The privateers were government sanctioned and sponsored pirates who stored their booty here. Among

the other vintage buildings are the wooden **Old Red Store**, once used for shipping operations and as a sail loft, and **Simon's Warehouse**, built in 1854.

Alexander Keith's Nova Scotia Brewery
BREWERY

(☑902-455-1474; www.keiths.ca; Brewery Market, 1496 Lower Water St; adult/child $16/8; ☺11am-8pm Mon-Thu, to 9pm Fri & Sat, noon-4pm Sun) A tour of this brewery takes you to 19th-century Halifax via costumed thespians, quality brew and dark corridors. Finish your hour-long tour with a party in the basement pub with beer on tap and ale-inspired yarns. Note that you'll need your ID. Kids are kept happy with lemonade.

Maritime Museum of the Atlantic
MUSEUM

(☑902-424-7490; http://maritimemuseum.novascotia.ca/; 1675 Lower Water St; adult/child $9.25/5; ☺9:30am-5pm Wed-Mon, to 8pm Tue) Part of this fun waterfront museum used to be a chandlery, where all the gear needed to outfit a vessel was sold. You can smell the charred ropes, cured to protect them from saltwater. There's a wildly popular display on the *Titanic* and another on the Halifax Explosion. The 3D film about the *Titanic* costs $5. Outside at the dock you can explore the CSS *Acadia,* a retired hydrographic vessel from England.

The last WWII corvette **HMCS Sackville** (adult/child $3/2; ☺10am-5pm) is docked nearby and staffed by the Canadian navy.

Canadian Museum of Immigration at Pier 21
MUSEUM

(☑902-425-7770; www.pier21.ca; 1055 Marginal Rd; adult/child $8.60/5; ☺9:30am-5:30pm) Named by CBC (Canadian Broadcasting Company) as one of the Seven Wonders of Canada, Pier 21 was to Canada what Ellis Island was to the USA. Between 1928 and 1971 over a million immigrants entered Canada through Pier 21. Their stories and the historical context that led them to abandon their homelands are presented in this museum.

Researchers fanned out across Canada to get firsthand testimonials from immigrants who passed through Pier 21. These moving videos are shown in screening rooms off a railcar – bring your hankie. The museum became a national museum in 2012 and, with the new funding that brings, expansion and upgrades are expected.

Citadel Hill National Historic Site
HISTORIC SITE

(☑902-426-5080; off Sackville St; adult/child $11.70/5.80; ☺9am-6pm) Canada's most visited national historic site, the huge and arguably spooky Citadel, is a star-shaped fort atop Halifax' central hill. Construction began in 1749 with the founding of Halifax; this version of the Citadel is the fourth, built from 1818 to 1861. Guided tours explain the fort's shape and history. The grounds inside the fort are open year-round, with free admission when the exhibits are closed.

Art Gallery of Nova Scotia
GALLERY

(☑902-424-7542; www.artgalleryofnovascotia.ca; 1723 Hollis St; adult/child $12/5; ☺10am-5pm Wed, Fri & Sat, to 9pm Thu, noon-5pm Sun) Don't miss the permanent, tear-jerking Maud Lewis Painted House exhibit that includes the 3m-by-4m house that Lewis lived in most of her adult life. The main exhibit in the lower hall changes regularly, featuring anything from ancient art to the avant-garde. Free tours are given at 2pm Sunday year-round and daily during July and August.

Halifax Public Gardens
GARDENS

At the corner of Spring Garden Rd and South Park St, these are considered the finest Victorian city gardens in North America. Oldies bands perform off-key concerts in the gazebo on Sunday afternoons in summer, tai chi practitioners go through their paces, and anyone who brings checkers can play on outside tables.

Titanic Burial Grounds
HISTORIC SITE

When the *Titanic* sank, the bodies not buried at sea were brought to Halifax. Today there are 19 graves at **Mt Olivet Catholic Cemetery** (7076 Mumford Rd), 10 in the **Baron de Hirsch Jewish Cemetery** at the north end of Windsor St, and 121 in the adjacent **Fairview Lawn Cemetery**; 40 graves are still unidentified. J Dawson, whose name was the basis for Leonardo DiCaprio's character in the film *Titanic,* is buried at Fairview Cemetery.

Anna Leonowens Gallery
GALLERY

(☑902-494-8184; http://nscad.ca; 1891 Granville St; ☺11am-5pm Tue-Fri, noon-4pm Sat, show openings 5:30-7:30pm Mon) **FREE** Off the pedestrian area on Granville St, this gallery shows work by students and faculty of the Nova Scotia College of Art & Design. The gallery is named for the founder of the college, who

Halifax

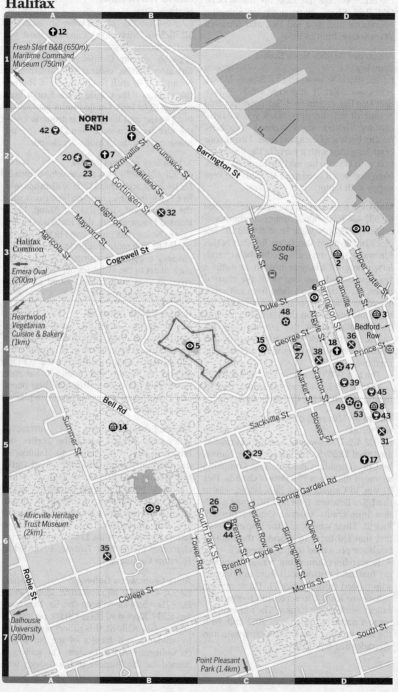

Fresh Start B&B (650m);
Maritime Command
Museum (750m)

NORTH
END

Halifax
Common

Emera Oval
(200m)

Heartwood
Vegetarian
Cuisine & Bakery
(1km)

Africville Heritage
Trust Museum
(2km)

Dalhousie
University
(300m)

Point Pleasant
Park (1.4km)

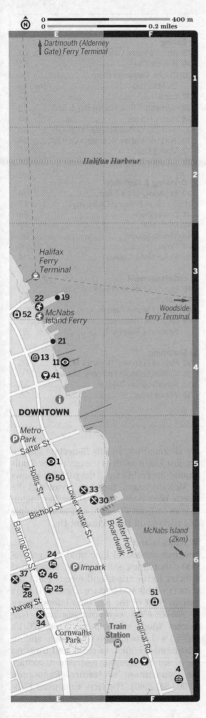

was immortalized in *The King and I* for her relationship with the king of Siam.

St Paul's Church
CHURCH

(☏902-429-2240; 1749 Argyle St; ⊙9am-4pm Mon-Fri) Established in 1749 with the founding of Halifax, Anglican St Paul's Church once served parishioners from Newfoundland to Ontario. Across the square, Halifax' **City Hall** is a true gem of Victorian architecture.

St Mary's Cathedral Basilica
CHURCH

(☏902-423-4116; 1508 Barrington St; ⊙free tours 10am & 2pm Jul-Sep) You can't miss this cathedral which purportedly has the largest free-standing spire in North America.

Old Town Clock
NOTABLE BUILDING

At the top of George St, at Citadel Hill, the Old Town Clock has been keeping time for 200 years. The inner workings arrived in Halifax from London in 1803, after being ordered by Prince Edward, the Duke of Kent.

⊙ North End

The North End has been a distinct neighborhood for almost as long as Halifax has existed. In the early 1750s the 'North Suburbs' area became popular and subsequently grew because of its larger building lots.

Africville Heritage Trust Museum
MUSEUM

(www.africvillemuseum.org; 5795 Africville Rd; adult/child $3.30/2; ⊙10am-4pm Tue-Sun) Learn the story of Africville, an African Nova Scotian part of town that was destroyed in the 1960s. Poignantly, the museum is housed in a replica of the Seaview United Baptist Church that was once the center of the community. If Eddie Carver is around, he'll have some stories to tell you.

Maritime Command Museum
MUSEUM

(☏902-427-0550, ext 6725; 2725 Gottingen St; ⊙9:30am-3:30pm Mon-Fri) **FREE** The admiral of the British navy for all of North America was based in Halifax until 1819 and threw grand parties at Admiralty House, now the Maritime Command Museum. Apart from the beautiful Georgian architecture, the museum is worth a visit for its eclectic collections: cigarette lighters, silverware and ship's bells, to name a few.

St George's Round Church
CHURCH

(☏902-423-1059; www.roundchurch.ca; 2222 Brunswick St) St George's Round Church was built in 1800 and is a rare circular Palladian

Halifax

church with a main rotunda 18m in diameter. Tours are by arrangement.

Cornwallis Street Baptist Church CHURCH
(5457 Cornwallis St) The Cornwallis Street Baptist Church has been serving African Nova Scotians since the 1830s. Walk by on Sunday morning and hear the gospel music flow through its walls.

Little Dutch Church CHURCH
(2405 Brunswick St) Tours of the 1756 Little Dutch Church, the second-oldest building in Halifax, can be arranged through St George's Round Church (p335).

◉ Outside the Center

Point Pleasant Park PARK
Some 39km of nature trails, picnic spots and the **Prince of Wales Martello Tower** (a round 18th-century defensive structure)

are all found within this 75-hectare sanctuary, just 1.5km south of the city center. Trails around the perimeter of the park offer views of McNabs Island, the open ocean and the North West Arm. Bus 9 along Barrington St goes to Point Pleasant, and there's ample free parking off Point Pleasant Dr.

McNabs Island ISLAND
(www.mcnabsisland.ca) Fine sand and cobblestone shorelines, salt marshes, abandoned military fortifications and forests paint the scenery of this 400-hectare island in Halifax harbor. Staff of the **McNabs Island Ferry** (☑ 902-465-4563; www.mcnabsisland.com; Government Wharf; round-trip adult/child $20/10; ☺ 24hr) will provide you with a map and an orientation to 30km of roads and trails on the island. For camping reservations contact the **Department of Natural Resources** (☑ 902-861-2560). The ferry runs from Fish-

erman's Cove in Eastern Passage, a short drive through Dartmouth.

🏃 Activities

Cycling

Cycling is a great way to see sites on the outskirts of Halifax. You can take bikes on the ferries to Dartmouth or cycle over the MacDonald Bridge. There are usually a few places renting out bikes by Bishop's Landing (at the end of Bishop St) along the waterfront for $9 per hour or $15 for a half day from mid June through August.

Otherwise, **Pedal & Sea Adventures** (☑877-772-5699, 902-857-9319; www.pedaland-seaadventures.com; bicycle rental per day/week from $35/140) will deliver the bike to you, complete with helmet, lock and repair kit. It also leads good-value self-guided tours; five-day trips including lodging and meals cost from $1099.

Hiking

There are both short and long hikes surprisingly close to downtown. **Hemlock Ravine** is an 80-hectare wooded area that has five trails, suitable for all levels. To get there, take the Bedford Hwy from central Halifax then turn left at Kent Ave; there's parking and a map of the trail at the end of this road. See www.novatrails.com for more detailed trail descriptions and directions to other trailheads. There's also hiking in Point Pleasant Park and on McNabs Island.

🧭 Tours

Check whether the two-masted schooner *Bluenose II* (p348) is in town for a harbor tour.

Tall Ship Silva   BOAT TOUR

(☑902-429-9463; www.tallshipsilva.com; Queen's Wharf, Prince St; cruises adult/child $22/15; ☺noon, 2pm, 4pm, 6pm & 10:30pm daily May-Oct) Lend a hand or sit back and relax while taking a 1½-hour daytime cruise or a two-hour evening party cruise on Halifax' square-masted tall ship.

East Coast Balloon Adventures   SCENIC FLIGHTS

(☑902-306-0095; www.eastcoastballoonadventures.com; 45min flights per person $250) Float from Halifax over the patchwork fields of Annapolis Valley at sunrise or sunset for the ultimate, peaceful views of this stunning province. Only available for ages eight and upwards.

Bluenose Sidecar Tours   DRIVING TOUR

(☑902-579-7433; www.bluenosesidecartours.com; tours $74-189) Enjoy free and breezy views from fun, old-school motorcycle sidecars on tours around Halifax or to Peggy's Cove, Lunenburg and the South Shore.

Tattle Tours   WALKING TOUR

(☑902-494-0525; www.tattletours.ca; per person $10; ☺7:30pm Wed-Sun) Lively two-hour tours depart from the Old Town Clock and are filled with local gossip, pirate tales and ghost stories. Walking tours are also available on demand – ask at any visitors information center (p342).

Salty Bear Adventure Travel   BUS TOUR

(☑902-224-1313; www.saltybear.ca; tours from $299) A sociable backpacker's choice for touring the province.

Great EARTH Expeditions   ECOTOUR

(☑902-223-2409; www.greatearthexpeditions.com; half-/full-day tours from $75/100) Half- and full-day ecotours led from Halifax can include hiking, kayaking or historical themes, including a tour to McNabs Island in Halifax Harbour. Longer four-day tours up the Cabot Trail and through Kejimkujik are also on offer.

Murphy's Cable Wharf   BOAT TOUR

(☑902-420-1015; www.mtcw.ca; 1751 Lower Water St) This tourism giant runs a range of tours on Halifax Harbour, from deep-sea fishing and two-hour scenic cruises to the popular 55-minute Harbour Hopper Tours (adult/child $30/17) on an amphibious bus.

NOVA SCOTIA HALIFAX

LOCAL KNOWLEDGE

FREE SKATING ON THE COMMON

The **Emera Oval** (www.halifax.ca/skate-hrm; ⊙7am-late) FREE on the Halifax Common serves as a speed-skating rink in winter and morphs into an inline-skating rink in summer. Skates, helmets and sledges (for use on the outside lane only) are free to borrow and there are even free lessons. Check the website and bring a valid ID.

⚝ Festivals & Events

Halifax is most vibrant during its jovial festivals. Check out volunteering opportunities through festival websites.

Nova Scotia Multicultural Festival CULTURE
(www.mans.ns.ca; ⊙late Jun) Performers, artisans, chefs and more entertain, promote and explore the province's multiculturalism at this huge festival.

Nova Scotia Tattoo CULTURE
(www.nstattoo.ca; tickets $27-65; ⊙early Jul) The world's 'largest annual indoor show' is a military-style event with lots of marching bands.

Atlantic Jazz Festival MUSIC
(www.jazzeast.com; evening tickets $15-30; ⊙mid-Jul) A full week of free outdoor jazz concerts each afternoon, plus evening performances ranging from world music to classic jazz trios.

Halifax International Busker Festival PERFORMING ARTS
(www.buskers.ca; ⊙early Aug) Comics, mimes, daredevils and musicians from all over the world perform along the Halifax waterfront.

Atlantic Fringe Festival THEATER
(www.atlanticfringe.com; ⊙mid-Sep) Offbeat and experimental theater from both emerging and established artists.

Atlantic Film Festival FILM
(www.atlanticfilm.com; tickets $10-15; ⊙mid-Sep) Ten days of great flicks from the Atlantic region and around the world.

Halifax Pop Explosion MUSIC
(www.halifaxpopexplosion.com; wristbands $50; ⊙mid-Oct) Some 130 concerts are spread out over 12 clubs during a five-day period and include hip-hop, punk, indie rock and folk.

A wristband gets you into as many shows as you can manage to see.

🛏 Sleeping

Halifax Backpackers Hostel HOSTEL $
(☎902-431-3170, 888-431-3170; www.halifax-backpackers.com; 2193 Gottingen St; dm/d/ste $20/57.50/80; 🐾) Coed dorms at this hip, 36-bed North End hostel hold no more than six beds. It draws a funky young crowd and everyone congregates at the downstairs cafe to swill strong coffee, eat cheap breakfasts and mingle with the eclectic local regulars. City buses stop right in front, but be warned: it's a slightly rough-edged neighborhood.

HI Nova Scotia HOSTEL $
(☎902-422-3863; www.hihostels.ca; 1253 Barrington St; HI member/nonmember dm $26/30, r $57; 🐾) Expect a dark and dormy night and a bright and cheery do-it-yourself breakfast at this exceptionally central, 75-bed hostel set in a Victorian house. The staff are friendly, and the shared kitchen is lively. Reserve ahead in summer.

Dalhousie University HOSTEL $
(☎902-494-8840; www.dal.ca/dept/summer-accommodations.html; s/d $48.50/75; ⊙May-Aug; 🐾♿) Dorm rooms with shared bathrooms are nearly sterile (read: no posters or beer bottles). Most people stay at **Howe Hall** (6230 Coburg St), which is adjacent to all the included university amenities and is a short walk to the Spring Garden Rd area.

★ Waverley Inn INN $$
(☎902-423-9346, 800-565-9346; www.waverley-inn.com; 1266 Barrington St; d incl breakfast $135-235; ❋@🐾) Every room here is furnished uniquely and nearly theatrically with antiques and dramatic linens. Both Oscar Wilde and PT Barnum once stayed here and probably would again today if they were still living. The downtown location can't be beat.

Fresh Start B&B B&B $$
(☎888-453-6616, 902-453-6616; www.bbcanada.com/2262.html; 2720 Gottingen St; r $110-130; @🐾) Run by two retired nurses, this majestic yet lived-in-feeling Victorian is in a gay-friendly part of the North End. Rooms with en-suite bathrooms are the best value.

Marigold B&B B&B $$
(☎902-423-4798; www.marigoldbedandbreakfast.com; 6318 Norwood St; s/d $75/85) Feel at home in this artist's nest full of bright floral paintings and fluffy cats. It's in a tree-lined

residential area in the North End with easy public transport access.

Pebble Bed & Breakfast
B&B $$$

(☑888-303-5056, 902-423-3369; www.thepebble.ca; 1839 Armview Tce; r $175-225; 🕿🌐) Bathroom aficionados will find heaven at this luxurious B&B. The tub and shower are in a giant room that leads to a terrace overlooking a leafy garden. The bedrooms are equally generous with plush, high beds and a modern-meets-antique decor. Irish owner Elizabeth O'Carroll grew up with a pub-owning family and brings lively, joyous energy from the Emerald Isle to her home in a posh, waterside residential area.

Halliburton
INN $$$

(☑902-420-0658; www.thehalliburton.com; 5184 Morris St; r $159-350; ❄@🕿) Pure, soothing class without all that Victorian hullabaloo can be found at this exceedingly comfortable and well-serviced historic hotel right in downtown.

Lord Nelson Hotel
HOTEL $$$

(☑902-423-5130, 800-565-2020; www.lordnelsonhotel.com; 1515 S Park St; d $130-360; ❄@🕿) When rock stars such as the Rolling Stones come to Halifax, they stay here. It's an elegant yet not stuffy 1920s building right across from Halifax Public Gardens. Rates drop dramatically in the off-season.

Prince George Hotel
HOTEL $$$

(☑800-565-1567, 902-425-1986; www.princegeorgehotel.com; 1725 Market St; d $160-350; ❄@❄🌐) A suave and debonair gem, central Prince George has all the details covered. Garden patios are a great place to take a drink or a meal, or even work, as an alternative to indoor meeting areas. Parking is $15.

Eating

Bars and pubs often serve very good food; kitchens close around 10pm.

Heartwood Vegetarian Cuisine & Bakery
VEGETARIAN $

(☑902-425-2808; 6250 Quinpool Rd; light meals from $5; 🕙10am-8pm Mon-Sat; 🍴) Try the local organic salad bar or amazing baked goods, along with a cup of fair-trade coffee.

Annie's Place Café
BREAKFAST $

(1592B Queen St; breakfasts $3-8; 🕙7am-3pm Mon-Fri, to 2pm Sat) A slice of small town in the heart of Halifax, Annie welcomes you in

and cooks up a hearty breakfast, including freshly baked bread and homemade chai. You'll have a whole new set of friends by the time you leave.

Just Us! Coffee Roaster's Co-Op
CAFE $

(1715 Barrington St; 🕙7am-5:30pm Mon-Thu, to 9pm Fri & Sat; 🕿) This bright yet cozy cafe serves up fair-trade, house-roasted coffee and baked goods made from locally sourced ingredients. It has free wi-fi and a central location; there's also a **second branch** (5896 Spring Garden Rd) nearby.

★ Edna
MODERN CANADIAN $$

(www.ednarestaurant.com; 2053 Gottingen St; mains $14-22; 🕙from 5pm Tue-Sun) Everything here is delicious, from the Southern fried rock hen to the filled-with-everything-good-from-the-sea Atlantic bouillabaisse. You can dine at a big wooden table where guests from everywhere chat and mingle, at the bar for a little less socializing or at a regular old table for two. It's a unique, vivacious, food-and-drink-loving atmosphere.

HALIFAX FOR CHILDREN

Discovery Centre (☑902-492-4422; www.discoverycentre.ns.ca; 1593 Barrington St; adult/child $8.50/6; 🕙10am-5pm Mon-Sat, 1-5pm Sun) Hands-on exhibits, live shows and movies make science fun for all ages. In 2014 the center will change locations to a modern new venue on the waterfront.

Museum of Natural History (☑902-424-7353; http://naturalhistory.novascotia.ca/; 1747 Summer St; adult/child $5.75/3.75; 🕙9am-5pm Mon, Tue & Thu-Sat, to 8pm Wed, noon-5pm Sun) Daily summer programs introduce children to Gus the toad and demonstrate the cooking of bugs. Exhibits on history and the natural world will keep parents engaged, too.

Theodore Too Big Harbour Tours (☑902-492-8847; www.mtcw.ca/theodoretugboat; 1751 Lower Water St; adult/child $20/15; 🕙11am, 12:30pm, 2pm, 3:30pm & 5pm daily Jun-Sep) One-hour tours on this funny-looking cartoon-character boat of book and television fame are particularly good for children under six.

★**Bicycle Thief**   MODERN CANADIAN $$
(☎902-425-7993; 1475 Lower Water St; lunch mains $14-18, dinner mains $15-29; ☻11.30am-late Mon-Fri, 5:30pm-late Sat) Named for the 1948 classic Italian film, this shabby-chic waterfront restaurant has won similar critical acclaim by local foodies – and with good reason. Start with regional oysters or polenta with wild mushroom ragout, then continue with dishes like pistachio-honey roasted salmon or pancetta wrapped pork tenderloin. The wine and cocktail list is several pages longer than the food menu.

Brooklyn Warehouse   CANADIAN $$
(☎902-446-8181;   www.brooklynwarehouse.ca; 2795 Windsor St; lunch mains $8-15, dinner mains around $20; ☻11:30am-10pm Mon-Sat; ☛) This North End hot spot is loaded with vegetarian and vegan options – the eggplant moussaka stack is excellent. It has a huge beer and cocktail menu, and an atmosphere that feels like a modern, hip version of *Cheers* – but with way better food.

Morris East   ITALIAN $$
(☎902-444-7663; www.morriseast.com; 5212 Morris St; pizzas $14-17; ☻11:30am-2:30pm Tue-Sat & 5-10pm Tue-Sun) At this cosmopolitan cafe, you'll find creative wood-fired pizzas on your choice of white, whole-wheat or gluten-free dough; try the peach, rosemary aioli and prosciutto pizza. They also have snazzy cocktails, like basil, lime and vodka punch.

Epicurious Morcels   FUSION $$
(☎902-455-0955; Hydrostone Market, 5529 Young St; mains around $12; ☻11:30am-8pm Tue-Thu, 10:30am-8pm Fri & Sat, 10:30am-2:30pm Sun) The specialties are smoked salmon, gravlax (dill-cured salmon) and unusual but extremely tasty homemade soups. The rest of the internationally inspired menu is also fantastic.

Hamachi Steak House
Bar & Grill   JAPANESE, FUSION $$
(☎902-425-1600; 1477 Lower Water St; teppanyaki $11-26; ☻11:30am-10pm Mon-Sat, 4-10pm Sun) Watch the show grill-side, while your chef slices, dices and sets the stove aflame to cook up the meats, seafood and veggies that make a crowd-pleasing Japanese teppanyaki. For a less theatrical experience, grab a table and enjoy the teppanyaki, sushi or Alberta steaks quietly, with a beautiful view of the harbor.

Wooden Monkey   CANADIAN $$
(☎902-444-3844; 1707 Grafton St; mains $14-23; ☻11am-10pm; ☛) ✿ This dark, cozy nook

with outdoor sidewalk seating on sunny days adamantly supports local organics and is a fab place to get superb gluten-free and vegan meals, as well as humane meat dishes.

Henry House   PUB $$
(1222 Barrington St; mains $11-20; ☻11:30am-midnight) Yeah, it's a pub, but the fish cakes are consistently rated the best in town and the bread pudding is legendary. Nosh all this with a frothy pint in a dimly lit and distinctly English-feeling basement or outside on the deck when the sun's out.

Chives Canadian Bistro   CANADIAN $$$
(☎902-420-9626; 1537 Barrington St; mains $17-35; ☻5-9:30pm) The menu changes with what's seasonably available and uses mostly local ingredients. The food is fine dining, while the low-lit cozy ambience is upscale casual.

Da Maurizio   ITALIAN $$$
(☎902-423-0859; 1496 Lower Water St; mains $28-34; ☻5-10pm Mon-Sat) Many locals cite this as their favorite Halifax restaurant. The ambience is as fine as the cuisine; exposed brick and clean lines bring out all the flavors of this heritage brewery building. Reservations are strongly recommended.

☕ Drinking & Nightlife

Halifax rivals Saint John's, Newfoundland, for the most drinking holes per capita. The biggest concentration of attractive bars is on Argyle St, where temporary street-side patios expand the sidewalk each summer. Pubs and bars close at 2am (a few hours earlier on Sunday).

Lower Deck   PUB
(☎902-422-1501; 1869 Lower Water St) A first stop for a real Nova Scotian knee-slapping good time. Think pints in frothy glasses, everyone singing, and live music all spilling out over the sidewalks on summer nights. When someone yells 'sociable!' it's time to raise your glass.

Economy Shoe Shop   PUB
(☎902-423-8845; 1663 Argyle St) This has been the 'it' place to drink and people-watch in Halifax for well over a decade. On weekend nights, actors and journalists figure heavily in the crush. It's a pleasant place for afternoon drinks and the kitchen dishes out tapas until last call at 1:45am.

Middle Spoon
COCKTAIL BAR

(www.themiddlespoon.ca; 1559 Barrington St; cocktails around $11; ⊘4-11pm Mon-Thu, to 1am Fri & Sat) What could be better than a place that serves only beer, wine, creative cocktails and decadent desserts? How about one with a super secret – should we even be writing this? It has a speakeasy-inspired lounge downstairs that serves even better cocktails. Get the password by clicking on the >: symbol on the website and don't tell.

Garrison Brewing Company
BREWERY

(1149 Marginal Rd; ☉10am-8pm Sun-Thu, to 10pm Fri & Sat) Not much beats a $2 taster glass of craft beer on a sunny patio except maybe five varieties of tasters, which is how many the brewery serves on tap each day. Other bottled beers are sold in the shop but, because they're not legally a bar (and Canada has complicated liquor laws), you can't drink them on the premises.Brewery tours are available by reservation.

Onyx
COCKTAIL BAR

(☑902-428-5680; 5680 Spring Garden Rd) A sultry place for a chic cocktail, the Onyx has a backlit white onyx bar that serves a huge selection of fine wines, single malt whiskeys and nine signature fresh-fruit mojitos, among other options. Imbibe small plates of Asian-French cuisine made with local ingredients.

☆ Entertainment

Check out *Coast* (www.thecoast.ca) to see what's on. A free weekly publication available around town, it's the essential guide for music, theater, film and events.

Live Music

Halifax seems to be fueled by music, with folk, hip-hop, alternative, country and rock gigs around town every weekend. Cover charge depends on the band.

Carelton
LIVE MUSIC

(☑902-422-6335; 1685 Argyle St) Catch acoustic sets, then enjoy the reasonable meals including a late-night menu.

Seahorse Tavern
LIVE MUSIC

(☑902-423-7200; 1665 Argyle St) The place to see punk, indie and metal bands.

Bearly's House of Blues & Ribs
LIVE MUSIC

(☑902-423-2526; 1269 Barrington St; cover $3) The best blues musicians in Atlantic Canada play here at incredibly low cover charges. Wednesday karaoke nights draw a crowd and some fine singers.

Theater

The two professional theaters in and around Halifax – Neptune Theatre and Eastern Front Theatre in Dartmouth – take a break in summer, with their last shows typically playing in May. However, Shakespeare by the Sea provides diversion through the summer.

Neptune Theatre
THEATER

(☑902-429-7070; www.neptunetheatre.com; 1593 Argyle St) This downtown theater presents musicals and well-known plays on its main stage (from $35), and edgier stuff in the studio (from $15).

Shakespeare by the Sea
THEATER

(☑902-422-0295; www.shakespearebythesea.ca; Point Pleasant Park; suggested donation $15; ☉Jun-Sep) Fine performances of the Bard's works at the Cambridge Battery, an old

NOVA SCOTIA HALIFAX

GAY & LESBIAN HALIFAX

Halifax has a thumping and thriving gay and lesbian scene, with most of the nightlife action concentrated around Gottingen St. In the city center, **Reflections Cabaret** (☑902-422-2957; 5184 Sackville St) is a wild disco that attracts a mixed crowd. It opens at 4pm, but the action really starts after 10pm (it stays open until 3am).

Lesbian travelers can stop by **Venus Envy** (☑902-422-0004; 1598 Barrington St; ☉10am-6pm Mon-Wed & Sat, to 7pm Thu & Fri, noon-5pm Sun) to network, browse books and check out fun toys. Squeaky clean **Seadog's Sauna & Spa** (☑902-444-3647; www.seadogs.ca; 2199 Gottingen St; ☉4pm-1am Mon-Thu, from 4pm Fri through 1am Mon) is the largest private men's club east of Québec City and has all the spa fixings. The same folks have opened **Menz Bar** (2182 Gottingen St; ☉3pm-2am), which offers its own Menz Pale Ale on tap.

Halifax Pride Week (www.halifaxpride.com) takes place every year around mid-July. Don't miss the Dykes versus Divas softball game that usually kicks off the week.

fortification in the middle of Point Pleasant Park. Check the website for details.

Sports

Halifax Metro Centre
STADIUM
([☑902-451-1221; 5284 Duke St; tickets $15) Halifax Mooseheads junior hockey team plays here.

Shopping

Halifax has some truly quirky shops to discover in the city center between Spring Garden Rd and Duke St.

★ Halifax Seaport Farmers Market
MARKET
(www.halifaxfarmersmarket.com; Marginal Rd; ☺10am-5pm Tue-Sun) The old Halifax Brewery Farmers Market was so popular this larger edifice was built to expand the fun. Find over 250 vendors selling everything from artisanal soaps to fresh carrots and baked goods. The market is biggest on Friday, Saturday and Sunday, but it's a great lunch stop anytime it's open.

Halifax Farmers Brewery Market
MARKET
([☑902-492-4043; 1496 Lower Water St; ☺7am-1pm Sat) North America's oldest farmers market, in the 1820s Keith's Brewery Building, has been overshadowed by the Seaport Market, but it's still worth checking this place out for the beautiful old building and longtime artisan vendors.

Nova Scotian Crystal
ARTS & CRAFTS
([☑888-977-2797; 5080 George St; ☺9am-6pm Mon-Fri, 10am-5pm Sat & Sun) It's as much of a show as a place to shop. Watch glass blowers form beautiful crystal glasses and vases, then pick the ones you want in the classy adjacent shop.

Orientation

The downtown area, three universities and older residential neighborhoods are contained on a compact peninsula cut off from mainland Halifax by an inlet called the North West Arm. Almost all sights of interest to visitors are concentrated in this area, making walking the best way to get around. Point Pleasant Park is at the extreme southern end of the peninsula, and the lively North End neighborhood – home to African Nova Scotians, art-school students and most of Halifax' gay bars – stretches from the midpoint to the northern extreme.

Two bridges span the harbor, connecting Halifax to Dartmouth and leading to highways

north (for the airport) and east. The MacDonald Bridge at the eastern end of North St is closest to downtown. The airport is 40km northeast of town on Hwy 102.

Information

INTERNET ACCESS
Many cafes, restaurants and public spaces have wi-fi. The new **Halifax Central Library** (Spring Garden Rd; ☺10am-9pm Tue-Thu, to 5pm Fri & Sat, 2-5pm Sun) has free wi-fi and computers on a first-come, first-served basis.

MEDICAL SERVICES
Family Focus ([☑902-420-2038; 5991 Spring Garden Rd; consultation $65; ☺8:30am-9pm Mon-Fri, 11am-5pm Sat & Sun) Walk-in or same-day appointments.

Halifax Infirmary ([☑902-473-7605, 902-473-3383; 1796 Summer St; ☺24hr) For emergencies.

MONEY
Bank branches cluster around Barrington and Duke Sts.

POST
Lawton's Drugs ([☑902-429-0088; 5675 Spring Garden Rd; ☺8am-9pm Mon-Fri, to 6pm Sat, noon-5pm Sun) Post office inside.

Main Post Office ([☑902-494-4670; 1680 Bedford Row; ☺7:30am-5:15pm Mon-Fri) Pick up mail sent to General Delivery, Halifax, NS B3J 2L3.

TOURIST INFORMATION
Check out posters for performances and events on the bulletin boards just inside the door of the Spring Garden Road Memorial Library.

Tourism Nova Scotia ([☑902-425-5781, 800-565-0000; www.novascotia.com) Operates visitors information centers in Halifax and other locations within Nova Scotia province, plus a free booking service for accommodations, which is useful when rooms are scarce in midsummer. It publishes the *Doers & Dreamers Guide* that lists places to stay, attractions and tour operators.

Visitors Information Centre (VIC) Halifax International Airport ([☑902-873-1223; ☺9am-9pm); Waterfront ([☑902-424-4248; 1655 Lower Water St; ☺8:30am-8pm).

USEFUL WEBSITES
Destination Halifax (www.halifaxinfo.com) Halifax' official tourism site has information on everything from events to package bookings.

Halifax Regional Municipality (www.halifax.ca) Info on everything from bus schedules to recreation programs.

❶ Getting There & Away

AIR
Most air services in Nova Scotia go to/from Halifax and there are multiple daily flights to Toronto, Calgary and Vancouver.

BUS
The only province-wide (and beyond) bus company is **Maritime Bus** (www.maritimebus.com), which services the main highways from Kentville to Halifax and up to Truro. From Truro the routes fork: towards North Sydney in one direction and towards Amherst and onto New Brunswick in the other.

Private shuttle buses compete with the major bus companies. Shuttles usually pick you up and drop you off from your hotel; with fewer stops, they travel faster, but the trade-off is a more cramped ride. They also tend to go out of business or change names frequently, so check online or ask around. Some of the more reliable companies include the following:

Cloud Nine Shuttle (✆902-742-3992, 888-805-3335; www.thecloudnineshuttle.com) Does the Yarmouth–Halifax route ($75, 3½ hours), stopping along the South Shore; airport pickup or drop-off is an extra $5.

Kathleen's Shuttle & Tours (✆903-834-2024; www.digbytoursandshuttle.webs.com) Halifax airport to Digby and Annapolis areas for around $65.

PEI Express Shuttle (✆902-462-8177, 877-877-1771; www.peishuttle.com) Goes to Charlottetown (PEI; $69), with early morning pickups.

TRAIN
One of the few examples of monumental Canadian train station architecture left in the Maritimes is found at 1161 Hollis St. Options with **VIA Rail** (www.viarail.ca) include overnight service to Montréal (21 hours, daily except Tuesdays).

❶ Getting Around

TO/FROM THE AIRPORT
Halifax International Airport is 40km northeast of town on Hwy 102 toward Truro. The cheapest way to get there is by Metro Transit public bus 320, which runs half-hourly to hourly between 5am and midnight from the Metro X bus stop on Albemarle St between Duke and Cogswell Sts. If you arrive in the middle of the night, as many flights do, your only choice is a taxi, which costs $56 to downtown Halifax. There are often not enough taxis, so it's prudent to reserve one in advance. Try **Halifax Airport Taxi** (✆902-999-2434; www.halifaxairportlimotaxi.com), which has 24-hour airport service.

CAR & MOTORCYCLE
Pedestrians almost always have the right-of-way in Halifax, so watch out for cars stopping suddenly!

Outside the downtown core, you can usually find free on-street parking for up to two hours. Otherwise, try private **Impark** (1245 Hollis St; per 1/12hr $1.50/8) or the municipally owned **Metro-Park** (✆902-830-1711; 1557 Granville St; per 1/12hr $2.25/15). Halifax' parking meters are enforced from 8am to 6pm Monday to Friday.

All the major national rental chains are represented at the airport and in downtown Halifax. Some will let you pick up in town and drop off at the airport free of charge.

PUBLIC TRANSPORTATION
Metro Transit (✆902-490-6600; www.halifax.ca/metrotransit; one-way fare $3.25) runs the city bus system and the ferries to Dartmouth. Maps and schedules are available at the ferry terminals and at the information booth in Scotia Sq mall.

Bus 7 cuts through downtown and North End Halifax via Robie St and Gottingen St, passing both hostels. Bus 1 travels along Spring Garden Rd, Barrington St, and the south part of Gottingen St before crossing the bridge to Dartmouth. **Fred** is a free city bus that loops around downtown every 30 minutes in the summer.

Taking the **ferry to Dartmouth** (one-way fare $2.25; every 15 to 30 minutes from 6am to 11:30pm) from the Halifax Ferry Terminal is a nice way of getting on the water, even if it's just for 12 minutes. Woodside, where another ferry goes in peak periods, is a good place to start a bike ride to Eastern Passage or Lawrencetown.

AROUND HALIFAX

Dartmouth
Founded in 1750, one year after Halifax, Dartmouth is Halifax' counterpart just across the harbor. It is more residential than Halifax, and the downtown area lacks the capital's charm and bustle, but it can make a pleasant base, since getting to Halifax by bus or ferry is so easy.

It's definitely worth a day trip just for the short cruise across the harbor on the ferry, the oldest saltwater ferry system in North America. Alderney Gate houses Dartmouth's ferry terminal.

Dartmouth Heritage Museum (✆902-464-2300; www.dartmouthheritagemuseum.ns.ca; 26 Newcastle St; admission $3; ◷10am-5pm

Tue-Sun mid-Jun–Aug, 1:30-5pm Wed-Sat Sep–mid-Jun) displays an eclectic collection in **Evergreen House**, the former home of folklorist Helen Creighton, who traversed the province in the early 20th century recording stories and songs. Tickets include same-day admission to the 1786 **Quaker House** (59 Ochterloney St; ⏱10am-5pm Tue-Sun Jun-Aug), the oldest house in the Halifax area, which was built by Quaker whalers from Nantucket who fled the American Revolution.

Shubie Campground (☎800-440-8450, 902-435-8328; www.shubiecampground.com; Jaybee Dr, off Waverley Rd; campsites from $33.50), the only campground accessible from Halifax on public transportation, is privately run and municipally owned. Facilities include showers and a laundry.

Haligonians head to Dartmouth just for the massive buttery chocolate croissants at **Two If By Sea** (66 Ochterloney St; chocolate croissants $3; ⏱7am-6pm Mon-Fri, 8am-5pm Sat & Sun). But be warned, they are usually sold out by about 1pm. Even sans pastries, it's a hip place to stop for coffee and people-watching on a sunny day, with a distinctly Dartmouth atmosphere.

Eastern Shore Beaches

When downtown dwellers venture over the bridge to Dartmouth on a hot summer's day, it's most likely en route to a beach. There are beautiful, long, white-sand beaches all along the Eastern Shore, and although the water never gets very warm, brave souls venture in for a swim or a surf, particularly if the fog stays offshore.

The closest – and therefore busiest – of the Eastern Shore beaches, **Rainbow Haven**, is 1km long. It has washrooms, showers, a canteen and a boardwalk with wheelchair access to the beach. Lifeguards supervise a sizable swimming area.

The most popular destination for surfers, cobblestone **Lawrencetown Beach** faces directly south and often gets big waves compliments of hurricanes or tropical storms hundreds of kilometers away. It boasts a supervised swimming area, washrooms and a canteen. To surf, learn to surf or just enjoy the view, stay at **Lawrencetown Beach House** (☎902-827-2345; www.lawrencetown-beachhouse.com; dm/d $28/75), a comfy hostel with 10 beds and three private rooms. It's beautifully nestled in the beach grass above one of the only stretches of real sand and often books up months before summer even begins, so plan in advance. There are several places in the area to rent surfboards (around $15 per day) and wet suits (also $15 per day). Surf lessons are around $75 for 1½ hours including equipment; try **Dacane Sports** (☎902-431-7873; http://dacanesurfshop.com), **Nova Scotia Surf School** (www.ecsurfschool.com) or the all-women-run **One Life Surf School** (☎902-880-7873; www.onelifesurf.com).

With more than 3km of white sand backed by beach grass, **Martinique** is the longest beach in Nova Scotia and one of the prettiest in the area. Even if you find the water too cold for a swim, it's a beautiful place to walk, watch birds or play Frisbee.

Sambro

Just 18km south of Halifax, **Crystal Crescent Beach** is on the outskirts of the fishing village of Sambro. There are actually three beaches here in distinct coves; the third one out, toward the southwest, is clothing optional and gay friendly. An 8.5km **hiking trail** begins just inland and heads through barrens, bogs and boulders to Pennant Point; to get to the trailhead, take Herring Cove Rd from the traffic circle in Halifax all the way to Sambro, then follow the signs.

Peggy's Cove

Peggy's Cove is one of the most visited fishing towns in Canada and for a good reason: the rolling granite cove highlighted by a

---

DON'T MISS

FISHERMAN'S COVE

If you're heading up the Eastern Shore from Dartmouth or Halifax, detour onto Hwy 322 to Fisherman's Cove in Eastern Passage, a Popeye-esque fishing port with some of the region's best seafood samplings. **Wharf Wraps** (104 Government Wharf Rd; fish & chips $12; ⏱10am-6pm Jun-Sep) has an outdoor seating area and deservedly famous (and huge) portions of fish and chips, or head next door to the **Fish Basket** (100 Government Wharf Rd; ⏱9am-6pm) for fish and lobster by the pound or a delicious fresh lobster sandwich ($8) for the road.

perfect red-and-white lighthouse exudes a dreamy seaside calm, even through the parading tour buses. Most visitors hop off their air-con bus, snap a few pictures, then get right back on the bus. If you stick around, you'll find it surprisingly easy to chat with the friendly locals (there are only 45 of them) and settle into fishing-village pace. At 43km west of Halifax on Hwy 333, it makes a mellow day trip from the city.

It's best to visit before 10am in the summer, as tour buses arrive in the middle of the day and create one of the province's worst traffic jams.

◎ Sights

Peggy's Cove Lighthouse NOTABLE BUILDING
(◎ 9:30am-5:30pm May-Oct) The highlight of the cove is this picture-perfect lighthouse, which for many years was a working post office. Meander around the granite landscape that undulates much like the icy sea beyond.

DeGarthe Gallery GALLERY
(✆ 902-823-2256; admission $2; ◎ on demand) See paintings by local artist William deGarthe (1907–83), who sculpted the magnificent 30m-high *Fishermen's Monument* into a rock face in front of the gallery.

🛏 Sleeping & Eating

Wayside Camping Park CAMPGROUND $
(✆ 902-823-2271; www.waysidecampground.com; 10295 Hwy 333, Glen Margaret; campsites/RV sites $25/35; ◎ May-Oct; 🐾🛜) About 10km north of Peggy's Cove and 36km from Halifax, this camping park has lots of shady sites on a hill. It gets crowded in midsummer.

Peggy's Cove Bed & Breakfast B&B $$
(✆ 902-823-2265, 877-725-8732; www.peggyscove-bb.com; 17 Church Rd; r $120-145; ◎ Apr-Oct) The only place to stay in the cove itself, this B&B has an enviable position with one of the best views in Nova Scotia, overlooking the fishing docks and the lighthouse; it was once home to artist William deGarthe. You'll definitely need advance reservations.

Oceanstone Inn & Cottages INN $$
(✆ 866-823-2160, 902-823-2160; www.oceanstone.ns.ca; 8650 Peggy's Cove Rd, Indian Harbour; r $95-145, cottages $185-365; @🛜🐾) Whimsically decorated cottages are a stone's throw from the beach and just a short drive from Peggy's Cove. Guests can use paddleboats to venture to small islands. Rhubarb, the inn's dining

PROSPECT

As pretty as Peggy's Cove, Prospect doesn't attract a fraction of the tourist traffic. An undeveloped **trail** starts at the end of Indian Point Rd and leads 3km along the coast past plenty of perfect picnic spots. There's not a lot of room to park at the trailhead, so you may need to leave your vehicle on the side of the road heading into the village.

If you enjoy Prospect, consider exploring more by taking other roads off Hwy 333 to the other incredibly scenic, less-visited cove villages in the area.

room, is considered one of the best seafood restaurants in the region.

Dee Dee's ICE CREAM $
(◎ noon-6pm May-Sep) On hot days, explore the area licking a delicious homemade-with-local-ingredients ice-cream cone from Dee Dee's, near the tourist information center.

☆ Entertainment

Old Red Schoolhouse THEATER
(✆ 902-823-2099; www.beales.ns.ca; 126 Peggy's Point Rd; suggested donation $10) This performance venue puts on comedies and music performances through the high season. A few shows per season are serviced by shuttle vans that offer round-trips to Halifax hotels. Check the website for details.

❶ Information

There's a free parking area with washrooms and a **tourist information office** (✆ 902-823-2253; 109 Peggy's Cove Rd; ◎ 9am-7pm May-Oct) as you enter the village. Free 45-minute walking tours are led from the tourist office daily from mid-June through August.

SOUTH SHORE

This is Nova Scotia's most visited coastline and it's here you'll find all those quintessential lighthouses, protected forested coves with white beaches, and plenty of fishing villages turned tourist towns. The area from Halifax to Lunenburg is cottage country for the city's elite and is quite popular with day-tripping tourists and locals. Hwy 3 – labeled the 'Lighthouse Route' by tourism officials –

can be slow as a result. Take this scenic route if you're not pressed for time and want to check out antique shops or artisans' wares en route. Travel times can be halved by taking Hwy 103 directly to the closest exit for your destination.

Chester

Established in 1759, the tiny town of Chester has today become a choice spot for well-to-do Americans and Haligonians to have a summer home. It's had a colorful history as the haunt of pirates and Prohibition-era bathtub-gin smugglers and it keeps its color today via the many artists' studios about town. There's a large **regatta** in the tranquil harbor in mid-August.

◉ Sights & Activities

Lordly House Museum   MUSEUM
(☑902-275-3842; 133 Central St; ☺10am-4pm Tue-Sat Jun-Sep) **FREE** A fine example of Georgian architecture from 1806, the Lordly House Museum has three period rooms illustrating 19th-century upper-class life and Chester history. The museum is also an artists' studio.

Tancook Island   ISLAND
This island (population 190) is a 45-minute ferry ride from Chester's government wharf (round-trip $5.50, four services daily Monday to Friday, two daily on weekends). **Walking trails** crisscross the island. Settled by Germans and French Huguenots in the early 19th century, the island is famous for its sauerkraut. The last ferry from Chester each day overnights in Tancook Island.

🛏 Sleeping & Eating

Graves Island Provincial Park CAMPGROUND $
(☑902-275-4425; www.parks.gov.ns.ca; campsites $24) An island in Mahone Bay connected by a causeway to the mainland has 64 wooded and open campsites. RVs usually park in the middle of the area, but some shady, isolated tent sites are tucked away on the flanks of the central plateau. It's 3km northeast of Chester off Hwy 3.

Mecklenburgh Inn B&B   B&B $$
(☑902-275-4638; www.mecklenburghinn.ca; 78 Queen St; r $115-155; ☺May-Jan; 🖥) This casual four-room inn, built in 1890, has a breezy 2nd-floor veranda. Some rooms have private adjacent balconies; most have private bath-

rooms. The owner is a cordon-bleu chef, so expect an excellent breakfast.

Kiwi Café   CAFE $
(☑902-275-1492; 19 Pleasant St; lunch mains $9-14; ☺8am-4pm Sun-Wed, to 8pm Thu-Sat; 🖥🖉) A New Zealand chef prepares excellent soups, salads, sandwiches and baked goods that you can eat in or take away in recyclable containers. The walls are painted kiwi green and there's beer, wine and a relaxed atmosphere.

Rope Loft   PUB $$
(☑902-275-3430; 36 Water St; mains around $15; ☺11:30am-11pm) You couldn't find a better setting than this bay-side pub. Hearty pub food is served indoors or out.

☆ Entertainment

Chester Playhouse   THEATER
(☑902-275-3933; www.chesterplayhouse.ca; 22 Pleasant St; tickets around $25) This older theater space has great acoustics for live performances. Plays or dinner theater are presented most nights in July and August, with occasional concerts during spring and fall.

ℹ Information

Tourist Office (☑902-275-4616; Hwy 3; ☺9:30am-5:30pm) In the old train depot near the Chester turnoff.

Mahone Bay

The sun shines more often here than anywhere else along the coast. With more than 100 islands only 100km from Halifax, it's a great base for exploring this section of the South Shore. Take out a kayak or a bike or simply stroll down Main St, which skirts the harbor and is scattered with shops selling antiques, quilts, pottery and works by local painters.

◉ Sights & Activities

Mahone Bay's skyline is dotted with three magnificent old churches along the seafront that draw in many keen photographers and host live music (tickets cost $20) in the summer.

Mahone Bay Settlers' Museum   MUSEUM
(☑902-624-6263; 578 Main St; ☺10am-5pm Tue-Sun Jun–mid-Oct) **FREE** Exhibits on local architecture and the settlement of the area by 'Foreign Protestants' in 1754.

You can rent boats at **Paddle South Kayaks** (617 Main St; 1hr/daily rentals from $30/70; ⊙9am-8pm Jun-Oct) or bikes at **Sweet Rides Cycling** (523 Main St; half-/full-day rentals $20/30; ⊙10am-5pm Mon-Sat, noon-5pm Sun).

☞ Tours

South Shore Boat Tours   BOAT TOUR
(☑902-543-5107; www.southshoreboattours.com; ⊙Jul & Aug) Offers boatbuilding and nature tours (1¾ hours, adults $35).

✪ Festivals & Events

Mahone Bay Pirate Festival & Regatta   REGATTA
(http://mahonebayregatta.wordpress.com) On the weekend prior to the first Monday in August, this pirate-themed festival includes lots of costumed thespians and ends with the dramatic burning of a model ship out on the bay.

Great Scarecrow Festival & Antiques Fair   CULTURE
(⊙1st weekend Oct) Locals make outlandish scarecrows and carved pumpkins to display them outside their homes. Meanwhile, a popular antique fair rages on.

🛏 Sleeping & Eating

Kip & Kaboodle Backpackers Hostel   HOSTEL $
(☑902-531-5494, 866-549-4522; www.kiwikaboodle.com; Hwy 3; dm $30; ⊙Apr-Oct; 🐾) This friendly nine-bed hostel is superbly located, 3km from the attractions of Mahone Bay

and 7km from Lunenburg. Owners offer town pickup, as well as economical tours, a shuttle service, BBQs and bonfires, and excellent area tips. There is also bike rental and one private room.

Fisherman's Daughter   B&B $$
(☑902-624-0483; www.fishermans-daughter.com; 97 Edgewater St; r $115-145; 🐾🐾) Set on the bay by the three beautiful churches, this very old house (1840) has been meticulously remodeled for comfort, while retaining all the charm. Two rooms have views through sharply pitched Gothic-style windows and all four rooms have good-sized attached bathrooms. It has all the friendly service you'd want from a top B&B.

Three Thistles B&B   B&B $$
(☑902-624-0517; www.three-thistles.com; 389 W Main St; r $100-150; 🐾) 🌿 Owner Ama Phyllis uses environmentally conscious cleaning agents and cooks with organic foods. Rooms are sparkling and clean and there's a back garden that stretches to a wooded area.

LaHave Bakery   DELI $
(cnr Edgewater & Main Sts; sandwiches from $4; ⊙9am-6pm; 🐾) This bakery is famous for its hearty bread. Sandwiches are made on thick slabs of it.

★Mateus Bistro   MODERN CANADIAN $$$
(☑902-531-3711; 533 Main St; mains $22-35; ⊙5-9pm Mon, Thu & Fri, 10am-9pm Sat & Sun) Tucked into a little gallery with an outdoor patio, this place may miss the sea views but once you hit the cocktails, wine and food, you'll

A PIRATE'S TREASURE

Oak Island, near Mahone Bay, is home to a so-called 'money pit' that has cost over $2 million in excavation expenses and six lives. There is still not a shred of information about what the pit is or what might be buried there.

The mystery began in 1795 when three inhabitants of the island came across a depression in the ground. Knowing that pirates had once frequented the area, they decided to dig and see what they could find. Just over half a meter down, they hit a layer of neatly placed flagstone; another 2.5m turned up one oak platform, then another. After digging to 9m, the men temporarily gave up but returned eight years later with the Onslow Company, a professional crew.

The Onslow excavation made it down 27.5m; when the crew returned the next morning, the shaft had flooded and they were forced to halt the digging. A year later, the company returned to dig 33.5m down in a parallel shaft, which also flooded. It was confirmed in 1850 that the pit was booby-trapped via five box drains at Smith Cove, 150m from the pit. The beach was found to be artificial.

Ever since, people have come to seek their fortune from far and wide at the 'money pit.' Only a few links of gold chain, some parchment, a cement vault and an inscribed stone have been found.

likely not care. The European-inspired menu changes with what's fresh locally, from oysters and Fundy scallops to duck and a rainbow of veggies.

🛍 Shopping

Amos Pewter
ARTS & CRAFTS

(☎800-565-3369; www.amospewter.com; 589 Main St; ⊙9am-7pm Mon-Sat, 10am-7pm Sun) Watch demonstrations in the art of pewter making, then buy wares at the attached store.

ℹ Information

Biscuit Eater Booktrader & Cafe (☎902-624-2665; 16 Orchard St; internet per hr $5; ⊙9am-5pm Wed-Sat, 11am-5pm Sun; 🛜) The best place to check email, with a fair-trade coffee and a light organic meal. Free wi-fi.

Mahone Bay (www.mahonebay.com) Links to restaurants and accommodations.

Visitors Information Centre (VIC; ☎902-624-6151; 165 Edgewater St; ⊙9am-7pm May-Oct) Has do-it-yourself walking-tour brochures.

Lunenburg

The largest of the South Shore fishing villages is historic Lunenburg, the region's only Unesco World Heritage site and the first British settlement outside Halifax. The town is at its most picturesque viewed from the sea around sunset, when the boxy, brightly painted old buildings literally glow behind the ship-filled port. Look for the distinctive 'Lunenburg Bump,' a five-sided dormer window on the 2nd floor overhanging the 1st floor.

Lunenburg was settled largely by Germans, Swiss and Protestant French, who were first recruited by the British as a workforce for Halifax, then later became fishermen. Today Nova Scotia has been hard hit by dwindling fish stocks, but Lunenburg's burgeoning tourism trade has helped shore up the local economy.

◉ Sights & Activities

Fisheries Museum of the Atlantic   MUSEUM
(☎902-634-4794; http://fisheriesmuseum.novascotia.ca; 68 Bluenose Dr; adult/child $10/3; ⊙9:30am-5pm) The knowledgeable staff at the Fisheries Museum of the Atlantic includes a number of retired fisherfolk who can give firsthand explanations of the fishing industry. A cute aquarium on the 1st floor lets you get eye-to-eye with halibut, a

6kg lobster and other sea creatures. Film screenings and talks are scheduled throughout the day.

Knaut-Rhuland House   MUSEUM
(☎902-634-3498; 125 Pelham St; admission $3; ⊙11am-5pm Tue-Sat, 1-5pm Sun Jun-Sep) Knaut-Rhuland House is considered the finest example of Georgian architecture in the province. This 1793 house has costumed guides who point out its features.

Ironworks Distillery   DISTILLERY
(www.ironworksdistillery.com; 2 Kempt St; ⊙noon-5pm Wed-Mon) Tastings are free but good luck getting out of this old ironworks building without buying a bottle of something amazing. Local ingredients craft a changing selection of liquors, a strong apple brandy, apple vodkas and a very quaffable black spiced rum.

Bike Barn   CYCLING
(☎902-634-3426; www.bikelunenburg.com; 579 Blue Rocks Rd; bicycle rental per day $25) About 2km east of town, the Bike Barn rents bikes. On a small peninsula, this area is a cyclist's dream, with few hills, great ocean views and little vehicle traffic. Owners Merrill and Al will gladly help you plan your trip.

Pleasant Paddling   KAYAKING
(www.pleasantpaddling.com; 221 The Point Rd; kayak rental 2hr/day $30/70, half-/full-day tours $65/110) The knowledgeable folks at this beautiful place to paddle offer rentals and tours in double or single kayaks.

☞ Tours

Numerous fishing, sailing and whale-watching tours depart from the wharf adjacent to the Fisheries Museum on Bluenose Dr. Book on the dock or at the visitor information center (p350).

Bluenose II   SAILING
(☎800-763-1963, 902-634-1963; www.bluenose.novascotia.ca; 2hr cruise adult/child $20/10) This classic replica of the *Bluenose* racing schooner is sometimes in Halifax and sometimes in Lunenburg. The boat was getting worked on in 2013 but should reopen in 2014. Check the website for details.

Lunenburg Town Walking Tours WALKING TOUR
(☎902-634-3848) Enthusiastic and very experienced Sheila Allen leads leisurely tours during the day or spooky lantern-lit ones at night; call for more information.

Lunenburg

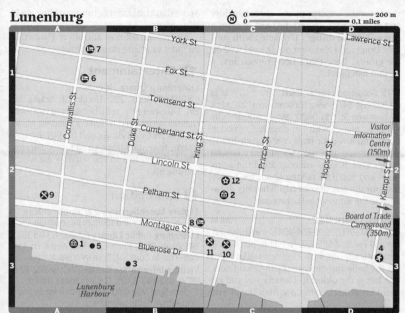

N 0 ——— 200 m / 0 ——— 0.1 miles

Trot in Time TOUR

(adult/child $20/8; ⊘ Jun–mid-Oct) Take a half-hour tour of town in a horse-drawn cart. Leaves from outside the Fisheries Museum of the Atlantic.

✨ Festivals & Events

Boxwood Festival MUSIC

(www.boxwood.org; festival pass $50; ⊘ late Jul) Flautists and pipers from around the world put on stellar public concerts.

Lunenburg Folk Harbour Festival MUSIC

(☑ 902-634-3180; www.folkharbour.com; ⊘ Aug) Singer-songwriters from Canada and beyond, plus traditional music and gospel.

Nova Scotia Folk Art Festival ARTS

(www.nsfolkartfestival.com; ⊘ 1st Sun Aug) Buffet dinner, artist talks and then a big art show and sale.

🛏 Sleeping

Make reservations as far ahead as possible, especially during summer festivals. Kip & Kaboodle Backpackers Hostel (p347), 7km north of town, is the best budget option.

Board of Trade Campground CAMPGROUND $

(☑ 902-634-3656, 902-634-8100; lbt@aliantz-inc.ca; 11 Blockhouse Hill Rd; campsites/RV sites

Lunenburg

$23/30; @) This campground, beside the visitor information center, has great views and a lot of gravel RV sites. Grassy tent sites are closely packed together and lack shade.

Sail Inn B&B B&B $$

(☑ 877-247-7075, 902-634-3537; www.sailinn.ca; 99 Montague St; r $100-140; ☎) Rooms have a view over the waterfront and are bright, airy and modern with an antique twist. You get a free sail on the owner's 15m ketch with your stay. Don't miss checking out the old well on the ground floor that's been turned into a lighted fish pond.

1775 Solomon House B&B B&B $$
(☑ 902-634-3477; www.bbcanada.com/5511.html; 69 Townsend St; r $110-130; ☏) A wonderfully antique place with undulating wooden floors and low door jams (watch your head), this B&B has the nicest and most helpful owner ever. Rooms are cozy amid the aging walls and you'll be talking about the breakfasts for the rest of your trip. The only drawback is the minuscule bathrooms.

Lennox Tavern B&B B&B $$
(☑ 888-379-7605, 902-634-4043; www.lennoxinn. com; 69 Fox St; r $85-140; ☏) This place feels authentically old, with electric candles lighting the halls and massive plank-wood floors. The inn is the oldest in Canada and you get to eat breakfast in what was once the tavern.

✖ Eating

Try some offbeat Lunenburg specialties. Solomon Gundy is pickled herring with onions. Lunenburg pudding – pork and spices cooked in the intestines of a pig – goes well with Scotch and water.

Salt Shaker Deli DELI $
(☑ 902-640-3434; 124 Montague St; meals $8-15; ⊙ 11am-9pm Tue-Sat, to 3pm Sun) With a clean-cut modern atmosphere, a waterfront deck and amazing food, it's no wonder this new deli-restaurant is always packed. Try the thin-crust pizzas or a pound of mussels cooked to the style of your choosing.

Magnolia's Grill DINER $
(☑ 902-634-3287; 128 Montague St; mains $8-16; ⊙ lunch & dinner) Try one of the many soups of the day at this diner-style locals' favorite. Seafood, including Solomon Gundy, and an extensive wine list are available.

★ Fleur de Sel FRENCH $$$
(☑ 902-640-2121; 53 Montague St; mains $22-38; ⊙ 11am-2pm & 5-10pm; ✐) This is by far the most elegant eating option in the region. French-inspired seafood, meat and vegetarian dishes made from organic produce are served in the classic, bright dining area. For one of the best culinary treats ever, indulge in the $90 several-course tasting menu.

Make that treat even better by adding a $58 wine pairing.

The restaurant now also offers a suite that includes exquisite meal packages.

☆ Entertainment

Lunenburg Opera House THEATER
(☑ 902-634-4010; 290 Lincoln St; tickets $5-25) This recently refurbished old 400-seat theater is rumored to have a resident ghost. Built as an Odd Fellows hall in 1907, it's now a favorite venue for rock and folk musicians. Check the posters in the window for what's coming up.

❶ Information

Explore Lunenburg (www.explorelunenburg. ca) Local history and tourism information.
Lunenburg Public Library (☑ 902-634-8008; 19 Pelham St; ⊙ 10am-6pm Tue, Wed & Fri, to 8pm Thu, to 5pm Sat) Free internet access.
Visitors Information Centre (VIC; ☑ 902-634-8100, 888-615-8305; 11 Blockhouse Hill Rd; ⊙ 9am-8pm May-Oct) Walking-tour maps and help with accommodations.

❶ Getting There & Away

At the time of writing, there were no public buses. Your best bet from Halifax is with **Kiwi Kaboodle** (☑ 902-531-5494; www.novascotia-toursandtravel.com), who run shuttles for $35.

Liverpool

There is plenty to do in Liverpool and it's well situated for exploring several gorgeous beaches, as well as Kejimkujik National Park (68km north) and its Seaside Adjunct (15km southwest). That said, it lacks the seaside quaintness of the villages to its north.

◉ Sights

Rossignol Cultural Centre MUSEUM
(☑ 902-354-3067; www.rossignolculturalcentre. com; 205 Church St; adult/child $5/3; ⊙ 10am-5:30pm Mon-Sat) Local character Sherman Hines' most fabulous endeavor is a must-see for anyone who enjoys the offbeat. There are halls of taxidermy animals, cases of gorgeous aboriginal beadwork, walls of Hines' beautiful photography (including from his Mongolian adventures) and a room dedicated to outhouses around the world.

If you love it so much you don't want to leave, an authentic Mongolian yurt (with en-suite bathroom) is for rent adjacent to the museum for a $100 per night donation.

Admission to the museum includes entry to the **Sherman Hines Museum of Photography** (☑ 902-354-2667; www.shermanhinesphotographymuseum.com; 219 Main St; ⊙ 10am-5:30pm Mon-Sat).

Perkins House Museum   MUSEUM
(☑ 902-354-4058; http://perkinshouse.novascotia.ca; 105 Main St; adult/child $4/2; ⊙ 9:30am-5:30pm Mon-Sat, 1-5:30pm Sun Jun-Oct) Perkins House Museum displays articles and furniture from the colonial period. Built in 1766, it's the oldest house belonging to the Nova Scotia Museum.

Queen's County Museum   MUSEUM
(☑ 902-354-4058; www.queenscountymuseum.com; 109 Main St; admission $4; ⊙ 9:30am-5:30pm Mon-Sat, 1-5:30pm Sun) This museum has First Nations artifacts and materials relating to town history, as well as some writings by early citizens.

Fort Point   LIGHTHOUSE
(☑ 902-354-5260; 21 Fort Lane; ⊙ 10am-6pm May-Oct) FREE At Fort Point a cairn marks the site where Frenchman Samuel de Champlain landed in 1604. You can blow the hand-pumped foghorn in the **lighthouse** at the end of Main St.

Hank Snow Home Town Museum   MUSEUM
(☑ 902-354-4675; www.hanksnow.com; 148 Bristol Ave; admission $3; ⊙ 9am-5pm Mon-Sat, noon-5pm Sun) This museum sheds light on Nova Scotia's status as a northern Nashville. In the old train station, it captures the history of Snow, Wilf Carter and other crooners and yodelers.

🎊 Festivals & Events

Privateer Days   HISTORY
(www.privateerdays.com; ⊙ early Jul) A celebration of piracy and history.

🛏 Sleeping & Eating

Geranium House   B&B $
(☑ 902-354-4484; 87 Milton Rd; r $60) This B&B on a large wooded property next to the Mersey River has three rooms with shared bathroom, ideal for cyclists and families.

Lane's Privateer Inn   INN $$
(☑ 902-354-3456, 800-794-3332; www.lanesprivateerinn.com; 27 Bristol Ave; r incl breakfast $95-150, mains $9-25; ⊙ dining room 7am-10pm; 🛜) Originally the home of a swashbuckling privateer, this 200-year-old inn now looks more 1980s than anything else, but it's a clean and pleasant place to stay. It's the center of action in summer, with live music on weekends and special events like wine tastings. There's also a **dining room** that serves the best food in town.

☆ Entertainment

Astor Theatre   THEATER
(☑ 902-354-5250; www.astortheatre.ns.ca; 59 Gorham St) The Astor is the oldest continuously operating performance venue in the province. Built in 1902 as the Liverpool Opera House, it presents films, plays and live music.

ℹ Information

Located near the river bridge, the **tourist office** (☑ 902-354-5421; 28 Henry Hensey Dr; ⊙ 9:30am-5:30pm May-Oct) has a walking-tour pamphlet.

Kejimkujik National Park

Less than 20% of Kejimkujik's 381-sq-km wilderness is accessible by car; the rest is reached either on foot or by canoe. Birdwatchers can hope to see plenty of water fowl, barred owls and pileated woodpeckers, while wildlife ranges from porcupines to black bear. On a less joyful note, biting insects are rampant; watch out for mosquitoes the size of hummingbirds and eel-like leeches in the lakes.

🥾 Activities

The main **hiking** loop is a 60km trek that begins at the east end of George Lake and ends at the Big Dam Lake trailhead. A shorter loop, ideal for an overnight trek, is the 26km Channel Lake Trail that begins and ends at Big Dam Lake. September to early October is prime hiking time; the bugs in the spring would drive you mad. More than a dozen lakes are connected by a system of portages, allowing canoe trips of up to seven days. A topographical map ($10) may be required for ambitious multi-day trips.

Rent canoes and other equipment in the park at **Jakes Landing** (☑ 902-682-2289; ⊙ 8am-9pm Jun-Sep). One-/24-hour hire of a double kayak, canoe or rowboat is $8/35; kayak or bike, $7/30. One-week hire for any of these is $125. It's open during the off-season by appointment.

Sleeping & Eating

Forty-five backcountry campsites ($24.50 per night including firewood) are scattered among the lakes of Kejimkujik. You must book them in advance by contacting the park's visitors center. There's a 14-day maximum; you can't stay more than two nights at any site.

Caledonia Country Hostel　　HOSTEL $
(☎ 902-682-3266, 877-223-0232; www.caledonia-countryhostel.com; 9960 Hwy 8, Caledonia; dm/d $25/60; ☜) In the heart of Caledonia – the only town near the park that has an internet cafe, a VIC, a gas station and a grocery store – this spotless hostel has beds on the 2nd floor of an adorable Victorian-style home. Cozy nooks with TV, books, old-style upholstered chairs and country linens abound. The owners also have tours and shuttle services available.

Raven Haven Hostel
& Family Park　HOSTEL, CAMPGROUND $
(☎ 902-532-7320; www.hihostels.ca; 2239 Virginia Rd, off Hwy 8, South Milford; dm HI member/nonmember $22/24, campsites/RV sites $20/24, cabins $72; ☜ Jun-Aug) This HI hostel and campground is 25km south of Annapolis Royal and 27km north of the national park. The four-bed hostel is in a cabin near the white-sand beach and rustic two-bedroom cabins have equipped kitchens but no linens. There are 15 campsites, but the camping in the park is better. Canoes and paddleboats can be rented.

Jeremy's Bay Campground　CAMPGROUND $
(☎ 877-737-3783; campsites/RV sites $25.50/29.40) Of the 360 campsites within the park, 30% are assigned on a first-come, first-served basis. There is only one shower area for the whole camp, so be prepared to wait for a stall. It costs from $10 to reserve a site.

Mersey River Chalets　CABIN $$
(☎ 902-682-2447, 877-667-2583; www.mersey-riverchalets.ns.ca; tepees $90, cabins $170-250; ☜) Comfy cabins have pine floors, wood-burning stoves and very private porches complete with barbecue; rooms in the lodge have private decks with lake views; and cozy tepees have fully equipped kitchens. Free canoes and kayaks are available for guests.

M&W Restaurant & Variety Store　DINER $
(☎ 902-682-2189; Hwy 8; mains $4-12; ☜ 9am-8pm May-Oct) Only 500m from the park entrance, this place serves 'hungry camper'

breakfasts ($6), as well as lunch and dinner. It's also a general store stocked with camping supplies, including firewood, and a Laundromat.

❶ Information

Get an entry permit and reserve backcountry sites at the **visitors center** (☎ 902-682-2772, 800-414-6765; www.parkscanada.gc.ca/keji; Hwy 8; park entrance adult/child $5.80/2.90; ☜ 8:30am-8pm).

Seaside Adjunct (Kejimkujik National Park)

The 'Keji Adjunct' protects angelic landscapes of rolling low brush, wildflowers, white sandy coves and the granite outcrops spreading between Port Joli and Port Mouton Bay. The only access from Hwy 103 is along a 6.5km gravel road. From the parking lot, two mostly flat trails lead to the coast. **Harbour Rocks Trail** (5.2km return) follows an old cart road through mixed forest to a beach where seals are often seen. A loop trail around **Port Joli Head** is 8.7km.

The Port Joli Basin contains **Point Joli Migratory Bird Sanctuary** with waterfowl and shorebirds in great numbers; *Nova Scotia Birding on the Lighthouse Route* is an excellent resource available at the visitor information centers. It's only easily accessible by kayak. The **Rossignol Surf Shop** (☎ 902-683-2550; www.surfnovascotia.com; White Point Beach Resort) in nearby White Point rents kayaks (half-/full-day rental $30/45), surfboards and bodyboards ($20/40), and offers kayak tours ($65/110) and surfing lessons ($75).

Thomas Raddall Provincial Park (☎ 902-683-2664; www.parks.gov.ns.ca; campsites $24; ☜ May-Oct), across Port Joli Harbour from Keji Adjunct, has large, private campsites, eight of which are walk-in. The forested campground extends out onto awesome beaches.

Port Mouton International Hostel (☎ 902-947-3140; www.wqccda.com/PMhostel; 8100 Hwy 3; dm $30; ☜), only five minutes from Keji Adjunct, is run on a volunteer basis by the community in a former school. There are 30 beds plus one private room, a good kitchen and a washer and dryer. Call in advance or, if you arrive between 10am and 5pm, you can usually check in at the crafts store next door.

Shelburne

Shelburne's historic waterfront area bobs with sailboats and has 17 pre-1800 homes – it feels like a historical recreation but it's real. The wonderfully maintained, low-in-the-earth buildings once housed Loyalists who retreated here from the American Revolution. In 1783 Shelburne was the largest community in British North America, with 16,000 residents, many from the New York aristocracy, who exploited the labor of Black Loyalists living in nearby Birchtown. Shelburne's history is celebrated with **Founders' Days** during the last weekend of July.

◉ Sights & Activities

Shelburne has started organizing a slew of activities from mid-June to mid-August, including daily demonstrations around town by folks in period costumes of old-style cooking, sewing, music, military exercises, carving and more; schedules change daily but start around 1pm. Check at the visitor information center for more information.

There's a **trail** for hiking or biking the 6km to Birchtown across from Spencer's Garden Centre at the far south end of Main St. Pick up an excellent self-guided walking-tour map at the visitor information center.

Admission to the following museums is $4, but you can buy a pass that covers all four for $10.

Ross-Thomson House   MUSEUM
(✆902-875-3141; http://rossthomson.novascotia.ca; 9 Charlotte Lane; ⊙9:30am-5:30pm Jun-Oct)

Built in 1784, Ross-Thomson House belonged to well-to-do Loyalist merchants who arrived in Shelburne from Cape Cod. Furniture, paintings and original goods from the store are on display. The house is surrounded by authentic period gardens. Admission is free on Sunday mornings.

Shelburne County Museum   MUSEUM
(✆902-875-3219;   www.historicshelburne.com; cnr Maiden Lane & Dock St; ⊙9:30am-5:30pm) A Loyalist house (c 1787) is now the Shelburne County Museum. It has a collection of Loyalist furnishings, displays on the history of the local fishery and a small collection of Mi'kmaw artifacts.

Muir-Cox Shipyard   MUSEUM
(✆902-875-1114;   www.historicshelburne.com/muircox.htm; 18 Dock St; ⊙9:30am-5:30pm) The Muir-Cox Shipyard has been in almost continuous operation since 1820, turning out barks, yachts and fishing boats. It's still active year-round, but the interpretive center is seasonal.

Dory Shop Museum   MUSEUM
(✆902-875-3219; http://doryshop.novascotia.ca; 11 Dock St; ⊙9:30am-5:30pm Jun-Sep) Shelburne dories (small open boats once used for fishing from a mother schooner) are still made to order at the Dory Shop Museum for use as lifeboats.

🛏 Sleeping & Eating

Water Street Lighthouse B&B   B&B $
(✆902-875-2331; www.shelburnelighthouse.com; 263 Water St; r $60-80; 🛜) Not really luxurious,

NOVA SCOTIA SHELBURNE

BLACK LOYALIST BIRCHTOWN

Just as Shelburne was once the largest settlement in British North America, so Birchtown was once the largest settlement of freed African slaves in North America. After the American Revolution, about 3500 Black Loyalists were rewarded by the British with land for settlements near Shelburne, Halifax, Digby and Guysborough. Nine years later, in 1792, after barely surviving harsh winters and unequal treatment, 1200 of them boarded 15 ships bound for Sierra Leone, in West Africa, where they founded Freetown. An additional 2000 from the USA settled in the Maritimes after the War of 1812, and others came from the Caribbean in the 1890s to work in the Cape Breton Island coal mines.

The future was no brighter. Underfunded, segregated schools existed until the 1950s. Birchtown's **Black Loyalist Heritage Society Historical Site & Museum** (✆902-875-1381, 888-354-0722; www.blackloyalist.com; 104 Birchtown Rd; admission $3; ⊙11am-6pm Tue-Fri, noon-6pm Sat, to 5pm Sun) includes a museum and a walking trail that leads to a 'pit house,' which archaeologists think was once a temporary shelter. There is also a **trail** for hiking or cycling the 6km to Shelburne.

A self-guided tour of African heritage in Nova Scotia is available online (www.gov.ns.ca/nsarm/virtual/africanns).

but comfy and friendly, this is a great B&B to shack up your bike for the night. A lighthouse theme runs through the house.

Islands Provincial Park CAMPGROUND $
(☑ 902-875-4304; www.parks.gov.ns.ca; off Hwy 3; campsites $20) Across the harbor from Shelburne are 65 campsites in mature forest and a beach for swimming.

★ Cooper's Inn B&B B&B $$
(☑ 902-875-4656, 800-688-2011; www.thecoopers-inn.com; 36 Dock St; r $100-185; ☎) Part of this waterfront building dates to 1784 and was brought here from Boston. Now it's a relatively modern but still charmingly heritage-style inn with six rooms and a flower-filled garden, where you can drink your complimentary bottle of Jost wine at sunset.

Bean Dock CAFE $
(☑ 902-875-1302; sandwiches from $5; ☉ 10am-4pm Mon, Tue & Thu-Sat, to 8pm Wed) Snuggle over to a wood table overlooking the bay for coffee, grilled sandwiches and light mains, from fish cakes to sun-dried-tomato pasta salad. The giant Adirondack chair out front is worth chatting about.

★ Charlotte Lane MODERN CANADIAN $$$
(☑ 902-875-3314; 13 Charlotte Lane; mains $16-35; ☉ 11:30am-2:30pm & 5-8pm Tue-Sat) People drive from Halifax to eat here, and rave about it; evening reservations are highly recommended. Swiss chef Roland Glauser is constantly revising an extensive annotated wine list to accompany his ever-changing menu of local seafood, meat and pasta dishes.

❶ Information

Visitors Information Center (VIC; ☑ 902-875-4547; 31 Dock St; ☉ 8am-8pm May-Sep) Has copies of a self-guided historic-district walking tour.

Barrington to West Pubnico

At Barrington you can choose to take the fast, not-very-scenic Hwy 103 to Yarmouth or meander along about 100km of interesting coastline via Hwy 3. It's worth taking a detour to **Cape Sable Island** (not to be confused with Sable Island), a puddle-flat appendage that is Nova Scotia's southernmost point. Many of the island's windy, white-sand beaches are designated as 'important

bird areas,' and a few are piping plover nesting grounds. The whole island tends to get banked in fog, which might explain why its lighthouse is 31.1m tall, the tallest in Nova Scotia.

Not to be confused with all the other nearby Pubnicos, West Pubnico is an old Acadian community. **Le Village Historique Acadien** (☑ 902-762-2530; Old Church Rd; adult/child $6/2; ☉ 9am-5pm Jun-Oct) re-creates an Acadian village, with a blacksmith shop, a timber-frame house and a fish store.

Yarmouth

Yarmouth is the biggest town in southern Nova Scotia, due mostly to the ferry that linked the province to Bar Harbor (Maine) since the 1950s. Sadly, the ferry service stopped in 2010, although the area has been fighting to get it back ever since. Without the ferry, Yarmouth has had a tough time. The only really pretty area is out beyond town around the lighthouse but, like anywhere in the province, stay awhile and the people will win you over.

❂ Sights & Activities

First settled by New Englanders from Massachusetts in 1761, Yarmouth reached its peak of growth and prosperity in the 1870s. The Collins Heritage Conservation District protects many fine Victorian homes built around that time. Check at the visitor information center (p355) for a self-guided walking tour.

Yarmouth Light NOTABLE BUILDING
(☑ 902-742-1433; Hwy 304; ☉ 9am-9pm) FREE
Yarmouth Light is at the end of Cape Forchu, left on Hwy 304 from Main St. The lighthouse affords spectacular views and there's a tearoom below. Stop at **Stanley Lobster Pound** (Hwy 304; ☉ 11am-7pm Mon-Sat, 2-7pm Sun), where you can get a fresh-cooked lobster at market-value price to take and eat on the beach.

Art Gallery of Nova Scotia GALLERY
(☑ 902-749-2248; www.artgalleryofnovascotia.ca; 341 Main St; adult/child $12/7; ☉ 10am-5pm) Practical Yarmouth is the unexpected home to the refreshingly cosmopolitan Art Gallery of Nova Scotia. The new three-storey building has well-selected works from mostly Maritime artists.

Yarmouth County Museum   MUSEUM

(☑902-742-5539; http://yarmouthcountymuseum.ednet.ns.ca; 22 Collins St; adult/student $5/2; ☺9am-5pm Mon-Sat, 2-5pm Sun) This museum, in a former church, contains five period rooms related to the sea. The ticket includes **Pelton-Fuller House** (☺9am-5pm Mon-Sat Jun-Oct) next door, which is filled with period artwork, glassware and furniture.

⊨ Sleeping & Eating

Lakelawn B&B Motel   MOTEL $

(☑902-742-3588; www.lakelawnmotel.com; 641 Main St; r $59-99; ☎☀) This place is as cute and service oriented as motels come. Rooms are clean and basic; the owner Mathew is a well of local info; and some of the better meals in town are available in the country-style dining area. Go even classier in the four B&B-style rooms in the central Victorian house.

★MacKinnon-Cann House Historic Inn   INN $$

(☑902-742-0042; www.mackinnoncanninn.com; 27 Willow St; r $140-185; ☎) Each of the six rooms represents a decade from the Victorian 1900s to the groovy '60s, depicting the decade at its most stylish, while managing to stay calming and comfortable. Two rooms can be joined to create a family suite.

Rudder's Brew Pub   PUB $$

(☑902-742-7311; 96 Water St; pub menu $8-14, dinner mains $14-32; ☺11am-late) The 300 seats at this waterfront pub and restaurant fill fast. A mean ale is brewed on-site and there's a wide-ranging menu. Drinks are poured until the wee hours on busy summer nights.

ⓘ Information

Visitors Information Centre (VIC; ☑902-742-5033; 228 Main St; ☺7:30am-9pm May-Oct) Also has a money-exchange counter.

Yarmouth Public Library (☑902-742-2486; 405 Main St; ☺10am-8pm Mon-Thu, to 5pm Fri, to 4pm Sat, 1-4pm Sun) Free internet access.

ⓘ Getting There & Away

Cloud Nine Shuttle (p343) runs to Halifax.

A nightly ferry service to Portland, Maine is expected to begin in May 2014 with **NS-USA Ferry Service** (www.nsusaferry.com). Check the website for details.

ANNAPOLIS VALLEY & FRENCH SHORE

Heading up the French Shore, you'll be regularly waved to by the Stella Maris, the single-starred, tricolored Acadian flag. Admire the many elaborate Catholic churches, stop at a roadside eatery to sample Acadian rappie pie (a type of meat pie topped with grated pastelike potato from which all the starch has been drawn) and take a walk along a fine-sand beach. If you stay longer, don't miss the chance to sample the region's foot-tapping music performances that take place frequently in summer.

Continuing northeast, the Annapolis Valley was the main breadbasket for colonial Canada and still produces much of Nova Scotia's fresh produce, especially apples. Recently, wineries have taken advantage of the sandy soil. Make sure to get to the Fundy coast at Annapolis Royal and eastwards for tidal vistas over patchwork farmland, red sands and undulating hills.

Cape St Mary to Meteghan

A long, wide arc of fine sand, just 900m off Hwy 1, **Mavilette Beach** is great for collecting seashells, and the marsh behind it is good for bird-watching. At the southern edge of Meteghan, the largest community on the French Shore, **Smuggler's Cove Provincial Park** is named for its popularity with 19th-century pirates. A hundred wooden stairs take you down to a rocky beach and a good cave for hiding treasure. There are picnic sites containing barbecue pits at the top of the stairs, with a view across St Mary's Bay to Brier Island.

Stop for lunch at **La Cuisine Robicheau** (9651 Hwy 1, Saulnierville; mains $8-29; ☺8am-9pm Tue-Sun), which serves this area's most *haute* Acadian cuisine. The rappie pie, seafood lasagna and chocolate pie may make you exclaim '*sacré bleu!*' they're so good and affordable. There's often live music at suppertime during summer.

À la Maison d'Amitié B&B (☑902-645-2601; www.houseoffriendship.ca; 169 Baseline Rd; r $140-175; ☎) is perched dramatically on a cliff close to the beach on six private hectares. The huge, American-style home has cathedral ceilings and sky-high windows with views on all sides.

Church Point to St Bernard

The villages of Church Point, Grosses-Coques, Belliveau Cove and St Bernard, on the mainland directly across St Mary's Bay from Digby Neck, make up the heart of the French Shore. This is where Acadians settled when, after trekking back to Nova Scotia following deportation, they found their homesteads in the Annapolis Valley already occupied. Now linked by Hwy 1 – pretty much the only road in town – these are small fishing communities.

◉ Sights & Activities

Rendez-Vous de la Baie　　CULTURAL BUILDING
(www.rendezvousdelabaie.com; Université Ste-Anne, Church Point; ⊙7am-7pm Mon-Fri, 9am-5pm Sat & Sun) If there's one essential stop along this coast, this is it. Learn about Acadian history and culture at the museum; check out local art at the gallery; watch musical performances and more at the theater; and get tourist tips at the information center – and all this is under one roof. The center also runs Acadian-themed tours of the area for $50 per person including lunch.

Église Ste-Marie　　CHURCH
(☑902-769-2808; Hwy 1; admission incl guide $2; ⊙9am-5pm May-Oct) The town of Church Point, also commonly known as Pointe de l'Église, takes its name from Église Ste-Marie, which towers over the town. Built between 1903 and 1905, the church is said to be the tallest wooden church in North America. An informative guide will show you around. Adjacent is the **Université Ste-Anne**, the only French university in the province and a center for Acadian culture, with 300 students.

Belliveau Beach　　BEACH
Belliveau Beach, near the southern end of Belliveau, is reached by turning right onto Major's Point. The beach is made up of masses of sea-polished stones broken only by small clumps of incredibly hardy fir trees. Just behind the beach, a cemetery and monument recall the struggles of the early Acadian settlers of the French Shore.

St Bernard Church　　CHURCH
(☑902-837-5637; Hwy 1; ⊙tours Jun-Sep) St Bernard is known for its church, a huge granite structure built by locals who added one row of blocks each year between 1910 and 1942. It has incredible acoustics, which are showcased each summer through the **Musique St-Bernard** (www.musiquesaintbernard.ca; adult/child $15/5) concert series.

Hinterland Adventures & Gear　　KAYAKING
(☑902-837-4092; www.kayakingnovascotia.com; 54 Gates Lane, Weymouth; kayak rentals per 1hr/day $7/40, half-/full-day tours $45/115) Running tours for over 15 years, this respected kayaking and canoeing outfit specializes in paddling tours of St Mary's Bay and the Sissiboo River.

✸ Festivals & Events

Festival Acadien de Clare　　CULTURE
(www.festivalacadiendeclare.ca; ⊙late Jul) The oldest of the annual Acadian cultural festivals, Festival Acadien de Clare is held at Church Point.

Théâtre Marc-Lescarbot　　THEATER
(☑902-769-2114; adult/child $25/15) In July and August, the musical *Évangéline*, based on Henry Wadsworth Longfellow's romantic poem about the Acadian deportation, is presented at the Théâtre Marc-Lescarbot at Church Point. Performances are given in English on Saturday; in French with English headset translation on Tuesday and Friday; and outdoors in French on Wednesday.

🛏 Sleeping & Eating

Several Acadian-style eateries have opened up along this stretch, so you'll be spoiled for choice.

DON'T MISS

LIVING WHARVES

Between mid-June and the end of September, the Acadian coast, from Dennis Point to Belliveau Cove and five points between, invites you to get a hands-on appreciation for what this area is all about: fishing. Each day of the week, one of the seven wharves opens up for visitors from 1pm to 4pm. During this time, active and retired fisherfolk tell yarns about their sea adventures and let you try your hand at a few odd jobs. More than anything, it's a great place to meet locals, hear stories and get closer to the salty lifestyle of Nova Scotia's south. More information is available at www.livingwharves.com.

Barn at the Point   B&B $
(www.thebarnatthepoint.ca; 63 Lighthouse Rd,
Gilbert's Cove; r $75-100; 🕸) Quietly situated
on 90 acres near Gilbert's Cove Lighthouse,
only 20 minutes from Digby, this affordable retreat offers the relaxation of rural
forest, the thrill of the coast and the convenience of town. The on-site cafe gets rave
reviews and serves the owners' own special
blend of coffee.

Roadside Grill   ACADIAN $
(📞902-837-5047; 3334 Hwy 1; meals $7-15;
⊙8am 9pm) At this pleasantly old-fashioned
and long-running local restaurant in Belliveau Cove, try the steamed clams or the
rappie pie. It also rents out three small
cabins (singles/doubles $60/80) with ca-
ble TV and microwaves. There's live Acadian music Tuesday nights from 5:30pm to
7:30pm June through August.

Digby Neck

Craning out to take a peek into the Bay
of Fundy, Digby Neck is a giraffe's length
strip of land that's a haven for whale- and
seabird-watchers. At the far western end of
the appendage are Long and Brier Islands,
connected by ferry with the rest of the
peninsula.

Plankton stirred up by the strong Fundy
tides attracts finback, minke and humpback whales and this is the best place in
the world to see the endangered North
Atlantic right whale. Blue whales, the
world's largest animal, are also sighted on
occasion, plus you're almost certain to see
plenty of seals.

Bring plenty of warm clothing (regardless of how hot a day it seems), sunblock
and binoculars; motion-sickness pills are
highly recommended.

❶ Getting There & Away

Two ferries connect Long and Brier Islands to
the rest of Digby Neck. The *Petit Passage* ferry
leaves East Ferry (on Digby Neck) 25 minutes
after the hour and Tiverton (on Long Island) on
the hour; ferries are timed so that if you drive
directly from Tiverton to Freeport (18km)
there is no wait for the *Grand Passage* ferry to
Westport (on Brier Island). Both ferries operate
hourly, 24 hours a day, year-round. Round-trip
passage on each ferry is $5.50 for a car and all
passengers. Pedestrians ride free.

Long Island

Most people head straight to Brier Island,
but Long Island has better deals on whale-
watching, as well as a livelier community. At
the northeastern edge of Long Island, **Tiverton** is an active fishing community.

The **Island Museum** (📞902-839-2853;
3083 Hwy 217; ⊙9:30am-7:30pm Jun-Oct) FREE,
2km west of the Tiverton ferry dock, has exhibits on local history and a tourist information desk.

One of the best whale-watching tours in
the province is found just near the Tiverton
ferry dock. **Ocean Explorations Whale
Cruises** (📞877-654-2341, 902-839-2417; www.
oceanexplorations.ca; half-day tours adult/child
$59/40; ⊙Jun-Oct), led by biologist Tom
Goodwin, has the adventurous approach
of getting you down low to whale level in a
Zodiac. Shimmy into an orange coastguard-
approved flotation suit and hold on tight!
Goodwin has been leading whale-watching
tours since 1980 and donates part of his pro-
ceeds to wildlife conservation and environmental education organizations. Discounts
are given for groups of three or more; tour
times depend on weather and demand.

A 4km round-trip trail to the **Balancing
Rock** starts 2km southwest of the museum.
The trail features rope railings, boardwalks
and an extensive series of steps down a
rock bluff to the bay. At the time of writing, a longer but easier-to-walk trail was in
the works as an alternate route. At the end
there's a viewing platform where you can
see a 7m-high stone column perched pre-
cariously just above the pounding surf of St
Mary's Bay.

Near the center of Long Island, **Central
Grove Provincial Park** has a 2km-long hiking trail to the Bay of Fundy.

At the southwestern end of Long Island,
Freeport is central for exploring both Brier
and Long Islands.

Lavena's Catch Café (📞902-839-2517;
15 Hwy 217; mains $5-15; ⊙11:30am-8pm) is a
country-style cafe directly above the wharf
at Freeport; it's the perfect spot to enjoy a
sunset and you might even see a whale from
the balcony. There's occasional live music in
the evenings.

Brier Island

Westport was the home of Joshua Slocum,
the first man to sail solo around the world,
and is the only community on Brier Island.

It's a quaint little fishing village and a good base to explore the numerous excellent, if rugged and windy, hiking trails around the island; don't miss a trip to the West Lighthouse. Columnar basalt rocks are seen all along the coast and agates can be found on the beaches.

The **Brier Island Backpackers Hostel** (902-839-2273; www.brierislandhostel.com; 223 Water St; dm/ ste $20/100;) is a tiny, spotless place about 1.5km to the left as you come off the ferry. The common room and kitchen area has big windows with views over the water. There's a general store, gas station and basic **cafe** (mains $5-8; 8am-9pm Mon-Sat, 10am-8pm Sun) next door, owned by the same people. You can book excellent whale-watching tours (2½ to five hours, depending on where the whales are) with eco-conscious **Brier Island Whale & Seabird Cruises** (800-656-3660, 902-839-2995; www.brierislandwhalewatch.com; adult/child $49/27; Jun-Oct).

Atop cliffs 1km east of Westport, **Brier Island Lodge** (800-662-8355, 902-839-2300; www.brierisland.com; r $90-140;) has four rooms, some with ocean views. Its **restaurant** (mains $8-29) is the best dining option, with views on two sides, perfect service and fabulously fresh seafood. Boxed lunches are available.

Digby

Known for its scallops, mild climate and daily ferry to Saint John, New Brunswick, Digby (www.digby.ca) is nestled in a protected inlet off the Bay of Fundy. Settled by United Empire Loyalists in 1783, it's now home to the largest fleet of scallop boats in the world.

Digby has been a tourist mecca for more than a century, and although the town itself doesn't offer the architectural charm of starlets such as Lunenburg or Annapolis Royal, it's a pleasant and convenient base from which to explore Digby Neck, the French Shore and some beautiful, lesser-known hiking trails in the area (hint: get out to Point Prim). If you're here in passing, the best things to do are to stroll the waterfront, watch the scallop draggers come and go, and eat as much of their catch as your belly can hold.

If you're in town mid-August, reserve even more space in your gut for the delicious **Digby Scallop Days** (www.digbyscallopdays.com) festival. Another of the year's highlights is the **Wharf Rat Rally** (www.wharfratrally.com) at the end of August, where at last count 30,000 bikers buzz in for motorcycle-oriented contests, tours and general mingling.

The only real sight in town is the **Admiral Digby Museum** (902-245-6322; www.admuseum.ns.ca; 95 Montague Row; admission by donation; 9am-5pm Mon-Sat), a mid-19th century Georgian home which contains exhibits of the town's marine history and early settlement.

Sleeping & Eating

★ Digby Backpackers Hostel HOSTEL $
(902-245-4573; www.digbyhostel.com; 168 Queen St; dm/r $28/65;) Arguably the nicest hostel in Nova Scotia; Saskia and Claude keep the solid four-bed dorm rooms spotless and often spontaneously take the whole hostel out to see the sunset or throw barbecues. The heritage house has plenty of communal areas, including a deck, and there's a lively vibe. Internet access, a light breakfast and towels are included in the price.

Bayside Inn B&B B&B $$
(888-754-0555, 902-245-2247; www.baysideinn.ca; 115 Montague Row; r $64-108;) In continuous operation since the late 1800s, the historic 11-room Bayside is Digby's oldest inn. Centrally located in town, it has views over the scallop fleet and Fundy tides. The cheaper rooms have shared bathrooms.

Digby Pines Golf Resort & Spa HOTEL $$$
(902-245-2511, 800-667-4637; www.digbypines.ca; 103 Shore Rd; r $160-442; May-Oct;) At the posh Pines, you almost expect Jay Gatsby to come up and slap you on the back with a hearty 'old sport.' Rooms are elegantly furnished with dark woods and lush beds, but are small for the price. The family-friendly grounds include a golf course, a spa, a good restaurant, walking trails and a playground.

Boardwalk Café CAFE $
(902-245-5497; 40 Water St; lunch mains $8-15; 11am-2pm & 5-8pm Mon-Fri, noon-3pm Sat) This little waterfront cafe serves delicious light mains, such as chicken rappie pie and shrimp jambalaya. Dinner is a more upscale experience, with mains around $18.

★ Mag Pye's CAFE $$
(Water St; lunch mains around $12; breakfast & lunch daily, dinner Thu-Sat in summer) Furnished like a posh granny's house, this comfortable-as-your-own-living-room cafe sells delicious

baked goods, coffee, breakfasts, and the best lunches in town. Dinners are even more special, with $30 set menus including starters like scallop ceviche, mains that often involve more of the local catch and amazing bakery desserts.

ℹ️ Information

Visitors Information Centre (VIC; ☑902-245-2201; Shore Rd; ⊙8:30am-8:30pm May-Oct) A large provincial tourist office, 2km from the ferry wharf, with hundreds of brochures.

Western Counties Regional Library (☑902-245-2163; 84 Warwick St; ⊙12:30-5pm & 6-8pm Tue-Thu, 10am-5pm Fri, 10am-2pm Sat) Free internet access.

ℹ️ Getting There & Away

Kathleen's Shuttle & Tours (p343) and a few other shuttle companies run to Halifax airport for $65 per person. Digby is also the port for Bay Ferries (p329) boats to New Brunswick.

Bear River

This country haven for offbeat artists is only minutes from the coast but enjoys inland, fogless temperatures. There's a strong Mi'kmaq presence mixed in with Scottish roots, giving Bear River a unique vibe. Some buildings near the river are on stilts, while other historic homes nestle on the steep hills of the valley. A few wineries are starting to pop up just out of town.

◎ Sights & Activities

Bear River Vineyards WINERY
(☑902-467-4156; www.wine.travel; 133 Chute Rd) 🍃 All estate-produced, award-winning wines made at this adorable little winery use solar energy, biodiesel, wind power and the natural slope of the property. Stop by to take a free tour and tasting (July to September) or stay longer at friendly hosts Chris and Peggy's one-room B&B ($130 per night) to enjoy wine-making workshops and retreats.

Annapolis Highland Vineyards WINERY
(☑902-467-0917; www.novascotiawines.com; 2635 Clementsvale Rd; ⊙10am-5pm Mon-Sat, noon-5pm Sun) Don't miss the gold-medal White Wedding dessert wine if you come in for a free tasting at this rather commercial winery. Delicious fruit wines are available.

Bear River First Nation FIRST NATION
Bear River First Nation is a five-minute drive from the heart of town: turn left after crossing the bridge, then take a left where the road forks. In a beautiful building, with a wigwam-shaped foyer, the **Heritage & Cultural Centre** (☑902-467-0301; 194 Reservation Rd; admission $3) offers demonstrations of traditional crafts and hands-on workshops, but unfortunately it's rarely open.

A 1km trail starts behind the center and highlights plants with traditional medicinal uses.

✕ Eating

Bear River Cafe CAFE $
(☑902-467-3008; 1870 Clementsvale Rd; mains $7-14; ⊙10am-5pm Tue-Sun) Stop in to chat with locals, drink a cup of coffee over a slice of pie, and enjoy the view of Bear River.

🔒 Shopping

Flight of Fancy SOUVENIRS
(☑902-467-4171; Main St; ⊙9am-7pm Mon-Sat, 11am-7pm Sun) This exquisitely curated craft store and gallery has work by more than 200 artists and craftspeople. If you want to buy just one unique treasure to take away from Nova Scotia, this is a good place to find it.

Bear Town Baskets SOUVENIRS
(☑902-467-3060; 44 Maple Ave, Bear River First Nation; ⊙10am-10pm) Baskets sold here are made by a retired chief of the Bear River First Nation, who is often there working away and is always happy to welcome visitors. Follow the signs to the studio in his front yard where he makes traditional ash baskets.

Annapolis Royal & Around

The community's efforts of village restoration have made this one of the most delightful places to visit in the region. In fact, Annapolis Royal is one of the only well-trodden towns of its size in Nova Scotia without a Tim Hortons (a ubiquitous fast-food franchise).

The site was Canada's first permanent European settlement. Formerly called Port Royal, it was founded by French explorer Samuel de Champlain in 1605. As the British and French battled, the settlement often changed hands. In 1710 the British had a decisive victory and changed the town's name to Annapolis Royal in honor of Queen Anne.

⊙ Sights & Activities

Most sights are on or near long, curving St George St. A waterfront boardwalk behind King's Theatre on St George St provides views of the village of Granville Ferry across the Annapolis River.

Fort Anne National Historic Site
HISTORIC SITE

(☑902-532-2397;www.parkscanada.gc.ca/fortanne; Upper St George St; adult/child $4/2; ⊙9am-5:30pm) This historic site in the town center preserves the memory of the early Acadian settlement, plus the remains of the 1635 French fort. Entry to the extensive grounds is free, but you'll also want to visit the museum, where artifacts are contained in various period rooms. An extraordinary four-panel tapestry, crafted in needlepoint by more than 100 volunteers, depicts 400 years of history.

Annapolis Royal Historic Gardens
GARDENS

(☑902-532-7018; www.historicgardens.com; 441 St George St; adult/student $10/8.50; ⊙9am-8pm May-Oct) Gorgeous Annapolis Royal Historic Gardens covers a rambling 6.5 hectares with various themed gardens, such as an Acadian kitchen garden one might have seen in the late 1600s and an innovative modern one. Munch on blueberries, ogle the vegetables and look for frogs. The **Secret Garden Café** offers lunches and German-style baked goods.

Port Royal National Historic Site
HISTORIC SITE

(☑902-532-2898; 53 Historic Lane; adult/child $4/2; ⊙9am-6pm) Some 14km northwest of Annapolis Royal, Port Royal National Historic Site is the actual location of the first permanent European settlement north of Florida. The site is a replica of de Champlain's 1605 fur-trading habitation, where costumed workers help tell the story of this early settlement.

Tidal Power Project
MUSEUM

(☑902-532-5454; ⊙10am-6pm) **FREE** A hydroelectric prototype at the Annapolis River Causeway, Tidal Power has been harnessing power from the Bay of Fundy tides since 1984. An interpretive center includes models, exhibits and a video.

★ Tour Annapolis Royal
WALKING TOUR

(www.tourannapolisroyal.com; Fort Anne National Historic Site; ⊙9:30pm Tue-Sun) Runs several history-oriented tours. The best is where

an undertaker-garbed guide leads a creepy tour (adult/child $7/3) of the Fort Anne graveyard. Everyone carries a lantern to wind through the headstones and discover the town's history through stories of those who've passed. Proceeds go to the Annapolis Royal Historical Society.

Delap's Cove Wilderness Trail
HIKING

Over the North Mountain from Annapolis Royal, Delap's Cove Wilderness Trail lets you get out on the Fundy shore. It consists of two loop trails connected by an old inland road that used to serve a Black Loyalist community, now just old foundations and apple trees in the woods. Both the loop trails are 9km return.

🛏 Sleeping & Eating

Many of the B&Bs, such as the Queen Anne, are open for elegant lunches and dinners.

Croft House B&B
B&B $

(☑902-532-0584; www.crofthouse.ca; 51 Riverview Lane; r $55-85; 🐾🖥) This farmhouse stands on about 40 hectares of land, about a five-minute drive from Annapolis Royal across the river. One of the enthusiastic owners is a chef, and he whips up a fine breakfast with organic ingredients.

Dunromin Campground
CAMPGROUND $

(☑902-532-2808; www.dunromincampground.ca; Hwy 1, Granville Ferry; campsites/RV sites $28/42, tepees/caravans $53/58, cabins $65-120; ⊙May-Oct; 🐾🖥) This offbeat campground has some secluded riverside sites, as well as nifty options such as a tepee for up to six people and a gypsy caravan. You can rent canoes for $10 per hour.

★ Queen Anne B&B
B&B $$

(☑902-532-7850, 877-536-0403; www.queenanneinn.ns.ca; 494 St George St; r $99-200, carriage house $239; ⊙May-Nov; 🖥) Arguably the most elegant property in Annapolis Royal, this B&B is the perfect balance of period decor and subtle grace. It's so beautiful, with the Tiffany lamp replicas, manicured grounds and sweeping staircases, that it might seem stuffy were it not for the friendly owners, who make you feel like you could (almost) kick your feet up on the antique coffee table.

★ Bailey House B&B
B&B $$

(☑902-532-1285, 877-532-1285; www.baileyhouse.ca; 150 Lower St George St; r $100-250; 🖥) The only B&B on the waterfront, Bailey House is also the oldest inn and one of the best in the area. The friendly owners have managed to keep the vintage charm (anyone over 6ft might hit their head on the doorways!), while adding all the necessary modern comforts and conveniences.

Ye Olde Pub
PUB $

(☑902-532-2244; 9-11 Church St; mains $5-15; ⊙11am-11pm Mon-Sat, noon-8pm Sun) On sunny days, eat gourmet pub fare on the outdoor terrace; when it's cooler, slip into the dark and cozy old bar. Try the marinated scallop appetizer.

Cafe Compose
EUROPEAN $$

(St George St; lunch $9-15, dinner $16-26; ⊙lunch & dinner; 🗢) This cafe is Austrian-German run, so you can finish your meal of European-style meats and seafood with a strudel or linzer torte. Reflections off the water light up the mustard-yellow interior. Dine on the outdoor garden patio to get even closer to the beach.

☆ Entertainment

King's Theatre
THEATER

(☑902-532-7704; www.kingstheatre.ca; 209 St George St; movies $8, live shows $14-25) Right on the waterfront, this nonprofit theater presents musicals, dramas and concerts most evenings in July and August, and occasionally during the rest of the year. Hollywood films are screened on most weekends and independent films most Tuesdays year-round.

🛍 Shopping

Farmers & Traders Market
MARKET

(cnr St George & Church Sts; ⊙10am-3pm Wed, 8am-noon Sat) Annapolis Royal's thriving community of artists and artisans offer their wares alongside local farmers at this popular market. There's live entertainment most Saturday mornings.

ℹ Information

Annapolis Royal (www.annapolisroyal.com) Links to history, festivals and everything else.

Visitors Information Centre (VIC; ☑902-532-5769; 209 St George St; ⊙10am-6pm May-Oct) At the Tidal Power Project; pick up a historic walking tour pamphlet.

ℹ Getting There & Away

Nelson's Shuttle (☑902-532-0441; www.nelsonsshuttle.com) Runs to/from Halifax and the Halifax airport for $60.

> ### ℹ KINGS TRANSIT
>
> The local **Kings Transit** (☑888-546-4442, 902-628-7310; www.kingstransit.ns.ca) bus line runs every other hour from 6am to around 7pm from Weymouth (just north of Church Point) to Bridgetown (just north of Annapolis Royal), stopping in every little town along the way. Tickets cost around $3.50 depending on the distance traveled.

Kentville

Kentville is the county seat for this area, with a number of government offices and stately old homes.

During the colorful spring bloom of the valley, the **Annapolis Valley Apple Blossom Festival** (www.appleblossom.com) in early June brings folks together with concerts, a parade, barbecues and art shows.

At the eastern end of town, the **Agriculture Research Station** (☑902-678-1093; off Hwy 1; ⊙8:30am-4:30pm) **FREE** includes a museum on the area's farming history and the apple industry in particular. Guided museum tours are offered during summer.

Local artifacts, history and an art gallery can be seen at the **Old King's County Museum** (☑902-678-6237; 37 Cornwallis Ave; ⊙9am-4pm Mon-Sat) **FREE**.

North of Highway 1

The North Mountain, which ends at the dramatic Cape Blomidon, defines one edge of the Annapolis Valley. On the other side of the mountain are fishing communities on the Bay of Fundy. The valley floor between Hwy 1 and the North Mountain is crisscrossed with small highways lined with farms and orchards. It's a great place to get out your road map – or throw it away – and explore. To start the adventure, turn north on Hwy 358 just west of Wolfville (at exit 11 off Hwy 101). The quaint, historic town of Canning is en route to Scots Bay, where Hwy 358 ends and a dramatic hiking trail leads to views of the Minas Basin and the Bay of Fundy.

Port Williams

Only a blink away from Wolfville on Hwy 358 is **Tin Pan** (☑902-691-0020; 978 Main St;

mains $3-11; ⊘ breakfast, lunch & dinner Mon-Sat), a favorite for motorcyclists who congregate here Saturday mornings for hearty breakfasts.

Prescott House Museum (✆ 902-542-3984; http://prescotthouse.novascotia.ca; 1633 Starr's Point Rd; adult/student $4/2.75; ⊘ 10am-5pm Mon-Sat, 1-5pm Sun Jun-Oct), c 1814, is one of the finest examples of Georgian architecture in Nova Scotia and is the former home of the horticulturalist who introduced many of the apple varieties grown in the Annapolis Valley. To get here, turn right on Starr's Point Rd at the flashing light in Port Williams, 2km north of Hwy 1, and follow it for 3.25km.

Canning

From November to March, hundreds of **bald eagles** – a photographer's and nature lover's dream – gather in the Canning area, attracted by local chicken farms. Just west of Canning on Hwy 221, Blomidon Estate Winery (p364) offers tastings and free tours. Further along Hwy 358, stop at the **Look-Off**. About 200m above the Annapolis Valley, this is the best view of its rows of fruit trees and picturesque farmhouses.

Art Can Gallery & Café (✆ 902-582-7071; www.artcan.com; 9850 Main St; mains $10-14; ⊘ 10am-5pm Tue-Thu, to 10pm Fri & Sat, to 4pm Sun) is an art-store-cum-cafe. Enjoy fairtrade coffee and delicious baked goods with views over the valley. Check the website for the availability of art classes and workshops.

Scots Bay

The hike to the end of **Cape Split** starts in Scots Bay. This is one of the most popular hiking trails in Nova Scotia. It's about 14km return, taking three to five hours, with little elevation change through a tunnel of forest. The hike ends in a dramatic, often windy clearing on cliffs high above the Bay of Fundy, where seabirds nest and squawk. Wander down to the rocky outcrop at the vertiginous end of the trail to see the tides creating waves called tidal rips that flow through a cluster of rock pinnacles.

Take time before or after the hike to look for agates along the beach at Scots Bay.

Blomidon Provincial Park (✆ 902-582-7319; www.parks.gov.ns.ca; off Hwy 358; campsites $24) is on the opposite side of Cape Blomidon from Scots Bay. There are a number of routes to get here from Hwy 358, all well signed. One route begins 15km south of Scots Bay and involves driving 10km along the Minas Basin. The campground is set atop high cliffs that overlook the basin. There's a beach and picnic area at the foot of the hill and a 14km system of hiking trails within the park.

Hall's Harbour

Further southeast on the Bay of Fundy, **Hall's Harbour** is a great spot to spend an afternoon hiking along the beach and in the surrounding hills. It's also one of the best places in Nova Scotia to eat lobster.

Pick your own lobster at **Hall's Harbour Lobster Pound** (✆ 902-679-5299; ⊘ noon-8pm May-Oct). The prices are determined by the market, but this is definitely a somewhat gentrified seafood shack and prices rival those of the restaurants in Wolfville. Still, it's arguably more fun to eat lobster closer to the source.

To get to Hall's Harbour, take any route west from Hwy 358 until you hit Hwy 359, then take it over the North Mountain.

Wolfville

Wolfville has a perfect blend of old college-town culture, small-town homeyness, and the fine food and drink scene that's grown around the surrounding wine industry. The students and faculty of Acadia University make up about 50% of the town's 7000-plus residents. Just outside town, you'll find Acadian dikes, scenic drives and some of the best hiking along the Fundy Coast. It's considered one of the most livable and diverse towns in the province; some 12% of the residents have moved here from outside Canada.

⊙ Sights & Activities

Waterfront Park   PARK
(cnr Gaspereau Ave & Front St) Waterfront Park offers a stunning view of the tidal mudflats, Minas Basin and the red cliffs of Cape Blomidon. Displays explain the tides, dikes, flora and fauna, and history of the area. This is an easy spot to start a walk or cycle on top of the dikes.

Randall House Museum   MUSEUM
(✆ 902-542-9775; 171 Main St; admission by donation; ⊘ 10am-5pm Mon-Sat, 2-5pm Sun Jun-Sep) Randall House Museum relates the history

of the New England planters and colonists who replaced the expelled Acadians.

Rent bikes at **Valley Stove & Cycle** (☑902-542-7280; 234 Main St; half-/full-day bicycle rental $25/30).

✴ Festivals & Events

Canadian Deep Roots Festival　　MUSIC (www.deeprootsmusic.ca) If you're in town in early fall, rock out to modern roots music at the annual Canadian Deep Roots Festival.

🛏 Sleeping & Eating

★Garden House B&B　　B&B $$ (☑902-542-1703; www.gardenhouse.ca; 220 Main St; r $65-110; 🛜) This antique house retains its old-time feel in the most comfortable way. Creaky floors, a rustic breakfast table decorated with wildflowers, and that everyone is encouraged to take off their shoes creates a lived-in vibe you instantly feel a part of. Bathrooms are shared.

Blomidon Inn　　INN $$ (☑902-542-2291, 800-565-2291; www.theblomidon.net; 195 Main St; d $120-160, ste $160-269; ✳@🛜) Lofty Victorian architecture and old-world extravagance make this a very upper-crust-feeling inn. On 2.5 hectares of perfectly maintained gardens, the rooms are just as well groomed. Check the website for package deals.

Gingerbread House Inn　　INN $$ (☑902-542-1458; www.gingerbreadhouse.ca; 8 Robie Tufts Dr; d $125-135, ste $145-215; 🛜🐾) The exterior of this unique B&B is like a big pink birthday cake with lacy white edging. Rooms, several of which have a hot tub, are like your own candlelit spa.

★Front & Central　　FUSION $$ (☑866-542-0588; 117 Front St; small plates $8-15; ⊙lunch Thu-Sun, dinner Tue-Sun) Choose creative small plates, from a delicious vegetarian 'faux pho' to scallops with a maple glazed pork belly. Share the plates, mix and match and have fun with it. Light eaters may find one is enough, while big appetites may devour four or more. Whatever you choose, waitstaff will pair it with the perfect wine.

Privet House　　FUSION $$ (☑902-542-7525; 268 Main St; lunch mains $11-18, dinner mains $19-36; ⊙11:30am-9pm) The finest dining in town serves up aged Atlantic beef, local seafood and game (ingredients are all

Canadian) prepared with everything from European to Indian and Thai influences. The tablecloths are white; the wine list is long and the service is excellent.

Coffee Merchant & Library Pub　　CAFE, PUB (☑902-542-4315; 472 Main St; ⊙11:30am-midnight Mon-Sat) Downstairs, the cafe serves up good fair-trade coffee and baked goods. Upstairs, you can get a pint and a square meal at the cozy pub.

ℹ Information

Tourist Office (☑902-542-7000; 11 Willow Ave; ⊙9am-9pm May-Oct) A very helpful office at the east end of Main St.

Wolfville (www.wolfville.info) Information on Wolfville, Acadia University and exploring Nova Scotia.

Wolfville Memorial Library (☑902-542-5760; 21 Elm Ave; ⊙11am-5pm Tue-Sat, 6:30-8:30pm Tue-Thu, 1-5pm Sun) Free internet access.

ℹ Getting There & Away

Maritime Bus (www.maritimebus.com) stops at Acadia University in front of Wheelock Hall off Highland Ave. **Kings Transit** (☑888-546-4442, 902-678-7310; www.kingstransit.ns.ca) buses run between Cornwallis (southwest of Annapolis Royal) and Wolfville and stop at 209 Main St.

Grand Pré

Grand Pré feels like the bucolic fringe of Wolfville. Today it's a very small English-speaking town, but in the 1750s, it was the site of one of the most tragic but compelling stories in eastern Canada's history, the Acadian deportation. Learn all about it at the Grand Pré National Historic Site.

⊙ Sights

Grand Pré National Historic Site　　HISTORIC SITE (☑902-542-3631; 2205 Grand Pré Rd; adult/child $8.50/4.20; ⊙9am-6pm May-Oct) At the Grand Pré National Historic Site, a modern interpretive center explains the historical context for the deportation from Acadian, Mi'kmaw and British perspectives and traces the many routes Acadians took from, and back to, the Maritimes. In 2012, the landscapes of this area became a Unesco World Heritage site.

Beside the center, a serene **park** contains gardens and an Acadian-style stone church.

WOLFVILLE REGION WINE TOUR

The wine-making tradition in Nova Scotia goes back to the early 1600s and it's possible that this was the first place in North America where wine grapes were grown. Today wineries are springing up everywhere. There are six distinct wine-growing regions in the province, although most wineries are found in the Annapolis Valley and on the Malagash Peninsula.

L'Acadie Blanc, a French hybrid grape, grows particularly well in Nova Scotia and has become the province's signature grape. It makes a medium-bodied, citrusy white wine that pairs well with scallops or smoked salmon. New York Muscat also grows well and is often used for dry white and ice wines. Most wineries make a blend of local varieties called Tidal Bay, an appellation specific to the region.

This tour of our favorite wineries starts at Blomidon Estate Winery in Canning, north of Hwy 1. From here go into downtown Wolfville and turn inland on Gaspereau Dr across from Tim Hortons. Follow the signs to the next three vineyards. Then, once you've left Luckett's, take a right when you reach the bottom of the hill, then take the first left, which will bring you back to Hwy 101 almost directly in front of Domaine de Grand Pré.

If you don't want to drive, hop on the **Wolfville Magic Winery Bus** (✆ 902-542-4093; www.wolfvillemagicwinerybus.ca; hop-on, hop-off bus passes $10; ⊙ 10:30am-5:30pm Sat & Sun) that runs from September through mid-October.

Blomidon Estate Winery (✆ 902-582-7565; www.blomidonwine.com; 10318 Hwy 221; tastings $4; ⊙ 10am & 6pm Jun-Sep) The friendly and laid-back winemaker comes out to chat to those tasting wines. The sparkling wines and Tidal Bay are probably the best, but the oaky red is worth a try. It's worth the trip just for the pretty drive to Canning.

There's also a bust of American poet Henry Wadsworth Longfellow, who chronicled the Acadian saga in *Evangeline: A Tale of Acadie,* and a statue of his fictional Evangeline, now a romantic symbol of her people.

Beyond the park, you can see the farmland created when the Acadians built dikes along the shoreline as they had done in northwest France for generations. There are 12 sq km below sea level here, protected by just over 9km of dike.

🛏 Sleeping & Eating

Olde Lantern Inn & Vineyard　　INN $$
(✆ 902-542-1389, 877-965-3845; www.oldlantern-inn.com; 11575 Hwy 1; r $100-155; 🕾) Clean lines, a friendly welcome and attention to every comfort makes this a great place to stay. The vineyard grounds overlook Minas Basin, where you can watch the rise and fall of the Fundy tides and gaze over the Grand Pré Unesco landscape.

★ Le Caveau　　EUROPEAN $$
(✆ 902-542-1753; 11611 Hwy 1; mains $16-32; ⊙ lunch & dinner) Considered to be the finest Northern European–style restaurant in the province, this Swiss restaurant is on the grounds of Domaine de Grand Pré. The beautiful outdoor patio is paved with fieldstones and shaded with grapevines.

🔒 Shopping

Tangled Garden　　FOOD, DRINK
(✆ 902-542-9811; 11827 Hwy 1; ⊙ 10am-6pm) Impossible to classify, this is probably the best-smelling shopping experience in Nova Scotia. Buy a bottle of herb-infused vinegar or jelly to take away, or stroll the gardens and meditative labyrinth while licking herb-flavored ice cream.

Windsor

Windsor was once the only British stronghold in this region, but today it's just a graying little town eking out an existence between the highway and the Avon River. Windsor is a place to enjoy bluegrass music – think lots of fast banjo picking. Avon River Park hosts two bluegrass festivals, one in June and one in July, and is a hangout for aficionados all summer long. The **tourist office** (✆ 902-798-2690; 31 Colonial Rd; ⊙ 8:30am-6:30pm daily Jul & Aug, Sat & Sun Jun, Sep & Oct) is just off exit 6 from Hwy 101. The dike beside the tourist office offers a view of the tidal river flats.

Gaspereau Vineyards (☎ 902-542-1455; www.gaspereauwine.com; 2239 White Rock Rd; ⊙ 10am-5pm May-Oct, tours noon, 2pm & 4pm) This is one of the province's best-known wineries, with award-winning ice wine. Definitely also try the Estate Riesling. The tasting room in a big red barn is posh on the inside and the staff is extra friendly.

L'Acadie Vineyards (☎ 902-542-8463; www.lacadievineyards.ca; 310 Slayter Rd; cottages $150; ⊙ 10am-5pm May-Oct) Overlooking Gaspereau Valley, this geothermally powered winery grows certified-organic grapes to make traditional-method sparkling and dried-grape wines. You can also stay in one of three country-style two-bedroom, kitchen-equipped cottages, which, of course, include a free bottle of wine.

Luckett Vineyards (www.luckettvineyards.com; 1293 Grand Pré Rd, Wolfville, tastings $7, lunch mains $9-15; ⊙ 10am-5pm May-Oct) This is one of the best destination wineries in the region, with palatial views over the vines and hillsides down to the Bay of Fundy cliffs. After sampling the red, white, fruit and dessert wines, and the particularly good ice wine, chill on the patio and dine on gourmet sandwiches, soups and salads at lunch or, in summer, on fine set meals at dinner. There's also an old British phone box in the vineyards, from where you can make free calls to anywhere in Canada!

Domaine de Grand Pré (☎ 902-542-1753; http://grandprewines.ns.ca; 11611 Hwy 1; tours $9; ⊙ 10am-6pm, tours 11am, 3pm & 5pm) A great destination winery and one of the best known in the province, it has a delicious spicy muscat and a nice sparkling Champlain Brut. The tours take about 45 minutes or you can do tastings and stroll through the vines by yourself. Le Caveau Restaurant has been named one of the 20 best winery restaurants in the world by *Wine Access* magazine.

While in town, check out **Haliburton House** (☎ 902-798-2915; 414 Clifton Ave; adult/student $3.60/2.55; ⊙ 10am-5pm Mon-Sat, 1-5pm Sun), once home to Judge Thomas Chandler Haliburton (1796–1865), writer of the Sam Slick stories. Many of Haliburton's expressions, such as 'quick as a wink' and 'city slicker', are still used.

Stay the night at the **Clockmaker's Inn** (☎ 866-778-3600, 902-792-2573; www.theclockmakersinn.com; 1399 King St; d $99-179; ☎), a French-château-style mansion with curved bay windows, lots of stained glass and sweeping hardwood staircases. It's gay friendly and afternoon tea is served daily, as is breakfast.

CENTRAL NOVA SCOTIA

Hiking, rafting and rockhounding are the activities of choice around this mildly touristed region. For those traveling overland from the rest of Canada, this is your first taster of Nova Scotia – do not let it pass you by on bleak Hwy 104.

Called the 'Glooscap Trail' in provincial tourism literature, the area is named for the figure in Mi'kmaw legend who created the unique geography of the Bay of Fundy region. Unfortunately, stories and representations of Glooscap are easier to come across than genuine acknowledgments of present-day Mi'kmaq people.

Shubenacadie

Shubenacadie, or simply 'Shube,' is best known for the **Shubenacadie Provincial Wildlife Park** (☎ 902-758-2040; https://wildlifepark.novascotia.ca; 149 Creighton Rd; adult/child $4.50/2; ⊙ 9am-6:30pm), the place to commune with Nova Scotia's wildlife. You can hand-feed the deer and, if you're lucky, pet a moose. The animals were either born in captivity or once kept as 'pets' and, as a result, cannot be released into the wild – they live in large enclosures. Turn off Hwy 102 at exit 11 and follow Hwy 2 to the park entrance.

Maitland

Tiny Maitland is the place to go rafting on the white water that is created by the outflow of the Shubenacadie River meeting the blasting force of the incoming Fundy tides. It's also one of the oldest towns in Canada.

Wave heights are dependent on the phases of the moon; get information from your rafting company about the tides for your chosen day since your experience (either mild or exhilarating) will be dictated by this. Outboard-powered Zodiacs plunge right through the white water for the two to three hours that the rapids exist. Prepare to get very, very wet – no experience is needed.

☆ Activities

Shubenacadie River Runners   RAFTING
(☎902-261-2770, 800-856-5061; www.tidalbore-rafting.com; 8681 Hwy 215; half-day $60-70) The biggest rafting company is organized and professional in every way. Prices depend on how big the tide and waves are.

Shubenacadie River Adventures   RAFTING
(☎902-261-2222, 800-878-8687; www.shubie.com; 10061 Hwy 15; rafting per day incl lunch adult/child $85/80) Besides the exciting tidal bore rafting day trips, mellow half-day river tours ($65) are also on offer.

🛏 Sleeping

There are a handful of places to sleep in Maitland, but the few eating options have unpredictable opening hours. Bring your own food or a full belly.

Tidal Life Guesthouse   B&B $$
(☎902-261-2583; www.thetidallife.ca; 9568 Cedar St; dm $35, r $90-120; ⊙May-Oct; ☎⊛) This

---

THE POWER OF THE BORE

The **tidal bore** phenomenon occurs when the first surge of the extreme Bay of Fundy tides flows upriver at high tide. Sometimes the advancing wave is only a ripple but, with the right phase of the moon, it can be a meter or so in height, giving the impression that the river is flowing backwards. You'll have to sit awhile to see the changes in the tide, but a good place to watch is from the lookout on Tidal Bore Rd, off Hwy 236 just west of exit 14 from Hwy 102 on the northwest side of Truro. Staff in the adjacent Palliser Motel **gift shop** (☎902-893-8951) can advise when the next tidal bore will arrive. There's another viewpoint in Moncton, New Brunswick.

---

backpackers-B&B hybrid in an old beauty of a house has grand airy rooms and large windows overlooking grassy fields. Artistically designed communal spaces are everywhere, including a hammock on the back porch. All options include a big healthy breakfast and bathrooms are shared. The drawback is that it can be hard to get in touch with the place, so contact them early.

Cresthaven by the Sea   B&B $$
(☎902-261-2001,   866-870-2001; www.cresthavenbythesea.com; r $140-150; ☎) Stay here for what is possibly the best view over the Fundy tides. The immaculate white Victorian house sits on a bluff right over the point where the Shubenacadie River meets the bay. All the rooms have river views and the lower ones are wheelchair accessible.

Truro

Several major highways converge here, along with a VIA Rail line, so it's no wonder Truro is known as the hub of Nova Scotia. While the town does look somewhat like an aging shopping mall, it's exceptionally well serviced and can make a good stop to pick up that nagging item you need or just stock up on food.

◉ Sights

Victoria Park   PARK
(Park St, off Brunswick St) Escape Truro's busy streets at Victoria Park, 400 hectares of green space in the very center of town, including a deep gorge and two waterfalls. The park attracts dozens of bird species.

🎉 Festivals & Events

Millbrook Annual Powwow   CULTURE
(☎902-897-9199; www.millbrookfirstnation.net; ⊙2nd weekend Aug) The best time to visit Truro is when Millbrook First Nation hosts its annual powwow. Campsites and showers are available; drugs and alcohol are prohibited.

🛏 Sleeping & Eating

Baker's Chest B&B   B&B $$
(☎902-893-4824, 877-822-5655; www.bakerschest.ca; 53 Farnham Rd; r/ste $100/120; ☎⊛) This newly restored classic older home has contemporary decor, a fitness room, a pool and a hot tub. The famous tearoom is open from noon to 2pm on weekdays and

is an adorable stop for soups, snacks and, of course, a nice cup of tea.

Wooden Hog
CANADIAN $$

(☑902-895-0779; 627 Prince St; lunch mains $8, dinner mains $11-17; ☺9am-4pm Mon, to 9pm Tue-Fri, 11am-9pm Sat) Named for the huge, sculpted Harley that hangs off the back wall, this popular restaurant cooks up local and Mexican specialties, plus decadent desserts.

ℹ Information

Tourist Office (☑902-893-2922; Victoria Sq, cnr Prince & Commercial Sts; ☺8.30am-7:30pm May-Oct) This place offers internet access and a terrific guide to the tree sculptures around town. The trees were carved after the region was affected by Dutch elm disease more than 30 years ago.

ℹ Getting There & Away

Maritime Bus stops en route to Amherst and Halifax.

Economy to Five Islands

Hwy 2 hugs the shore of the Minas Basin, the northeast arm of the Bay of Fundy, and Economy is the first sizable community that you'll arrive at. There's great **hiking** and several interesting sites around Economy.

◉ Sights & Activities

Cobequid Interpretation
Centre
MUSEUM, HIKING

(☑902-647-2600; 3248 Hwy 2, near River Phillip Rd; by donation; ☺9am-4:30pm Jun-Sep) Stop here for good exhibits on the area's ecology and history. Climb a WWII observation tower for a bird's-eye view of the surrounding area and pick up hiking information from the staff.

The nearby **Thomas Cove Coastal Trail** is actually two 3.5km loops with great views across the Minas Basin and the Cobequid Mountains. They begin down Economy Point Rd, 500m east of the Cobequid Interpretation Centre. Follow the signs to a parking area.

Economy Falls
HIKING

The most challenging hikes in the area are around Economy Falls. The **Devil's Bend Trail** begins 7km up River Phillip Rd toward the Cobequid Mountains. Turn right and park; the 6.5km (one-way) trail follows the river to the falls.

The **Kenomee Canyon Trail** begins further up River Phillip Rd, at the top of the falls. A 20km loop, it takes you up the river to its headwaters in a protected wilderness area. Several streams have to be forded. There are designated campsites, making this a good two-day adventurous trek.

Five Islands Provincial Park
HIKING

(☑902-254-2980; http://parks.gov.ns.ca) Just 7km west of Economy, there are several hikes in Five Islands Provincial Park. The 4.5km **Red Head Trail** is well developed, with lookouts, benches and great views.

🛏 Sleeping & Eating

Several takeaway stands selling fried clams pop up along the highway near Five Islands Provincial Park in the summer.

Mo's at Five Islands
HOSTEL, CAFE $

(☑902-254-8088; www.mosatfiveislands.com; 951 Hwy 2, Five Islands; dm/r $28/65, light meals from $4; ☺May-Sep; 🛜🐾) You can usually count on an interesting crowd at this spotless hostel and the large homey cafe out front. The owner also owns one of the five islands (of the eponymous town) and holds a running race each year from the mainland to the island when the tide goes out high enough – the race and the hostel are named after Moses and his parting of the Red Sea.

Four Seasons Retreat
RESORT $$

(☑902-647-2628, 888-373-0339; www.fourseasonsretreat.ns.ca; 320 Cove Rd, Upper Economy; 1-/2-bedroom cottages $109/225; 🛜🐾🐾) Fully equipped cottages are surrounded by trees and face the Minas Basin. In summer, there's a hot tub near the pool; in winter – or on a chilly night – there are woodstoves.

High Tide B&B
B&B $$

(☑902-647-2788; www.hightidebb.com; 2240 Hwy 2, Lower Economy; d $85-95; 🛜) This friendly, modern bungalow has great views. Janet, one of the owners, will have you down on the beach for a clam boil in no time.

That Dutchman's Farm
CAFE $

(☑902-647-2751; www.thatdutchmansfarm.com; 112 Brown Rd, Upper Economy; lunch $8; ☺11am-5pm Jul & Aug) The yummy cafe here offers sandwiches, soups and plates of the eccentric farmer's own Gouda. You can tour the farm for a small fee.

NOVA SCOTIA ECONOMY TO FIVE ISLANDS

Parrsboro

Rock hounds come from far and wide to forage the shores of Parrsboro, the largest of the towns along the Minas Basin. The Fundy Geological Museum has wonderful exhibits and good programs that take you to the beach areas known as Nova Scotia's 'Jurassic Park.' For more serious rock lovers, the annual **Gem & Mineral Show** is in mid-August.

👁 Sights

Fundy Geological Museum   MUSEUM
(📞 902-254-3814; http://fundygeological.novascotia.ca; 162 Two Islands Rd; adult/child $8/4.50; ⊙ 9:30am-5:30pm) This award-winning museum got a $1 million makeover in 2010 and uses interactive exhibits to help its visitors 'time travel' to when the fossils littering Parrsboro's beaches were alive. You can see a lab where dinosaur bones are being cleaned and assembled.

Beach tours are included in the admission price and focus on minerals or fossils. Times, length and frequency are dependent on the tides.

Partridge Island   ISLAND
Steeped in history, Partridge Island is the most popular shoreline to search for gems, semiprecious stones and fossils. Connected to the mainland by an isthmus, the island is 4km south of town on Whitehall Rd. From the end of the beach, a 3km **hiking trail** with explanatory panels climbs to the top of the island for superb views of Cape Blomidon and Cape Split.

Ottawa House Museum   MUSEUM
(📞 902-254-2376; www.ottawahousemuseum.ca; 1155 Whitehall Rd; admission $2; ⊙ 10am-6pm) Just before the beach is Ottawa House Museum, a 21-room mansion that was once the summer home of Sir Charles Tupper (1821–1915), who served as both premier of Nova Scotia and prime minister of Canada. The museum has exhibits on shipbuilding, rum-running and the former settlement on Partridge Island.

🛏 Sleeping & Eating

Riverview Cottages   COTTAGES $
(📞 902-254-2388; www.riverviewcottages.ca; 3575 Eastern Ave; cottages $60-100; ⊙ May-Nov; 🐾🖥) These rustic, country-cute, completely equipped cottages are a steal. You can canoe and fish on the bordering river and there's a big lawn perfect for a barbecue.

Mad Hatter Hostel   HOSTEL $
(📞 902-254-3167; madhatterhostel@hotmail.com; 16 Prince St; dm/s/d $20/35/50; 🖥) More like a few rooms and beds upstairs in an inviting home, this 'hostel' offers a ton of hospitality, kitchen use and a great location right in town.

Evangeline's Tower B&B   B&B $$
(📞 902-254-3383, 866-338-6937; www.evangelinestower.ca; 322 Main St; d $70-150; 🖥🐾) This elegantly decorated 1890s Victorian home has three rooms; two can be combined into a two-room suite for families. The generous, home-cooked breakfasts are delicious and cyclists are welcome.

LOCAL KNOWLEDGE

RODD & HELEN TYSON: GEOLOGISTS & MINERAL DEALERS

Rodd Tyson is considered one of the most successful mineral dealers in Canada. He and his wife Helen moved to Parrsboro several years ago and opened a small shop that displays some of their finest pieces.

Why Parrsboro? The tides and rains are moving things all the time, so on any given day we could still potentially find something suitable for our own private collection in one of several places.

Where to Go Partridge Island is the easiest place to go. Just remember to wear good footwear, be careful of the cliffs and be vigilant about checking the tides, so you don't get stuck somewhere.

What to Look For You're looking for color. Stilbite is amber-gold; chabazite is orange; agates have banded colors and patterns; and jasper is a deep brick red or forest green. You won't find much amethyst here, no matter what anyone tells you, unless it's pretty pale. It's illegal to take fossils.

Harbour View Restaurant   CANADIAN $$
(145 Pier Rd; mains $9-16; ⊘7am-8pm) Hang out with the local fishers devouring Parrsboro's best I-worked-hard-all-day portions of fish and chips, chowder, homemade pies and more. It's right on the water, but the set-up blocks most of the view.

☆ Entertainment

Ship's Company Theatre   THEATER
(☑800-565-7469, 902-254-3000; www.shipscompany.com; 18 Lower Main St; tickets $12-28; ⊘Jul-Sep) This innovative theater company performs new Canadian and Maritime works 'on board' the MV *Kipawo*, the last of the Minas Basin ferries, now integrated into a new theater. There's high-quality theater for kids, improv comedy, readings and concerts.

🛍 Shopping

Parrsboro Rock & Mineral Shop   ROCKS & MINERALS
(☑902-254-2981; 39 Whitehall Rd; ⊘9am-9pm Mon-Sat, to 5pm Sun May-Nov) Browse the collection of prehistoric reptile fossils and semiprecious stones from Parrsboro and around the world. There's even a one-of-a-kind fossilized footprint of the world's smallest dinosaur, found by the proprietor, Eldon George. If Eldon is there, don't miss the chance to chat with him – he's one of Parrsboro's favorite characters.

Tysons' Fine Minerals   ROCKS & MINERALS
(☑902-254-2376; 249 Whitehall Rd; ⊘from 10am) This place is more like a museum than a shop, with some of the most sparkling, massive and colorful minerals on display you're likely to see anywhere. Sometimes Helen takes visitors in to see the Tysons' private collection, which is even more breathtaking.

ℹ Information

Tourist Office (☑902-254-3266; Fundy Geological Museum, 162 Two Islands Rd; ⊘10am-7pm Jun-Oct) Tide information and free internet access.

Cape d'Or

This spectacular cape of sheer cliffs was misnamed Cape d'Or (Cape of Gold) by Samuel de Champlain in 1604 – the glittering veins he saw in the cliffs were actually made of copper. Mining took place between 1897 and 1905 and removed the sparkle.

★**Lightkeeper's Kitchen & Guest House** (☑902-670-0534; www.capedor.ca; s/d $85/125; ⊘May-Oct; 🛜🍽), an original light-

AGE OF SAIL HERITAGE CENTRE

Stop for tea, baked goods and a tour at the **Age of Sail Heritage Centre** (☑902-348-2030; Rte 209; adult $3; ⊘10am-6pm Jun-Sep) in Port Greville, about 20km to the west of Parrsboro on Rte 209. It captures the area's ship-building heritage. The site also includes a restored 1857 Methodist church and a working blacksmith shop.

house keeper's residence, is now a laid-back four-room guesthouse at what is perhaps one of the most perfect spots in Nova Scotia (even more so when the sun's out). Take the side road off Hwy 209 to Cape d'Or, then hike down the dirt trail. Its cosmopolitan **restaurant** (lunch mains $9-16, dinner mains $22-28; ⊘noon-7pm; ☑) pumps out low-volume techno music and serves original seafood, meat and vegetarian creations.

Cape Chignecto Provincial Park & Advocate Harbour

The **Cape Chignecto Coastal Trail** is a rugged 60km loop with backcountry – nay, old-growth – campsites. Allow four days and three nights for the hike. The **Mill Brook Canyon Trail** (15km return) and the hike to **Refugee Cove** (20km return) are other challenging overnight hikes. There are some easier hikes and more are being developed – the newest is the **Eatonville Trail** (5.6km return) that begins at a new 'Phase 2' entrance to the park about 15km north of the main entrance. Some hikers have tried to avoid the ups and downs of the trails by taking shortcuts along the beach at low tide and have been cut off by Bay of Fundy tides. Get a tide table and follow advice from park staff to avoid being trapped on the cliffs.

Park visitors must register and leave an itinerary at the **visitors center** (☑902-392-2085; www.capechignecto.net; 1108 West Advocate Rd; day/annual hiking permits $5/25, campsites $24; ⊘8am-7pm Mon-Thu, to 8pm Fri & Sat). Camping in the backcountry requires reservations. In addition to 51 wilderness campsites at six points along the coastal trail and 27 walk-in sites near the visitors center, there is also a bunkhouse ($55, up to four people) and a wilderness cabin ($55, up to four people).

Advocate Harbour is the nearest town, about 2km southeast of the park entrance. It's a breathtaking place with a 5km-long beach piled high with driftwood that changes dramatically with the tides. Behind the beach, salt marshes reclaimed with dikes by the Acadians are now replete with birds.

Kayak through Cape Chignecto Provincial Park with **Nova Shores Adventures** (☎866-638-4118; www.novashores.com; Hwy 33, Advocate Harbour; 1-/2-day tours $95/350; ☎). You'll often see seals and bears. Overnight tours include accommodations and food.

★**Wild Caraway Restaurant & Cafe** (☎902-392-2889; www.wildcaraway.com; 3721 Hwy 209; lunch mains $6-15, dinner mains $18-24; ☽11am-8pm Thu-Mon; ☎) is inviting, cozy, overlooks the harbor, and is the best place to eat along this coast. Try the ploughman's lunch with house-smoked pork and cheese from local That Dutchman's Farm, or dine on applewood-smoked mackerel or a selection of seasonal specials. There are also two charming B&B rooms ($90) upstairs in this beautiful Victorian home.

Joggins

Between Amherst and Advocate Harbour on Chignecto Bay, Joggins is famous for its Unesco World Heritage fossil cliffs, said to be the best place on Earth to see what life was like over 300 million years ago in the late Carboniferous period. The wealth of fossils in the 15km of seaside cliffs are preserved in their original setting and include rare land species. The state-of-the- art **Joggins Fossil Centre** (www.joggensfossilcliffs.net; 100 Main St; admission from $10.50; ☽9:30am-5:30pm May-Nov) is the place to start your visit and explains through displays and film what you can see in the cliffs below. Ticket price includes a half-hour tour, but you can also opt for a ticket including a two- ($25) or four-hour ($55) tour. The best time to visit the cliffs is at low tide when all of the beaches can be accessed – otherwise you'll be cut off from some of the more interesting sites by high water. Tours leave on an irregular schedule, depending on the tides; you can reserve in advance on the website.

Amherst

Amherst is the geographic center of the Maritimes and a junction for travelers to Nova Scotia, PEI and New Brunswick. There's little reason to dawdle here, as you're just a short drive from either the Bay of Fundy shore or the Northumberland Strait (between Nova Scotia and PEI). The historic downtown does have some stately buildings and there's bird-watching at the 490-hectare **Amherst Point Migratory Bird Sanctuary** nearby (off exit 3 from the Trans-Canada Hwy). The massive **visitors information center** (VIC; ☎902-667-8429; ☽8:30am-8pm) is at exit 1 off Hwy 104, just as you cross the border from New Brunswick.

Maritime Bus has bus services to Halifax that leave from the Circle K at 213 S Aubion St. The Trans-Canada Hwy east of Amherst charges a toll of $4. It's an incentive to use scenic Hwy 2 through Parrsboro instead of dull – but fast – Hwy 104. The Sunrise Trail (Hwy 6) through Pugwash and Tatamagouche to Pictou also avoids the toll.

SUNRISE TRAIL

It's claimed that the Northumberland Strait between Nova Scotia's north shore and PEI has some of the warmest waters north of the US Carolinas, with water temperatures averaging slightly over 20°C during summer. It's a prime area for beach-hopping, cycling and exploring friendly countryside towns.

Wallace

Wallace is perfect territory for birding and beachcombing. The tourist information center is at the **Wallace Museum** (☎902-257-2191; Hwy 6; ☽9am-5pm Mon-Sat, 1-4pm Sun), where collections of baskets woven by the Mi'kmaq, period dresses and ship-building memorabilia are displayed.

Wallace Bay Wildlife Bird Sanctuary (1km north of Hwy 6 on Aboiteau Rd) protects 585 hectares, including tidal and freshwater wetlands. In the spring, keep your eyes peeled for bald eagles nesting near the parking lot, which is on the left just before the causeway.

Wentworth

The Wentworth Valley is a detour off the shore, 25km south of Wallace via Hwy 307, and is particularly pretty in fall when the deciduous trees change color. The 24-bed, cabin-like **Wentworth Hostel** (☎902-548-2379; www.hihostels.ca; 249 Wentworth Station Rd; HI member/nonmember dm $25/30, r $45/50; ☎) is 1.3km west of Hwy 4 on Valley Rd, then straight up steep, dirt Wentworth Station Rd. The rambling farmhouse, built in 1866, has been used as a hostel for half a century. It's central enough to be a base for both the Sunrise Trail and much of the Minas Basin shore. Trails for hiking and mountain biking start just outside the door. It gets particularly booked up in winter for the cross-country and downhill skiing nearby.

Tatamagouche

The Malagash Peninsula, which juts out into protected Tatamagouche Bay, is a low-key, bucolic loop for a drive or bike ride. Stop at the local winery for tastings, explore beaches galore or take a peek in some interesting museums found just inland. Tatamagouche is the largest town on the Northumberland Shore coast west of Pictou and makes a great base for exploring.

◎ Sights

Jost Winery WINERY
(☎902-257-2636; www.jostwine.com; off Hwy 6, Malagash; ⊙tours noon & 3pm Jun-Sep) Take a free tour of the scenically located Jost Winery. While regular wine is free to taste, the ice wine costs $5. If you want to try all three ice wine varieties, ask to have three small glasses for the price of one large one. Winery signs direct you about 5km off Hwy 6.

Balmoral Grist Mill HISTORIC SITE
(☎902-657-3016; 660 Matheson Brook Rd; adult/child $3/2; ⊙9:30am-5:30pm Mon-Sat, 1-5:30pm Sun) In a gorgeous setting on the stream that once provided it with power, the Balmoral Grist Mill still grinds wheat in summer. From Tatamagouche, turn south on Hwy 311 (at the east edge of town) and then east on Hwy 256.

Sutherland Steam Mill HISTORIC SITE
(☎902-657-3365; off Hwy 326, Denmark; adult/child $3/2; ⊙9:30am-5:30pm Mon-Sat, 1-5:30pm Sun) Built in 1894, the Sutherland Steam Mill produced lumber, carriages, wagons and windows until 1958. To get here from Hwy 256, drive east, and then north on Hwy 326.

Blue Sea Beach BEACH
Blue Sea Beach on the Malagash Peninsula has warm water and fine sand, and a marsh area just inland that's ideal for bird-watching. There are picnic tables and shelters to change in.

Rushton's Beach BEACH
Small cottages crowd around Rushton's Beach, just east of Tatamagouche in Brule. It's worth a visit to look for seals (turn left at the end of the boardwalk and walk toward the end of the beach) and birdlife in the adjoining salt marsh.

⭐ Festivals & Events

Oktoberfest BEER
(☎902-657-2380; tickets $10-20; ⊙Sep) The wildly popular Oktoberfest is held the last weekend in September – yes, September.

🛏 Sleeping & Eating

Train Station Inn INN $$
(☎902-657-3222, 888-724-5233; www.trainstation.ca; 21 Station Rd; carriages $99-179; ⊙May-Nov; ☎☎) It's a museum, it's a kooky gift shop, it's a restaurant, it's a hotel and…it's a stationary train. Each unique carriage suite is an eight-year-old boy's dream decorated with period train posters, toy trains and locomotive books.

The dreamer behind the inn, James Le-Fresne, grew up across the tracks and saved the train station from demolition when he was just 18. Dine on delicious seafood, meat and salads in the c 1928 dining car or have a blueberry pancake breakfast in the station house. Free self-guided tours are available from the gift shop.

Sugar Moon Farm CANADIAN $$
(☎902-657-3348, 866-816-2753; www.sugarmoon.ca; Alex Macdonald Rd, off Hwy 311, Earltown; mains $10-30; ⊙9am-5pm Thu-Mon Jul & Aug, Sat & Sun Sep-Jun) The food – simple, delicious pancakes and locally made sausages served with maple syrup – is the highlight of this working maple farm and woodlot. Check online for special happenings.

🛍 Shopping

Lismore Sheep Farm   SOUVENIRS
(✆902-351-2889; 1389 Louisville Rd, off Hwy 6; ⊙9am-5pm) A working farm with more than 300 sheep, this is a fun destination even if you don't buy a rug, blanket or socks. From May to October, the barn is open for visitors to pat the lambs and learn all about producing wool.

❶ Information

Fraser Cultural Centre (✆902-657-3285; 362 Main St; ⊙10am-5pm Mon-Fri, to 4pm Sat, 11am-3pm Sun Jun-Sep) Has tourist information, internet access and local history displays.

Pictou

Many people stop in Pictou for a side trip or as a stopover via the ferry from PEI, but it's also an enjoyable base for exploring Northumberland Strait. Water St, the main street, is lined with interesting shops and beautiful old stone buildings but, unfortunately, the sea views are blighted by a giant smoking mill in the distance. The town is known as the 'Birthplace of New Scotland' because the first Scottish immigrants to Nova Scotia landed here in 1773.

◉ Sights & Activities

You can picnic and swim at Caribou/Munroes Island Provincial Park.

Hector   SHIP
(admission $7.50; ⊙9am-7pm Jun-Oct) A replica of the ship *Hector* that carried the first 200 Highland Scots to Nova Scotia is tied up for viewing. Descend into the large hull crammed with bunks to get a feel of how challenging the crossing was. The ticket includes admission to **Hector Heritage Quay** (✆902-485-4371; 33 Caladh Ave; adult/student $5/2; ⊙9am-5pm Mon-Sat, noon-5pm Sun May-Sep), which has an interpretive center, a re-created blacksmith shop, a collection of shipbuilding artifacts and displays about the *Hector* and its passengers.

Northumberland Fisheries Museum   MUSEUM
(✆902-485-4972; 71 Front St; admission $5; ⊙10am-6pm Mon-Sat) In the old train station, this museum explores the area's fishing heritage. Exhibits include strange sea creatures and the spiffy *Silver Bullet,* an early-1930s lobster boat.

🎆 Festivals & Events

Pictou Landing First Nation Powwow   CULTURE
(✆902-752-4912; ⊙1st weekend Jun) Across the Pictou Harbour (a 25-minute drive through New Glasgow), this annual powwow features sunrise ceremonies, drumming and craft demonstrations. Camping and food are available on-site; it's strictly alcohol and drug free.

Lobster Carnival   FOOD
(✆902-485-5150; www.townofpictou.ca; ⊙mid-Jul) Begun in 1934 as the Carnival of the Fisherfolk, this four-day event now offers free entertainment, boat races and lots of chances to feast on lobster.

Hector Festival   MUSIC
(✆902-485-8848; www.decostecentre.ca; ⊙mid-Aug) Free daily outdoor concerts, Highland dancing and piping competitions, and a *Hector* landing reenactment.

🛏 Sleeping & Eating

Pictou is no culinary center, but there are some excellent dining options 20km away in New Glasgow. Plenty of pub-food and fish-and-chip-style joints line the waterfront and main drags.

Caribou/Munroes Island Provincial Park   CAMPGROUND $
(✆902-485-6134; www.parks.gov.ns.ca; 2119 Three Brooks Rd; campsites $24) Less than 5km from Pictou, this park is set on a gorgeous beach. Sites 1 to 22 abut the day-use area and are less private; sites 78 to 95 are gravel and suited for RVs. The rest are wooded and private.

Pictou Lodge   HOTEL $$
(✆888-662-7484, 902-485-4322; www.pictoulodge.com; 172 Lodge Rd, off Braeshore Rd; r/cottages from $109/159; 🕸🐾🐕) This atmospheric 1920s resort is on more than 60 hectares of wooded land between Caribou/Munroes Island Provincial Park and Pictou. Beautifully renovated ocean-side log cabins have original stone fireplaces. Motel rooms are also available. There's a life-sized checkerboard, paddleboats, a private beach and the best restaurant in town.

Willow House Inn   B&B $$
(✆902-485-5740; www.willowhouseinn.com; 11 Willow St; r with shared/private bathroom $60/120; 🕸🐕) This historic c 1840 home is a labyrinth of staircases and cozy, antique rooms.

The owners whip up great breakfasts, as well as conversation and tips for what to do around town.

Customs House Inn INN $$
(☑ 902-485-4546; www.customshouseinn.ca; 38 Depot St; r incl breakfast $80-170; 🐟) The tall stone walls here are at once imposingly chic and reassuringly solid. The chunky antique decor is as sturdy and elegant as the walls and many rooms have waterfront views. You'll be left pretty much to your own devices, including at the continental breakfast in the basement, which can be a nice break after days of B&B chitchat.

Carver's Coffeehouse & Studio CAFE $
(☑ 902-382-3332; 41 Coleraine St; light meals around $8; ⊙ 8am-9pm) This bright and inviting cafe used to be the carving studio for Keith Matheson, who did the detail work on the *Hector*. Nowadays it's a mellow stop for soup, sandwiches, coffee and pastries.

☆ Entertainment

deCoste Centre MUSIC, THEATER
(☑ 902-485-8848; www.decostecentre.ca; 91 Water St; tickets about $18; ⊙ box office 11:30am-5pm Mon-Fri, 1-5pm Sat & Sun) Opposite the waterfront, this impressive performing arts center stages a range of live shows. Experience some top-notch Scottish music during a summer series of ceilidhs (*kay*-lees; adult/child $15/7) at 2pm from Tuesday to Thursday.

❶ Information

Pictou Public Library (☑ 902-485-5021; 40 Water St; ⊙ noon-9pm Tue & Thu, to 5pm Wed, 10am-5pm Fri & Sat) Free internet access.

Town of Pictou (www.townofpictou.ca) Links to sights and festivals.

Visitors Information Centre (VIC; ☑ 902-485-6213; Pictou Rotary; ⊙ 8am-9:30pm May-Dec) A large information center situated northwest of town to meet travelers arriving from the PEI ferry.

❶ Getting There & Away

Northumberland Ferries (p434) to PEI leave from a terminal a few kilometers from Pictou.

New Glasgow

The largest town on the Northumberland Shore, New Glasgow has always been an industrial center; the first mine opened in neighboring Stellarton in 1807. Still, it's a pleasant town with plenty of aging architecture, a river running through the center and some good places to eat. The few major local attractions are in Stellarton, a 5km drive south.

◉ Sights & Activities

Crombie Art Gallery GALLERY
(☑ 902-755-4440; 1780 Abercrombie Rd; ⊙ tours hourly 9-11am & 1-4pm Wed Jul & Aug) **FREE** In the personal residence of the founder of the Sobeys supermarket chain, this private gallery has an excellent collection of 19th- and early-20th-century Canadian art, including works by Cornelius Krieghoff and the Group of Seven.

Museum of Industry MUSEUM
(☑ 902-755-5425; http://museumofindustry.novascotia.ca; Hwy 104 at exit 24; adult/child $7/3; ⊙ 9am-5pm Mon-Sat, 10am-5pm Sun; 🖝) This is a wonderful place for kids. There's a hands-on water-power exhibit and an assembly line to try to keep up with.

Anchors Above Zipline Adventure ZIP LINE
(www.anchorsabovezipline.ca; 464 McGrath Mountain Rd, French River; 1 ride $30; ⊙ 10am-5pm) Nova Scotia's only zip line is found off Hwy 104 (exit 27) on the way to Antigonish. Two lines total 600m (2000ft) and dangle 75m (250ft) up in the trees. The first is a bit slower and lets you get the hang of it, while the second drops down about 60m (190ft) and goes quite fast!

✗ Eating

The Bistro MODERN CANADIAN $$
(☑ 902-752-4988; 216 Archimedes St; mains $19-32; ⊙ from 5pm Tue-Sat) The only constant on the menu is creativity in spicing and sauces. The menu changes daily according to what's available and in summer everything is organic. Try the Thai grilled salmon, or pork tenderloin with black-mission-fig butter. Enjoy the local art on display that's also for sale.

Hebel's INTERNATIONAL $$$
(☑ 902-695-5955; 71 Stellarton Rd; lunch mains $9-14, dinner mains $22-36; ⊙ 11:30am-2pm Tue-Fri, 5-9pm Tue-Sat) Flavors from all over the world are mingled with fresh Nova Scotian ingredients at this bright and homey, fire-warmed spot in an elegant Victorian. Choices may include anything from seafood creole or beef stroganoff to miso-glazed salmon on Japanese noodles.

Antigonish

Beautiful beaches and hiking possibilities north of town could easily keep you busy for a couple of days, but Antigonish town is lively enough and has some great places to eat. Catholic Scots settled and established St Francis Xavier University and today the university still dominates the ambience of the town. Antigonish is known for the Highland Games held each July since 1861.

◉ Sights & Activities

St Francis Xavier University NOTABLE BUILDING
The attractive campus of 125-year-old St Francis Xavier University is behind the Romanesque **St Ninian's Cathedral** (120 St Ninian St; ⊙7:30am-8pm). The **Hall of the Clans** is on the 3rd floor of the old wing of the Angus L MacDonald Library, just beyond the St Ninian's Cathedral parking lot. In the hall, crests of all the Scottish clans that settled this area are displayed. Those clans gather each July for the Antigonish Highland Games.

Antigonish Landing HIKING, CYCLING
A 4km hiking and cycling trail to the nature reserve at Antigonish Landing begins just across the train tracks from the museum, then 400m down Adam St. The landing's estuary is a good bird-watching area where you might see eagles, ducks and ospreys.

✬ Festivals & Events

Antigonish Highland Games CULTURE
(www.antigonishhighlandgames.ca; ⊙mid-Jul) An extravaganza of dancing, pipe playing, and heavy-lifting events involving hewn logs and iron balls.

Evolve MUSIC
(www.evolvefestival.com; ⊙late Jul) Five stages of funk, bluegrass, hip-hop and more, plus workshops on everything from puppetry to media literacy.

⌦ Sleeping & Eating

Shebby's Tourist Home B&B $$
(Antigonish Highland Heart; ☑902-863-1858, 800-863-1858; www.bbcanada.com/3241.html; 135 Main St; r $90-110; ⊙May-Oct; ☜) Smiling Shebby, the friendly owner of this c 1854 house, brightens her centrally located home with special touches such as rag dolls on the beds.

★ **Gabrieau's Bistro** MODERN CANADIAN $$
(☑902-863-1925; 350 Main St; lunch mains $8-16, dinner mains $16-32; ⊙10am-9pm Mon-Fri, 4-9:30pm Sat; ☑) Dine on any of a number of imaginative vegetarian dishes, salads, meats and seafood for lunch or dinner. Locals credit chef Mark Gabrieau for setting the culinary high-water mark in Antigonish. The Thai shrimp and lobster risotto is divine.

❶ Information

Antigonish Public Library (☑902-863-4276; 274 Main St; ⊙10am-9pm Tue & Thu, to 5pm Wed, Fri & Sat) Free internet access. Enter off College St.

Visitors Information Centre (VIC; ☑902-863-4921; 56 West St; ⊙10am-8pm Jun-Sep) Brochures, free local calls and free internet access. It's in the Antigonish Mall parking lot at the junction of Hwys 104 and 7.

❶ Getting There & Away

Maritime Bus services stop at Bloomfield Centre at St Francis Xavier University.

Pomquet

About 16km east of Antigonish, this tiny Acadian community is on a stunning **beach** with 13 dunes that keep growing; waves dump the equivalent of more than 4000 truckloads of sand on the beach each year. Many bird species frequent the salt marshes behind the dunes.

Cape George

It's a pleasant day cruising this 72km route that loops up Hwy 245 from Antigonish to Malignant Cove and around Cape George. It's been dubbed a 'mini Cabot Trail' but really the two routes are quite different; Cape George is much less mountainous and forested and has more beaches.

From a well-marked picnic area close to **Cape George Point Lighthouse**, a 1km walk leads to the lighthouse itself. It's automated and not that big, but there are lovely views to Cape Breton Island and PEI. Signs at the picnic area point to longer hikes through forests and coastal areas, including one 32km loop.

You can also start exploring these trails from the wharf at **Ballantyne's Cove**, one of the prettiest communities in Nova Scotia. To walk from the wharf to the lighthouse and back again is an 8km trip. Also stop in at the **Ballantyne's Cove Tuna Interpretive Centre** (☑902-863-8162; 57 Ballantyne's Cove Wharf Rd; ⊙10am-7:30pm Jul-Sep) FREE for displays on both the fish and the fishery. A fish-and-chip van parks nearby.

CAPE BRETON ISLAND

Floating over the rest of Nova Scotia like an island halo, Cape Breton is a heavenly, forested realm of bald eagles, migrating whales, palpable history and foot-tapping music. Starting up the Ceilidh Trail along the western coastline, Celtic music vibrates through the pubs and community centers, eventually reaching the Cabot Trail where more-eclectic Acadian-style tunes ring out around Chéticamp.

The 300km Cabot Trail continues around Cape Breton Highlands National Park. It winds and climbs around and over coastal mountains, with heart-stopping ocean views at every turn, moose on the roads (watch out!) and plenty of trails to stop and hike.

Take a side trip to Glace Bay to learn firsthand about the region's coal-mining history; Fortress Louisbourg in the east, to get a taste of 18th-century military life; or the Highland Village Museum in Iona, to get some visuals of what life was like for early Scottish immigrants. The region around Bras d'Or Lake offers opportunities to explore the past and present of the Mi'kmaq First Nation and in Baddeck you can learn everything you ever wanted to know about Alexander Graham Bell.

Most tourists visit in July and August, and many restaurants, accommodations and VICs are only open from mid-June through September. **Celtic Colours** (www.celtic-colours.com; ⊙Oct), a wonderful roving music festival that attracts top musicians from Scotland, Spain and other countries with Celtic connections, helps extend the season into the fall, a superb time to visit.

Port Hastings & Port Hawkesbury

Cape Breton Island ceased to be a true island when the Canso Causeway was built across the Strait of Canso in 1955. A big and busy **visitors information center** (VIC; ☑902-625-4201; 96 Hwy 4; ⊙9am-8pm) is on your right as you drive onto Cape Breton Island. This is definitely worth a stop: there are few other information centers on Cape Breton, especially outside of July and August; the staff is very well informed; and one wall is covered with posters advertising square dances and ceilidhs.

If you need lunch or a kick of caffeine, stop in at **Haven Coffee Bar** (3 Water St, Port Hawkesbury; sandwiches $6.75; ⊙8am-5pm Mon-Fri). They bake their own bread, brew a fine cup of joe and provide a cozy place to enjoy it all on the waterfront, although there's not much of a view.

Ceilidh Trail

Take a hard left immediately after leaving the Port Hastings VIC to get on the Ceilidh Trail (Hwy 19), which snakes along the western coast of the island. Then put on your dancing shoes: this area was settled by Scots with fiddles in hand and is renowned for its ceilidh music performances, square dances and parties.

For a great introduction to local culture, visit the **Celtic Music Interpretive Centre** (☑902-787-2708; www.celticmusiccentre.com; 5473 Hwy 19, Judique; admission $12; ⊙9am-5pm Mon-Fri Jun-Aug). Half-hour tours (which can be self-guided if you arrive when no guides are available) include a fiddle lesson and a dance step or two. Square dances are advertised around the admissions desk – try a Saturday dance at the community hall in West Mabou or a Thursday evening dance in Glencoe Mills. Ceilidhs at the music center itself are held at 11:30am Monday to Friday during summer.

Creignish B&B (☑902-625-5709; www.bb-canada.com/159.html; 2154 Hwy 19; s/d $30/60; ⊙Jun-Nov) is a 'recycled school house' that's been turned into a guesthouse and artist's haven. Wildflowers, shells and bones are everywhere and there's even a giant stuffed tuna hanging on the ceiling. 'Improvised' arts and crafts classes are offered and owner Sandra can point you to the best-hidden secrets of Cape Breton Island. Rooms are large and comfortable, and the B&B is only a 10-minute drive from the causeway.

Mabou

Although it looks unlikely at first glance, micro Mabou is the not-so-underground hot spot of Cape Breton's Celtic music scene. Among lush hills and quiet inlets you can hike away your days and dance away your nights – and don't forget to scorch your tonsils with single malt whiskey at the distillery down the road.

Sights & Activities

Mabou is more a place to experience than to see specific sights. Take any turn off Hwy 19 and see where it takes you.

Glenora Inn & Distillery DISTILLERY
(902-258-2662, 800-839-0491; www.glenoradistillery.com; Hwy 19; guided tours incl tasting $7; tours hourly 9am-5pm Jun-Oct) Take a tour and taste the rocket fuel at the only distillery making single malt whiskey in Canada. Then, stop for an excellent meal at the gourmet pub (there are daily lunchtime and dinner ceilidhs) or even for the night. Cave-like rooms ($125 to $150 per night) are perfect for sleeping it off if you've been drinking the local beverage; the chalets ($175 to $240) are a better choice if you want brighter surroundings. It's 9km north of Mabou.

Cape Mabou Highlands HIKING
Within the Cape Mabou Highlands, an extensive network of hiking trails extends between Mabou and Inverness toward the coast west of Hwy 19. The trails are sometimes closed when the fire danger is high; otherwise, hikes ranging from 4km to 12km start from three different trailheads. An excellent trail guide ($5) is available at the grocery store across the road from the Mull Café & Deli when the trails are open. Maps are also posted at the trailheads.

Sleeping & Eating

Clayton Farm B&B B&B $$
(902-945-2719; 11247 Hwy 19; s/d $75/100; May-Nov; @) This 1835 farmhouse sits on a working red-angus ranch and is run by hardworking Isaac Smith. Paraphernalia of old Cape Breton life and of Isaac's family are casually scattered throughout the common areas and comfortable guest rooms. It's rustically perfect.

Duncreigan Country Inn INN $$
(902-945-2207, 800-840-2207; www.duncreigan.ca; Hwy 19; r incl breakfast $135-195;) Nestled in oak trees on the banks of the river, this inn has private, spacious rooms, some with terraces and water views. Bikes are available to guests and there's a licensed dining room that

serves breakfast to guests or dinner by reservation (mains $10 to $23).

Red Shoe Pub PUB $$
(902-945-2996; www.redshoepub.com; 11533 Hwy 19; mains $9-22; 11:30am-11pm Mon-Wed, to 2am Thu-Sat, noon-11pm Sun) Straddling the spine of the Ceilidh Trail, this pub is the beating heart of Mabou. Gather round a local fiddle player (often from the Rankin family) while enjoying a pint and a superb meal. The desserts, including the gingerbread with rum-butterscotch sauce and fruit compote, are divine. Don't be afraid to stay on after dinner to get to know some locals and maybe a few travelers, too. Check the website for details of performances.

Inverness

Row upon row of company housing betrays the history of coal mining in Inverness, the first town of any size on the coast. Its history and people are captured evocatively by writer Alistair MacLeod. His books are for sale at the **Bear Paw** (902-258-2528; Hwy 19), next to the Royal Bank.

Beginning near the fishing harbor, there are kilometers of sandy **beach** with comfortable water temperatures in late summer. A **boardwalk** runs 1km along the beach.

In the old train station just back from the beach, the **Inverness Miners' Museum** (902-258-3822; 62 Lower Railway St; admission by donation; 9am-5pm Mon-Fri, noon-5pm Sat & Sun) presents local history. **Inverness County Centre for the Arts** (902-258-2533; www.invernessarts.ca; 16080 Hwy 19; 10am-5pm) is a beautiful establishment with several galleries and an upmarket gift shop featuring work by local and regional artists. It's also a music venue with a floor built for dancing, of course.

MacLeods Inn B&B (902-253-3360; www.macleods.com; Broad Cove Rd, off Hwy 19; r $75-125; mid-Jun-mid-Oct;) is a high-end B&B for a not-so-high-end price about 5km north of Inverness. The house is big and modern, but the decoration is in keeping with Cape Breton heritage.

Cabot Trail & Cape Breton Highlands National Park

One of Canada's most dramatic parks and its lively surrounds are accessible via the famous Cabot Trail. The drive is at its best along the northwestern shore of Cape Breton and then down to Pleasant Bay. Be sure to take advantage of the many stops for scenic views; otherwise, keep your eyes on this very circuitous road. Of course, it's even better if you can explore on foot, hiking through a tapestry of terrain to reach vistas looking out over an endless, icy ocean.

Chéticamp

While Mabou is the center of Celtic music, lively Chéticamp throws in some folky notes and French phrases to get your feet moving to Acadian tunes. The town owes much of its cultural preservation to its geographical isolation; the road didn't make it this far until 1949. Today, it's a gateway to Cape Breton Highlands National Park, and has some top-notch museums and live-music opportunities – there's always something going on. The 1893 Church of St Pierre dominates the town with its silver spire and colorful frescoes, but the rest of this seaside town is modern and drab.

Chéticamp is also known for its crafts, particularly hooked rugs, and as a pioneer of the cooperative movement. Check out the rug displays at Les Trois Pignons and take notice of all those co-ops around town: the Credit Union, co-op grocery store, and more.

Visitors information and internet access are available at Les Trois Pignons.

⊙ Sights & Activities

Les Trois Pignons   MUSEUM
(☑ 902-224-2642;   www.lestroispignons.com; 15584 Cabot Trail; admission $5; ⊙ 9am-5pm) This excellent museum explains how rug hooking went from being a home-based activity to an international business. Artifacts, including hooked rugs, illustrate early life and artisanship in Chéticamp. Almost everything here – from bottles to rugs – was collected by one eccentric local resident.

Centro de la Mi-Carême   MUSEUM
(☑ 902-224-1016; www.micareme.ca; 12615 Cabot Trail; admission $5; ⊙ 9am-5pm) Mi-Carême, celebrated in the middle of Lent, is Chéticamp's answer to Mardi Gras. Locals wear masks and disguises and visit houses, trying to get people to guess who they are. This museum covers the history of the celebration and displays traditional masks.

Whale Cruisers   BOAT TOUR
(☑ 902-224-3376, 800-813-3376; www.whalecruisers.com; Government Wharf; adult/child $38/17) Several operators sell tours from the Government Wharf, across and down from the church. Captain Cal is the most experienced and offers three-hour expeditions up to four times daily. It's wise to reserve your trip a day in advance in midsummer.

🛏 Sleeping & Eating

Accommodations are tight throughout July and August. It's advisable to call ahead or arrive early in the afternoon.

THE ACADIANS

When the French first settled the area around the Minas Basin, they called the region Arcadia, a Greek and Roman term for 'pastoral paradise.' This became Acadia and by the 18th century, the Acadians felt more connection with the land here than with the distant Loire Valley they'd come from.

To the English, however, they would always be French, with whom rivalry and suspicion was constant. Considering it an affront to their Catholic faith, the Acadians refused to take an oath of allegiance to the English king after the Treaty of Utrecht granted Nova Scotia to the British. When hard-line lieutenant governor Charles Lawrence was appointed in 1754, he became fed up with the Acadians and ordered their deportation. The English burned many villages and forced some 14,000 Acadians onto ships.

Many Acadians headed for Louisiana and New Orleans; others went to various Maritime points, New England, Martinique in the Caribbean, Santo Domingo in the Dominican Republic, or back to Europe. Not once were they greeted warmly with open arms. Some hid out and remained in Acadia. In later years many of the deported people returned but found their lands occupied. In Nova Scotia, Acadians resettled the Chéticamp area on Cape Breton Island and the French Shore north of Yarmouth. New Brunswick has a large French population stretching up the east coast past the Acadian Peninsula at Caraquet.

Maison Fiset House
B&B $$

(☎902-224-1794, 855-292-1794; www.maisonfiset-house.com; 15050 Cabot Trail; r $169-219; ☎) A little luxury in Chéticamp is found in this grand old 1895 home, once owned by the town's first doctor. If you're in a suite, lounge in your Jacuzzi tub and enjoy the ocean views. Most importantly, experience the full-fledged Acadian hospitality from your host Lyne.

Chéticamp Outfitters Inn B&B
B&B $$

(☎902-224-2776; www.cheticampns.com/cheti-campoutfitters; 13938 Cabot Trail; r $65-120, chalet with kitchen $135; ☺Apr-Nov; ☎) Just 2km south of town, this place offers a range of well-priced choices in Acadian style. Views stretch from the sea to the mountain, wildflowers burst from every corner of the garden, and you might even see a passing moose. Very full breakfasts are served in the panoramic dining area by energetic hosts.

Acadian Crafts & Cuisine
ACADIAN $$

(☎902-224-2170; 15067 Main St; mains $10-15; ☺9am-9pm) This Acadian-only restaurant serves home-style dishes, such as Laurette's meat pie (an Acadian-style pork pie) or get a sample plate to try a bit of everything. Ruddy-cheeked serving ladies wear traditional Acadian bonnets and treat everyone like kin.

☆ Entertainment

Doryman's Beverage Room
LIVE MUSIC

(☎902-224-9909; 15528 Cabot Trail) This drinking establishment hosts 'sessions' (cover $8), with a fiddler and piano players from Mabou each Saturday (2pm to 6pm), and an acoustic Acadian group at 8pm Sunday, Tuesday, Wednesday and Friday.

Cape Breton Highlands National Park

One-third of the Cabot Trail runs through this extensive **park** (www.pc.gc.ca/capebreton; adult/child/vehicle & passengers $7.80/3.90/19.60) of woodland, tundra, bog and startling sea views. Established in 1936 and encompassing 20% of Cape Breton's landmass, it's the fancy feather in Nova Scotia's island cap.

There are two park entrances: one at Chéticamp and one at Ingonish. Purchase an entry permit at either park entrance. A one-day pass is good until noon the next day. Wheelchair-accessible trails are indicated on the free park map available at either entrance.

🏃 Activities

Hiking

Two trails on the west coast of the park have spectacular ocean views. **Fishing Cove Trail** gently descends 330m over 8km to the mouth of rugged Fishing Cove River. You can opt for a steeper and shorter hike of 2.8km from a second trailhead about 5km north of the first. Double the distances if you plan to return the same day. Otherwise, you must preregister for one of eight backcountry sites ($9.80) at the Chéticamp Information Centre (p379). Reviews of trails in and near the park are available at www.cabottrail.com.

Most other trails are shorter and close to the road, many leading to ridge tops for impressive views of the coast. The best of these is **Skyline Trail**, a 7km loop that puts you on the edge of a headland cliff right above the water. The trailhead is about 5.5km north of Corney Brook Campground.

Just south of Neil's Harbour, on the eastern coast of the park, the **Coastal Trail** runs 11km round-trip and covers more gentle coastline.

Cycling

Don't make this your inaugural trip: the riding is tough, there are no shoulders in many sections and you must be comfortable sharing the incredible scenery with RVs. Alternatively, you can mountain bike on four inland trails in the park. Only **Branch Pond Lookoff Trail** offers ocean views.

Sea Spray Outdoor Adventures (☎902-383-2732; www.cabot-trail-outdoors.com; 1141 White Point Rd; bicycle rental per day/week $45/160; ☺9am-5pm Jun-Oct) in Smelt Brook near Dingwall rents bikes and will do emergency repairs on the road. It also offers help planning trips and leads organized cycling, kayaking and hiking tours.

🛏 Sleeping

Towns around the park offer a variety of accommodations. Cape Breton Highlands National Park has six drive-in **campgrounds** (campsites/RV sites from $17.60/29.40) with discounts after three days. Most sites are first-come, first-served, but wheelchair-accessible sites, group campsites and backcountry sites can be reserved for $9.80. In the smaller campgrounds, further from the park entrances, just pick a site and self-register. To camp at any of the three larger ones near the park entrances, register at the closest information center.

The 162-site **Chéticamp Campground** is behind the information center. There are no 'radio free' areas, so peace and quiet is not guaranteed.

Corney Brook (20 sites), 10km further north, is a particularly stunning campground high over the ocean. There's a small playground, but it would be a nerve-racking place to camp with small kids. **MacIntosh Brook** (10 sites) is an open field 3km east of Pleasant Bay. It has wheelchair-accessible sites. **Big Intervale** (10 sites) is near a river 11km west of Cape North.

Near the eastern park entrance, you have a choice of the 256-site **Broad Cove Campground** at Ingonish and the 90-site **Ingonish Campground**, near Keltic Lodge at Ingonish Beach. Both have wheelchair-accessible sites. These large campgrounds near the beach are popular with local families in midsummer.

From late October to early May, you can camp at the Chéticamp and Ingonish Campgrounds for $22, including firewood. In truly inclement weather, tenters can take refuge in cooking shelters with woodstoves.

ℹ️ Information

Chéticamp Information Centre (☎902-224-2306; www.parkscanada.gc.ca; 16646 Cabot Trail; ◉8:30am-7pm) Has displays and a relief map of the park, plus a bookstore. Ask the staff for advice on hiking or camping.

Ingonish Information Centre (☎902-285-2535; 37677 Cabot Trail; ◉8am-8pm May-Oct) On the eastern edge of the park, it's much smaller than the center at Chéticamp and has no bookstore.

Pleasant Bay

A perfect base for exploring the park, Pleasant Bay is a carved-out bit of civilization hemmed in on all sides by wilderness. It's an active fishing harbor known for its whale-watching tours and Tibetan monastery. If you are in the area on Canada Day (July 1), try to be in the stands for the annual monks versus townspeople baseball game. There are lots of fish-and-chip and burger places around town, but no really special places to eat.

◉ Sights & Activities

Gampo Abbey　　　　　　　MONASTERY
(☎902-224-2752; www.gampoabbey.org; ◉tours 1:30-3:30pm Mon-Fri Jun-Sep) This abbey, 8km north of Pleasant Bay past the village of Red River, is a monastery for followers of Tibetan Buddhism. Ane Pema Chödrön is the founding director of the abbey and a noted Buddhist author, but you aren't likely to see her here as she is often on the road. You can visit the grounds any time during the day, but you get a more authentic experience with a tour – a friendly monk escorts you.

Whale Interpretive Centre　　　MUSEUM
(☎902-224-1411; www.whalecentre.ca; 104 Harbour Rd; adult/child $5/4; ◉9am-5pm Jun-Oct) Stop here before taking a whale-watching tour from the adjacent wharf. Park entrance permits are for sale, and internet access is available at the C@P site downstairs.

Pollett's Cove　　　　　　　　HIKING
The popular, challenging 20km-return hiking trail to Pollett's Cove begins at the end of the road to Gampo Abbey. There are great views along the way and perfect spots to camp when you arrive at the abandoned fishing community. This is not a Parks Canada trail, so it can be rough underfoot.

Captain Mark's Whale & Seal Cruise　　　　　　　BOAT TOUR
(☎902-224-1316, 888-754-5112; www.whaleandsealcruise.com; adult $35-44, child $15-22; ◉May-Sep) Depending on the season, two to five daily tours can be taken in the lower-priced 'Cruiser' motorboat or closer to the action in a Zodiac. Captain Mark promises not only guaranteed whales, but also time to see seabirds and seals, as well as Gampo Abbey. There's a discount of up to 10% if you reserve a spot on the earliest (9:30am) or latest (5pm) tour. Tours leave from the wharf next to the Whale Interpretive Centre.

🛏️ Sleeping

Cabot Trail Backpackers　　HOSTEL $
(☎902-224-1976; www.cabottrail.com/hostel; 23349 Cabot Trail; dm/r $28/68; @🤶) Bright and basic, this very friendly 18-bed hostel has a common kitchen and barbecue area. The office for Cabot Trail Whale Watching is here.

Bay St Lawrence

Bay St Lawrence is a picturesque little fishing village at the very north edge of Cape Breton Island.

Captain Cox (☑888-346-5556, 902-383-2981; Bay St Lawrence Wharf; adult/child $45/25) has been taking people to see whales aboard the 35ft *Northern Gannet* since 1986. He does trips at 10:30am, 1:30pm and 4:30pm in July and August. Call for spring and fall schedules.

Jumping Mouse Campground (☑902-383-2914; www.ecocamping.ca; 3360 Bay St Lawrence Rd; campsites/cabins $25/40; ☉ Jun-Sep) is an ecofriendly campground with 10 oceanfront sites (no cars allowed). Reservations are accepted for multinight stays and for a beautifully built four-bunk cabin. There are hot showers, a cooking shelter, frequent whale sightings and the whole place is nearly bug-free.

To enjoy Aspy Bay and its spectacular beach just for an afternoon, stop at nearby **Cabot's Landing Provincial Park** (www.parks.gov.ns.ca).

Meat Cove

The northernmost road in Nova Scotia finishes at the steep, emerald coast of Meat Cove, 13km northwest of Bay St Lawrence (the last 7km of the road is gravel). As well as watching for frolicking whales in unbelievably clear water, keep an eye on the earth for orchids – some rare species here aren't found anywhere else in Nova Scotia.

🏃 Activities

Cape St Lawrence Lighthouse   HIKING

From Meat Cove, a 16km hiking trail continues west to Cape St Lawrence lighthouse and Lowland Cove. Spend an hour gazing over the ocean and you're guaranteed to see pods of pilot whales. They frolic here all spring, summer, and into the fall. Carry a compass and refrain from exploring side paths; locals have gotten lost in this area.

Grassy Point   HIKING

For a shorter hike, you can't beat the views over the coast from Grassy Point. The small foot trail (about 40 minutes return) starts just past the campground. Sit for a while at the point to look for whales and nesting bald eagles.

🛏 Sleeping

At the time of research, the old Meat Cove Lodge across from the Welcome Center had been torn down and the owner had plans to build a new structure. Check online or ask around starting from the 2014 summer season.

Meat Cove Campground   CAMPGROUND $

(☑902-383-2379, 902-383-2658; www.meatcove-campground.com; 2475 Meat Cove Rd; campsites $25-30, cabins $60; ☉ Jun-Nov) Meat Cove Campground is spectacular, perched on a grassy bluff high above the ocean out in the middle of nowhere. Four cabins with no electricity or plumbing share the magnificent view; bring your own bedding. Be prepared for high winds.

Hine's Ocean View Lodge   HOSTEL $

(☑902-383-2512; www.hinesoceanviewlodge.ca; r $60; 🖥🐾) This isolated spot, high up its own road (signposted off Meat Cove Road), has plain almost-dormitory style rooms and a shared kitchen. Cash only.

ℹ Information

Meat Cove Welcome Center (☑902-383-2284; 2296 Meat Cove Rd; ☉8am-8:30pm Jul-Sep) Stop by the Meat Cove Welcome Center to get excellent information on hiking trails, check email and grab a bite to eat (from sandwiches to lobster suppers). Leave your car here if there's no room at the trailhead.

Ingonish

At the eastern entrance to Cape Breton Highlands National Park are Ingonish and Ingonish Beach, small towns lost in the background of motels and cottages. This is a long-standing popular destination, but there are few real attractions. There are several hiking trails and an information center nearby in the national park.

👁 Sights & Activities

Ingonish Beach   BEACH

This long, wide strip of sand is tucked in a bay surrounded by green hills.

Highlands Links Golf Course   GOLF

(☑800-441-1118, 902-285-2600; www.highlandslinksgolf.com; per round $91) Reputed to be one of the best golf courses in the world.

🍽 Sleeping & Eating

Driftwood Lodge
INN $

(☑902-285-2558; www.driftwoodlodge.ca; 36125 Cabot Trail; r $55, ste with kitchen $85-100; ⊘May-Nov; 🐾) Located 8km north of the Ingonish park entrance, this funky cabin-meets-hotel establishment is a steal. The owner works at the park and is a mine of info about hiking and activities. There's a fine-sand beach just below the lodge.

Keltic Lodge
HOTEL $$$

(☑902-285-2880, 800-565-0444; www.signature-resorts.com; Ingonish Beach; r $155-280, cottages $315-395; ⊘May-Oct; 🎧🐾🏊) The finest digs in the area are scattered within this theatrical Tudor-style resort erected in 1940. It shares Middle Head Peninsula with the famous **golf course** and the **Ingonish Campground**. The lodge is worth visiting even if you're not a guest for its setting and the **hiking trail** to the tip of the peninsula just beyond the resort.

You must have a valid entry permit to the national park, as the lodge, the golf course and the hiking trail are all within park boundaries.

★Main Street Restaurant & Bakery
CANADIAN $$

(☑902-285-2225; 37764 Cabot Trail, Ingonish Beach; lunch around $10, dinner $10-24; ⊘7am-9pm Tue-Sat) By far the best breakfast stop (from $6) near the park and also a great stop for lunch and dinner. Sandwiches and French toast are made with thick fresh bread and the seafood plates are immense.

The specialty is the lobster angel-hair pasta with crab and mussels in a brandy cream sauce, but the lobster dinners get our vote for best value of its kind on the island.

White Point to Neil's Harbour

On your way south to Ingonish, leave the Cabot Trail to follow the rugged, windswept White Point Rd via Smelt Brook to the fishing villages of **White Point** and **Neil's Harbour**. These are gritty, hard-working towns, but there is some nice architecture, colorful homes, and illuminated, slightly disorienting views of Cape North to Meat Cove when the sun hits them at the end of the day. These are villages where there are as many fishing boats as houses – the area feels distinctly off the beaten tourist track.

Stay the night at homey **Two Tittle** (☑866-231-4087, 902-383-2817; www.twotittle.

com; 2119 White Point Rd, White Point; r $60-100; 🎧), which smells like supper and whose grandparent-like proprietors are in most evenings watching *Wheel of Fortune*. Don't miss the short but gorgeous walk out back to the Two Tittle Islands the B&B is named for and look out for whales and eagles.

The perfect stop for lunch or dinner is **Chowder House** (chowder from $6, suppers from $14; ⊘11am-8:30pm), out beyond the lighthouse at Neil's Harbour. It's famous for its chowder, but also serves great-value suppers of snow crab, lobster, mussels and more. There are plenty of dining locals, who like to chat with folks from far away while they splatter themselves with seafood juice.

Around St Ann's Bay

Settle into the artsy calm of winding roads, serene lakes, eagles soaring overhead and a never-ending collection of artists' workshops that dot the Cabot Trail like Easter eggs. Although you could skip the drive around St Ann's Bay and take a $5.50 ferry to Englishtown, you'd be missing a unique leg of the trail. If you explore deeper, you'll discover walking trails to waterfalls, and scenic vistas, Mi'kmaw culture and a decidedly interesting mishmash of characters.

◎ Sights & Activities

Don't leave the area without stopping in at an **artist's workshop** or two; you'll find pottery, leather and pewter workers, a crazy wonderful hat shop and more. The artists are easy to find – just keep an eye out for the signs along the main road.

Gaelic College of Celtic Arts & Crafts
CULTURAL BUILDING

(☑902-295-3411; www.gaeliccollege.edu; 51779 Cabot Trail; 5-day course incl lodging $705-805; ⊘9am-5pm Jun-Oct) At the end of St Ann's Bay, the college teaches Scottish Gaelic, bagpipe playing, Highland dancing, weaving and more. The college's **Great Hall of the Clans Museum** (admission $3) traces Celtic history from ancient times to the Highland clearances.

🍽 Sleeping & Eating

The Maven Gypsy B&B & Cottages
B&B $$

(☑902-929-2246; www.themavengypsy.com; 41682 Cabot Trail, Wreck Cove; r $92-117; ⊘Jun-Nov; 🎧🐾) At this adorable butter-yellow cottage three minutes' walk to the beach, enjoy friendly hosts and fresh baked goods for breakfast.

Chanterelle Country Inn & Cottages INN $$

(📞 902-929-2263, 866-277-0577; www.chanterelle-inn.com; 48678 Cabot Trail, North River; r $145-225, restaurant mains $20-28, 4-course set menu veg/nonveg $38/45; ⊙ May-Nov; 🎇) 🍴 Unparalleled as an environmentally friendly place to stay, the house and cabins are on 60 hectares overlooking rolling pastures and bucolic bliss. Meals (breakfast and dinner) are served on the screened-in porch. If you're not staying, you can reserve for dinner at the highly reputed restaurant.

Clucking Hen Deli & Bakery CAFE $

(📞 902-929-2501; 45073 Cabot Trail; mains $5-15; ⊙ 7am-7pm May-Oct) A sign reads 'no fowl moods in here.' Listen to the local 'hens' cluck away while you eat a delicious meal of homemade breads, soup and salad.

Bras d'Or Lake & Around

The highlands meet the lowlands along the shores of this inland saltwater sea, where eagles nest and puffins play. At 1099 sq km, it's the biggest lake in Nova Scotia and all but cleaves Cape Breton Island in two.

Baddeck

An old resort town in a pastoral setting, Baddeck is on the north shore of Bras d'Or Lake, halfway between Sydney and the Canso Causeway. It's the most popular place to stay for those who intend to do the Cabot Trail as a one-day scenic drive.

⊙ Sights & Activities

⭐ Alexander Graham Bell
National Historic Site MUSEUM
(📞 902-295-2069; www.parkscanada.gc.ca; 559 Chebucto St; adult/child $7.80/3.90; ⊙ 9am-6pm) The inventor of the telephone is buried near his summer home, Beinn Bhreagh, which is visible across the bay from Baddeck. The excellent museum of the Alexander Graham Bell National Historic Site, at the eastern edge of town, covers all aspects of his inventions and innovations.

Although nothing looks spectacular at first glance, it's the story of the man that will hook you. See medical and electrical devices, telegraphs, telephones, kites and seaplanes and then learn about how they all work.

Bras d'Or Lakes & Watershed
Interpretive Centre MUSEUM
(📞 902-295-1675; www.brasdor-conservation.com; 532 Chebucto St; admission by donation; ⊙ 11am-7pm Jun-Oct) This center explores the unique ecology of the enormous saltwater lake.

Amoeba SAILING

(www.amoebasailingtours.com; 2hr tours $25; ⊙ Jun-Oct) Classic schooner sailing tours on the Bras d'Or Lake bring you past Alexander Graham Bell's grand Beinn Bhreagh mansion and under soaring bald eagles.

🛏 Sleeping & Eating

Broadwater Inn & Cottages INN $$

(📞 902-295-1101, 877-818-3474; www.broadwater.baddeck.com; 975 Bay Rd; r $95-150, ste $225, cottages $105-225; ⊙ May-Nov; 🎇🐾) In a tranquil spot 1.5km east of Baddeck, this c 1830 home once belonged to JAD McCurdy, who worked with Alexander Graham Bell on early aircraft designs. The rooms in the inn are full of character, have bay views and are decorated with subtle prints and lots of flair. Modern self-contained cottages are set in the woods and are great for families.

Only the B&B rooms include breakfast.

Mother Gaelic's B&B $$

(📞 902-295-2885, 888-770-3970; www.mother-gaelics.com; 26 Water St; d $105, with shared bath $60-80; ⊙ May-Oct) Named for the owner's great-grandmother, who was a bootlegger patronized by Alexander Graham Bell, this sweet cottage opposite the waterfront has the feel of an uncluttered summer home.

Lynwood Inn INN $$

(📞 902-295-1995; www.lynwoodinn.com; 441 Shore Rd; r $100-230; 🎇) Rooms in this enor-

---

DON'T MISS

HIGHLAND VILLAGE MUSEUM

Explore Scottish heritage through the **Highland Village Museum** (📞 902-725-2272; http://highlandvillage.novas-cotia.ca; 4119 Hwy 223 Iona; adult/child $9/4; ⊙ 9:30am-5:30pm), a living history museum perched on a hilltop overlooking the Bras d'Or Lake. Costumed Scots demonstrate day-to-day activities of early settlers' lives and there are Celtic-inspired workshops from spring through fall – check the website for scheduling.

mous inn go far beyond the hotel standard, with Victorian wooden beds, muted color schemes and airy, spacious living spaces. There's a family-style restaurant downstairs that serves breakfast, lunch and dinner; breakfast is not included in room rates.

Highwheeler Cafe & Deli CAFE $
(486 Chebucto St; sandwiches $9; ⏲6am-8pm) This place bakes great bread and goodies (some gluten-free), and makes big tasty sandwiches (including vegetarian), quesadillas, soups and more. Finish off on the sunny deck licking an ice-cream cone. Box lunches for hikers are also available.

Baddeck Lobster Suppers SEAFOOD $$$
(☎902-925-3307; 17 Ross St; dinners $33; ⏲4-9pm Jun-Oct) In the former legion hall, this high production, arguably high-priced institution gets live lobsters in the pot then to you lickety-split. Meals come with just about everything and, although not spectacularly prepared, could fuel you for days.

☆ Entertainment

Baddeck Gathering Ceilidhs LIVE MUSIC
(☎902-295-2794; www.baddeckgathering.com; St Michael's Parish Hall, 8 Old Margaree Rd; adult/child $10/5; ⏲7:30pm Jul & Aug) Nightly fiddling and dancing. The parish hall is just opposite the VIC right in the middle of town.

ℹ Information

Visit Baddeck (www.visitbaddeck.com) Has maps, and info on tour operators, golf courses and more.

Visitors Information Centre (VIC; ☎902-295-1911; 454 Chebucto St; ⏲9am-7pm Jun-Sep)

Wagmatcook & Around

Stop in the Mi'kmaw community of Wagmatcook just west of Baddeck to visit the **Wagmatcook Culture & Heritage Centre** (☎902-295-2492, 902-295-2999; www.wagmatcook.com; Hwy 105; ⏲9am-8pm May-Oct, call for hours Nov-Apr). This somewhat empty cultural attraction offers an entryway into Mi'kmaw culture and history.

★**Bear on the Lake Guesthouse** (☎866-718-5253; www.bearonthelake.com; 10705 Hwy 105; dm/r $32/78; 📶), between Wagmatcook and the next town of Whycocomagh, is a fun place overlooking the lake. Everything is set up for backpacker bliss, from the drive-share board to the big sunny deck and inviting communal areas. This place is so popular that a whole other building of two dorm rooms and a kitchen was being built in a beautiful forest when we passed; there are also rooms with private sitting areas on the top level of the house. Owner Carmen is the perfect social soldier.

Also on Hwy 105, 12km southwest of Baddeck, is **Herring Choker Deli** (☎902-295-2275; 1958 Hwy 105; sandwiches $4.85; ⏲9am-5pm). Arguably the region's best pit stop, the deli serves gourmet sandwiches, soups and salads. Or drive a little farther to the **Dancing Goat** (6289 Cabot Trail, Northeast Margaree; sandwiches $8; ⏲8am-5pm Sat-Thu, to 8pm Fri), which is out of the way (it's 32 km from the Margaree Forks turnoff from Hwy 105), but worth the drive. Everything is homemade, most ingredients are local and hearty breakfasts are as good as you'll get on Cape Breton. Big sandwiches and salads can be eaten in or taken away for hiking. A second, more convenient location is planned in Inverness.

North Sydney

North Sydney is a small, friendly industrial town with few sites, though there are some excellent-value places to stay and eat.

Reserve accommodations if you're coming in on a late ferry or going out on an early one. Most North Sydney motels and B&Bs are open year-round, and it's understood that guests will arrive and leave at all hours. Most places to stay are along Queen St about 2km west of the ferry terminal.

🛏 Sleeping & Eating

Heritage Home B&B B&B $
(☎866-601-4515, 902-794-4815; www.bbcanada.com/3242.html; 110 Queen St; r $60-100; 📶🐾) This exceptionally well decorated and maintained Victorian home is an extremely elegant place to stay for the price. Breakfasts are home cooked and most rooms have private bathrooms.

A Boat to Sea B&B $$
(☎902-794-8326, 855-580-9540; www.aboattosea.com; 61 Queen St; r $95-105; 📶🐾) Right on the waterfront and surrounded by beautiful gardens (look for bald eagles), this grand home is decorated with stained glass and a quirky antiques collection. Relax on the waterfront patio and enjoy hearty breakfasts. There are only three rooms, so book ahead in high season.

★**Lobster Pound & Moore**　SEAFOOD $$

(☑902-794-2992; 161 Queen St; mains $15-35; ⊙lunch & dinner Tue-Sun) With the standard lobster here weighing in at almost a kilo (2lb), show up hungry because portions are massive. But big quantity doesn't affect the freshness, high quality and all around deliciousness of the food. Try Korean grilled steaks, seafood stew, or the ravioli stuffed with fresh lobster and topped with even more. Decor is chic bistro meets seafood shack.

★**Black Spoon**　MODERN CANADIAN $$

(☑902-241-3300; 320 Commercial St; mains $10-17; ⊙11am-8pm Mon-Thu, to 9pm Fri & Sat) At this hip black and beige restaurant, dine on local faves with a delectable twist, like breaded haddock with mango salsa, or the colorful grilled vegetable salad with goat cheese. There's also espresso drinks, cocktails and a reasonable wine list.

ⓘ Getting There & Away

Marine Atlantic ferry (☑800-341-7981; www.marine-atlantic.ca) services Newfoundland. Maritime Bus runs regular services to Halifax (one-way $68.50).

Bay Luxury Shuttle (☑855-673-8083; www.capebretonshuttle.ca) runs from Glace Bay to Halifax (one-way $65) via North Sydney, Sydney and Hwy 105; you can get it to stop or pick up along the way.

Sydney

POP 31,597

The second-biggest city in Nova Scotia and the only real city on Cape Breton Island, Sydney is the embattled core of the island's collapsed industrial belt. The now-closed steel mill and coal mines were the region's largest employers and now the city feels a bit empty, but there are some lovely older houses, especially in the North End residential areas where most of the B&Bs are found. Overall, the city is well serviced and you get more bang for your buck staying here as a base to explore Louisbourg and the Cabot Trail than you would in more scenic areas.

⊙ Sights

Downtown, Charlotte St is lined with stores and restaurants and there's a pleasant boardwalk along Esplanade.

The North End historic district has a gritty charm. There are eight buildings older

than 1802 in a two-block radius in North End. Three are open to the public.

St Patrick's Church Museum　HISTORIC BUILDING

(☑902-562-8237; 87 Esplanade; admission $2; ⊙9am-5pm) St Patrick's Church Museum is the oldest Catholic church on Cape Breton Island.

Cossit House　HISTORIC BUILDING

(☑902-539-7973; http://cossithouse.novascotia.ca; 75 Charlotte St; adult/concession $2/1; ⊙9am-5pm Mon-Sat, 1-5pm Sun Jun-Oct) The 1787 Cossit House is the oldest house in Sydney.

Jost Heritage House　HISTORIC BUILDING

(☑902-539-0366; 54 Charlotte St; admission $3; ⊙9am-5pm Mon-Sat, 1-5:30pm Sun) Just down the road from Cossit House, Jost Heritage House features a collection of model ships and an assortment of medicines used by an early-20th-century apothecary.

Cape Breton Centre for Heritage & Science　MUSEUM

(☑902-539-1572; 225 George St; admission $2; ⊙9am-5pm Mon-Sat) In the lyceum, this center explores the social and natural history of Cape Breton Island.

ⓒ Tours

Ghosts & Legends of Historic Sydney　WALKING TOUR

(☑902-539-1572; www.oldsydney.com; tours per person $12; ⊙7pm Tue & Wed Jul & Aug) This recommended walking tour leaves from St Patrick's Church Museum, does the loop of historic buildings and finishes with tea and scones at the lyceum.

🛏 Sleeping & Eating

Most establishments in Sydney are open year-round.

★**Colby House**　B&B $$

(☑902-539-4095; www.colbyhousebb.com; 10 Park St; r $100-120; 🐾) It's worth staying in Sydney for the affordable luxe of this exceptional B&B. The owner used to travel around Canada for work and she decided to offer everything she wished she'd had while on the road. The result is a mix of heritage and modern design, the softest sheets you can imagine, guest bathrobes, plenty of delicious-smelling soaps, chocolates next to the bed and so many other comfort-giving details we can hardly begin to list them.

Gathering House B&B   B&B **$$**
(📞866-539-7172, 902-539-7172; www.gathering-house.com; 148 Crescent St; r $75-150; 🖥🅿) This welcoming, ramshackle Victorian home is close to the heart of town. Staying here makes you feel like you're part of a big, lively family.

Flavors   MODERN CANADIAN **$$**
(📞902-562-6611; 6 Pitt St; lunch/dinner mains around $10/20; ⊙8:30am-8:30pm Mon-Sat; 🖊) What the setting lacks in feng shui – it has small tables and a strange street-side patio setup – the restaurant makes up for in delicious food prepared from locally sourced ingredients. Start with mains like maple-seared salmon or roast pork loin with wild-blueberry sauce, then finish with a homemade ice-cream sandwich with coconut cookies rolled in toffee bits. Vegan and gluten-free options are also available.

Allegro Grill   MODERN CANADIAN **$$**
(📞902-562-1623; 222 Charlotte St; mains $9-25; ⊙11am-3pm Mon-Fri, 5-9pm Tue-Fri, 11am-10pm Sat) Seafood and meat lovers should go here. This simple-looking spot serves not-so-simple specialties, including their famous, handmade turkey andouille sausages.

🍷 **Drinking & Entertainment**

A lot of touring bands make the trek to Sydney. Fiddlers and other traditional musicians from the west coast of the island perform here or at the Savoy in Glace Bay. Gigs are about $12.

Governors Pub & Eatery   PUB
(www.governorseatery.com; 233 Esplanade; mains $9-22; ⊙11am-11pm) Easily the most popular place in Sydney, stop in to mingle with the after-work crowd for drinks, dine on gourmet pub grub made with local ingredients, and stay on for live-music events like Wednesday night Irish jam sessions. Check the website for what's on.

ℹ️ **Information**

Visitors Information Centre (VIC; 20 Keltic Dr; ⊙8:30am-6pm) Off Kings Rd, just south of town.

ℹ️ **Getting There & Away**

The Sydney airport is none too busy. Air Canada flies between Sydney and Halifax, while Westjet has direct Toronto flights. **Air St-Pierre** (📞877-277-7765, 902-562-3140; www.airsaintpierre.com) flies to St-Pierre ($250 one-way, two

hours) on Thursdays and Sundays from early July to early September.

Bay Luxury Shuttle (p384) has shuttle services to Halifax.

Glace Bay

Glace Bay, 6km northeast of Sydney, would be just another fading coal town were it not for its exceptional **Cape Breton Miners' Museum** (📞902-849-4522; www.minersmuseum.com; 42 Birkley St; tour & mine visit adult/child $12/10, restaurant mains $8-14; ⊙museum 10am-6pm, restaurant 11am-8pm); it's off South St less than 2km east from the town center. The highlight of this museum is the adventure under the seafloor to visit closed-down mines with a retired miner as a guide (it's your lucky day if you get Abbie). The museum's **restaurant** is highly recommended and offers seafood, sandwiches and burgers; there's a daily lunch buffet from noon to 2pm.

The town's grand 1920 **Savoy Theatre** (📞902-842-1577; www.savoytheatre.com; 116 Commercial St) is the region's premier entertainment venue.

Louisbourg

Louisbourg, 37km southeast of Sydney, is famous for its historic fortress. The town itself has plenty of soul, with its working fishing docks, old-timers and a friendly vibe.

◎ **Sights & Activities**

Starting from the trailhead at the lighthouse at the end of Havenside Rd, a rugged 6km **trail** follows the coast over bogs, barrens and pre-Cambrian polished granite. Bring your camera to capture the views back toward the fortress at the national historic site.

Louisbourg National Historic Site   HISTORIC SITE
(📞902-733-2280; 259 Park Service Rd; adult/child $17.60/8.80; ⊙9am-5:30pm) Budget a full day to explore this extraordinary historic site that faithfully re-creates Fortress Louisbourg as it was in 1744, right down to the people – costumed thespians take their characters and run with them. Built to protect French interests in the region, it was also a base for cod fishing and an administrative capital. Louisbourg was worked on continually from 1719 to about 1745. The British took it in a 46-day siege in 1745 but

it would change hands twice more. In 1760, after British troops under the command of General James Wolfe took Québec City, the walls of Louisbourg were destroyed and the city was burned to the ground.

In 1961, with the closing of many Cape Breton Island coal mines, the federal government funded the largest historical reconstruction in Canadian history as a way to generate employment, resulting in 50 buildings open to visitors. Workers in period dress take on the lives of typical fort inhabitants.

Free guided tours around the site are offered throughout the day. Travelers with mobility problems can ask for a pass to drive their car up to the site; there are ramps available to access most buildings. Be prepared for lots of walking, and bring a sweater and raincoat even if it's sunny when you start out. There's also an ever-changing array of tours and activities on offer, from nighttime candlelit walks to period dinner theater; check the website for what's on each season.

Though the scale of the reconstruction is massive, three-quarters of Louisbourg is still in ruins. The 2.5km **Ruins Walk** guides you through the untouched terrain and out to the Atlantic coast. A short **interpretive walk** opposite the visitors center discusses the relationship between the French and the Mi'kmaq and offers some great views of the whole site.

Three restaurants in the site serve food typical of the time. **Hotel de la Marine** and the adjacent **L'Épée Royale** (grilled cod with soup $14, 3-course meal $20) are where sea captains and prosperous merchants would dine on fine china with silver cutlery. Servers in period costume also dish out grub at **Grandchamps House** (meals $9-15), a favorite of sailors and soldiers. Wash down beans and sausage with hot buttered rum ($4). Otherwise buy a 1kg ration ($4) of soldiers' bread at the Destouches Bakery. There's also a small coffee shop between the restaurants serving hot drinks and a few snacks.

🛏 Sleeping & Eating

Stacey House B&B B&B $
(☑ 902-733-2317; www.bbcanada.com/thestaceyhouse; 7438 Main St; r $60-90; ☺ Jun-Oct; 🛜) Interesting knickknacks, such as antique teddy bears, dolls and model ships, are harmoniously placed throughout this pretty house.

★ Cranberry Cove Inn INN $$
(☑ 800-929-0222, 902-733-2171; www.cranberrycoveinn.com; 12 Wolfe St; r $105-160; ☺ May-Nov; 🛜) From the dark pink facade to the period-perfect interior of mauves, dusty blues and antique lace, you'll be transported back in time through rose-colored glasses at this stunning B&B. Each room is different and several have Jacuzzis and fireplaces.

Spinning Wheel B&B B&B $$
(☑ 902-733-3332, 866-272-3222; www.spinningwheelbedandbreakfast.com; 5 Riverdale St; d with shared bathroom $65-75, d with private bathroom $90; ☺ May-Nov; 🛜) Try this place if everything else in town is full, which it will be during high season. It's not a looker, but the cleanliness, friendly hosts and made-to-order breakfasts more than make up for it.

Grubstake CANADIAN $$
(☑ 902-733-2308; 7499 Main St; lunch mains $8-17, dinner mains $16-32; ☺ lunch & dinner) This informal restaurant is the best place to eat in town. The menu features burger platters at lunch and pastas and fresh seafood for dinner.

★ Beggar's Banquet SEAFOOD $$$
(☑ 888-374-8439; Point of View Suites, 15 Commercial St Extension; meals $38; ☺ 6-8pm Jul-Sep) Finally, here's a chance for you to get into period costume and gorge on a feast of local seafood in a replicated 18th-century tavern. There's a choice of four delicious and copious mains including crab and lobster. It's located at the Point of View Suites.

☆ Entertainment

Louisbourg Playhouse THEATER
(☑ 902-733-2996; 11 Lower Warren St; tickets from $15; ☺ 8pm-late Jun-Aug) A cast of young, local musicians entertain all summer long in this 17th-century-style theater.

❶ Information

Tourist Information Office (☑ 902-733-2720; 7535 Main St; ☺ 9am-7pm) Right in the center of town.

EASTERN SHORE

If you want to escape into the fog, away from summer tourist crowds, this is the place to do it. Running from Cape Canso at the extreme eastern tip of the mainland to the outskirts of Dartmouth, the Eastern Shore has no large towns and the main road is almost as convoluted as the rugged shoreline it follows. If you want to experience wilderness and are willing to hike or kayak, this is your heaven.

Guysborough

Guysborough was settled by United Empire Loyalists after the American Revolution. Over the years it became another particularly scenic yet economically challenged Eastern Shore village until Glynn Williams and his brand Authentic Seacoasts came to town. With an estimated $8 million investment, the town is now home to a charming waterfront golf course, a craft brewery, a fair-trade coffee company, a bakery-cafe, Debarres Manor inn and the Rare Bird Pub; a huge distillery was planned for construction when we passed. Not only has Guysborough become an activity-filled holiday hamlet, but the community has jobs they may have never had otherwise. Meanwhile, the old-time charm and natural beauty of the place has remained wonderfully intact.

◉ Sights & Activities

The 26km **Guysborough Trail**, part of the Trans Canada Trail (TCT), is great for biking and hiking and the sheltered coves beg to be kayaked.

Old Court House Museum MUSEUM
(☑902-533-4008; 106 Church St; ⊙9am-5pm Mon-Fri, 10am-4pm Sat & Sun) FREE The Old Court House Museum displays artifacts related to early farming and housekeeping. It also offers tourist information and guides to hiking trails.

🛏 Sleeping & Eating

Boylston Provincial Park CAMPGROUND $
(☑902-533-3326; www.parks.gov.ns.ca; off Hwy 16; campsites $18) The 36 shaded sites are never all taken. From the picnic area on the highway below the campground, a footbridge leads to a small island on the coast about 12km north of Guysborough.

★**Desbarres Manor** INN $$$
(☑902-533-2099; www.desbarresmanor.com; 90 Church St; r from $199; 🖥) This tastefully renovated 1830 grand mansion with massive, opulent rooms is reason enough to come to Guysborough. With extraordinary service, fine dining and a range of activities on of-

fer including canoeing, walking and golfing, it's one of the most luxurious properties in Nova Scotia.

Rare Bird Pub PUB $$
(☑902-533-2128; www.rarebirdpub.com; 80 Main St; mains $9-15; ⊙11am-2am) The Bird is a quintessential stop for a swig of local ale, a pot of mussels, rocking live east coast music on weekends and fiddlers on the wharf below on Wednesdays. Check the website for schedules.

Canso

Mainland North America's oldest seaport is a cluster of boxy fishermen's houses on a treeless bank of Chedabucto Bay. Long dependent on the fishery, Canso has been decimated by emigration and unemployment since the northern cod stocks collapsed around 1990.

◉ Sights & Activities

The cape surrounding the village has some very off-the-beaten-track opportunities for hiking, kayaking, bird-watching and surfing.

Grassy Island National Historic Site HISTORIC SITE
(☑902-366-3136; 1465 Union St; admission $3; ⊙10am-6pm Jun-Sep) An interpretive center on the waterfront tells the story of Grassy Island National Historic Site, which lies just offshore and can be visited by boat until 4pm. In 1720 the British built a small fort to offset the French who had their headquarters in Louisbourg, but it was totally destroyed in 1744. Among the ruins today, there's a self-guided **hiking trail** with eight interpretive stops explaining the history of the area. The boat to Grassy Island departs from the center upon demand, weather permitting.

Whitman House Museum MUSEUM
(☑902-366-2170; 1297 Union St; ⊙9am-5pm Jun-Sep) FREE The **tourist office** is at the 1885 Whitman House Museum, which holds reminders of the town's history and offers a good view from the widow's walk on the roof.

Chapel Gully Trail HIKING
This is a 10km boardwalk and hiking trail along an estuary and out to the coast. It begins near the lighthouse on the hill behind

WORTH A TRIP

SABLE ISLAND

This ever-shifting, 44km-long spit of sand lies some 300km southeast of Halifax and has caused more than 350 documented shipwrecks. But what makes Sable Island most famous is that it's home to one of the world's only truly wild horse populations.

The first 60 ancestors of today's Sable Island horses were shipped to the island in 1760 when Acadians were being deported from Nova Scotia by the British. The Acadians were forced to abandon their livestock and it appears that Boston merchant ship owner Thomas Hancock helped himself to their horses then put them to pasture on Sable Island to keep it low profile. The horses that survived became wild.

Today the island works as a research center; scientists come every year, mostly to study the birds, seals and horses. Since 2003, natural gas fields run by Exxon have been working only 10km from the island but, so far, there has been little environmental conflict.

It's complicated and expensive but not impossible to visit Sable Island as a layperson – in fact, about 50 to 100 adventurous souls make it there each year. Contact **Sable Island Station** (📞902-453-9350; gforbes@ca.inter.net), in conjunction with Environment Canada, for information about where to get necessary permissions and independently arrange transport.

---

the hospital at the eastern end of Canso. A large map is posted at the trailhead.

✦✦ Festivals & Events

★ **Stan Rogers Folk Festival** MUSIC
(www.stanfest.com; ☉1st weekend Jul) Most people who come to Canso come for the Stan Rogers Folk Festival, the biggest festival in Nova Scotia. It quadruples the town's population, with six stages showcasing folk, blues and traditional musicians from around the world. Accommodations are pretty much impossible to get unless you reserve a year ahead. Locals set up 1000 campsites for the festival; check the website for details and try to get a campsite away from the festival site if sleep is a priority.

🛏 Sleeping

Last Port Motel MOTEL $$
(📞902-366-2400; www.lastportmotel.ca; 10 Hwy 16; r $80-100) The only place to stay is the basic Last Port Motel just out of town.

Sherbrooke

The pleasant little town of Sherbrooke, 123km west of Canso and 63km south of Antigonish, is overshadowed by its historic site, which is about the same size.

The local tourist office is at **Sherbrooke Village** (📞902-522-2400; http://sherbrookevillage.novascotia.ca; Hwy 7; adult/child $10.75/4.75; ☉9:30am-5:30pm Jun-Oct), which re-creates everyday life from 125 years ago through

buildings, demonstrations and costumed workers. There are 25 buildings to visit in this living museum that effectively helps its visitors step back in time.

On a quiet farm, **Days Ago B&B** (📞866-522-2811, 902-522-2811; www.bbcanada.com/daysago; 15 Cameron Rd; r $70-80, chalet $80-90; 📶) will lull you with its slower pace. There's a sunporch for sitting on, or you can take out a kayak. Rooms in the house have a shared bathroom, while the loft-style chalet has its own bathroom.

You'll find coffee and good food at godsend **Village Coffee Grind** (sandwiches around $9; ☉8am-6pm Tue-Sat, 10am-2pm Sun) on the town's minuscule main drag.

Taylor Head Provincial Park

A little-known scenic highlight of Nova Scotia, this spectacular **park** (📞902-772-2218; www.parks.gov.ns.ca; 20140 Hwy 7) encompasses a peninsula jutting 6.5km into the Atlantic. On one side is a long, very fine, sandy beach fronting a protected bay. Some 17km of hiking trails cut through the spruce and fir forests. The **Headland Trail** is the longest at 8km round-trip and follows the rugged coastline to scenic views at Taylor Head. The shorter **Bob Bluff Trail** is a 3km round-trip hike to a bluff with good views. In spring you'll see colorful wildflowers, and this is a great bird-watching venue. Pack the picnic cooler and plan on spending a full day hiking, lounging and, if you can brave the cool water, swimming.

Tangier

About 10km southwest of Taylor Head Provincial Park, Tangier is one of the best settings for kayaking in the Maritimes. Highly recommended **Coastal Adventures Sea Kayaking** (✆902-772-2774; www.coastaladventures.com; off Hwy 7; ☉Jun-Sep) offers introductions to sea-kayaking (half-/full-day $75/115), rentals (single/double kayaks $45/65) and guided trips. The establishment also has a cozy, excellent-value B&B, **Paddlers Retreat** (s $50, d $60-85; ☉mid-Jun–mid-Oct; 🛜🍴).

Murphy's Camping on the Ocean (✆902-772-2700; www.murphyscampingontheocean.ca; 291 Murphy's Rd; campsites/RV sites $27/39, trailer rental $70-90; ☉mid-May–mid-Oct; 🛜🍴) gets you out of your tent and into the water to collect mussels; you eat your labors at a beach barbecue to the music of yarns told by Brian the owner. There are RV sites, RV rental, secluded tent sites and a very rudimentary room above the dock that can sleep four people. Boat rental is $75 per hour and there's also drop-off and pickup services for camping on the islands.

Don't miss a snack stop at **J Willy Krauch & Sons Ltd** (✆902-772-2188; 35 Old Mooseland Rd, off Hwy 7; ☉10am-5pm Mon-Fri, 9am-5pm Sat & Sun), famed for making the tastiest smoked fish in the province. Choose from a variety of salmon, eel, mackerel and more – don't forget to bring some crackers.

Charlotte Lake to Jedore

The tiny **Fisherman's Life Museum** (✆902-889-2053; http://fishermanslife.novascotia.ca; 58 Navy Pool Loop; adult/child $4/2.75; ☉10am-5pm Jun-Oct), 45km toward Halifax from Tangier, should really be renamed. The man of the house used to row 16km to get to his fishing grounds, leaving his wife and 13 daughters at home. The museum really captures women's domestic life of the early 20th century. Costumed local guides offer tea and hospitality.

Some 6km down the highway towards Halifax, **Memory Lane Heritage Village** (5435 Clam Harbour Rd, Lake Charlotte; adult/child $6/4; ☉11am-4pm Jun-Oct) re-creates the 1940s via antique cars, a farmstead with animals (great for kids), mid-century-style meals and displays of then new fangled (but now old) washing machines, appliances and more.

New Brunswick

Includes ➡

Best Places to Eat

➡ Rossmount Inn Restaurant (p406)

➡ North Head Bakery (p412)

➡ East Coast Bistro (p416)

Best Places to Stay

➡ Carriage House Inn (p395)

➡ Algonquin Resort (p406)

➡ Inn at Whale Cove (p411)

➡ Mahogany Manor (p415)

Why Go?

In the early 20th century, New Brunswick was a Very Big Deal. Millionaire businesspeople, Major League Baseball players and US presidents journeyed here to fish salmon from its silver rivers and camp at rustic lodges in its deep primeval forests. But over the decades, New Brunswick slipped back into relative obscurity. Today, some joke that it's the 'drive-through province,' as vacationers tend to hot-foot it to its better-known neighbors Prince Edward Island (PEI) and Nova Scotia.

But the unspoiled wilderness is still here. There are rivers for fly-fishing, coastal islands for kayaking, snowy mountains for skiing and quaint Acadian villages for exploring. So do yourself a favor, and don't just drive through. Prince Edward Island will still be there when you're done, we promise.

When to Go
Fredericton

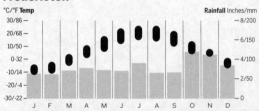

Jul–Sep St Andrews by-the-Sea bustles with crowds of whale-watchers.

Aug Acadians unleash their Franco-Canadian spirit for the Festival Acadien in Caraquet.

Nov–Mar Cross-country skiers hit the groomed trails of Fundy National Park.

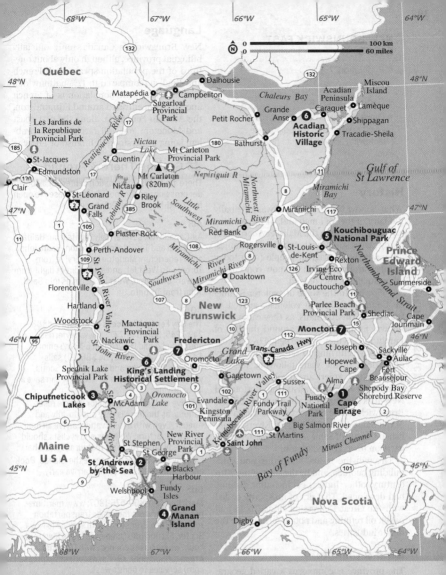

New Brunswick Highlights

❶ Feel the power of the highest tides in the world at **Cape Enrage** (p420).

❷ Discover the history of picturesque **St Andrews by-the-Sea** (p403).

❸ Dip your canoe paddle in the **Chiputneticook Lakes** (p402).

❹ Breathe in the fresh sea air and unwind on peaceful, isolated **Grand Manan Island** (p410).

❺ Stretch out on the sandy beach or splash in the lagoon at **Kouchibouguac National Park** (p426).

❻ Live history at **King's Landing Historical Settlement** (p398) and **Acadian Historic Village** (p429).

❼ Taste the delicacies at weekly farmers markets in **Fredericton** (p396) and **Moncton** (p423).

NEW BRUNSWICK FAST FACTS

➡ Population: 751,000

➡ Area: 73,400 sq km

➡ Capital: Fredericton

➡ Quirky fact: Home to the world's biggest fake lobster (Shediac), axe (Nackawic) and fiddlehead (Plaster Rock).

History

What is now New Brunswick was originally the land of the Mi'kmaq and, in the western and southern areas, the Maliseet Aboriginals. Many places still bear their aboriginal names, although the Aboriginal people (who today number around 17,000) are now concentrated on small pockets of land.

Following in the wake of explorer Samuel de Champlain, French colonists arrived in the 1600s. The Acadians, as they came to be known, farmed the area around the Bay of Fundy. In 1755 they were expelled by the English, many returning to settle along the Bay of Chaleur. In the years following, the outbreak of the American Revolution brought an influx of British Loyalists from Boston and New York seeking refuge in the wilds of New Brunswick. These refugees settled the valleys of the Saint John and St Croix Rivers, established the city of Saint John and bolstered the garrison town at Fredericton.

Through the 1800s, lumbering and shipbuilding boomed, and by the start of the 20th century, other industries, including fishing, had developed. That era of prosperity ended with the Great Depression. Today, pulp and paper, oil refining and potato farming are the major industries.

Land & Climate

The province encompasses a varied geography of moist, rocky coastal areas, temperate inland river valleys and a heavily forested and mountainous interior. There are four distinct seasons. Summers are generally mild with occasional hot days. The Fundy shore is prone to fog, particularly in the spring and early summer. The primary tourist season lasts from late June to early September. Many tourist facilities (beaches, organized tours and some accommodations in resort areas) shut down for the remainder of the year.

Language

New Brunswick is Canada's only officially bilingual province, although only about one-third of the population speaks both French and English (compared to 17% nationwide). Around 34% of the population is of French ancestry, concentrated around Edmundston, the Acadian Peninsula, along the east coast and Moncton. You will rarely have a problem being understood in English or French.

ℹ Getting There & Around

There are tourist information centers at all border crossings and in most towns. These are open from mid-May to mid-October only.

AIR

Air Canada has several daily flights from Halifax, Montréal and Toronto into Moncton, Saint John and Fredericton. Moncton has service from Toronto on WestJet; and a daily direct flight from Newark on United. WestJet also flies into Saint John from Toronto.

BOAT

The Bay Ferries' **Princess of Acadia** (☑888-249-7245, 506-649-7777; www.bayferries.com; adult/child 0-5yr/child 6-13yr/senior $43/5/28/33, car/bicycle $86/10) sails between Saint John and Digby, Nova Scotia, year-round. The three-hour crossing can save a lot of driving.

Arrive early or call ahead for vehicle reservations, as the ferry is very busy in July and August. Even with a reservation, arrive an hour before departure. Walk-ons and cyclists should be OK any time. There's a restaurant and a bar.

Fundy Isles ferries also serve the islands. Book ahead where possible and/or arrive early.

BUS

Maritime (☑1-800-575-1807; www.maritimebus.com) services the major transportation routes in New Brunswick, with service to Nova Scotia, PEI and into Québec as far as Rivière-du-Loup, where buses connect with **Orléans Express** (☑888-999-3977; www.orleansexpress.com) services to points west.

REGIONAL DRIVING DISTANCES

Edmundston to Saint John: 375km

Fredericton to Miramichi: 180km

St Andrews by-the-Sea to Moncton: 254km

CAR & MOTORCYCLE

For drivers, the main access points into New Brunswick are Edmundston, Maine, Houlton, Nova Scotia or PEI. If you're going to PEI, there's no charge to use the Confederation Bridge eastbound from Cape Jourmain – you pay on the way back. Traffic is generally light, although crossing the Maine border usually means a delay at customs.

TRAIN

VIA Rail (☑ 888-842-7245; www.viarail.ca) operates passenger services between Montréal and Halifax ($219, 15½ hours, daily except Tuesday), with stops in Campbellton, Miramichi and Moncton.

FREDERICTON

POP 50,600

This sleepy provincial capital does quaint very well. The St John River curves lazily through Fredericton, past the stately government buildings on the waterfront and the university on the hill. Its neatly mowed, tree-lined banks are dotted with fountains, walking paths and playing fields. On warm weekends, 'The Green,' as it's known, looks like something out of a watercolor painting – families strolling, kids kicking soccer balls, couples picnicking.

On a flat, broad curve in the riverbank, the small downtown commercial district is a neat grid of redbrick storefronts. Surrounding it are quiet residential streets lined with tall, graceful elms shading beautifully maintained Georgian and Victorian houses and abundant flower beds. A canopy of trees spreads over the downtown, pierced here and there by church spires.

⊙ Sights

The two-block strip along Queen St between York and Regent Sts is known as the Historic Garrison District. In 1875, Fredericton became the capital of the newly formed province of New Brunswick, and the garrison housed British soldiers for much of the late 18th and early 19th centuries. It's now a lively multi-use area with impressive stone architecture.

Old Government House   HISTORIC BUILDING
(www.gnb.ca/lg/ogh; 51 Woodstock Rd; ⊙10am-4pm Mon-Sat, noon-4pm Sun) **FREE** This magnificent sandstone palace was erected for the British governor in 1826. The representative of the queen moved out in 1893 after the

province refused to continue paying his expenses, and during most of the 20th century the complex was a Royal Canadian Mounted Police (RCMP) headquarters. It now evocatively captures a moment in time with tours led by staff in period costume. New Brunswick's current lieutenant governor (Graydon Nicholas, a member of the Maliseet Nation and the first aboriginal lawyer in Atlantic Canada) lives on the 3rd floor.

★**Beaverbrook Art Gallery**   MUSEUM
(www.beaverbrookartgallery.org; 703 Queen St; adult/child $10/5, pay as you wish Thu after 5pm; ⊙10am-5pm Mon-Wed, Fri & Sat, to 9pm Thu, noon-5pm Sun) This relatively small but excellent gallery was one of Lord Beaverbrook's gifts to the town. The exceptional collection includes works by international heavyweights and is well worth an hour or so. Among others you will see Constable, Dali, Gainsborough and Turner, Canadian artists Tom Thompson, Emily Carr and Cornelius Kreighoff as well as changing contemporary exhibits of Atlantic art.

Officers' Square   HISTORIC SITE
(www.downtownfredericton.ca; btwn Carleton & Regent Sts; ⊙ceremonies 11am & 4pm daily & 7pm Tue & Thu Jul & Aug) Once the military parade ground, the Garrison District's Officers' Square now hosts a full-uniform changing of the guard ceremony in summertime. Also in summer the Calithumpians Outdoor Summer Theatre performs daily at 12:15pm weekdays and 2pm weekends. The free historical skits are laced with humor. Summer evenings bring jazz, Celtic and rock concerts – see the website for schedules.

York Sunbury Historical Museum   MUSEUM
(☑506-455-6041; www.yorksunburymuseum.com; Officers' Sq; adult/student $5/2; ⊙10am-5pm Apr-Nov, by appointment Dec-Mar) Housed in the 19th-century officers' quarters on the west side of Officers' Sq, this museum's collection preserves the city's past. Displays feature military pieces used by local regiments and by British and German armies from the Boer War and both world wars, furniture from a Loyalist sitting room and a Victorian bedroom, and aboriginal and Acadian artifacts. Don't miss the Coleman Frog, a 42lb creature of Fredericton legend. Real or plaster? Decide for yourself.

Soldiers' Barracks   HISTORIC BUILDING
(cnr Queen & Carleton Sts; ⊙10am-5pm Tue-Sun) **FREE** See how the common soldier lived in

NEW BRUNSWICK FREDERICTON

Fredericton

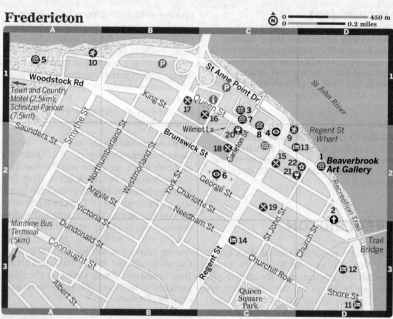

Fredericton

◎ Top Sights

1 Beaverbrook Art Gallery D2

◎ Sights

2 Christ Church Cathedral....................... D2
3 Guard House...C1
4 Officers' Square C2
5 Old Government House A1
6 Old Loyalist Burial Ground C2
7 Soldiers' Barracks C1
8 York Sunbury Historical Museum C2

⊕ Activities, Courses & Tours

9 Lighthouse on the Green C2
10 Small Craft Aquatic Centre A1

⊟ Sleeping

11 Brennan's B&B..D3
12 Carriage House Inn.................................D3

13 Crowne Plaza Lord
Beaverbrook C2
14 Fredericton International
Hostel...C3

⊗ Eating

15 Blue Door..C2
16 Caribbean Flavas.....................................C1
17 Chez Riz B1
18 Second Cup...C2
19 WW Boyce Farmers
Market..C2

⊙ Drinking & Nightlife

20 Boom! Nightclub C2
21 Lunar Rogue Pub......................................D2

⊙ Entertainment

22 Playhouse..D2

---

the 1820s (lousy food, too much drink) at this grim stone barracks in the Garrison District. The adjacent 1828 **Guard House** was also unpleasant (plank beds, thin straw mattresses), but the conditions for those held in cells were truly nasty. Threaten your kids! The lower section of the barracks is now used as artisan studios.

Old Loyalist Burial Ground CEMETERY
(Brunswick St; ⊙ 8am-9pm) This Loyalist cemetery, dating back to 1784, is an atmospheric, thought-provoking history lesson of its own, revealing large families and kids dying tragically young. The Loyalists arrived from the 13 colonies after the American Revolution of 1776.

Christ Church Cathedral   CHURCH
(www.christchurchcathedral.com; 168 Church St)
Built in 1853, this cathedral is a fine early
example of 19th-century Gothic Revival style
and has exquisite stained glass. It was modeled after St Mary's in Snettisham, Norfolk.

🏄 Activities

Small Craft Aquatic Centre   BOATING
(off Woodstock Rd; boat hire per hour $10; ⊘ May-
Sep) This small center, on the St John River
beside Old Government House, rents out
canoes, kayaks and rowboats. On offer are
weekly passes, guided canoe and kayak
tours, one-hour to three-day river ecology
trips, and instruction in either canoeing or
kayaking.

Lighthouse on the Green   HIKING, BIKING
(cnr Regent St & St Anne Point Dr; ⊘ 9am-6pm)
There are 70km of recreational trails around
town and along the river that either begin
or intersect at this riverfront lighthouse,
which doubles as an info center and small
museum. Pick up a map inside. In summer,
enjoy weekend concerts and Wednesday
night yoga on the lighthouse deck.

☞ Tours

Heritage Walking Tours   WALKING TOUR
(⊘ 10am, 2:30pm & 5pm daily Jul & Aug, 4pm Jun
& Sep-Nov) FREE Enthusiastic young people
wearing historic costumes lead good, free
hour-long tours of the river, the government
district or the Historic Garrison District, departing from City Hall.

Haunted Hikes   WALKING TOUR
(www.calithumpians.com; 796a Queen St; adult/
child $14/9; ⊘ 9:15pm Mon-Sat Jul & Aug) Actors
masquerading as ghoulish thespians run entertaining Fredericton ghost tours.

🎉 Festivals & Events

Notable Acts Summer Theatre
Festival   THEATER
(www.nbacts.com; ⊘ end Jul) Showcases new
and noted playwrights with street and theater presentations.

Harvest Jazz & Blues Festival   MUSIC
(www.harvestjazzandblues.com; ⊘ Sep) This
weeklong event transforms the downtown
area into the 'New Orleans of the North.'
Jazz, blues and Dixieland performers arrive
from across North America.

Silver Wave Film Festival   FILM
(www.swfilmfest.com; ⊘ early Nov) Three days
of New Brunswick, Canadian and international films and lectures organized by the
NB Filmmakers' Cooperative.

🛏 Sleeping

There are a number of budget and midrange
motels on the Fredericton Bypass and its
parallel Prospect St (southwest of town).

Fredericton International Hostel   HOSTEL $
(☎ 506-450-4417; fredericton@hihostels.ca; 621
Churchill Row; dm members/nonmembers $30/35;
⊘ office 8am-noon & 6-10pm; ⊜ @) This dark,
rambling residence hall is part university
student housing, part travelers' lodging. The
big, slightly creepy basement has a laundry
and pool tables.

Town and Country Motel   MOTEL $
(☎ 506-454-4223; 967 Woodstock Rd; s & d $90, tw
$100; ❋) In a quiet riverside setting, you'll
find sparkling clean and bright modern
rooms with kitchenettes and big picture
windows framing a gorgeous view of the
river. It's on the walking/cycling path 3km
west from the city center.

★ Carriage House Inn   B&B $$
(☎ 506-452-9924, 800-267-6068; www.carriage-
house-inn.net; 230 University Ave; r incl breakfast $105-139; ⊜ ❋ 🛜) In a shady Victorian
neighborhood near the Green, this beautifully restored 1875 Queen Anne was built
for a lumber baron and former Fredericton mayor. The grand common room has
polished hardwood floors, antiques, comfy
sofas, fireplaces and a grand piano. Upstairs, the guest rooms have high ceilings,
four-posters, period wallpapers and vintage artwork. There is a deep veranda for
lounging.

Brennan's B&B   B&B $$
(☎ 506-455-7346; www.bbcanada.com/3892.
html; 146 Waterloo Row; r incl breakfast $95-135;
⊜ ❋ @) Built for a wealthy merchant family in 1885, this turreted white riverfront
mansion is now a handsome four-room
B&B. The better rooms have hardwood
floors and water views.

Crowne Plaza Lord Beaverbrook   HOTEL $$$
(☎ 506-455-3371; www.cpfredericton.com; 659
Queen St; r $120-270; ❋ 🛜) Always bustling
with weddings, conventions and business
travelers, this 1948 downtown hotel is another one of Lord Beaverbrook's legacies to

the city. The lobby has a touch of vintage glamour, and the 168 rooms are modern and comfortable. Check out the beaver mosaics on the facade.

✗ Eating

For a small city, Fredericton offers a wide, cosmopolitan cross section of restaurants, most in the walkable downtown. Fredericton has also embraced coffee culture in several appealing venues.

WW Boyce Farmers Market   MARKET $
(www.boycefarmersmarket.com; 665 George St; ☺6am-1pm Sat) This Fredericton institution is great for picking up fresh fruit, vegetables, meat, cheese, handicrafts, dessert and flowers. Many of the 150 or so stalls recall the city's European heritage, with everything from German-style sausages to French duck pâtés to British marmalade. There is also a restaurant where Frederictonians queue to chat and people-watch.

Second Cup   CAFE $
(www.secondcup.com; Kings Place Mall, 440 King St; snacks $3-7; ☺6:30am-9pm Mon-Sat, 9am-10pm Sun; ☺) Warm lighting, world music and the aroma of fresh-roasted coffee beans draw a loyal clientele of office workers, passers-by and aspiring novelists toiling away on their laptops.

Caribbean Flavas   CARIBBEAN $$
(www.caribbeanflavas.ca; 123 York St; mains $16-25; ☺11:30am-2:30pm Tue-Fri & 4:30-8:30pm Tue-Sat) A bright nook dishing up the tastes and colors of the Caribbean. Great for a casual, flavorful meal. BYOB.

Chez Riz   INDIAN $$
(☎506-454-9996; 366 Queen St; mains $16-23; ☺11:30am-2:30pm Mon-Fri, 5-9pm Mon-Sat) Delicious Indian and Pakistani cuisine in a darkly stylish, romantically lit cave of a place.

Schnitzel Parlour   GERMAN $$
(☎506-450-2520; www.facklemanschocolateheaven.com; 3136 Woodstock Rd; mains $19-24; ☺5:30-10pm Tue-Sat) Specializing in hearty, old-fashioned German fare, this cozy countryside restaurant has richly spiced goulash (the secret ingredient is chocolate), wild-boar stew and six kinds of schnitzel on homemade *spätzle* (soft egg noodles). BYOB. The on-site **Chocolaterie Fackleman** (open from noon) sells truffles and traditional central European tortes. The

restaurant is about 8km west of town on Woodstock Rd.

Blue Door   FUSION $$$
(☎506-455-2583; www.thebluedoor.ca; 100 Regent St; mains $14-28; ☺11:30am-2pm Tue-Fri, 5-9pm Mon-Sat) This local hot spot serves upscale fusion dishes such as Gorgonzola bruschetta, maple-miso cod and chicken curry in a dim, urban-chic dining room. Retro cocktails such as Singapore slings and Harvey Wallbangers are real favorites.

🍷 Drinking & Nightlife

In the evenings, the bars, pubs and rooftop patios of King and Queen Sts come alive.

Lunar Rogue Pub   PUB
(www.lunarrogue.com; 625 King St; ☺10am-late Mon-Sat, 11am-10pm Sun) This jolly locals' joint has a good beer selection and a fine assortment of single malts. The patio is wildly popular during the warmer weather.

Boom! Nightclub   CLUB
(www.boomnightclub.ca; 474 Queen St; cover charge $5-8; ☺8pm-late Wed-Sun) A hip gay bar and dance club welcoming folks of all stripes.

☆ Entertainment

For the scoop on concerts, art gallery openings and other happenings around town, pick up a copy of *here*, a free entertainment weekly available all over town.

Outdoor Summer Concerts   LIVE MUSIC
(www.tourismfredericton.ca) FREE In summer, downtown venues from Officers' Sq to the Lighthouse on the Green feature live local music ranging from highland bagpipes and drums to country and blues. Check the website for schedules.

Playhouse   THEATER
(www.theplayhouse.nb.ca; 686 Queen St) The Playhouse stages concerts, theater, ballet and shows throughout the year.

ℹ Information

Dr Everett Chalmers Hospital (☎506-452-5400; 700 Priestman St) Located 2km south of the city center.

Fredericton Public Library (12 Carleton St; ☺10am-5pm Mon, Tue, Thu & Sat, to 9pm Wed & Fri) Free internet access is first-come, first-served.

Main Post Office (☎506-444-8602; 570 Queen St; ☺8am-5pm Mon-Fri) General

NEW BRUNSWICK ITINERARIES

Four Days

Spend the first day at **King's Landing Historical Settlement** (p398). Land in **Fredericton** on Saturday morning – peruse the stalls at the **WW Boyce Farmers Market** (p396), and nip into the **Beaverbrook Art Gallery** (p393) to see a few old masters and contemporary Canadian art. Follow the **Old River Road** through Gagetown to the port city of **Saint John**, stopping at a few pottery studios on the way. Hit Saint John on a Saturday night – catch some live Maritime music at **O'Leary's pub** (p416) or a play at the **Imperial Theatre** (p416). The next morning, head west along the Fundy coast to catch the ferry to **Grand Manan Island**. Take your pick of whale-watching tours, hiking, cycling or relaxing on the veranda with a book.

One Week

Back on the mainland from Grand Manan, take the scenic route east through **St Martins, Sussex** and **Fundy National Park** (p418). Stop for a dip in the ocean at **Parlee Beach** near Shediac, then head north toward Bouctouche. Get a taste of Acadian culture at **Le Pays de la Sagouine** (p425), then round out the experience with a visit to the modern village of **Caraquet** and a time trip to the early 19th c**entury at Acadian Historic Village (p429). Alternatively, head up to the Miramichi** for a few days of salmon fishing and tubing on the famed river.

Outdoor Adventures

Start with a couple of days camping by the ocean, kayaking along the dunes and exploring the cycling and hiking trails at **Kouchibouguac National Park**. Spend a day or a week hiking the northern end of the **International Appalachian Trail** up over Mt Carleton, around **Grand Manan** or along the **Fundy Trail Parkway** (p420). Take a sea-kayaking expedition in **Passamaquoddy Bay** (p407), then spend a week canoe-tripping through the **Chiputneticook Lakes**. Do a week-long cycling trip up the **St John River Valley** or day trips around **Grand Manan, Fredericton** and **Sussex**. Leave a couple of days for whale-watching and a boat excursion to **Machias Seal Island** to see the puffins.

Canoe maps for the Nepisiquit, Restigouche, Southwest Miramichi, St Croix and Tobique Rivers are available from **Service New Brunswick** (www.snb.ca; $7 each). It also distributes a guide to the **New Brunswick Trail** ($13) and a snowmobile trail map (free).

delivery mail addressed to Fredericton, NB E3B 4Y1, is held here.

Visitors Center (☑888-888-4768, 506-460-2129; www.tourismfredericton.ca; City Hall, 397 Queen St; ☺9am-8pm) Free city parking passes provided here.

① Getting There & Away

AIR

Fredericton International Airport (YFC; www.yfcmobile.ca) is on Hwy 102, 14km southeast of town.

BUS

The **Maritime Bus Terminal** (☑1-800-575-1807; www.maritimebus.com; 150 Woodside Lane) is a few kilometers southwest of downtown. Some useful destinations:

Moncton ($44, 2¼ hours, two daily)
Charlottetown, PEI ($69, 5½ hours, two daily)

Bangor, Maine ($58, 7½ hours, one daily)
Saint John ($31, 1½ hours, two daily)

CAR & MOTORCYCLE

Cars with out-of-province license plates are eligible for a free three-day parking pass for downtown Fredericton May to October, available at the visitors center at City Hall. In-province visitors can get a one-day pass.

Avis, Budget, Hertz and National car-rental agencies all have desks at the airport.

① Getting Around

A taxi to the airport costs $18 to $22.

Bicycle rentals are available at **Radical Edge** (☑506-459-3478; www.radicaledge.ca; 386 Queen St; rental per day $25).

The city has a decent bus system, **Fredericton Transit** (☑506-460-2200); tickets cost $2 and include free transfers. Service runs Monday through Saturday from 6:15am to 11pm. Most city bus routes begin at King's Place Mall, on King St between York and Carleton.

UPPER ST JOHN RIVER VALLEY

The St John River rises in the US state of Maine, then winds along the western border of the province past forests and beautiful lush farmland. It then drifts through Fredericton between tree-lined banks and flows around flat islands between rolling hills before emptying into the Bay of Fundy 700km later. The broad river is the province's dominant feature and for centuries has been its major thoroughfare. The valley's soft, eye-pleasing landscape makes for scenic touring by car, or by bicycle on the Trans Canada Trail (TCT), which follows the river for most of its length.

Two automobile routes carve through the valley: the quicker Trans-Canada Hwy (Hwy 2), mostly on the west side of the river, and the more scenic old Hwy 105 on the east side, which meanders through many villages. Branching off from the valley are Hwy 17 (at St-Léonard) and Rte 385 (at Perth-Andover), which cut northeast through the Appalachian highlands and lead to rugged Mt Carleton Provincial Park.

King's Landing Historical Settlement

One of the province's best sites is this worthwhile recreation of an early-19th-century Loyal-ist village (☑506-363-4999; www.kingslanding.nb.ca; adult/child/family $16/11/38; ☉10am-5pm Jun-Oct), 36km west of Fredericton. A community of 100 costumed staff create a living museum by role-playing in 11 houses, a school, church, store and sawmill typical of those used a century ago, providing a glimpse and taste of pioneer life in the Maritimes. Demonstrations and events are staged throughout the day and horse-drawn carts shunt visitors around. The prosperous Loyalist life reflected here can be tellingly compared to that at the Acadian Historic Village in Caraquet. The King's Head Inn, a mid-1800s pub, serves traditional food and beverages, with a nice authentic touch – candlelight. The children's programs make King's Landing ideal for families, and spe-

cial events occur regularly. It's not hard to while away a good half-day or more here.

About 10km south, busy, resortlike Mactaquac Provincial Park (day use per vehicle $7) has swimming, fishing, hiking, picnic sites, camping, boat rentals and a huge campground (☑506-363-4747; 1256 Hwy 105; campsites/RV sites $24/28; ☉Jun-Oct).

Hartland

This tiny country hamlet has the granddaddy of New Brunswick's many wooden covered bridges. The photogenic 390m-long Hartland covered bridge over the St John River was erected in 1897 and is a national historic site. The picnic tables overlooking the river and the bridge at the tourist information center are five-star lunch spots (fixings at the grocery store across the road). Otherwise, the village has a rather forlorn atmosphere.

Rebecca Farm B&B (☑506-375-1699; 656 Rockland Rd; d incl breakfast $100-130; ☻❋☎), about 4km from the town center, is a scrupulously maintained 19th-century farmhouse that sits in the midst of gorgeously hilly potato fields.

Florenceville & Around

The tidy and green riverside village of Florenceville is ground zero of the global french-fry industry. It's home to the McCain Foods frozen-foods empire, which is sustained by the thousands of hectares of potato farms that surround it in every direction. Started by the McCain brothers in 1957 and still owned by the family, the company produces one-third of the world's french-fry supply at its Florenceville factory and 54 like it worldwide. That adds up to one million pounds of chips churned out every hour and $5.8 billion in annual net sales.

Worth a stop is the Potato World Museum (www.potatoworld.ca; Rte 110; tours adult/child $5/4, experiential tours $10/8; ☉9am-6pm Mon-Fri, to 5pm Sat & Sun). It's a cheesy name, but the museum is a tasteful, top-class interactive exposition of the history of the humble potato in these parts and its continuing centrality to the provincial economy. In this area, school kids are still given two weeks off in the autumn to help bring in the harvest. The museums' new experiential tour lets you get your hands

SCENIC DRIVE: LOWER ST JOHN RIVER VALLEY

The main Hwy (Rte 7) between the capital and the port city of Saint John barrels south through a vast expanse of trees, trees and more trees. A far more scenic route (albeit about twice as long) follows the gentle, meandering St John River through rolling farmland and a couple of historic villages down to the Fundy coast.

Start on the north side of the river in Fredericton, and follow Rte 105 south through Maugerville to Jemseg. At Exit 339, pick up Rte 715 South which will take you to the **Gagetown ferry landing** (⊙24hr year-round) **FREE**. This is the first of a system of eight free cable ferries that crisscross the majestic St John River en route to the city of Saint John. You will never have to wait more than a few minutes for the crossing, which generally takes five to 10 minutes.

When you reach the opposite bank, head north a couple of miles to visit the pretty 18th-century village of **Gagetown** – well worth a look-see. Front St is lined with craft studios and shops and a couple of inviting cafes. Stop into the excellent **Queen's County Museum** (69 Front St; adult/child $3/free; ⊙10am-5pm) housed in Sir Leonard Tilley's childhood home, built in 1736. The top-notch staff will show you through the exhibits spanning pre-Colonial aboriginal history in the area, 18th-century settler life, and up to WWII. **Gagetown Cider Company** (☑506-488-2147; 127 Fox Rd; ⊙1-6pm) offers tours by appointment.

Explore scenic Gagetown Creek by boat. **Village Boatique** (☑877-488-1992; 50 Front St) has canoe/kayak rentals for $10/15 per hour, $50/75 per day. Homey **Step-Aside Inn** (☑506-488-1808; stepamau@nbnet.nb.ca; 58 Front St; s/d incl breakfast $80/95; ⊙May-Dec; ⊖❄☎) has four bright rooms with views of the river. To eat, grab a smoked-meat sandwich and a beer at the **Old Boot Pub** (48 Front St; ⊙11am-10pm) on the riverfront.

From Gagetown, head south on Rte 102, known locally as 'the Old River Road,' denoting its status as the major thoroughfare up the valley in the kinder, simpler era between the decline of the river steamboats and the construction of the modern, divided highway. The grand old farmhouses and weathered hay barns dotted at intervals along the valley belong to that earlier age. The hilly 42km piece of road between Gagetown and the **Evandale ferry landing** (⊙24hr year-round) **FREE** is especially picturesque, with glorious panoramic views of fields full of wildflowers, white farmhouses and clots of green and gold islands set in the intensely blue water of the river.

A hundred years ago, tiny Evandale was a bustling little place, where a dance band would entertain riverboat passengers stopping off for the night at the **Evandale Resort** (☑506-468-2222; ferry landing; r $139-199), now restored to its Victorian grandeur. It has six rooms and a fine-dining restaurant. On the other side of the water, Rte 124 takes you the short distance to the **Belleisle ferry** (⊙24hr year-round) **FREE**. The ferry deposits you on the rural Kingston Peninsula, where you can cross the peninsula to catch the **Gondola Point Ferry** (signposted off Hwy 1 at Exit 141) **FREE** and head directly into Saint John.

dirty – literally – by planting potato seeds and cutting your own french fries. If all the spud talk leaves you peckish, slip into a potato barrel chair at the on-site **Harvest Cafe** (lunch $5-7; ⊙11am-4pm Mon-Fri). The museum is 2km off Hwy 2 at Exit 152 toward Centreville on Rte 110.

Just outside Florenceville is the **Tannaghtyn B&B** (☑866-399-6966, 506-392-6966; www.tannaghtyn.ca; 4169 Rte 103, off Rte 110, Connell; r incl breakfast $95-140; ❄☎), set high on a ridge with a spectacular view of the St John River and the green and gold patchwork of farms on the opposite side.

Both stylish and cozy, the house is furnished with dramatic Canadian art, comfy sofas and beds made up with linens dried in the fresh country air. Plus, there's a hot tub under the stars. Besides the Harvest Cafe, Florenceville has a half-dozen middle-of-the-road restaurants serving three meals a day.

Maritime (☑1-800-575-1807; www.maritimebus.com; 8738 Main St) buses stop at the Irving gas station in Florenceville.

Mt Carleton Provincial Park & the Tobique Valley

From his workshop on the forested banks of the Tobique River at the foot of Mt Carleton, Nictau canoe-maker Bill Miller rhapsodizes that 'If you telephone heaven, it's a local call.' He may be right.

The 17,427-hectare **provincial park** offers visitors a wilderness of mountains, valleys, rivers and wildlife including moose, deer, bear and, potentially, the 'extinct' (but apparently regularly seen) eastern cougar. The main feature of the park is a series of rounded glaciated peaks and ridges, including Mt Carleton, which at 820m is the Maritimes' highest. This range is an extension of the Appalachian Mountains, which begin in the US state of Georgia and end in Québec. Mt Carleton is little known and relatively unvisited, even in midsummer. It could be the province's best-kept secret.

The park is open from mid-May to October; entry is free. Hunting and logging are prohibited in the park, and all roads are gravel-surfaced. The nearest town is **Riley Brook**, 30km away, so bring all food and a full tank of gas.

🏃 Activities

Canoeing

The Mt Carleton area boasts superb wilderness canoeing. In the park itself, the Nictau and Nepisiguit chains of lakes offer easy day-tripping through a landscape of tree-clad mountains. For experienced canoeists, the shallow and swift Little Tobique River rises at Big Nictau Lake, winding in tight curls through dense woods until it joins the Tobique itself at Nictau. The more remote Nepisiguit River flows out of the Nepisiguit Lakes through the wilderness until it empties into the Bay of Chaleur at Bathurst, over 100km away.

The lower reaches of the Tobique, from Nictau, through minute Riley Brook and down to Plaster Rock is a straight, easy paddle through forest and meadow that gives way to farmland as the valley broadens, with a couple of waterfront campgrounds along the way. The easy 10km between Nictau and the Bear's Lair landing in Riley Brook makes for a relaxing afternoon paddle.

Don McAskill at **Bear's Lair** (☑506-356-8351; www.bearslairhunting.com; 3349 Rte 385, Riley Brook; boats per day $40) has boats and can provide expert knowledge on canoeing

in these parts. He also offers a shuttle service between your put-in and take-out point (eg boat delivery to Mt Carleton Provincial Park and transport of your vehicle down to Riley Brook is $45). In the park, **Guildo Martel** (☑506-235-2499) rents canoes and kayaks for the day on the edge of Big Nictau Lake at Armstrong Campground.

Fiddles on the Tobique (☑506-356-2409; ⊙late Jun) is a weekend festival held annually in Nictau and Riley Brook. It is a magical idea: a round of community-hall suppers, jam sessions and concerts culminating in a Sunday afternoon floating concert down the Tobique River from Nictau to Riley Brook. Upward of 800 canoes and kayaks join the flotilla each year – some stocked with musicians, some just with paddlers – and 8000 spectators line the river banks to watch. By some accounts, the event has been damaged by its own popularity, devolving into a boisterous booze cruise. Others call it a grand party and good fun.

On land, **Bill Miller** (☑506-356-2409; www.millercanoes.com; 4160 Rte 385, Nictau) welcomes visitors to his cluttered canoe-making workshop in Nictau (population roughly 12), where he and his father and grandfather before him have handcrafted wooden canoes since 1922. Also worth a stop is the **Tobique Salmon Barrier** (⊙9am-5pm) **FREE**, signposted from the road at Nictau, located at the confluence of the Little Tobique and Campbell Rivers. There is a spectacular view from the Department of Fisheries office situated on a bluff overlooking the water. From here, officers keep a 24-hour watch on the Atlantic salmon, which are trucked up by road from below the Mactaquac Dam at Fredericton and held here until spawning time, in order to protect their dwindling numbers from poachers.

Hiking

The best way to explore Mt Carleton is on foot. The park has a 62km network of trails: most of them are loops winding to the handful of rocky knobs that are the peaks. The International Appalachian Trail (IAT) passes through here.

The easiest peak to climb is Mt Bailey; a 7.5km loop trail to the 564m hillock begins near the day-use area. Most hikers can walk this route in three hours. The highest peak is reached via the Mt Carleton Trail, a 10km route that skirts over the 820m knob, where there's a fire tower. Plan on three to four hours for the trek and pack your parka; the wind above the tree line can be brutal.

The most challenging hike is the Sagamook Trail, a 6km loop to a 777m peak with superlative vistas of Nictau Lake and the highlands area to the north of it; allow three hours for this trek. The Mountain Head Trail connects the Mt Carleton and Sagamook Trails, making a long transit of the range possible.

All hikers intending to follow any long trails must register at the visitors center or park headquarters before hiking the trail. Outside the camping season (mid-May to mid-September), you should call ahead to make sure the main gate will be open, as the Mt Carleton trailhead is 13.5km from the park entrance. Otherwise park your car at the entrance and walk in – the Mt Bailey trailhead is only 2.5km from the gate.

🛏 Sleeping & Eating

There is lodging, a general store, gas station and restaurant in Riley Brook. The park has four public-use **campgrounds** (☑506-235-0793; www.friendsofmountcarleton.ca). In addition to Armstrong Brook, there are the semiwilderness campgrounds of Franquelin and Williams Brook, with outhouses and fire pits (bring your own water), and the ultraremote Headwaters campground on the slopes of Mt Carleton.

The town of Plaster Rock, situated 54km downriver toward the Trans-Canada Hwy (Rte 385), also has several serviceable motels and a couple of casual restaurants.

Bear's Lair INN $
(☑506-356-8351; www.bearslairhunting.com; 3349 Rte 385, Riley Brook; r from $60; ☻) If any place in the province captures the essence of life in the north woods, this is it. A cozy log hunting lodge set on the banks of the Tobique River, it is busiest during fall hunting season – the high-ceilinged main lodge is adorned with numerous taxidermied specimens – but is also a relaxing base for outdoor enthusiasts year-round. The guest rooms are spick and span and the lodge's friendly owners offer meals, canoe/kayak rentals and guided hunting trips.

Armstrong Brook Campground CAMPGROUND $
(☑506-235-0793; campsites/RV sites $10/18; ☻May-Oct) The park's largest campground has 89 sites nestled among the pines on the north side of Nictau Lake, 3km from the entrance. It has toilets, showers and a kitchen shelter, but no sites with hookups. RV drivers often have their noisy generators running, so tenters should check out the eight tent-only sites along Armstrong Brook on the north side of the campground.

❶ Information

At the entrance to the park is a **visitors center** (☑506-235-0793; www.friendsofmountcarleton.ca; off Rte 385; ☻8am-8pm May-Oct) for maps and information.

WORLD CLASS (POND) HOCKEY

As anyone who has been in the country for more than five minutes knows, Canadians love their hockey. For many, this affection (obsession?) is wrapped up in happy childhood memories of bright winter afternoons chasing a puck up and down a frozen pond or backyard rink.

Every February, the small forest town of Plaster Rock (population 1200), 84km from Mt Carleton, hosts the **World Pond Hockey Tournament** (www.worldpondhockey.com; Rte 109, Plaster Rock) FREE. Twenty rinks are plowed on Roulston Lake, which is ringed by tall evergreens, hot-chocolate stands and straw-bale seating for the 8000-odd spectators drawn to the four-day event. The tournament is wildly popular, with 120 amateur four-person teams traveling in from places as far flung as England, Egypt and the Cayman Islands. Anyone can register to play, but they will have to defeat the Boston Danglers, who have scrambled over squads such as the Skateful Dead, the Raggedy Ass River Boys and the Boiled Owls to put a lock on the championship trophy several years running.

If you want to play, register early. If you want to watch, pack your long johns and a toque (wool hat) and book your accommodations early. If the motels are full, the organizers keep a list of local folks willing to billet out-of-towners in their homes for the weekend.

There is also an **office** at the park head-quarters in St Quentin(☑506-235-6040; dnr. Mt.carleton@gnb.ca; 11 Gagnon St).

Grand Falls

With a drop of around 25m and a 1.6km-long gorge with walls as high as 80m, these falls merit a stop in this otherwise un-scenic town. The Grand Falls are best in spring or after heavy rain – in summer, much of the water is diverted for generating hydro-electricity – yet the gorge is appealing any time.

In the middle of town, overlooking the falls, the **Malabeam Reception Centre** (25 Madawaska Rd; ⊙9am-9pm Jul & Aug, 10am-6pm May, Jun & Sep) FREE doubles as a tourist office. Among the displays is a scale model of the gorge showing its extensive trail system.

A 253-step stairway down into the gorge begins at **La Rochelle** (1 Chapel St; tours adult/child $4/2; self-guided tours per family $5; boat trips adult/family $12/28; ⊙May-Oct), across the bridge from the Malabeam Reception Centre and left on Victoria St. Boats maneuver for 45-minute trips up the gorge. These run up to eight times a day but only in midsummer when water levels are low (it's too dangerous when the river is in full flood). Buy the boat ticket at La Rochelle first, as it includes admission to the stairway to the base of the gorge.

There are dramatically situated tent and RV sites at the **Falls and Gorge Campground** (☑877-475-7769; 1 Chapel St; campsites/RV sites $18/25). **Côté's** (☑877-444-2683; www.cotebb-inn.com; 575 Broadway Blvd West; r incl breakfast $103-175) is a homey, five-room B&B with a patio and hot tub.

Le Grand Saut (www.legrandsautristorante.com; 155 Broadway Blvd; mains $11-22; ⊙10:30am-10pm), a popular, two-tiered spot with an inviting deck out front, serves up salads, pastas, pizzas and steaks.

❶ Getting There & Away

Maritime (☑1-800-575-1807; www.maritime-bus.com; 555 Madawaska Rd) buses stop at the Esso station, just west of downtown.

Hwy 108 (known locally as the Renous Hwy) cuts across the province through Plaster Rock to the east coast, slicing through forest for nearly its entirety. It is tedious, but fast. Watch out for deer and moose.

OFF THE BEATEN TRACK

CHIPUTNETICOOK LAKES

Tucked away on New Brunswick's southwest border with the USA state of Maine is a little-known but spectacular chain of wilderness lakes. Stretching for 180km along the international border, the forest-ringed Chiputneticook Lakes offer canoeing enthusiasts the chance to slip away into the wild for a few weeks. The nonprofit **St Croix International Waterway Commission** (www.stcroix.org; 5 Rte 1, St Stephen) maintains a network of backcountry campsites on the islands and lakeshores along the chain and publishes a detailed map of the waterway ($10). It includes the St Croix River, a popular three- to four-day paddling route beginning south of the lakes. Canoe rentals are available in Saint John and Fredericton. Note: the lakes are not patrolled by the park service, and paddlers should be experienced and well equipped.

There are a couple of fishing lodges on Palfrey Lake accessible via Rte 630. Day-trippers can use the scenic lakeshore campsites at **Spednik Lake Provincial Park** (free; maintained by volunteers), where there is a hiking trail through the woods, primitive toilets and fire rings. Bring your own water. Take Rte 3 north from St Stephen, then bear left on Rte 630 to reach the park gate.

Edmundston

Working-class Edmundston, with a large paper mill, a utilitarian town center and a mainly bilingual French citizenry, doesn't bother much with tourism. Nevertheless, it makes a convenient stopover for those traveling east from Québec.

Halfway between the Québec border and Edmundston in the small community of St-Jacques is the **New Brunswick Botanical Garden** (www.jardinbotaniquenb.com; off Rte 2; adult/child $14/7; ⊙9am-8pm). Here, there are 80,000 plants to brighten your day, all accompanied by classical music. Kids might prefer the neat temporary exhibitions, such as a butterfly garden.

Edmundston is the eastern terminus of the **Petis Témis Interprovincial Linear Park** (www.petit-temis.com), a 134km cycling/hiking trail between Edmundston and Rivière-du-Loup, Québec. It follows an old railbed along the Madawaska River and the shores of Lake

Témiscouata, passing by several small villages and campgrounds along the way.

Get out of gritty Edmundston and sleep next to the botanical gardens at **Auberge Les Jardins** (506-739-5514; www.lesjardinsinn.com; 60 Rue Principale, St-Jacques; r $89-180;), a gracious inn whose 17 rooms are each decorated with a different Canadian flower or tree theme. There's also a modern motel in back, and a wood-and-stained-glass **dining room** that's considered one of the best restaurants in the province (check out the fabulous wine list). Several motels line the highway and old Hwy 2 (Blvd Acadie).

For eats, head to **Bel Air** (506-735-3329; 174 Victoria St, cnr Blvd Hébert; mains $6-15; 24hr). A city landmark since the 1950s, this is a total classic, right down to the seasoned, uniformed servers. The you-name-it menu includes acceptable Italian, Chinese, seafood and basic Canadian fare.

The **Provincial Tourist Office** (Hwy 2; 8am-9pm Jun-Sep) is about 20km north at the Québec border.

Maritime (www.maritimebus.com; 191 Victoria St) buses depart from the downtown terminal.

WESTERN FUNDY SHORE

Almost the entire southern edge of New Brunswick is presided over by the constantly rising and falling, always impressive waters of the Bay of Fundy.

The resort town of St Andrews by-the-Sea, the serene Fundy Isles, fine seaside scenery and rich history make this easily one of the most appealing regions of the province. Whale-watching is a thrilling area activity. Most commonly seen are the fin, humpback and minke, and less so, the increasingly rare right whale. Porpoises and dolphins are plentiful. And let's not overlook the seafood – it's bountiful and delicious.

St Stephen

Right on the US border across the river from Calais, Maine, St Stephen is a busy entry point with small-town charm and one tasty attraction. It is home to Ganong, a family-run chocolate business, operating since 1873, whose products are known around eastern Canada. The five-cent chocolate nut bar was invented by the Ganong brothers in 1910, and they can also be credited with developing the heart-shaped box of chocolates seen everywhere on Valentine's Day.

The old Ganong chocolate factory on the town's main street is now the **Chocolate Museum** (www.chocolatemuseum.ca; 73 Milltown Blvd; adult/student/family $10/8.50/30; 9:30am-6:30pm Mon-Sat, 11am-3pm Sun), with tasteful (and tasty) interactive displays of everything from antique chocolate boxes to manufacturing equipment. The adjacent **shop** sells boxes of Ganong hand-dipped chocolates and is free to visit. Try the iconic chicken bone (chocolate-filled cinnamon sticks) or the old-fashioned Pal-O-Mine candy bar.

The museum also offers a **guided heritage walking tour** (adult/child/family $13/10/40; Jun-Aug) of St Stephen. Once a year, during **Chocolate Fest** (www.chocolate-fest.ca; 1st week Aug), the town celebrates all things chocolate with a parade, tours of the factory with unlimited sampling of the goods, and games for the kids.

There are five very comfortable rooms complemented by a quiet garden at **Blair House** (888-972-5247, 506-466-2233; www.blairhouseinn.nb.ca; 38 Prince William St; s/d incl breakfast from $90/110;), a fabulous Victorian home. You can walk the main street easily from here. There are also a few run-down motels on the outskirts of town if you are desperate.

Home cooking is served up at **Carman's Diner** (506-466-3528; 164 King St; mains $4-16; 7am-10pm), a 1960s throwback with counter stools and jukeboxes at the tables.

The **tourist office** (cnr Milltown Blvd & King St; 8am-9pm Jun-Sep) is in the old train station.

ⓘ Getting There & Away

Across the border in Calais, Maine, **West's Coastal Connection** (800-596-2823) buses connect to Bangor. They usually leave from Carmen's Hometown Pizzeria on Main St, but call ahead to confirm. In Bangor, buses use the Greyhound terminal and connect to Bangor airport.

St Andrews by-the-Sea

St Andrews is a genteel summer resort town. Blessed with a fine climate and picturesque beauty, it also has a colorful history. Founded by Loyalists in 1783, it's one of the oldest towns in the province. It's busy with holidaymakers and summer residents in July and August, but the rest of the year there are more seagulls than people.

The town sits on a peninsula pointing southward into the Bay of Fundy. Its main drag, Water St, is lined with restaurants and souvenir and craft shops.

St Andrews by-the-Sea

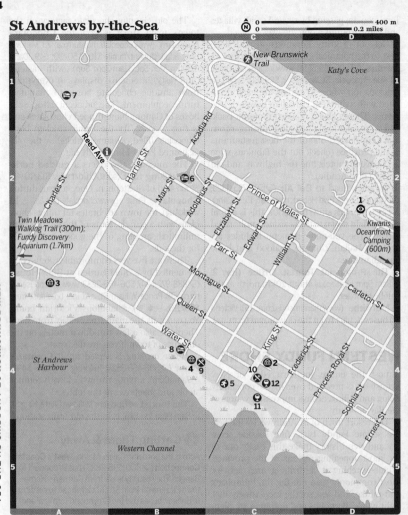

👁 Sights

Fundy Discovery Aquarium AQUARIUM
(www.huntsmanmarine.com/aquarium; 1 Lower
Campus Rd; adult/child $12/9; ⏱10am-5pm)
This aquatic center focuses on the local
marine ecology; a 20,000-sq-ft aquarium
has most specimens that are found in Bay
of Fundy waters, including seals (feedings
at 11am and 4pm), lobsters and sturgeon.
Kids (and parents) love the touch pool reserved just for slippery skates.

Minister's Island ISLAND
(www.ministersisland.ca; adult/child $15/10;
⏱May-Oct) This picturesque tidal island was
once used as a summer retreat by William
Cornelius Van Horne, builder of the Canadian Pacific Railway and one of Canada's
wealthiest men. **Covenhoven**, his splendid
50-room Edwardian cottage, is now open
to visitors – check out the tower-like stone
bathhouse, the tidal swimming pool and the
château-like barn.

The island can be visited at low tide, when
you can drive (or walk, or bike) on the hard-
packed sea floor. A few hours later it's 3m

St Andrews by-the-Sea

under water, so you need to be careful! During high tide, a ferry departs from Bar Rd. To get to Minister's Island from downtown St Andrews, follow Rte 127 northeast for about 1km and then turn right on Bar Rd.

Kingsbrae Garden   GARDEN
(www.kingsbraegarden.com; 220 King St; adult/student/family $16/12/38, tours per person $3; ◎9am-6pm May-Oct) Extensive, multihued Kingsbrae Garden is considered one of the best horticultural displays in Canada. Check out the wollemi pine, one of the world's oldest and rarest trees.

Sunbury Shores Arts & Nature
Centre   GALLERY
(www.sunburyshores.org; 139 Water St; ◎9am-4:30pm Mon-Fri, noon-4pm Sat & Sun) **FREE** This nonprofit educational and cultural center offers courses in painting, weaving, pottery and other crafts for a day, weekend or week, as well as natural science seminars. Various changing exhibits run through summer.

St Andrews Blockhouse   HISTORIC BUILDING
(Joe's Point Rd; ◎9am-8pm Jun-Aug, to 5pm early Sep) **FREE** The restored wooden Blockhouse Historic Site is the only one left of several that were built here for protection in the War of 1812. If the tide is out, there's a path that extends from the blockhouse out across the tidal flats.

Sheriff Andrew House   HISTORIC BUILDING
(cnr King & Queen Sts; admission by donation; ◎9:30am-4:30pm Mon-Sat, 1-4:30pm Sun Jul-Sep) This 1820 neoclassical house has been restored to look like a middle-class home in the 1800s, and it's attended by lively and informative costumed guides.

Atlantic Salmon
Interpretive Centre   MUSEUM, AQUARIUM
(www.salarstream.ca; Chamcook Lake No 1 Rd, off Rte 127; adult/student/child $6/4/3; ◎9am-5pm) This handsome lodge has an in-stream aquarium, guided tours and displays devoted to the life and trials of the endangered wild Atlantic salmon, once so plentiful in provincial rivers and bays.

🏃 Activities

Eastern Outdoors   BIKING, KAYAKING
(☑506-529-4662; www.easternoutdoors.com; 165 Water St; mountain bikes per hr/day $20/35, kayaks per day $55; ◎May-Oct) This St Andrews–based outfitter offers a variety of trips, including two-hour sunset paddles ($49) and multiday camping expeditions (from $145 per day).

Twin Meadows Walking Trail   WALKING
The 800m Twin Meadows Walking Trail, a boardwalk and footpath through fields and woodlands, begins opposite 165 Joe's Point Rd beyond the blockhouse.

☞ Tours

Several companies offering boat trips and whale-watching cruises have offices by the wharf at the foot of King St. They're open from mid-June to early September. The cruises (around $60) take in the lovely coast. Seabirds are commonplace and seeing whales is the norm. The ideal waters for watching these beasts are further out in the bay, however, so if you're heading for the Fundy Isles, do your trip there.

Jolly Breeze   BOAT TOUR
(☑506-529-8116; www.jollybreeze.com; adult/child $55/39; ◎tours 9am, 12:45pm, 4:30pm Jun-Oct) This antique-style tall ship sails around Passamaquoddy Bay looking for seals and whales.

Quoddy Link Marine   BOAT TOUR
(☑506-529-2600; adult/child $58/36; ◎Jul-Oct) Serious whale-watchers should hop aboard this catamaran, staffed by trained marine biologists. There are one to three tours daily.

📖 Sleeping

Kiwanis Oceanfront Camping CAMPGROUND $

(📞 877-393-7070; www.kiwanisoceanfrontcamping.
com; 550 Water St; campsites/RV sites $31/38;
⊙ Apr-Oct) Situated at the far eastern end of
town on Indian Point, this is mainly a gravel
parking area for trailers, although there are
some grassy spots.

Picket Fence Motel MOTEL $

(📞 506-529-8985; www.picketfencenb.com; 102
Reed Ave; r $90-105; ❋ ❋ 🛜) Modern, neat-as-a-
pin motel rooms within walking distance of
the main drag. Ultrafriendly management
to boot.

⭐ Rossmount Inn INN $$

(📞 506-529-3351; www.rossmountinn.com; 4599
Rte 127; r incl breakfast $125-138; ⊙ Apr-Dec;
🛜) Flags flap in the breeze in front of this
stately yellow summer cottage, perched
atop a manicured slope overlooking Passamaquoddy Bay. Inside, the 18 rooms have a
stylish mix of antiques and modern decor,
with hand-carved wooden furniture and
snowy white linens. Many people consider
the hotel restaurant to be the town's best.
Rossmount Inn is about 3km north of
downtown St Andrews on Rte 127.

⭐ Algonquin Resort HOTEL $$$

(📞 855-529-8693, 506-529-8823; www.algon-
quinresort.com; 184 Adolphus St; r $189-389;
❋ 🛜 ⛲) The doyenne of New Brunswick
hotels, this Tudor-style 'Castle-by-the-Sea'
has sat on a hill overlooking town since
1889. With its elegant veranda, gardens,
rooftop terrace, golf course, tennis courts
and indoor pool with waterslides, it's
worth a look even if you're not spending
the night. A revamped spa is due to open
in early 2014.

Treadwell Inn B&B $$$

(📞 888-529-1011, 506-529-1011; www.treadwell-
inn.com; 129 Water St; r incl breakfast $150-250;
😊 ❋ 🛜) Big, handsome rooms in an 1820
ship chandler's house, some with private
decks and ocean views.

🍴 Eating

In keeping with its genteel atmosphere, St
Andrews has embraced the custom of afternoon cream tea. For lunch and dinner,
there are a range of nice options, mostly
clustered around Water St.

Sweet Harvest Market CAFE $

(182 Water St; mains $5-11; ⊙8am-5pm Mon-Sat,
9am-3pm Sun) Cheerful counter staff create
wholesome soups, salads, sandwiches and
sweets that are way beyond average standard, and chowder that is truly outstanding.
The coffee's good, too.

Clam Digger SEAFOOD $

(4468 Hwy 127, Chamcook; mains $6-15;
⊙11:30am-3pm & 5-9pm Apr-Sep) Cars park
three-deep outside this teeny red-and-
white seafood shack that's a summertime
tradition in these parts. Order your clam
platter or juicy, dripping cheeseburger,
and claim one of the red-painted picnic
tables. Don't forget an ice cream cone! It's
in Chamcook, about 9 km north of St Andrews.

⭐ Rossmount Inn
Restaurant MODERN CANADIAN $$

(📞506-529-3351; www.rossmountinn.com; 4599
Rte 127; mains $18-30; ⊙5-9:30pm) The Swiss
chef-owner makes wonderful use of local
bounty in this warm, art-filled dining room.
The ever-changing menu might include
foraged goose-tongue greens and wild
mushrooms, periwinkles (a small shellfish)
or New Brunswick lobster. They each play
a part in complex, exquisite dishes – say,
lobster with nasturtium flower dumplings
and vanilla bisque, or foie gras with cocoa
nibs and bee balm–poached peach. Reservations are crucial. The restaurant is 3km
north of town.

Garden Cafe CAFE $$

(www.kingsbraegarden.com; 220 King St; mains
$9-17, cream teas $13, plus admission to Kingsbrae
Garden; ⊙10am-5pm May-Oct) At Kingsbrae
Garden, the terrace cafe serves high tea
and sandwiches and salads for lunch with
a glass of wine or local ale.

Gables SEAFOOD $$

(📞506-529-3440; 143 Water St; mains $10-20;
⊙11am-10pm) Seafood and views of the
ocean through a row of tall windows dominate this comfortable place. To enter, head
down the alley onto a gardenlike patio on
the water's edge.

🍷 Drinking & Nightlife

Afternoon cocktails at the Algonquin Resort are a must. In the evenings, several
downtown pubs serve up beer, music and
camaraderie.

Shiretown Pub
PUB

(www.kennedyinn.ca; 218 Water St; ⊘11am-2am)
On the ground floor of the delightfully
creaky Kennedy Inn, this old-school English pub draws a mixed-age crowd of par-
tiers. Early afternoons mean sipping New
Brunswick–brewed Picaroons bitter on the
porch, while late nights bring live music
and raucous karaoke.

Red Herring Pub
PUB

(211 Water St; ⊘noon-2am) A fun, slightly divey downtown bar with pool tables, live
music and frosty Canadian beers.

ℹ Information

The main **tourist office** (www.townofstandrews.
ca; 46 Reed Ave; ⊘8am-8pm May-Sep; 📶) has
free walking-tour brochures that include a map
and brief description of some of the most noteworthy places. It also has free internet access.

ℹ Getting There & Around

HMS Transportation (www.hmstrans.com; 260
Water St) rents cars for $60 to $80 per day with
200 free kilometers; you must arrange your own
collision insurance coverage.

New River Provincial Park

Just off Hwy 1, about 35km west of Saint
John on the way to St Stephen, this large
park has one of the best beaches along the
Fundy shore, a wide stretch of sand bordered on one side by the rugged coastline of
Barnaby Head. During camping season the
park charges a $7 fee per vehicle for day use,
which includes parking at the beach and
Barnaby Head trailhead.

You can spend an enjoyable few hours
hiking Barnaby Head along a 6km network
of nature trails. The **Chittick's Beach Trail**
leads through coastal forest and past four
coves, where you can check the catch in a
herring weir or examine tidal pools for marine life. Extending from this loop is the
2.5km **Barnaby Head Trail**, which hugs
the shoreline most of the way and rises
to the edge of a cliff 15m above the Bay of
Fundy.

The park's **campground** (⌨ 506-755-4042;
newriver@gnb.ca; 78 New River Beach Rd; camp-
sites/RV sites $22/24.50; ⊘May-Sep) is across
the road from the beach and features 100 secluded sites, both rustic and with hookups,
in a wooded setting. Drawbacks are the
gravel emplacements and traffic noise.

FUNDY ISLES

The thinly populated, unspoiled Fundy Isles
are ideal for a tranquil, nature-based escape.
With grand scenery, colorful fishing wharves
tucked into coves, supreme whale-watching,
uncluttered walking trails and steaming
dishes of seafood, the islands will make
your everyday stresses fade away and your
blood pressure ease. The three main islands
each have a distinct personality and offer a
memorable, gradually absorbed peace. Out
of the summer season, all are nearly devoid
of visitors and most services are shut.

Deer Island

Deer Island, the closest of the three main
Fundy Isles, is a modest fishing settlement
with a lived-in look. The 16km-by-5km
island has been inhabited since 1770, and
1000 people live here year-round. It's well
forested, and deer are still plentiful. Lobster
is the main catch and there are half a dozen
wharves around the island.

Deer Island can be easily explored on a
day trip. Narrow, winding roads run south
down each side toward Campobello Island
and the ferry (drive defensively).

◉ Sights & Activities

At **Lamberts Cove** is a huge lobster pound
used to hold live lobster (it could well be
the world's largest). Another massive pound
squirms at **Northern Harbor**.

At the other end of the island is the
16-hectare **Deer Island Point Park** where
Old Sow, the world's second-largest natural
tidal whirlpool, is seen offshore a few hours
before high tide. Whales pass occasionally.

At the end of Cranberry Head Rd is a deserted **beach**. Most land on the island is privately owned, so there are no hiking trails.

☞ Tours

Whales usually arrive in mid-June and stay
until October. Ask at any motel or restaurant
about whale-watching tours.

Seascape Kayak Tours
KAYAKING

(⌨ 866-747-1884, 506-747-1884; www.seascape
kayaktours.com; 40 NW Harbour Branch Rd,
Richardson; half-/full-day trips $85/150) Offers
guided paddling excursions around Deer
Island and Passamaquoddy Bay. Multiday island-jumping camping trips are also
available.

Fundy Isles

🛏 Sleeping & Eating

Deer Island Point Park CAMPGROUND $
(☏506-747-2423; www.deerislandpointpark.com; 195 Deer Island Point Rd; campsites $25-30; ⊙ Jun-Sep) Set up your tent on the high bluff and spend an evening watching the Old Sow whirlpool. The campground is directly above the Campobello ferry landing.

Sunset Beach Cottage & Suites INN $$
(☏506-747-2972; www.cottageandsuites.com; 21 Cedar Grove Rd, Fairhaven; r $80, cottage per week $840; ⊙ May-Oct; 🐾) On a secluded cove, this two-story unit has five tidy, basic suites with carpet and unstylish plaid bedding. Upper floors have better views. The private barbecues and the pool and hot tub overlooking the bay are major draws. The furnished cottage (sleeps four maximum) is nice for families.

45th Parallel Motel & Restaurant
SEAFOOD $
(☏506-747-2222; www.45thparallel.ca; 941 Hwy 772, Fairhaven; mains $6-25; ⊙7:30am-9pm) The specialty is seafood at this small, rustic country classic with a homey feel and great food. Ask to see Herman, the monster lobster. The creaky-but-clean motel rooms (from $62) are a fine bargain, too.

ⓘ Information

There's a summertime **tourist information kiosk** (www.deerisland.nb.ca; ⊙10am-3pm Thu-Tue) at the ferry landing.

ⓘ Getting There & Away

A free government-run ferry (25 minutes) runs to Deer Island from Letete, which is 14.5km south of St George on Hwy 172 via Back Bay. The ferries run year-round every half-hour from 6am to 7pm, and hourly from 7pm to 10pm. Get in line early on a busy day.

The private **East Coast Ferries** (www.east-coastferries.nb.ca; car & driver $16, additional passenger $3; ⊙9am-6pm end Jun–mid-Sep) links Deer Island Point to Eastport, Maine, an attractive seaside town. It leaves for Eastport every hour on the hour.

Campobello Island

The atmosphere on Campobello is remarkably different from that of Deer Island. It's a gentler and more prosperous island, with straight roads and better facilities. The wealthy have long been enjoying Campobello as a summer retreat. Due to its accessibility and proximity to New England, it feels as much a part of the USA as of Canada, and most of the tourists here are Americans.

Like many moneyed families, the Roosevelts bought property in this peaceful coastal area at the end of the 1800s, and it is for this that the island is best known. The southern half of Campobello is almost all park, and a golf course occupies still more.

Come to the island prepared. There's a single grocery store, two ATMs, a liquor store and a pharmacy, but no gas station – the 1200 residents of the 16km-long Campobello must cross the bridge to Lubec, Maine, to fill their tanks. They generally use the same bridge to go elsewhere in New Brunswick, as the Deer Island ferry only operates in the summer.

⊙ Sights & Activities

★ Roosevelt Campobello International Park
PARK

(www.fdr.net; Hwy 774; ☼sunrise-sunset year-round, cottage tours Jun-Sep) The southernmost green area of Campobello Island is this 1200-hectare park. Its biggest visitor attraction is the **Roosevelt Cottage**, the 34-room lodge where Franklin D Roosevelt grew up (between 1905 and 1921) and visited periodically throughout his time as US president (1933–45). The tomato-red Arts and Crafts–style structure is furnished with original Roosevelt furniture and artifacts. Adjacent **Hubbard House**, built in 1898, is also open to visitors. The grounds are open all the time, and you can peek through the windows when the doors are closed.

The park is just 2.5km from the Lubec bridge, and from the Roosevelt mansion's front porch you can look directly across to Eastport, Maine. You'd hardly know you were in Canada.

Unlike the manicured museum area, most of the international park has been left in its natural state to preserve the flora and fauna that Roosevelt appreciated so much. A couple of gravel roads meander through it, leading to beaches and 7.5km of nature trails. It's a surprisingly wild, little-visited part of Campobello Island. Deer, moose and coyote call it home, and seals can sometimes be seen offshore on the ledges near Lower Duck Pond, 6km from the visitors center. Look for eagles, ospreys and loons.

Herring Cove Provincial Park
PARK

Along the northern boundary of Roosevelt Campobello International Park is Herring Cove Provincial Park. This park has 10km of walking trails as well as a campground and a picnic area on an arching 1.5km beach. It makes a fine, picturesque place for lunch.

Wilson's Beach
VILLAGE

Ten kilometers north of Roosevelt Park, Wilson's Beach has a large pier with fish for sale, and a sardine-processing plant with an adjacent store. There are various services and shops here in the island's biggest community.

East Quoddy Head Lighthouse
LIGHTHOUSE

Four kilometers north of Wilson's Beach is East Quoddy Head Lighthouse. Whales browse offshore and many people sit along the rocky shoreline with binoculars enjoying the sea breezes.

⚐ Tours

Island Cruises
CRUISE

(☏506-752-1107, 888-249-4400; www.bayof-fundywhales.com; 62 Harbour Head Rd, Wilson's Beach; adult/child $52/42; ☼Jul-Oct) Offers 2½-hour whale-watching cruises.

🛏 Sleeping & Eating

There are very few restaurants on Campobello, and the pickings across the bridge in Lubec, Maine, aren't much better. For self-catering, there's a Valufoods supermarket in Welshpool.

Herring Cove Provincial Park
CAMPGROUND $

(☏506-752-7010; www.tourismnewbrunswick.ca; 136 Herring Cove Rd; campsites/RV sites $22/24; ☼Jun-Sep) This 76-site park on the east side of the island, 3km from the Deer Island ferry, has some nice secluded sites in a forest setting, plus there's a sandy beach and ample hiking.

Pollock Cove Cottages
COTTAGES $$

(☏506-752-2300; senewman@nbnet.nb.ca; 2455 Rte 774, Wilson's Beach; cottages $75-175; @) Simple, clean one- and two-bedroom cottages with million-dollar views.

Owen House B&B
B&B $$

(☏506-752-2977; www.owenhouse.ca; 11 Welshpool St, Welshpool; d incl breakfast with/without bathroom from $122/114) A classic seaside vacation home of yesteryear, complete with antique spool beds made up with quilts, cozy reading nooks and lots of windows on the ocean.

Family Fisheries Restaurant
SEAFOOD $$

(Hwy 774, Wilson's Beach; mains $9-23; ☼8am-7:30pm, later in summer) Part of a fresh fish market, this ultracasual seafood shack specializes in fish-and-chips, lip-smacking chowders, and lobster rolls.

ⓘ Information

For further information see www.visitcampobello.com. There's also a **visitors center** (Hwy 774; ☼10am-5pm) at Roosevelt Campobello International Park.

ⓘ Getting There & Away

East Coast Ferries (www.eastcoastferries.nb.ca; car & driver $16, additional passenger $3; ☼9am-7pm) connects Deer Island to Welshpool on Campobello Island (25 minutes, half-hourly).

NEW BRUNSWICK CAMPOBELLO ISLAND

Grand Manan Island

Cue the Maritime fiddle music. As the ferry from the mainland rounds the northern tip of Grand Manan Island (population 2700), Swallowtail Lighthouse looms into view, poised atop a rocky, moss-covered cliff. Brightly painted fishing boats bob in the harbor. Up from the ferry dock, the tidy village of North Head spreads out along the shore: a scattering of clapboard houses and shops surrounded by well-tended flower gardens and tall, leafy trees.

Grand Manan is a peaceful, unspoiled place. There are no fast-food restaurants, no trendy coffeehouses or nightclubs, no traffic lights and no traffic. Just a ruggedly beautiful coastline of high cliffs and sandy coves interspersed with spruce forest and fields of long grass. Along the eastern shore and joined by a meandering coastal road sit a string of pretty and prosperous fishing villages. There is plenty of fresh sea air and that rare and precious commodity in the modern world: silence, broken only by the rhythmic ocean surf. Some people make it a day trip, but lingering is recommended.

The ferry disembarks at the village of North Head at the north end of the island. The main road, Rte 776, runs 28.5km down the length of the island along the eastern shore. It connects all of Grand Manan's settlements en route to the lighthouse, which is perched atop a bluff at South Head. You can drive from end to end in about 45 minutes. The western side of Grand Manan is uninhabited and more or less impenetrable: a sheer rock wall rising out the sea, backed by dense forest and bog, broken only at Dark Harbour where a steep road drops down to the water's edge. A hiking trail provides access to this wilderness.

Sights

Swallowtail Lighthouse   LIGHTHOUSE
Whitewashed Swallowtail Lighthouse (1860) is the island's signature vista, cleaving to a rocky promontory about 1km north of the ferry wharf. Access is via steep stairs and a slightly swaying suspension bridge. Since the light was automated in 1986, the site has been left to the elements. Nevertheless, the grassy bluff is a stupendous setting for a picnic. It has a wraparound view of the horizon and seals raiding the heart-shape fishing weirs (an ancient type of fishing trap made from wood posts) below.

All of the approximately 30 weirs dotting the waters around Grand Manan are named, some dating back to the 19th century. They bear labels such as 'Ruin,' 'Winner,' 'Outside Chance' and 'Spite,' evoking the heartbreak of relying on an indifferent sea for a living. A tear made by a marauding seal in a net can free an entire catch of herring in a single night.

Grand Manan Historical Museum   MUSEUM
(www.grandmananmuseum.ca; 1141 Rte 776, Grand Harbour; adult/student & senior $5/3; ⊙9am-5:30pm Mon-Sat) This museum makes a good destination on a foggy day. Its diverse collection of local artifacts provides a quick primer on island history. Here you can see a display on shipwreck lore and the original kerosene lamp from nearby Gannet Rock lighthouse (1904). There is also a room stuffed with 200-plus taxidermied birds (including the now-extinct passenger pigeon). The museum hosts a number of evening lectures and community classes and activities.

Seal Cove   HISTORIC SITE
Seal Cove is the island's prettiest village. Much of its charm comes from the fishing boats, wharves and herring-smoking sheds clustered around the tidal creek mouth. For a century, smoked herring was king on Grand Manan. A thousand men and women worked splitting, stringing and drying fish in 300 smokehouses up and down the island. The last smokehouse shut down in 1996. Although herrings are still big business around here, they're now processed at a modern cannery. Today, the sheds house an informal **Sardine Museum** (admission by donation; ⊙11am-4pm Tue-Sat). On display are the world's largest sardine can (alleged) and an authentically smelly exhibit on the smoking process.

Activities

Sea Watch Tours   BIRDWATCHING
(☎506-662-8552, 877-662-8552; www.seawatchtours.com; Seal Cove fisherman's wharf; adult/child $86/48; ⊙Mon-Sat Jul & Aug) Make the pilgrimage out to isolated Machias Seal Island to see the Atlantic puffins waddle and play on their home turf. Access is limited to 15 visitors a day, so reserve well in advance. Getting onto the island can be tricky, as the waves are high and the rocks slippery. Wear sturdy shoes.

Whales-n-Sails Adventures BOAT TOUR
(2 506-662-1999, 888-994-4044; www.whales-n-sails.com; North Head fisherman's wharf; adult/child $66/46; ☉Jul-Sep) A marine biologist narrates these exhilarating whale-watching tours aboard the sailboat *Elsie Menota*. You'll often see puffins, razorbills, murre and other seabirds.

Hiking Trails HIKING
Seventy kilometers of hiking trails crisscross and circle the island. Grab the comprehensive guide, *Heritage Trails and Footpaths on Grand Manan* ($5), available at most island shops. Stay well away from the cliff edges; unstable, undercut ground can give way beneath your feet.

For an easy hike, try the 1.6km shoreline path from Long Pond to Red Point (about a one-hour round-trip; suitable for children). In Whale Cove, the Hole-in-the-Wall is an often photographed natural arch jutting into the sea. It's a short hike from the parking area.

Adventure High KAYAKING, CYCLING
(2 506-662-3563; www.adventurehigh.com; 83 Rte 776, North Head; day tours $45-110, bicycles per half-day/day/week $16/22/130; ☉May-Oct) This outfitter offers tours of the Grand Manan coastline ranging from two-hour sunset paddles to multiday Bay of Fundy adventures.

🛏 Sleeping

Anchorage Provincial Park CAMPGROUND $
(2 506-662-7022; Rte 776 btwn Grand Harbour & Seal Cove; campsites/RV sites $24/26; ☉May-Sep) Family-friendly camping in a large field surrounded by tall evergreens, located 16km from the ferry. There's a kitchen shelter for rainy days, a playground, laundry and a long pebbly beach. Get down by the trees to block the wind. Anchorage adjoins some marshes, which comprise a migratory bird sanctuary, and there are several short hiking trails.

Hole-in-the-Wall Campground CAMPGROUND $
(2 506-662-3152, 866-662-4489; www.grandmanancamping.com; 42 Old Airport Rd, North Head; campsites/cabins $27/40; ☉May-Oct) These spectacular cliff-top campsites are secluded among the rocks and trees, with fire pits, picnic tables and breathtaking views. Choose an inland site if you sleepwalk or suffer from vertigo. Showers and laundry facilities are available, as well as a couple of spotless, simple cabins, furnished with bunk beds and a microwave.

Shorecrest Lodge INN $$
(2 506-662-3216; www.shorecrestlodge.com; 100 Rte 776, Seal Cove; r $90-135; 🖥) Near the ferry landing, this big, comfy farmhouse has 10 sunny rooms with quilts and antique furniture. A rec room has a TV and a toy train set for the kids. The Austrian owners cook up fresh seafood dinners (mains $18 to $28) and takeout lunches; nonguests can call ahead to order.

★ Inn at Whale Cove INN $$
(2 506-662-3181; www.whalecovecottages.ca; Whistle Rd, North Head; s/d incl breakfast $135/145;

NEW BRUNSWICK GRAND MANAN ISLAND

WHOSE ROCK IS IT ANYWAY?

Though Canada and the US share nearly 9000km of border, they manage to play nicely most of the time. So nicely, in fact, that today the sole remaining land dispute between the two countries is over an uninhabited 8-hectare chunk of rock called Machias Seal Island, and a neighboring (and even smaller) island so undistinguished it's referred to only as 'North Rock.'

Foggy, barren and treeless, Machias Seal Island is best known as a nesting site for Atlantic puffins. North Rock is best known for...being a rock. Yet the two tiny islands are part of a dispute that dates back to the 1783 Treaty of Paris, which attempted to draw a border between the newly formed USA and what was then called 'British North America.' Machias Seal Island, approximately equidistant between Maine and New Brunswick's Grand Manan Island, was not directly addressed in the treaty (imagine that!), and has remained part of a 'gray zone' ever since. Canada operates a lighthouse on the island and attempts to maintain it as a bird sanctuary, while some American puffin-boat tour operators challenge Canadian sovereignty. One, the late Captain Barna Nelson of Jonesport, Maine, would parade around the island once a year, waving an American flag. Canada and the US have had the opportunity to resolve the border dispute in international courts, but have declined.

☺ May-Oct) 'Serving rusticators since 1910,' including writer Willa Cather, who wrote several of her novels here in the 1920s and '30s. The main lodge (built in 1816) and half a dozen vine-covered and shingled cottages retain the charm of that earlier era. They are fitted with polished pine floors and stone fireplaces, antiques, chintz curtains and well-stocked bookshelves. Some have kitchens.

Compass Rose B&B **$$**
(☎ 506-662-8570, off-season 613-471-1772; www.compassroseinn.com; 65 Rte 776, North Head; r incl breakfast $105-149) Cheerful, comfortable guest rooms with a seashore motif and harbor views. Within walking distance of the ferry dock, it has one of the island's most atmospheric restaurants (mains $12-$18) attached.

✖ Eating

The island's scant options are nearly non-existent in the off-season (October to early June). That said, there is some fine eating on Grand Manan. Reservations are essential for dinner due to limited table space island-wide.

★ North Head Bakery BAKERY **$**
(www.northheadbakery.ca; 199 Rte 776, North Head; baked goods $1-5; ☺ 6:30am-5:30pm Tue-Sat May-Oct) Scrumptious Danish pastries, fruit pies and artisanal breads made with organic flour make this cheerful red-and-white bakery the first stop for many folks just off the ferry. Sit at the lunch counter with a coffee and sandwich and watch the parade.

Sailors Landing CANADIAN **$**
(☎ 506-662-9620; 1 Ferry Wharf Rd, North Head; mains $5-10; ☺ 6am-10pm Mon-Fri, to 11pm Sat, 7am-9pm Sun) In a hangarlike corrugated metal building by the ferry dock, this updated restaurant offers a 'featured menu' daily, plus fresh, locally caught seafood and homemade desserts.

★ Inn at Whale Cove MODERN CANADIAN **$$$**
(☎ 506-662-3181; www.whalecovecottages.ca; Whistle Rd, North Head; mains $22-28; ☺ 5-9pm) Absolutely wonderful food in a relaxed country setting on the cove. The menu changes daily, but includes mouth-watering upscale meals such as Provençal-style rack of lamb, scallop ravioli and a to-die-for hazelnut crème caramel for dessert. Come early and have a cocktail by the fire in the cozy, old-fashioned parlor.

🛍 Shopping

Roland's Sea Vegetables MARKET
(www.rolandsdulse.com; 174 Hill Rd; ☺ 9am-6pm) Grand Manan is one of the few remaining producers of dulse, a type of seaweed that is used as a snack food or seasoning in Atlantic Canada and around the world. Dark Harbour, on the west side of the island, is said to produce the world's best. Dulse gatherers wade among the rocks at low tide to pick the seaweed, then lay it out on beds of rocks to dry just as they've been doing for hundreds of years. Buy some at this little roadside market, which sells various types of edible local seaweeds from nori to sea lettuce to Irish moss. Sandy, Roland's son, recommends sprinkling powdered dulse on fried eggs or baked fish.

❶ Information

Tourist Information Office (www.grand-manannb.com; 130 Rte 776, North Head; ☺ 8am-4pm Mon-Fri, 9am-noon Sat)

❶ Getting There & Around

The only way to get on and off the island from Blacks Harbour on the mainland to North Head on Grand Manan is by the **government ferry** (☎ 506-662-3724; www.coastaltransport.ca; adult/child/car/bicycle $12/6/33/4; 🎫 ticket office at North Head ferry terminal). The crossing takes 1½ hours, and there are seven departures daily in summer. Service is first-come, first-served at Blacks Harbour; plan on arriving at least 45 minutes before departure. In July and August especially there can be long queues for vehicles to board, but cyclists and pedestrians can walk on at any time. No ticket is required for the trip over; book and pay for your return trip in North Head the day before you plan to leave for the mainland. Watch for harbor porpoises and whales en route.

The ferry dock is within walking distance of several hotels, restaurants, shops and tour operators. To explore the whole of the island, bring your own car, as there is no rental company on Grand Manan.

Adventure High (p411) rents bicycles.

SAINT JOHN

POP 70,500

Saint John is the economic engine room of the province, a gritty port city with a dynamism that's missing from the demure capital. The setting is spectacular – a ring of rocky bluffs, sheer cliffs, coves and peninsulas surrounding a deep natural harbor where the mighty Saint John and Kennebecasis Rivers empty into the Bay of Fundy. It can take a bit of imagination to appreciate this natural beauty, obscured as it is by the smokestacks of a pulp mill, oil refinery and garden-variety urban blight. The city is surrounded by an ugly scurf of industrial detritus and a tangle of concrete overpasses. But those who push their way through all this to the historic core are rewarded with beautifully preserved red-brick and sandstone 19th-century architecture and glimpses of the sea down steep, narrow side streets.

Originally a French colony, the city was incorporated by British Loyalists in 1785 to become Canada's first legal city. Thousands of Irish immigrants arrived during the potato famine of the mid-1800s and helped build the city into a prosperous industrial town, important particularly for its wooden shipbuilding. Today, a large percentage of the population works in heavy industry, including pulp mills, refineries and the Moosehead Brewery.

Downtown (known as Uptown) Saint John sits on a square, hilly peninsula between the mouth of the St John River and Courtenay Bay. Kings Sq marks the nucleus of town, and its pathways duplicate the pattern of the Union Jack.

West over the Harbour Bridge (50¢ toll) is Saint John West. Many of the street names in this section of the city are identical to those of Saint John proper, and to avoid confusion, they end in a west designation, such as Charlotte St W. Saint John West has the ferries to Digby, Nova Scotia.

◎ Sights

New Brunswick Museum
MUSEUM

(www.nbm-mnb.ca; 1 Market Sq; adult/student/family $8/4.50/17; ◎9am-5pm Mon-Wed & Fri, to 9pm Thu, 10am-5pm Sat, noon-5pm Sun) This is a quality museum with a varied collection. There's a captivating section on marine wildlife with an outstanding section on whales, including a life-size specimen. There are also hands-on exhibits, models of old sailing ships and an original copy of *The Night Before Christmas* written in author Clement Clarke Moore's own hand, which was sent to his godfather Jonathan Odell's family in New Brunswick.

Reversing Rapids
RIVER

The Bay of Fundy tides and their effects are a predominant regional characteristic. The rapids here on the St John River are part of that and are one of the best-known sites in the province. However, 'reversing rapids' is a bit of a misnomer. When the high Bay of Fundy tides rise, the current in the river reverses, causing the water to flow upstream. When the tides go down, the water flows in the normal way. Generally, it looks like rapids. **Reversing Rapids Visitors Centre** (200 Bridge Rd; ◎8am-7pm May-Oct), next to the bridge over the river, can supply a 'Reversing Rapids Tide Table' brochure that explains where in the cycle you are.

Loyalist House
HISTORIC BUILDING

(120 Union St; adult/child/family $5.50/2.50/7.50; ◎10am-5pm May-Sep) Dating from 1810, the Georgian-style Loyalist House is one of the city's oldest unchanged buildings. It's now a museum, depicting the Loyalist period, and contains some fine carpentry.

Loyalist Burial Ground
CEMETERY

This solemn cemetery, with fading tombstones from as early as 1784, is just off Kings Sq, in a park-style setting in the center of town.

Carleton Martello Tower
HISTORIC BUILDING

(454 Whipple St; adult/child $3.90/1.90; ◎10am-5:30pm Jun-Sep) Built during the War of 1812, this round stone fort features a restored barracks and other historical displays, but the real reason to go is the panoramic view over Saint John and the Bay of Fundy from the hilltop locale.

Saint John Jewish Historical Museum
MUSEUM

(91 Leinster St; admission by donation; ◎10am-4pm Mon-Fri, 1-4pm Sun) This modest museum traces the history of Saint John's once-thriving Jewish community, whose members included Louis B Mayer of Metro-Goldwyn-Mayer Hollywood fame.

⋔ Activities

Reversing Falls Jet Boat Rides
BOAT TOUR

(☏506-634-8987; www.jetboatrides.com; Fallsview Ave; adult/child $39/29; ◎Jun-Oct) Offers two types of boat trips. One is a leisurely one-hour sightseeing tour to the Reversing Rapids and around the harbor. The other is a 20-minute 'thrill ride' through the white water at the rapids. Count on getting soaked.

Saint John

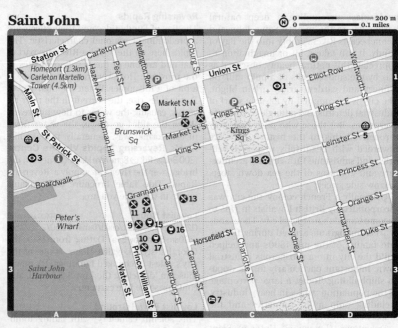

Saint John

◎ Sights
1 Loyalist Burial Ground C1
2 Loyalist House B1
3 Market Square A2
4 New Brunswick Museum A2
5 Saint John Jewish Historical
   Museum D2

🛏 Sleeping
6 Chipman Hill Suites A1
7 Mahogany Manor C3

⊗ Eating
8 Billy's Seafood Company B1
9 Bourbon Quarter & Magnolia Cafe B3

10 East Coast Bistro B3
   Infusion ....(see 12)
11 Java Moose B2
12 Old City Market B1
13 Taco Pica B2
14 Thandi B2

⊖ Drinking & Nightlife
15 Big Tide Brewing Company B3
16 Happinez Wine Bar B3
17 O'Leary's B3

✪ Entertainment
18 Imperial Theatre C2

Irving Nature Park   HIKING
(◎8am-dusk May-Oct) For those who have
vehicles and an appreciation for nature,
Irving Nature Park is a must for its rugged, unspoiled coastal topography. It's
also a remarkable place for birdwatching,
with hundreds of species regularly spotted.
Seals may be seen on the rocks offshore.
Seven trails of varying lengths lead around
beaches, cliffs, woods, mudflats, marsh and
rocks. Good footwear is strongly recommended.

It's well worth the 5km drive southwest
from downtown to get here. Take Hwy 1
west from town and turn south at Exit 107,
Bleury St. Then take a right on Sand Cove
Rd and continue for 2km to the entrance.

Harbour Passage   WALKING
Beginning on a boardwalk at **Market Sq**
(behind the Hilton Hotel), Harbour Passage is a red-paved walk- and cycle-trail
that leads around the harbor, up Bennett
St and down Douglas Ave to the Reversing Falls bridge and lookout. Informative

plaques line the route and it's about a one-hour walk one-way.

Gibson Creek Canoeing CANOEING

(☑506-672-8964; www.gibsoncreek.ca; tours per day from $65) This company offers guided canoe trips through the numerous inter-tidal marshes and peaceful rivers close to the city.

👉 Tours

As a popular stop for cruise-ship travelers, Saint John has a surprisingly large range of tour options. Whale-watching, unfortunate-ly, is not an attraction in Saint John, save for the very occasional, very wayward minke.

Saint John Transit Commission BUS TOUR

(☑506-658-2855; www.saintjohntransit.com; adult/child $22/6; ☺Jun-Sep) Runs two-hour bus tours around the city. Departures and tickets from Reversing Rapids Visitors Centre, Barbour's General Store at Market Sq, and Rockwood Park Campground. Two tours daily.

Words, Walks & Workshops WALKING TOUR

(☑506-672-8601; walks free-$5; ☺7pm Tue Jun-Sep) For nearly 30 years David Goss, travel and outdoor columnist, has led themed walks throughout the city and natural environments. The walks have so much flair that locals as well as visitors frequent the fun. Departure locations and hours vary; check with the visitors center.

Roy's Tour DRIVING TOUR

(www.roystours.webs.com; tours per group per hr $50) Knowledgeable local Roy Flowers nar-rates personalized five- to six-hour taxi tours of the city and surrounds.

🛏 Sleeping

Saint John motels sit primarily along Mana-wagonish Rd, 7km west of uptown. There are also a couple of upscale chain hotels up-town.

Rockwood Park CAMPGROUND $

(☑506-652-4050; www.rockwoodparkcamp-ground.com; Lake Dr S; campsites/RV sites $25/35; ☺May-Sep; ☎) A couple of kilometers north of the downtown area is huge Rockwood Park, with small lakes, a woodland criss-crossed by walking paths, and a camp-ground in a small open field. Bus 6 to Mt Pleasant from Kings Sq goes within a few blocks Monday to Saturday.

University of New Brunswick Summer Residences RESIDENCE HALL $

(☑506-648-5755; www.unbsj.ca; off Sandy Point Rd near Rockwood Park; s/d/ste $35/48/72; ☎) From May to August, the University of New Brunswick's Saint John campus offers sim-ple rooms and rather spartan kitchenette suites in two residence halls. The univer-sity is 6km north of the city center (take bus 15 from Kings Sq).

★Mahogany Manor B&B $$

(☑800-796-7755, 506-636-8000; www.sinow.com/mm; 220 Germain St; d incl breakfast $105-115; ☺@☎) On the loveliest street in Saint John, this gay-friendly, antique-filled Vic-torian is a wonderful place to temporarily call home. Five rooms are a comfy mix of antiques and plush, modern bedding. The upbeat owners know more about the city than you'll be able to absorb – even which meal to order at which restaurant!

Homeport B&B $$

(☑506-672-7255, 888-678-7678; www.homeport.nb.ca; 60 Douglas Ave; r incl breakfast $109-175; ☺❄☎) Perched above once-grand Doug-las Ave, this imposing Italianate-style B&B was once two separate mansions belonging to shipbuilder brothers. It has a boutique-hotel vibe, with a stately parlor, a full bar and 10 sunny guest rooms. Try to snag one with a clawfoot tub. It's about 1km west of the uptown peninsula.

Chipman Hill Suites APARTMENTS $$

(☑506-693-1171; www.chipmanhill.com; 9 Chip-man Hill; ste $79-299; ☺❄☎) Chipman has taken historic properties around downtown, renovated them into mini-apartments with kitchens while retaining all the character, and rents them out by the day, week or month. Size and features determine price, but all are a steal.

🍴 Eating

★Old City Market MARKET $

(www.sjcitymarket.ca; 47 Charlotte St; lunches $5-10; ☺7:30am-6pm Mon-Fri, to 5pm Sat) Wedged between North and South Market Sts, this sense-stunning food hall has been home to wheeling and dealing since 1876. The interi-or of the impressive brick building is packed with produce stalls, bakeries, fishmongers and butcher shops, as well as numerous counters selling a range of delectable pre-pared meals. Locals head to the lunch coun-ter at Slocum and Ferris.

Look out for bags of dulse, a dried Atlantic seaweed that's eaten like potato chips in these parts.

Java Moose
CAFE $

(www.javamoose.com; 84 Prince William St; snacks $2-5; ☺8am-6pm; 🐾) Get your caffeine fix at this home-grown coffeehouse with a groovy North Woods vibe.

Infusion
CAFE $

(www.infusiontearoom.ca; Old City Market; snacks $3-6; ☺7am-7pm; 🐾) In the Old City Market, this warmly lit urban-chic cafe offers dozens of rare and exceptional teas, along with sandwiches and other light fare.

★ East Coast Bistro
INTERNATIONAL $$

(☑506-696-3278; www.eastcoastbistro.com; 60 Prince William St; mains $18-25; ☺11am-4pm Mon, to 9pm Tue-Thu, to 10pm Fri & Sat) Sustainable, local cuisine (they even make their own bread) is the real deal here. East Coast Bistro is one of the standout restaurants in Saint John, offering top-notch cuisine at digestible prices. Pan-fried New Brunswick goat cheese, molasses-glazed Atlantic salmon, and brown-butter apple crumble are just a few of the luscious dishes whipped up in this casual space.

Bourbon Quarter & Magnolia Cafe
CAJUN $$

(☑506-214-3618; Prince William St; mains $10-35; ☺8am-11pm Mon-Fri, 9am-midnight Sat, to 8pm Sun) Cajun food in Canada? Hip, young Saint Johners don't seem to find anything odd about the idea, flocking to eat fried oysters and muffuletta sandwiches at this recently opened pair of adjacent New Orleans–style restaurants. Bourbon Quarter is more formal, Magnolia a casual lunch spot. Both have live music.

Splash Thai Cuisine
THAI $$

(www.splashthaicuisine.com; 419 Rothesay Ave; mains $18-23; ☺4-10pm Tue-Sun) Killer Thai specialties that bring back the locals over and over again. Go for the usual suspects or more inventive twists on the old, like mango chicken curry. Soothing low lights and minimalist decor lend the space an upscale, relaxing vibe.

Taco Pica
MEXICAN, GUATEMALAN $$

(www.tacopica.ca; 96 Germain St; mains $10-17; ☺10am-10pm Mon-Sat) A fusion of authentic Guatemalan and Mexican fare is served in this colorful cantina. An economical introduction to the cuisine is Taco Pica's *pepian* – a simple but spicy beef stew that is as good as you'll find in any Guatemalan household.

Billy's Seafood Company
SEAFOOD $$$

(www.billysseafood.com; 49 Charlotte St; mains $16-32; ☺11am-10pm Mon-Sat, 4-10pm Sun) Since we are on the east coast after all...this popular casual restaurant at the top of the City Market does seafood with flair.

Thandi
INDIAN $$$

(☑506-648-2377; www.singhdining.com; 33 Canterbury St; mains $17-38; ☺11am-10pm Mon-Fri, 4pm-midnight Sat, to 10pm Sun) Thandi gets an A+ for atmosphere, with exposed brick, heavy timbers and warm lighting, a stylish backlit bar downstairs, and cozy fireplaces upstairs. The food is good, too – try Indian classics such as lamb korma or shrimp vindaloo, or fusion specialties such as tandoori strip loin or snapper with mango salsa.

🍷 Drinking & Entertainment

There isn't much of a nightclub scene here, but pub culture and live music thrive in a handful of atmospheric waterfront bars in the uptown core. For weekly goings on, pick up the free *here* entertainment paper, available around town.

Big Tide Brewing Company
BREWERY

(www.bigtidebrew.com; 47 Princess St; ☺11am-midnight Mon-Sat, 3-9pm Sun) This subterranean brewpub is a cozy spot for a pint (try the Confederation Cream Ale or the Whistlepig Stout), a plate of beer-steamed mussels or a friendly game of trivia.

Happinez Wine Bar
BAR

(www.happinezwinebar.com; 42 Princess St; ☺4pm-midnight Wed & Thu, to 1am Fri, 5pm-1am Sat) For a quiet tipple in a sleek urban environment, duck into this intimate little wine bar.

O'Leary's
PUB

(www.olearyspub.com; 46 Princess St; ☺11:30am-11pm Mon & Tue, to 2am Wed-Fri, 3pm-2am Sat) Shoot the breeze with local barflies at this pleasantly divey downtown institution.

Imperial Theatre
THEATER

(☑506-674-4100; www.imperialtheatre.nb.ca; 24 Kings Sq S) Now restored to its original 1913 splendor, this is the city's premier venue for performances ranging from classical music to live theater.

ⓘ Information

Main Post Office (41 Church Ave W, Saint John West) Send general delivery mail here (Postal Station B, E2M 4X6).

Saint John Library (1 Market Sq; ⏱9am-5pm Mon & Sat, 10am-5pm Tue & Wed, to 9pm Thu & Fri) Free internet access.

Saint John Regional Hospital (☏506-648-6000; 400 University Ave; ⏱24hr) Northwest of the town center.

Visitor & Convention Bureau (☏506-658-2990, 888-364-4444; www.tourismsaintjohn. com; Market Sq; ⏱9:30am-8pm) Knowledgeable, friendly staff. Ask for the self-guided walking-tour pamphlets.

ⓘ Getting There & Away

AIR

The airport is 5km east of town on Loch Lomond Rd toward St Martins. Air Canada runs daily flights to Toronto, Montréal and Halifax.

BOAT

There's a daily ferry service between Saint John and Digby, Nova Scotia ($43, three hours).

BUS

The **bus station** (300 Union St; ⏱7:30am-9pm Mon-Fri, 8am-9pm Sat & Sun) is a five-minute walk from town. Routes include Fredericton ($29, 1½ hours) and Moncton ($33, two hours). There's a daily direct bus to Bangor, Maine ($55, 3½ hours), but you'll need to buy your ticket in person.

ⓘ Getting Around

TO/FROM THE AIRPORT

City bus 22 links the airport and Kings Sq. A taxi costs around $35.

ⓘ MOOSE ON THE LOOSE

Every year, there are around 300 collisions involving moose on the roads in New Brunswick. These accidents are almost always fatal for the animal and about five people a year die this way. Eighty-five percent of moose-vehicle collisions happen between May and October, and most occur at night. Slow down when driving after dusk and scan the verges for animals, using your high beams when there is no oncoming traffic. High-risk zones are posted.

BUS

Saint John Transit (☏506-658-4700) charges $2.50. The most important route is the east–west bus service, which is either bus 1 or 2 eastbound to McAllister Dr and bus 3 or 4 westbound to Saint John West near the ferry terminal. It stops at Kings Sq in the city center. Another frequent service is bus 15 or 16 to the university.

CAR & MOTORCYCLE

Discount Car Rentals (☏506-633-4440; www. discountcar.com; 255 Rothesay Ave) is opposite the Park Plaza Motel. Avis, Budget, Hertz and National all have car rental deals at the airport.

Parking meters in Saint John require $1 an hour from 8am to 6pm weekdays only. You can park free at meters on weekends, holidays and in the evening. Park free any time on back streets such as Leinster and Princess Sts, east of Kings Sq. The **city parking lot** (11 Sydney St) is free on weekends.

EASTERN FUNDY SHORE

Much of the rugged, unspoiled Eastern Fundy Shore from Saint John to Hopewell Cape remains essentially untouched. Indeed, hikers, cyclists, kayakers and all nature-lovers will be enchanted by this marvelous coast, edged by dramatic cliffs and tides. It's not possible to drive directly along the coastline from St Martins to Fundy National Park; a detour inland by Sussex is necessary, unless you're prepared to hike.

St Martins

A 40km drive east of Saint John, St Martins is a winsome seaside hamlet surrounded by steep cliffs and flower-studded pastureland. Once a sleepy wooden shipbuilding center, it now draws hikers, bikers and scenic-drive takers to the 11km **Fundy Trail Parkway** (www.fundytrailparkway.com), which winds along a jaw-dropping stretch of coastline. In town, check out the impressive red sandstone sea caves of Mac's Beach, accessible by foot when the tide is low. The village's twin covered bridges are a popular photo op, so bring your camera.

River Bay Adventures (☏506-663-9530; www.riverbayadventures.com; tours from $50, kayaks half-/full day $33/52) runs two- to three-hour guided sea-kayaking trips to the caves and islands along the coast.

St Martin's Country Inn (☏800-566-5257, 506-833-4534; www.stmartinscountryinn.ca;

WORTH A TRIP

SCENIC DRIVE: KENNEBECASIS RIVER VALLEY

On a Saturday in summer, do what loads of Saint Johners do and take the Gondola Point Ferry (p399) to the bucolic Kingston Peninsula, then follow Rte 845 east to the **Kingston Farmers Market** (Rte 845, Kingston; ⊗ 8am-1pm Sat). Sample the fresh fruits and vegetables and various ethnic foods on offer or stop for lunch at the restored 1810 **Carter House Tea Room** (874 Rte 845; cakes & teas $4-8; ⊗ 9:30am-4:30pm Tue-Sat), which is, of course, haunted – by a ghost who likes to tidy up and rearrange the books.

Leave the city folk behind, continuing on Rte 845 into the bustling community of Hampton, where you pick up Rte 121, which follows the north side of the Kennebecasis River through farm country and the villages of Norton and Apohaqui into **Sussex** (population 4200).

Sussex is a working farming community nestled in a green valley dotted with dairy farms. The old-fashioned main street could be a movie set for a heartwarming 1950s coming-of-age story (but please, enough with the outdoor murals!). The well-preserved railway station houses the tourist information center, a small museum devoted to the area's military regiment, and Sully's Ice Cream Parlour.

If you stick around until evening, keep up the 1950s time trip with a double-bill at the **Sussex Drive-In** (☎ 506-432-9114; www.sussexdrivein.com; Rte 2; adult/child $10/6; ⊗ dusk Fri-Sun May-Sep). You can pitch your tent at the attached **Town & Country Campark** (☎ 506-432-9114; www.sussexdrivein.com; campsites/RV sites $24/31). You can also bed down at **Jonah Place B&B** (☎ 866-448-8800, 506-433-6978; www.jonahplace.com; 977 Main St; r incl breakfast from $99; ⊝ @ 🕾). The classy and cozy **Broadway Cafe** (☎ 506-433-5414; 73 Broad St; mains lunch $8, dinner $17-35; ⊗ 10am-3pm Mon & Tue, to 9pm Wed-Sat) is the place to eat in town.

Gasthof Old Bavarian (☎ 506-433-4735; www.oldbavarian.ca; 1130 Knightville Rd; mains $10-24; ⊗ noon-10pm Fri-Sun) is the place for a truly memorable meal in the countryside. On a country road in a quiet valley settled by German and Dutch farmers, this place could have been transported – beer steins and all – from the Black Forest. The decor is Bavarian hunting lodge, with low timbered ceilings, heavy wooden furniture and cheerful blue-and-white-checked tablecloths. The plates of schnitzel and sausages made on the family farm are plain beautiful: they're decorated with purple cabbage, fresh-picked greens and creamy white dumplings, with hearty flavors to match. Despite being more or less in the middle of nowhere, this place is always packed for dinner, so reservations are recommended. It's cash only.

Hang a left out of Gasthof's back onto the Knightville Rd, then left again onto Country View Rd at Anagance Ridge, then right onto Rte 890 into Petitcodiac. This stretch of road affords breathtaking vistas of rolling green countryside that'll make you want to sell up, move here and raise chickens. If you can work up an appetite, stroll through the greenhouses and have a healthy organic lunch or tea and cake at **Cornhill Nursery & Cedar Cafe** (www.cornhillnursery.com; 2700 Rte 890; mains $8-12; ⊗ 8am-4pm May-Oct). From Petitcodiac you can rejoin Hwy 1, heading east to Moncton or west back to Fundy Park and Saint John. The views of the valley from Hwy 1 between Hampton and Sussex are also lovely.

303 Main St; r $110-165; ⊝ ✳ 🕾), the towering mansion overlooking the bay, is the most deluxe place in town and also offers delectable meals (mains $19 to $24) in its delightful, caught-in-time dining room.

Right on Mac's Beach, the resort-style **Seaside Restaurant** (81 Mac's Beach; mains $8-18; ⊗ 11am-7pm) serves fish and chips, scallops, chowder and more. Now you know you are on holiday.

Fundy National Park

This **national park** (www.pc.gc.ca/fundy; daily permits adult/child/family $7.80/3.90/19.60) is one of the country's most popular. Highlights are the world's highest tides, the irregularly eroded sandstone cliffs and the wide beach at low tide that makes exploring the shore for small marine life and debris such a treat. The park features an extensive network of impressive hiking trails.

🏃 Activities

Cycling

Mountain biking is permitted on six trails: Goose River, Marven Lake, Black Hole, East Branch, Bennett Brook (partially open) and Maple Grove. Surprisingly, at last report there were no bicycle rentals in Fundy National Park or in nearby Alma. Contact the visitors centers to find current information on this.

Hiking

Fundy features 120km of walking trails, where it's possible to enjoy anything from a short stroll to a three-day trek. Several trails require hikers to ford rivers, so be prepared.

The most popular backpacking route is the **Fundy Circuit**, a three-day trek of 45km through the heart of the park. Hikers generally spend their first night at Marven Lake and their second at Bruin Lake, returning via the Upper Salmon River. First, stop at the visitors center to reserve your wilderness campsites ($10 per night; call ahead for reservations).

Another overnight trek is the **Goose River Trail**. It joins the Fundy Circuit, and is accessible by road from St Martins. This undeveloped three-day trek is one of the most difficult in the province. While you can cycle to Goose River, the trail beyond can only be done on foot.

Enjoyable day hikes in Fundy National Park include the **Coppermine Trail**, a 4.4km loop which goes to an old mine site; and the **Third Vault Falls Trail**, a challenging one-way hike of 3.7km to the park's tallest falls. In summer, rangers lead a variety of family-friendly educational programs, including night hikes.

Skiing

In the winter, 25km of park trails are groomed for fantastic cross-country skiing, with additional snowshoeing tracks through the forest.

Swimming

The ocean is pretty bracing here; luckily, there's a heated saltwater **swimming pool** (adult/child $3/1.50; ☻11am-6:30pm Jul & Aug) not far from the park's southern entrance.

🛏 Sleeping

The park has three campgrounds and 13 wilderness sites. **Camping reservations** (☎877-737-3783; www.pccamping.ca) must be made at least three days in advance. The park entry fee is extra and is paid upon arrival.

With bathhouses and showers, **Chignecto North** (campsites/RV sites $26/36) is a good pick for families. The 131-site **Headquarters Campground** (campsites/RV sites $26/37) is near the visitors center. It's the only area open for winter camping. Along the coast, 8km southwest of the visitors center, is **Point Wolfe Campground** (campsites $26) and its 181 sites with sea breezes and cooler temperatures. To reserve a backcountry site ($10), call either of the visitors centers.

Fundy Highlands Inn & Chalets
CABINS, MOTEL **$$**

(☎506-887-2930, 888-883-8639; www.fundyhighlandchalets.com; 8714 Hwy 114; r $95-105, cabins from $115; ☻May-Oct) Simple but charming little cabins, all with decks, kitchenettes and superlative views, and a small, well-kept motel.

ℹ Information

Headquarters Visitors Centre (☎506-887-6000; ☻10am-6pm) At the park's south entrance.

Wolfe Lake Information Centre (☎506-432-6026; Hwy 114; ☻10am-6pm Jul & Aug) At the park's north entrance.

THE TIDES OF FUNDY

The tides of the Bay of Fundy are the highest in the world. A Mi'kmaq legend explains the tide as the effect of a whale's thrashing tail sending the water forever sloshing back and forth. A more prosaic explanation is in the length, depth and gradual funnel shape of the bay itself.

The contrasts between the high and ebb tide are most pronounced at the eastern end of the bay and around the Minas Basin, with tides of 10m to 15m twice daily 12½ hours apart. The highest tide ever recorded anywhere was 16.6m, the height of a four-story building, at Burncoat Head near Noel, Nova Scotia.

SCENIC DRIVE: FUNDY TRAIL PARKWAY

This magnificent **parkway** (www.fundytrailparkway.com; adult/child/family $5.50/3.50/13; ⊘ 6am-8pm May-Oct) traverses a rugged section of what has been called the only remaining coastal wilderness between Florida and Newfoundland. The 11km-long parkway to Big Salmon River put an end to the unspoiled wilderness part. There is now a lovely stretch of pavement with numerous viewpoints, picnic areas and parking lots. Eventually, it will extend to Fundy National Park. Nova Scotia is visible across the bay. There is also a separate 16km-long very steep and hilly hiking/biking trail.

On Saturdays, Sundays and holidays, a free hourly **shuttle bus** operates from noon to 6pm, ferrying hikers up and down the trail between the parkway entrance and Big Salmon River. In the off-season, the main gate is closed, but you can park at the entrance and hike or pedal in.

At Big Salmon River a suspension bridge leads to a vast wilderness hiking area beyond the end of the road. Hikers can make it from Big Salmon River to Goose River in Fundy National Park in three to five days. At last report, no permits or permissions were required to do so. But beyond Big Salmon River, be prepared for wilderness, rocky scree and even a rope ladder or two.

You can spend the night here, too, at **Hearst Lodge** (r incl breakfast & dinner per person $109; ⊘ Jun-Sep), a cabin-on-steroids built by newspaper magnate J Randolph Hearst.

Alma

The tiny village of Alma is a supply center for the park. It has accommodations, restaurants, a small gas station, grocery store, liquor outlet and laundry. Most facilities close in winter, when it becomes a ghost town. Down on the beach is a statue of Molly Kool, the first female sea captain on the continent.

Fresh Air Adventure (☏800-545-0020, 506-887-2249; www.freshairadventure.com; 16 Fundy View Dr; tours from $55; ⊘ Jun-Sep) offers myriad kayaking tours, from two-hour trips to multiday excursions, in and around Fundy.

For accommodations, **Parkland Village Inn** (☏506-887-2313; www.parklandvillageinn.com; 8601 Hwy 114; r incl breakfast $95-160) is a busy 60-year-old inn with comfy, renovated rooms, some with killer Bay of Fundy views. At the inn, **Tides Restaurant** (8601 Hwy 114; mains $12-22; ⊘ noon-8pm) is a beachy, fine-dining place that does top-rate seafood and excellent ribs. The casual takeout patio has fish-and-chips and cold beer.

Cape Enrage & Mary's Point

From Alma, old Rte 915 yields two sensational, yet relatively isolated, promontories high over the bay.

See the 150-year-old lighthouse at the windblown, suitably named **Cape Enrage** (www.capenrage.ca; off Rte 905; adult/child $5/3; ⊘ 9am-8pm). The cape was restored and is still expertly run by local high-school students and volunteer mentors from the area. On-site guides offer **climbing** ($85 for two hours) and **rappelling** ($90 for two hours) off the steep rock faces. Or you can simply wander the beach looking for fossils (low tide only!).

When all that activity gets you hungry, head to the **Cape House Restaurant** (mains $13-28; ⊘ 11:30am-11pm). Here in the original lighthouse-keeper's house you can enjoy the dramatic view while dining on pan-seared local scallops, foraged fiddlehead ferns and lobster tacos.

At Mary's Point, 22km east, is the **Shepody Bay Shorebird Reserve** (Mary's Point Rd, off Hwy 915) **FREE**. From mid-July to mid-August hundreds of thousands of shorebirds, primarily sandpipers, gather here. Nature trails and boardwalks lead through the dikes and marsh. The interpretive center is open from late June to early September, but you can use the 6.5km of trails any time.

Hopewell Rocks

At Hopewell Cape, where the Petitcodiac River empties into Shepody Bay, are the **Hopewell Rocks** (www.thehopewellrocks.ca; off Hwy 114; adult/child/family $9/6.75/24; shuttle per person $2; ⊘ 8am-8pm; 🚻). The 'rocks' are bizarre sandstone erosion formations known as 'flowerpots,' rising several stories from the ocean floor. Some look like arches, others like massive stone mushrooms, still others like enormous ice-cream cones. Crowds come from all over the world to marvel at their Dr Seussian look, making the rocks New Brunswick's top attraction (and certainly one of its most crowded). You can only walk amid the rocks at low tide – check the tide tables at any tourist office or area hotel. At high tide, the rock towers are still visible from the trails that wind through the woods above.

The park features a large interpretive center with educational displays, two cafes, picnic areas and several kilometers of well-trafficked trails. In high season, the massive parking lot is choked with cars and the staircases down to the beaches suffer human traffic jams.

Another way to visit the rocks is by kayak. **Baymount Outdoor Adventures** (☑877-601-2660; www.baymountadventures.com; tours adult/child $62/52; ☺Jun-Sep) offers two-hour paddling tours.

There are several motels in the Hopewell Rocks vicinity, including the family-run **Hopewell Rocks Motel** (☑506-734-2975; www.hopewellrocksmotel.com; 4135 Hwy 114; r incl breakfast $110; �j☷), with 39 tidy rooms, a heated pool and an adjacent lobster restaurant. Prices are halved in the low season.

SOUTHEASTERN NEW BRUNSWICK

The southeastern corner of New Brunswick province is a flat coastal plain sliced by tidal rivers and salt marshes. Moncton, known as 'Hub City,' is a major crossroads with two well-known attractions where nature appears to defy gravity. Southeast, toward Nova Scotia, are significant historical and bird-life attractions.

Moncton

POP 64,100

Once a major wooden shipbuilding port, Moncton is now the fastest-growing city in the Maritimes, with an economy built on transportation and call centers drawn here by the bilingual workforce. It's a pleasant, suburban city, with a small redbrick

downtown along the muddy banks of the Petitcodiac River. There are some decent restaurants, bars and a bustling Acadian farmers market. Apart from that, there is little to detain the visitor.

◉ Sights

Magnetic Hill   AMUSEMENT PARK
(www.magnetichill.com; cnr Mountain Rd & Hwy 2; admission per car $5; ☺8am-8pm May-Sep) At Magnetic Hill, one of Canada's best-known (though not best-loved) attractions, gravity appears to work in reverse. Start at the bottom of the hill in a car and you'll drift upward. You figure it out. After hours and out of season, it's free. It's a goofy novelty, worth the head-scratching laugh, but all the money-generating, spin-off hoopla now surrounding the hill is a bit much. Family-oriented attractions include a zoo, faux village hawking ice cream and souvenirs, and a water park. Magnetic Hill is about 10km northwest of downtown off Mountain Rd.

Tidal Bore Park   PARK
(Main St; ☺24hr) The tourist literature talks up the twice-daily return of the waters of the tidal Petitcodiac River. In theory, the tide comes in as one solid wave, unfurled like a carpet across the muddy riverbed in one dramatic gesture; the height of this on-coming rush can allegedly vary from just a few centimeters to about 1m. In reality, it usually just looks like a big mud seep, and is, well...boring.

Casino New Brunswick   CASINO
(www.casinonb.ca; 21 Casino Dr; ☺10am-3am) The province's first full-service casino, this 24,000-sq-foot gambling palace brings a touch of Vegas to Moncton. It packs in crowds with its 500 slot machines, poker room, numerous bars and buffets, and an entertainment venue boasting big-name performers such as the Beach Boys and Bill Cosby. The casino is about 9km northwest of the town center off Mountain Rd.

☞ Tours

Roads to Sea   BUS TOUR
(☑506-850-7623; www.roadstosea.com; ☺May-Oct) Roads to Sea offers 3½-hour bus tours ($85) to Hopewell Rocks (p420), an eight-hour guided trip that takes in the Rocks, Fundy National Park, Cape Enrage and a few covered bridges and lighthouses ($160),

Moncton

Moncton

⊙ Sights

🛏 Sleeping

⊗ Eating

⊛ Entertainment

as well as a two-hour tour of the Moncton sights ($45).

🛏 Sleeping

Reservations are a good idea as the city is a major conference destination and often gets packed solid. Most of the chain hotels are clustered around Magnetic Hill.

C'mon Inn HOSTEL **$**
(☎506-854-8155, 506-530-0905; www.moncton-hostel.ca; 47 Fleet St; dm/r $35/70; 🛜) Moncton's only hostel is housed in a rambling Victorian two blocks from the bus station. The five-bunk dorm rooms and private singles and doubles with shared bathroom are nothing fancy, but they are clean and comfortable. There is a kitchen for guest use and lots of space for lounging on the verandas.

Auberge au Bois Dormant Inn
B&B $$

(☎506-855-6767, 866-856-6767; www.auberge-auboisdormant.com; 67 John St; s $85-120, d $95-130; ⊗⊞@⊗) A gracious Victorian renovated with crisp modern flair. This gay-friendly establishment is on a quiet, tree-lined residential street and puts on a three-course breakfast spread. Some rooms have private balconies.

L'Hotel St James
BOUTIQUE HOTEL $$$

(☎888-782-1414; www.stjamesgatecanada.com; 14 Church St; r $150-280; ☎) On the 2nd floor of a 19th-century brick shop building, this downtown boutique hotel has 10 stylish urban-chic guest rooms that wouldn't look a bit out of place in Montréal or New York. Swank design touches include mod tile walls, crisp white linens, huge flatscreen TVs and iPod docks. There's a popular pub and restaurant downstairs.

Eating

Cafe Archibald
FRENCH, CANADIAN $

(221 Mountain Rd; mains $8-12; ⊙7am-11pm) At this stylish bistro, crepes are the house specialty, whipped up in the open stainless-steel kitchen and served at redwood and zebra-print banquettes or on the inviting screened-in porch. Alternatively, feast on the wild mushroom and basil pizza with a leafy salad.

Café Cognito
CAFE $

(700 Main St; snacks $3-8; ⊙7:30am-5:30pm Mon-Fri, 9am-4pm Sat) Get your morning joe at downtown's Café Cognito, a tiny European-style cafe with exposed brick walls and a handful of bistro tables.

Calactus
VEGETARIAN $

(☎506-388-4833; www.calactus.ca; 125 Church St; mains $10-13; ⊙11am-10pm; ☑) Shangri-la for vegetarians! Enjoy the freedom to order anything off the globally inspired menu, which contains everything from felafel plates, to tofu cheese pizza, to fried Indian *pakoras*. The natural wood, warm earth colors and burbling fountain create a soothing atmosphere.

Pump House
BREWERY $$

(www.pumphousebrewery.ca; 5 Orange Lane; mains $8-15; ⊙11:30am-late) The Pump is where the locals unwind and you can get a good burger, steak-based meal or wood-fired pizza. Of the brews made on the premises, the Muddy River stout is tasty – or try the beer sample tray.

Little Louis'
MODERN CANADIAN $$$

(☎506-855-5022; www.littlelouis.ca; 245 Collishaw St; mains $24-34; ⊙5-10pm) The odd location of this nouvelle-cuisine bistro – upstairs in a faceless industrial strip mall – only adds to its speakeasy vibe. The atmosphere is cozy, with low lights, white tablecloths and jazzy live music. Local foodies rave about dishes such as foie gras with apple-wine jelly, or crispy steelhead trout with shitake and saffron-vanilla butter. Whatever you do, always start with raw local oysters on the half shell with fresh horseradish. The wine list racks up awards on a regular basis.

Drinking & Entertainment

Moncton has a lively little rock and indie music scene, with several bars and clubs clustered around central Main St. The free *here* has the rundown on the city's vibrant (read: raucous) nightlife.

Capitol Theatre
THEATER

(www.capitol.nb.ca; 811 Main St) You can sip a glass of wine during the interval at the grand Capitol Theatre, a 1922 vaudeville house that has been restored to its original glory. It is the venue for concerts and live theater throughout the year.

Shopping

Dieppe Farmers Market
MARKET

(www.marchedieppemarket.com; cnr Acadie Ave & Gauvin Rd, Dieppe; ⊙7am-1:30pm Sat) A great place to get a taste of New Brunswick's vibrant Acadian culture is this weekly market. Stalls overflow with locally made cheeses, cottage wines and homemade preserves as well as Acadian dishes such as *tourtière* (a meat pie), *fricot à la poule* (home-style chicken stew) and rabbit pie. You can nibble sweet pastries such as *plogues* and *guaffres* while browsing the craft stalls. To get there from downtown, head 2km east on Main St, which becomes Champlain, to Acadie Ave. Look for the yellow roof.

Information

Moncton Hospital (☎506-857-5111; 135 MacBeath Ave) Emergency room.

Moncton Public Library (644 Main St; ⊙9am-8:30pm Tue-Thu, to 5pm Fri & Sat; ☎) Free internet access.

St George St After Hours Medical Clinic (☎506-856-6122; 404 St George Blvd; ⊙5:30-8pm Mon-Fri, noon-3pm Sat, Sun & holidays) No appointment is required to see a doctor here. Adjacent to Jean Coutu Pharmacy.

Visitors Information Center (www.gomonc-ton.com; Bore Park, Main St E; ⊙8:30am-6:30pm)

ℹ Getting There & Away

AIR

Greater Moncton International Airport (YQM; www.gmia.ca) is about 6km east of Champlain Place Shopping Centre via Champlain St. Air Canada runs daily flights to Toronto and Montréal.

BUS

Maritime (☑1-800-575-1807; www.maritime-bus.com; 92 Lester St) runs to Fredericton ($34, two hours), Saint John ($34, two hours), Char-lottetown, PEI ($34, three hours) and Halifax ($49, four hours).

CAR & MOTORCYCLE

If you need wheels, Avis, Budget, Hertz and National all have car-rental desks at the airport, or try **Discount Car Rentals** (☑506-857-2323; www.discountcar.com; 1543 Mountain Rd).

Parking can be a hassle in Moncton: the parking meters ($1 per hour) and 'no parking' signs extend far from downtown. The municipal parking lot at Moncton Market on Westmorland St charges $1/$8 per hour/day and is free on Saturday, Sunday and evenings after 6pm. High-field Sq Mall on Main St provides free parking for its clients.

TRAIN

With **VIA Rail** (www.viarail.ca; 1240 Main St), the Ocean line goes through northern New Bruns-wick, including Miramichi and Campbellton, and into Québec, on its way to Montréal (from $135). The train to Halifax (from $39) departs six days a week.

ℹ Getting Around

The airport is served by bus 20 from Champlain Pl nine times a day on weekdays. A taxi to the center of town costs about $15.

Codiac Transit (www.codiactranspo.ca) is the local bus system, with 40 wi-fi-equipped buses going all over town.

Sackville

Sackville is a small university town that's in the right place for a pit stop – for birds and people. The **Sackville Waterfowl Park**, across the road from the university off East Main St, is on a major bird migration route. Boardwalks with interpretive signs rise over portions of it. The **Wildlife Service** (17 Water-fowl Lane, off E Main St; ⊙8am-4pm Mon-Fri) has

information and a wetlands display at one of the entrances. Enthusiasts should also see the **Tantramar Wetlands Centre** (www.wet-ed.com; 223 Main St; ⊙8am-4pm Mon-Fri) **FREE**, with its walking trail and educational office, behind the high school.

Mel's Tea Room (17 Bridge St; mains $4-10; ⊙7:30am-8pm) has been operating in the center of town since 1919, now with the charm of a 1950s diner – with a jukebox and prices to match.

Fort Beauséjour National Historic Site

Right by the Nova Scotia border, this **national historic site** (www.pc.gc.ca/fort-beausejour; adult/child/family $3.90/1.90/9.50; ⊙interpretive center 9am-5pm Jun-Oct), 1.5km west of the visitors center, preserves the re-mains of a French fort built in 1751 to hold the British back. It didn't work. Later it was used as a stronghold during the American Revolution and the War of 1812. Only earth-works and stone foundations remain, but the view is excellent, vividly illustrating why these crossroads of the Maritimes were forti-fied by two empires.

To find out more, visit the **New Bruns-wick Visitors Centre** (☑506-364-4090; 158 Aulac Rd; ⊙9am-9pm), off Hwy 2 in Aulac, at the junction of roads leading to all three Maritime provinces.

NORTHUMBERLAND SHORE

New Brunswick's Northumberland Shore stretches from the Confederation Bridge to Kouchibouguac National Park and is dotted with fishing villages and summer cottages. Shediac, on all lobster-lovers' itineraries, is a popular resort town in a strip of summer seaside and beach playgrounds. A good part of the population along this coast is French-speaking, and Bouctouche is an Acadian stronghold. Further north, Kouchibouguac National Park protects a large swath of sce-nic coastal ecosystems.

Cape Jourimain

Near the bridge to PEI, the **Cape Jouri-main Nature Centre** (www.capejourimain. ca; Rte 16; ⊙8am-7pm May-Oct) **FREE** sits in a 675-hectare national wildlife area that protects this undeveloped shoreline and its migratory birds. Seventeen kilometers of trails wind through salt marshes, dunes, woods and beach. A four-story lookout provides views of the surroundings and Confederation Bridge.

There's a **visitors center** (Hwy 16; ⏱8am-9pm May-Sep) by the bridge.

Shediac

Shediac, a self-proclaimed lobster capital, is a busy summer beach town and home of the annual July lobster fest. The many white lights sprinkled around town all summer lend a festive air. Don't fail to have your picture taken with the 'World's Largest Lobster' sculpture – you can't miss it!

It seems on any hot weekend that half the province is flaked out on the sand at **Parlee Beach**, turning the color of cooked lobster. South at Cap Pelé are vast stretches of more sandy shorelines. Terrific **Aboiteau Beach** comprises over 5km of unsupervised sand, while others have all amenities and lifeguards.

Shediac Bay Cruises (☎888-894-2002, 506-532-2175; www.lobstertales.ca; Pointe-du-Chene wharf; adult/child $68/46) takes passengers out on the water, pulls up lobster traps, then shows you how to cook and eat 'em.

Shediac is ringed with shantytown-like RV campgrounds whose only appeal is their proximity to Parlee Beach. More upscale lodgings are found at **Maison Tait** (☎506-532-4233; www.maisontaithouse.com; 293 Main St; r incl breakfast from $189; 🐾), a luxurious 1911 mansion with nine sun-drenched rooms, and **Auberge Gabriele Inn** (☎877-982-7222, 506-532-8007; www.aubergegabrieleinn.com; 296 Main St; r $110-165; ♨🐾), with simple, country-chic rooms above a popular restaurant.

Tops for dining out are **Paturel's Shore House** (☎506-532-4774; Rte 133; mains $18-27; ⏱4-10pm) for fresh seafood, or the restaurant at Maison Tait for fine dining and romantic ambience. Grab fresh seafood and strawberry daiquiris at always-packed **Captain Dan's** (www.captaindans.ca; mains $11-28) at the busy Pointe-du-Chene wharf. After dinner, catch a flick at the wonderfully retro **Neptune Drive-In** (www.neptunedrivein.ca; 691 Main St; ⏱Jun-Sep).

Bouctouche

This small, surprisingly busy waterside town is an Acadian cultural focal point with several unique attractions. The **visitors information center** (Hwy 134; ⏱9am-5pm Jun-Sep) at the town's south entrance features a boardwalk out over the salt marsh.

⊙ Sights

Le Pays de la Sagouine　HISTORIC PARK
(www.sagouine.com; 57 Acadie St; adult/child/family $20/12/45; ⏱10am-5:30pm Jul & Aug) Sitting on a small island in the Bouctouche River, this reconstructed Acadian village has daily programs in English and French. There are interactive cooking and craft demos, historical house tours and live music, as well as several cafes in which to sample old-fashioned Acadian cuisine. In July and August there's a supper theater at 7pm Monday to Saturday ($66).

Irving Eco Centre　PARK
(www.irvingecocentre.com; 1932 Hwy 475; ⏱interpretive center 10am-6pm May-Oct) On the coast 9km northeast of Bouctouche, this nature center protects and makes accessible 'La Dune de Bouctouche,' a beautiful, long sandspit jutting into the strait. The interpretive center has displays on the flora and fauna, but the highlight is the **boardwalk** that snakes above the sea grass along the dunes for 2km. The peninsula itself is 12km long, taking four to six hours to hike over the loose sand and back. There are several naturalist-led tours daily. There's a 12km hiking/cycling trail through mixed forest to Bouctouche town, which begins at the Eco Centre parking lot.

KC Irving, founder of the Irving empire, was from Bouctouche, and there's a large bronze statue of him in the town park.

Olivier Soapery
MUSEUM

(www.oliviersoaps.com; 831 Rte 505, Ste-Anne-de-Kent) This old-fashioned soap factory advertises its 'museum' on what seems like every highway in New Brunswick. It's really more of a store, with tons of luscious-smelling hand-molded soaps, but it does have regular talks on the soap-making process and a few interesting historical displays.

🛏 Sleeping & Eating

Chez les Maury
CAMPGROUND $

(☎506-743-5347; www.fermemaury.com; 2021 Rte 475; campsites $25; ⊙May-Oct) On the grounds of a family-run vineyard, this small, basic campground has toilets, showers and a tiny private beach across the way.

Le Vieux Presbytère
INN $$

(☎506-743-5568; www.vieuxpresbytere.nb.ca; 157 Chemin du Couvent; d incl breakfast $119-165; 🛜) This former priest's residence was once a popular religious retreat for Acadians from across the province. The best rooms, with high molded ceilings and simple, sunny decor, are in the older part of the building.

Restaurant La Sagouine
ACADIAN $

(43 Blvd Irving; mains $8-18; ⊙6am-10pm) Fried clams or a traditional Acadian dinner are on offer here. Be sure to get a seat on the outdoor patio.

Kouchibouguac National Park

Beaches, lagoons and offshore sand dunes extend for 25km here, inviting strolling, birdwatching and clam-digging. The **park** (www.pc.gc.ca; adult/child $7.80/3.90; ⊙8am-dusk) encompasses hectares of forest and salt marshes, crisscrossed or skirted by bike paths, hiking trails and groomed cross-country ski tracks. Kouchibouguac (*koosh-e-boo-gwack*), a Mi'kmaq word meaning 'river of long tides,' also has moose, deer and black bear.

🏃 Activities

Cycling & Kayaking

Kouchibouguac has 60km of bikeways – crushed gravel paths that wind through the park's backcountry. **Ryan's Rental Centre** (☎506-876-3733; bicycles per hour/day $6/28,

canoes/kayaks per day $30/50), near the South Kouchibouguac campground, rents out bicycles, canoes and kayaks. From Ryan's you can cycle a 23km loop and never be on the park road. The calm, shallow water between the shore and the dunes, which run for 25km north and south, makes for a serene morning paddle.

Hiking

The park has 10 trails, mostly short and flat. The excellent **Bog Trail** (1.9km) is a boardwalk beyond the observation tower, and only the first few hundred meters are crushed gravel. The **Cedars Trail** (1.3km) is less used. The **Osprey Trail** (5.1km) is a loop trail through the forest. **Kelly's Beach Boardwalk** (600m one-way) floats above the grass-covered dunes. When you reach the beach, turn right and hike 6km to the end of the dune. Take drinking water.

Swimming

The lagoon area is shallow, warm and safe for children, while adults will find the deep water on the ocean side invigorating.

🛏 Sleeping & Eating

Kouchibouguac has two drive-in campgrounds and three primitive camping areas totaling 359 sites. The camping season is from mid-May to mid-October, and the park is very busy throughout July and August, especially on weekends. **Camping reservations** (☎877-737-3783; www.pccamping.ca) are taken for 60% of the sites. Otherwise, get on the lengthy 'roll call' waiting list – it can take two or three days to get a site. The park entry fee is extra.

South Kouchibouguac (campsites $28) is the largest campground. It's 13km inside the park near the beaches in a large open field ringed by trees, with sites for tents and RVs, showers and a kitchen shelter.

On the north side of Kouchibouguac River, **Cote-a-Fabien** (campsites $19) is the best choice for those seeking a bit of peace and privacy. There is water and vault toilets, but no showers. Some sites are on the shore, others nestled among the trees, with a dozen walk-in sites (100m; wheelbarrows are provided for luggage) for those who want a car-free environment. The Osprey hiking trail starts from here. No reservations accepted.

The three primitive campgrounds cost $10 per person per night; they have only vault toilets. **Sipu** and **Petit-Large** have water pumps. **Pointe-a-Maxime** is the most difficult to get to (access by water only), but this does not translate into remote seclusion. There is a constant stream of passing motorized boat traffic from the fishing wharf nearby.

There are a couple of snack bars and a restaurant in the park, but you should stock up on groceries in nearby St-Louis-de-Kent.

ℹ Information

Visitors Center (www.pc.gc.ca/kouchibouguac, 186 Hwy 117; ⊙ 8am-8pm)

ℹ Getting There & Away

It is difficult to get to and around the park without a car or bicycle. The distance from the park gate to the campgrounds and beaches is at least 10km. The nearest bus stop is in Rexton, 16km south of the park, where **Maritime** (☑ 1-800-575-1807; www.maritimebus.com; 126 Main St) buses stop at the Circle K gas station. There is one bus a day heading south to Moncton ($16), and one a day heading north to Miramichi ($23).

MIRAMICHI RIVER VALLEY AREA

In New Brunswick, the word Miramichi refers to both the city and the river, but it connotes even more: an intangible, captivating mystique. The spell the region casts emanates partially from the Acadian and Irish mix of folklore, legends, superstitions and tales of ghosts. It also seeps from the dense forests and wilderness of the area and from the character of the residents, who wrestle a livelihood from these natural resources. The fabled river adds its serpentine cross-country course, crystal tributaries and world-renowned salmon fishing. The region produces some wonderful rootsy music and inspires artists, including noted writer David Adams Richards, whose work skillfully mines the temper of the region.

Miramichi

The working-class river city of Miramichi is an amalgam of the towns of Chatham, Newcastle, Douglastown, Loggieville, Nelson and several others along a 12km stretch of the Miramichi River near its mouth. Miramichi, with its Irish background, is an English-speaking enclave in the middle of a predominantly French-speaking region.

Though surrounded by two paper mills and sawmills, central Newcastle is pleasant enough. In the central square is a statue to Lord Beaverbrook (1879–1964), one of the most powerful press barons in British history and a major benefactor of his home province. His ashes lie under the statue presented as a memorial to him by the town. Beaverbrook's boyhood home, the 1879 **Beaverbrook House** (www.beaverbrookhouse. com; 518 King George Hwy; ⊙ 9am-5pm Mon-Fri, 10am-5pm Sat, 1-5pm Sun Jun-Aug) **FREE**, is now a museum.

Miramichi is a mill town, not a tourist center, but traditional folk-music enthusiasts might want to pay a visit for the **Irish Festival** (www.canadasirishfest.com; ⊙ mid-Jul) and the **Miramichi Folksong Festival** (www. miramichifolksongfestival.com; ⊙ early Aug), the oldest of its kind in North America.

🛏 Sleeping & Eating

Enclosure Campground   CAMPGROUND $
(☑ 506-622-0680; 8 Enclosure Rd, Derby Junction; campsites/RV sites $31/36; ⊙ May-Oct) Southwest of Newcastle off Hwy 8, this former provincial park includes a nice wooded area with spacious quasi-wilderness sites for tenters.

Governor's Mansion   B&B $$
(☑ 506-622-3036, 877-647-2642; www.governorsmansion.ca; 62 St Patrick's St, Miramichi; r incl breakfast from $80) On the south side of the river overlooking Beaubears Island is the creaky-but-elegant Victorian Governor's Mansion (1860), onetime home of the first Irish lieutenant governor of the province. Rooms are a tad frilly but provide a cozy place to rest your head.

Cunard   CHINESE $$
(www.cunardrestaurant.com; 32 Cunard St, Chatham; mains $11-23; ⊙ noon-10pm) Surprisingly decent Canadianized Chinese food, such as chicken chow mein and honey-garlic spareribs, in a classic, lacquer-and-dragon-print dining room.

ℹ Information

Tourist Information Center (www.discover-miramichi.com; 199 King St; ⊙ 10am-5pm Jun-Sep) The tourist information center is downtown at Ritchie's Wharf, a down-at-heel riverfront boardwalk park.

ℹ️ Getting There & Away

Maritime (☎1-800-575-1807; www.maritime-bus.com; 201 Edward St) buses depart from the Best Value Inn. Daily buses leave for Fredericton ($54, 2½ hours), Saint John ($49, five hours) and Campbellton ($44, three hours).

The **VIA Rail station** (www.viarail.ca; 251 Station St at George St) is in Newcastle. Trains from Montréal and Halifax stop here.

Miramichi River Valley

The Miramichi is actually a complex web of rivers and tributaries draining much of central New Brunswick. The main branch, the 217km-long Southwest Miramichi River, flows from near Hartland through forest to Miramichi where it meets the other main fork, the Northwest Miramichi. For over a hundred years, the entire system has inspired reverent awe for its tranquil beauty and incredible Atlantic salmon fly-fishing. Famous business tycoons, international politicians, sports and entertainment stars and Prince Charles have all wet lines here. Even Marilyn Monroe is said to have dipped her toes in the water. The legendary fishery has had some ups and downs with overfishing, poaching and unknown causes (perhaps global warming) affecting stocks, but they now seem back at sustainable levels.

⊙ Sights

Atlantic Salmon Museum   MUSEUM (www.atlanticsalmonmuseum.com; 263 Main St, Doaktown; adult/child $5/3; ⊙9am-5pm Apr-Oct) Learn about historic Doaktown's storied fishing history and check out the salmon and trout aquarium.

Metepenagiag Heritage Park   HISTORIC SITE (☎506-836-6118; www.metpark.ca; 2156 Micmac Rd, Red Bank; adult/child $8/6; ⊙10am-5pm) On the Esk River, the Metepenagiag Heritage Park has interpretive tours of Mi'kmaq culture and history on a 3000-year-old archaeological site.

🏃 Activities

Sport fishing remains the main activity, but is tightly controlled for conservation. Licenses are required and all anglers must employ a registered guide. A three-day license for nonresidents is $60. All fish under 35cm or over 63cm must be released. Salmon fishing on the Miramichi is primarily hook and release, to preserve the precious and endan-

gered species. (Most of the salmon served up in the province is, in fact, salmon farmed in the Bay of Fundy.)

WW Doak & Sons (www.doak.com; 331 Main St, Doaktown) is one of Canada's best fly-fishing shops. It sells a huge number of flies annually, some made on the premises. A wander around will get an angler pumped.

Despite the presence of the king of freshwaters, there are other pastimes to enjoy. The **Miramichi Trail**, a walking and cycling path along an abandoned rail line, is now partially complete, with 75km of the projected 200km usable.

At McNamee, the pedestrian Priceville Suspension Bridge spans the river. It's a popular put-in spot for canoeists and kayakers spending half a day paddling downriver to Doaktown. Several outfitters in Doaktown and Blackville offer equipment rentals, shuttle services and guided trips for leisurely canoe, kayak or even tubing trips along the river. Try **Gaston Adventure Tours** (bgaston@nbnet.nb.ca; canoe tours $60-180), with personalized fishing trips and falls tours run by Bev Gaston of the Atlantic Salmon Museum.

🛏️ Sleeping & Eating

Beautiful rustic lodges and camps abound, many replicating the halcyon days of the 1930s and '40s. Check out www.miramichirivertourism.com for links to more accommodations and fishing outfitters. Restaurants are few and far between – plan to pack in your own supplies.

O'Donnell's Cottages & Expeditions   MOTEL, COTTAGES $$ (☎800-563-8724, 506-365-7636; www.odonnellscottages.com; 439 Storeytown Rd, Doaktown; cottages from $129) Cozy log cabins on the riverbank. Offers a variety of outdoor activities.

ℹ️ Information

Tourist Office (www.doaktown.com; 263 Main St; ⊙10am-5pm) The tourist office is in the Salmon Museum in Doaktown, the center of most valley activity.

NORTHEASTERN NEW BRUNSWICK

The North Shore, as it is known to New Brunswickers, is the heartland of Acadian culture in the province. The region was settled 250 years ago by French farmers and fishers, starting from scratch again after the upheaval of the Expulsion, frequently intermarrying with the original Mi'kmaq inhabitants. The coastal road north from Miramichi, around the Acadian Peninsula and along Chaleurs Bay to Campbellton passes through small fishing settlements and peaceful ocean vistas. At Sugarloaf Provincial Park, the Appalachian Mountain Range comes down to the edge of the sea. Behind it, stretching hundreds of kilometers into the interior of the province, is a vast, trackless wilderness of rivers and dense forest, rarely explored.

Tracadie-Sheila

Unmasking a little-known but gripping story, the **Historical Museum of Tracadie** (Rue du Couvent; adult/child $3/free; ☺9am-5pm Mon-Fri, noon-5pm Sat & Sun) focuses on the leprosy colony based here from 1868 to as late as 1965. The nearby cemetery has the graves of 60 victims of Hansen's Disease (leprosy).

Caraquet

The oldest of the Acadian villages, Caraquet was founded in 1757 by refugees from forcibly abandoned homesteads further south. It's now the quiet, working-class center of the peninsula's French community. Caraquet's colorful, bustling fishing port, off Blvd St-Pierre Est, has an assortment of moored vessels splashing at the dock. East and West Blvd St-Pierre are divided at Rue le Portage.

The tourist office and all of the local tour operators are found at the **Carrefour de la Mer** complex, with its Day Adventure Centre, restaurant and views down on the waterfront near the fishing harbor.

◉ Sights

Acadian Historic Village   HISTORIC PARK (www.villagehistoriqueacadien.com; 14311 Hwy 11; adult/student/family $17.50/15.50/42; ☺10am-6pm Jun-Sep) Acadian Historic Village, 15km west of Caraquet, is a major historical reconstruction set up like a village of old. Thirty-three original buildings relocated to the site and animators in period costumes reflect life from 1780 to 1880. A good three to four hours is required. To eat there are old-fashioned sit-down Acadian meals at La Table des Ancêtres, the 1910 historical menu at the Château Albert dining room, and several snack bars. The village has a program for kids ($35), which provides them with a costume and seven hours of supervised historical activities.

★ Festivals & Events

The largest annual Acadian cultural festival, **Festival Acadien** (www.festivalacadien.ca), is held here the first two weeks of August. It draws 100,000 visitors; over 200 performers including singers, musicians, actors, dancers from Acadia and other French regions (some from overseas) entertain. Especially picturesque is the annual blessing of the fleet, when a flotilla of fishing vessels cruises the harbor with ribbons and flags streaming from their rigging. The culminating Tintamarre Parade is a real blowout.

🛏 Sleeping & Eating

Maison Touristique Dugas   INN, CAMPGROUND $ (☎506-727-3195; www.maisontouristiquedugas. ca; 683 Blvd St-Pierre W; campsites/r/ste from $20/85/119, cabins $99) A few miles west of Caraquet, five generations of the friendly Dugas family have run this rambling, something-for-everyone property. The homey,

NEW BRUNSWICK TRACADIE-SHEILA

WORTH A TRIP

SCENIC DRIVE: THE ACADIAN PENINSULA

Take a run out to the very northeastern tip of the province – a chain of low, flat islands pointing across the Gulf of St Lawrence to Labrador. Rte 113 cuts across salt marsh and scrub arriving first in **Shippagan**, home of the province's largest fishing fleet, where crab is king. Visit the sea creatures at the **Aquarium & Marine Centre** (www.aquarium-nb.ca; 100 Aquarium St; adult/child $8.50/5.50; ☺10am-6pm Jul-Sep). Kids will love the touch tanks full of sea creatures, and the seals (fed at 11am and 4pm).

Hop the bridge to **Lamèque**, a tidy fishing village that has hosted the **Lamèque International Baroque Festival** (☎800-320-2276, 506-344-5846; www.festivalbaroque. com; ☺late Jul) for over 30 years. Note the red, white and blue Acadian flags flying from nearly every porch. Rte 113 continues north to **Miscou Island**. Stop to walk the boardwalk trail over a cranberry bog before the road dead-ends at the lighthouse.

antique-filled 1926 house has 11 rooms with shared bathrooms. There are five clean, cozy cabins with private bathrooms and cooking facilities in the backyard, a small field for RVs beyond that, and a quiet, tree-shaded campground for tenters.

★**Hotel Paulin**   HOTEL $$
(📞866-727-9981, 506-727-9981; www.hotelpaulin. com; 143 Blvd St-Pierre W; r incl breakfast $128, r incl breakfast & 4-course dinner from $195) Scrimp elsewhere and splurge on a night at the exquisite Hotel Paulin. This vintage seaside hotel overlooking the bay was built in 1891 and has been run by the Paulin family since 1907. The rooms are sunny and polished, done up in crisp white linens, lace and antiques. If you are staying elsewhere, make reservations for dinner; the hotel has earned a reputation for fine cuisine. An example: fiddlehead fern soup followed by Acadian chicken fricot with herb dumplings (table d'hôte $45).

Château Albert   INN $$$
(📞506-726-2600; www.villagehistoriqueaca-dien.com/chateauanglais.htm; Acadian Historic Village; d incl dinner & theater package $275) For complete immersion in the Acadian Historic Village, spend the night in early-20th-century style – no TV, no phone, but a charming, quiet room restored to its original 1909 splendor (with a modern bath). The original Albert stood on the main street in Caraquet until it was destroyed by fire in 1955. Packages are available that include dinner in the period dining room downstairs and a ride in a Ford Model T.

Le Caraquette   CANADIAN $$
(89 Blvd St-Pierre; mains $8-14) Overlooking the harbor, this casual family-run restaurant serves Maritime standards such as fried clams and mayonnaise shrimp salad along with French-Canadian specialties such as poutine and smoked-meat sandwiches.

ⓘ Information

Tourist Office (www.ville.caraquet.nb.ca; 51 Blvd St-Pierre Est; ⏰9am-5pm Jun-Sep)

ⓘ Getting There & Away

Public transportation around this part of the province is very limited as Maritime buses don't pass this way. Van shuttles connect with the bus or train in Miramichi or Bathurst. Ask for details at the tourist office.

Campbellton

Campbellton is a pleasant but unremarkable mill town on the Québec border. There are really only two reasons to come here: to transit to or from Québec, or to hike, ski and camp at Sugarloaf Provincial Park. The lengthy Resti-gouche River, which winds through northern New Brunswick and then forms the border with Québec, empties to the sea here. The Bay of Chaleur is on one side and dramatic hills surround the town on the remaining sides.

Dominated by Sugarloaf Mountain, which looks vaguely like one of its other namesakes in Rio, **Sugarloaf Provincial Park** (www.parc-sugarloafpark.ca; 596 Val d'Amours Rd) FREE is off Hwy 11 at Exit 415. From the base, it's just a half-hour walk to the top – well worth the extensive views.

The last naval engagement of the Seven Years' War was fought in the waters off this coast in 1760. The Battle of Restigouche marked the conclusion of the long struggle for Canada by Britain and France. Sugarloaf Provincial Park has 76 **campsites** (📞506-789-2366; www.parcsugarloafpark.ca; 596 Val d'Amours Rd; campsites/RV sites $25/32; ⏰May-Sep) in a wooded setting 4km from Campbellton.

You can also crash comfortably at **Campbellton Lighthouse Hostel** (📞506-759-7044; campbellton@hihostels.ca; 1 Ritchie St; dm $27; ⏰Jun-Aug; 📶). This clean hostel is in a converted lighthouse by the Restigouche River, near the Maritime bus stop and Campbellton's 8.5m **salmon sculpture**.

Alternatively, **Maison McKenzie House B&B** (📞506-753-3133; www.bbcanada.com/4384. html; 31 Andrew St; r with shared bathroom incl breakfast $75-100; ⊜📶) is a homey 1910 house handy to downtown. For $60, the folks here will rent you a kayak and drop you off upriver.

The helpful provincial **tourist office** (📞506-789-2367; 56 Salmon Blvd; ⏰8am-9pm May-Sep) is next to City Centre Mall.

ⓘ Getting There & Away

Maritime (📞1-800-575-1807; www.maritimebus. com; 46 Water St) stops at the Pik-Quik convenience store, near Prince William St. The bus departs daily for Fredericton ($82, six hours) and Moncton ($59, six hours). Twice a day (once in the morning and once in the afternoon), an **Orléans Express** (www.orleansexpress.com) bus leaves from the Pik-Quick for Gaspé ($41, six hours) and Québec City ($91, seven hours). The **VIA Rail station** (www.viarail.ca; 99c Roseberry St) is conveniently central.

Prince Edward Island

Best Places to Eat

➡ Lot 30 (p440)

➡ Shipwright's Café (p453)

➡ Inn at Bay Fortune (p444)

➡ Pearl (p452)

➡ Lobster suppers at town halls and churches around the province

Best Places to Stay

➡ Fairholm Inn (p438)

➡ Barachois Inn (p449)

➡ Great George (p438)

➡ Maplehurst Properties (p443)

➡ Willowgreen Farm (p454)

Why Go?

Prince Edward Island (PEI) is as pretty as a storybook, and it just so happens that the island's depiction in a storybook – Lucy Maud Montgomery's *Anne of Green Gables* – is what has made the place famous. And like Anne Shirley, the heroine of that book, the island is a red-head – from tip to tip, sienna-colored soil peeks out from under potato plants, and the shores are lined with rose and golden sand. Meanwhile the Green Gables–esque landscape is a pastoral green patchwork of rolling fields, tidy gabled farmhouses and seaside villages.

Yet despite the pervasive splendor of the province, the first thing most visitors notice, and fall in love with, is PEI's charm and relaxed atmosphere. The 'Gentle Island' really lives up to its nickname, and the least authentic things you'll find here are the orange nylon braids of little girls in tourist spots dressed up as 'Anne.'

When to Go
Charlottetown

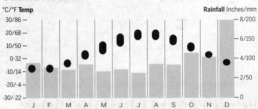

Jun Enjoy the spring calm and blooming wildflowers before the crowds hit.

Jul & Aug The entire island is in festival mode with live music and lobster suppers nightly.

Sep Traditional music and a bevy of food events mark PEI's Fall Flavours Festival.

Prince Edward Island Highlights

1 Be transported into the pages of *Anne of Green Gables* while visiting the Green Gables House in **Cavendish** (p451).

2 Eat your fill of lobster with all the fixings at **New Glasgow** (p449) or **St Ann** (p450).

3 Follow the floating boardwalk across the salt marsh and over the sand dunes onto the empty beach at **Greenwich** (p445).

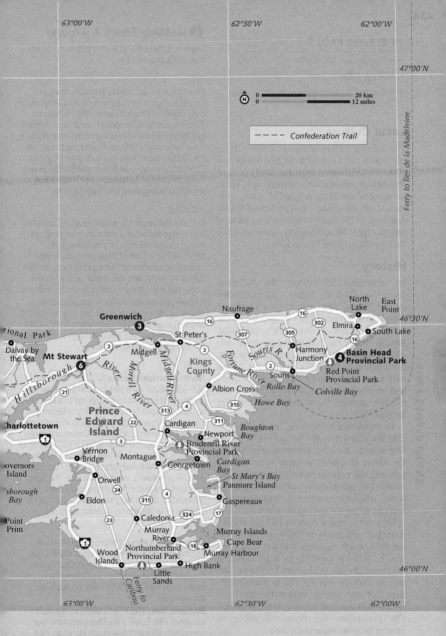

4 Wiggle your feet and hear a squeak at the 'singing sands' of **Basin Head Provincial Park** (p444).

5 Stay in a heritage B&B, wander the scenic waterfront and enjoy the charms of **Charlottetown** (p435).

6 Revel with the locals to rocking live music at homey venues like the **Trailside Cafe** (p445) in Mt Stewart.

PEI FAST FACTS

➡ Population: 145,000

➡ Area: 5700 sq km

➡ Capital: Charlottetown

Local Culture

The defining feature of island culture is its rural roots – most islanders are just one or two generations removed from the family farm or fishing boat, or are still there working it. There are descendants of the original Mi'kmaq (mig-*maw*) population and small pockets of French Acadians in the eastern and western parts of the province. Most islanders, however, trace their heritage to the British Isles.

History

Its Aboriginal inhabitants, the Mi'kmaq, knew the island as Abegeit – 'Land Cradled on the Waves.' Although Jacques Cartier of France first recorded PEI's existence in 1534, European settlement didn't begin until 1603. Initially small, the French colony grew only after Britain's expulsion of the Acadians from Nova Scotia in the 1750s. In 1758 the British took the island, known then as Île St Jean, and expelled the 3000 Acadians. Britain was officially granted the island in the Treaty of Paris of 1763.

To encourage settlement, the British divided the island into 67 lots and held a lottery to give away the land. Unfortunately, most of the 'Great Giveaway' winners were speculators and did nothing to settle or develop the island. The questionable actions of these absentee landlords hindered population growth and caused unrest among islanders.

One of the major reasons PEI did not become part of Canada in 1867 was because union did not offer a solution to the land problem. In 1873 the Compulsory Land Purchase Act forced the sale of absentee landlords' land and cleared the way for PEI to join Canada later that year. Foreign land ownership, however, is still a sensitive issue in the province. The population has remained stable, at around 140,000, since the 1930s.

In 1997, after much debate, PEI was linked to New Brunswick and the mainland by the Confederation Bridge – at almost 13km, it's the world's longest artificial bridge over ice-covered waters.

ℹ Getting There & Around

There is little public transportation on PEI so most people rent a car.

AIR

Charlottetown's airport is 8km from town and serves all flights for the province. Air Canada has daily flights to Charlottetown from Halifax and Toronto, and from Montréal from June to September. WestJet offers direct flights to Charlottetown from Toronto and Ottawa. From June to September, Delta Airlines runs one daily direct flight to Charlottetown from New York and Boston, respectively. In summer **Sunwing** (📞877-786-9464; www.flysunwing.com) flies from Toronto.

BICYCLE

Cyclists and pedestrians can't use the Confederation Bridge and must use the 24-hour, demand-driven shuttle service (bicycle/pedestrian $8.25/4.25). On the PEI side, go to the bridge operations building at Gateway Village in Borden-Carleton; on the New Brunswick side, go to the Cape Jourimain Nature Centre at exit 51 on Rte 16.

While your easiest option to get around the island is by car, bicycle is also a fine choice. The flat and well-maintained Confederation Trail (p439) runs the length of the island through some beautiful countryside and small towns.

BOAT

Northumberland Ferries (📞888-249-7245, 902-566-3838; www.peiferry.com) runs the ferry service that links Wood Islands, in PEI's southeast, to Caribou, Nova Scotia, from May to December. There are up to nine daily sailings in each direction during the summer, and five in the fall and spring (car/pedestrian/motorcycle $67.50/17/40). Note that vehicle fees include all passengers for the 1¼-hour trip. All tickets are round-trip fares even if you're only taking the ferry one way. The ferry operates on a first-come, first-served basis. For information on the ferry service between Souris and Îles de la Madeleine, Québec, see p321.

BUS

Trius Transit Lines (📞902-566-5664; www.triustransit.ca) Runs local services within Charlottetown and Summerside and its County Line Express runs between the two ($9 each way) three times a day via Rte 2. Schedules are available on the website.

Maritime Bus (📞800-575-1807; www.maritimebus.com; 7 Mt Edward Rd, Charlottetown) Has services to Charlottetown from Moncton, New Brunswick ($42.87 one-way, three hours) two times a day, with stops at Borden-Carleton and Summerside en route. There are two buses a day to Halifax ($72.35 one-way, 5½ hours), with a transfer in Amherst, Nova Scotia.

Advanced Shuttle (📞877-886-3322; www.advancedshuttle.ca; Nassau St, University Ave,

REGIONAL DRIVING DISTANCES

North Cape to East Point: 273km

Halifax to Charlottetown: 227km

Charlottetown to Montréal: 1199km

Charlottetown) A convenient service from Charlottetown or Summerside to Halifax or any point along the way (adult one-way $69). The van has a bicycle carrier.

East Connection (☑902-393-5132) Departs Charlottetown daily around noon for Souris, arriving at 1pm in time for the 2pm ferry. The shuttle van leaves Souris at 1:30pm, arriving at Charlottetown an hour later.

CAR & MOTORCYCLE

The **Confederation Bridge** (☑888-437-6565, 902-437-7300; www.confederationbridge.com; car/motorcycle $43/17; ◔24hr) is the quickest way to get to PEI from New Brunswick and east central Nova Scotia. Unfortunately, the 1.1m-high guardrails rob you of any hoped-for view. The toll is only charged on departure from PEI, and includes all passengers.

If you're planning to travel one way on the bridge and the other way by ferry, it's cheaper to take the ferry to PEI and return via the bridge.

CHARLOTTETOWN

POP 34,562

PEI's capital is just about the perfect size, with a collection of stylish eateries and a lively cultural scene. Couple this with quiet streets for strolling, abundant greenery and a well-preserved historical core, and you have plenty of small-town appeal.

History

Charlottetown is named after the exotic consort of King George III. Her African roots, dating back to Margarita de Castro Y Sousa and the Portuguese royal house, are as legendary as they are controversial.

While many believe the city's splendid harbor was the reason Charlottetown became the capital, the reality was less glamorous. In 1765 the surveyor-general decided on Charlottetown because he thought it prudent to bestow the poor side of the island with some privileges. Thanks to the celebrated 1864 conference, however, Charlottetown is etched in Canadian history as the country's birthplace.

⊙ Sights

All of the major sights are within the confines of Old Charlottetown, which makes wandering between them as rewarding as wandering through them.

Province House National Historic Site · HISTORIC SITE

(☑902-566-7626; http://www.pc.gc.ca/lhn-nhs/pe/provincehouse/index.aspx; 165 Richmond St; admission $3.40; ◔8:30am-5pm) Charlottetown's centerpiece is the imposing, yet welcoming, neoclassical Province House. The symmetry of design is carried throughout, including two brilliant skylights reaching up through the massive sandstone structure. It was here in 1864, within the Confederation Chamber, that 23 representatives of Britain's North American colonies first discussed the creation of Canada. Along with being the 'birthplace of Canada,' the site is home to Canada's second-oldest active legislature.

Several rooms have been restored, and in July and August actors in period garb wander the halls and regularly come together to perform reenactments of the famous conference. Enjoy the *Great Dream*, a 17-minute film about the monumental 1864 conference.

Founders' Hall · MUSEUM

(☑800-955-1864, 902-368-1864; www.founders-hall.ca; 6 Prince St; adult/child $9.50/6.25; ◔8:30am-8pm) Opened in 2001, this high-tech multimedia exhibit, housed in an old train station, swamps your senses with facts and fun about Canada's history since 1864. It's sure to entertain children and the child in you.

Beaconsfield Historic House · NOTABLE BUILDING

(☑902-368-6603; 2 Kent St; adult/student/family $5/4/14; ◔10am-5pm) With its crowning belvedere, intricate gingerbread trim and elegant 19th-century furnishings, Beaconsfield House is the finest Victorian mansion in Charlottetown. Have a wander or sit on the verandah and be stunned by the view.

Government House · NOTABLE BUILDING

(☑902-368-5480; ◔10am-4pm Mon-Fri Jul & Aug) **FREE** Within the sprawling gardens of Victoria Park is Government House. This striking colonial mansion, with its grand hall, Palladian window and Doric columns, has been home to PEI's lieutenant governors since 1835. In 2003 the Hon JL Bernard

Charlottetown

400 m
0.2 miles

East (Hillsborough) River

Peake's Wharf

Maritime Bus (900m)

Papa Joe's (700m);
Farmers Market (2km)

Victoria Park

Terry Fox Rd
Park Rdwy

East St
West St
Union St
Kent St
Rochford St
Chestnut St
Passmore St
Churchill Ave
Victoria St
Ambrose St
Pownal St
Bayfield St
Euston St

Grafton St
University Ave
Fitzroy St
Prince St
Kent St
Queen St
Grafton St
Richmond St
Dorchester St
King St
Water St
Pownal St

Great George St
Sydney St
Hillsborough St
Victoria Row
Cumberland St
Weymouth St

Charlottetown

broke with an almost 170-year-old tradition and opened its doors to the public.

St Dunstan's Basilica NOTABLE BUILDING
(☑902-894-3486; 45 Great George St; ⊘9am–5pm) **FREE** Rising from the ashes of a 1913 fire, the three towering stone spires of this neo-Gothic basilica are now a Charlottetown landmark. The marble floors, Italianate carvings and decoratively embossed ribbed ceiling are surprisingly ornate.

🖙 Tours

Self-guided walking tour booklets are available for just a Loonie ($1) at the tourist office.

Confederation Players WALKING TOUR
(☑1800-565-0278; 6 Prince St; adult/child $15/8; ⊘daily Jul & Aug) There is no better way to tour Charlottetown. Playing the fathers and ladies of Confederation, actors garbed in 19th-century dress educate and entertain through the town's historic streets. Tours leave from Founders' Hall, and there are three variations on the theme: historic Great George St, Island Settlers and the haunts of local ghosts.

Peake's Wharf Boat Cruises BOAT CRUISE
(☑902-566-4458; www.peakeswharfboattours. com; 1 Great George St; 70min cruise $20; ⊘2:30pm, 6:30pm & 8pm Jun-Aug) Observe sea life, hear interesting stories and witness a wonderfully different perspective of Charlottetown from the waters of its harbor. An

excellent seal-watching trip ($28) departs at 2:30pm, returning at 5pm.

Harbour Hippo Hippopotabus BUS & BOAT TOUR
(☑902-628-8687; www.harbourhippo.com; 2 Prince St; 1hr tour adult/child $24/16) Want to explore historic Charlottetown but afraid the kids will get bored? Hop on this amphibious bus that takes you to all the sights on land, then floats in the water.

🎎 Festivals & Events

Charlottetown Festival THEATER
(☑800-565-0278; www.charlottetownfestival.com; ⊘mid-May–mid-Oct) This theatrical festival features free outdoor performances, a children's theater and dance programs.

Festival of Small Halls MUSIC
(www.smallhalls.com; ⊘mid-Jun) Island musicians, dancers and storytellers who have 'made it' out of the province return to their homeland to perform in rural community halls around PEI during this 11-day festival.

Old Home Week CULTURE
(☑902-629-6623; www.oldhomeweekpei.com; ⊘mid-Aug) Held at the Provincial Exhibition grounds, this event features carnival rides, musical entertainment, games of chance, harness racing and traditional livestock shows.

Fall Flavours   FOOD

(☎866-960-9912; www.fallflavours.ca; ☉last 3 weeks of Sep) Now one of the island's largest festivals, this massive kitchen party, set on the Charlottetown waterfront, merges great traditional music with incredible seafood. Don't miss the oyster-shucking championships or the chowder challenge.

🛏 Sleeping

Old Charlottetown's charms and proximity to major sights and restaurants makes it the most enviable area to rest your head. During summer, Charlottetown hums with activity, so it's wise to book ahead. In the off-season, accommodations are plentiful and most places reduce their rates. Parking is freely available at, or close to, all accommodations.

Spillett House B&B   B&B $

(☎902-892-5494; www.spilletthouse.pe.ca; 157 Weymouth St; s/d without bathroom incl breakfast $50/60; ☎) This lovely heritage home is scrupulously clean, with polished hardwood floors and antique furnishings, homemade quilts on the beds and lace curtains on the windows. Kids are welcome and there are storage facilities for bicycles.

Charlottetown Backpackers   B&B $

(☎902-367-5749; www.charlottetownbackpackers.com; 60 Hillsborough St; dm/r incl breakfast $32/80; ☎) Impossible to miss with its bright red-and-white paint job and happy hostellers milling about on the lawn, this superbly happening backpackers has cozy single-sex or mixed dorms, a good kitchen and a quirky common room with a turntable and a rather epic vinyl collection. Be prepared for spontaneous barbecues and pub outings.

Charlotte's Rose Inn   INN $$

(☎888-237-3699, 902-892-3699; www.charlottesrose.ca; 11 Grafton St; r incl breakfast $120-195, apt $195; ✳☎) Miss Marple must be around here somewhere. This decadent Victorian has true English flair with bodacious rose-printed wallpaper, lace canopies, big fluffy beds and grand bathrooms. There's a fire in the parlor for guests to enjoy along with complimentary tea and cakes. A modern loft apartment can accommodate five and has its own private rooftop deck.

Aloha Tourist Home   B&B $$

(☎855-892-5642, 902-892-5642; www.alohaamigo.com; 234 Sydney St; r incl breakfast $90-150; ☎) A welcoming choice that's really a heritage B&B complete with antiques and comfy beds, but without the hefty price tag. The serve-yourself breakfasts are gourmet, the location is central and the owner is sweet and helpful. Lower-end rooms have shared bathrooms. There's one family-sized room for $225 and all prices drop considerably outside the high season.

★ Fairholm Inn   B&B $$$

(☎888-573-5022, 902-892-5022; www.fairholm.pe.ca; 230 Prince St; ste incl breakfast $129-289; ☎) This historic inn was built in 1838 and is a superb example of the picturesque movement in British architecture. Take tea while enjoying the morning sun in the beautiful conservatory, wander the gardens or hole up with a book in the library. Luxurious English fabrics, beautiful PEI artwork and grand antiques fill each suite. Light a fire, soak in your tub and sink back into the elegant days of the 19th century.

★ Great George   INN $$$

(☎800-361-1118, 902-892-0606; www.thegreatgeorge.com; 58 Great George St; d incl breakfast $175-219, ste $269-899; ✳☎) This colorful collage of celebrated buildings along Charlottetown's most famous street has rooms ranging from plush and historic to bold and contemporary – but all are simply stunning. It's both gay- and family-friendly. A babysitting service is available, as is a fitness room.

Fitzroy Hall B&B   B&B $$$

(☎866-627-9766; www.fitzroyhall.com; 45 Fitzroy St; d $99-190, ste $225-300; ☎) A perfect blend of elegance and comfort, this house is as grand as they come, while the welcome is warm and down to earth. The innkeepers have put some serious thought into how to make their guests comfortable: the answer is found with refined antiques, muted color schemes, and details like hidden alcoves with fridges and hot pots for guests to keep cold drinks or make tea.

🍴 Eating

Thanks largely to the Culinary Institute at Charlottetown's Holland College, which keeps churning out talented chefs, the city has a heaped helping of fine eateries. During summer, Victoria Row's pedestrian mall and the waterfront are hot spots for diners and drinkers. Pubs are also a great place to go for good-value eating.

★ Leonard's
CAFE $

(University Ave; sandwiches from $5; ⊘9am-5pm Tue-Sat) Find absolute comfort in this little cafe full of cushioned seating and soothing country-style muted hues. Treat yourself to excellent German pastries, salads and creative sandwiches as well as all-day breakfasts made with free-range eggs, a great cheese selection and cold cuts like Black Forest ham. Wash it down with farmers market teas and espresso.

Young Folk & the Kettle Black
CAFE $

(98 Water St; light lunches $9; ⊘8am-8pm Mon-Thu, to 10pm Fri & Sat, 11am-6pm Sun) A cozy bakery and cafe that feels like a mix between a rural farmhouse and an urban art gallery. Enjoy great coffee, breakfasts and light lunches.

Splendid Essence
TAIWANESE $

(☑902-566-4991; 186 Prince St; mains $6-12; ⊘11:30am-3pm & 5-8pm; ☑) Savory Taiwanese vegetarian dishes are served in this cozy Victorian, fitted out with warm wood paneling and intimate booths upholstered in red, green and gold and accented with Chinese art. Recommended are the spicy vegetables and fried rice chased with a steaming mug of hot almond milk.

Farmers Market
MARKET $

(☑902-626-3373; 100 Belvedere Ave; ⊘9am-2pm Sat, also Wed Jul & Aug) Come hungry and empty-handed. Enjoy some prepared island foods or peruse the cornucopia of fresh organic fruit and vegetables. The market is north of the town center off University Ave.

Papa Joe's
CANADIAN $

(345 University Ave; mains $10-15; ⊘11am-9pm) This family-style restaurant is superpopular with locals. Here, all pretensions are checked at the door as you dine on bacon-wrapped meatloaf, turkey pot pie or a steak sandwich. Wednesdays go exotic with Indian cuisine served all day.

Water Prince Corner Shop
SEAFOOD $$

(☑902-368-3212; 141 Water St; meals $10-27; ⊘9:30am-8pm) When locals want seafood they head to this inconspicuous, sea-blue eatery near the wharf. It is deservedly famous for its scallop burgers, but it's also the best place in town for fresh lobster. You'll probably have to line up for a seat, otherwise order takeout lobster, which gets you a significant discount.

Sirinella
ITALIAN $$

(☑902-628-2271; 83 Water St; lunch $8-17, dinner $15-28; ⊘11:30am-2pm & 5-10pm Mon-Fri, 5-10pm Sat) Cross the threshold of this charming restaurant and you are transported to seaside Italy. It's nothing fancy, just little round white-clothed tables, some Mediterranean oil paintings and incredibly authentic Italian fare.

Daniel Brennan Brick House
MODERN CANADIAN $$

(☑902-566-4620; 125 Sydney St; mains $13-32; ⊘11am-9pm Mon-Thu, to 10pm Fri & Sat, 4-10pm Sun) The chic ambience of this heritage brick building is matched by creative dishes inspired by island culture and made with local ingredients. Try the lobster poutine, seafood bouillabaisse, Thai curry chicken or just a good PEI beef burger. Don't leave without enjoying a cocktail or dessert in the upstairs lounge.

CYCLING THE CONFEDERATION TRAIL

Following the rail-bed of Prince Edward Island's erstwhile railway, the 357km-long Confederation Trail is almost entirely flat as it meanders around hills and valleys. There are some sections of the trail that are completely canopied by lush foliage, and in late June and the early weeks of July the trail is lined with bright, flowering lupines. There's perhaps no better way to enjoy the fall's change of colors than by riding the trail.

The 279km tip-to-tip route from Tignish, near North Cape, to Elmira, near East Point, is a rewarding workout, passing through idyllic villages, where riders can stop for meals or rest for the night. Note that the prevailing winds on PEI blow from the west and southwest, so cycling in this direction is easier. Branches connect the trail to the Confederation Bridge, Charlottetown, Souris and Montague.

Provincial **tourist offices** (www.gov.pe.ca/visitorsguide) have excellent route maps and their website offers a plethora of planning and trail information. The bicycle rental shops in Charlottetown also run superb island-wide tours.

Pilot House

MODERN CANADIAN $$

(☎902-894-4800; 70 Grafton St; mains $19-37; ☉11am-10pm Mon-Sat) The oversized wood beams and brick columns of the historic Roger's Hardware building provide a bold setting for fine dining or light pub fare. A loyal clientele tucks into lobster-stuffed chicken, vegetarian pizza or seafood torte. Lunch specials start at $10.

★ Lot 30

MODERN CANADIAN $$$

(☎902-629-3030; 151 Kent St; mains $22-55; ☉from 5pm Tue-Sun) Anyone who's anyone goes to Lot 30, but show up unknown and in jeans and you'll be treated just as well. Tables are in view of each other so you can see the ecstatic expressions of food bliss on the merry diners' faces; dishes from *beurre blanc* to curry are spiced to perfection.

For a treat, try the excellent-value five-course tasting menu ($60) – small servings of a starter, three mains and a dessert sampler. Staff are wine-pairing masters, the eclectic ever-changing menu is made with local seasonal ingredients and the chef is happy to cater to food allergies and special needs. This really is a Charlottetown highlight.

Claddagh Room

SEAFOOD $$$

(☎902-892-6992; 131 Sydney St; mains $19-45; ☉5-10pm Mon-Sat) Locals herald the Claddagh Room as one of the best seafood restaurant in Charlottetown. Trust 'em! The Irish-inspired Galway Bay Delight features a coating of fresh cream and seasonings over scallops and shrimp that have been sautéed with mushrooms and onions, then flambéed with Irish Mist liqueur.

🍷 Drinking

Charlottetown has an established and burgeoning drinking scene. Historic pubs dot the old part of town. Most bars and pubs have a small cover charge (about $5) on weekends, or when there is live music. People spill into the streets at 2am when things wrap up.

★ Gahan House

PUB

(☎902-626-2337; 126 Sydney St; ☉11am-10pm or 11pm Sun-Thu, to midnight or 1am Fri & Sat) Within these homey, historic walls the pub owners brew PEI homegrown ales. Sir John A's Honey Wheat Ale is well worth introducing to your insides, as is the medium- to full-bodied Sydney Street Stout. The food here is also great – enjoy with friends old and new.

Marc's Studio

BAR

(☎902-566-4620; 125 Sydney St; ☉4:30pm-midnight) Climb the stairs for a cocktail or a nightcap. Think plenty of art by the late, local artist Marc Gallant (who restored this building in the 1980s) and cozily grouped sofas set against exposed brick walls. It usually closes around midnight, but will stay open until the crowd thins out.

☆ Entertainment

From early evening to the morning hours, Charlottetown serves up a great mix of theater, music, island culture and fun. Throughout the city and across PEI, various venues host traditional ceilidhs (*kay*-lees). They are sometimes referred to as 'kitchen parties' and usually embrace gleeful Celtic music and dance. If you have the chance to attend one, don't miss it. The Friday edition of the *Guardian* newspaper and the free monthly *Buzz* list times and locations of upcoming ceilidhs, along with other details of the entertainment scene.

City Cinema

CINEMA

(☎902-368-3669; 64 King St) A small independent theater featuring Canadian and foreign-language films.

Confederation Centre of the Arts

THEATER

(☎800-565-0278, 902-566-1267; www.confederationcentre.com; 145 Richmond St) This modern complex's large theater and outdoor amphitheater host concerts, comedic performances and elaborate musicals. *Anne of Green Gables – The Musical* has been entertaining audiences here as part of the Charlottetown Festival since 1964, making it Canada's longest-running musical. You'll enjoy it, and your friends will never have to know.

Mack

THEATER

(www.charlottetownfestival.com/theatres-themack.php; 28 University Ave) An intimate venue where guests sit at round tables. *O Come Ye* is a comedy about PEI shown through summer, while *Late Night at the Mack* (selected dates through summer) gets performers from the Confederation Centre of the Arts at a sort of open-mike show where they can show off their talents.

Olde Dublin Pub

LIVE MUSIC

(☎902-892-6992; 131 Sydney St; admission $8) A traditional Irish pub with a jovial spirit and live entertainment nightly during the summer months. Celtic bands and local notables take to the stage and make for an engaging night out.

Baba's Lounge

LIVE MUSIC

(☑902-892-7377; 81 University Ave; admission $8) Located above Cedar's Eatery, this welcoming, intimate venue hosts great local bands playing their own tunes. Occasionally there are poetry readings.

Benevolent Irish Society
LIVE MUSIC

(☑902-963-3156; 582 North River Rd; admission $10; ☺8pm Fri) On the north side of town, this is a great place to catch a ceilidh. Come early, as seating is limited.

❶ Information

Main Post Office (☑902-628-4400; 135 Kent St)

Police, Ambulance & Fire (☑911)

Polyclinic Professional Centre (☑902-629-8810; 199 Grafton St; ☺5:30-8pm Mon-Fri, 9:30am-noon Sat) Charlottetown's after-hours, walk-in medical clinic.

Queen Elizabeth Hospital (☑902-8894-2111; 60 Riverside Dr; ☺24hr) Emergency room.

Royal Canadian Mounted Police (☑902-368-9300; 450 University Ave) For nonemergencies only.

Visit Charlottetown (www.visitcharlotte-town.com) A helpful website with upcoming festival information, city history and visitor information.

Visitors Centre (☑888-734-7529, 902-368-4444; www.peiplay.com; 6 Prince St; ☺9am-10pm Jul & Aug, reduced hours Sep-Jun) Located in Founders' Hall, this visitors center is the island's main tourist office. It has all the answers, a plethora of brochures and maps, and free internet access.

❶ Getting There & Away

AIR

Charlottetown Airport (YYG; ☑902-566-7997; www.flypei.com) is 8km north of the city center at Brackley Point and Sherwood Rds. A taxi to/from town costs $12, plus $3.50 for each additional person.

CAR & MOTORCYCLE

With next to no public transportation available, rental cars are the preferred method for most travelers going to/from Charlottetown. During the summer cars are in short supply, so make sure you book ahead.

Nationwide companies such as Avis, Budget, National and Hertz have offices in town and at the airport. Note that the airport desks are strictly for people with reservations.

BUS

For information, see p434.

❶ Getting Around

BICYCLE

Riding is a great way to get around this quaint town. **MacQueen's Bicycles** (☑902-368-2453; www.macqueens.com; 430 Queen St; per day/week $25/125) rents a variety of quality bikes. Children's models are half price. **Smooth Cycle** (☑902-566-5530; www.smoothcycle.com; 330 University Ave; per day/week $26/110) also provides super service. Both of these operators also offer excellent customized island-wide tours of the Confederation Trail.

CAR & MOTORCYCLE

The municipal parking lots near the tourist office and Peak's Wharf charge $6 per day. One Loonie gets you two hours at any of the town's parking meters, which operate between 8am and 6pm on weekdays.

PUBLIC TRANSPORTATION

Trius Transit Lines (www.triustransit.ca) operates the anemic city transit within Charlottetown (one-way fare $2.25). One bus makes various loops through the city, stopping sporadically at the Confederation Centre between 9:20am and 2:40pm.

TAXI

Fares are standardized and priced by zones. Between the waterfront and Hwy 1 there are three zones. Travel within this area is about $11, plus $3 per extra person. Try **City Taxi** (☑902-892-6567; www.citytaxipei.com) and **Yellow Cab PEI** (☑902-566-6666; www.yellowcabpei.com).

EASTERN PRINCE EDWARD ISLAND

You can make your own tracks across Kings County, the eastern third of the province and PEI's most under-touristed region. From stretches of neatly tended homesteads to the sinuous eastern shore with its protected harbors, sweeping beaches and country inns, majestic tree canopies seem to stretch endlessly over the scenic heritage roads. The 338km Points East Coastal Drive winds along the shore, hitting the highlights.

Orwell

Situated 28km east of Charlottetown, via Hwy 1, is **Orwell Corner Historic Village** (☑902-651-8510; www.orwellcorner.ca; off

Hwy 1; adult/child $7.50/4.50; ⊙9am-4:30pm), a living re-creation of a 19th-century farming community, complete with bonneted school teacher and a blacksmith. Check the website for special events. The **Sir Andrew MacPhail Homestead** (☑902-651-2789; www.macphailhomestead.ca; 271 MacPhail Park Rd; ⊙9am-5pm Wed & Sun Jun-Dec), a further 1km down the road, is open for tea on summer afternoons (light lunches around $12).

Point Prim

This skinny bucolic spit of land is covered in wild rose, Queen Anne's lace and wheat fields through summer and has views of red sand shores on either side. At the tip is the province's oldest **lighthouse** (adult/child $7/2; ⊙9am-6pm); we think it's one of the prettiest spots on the island. Climb up the steep lighthouse steps to pump the foghorn and for panoramas over the south coast on sunny days.

Many folks come out this way to dig razor, soft shell, bar and quahog clams with **Happy Clammers** (☑866-887-3238; www.experiencepei.ca; adult/child $90/25 minimum 4 people). Once you've filled your buckets, go home to Gilbert and Goldie's house to steam up your catch and to dine on other treats cooked up by this charming local family.

Get even more into the treasures of this coast with **Seaweed Secrets** (☑866-887-3238; www.experiencepei.ca; adult/child $90/25, min/max 4/8 people; ⊙Mon, Tue, Thu & Fri), where you can harvest seaweed and learn about which types are edible or have medicinal qualities; it's all led by a local family who have been in the industry for generations, plus a knowledgeable marine botanist.

Eat at **Chowder House** (chowder with a biscuit $8; ⊙11am-7pm), a homey cafe near the lighthouse reminiscent of Cape Cod circa 1950; it serves a mean chowder and homemade pie.

Wood Islands

Wood Islands is the jumping-off point for ferries to Nova Scotia. A **visitors information center** (☑902-962-7411; Plough Waves Centre, cnr Hwy 1 & Rte 4; ⊙10:30am-9pm) is just along the road from the terminal.

If you'll be waiting a while at the terminal, **Wood Islands Provincial Park** and its 1876 lighthouse are well worth the short walk. Munch a rock crab sandwich or a lobster roll at **Crabby's Seafood** (snacks $4-7; ⊙noon-6pm Jun-Sep) near the ferry terminal.

Murray River & Around

From Wood Islands, Rte 4 heads east along the Northumberland Strait, veering inland at High Bank toward the lively and surprisingly artsy fishing settlement of Murray River. The coastal road becomes Rte 18, keeping the sea in view as it rounds Cape Bear, passing the lighthouse before looping back through the village of Murray Harbour and into Murray River. This stretch of flat, empty road offers superbly serene scenery and excellent cycling possibilities. Cyclists can follow the coastal road from Murray River, then loop back on the extension of the Confederation Trail at Wood Islands.

Head towards the coast from Murray River along Rte 348 (Gladstone Rd) to find **Newman Estate Winery** (☑902-962-4223; www.newmanestatewinery.com; 9404 Gladstone Rd, Gladstone; ⊙by appointment). This lovely place specializes in blueberry wines, but has recently began making white wine from grapes.

For more wine tasting on a grander scale, cruise over to Little Sands, 9km from the Wood Islands Ferry, where **Rossignol Estate Winery** (☑902-962-4193; Rte 4; ⊙10am-5pm Mon-Sat, 1-5pm Sun May-Oct) has free tastings and specializes in fruit wines. The divine blackberry mead has won a string of gold medals and the wild rose liquor made from rose hips is also well worth a try; call ahead for winter hours.

Brehaut's Restaurant (☑902-962-3141; Murray Harbour; dinner under $8; ⊙8am-9pm Mon-Sat, 11am-9pm Sun) is the place to stop in the area for a hearty meal. There are cozy booths and nooks filled with happy diners in this big, red wooden house. The seafood chowder gets rave reviews.

Panmure Island

Duck off Hwy 17 and ride the tarmac to the tip of Panmure Island, known for its variety of beaches: white sand and cold water line the ocean side, while pink sands and warmer water run along the St Mary's Bay side. Joined to the main island by a causeway, the island offers sweeping vistas of sand dunes and ocean surf, grazing horses and a gaily painted **lighthouse** (☑902-838-3568; tours $5; ⊙9:30am-5pm Jul & Aug, hours vary

Jun & Sep). You can climb the tower for $4. There's an annual **powwow** (☑902-892-5314; www.ncpei.com/powwow-trail.html; ☺mid-Aug) held each year with drumming, crafts and a sweat tent – it attracts around 5000 visitors, so don't expect any secluded beaches!

Bring a picnic for the supervised beach at **Panmure Island Provincial Park** (☑902-838-0668; Hwy 347; campsites $21; ☺ Jun-Sep). The park campground has every amenity for its 44 sites (most unserviced) tucked under the trees and along the shore. For something more luxurious stay at the grand **Maplehurst Properties** (☑902-838-3959; www.maplehurstproperties.com; Rte 347; d $145-190, cottage $1500 per week; ☺May-Nov; ☎). Marsha Leftwich has mustered every glimmer of her native Southern hospitality to create this exceptional B&B that drips with gorgeous chandeliers as well as fresh baked muffins and treats.

Montague & Around

The fact that Montague isn't flat gives it a unique, inland feel. Perched on either side of the Montague River, the busy little town is the service center for Kings County; its streets lead from the breezy, heritage marina area to modern shopping malls, supermarkets and fast-food outlets.

In the old train station on the riverbank there's an **Island Welcome Center** (☑902-838-0670; cnr Rtes 3 & 4; ☺8am-7pm Jul & Aug,

9am-4:30pm May, Jun, Sep & Oct). Here, you can hop on the Confederation Trail, which follows the former rail line; rent bikes at **Pines Bicycle Rentals** (☑902-838-3650; 31 Riverside Dr; bike rental half-/full day $20/30; ☺8am-8pm).

On the other side of the river, the statuesque former post office and customs house (1888) overlooks the marina, and houses the **Garden of the Gulf Museum** (☑902-838-2467; 564 Main St S; adult/child under 12yr $3/free; ☺9am-5pm Mon-Fri Jun-Sep). Inside are several artifacts illustrating local history.

Just north of town, development meets nature at **Brudenell River Provincial Park** (☑902-652-8966; off Rte 3; campsites $21, RV sites $24-28; ☺May-Oct), which is a park and resort complex. Options range from kayaking to nature walks and golf on two championship courses. You can also take a one-hour horseback trail ride through the sun-dappled forest and onto the beach with **Brudenell Riding Stables** (☑902-652-2396; www.brudenellridingstables.com; 1hr ride $35; ☺Jun-Sep).

🛏 Sleeping & Eating

⭐**Knox's Dam B&B**   B&B $$
(☑866-245-0037, 902-838-4234; www.bbcanada.com/3963.html; cnr Rtes 353 & 320; r incl breakfast $85-100; ☺Apr-Nov; ☎) This cheerful, red Victorian country home is constantly serenaded by the babble and flow of Knox dam on the Montague River. Guest rooms are thoughtfully appointed with soft linens, the old-fashioned elegance of a claw-foot tub and

---

WORTH A TRIP

DISTILLERIES

Two distinctly different distilleries operate on PEI, echoing the province's fame for bootlegging during Prohibition. Even today many families distill their own moonshine (which is technically illegal) and this is what is often mixed in punch and cocktails at country weddings and parties.

Prince Edward Distillery (☑902-687-2586; www.princeedwarddistillery.com; Rte 16, Hermanville; ☺11am-6pm) specializes in potato vodka that, even in its first year of production, has turned international heads (some calling it among the finest of its class). Stop in for tours of the immaculate distillery and to taste the different vodkas (potato, grain and blueberry) as well as the newer products such as bourbon, rum, whiskey, pastis and a very interesting and aromatic gin.

Myriad View Distillery (☑902-687-1281; www.straightshine.com; 1336 Rte 2, Rollo Bay; ☺11am-6pm Mon-Sat, 1-5pm Sun) produces Canada's first and only legal moonshine. The hardcore Straight Lightning Shine is 75% alcohol and so potent it feels like liquid heat before it evaporates on your tongue. Take our advice and start with a micro-sip! A gulp could knock the wind out of you. The 50% alcohol Straight Shine lets you enjoy the flavor a bit more. Tours and tastings are free and the owner is happy to answer any questions.

It's about a 10-minute drive on Hwy 307 between the two places.

modern amenities such as satellite TV. Rooms overlook the prize-winning flower gardens or the bountiful vegetable patch, there's good trout fishing at the dam and your hosts couldn't be kinder.

Windows on the Water
Café
MODERN CANADIAN **$$**

(☑902-838-2080; cnr Sackville & Main Sts; mains $9-17; ☺11:30am-9:30pm May-Oct) Enjoy a flavorful array of seafood, chicken and vegetarian dishes on the deck overlooking the water and, sort of, the road. Try the lobster quiche and leave room for a freshly baked dessert.

Georgetown

The many heritage buildings in Georgetown are testament to the town's importance as a shipbuilding center in the Victorian era. Today it's a sleepy village cum tourist spot thanks to its great places to eat and waterfront setting. It's also the site of **Tranquility Cove Adventures** (☑902-969-7184; www.tranquilitycoveadventures.com; Fisherman's Wharf, 1 Kent St; half-/full day tours $55/98) that leads excellent fishing and clamming trips as well as kundalini yoga on a deserted island. Check the website for details on other exciting packages.

🛌 Sleeping & Eating

★**Georgetown Inn & Dining Room** INN **$$**
(☑877-641-2414, 902-652-2511; www.peigeorge-townhistoricinn.com; 62 Richmond St; r incl breakfast $105-155; ☎) Right in the center of Georgetown, this place is as equally well known for its PEI-themed rooms (including a Green Gables room) as for its fine casual island-fare dining.

Clamdigger's Beach House & Restaurant
SEAFOOD **$$**
(☑902-652-2466; 7 West St; mains $12-37; ☺11am-9pm) Some claim this place serves PEI's best chowder, but no matter what your opinion, you can't help but ooh and aah about the water view from the deck or through the dining room's giant windows.

Cardigan Lobster Suppers
LOBSTER SUPPER **$$**
(☑902-583-2020; www.peicardiganlobster-suppers.com; Rte 311; adult/child $39/26; ☺5-9pm Jun-Oct) In tiny Cardigan, enjoy a five-course lobster supper in a heritage building on Cardigan Harbor.

DON'T MISS

BASIN HEAD PROVINCIAL PARK
....

While this park (off Rte 16) is home to the **Basin Head Fisheries Museum** (☑902-357-7233; adult/student $4.50/2; ☺9am-6pm Jun-Sep), its star attraction is the sweeping sand of golden **Basin Head Beach**. Many islanders rank this as their favorite beach and we have to agree. The sand is also famous for its singing – well, squeaking – when you walk on it. Unfortunately, the sand only performs when dry, so if it's been raining, it's no show. Five minutes of joyous 'musical' footsteps south from the museum and you have secluded bliss – enjoy!

Souris

Wrapped around the waters of Colville Bay is the bustling fishing community of Souris (*sur*-rey). It owes its name to the French Acadians and the gluttonous mice who repeatedly ravaged their crops. It's now known more for its joyous annual music festival than for the hungry field rodents of old. The **PEI Bluegrass & Old Time Music Festival** (☑902-569-3153; www.bluegrasspei.com/rollobay; Rte 2; ☺early Jul) draws acts from as far away as Nashville. Come for just a day, or camp out for all three.

This is a working town that's a friendly jumping-off point for cycling the coastal road (Rte 16) and the Confederation Trail, which comes into town. Souris is also the launching point for ferries to the Îles de la Madeleine in Québec (see p321).

🛌 Sleeping & Eating

Inn at Bay Fortune
INN **$$**
(☑902-687-3745; www.innatbayfortune.com; 758 Rte 310; r from $135, ste $225-335; ☒☎) Find some of PEI's most upscale rooms at this waterside inn about 12km south of Souris, as well as one of the island's best restaurants (meals from $60). Chef Domenic Serio has created a menu that captures the essence of PEI flavors; highlights include tartar of PEI scallops with strawberry and balsamic salsa or crispy beef short ribs with roasted organic shiitake mushrooms. Rooms are modern with country flair; the most fun rooms, tiny units in a tower with nearly 360-degree

views, are the least expensive. The price goes up with size, culminating in private cottages.

21 Breakwater CANADIAN $$
(21 Breakwater St; mains $10-20; ☻11:30am-8pm Mon-Sat) Souris' most elegant option is in a bright, historic mansion overlooking the industrial waterfront. The menu focuses on the usual suspects such as burgers, pasta with scallops, steamed mussels or chowder, but the preparation is top notch as is the service.

East Point to Naufrage

Built the same year Canada was unified, the **East Point Lighthouse** (☏902-357-2106; adult/child $4/2; ☻10am-6pm Jun-Aug) still stands guard over the northeastern shore of PEI. After being blamed for the 1882 wreck of the British *Phoenix*, the lighthouse was moved closer to shore. The eroding shoreline is now chasing it back. There's a gift shop and a little cafe next to the lighthouse that serves good-value lobster rolls ($9.50), hearty chowder and nice sandwiches.

The wooded coast and lilting accents of the north shore make for an interesting change of pace. Giant white windmills march across the landscape. **North Lake** and Naufrage harbors are intriguing places to stop and, if you feel so inclined, join a charter boat in search of a monster 450kg tuna.

The **railway museum** (☏902-357-7234; Rte 16A; adult/student/family $3/2/10; ☻10am-6pm Jun-Sep) in Elmira includes a quirky miniature train ride (adult/student/family $8/5/16) that winds through the surrounding forest. The station marks the eastern end of the Confederation Trail.

Treat yourself to one of the most luxurious stays on the island at **Johnson Shore Inn** (☏902-687-1340; www.johnsonshoreinn.com; 9984 Northside Rd, Hermanville; r $175-350; ☻May-Feb; ☎), run by the same effervescent couple who own Prince Edward Distillery (p443). Besides being impeccably run, the inn is blessed with a stunning setting on a red bluff that looks over endless sea.

St Peter's to Mt Stewart

The area between these two villages is a hot-bed for cycling. The section of the Confederation Trail closest to St Peter's flirts with the shoreline and rewards riders with an eyeful of the coast. In Mt Stewart three riverside sections of the Confederation Trail converge, giving riders and hikers plenty of attractive options within a relatively compact area. Both the Confederation Trail and a **provincial tourist office** (☏902-961-3540; Rte 2; ☻8am-7pm Jul & Aug, 9am-4:30pm Jun, Sep & Oct) are found next to the bridge in St Peter's.

🛏 Sleeping & Eating

Inn at St Peters Village INN $$$
(☏800-818-0925, 902-961-2135; www.innatstpeters.com; 1168 Greenwich Rd; d $125-265; ☎) Even with its large, comfortable rooms and stunning water views, the main reason to come to this inn is to dine on some of PEI's finest fare at the sunset-facing restaurant (lunch mains from $17, dinner mains from $22). Rooms are simply and elegantly decorated with antique furniture, but even if you don't stay here we highly recommend stopping in for a meal (even you, sweaty bikers).

★**Trailside Cafe & Inn** CAFE $$
(☏902-628-7833; www.trailside.ca; 109 Main St, Mt Stewart; mains $12-17) It's a cafe, it's a music venue, it's a cozy and affordable inn (rooms $89). In all ways this place exudes the best of PEI. Grab a pot of mussels or a taster plate of local cheeses and a beer and let the live local music tingle your spine. Check the website for showtimes and ticket sales.

WORTH A TRIP

GREENWICH

Massive, dramatic and ever-shifting sand dunes epitomize the amazing area west of Greenwich. These rare parabolic giants are fronted by an awesome, often empty beach – a visit here is a must. Preserved by Parks Canada in 1998, this 6km section of shore is now part of Prince Edward Island National Park.

Avant-garde meets barn at the **Greenwich Interpretation Centre** (☏902-961-2514; Hwy 13; ☻9:30am-7pm Jul & Aug, to 4:30pm May, Jun, Sep & Oct), where an innovative audiovisual presentation details the ecology of the dune system and the archaeological history of the site. The highlight though is getting out into the tree-eating dunes. Four walking trails traverse the park; the **Greenwich Dunes Trail** (4.5km return, 1½ hours) is especially scenic.

If you can't make a nighttime show, try and make it to the Hillsborough River Gospel Brunch, on every Sunday May through September for $20 including brunch.

CENTRAL PRINCE EDWARD ISLAND

Central PEI contains a bit of all that's best about the island – verdant fields, quaint villages and forests undulating north to the dramatic sand-dune-backed beaches of Prince Edward Island National Park. Anne of Green Gables, the engaging heroine of Lucy Maud Montgomery's 1908 novel, has spawned a huge global industry focused on the formerly bucolic hamlet of Cavendish. However, this being PEI, even its most savagely developed patch of tourist traps and commercial detritus is almost quaint – freshly painted and flower bedecked.

For those entering central PEI via the Confederation Bridge, it's worth stopping at the **Gateway Village Visitors Information Centre** (902-437-8570; Hwy 1; 8:30am-8pm), just off the bridge on the PEI side, for its free maps, restrooms and an excellent introductory exhibit called *Our Island Home* (open May to November). Staff can point you to the Confederation Trail, which starts nearby.

Victoria

The shaded, tree-laden lanes of this lovely little fishing village – a place to wander and experience more than 'see' – scream out character and charm. The entire village still fits neatly in the four blocks laid out when the town was formed in 1819. Colorful clapboard and shingled houses are home to more than one visitor who was so enthralled by the place they decided to stay. There's a profusion of art, cafes and eateries, as well as an excellent summer theater festival.

Sights & Activities

Lighthouse Museum   MUSEUM
(admission by donation; 9am-5:30pm Jun-Aug) This museum has an interesting exhibit on local history. If it's closed, get the key from the shop across the road.

By the Sea Kayaking   KAYAKING
(877-879-2572, 902-658-2572; www.bytheseakayaking.ca; kayak rentals per hr/day $25/50) Paddle round the bay on your own or on a guided tour, then take a dip off the beach at **Victoria Harbour Provincial Park** FREE, where there are change rooms available. The outfit also operates popular 'I Dig Therefore I Clam' clamming expeditions ($7) and offers bike rentals (per hour/day $15/30).

Sleeping & Eating

Orient Hotel B&B   B&B $$
(800-565-6743, 902-658-2503; www.theorienthotel.com; 34 Main St; r incl breakfast $85-105, ste $125-160;) A delightful Victorian confection of buttercup yellow, red and blue, this historic seaside inn is a perfect jewel.

★ Landmark Café   CAFE $$
(902-658-2286; 12 Main St; mains $12-25; 11:30am-10pm May-Sep) People come from miles around for the wonderful imaginative food at this family-run cafe. Prepared with wholesome ingredients, every colorful menu item from lasagnas and homemade soups to Cajun stir-fries and feta-stuffed vine leaves is a winner. Enjoy the photos on the wall of the family's annual exotic trips and their equally multicultural music selection, softly pumping through the cafe.

☆ Entertainment

Victoria Playhouse   THEATER
(902-658-2025, 800-925-2025; www.victoriaplayhouse.com; 20 Howard St; tickets $30; 8pm Jun-Sep) The ornate red velvet and gold theater at Victoria Playhouse presents a series of plays over the summer, with concerts from some of the region's finest musicians on Monday nights.

Prince Edward Island National Park

Heaving dunes and red sandstone bluffs provide startling backdrops for some of the island's finest stretches of sand; welcome to **Prince Edward Island National Park** (902-672-6350; www.pc.gc.ca/pei; day pass adult/child $7.80/3.90). This dramatic coast, and the narrow sections of wetland and forests behind it, is home to diverse plants, animals and birdlife, including the red fox and endangered piping plover.

The park is open year-round, but most services only operate between late June and the end of August. Entrance fees are charged between mid-June and mid-September, and admit you to all park sites, except the House of Green Gables (p451). If you're planning to stay longer than five days, look into a seasonal pass. The park maintains an information desk at the Cavendish Visitor Centre (p452).

The following sights and sleeping and eating options are organized from east to west covering the park-run facilities and private operations inside and out of the park.

◎ Sights & Activities

Beaches lined with marram grasses and wild rose span almost the entire length of the park's 42km coastline. In most Canadians' minds, the park is almost synonymous with these strips of sand. **Dalvay Beach** sits to the east, and has some short hiking trails through the woods. The landscape flattens and the sand sprawls outward at **Stanhope Beach**. Here, a boardwalk leads from the campground to the shore. Backed by dunes, and slightly west, is the expansive and popular **Brackley Beach**. On the western side of the park, the sheer size of **Cavendish Beach** makes it the granddaddy of them all. During summer this beach sees copious numbers of visitors beneath its hefty dunes. If crowds aren't your thing, there are always the pristine sections of sand to the east. Lifeguards are on duty at Cavendish, Brackley and Stanhope Beaches in midsummer. A beautiful bike lane runs all the way along this coast.

🛏 Sleeping

Parks Canada operates three highly sought-after **campgrounds** (☎800-414-6765; campsites/RV sites $28/36; ⊙Jun-Aug), which are spread along the park's length. They all have kitchen shelters and showers. For an additional fee of $11, you can reserve a campsite online at www.reservation.parkscanada.gc.ca (or it's $13.50 by phone). You can request a campground, but not a specific site; you must accept whatever is available when you arrive. While 80% of sites can be booked in advance, the remaining sites are first-come, first-served, so it's wise to arrive early.

Stanhope Campground, on Gulfshore East Pkwy, is nestled nicely in the woods behind the beach of the same name. There is a well-stocked store on-site.

Robinsons Island Campground, also on Gulfshore East Pkwy, is open from late June. The most isolated of the three sites, it's set at the end of Brackley Point. It's not too much fun if the wind gets up.

The proximity of **Cavendish Campground**, off Rte 6, to the sights makes it the most popular. It has exposed oceanfront sites and ones within the shelter and shade of the trees. Don't be lured by the view – it's nice, but sleep is better.

Dalvay by the Sea

Standing proudly near the east end of the park, and overlooking the beach named after it, is Dalvay, a historic mansion. Built in 1895 this majestic building is now owned by Parks Canada and operated as an **inn** (☎888-366-2955, 902-672-2048; www.dalvaybythesea.com; Gulfshore East Pkwy; r incl breakfast $174-344, cottages $404-444; ❋ 🛜 🛜). It's easily the most luxurious and stunning accommodations on the north shore. Each plush room's view and antique furnishings are refreshingly unique. The majestic **dining room** (dinner $18-36; h breakfast, lunch and dinner Jul-Aug) prepares remarkable dishes ranging from hazelnut- and sage-crusted rack of lamb to fresh island lobster. It is open to nonguests, and both lunch and afternoon tea (from 2pm to 4pm) are reasonably priced. The inn also rents bicycles ($9/26 per hour/day).

Brackley Beach

Brackley Beach isn't so much a town as a rural area with a few scattered amenities and the main beach access to the central eastern beaches of Prince Edward Island National Park. It's a short enough drive from Charlottetown (21km) so that even if you're not staying overnight, it's fun to catch a movie at **Brackley Beach Drive-In** (☎902-672-3333; www.drivein.ca; 3164 Rte 15; adult/child $9/6; ⊙May-Sep). Check the website for what's showing.

Shaw's Hotel & Cottages (☎902-672-2022; www.shawshotel.ca; Rte 15, 99 Apple Tree Rd; d $85-260, cottages $155-500; ❋ 🛜), open since 1860, is Canada's oldest family-operated inn. The hotel occupies 30 hectares of the family farm, with a private lane leading to Brackley Beach, a 600m walk away. Rooms in the inn have old-fashioned simplicity. One- to four-bedroom cottages, ranging from rustic to modern, are scattered around the property. A children's program runs in July and August, with hay rides, games, trips to the beach and a supervised supper hour. The **dining room** (☎902-672-2022; mains $22-33; ⊙8-10am & 5:45-9:30pm) is open to outside guests;

Around PEI National Park

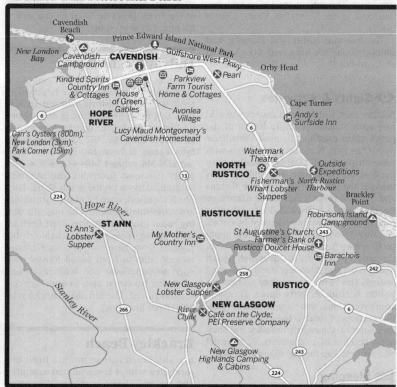

reservations are recommended for the popular Sunday evening buffet ($40; held in July and August).

For near-the-beach budget digs you won't find better than the clean and superfriendly **Brackley Beach Hostel** (☎902-672-1900; www.brackleybeachhostel.com; 37 Britain Shore Rd; dm/q $27/59; ☎) housed in a big barn about 2km from the shoreline. There are several eight-bed dorm rooms and a few quads as well as plenty of showers and an equipped kitchen.

While over-the-top springs to mind, **Dunes Café & Gallery** (☎902-672-2586; Rte 15; dinner mains $16-25; ☎11:30am-10pm) is a nice change of pace. Honestly, where else on the island can you enjoy Vietnamese rice-noodle salad in the shade of a giant Buddha? Come in for a coffee, a meal or just to roam the eclectic mix of Asian and island art in the sprawling glass gallery and garden.

Rustico

The seafront Acadian settlement at Rustico dates back to 1700, and several fine historic buildings speak of this tiny village's former importance. Most prominent is **St Augustine's Church** (1830), the oldest Catholic church on PEI. The old cemetery is on one side of the church, the solid red-stone **Farmer's Bank of Rustico** is on the other. The bank operated here from 1864 to 1894; it was a forerunner of the credit-union movement in Canada. Beside the bank is **Doucet House**, an old Acadian dwelling that was relocated here. A **museum** (☎902-963-2194; adult/student $4/2; ☎9:30am-5:30pm Mon-Sat, 1-5pm Sun) describing the settlement of the community and the establishment of the bank is now housed in the two secular buildings.

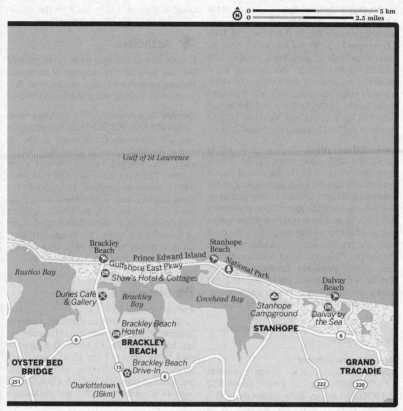

N
0 _____ 5 km
0 _____ 2.5 miles

Gulf of St Lawrence

Brackley
Beach

Prince Edward Island
Gulfshore East Pkwy

Rustico Bay

Stanhope
Beach

National Park

Dalvay
Beach

Shaw's Hotel & Cottages

Dunes Café
& Gallery

*Brackley
Bay*

Covehead Bay

Stanhope
Campground

Dalvay by
the Sea

Brackley Beach
Hostel

STANHOPE

**BRACKLEY
BEACH**

6

**OYSTER BED
BRIDGE**

251

15

Brackley Beach
Drive-In

6

6

**GRAND
TRACADIE**

222

220

*Charlottetown
(16km)*

In a prime location just across the street from the towering old church, **Barachois Inn** (☎800-963-2194, 902-963-2906; www.barachoisinn.com; 2193 Church Rd; d incl breakfast $140-275; ❋🛜) is one of the finest B&Bs on PEI. The grand Acadian-style mansion is decorated not only with the standard sublime selection of antiques, but also with very eclectic paintings, which makes walking around the many common areas like touring an art museum. Bathrooms are nearly equal in size to the enormous rooms, and hidden in the basement of the newer annex (built to copy the older building to perfection) is an exercise room, sauna and conference area.

New Glasgow

New Glasgow is a quiet town that spreads elegantly across the shores of the River Clyde. This is the favorite lobster supper getaway for folks from Charlottetown, although it's becoming equally respected for its luscious preserves.

🛏 Sleeping & Eating

New Glasgow Highlands
Camping & Cabins   CAMPGROUND $
(☎902-964-3232; www.campcabinpei.com; Rte 224; campsites/RV sites $32/38, cabins $60; ☺Apr-Nov; 🛜🏊) The 20-odd sites here are properly spaced in the forest, each with its own fire pit. For rainy days there are simple cooking facilities in the lodge. Add a laundry, a small store, a heated swimming pool and a mystifying absence of bugs, and you're laughing. There are also bright cabins, each with two bunks, a double bed, a sofa and a picnic table, but no linen or pillows; bathrooms are shared. Be sure to book ahead and don't even think about making late-night noise – peace is the word.

My Mother's Country Inn
B&B $$

(☑800-278-2071, 902-964-2508; www.mymoth-erscountryinn.com; Rte 13; d incl breakfast $110-225, cottages $125-250; ☎) An oasis within 20 hectares of rolling hills, brisk streams and enchanting woodlands, this is pure, rural delight. The house is the essence of country style with sea-green and ochre painted walls, bright pastel quilts, wood floors and plenty of light. A big red barn just begs to be photographed beside a storybook brook.

Café on the Clyde
CAFE $$

(☑902-964-4300; dinner mains $13-20; ☻9am-8pm) This is one of the better casual dining options near the national park as long as the tour buses haven't arrived before you have. Sun reflects in off the River Clyde and makes this place glow. The vegetarian wraps with a hint of feta truly hit the spot; finish the meal with the house specialty, raspberry cream cheese pie. The cafe is an addition to the famous **PEI Preserve Company** (☻9am-8pm Jun-Sep). While the preserves are a tad pricey, we think they're worth every penny; if you're not going to buy, at least come in to browse the free samples. Don't pass the orange ginger curd or the raspberry champagne preserves.

New Glasgow Lobster Supper
LOBSTER SUPPER $$

(☑902-964-2870; Rte 258; lobster dinners $32; ☻4-8:30pm) You can make a right mess with the lobster here, while also gorging on an endless supply of great chowder, mussels, salads, breads and homemade desserts.

St Ann

St Ann is so small you hardly even know you've arrived. Yet on a summer evening, follow the traffic and wafts of lobster steam to **St Ann's Lobster Supper** (☑902-621-0635; Rte 224; lobster dinners $32; ☻4:30-8:30pm), which rivals New Glasgow as PE Islanders' favorite lobster supper.

North Rustico

Within a few minutes of arrival, it is pretty obvious that this is not simply a tourist town. Rickety, boxy fishermen's houses painted in navies, brick reds and beiges, line a deep harbor that is simply packed with fishing vessels. A walk east from the pier along the boardwalk, and out to North Rustico Harbour, is a great way to take in the sights, sounds and smells of this little village.

🏃 Activities

If your idea of ocean activity is reeling in a big one, look for the plethora of **deep-sea fishing operators** (three to 3½ hour trip adult/child $45/35) along Harbourview Dr.

Outside Expeditions
CYCLING, KAYAKING

(☑800-207-3899, 902-963-3366; www.getoutside.com; 374 Harbourview Dr) Situated at the far end of the harbor in a bright-yellow fishing shed, this company runs a 1½-hour introductory 'Beginner Bay' tour ($39) that starts with a lesson in kayaking techniques. The most popular trip is the three-hour 'Harbour Passage' tour ($59), which operates two times daily. It also offers guided 'Land of Anne' bicycle tours ($120) and bike rentals ($20/35 per half-/full day). Trips are operated in the off-season, whenever at least four people want to go.

🛏 Sleeping & Eating

Andy's Surfside Inn
INN $

(☑902-963-2405; andyssurfsideinn@gmail.com; Gulfshore West Pkwy; d with shared bathroom incl light breakfast $50-75; ☎) Inside the national park, 2.7km toward Orby Head from North Rustico, is this very rustic, rambling house overlooking beautiful Doyle's Cove. It has been an inn since the 1930s, and the kitchen is open to those who want to bring home a few live lobsters. Sit back on the porch, put your feet up and thank your lucky stars.

Fisherman's Wharf Lobster Suppers
LOBSTER SUPPER $$$

(☑902-963-2669; 7230 Main St; lobster dinners $32; ☻noon-9pm) During the dinner rush in July and August this huge place has lines of people out the door. It's a fun, casual, holiday-style restaurant offering excellent value – that is if you don't wreck your shirt! Come hungry, as there are copious servings of chowder, tasty local mussels, rolls and a variety of desserts to go with your pound of messy crustacean. If things go your way, you may get a table with an ocean view.

☆ Entertainment

Watermark Theatre
THEATER

(☑902-963-3963; www.watermarktheatre.com; North Rustico Village; tickets $28-39) Opened in 2008 in honor of the 100th anniversary of the publication of *Anne of Green Gables*, this theater presents plays from the life and times of Lucy Maud Montgomery. Performances are in a renovated 19th-century church that Montgomery herself attended. Seats sell out fast, so book in advance!

Cavendish

Anyone familiar with *Anne of Green Gables* might have lofty ideas of finding Cavendish as a quaint village bedecked in flowers and country charm; guess again. While the Anne and Lucy Maud Montgomery sites are right out of the imagination-inspiring book pages, Cavendish itself is a mishmash of manufactured attractions with no particular town center. The junction of Rte 6 and Hwy 13 is the tourist center and the area's commercial hub. When you see the service station, wax museum, church, cemetery and assorted restaurants, you know you're there. This is the most-visited community on PEI outside of Charlottetown and, although an eyesore in this scenic region, it is a kiddie wonderland. To get out of the world of fabricated and fictional free-for-all, head to beautiful **Cavendish Beach**; it gets crowded during summer months, but with perfect sand and a warm(ish) ocean in front, you won't really care.

If you haven't read the 1908 novel, this is the place to do it – not just to enjoy it, but to try and understand all the hype. The story revolves around Anne Shirley, a spirited 11-year-old orphan with red pigtails and a creative wit, who was mistakenly sent from Nova Scotia to PEI. The aging Cuthberts (who were brother and sister) were expecting a strapping boy to help them with farm chores. In the end, Anne's strength of character wins over everyone in her path.

⊙ Sights

House of Green Gables HISTORIC SITE
(☑902-672-7874; Rte 6; adult/child $6.30/3.15; ☺10am-5pm Mon-Sat) Cavendish is the home town of Lucy Maud Montgomery (1874–1942), author of *Anne of Green Gables*. Here she is simply known as Lucy Maud or LM. Owned by her grandfather's cousins, the now-famous House of Green Gables and its Victorian surrounds inspired the setting for her fictional tale.

In 1937 the house became part of the national park and it's now administered as a national heritage site, celebrating Lucy Maud and Anne with exhibits and audiovisual displays.

❶ IN LUCY MAUD'S FOOTSTEPS

To really get a feel for the *Anne of Green Gables* scenery get out and walk the green, gentle creek-crossed woods that Lucy Maud herself knew like the back of her hand. The best way is to start at the Lucy Maud Montgomery's Cavendish Homestead where you can buy a combo ticket that includes the House of Green Gables for $8.50. Then walk the 1.1km return trail to the House of Green Gables through the 'Haunted Wood.' In this way you arrive to a magical view from below the house rather than via a big parking lot and modern entrance. Once you're at the House of Green Gables you can enjoy the site plus many other surrounding trails including 'Lover's Lane,' before hoofing it back to the homestead.

Lucy Maud Montgomery's Cavendish Homestead HISTORIC SITE
(☑902-963-2231; Rte 6; adult/child $4/2; ☺9am-6pm) This is considered hallowed ground to Anne fans worldwide. Raised by her grandparents, Lucy Maud lived in this house from 1876 to 1911 and it is here that she wrote *Anne of Green Gables*. You'll find the old foundation of the house, many interpretive panels about Lucy Maud, a small on-site museum and a bookshop.

Avonlea Village AMUSEMENT PARK
(☑902-963-3050; www.avonlea.ca; Rte 6; adult/family $19/70; ☺10am-5pm) Delve deeper into Anne fantasy at this theme park where costumed actors portray characters from the book and perform dramatic moments and scenes from Green Gable chapters. Beyond the theatrical exploits, the park offers you cow-milking demonstrations, a ride in a horse-drawn wagon and other period farm activities. Check the website for the day's schedule.

🍴 Sleeping & Eating

While accommodations are numerous, remember that this is the busiest and most expensive area you can stay. There are bargains and more bucolic settings east, toward North Rustico.

Parkview Farm Tourist Home & Cottages
B&B $

(📞 800-237-9890, 902-963-2027; www.peion-line.com/al/parkview; 8214 Rte 6; r with shared bathroom incl light breakfast $65-70, 2-bedroom cottages $165-265; 🛜🐾) This fine choice is set on a working dairy farm, 2km east of Cavendish. Ocean views, bathrooms and the prerequisite flowered wallpaper and frills abound in this comfortable and roomy tourist home. Each of the seven cottages, which are available May to mid-October (the B&B is open year-round), contains a kitchen and a barbecue, as well as a balcony to catch those dramatic comings and goings of the sun.

Kindred Spirits Country Inn & Cottages
INN $$

(📞 800-461-1755, 902-963-2434; www.kindred-spirits.ca; Rte 6; d $85-320, cottages $105-500; ❄🛜🐾) A huge, immaculate complex, this place has something for everyone from a storybook-quality inn-style B&B to deluxe suites. Rooms are every Anne fan's dream, with dotty floral prints, glossy wood floors and fluffy, comfy beds. Downstairs the lounge has a fireplace that will make you wish it would snow and couches perfect for snuggling up with a mug of cocoa.

Carr's Oysters
SEAFOOD $$

(📞 902-886-3355; Stanley Bridge Wharf, Rte 6; mains $14-32; ⏱10am-7pm) Dine on oysters straight from Malpeque Bay or lobster, mussels and seafood you've never even heard of like quahogs from this place's saltwater tanks. There are also plenty of fish on offer from salmon to trout. The setting over the bay is sociable and bright and there's also an on-site market selling fresh and smoked sea critters.

★ Pearl
MODERN CANADIAN $$$

(📞 902-963-2111; 7792 Cavendish Rd; mains $22-32, brunch $8-12; ⏱from 4:30pm daily, 10am-2pm Sun) This shingled house just outside Cavendish is surrounded by flowers and is an absolutely lovely place to eat. There are plenty of unusual and seasonally changing options like ice-wine-infused chicken liver pâté on a Gouda brioche for starters and locally inspired mains such as delicious butter-poached scallops.

ⓘ Information

Cavendish Visitor Centre (📞 902-963-7830; cnr Rte 6 & Hwy 13; ⏱9am-9pm)

New London & Park Corner

New London and Park Corner both have strong ties to Lucy Maud Montgomery, and are thus caught up in the everything-Anne pandemonium. The most charming place to stop for a bite to eat and a cup of tea is the **Blue Winds Tea Room** (📞 902-886-2860; 10746 Rte 6, New London; meals $10-14; ⏱11am-6pm Mon-Thu, to 8pm Fri-Sun) about 500m southwest of Lucy Maud Montgomery's birthplace and surrounded by English gardens. Of course like everything else in this region, they've got to be 'Anne,' so order a raspberry cordial or some New Moon Pudding – both recipes have been taken from Lucy Maud's journals.

⊙ Sights & Activities

Lucy Maud Montgomery Birthplace
MUSEUM

(📞 902-886-2099; cnr Rtes 6 & 20; admission $4; ⏱9am-5pm) This house is now a museum that contains some of Lucy Maud's personal belongings, including her wedding dress.

Anne of Green Gables Museum
MUSEUM

(📞 902-886-2884; 4542 Rte 20; adult/child $5/1; ⏱9am-6pm May-Oct) Surrounded by a luscious 44-hectare property, this is the charming home Lucy Maud liked to call Silver Bush. It was always dear to her and she chose the parlor for her 1911 wedding. Silver Bush hosts the Anne of Green Gables Museum. It contains such items as her writing desk and autographed first-edition books.

Lucy Maud Montgomery Heritage Museum
MUSEUM

(📞 902-886-2807; 4605 Rte 20; admission $4; ⏱9:30am-6pm) The building that houses this museum is believed to be the home of Lucy Maud's grandfather and there's a lot of Anne paraphernalia. Take a guided tour; there's a guarantee that if you're not absolutely fascinated, you don't pay the admission.

Annie's Table
COOKERY

(📞 902-314-9666; www.annies-table.com; 4295 Graham's Rd, New London; 2hr course $50) Learn the secrets of local lavender, discover how to make PEI spuds spectacular, wrangle seafood into deliciousness or get acquainted with Acadian food at a cookery course in this remodeled antique church. On staff are several chefs and a sommelier to make sure the food is as beautiful as the setting.

Kensington & Around

Kensington is a busy market town about half-way between Cavendish and Summerside. It's a good place to replenish supplies and the closest service center for those attending the **Indian River Festival** (www.indianriverfestival.com) when some of Canada's finest musicians (from Celtic to choral) play in the wonderfully acoustic St Mary's Church, from June through September.

Home Place Inn & Restaurant (☑866-522-9900, 902-836-5686; www.thehomeplace.ca; 21 Victoria St E; d incl breakfast $89-109, ste $149; ☺May-Oct; ☎) exudes country elegance at its finest. In the morning you may be awakened with scents of freshly baking cinnamon rolls and there's a licensed pub and restaurant on the premises.

In nearby Margate, **Shipwright's Café** (☑902-836-3403; cnr Rtes 6 & 233; dinner mains $25-35; ☺11:30am-3:30pm Mon-Fri, from 5pm daily) is housed in an 1880s farmhouse overlooking rolling fields and flower gardens. It earns rave reviews for its seafood dishes and vegetarian fare concocted from organic herbs and vegetables from the gardens. Try the 'Salute to Our Greenhouse' salad, a paella endowed with the island's best seafood and creations with PEI beef.

WESTERN PRINCE EDWARD ISLAND

Malpeque and Bedeque Bays converge to almost separate the western third of PEI from the rest of the province. This region sits entirely within the larger Prince County, and it combines the sparse pastoral scenery of Kings County's interior with some of Queens County's rugged coastal beauty.

The cultural history here stands out more than elsewhere on the island. On Lennox Island a proud Mi'kmaq community is working to foster knowledge of its past, while French Acadians are doing the same in the south, along Egmont and Bedeque Bays.

Summerside

While it lacks the elegance and cosmopolitan vibe of Charlottetown, Summerside is a simpler, seaside-oriented place with everything you need in one small, tidy package. Recessed deep within Bedeque Bay and PEI's second-largest 'city,' this tiny seaside village has a modern waterfront and quiet streets lined with trees and grand old homes. The two largest economic booms in the province's history, shipbuilding and fox breeding, shaped the city's development in the 19th and early 20th centuries. Like Charlottetown, its outskirts are plagued with unsightly development – you'll find most of the interesting bits along, or near to, Water St, parallel to the waterfront.

◉ Sights & Activities

The Confederation Trail makes its journey right through town and passes behind the library on Water St.

Spinnaker's Landing BOARDWALK
This redeveloped waterfront is the highlight of Summerside. A boardwalk allows you to wander and enjoy the harbor and its scenic surrounds. There are some very nice eateries, a stage for live music in the summer and numerous shops. A mock lighthouse provides adults with a nice lookout and some local information, while a large model ship is a

PRINCE EDWARD ISLAND KENSINGTON & AROUND

WORTH A TRIP

MALPEQUE

So where is this place where all the oysters come from, you might ask. The tiny hamlet of Malpeque takes you off the beaten path, past shadeless, rolling farmland to a tiny bay simply jam-packed with fishing boats and their colorfully painted storage barns. Don't miss lunch at **Malpeque Oyster Barn** (Malpeque Wharf; 6 oysters $14; ☺11am-9pm Mon-Sat, noon-9pm Sun), one of PEI's more authentically ambient cafes, in the top of a fisherman's barn and overlooking the bay and its oyster-filled action. Downstairs is a seafoodmonger where you can pick up fresh local sea critters to take away.

To get even closer to the crustaceans, hop in a sea kayak or on a stand up paddle board with **Malpeque Bay Kayak Tour Ltd** (☑866-582-3383; www.peikayak.ca; 3hr kayak tour $55).

Summerside

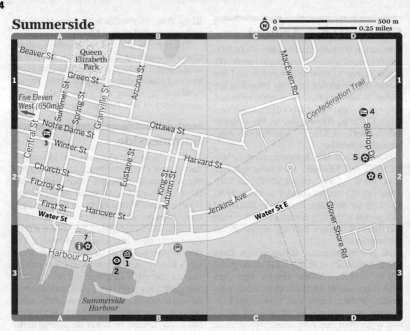

Summerside

⊙ Sights
1 Eptek Exhibition Centre	B3
2 Spinnaker's Landing	B3

🛏 Sleeping
3 Summerside Bed & Breakfast	A2
4 Willowgreen Farm	D1

✪ Entertainment
5 College of Piping & Celtic Performing Arts	D2
6 Feast Dinner Theatres	D2
7 Harbourfront Theatre	A3

dream playground for kids. Backing all of this is the modern **Eptek Exhibition Centre** (☑ 902-888-8373; 130 Harbour Dr; admission by donation; ◷ 10am-4pm), which features local and traveling art exhibitions.

🛏 Sleeping & Eating

★ Willowgreen Farm   B&B $$
(☑ 888-436-4420, 902-436-4420; www.willow-greenfarm.com; 117 Bishop Dr; d incl breakfast $60-118; ☎) With the Confederation Trail at its back door, and the College of Piping & Celtic Performing Arts out its front door, this rambling farmhouse is an incredibly great-value place to stay; you feel like you're in the coun-

try, but actually you're in central Summerside. Rooms are bright, and the bold country interior is a refreshing change from busy period decors. Read beside the woodstove or check out some of the more interesting farm animals.

Summerside Bed & Breakfast   B&B $$
(☑ 902-620-4993;www.summersideinnbandb.com; 98 Summer St; r $115; ❋ ☎) Poetically located on the corner of Summer and Winter Sts; the room you should obviously angle for is the bright and spacious Spring Room. This fine heritage building has been home to two Canadian premiers and boasts plenty of sitting areas and charm. Your friendly hosts prepare delicious hot breakfasts.

Five Eleven West   CANADIAN $$
(Credit Union Place, 511 Notre Dame St; mains $10-19; ◷ 11:30am-2pm Mon-Fri, 5-8pm daily) Summerside's most modern eatery is tucked into a very unlikely corner of the town's multi-purpose sports complex. Once you find it (to the left of the snack bar) be prepared to be impressed. Everything from the massive portion of beer-battered fish and chips to Madras chicken over rice, steamed mussels and prime rib is beautifully prepared, and the ambience is chic.

☆ Entertainment

Harbourfront Theatre   THEATER
(📞800-708-6505, 902-888-2500; www.harbour-frontheatre.com; 124 Harbour Dr) This modern theater is in the same complex as the Eptek Exhibition Centre and is the venue for a changing series of plays, comedy and more. It also hosts the **Summer on the Waterfront Festival** (☉Jul- mid-Sep), which showcases local and well-known Canadian musical acts.

Feast Dinner Theatres   THEATER
(📞902-888-2200, 888-748-1010; 618 Water St E; dinner & show $40; ☉6:30pm Mon-Sat Jun-Dec) Most locals start to giggle when they speak of their last time at Feast Dinner Theatres. You will find it below Brothers Two Restaurant and it is the longest-running theater restaurant in Atlantic Canada. Music, script and improvisation combine with audience participation to make for a truly memorable evening. And that's not all: the food's not too shabby, either.

College of Piping & Celtic Performing Arts   MUSIC
(📞902-436-5377; 619 Water St E; ceilidhs adult/student $12/7; ☉9am-9pm, ceilidhs 7pm) In celebration of Celtic dance and music, this school provides visitors with free 20-minute miniconcerts from Monday to Friday at 11:30am, 1:30pm and 3:30pm – expect bagpipes, singing and dancing. Inspired? Then get yourself out to the 'Highland Storm,' a Celtic music and dance extravaganza with a cast of 30 of the island's best performers. The show is on three days a week through summer.

❶ Information

Provincial Tourist Office (📞902-888-8364; Harbourfront Theatre, 124 Harbour Dr; ☉9am-7pm Jul & Aug, reduced hours May, Jun, Sep & Oct) Pick up a copy of the useful walking-tour pamphlet, which details the town's finer 19th-century buildings.

❶ Getting There & Away

Maritime Bus (p434) stops at the **Irving gas station** (📞902-436-2420; 96 Water St) in the center of town and has services to Charlottetown ($14.25, one hour), Moncton ($29.50, two hours) and Halifax ($53.25, 3½ hours). On request, bus shuttles pick up at the Esso station on Hwy 1A at the end of Water St E.

Région Évangéline

The strongest French Acadian ancestry on the island is found here, between Miscouche and Mont Carmel. Some 6000 residents still speak French as their first language, although you'll have trouble discerning this region from others in the province. There is one notable exception: the red, white, blue and yellow star of the Acadian flag hangs proudly from many homes. It was in Miscouche, on August 15, 1884, that the Acadian flag was unfurled for the very first time. The yellow star represents the patron saint of the Acadians, the Virgin Mary.

A favorite stop on this stretch is the **Bottle Houses** (📞902-854-2987; Rte 11, Cape Egmont; adult/child $5/2; ☉9am-8pm), the artful and monumental recycling project of Edouard Arsenault. Over 25,000 bottles of all shapes and sizes (that Edouard collected from the community) are stacked in white cement to create a handful of buildings with light-filled mosaic walls.

The very worthwhile **Acadian Museum** (📞902-432-2880; 23 Maine Dr E; admission $5; ☉9:30am-7pm), in Miscouche, uses 18th-century Acadian artifacts, texts, visuals and music to enlighten visitors about the tragic and compelling history of the Acadians on PEI since 1720. The introspective video introduces a fascinating theory that the brutal treatment of the Acadians by the British may have backhandedly helped preserve a vestige of Acadian culture on Prince Edward Island.

Tyne Valley

This area, famous for its Malpeque oysters, is one of the most scenic in the province. The village, with its cluster of ornate houses, gentle river and art studios, is definitely worth a visit.

Green Park Provincial Park, 6km north of the village, hosts the **Green Park Shipbuilding Museum & Historic Yeo House** (📞902-831-7947; Rte 12; adult $5; ☉9am-5pm). The museum and restored Victorian home, along with a re-created shipyard and partially constructed 200-tonne brigantine, combine to tell the story of the booming shipbuilding industry in the 19th century.

The park has 58 **campsites** (📞902-831-7912; off Rte 12; campsites $23-25, with hookups $30, cabins with shared bathroom $45; ☉Jun-Sep) spread within a mixed forest. The dozen cabins just beyond the campground are a steal.

Not surprisingly, the specialty at **Landing Oyster House & Pub** (☑902-831-3138; 1327 Port Hill Station Rd; mains $8-13; ⊙11am-9pm Mon & Tue, to 11pm Wed, to midnight Thu-Sat, 8am-8pm Sun) is deep-fried oysters – definitely indulge. Live bands (cover $4 to $8) play here on Friday night, and also on Saturday during July and August.

Lennox Island

Set in the mouth of Malpeque Bay, sheltered behind Hog Island, is Lennox Island and its 250 Mi'kmaq people. The island is connected by a causeway, making it accessible from the town of East Bideford off Rte 12.

The **Lennox Island Aboriginal Ecotourism Complex** (☑866-831-2702; 2 Eagle Feather Trail; adult/student $4/3; ⊙10am-6pm Mon-Sat Jun-Sep) opened its doors in June 2004. Inside there are small, changing exhibits and information about the two excellent **interpretive trails** around the island. These trails consist of two loops, forming a total of 13km, with the shorter one (3km) being accessible to people in wheelchairs – if you're lucky and someone's around, a local will guide you for a small fee. Also ask at the center if anything else is on offer, as it seems to change frequently.

Tignish

Tignish is a quiet town tucked up near the North Cape; it sees only a fraction of PEI's visitors. The towering **Church of St Simon & St Jude** (1859) was the first brick church built on the island. Have a peek inside – its ceiling has been restored to its gorgeous but humble beginnings, and the organ (1882) is of gargantuan proportions.

The Confederation Trail begins (or ends!) two blocks south of the church on School St. The **Tignish Cultural Centre** (☑902-882-1999; 305 School St; ⊙8am-4pm Mon-Fri) **FREE**, near the church, has a good exhibition of old maps and photos and tourist information.

North Cape

The drive toward North Cape seems stereotypically bucolic, until the moment your eyes rise above the quaint farmhouses to see the heavens being churned by dozens of sleek behemoth-sized white blades.

The narrow, windblown North Cape is not only home to the **Atlantic Wind Test**, but also to the longest **natural rock reef** on the continent. At low tide, it's possible to walk out 800m, exploring tide pools and searching for seals. The expanded **interpretive center** (☑902-882-2991; admission $6; ⊙9:30am-8pm), at the northern end of Rte 12, provides high-tech displays dedicated to wind energy, and informative displays on the history of the area. The aquarium is always a hit with kids. The **Black Marsh Nature Trail** (2.7km) leaves the interpretive center and takes you to the west side of the cape – at sunset these crimson cliffs simply glow against the deep-blue waters.

Above the interpretive center, the atmospheric **Wind & Reef Restaurant & Lounge** (☑902-882-3535; mains $9-29; ⊙lunch & dinner) attracts visitors and locals out for a treat. The menu and view are equally vast and pleasing.

West Coast

In Miminegash, stop into the **Seaweed Cafe** (meals $5-12) that serves a special seaweed pie, although nothing about this fluffy, creamy creation reeks of the beach.

Inland at O'Leary is the **Canadian Potato Museum** (☑902-859-2039; 1 Dewar Lane; admission $8; ⊙9am-5pm Mon-Sat, 1-5pm Sun May-Oct). It's a bit like a giant school science fair project with hallways of information panels and pictures on the walls.

Between Miminegash and West Point, Rte 14 hugs the shore and provides stunning vistas. It's perhaps the finest drive on the island. Off Hwy 14, the striking black-and-white-striped **West Point Lighthouse** (☑800-764-6854, 902-859-3605; www.westpointlighthouse.com; ⊙8am-9:30pm) dates from 1875. There's a small **museum** (admission $4; ⊙9am-9pm), where you can climb the tower for a breathtaking view. Part of the former lighthouse keepers' quarters have been converted into a nine-room **inn** (www.westpointlighthouse.com; d $170; ⊙Jun-Sep; ❀❀); the Tower Room is actually in the old lighthouse tower. The **restaurant** (meals $8-18; ⊙8am-8pm) is locally famous for its clam chowder.

Cedar Dunes Provincial Park (☑902-859-8785; campsites $23-25, RV sites $26-27) has tent space in an open grassy field adjacent to West Point Lighthouse. Its red-sand beach is an island gem.

Newfoundland & Labrador

Best Places to Eat

➡ Chinched (p467)
➡ Bonavista Social Club (p479)
➡ Lighthouse Picnics (p473)

Best Places to Stay

➡ Tuckamore Lodge (p495)
➡ Artisan Inn (p477)
➡ Skerwink Hostel (p477)
➡ The Cliffhouse (p476)

Why Go?

Canada's easternmost province floats in a world of its own. Blue icebergs drift by. Puffins flap along the coast. Whales spout close to shore. The island even ticks in its own offbeat time zone (a half-hour ahead of the mainland) and speaks its own dialect (the *Dictionary of Newfoundland English* provides translation, me old cock).

Outside of the good-time capital St John's, it's mostly wee fishing villages that freckle the coast, some so isolated they're reached only by boat. They offer plenty of hiking and kayaking escapes where it will just be you, the local family who's putting you up for the night and the lonely howl of the wind.

If you're looking to get off the beaten path – to see Viking vestiges, eat meals of cod tongue and partridgeberry pie, and share fish tales over shots of rum – set a course for this remote hunk of rock.

When to Go

St John's

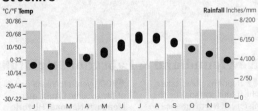

Jun Icebergs glisten offshore, though the weather can be wet and foggy.

Jul & Aug Whales swim by, festivals rock most weekends, and the province is at its sunniest.

Dec & Jan Skiers hit the slopes as Marble Mountain receives most of its 5m of snow.

Newfoundland & Labrador Highlights

❶ Hear live music, take a ghost tour and soak up the history of North America's oldest city, **St John's** (p460).

❷ Share the waves with whales and puffins at **Witless Bay Ecological Reserve** (p472).

❸ Explore Leif Eriksson's 1000-year-old Viking pad at the sublime **L'Anse aux Meadows National Historic Site** (p493).

❹ Hike the mountains and kayak the lakes at **Gros Morne National Park** (p488).

❺ Try out the modern outport life in **Fogo** (p486).

❻ Hike, ogle icebergs and sip Moose Joose in **Twillingate** (p484).

❼ Get your French fix – wine, éclairs and baguettes – in **St-Pierre** (p480).

❽ Learn Basque whaling history and see ancient whale bones at **Red Bay** (p506).

History

The Paleoindians walked into Labrador 9000 years ago. They hunted seals, fished for salmon and tried to stay warm. The Vikings, led by Leif Eriksson, washed ashore further south at L'Anse aux Meadows in Newfoundland in AD 1000 and established North America's first European settlement.

John Cabot (Italian-born Giovanni Caboto) sailed around the shores of Newfoundland next. It was 1497, and he was employed by England's Henry VII. Cabot's stories of cod stocks so prolific that one could nearly walk on water spread quickly throughout Europe. Soon the French, Portuguese, Spanish and Basques were also fishing off Newfoundland's coast.

The 1713 Treaty of Utrecht ceded all of Newfoundland to England. The land remained a British colony for most of the next two centuries, with life revolving around the booming fishing industry. Newfoundland's Aboriginal people, the Beothuk, did not fare well after settlement began. Diseases and land conflicts contributed to their demise by 1829.

Ever true to its independent spirit, Newfoundland was the last province to join Canada, doing so in 1949. While Labrador was always part of the package, it wasn't until 2001 that it became part of the provincial name.

Language

Two hundred years ago, coastal fishing families from Ireland and England made up almost the entire population. Since then, as a result of living in isolated outposts, their language has evolved into almost 60 different dialects. Strong, lilting inflections, unique slang and colorful idioms pepper the language, sometimes confounding even residents.

The authoritative source is the *Dictionary of Newfoundland English* (www.heritage.nf.ca/dictionary).

Land & Climate

They don't call it the Rock for nothing. Glaciers tore through, leaving behind a rugged landscape of boulders, lakes and bogs. The interior remains barren, while the island's cities and towns congregate at its edges near the sea.

Labrador is more sparse than Newfoundland, puddled and tundralike, with mountains thrown in for good measure.

---

❶ PLANNING YOUR TRIP

➡ Book ahead for rental cars and accommodations. If you're arriving during the mid-July to early August peak, secure a car by April or May and don't wait much longer to book a room. **Newfoundland & Labrador Tourism** (www.newfoundlandlabrador.com) has listings.

➡ Driving distances are lengthy so have realistic expectations of what you can cover. For instance, it's 708km between St John's and Gros Morne National Park. The **Road Distance Database** (www.stats.gov.nl.ca/DataTools/RoadDB/Distance) is a good reference.

➡ Know your seasons for puffins (May to August), icebergs (June to early July) and whales (July to August). Icebergs, in particular, can be tricky to predict. Check **Iceberg Finder** (www.icebergfinder.com) to get the drift.

Temperatures peak in July and August, when daytime highs average 20°C. These are also the driest months; it rains or snows about 15 out of every 30 days. Wintertime temperatures hover at 0°C. Fog and wind plague the coast much of the year (which makes for a lot of canceled flights).

Parks & Wildlife

Whales, moose and puffins are Newfoundland's wildlife stars, and most visitors see them all. Whale-watching tours depart from all around the province and will take you close to the sea mammals (usually humpback and minke). Puffins – the funny-looking love child of the penguin and parrot – flap around Witless Bay and Elliston. Moose nibble shrubs near roadsides throughout the province, so keep an eye out while driving. Some visitors also glimpse caribou near the Avalon Wilderness Reserve, which is special because usually these beasts can only be seen in the High Arctic. Caribou herds also roam in Labrador, though their numbers have been declining sharply in recent years.

❶ Getting There & Around

AIR

St John's International Airport (YYT; www.stjohnsairport.com) is the main hub for the region, though Deer Lake Airport (p488) is an

REGIONAL DRIVING DISTANCES

St John's to Port aux Basques: 905km

St John's to Gros Morne: 708km

Gros Morne to St Anthony: 372km

excellent option for visitors focusing on the Northern Peninsula. Airlines flying in include **Air Canada** (www.aircanada.com), **Provincial** (www.provincialairlines.ca), **Porter** (www.fly-porter.com) and **United** (www.united.com).

BOAT

Marine Atlantic (☑ 800-341-7981; www.marine-atlantic.ca) operates two massive car/passenger ferries between North Sydney, Nova Scotia and Newfoundland. There's a daily, six-hour crossing to Port aux Basques (western Newfoundland) year-round, and a thrice-weekly, 14-hour crossing to Argentia (on the Avalon Peninsula) in summer. Reservations are recommended, especially to Argentia.

Provincial Ferry Service (www.gov.nl.ca/ferryservices) runs the smaller boats that travel within the province to various islands and coastal towns. Each service has its own phone number with up-to-the-minute information; it's wise to call before embarking.

BUS

DRL (☑ 709-263-2171; www.drl-lr.com) sends one bus daily each way between St John's and Port aux Basques (13½ hours), making 25 stops en route. Other than DRL, public transportation consists of small, regional shuttle vans that connect with one or more major towns. Although not extensive, the system works pretty well and will get most people where they want to go.

CAR

The Trans-Canada Hwy (Hwy 1) is the main cross-island roadway. Driving distances are deceptive, as travel is often slow-going on heavily contorted, single-lane roads. Watch out for moose, especially at dusk.

ST JOHN'S

POP 106,200

Encamped on the steep slopes of a harbor, with jelly-bean-colored row houses popping up from hilly streets, St John's is often described as looking like a mini San Francisco. And like its American counterpart, it's home to artists, musicians, inflated real estate prices and young, iPhone-using denizens. Yet the vibe of Newfoundland's largest city and capital remains refreshingly small-town. At some point, locals will be sure to let you know St John's is North America's oldest city.

Highlights include view-gaping from Signal Hill and listening to live music and hoisting a pint (or shot of rum) in George St's pubs. Many visitors take advantage of the city's beyond-the-norm eating and lodging options by making St John's their base camp for explorations elsewhere on the Avalon Peninsula. Cape Spear, Witless Bay Ecological Reserve and Ferryland are among the easy day trips.

History

St John's excellent natural harbor, leading out to what were once seething seas of cod, prompted the first European settlement here in 1528. During the late 1600s and much of the 1700s, St John's was razed and taken over several times as the French, English and Dutch fought for it tooth and nail. Britain won the ultimate victory on Signal Hill in 1762.

The harbor steadfastly maintained its position as the world trade center for salted cod well into the 20th century. By mid-century, warehouses lined Water St, and the merchants who owned them made a fortune. Come the early 1960s, St John's had more millionaires per capita than any other city in North America.

Today the city's wharves still act as service stations to fishing vessels from around the world and the occasional cruise ship, though the cod industry suffered mightily after a 1992 fishing moratorium. The offshore oil industry now drives the economy.

◉ Sights

Most sights are downtown or within a few kilometers, though be prepared for some serious uphill walking.

Signal Hill National Historic Site

HISTORIC SITE

(☑ 709-772-5367; www.pc.gc.ca/signalhill; ⊘ grounds 24hr) The city's most famous landmark is worth it for the glorious view alone, though there's much more to see. The tiny castle atop the hill is **Cabot Tower** (⊘ 8:30am-5pm Apr-Nov) **FREE**, built in 1900 to honor both John Cabot's arrival in 1497 and Queen Victoria's Diamond Jubilee. In midsummer, soldiers dressed as the 19th-century Royal Newfoundland Company perform a **tattoo** (www.rnchs.ca/tattoo; admission $5; ⊙11am & 3pm Wed-Thu, Sat & Sun Jul & Aug) and fire cannons.

An **interpretive center** (adult/child $3.90/1.90; ⊙10am-6pm May-Oct) features interactive displays on the site's history. The last North American battle of the Seven Years' War took place here in 1762, and Britain's victory ended France's renewed aspirations for control of eastern North America. The tattoo takes place next to the center at O'Flaherty Field.

You can see cannons and the remains of the late-18th-century British battery at **Queen's Battery & Barracks** further up the hill. Inside Cabot Tower, educational displays relay how Italian inventor Guglielmo Marconi received the first wireless transatlantic message from Cornwall, England at the site in 1901. An amateur radio society operates a station in the tower in July and August.

Signal Hill also offers guided tours around the grounds, Thursday lunches where you eat like an 18th-century soldier (complete with rum pairings) and sunset concerts. Check the website's 'Activities' section for details and costs.

An awesome way to return to downtown is along the **North Head Trail** (1.7km) which connects Cabot Tower with the harborfront Battery neighborhood. The walk departs from the tower's parking lot and traces the cliffs, imparting tremendous sea views and sometimes whale spouts. The trailhead isn't marked; look for it right before you enter the lot. It's the path leading furthest to the right. Because much of the trail runs along the bluff's sheer edge, this walk is not something to attempt in icy, foggy or dark conditions. Free maps are available at Cabot Tower.

The site sits 1.5km from downtown, up Signal Hill Rd.

Rooms MUSEUM
(☎709-757-8000; www.therooms.ca; 9 Bonaventure Ave; adult/child $7.50/4, 6-9pm Wed free; ⊙10am-5pm Mon, Tue & Thu-Sat, to 9pm Wed, noon-5pm Sun; ☎) Not many museums offer the chance to see a giant squid, hear avant-garde sound sculptures and peruse ancient weaponry all under one roof. But that's the Rooms, the province's all-in-one historical museum, art gallery and archives. Frankly, the building is much more impressive to look at than look in, since its frequently changing exhibits are sparse.

But whoa! The views from this massive stone-and-glass complex, which lords over the city from a breath-sapping hilltop, are eye-poppers; try the 4th-floor cafe for the best vistas.

Johnson Geo Centre MUSEUM
(☎709-737-7880; www.geocentre.ca; 175 Signal Hill Rd; adult/child $12/6; ⊙9:30am-5pm) Nowhere in the world can geo-history, going back to the birth of the earth, be accessed so easily as in Newfoundland, and the Geo Centre does a grand job of making snore-worthy geological information perk up with appeal via its underground, interactive displays.

The center also has an exhibit on the *Titanic,* and how human error and omission, not just an iceberg, caused the tragedy. For instance, the ship's owners didn't supply her with enough lifeboats so as not to 'clutter the deck,' and the crew ignored myriad ice warnings. What any of this has to do with geology remains unclear, but who cares? It's fascinating.

Trails with interpretive panels wind around outside. The Geo Centre is up Signal Hill Rd, about 1km beyond downtown.

Basilica of St John the Baptist CHURCH
(☎709-754-2170; www.thebasilica.ca; 200 Military Rd; ⊙9:30am-5pm) Built in 1855, the soaring twin spires of the basilica pierce the sky and are visible all the way from Signal Hill. Its design marks the revival of classical architecture in North America. Inside, 65 stained-glass windows illuminate the remarkable polychromatic Italianate ceiling and its gold-leaf highlights.

The honor of being named a 'basilica' was bestowed on the church by Pope Pius XII on its centennial anniversary. Free half-hour tours are offered from 10am Monday to Saturday in July and August, according to demand. The convent behind

NEWFOUNDLAND FAST FACTS

➡ Population: 484,700

➡ Area: 111,390 sq km

➡ Capital: St John's

➡ Quirky fact: Newfoundland has 82 places called Long Pond, 42 called White Point and one called Jerry's Nose

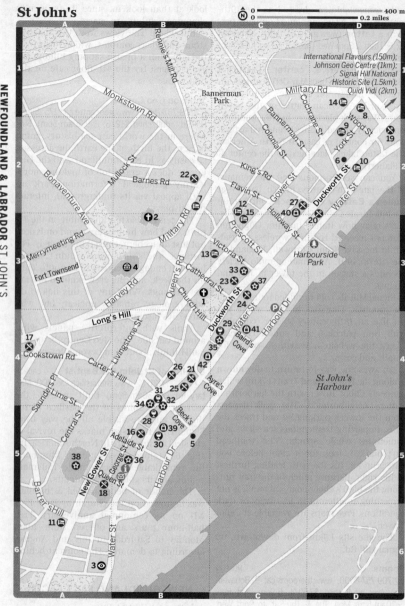

the church holds the 'Veiled Virgin,' a one-of-a-kind marble statue that spiritual types come to view. Ring the buzzer for entry. to the convent.

Anglican Cathedral of St John the Baptist   CHURCH

(☎ 709-726-5677; www.stjohnsanglicancathedral. org; 16 Church Hill; ⊗ 9:30am-4pm) Serving Canada's oldest parish (1699), the Anglican cathedral is one of the finest examples of

St John's

ecclesiastical Gothic architecture in North America. Although originally built in the 1830s, all but its exterior walls were reduced to ashes by the Great Fire of 1892. It was rebuilt in 1905. The Gothic ribbed ceiling, graceful stone arches and long, thin, stained-glass windows are timeless marvels.

A gargoyle dating from the 12th century – a gift from the Diocese of Bristol – stands guard over the south transept. Students offer tours (in July and August), organists play concerts (1:15pm Wednesdays year-round) and church ladies serve tea and crumpets.

Quidi Vidi　　　　　　　　　HISTORIC SITE

Over Signal Hill, away from town, is the tiny picturesque village of Quidi Vidi. Check out the 18th-century battery and the lakeside regatta museum, but make your first stop **Quidi Vidi Brewery** (☏ 709-738-4040; www. quidividibrewery.ca; 35 Barrows Rd; tours $15; ⊙ 10am-4pm), which cooks up Newfoundland's most popular microbrews. Located in an old fish-processing plant on the small wharf, it's a scenic place to slake one's thirst.

The fee includes ample tastings and a bottle to sip while touring. Be sure to try the Iceberg brand, made with water from the big hunks.

Nearby you'll find the oldest cottage in North America, the 1750s-era **Mallard Cottage** (www.mallardcottage.ca; 2 Barrows Rd). At press time it was being converted into a restaurant serving Newfoundland comfort foods.

The 1762 **Quidi Vidi Battery**, atop the hill end of Cuckhold's Cove Rd, was built by the French after they took St John's. The British quickly claimed it, and it remained in military service into the 1800s.

Inland from the village, **Quidi Vidi Lake** is the site of the city-stopping St John's Regatta. The **Royal St John's Regatta Museum** (☏ 709-576-8921; cnr Lakeview Ave & Clancy Dr, off Forest Rd; ⊙ by appointment) FREE is on the 2nd floor of the boathouse. A popular walking trail leads around the lake.

Quidi Vidi is about 2km from the northeast edge of downtown. Take Plymouth Rd, go left on Quidi Vidi Rd, then right on Forest Rd (which becomes Quidi Vidi Village Rd).

TEA TOMB

All around the Anglican Cathedral of St John the Baptist you'll see signs for 'tea in the crypt.' Sound spooky? It is a bit when you first arrive at the church's basement, what with all the women in flowery dresses and sensible shoes flurrying to and fro. But give it a chance, and **high tea** ($9; 2:30-4pm Mon-Fri Jul & Aug) here becomes more than home-baked cookies and mini-scones. It's a chance to chat with the older genera-tion about jam recipes, tips for summer holidays and the way things used to be (actually, you'll be listening and eating, and they'll do all the talking). The crypt, by the way, has never been used for burials.

For the brewery, bear right onto Barrows Rd. For the battery, veer off on Cuckold's Cove Rd. For the regatta museum, take a left off Forest Rd onto Lakeview Ave. You can also walk from Signal Hill via the Cuckold's Cove Trail, which takes about 30 minutes.

Newman Wine Vaults   HISTORIC SITE
(☑709-739-7870; www.seethesites.ca; 436 Water St; admission by donation; ☺by appointment) Dat-ing from the 1780s, these dark, cool wine vaults are where the Newman company aged its port until 1996 (when EU regula-tions forced the process back to Portugal). Guides used to give tours, but at press time they were on hold. The vaults often host mu-sic, literary and foodie events.

CA Pippy Park   PARK
(www.pippypark.com) The feature-filled, 1343-hectare CA Pippy Park coats down-town's northwestern edge. Recreational facilities include walking trails, picnic areas, playgrounds, a golf course and a campground. **Memorial University**, the province's only university, is here too. The university's **botanical garden** (☑709-737-8590; www.mun.ca/botgarden; adult/child $7/3; ☺10am-5pm May-Aug, reduced hours Sep-Apr) is at Oxen Pond, at the park's western edge off Mt Scio Rd.

Cultivated areas and a nature reserve fill the botanical landscape. Together, these and the park's **Long Pond** marsh give visitors an excellent introduction to Newfoundland's flora, habitats (including boreal forest and bogs) and animals (look for birds at Long Pond and the occasional moose). Take the 3km **Long Pond Walk** for the full effect.

The **Fluvarium** (☑709-754-3474; www.flu-varium.ca; 5 Nagle's Pl; adult/child/family $7/4/20; ☺9am-5pm Mon-Fri, from 10am Sat & Sun Jul & Aug, reduced hours Sep-Jun), a glass-sided cross-section of a 'living' river, is located across the street from the campground. Viewers can peer through large windows to observe the undisturbed goings-on beneath the sur-face of Nagle's Hill Brook. Numerous brown trout and the occasional eel can be seen. If there has been substantial rain or high winds, all visible life is completely lost in the murkiness.

To get here from downtown, take Bon-aventure Ave north to Allandale Rd and fol-low the signs; it's about 2km.

🏃 Activities

Golf and cross-country skiing enthusiasts can partake in CA Pippy Park.

Excellent walking trails zigzag across the area. The **Grand Concourse** (www.grandcon-course.ca) is an ambitious 160km-long trail network throughout St John's and environs. Many hikes are in the CA Pippy Park and Quidi Vidi Lake areas. Definitely make time for the sea-hugging North Head Trail on Sig-nal Hill. The concourse website has route details for all walks.

The epic **East Coast Trail** (www.eastcoast-trail.ca) stretches 265km from Cape St Francis south to Cappahayden; a further 275km is to be developed. It's part easy coastal walking, part tough wilderness trail. The website has details on free weekly guided hikes; on some you can also volunteer to do trail cleanup. An excellent stretch runs along the coast from Cape Spear.

👉 Tours

Boat

For most tours, you need to head south of town to Witless Bay.

Iceberg Quest   BOAT TOUR
(☑709-722-1888; www.icebergquest.com; Pier 6; 2hr tour adult/child $60/28) Departs from St John's harbor and makes a run down to Cape Spear in search of icebergs in June, whales in July and August.

O'Brien's   BOAT TOUR
(☑709-753-4850, 877-639-4253; www.obriens-boattours.com; 126 Duckworth St; 2hr tour adult/child $55/25) See whales, puffins and ice-bergs at Witless Bay. Boats launch from Bay

Bulls 31km south, but O'Brien's has a shuttle service (round-trip $25) that picks up from hotels throughout St John's. Buy tickets at O'Brien's shop.

Outfitters
KAYAKING

(☑709-579-4453, 800-966-9658; www.theoutfitters.nf.ca; 220 Water St; half-/full-day tour $69/169) Popular kayak tours at Bay Bulls, with shuttle service (round-trip $25) from Outfitters' store downtown.

Bus

Jellybean Tours
BUS TOUR

(☑709-754-4789; www.jellybean-tours.com; 8 Gower St) This group, based out of the HI St John's hostel, arranges city tours ($49, four hours) and Cape Spear/Witless Bay tours ($99, six hours) daily, if enough people sign up for it.

Legend Tours
BUS TOUR

(☑709-753-1497; www.legendtours.ca; 3hr tour $49-59) This award-winning operator covers St John's, Cape Spear and the northeast Avalon Peninsula. The commentary is richly woven with humor and historical tidbits. Call to reserve; they'll pick you up at your hotel or B&B.

Walking

The visitors center has brochures for self-guided walking tours in town. Also check the East Coast Trail website (www.eastcoasttrail.ca) for free guided hikes in the area.

★St John's Haunted Hike
WALKING TOUR

(www.hauntedhike.com; tours $10; ☺9:30pm Sun-Thu Jun-Sep) The black-caped Reverend Thomas Wyckham Jarvis Esq leads these super-popular explorations of the city's dark corners. He'll spook you with tales of headless captains, murderers and other ghosts. Departure is from the Anglican Cathedral's west entrance. On midsummer Fridays and Saturdays, the spine-tingling action moves to Signal Hill for a seated, indoor show of ghost stories (8pm, tickets $15).

★彡 Festivals & Events

Festival 500
MUSIC

(www.festival500.com; ☺early Jul) Choirs and beatboxers from around the globe let their voices soar in cool venues citywide. It takes place every other year; upcoming fests are in 2015 and 2017.

Sound Symposium
PERFORMING ARTS

(www.soundsymposium.com; ☺early Jul) Held every other year, it's a big, avant-garde week of concerts, workshops, dance, theater and film experiments; next symposiums are in 2014 and 2016.

George Street Festival
MUSIC

(www.georgestreetlive.ca; ☺late Jul/early Aug) The mighty George St becomes one big nightclub for a fabulous week of daytime and nighttime musical performances.

Royal St John's Regatta
SPORTS

(www.stjohnsregatta.org; ☺1st Wed Aug) The streets are empty, the stores are closed and everyone migrates to the shores of Quidi Vidi Lake. This rowing regatta officially began in 1825 and is now the oldest continuously held sporting event in North America.

Newfoundland & Labrador Folk Festival
MUSIC

(www.nlfolk.com; ☺early Aug) This three-day event celebrates traditional Newfoundland music, dancing and storytelling. It's held the weekend after the regatta.

Downtown Busker Festival
CARNIVAL

(www.downtownstjohns.com; ☺early Aug) Jugglers, magicians, acrobats, comedians and more take their performances to the streets for a long weekend.

NEWFOUNDLAND & LABRADOR ST JOHN'S

ST JOHN'S FOR CHILDREN

St John's will keep the wee ones entertained, rain or shine. CA Pippy Park is a kids' haven, with a huge playground, lots of trails and, of course, the Fluvarium. The ever-hungry ducks at the pond in **Bowring Park** (www.bowringpark.com; Waterford Bridge Rd) love company, as do the sea creatures at the Ocean Sciences Centre (p471).

Just knowing a cannon will blast at the end of the tattoo should keep kids riveted at Signal Hill (p460). The various boat tours are also a great bet, but inquire if there are icebergs and whales in the area first. While geology may not initially spark their interest, the fact that the Johnson Geo Centre (p461) is underground may do the trick. Older kids will enjoy the ghostly tales of the St John's Haunted Hike..

🛏 Sleeping

Scores of B&Bs offer a place to rest your head in the heart of St John's; they're usually better value than the hotels and motels. They fill fast, so book ahead. Many have a two-night minimum stay requirement. The ones listed here all serve a hot breakfast. The city's 17% tax is not included in prices listed here. Parking is available at or near all accommodations.

HI St John's   HOSTEL $

(📞709-754-4789; www.hihostels.ca; 8 Gower St; dm $28-33, r $75-89; 🌐@🛜) It's everything a good hostel should be: well located near the action, spic 'n' span facilities, not too big (16 beds in all), and helpful. A white-board lists everything of interest happening in town each day. The hostel also books reasonably priced tours.

Chef's Inn   B&B $$

(📞709-753-3180, 877-753-3180; www.thechefs-inn.ca; 29 Gower St; r $140-170; 🌐❄🛜) TV chef Todd Perrin owns this snug B&B, and his parents run it. The four rooms are done up in modern, minimalist decor, and each has an en suite bathroom. As you might expect, breakfast is a hearty feed with house-cured bacon and herbs from the garden.

Balmoral House   B&B $$

(📞877-428-1055, 709-754-5721; www.balmoral-house.com; 38 Queen's Rd; r $129-209; 🌐❄@) While the Balmoral is a typical B&B in many ways (cherub statues, long wooden antique tables), its owners live off-site and breakfast is self-serve, so it's more relaxed and private than many B&Bs. The beds are bestowed with super-comfy mattresses.

Abba Inn   B&B $$

(📞800-563-3959, 709-754-0058; www.abbainn.com; 36 Queen's Rd; r $139-189; 🌐❄@🛜) The Abba shares the same building as the Balmoral, and it even shares reservations (ie if one is full, it'll hook you up with the other). Both B&Bs have similar amenities and ambience. If Abba is full, the owner also has nearby Gower House, which is comparable.

Gower House   B&B $$

(📞709-754-0058; www.newfoundland-hotels.com; 180 Gower St; r $129-139; ❄🛜) Gower House is more like a boarding house than frilly B&B. Rooms are small, but with restful bedding, a flatscreen TV and amenity-laden en suite bathroom. A university student lives on-site and manages opera-tions (he also cooks the egg-filled breakfast). Gower has the same owner as Abba Inn, but with an even better location.

Narrows B&B   B&B $$

(📞866-739-4850, 709-739-4850; www.thenar-rowsbb.com; 146 Gower St; r $130-175; 🌐🛜) Warm colors mix with elegant trims and large wooden beds in the rooms of this welcoming B&B. There are modern amenities throughout and a gorgeous sitting room and balcony where guests can mingle and swap whale stories.

At Wit's Inn   B&B $$

(📞877-739-7420, 709-739-7420; www.atwitsinn.ca; 3 Gower St; r $129-149; 🌐❄@🛜) Polished floorboards, plasterwork ceilings, ornate fireplaces, bright-colored walls and beds you'll have trouble leaving make this B&B memorable. The living and dining rooms are as swank as they are comfy.

Foggy Rock B&B   B&B $$

(📞709-697-0077; www.foggyrock.ca; 50 Prescott St; r from $99; 🌐🛜) Foggy Rock ranks between a B&B and hostel. The four rooms share a couple of bathrooms, and breakfast is do-it-yourself continental. It's not the best value for money in town, but when everything is else is booked up, you'll be glad it's there.

Courtyard St John's   HOTEL $$

(📞709-722-6636; www.marriott.com/yytcy; 131 Duckworth St; r $159-199; ❄@🛜) It's the Marriott chain's typical property, with comfy beds. Some rooms have harbor views (about $10 extra).

Leaside Manor   B&B $$

(📞877-807-7245, 709-722-0387; www.leaside-manor.com; 39 Topsail Rd; r $139-249; 🌐❄@🛜) The higher-end rooms in this old merchant's home have a canopied bed, fireplace and Jacuzzi, which explains why the *Globe and Mail* designated Leaside as one of Canada's 'most romantic destinations.' It's about a half-hour walk from downtown; if you want to be closer, inquire about the downtown apartments.

Delta Hotel   HOTEL $$$

(📞709-739-6404; www.deltahotels.com; 120 New Gower St; r $189-269; ❄@🛜🏊) The Delta is the main, amenity-laden business hotel in town; it's located next to the convention center. Parking costs $12.

Eating

Japanese, Indian, Latin and even vegetarian restaurants pop up along Water and Duckworth Sts, providing a variety of food you won't find elsewhere in the province. You'll need reservations several days in advance for high-end and foodie hot spots.

Rocket Bakery BAKERY $
(www.rocketfood.ca; 272 Water St; mains $5-9; ⏱7:30am-10pm Mon-Sat, 8am-6pm Sun; 🛜) Cheery Rocket is the perfect spot for a cuppa joe, groovy sandwich or sweet treat. Try the hummus on multigrain bread, or maybe a croissant with lemon curd. The fish cakes also win raves. Order at the counter, then take your goodies to the tables in the bright-hued adjoining room.

International Flavours PAKISTANI $
(☑709-738-4636; 4 Quidi Vidi Rd; mains $8-12; ⏱noon-7pm Tue-Sat; 🖋) Pakistani owner Talat ladles out a whopping spicy plateful of dahl or curry with basmati rice for her daily set meal (one with meat, the other without). She's just beyond downtown, a few minutes' walk up Signal Hill Rd.

Ches's FAST FOOD $
(☑709-726-2373; www.chessfishandchips.ca; 9 Freshwater Rd; mains $8-15; ⏱11am-2am Sun-Thu, to 3am Fri & Sat) Ches's and its fish and chips are an institution in Newfoundland. No frills, just cod that will melt in your mouth.

Hava Java CAFE $
(258 Water St; baked goods $3-7; ⏱7:30am-6pm Sun-Wed, to 9pm Thu-Sat; 🛜) The atmosphere at this place is refreshingly antifranchise and pro-tattoo; it just focuses on making the best coffee in town.

Fixed Coffee & Baking CAFE $
(www.fixedcoffee.com; 183 Duckworth St; baked goods $3-8; ⏱7am-6pm Mon-Fri, from 9am Sat & Sun; 🛜) Fixed pours the city's best hot chocolate and mighty fine coffee and chai, plus it's cheaper than elsewhere. House-made bagels and breads add to the divine aroma.

Sun Sushi JAPANESE $
(☑709-726-8688; 186 Duckworth St; sushi rolls $4.50-7.50; ⏱noon-10pm Mon-Sat) This unadorned spot tops the townsfolks' list for reasonably priced sushi. The spicy tuna wins raves.

Hungry Heart CAFE $$
(☑709-738-6164; www.hungryheartcafe.ca; 142 Military Rd; mains $7-15; ⏱10am-2pm Mon-Sat) Eat in this warm-toned cafe and you're helping abused women and others in need to train in food service and get back on their feet. Try the curry mango chicken or pulled- pork sandwiches. Saturday brunch brings out the cheese scones with peameal bacon and cherry bread pudding. Lots of baked goodies, too.

Sprout VEGETARIAN $$
(☑709-579-5485; www.thesproutrestaurant.com; 364 Duckworth St; mains $10-15; ⏱11:30am-9pm Mon-Fri, from 10am Sat; 🖋) It's almost unheard of in Newfoundland: full-on vegetarian food. So savor your marinated tofu burger, walnut-pesto-melt sandwich and brown rice poutine (fries served under miso gravy) before leaving town.

Classic Cafe CAFE $$
(☑709-726-4444; 73 Duckworth St; mains $14-22; ⏱8am-2:30pm Sun-Tue, to 9pm Wed-Sat) Yes, many tourists eat here, but it's still a swell place to soak up harbor views and fork into Newfie standards like toutons, fish 'n' brewis, seafood chowder and fishcakes, plus omelettes and sandwiches.

India Gate INDIAN $$
(☑709-753-6006; www.indiagatenl.com; 286 Duckworth St; mains $12-17; ⏱11:30am-2pm Mon-Fri, 5-10pm daily; 🖋) This is the local Indian favorite, with loads of vegetarian options. Fill up at the weekday all-you-can-eat lunch special for $15.

★**Chinched** MODERN CANADIAN $$$
(☑709-722-3100; www.chinchedbistro.com; 7 Queen St; mains $30-35; ⏱6-9:30pm Tue-Sat) 🖋 Chinched is St John's first real foodie restaurant, the kind that offers mega-quality dishes but without the white-tablecloth pretense. So belly up in the warm, dark-wood room for octopus tacos or Newfoundland wild mushroom risotto. The meaty menu changes regularly. The young chefs' creativity extends to the singular desserts (say, wild nettle ice cream) and spirits (partridgeberry vodka) made in-house.

If you don't want to commit to a full meal, the bar menu lets you sample dishes for $6 to $7.

★**Reluctant Chef** MODERN CANADIAN $$$
(☑709-754-6011; www.facebook.com/TheReluctantChefRestaurant; 281 Duckworth St; set menu $60; ⏱noon-3:30pm Wed-Fri, 5pm-midnight Mon-Sat) 🖋 Perhaps it should be renamed the 'passionate chef,' given the lovingly pre-

SCRUNCHEONS, TOUTONS & FLIPPER PIE: A GASTRONOMIC GUIDE

Get ready for a whole new culinary vocabulary when you enter Newfoundland. Lesson number one: having a 'scoff' is local parlance for eating a big meal.

Two of Newfoundland's favorite dishes are fish 'n' brewis and Jiggs dinner. Fish 'n' brewis is a blend of salted fish, onions, scruncheons (aka fried pork fat) and a near-boiled bread. Jiggs dinner is a right feast comprising a roast (turkey or possibly moose) along with boiled potatoes, carrots, cabbage, salted beef and pea-and-bread pudding. A touton is fried dough that you dip in gooey molasses.

Cod tongues are the tender, fleshy bits between the lower jaws served battered and fried, while cod cheeks are just that: cheeks from the fish. Fishcakes are a blend of cod, potato and onion mashed together and fried – delicious. Seal flipper pie, on the other hand, is for the brave; the strong flavor of seal meat is definitely an acquired taste.

To finish off your meal, try figgy duff, a thick fig pudding boiled in a cloth bag.

pared, eight-course (give or take) menu that hits the toasty tables here. The dishes always vary; check the Facebook page to see what's cooking. Then plan on a three-hour flavor-gasm with 30 other chowhounds under a sparkly chandelier.

Bacalao MODERN CANADIAN $$$
(☑709-579-6565; www.bacalaocuisine.ca; 65 Le-marchant Rd; mains $26-36; ☺noon-2:30pm Tue-Fri, from 11am Sat & Sun, 6-10pm Tue-Sun) 🍴 Cozy Bacalao sources local, sustainable ingredients for its 'nouvelle Newfoundland cuisine.' Dishes include salt cod *du jour* and caribou in partridgeberry sauce, washed down by local beer and wines. Located 1.5km west of downtown; take Water St south to Walde-grave St, then Barters Hill Rd.

Bistro Sofia CAFE $$$
(☑709-738-2060; www.bistrosofia.net; 320 Water St; mains $26-36; ☺9am-11pm; 🛜) Bistro Sofia cooks up high-quality food and serves it casually in a bright, classy coffee shop ambience. Order at the counter, plop down at a roomy table, and wait for your lunch (grilled sandwiches plumped to perfection) or dinner (braised lamb shank or salmon and squash risotto) while sipping coffee or wine.

🍷 Drinking & Nightlife

George St is the city's famous party lane. Water and Duckworth Sts also have plenty of drinkeries, but the scene is slightly more sedate. Bars stay open until 2am (3am on weekends). Expect many places to charge a small cover (about $5) on weekends or when there's live music. Don't forget to try the local Screech rum.

★**Duke of Duckworth** PUB
(www.dukeofduckworth.com; McMurdo's Lane, 325 Duckworth St; ☺noon-late; 🛜) 'The Duke,' as it's known, is an unpretentious English-style pub that represents all that's great about Newfoundland and Newfoundlanders. Stop in on a Friday night and you'll see a mix of blue-collar, white-collar, young and old, perhaps even band members from Great Big Sea plunked down on the well-worn, red-velour bar stools.

The kitchen cooks the ultimate in chicken pot pie, fish and chips and other comfort foods, and 14 beers (including the local Qui-di Vidi) flow through the taps. The popular *Republic of Doyle* CBC TV series films here, which explains all the people taking photos of the sign by the door.

Trapper John's Museum & Pub PUB
(www.trapperjohns.com; 2 George St; ☺noon-2am Mon-Wed, to 3am Thu-Sun) It's not the most refined pub in town, but it sure is the most fun place to become an Honorary Newfound-lander, which happens after you kiss Stubby the Puffin (a variation on the usual codfish). The animal traps enshrined throughout grant the 'museum' status.

Gypsy Tea Room BAR
(www.gypsytearoom.ca; 315 Water St; ☺from 11:30am) It holds a well-regarded Mediterranean restaurant and chic lounge, but the courtyard is where you want to be, sipping wine, cocktails and other refreshing beverages under the stars.

Celtic Hearth PUB
(www.theceltichearth.com; 298 Water St; ☺24hr) Get your Guinness and pub grub 24/7.

Velvet CLUB
(twitter.com/Velvetniteclub; 208 Water St; ☺11pm-3am Fri & Sat) This is the premier gay dance bar in Newfoundland. Straights are equally welcome to soak up the fun energy. Located above Rose & Thistle; the entrance is via Mc-Murdo's Lane.

☆ Entertainment

The Scope (www.thescope.ca) has the daily lowdown. Perhaps because this is such an intimate city, word-of-mouth and flyers slapped on light poles are also major vehicles for entertainment information. Venues are close together – have a wander and enjoy.

Live Music

Cover charges range from $5 to $10. **Mighty Pop** (www.mightypop.ca) lists cool upcoming shows.

Ship Pub LIVE MUSIC
(☎709-753-3870; 265 Duckworth St; ☺noon-late) Attitudes and ages are checked at the door of this little pub, tucked down Solomon's Lane. You'll hear everything from jazz to indie, and even the odd poetry reading. Wednesday is folk music night.

Shamrock City LIVE MUSIC
(www.shamrockcity.ca; 340 Water St; ☺noon-late) Bands, most playing Irish and Newfoundland-style music, take the stage nightly at this all-ages pub.

Rose & Thistle LIVE MUSIC
(☎709-579-6662; 208 Water St; ☺9am-late) Pub where well-known local folk musicians strum.

Fat Cat BLUES
(www.fatcatbluesbar.com; George St; ☺8pm-late Tue-Sun) Blues radiates from the cozy Fat Cat nightly during the summer months.

Rock House LIVE MUSIC
(☎709-579-6832; 8 George St) When indie bands visit town, they plug in here.

Theater

Resource Centre for the Arts PERFORMING ARTS
(☎709-753-4531; www.rca.nf.ca; 3 Victoria St) Sponsors indie theater, dance and film by Newfoundland artists, all of which plays downtown in the former longshoremen's union hall (aka LSPU Hall).

Shakespeare by the Sea Festival THEATER
(www.shakespearebytheseafestival.com; tickets $20; ☺early Jul–mid-Aug) Live outdoor productions are presented at Signal Hill, local parks and other venues. Buy all tickets on-site; cash only. Some performances are free.

Sports

St John's IceCaps HOCKEY
(www.stjohnsicecaps.com; 50 New Gower St; ☺Oct-May) The popular IceCaps, part of the American Hockey League, slap the puck at Mile One Centre.

Shopping

You'll find traditional music, berry jams and local art in the nooks and crannies of Water and Duckworth Sts.

Fred's MUSIC
(☎709-753-9191; www.fredsrecords.com; 198 Duckworth St; ☺9:30am-9pm Mon-Fri, to 6pm Sat, noon-5pm Sun) The town's premier music shop features local music such as Hey Rosetta, Buddy Wasisname, Ron Hynes, The Navigators and Great Big Sea.

Living Planet SOUVENIRS
(☎709-739-6810; www.livingplanet.ca; 181 Water St; ☺10am-5pm Mon-Sat, noon-5pm Sun) For quirky

---

GETTING SCREECHED IN

Within a few days of your arrival in St John's, you'll undoubtedly be asked by everyone if you've been 'screeched in,' or in traditional Newfoundland slang, 'Is you a screecher?' It's not as painful as it sounds, and is, in fact, locals' playful way to welcome visitors to the province.

Screeching derives from the 1940s when new arrivals were given their rites of passage, and from pranks played on sealers heading to the ice for the first time. Today the ceremony takes place in local pubs, where you'll gulp a shot of rum (there's actually a local brand called Screech), recite an unpronounceable verse in the local lingo, kiss a stuffed codfish and then receive a certificate declaring you an 'Honorary Newfoundlander.' Sure it's touristy, but it's also good fun. The more the merrier, so try to get screeched in with a crowd.

tourist T-shirts and buttons even locals are proud to wear.

Downhome SOUVENIRS
(☑709-722-2070; 303 Water St; ☺10am-5:30pm Mon-Sat, noon-5pm Sun) It's touristy, but it does have a fine selection of local goods such as jams, woolen wear, moose cookbooks and the coveted *How to Play the Musical Spoons* CD.

Outfitters OUTDOOR EQUIPMENT
(☑709-579-4453; www.theoutfitters.nf.ca; 220 Water St; ☺10am-6pm Mon-Wed & Sat, to 9pm Thu & Fri, noon-5pm Sun) A camping and gear shop where you can get the local outdoorsy lowdown (check the bulletin board).

ⓘ Information

INTERNET ACCESS

Almost all coffee shops and bars have free wi-fi, including Fixed, Hava Java and Duke of Duckworth.

MEDIA & INTERNET RESOURCES

City of St John's (www.stjohns.ca) The 'Visiting Our City' category has descriptions of attractions, accommodations, eateries and events.

Downhome (www.downhomelife.com) A folksy, *Reader's Digest*–style monthly for the region.

Scope (www.thescope.ca) Free alternative newspaper covering local arts and politics.

St John's Telegram (www.thetelegram.com) The city's daily newspaper.

MEDICAL SERVICES

Health Sciences Complex (☑709-777-6300; 300 Prince Phillip Dr) A 24-hour emergency room.

Water St Pharmacy (☑709-579-5554; 335 Water St; ☺Mon-Sat)

MONEY

Banks stack up near the Water St and Ayre's Cove intersection.

CIBC (215 Water St)

Scotia Bank (245 Water St)

POST

Central Post Office (☑709-758-1003; 354 Water St)

TOURIST INFORMATION

Visitors Centre (☑709-576-8106; www.stjohns. ca; 348 Water St; ☺9am-4:30pm) Excellent resource with free provincial and city roadmaps, and staff to answer questions and help with bookings.

ⓘ Getting There & Away

AIR

Air Canada (www.aircanada.com), **WestJet** (www.westjet.com), **Provincial Airlines** (www.

provincialairlines.ca) and **Porter Airlines** (www. flyporter.com) are the main carriers. United Airlines schedules the only direct flight from the US. Air Canada offers a daily direct flight to and from London.

BUS

DRL (☑709-263-2171; www.drl-lr.com) sends one bus daily each way between St John's and Port aux Basques ($123, cash only, 13½ hours) via the 905km-long Hwy 1, making 25 stops en route. It leaves at 7:30am from Memorial University's Student Centre, in CA Pippy Park.

CAR & MOTORCYCLE

Avis, Budget, Enterprise, Hertz, National and Thrifty have offices at the airport. **Practicar** (☑709-753-2277; www.practicar.ca; 909 Topsail Rd) is a 20-minute drive from the airport but often has lower rates.

SHARE TAXI

These large vans typically seat 15 and allow you to jump on or off at any point along their routes. You must call in advance to reserve. They pick up and drop off at your hotel. Cash only.

Foote's Taxi (☑800-866-1181, 709-832-0491) Travels daily down the Burin Peninsula as far as Fortune ($45, 4½ hours).

Newhook's Transportation (☑709-682-4877, in Placentia 709-227-2552) Travels down the southwestern Avalon Peninsula to Placentia, in sync with the Argentia ferry schedule ($30, two hours).

Shirran's Taxi (☑709-468-7741) Plies the Bonavista Peninsula daily, making stops at Trinity ($50, 3½ hours) and Bonavista ($40, four hours), among others.

ⓘ Getting Around

TO/FROM THE AIRPORT

St John's International Airport is 6km north of the city on Portugal Cove Rd (Rte 40). A government-set flat rate of $25 (plus $3 for each extra passenger) is charged by taxis to go from the airport to downtown hotels and B&Bs; **Citywide Taxi** (☑709-722-7777) provides the official service. However, when you make the trip in reverse – ie from town to the airport – taxis run on meters and should cost a few bucks less.

CAR & MOTORCYCLE

The city's one-way streets and unique intersections can be confounding. Thankfully, citizens are incredibly patient. The parking meters that line Water and Duckworth Sts cost $1.25 per hour. **Sonco Parking Garage** (cnr Baird's Cove & Harbour Dr; ☺6:30am-11pm) charges $1.50 for 30 minutes or $11 per day.

ℹ THE RENTAL CAR CRUNCH

Be warned: rental car fleets are small (thanks to the island's remoteness and short tourist season), which means loads of visitors vie for limited vehicles in midsummer. Costs can rack up to $100 per day (including taxes and mileage fees). Reserve well in advance – April or May is recommended if you're traveling during the mid-July to early August peak – and confirm the booking before you arrive.

PUBLIC TRANSPORTATION

The **Metrobus** (www.metrobus.com) system covers most of the city (fare $2.25). Maps and schedules are online and in the visitors center. Bus 3 is useful; it circles town via Military Rd and Water St before heading to the university. The new 'trolley line' (it's actually a bus) loops around the main tourist sights, including Signal Hill. It costs $5/20 per person/family per day.

TAXI

Except for the trip from the airport, all taxis operate on meters. A trip within town should cost around $8. **Jiffy Cabs** (☎709-722-2222; www.jiffycabs.com) provides dependable service.

AROUND ST JOHN'S

North of St John's

Right out of *20,000 Leagues Under the Sea*, the **Ocean Sciences Centre** (☎709-737-3708; www.mun.ca/osc; ☉10am-5pm Jun-Aug) **FREE** is operated by Memorial University and examines the salmon life cycle, seal navigation, ocean currents and life in cold oceanic regions. The outdoor visitors area consists of local sealife in touch tanks. It's about 8km north of St John's, just before Logy Bay. From the city, take Logy Bay Rd (Rte 30), then follow Marine Dr to Marine Lab Rd and take it to the end.

Secluded and rocky, **Middle Cove** and **Outer Cove** are just a bit further north on Rte 30 – they're perfect for a beach picnic.

North at the head of **Torbay Bight** is the enjoyably short **Father Troy Path**, which hugs the shoreline. The view from **Cape St Francis** is worth the bumpy gravel road from Pouch Cove. There's an old battery and you may just be lucky and see a whale or two.

West of St John's

West of town on Topsail Rd (Rte 60), just past Paradise, is **Topsail Beach** with picnic tables, a walking trail and panoramic views of Conception Bay and its islands.

Bell Island (www.tourismbellisland.com) is the largest of Conception Bay's little landmasses, and it makes an interesting day trip. It's a 14km drive northwest from St John's to Portugal Cove to the **ferry** (☎709-895-6931) and then a 20-minute crossing (per passenger/car $2.50/7, hourly 6am to 10:30pm). Bell Island has the distinction of being the only place on the continent to have been nailed by German forces in WWII. Its pier and 80,000 tonnes of iron ore were torpedoed by U-boats in 1942. At low tide, you can still see the aftermath. The island sports a pleasant mélange of beaches, coastal vistas, lighthouses and trails. Miners here used to work in shafts under the sea at the world's largest submarine iron mine. The **Iron Ore Mine & Museum** (☎709-488-2880; adult/child $12/5; ☉11am-6pm Jun-Sep) details the operation and gives visitors the chance to go underground; dress warmly.

South of St John's

Cape Spear

A 15km drive southeast of town leads you to the most easterly point in North America. The coastal scenery is spectacular, and you can spot whales through much of the summer. The area is preserved as the **Cape Spear National Historic Site** (☎709-772-5367; www.pc.gc.ca/capespear; Blackhead Rd; adult/child $3.90/1.90; ☉grounds year-round) and includes an **interpretive center** (☉10am-6pm May-Oct), the refurbished 1835 **lighthouse** (☉10am-6pm Jun-Aug, reduced hours May, Sep & Oct) and the heavy gun batteries and magazines built in 1941 to protect the harbor during WWII. A **trail** leads along the edge of the headland cliffs, past 'the most easterly point' observation deck and up to the lighthouse. You can continue all the way to Maddox Cove and Petty Harbour along the East Coast Trail; even walking it a short way is tremendously worthwhile.

Heed all signs warning visitors off the rocks by the water, as rogue waves have been known to sweep in.

You reach the cape from Water St by crossing the Waterford River south of town and then following Blackhead Rd for 11km.

Goulds & Petty Harbour

In Goulds, at the junction of Rte 10 and the road to Petty Harbour, is **Bidgood's** (www.bidgoods.ca; Bidgood's Plaza; ⊙ 9am-7pm Mon-Sat, 10am-5pm Sun). It's just a normal-looking supermarket, except for the fresh seal flipper (in pies, jars or jerky-like strips) and caribou steak purveyed at the back of the store. For the faint of heart, partridgeberry and bakeapple jams are the other Newfoundland specialties on hand.

Its back lapping up against steep rocky slopes, movie-set-beautiful Petty Harbour is filled with weathered boats, wharves and sheds on precarious stilts. **North Atlantic Ziplines** (www.zipthenorthatlantic.com; 2½hr trips adult/child $115/90) is quite scenic. Depending on when you go, you might see whales or moose. There are five trips per day.

AVALON PENINSULA

The landscape along the coastline's twisting roads is vintage fishing-village Newfoundland. Many visitors make day trips here from St John's, which is easily doable, but there's something to be said for burrowing under the quilt at night, with the sea sparkling outside your window, in Cupids or Branch. Four of the province's six seabird ecological reserves are in the region, as are 28 of its 41 national historic sites.

Much of the **East Coast Trail** (www.eastcoasttrail.ca) runs through the area; keep an eye out for free guided hikes. The ferry to Nova Scotia leaves from Argentia.

Southeastern Avalon Peninsula

This area, sometimes called the South Shore, is known for its wildlife, archaeology, boat and kayak tours and unrelenting fog. Scenic Rtes 10 and 90, aka the **Irish Loop** (www.theirishloop.com), lasso the region.

Witless Bay Ecological Reserve

This is a prime area for whale-, iceberg- and bird-watching, and several boat tours will take you to see them from the towns of **Bay Bulls** (31km south of St John's) and around **Bauline East** (15km south of Bay Bulls).

Four islands off Witless Bay and southward are preserved as the **Witless Bay Ecological Reserve** (www.env.gov.nl.ca/parks) and represent one of the top seabird breeding areas in eastern North America. Every summer, more than a million pairs of birds gather here, including puffins, kittiwakes, storm petrels and the penguinlike murres. Tour boats sail to the islands, hugging the shore beneath sheer cliffs and giving you a shrieking earful as well as an eyeful.

The best months for trips are late June and July, when the humpback and minke whales arrive to join the birds' capelin (a type of fish) feeding frenzy. If you really hit the jackpot, in early summer an iceberg might be thrown in too.

☞ Tours

Tours from Bay Bulls (ie the big operators O'Brien's and Gatherall's) visit Gull Island, which has the highest concentration of birds. Tours that depart to the south around Bauline East head to nearby Great Island, home to the largest puffin colony. Bauline East is closer to the reserve, so less time is spent en route, but you see the same types of wildlife on all of the tours.

Kayaking is also popular in the area. You don't just see a whale while paddling, you feel its presence.

You can't miss the boat operators – just look for signs off Rte 10. Sometimes the smaller companies cancel tours if there aren't enough passengers; it's best to call ahead to reserve and avoid such surprises. The following are recommended tour companies, all operating from mid-May through mid-September. Most depart several times daily between 9:30am and 5pm.

Colbert's Tours   BOAT TOUR
(☎709-334-2098; Rte 10, Bauline East; 1hr tour adult/5-15yr $30/15) It's a 10-minute ride on a 40ft boat to see the puffins and whales.

Gatherall's   BOAT TOUR
(☎800-419-4253; www.gatheralls.com; Northside Rd, Bay Bulls; 1½hr tour adult/child $56/16) A large, fast catamaran gives you as much time at the reserve as O'Brien's. It's also a good choice for people prone to seasickness.

Molly Bawn Tours · BOAT TOUR

(☑709-334-2621; www.mollybawn.com; Rte 10, Mobile; 1hr tour adult/child $40/35) These tours cruise over the waves on a small, 35ft boat. Mobile is halfway between Bay Bulls and Bauline East.

O'Brien's · BOAT TOUR

(☑709-753-4850, 877-639-4253; www.obriens-boattours.com; 2hr tour adult/child $55/25) O'Brien's, on the south side of Bay Bulls, is the granddaddy of tours and includes story-telling, music and more on its nice, big boat. A more expensive but exhilarating option is the two-hour tour in a high-speed Zodiac ($85). There's a shuttle service from St John's (round-trip $25).

Outfitters · KAYAKING

(☑709-579-4453, 800-966-9658; www.theoutfitters.nf.ca; Bay Bulls; half-/full-day tour $69/169) Popular half-day kayak tours leave at 9am and 2pm; full-day tours depart at 9:30am and travel beyond the inner bay of Bay Bulls to the top of the eco reserve. There is a shuttle service (round-trip $25) from St John's that leaves from Outfitters at 220 Water St.

Stan Cook Sea Kayak Adventures · KAYAKING

(☑709-579-6353, 888-747-6353; www.wildnfld.ca; Harbour Rd, Cape Broyle; 2½hr tour from $59) Located further south near Ferryland, this company offers great guided tours for beginners and advanced paddlers.

La Manche Provincial Park

Diverse bird life, along with beaver, moose and snowshoe hare, can be seen in this lush park only 53km south of St John's. A highlight is the 1.25km trail to the remains of La Manche, a fishing village that was destroyed in 1966 by a fierce winter storm. Upon arrival, you'll see the beautiful newly built suspension bridge dangling over the narrows – it's part of the East Coast Trail. The trailhead is situated at the park's fire-exit road, past the main entrance.

There is excellent **camping** (☑709-685-1823; www.nlcamping.ca; Rte 10; campsites $15-23, per vehicle $5; ☉May-Sep), with many sites overlooking large La Manche Pond; the latter is good for swimming.

Ferryland

Ferryland, one of North America's earliest settlements, dates to 1621, when Sir George Calvert established the Colony of Avalon. A few Newfoundland winters later he was scurrying for warmer parts. He settled in Maryland and eventually became the first Lord Baltimore. Other English families arrived later and maintained the colony despite it being razed by the Dutch in 1673 and by the French in 1696.

The seaside surrounds the **Colony of Avalon Archaeological Site** (☑709-432-3200; www.colonyofavalon.ca; Rte 10; adult/child $9.50/7.50; ☉10am-6pm Jun-Sep) only add to the rich atmosphere, where you'll see archaeologists unearthing everything from axes to bowls. The **visitors center** (☑709-432-3207) houses interpretive displays and many of the artifacts that have been recovered.

The village's former courthouse is now the small **Historic Ferryland Museum** (☑709-432-2711; Rte 10; admission $2; ☉10am-4pm Mon-Sat, 1-4pm Sun Jul & Aug). The towering hill behind the museum was where settlers climbed to watch for approaching warships, or to escape the Dutch and French incursions. After seeing the view, you'll understand why the settlers named the hill 'the Gaze.'

★ **Lighthouse Picnics** (☑709-363-7456; www.lighthousepicnics.ca; Lighthouse Rd, off Rte 10; per person $25; ☉11:30am-4:30pm Wed-Sun Jun-Sep; 🐾) 🍴 has hit upon a winning concept: it provides a blanket and organic picnic meal (say, a curried chicken sandwich, mixed-green salad and lemonade from a Mason jar) that visitors wolf down while sitting in a field overlooking the ocean. It's at Ferryland's old lighthouse; you have to park and hike 2km to reach it, but ooh is it worth it. Reserve in advance.

Avalon Wilderness Reserve

Dominating the interior of the region is the 1070-sq-km **Avalon Wilderness Reserve** (☑709-635-4520; www.env.gov.nl.ca/parks; free permit required). Illegal hunting dropped the region's caribou population to around 100 in the 1980s. Thirty years later, a couple of thousand now roam the area. Permits for hiking, canoeing and birdwatching in the reserve are available at La Manche Provincial Park.

Even if you don't trek into the wilds, you still might see caribou along Rte 10 between Chance Cove Provincial Park and St Stevens.

Mistaken Point Ecological Reserve

This **ecological reserve** (www.env.gov.nl.ca/parks), which Unesco has short-listed for World Heritage site designation, protects 575-million-year-old multicelled marine fossils – the oldest in the world. The only way to reach it is via a free, ranger-guided, 45-minute hike from the **Edge of Avalon Interpretive Centre** (☑709-438-1100; www.edgeofavalon.ca; Rte 10; ☺May-Oct) in Portugal Cove South.

You can also drive the bumpy gravel road between here and Cape Race. At the end, a lighthouse rises up beside an artifact-filled, replica 1904 Marconi wireless station. It was the folks here who received the fateful last message from the *Titanic*.

The 'Mistaken Point' name, by the way, comes from the blinding fog that blankets the area and has caused many ships to lose their way over the years.

Along Route 90

The area from St Vincent's to St Mary's provides an excellent chance of seeing whales, particularly humpbacks, which feed close to shore. The best viewing is from **St Vincent's beach**. Halfway between the two villages is **Point La Haye Natural Scenic Attraction**, a dramatic arm of fine pebbles stretching across the mouth of St Mary's Bay – it's perfect for a walk.

Salmonier Nature Park (☑709-229-7189; www.env.gov.nl.ca/snp; Rte 90; ☺10am-5pm Jun-Aug, to 3pm Sep & Oct) **FREE** rehabilitates injured and orphaned animals for release back into the wild. A 2.5km trail through pine woods takes you past indigenous fauna and natural enclosures with moose, caribou and cavorting river otters. There's an **interpretive center** and touch displays for children. The park is on Rte 90, 12km south of the junction with Hwy 1.

Conception Bay

Fishing villages stretch endlessly along Conception Bay's scenic western shore, a mere 80km from St John's. Highlights include Brigus, in all its Englishy, rock-walled glory combined with North Pole history, and Cupids, a 1610 settlement complete with an archaeological dig to explore.

Brigus

Resting on the water and surrounded by rock bluffs is the heavenly village of **Brigus** (www.brigus.net). Its idyllic stone-walled streams meander slowly past old buildings and colorful gardens before emptying into the serene Harbour Pond. During WWI, American painter Rockwell Kent lived here, before his eccentric behavior got him deported on suspicion of spying for the Germans in 1915. The path toward his old cottage makes a great walk.

Captain Robert Bartlett, the town's most famous son, is renowned as one of the foremost Arctic explorers of the 20th century. He made more than 20 Arctic expeditions, including one in 1909, when he cleared a trail in the ice that enabled US commander Robert Peary to make his celebrated dash to the North Pole. Bartlett's house, **Hawthorne Cottage** (☑709-528-4004; www.pc.gc.ca/hawthornecottage; cnr Irishtown Rd & South St; adult/child $5/4; ☺10am-6pm daily Jul & Aug, Wed-Sun Jun), is a national historic site and museum.

On the waterfront, below the church, is the **Brigus Tunnel**, which was cut through rock in 1860 so Robert Bartlett could easily access his ship in the deep cove on the other side.

Every perfect village needs a perfect eatery. At **North St Cafe** (☑709-528-1350; 29 North St; light meals $6-9; ☺11am-6pm May-Oct), quiche, fishcakes, scones and afternoon tea are all on order. Brigus has a couple of B&Bs, but we suggest sleeping down the road in Cupids.

Cupids

Merchant John Guy sailed here in 1610 and staked out England's first colony in Canada. It's now the **Cupids Cove Plantation Provincial Historic Site** (☑709-528-3500; www.seethesites.ca; Seaforest Dr; adult/child $6/3; ☺9:30am-5pm May-Oct). An active archaeological dig is ongoing, and you can take a tour of it. A stone's throw down the road is the **Cupids Legacy Centre** (www.cupidslegacycentre.ca; Seaforest Dr; adult/child $8.50/4.25; ☺9:30am-5pm Jun-Oct), stuffed with silver coins, bottle shards and some of the other 150,000 artifacts unearthed on-site so far.

Afterward, head to the town's northern edge and hike the **Burnt Head Trail**. Climb to the rocky headlands, past blueberry thickets and stone walls that once fenced settlers' gardens, and look out over the same sea-buffeted coast that drew Guy.

The trail departs from an old Anglican church that has been converted into the divine **Cupid's Haven B&B and Tea Room** (☑709-528-1555; www.cupidshaven.ca; 169 Burnt Head Loop; r $99-149; ☻☎). Each of the four rooms has a private bathroom, vaulted ceilings and Gothic arched windows that let light stream in.

Harbour Grace & Around

A mixed crowd of historic figures has paraded through Harbour Grace over the past 500 years. Notables include the pirate Peter Easton and aviator Amelia Earhart. Learn about them at the redbrick customs house that is now the small **Conception Bay Museum** (☑709-596-5465; www.hrgrace.ca/museum.html; Water St; adult/child $3/2; ☺10am-6pm Jun-Aug). You can visit the airstrip Amelia launched from in 1932 – **Harbour Grace Airfield** (www.hrgrace.ca/air.html; Earhart Rd) – when she became the first woman to cross the Atlantic solo.

It's hard to miss the large ship beached at the mouth of the harbor. This is the **SS Kyle** (1913), wrecked during a 1967 storm. Locals liked the look of it so much they paid to have it restored instead of removed.

Clinging to cliffs at the northern end of the peninsula are the remote and striking villages of **Bay de Verde** and **Grates Cove**. Hundreds of 500-year-old rock walls line the hills around Grates Cove and have been declared a national historic site. Further offshore, in the distance, is the inaccessible **Baccalieu Island Ecological Reserve**, which is host to three million pairs of Leach's storm petrel, making it the largest such colony in the world.

Trinity Bay

Thicker forests, fewer villages and subdued topography typify the shores of Trinity Bay and give the west coast of the peninsula a much more serene feeling than its eastern shore.

Heart's Content

The **Cable Station Provincial Historic Site** (☑709-583-2160; www.seethesites.ca; Rte 80; adult/child $6/3; ☺9:30am-5:30pm May-Oct) tells the story of the first permanent transatlantic cable that was laid here in 1866. The word 'permanent' is significant, because the first successful cable (connected in 1858 to Bull Arm, on Trinity Bay) failed shortly after Queen Victoria and US President James Buchanan christened the line with their congratulatory messages.

Dildo

Oh, go on – take the obligatory sign photo. For the record, no one knows definitively how the name came about; some say it's from the phallic shape of the bay.

Joking aside, Dildo is a lovely village and its shore is a good spot for whale-watching. The **Dildo Interpretation Centre** (☑709-582-3339; Front Rd; adult/child $2/1; ☺10am-4:30pm Jun-Sep) has a whale skeleton and exhibits on the ongoing Dorset Eskimo archaeological dig on Dildo Island. It's not terribly exciting, but outside are excellent photo opportunities with Captain Dildo and a giant squid. Across the street, **Kountry Kravins 'n' Krafts** (☑709-582-3888; ☺9am-8pm Mon-Sat, 10am-6pm Sun Jun-Sep) sells fruit pies and knickknacks (including many 'Dildo' logoed items – always a fine souvenir for folks back home).

Cape Shore

The ferry, French history and lots of birds fly forth from the Avalon Peninsula's southwesterly leg. Newhook's Transportation (p470) connects the towns of Argentia and Placentia to St John's.

Argentia

Argentia's main purpose is to play host to the **Marine Atlantic ferry** (☑800-341-7981; www.marine-atlantic.ca; adult/child $112/54, per car/motorcycle $225/113), which connects Argentia with North Sydney in Nova Scotia – a 14-hour trip. It operates from mid-June to late September with three crossings per week. The boat leaves North Sydney at 5pm Monday, Wednesday and Friday. It returns from Argentia at 5pm Tuesday, Thursday and Saturday. Cabins (four-berth $172) are available. Vehicle fares do not include drivers.

A provincial **visitors center** (☑709-227-5272; Rte 100) is 3km from the ferry on Rte 100. Its opening hours vary to coincide with ferry sailings.

Placentia

In the early 1800s, **Placentia** (www.placentia-tourism.ca) – then Plaisance – was the French capital of Newfoundland, and the French attacks on the British at St John's were based here. Near town, lording over the shores, is **Castle Hill National Historic Site** (☑709-227-2401; www.pc.gc.ca/castlehill; adult/child $3.90/1.90; ◷10am-6pm Jun-Aug), where remains of French and British fortifications from the 17th and 18th centuries provide panoramic views over the town and the surrounding waters.

The fascinating **graveyard** next to the Anglican church holds the remains of people of every nationality who have settled here since the 1670s. The **O'Reilly House Museum** (☑709-227-5568; 48 Orcan Dr; admission $2; ◷11:30am-7:30pm Jun-Aug), within a century-old Victorian home, gives you more of an inside look at the town and its past luxuries. Wander past the other notable buildings, including the **Roman Catholic church** and the **stone convent**. A boardwalk runs along the stone-skipper's delight of a beach.

Philip's Cafe (170 Jerseyside Hill; mains $3-7; ◷7:30am-3:30pm Tue-Sat; ☏) is a must pre- or post-ferry ride for yummy baked goods and creative sandwiches such as apple and sharp cheddar on molasses-raisin bread. The chef also owns the five-room **Rosedale Manor B&B** (☑877-999-3613; www.rosedalemanor.ca; 40 Orcan Dr; r $99-129; ◖☏). It's a 10-minute drive from the Argentia ferry.

Cape St Mary's Ecological Reserve & Around

At the southwestern tip of the peninsula is **Cape St Mary's Ecological Reserve** (www.env.gov.nl.ca/parks) FREE, one of the most accessible bird colonies on the continent. Birders swoon over it, and it's impressive even for those who aren't bird crazy. Stop at the **Interpretive Centre** (☑709-277-1666; ◷9am-5pm May-Oct) and get directions for the 1km trail to Bird Rock. It's an easy footpath through fields of sheep and blue irises, and then suddenly you're at the cliff's edge facing a massive, near-vertical rock swarmed by squawking birds. There are 70,000 of them, including gannets, kittiwakes, murres and razorbills. The reserve is isolated, so you'll have to travel for lodging.

The **Cliffhouse** (☑709-338-2055; www.thecliffhouse.ca; Rte 100; r $100), in the wee town of Branch 22km away, is strongly recommended. Set high on a hill, you can see the ocean and spouting whales from everywhere: the front yard's Adirondack chairs, the porch, the front picture window and all three guest rooms. It's owned by a local family – Chris is a naturalist at the reserve, wife Priscilla is the town mayor and mum Rita cooks breakfast.

Near the reserve turnoff is **Gannet's Nest Restaurant** (☑709-337-2175; Rte 100; mains $8-15; ◷8am-8pm), frying some of the province's crispiest fish and chips and baking a mean rhubarb pie.

EASTERN NEWFOUNDLAND

Two peninsulas seem to grasp awkwardly out at the sea and comprise the sliver that is Eastern Newfoundland. The beloved, well-touristed Bonavista Peninsula projects northward. Historic fishing villages freckle its shores, and windblown walking trails swipe its coast. **Clarenville** (www.clarenville.net) is the Bonavista Peninsula's access point and service center, though there's not much for sightseers.

To the south juts the massive but less-traveled Burin Peninsula, another region of fishing villages. These towns are struggling to find their way in the post-cod world. The ferry for France – yes, France, complete with wine, éclairs and Brie – departs from Fortune and heads to the nearby French islands of St-Pierre and Miquelon, a regional highlight.

Trinity

POP 250

Let's set the record straight: Trinity is the Bonavista Peninsula's most popular stop, a historic town of crooked seaside lanes, storybook heritage houses and gardens with white picket fences. Trinity Bight is the name given to the 12 communities in the vicinity, including Trinity, Port Rexton and New Bonaventure.

While Trinity is movie-set lovely, some visitors have complained that its perfection is a bit boring. But if you like historic buildings and theater along with your scenery – and you're keen for a whale-watch tour – this is definitely your place. It's a tiny town and easily walkable.

First visited by Portuguese explorer Miguel Corte-Real in 1500 and established as a town in 1580, Trinity is one of the oldest settlements on the continent.

Sights & Activities

Trinity Historic Sites
HISTORIC SITE

(☑709-464-3599; adult/child $15/free; ⊙9:30am-5pm Jun-Sep) One admission ticket lets you gorge on seven buildings scattered throughout the village.

The **Trinity Historical Society** (www.trinityhistoricalsociety.com) runs four of the sites. The **Lester Garland House** (West St) was rebuilt to celebrate cultural links between Trinity and Dorset, England – major trading partners in the 17th, 18th and 19th centuries. The **Cooperage** (West St) brings on a real live barrel-maker; the **Green Family Forge** (West St) is an iron-tool-filled blacksmith museum and the **Trinity Museum** (Church Rd) displays more than 2000 pieces, including North America's second-oldest fire wagon.

The provincial government operates the other trio of **sites** (www.seethesites.ca), which include costumed interpreters. The **Lester Garland Premises** (West St) depicts an 1820s general store; the **Interpretation Centre** (West St) provides a comprehensive history of Trinity; and **Hiscock House** (Church Rd) is a restored merchant's home from 1910.

Fort Point
HISTORIC SITE

Further afield is Fort Point (aka Admiral's Point), where you'll find a pretty lighthouse and four cannons, the remains of the British fortification from 1745. There are 10 more British cannons in the water, all compliments of the French in 1762. An interpretive center and trail tells the tale. It's accessible from Dunfield, a few kilometers south on Rte 239.

Skerwink Trail
HIKING

The Skerwink Trail (5km) is a fabulous (though muddy) loop that reveals picture-perfect coastal vistas. The trailhead is near the church in Trinity East, off Rte 230.

Tours

Rugged Beauty Tours
BOAT TOUR

(☑709-464-3856; www.ruggedbeautyboat-tours.net; 3hr tour $70; ⊙10am & 2pm May-Oct) Unique trips with Captain Bruce, who takes you to abandoned outports and makes their history come alive. You might even see an eagle along the way.

Sea of Whales
BOAT TOUR

(☑709-464-2200; www.seaofwhales.com; 1 Ash's Lane; 3hr tour adult/child $80/50) Zodiac boats head out in search of whales three times per day.

Trinity Historical Walking Tours
WALKING TOUR

(☑709-464-3723; www.trinityhistoricalwalking-tours.com; Clinch's Lane; adult/child $10/free; ⊙10am Mon-Sat Jul & Aug) These entertaining and educational tours start behind Hiscock House.

Sleeping & Eating

There are numerous fine inns and B&Bs. Space gets tight in summer, so book ahead. Several snack shops and grocery stores have popped up and are good places to pick up a sandwich or cheese plate that you can take to the picnic tables near the Lester Garland Premises.

★Skerwink Hostel
HOSTEL $

(☑709-557-2015; www.skerwinkhostel.com; dm $25-29, r $55-59; ⊙May-Oct; 🛜) The homey Skerwink, with two six-bed dorms and two private rooms, is part of Hostelling International. All ages of travelers stay here, and a community vibe pervades as lots of locals drop by to chat and play guitar with the staff. Fresh bread and coffee are included for breakfast, and there are bicycles you can use for free.

The hostel also arranges kayak tours (per person $50 for two hours). It's off Rte 230, about 500m from the Skerwink Trail.

★Artisan Inn & Campbell House B&B
B&B $$

(☑709-464-3377, 877-464-7700; www.trinity-vacations.com; High St; r incl breakfast $125-179; ⊙May-Oct; ⊛🛜) Adjacent to each other and managed by the same group, these places are gorgeous. The three-room inn hovers over the sea on stilts; the flower-surrounded, three-room B&B also provides ocean vistas. The inn's Twine Loft restaurant serves a three-course, prix-fixe meal ($39) of local specialties; check the menu posted out front, which changes daily.

Eriksen Premises
B&B $$

(☑877-464-3698, 709-464-3698; www.trinity-experience.com; West St; r incl breakfast $105-170; ⊙May-Oct; ⊛🛜) This Victorian home offers elegance in accommodations and dining (mains $20 to $30, open lunch and dinner). It also books two nearby B&Bs: Kelly's

Landing (four rooms) and Bishop White Manor (nine rooms).

Trinity Mercantile
CAFE $

(www.trinitymercantile.ca; 24 West St; mains $6-15; ⊙8am-9pm; 🕸) It's a great spot for a cup of coffee, baked goods, sandwiches, chowder, salt cod or cold beer.

☆ Entertainment

Rocky's Place Lounge
LIVE MUSIC

(☑709-464-3400; High St; ⊙from 7pm) Rocky's hosts bands from time to time, but even if the mics are quiet it's a friendly place to hoist a brew.

Rising Tide Theatre
THEATER

(☑709-464-3232; www.risingtidetheatre.com; Water St; tickets $27; ⊙Jun-Sep) Alongside the Lester Garland Premises is the celebrated Rising Tide Theatre, which hosts the 'Seasons in the Bight' theater festival and the **Trinity Pageant** (adult/child $19/free; ⊙2pm Wed & Sat), an entertaining outdoor drama on Trinity's history.

ⓘ Information

RBC Royal Bank (West St; ⊙10:30am-2pm Mon-Thu, to 5pm Fri) No ATM.

Town of Trinity (www.townoftrinity.com) Tourism info.

ⓘ Getting There & Around

Trinity is 259km from St John's and is reached via Rte 230 off Hwy 1. **Shirran's Taxi** (☑709-468-7741) makes the trip daily from St John's ($50).

Bonavista

POP 3700

'O buona vista!' (Oh, happy sight!), shouted John Cabot upon spying the New World from his boat on June 24, 1497. Or so the story goes. From all descriptions, this pretty spot is where he first set foot in the Americas. Today Bonavista's shoreline, with its lighthouse, puffins and chasms, continues to rouse visitors.

⊙ Sights

Cape Bonavista Lighthouse
LIGHTHOUSE

(☑709-468-7444; www.seethesites.ca; Rte 230; adult/child $6/3; ⊙9:30am-5pm May-Oct) Cape Bonavista Lighthouse is a brilliant red-and-white-striped lighthouse dating from 1843. The interior has been restored to the 1870s

and is now a provincial historic site. A **puffin colony** lives just offshore; the birds put on quite a show around sunset.

Dungeon Park
PARK

(Cape Shore Rd, off Rte 230) Nowhere is the power of water more evident than at the Dungeon, a deep chasm 90m in circumference that was created by the collapse of two sea caves, through which thunderous waves now slam the coast.

Ryan Premises National Historic Site
HISTORIC SITE

(☑709-468-1600; www.pc.gc.ca/ryanpremises; Ryans Hill Rd; adult/child $3.90/1.90; ⊙10am-6pm Jun-Sep) Ryan Premises National Historic Site is a restored 19th-century saltfish mercantile complex. The slew of white clapboard buildings honors five centuries of fishing in Newfoundland via multimedia displays and interpretive programs.

Ye Matthew Legacy
HISTORIC SITE

(☑709-468-1493; www.matthewlegacy.com; Roper St; adult/child $7.25/3; ⊙9:30am-4:45pm Jun-Sep) The site has an impressive full-scale replica of the ship on which Cabot sailed into Bonavista.

🛏 Sleeping & Eating

HI Bonavista
HOSTEL $

(☑877-468-7741, 709-468-7741; www.hihostels.ca; 40 Cabot Dr; dm $26-30, r $75-120; @🕸) This tidy white-clapboard hostel offers four private rooms, two shared dorm rooms, free bike use and kitchen and laundry facilities. It's a short walk from the center.

Harbourview B&B
B&B $

(☑709-468-2572; 21 Ryans Hill Rd; r incl breakfast $70; ⊙May-Sep; 🐾) The name doesn't lie: you get a sweet view at this simple, four-room B&B, plus an evening snack (crab legs) with owners Florence and Albert.

White's B&B
B&B $

(☑709-468-7018; www.bbcanada.com/3821.htm; 21 Windlass Dr; r incl breakfast $75-85; 🐾@🕸) Low-key White's has three rooms to choose from, all with either private bathroom or en suite. Enjoy the bike rentals, barbecue use and ocean view.

Neil's Yard
CAFE $

(www.neilsyard.org; 27-29 Church St; mains $5-10; ⊙10am-8pm May-Oct; 🕸) A tea lounge serving buckwheat crepes? Neil's Yard is not your usual Newfoundland cafe. The gregarious

ELLISTON: ROOT CELLARS & PUFFINS

The Root Cellar Capital of the World, aka Elliston, lies 6km south of Bonavista on Rte 238. The teeny town was struggling until it hit upon the idea to market its 135 subterranean veggie storage vaults, and then presto – visitors came a knockin'. Actually, what's most impressive is the **puffin colony** just offshore and swarming with thousands of chubby-cheeked, orange-billed birds from mid-May to mid-August. A quick and easy path over the cliffside brings you quite close to them and also provides whale and iceberg views.

Stop at the **visitors center** (✆709-468-7117; www.townofelliston.ca; Main St) as you enter town, and the kindly folks will give you directions to the site along with a map of the cellars (which you're welcome to peek inside).

Work up an appetite while you're here, because **Nanny's Root Cellar Kitchen** (✆709-468-7998; ⊙8am-10pm) in historic Orange Hall cooks a mighty fine lobster, Jiggs dinner and other traditional foods, plus she's licensed.

The **Roots, Rants and Roars Festival** (www.rootsrantsandroars.ca) brings crowds in late September. The province's top chefs serve dishes alfresco along a 5km shoreline hiking route.

From the adjoining hamlet of **Maberly** a gorgeous 17km **coastal hiking trail** winds over the landscape to Little Catalina.

English owner will set you up with a steaming mug of exotic tea, while his wife cooks up the crepes, carrot ginger soup, cheesecake with local berries and other healthy fare. Service can be slow, but there's plenty to look at in the attached craft shop.

Walkham's Gate   CAFE $
(✆709-468-7004;   www.walkhamsgatepub.ca; mains $5-9; ⊙24hr; 🔊) One side is a coffee shop with whopping pies and hearty soups, the other side a congenial pub tended by music-lover Harvey. Located in the town center, near the courthouse.

★ **Bonavista Social Club**   MODERN CANADIAN $$
(✆709-445-5556; www.bonavistasocialclub.com; Upper Amherst Cove; mains $12-23; ⊙11am-8pm Tue-Sun) 🌿 Incredible breads and pizzas emanate from the wood-fired oven. Other highlights include the famed rhubarb lemonade and moose burger with partridgeberry ketchup. The young couple who own the restaurant grow many of their ingredients in the surrounding gardens. The goats roaming the grounds provide milk for cheese, while the chickens lay the eggs. Reserve ahead.

The rustic restaurant, complete with ocean-view terrace, is about 15 minutes from Bonavista via Rte 235 (turn left when you see the sign for Upper Amherst Cove). The chef's dad carved all the beautiful wood decor in his workshop next door.

☆ Entertainment

Garrick Theatre   THEATER
(www.garricktheatre.ca; 18 Church St) The artfully restored Garrick shows mainstream and indie films and hosts live music performances.

ℹ Information

Bonavista Community Health Centre (✆709-468-7881; Hospital Rd)
Scotiabank (✆709-468-1070; 1 Church St)
Town of Bonavista (www.townofbonavista. com) Tourism info.

ℹ Getting There & Around

Bonavista is a scenic 50km drive north of Trinity along Rte 230. **Shirran's** (✆709-468-7741) drives up daily from St John's ($40).

Burin Peninsula

It's not exactly lively on the Burin Peninsula, as the besieged fishing economy is felt. Still, the coastal walks inspire, and the region is a low-key place to spend a day or two before embarking toward the baguettes of France (aka St-Pierre).

Marystown is the peninsula's largest town; it's jammed with big-box retailers but not much else. **Burin** is the area's most attractive town, with a gorgeous elevated boardwalk over the waters of its rocky shoreline. **St Lawrence** is known for fluorite mining and scenic coastal hikes. In **Grand**

Bank, there's an interesting self-guided walk through the historic buildings and along the waterfront. Just south is fossil-rich **Fortune**, the jump-off point for St-Pierre.

◉ Sights & Activities

Provincial Seamen's Museum   MUSEUM
(☏709-832-1484;   www.therooms.ca/museum; Marine Dr, Grand Bank; admission $2.50; ⊙9:30am-4:45pm May-Oct) The impressive-looking Seamen's Museum depicts both the era of the banking schooner and the changes in the fishery over the years.

Burin Heritage Museums   MUSEUM
(☏709-891-2217; Seaview Dr, Burin; ⊙9am-6pm Mon-Fri, 10:30am-6pm Sat & Sun Apr-Sep) **FREE** Displays in two historic homes tell of life's highs and lows in remote outports.

Fortune Head Ecological Reserve   PARK
(www.env.gov.nl.ca/parks; off Rte 220; ⊙24hr) The reserve protects fossils dating from the planet's most important period of evolution, when life on earth progressed from simple organisms to complex animals some 550 million years ago. The reserve is about 3km west, by the Fortune Head Lighthouse. Kids will appreciate the **Interpretation Centre** (☏709-832-3569; adult/child $5/3; ⊙9am-5pm Jun-Aug) with fossils to touch; it's in town by the St-Pierre ferry dock.

Hiking Trails   HIKING
Ask at the Burin Heritage Museum about locating the **Cook's Lookout** trailhead. It's a 20-minute walk from town to the panoramic view. Off Pollux Cres in St Lawrence, the rugged, breath-draining **Cape Trail** (4km) and **Chamber Cove Trail** (4km) shadow the cliff edges and offer amazing vistas to rocky shores and some famous WWII shipwrecks. Another good (and easier) trail is the **Marine Hike** (7km) that traces Admiral's Beach near Grand Bank. It leaves from Christian's Rd off Rte 220.

🛏 Sleeping & Eating

Options are spread thinly. For those heading to St-Pierre, Grand Bank and Fortune are the best bases. Grand Bank has better lodging but it's further, at 8km from the ferry dock. Fortune has a sweet bakery by its dock. For more choices check the **Heritage Run** (www.theheritagerun.com).

Thorndyke B&B   B&B $$
(☏877-882-0820,   709-832-0820;   www.thethorndyke.ca; 33 Water St, Grand Bank; r $95-120;

⊙May-Oct; ☉) This handsome old captain's home overlooks the harbor. Antique wood furnishings fill the four light and airy rooms (each with private bathroom). The hosts will provide dinner with advance notice.

Fortune Harbourview B&B   B&B $$
(☏709-832-7666;   www.fortuneharbourview.com; 74 Eldon St, Fortune; r $99; ☏) The five rooms aren't fancy, and they're perched on top of a beauty salon, but they're tidy and best of all, located near the ferry to St-Pierre. It's a serve-yourself, continental-style breakfast.

Sharon's Nook & the Tea Room   CAFE $
(☏709-832-0618; 12 Water St, Grand Bank; mains $7-10; ⊙7:30am-9pm Mon-Sat, 11am-7:30pm Sun) This countrified eatery serves up lasagna, chili, sandwiches and heavenly cheesecake.

❶ Getting There & Around

The Burin Peninsula is accessed via Rte 210 off Hwy 1. The drive from St John's to Grand Bank is 359km and takes just over four hours. **Foote's Taxi** (☏800-866-1181, 709-832-0491) travels from St John's down the peninsula as far as Fortune ($45, 4½ hours).

ST-PIERRE & MIQUELON

POP 6100

Twenty-five kilometers offshore from the Burin Peninsula floats a little piece of France. The islands of St-Pierre and Miquelon aren't just Frenchlike with their berets, baguettes and Bordeaux, they *are* France, governed and financed by the *tricolore*.

Locals kiss their hellos and pay in euros, while sweet smells waft from the myriad pastry shops. French cars – Peugeots, Renaults and Citroëns – crowd the tiny one-way streets. It's an eye-rubbing world away from Newfoundland's nearby fishing communities.

St-Pierre is the more populated and developed island, with most residents of its 5500 living in the town of St-Pierre. Miquelon is larger geographically but has only 600 residents overall.

The fog-mantled archipelago has a 20th-century history as colorful as its canary-yellow, lime and lavender houses. Going further back, Jacques Cartier claimed the islands for France in 1536, after they were discovered by the Portuguese in 1520. At the end of the Seven Years' War in 1763, the islands were turned over to Britain, only to

ST-PIERRE'S BOOZY BACKSTORY

When Prohibition dried out the USA's kegs in the 1920s, Al Capone decided to slake his thirst – and that of the nation – by setting up shop in St-Pierre.

He and his mates transformed the sleepy fishing harbor into a booming port crowded with imported-booze-filled warehouses. Bottles were removed from their crates, placed in smaller carrying sacks and taken secretly to the US coast by rumrunners. The piles of Cutty Sark whiskey crates were so high on the docks that clever locals used the wood both to build and heat houses. At least one house remains today and is known as the 'Cutty Sark cottage'; most bus tours drive by.

The visitors center offers a special **Prohibition tour** (per person $25) that covers sites related to the theme. If nothing else, drop by the Hotel Robert near the tourist information center and check out Al Capone's hat; it hangs in the gift shop.

be given back to France in 1816. And French they've remained ever since.

◉ Sights & Activities

In St-Pierre, the best thing to do is just walk around and soak it up – when you're not eating, that is. Pop into stores and sample goods you'd usually have to cross an ocean for. Or conduct research as to the best choc-olate-croissant maker. A couple of **walking trails** leave from the edge of town near the power station.

Île aux Marins HISTORIC SITE
(3hr tour €24; ⊙9am & 1:30pm May-Sep) The magical Île aux Marins is a beautiful aban-doned village on an island out in the har-bor. A bilingual guide will walk you through colorful homes, a small schoolhouse muse-um and the grand church (1874). Book tours at the visitors center. You can also go over on the boat (€3) *sans* guide, but be aware most signage is in French.

L'Arche Museum MUSEUM
(☑508-410-435; www.arche-musee-et-archives. net; Rue du 11 Novembre; adult/child €4/2.50; ⊙10am-noon & 1:30-5pm Tue-Sun Jun-Sep) The well-done exhibits cover the islands' history, including Prohibition times. The showstop-per is the **guillotine** – the only one to slice in North America. Islanders dropped the 'timbers of justice' just once, in 1889, on a murderer. The museum also offers bilingual **architectural walking tours** (€6.50 to €8.50).

Miquelon & Langlade ISLANDS
The island of Miquelon, 45km away, is less visited and less developed than St-Pierre. The village of **Miquelon**, centered on the church, is at the northern tip of the island. From nearby **l'Étang de Mirande** a walking

trail leads to a lookout and waterfall. From the bridge in town, a scenic 25km road leads across the isthmus to the wild and uninhab-ited island of Langlade. There are some wild horses, and around the rocky coast you'll see seals and birds.

Cemetery CEMETERY
(Ave Commandant Roger Birot) The cemetery, with its above-ground mausoleums, pro-vides an atmospheric wander.

Les Salines NEIGHBORHOOD
(Rue Boursaint & the waterfront) Old-timers hang out around this scenic cluster of multi-hued fishing shacks.

Fronton PELOTE
(Rue Maître Georges Lefèvre & Rue Gloanec) Watch locals play the Basque game of *pelote* (a type of handball) at the outdoor court here.

☞ Tours

Chez Janot BOAT TOUR
(www.chezjanot.fr; adult/child €73/50; ⊙Jun-Sep) It offers full-day, bilingual tours by Zodiac covering both Miquelon and Langlade. Book at the visitors center.

Festivals & Events

From mid-July to the end of August, folk dances are often held in St-Pierre's square.

Bastille Day CULTURAL
(⊙Jul 14) The largest holiday of the year.

Basque Festival CULTURAL
(⊙mid-Aug) A weeklong festival with music, marching and invigorating street fun.

🛏 Sleeping & Eating

There are about a dozen accommoda-tions on St-Pierre; all include continental breakfast. Book ahead in summer. Great eateries abound, not surprisingly; make reservations to ensure a table. Several bars and restaurants are on Rue Albert Briand.

Bernard Dodeman B&B
B&B $

(☑508-413-060; www.pensiondodeman.com; 15 Rue Paul Bert; r €55; ⊜@🛜) The Dodeman's three simple rooms share two bathrooms and a communal TV parlor. It's a 15-minute walk from the ferry, on a hill above town.

Auberge Quatre Temps B&B
B&B $

(☑508-414-301; www.quatretemps.com; s/d €70/78; @🛜) Quatre Temps is a 15-minute schlep from the ferry dock, but don't let that deter you. All six rooms have their own bathroom. There's a fine terrace where you can buy drinks and sip alfresco. The owner also runs the Saveurs des Îles restaurant.

Nuits St-Pierre
B&B $$

(☑508-412-720; www.nuits-saint-pierre.com; 10 Rue du Général Leclerc; r €125-150; ⊜🛜) St-Pierre's most upscale lodging aims for the honeymoon crowd. The five rooms, each with private bathroom and downy, above-the-norm beds, are named after famous French authors. There's free pickup from the airport or ferry. The attached tea salon is open every afternoon from 2pm to 6pm and is a must for a restorative beverage and slice of cake.

★ Guillard Gourmandises
BAKERY $

(23 Rue Boursaint; pastries €1-3; ⊙7am-noon & 2-5:30pm Tue-Sat, to 4:30pm Sun) Holy mother! These cream-plumped chocolate éclairs, macarons and gateaux are the reason you came to France, right?

Saveurs des Îles
FRENCH $$$

(☑508-410-360; www.restaurant-saveursdesiles. com; 6 Rue Maître Georges Lefèvre; mains €16-20; ⊙11:30am-2pm & 6:30-10pm) The candlelit wood bar, gauzy curtains, crooners on the stereo and cocktail list lend a sexy vibe to this restaurant. Staff chalk the daily specials on the board, say, of fresh-plucked fish or snails with garlic cream. A fine wine selection, of course, washes it down.

L'Atelier Gourmand
FRENCH $$$

(☑508-415-300; www.lateliergourmandspm.com; 12 Rue du 11 Novembre; mains €15-26; ⊙noon-2pm & 6-10:30pm; 🛜) Crowds of diners tuck into classic, delicious, French fare at this cozy restaurant with a streetfront patio. The heaping bowl of mussels, toasted goat cheese salad and white chocolate crème brûlée are among the dishes that will haunt your dreams.

ℹ Information

Americans, EU citizens and all visitors except Canadians need a passport for entry. Those staying longer than 30 days also need a visa. Other nationalities should confirm with their French embassy if a visa is needed prior to arrival. Canadians can enter with a driver's license.

Business Hours Most shops and businesses close between noon and 1:30pm. Some stores also close on Saturday afternoons, and most are closed on Sunday.

Customs To merit the duty-free waiver on alcohol, you must stay on the islands at least 48 hours.

Language French, but many people also speak English.

Money Many merchants accept the loonie, though they return change in euros. If you're staying more than an afternoon, it's probably easiest to get euros from the local ATMs.

Telephone Calling the islands is an international call, meaning you must dial 011 in front of the local number. Phone service links in to the French system, so beware of roaming charges on your mobile.

Time Half an hour ahead of Newfoundland Time.

Tourist Information (www.st-pierre-et-mique-lon.com) The visitors center, near the ferry dock, provides a map showing all the banks, restaurants etc. Staff also provides information on the islands' hotels and tours and make bookings for free.

Voltage 220V; Canadian and American appliances need an electrical adapter.

ℹ Getting There & Away

AIR

Air St-Pierre (www.airsaintpierre.com) flies to St John's, Montréal and Halifax. There are two to three flights weekly to each city. Taxis to/from the airport cost around €5.

BOAT

From Fortune on Newfoundland, the **St-Pierre Ferry** (☑709-832-3455; www.saintpierreferry. ca; 14 Bayview St; adult/child return $93/58) makes the hour-long trip to and from the island once daily (twice on Wednesdays) in July and August. It runs less often the rest of the year. Departure times vary, so check the schedule. The boats carry foot passengers only. You can leave your car in the parking lot by the dock (per day $9).

❶ Getting Around

Much can be seen on foot. Roads are steep, so prepare to huff and puff. The visitors center rents bicycles (per half/full day €10/15). Local ferries head to Miquelon and Langlade; check with the visitors center for schedules and costs.

CENTRAL NEWFOUNDLAND

Central Newfoundland elicits fewer wows per square kilometer than the rest of the province, but that's because huge chunks of the region are pure bog land and trees. The islands of Notre Dame Bay – particularly Twillingate, when icebergs glide by – are exceptional exceptions.

Terra Nova National Park

Backed by lakes, bogs and hilly woods, and fronted by the salty waters of Clode and Newman Sounds, **Terra Nova National Park** (✎ 709-533-2801; www.pc.gc.ca/terranova; adult/child/family per day $5.80/2.90/14.70) is spliced by Hwy 1 running through its interior. It's not nearly as dramatic as the province's other national parks, though it does offer moose, bear, beaver and bald eagles, as well as relaxed hiking, paddling, camping and boat tours.

Make your first stop the **visitors center** (✎ 709-533-2942; Hwy 1; ☉ 10am-6pm Jul & Aug, to 4pm May, Jun & Sep), which has oodles of park information, ranger-guided programs and marine displays with touch tanks and underwater cameras. It's 1km off Hwy 1 at Salton's Day-Use Area, 80km east of Gander.

❍ Sights & Activities

Terra Nova's 14 hiking trails total almost 100km; pick up maps at the visitors center. Highly recommended is the **Malady Head Trail** (5km), which climaxes at the edge of a headland cliff offering stunning views of Southwest Arm and Broad Cove. **Sandy Pond Trail** (3km) is an easy loop around the pond – your best place to spot a beaver. The area is also a favorite for **swimming**, with a beach, change rooms and picnic tables. In winter, the park grooms trails here for cross-country skiing.

The epic **Outport Trail** (48km) provides access to backcountry campgrounds and abandoned settlements along Newman Sound. The loop in its entirety is rewarding, but be warned: parts are unmarked, not to mention mucky. A compass, a topographical map and ranger advice are prerequisites for this serious route.

Kayak rentals are available at the kiosk by the visitors center. Inquire about the **Sandy Pond-Dunphy's Pond Route** (10km), a great paddle with only one small portage.

About 15km from the park's western gate, the **Burnside Archaeology Centre** (✎ 709-677-2474; www.digthequarry.com; Main St; adult/child $2/1; ☉ 9am-6pm Jul-Oct) catalogs artifacts found at local Beothuk sites; ask about **boat tours** (per adult/child $45/25) to the more far-flung settlements. Also in the region is **Salvage**, a photographer's-dream fishing village with well-marked walking trails. It's near the park's north end on Rte 310, about 26km from Hwy 1.

❒ Tours

Departures are from the visitors center.

Coastal Connections BOAT TOUR
(✎ 709-533-2196; www.coastalconnections.ca; 2½hr tours adult/child $65/35; ☉ 9:30am & 1pm May-Oct) Climb aboard for a trip through Newman Sound, where you'll pull lobster pots, examine plankton under the microscope and engage in other hands-on activities. It's common to see eagles, less so whales.

⌂ Sleeping

Camping is the only option within the park itself. Those with aspirations of a bed should head to Eastport; it's near the park's north end on Rte 310, about 16km from Hwy 1. For camping reservations (recommended on summer weekends), call **Parks Canada** (✎ 877-737-3783; www.pccamping.ca; reservation fee $10.80) or go online.

Backcountry Camping CAMPGROUND $
(free permit required, campsites $16) There are several backcountry sites around the Outport Trail, Beachy Pond, Dunphy's Island and Dunphy's Pond, reached by paddling, hiking or both. Register at the visitors center.

Newman Sound Campground CAMPGROUND $
(campsites $26-30) This is the park's main (noisier) campground, with 343 sites, a grocery store and laundromat. It's open for winter camping, too.

Malady Head Campground   CAMPGROUND $
(campsites $17-22) Located at the park's northern end, Malady Head is smaller, quieter and more primitive (though it does have showers).

Gander

POP 11,000

Gander sprawls across the juncture of Hwy 1 and Rte 330, which leads to Notre Dame Bay. It is a convenient stopping point and offers a couple of sights for aviation buffs.

There is a **visitors center** (www.gander-canada.com; ◷8am-8pm Jun-Sep, 8:30am-5pm Oct-May) on Hwy 1 at the central entry into town. For aviation fanatics, the **North Atlantic Aviation Museum** (☑709-256-2923; www.northatlanticaviationmuseum.com; Hwy 1; adult/child $6/5; ◷9am-7pm daily Jul & Aug, to 4pm Mon-Fri Sep-Jun) has exhibits detailing Newfoundland's air contributions to WWII and the history of navigation. Just east on Hwy 1 is the sobering **Silent Witness Monument**, a tribute to 248 US soldiers whose plane crashed here in December 1985.

Sinbad's Hotel & Suites (☑709-651-2678; www.steelehotels.com; Bennett Dr; r $95-130) has clean, basic hotel rooms within the center of Gander. Big box retailers are everywhere, as this is the region's main town. If you need to stock up on anything, do it here.

The **Gander Airport** (YQX; www.gander-airport.com) gets a fair bit of traffic. **DRL** (☑709-263-2171; www.drl-lr.com) buses stop at the airport en route to St John's (four hours) and Port aux Basques (nine hours).

Twillingate Island & New World Island

POP 2600

This area of Notre Dame Bay gets the most attention, and deservedly so. Twillingate (which actually consists of two barely separated islands, North and South Twillingate) sits just north of New World Island. The islands are reached from the mainland via an amalgamation of short causeways. It's stunningly beautiful, with every turn of the road revealing new ocean vistas, colorful fishing wharves or tidy groups of pastel houses hovering on cliffs and outcrops. An influx of whales and icebergs every summer only adds to the appealing mix.

◉ Sights

The sights below are roughly in order of how you will come across them as you drive through Twillingate.

★**Prime Berth/Twillingate Fishing Museum**   MUSEUM
(☑709-884-5925; www.primeberth.com; Walter Elliott Causeway; admission $5, tour $8; ◷10am-5pm Jul & Aug) Make this your first stop. Run by an engaging fisherman, the private museum, with its imaginative and deceivingly simple concepts (a cod splitting show!), is brilliant, and fun for mature scholars and school kids alike. It's the first place you see as you cross to Twillingate.

Little Harbour   WATERFRONT
In Little Harbour, en route to the town of Twillingate, a 5km trail leads past the vestiges of a resettled community and rock arch to secluded, picturesque **Jone's Cove**.

Auk Island Winery   WINERY
(☑709-884-2707; www.aukislandwinery.com; 29 Durrell St; tastings $3, with tour $5; ◷9:30am-6:30pm Jul & Aug, reduced hours Sep-Jun) Visit the grounds that produce Moose Joose (blueberry-partridgeberry), Funky Puffin (blueberry-rhubarb) and other fruity flavors using iceberg water and local berries. There's also ice cream made from iceberg water and bicycle rentals (per day $25).

Durrell Museum   MUSEUM
(☑709-884-2780; Museum St, off Durrell St; adult/child $2/1; ◷9am-5pm Jun-Sep) Don't neglect to see scenic Durrell and its museum, dwelling atop Old Maid Hill. The polar bear is a bonus. Bring your lunch; there are a couple of picnic tables and a spectacular view.

Twillingate Museum   MUSEUM
(☑709-884-2825; www.tmacs.ca; off Main St; admission by donation; ◷9am-5pm May-Sep) Housed in a former Anglican rectory, the museum tells the island's history since the first British settlers arrived in the mid-1700s. One room delves into the seal hunt and its controversy. There's a historic **church** next door.

Long Point Lighthouse   LIGHTHOUSE
(☑709-884-2247; ◷10am-6pm) **FREE** Long Point provides dramatic views of the coastal cliffs. Travel up the winding steps, worn from lighthouse keepers' footsteps since 1876, and gawk at the 360-degree view. Located at the tip of the north island, it's an

ideal vantage point for spotting icebergs in May and June.

Tours

Fun two-hour tours (per adult/child $44/22) to view icebergs and whales depart daily from mid-May to early September.

Twillingate Adventure Tours   BOAT TOUR
(☎888-447-8687; www.twillingateadventuretours.com; off Main St) Depart from Twillingate's wharf at 10am, 1pm and 4pm (and sometimes 7pm).

Twillingate Island Boat Tours   BOAT TOUR
(☎709-884-2242; www.icebergtours.ca; Main St) Depart from the Iceberg Shop (itself worth a peek, with its iceberg pictures and crafts) at 9:30am, 1pm and 4pm.

Festivals & Events

Fish, Fun & Folk Festival   MUSIC
(www.fishfunfolkfestival.com; ⊙late Jul) Traditional music and dance, some of which goes back to the 16th century, merrily take over Twillingate during this weeklong festival.

Sleeping & Eating

Despite having about 20 lodging options, Twillingate gets very busy in the summer. Book early.

Captain's Legacy B&B   B&B $$
(☎709-884-5648; www.captainslegacy.com; Hart's Cove; r $95-125; ⊙May-Oct; ❀🐾) A real captain named Peter Troake once owned this historic 'outport mansion,' now a gracious four-room B&B overlooking the harbor.

Paradise B&B   B&B $$
(☎877-882-1999, 709-884-5683; www.capturegaia.com/paradiseb&b.html; 192 Main St; r $100; ⊙May-Sep; ❀🐾) Set on a bluff overlooking Twillin-

gate's harbor, Paradise offers the best view in town. You can wander down to the beach below, or relax on a lawn chair and soak it all up. Oh, the three rooms are comfy too. Angle for room 1. Cash only.

Anchor Inn Hotel   HOTEL $$
(☎800-450-3950, 709-884-2777; www.anchorinntwillingate.com; 3 Path End; r $120-180; ⊙Mar-Dec; 🐾) The waterfront Anchor has rooms with deliciously soft beds. Amenities include the hotel's view-worthy deck and the barbecue grill for do-it-yourself types. There's also an excellent on-site restaurant.

J & J Fish Market   SEAFOOD $
(98 Main St; mains $8-16; ⊙11am-7pm) It only has six tables, but they're filled with diners shoveling fresh fish, lobster and crab in their gobs.

R&J Restaurant   SEAFOOD $
(☎709-884-2212; 110 Main St; mains $8-14; ⊙8am-11pm) Sink your teeth into fish 'n' brewis, shrimp, scallops or battered fish. Pizzas and burgers are also available.

Entertainment

All Around the Circle Dinner Theatre   THEATER
(☎709-884-5423; Crow Head; adult/child $32/16; ⊙6pm Mon-Sat Jun-Sep) Six of Newfoundland's best will not only cook you a traditional meal, they'll also leave you in stitches with their talented performances. It's just south of the Long Point Lighthouse.

Information

Town of Twillingate (www.townoftwillingate.ca)
Twillingate Tourism (www.visittwillingate.com)

NEWFOUNDLAND & LABRADOR TWILLINGATE ISLAND & NEW WORLD ISLAND

DRIFTING DOWN ICEBERG ALLEY

Each year 10,000 to 40,000 glistening icebergs break off Greenland's glaciers and enter the Baffin and Labrador currents for the three-year trip south to Newfoundland's famed 'Iceberg Alley.' This 480km-long, 98km-wide stretch of sea runs along the province's north and east coasts and is strewn with 'bergs in late spring and early summer. Fogo and Twillingate Islands in Notre Dame Bay and St Anthony on the Northern Peninsula are some of the best places for sightings. Even St John's is graced with a few hundred of the blue-and-white marvels most years (though sometimes the waters remain barren due to climate and current shifts).

To see where the behemoths lurk, check www.icebergfinder.com, the provincial tourism association's website showing where icebergs are floating; you can get weekly email updates on their locations and plan your trip accordingly.

① Getting There & Away

From the mainland, Rte 340's causeways almost imperceptibly connect Chapel Island, tiny Strong's Island, New World Island and Twillingate Island.

Fogo Island & Change Islands

POP 2900

Settled in the 1680s, Fogo is an intriguing and rugged island to poke around. Keep an eye on this place: it has embarked on an ambitious, arts-oriented sustainable tourism plan that's quite progressive for the region. The rare Newfoundland pony roams the Change Islands, which float to the west.

◉ Sights & Activities

On Fogo, the village of **Joe Batt's Arm**, backed by rocky hills, is a flashback to centuries past – though it now has a mod twist thanks to the luxe new Fogo Island Inn. A **farmers market** takes place at the ice rink on Saturday mornings.

Nearby is **Tilting**, perhaps the most engaging village on the island. The Irish roots run deep here and so do the accents. The inland harbor is surrounded by picturesque fishing stages and flakes, held above the incoming tides by weary stilts. There's also the great coastal **Turpin's Trail** (9km) that leaves from Tilting, near the beach at **Sandy Cove**.

On the opposite end of the island is the village of **Fogo** and the indomitable **Brimstone Head**. After you take in the mystical rock's view, do another great hike in town: the **Lion's Den Trail** (5km), which visits a Marconi radio site. Keep an eye out for the small group of caribou that roams the island.

As part of the new development plan, the island is stringing **art studios** along its walking trails, and inviting painters, filmmakers and photographers from around the world for residencies. Ask about the **digital cinema's** current location.

The Change Islands are home to the **Newfoundland Pony Sanctuary** (☑709-621-6381; 12 Bowns Rd; admission by donation; ⊗by appointment), established to increase numbers of the native, endangered Newfoundland pony. Less than 100 registered beasts of breeding age remain in the province, and this humble stable of 11 ponies is the largest herd. The small creatures are renowned as hardy workers (especially in winter) with gentle temperaments. Pony rides are available for $5 to $10. Call first to make sure someone is on-site before visiting.

✻ Festivals & Events

Great Fogo Island Punt Race CULTURAL
(www.fogoislandregatta.com; ⊗late Jul) Locals row traditionally built wooden boats (called punts) 16km across open sea to the Change Islands and back.

Brimstone Head Folk Festival MUSIC
(www.brimstoneheadfestival.com; ⊗mid-Aug) A three-day hootenanny; Irish and Newfoundland music.

⊨ Sleeping & Eating

Peg's B&B B&B $
(☑709-266-2392; www.pegsbb.com; 60 Main St, Fogo; r from $80; ⊗May-Oct; ⊜🕸) Right in the heart of Fogo village, Peg's four-room place offers up a friendly atmosphere and harbor views.

Foley's Place B&B B&B $
(☑866-658-7244, 709-658-7288; www.foleysplace. ca; 10A Kelley's Island Rd, Tilting; r $85; ⊜🕸) The four rooms in this traditional, 100-year-old home are brightly colored, furnished in modern style and have en suite bathrooms.

ROUND OR FLAT?

Despite Columbus' stellar work in 1492 (when he sailed the ocean blue without falling off the earth's edge), and despite modern satellite photos that confirm his findings of a rounded orb, the folks at the Flat Earth Society aren't buying it. A spinning, spherical world hurtling through space would only lead to our planet's inhabitants living a confused and disorientated life, they say.

In 'reality', the stable and calming flat earth is said to have five striking corners: Lake Mikhayl in Tunguska (Siberia); Easter Island; Lhasa (Tibet); the South Pacific island of Ponape; and Brimstone Head on Fogo Island, right here in Newfoundland. So climb up the craggy spine of Brimstone Head, stare off the abyss to earth's distant edge and judge for yourself if the earth is round or flat. If nothing else, you're guaranteed a stunning view of Iceberg Alley.

Fogo Island Inn INN $$$
(☑ 709-658-3444; www.fogoislandinn.ca; Joe Batt's Arm; r incl meals $850-2700) ◢ Opened in 2013, this 29-room, ecofriendly inn is a gorgeous architecturual wonder clasping the edge of the world. Each room has phenomenal views, as does the on-site restaurant (mains $40 to $49, open 7am to 9pm). The chef sources almost everything from island forages. If staff aren't busy, they'll give you a tour of the mod building.

Nicole's Cafe CAFE $$
(☑ 709-658-3663; www.nicolescafe.ca; 159 Main Rd, Joe Batt's Arm; mains $16-22; ☺10am-9pm) ◢ Nicole uses ingredients from the island – sustainably caught seafood, root vegetables and wild berries – for her contemporary take on dishes like Jiggs dinner, caribou pâté and the daily vegetarian plate. It's a sunny spot with big wood tables and local artwork and quilts on the walls.

❶ Information

Change Islands (www.changeislands.ca)
Fogo Tourism (www.townoffogoisland.ca)

❶ Getting There & Away

Rte 335 takes you to the town of Farewell, where the ferry sails to the Change Islands (20 minutes) and then onward to Fogo (45 minutes). Five boats leave between 7:45am and 8:30pm. Schedules vary, so check with **Provincial Ferry Services** (☑ 709-627-3492; www.gov.nl.ca/ferryservices). The round-trip fare to Fogo is $18 for car and driver, and $6 for additional passengers. It's $7 to the Change Islands. Note it is about 25km from Fogo's ferry terminal to Joe Batt's Arm.

Grand Falls-Windsor

POP 13,700

The sprawl of two small pulp-and-paper towns has met and now comprises the community of Grand Falls-Windsor. The Grand Falls portion, south of Hwy 1 and near the Exploits River, is more interesting for visitors. The five-day **Salmon Festival** (www.salmonfestival.com; ☺mid-Jul) rocks with big-name Canadian bands.

◉ Sights

Mary March Provincial Museum MUSEUM
(☑ 709-292-4522; www.therooms.ca/museum; 24 St Catherine St; adult/child $2.50/free; ☺9am-4:45pm Mon-Sat, from noon Sun May-Oct) This

is worth visiting. Exhibits concentrate on the recent and past histories of Aboriginal peoples in the area, including the extinct Beothuk tribe. Take exit 18A south to reach it. Admission includes the loggers' museum.

Loggers' Life Provincial Museum MUSEUM
(☑ 709-292-0492; www.therooms.ca/museum; exit 17, Hwy 1; adult/child $2.50/free; ☺9am-4:45pm Mon-Sat, from noon Sun Jun-Sep) Here you can experience the life of a 1920s logging camp – smells and all. Admission includes the provincial museum.

Salmonid Interpretation Centre PARK
(☑ 709-489-7350; www.exploitsriver.ca; adult/child $6.50/3; ☺8am-8pm Jun-Sep) Watch Atlantic salmon start their mighty struggle upstream to spawn. Unfortunately, they do so under the pulp mill's shadow. To get there, cross the river south of High St and follow the signs.

⬛ Sleeping & Eating

Hill Road Manor B&B B&B $$
(☑ 866-489-5451, 709-489-5451; www.hillroadmanor.com; 1 Hill Rd; r $119-129; ☎) Elegant furnishings, cushiony beds that will have you gladly oversleeping and a vibrant sunroom combine for a stylish stay. Kids are welcome.

Kelly's Pub & Eatery BURGERS $
(☑ 709-489-9893; 18 Hill Rd; mains $8-12; ☺9am-2am) Hidden neatly behind the smoky pub is this great countrified spot. It makes the best burgers in town and the stir-fries are not too shabby either.

❶ Information

Town of Grand Falls-Windsor (www.townofgrandfallswindsor.com)

❶ Getting There & Away

DRL (☑ 709-263-2171; www.drl-lr.com) has its bus stop at the Highliner Inn on the Hwy 1 service road. The drive to St John's is 430km, to Port aux Basques it's 477km.

Central South Coast

Rte 360 runs 130km through the center of the province to the south coast. It's a long way down to the first settlements at the end of **Bay d'Espoir**, a gentle fjord. Note there is no gas station on the route, so fill up on Hwy 1. **St Alban's** is set on the west side of the fjord. You'll find a few motels with dining rooms and lounges around the end of the bay.

Further south is a concentration of small fishing villages. The scenery along Rte 364 to **Hermitage** is particularly impressive, as is the scenery around **Harbour Breton**. It's the largest town (population 1700) in the region and huddles around the ridge of a gentle inland bay.

Southern Port Hotel (🖉 709-885-2283; www.southernporthotel.ca; Rte 360, Harbour Breton; r $93-97; 🕸) provides spacious, standard-furnished rooms; even-numbered ones have harbor views. Two doors down is **Scott's Snackbar** (🖉 709-885-2406; mains $7-15; ☺ 10:30am-11pm Sun-Thu, to 1am Fri & Sat), serving burgers and home-cooked dishes; it's licensed.

Thornhill Taxi Service (🖉 866-538-3429, 709-885-2144) connects Harbour Breton with Grand Falls ($40, 2½ hours), leaving at 7:15am. Government passenger ferries serve Hermitage, making the western south-coast outports accessible from here.

NORTHERN PENINSULA

The Northern Peninsula points upward from the body of Newfoundland like an extended index finger, and you almost get the feeling it's wagging at you saying, 'Don't you dare leave this province without coming up here.'

Heed the advice. This area could well be crowned Newfoundland's star attraction. Two of the province's World Heritage–listed sites are here: Gros Morne National Park, with its fjordlike lakes and geological oddities, rests at the peninsula's base, while the sublime, 1000-year-old Viking settlement at L'Anse aux Meadows stares out from the peninsula's tip. Connecting these two famous sites is the **Viking Trail** (www.vikingtrail.org), aka Rte 430, an attraction in its own right that holds close to the sea as it heads resolutely north past the ancient burial grounds of Port au Choix and the ferry jump-off point to big, brooding Labrador.

The region continues to gain in tourism, yet the crowds are nowhere near what you'd get at Yellowstone or Banff, for example. Still, it's wise to book ahead in July and August.

It's a five- to six-hour drive from Deer Lake at the peninsula's southern edge to L'Anse aux Meadows at its northern apex.

Towns and amenities are few and far between so don't wait to fuel up.

Deer Lake

There's little in Deer Lake for the visitor, but it's an excellent place to fly into for trips up the Northern Peninsula and around the west coast.

Those looking for B&B comfort can hunker down at plain-and-simple **Auntie M's Lucas House** (🖉 709-635-3622; www.lucashousebb.net; 22 Old Bonne Bay Rd; r $65-75; ☺ May-Sep; ➡ @ 🕸); it's a five-minute ride from the airport. The biggest show in town is new, 88-room **Holiday Inn Express** (🖉 709-635-3232; www.ihg.com; 38 Bennett's Ave; r $130-180; ✳ @ 🕸 ≈ 🐾); it's a 10-minute ride from the airport.

The **visitors center** (☺ 9am-7pm) and the **DRL** (🖉 709-263-2171; www.drl-lr.com) bus stop at the Irving gas station sit beside each other on Hwy 1. A taxi from the airport to any of these spots costs about $10.

Deer Lake Airport (YDF; www.deerlakeairport.com) is a stone's throw off Hwy 1. It's a well-equipped little place with ATMs, food, free wi-fi and internet access, and a staffed tourism desk. Flights arrive regularly from St John's, Halifax, Toronto and even London. Avis, Budget and National are among the companies renting cars at the airport.

Gros Morne National Park

This **national park** (🖉 709-458-2417; www.pc.gc.ca/grosmorne; adult/child/family per day $9.80/4.90/19.60) stepped into the world spotlight in 1987, when Unesco granted it World Heritage designation. To visitors, the park's stunning flat-top mountains and deeply incised waterways are simply supernatural playgrounds. To geologists, this park is a blueprint for the planet and supplies evidence for theories such as plate tectonics. Specifically, the bronze-colored Tablelands are made of rock that comes from deep within the earth's crust. Nowhere in the world is such material as easily accessed as in Gros Morne (it's usually only found at unfathomable ocean depths). Such attributes have earned the park its 'Galapagos of Geology' nickname.

There is enough to do in and around the park to easily fill several days. The hiking, kayaking, camping, wildlife-spotting and boat tours are fantastic.

Several small fishing villages dot the shoreline and provide amenities. Bonne Bay swings in and divides the area: to the south is Rte 431 and the towns of **Glenburnie**, **Woody Point** and **Trout River**; to the north is Rte 430 and **Norris Point**, **Rocky Harbour**, **Sally's Cove** and **Cow Head**. Centrally located Rocky Harbour is the largest village and most popular place to stay. Nearby Norris Point and further-flung Woody Point also make good bases.

◎ Sights

The park is quite widespread – it's 133km from Trout River at the south end to Cow Head in the north – so it takes a while to get from sight to sight. We've listed the following places from south to north. Don't forget to stop in the park's visitors centers, which have interpretive programs and guided walks.

Tablelands   GEOGRAPHIC FEATURE

(Rte 431, near Trout River) Dominating the southwest corner of the park are the unconquerable and eerie Tablelands. This massive flat-topped massif was part of the earth's mantle before tectonics raised it from the depths and planted it squarely on the continent. Its rock is so unusual that plants can't even grow on it. You can view the barren golden phenomenon up close on Rte 431, or catch it from a distance at the stunning **photography lookout** above Norris Point. West of the Tablelands, dramatic volcanic sea stacks and caves mark the coast at **Green Gardens**.

Bonne Bay Marine Station   AQUARIUM

(☑709-458-2550; www.bonnebay.mun.ca; Rte 430, Norris Point; adult/child/family $6.25/5/15; ⊙9am-5pm Jun-Aug) At the wharf in Norris Point is the Bonne Bay Marine Station, a research facility that's part of Memorial University. Every half-hour there are interactive tours, and the aquariums display the marine ecological habitats in Bonne Bay. For children, there are touch tanks and a rare blue lobster lurking around.

SS Ethie   SHIPWRECK

(Rte 430, past Sally's Cove) Follow the sign off the highway to where waves batter the rusty and tangled remains of the SS *Ethie*. The story of this 1919 wreck, and the subsequent rescue, was inspiration for a famous folk song.

Broom Point Fishing Camp   HISTORIC SITE

(Rte 430, Broom Point; ⊙10am-5:30pm May-Oct) **FREE** This restored fishing camp sits a short distance north of Western Brook Pond. The three Mudge brothers and their families fished here from 1941 until 1975, when they sold the entire camp, including boats, lobster traps and nets, to the national park. Everything has been restored; it's staffed by guides.

Shallow Bay   BEACH

The gentle, safe, sand-duned beach at Shallow Bay seems out of place, as if transported from the Caribbean by some bizarre current. The water, though, provides a chilling dose of reality, rarely getting above 15°C.

The Arches   PARK

These scenic arched rocks on Rte 430 north of Parsons Pond are formed by pounding waves and worth a look-see.

🏃 Activities

Hiking and kayaking can also be done via guided tours.

Hiking

Twenty maintained trails of varying difficulty snake through 100km of the park's most scenic landscapes. The gem is the **James Callahan Gros Morne Trail** (16km) to the peak of Gros Morne, the highest point at 806m. While there are sections with steps and boardwalks, this is a strenuous seven-to eight-hour hike, and includes a steep rock gully that must be climbed to the ridge line of the mountain. Standing on the 600m precipice and staring out over **10 Mile Pond**, a sheer-sided fjord, can only be described as sublime.

Green Gardens Trail (16km) is almost as scenic and challenging. The loop has two trailheads off Rte 431, with each one descending to Green Gardens along its magnificent coastline formed from lava and shaped by the sea. Plan on six to eight hours of hiking or book one of the three backcountry camping areas, all of them on the ocean, and turn the hike into an overnight adventure. A less strenuous day hike (9km) to the beach and back is possible from this trail's Long Pond Trailhead.

Shorter scenic hikes are **Tablelands Trail** (4km), which extends to Winterhouse Brook Canyon; **Lookout Trail** (5km), which starts behind the Discovery Centre and loops to the site of an old fire tower above the tree line; **Lobster Cove Head Trail** (2km), which loops through tidal pools; and Western Brook Pond Trail, the most popular path.

The granddaddies of the trails are the **Long Range Traverse** (35km) and **North Rim Traverse** (27km), serious multiday treks over the mountains. Permits and advice from park rangers are required.

If you plan to do several trails, invest $20 in a copy of the *Gros Morne National Park Trail Guide,* a waterproof map with trail descriptions on the back, which is usually available at the visitors centers.

Western Brook Pond
HIKING

(Rte 430) Park your car in the lot off the highway, then take the 3km easy path inland to Western Brook Pond. 'Pond' is a misnomer, since the body of water is huge. Many people also call it a fjord, which is technically incorrect, since it's freshwater versus saltwater. Here's the thing everyone agrees on: it's flat-out stunning. Western Brook's sheer 700m cliffs plunge to the blue abyss and snake into the mountains. The best way to experience it is on a boat tour (p490).

Kayaking

Kayaking in the shadow of the Tablelands and through the spray of whales is truly something to be experienced. Gros Morne Adventures provides rentals (single/double per day $55/65) for experienced paddlers.

Skiing

Many trails in the park's impressive 55km cross-country ski-trail system were designed by Canadian Olympic champion, Pierre Harvey. Contact the Main Visitor Centre for trail information and reservations for backcountry huts.

☞ Tours

Most tours operate between June and mid-September; book in advance. Kayaking is best in June and July.

Bon Tours
BOAT TOUR

(☎709-458-2016; www.bontours.ca; Ocean View Motel, Main St, Rocky Harbour) Bon runs the phenomenal **Western Brook Pond boat tour** (2hr trip per adult $53-60, child $20-26) every hour between 10am and 5pm. The dock is a 3km walk from Rte 430 via the easy Western

---

THE SEAL HUNT DEBATE

Nothing ignites a more passionate debate than Canada's annual seal hunt, which occurs in March and April off Newfoundland's northeast coast and in the Gulf of St Lawrence around the Îles de la Madeleine and Prince Edward Island.

The debate pits animal rights activists against sealers (typically local fishers who hunt seals in the off-season), and both sides spin rhetoric like a presidential press secretary. The main issues revolve around the following questions.

Are baby seals being killed? Yes and no. Whitecoats are newborn harp seals, and these are the creatures that have been seen in horrifying images. But it's illegal to hunt them and has been for 20 years. However, young harp seals lose their white coats when the seals are about 12 to 14 days old. After that, they're fair game.

Are the animals killed humanely? Sealers say yes, that the guns and/or clubs they use kill the seals humanely. Animal activists dispute this, saying seals are shot or clubbed and left on the ice to suffer until the sealers come back later and finish the job.

Is the seal population sustainable? The Canadian government says yes, and sets the yearly quota based on the total seal population in the area (estimated at 7.3 million). For 2013, the harp seal quota was 400,000. The 2012 quota was the same. Activists say the quotas don't take into account the actual number of seals killed in the hunt, such as those that are 'struck and lost,' or discarded because of pelt damage.

Is the seal hunt really an important part of the local economy? Activists say no, that it represents a fraction of Newfoundland's income. The province disagrees, saying for some sealers it represents up to one-third of their annual income. And in a province with unemployment near 12%, that's significant.

In 2009 the European Union banned the sale of seal products, which hurt the industry considerably. For further details on the two perspectives, see the websites of the **Canadian Sealers Association** (www.sealharvest.ca) and the **Humane Society of the United States** (www.protectseals.org).

Brook Pond Trail. If you haven't purchased a **park pass** ($9.80), you must do so before embarking. Reserve in advance, either online or at Bon's office in the Ocean View Hotel. It's about a 25-minute drive from Bon's office to the trailhead.

Bon also runs **Bonne Bay boat tours** (2hr trip per adult/child $40/14) departing from Norris Point wharf, as well as a water taxi (adult/child $14/10 round-trip, foot passengers and bikes only) from Norris Point to Woody Point.

Gros Morne Adventures
GUIDED TOUR

(☎ 800-685-4624, 709-458-2722; www.grosmorneadventures.com; Norris Point wharf) It offers daily guided sea-kayak tours (two/three hours $55/65) in Bonne Bay, plus full-day and multiday kayak trips and various hiking tours.

Cycle Solutions
CYCLING TOUR

(☎ 866-652-2269, 709-634-7100; www.cyclesolutions.ca; Rte 430, Rocky Harbour) The Corner Brook-based bike shop offers all manner of cycling tours through Gros Morne, from easy half-day rides to hard-core, multiday trips. Prices vary. The office is next to Rocky Harbour's town information center.

Ocean Quest Adventures
BOAT TOUR

(☎ 270-326-8687; www.oceanquestadventures.com; Trout River Pond; 1½hr tour $89; ☉ Jun-Sep) Offers geologic-themed Zodiac tours from Trout River Pond, as well as kayak rentals and shuttle service to hike the Overfalls Trail (a moderate 5km section of the International Appalachian Trail).

★ Festivals & Events

Gros Morne Theatre Festival
THEATER

(☎ 709-243-2899; www.theatrenewfoundland.com; tickets $15-30; ☉ late-May–mid-Sep) Eight productions of Newfoundland plays, staged both indoors and outdoors at various locations throughout the summer.

Writers at Woody Point Festival
LITERATURE

(☎ 709-453-2900; www.writersatwoodypoint.com; tickets $30; ☉ mid-Aug) Authors from across Newfoundland, Canada and the world converge at the Woody Point Heritage Theatre to do readings.

⬛ Sleeping

Rocky Harbour has the most options. Woody Point and Norris Point are also good bets. Places fill fast in July and August.

Park Campgrounds
CAMPGROUND $

(☎ 877-737-3783; www.pccamping.ca; campsites $19-26, reservation fee $11) Four developed campgrounds lie within the park: **Berry Hill** (☉ Jun-Sep), the largest, is most central; **Lomond** (☉ Jun-Oct) is good and closest to the southern park entrance; **Trout River** (☉ Jun-Sep) is average and closest to the Tablelands; and **Shallow Bay** (☉ Jun-Sep) has ocean swimming (and mosquitoes). There's also a **primitive campground** (☉ year-round) at superb Green Point.

Numerous **backcountry campsites** (campsites $10) are spread along trails; reserve them at the Main Visitor Centre. Berry Hill and Shallow Bay campgrounds also have **oTENTik units** (per night $120), a sort of tent-cabin hybrid equipped with beds and furniture on a raised wooden floor.

Aunt Jane's Place B&B
B&B $

(☎ 709-453-2485; www.grosmorne.com/victorianmanor; Water St, Woody Point; d without/with bathroom $75/85; ☉ May-Oct; ☻) This historic house oozes character. It sits beachside, so you may be woken early in the morning by the heavy breathing of whales.

Gros Morne Accommodations & Hostel
HOSTEL $

(☎ 709-458-3396; www.grosmorneaccommodationsandhostel.com; 8 Kin Pl, Rocky Harbour; dm/r $30/70; ☻☎) At this small, well-kept, newish hostel, the dorms have pinewood bunk beds, and there's a common area with cable TV and a shared kitchen. Towels are provided for a small fee. Check-in is at the Gros Morne Wildlife Museum at 76 Main St, which is a bit of a walk if you're without a car.

Anchor Down B&B
B&B $$

(☎ 800-920-2208, 709-458-2901; www.theanchordown.com; Pond Rd, Rocky Harbour; r $90-100; ☻@) The home and its five rooms are pretty simple, but guests have raved about excellent hospitality and cooking from the friendly hosts.

Middle Brook Cottages
CABIN $$

(☎ 709-453-2332; www.middlebrookcottages.com; off Rte 431, Glenburnie; cabins $115-149; ☉ Mar-Nov; ☻☎) These all-pinewood, spick-and-span cottages are both perfectly romantic and perfectly kid-friendly. They have kitchens and TVs, and you can splash around the swimming hole and waterfalls behind the property.

Gros Morne Cabins
CABIN $$

(☑709-458-2020; www.grosmornecabins.com; Main St, Rocky Harbour; cabins $159-199; 🐾) While backed by tarmac, most of these beautiful log cabins are fronted by nothing but ocean (ask when booking to ensure a view). Each has a full kitchen, TV and pullout sofa for children. Bookings can be made next door at Endicott's variety store.

✖ Eating

Rocky Harbour and Woody Point have the most options. There's a good chip van in Sally's Cove.

Earle's
CANADIAN $

(☑709-458-2577; Main St, Rocky Harbour; mains $8-14; ⊙9am-11pm) Earle is an institution in Rocky Harbour. Besides selling groceries and renting DVDs, he has great ice cream, pizza, moose burgers and traditional Newfoundland fare that you can chomp on the patio.

Java Jack's
CAFE $$

(☑709-458-3004; www.javajacks.ca; Main St, Rocky Harbour; mains $9-19; ⊙7:30am-8:30pm Wed-Mon May-Sep; 🍽) Art-filled Jack's provides Gros Morne's best coffees, wraps and soups by day. By night, the upstairs dining room fills hungry, post-hike bellies with fine seafood, caribou and vegetarian fare. Greens come fresh from the property's organic garden.

Justin Thyme
CAFE $$

(☑709-458-2326; www.justinthymebeanandbistro. ca; 216 Main St, Norris Point; mains $17-24; ⊙9am-9pm, from 5pm Tue) This casual, red-walled bistro serves coffee and baked goods for breakfast, eclectic sandwiches for lunch and lemon-cream cod and pesto mussels among its dinner line-up.

Old Loft Restaurant
SEAFOOD $$

(☑709-453-2294; www.theoldloft.com; Water St, Woody Point; mains $15-21; ⊙11:30am-9pm Jul & Aug, to 7pm May, Jun & Sep) Set on the water in Woody Point, this tiny place is popular for its traditional Newfoundland meals and seafood.

❶ Information

Park admission includes the trails, Discovery Centre and all day-use areas.

Discovery Centre (☑709-453-2490; Rte 431, Woody Point; ⊙9am-6pm May-Oct) Has interactive exhibits and a multimedia theater explaining the area's ecology and geology.

There's also an information desk with maps, daily interpretive activities and a small cafe.

Main Visitor Centre (☑709-458-2066; Rte 430, near Rocky Harbour; ⊙8am-8pm May-Oct) As well as issuing day and backcountry permits, it has maps, books, Viking Trail materials and an impressive interpretive area.

Park Entrance Kiosk (Rte 430; ⊙10am-6pm May-Oct) Near Wiltondale.

Rocky Harbour (www.rockyharbour.ca)

Western Newfoundland Tourism (www. gowesternnewfoundland.com)

❶ Getting There & Around

Deer Lake Airport is 71km south of Rocky Harbour. There are shuttle bus services to Rocky Harbour, Woody Point and Trout River; see Corner Brook for details (p498).

Port au Choix

Port au Choix, dangling on a stark peninsula 13km off the Viking Trail, houses a large fishing fleet, quirky museum and a worthy archaeological site that delves into ancient burial grounds.

◉ Sights

Port au Choix National Historic Site
HISTORIC SITE

(☑709-861-3522; www.pc.gc.ca/portauchoix; Point Riche Rd; adult/child $3.90/1.90; ⊙9am-6pm Jun-Sep) The Port au Choix National Historic Site sits on ancient burial grounds of three different Aboriginal groups, dating back 5500 years. The modern visitors center tells of these groups' creative survival in the area and of one group's unexplained disappearance 3200 years ago. Several good trails around the park let you explore further.

Phillip's Garden, a site with vestiges of Paleo-Eskimo houses, is a highlight. Two trails will take you there. One is the **Phillip's Garden Coastal Trail** (4km), which leaves from Phillip Dr at the end of town. From here you hopscotch your way over the jigsaw of skeletal rock to the site 1km away.

If you continue, it's another 3km to the **Point Riche Lighthouse** (1871). It's also accessible via the visitors center road.

Another way to reach Phillip's Garden is the **Dorset Trail** (8km). It leaves the visitors center and winds across the barrens past stunted trees, passing a Dorset Paleo-Eskimo burial cave before finally reaching the site and linking to the Coastal Trail.

Ben's Studio
GALLERY

(☑709-861-3280; www.bensstudio.ca; 24 Fisher St; ⊙9am-5pm Mon-Fri Jun-Sep) **FREE** At the edge of town is Ben Ploughman's capricious studio of folk art. Pieces like *Crucifixion of the Cod* are classic.

🛏 Sleeping & Eating

Jeannie's Sunrise B&B
B&B $$

(☑877-639-2789, 709-861-2254; www.jeanniessunrisebb.com; Fisher St; r $79-99; ☺🐾) Jeannie radiates hospitality through her spacious rooms, bright reading nook and demeanor as sweet as her breakfast muffins. Rooms at the lower end of the price spectrum share a bathroom.

Anchor Cafe
SEAFOOD $$

(☑709-861-3665; Fisher St; mains $12-18; ⊙11am-9pm) You can't miss this place – the front half is the bow of a boat – and don't, because it has the best meals in town. The luncheon specials offer good value and the dinner menu has a wide array of seafood.

St Barbe to L'anse aux Meadows

As the Viking Trail nears St Barbe, the waters of the gulf quickly narrow and give visitors their first opportunity to see the desolate shores of Labrador. Ferries take advantage of this convergence and ply the route between St Barbe and the Labrador Straits (p503). At Eddies Cove, the road leaves the coast and heads inland.

As you approach the northern tip of the peninsula, Rte 430 veers off toward St Anthony, and two new roads take over leading to several diminutive fishing villages that provide perfect bases for your visit to L'Anse aux Meadows National Historic Site. Route 436 hugs the eastern shore and passes through (from south to north) St Lunaire-Griquet, Gunners Cove, Straitsview and L'Anse aux Meadows village. Route 437 heads in a more westerly direction through Pistolet Bay, Raleigh and Cape Onion.

⊙ Sights

★ L'Anse aux Meadows National Historic Site
HISTORIC SITE

(☑709-623-2608; www.pc.gc.ca/lanseauxmeadows; Rte 436; adult/child/family $11.70/5.80/29.40; ⊙9am-6pm Jun-Sep) Leif Eriksson and his Viking friends lived here circa AD 1000. The remains of their waterside settlement – eight wood-and-sod buildings, now just vague outlines left in the spongy ground – are what visitors can see, plus three replica buildings inhabited by costumed docents. The latter have names such as 'Thora' and 'Bjorn' and simulate Viking chores such as spinning fleece and forging nails. Allow two or three hours to walk around and absorb the ambience.

The premise may seem dull – visiting a bog in the middle of nowhere and staring at the spot where a couple of old sod houses once stood – but somehow this site lying in a forlorn sweep of land turns out to be one of Newfoundland's most stirring attractions.

Be sure to browse the interpretive center and watch the introductory film, which tells the captivating story of Norwegian explorer Helge Ingstad, who discoverd the site. Also worthwhile is the 3km trail that winds through the barren terrain and along the coast surrounding the interpretive center.

Norstead
HISTORIC VILLAGE

(☑709-623-2828; www.norstead.com; Rte 436; adult/child/family $10/6.50/30; ⊙9:30am-5:30pm Jun-Sep) Can't get enough of the long-bearded Viking lifestyle? Stop by Norstead, just beyond the turnoff to the national historic site. It's a recreation of a Viking village with costumed interpreters (more than at L'Anse aux Meadows) smelting, weaving, baking and telling stories around real fires throughout four buildings. Sounds cheesy, but they pull it off with class. There's also a large-scale replica of a Viking ship on hand.

🛏 Sleeping & Eating

Straitsview, Gunners Cove and St Lunaire-Griquet are all within 12km of the national historic site.

Tickle Inn
B&B $

(☑709-452-4321; www.tickleinn.net; Rte 437, Cape Onion; r with shared bathroom $70-90; ⊙Jun-Sep; ☺) This delightful seaside inn, built in 1890, is surrounded by a white picket fence, oodles of grass and your own private beach. Sit in the parlor, feel the warmth of the Franklin woodstove and enjoy great home-cooked meals. The location is wonderfully remote.

Viking Village B&B
B&B $

(☑709-623-2238; www.vikingvillage.ca; Hay Cove, L'Anse aux Meadows village; d $72-78; ☺🐾) A timbered home with ocean views, Viking Village offers comfy, quilted rooms just 1km from

THE VIKINGS

Christopher Columbus gets the credit for 'discovering' North America, but the Vikings were actually the first Europeans to walk upon the continent. Led by Leif Eriksson, they sailed over from Scandinavia and Greenland some 500 years before Columbus and landed at L'Anse aux Meadows. They settled, constructed houses, fed themselves and even smelted iron out of the bog to forge nails, attesting to their ingenuity and fortitude. That it was all accomplished by a group of young-pup 20-somethings is even more impressive.

Norse folklore had mentioned a site called 'Vinland' for centuries. But no one could ever prove its existence – until 1968, when archaeologists found a small cloak pin on the ground at L'Anse aux Meadows. Archaeologists now believe the site was a base camp, and that the Vikings ranged much further along the coast.

the Viking site. Ask for one of the rooms with balcony access and watch the sun rise.

Snorri Cabins
CABIN $$

(☑709-623-2241; www.snorricabins.com; Rte 436, Straitsview; cabins $89; ☺Jun-Sep; ☜) These modern cabins offer simple comfort and great value. They're perfect for families, with a full kitchen, sitting room and a pull-out sofa. There's a convenience store on-site.

Valhalla Lodge B&B
B&B $$

(☑709-623-2018, 877-623-2018; www.valhalla-lodge.com; Rte 436, Gunners Cove; r $95-110; ☺May-Sep; ☜☜) Set on a hill overlooking the ocean, the five-room Valhalla is only 8km from the Viking site. Put your feet up on the deck and watch icebergs in comfort. This very view inspired E Annie Proulx, Pulitzer Prize–winning author, while she wrote *The Shipping News* here.

Daily Catch
SEAFOOD $$

(☑709-623-2295; www.thedailycatch.ca; 112 Main St, St Lunaire-Griquet; mains $16-20; ☺11am-9pm) Set on the water overlooking a pretty bay, the Daily Catch is a stylish little restaurant serving finely prepared seafood and wine. The basil-buttered salmon gets kudos. Fish

cakes, crab au gratin and cod burgers also please the palate.

Northern Delight
SEAFOOD $$

(☑709-623-2220; Rte 436, Gunners Cove; mains $10-16; ☺8am-9pm) Dine on local favorites such as turbot cheeks and pan-fried cod, fresh lobster and mussels, or just have a 'Newfie Mug-up' (bread, molasses and a strong cup of tea). There's live music on some evenings.

★Norseman Restaurant & Art Gallery
SEAFOOD $$$

(☑709-623-2018; www.valhalla-lodge.com; Rte 436, L'Anse aux Meadows village; mains $20-38; ☺noon-9pm May-Sep) This casual, waterfront restaurant may be Newfoundland's best. Relish the butternut squash soup, peruse a few vegetarian options or sink your teeth into tender Labrador caribou tenderloin. Norseman chills all its drinks with iceberg ice. Patrons who order lobster hand-pick their dinner by donning rubber boots and heading out front to the ocean, where the freshly caught crustaceans await in crates.

St Anthony

Yeehaw! You've made it to the end of the road, your windshield has helped control the insect population and you have seen two World Heritage sites. After such grandeur, St Anthony may be a little anticlimactic. It's not what you'd call pretty, but it has a rough-hewn charm. And the hiking and whale- and iceberg-watching are inspiring.

Grenfell is a big name around here. Sir Wilfred Grenfell was a local legend and, by all accounts, quite a man. This English-born and educated doctor first came to Newfoundland in 1892 and, for the next 40 years, traveling by dogsled and boat, built hospitals and nursing stations and organized much-needed fishing cooperatives along the coast of Labrador and around St Anthony.

☉ Sights

Grenfell Historic Properties
HISTORIC BUILDING

(www.grenfell-properties.com; West St; adult/child/family $10/3/22; ☺8am-5pm Jun-Sep) A number of local sites pertaining to Wilfred Grenfell are subsumed under Grenfell Historic Properties. The **Grenfell Interpretation Centre**, opposite the hospital, is a modern exhibit recounting the historic and sometimes dramatic life of Grenfell. Its **handicraft shop** has some high-quality carvings and artwork, as well as embroidered parkas made by locals – proceeds go to maintenance of the historic properties.

Grenfell Museum   MUSEUM
(www.grenfell-properties.com; ⊙9am-6pm Jun-Sep) Admission to the Grenfell Historic Properties also includes Grenfell's beautiful mansion, now the Grenfell Museum. It's behind the hospital, about a five-minute walk from the waterfront. Dyed burlap walls and antique furnishings envelop memorabilia, including a polar-bear rug and, if rumors are correct, the ghost of Mrs Grenfell.

Fishing Point Park   PARK
The main road through town ends at Fishing Point Park, where a lighthouse and towering headland cliffs overlook the sea. The **Iceberg Alley Trail** and **Whale Watchers Trail** both lead to clifftop observation platforms – the names say it all.

A **visitors center,cafe** and **craft shop** is also out here; in the side room there's a **polar bear display** (adult/child $3/2). Creatures like this guy have been known to roam St Anthony from time to time as pack ice melts in the spring.

☞ Tours

Northland Discovery Tours   BOAT TOUR
(☎709-454-3092, 877-632-3747; www.discover-northland.com; 2½hr tour adult/child $58/25; ⊙9am, 1pm & 4pm Jun-Sep) Northland offers highly recommended cruises for whale- or iceberg-viewing that leave from the dock behind the Grenfell Interpretation Centre on West St. If you tend to get seasick, medicate before this one.

🛏 Sleeping & Eating

Fishing Point B&B   B&B $$
(☎866-454-2009, 709-454-3117; www.bbcanada.com/6529.html; Fishing Point Rd; r $90; ⊛🐾🤶) This tiny place clings to the rocks en route to the lighthouse and offers the best harbor view in St Anthony. Get up early, enjoy a bountiful breakfast and watch the boats head out to sea. The three rooms each have their own bathroom.

Lightkeeper's Seafood
Restaurant   SEAFOOD $$
(☎709-454-4900; Fishing Point Park; mains $12-20; ⊙11:30am-8pm Jun-Sep) This little gem of an eatery sits in the shadow of the lighthouse and is often graced by the sight of icebergs and whales. The chowder and scallops are legendary.

ℹ Getting There & Away

Flying to St Anthony is technically possible, but the airport is nearly an hour away. **Provincial Airlines** (www.provincialairlines.ca) makes the trip from St John's daily. If you're leaving St Anthony by car, you have two options: backtrack entirely along Rte 430, or take the long way via Rte 432 along the east coast and Hare Bay. This will meet up with Rte 430 near Plum Point, between St Barbe and Port aux Choix.

NEWFOUNDLAND & LABRADOR ST ANTHONY

WORTH A TRIP

ROUTE 432 & THE FRENCH SHORE

Surprises await along lonely Rte 432. First is **Tuckamore Lodge** (☎888-865-6361, 709-865-6361; www.tuckamorelodge.com; r incl breakfast $150-180; ⊛@🤶), a wood-hewn, lakeside retreat with ridiculously comfortable beds and home-cooked meals, located smack in the middle of nowhere. You'll pass about 20 moose on your way out to it. Owner Barb Genge arranges all manner of activities (fishing, birdwatching, hunting, photography classes) with first-rate guides.

The little towns along the coast are known as the **French Shore** (www.frenchshore.com) for the French fishers who lived in the area from 1504 to 1904. Top of the heap is **Conche** with its intriguing gaggle of sights: a **WWII airplane** that crashed in town in 1942, the seaside **Captain Coupelongue walking trail** past old French gravemarkers, and a crazy-huge **tapestry** in the local interpretation center. A woman named Delight runs the sunny **Bits-n-Pieces Cafe** (☎709-622-5400; mains $10-15; ⊙8am-8pm, to 9pm Thu-Sat), ladling out cod cakes, Thai chicken and other fare that's, well, delightful. Two simple rooms above the cafe comprise the **Stage Cove B&B** (r $95; 🤶) if you want to spend the night. It's about 68km from Tuckamore Lodge; take Rte 433 to unpaved Rte 434.

WESTERN NEWFOUNDLAND

Western Newfoundland presents many visitors with their first view of The Rock, thanks to the ferry landing at Port aux Basques. It's big, cliffy, even a bit forbidding with all those wood houses clinging to the jagged shoreline against the roaring wind. From Port aux Basques, poky fishing villages cast lines to the east, while Newfoundland's second-largest town, Corner Brook, raises its wintry head (via its ski mountain) to the northeast.

Corner Brook

POP 19,900

Newfoundland's number-two town is pretty sleepy, though skiers, hikers and anglers will find plenty of action. The handsome Humber Valley, about 10km east, is where it's going on. Centered on the Marble Mountain ski resort, the area experienced a huge development boom until the bottom fell out of the international economy. But now the area is heating up again. The valley offers adventure-sport junkies places to play, while the city itself sprawls with big-box retailers and a smoke-belching pulp and paper mill.

◉ Sights & Activities

Captain James Cook Monument MONUMENT
(Crow Hill Rd) While this clifftop monument is admirable – a tribute to James Cook for his work in surveying the region in the mid-1760s – it's the panoramic view over the Bay of Islands that is the real payoff. Cook's names for many of the islands, ports and waterways you'll see, such as the Humber Arm and Hawke's Bay, remain today.

The site is northwest of downtown via a convoluted route. Ready? Take Caribou Rd to Poplar Rd to Country Rd, then go right on Atlantic Ave, left on Mayfair Ave and follow the signs.

Railway Society of Newfoundland MUSEUM
(☎709-634-2720; Station Rd, off Humber Rd; admission $2; ⊙9am-8pm Jun-Aug) Within historic Humbermouth Station, the Railway Society of Newfoundland has a good-looking steam locomotive and some narrow-gauge rolling stock that chugged across the province from 1921 to 1939.

Marble Mountain SKIING
(☎709-637-7616; www.skimarble.com; Hwy 1; day pass adult/child $59/32; ⊙10am-4:30pm Sat-Thu, 9am-9:30pm Fri Dec-Apr) Marble Mountain is the lofty reason most visitors come to Corner Brook. With 35 trails, four lifts, a 488m vertical drop and annual snowfall of 5m, it offers Atlantic Canada's best skiing. There are snowboarding and tubing parks, as well as night skiing on Friday, plus there's Oh My Jesus (you'll say it when you see the slope).

When the white stuff has departed, the **Steady Brook Falls Trail** (500m) leads from the ski area's rear parking lot, behind the Tim Hortons, to a cascade of water that tumbles more than 30m.

Marble Zip Tours ZIPLINING
(☎709-632-5463; www.marbleziptours.com; Thistle Dr; 2hr tour adult/child $99/89) It's the highest zip-line in Canada. Strap in near the mountaintop, and zigzag platform to platform down a gorge traversing Steady Brook Falls. It'll take your breath away. Tours depart four to five times daily. The office is past Marble Mountain's lodge, behind the Tim Hortons.

My Newfoundland Adventures ADVENTURE SPORTS
(☎800-686-8900, 709-638-0110; www.mynewfoundland.ca) If skiing doesn't get the adrenaline flowing, you must try snow-kiting (a windsurfing-meets-snowboarding endeavor). Or there's snowshoeing, ice fishing and even ice climbing. Canoeing, salmon fishing and caving all take place in the warmer seasons. There again, pretty much anything is possible with these patient folks; no experience is required. The office is at Marble Mountain's base by the Tim Hortons.

Blow-Me-Down Cross-Country Ski Park SKIING
(☎709-639-2754; www.blowmedown.ca; Lundigran Dr; day pass $13; ⊙sunrise-9pm Dec-Apr) It has 50km of groomed trails; ski rentals (per day $12) are available. It's about 6km southwest of downtown.

Cycle Solutions CYCLING
(☎709-634-7100, 866-652-2269; www.cyclesolutions.ca; 35 West St; ⊙9am-5:30pm Mon-Thu, to 9pm Fri, to 6pm Sat) This sweet bike shop runs local cycling and caving tours; it's attached to the Brewed Awakening coffee shop.

Corner Brook

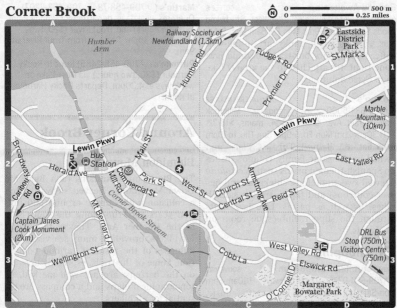

📖 Sleeping & Eating

Brookfield Inn   B&B $
(☏709-639-3111, 877-339-3111; brookfieldinn@
gmail.com; 2 Brookfield Ave; r $60-85; ⊖🐾) A
cool couple runs this B&B in their white-
frame house. The homey rooms have
hardwood floors and plump beds. In the
morning make your own breakfast from
the eggs, bacon, cheeses and breads in the
well-stocked kitchen. In the evening watch
the sun set from the deck. The house dogs
will amble up for a scratch if you want.

Glynmill Inn   HOTEL $$
(☏800-563-4400, 709-634-5181; www.steele-
hotels.com; 1 Cobb Lane; r $130-160; ❄@🐾)
Lawns, gardens and graciousness surround
the Tudor-style Glynmill. It was built origi-
nally for the engineers supervising the
pulp mill's construction in the 1920s, at
that time the largest project in the history
of paper making. The inn retains an ele-
gant, if somewhat faded, ambience.

Bell's Inn   B&B $$
(☏888-634-1150, 709-634-1150; www.bellsinn.
ca; 2 Ford's Rd; r $80-120; ⊖🐾) Gordon Bell's
rambling green house tops a hill that's
a 15-minute walk from downtown. The
eight smallish, comfy rooms all have pri-

Corner Brook

vate bathroom; rooms 1 and 4 have harbor
views. Breakfast is a do-it-yourself, conti-
nental-style affair.

Thistle's Place   CAFE $
(☏709-634-4389; www.thistledownflorist.com;
Millbrook Mall, Herald Ave; sandwiches $6-11;
⊕9am-5pm Mon-Sat; 🐾) Walk through the
front flower shop to reach the smoked
meat, curried chicken and whole-wheat
vegetable wraps at the wee cafe out the
back.

Brewed Awakening
COFFEE $

(www.brewedawakening.ca; 35 West St; baked goods $3-7; ⊙7am-9pm Mon-Fri, 8am-9pm Sat & Sun; 🐾) This small, funky, art-on-the-wall coffee shop pours fair-trade, organic java done right. It's attached to the groovy bike shop Cycle Solutions.

Gitano's
MEDITERRANEAN $$

(☑709-634-5000; www.gitanos.ca; Millbrook Mall, Herald Ave; tapas $8-14, mains $18-32; ⊙11:30am-2pm Mon-Fri, 5-9pm Sun-Thu, to 10pm Fri & Sat; 🐾) Behind Thistle's Place and owned by the same family, Gitano's dishes up Spanish-themed mains such as *estofado* (stewed sweet potatoes, chickpeas and figs over couscous) and tapas (try the saltfish cakes) as well as pastas. Live jazz wafts through the supper club-esque room on weekends.

🛍 Shopping

Newfoundland Emporium
SOUVENIRS

(☑709-634-9376; 11 Broadway; ⊙10am-5pm Mon-Sat) It's a trove of local crafts, music, antiques and books.

ℹ Information

CIBC Bank (☑709-637-1700; 9 Main St)

Post Office (14 Main St)

Visitors Centre (☑709-639-9792; www.cornerbrook.com; 15 Confederation Dr; ⊙9am-5pm) Just off Hwy 1 at exit 5. Has a craft shop.

ℹ Getting There & Away

Corner Brook is a major hub for bus services in Newfoundland. **DRL** (☑709-263-2171; www.drl-lr.com) stops on the outskirts of town at the **Irving gas station** (Confederation Dr), just off Hwy 1 at exit 5 across from the visitors center.

All other operators use the **bus station** (☑709-634-2659; Herald Ave) in the Millbrook Mall building. The following are shuttle vans. Prices are one way. You must make reservations.

Burgeo Bus (☑709-634-7777) Runs to Burgeo ($38 cash only, two hours) departing at 3pm Monday through Friday. Leaves Burgeo between 8am and 9am.

Deer Lake Airport Shuttle (☑709-634-4343) Picks up from various hotels en route to Deer Lake Airport ($22, 45 minutes) three to five times daily.

Eddy's (☑709-643-2134) Travels to/from Stephenville ($22, 1¼ hours) twice daily on weekdays, once daily on weekends.

Gateway (☑709-695-9700) Runs to Port aux Basques ($36, three hours) on weekdays at 3:45pm. Departs Port aux Basques at 7:45am.

Martin's (☑709-458-7845, 709-453-2207) Operates weekdays, departing for Woody Point ($18, 1½ hours) and Trout River ($20, two hours) at 4:30pm. Returns from Trout River at 9am.

Pittman's (☑709-458-2486) Runs to Rocky Harbour ($30, two hours) via Deer Lake on weekdays at 4:30pm. Departs Rocky Harbour at noon.

Around Corner Brook

Blomidon Mountains

The Blomidon Mountains (aka Blow Me Down Mountains), heaved skyward from a collision with Europe around 500 million years ago, run along the south side of the Humber Arm. They're tantalizing for hikers, providing many sea vistas and glimpses of the resident caribou population. Some of the trails, especially ones up on the barrens, are not well marked, so topographical maps and a compass are essential for all hikers.

Many trails are signposted off Rte 450, which runs west from Corner Brook along the water for 60km. One of the easiest and most popular is **Blow Me Down Brook Trail** (5km), which begins west of Frenchman's Cove at a parking lot. The trail can be followed for an hour or so; for more avid hikers it continues well into the mountains, where it becomes part of the International Appalachian Trail (IAT). The moderately difficult **Copper Mine Trail** (7km), by York Harbour, provides awesome views of the Bay of Islands and also links to the IAT.

Further on, **Blow Me Down Provincial Park** (☑709-681-2430; www.nlcamping.ca; Rte 450; campsites $15, per vehicle $5; ⊙Jun-Aug) has beaches and scenery.

Stephenville

As the drive into town past deserted hangars, piles of rusted pipes and tract housing portends, Stephenville is in the running for Newfoundland's least appealing town. There's not much reason to stop, except for the **Stephenville Theatre Festival** (www.stephenvilletheatrefestival.com; ⊙Jul & Aug). It sweeps into town in summer toting along the Bard, Broadway and – to stir the pot – some cutting-edge Newfoundland plays.

Port au Port Peninsula

The large peninsula west of Stephenville is the only French-speaking area of the province, a legacy of the Basque, French and Acadians who settled the coast starting in the 1700s. Today, the culture is strongest along the western shore between **Cape St George** and **Lourdes**. Here children go to French school, preserving their dialect, which is now distinct from the language spoken in either France or Québec.

In **Port au Port West**, near Stephenville, the gorgeous **Gravels Trail** (3km) leads along the shore, passing secluded beach after secluded beach. Nearby in Felix Cove, stop at **Alpacas of Newfoundland** (www.alpacasofnfld.ca; Rte 460; ☺9am-6pm) **FREE** and meet the fluffy namesake critters on a farm tour.

Barachois Pond Provincial Park

This popular **park** (☎709-649-0048; www.nlcamping.ca; Hwy 1; campsites $15, per vehicle $5; ☺May-Sep), sitting just south of Rte 480 on Hwy 1, is one of the few in the province to offer a backcountry experience. From the campground, the **Erin Mountain Trail** (4.5km) winds through the forest and up to the 340m peak, where there are backcountry campsites and excellent views. Allow two hours for the climb.

Not far away are a couple of leisurely nature trails and a nice swimming area.

Port aux Basques

POP 4170

It's all about the ferry in Port aux Basques. Most visitors come here to jump onto the Rock from Nova Scotia, or jump off for the return trip. That doesn't mean the town isn't a perfectly decent place to spend a day or night. Traditional wood houses painted brightly in aqua, scarlet and sea-green clasp the stony hills. Laundry blows on the clotheslines, boats moor in backyard inlets and locals never fail to wave hello to newcomers.

Port aux Basques (occasionally called Channel-Port aux Basques) was named in the early 16th century by Basque fishers and whalers who came to work the waters of the Strait of Belle Isle.

The town is a convenient place to stock up on food, fuel and/or money before journeying onward.

◉ Sights

Several scenic fishing villages lie to the east.

Grand Bay West Beach   BEACH
(Kyle Lane) Located a short distance west of town, the long shore is backed by grassy dunes, which are breeding grounds for the endangered piping plover. The **Grand Bay West Trail** leaves from here and flirts with the coast for 10km.

Scott's Cove Park   PARK
(Caribou Rd) This park, with its restored boardwalk, candy-colored snack shacks and boat-shaped amphitheater, is the place to mingle with townsfolk and listen to live music.

Railway Heritage Centre   MUSEUM
(☎709-695-7560; off Hwy 1; museum $2, railcars $5; ☺10am-8pm Jul & Aug) The center has two things going on. One is a museum stuffed with shipwreck artifacts. Its showpiece is the astrolabe, a striking brass navigational instrument made in Portugal in 1628. The device is in remarkable condition and is one of only about three dozen that exist in the world. Restored railway cars are the center's other facet.

🛏 Sleeping & Eating

With all the ferry traffic, accommodation reservations are a good idea.

> **ⓘ NEWFOUNDLAND APPALACHIAN**
>
> Think the **International Appalachian Trail** ends in Québec just because it runs out of land at Cap Gaspé? Think again. It picks up in Newfoundland, where another 1200km of trail swipes the west coast from Port aux Basques to L'Anse aux Meadows. The province has linked existing trails, logging roads and old rail lines through the Long Range Mountains, part of the Appalachian chain. It's a work in progress, but some of the most complete sections are around Corner Brook and the Blomidon Mountains. See www.iatnl.com for trail details.

Port aux Basques

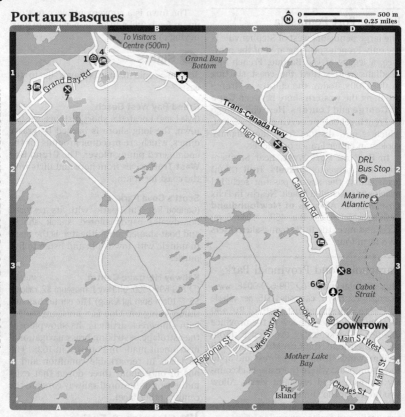

Port aux Basques

Radio Station B&B
B&B $$

(📞709-695-2906; jggillam@hotmail.com; 100 Caribou Rd; r from $89; ☾May-Oct) Up on the bluff overlooking the harbor, the five-room Radio Station is one of the closest lodgings to the ferry (a 10-minute walk). Three rooms have their own bathroom, the other two share, and there's a kitchen for guest use.

Caribou B&B
B&B $$

(📞709-695-3408; www.bbcanada.com/2225. html; 42 Grand Bay Rd; r $90; ☾May-Sep; ☞🛜) There's nothing fancy going on here, but the five rooms are clean, bright and carpeted; two of the rooms share a bathroom between them.

St Christopher's Hotel
HOTEL $$

(📞800-563-4779, 709-695-3500; www.stchris-hotel.com; Caribou Rd; r $93-140; ❄🛜) This is the most professional digs in town, with a small fitness room and a fine seafood restaurant called the Captain's Room (meals $10 to $16, open 7am to 1:30pm and 5pm to 10pm). Odd-numbered rooms have harbor views.

Hotel Port aux Basques
HOTEL **$$**

(☑877-695-2171, 709-695-2171; www.hotelpab.com; 1 Grand Bay Rd; r $85-120, ste $130; ❋☎) The closest competition to St Christopher's, this hotel is older but has more character. Kids stay for free.

Harbour Restaurant
CANADIAN **$**

(☑709-695-3238; 121 Caribou Rd; mains $8-15; ☺8am-midnight) While you'll get better food and service elsewhere, you can't beat the harborside view here. Pizzas and *donairs* (spiced beef in pita bread) share the menu with fried chicken. It's licensed, too.

Alma's
CANADIAN **$**

(☑709-695-3813; Mall, Grand Bay Rd; mains $7-13; ☺8am-8pm Mon-Sat) Follow the locals into this no-frills family diner for heaping portions of cod, scallops, fishcakes and berry pies. It serves breakfasts, burgers and sandwiches, too.

Tai Hong
CHINESE **$**

(☑709-695-3116; 77 High St; mains $7-12; ☺11am-10:30pm) Tai Hong stir-fries standard Chinese fare. Vegetarians will find a couple of fried rice options.

ℹ Information

Bank of Montréal (83 Main St)

Hospital (☑709-695-2175; Grand Bay Rd)

Post Office (3 Main St)

Visitors Centre (☑709-695-2262; www.portaux-basques.ca; Hwy 1; ☺6am-8pm May-Oct) Information on all parts of the province; sometimes open later to accommodate ferry traffic.

ℹ Getting There & Away

The **Marine Atlantic Ferry** (☑800-341-7981; www.marine-atlantic.ca) connects Port aux Basques with North Sydney in Nova Scotia (adult/child/car $42/20/110). It operates year-round, typically with two sailings daily during winter and three or four sailings between mid-June and mid-September. Crossings take about six hours. The ferry terminal has no ATMs or car rentals.

DRL (☑709-263-2171; www.drl-lr.com) has its stop at the ferry terminal. Buses leave at 8am for Corner Brook ($42, 3½ hours) and St John's ($123, 13½ hours); cash only.

Around Port aux Basques

Cape Ray

Adjacent to John T Cheeseman Provincial Park 14km north of town is Cape Ray. The coastal scenery is engaging, and the road leads up to the windblown **Cape Ray Lighthouse** (☺8am-8pm Tue-Sun Jul & Aug) **FREE**. This area is the southernmost known Dorset Paleo-Eskimo site, dating from 400 BC to AD 400. Thousands of artifacts have been found here and some dwelling sites can be seen.

There are also some fine **hikes** in the area. The **Table Mountain Trail** (12km) is more like a rugged road (but don't even think about driving up it) and begins on Hwy 1 opposite the exit to Cape Ray. The hike leads to a 518m plateau, where there are ruins from a secret US radar site and airstrip from WWII. It's not a hard hike, but allow three or four hours.

John T Cheeseman Provincial Park (☑709-695-7222; www.nlcamping.ca; Rte 408; campsites $15-23, per vehicle $5; ☺Jun-Sep) rests next to the beach and has top-notch facilities.

South Coast

Visitors often ignore Rte 470, and that's a shame because it's a beauty. Heading east out of Port aux Basques for 45km and edging along the shore, the road rises and falls over the eroded, windswept terrain, looking as though it's following a glacier that plowed through yesterday.

Isle aux Morts (Island of the Dead) got its label compliments of the many shipwrecks that occurred just offshore over some 400 years. Named after a family famous for daring shipwreck rescues, the **Harvey Trail** (7km) twists along the rugged shore and makes a stirring walk. Look for the signs in town.

Another highlight is the last settlement along the road, **Rose Blanche**, an absolutely splendid, traditional-looking village nestled in a cove with a fine natural harbor – a perfect example of the classic Newfoundland fishing community. From here follow the signs to the restored **Rose Blanche Lighthouse** (www.roseblanchelighthouse.ca; admission $5; ☺9am-9pm May-Oct). Built in 1873, it's the last remaining granite lighthouse on the Atlantic seaboard. If you think it's too pretty to leave, stay the night at **Rose Sea Guest House** (☑709-956-2872; www.roseblanche.ca; r $85-95; ☺Jun-Oct). It offers five rooms in a recently refurbished traditional home right on the water.

SOUTH COAST OUTPORTS

If you have the time and patience, a trip across the south coast with its wee fishing villages – called outports – is the best way to witness Newfoundland's unique culture. These little communities are some of the most remote settlements in North America, reachable only by boat as they cling to the convoluted shore. An anomaly is Burgeo (population 1460), connected by an easy road trip; it has an unspoiled, isolated feel, yet good amenities for travelers. Ramea (population 525) is another uncomplicated option. It's an island just offshore from Burgeo with lodging and activities.

Other outports along the coast include Grey River, François and McCallum. But hurry: the villages are dwindling fast as government pressure and lack of employment force residents to relocate to more accessible areas. The community of Grand Bruit was the latest to call it quits. Down to just 18 residents, they packed up and left for good in 2010.

◉ Sights & Activities

When the sun is out and the sea shimmers between endless inlets and islands, **Burgeo** is a dream. Climb the stairs to **Maiden Tea Hill** and look out in admiration. The 7km of white-sand beaches at **Sandbanks Provincial Park** may be the best in the entire province (at least the piping plover who dawdle there think so).

Author Farley Mowat lived in Burgeo for several years, until he penned *A Whale for the Killing* and irked the locals. The book tells the story of how Burgeo's townsfolk treated an 80-tonne fin whale trapped in a nearby lagoon. Let's just say the whale's outcome was not a happy one. Locals can point out the lagoon and Mowat's old house, though expect to get an earful about it.

The other outports are great areas for remote **camping**, **hiking** and **fishing**; ask locals or at the visitors center in Port aux Basques about arranging a guide. Tiny **François**, surrounded by towering walls of rock, is particularly gorgeous.

🛏 Sleeping & Eating

Ramea Retreat   HOSTEL, B&B $
(☑ 709-625-2522; www.ramea.easternoutdoors. com; 2 Main St, Ramea; dm/r $39/79; ☺ May-Nov; ☎) The owners have 10 hostel beds at their lodge, where they arrange kayaking, birdwatching, hiking and fishing tours. In addition, they rent rooms in various vintage clapboard houses scattered around Ramea.

Sandbanks Provincial Park   CAMPGROUND $
(☑ 709-886-2331; www.nlcamping.ca; off Rte 480, Burgeo; campsites $15, per vehicle $5; ☺ Jun-Sep) Two-thirds of the 25 campsites here are nestled in the forest, while the remainder are in a grassy area. The flies can be brutal.

Burgeo Haven B&B   B&B $$
(☑ 709-886-2544; www.burgeohaven.com; 111 Reach Rd, Burgeo; r $100-110; @ ☎) Right across from Maiden Tea Hill, this large house backs onto an inlet and offers a serene setting. Some of the five rooms here have views.

Gillett's Motel   MOTEL $$
(☑ 709-886-1284; www.gillettsmotel.ca; 1 Inspiration Rd, Burgeo; r from $99; ☎) The sole motel in town is well, motel-like, with all the usual room amenities. It's just fine, as is the on-site Galley Restaurant (meals $8 to $15), where you'll eat cod likely caught that morning.

Joy's Place   CANADIAN $
(☑ 709-886-2569; Reach Rd, Burgeo; mains $6-11; ☺ 11am-10:30pm) Near Burgeo Haven B&B, Joy whips up fried chicken, Chinese dishes, burgers and pies in addition to her ever-present fish dishes.

ℹ Information

Burgeo (www.burgeonl.com) Official town website.

ℹ Getting There & Away

Lonely, 148km-long Rte 480 shoots off Hwy 1 south of Corner Brook and then runs straight into Burgeo. Note there is no gas station and barely any civilization, just glacier-cut boulders and ponds and a whole lotta moose.

The Burgeo Bus shuttle van runs between Corner Brook and Burgeo just once per day.

Access to the other towns is by boat only. While the ferries run all year, the routes described here are for mid-May through September. Schedules change, so check with **Provincial Ferry Services** (☑ 709-292-4302; www.tw.gov. nl.ca/ferryservices). Note that the ferries do not take vehicles (except Burgeo to Ramea).

With careful planning a trip through the islands is doable.

Burgeo to Ramea ($4, 1½ hours) Departs twice per day; times do vary but there is usually one at around 11am and another in the evening.

Burgeo to Grey River to François ($8.25, five hours) Goes daily (except Tuesday and Thursday) at 1:45pm.

François to McCallum to Hermitage ($7.50, four hours) Departs on Thursday, but only at 7am.

At Hermitage, you'll have to suss out transportation back to Rte 360. You can then hook up with Thornhill Taxi Service (p488), which runs between Harbour Breton and Grand Falls, and connects with DRL in the latter.

LABRADOR

POP 29,800

It's called the Big Land, and with 293,000 sq km sprawling north toward the Arctic Circle, it's easy to see why. Undulating, rocky, puddled expanses form the sparse, primeval landscape. If you ever wanted to see what the world looked like before humans stepped on it, this is the place to head.

Inuit and Innu have occupied Labrador for thousands of years, and until the 1960s the population was still limited to them and a few longtime European descendants known as 'liveyers.' They eked out an existence by fishing and hunting from their tiny villages that freckled the coast. The interior was virgin wilderness.

Over the past few decades, the economic potential of Labrador's vast natural resources has earned it a new degree of attention. Companies have tapped into the massive iron-ore mines in Wabush and Labrador City and the hydroelectric dam at Churchill Falls. It makes for a boom or bust economy, and right now it's booming big-time.

The simplest way to take a bite of the Big Land is via the Labrador Straits region, which connects to Newfoundland via a daily ferry. From there, a solitary road – the stark, rough Trans-Labrador Hwy – connects the interior's main towns. The aboriginal-influenced northern coast is accessible only by plane or supply ferry.

Labrador is cold, wet and windy, and its bugs are murderous. Facilities are few and far between throughout the behemoth region, so planning ahead is essential.

Labrador Straits

And you thought the Northern Peninsula was commanding? Sail the 28km across the Strait of Belle Isle and behold a landscape even more windswept and black-rocked.

Clouds rip across aqua-and-gray skies, and the water that slaps the shore is so cold it's purplish. Unlike the rest of remote Labrador, the Straits region is easy to reach and exalted with sights such as Red Bay and a slew of great walking trails that meander past shipwreck fragments and old whale bones.

'Labrador Straits' is the colloquial name for the communities that make the southern coastal region of Labrador. Note that your first stop in the area will not actually be in Labrador at all, as the ferry terminal and airport are both in Blanc Sablon, Québec. Once in Labrador, Rte 510 is the road that connects the Straits' communities. South of Red Bay, it is sealed and open all year. From Red Bay north, it's hard-packed gravel but in the process of being paved. Check conditions with the **Department of Transportation & Works** (☎709-729-2300; www.roads.gov.nl.ca).

Blanc Sablon to L'Anse au Clair

After arriving by ferry or plane in Blanc Sablon and driving 6km northeast on Rte 510 you come to Labrador and the gateway town of L'Anse au Clair. Here you will find the Straits' excellent **visitors center** (☎877-931-2013, 709-931-2013; www.labradorcoastaldrive.com; Rte 510, L'Anse au Clair; ⊙9am-5pm Jun-Oct) in an old church that doubles as a small museum. Be sure to pick up hiking trail information for the region.

The town makes a good pre-ferry base. Norm at **Beachside Hospitality Home** (☎709-931-2338; normanletto@nf.sympatico.ca; 9 Lodge Rd; r with shared bathroom $55-65; ⊛) plays the accordion for guests in the evening. Quilts await on the beds, while homemade jams await in the kitchen at this three-bedroom, two-bathroom B&B.

The modern, well-kept **Northern Light Inn** (☎800-563-3188, 709-931-2332; www.northernlightinn.com; 56 Main St; r $99-189; ❋☎) is a tour-bus favorite. Even-numbered rooms

---

LABRADOR FAST FACTS

➡ Population: 29,800

➡ Area: 294,330 sq km

➡ Biggest town: Labrador City

➡ Time zones: Labrador Straits are on Newfoundland Time, while the rest of Labrador (starting at Cartwright) is on Atlantic Time, ie 30 minutes behind Newfoundland.

have harbor views. The dining room (mains $12 to $18, open 7am to 9pm Sunday to Thursday, to 10pm Friday and Saturday) here is your best bet for food in town.

The **MV Apollo** (☑866-535-2567, 709-535-0810; www.labradormarine.com; adult/child/car $8.25/6.60/25) sails the two hours between St Barbe in Newfoundland and Blanc Sablon between May and early January. The boat runs one to three times daily between 8am and 6pm. Schedules vary from day to day. In July and August, it's not a bad idea to reserve in advance (though there's a $10 fee). Note that the ferry terminal in Blanc Sablon operates on Newfoundland Time and not Eastern Time (as in the rest of Québec).

Provincial Airlines (www.provincialairlines. ca) has flights to Blanc Sablon from St John's and St Anthony. Just to confuse you, departure times from the airport are on Eastern Time versus Labrador Straits (ie Newfoundland) Time.

Rental cars are available at the airport from **Eagle River Rent-a-Car** (☑709-931-2352, 709-931-3300).

Forteau to Pinware

Continuing northeast on Rte 510 you'll pass Forteau, L'Anse Amour, L'Anse au Loup, West St Modeste and Pinware.

Labrador Adventures (☑709-931-2055; www.tourlabrador.ca; tours $50-210) provides knowledgeable guides for Straits-oriented hikes or day tours by SUV. It also arranges all-inclusive overnight packages. This is a terrific way to see the area, especially if you're short on time or car-less.

In Forteau, the **Overfall Brook Trail** (4km) shadows the coast and ends at a 30m waterfall.

Six houses in total comprise the village of **L'Anse Amour**, but it holds more than its fair share of sights. **L'Anse Amour Burial Mound** (L'Anse Amour Rd), a pile of stones placed here by the Maritime Archaic Aboriginals, is the oldest burial monument in North America. A small roadside plaque marks the 7500-year-old site.

On the same road is **Point Amour Lighthouse** (☑709-927-5825; www.seethesites.ca; L'Anse Amour Rd; adult/child $6/3; ⊙9:30am-5pm May-Oct). It is the tallest lighthouse in Atlantic Canada, with 127 steps to climb. When you reach the top, you will be rewarded with a spectacular 360-degree view of the coastline. The lighthouse keeper's house has exhibits on maritime history. The HMS

SCENIC DRIVE: QUÉBEC'S ROUTE 138

This drive is most easily accessed from Québec. Rte 138 (the Québec incarnation of Labrador's Rte 510) runs down the Lower North Shore, the name given to the wild, remote chunk of La Belle Province that extends south of Blanc Sablon. From the ferry landing until the road ends abruptly 65km later at Vieux Fort, Rte 138 makes a beautiful swing past several roadside **waterfalls** and lookouts from which to see the crashing surf and offshore **puffin colonies**.

For those wanting to do more than just drive through the region, **Tourism Lower North Shore** (www.tourismlowernorthshore.com) provides information on attractions and accommodations.

Raleigh went aground here in 1922 and was destroyed in 1926. The **Raleigh Trail** (2km) takes you by the site and warship fragments on the beach.

Past L'Anse au Loup is the **Battery Trail** (4km), which meanders through a stunted tuckamore forest to the summit of the Battery, unfurling panoramic sea views.

The road veers inland at Pinware, and skirts along the western side of the Pinware River, until it crosses a one-lane iron bridge, and then runs along the eastern side, high above the rushing white water. This stretch of the Pinware is renowned for its **salmon fishing**. About 10km before reaching Red Bay, the land becomes rocky and barren, except for the superfluity of blueberries and bakeapples (and pickers) in August.

Forteau's **Grenfell Louie A Hall B&B** (☑709-931-2916; www.grenfellbandb.ca; Willow Ave; r $75-85; ⊙May-Oct) is in the old nursing station where generations of Labrador Straits folk were born. The five simple rooms (a couple with sea views) share two bathrooms.

The **Seaview Restaurant** (Rte 510; mains $10-20; ⊙9am-8pm) is nearby in Forteau. Chow down on the famous fried chicken and tender caribou. A grocery store and jam factory are also on-site.

Up and over the hills in L'Anse au Loup, **Dot's Bakery** (☑709-927-5311; Rte 510; breakfasts $4-6.50, pizzas $23; ⊙7am-11pm Mon-Sat) caters to all your needs with her doughnuts, pies, breakfast dishes and pizzas.

Labrador

Red Bay

Spread between two venues, **Red Bay National Historic Site** (709-920-2051; www.pc.gc.ca/redbay; Rte 510; adult/child/family $7.80/3.90/19.60; 9am-5pm Jun-Sep) – which was declared a Unesco World Heritage site in 2013 – uses different media to chronicle the discovery of three 16th-century Basque whaling galleons on the seabed here. Well preserved in the ice-cold waters, the vestiges of the ships tell a remarkable story of what life was like here some four centuries ago. Red Bay was the largest whaling port in the world, with more than 2000 people residing here. Have a look at the reconstructed *chalupa* (a small Basque dingy used for whale hunting) and some of the other relics in the museum. Then hop in a small boat ($2) to nearby **Saddle Island**, where there is a self-guided interpretive trail around the excavated land sites. Allow at least two or three hours for the museum and island.

Across the bay, the amazing **Boney Shore Trail** (2km) skirts along the coast and passes ancient whale bones (they pretty much look like rocks) scattered along it. The **Tracey Hill Trail** climbs a boardwalk and 670 steps to the top of American Rockyman Hill for a bird's-eye view of the harbor; it takes about 20 minutes each way.

Between the trails and the historic site, a 15m, 400-year-old **North Atlantic right whale skeleton** sprawls through the **Selma Barkham Town Centre** (admission $2; 9am-5pm Jul-Sep).

Basinview B&B (709-920-2002; blanchee-arle@hotmail.com; 145 Main St; r $55-90) is a simple four-room, shared bathroom home right on the water.

Remember, Red Bay is the end of the paved road... for now. Another 200km of the hard-packed gravel is scheduled to be paved by 2015.

Battle Harbour

Sitting on an island in the Labrador Sea is the elaborately restored village and saltfish premises of Battle Harbour. Now a national historic district, it used to be the unofficial 'capital' of Labrador during the early 19th century, when fishing schooners lined its docks. Another claim to fame: this is the place where Robert E Peary gave his first news conference after reaching the North Pole in 1909.

It's accessed by boat from Mary's Harbour (departure at 11am, one hour). Accommodations are spread among various heritage homes and cottages operated by the **Battle Harbour Inn** (709-921-6325; battleharbour-reservations@gmail.com; r $175; Jun-Sep). A store and **restaurant** (mains $9-18; 8am-6pm) are also on-site. At press time, trips were set up as an overnight package deal, but day trips are on the docket. Contact the inn for details.

Mary's Harbour to Cartwright

After departing Mary's Harbour you'll pass through Port Hope Simpson 53km up the road, and then there's nothing for 186km until Cartwright.

Cartwright-based **Experience Labrador** (709-938-7444; www.experiencelabrador.com; Jul & Aug) runs adventure trips that range from 2½-hour kayaking jaunts ($50) to day-long boat and hiking tours ($250). The latter go along the Wonderstrands' endless sands that mesmerized the Vikings so long ago.

In 2010, the federal government created the **Mealy Mountains National Park Reserve** from 11,000 sq km of caribou-crossed boreal forest between Cartwright and Happy Valley-Goose Bay. Once the park gets up and running (which is taking place slowly), paddlers, snowshoers, cross-country skiers and hikers will have access to an unblemished wilderness.

Other than that, Cartwright is about the ferry. Passenger boats depart for the remote villages that sprinkle the northern coast. **Labrador Marine** (866-535-2567, 709-535-0810; www.labradormarine.com) has the schedules.

Rte 510 continues west to Happy Valley-Goose Bay. Contact the **Department of Transportation & Works** (www.roads.gov.nl.ca) for the latest conditions.

Northern Coast

North of Cartwright up to Ungava Bay there are a half-dozen small, semitraditional Inuit communities accessible only by sea or air along the rugged, largely unspoiled mountainous coast. Torngat Mountains National Park is the (literal) high point.

In 1993 on the shores of Voisey's Bay, near Nain, geologists discovered stunningly rich concentrations of copper, cobalt and especially nickel. A giant mine has been built to extract the goods, and it is expected to pump $11 billion into the provincial economy over the next few decades. This is opening up the north – for better or worse.

◎ Sights & Activities

The first port of call on the northern coast is **Makkovik**, an early fur-trading post and a traditional fishing and hunting community. Both new and old-style crafts can be bought.

Further north in **Hopedale** visitors can look at the old wooden Moravian mission church (1782). This **national historic site** (☑ 709-933-3490; admission $5; ⊗ 8:30am-7pm Jul-Oct) also includes a store, residence, some huts and a museum collection.

Natuashish is a new town that was formed when the troubled village of Utshimassit (Davis Inlet) was relocated to the mainland in 2002. The move was made after a 2000 study showed that 154 of 169 youths surveyed had abused solvents (ie sniffed gasoline) and that 60 of them did it on a daily basis.

The last stop on the ferry is **Nain**, and it's the last town of any size as you go northward. Fishing has historically been the town's main industry, but this is changing due to the Voisey's Bay nickel deposit.

🛏 Sleeping & Eating

Most travelers use the ferry as a floating hotel. For those wishing to get off and wait until the next boat, it usually means winging it for a room, as only Postville, Hopedale and Nain have official lodging.

Atsanik Lodge   HOTEL $$
(☑ 709-922-2910; atsaniklabrador@msn.com; Sand Banks Rd, Nain; r $150-180; 🛜) This large, 25-room lodge and its restaurant (meals $15 to $22) are your best bet in Nain.

Amaguk Inn   HOTEL $$
(☑ 709-933-3750; Hopedale; r $140-200; 🛜) This 18-room inn also has a dining room (meals $15 to $20), and a lounge where you can get a cold beer.

ℹ Getting There & Away

Provincial Airlines (www.provincialairlines. ca) serves most of the northern coast's villages from Goose Bay.

The passenger-only MV *Northern Ranger* plies this section of coast from mid-June to mid-November. It leaves once per week, making the three-day (one way) journey between Happy Valley-Goose Bay and Nain, stopping in Mak-

---

TORNGAT MOUNTAINS NATIONAL PARK

From Nain, you can try to arrange boat transportation to otherworldly **Torngat Mountains National Park** (☑ 709-922-1290; www.pc.gc.ca/torngat) at Labrador's wintry tip. The park headquarters is in town, and staff can direct you to local Inuit guides. The mountains are popular with climbers because of their altitude (some of the highest peaks east of the Rockies) and isolation. The **Kaumajet Mountains**, south of the park, also make for an out-of-this-world hiking experience.

The Inuit-run **Torngat Mountains Base Camp and Research Station** (☑ 855-867-6428; www.torngatbasecamp. com; ⊗ Jul & Aug) offers package tours, including air transportation from Happy Valley-Goose Bay. At camp, activities include hiking, boating and flightseeing. An electrified fence keeps out polar bears.

---

kovik, Hopedale and Natuashish along the way. Check with **Labrador Marine** (www.labradormarine.com) for the ever-evolving schedule and fares.

Central Labrador

Making up the territorial bulk of Labrador, the central portion is an immense, sparsely populated and ancient wilderness. Paradoxically, it also has the largest town in Labrador, **Happy Valley-Goose Bay** (www. happyvalley-goosebay.com), home to a military base. The town (population 7600) has all the usual services, but unless you're an angler or hunter, there isn't much to see or do.

Goose Bay was established during WWII as a staging point for planes on their way to Europe, and has remained an aviation center. The airport is also an official NASA alternate landing site for the space shuttle.

◎ Sights

Northern Lights Building   MUSEUM
(☑ 709-896-5939; 170 Hamilton River Rd; ⊗ 10am-5:30pm Tue-Sat) **FREE** The Northern Lights Building hosts a military museum, interesting lifelike nature scenes and simulated northern lights.

Labrador Interpretation Centre MUSEUM
(☎709-497-8566; www.therooms.ca/lic; 2 Portage Rd, North West River; ◷10am-4pm daily Jul & Aug, 1-4pm Wed-Sun Sep-Jun) FREE Officially opened by Queen Elizabeth II in 1997, the Labrador Interpretation Centre is the provincial museum, which holds some of Labrador's finest works of art. It's in North West River, via Rte 520.

🛏 Sleeping & Eating

Everything listed here is in Happy Valley-Goose Bay.

Davis' B&B B&B $
(☎709-896-5077; davisbb@canada.com; 14 Cabot Crescent Rd; r $60-80; 🐱) Family atmosphere and caribou sausages await you at Davis' four-room home. It's near restaurants and amenities.

Royal Inn & Suites HOTEL $$
(☎709-896-2456; www.royalinnandsuites.ca; 5 Royal Ave; d incl breakfast $105-155; ❄🐱) The good-looking Royal has a variety of rooms to choose from; many of them have kitchens. The 'inn' side has wi-fi; the suites side has hard-wired high-speed access.

El Greco PIZZERIA $$
(☎709-896-3473; 133 Hamilton River Rd; pizzas $16-22; ◷4pm-1am Sun-Wed, to 3am Thu-Sat) This is a decent joint serving pizzas. It's near the Royal Inn.

❶ Getting There & Away

AIR
Air Canada (www.aircanada.com) flies to St John's and Gander. **Provincial Airlines** (www.provincialairlines.ca) flies to St John's, Deer Lake and most towns around Labrador.

BOAT
You can reach Goose Bay by the passenger-only MV *Northern Ranger*; see www.labradorferry.ca.

CAR & MOTORCYCLE
From Happy Valley-Goose Bay you can take gravel (but to be paved by 2015) Rte 500 west to Churchill Falls and then on to Labrador City. The drive to Labrador City takes about 10 hours. There are no services until Churchill Falls, so stock up. The Royal Inn & Suites has free satellite phones you can take on the road (part of a region-wide safety program). Rte 510 is the gravel road heading southeast toward Cartwright (383km) and L'Anse au Clair (623km); parts of it are also being paved. Before leaving, contact the **Department of Transportation & Works** (www.roads.gov.nl.ca) for the latest conditions.

Trucks can be rented at the airport from **National** (☎709-896-5575), but due to road conditions, you cannot buy insurance.

Labrador West
POP 9200

Just 5km apart and 15km from Québec, the twin mining towns of Labrador City (population 7400) and Wabush (population 1800) are referred to collectively as Labrador West, and this is where the western region's population is concentrated. The largest open-pit iron ore mine in the world is in Labrador City, and another mine operates in Wabush. The landscape is massive and the celestial polychromatic artwork can expand throughout the entire night sky.

◉ Sights & Activities

Gateway Labrador MUSEUM
(☎709-944-5399; ◷9am-4pm Mon-Fri, 10am-5pm Sat) FREE In the same building as the visitors center is Gateway Labrador and its Montague Exhibit Hall, where 3500 years of human history and culture, including the fur trade, are represented with intriguing artifacts and displays.

Grande Hermine Park PARK
(☎709-282-5369; admission $3; ◷Jun-Sep) From Wabush, 39km east on Rte 500 is Grande Hermine Park, which has a beach and some fine scenery. The **Menihek hiking trail** (15km) goes through wooded areas with waterfalls and open tundra. Outfitters can take anglers to excellent **fishing** waters.

Wapusakatto Mountains SKIING
The Wapusakatto Mountains are 5km from town, popping up off the vast landscape interspersed with flat northern tundra. A good, cold dry snow falls from late October to late April, so the ski season here is much longer than anywhere else in Canada. For trail information and fees for world-class cross-country skiing (the Canadian national team trains in the region), check with the **Menihek Nordic Ski Club** (☎709-944-5842; www.meniheknordicski.ca); for alpine skiing, check with the **Smokey Mountain Ski Club** (☎709-944-2129; www.smokeymountain.ca).

Tours

Mines   MINE TOUR
(☑709-944-7631; tours $10; ☉1:30pm Wed & Sun
Jul & Aug) If big holes and trucks the size of
apartment buildings make your heart flutter, you can tour the mines; call to make
reservations.

🛏 Sleeping & Eating

Wabush Hotel   HOTEL $$
(☑709-282-3221; www.wabushhotel.com; 9 Gren-
ville Dr, Wabush; r $165-175; ❇🤫) Centrally lo-
cated in Wabush, this chalet-style 68-room
hotel has spacious and comfortable rooms.
The dining room (meals $14 to $22, open
6:30am to midnight) has a popular dinner
buffet.

Carol Inn   MOTEL $$
(☑888-799-7736, 709-944-7736; www.carolinn.ca;
215 Drake Ave, Labrador City; d $110-130; ❇🤫) All
20 rooms here have a kitchenette. There's
also a fine dining room (meals $20 to $30,
open 5:30pm Tuesday to Saturday) and pub
(meals $11 to $14, open 8am to midnight).

❶ Information

Destination Labrador (www.destination-
labrador.com)
Visitors Centre (☑709-944-5399; www.
labradorwest.com; 1365 Rte 500) Just west of
Labrador City, in the Gateway Labrador
building.

❶ Getting There & Away

AIR

Air Canada (www.aircanada.com), **Provincial
Airlines** (www.provincialairlines.ca) and **Air
Inuit** (www.airinuit.com) fly into the twin cities'
airport (in Wabush).

CAR & MOTORCYCLE

Fifteen kilometers west from Labrador City
along Rte 500 is Fermont, Québec. From there
Rte 389 is mainly paved (with some fine gravel
sections) and continues south 581km to Baie
Comeau. Happy Valley-Goose Bay is a 10-hour
drive east on Rte 500.

  Budget (☑709-282-1234) has an office at
the airport; rental cars may not be driven on
Rte 500.

Manitoba

Best Places to Eat

➡ Tall Grass Prairie (p520)

➡ Deer + Almond (p520)

➡ Baked Expectations (p521)

➡ Reykjavik Bakery (p524)

➡ Gypsy's Bakery (p531)

Best Places to Stay

➡ Fort Garry Hotel (p519)

➡ Place Louis Riel Suite Hotel (p519)

➡ Solmundson Gesta Hus Bed & Breakfast (p524)

➡ Idylwylde Cabins (p527)

Why Go?

The two prominent stars of Manitoba are Winnipeg, with its big-city sophistication, and Churchill, with its profusion of natural wonders. But it's what lies between that truly defines this often misunderstood province. Open spaces of this prairie province seem to stretch forever – gently rolling fields of grain and sunflowers and wildflowers reach all the way north to Arctic tundra.

The magnitude of this land is only fully appreciated while standing on the edge of a vivid yellow canola field counting three different storms on the horizon, or on the edge of Hudson Bay's rugged coastline counting polar bears as beluga whales play in the distance. Wander its empty roads, stop in its evocative little towns, find the subtle dramas in the land and expect surprises, whether it's a moose mewling in a bog or a future pop legend performing on stage.

When to Go
Winnipeg

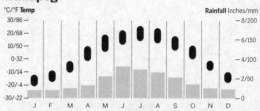

May Wildflowers spring up along the roads and signal the end of a long winter.

Jun–Aug Days *can* be balmy but cool nights rule; at Churchill, 18°C is considered hot.

Sep Fall comes early and days are crisp; by October the north is under snow.

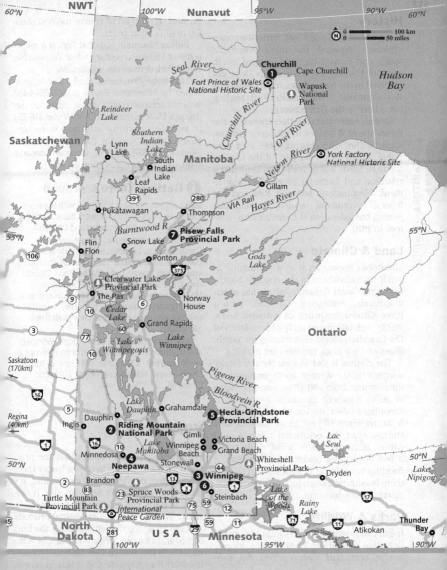

Manitoba Highlights

1 Revel in polar bears, beluga whales and even an ancient fort in **Churchill** (p528), the surprising subarctic city that's difficult to reach.

2 Hike and paddle Manitoba's best natural setting, **Riding Mountain National Park** (p526).

3 Enjoy big-city fun and world-class talent prairie-style in **Winnipeg** (p512).

4 Discover small-town gems like charming **Neepawa** (p525), where time seems to stand still.

5 Contemplate nature virtually surrounded by Lake Winnipeg at **Hecla-Grindstone Provincial Park** (p524).

6 Get caught up in raucous local culture with the screaming masses at a **Winnipeg Jets** (p521) hockey game.

7 Drive lonely roads and stop for natural wonders like **Pisew Falls** (p528).

History

Tired of being labeled soft, early European explorers shunned the more hospitable south and braved the cold, rugged north coast of Hudson Bay. Indigenous Dene got involved in the fur trade soon after Hudson's Bay Company (HBC) established trading posts here in the 17th century.

British agricultural settlers moved to the future site of Winnipeg in 1811, creating constant friction with existing Métis over land rights. When HBC sold part of the land to the feds, Métis leader Louis Riel launched a rebellion and formed a provisional government. Negotiations between Riel and the federal government resulted in Manitoba joining the federation as Canada's fifth province in 1870.

Land & Climate

Manitoba's geography is as wide-ranging as you'll find anywhere in the country. Southern agricultural flatlands blend into green woodlands embracing Canada's largest lakes. Glacial footprints of potholed lakes, stubby vegetation and scraped-bare lands of the Canadian Shield characterize the north. Everywhere you go, the skies are massive.

The climate is just as variable and totally unpredictable. Average northern temperatures range from -50°C to summer highs of 20°C. Southern summers average 25°C dropping to -15°C during winter. Notoriously strong winds all year create summer dust storms, even the occasional tornado, and winter blizzards where wind chills make it feel 30 degrees colder than it is. Spring flooding is common in southern areas, and there is nothing like an intense prairie summertime thunderstorm.

Parks & Wildlife

It can't be overstated: every kind of popular Canadian animal can be seen here. Moose, beaver, bear, lynx, deer, caribou, fox, rab-

bit and so on. And of course the real stars: Churchill's polar bears.

Riding Mountain National Park is a microcosm of Manitoba ecology, while Wapusk National Park defines raw wilderness.

Manitoba Provincial Parks Guide, published by **Manitoba Parks** (☏800-214-6497; www.manitobaparks.com; vehicle admission per day/year $5/40, campsites $12-24, RV sites $16-29), is available at visitor information centers. Reserve ahead with the **Parks Reservation System** (☏888-482-2267; www.manitobaparks. com), as campgrounds often fill up.

❶ Getting There & Around

Major airlines connect Winnipeg with the main Canadian cities and US Midwest hubs. Calm Air serves northern communities and Churchill.

Manitoba shares more than a dozen US–Canada vehicle border crossings with North Dakota and Minnesota. There are several routes into Saskatchewan, but only the Trans-Canada Hwy (Hwy 1) leads into Ontario. Southern Manitoba's extensive road network disappears heading north, where Hwy 10 or Hwy 6 are the only options and services are few (watch your gas gauge).

VIA Rail's *Canadian* passes through Winnipeg and southern communities two or three times a week. Also out of Winnipeg is the two- or three-times-a-week sclerotic service to Subarctic Churchill.

WINNIPEG

POP 663,600

Winnipeg surprises. Rising above the prairie, it's a metropolis where you least expect it. Cultured, confident and captivating, it's more than just a pit stop on the Trans-Canada haul, but a destination in its own right. Wander its historic neighborhoods and lap up a vibe that enjoys being the butt of a *Simpsons* joke ('That's it! Back to Winnipeg!'), is inspired by Guy Maddin's haunting 2011 film *Keyhole* and revels in one of the world's best fringe theater festivals.

History

An aboriginal hub for 6000 years and center of the 19th-century fur trade rivalry between HBC and North West Company, the confluence of the Assiniboine and Red Rivers had little choice in any other official name than the Europeanized *win nipee* (Cree for 'muddy waters').

MANITOBA FAST FACTS

➡ Population: 1,208,000

➡ Area: 649,950 sq km

➡ Capital: Winnipeg

➡ Quirky fact: Manitobans are the highest per capita consumers of 7-Eleven slurpees in the world

French settlers established the neighborhood of St-Boniface, birthplace of the controversial Métis leader Louis Riel.

The railroad's arrival in 1886 solidified Winnipeg's commercial importance, later rendered moot by the opening of the Panama Canal. Winnipeg subsequently stagnated, although a landmark general strike in 1919 helped raise union recognition across Canada. Today it has a diverse economy and modest growth. Its most notable brand is familiar to anyone with the munchies: Old Dutch, the potato chip maker.

Sights & Activities

Winnipeg is mostly concentrated around the walkable downtown area; other sights are reached most easily by vehicle.

'Portage and Main' marks the center of downtown and is famous for incredibly strong winds and frigid temperatures – Randy Bachman and Neil Young wrote a song about it, 'Prairie Town,' with the chorus repeating the line 'Portage and Main, 50 below.'

To the north, 1900s limestone architecture marks the warehouse-and-arts Exchange District. South of downtown is the Forks and across the Red River is the French neighborhood of St-Boniface; west of there is the very strollable Osborne Village and Corydon Ave.

Downtown

Manitoba Legislative Building   NOTABLE BUILDING
(Map p516; ☑ 204-945-5813; www.gov.mb.ca/legtour; 450 Broadway Ave; ☺ 8am-8pm, tours hourly 9am-6pm Jul & Aug) FREE Designed during Winnipeg's optimistic boom of the early 20th century, this 1920 building flaunts neoclassical beaux-arts design, limestone construction and governmental importance above the Red River. Surrounded by impeccable lawns and gardens, ancient gods and contemporary heroes are immortalized, including the Louis Riel monument facing St-Boniface. 'Eternal Youth and the Spirit of Enterprise' – aka Golden Boy – shines his 23½-carat gold-covered splendor atop the oxidized copper dome.

Upper Fort Garry Heritage Provincial Park   HISTORIC SITE
(Map p516; www.upperfortgarry.com; 130 Main St) Original 1830s oak, stone and mortar walls stand where four different forts have stood

since 1738. The entire site has had a drastic revamp and is set to open in 2014 as a rather lavish urban park, complete with trellises showing the course of some of the old walls. An interpretive center is set to open by 2017.

Winnipeg Art Gallery   GALLERY
(WAG; Map p514; ☑ 204-786-6641; www.wag.ca; 300 Memorial Blvd; adult/child $12/6; ☺ 11am-5pm Tue, Wed & Fri-Sun, to 9pm Thu) This ship-shaped gallery plots a course for contemporary Manitoban and Canadian artists, including the world's largest collection of Inuit work. Enjoy canvas-worthy views during lunch in the rooftop cafe.

Plug In Institute of Contemporary Art   GALLERY
(☑ 204-942-1043; www.plugin.org; 460 Portage Ave; ☺ noon-5pm Tue, to 9pm Wed & Thu, to 7pm Fri, 9am-5pm Sat & Sun) Contemporary art rules at this gallery with exhibitions from local and international artists.

The Forks

Strategically important and historically significant, the meeting place of the muddy and small Assiniboine River and the muddy and large Red River has been drawing people for millennia.

It's the focus for many visitors and combines several distinct areas. Parks Canada runs a historic site amid beautifully landscaped parks. Nearby, old railway shops have been converted into the **Forks** (☑ 204-957-7618; www.theforks.com), a touristy collection of shops, cafes and restaurants in renovated old buildings.

★ **Forks National Historic Site** HISTORIC SITE
(Map p516; ☑ 204-983-6757; www.parkscanada.ca/forks) In a beautiful riverside setting, modern amenities for performances and interpretive exhibits outline the area's

Greater Winnipeg

history. Footpaths line the riverbank; plaques offer historical context.

The rivers routinely overflow during spring runoff and flooded pathways are not uncommon, an event as exciting as it is dangerous. Follow the waterways with a canoe from **Splash Dash** (☑204-783-6633; www.splashdash.ca; rental per 30/60min $10/18; ⊙11am-9pm Jun-Sep).

Tours are available by foot and by boat. Kids can go nuts in the heritage-themed playground, the **Variety Heritage Adventure Park**.

Wintertime fun involves **ice skating** on the river and **cross-country skiing** the pathways.

Canadian Museum for Human Rights
MUSEUM

(Map p516; ☑204-289-2000; www.humanrightsmuseum.ca; Waterfront Dr & Provencher Blvd) Winnipeg's newest major attraction, the Canadian Museum for Human Rights, gleams on a high-profile site near Provencher Bridge. Housed in a stunning building, the $310 million complex is the first national museum outside of Ottawa. The focus will be human rights, as they relate to Canada, its culture and the rest of the world. Symbolism abounds, with an enormous glass cloud wrapping around the northern facade, modeled in the image of five dove wings wrapping one over the other.

Set to open in 2014, the museum promises not to duck controversy: an early program examined genocide in Nicaragua.

Winnipeg Railway Museum
MUSEUM

(Map p516; ☑204-942-4632; www.wpgrailwaymuseum.com; Union Station, 123 Main St; adult/child $5/3; ⊙11am-4pm daily May-Oct, Sat & Sun Mar, Apr & Nov) Winnipeg's gorgeous and underused Union Station (opened in 1911 and designed by the same firm that did New York's Grand Central Terminal) houses a small collection of historic Canadian railway cars, gear and model trains.

◉ Exchange District

Restored century-old brick buildings are the backdrop to the **Exchange District** (www.exchangedistrict.org), Winnipeg's most vibrant neighborhood downtown. Hipsters, tourists and vagrants congregate amid heritage buildings housing restaurants, clubs, boutiques and galleries. It's been declared a national historic site; walking tours provide context.

The grassy haven of **Old Market Square** is the neighborhood focal point. There's regular live music in summer at the controversially modern **Cube** (Map p516).

The Exchange District abounds in art galleries.

★ Manitoba Museum
MUSEUM

(Map p516; ☑ 204-956-2830; www.manitobamuseum.ca; 190 Rupert Ave; adult/child from $9/7.50; ⊙ 10am-5pm Jun-Aug, reduced hours Sep-May) Nature trips through the subarctic, history trips into 1920s Winnipeg, cultural journeys covering the past 12,000 years – if it happened in Manitoba, it's here. Amid the superb displays are a planetarium and an engaging science gallery. One exhibit shows what Churchill was like as a tropical jungle, a mere 450 million years ago.

Aceartinc
GALLERY

(Map p516; ☑ 204-944-9763; www.aceart. org; 290 McDermot Ave; ⊙ noon-5pm Tue-Sat) With several other galleries, focuses on contemporary art.

Graffiti Gallery
GALLERY

(Map p516; ☑ 204-667-9960; www.graffitigallery. ca; 109 Higgins Ave; ⊙ noon-5pm Mon-Sat) Aims to redirect young artists from vandalism to sanctioned public art.

Outworks Art Gallery
GALLERY

(Map p516; ☑ 204-479-4804; 290 McDermot Ave; ⊙ noon-4pm Thu-Sat) Artist-run exhibition space and gallery. Meet some of Winnipeg's best talent during their shows.

Urban Shaman Contemporary Aboriginal Art
GALLERY

(Map p516; ☑ 204-942-2674; www.urbanshaman. org; 290 McDermot Ave; ⊙ noon-5pm Tue-Sat) A noted gallery displaying contemporary Canadian aboriginal art.

◉ St-Boniface

Canada's oldest French community outside of Québec sits just across the Red River from the Forks.

Visitor information centers have an excellent historical self-guided walking map. **Taché Promenade** follows the Red River along Ave Taché, past many of St-Boniface's historical sites.

St-Boniface Basilica
HISTORIC SITE

(Map p516; 151 Ave de la Cathédrale) Mostly destroyed by fire in 1968, the original facade still stands as a 100-year, imposing, Godfearing reminder of the basilica that once stood here. A more current structure was rebuilt on the ruins and Louis Riel rests in the cemetery.

★ St-Boniface Museum
MUSEUM

(Map p516; ☑ 204-237-4500; www.msbm.mb.ca; 494 Ave Taché; adult/child $6/4; ⊙ 10am-4pm Mon-Fri, noon-4pm Sat & Sun) A mid-19th-century convent is Winnipeg's oldest building and the largest oak-log construction on the continent. The museum inside focuses on the establishment of St-Boniface, the birth of the Métis nation, and the Grey Nuns' 3000km journey.

Fort Gibraltar
HISTORIC PARK

(Map p516; ☑ 204-237-7692; www.fortgibraltar. com; 866 Rue St-Joseph; adult/child $8/5; ⊙ 10am-6pm Wed & Thu, 10am-4pm Fri & Sat) Behind wooden walls sits this re-created fur trade fort. Along with inspired interpreters, real clothes, tools, furs, bunks, bannock and blacksmith shops give a sense of 1810-era life at the Forks, the fort's original location.

◉ Greater Winnipeg

★ Assiniboine Park
PARK

(Map p514; www.assiniboinepark.ca; 2355 Corydon Ave) Winnipeg's emerald jewel, this 4.5-sq-km urban park is easily worth at least a half day's frolic. Besides the top-notch zoo (p518), there are playgrounds, gardens, a conservatory and much more. From 2014, look for the vast Journey to Churchill exhibit which explores Manitoba's nature.

Royal Canadian Mint
NOTABLE BUILDING

(Map p514; ☑ 204-257-3359; www.mint.ca; 520 Blvd Lagimodière; tours adult/child $5/2.50; ⊙ 9am-4pm Tue-Sat) Producing Loonies to the tune of billions of dollars, this high-tech mint produces money for Canada and 60 other nations. Tour the pyramid-shaped glass facility to see how money is made (the greatest action occurs on weekdays). It is 9km southeast of the center.

Riel House National Historic Site
HISTORIC SITE

(Map p514; ☑ 204-257-1783; www.parkscanada.ca/riel; 330 River Rd; adult/child $4/2; ⊙ 10am-5pm Jul & Aug) After Louis Riel's 1885 execution for treason, his body was brought to his family home before being buried in St Boniface

---

❶ WINNIPASS

To save Loonies, buy a **Winnipass** (www.heartlandtravel.ca/winnipass; adult $30), with access to six of Winnipeg's major attractions.

Central Winnipeg

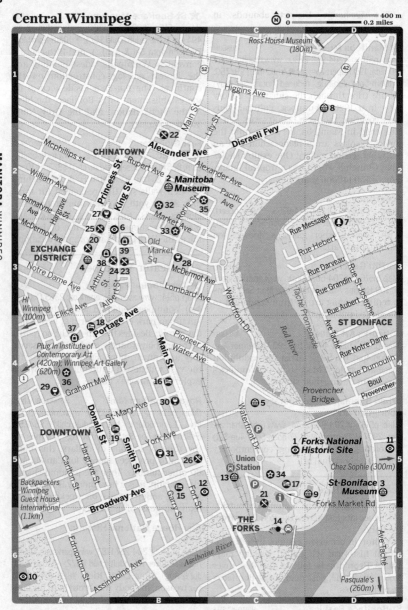

Basilica. Riel grew up on this farm in a cabin by the river; the 1880s house now on display housed his descendents as recently as the 1960s. Now surrounded by subdivisions, the house is 9km south of the center.

Living Prairie Museum   PARK
(Map p514; ☎ 204-832-0167; www.winnipegmuse-ums.org; 2795 Ness Ave; ⏰ 10am-5pm daily Jul & Aug, 10am-5pm Sun May, Jun, Sep & Oct) FREE
Protects 12 hectares of original, unplowed, now-scarce, tall prairie grass. Self-guided

Central Winnipeg

MANITOBA WINNIPEG

tours from the nature center show the seasons of wildflowers in what was once an ocean of color across the prairie provinces and which supported millions of bison.

Fort Whyte PARK
(Map p514; ☑204-989-8355; www.fortwhyte.org; 1961 McCreary Rd; adult/child $6/4; ⊙9am-5pm Mon-Fri, 10am-5pm Sat & Sun) A vast, trail-laced natural site with an eco-focus; here you can spot bison, deer and other wildlife. Learn about sod houses and rent seasonal activity gear such as snowshoes and canoes for modest rates. Even better, in winter, toboggans are free. It's 13km southwest of the center.

Ro-ss House Museum HISTORIC BUILDING
(off Map p516; ☑204-943-3958; www.mhs.mb.ca; Joe Zuken Heritage Park, 140 Mead St N; ⊙10am-5pm Wed-Sun Jun-Aug) **FREE** The small log cabin where William Ross ran the west's first post office is in a pretty setting and documents pioneer life in the 1850s.

☞ Tours

Tourisme Riel (p522) has themed self-guided tours; also check out **Routes on the Red** (www.routesonthered.ca), which has a variety of downloadable tours for the Winnipeg area.

★ **Historic Exchange District Walking Tours** WALKING TOUR
(☑204-942-6716; www.exchangedistrict.org; Old Market Sq; adult/child $8/free; ⊙9am-4:30pm Mon-Sat Jun-Aug) Themed and history tours departing from Old Market Sq. Book in advance.

★ **Muddy Water Tours** WALKING TOUR
(☑204-898-4678; www.muddywatertours.ca; adult/child from $12/6) Numerous entertaining and historically themed walking tours – including the popular 'Murder, Mystery & Mayhem' and 'Pestilence, Shamans & Doctors' – depart on regular schedules all summer.

'Symbols, Secrets & Sacrifices Under the Golden Boy' is a much-acclaimed look at the hidden meanings in the capital. A new hit is 'Beavers, Weavers & High Achievers.'

Splash Dash
BOAT TOUR

(Map p516; 204-783-6633; adult/child $11/9; 10am-sunset May-Oct) Has 30-minute tours of the river from the Forks.

Paddlewheel Riverboats
BOAT TOUR

(204-944-8000; www.paddlewheelcruises.com; cnr Redwood Ave/Rte 37 & Main St; adult/child $19/10) Afternoon (1pm), sunset and moonlight paddlewheel cruises.

Festivals & Events

Festival du Voyageur
CULTURE

(www.festivalvoyageur.mb.ca; Fort Gibraltar; mid-Feb) Winnipeg's signature event. Everyone gets involved in the 10-day winter festival celebrating fur traders and French voyageurs. Centered around Fort Gibraltar; enjoy concerts, dog-sled races and *joie de vivre*.

Pride Winnipeg
CULTURE

(www.pridewinnipeg.com; late May) Nine-day gay and lesbian celebration with a colourful parade.

★ Winnipeg Folk Festival
MUSIC

(204-231-0096; www.winnipegfolkfestival. ca; early Jul) More than 200 concerts on seven stages over five days in Birds Hill Provincial Park.

★ Winnipeg Fringe Theatre Festival
THEATER

(204-943-7464; www.winnipegfringe.com; mid-Jul) North America's second-largest fringe fest; the comedy, drama, music and cabaret are often wildly creative, raw and great fun.

Folklorama
CULTURE

(204-982-6230; www.folklorama.ca; early Aug) Longest-running multicultural event of its kind in the world. Performances, story-telling and more in pavilions representing various cultures across town.

Manito Ahbee
CULTURE

(204-956-1849; www.manitoahbee.com; late Aug) A huge celebration of aboriginal culture that draws participants from all across the globe.

WINNIPEG FOR CHILDREN

Right in the Forks, kids learn by doing at **Manitoba Children's Museum** (Map p516; 204-924-4000; www.childrensmuseum.com; 45 Forks Market Rd; admission $10; 9:30am-6pm), where 'hands off' is not part of the program. The colorful, interactive exhibits encourage tykes to act as train conductors, astronauts and empire builders. It has outdoor programs in summer.

Also in the Forks, the much-heralded **Manitoba Theatre for Young People** (Map p516; 204-942-8898; www.mtyp.ca; 2 Forks Market Rd; tickets $17; Oct-Apr) uses colorful sets for enthusiastic performances for kids without being too treacly for adults.

Over 2000 animals populate **Assiniboine Park Zoo** (Map p514; 204-927-6000; www.assiniboineparkzoo.ca; 460 Assiniboine Park Dr; adult/child $8.50/5.50; 9am-6pm), which specializes in animals that are indigenous to harsh climates. The new International Polar Bear Conservation Centre has exhibits on its namesake critters and often cares for orphaned cubs.It's part of the zoo's huge **Journey to Churchill**, which is set to open in 2014 and will combine exhibits and live animals. From bogs to Arctic beaches, it will cover the province's ecology.

Kids get the chance to play pilot or air traffic controller at the **Western Canadian Aviation Museum** (Map p514; 204-786-5503; www.wcam.mb.ca; 958 Ferry Rd; adult/child $7.50/3; 9:30am-4:30pm Mon-Fri, 10am-5pm Sat, noon-5pm Sun) amid planes from the past 90 years.

For old-fashioned thrills, **Tinkertown Family Fun Park** (204-257-8095; www. tinkertown.mb.ca; 621 Murdock Rd; unlimited ride ticket $15; noon-5pm, till 7pm some days May-Sep) has rides and games in a carnival setting. Play mini-golf and then have a miniature doughnut.

Kids also love the critters and activities at Fort Whyte (p517), while the Science Gallery at Manitoba Museum (p515) has kid-friendly fun, including a lab where you build a race car.

🛏 Sleeping

You'll find plenty of chain motels on main routes around Winnipeg and near the airport, but there's no reason not to stay downtown, where you can easily explore on foot.

Backpackers Winnipeg Guest House International
HOSTEL $

(☑ 800-743-4423, 204-772-1272; www.backpackerswinnipeg.com; 168 Maryland St; dm/r $30/60; ✹ @ 🖙) Creaky-floored Victorian turned hostel lives on a quiet, tree-lined street west of the center. The musty basement has a crowded games room and small showers. Pubs and shops are nearby.

HI Winnipeg
HOSTEL $

(Off map p516; ☑ 204-783-3000; www.hihostels.ca; 330 Kennedy St; dm/r from $35/70; ✹ @ 🖙) A remodeled '60s-era hotel downtown offers budget travelers 100 beds – two levels of dorms and another with private rooms. There's a restaurant and a courtyard; the train station is a 20-minute walk.

★ Place Louis Riel Suite Hotel
HOTEL $$

(Map p516; ☑ 204-947-6961; www.placelouisriel.com; 190 Smith St; r $120-250; ✹ 🖙 ✹) In a renovated 23-story building downtown, the 302 rooms here all include large, stylish kitchens. Sizes range from studio to two-bedroom and rooms on higher floors have great views. The parking is enclosed and the service is excellent.

★ Fort Garry Hotel
HOTEL $$

(Map p516; ☑ 204-942-8251, 800-665-8088; www.fortgarryhotel.com; 222 Broadway Ave; r $130-200; ✹ @ 🖙 ✹) Winnipeg history radiates from this locally owned 1913 limestone legacy that's like something out of a movie. Built as one of Canada's château-style railway stopovers, the grand foyer embodies the hotel's spirit: look for historical photographs lining the walls and lament that they really don't make them like this anymore.

Upstairs the rooms are comfortable if a tad fusty, although that only adds to the charm. Vintage touches include coffee requests you clip to your door.

Malborough Hotel
HOTEL $$

(Map p516; ☑ 800-667-7666, 204-942-6411; www.themarlborough.ca; 331 Smith St; r $80-120; ✹ 🖙 ✹) Goth-Renaissance design and open common spaces characterize this heritage building. Though parts of it smell, the building is almost 100 years old and it has a prime location. Improvements are ongoing; the best of the 148 rooms are on the corporate floor. Public spaces can be grand and the indoor pool has a slide.

Humphry Inn
HOTEL $$

(Map p516; ☑ 877-486-7479, 204-942-4222; www.humphryinn.com; 260 Main St; r $120-200; ✹ @ 🖙 ✹) This modern, six-story hotel is well located downtown. Rooms are large and nicely appointed with fridges and microwaves; get one facing east for good views. The free breakfast buffet is large.

Inn at the Forks
HOTEL $$$

(Map p516; ☑ 877-377-4100, 204-942-6555; www.innforks.com; 75 Forks Market Rd; r $130-250; ✹ @ 🖙) With a vaguely *Mad Men*–esque look, modern style comes to Winnipeg's oldest real estate. Funky bathrooms and solid colors are in 117 spacious rooms. Enjoy river views and the services of a high-end spa.

🍴 Eating

Winnipeg is an excellent place to dine, with a diverse choice. On a summer's evening stroll the Exchange District, St-Boniface, Osborne Village and the Corydon Ave strip, all of which are loaded with options.

In the Exchange District, there's a small **farmers market** (Old Market Sq; ⏲ 10am-2pm Thu & Sat Jul-Sep). To really explore the bounteous produce of the province, however, head 14km south to the **St Norbert Farmers Market** (www.stnorbertfarmersmarket.ca; 3514 Pembina Hwy; ⏲ 11am-4pm Wed, 8am-3pm Sat Jun-Aug), which has scores of vendors selling seasonal produce, prepared foods, crafts and more.

🍴 Downtown

★ VJ's Drive-In
FAST FOOD $

(Map p516; ☑ 204-943-2655; 170 Main St; mains $4-9; ⏲ 10am-1am) Across from Union Station, VJ's is a fave for takeout fixes. There may be a line at lunchtime, but overstuffed chili dogs, greasy cheeseburgers and bronze-hued fries consistently voted the best in Winnipeg won't disappoint. Seating is limited to outdoor picnic tables.

🍴 The Forks

The commercial area of the Forks has a number of indifferent restaurants aimed at tourists, but the market building offers great redemption.

★ **Forks Market** MARKET **$**
(Map p516; www.theforks.com; 1 Forks Market Rd; mains $4-12; ⊙9am-6pm) Vendors selling prepared foods and an array of stalls with well-priced and tasty ethnic dishes are the unbeatable draw here. Enjoy the bounty at tables scattered about inside or have a picnic outside.

★ **Tall Grass Prairie** BAKERY **$**
(Map p516; ✆204-957-5097; www.tallgrassbakery. ca; 1 Forks Market Rd; mains from $4; ⊙7am-9pm Mon-Sat, to 6:30pm Sun) 🍴 Spread over two stalls in the Forks Market, this local legend uses organic Manitoba fare to create lovely baked goods, sandwiches and prepared meals. The coffee's good, too.

✗ Exchange District & Around

On a summer evening, sitting outside at a funky place on the lively, historic streets of the Exchange District is a treat. The Kings Head pub has good pub food. Further north are the smells and tastes of Winnipeg's small Chinatown.

★ **Mondragón** CAFE **$**
(Map p516; ✆204-946-5241; www.mondragon.ca; 91 Albert St; mains $6-11; ⊙11am-2pm Mon, 8am-9pm Tue-Sat; 🖉) 🍴 Still true to the Exchange District's funky roots, the Mondragón is run by a workers collective and sells the kind of left-wing books you won't find on Amazon. The cafe is vegan and the creative menu of fresh fare changes daily. A small market within is named for Sacco & Vanzetti.

News Cafe CAFE **$**
(Map p516; www.winnipegfreepress.com/cafe; 237 McDermot Ave; mains $7-12; ⊙8am-6pm Sat-Thu, to 10pm Fri; 🛜) This great corner cafe is run by Winnipeg's major daily newspaper, the *Free Press*. Besides great breakfasts and lunches that include a famous pulled pork sandwich, there's a definite newsy vibe. Reporters can be spotted doing interviews at some tables and there is regular programming featuring talks on local issues and performances by local musicians.

★ **Deer + Almond** BISTRO **$$**
(Map p516; ✆204-504-8562; 85 Princess St; mains $12-25; ⊙11am-3pm & 5-11pm Mon-Sat) This fabulous recent addition to the Exchange District has a creative and ever-changing menu that features a Canadian accent on comfort food. Check the blackboards for dishes like a killer Reuben or an excellent

steak. It's a bright corner location; the beers and wines are some of the country's best.

Kum-Koon Garden CHINESE **$$**
(Map p516; ✆204-943-4655; www.kumkoongarden.com; 257 King St; mains $3-20; ⊙11:30am-10pm) Excellent dim sum draws legions of loyal fans to this Chinatown anchor. Service can be as abrupt as the whack of the blade on a duck in the kitchen but you'll barely notice as you navigate the huge menu. Mains are big enough for several people – the reason you see everybody leave with bags of little boxes.

Peasant Cookery BISTRO **$$**
(Map p516; ✆204-989-7700; www.peasantcookery.com; 100-283 Bannatyne Ave; mains $9-26; ⊙11am-2pm Mon-Fri & 5-9pm daily) In a high-ceilinged, high-profile corner space in a 1907 warehouse, this inviting bistro has a menu with ingredients drawn right from the fertile central Canada countryside. Meats and vegetables are offered seasonally, although you can always get a delicious roast chicken with hearty vegetables.

✗ St-Boniface

The charming old neighborhood of St-Boniface has some fine little restaurants, which, not surprisingly, reflect the local French accent. None are more than a 20-minute walk over the river from the center.

Chez Sophie FRENCH **$$**
(off Map p516; ✆204-235-0353; www.chezsophie. ca; 248 Av de la Cathédrale; meals $9-15; ⊙11am-9pm Wed-Sat) A neighborhood fixture for decades – corner store, launderette – has become a favorite neighborhood bistro. It's cozy and has a well-priced classic French menu of salads, crepes, quiche and more hearty fare such as mussels and frites. Pizzas and pasta add Italian flair.

Pasquale's ITALIAN **$$**
(✆204-231-1403; www.pasqualesrest.com; 109 Marion St; mains $12-25; ⊙11am-10pm Mon-Fri, from 4pm Sat) Classic red-sauce Italian fare keeps this family eatery packed. The mussels and the thin-crust pizza are standouts, although the cannelloni is a quiet contender. Portions are bounteous. When weather allows, head straight to a table on the rooftop patio and bathe in the twinkle of the prairie's stars.

Osborne Village & Corydon Ave

Some of Winnipeg's trendiest restaurants are in Osborne Village, close to the center.

All manner of places line the genteel climes of Corydon Ave, which runs through one of Winnipeg's oldest and nicest neighborhoods. Near the middle is a string of cafes that comprise **Little Italy**, most with terraces perfect for having a cup of strong coffee and solving the world's woes.

★Baked Expectations
CAFE $

(☏204-452-5176; www.bakedexpectations.ca; 161 Osborne St; mains $8-16; ☺noon-midnight) The cakes may weaken your knees as you enter this stylish palace of desserts. However, the foodie foreplay is just as good, with excellent burgers, pastas, omelettes and more. There's a cute kids' menu; Sunday brunch is worth the queue.

Sushi Ya
SUSHI $$

(☏204-452-3916; 659 Corydon Ave; mains $12-20; ☺11am-9pm; ☏) Typical of the vibrant storefronts along Corydon Ave, this sushi spot packs in locals for its classic rolls and other fare. The fried tofu wins plaudits and there's a taste of Korean, courtesy of the piquant kimchi.

Segovia
MEDITERRANEAN $$

(☏204-477-6500; www.segoviatapasbar.com; 484 Stradbrook Ave; small mains $8-15; ☺5-11pm Wed-Mon) This tapas place is as authentic as the house-made aioli. Set in a stylishly renovated old home in a quiet spot just off noisy Osborne St, Segovia has a long list of wines and cocktails you can savor on the patio while enjoying – and sharing – exquisite little dishes.

Drinking & Nightlife

Decent places for a drink are found throughout Winnipeg; most have a cheery neighborhood charm. Look for the local Fort Garry and Half Pints microbrews.

★King's Head Pub
PUB

(Map p516; ☏204-957-7710; www.kingshead.ca; 120 King St; ☺11am-2am) Vaguely British, the gregarious sidewalk tables are the place to be in the Exchange District on a balmy evening. Inside it's all rough and tumble wood. The long menu does pub standards like burgers and fish and chips quite well.

★Times Chang(d) High & Lonesome Club
CLUB

(Map p516; ☏204-957-0982; www.highandlonesomeclub.ca; 234 Main St; ☺7pm-late) Honkytonk/country/rock/blues weekend bands jam, and beer and whiskey flow, at this small, rough, raunchy and real throwback. Don't miss the Sunday night jam.

Windsor Hotel
BAR

(Map p516; ☏204-942-7528; www.windsorhotel.biz; 187 Garry St; ☺7pm-late) The well-worn Windsor is Winnipeg's definitive live blues bar. There's open stage some nights; bands perform at weekends.

Tavern United
BAR

(Map p516; ☏204-944-0022; 345 Graham Ave; ☺noon-late) The inside is huge and the rooftop patio massive, with views across to the MTS Centre. It bustles with a sports-bar vibe and rocks for Jets home games.

Liv in the Exchange
CLUB

(Map p516; ☏204-989-8080; www.aliveinthedistrict.com; 40 Bannatyne Ave; ☺9pm-2am Fri & Sat) Cool and glitzy club in the Exchange District.

Whiskey Dix
CLUB

(☏204-944-7539; www.whiskeydix.ca; 436 Main St; ☺9pm-2am Fri & Sat) Dress nice and get here by 10:30pm to enter this popular club. Outside there's a vast and hugely popular ever-thumping terrace; inside high ceilings open up the crowded dance floor. Watch for special events outside weekends.

☆ Entertainment

After hockey, Winnipeg's impressive arts and cultural scene earns the town well-deserved applause, not bad for the town that produced Neil Young.

★Winnipeg Jets
HOCKEY

(http://jets.nhl.com; MTS Centre; ☺Sep-Apr) They're back! There's Manitoba mania for the Jets (see p522) who play at the **MTS Centre** (Map p516; ☏204-987-7825; www.mtscentre.ca; 260 Hargrave St). Games are raucous and often sold out; ask around for tickets.

Centennial Concert Hall
CONCERT VENUE

(Map p516; www.centennialconcerthall.com; 555 Main St) Home to the **Winnipeg Symphony Orchestra** (Map p516; ☏204-949-3999; www.wso.mb.ca; tickets $20-60; ☺Sep-May), the **Royal Winnipeg Ballet** (Map p516; ☏204-956-2792; www.rwb.org) and the highly acclaimed

JETS FLY HOME

In 1996, the hearts of Winnipeg's hockey fans (basically everybody in town) were broken when the beloved local National Hockey League franchise, the Winnipeg Jets, headed south, not just for the winter, but for good. In search of TV revenues, the franchise moved to Phoenix and was renamed the Coyotes.

Meanwhile fans across Manitoba prayed, begged, hoped and schemed for a new team called the Jets. In 2011 a collective roar was heard around Winnipeg and the province when True North Sports & Entertainment bought the failing Atlanta NHL franchise, the glottal-stop-challenged Thrashers, and moved it to Winnipeg. As operators of the huge arena, MTS Centre, True North had good reason to buy a team guaranteed to sell tickets in hockey-mad Winnipeg. And what was barely a gamble paid off as season tickets for the newly reborn Jets sold out in record time.

Although success on the ice was elusive during the reborn Jet's early seasons, ticket sales are strong and Winnipeg is alive with excitement on any day there's a home game. A fan favorite is the mascot, Mick E Moose, a holdover from the minor-league team the Manitoba Moose, who played in Winnipeg during the Jet-less years. His costume now includes a vintage aviator helmet.

Another tradition, the 'White Out,' in which fans wear all-white when the Jets are in the play-offs, will require the Jets to actually make the play-offs.

Manitoba Opera (Map p516; ☑204-942-7479; www.manitobaopera.mb.ca; tickets $30-99; ☉Nov-Apr), complete with subtitles.

Manitoba Theatre Centre THEATER
(MTC; map p516; ☑204-942-6537; www.mtc.mb.ca; 174 Market Ave) This company produces popular shows on the main stage and more-daring works at the **MTC Warehouse** (Map p516; 140 Rupert Ave).

🔒 Shopping

The Exchange District practically groans with art galleries and funky stores. Osborne Village and Corydon Ave are excellent places to browse (especially around Lilac St along the latter). Academy Rd has top-end boutiques.

★ Winnipeg Folk Festival Music Store MUSIC
(Map p516; www.winnipegfolkfestival.ca; 103-211 Bannatyne Ave; ☉11am-6pm Tue-Sat) The retail storefront for Winnipeg's huge July music festival is a great year-round source for folk, blues, bluegrass, country, rock, alternative, jazz and much more. It's a good place to plug into the local music scene.

Red River Books BOOKS
(Map p516; ☑943-956-2195; 92 Arthur St; ☉10am-5pm Sat-Tue, to 7pm Wed-Fri) Literally piles of secondhand books; a treasure trove of literature.

Mountain Equipment Co-Op OUTDOOR EQUIPMENT
(MEC; Map p516; ☑204-943-4202; www.mec.ca; 303 Portage Ave; ☉10am-9pm) Canada's favorite outdoor store rents gear for hiking and camping plus kayaks, snowshoes and more.

ℹ Information

INTERNET ACCESS
Millennium Library (☑204-986-6450; wpl.winnipeg.ca/library; 251 Donald St; ☉10am-9pm Mon-Thu, to 6pm Fri & Sat; 🛜) Free wi-fi and internet computers.

TOURIST INFORMATION
Explore Manitoba Centre (Map p516; ☑800-665-0040, 204-945-3777; 25 Forks Market Rd; ☉10am-6pm) Provincial information center at the Forks; has Parks Canada and Winnipeg info.
Tourisme Riel (☑204-233-8343; www.tourismeriel.com; 219 Blvd Provencher; ☉9am-5pm) St-Boniface visitor information center, specializes in Francophone attractions. Usually has a summer booth at the base of Esplanade Riel, the pedestrian bridge over the river.

ℹ Getting There & Away

AIR
Winnipeg International Airport (www.waa.ca) has a flash terminal a convenient 10km west of downtown. It has service to cities across Canada and to major hubs in the US. Regional carriers handle remote excursions.

BUS

Greyhound buses stop at a **terminal** (2015 Wellington Ave) at Winnipeg International Airport. Services include Regina ($86, nine hours, two daily), Thunder Bay ($81, nine hours, two daily) and Thompson ($95, nine hours, two daily).

TRAIN

VIA Rail's transcontinental *Canadian* departs **Union Station** (123 Main St) two or three times weekly in each direction. The dismal service to Churchill runs two or three times a week via Thompson and may take 40 hours or more.

❶ Getting Around

Walking is easy and enjoyable from downtown to any of the surrounding neighborhoods. In poor weather, under- and above-ground walkways connect downtown buildings.

TO/FROM THE AIRPORT

A downtown taxi costs $25; some hotels have free shuttles. Winnipeg Transit's bus 15 runs between the airport and downtown every 20 minutes and takes 30 minutes.

CAR & MOTORCYCLE

Downtown street parking (free after 6pm) and parking lots are plentiful. Break-ins are common at Union Station, so enclosed lots downtown are a better option if you're taking the train.

If transiting Winnipeg by road, the slow Trans-Canada Hwy (Hwy 1) goes right through downtown. You can bypass this on looping Hwy 100, although suburban roads west, east and south of the city are often jammed.

PUBLIC TRANSPORTATION

Winnipeg Transit (☑204-986-5700; www.winnipegtransit.com; adult/child $2.50/2) runs extensive bus routes around the area, most converging on Fort St. Get a transfer and use exact change. Its free *Downtown Spirit* runs various routes serving the center.

WATER TAXI

See the city from a new perspective on the water taxi run by **River Spirit** (Map p516; ☑204-783-6633; one-way/day pass $3.50/15; ☺noon-9pm Mon-Wed, noon-11pm Thu-Sun Jul & Aug) between the Forks, the Legislature Building, Osborne Village, St-Boniface and the Exchange District.

AROUND WINNIPEG

Lower Fort Garry

Huge stone walls on the banks of the Red River bank surround the only stone **fort** (☑204-785-6050; www.parkscanada.ca/garry; 5925 Hwy 9; buildings adult/child $8/4; ☺buildings 9am-5pm daily Jul & Aug, Mon-Fri May & Jun, grounds open year-round) still intact from the fur-trading days. It's impeccably restored and reflective of the mid-19th century, with costumed interpreters adding color. The lovely park-like site is 32km northeast of Winnipeg.

Oak Hammock Marsh

Smack in the middle of southern Manitoba's wetlands is **Oak Hammock Marsh** (☑204-467-3300; www.oakhammockmarsh.ca; Rte 200, at Hwy 67; adult/child $6/4; ☺10am-8pm Sep & Oct, to 4pm Nov-Aug), home and migratory stopping point for hundreds of thousands of birds and one of the best sanctuaries around. Springtime has diversity and autumn sees 200,000 to 400,000

SPIRIT OF THE PRAIRIE: LOUIS RIEL

Born in 1844 on the Red River near today's Winnipeg, Louis Riel became a leader of the Métis, like him people of mixed Aboriginal and European backgrounds. He battled for their rights, and helped lead the Red River Rebellion, which gave the Métis political power but led to his exile in the US. Riel eventually returned to Canada; in 1885 he was tried for treason and hanged. For more on Riel, see p841.

The third Monday of February is a provincial holiday in Riel's honor. You can find numerous Riel legacies in Manitoba and Saskatchewan:

➡ Riel House (p515): His birthplace and the family house where he was taken after his execution.

➡ His grave at St-Boniface Basilica (p515).

➡ A seasonal play, *Trial of Louis Riel* (p539), which dramatizes his trial for treason.

➡ Batoche (p552), the haunting site of his last battle.

geese. Boardwalks, telescopes, remote-controlled cameras and canoes get you close.

LAKE WINNIPEG

The southern end of Canada's fifth-largest lake has been a resort destination since the 1920s. Sandy white beaches, constant sunshine and the oceanlike size of the lake made a visit like 'going to the coast' for all Winnipeggers. It's a tremendously popular summer destination; in winter, when snowy white beaches line the frozen lake, it's virtually deserted.

Popular places such as Winnipeg Beach on the western shore and Grand Beach on the east are typical...well...beach towns. Not that they have zero appeal, but they're predictable centers of summer fun, right down to the arcades, beach boardwalks, ice-cream shops, take-out burger joints and crowds of families, teenagers and vacationers sunning and splashing.

There is hiking in **Grand Beach Provincial Park** (204-754-2212; Hwy 12; campsites $12-24, RV sites $16-29), where hundreds of species of birds use the lagoon behind the beach and the nearby dunes reach 12m. It's also one of Manitoba's busiest campgrounds, meaning it can get loud.

Most land around and between Lake Winnipeg and Lakes Manitoba and Winnipegosis, aka Interlake, is privately owned and cottage rentals are possible. Plenty of small towns and villages are lived in year-round so standard motels and B&Bs can be found everywhere.

Gimli

On the surface it could be another clichéd tourist trap, but beneath the kitsch and tackiness is historic Gimli (Icelandic for 'Home of the Gods'). Settled as 'New Iceland' in 1875, this neat little town has retained its fascinating heritage.

The **New Iceland Heritage Museum** (204-642-4001; www.nihm.ca; 94 1st Ave; adult/child $6/5; 10am-4pm Jun-Aug) is packed with history and artifacts telling the story of an unlikely people settling an unlikelier part of Canada. It has tourist information. On the beach overlooking the lake, the huge **Viking statue** reinforces the town's Icelandic heritage.

Worth visiting simply for its creaky-floored history, **HP Tergesen & Sons** (204-642-5958; 82 1st Ave; 10am-6pm Mon-Sat) is a busy general store that's been in continuous operation since 1899.

It's all Iceland during **Islendingadagurinn** (204-642-7417; www.icelandicfestival.com; early Aug), a provincially popular fest including *Islendingadance,* Icelandic games, live music (no Björk) and, of course, an Iceland-themed parade with a lot of blonde people.

Just outside town, **Autumnwood Motel & RV Resort** (204-642-8565; www.autumnwoodresort.com; 19150 Gimli Park Rd; r $90-150;) has 18 standard rooms with polychromatic decor nestled in a quiet location among trees. Various lodges can be found by the water; they usually book up for summer weekends.

Pickerel, a mild lake fish, is served fresh at simple cafes along the lake. **Reykjavik Bakery** (Lighthouse Mall, Centre St; snacks from $2; 7am-6pm) sells sensational baked goods that are popular in Iceland. Try the *kleina,* a sort of trapezoidal doughnut. For heartier fare, try the creative pub food at **Ship and Plough** (204-642-5276; 42 Centre St; mains $10-20; noon-11pm Mon-Thu, to 2am Fri & Sat) downtown.

Hecla-Grindstone Provincial Park

On an island away from the tacky hustle of Lake Winnipeg's beaches sits a natural oasis featuring Manitoba the way it's meant to be seen. The islands, marshes and forests are full of deer, moose, beaver and bear. Stop at **Grassy Narrows Marsh**, which has trails close to the park's entrance leading to shelters and towers perfect for habitat viewing. The **park office** (www.manitobaparks.com; Hwy 8; campsites $12-24, RV sites $16-29) provides information for visitors.

Almost too picture-perfect to be real, Hecla Village has been a lived-in Icelandic settlement since 1876. You can go on a 1km **self-guided tour** of the old lakefront buildings. The **Heritage Historic Village** (Village Rd; admission free; 10am-6pm Thu-Sun Jun-Aug) lets you look inside a 1920s Icelandic immigrant village.

Solmundson Gesta Hus Bed & Breakfast (204-279-2088; www.hecla.ca; Riverton; r $85-90;) is a beautiful historic home with a hot tub surrounded by manicured gardens.

SOUTHEASTERN MANITOBA

Heading east from Winnipeg, the flat expanse typical of the prairies blends with forests and lakes typical of the Great Lakes region. While most visitors speed through toward Kenora and beyond, the eastern region of Manitoba has the same rugged woodland terrain as neighboring Ontario.

Whiteshell Provincial Park

Foreshadowing the green forests, clear lakes and Canadian Shield of northern Ontario, pine-covered hills erupt from the plains immediately inside **Whiteshell Provincial Park** (www.manitobaparks.com).

The park is fairly commercialized; resorts and stores are found every few kilometers and larger centers have **park offices**. However, there is still a sense of spirituality and you can get away via hiking trails of varying lengths – the longest being the six-day, 60km Mantario – and canoe routes, the most popular being the tunnels of **Caddy Lake**.

There are hundreds of **campsites** (campsites $12-24, RV sites $16-29) throughout the park. **Falcon Lakeshore Campground**, with trees and seclusion, is only a short walk from the lake's beaches.

Big Whiteshell Lodge (☑204-348-7623; www.bigwhiteshelllodge.com; Hwy 309; cottages $100-190) has cottages in a quiet, woodsy location on the shores of Big Whiteshell Lake at the end of Rte 309.

WESTERN MANITOBA

Between Winnipeg and Saskatchewan, Manitoba is a seemingly endless sea of agriculture until you decide to make a few detours here and there to often overlooked natural delights and some atmospheric towns.

Spruce Woods Provincial Park

Un-Manitoban shifting sand dunes in this 270-sq-km **park** (☑204-827-8850; www.manitobaparks.com; Hwy 5) provide a home for unlikely cacti and creatures including Manitoba's only lizard: the 20cm-long northern prairie skink. Stretch your legs on the 1.6km trail to the dunes at Spirit Sands.

Brandon

POP 46,100

Manitoba's second-largest center is an attractive residential city with a historic downtown bisected by the Assiniboine River.

Riverbank Discovery Centre (☑204-729-2141; www.brandontourism.com; 545 Conservation

---

FLOWERS OF THE PRAIRIE: SMALLTOWN MANITOBA

Manitoba's welter of rural roads are ideal for random explorations. Many lead to small towns that make the journey worthwhile. Here are a few of our favorites:

Carman Gorgeous river setting an hour southwest of Winnipeg with a 5km walking trail.

Minnedosa Perfect little Main St with Dairy Isle ice-cream stand and a bowling alley.

Morden Southern town with brick buildings, a grain elevator, the Canadian Fossil Discovery Centre and the Manitoba Baseball Hall of Fame; enough said.

Neepawa Tree-lined streets and old houses mean this town is often voted Manitoba's prettiest. Look for U-pick berry farms here.

Norway House A large Cree community steeped in history on Lake Winnipeg's isolated northern shore.

Snow Lake Fun little town on the shores of Snow Lake, just north of Hwy 10, with mining museum and roadside bear crap.

Stonewall Hanging baskets, peaceful atmosphere and limestone-quarry swimming hole, an hour north of Winnipeg.

Victoria Beach Greenest village ever. Cottage-centric with limited vehicle access (walk or bike) and Lake Winnipeg's sandiest beaches, located on the eastern shore.

Dr; ⊘ 8:30am-8pm) is both a tourist office and a hub for riverside walking paths.

On **CFB Shilo**, an active military base east of Brandon, the **Royal Canadian Artillery Museum** (☑ 204-765-3000; www.rca-museum.com; Hwy 340, Shilo; adult/child $5/3; ⊘ 10am-5pm) displays uniforms, guns, ammunition and 60-plus vehicles dating from 1796 through the Cold War. Sadly, there's no hands-on cannon demonstration.

Chain motels line the exits from Hwy 1, and eateries can be found downtown. Regular Greyhound buses plying the highway pause at the downtown **depot** (☑ 204-727-0643; 141 6th St).

International Peace Garden

The setting – a very quiet B-level Manitoba–North Dakota border crossing – is certainly appropriate for this cross-border **garden** (☑ 204-534-2510; www.peacegarden.com; Canada Hwy 10/US281; per vehicle $10; ⊘ 24hr), which honors the peaceful relations between Canada and the US. Yet nothing is as simple since 9/11 (you have to go through customs and immigration of either country just to reach the garden).

Riding Mountain National Park

Rising like a vision above the plains, **Riding Mountain National Park** (☑ 204-848-7275; www.parkscanada.ca/riding; adult/child $8/4) is more than 3000 sq km of boreal forest, deep valleys, lofty hills and alpine lakes. It rewards those with an hour or a week. You might even see a bear or a moose.

Most of the park is wilderness; **Wasagaming**, on the south shore of eponymously named Clear Lake, is such a perfect little summer town that it would be a cliché if it weren't so, well, perfect.

The beautiful 1930s **visitors center** (☑ 204-848-7275; Wasagaming Rd; ⊘ 9:30am-8pm Jul & Aug, to 5pm May, Jun, Sep & Oct) contains impressive dioramas, the invaluable *Visitor Guide* and backcountry permits.

⊙ Sights & Activities

Highway 10 cuts a 53km course down the middle of the park. It's fine if the only time you have is for a quick transit, but the park is at its best on any of the 400km of **walking**, **cycling** and **horseback-riding trails**. Hikes range from the 1km-long Lakeshore Trail to a 17km trek through forest and meadows to a cabin used by naturalist Grey Owl. **Elkhorn Riding Adventures** (☑ 204-848-4583; www.elkhornridingadventures.com; trail rides from $40) beside Elkhorn Resort offers a chance to honor the park's name atop a horse.

Canoeing and **kayaking** are excellent and offer shoreline glimpses at wildlife, though Clear Lake gets windy and also allows motorboats. Rentals are available from **Clear Lake Marina** (☑ 204-848-1770; www.theclearlakemarina.com; Wasagaming Pier; per hr from $15; ⊘ May-Sep).

⊨ Sleeping & Eating

Backcountry camping is possible; check with the visitors center. Motels and cabins are plentiful in Wasagaming; some open year-round.

GRAIN ELEVATORS

Barn-red or tractor-green; striking yet simple; function and form: characterizing prairie landscapes like the wheat they hold, grain elevators were once flagships of prairie architecture.

Introduced in 1880, more than 7000 of the vertical wooden warehouses lined Canadian train tracks by 1930. Their importance was invaluable, as the prairies became 'the breadbasket of the world,' and their stoic simplicity inspired Canadian painters, photographers and writers who gave them life.

Today's concrete replacements are as generic as their fast-food-chain neighbors. For a glimpse of the vanishing past, make the detour to **Inglis Grain Elevators National Historic Site** (☑ 204-564-2243; www.ingliselevators.com; ⊘ 10am-6pm Mon-Sat, noon-6pm Sun Jun-Aug) FREE . A stunning row of elevators has been restored to their original splendor. Inside the creaky interiors, exhibits capture the thin lives where success or failure rested with the whims of commodity brokers.

Inglis is 20km north of the Yellowhead Hwy (Hwy 16) near the Saskatchewan border.

There are 600 **campsites** (sites $16-40, yurts from $70) in the park. **Wasagaming Campground** is the most popular, **Lake Audy** has abundant wildlife and **Whirlpool Lake** has lakeside walk-in sites within thick forest a 50m hike from the parking lot.

For a little bit of dudeness in the wilderness, **Elkhorn Resort** (⏎204-848-2802; www.elkhornresort.mb.ca; Mooswa Dr W, Wasagaming; r $90-220; ❀☒) offers genteel comfort. Better yet, **Idylwylde Cabins** (⏎204-848-2383; www.idylwylde.ca; 136 Wasagaming Dr, Wasagaming; cabins from $100; ❀☒) offers short walk to the ice-cream stands in town and you can stay here for less than a week during the off-season. Enjoy the artisan baked goods and lunches at **Sparrow's Bakery** (144 Wasagaming Dr, Wasagaming; snacks from $2; ☺8am-5pm).

❶ Getting There & Away

You can drive through the park on Hwy 10 for free if you solemnly promise not to stop. Better to pay the fee and make a day of it.

NORTHERN MANITOBA

'North of 53' (the 53rd parallel), convenience takes a backseat to rugged beauty as lake-filled timberland dissolves into the treeless tundra of the far north. Here cell phones are useless and you're left to rely on your own wits for adventure and even survival. Churchill is justifiably the big draw and reason enough for a journey that leaves the life you know far behind.

The Pas

A traditional meeting place of Aboriginal and European fur traders, the Pas (pronounced pah) is a useful stop for services on northern trips.

The **Northern Manitoba Trappers' Festival** (⏎204-623-2912; www.trappersfestival.com; ☺mid-Feb) is one of the best-known parties of the Pas and Manitoba, featuring dog-sled races, snowmobiling, ice sculptures, torch-light parades and trapping games in a weekend of frosty anarchy.

Boreal forests surround the amazingly clear waters and there's camping with pelicans at **Clearwater Lake Provincial Park** (⏎204-624-5525; www.manitobaparks.ca; campsites $12-24, RV sites $16-29) near the airport. The scenic Caves Trail follows deep crevices and eroding cliffs.

Motels are strung out along Hwy 10. **Miss the Pass** (⏎204-623-3130; 158 Edwards St; mains from $6; ☺7am-7pm Mon-Sat) has the kind of tasty, hearty fare that will ready you for adventure and is almost a museum.

VIA Rail's Winnipeg–Churchill train stops at the **train station** (380 Hazelwood Ave).

Flin Flon

A worthy pause on a northern routing along lonely, pretty Hwy 10 into Saskatchewan, Flin Flon (www.cityofflinflon.ca) still has some of the 1930s character from when it was a mining boomtown. Straddling the border, it has a full slate of services.

Thompson

Carved out of the boreal forest by mining interests in the 1950s, Thompson is a necessary evil for northern itineraries. There's no way around it, the town lacks charm although the boom in minerals means that it has 24-hour fast-food chains, a Wal-Mart and plenty of services.

At the entrance to town, the **Heritage North Museum** (⏎204-677-2216; www.heritagenorthmuseum.ca; 162 Princeton Dr; ☺9am-5pm) is in a small log-cabin stuffed with stuffed local wildlife and history. It has tourist info.

McCreedy Campground (⏎204-778-8810; 114 Manasan Dr; campsites from $20; ☺May-Sep) is set up for recreational vehicles (RVs) and has a few campsites in the trees; it's just north of the river. Centrally located, **Interior Inn** (⏎204-778-5535; www.interiorinn.ca; 180 Thompson Dr N; r from $90; ✱☎) is typical of the raw-edged motels that abound in town.

Calm Air (p531) flies throughout Manitoba including Churchill to/from **Thompson Airport** (⏎204-778-5212; www.thompsonairport.ca), 10km north of town. Two daily Greyhound buses to/from Winnipeg ($95, nine hours) and other Hwy 6 destinations use the **bus station** (⏎204-677-0360; 81 Berens Rd) near the visitors center.

Thompson is the end of paved roads, and many people catch the lethargic VIA Rail Churchill train from here. The **station** (⏎204-677-2241; 1310 Station Rd), in an industrial area 1km from town, is not a safe spot to leave your vehicle. McReedy Campground offers vehicle storage and shuttles to the train.

Pisew Falls

Around 80km southwest of Thompson along Hwy 6, **Pisew Falls Provincial Park** (www.manitobaparks.ca; Hwy 6) is a must-stop for anyone passing. A short boardwalk runs from the parking area down to lookouts on the surging waters of the 13m falls. Water shoots over the wide precipice and then gushes through a rocky gorge while mist fills the air.

A trail from here leads to remote **Kwasitchewan Falls**. The partial looping route runs 22km there and back and offers prime backcountry hiking and camping.

Churchill

POP 820

Churchill lures people to the shores of Hudson Bay for polar bears, beluga whales, a huge old stone fort and endless subarctic majesty. But while these are reason enough for Churchill to be on any itinerary, there's something less tangible that makes people stay longer and keeps them coming back: a hearty seductive spirit that makes the rest of the world seem – thankfully – even further away than it really is.

Prime times to visit are July and August and then again during the peak polar bear viewing period of mid-October to November. At other times Churchill is often frozen and desolate, which has its own appeal.

History

Permafrost springs upwards about an inch per millennia chronicling old shorelines and leaving nearby evidence of aboriginal settlements up to 3000 years old. In European exploration, Churchill is one of the oldest places in Canada. The first outpost of HBC (said to stand for 'Here Before Christ') was built here in 1717. It was a stop in attempts to find the fabled Northwest Passage by explorers such as Samuel Hearne and Lord Churchill, former HBC governor and the town's namesake.

Churchill's strategic location ensured a military presence over centuries. The railway's arrival and opening of the huge port in 1929 has made the town a vital international grain shipping point for the prairie provinces.

⊙ Sights

The town itself is a typical assemblage of tattered northern structures. Wander the streets, stop and peruse the beach (!), visit the museum and then get out onto the land and water for nature at its most magnificent.

★ Eskimo Museum   MUSEUM

(🖉 204-675-2030; 242 La Verendrye Ave; admission by donation $3; ⊙1-5pm Mon, 9am-noon & 1-5pm Tue-Sat) This museum is really just a bunch of stuff in an unexciting room with linoleum floors, but like Churchill it sucks you in and soon an hour or two has passed.

The obvious standouts – stuffed polar bear and musk ox, narwhal horns and original hide-covered kayaks – are immediate attention-grabbers, but closer inspection reveals tiny arrowheads, big harpoon blades and hundreds of carvings showing intricate scenes of everyday life (look for the one titled *First Airplane*). A large range of Northern books are for sale.

Parks Canada   MUSEUM

(🖉 204-675-8863) There's a small but essential museum and nature center in the train station along with the Parks Canada info desk. It has a good model of the fort and excellent information on the many creatures you've come far to see. Check for opening hours and any scheduled lectures.

Fort Prince of Wales
National Historic Site   HISTORIC SITE

Parks Canada (www.parkscanada.ca; ⊙ Jul & Aug) administers three sites in the area documenting Churchill's varied history. Transportation to the sites across the water is handled by licensed tour operators and the entry fee is included in tour costs.

It took 40 years to build and its cannons have never fired a shot, but the star-shaped stone Fort Prince of Wales has been standing prominently on rocky Eskimo Point across the Churchill River since the 1770s. As English-French tensions mounted in the 1720s, HBC selected the site for presence and strategy, but surrendered during the first French attack in 1782, making it an Anglo Maginot Line forerunner. It's a boggy, buggy place with sweeping views and a real sense that duty here was best avoided.

Four kilometers south of the fort, **Sloop's Cove** was a harbor for European vessels during Churchill's harsh winters. The only indications of early explorers are simple yet profound: names such as Samuel Hearne, local 18th-century governor and first to make an overland trip to the Arctic Ocean, are carved into the seaside rocks.

★**Cape Merry**, at the national historic site, has a lone cannon and crumbling walls but the location astounds with vistas across the bay and river. In season, those aren't whitecaps, they're belugas. The site is an easy and pretty 2km-walk northwest of town, but get bear advice before setting out.

Fort Churchill   HISTORIC SITE

Amid the undulating rocks, late-season ice and scraggy, stunted trees looms a Cold War relic. Spotted long before you complete the 20km drive east from the airport, Fort Churchill was Canada's Cape Kennedy. Starting in 1954, over 3500 small rockets were launched from here on military and scientific missions. Pondering the abandoned and crumbling remains of the complex is both fascinating and eerie.

Wapusk National Park   PARK

(☎204-675-8863, 888-748-2928; www.parkscanada.ca/wapusk) Established primarily to protect polar bear breeding grounds (*wapusk* is Cree for 'white bear'), this remote park extends along Hudson Bay's shores 45km southeast of Churchill. Its location between boreal forests and arctic tundra gives it importance for monitoring the effects of climate change. Visits center on polar bears and are only possible through licensed operators.

York Factory National Historic Site   HISTORIC SITE

(www.parkscanada.ca/yorkfactory; ☉Jun-Sep) Around 250km southeast of Churchill and impossibly remote, this HBC trading post, near Hayes River, was an important gateway to the interior and active for 273 years until 1957. The stark-white buildings are an amazing sight contrasting with their barren setting. It's accessible only by air or boat.

🐚 Courses

Churchill Northern Studies Centre   RESEARCH

(CNSC; ☎204-675-2307; www.churchillscience.ca; Launch Rd; courses from $1100) Located at Fort Churchill, 23km east of town, CNSC is an active base for researchers. Learning vacations feature all-inclusive (dorms, meals and local transportation) multiday courses with scientists working on projects involving belugas, wildflowers, birds and polar bears. There are also courses in winter survival, northern lights and astronomy. It moved into a shiny new building in 2011.

👉 Tours

Independent exploration is not encouraged in Churchill, not just for reasons of safety but primarily due to expertise. Local guides have a wealth of knowledge that guide you to wildlife and provide vital context for exploring the area.

Polar Bear Tours

Polar bears overshadow Churchill's other draws. In summer, you may see them as part of other tours on land and even swimming in the river. Later in the year, however, is the main event. Special lightweight vehicles riding high on huge tires to protect the tundra venture out on day trips (about $400 per person). Heated cabins and open-air

---

FOR EVERY SEASON...

In climatological terms, Churchill has three seasons: July, August and winter. For visitors, it has five: bird, flower, beluga whale, polar bear and northern lights.

Bird (peak season: mid-May to September) Two hundred-plus species use Churchill as nesting grounds, including rare Ross's gulls, or as a stopover on their way further north. Granary Ponds by the port, Cape Merry or Bird Cove are good viewing spots.

Wildflower (June to August) As the ice melts and the sun hits the soil for the first time in months, Churchill explodes in colors and aromas.

Beluga whale (mid-June to August) Curious as dolphins and voluble as the label 'sea canaries' implies, about 3000 of these glossy white, 4m-long creatures summer in Churchill River. From Cape Merry they look like whitecaps; go snorkeling, kayaking or view them from a boat.

Polar bear (September to early November) Peak season is late in the year, but sightings begin in July.

Northern lights (October to March) The aqua-turquoise-yellow dance of the aurora borealis is nothing short of spectacular.

MONARCHS OF THE TUNDRA

Massive and graceful, ferocious and majestic, carnivorous and curious, polar bears are Churchill's most popular yet most misunderstood creatures. They're resilient enough to spend winters hunting ring seals on the frozen ocean, and smart and strong enough to get them through meter-thick ice. They return to land when the ice melts, where they wait and mate, then the females give birth in dens while the males head north waiting for the ice to reform. Churchill is right on their migration path.

Each year, polar bears arrive sooner, stay later and are more plentiful near town – climate change figures prominently in the reasons for this. Shorter winters mean the polar ice melts sooner and freezes later, making the hunting season shorter. About 900 of the world's roughly 20,000 polar bears live in the Churchill area, a population considered the most endangered as it lives the furthest south.

Weighing upwards of 600kg (those bears you saw roadside in the south rarely top 300kg), polar bears have razor-sharp claws and can run 50km/h. They are naturally curious and will attack humans out of hunger or boredom. Read Parks Canada's *You Are in Polar Bear Country* guide and heed the Polar Bear Alert signs around town. Those warning gunshots heard around the clock are the polar-bear patrols in action.

porches allow you to get good views of the marauding bears.

Great White Bear Tours
ADVENTURE TOUR

(☑ 866-765-8344, 204-487-7633; www.greatwhitebeartours.com; 266 Kelsey Blvd; from $400 per day; ⊙ Oct & Nov) Uses tundra coaches but only operates day tours; guests sleep in town.

Lazy Bear Lodge
ADVENTURE TOUR

(☑ 866-687-2327, 204-663-9377; www.lazybearlodge.com; 3-night fall tour from $3200) Has liveaboard tundra coaches; also operates multiday expeditions to study belugas and polar bears in the summer.

Tundra Buggy Adventure
ADVENTURE TOUR

(☑ 800-663-9832, 204-949-2050; www.tundrabuggy.com; 124 Kelsey Blvd; tours $2500-9000; ⊙ Oct & Nov) Longer overnight trips assemble caravans of tundra vehicles into mobile camps, complete with cabins and common areas. A manic one-day tour from Winnipeg costs $1500.

Land & Sea Tours

Several outfits offer land tours of the area in summer. These typically take in Cape Merry, CNSC and the disused missile site plus novelties such as a crashed plane and a grounded ship. The cost averages $75 for several hours and you may well see a bear or two.

Sea North Tours
ADVENTURE TOUR

(☑ 204-675-2195; www.seanorthtours.com; 39 Franklin St; tours from $105; ⊙ Jul & Aug) Summer beluga whale tours use a custom viewing boat, Zodiac inflatables and kayaks. Belugas are naturally curious and will be as curious about you as you are about them. You can even go snorkeling with pods of these gentle, 4m-long creatures. Many trips include a visit to Fort Prince of Wales.

Lazy Bear Lodge
ADVENTURE TOUR

(☑ 866-687-2327, 204-675-2869; www.lazybearlodge.com; 313 Kelsey Blvd; tours from $135; ⊙ Jul & Aug) Summer day tours include kayaking with belugas.

Nature 1st
WALKING TOUR

(☑ 204-675-2147; www.nature1sttours.ca; tours from $85; ⊙ Jun-Aug) Hiking, trekking and birding are combined in various nature tours that explore the four distinct ecosystems around Churchill.

Churchill Wild
ADVENTURE TOUR

(☑ 204-377-5090, 866-846-9453; www.churchillwild.com; multiday tours from $8000; ⊙ Jul-Oct) This outfit has remote lodges you reach from Churchill by float plane and boat. The highlight are their walks that get close to bears, which are otherwise oblivious.

🛏 Sleeping

Rates rise dramatically in polar-bear season when demand is high and people book a year in advance. Group cancellations do occur, so a lodge *may* get an opening. Don't expect luxury in Churchill, but you will be comfortable and all places are walkable and central. Camping is generally not possible as there are rules against feeding yourself to the bears.

Tundra House HOSTEL $

(☑204-675-8831; www.tundrainn.com; 51 Franklin St; dm/r from $35/80; ☺Dec-Sep; ☎) A much-needed addition to Churchill, this basic hostel is in a house that serves as a dorm for workers during peak polar bear season. But other times you can grab a bunk bed or private room at rates better than elsewhere in town. Bored? Try to find similarities in the polyglot furnishings.

Tundra Inn MOTEL $$

(☑800-265-8563, 204-675-2850; www.tundrainn.com; 34 Franklin St; r from $135, bear season from $235; @☎) The 31 motel-style rooms are large and comfortable and have fridges and microwaves. There's a laundry and shared kitchen with cereal and toast available in the morning.

Polar Inn MOTEL $$

(☑204-675-8878; www.polarinn.com; 153 Kelsey Blvd; r incl breakfast from $120, bear season from $200; ☎) Basic motel-style units come with fridges. There are also studios with small kitchens and full apartments.

✖ Eating & Drinking

Caribou and/or musk ox appear on many menus, especially those geared toward tour groups. Definitely seek out Arctic char, a delicious local fish that is like a cross between salmon and trout.

★Gypsy's Bakery CANADIAN $$

(☑204-675-2322; 253 Kelsey Blvd; mains $7-25; ☺7am-9pm; ☎) The best place to eat in Churchill. Luscious baked goods await in display cases and you can order from a full cafeteria-style menu. The breakfasts, sandwiches, burgers and more are tops. Departing by train? Load up on takeout vittles here in lieu of the VIA Rail offerings.

Pier Bar BAR

(☑204-675-8807; Kelsey Blvd; mains $7-18; ☺noon-1am) The Seaport Hotel's attached bar (with terrace!) is popular with summer workers and most anyone looking for a beer. The adjoining **Reef Dining Room** has daily specials and an excellent burger.

🛍 Shopping

Arctic Trading Company ARTS & CRAFTS

(☑204-675-8804; www.arctictradingco.com; 141 Kelsey Blvd; ☺9am-6pm Mon-Sat) Has locally made carvings, clothing, paintings and caribou-antler cribbage boards.

❶ Information

In summer it's war with the swarms of mosquitoes and black flies. Pack bug repellent with *at least* 30% DEET. Always keep warm clothing handy as it can get cold fast in summer. Heed all polar bear warnings.

Chamber of Commerce (☑204-675-2022; 211 Kelsey Blvd; ☺11am-3pm Mon-Sat Jul-Nov) Near the train station.

Everything Churchill (www.everythingchurchill.com)

Parks Canada (☑204-675-8863; train station) An essential first stop, but opening hours are variable.

Royal Bank (☑204-675-8894; La Verendrye Ave) One of several local ATMs.

Town of Churchill (www.churchill.ca)

❶ Getting There & Away

There is no road to Churchill; access is by plane or train only. A popular option is exploring Manitoba to Thompson and then catching a train or plane from there.

AIR

Calm Air (☑800-839-2256; www.calmair.com) serves Thompson and Winnipeg. Airfares can feel like the bite of a polar bear: round-trip from Winnipeg averages $1300, Thompson $750. On a few days each month the airline offers a few seats somewhat cheaper while on many days the seats cost much more.

Churchill Airport (☑204-675-8868) is 11km east of town. Most accommodations offer drop-off/pickup; a taxi is a pricey $20.

TRAIN

VIA Rail's Churchill train is slow; it runs two to three times per week and takes upwards of 45 hours from Winnipeg and 16 from Thompson (you can drive from Winnipeg to Thompson in seven). That said, there is a mesmerizing quality to the endless empty tracts of trees, muskeg and lakes from Thompson. You could fly one way and putter down the tracks the other. Try to get a sleeper compartment. Fares are one-way coach/sleeper from Winnipeg $185/470 and Thompson $65/230.

❶ Getting Around

Most locals walk or cycle around the compact town but you should proceed carefully and be bear aware. **Polar Inn** (☑204-675-8878; 15 Franklin St; per day $20) rents bicycles. **Tamarack Rentals** (☑204-675-2192; www.tamarackrentals.ca; 299 Kelsey Blvd) rents battered pickup trucks and SUVs and will meet you at the airport. Prices are $75 to $150 per day.

Arrange airport pickup with your lodging, otherwise you'll need to call a **taxi** (☑204-675-2517). Airport to town is $25, around town $9.

Saskatchewan

Best Places to Eat

➡ Calories (p549)

➡ Truffles Bistro (p549)

➡ Beer Bros. Gastropub & Deli (p538)

➡ Russell Up Some Grub (p543)

Best Places to Stay

➡ James (p548)

➡ Delta Bessborough (p548)

➡ Radisson Plaza Hotel Saskatchewan (p538)

➡ Elkwater Lake Lodge & Resort (p545)

Why Go?

Welcome to the 'Land of the Living Skies,' where proud locals are quick to correct the misconception that Saskatchewan is all flat. It's a place of rolling hills and coulees, sand dunes, rivers, forests and golden prairies stretching on forever beneath breathtakingly photogenic skies.

Friendly Saskatchewanians see more sunshine than any other province. Numbering one million, they're spread over small communities separated by vast swaths of land and sky, buffeted by long, harsh winters: no wonder they're happy to see you! If you're looking for impersonal big-city excitement, move on.

Come to Saskatchewan for awe-inducing landscapes and the warmth of her people. Get off the beaten track, run up a hill and hear your heartbeat pounding in the all-pervasive silence and enveloping isolation of the vast prairies. And don't forget your camera – studies in light and color don't get better than this.

When to Go
Saskatoon

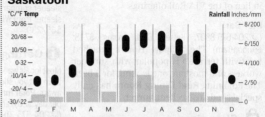

May Spring wildflowers paint the landscape and birdsong fills the air as life, post-winter, returns.

Jun–Aug Long sunny days draw happy locals to lakes, parks and patios.

Sep Crisp air, endless skies and dramatic fall colors herald the year's last harvests.

Saskatchewan Highlights

❶ Adjust your perspective from the breathtaking vantage points of **Cypress Hills Interprovincial Park** (p544).

❷ Step back in time aboard the Southern Prairie Railway and the Deep South Pioneer Museum in **Ogema** (p542).

❸ Marvel at the stunning architecture of Fransaskois **Gravelbourg** (p542) and contemplate a vanishing era.

❹ Enjoy a leisurely riverside ramble along Saskatoon's tranquil **Meewasin Trail** (p545).

❺ Remember the brave Métis revolutionaries at **Batoche** (p552).

❻ Hear the rustling of the long grass and the thunder of the bison (if you can find them) at **Grasslands National Park** (p543).

> ### SASKATCHEWAN FAST FACTS
>
> ➡ Population: 1,034,000
>
> ➡ Area: 586,561 sq km
>
> ➡ Capital: Regina
>
> ➡ Quirky fact: Hoodies are known throughout the province as 'bunny hugs' and no one's really sure why

History

For over 10,000 years, the region was populated by the Cree, Dene and Assiniboine people. In 1690, Henry Kelsey of the Hudson's Bay Company became the first European to approach these native cultures to buy furs. In 1774 a permanent settlement was established northeast of Saskatoon.

The Europeans demanded land, often resulting in bloody conflicts. As more Europeans arrived, tensions increased. In 1865 an estimated 60 million wild bison roamed Saskatchewan, providing food and materials for clothing and shelter for the Aboriginals. In one short decade, mass slaughter by homesteaders and hunters slashed that population to just 500: a staggering ecocide with drastic repercussions. By 1890 most Aboriginals lived on reserves.

Saskatchewan became a province in 1905. On June 30, 1912, its young capital Regina was decimated by Canada's deadliest tornado, which destroyed 500 buildings and claimed 28 lives.

Each of the two world wars and the Great Depression contributed to a meteoric increase in wheat production. Farming continues to be the lifeblood of the province, although massive natural gas and oil reserves and an increase in immigration help stimulate the economy. Saskatchewan is the world's top producer of potash and one of the largest exporters of uranium.

Land & Climate

Short, warm summers are ideal for traveling: days are long and nights are cool. Don't be fooled into thinking Saskatchewan's scenic beauty is limited to the mesmerizing tableau of grain and sky you whiz past as you traverse Hwy 1. If you're coming from other parts of Canada, you'll be interested in exploring the south, with its unique and contrasting scenery. The north's boreal forests, untouched wilderness and pristine lakes echo other provinces, but offer the perfect place to get off the grid.

Photographers will delight in watching summer storms roll in: the azure-blue sky turns dishwater gray, and if that gray turns to an eerie green, it can be a sign of imminent, significant hail. Southern Saskatchewan frequently produces supercell thunderstorms – several tornadoes touch down each year. Pay attention to weather forecasts when traveling large distances.

Winter can arrive in October and stay finger-numbingly cold (down to as low as -40°C) until April; it doesn't always snow buckets, but it can snow early and it does stick around. The reason all those parking spaces have electrical outlets is so people can plug in their engine-block heaters.

Parks

Saskatchewan has two contrasting national parks. Prince Albert National Park (p552) in the north is a forested sanctuary of lakes, untouched land and wildlife. Outdoor activities such as canoeing, hiking and camping are at their shining best. Deep in the south, Grasslands National Park (p543) contains thousands of hectares of grasses, undulating hills, wildflower accents and oodles of solitude. Virtually absent of trees, it's a splendid place to appreciate the bigger picture.

There are also numerous provincial parks. Cypress Hills Interprovincial Park (p544), jointly managed with Alberta, has spectacular vistas, abundant wildlife and a unique microclimate.

Camping is available in most parks, and some have backcountry sites. Go to www.saskparks.net for information and bookings.

❶ Getting There & Around

Saskatchewan has long been somewhere people drive through to get someplace else. That's changing as the province builds steam as a destination in itself. Hwy 1 runs across the

> ### REGIONAL DRIVING DISTANCES
>
> **Saskatoon to Prince Albert National Park:** 230km
>
> **Saskatoon to Regina:** 260km
>
> **Regina to Cypress Hills:** 490km
>
> **Cypress Hills to Grasslands:** 410km

south passing through Regina, Moose Jaw and Swift Current. Hwy 16 cuts diagonally across the province.

It's almost impossible to get to know Saskatchewan without the freedom of four wheels: if you plan to explore, renting a 4WD or SUV is strongly advised. Many provincial roads are unpaved and major highways can be riddled with potholes after the winter melt; pay attention to these potential hazards and that of wild deer, elk and moose. Be sure to have enough fuel, music and munchies before you set out; townships are small and separated by significant distances. Roads cross into Montana and North Dakota in the USA.

If you are without your own wheels, **Greyhound Canada** (☑ 800-661-8747; www.greyhound.ca) operates bus services into Alberta, Manitoba and beyond. Within the province, **Saskatchewan Transportation Company** (STC; ☑ 800-663-7181; www.stcbus.com) buses serve around 290 communities. In summer, monthly all-you-can-ride passes for those under 26 are only $45.

There are no longer any passenger rail services within the province.

REGINA

POP 193,100

Bisected by the Trans-Canada Hwy (Hwy 1; Victoria Ave, at this point), the provincial capital is by default the primary destination of visitors to Saskatchewan. Although there's some heady rivalry with her handsome bigger brother, Saskatoon, 230km to the north, this prairie queen has come far since her days as a hunting ground for the Cree, who called her Wascana, or 'pile of bones.'

Leafy parks make the capital a pleasant place to be: the Wascana Centre and Victoria Park, presided over by the elegant Hotel Saskatchewan are great spots to sit and ponder. You can walk to most areas of interest, including the gentrified Cathedral Village and the up-and-coming Regina Warehouse District, which oozes potential – especially at beer o'clock.

Regina's capital status and ties to transportation have given rise to some satisfying restaurants, bars and comfortable accommodations. These and location combined make Regina a good base from which to explore southern Saskatchewan and an appropriate place for a sojourn as you cross the Canadian interior.

❶ TOURIST INFO

Tourism Saskatchewan (☑ 877-237-2273; www.tourismsaskatchewan.com) will send out excellent maps and guides and has info centers near the provincial borders on Hwys 1 and 16. Tourist offices in larger towns have province-wide info as well.

◉ Sights & Activities

Wascana Centre   PARK

The geographic and cultural center of Regina, this sprawling public nature haven has miles of lakeside walking trails and is home to the Royal Saskatchewan Museum, Saskatchewan War Memorial and Saskatchewan Science Centre. Public events and celebrations are held by Wascana Lake's clear waters, which mirror such vistas as the stunning Provincial Legislature building and the Spruce Island bird sanctuary. Park residents include mink, hare, beaver and the occasional moose.

★ Provincial Legislature   NOTABLE BUILDING

(☑ 306-787-2376; Legislative Dr; ⊘ 8am-9pm) **FREE** Escaping significant damage from the devastating tornado in its year of completion (1912), the arresting 'Leg,' nestled in Wascana Centre's leafy embrace, stands as a proud symbol to the people of Regina. Ponder the rich marble and ornate carvings of this lavish example of beaux-arts architecture on free half-hourly tours or just play frisbee out front on the Great Lawn.

Royal Saskatchewan Museum   MUSEUM

(☑ 306-787-2667; www.royalsaskmuseum.ca; 2445 Albert St; suggested donation adult/child $6/3; ⊘ 9.30am-5pm) The Royal provides a great insight into the people and geography that make up Saskatchewan. Three galleries focus on earth and life sciences and aboriginal history. Prairie dioramas tell the story of the native flora, fauna and cultures that lived off the harsh land. Tipis, dinosaurs and deer all make an appearance.

MacKenzie Art Gallery   GALLERY

(☑ 306-584-4250; www.mackenzieartgallery.ca; 3475 Albert St; admission by donation welcomed; ⊘ 10am-5:30pm Mon-Sat, noon-5:30pm Sun) This gallery features a permanent outdoor sculpture garden, grazed by Joe Fafard's famed bronzed cows, and keeps things fresh with rotating and special exhibitions primarily

Regina

concerned with historical and contemporary Canadian art.

Saskatchewan Science Centre   MUSEUM
(☎306-522-4629; www.sasksciencecentre.com; 2903 Powerhouse Dr; adult/child $9/7, with IMAX feature $19/15; ☺9am-6pm Mon-Fri, 10am-6pm Sat & Sun) Science class was never this much fun! Try your hand at scoring a goal against a virtual goalkeeper, blow bubbles the size of a car or discover the secret to burping. Hands-on and a hit with kids, the center has an IMAX theater and an observatory.

RCMP Heritage Centre   MUSEUM
(☎306-522-7333; www.rcmpheritagecentre.com; 5907 Dewdney Ave W; adult/child $10/6; ☺11am-5pm) Exhibits chart the past, present and future of the iconic Canadian Mounties. This is also part of the RCMP (Royal Canadian Mounted Police) training center: check out the jutting jaws at the Sergeant Major's Parade.

Saskatchewan Sports Hall of Fame & Museum   MUSEUM
(☎306-780-9232; www.sshfm.com; 2205 Victoria Ave; adult/child $5/2; ☺10am-4.30pm Mon-Fri) With an emphasis on grassroots athletes,

Regina

⊚ Sights	
1 Royal Saskatchewan Museum	B4
2 Saskatchewan Sports Hall of Fame & Museum	B3
3 Wascana Centre	B5

🛏 Sleeping	
4 DoubleTree by Hilton	C3
5 Dragon's Nest B&B	A4
6 Holiday Inn Express	C2
7 Radisson Plaza Hotel Saskatchewan	B3
8 Wingate by Wyndham	C2

🍴 Eating	
9 Beer Bros. Gastropub & Deli	C2
10 Green Spot Cafe	C2
11 Italian Star Deli	D3

12 La Bodega	A4
13 Memories Fine Dining	C3
14 Michi	C2
15 Peking House	C2

🍷 Drinking & Nightlife	
16 Bushwakker Brewpub	B1
17 Casino Regina	C1
18 Cathedral Free House	A3
19 O'Hanlon's	C3
20 Outside Nightclub	C3
21 Pure Ultra Lounge	C1

🎭 Entertainment	
22 Globe Theatre	C2
23 Regina Public Library Film Theatre	B2
24 Saskatchewan Roughriders	A2

this museum tells the story of over 480 of the province's sporting heroes.

Wascana Canoe Kayak Rentals WATER SPORTS
(☎ 306-757-2628; www.wascanacanoekayak-rentals.com; Wascana Marina Rd; canoe/kayak/pedal boat rentals per hr $15/10/15; ☺ noon-8pm May-Sep) In the grounds of Wascana Centre at the Wascana Marina you'll find this seasonal provider of canoes, kayaks and pedal boats for use on Wascana Lake.

🎉 Festivals & Events

Regina comes alive in the warmer months. For a listing of events, go to www.tourism-regina.com/events.

First Nations University of Canada Pow-wow CULTURE
(www.fnuniv.ca/pow-wow) Held over a weekend in the spring, dancers from around North America converge for this, the largest and longest running celebration of First Nation's culture in the province.

Queen City Ex FIESTA
(☎ 306-781-9200; www.thequeencityex.com; ☺ Jul-Aug) Saskatchewan's favorite festival; people dress up in pioneer garb for six days of concerts, pancake breakfasts, amusement-park rides, a beard-growing contest and parades. Dates vary year to year – check the website for details.

🛏 Sleeping

There's plenty of decent accommodations in Regina, though rooms tend to be expensive.

Victoria Ave east of town has no shortage of highway motels.

DoubleTree by Hilton HOTEL $$
(☎ 306-525-6767; www.doubletree.hilton.com; 1975 Broad St; d from $169; ❄ @ 🖥) The former Regina Inn Hotel is set to be re-introduced to the world in late 2013 as the completely remodelled DoubleTree by Hilton. This brand-new product is sure to be the talk of the town. Check the website for the latest updates and pricing.

Homesuites by d3h MOTEL $$
(☎ 306-522-4434; www.homesuites.ca; 3841 Eastgate Dr; r incl breakfast $149-195) We love the practicality and good design of this new-in-2012 property outside town (but near a bunch of facilities and perfect if you're passing through). A variety of roomy suites include kitchenettes, heavy doors and bedding otherwise found in luxury hotels.

Dragon's Nest B&B B&B $$
(☎ 306-525-2109; www.dragonsnest.ca; 2200 Angus St; s/d incl breakfast from $100/125, with shared bathroom $70/85; ❄ ❄ 🖥) This stylish six-room B&B is run by a feng shui consultant, so it's all lined up for optimum comfort. Included breakfasts are country fresh and hearty.

Wingate by Wyndham HOTEL $$
(☎ 306-584-7400; www.wingatebywyndhamregina. com; 1700 Broad St; r incl breakfast from $169; ❄ @ 🖥) The central Wingate offers good-value, large and comfortable guest rooms decorated in an attractive pastel palette.

Holiday Inn Express HOTEL $$

(☑306-667-9922; www.hiexpress.com; 1907 11th Ave; r incl breakfast from $150; ✳@⊛) This low-rise hotel has 78 basic but comfortable rooms, a short walk to everything Regina has to offer.

Radisson Plaza Hotel
Saskatchewan HOTEL $$$

(☑306-522-7691; www.hotelsask.com; 2125 Victoria Ave; r from $219; ⊝✳@⊛) Overlooking Victoria Park, this 1927 former grand dame of the Canadian National Railroad maintains a lofty presence. There's a degree of wow-factor upon entry, but pricey rooms are on the small side. The period decor won't suit everybody. If not to spend the night, stop by to enjoy the old-world charm of the Monarch's Lounge.

✗ Eating

Regina has plenty of decent restaurants located in the downtown core and on the Victoria Ave and Albert St arterials.

Italian Star Deli DELI $

(☑306-757-6733; www.italianstardeli.com; 1611 Victoria Ave; panini $2.25-8; ☺9am-5pm Tue-Sat) Since 1966, this authentic Italian deli has brought the flavors of Europe to the prairies. Folks flock for the delicious panini and you're well advised to follow suit – they're great value and bursting with freshness. Perfect for your picnic basket.

13th Ave Coffee House CAFE $

(☑306-522-3111; www.13thavecoffee.com; 3136 13th Ave; sandwiches from $7.50, rice bowls $12; ☺8.30am-9pm Tue-Sat; ✎) 'Healthy, fresh and local' is the mantra of this Cathedral Village anchor. Come for your fix of locally roasted, fair-trade Java and get your daily dose of quinoa, free radicals and vitamins as well. Carnivores aren't excluded, but vegetarians will feel right at home.

Green Spot Cafe VEGETARIAN $

(☑306-757-7899; www.greenspotcafe.ca; 1838 Hamilton St; ☺7am-5pm Mon-Fri, 8am-3pm Sat; ✎) This 100% vegetarian cafe features a downtown location and a menu of healthy treats chock-full of good karma.

★ Beer Bros. Gastropub & Deli PUB, DELI $$

(☑306-586-2337; www.beerbros.ca; 1821 Scarth St; starters $6-18, mains $12-24; ☺11:30am-11pm Mon-Thu, to 1am Fri & Sat, 2-9pm Sun) It's hard not to love this clever pub in the heritage Northern Bank building for matching food with beer! Think hearty – cheese, carbs and lots of calories – but with a gourmet bent. Favorites include 'beerogies and sausage,' 'seafood mac and cheese' and 'cheddar ale soup.' Great value takeout salads, soups and sandwiches are available from the deli.

La Bodega TAPAS $$

(☑306-546-3660; www.labodegaregina.com; 2228 Albert St; tapas from $6, large plates $12-25; ☺11am-2am) Ambience is the word of the day, where a fantastic tri-level patio wraps around a huge tree: the liveliest of all treehouses! This style of dining is best enjoyed with at least one dining companion. Great for weekend brunch.

Spices of Punjab INDIAN $$

(☑306-585-8882; www.spicesofpunjab.com; 320 Victoria Ave E; lunch & dinner buffet $15; ☺11:30am-2:30pm & 4:30-9:30pm Mon-Thu, 11am-9:30pm Fri & Sat, from 1pm Sun) There's a full à la carte menu with vegetarian options, but the best value is in the excellent lunch and dinner buffet, plentifully refreshed with favorites like dahl, butter chicken and Goan fish curry.

Michi JAPANESE $$

(☑306-565-0141; www.michi.ca; 1943 Scarth St; sushi & small plates $4.50-10, dinner sets $10-25; ☺noon-2:30pm & 5-9pm Tue-Sat) Opposite Victoria Park, Michi has been serving real-deal Japanese cuisine for over 10 years. A range of staple dishes are represented well, from a variety of sushi, hand-rolls and chunky sashimi to tempura, *donburi* and delicious *gyoza* dumplings.

Peking House CHINESE $$

(☑306-757-3038; www.pekinghouse.ca; 1850 Rose St; mains $11-50; ☺11am-2pm & 4-10pm Mon-Fri, 4-11pm Sat & Sun) Authentic Cantonese cuisine can be found at this affable downtown Chinese restaurant. Peking duck fans must order a day in advance at $50 a pop. Otherwise, familiar Canadian-Chinese specials are good value.

Memories Fine Dining MODERN CANADIAN $$$

(☑306-522-1999; www.memoriesdining.com; 1717 Victoria Ave; mains $19-40; ☺11am-10pm Mon-Fri, 5-10pm Sat & Sun) Don't be put off by the 'fine dining' bit if you're travelling without your tux – in this context the 'fine' speaks more for the food than the smart-casual ambience. The extensive menu is executed with aplomb and accompanied by an impressive wine selection.

🍸 Drinking & Nightlife

Albert St in the center is a good place to carouse. Dewdney Ave, just north of downtown in the it'll-get-there-one-day up-and-coming Warehouse District, has a fun strip of pubs and clubs. Regina has some fantastic patios, but smoking is prohibited.

⭐ Bushwakker Brewpub PUB
(☎306-359-7276; www.bushwakker.com; 2206 Dewdney Ave; ⊙11am-late Mon-Sat) In an impressive 1913 warehouse, Bushwakker is reason enough to cross the tracks to the Warehouse District. There's live music many nights, but the real draw is the beer: scores of house brews in which to delight.

O'Hanlon's PUB
(☎306-566-4094; 1947 Scarth St; ⊙11.30am-late) O'Hanlon's has a grungy Irish pub vibe and a patio overlooking Victoria Park and Hotel Saskatchewan. It's the kind of place where you can find yourself eating, drinking and babbling on until the wee hours.

Cathedral Free House BAR
(☎306-359-1661; www.thefreehouse.com/cathedral; 2062 Albert St; ⊙11am-late Mon-Sat, noon-10pm Sun) The huge back deck is the place to be on a balmy night. Pub food is served late and goes beyond the usual fish-and-chips cliché. Live music includes acoustic early in the week, morphing to hard-edged stuff at weekends.

Pure Ultra Lounge CLUB
(☎306-543-7475; www.pureultralounge.ca; 2044 Dewdney Ave; ⊙10pm-late Sat) In the Warehouse District, Regina's premier nightclub heaves every Saturday night and some Fridays.

Outside Nightclub GAY
(☎306-569-1995; www.glcrclub.ca; 2070 Broad St; ⊙5pm-late) Ironically occupying a former church building, Regina's only gay bar/club is a welcoming, straight-friendly affair, run by a members co-op. The awesome rough-around-the-edges, multilevel space has an outdoor patio. Come along to meet the friendly locals – you're bound to turn some heads.

Casino Regina CASINO
(☎306-565-3000; www.casinoregina.com; 1880 Saskatchewan Dr; ⊙9am-4am) In a sad commentary on priorities, the beautiful old train station has been converted into a vast casino, where you can derail your budget on games of chance.

☆ Entertainment

Conexus Arts Centre THEATER
(☎306-565-4500; www.conexusartscentre.ca; 200A Lakeshore Dr) Home of the symphony orchestra and venue of choice for touring musicians and shows, the Arts Centre vaguely resembles vintage Saskatchewan grain elevators.

Globe Theatre THEATER
(☎306-525-6400; www.globetheatrelive.com; 1801 Scarth St;) The local cast of players puts on contemporary theatrical presentations in the round. Constantly garnering rave reviews, the Globe is a recognized cultural arts institution in Regina.

Regina Public Library Film Theatre CINEMA
(☎306-777-6027; www.reginalibrary.ca; 2311 12th Ave; adult/child $6/3) On the lower level of the Regina Public Library, the Repertory Cinema screens arthouse films, hot docs and more, at back-to-the-good-ol'-days prices.

Trial of Louis Riel THEATER
(☎306-728-5728; www.rielcoproductions.com; ⊙Jul & Aug) Actual transcripts from Riel's 1885 trial – which resulted in his hanging – are the basis of this, Canada's second-longest-running play, first performed in 1967. Performances take place in the Shumiatcher Theatre, at the MacKenzie Art Gallery (p535) over three weeks in the summer. Check the website for details.

McNally's Tavern LIVE MUSIC
(☎306-522-4774; www.mcnallystavern.ca; 2226 Dewdney Ave; ⊙5pm-late Tue-Sat) This is the pub to hit if you're looking for live entertainment. From bands to karaoke to open mike and jam nights, there's something live every night it's open.

Saskatchewan Roughriders FOOTBALL
(☎888-474-3377, 306-525-2181; www.riderville.com; Mosaic Stadium, 2940 10th Ave; ⊙Jun-Nov) Not to be confused with the Ottawa Rough Riders, the Green Riders, as they're known to legions of rabid locals, have achieved cult status within the Canadian Football League (CFL). Don't underestimate how crazy things get in this town, for this team.

Regina Pats

HOCKEY

(☑306-543-7800; www.reginapats.com; Brandt Centre, 1700 Elphinstone St; ⊙Sep-Mar) The younger, tougher, more eager players of the Western Hockey League (WHL) make for an exciting brand of hockey. It's about 3km west of the center.

❶ Information

Free wi-fi is available throughout much of the downtown and Cathedral Village areas.

Main Post Office (☑866-607-6301; 2200 Saskatchewan Dr)

Prairie Dog (www.prairiedogmag.com) Feisty, fun and free biweekly newspaper with good entertainment listings.

Regina General Hospital (☑306-766-4444; 1440 14th Ave; ⊙24hr) Emergency room.

Regina Public Library – Central Branch (☑306-777-6000; 2311 12th Ave; ⊙9:30am-9pm Mon-Thu, to 6pm Fri, to 5pm Sat, 1:30-5pm Sun; 🛜) Free internet access.

Tourism Regina (☑1-800-661-5099, 306-789-5099; www.tourismregina.com; 1925 Rose St; ⊙9am-5pm Mon-Fri) Useful local guides and maps.

❶ Getting There & Away

Regina International Airport (☑306-761-7555; www.yqr.ca; 5200 Regina Ave), 5km west of downtown, has services to major Canadian destinations and Minneapolis and Chicago in the US. Renting a car from airport branches of most major car-rental companies is the easiest way to get around.

Greyhound Canada (www.greyhound.ca) runs east to Winnipeg ($100, nine hours, two daily) and west to Calgary ($79, 11 hours, two daily). **STC** (☑306-787-3340; www.stcbus.com) runs buses in all directions, including to Saskatoon ($44, three hours, three daily). All depart from the revamped **bus station** (☑306-787-3340; 1717 Saskatchewan Dr).

❶ Getting Around

The airport is a 10-minute cab ride ($10) from downtown; there is no public transit service.
Regina Transit (☑306-777-7433; www.regina-transit.com; adult/child $2.50/2, day pass $7) operates city buses, most of which converge on 11th St downtown.

Metered street parking ($1 to $2 per hour, from 8am to 6pm) is limited to two-hour stays; there are many paid-parking garages.

Co-op Taxi (☑306-525-2727; www.cooptaxi-regina.com) comes when you call.

AROUND REGINA

Qu'Appelle Valley

The Qu'Appelle Valley's wide river and rolling hills highlight Saskatchewan's remarkable contrasts.

Heading northeast from Regina on Hwy 10, don't be afraid to get off the main road and explore. After 70km, pass through **Fort Qu'Appelle** and turn right on **Hwy 56** towards the village of **Lebret** and the beautiful fieldstone **Sacred Heart Church**, completed in 1925. Spin around and ponder the ominous **Stations of the Cross** and **Chapel on the Hill**. You can walk up there if you feel inspired. Otherwise, continue on the road until you see **Lebret Antiques** (☑306-322-5810; 36 Ellisboro Trail) on your left. Pop in and have a chat with the affable Roy Poitras; he might share some tales of the area's rich Métis history. Continuing on, you'll soon come to a left-hand turn. Follow this road until it reconnects with Hwy 10. Turn right here and continue on through the village of **Abernethy**, then south on Hwy 22. After 9km you'll reach **Motherwell Homestead National Historic Site** (☑306-333-2116; www.parkscanada.gc.ca/motherwell; adult/child $8/4; ⊙9am-5pm Jun-Aug), a fascinating early Saskatchewan farm where you can make hay with huge draft horses and meet characters dressed up in period costume. A small cafe serves homemade lunches.

Continue to follow the road until you reach provincial road 619. Turn left and follow it until you once again meet Hwy 56. A right-hand turn heads you back west and you'll soon find yourself in the little community of **Katepwa Beach**. There's a lovely grassy campground and swimming spot with walking trails, picnic areas and shady trees. If it's a sunny day, why not linger awhile at the **Main Beach Bar and Grill** (☑306-332-4696; mains from $9; ⊙noon-9pm). It's open year-round, serving cold beer and the best (and only) pub grub in town. There's a fantastic large patio overlooking the park and the lake. If you'd like to stay here longer still, **Sunday's Log Cabins** (☑306-783-7951; www.sundayslogcabins.com; cabins from $119; ⊙May-Oct) offers four handsome, nicely maintained cabins with all the comforts of home. They're in an almost beachfront setting, a hop, skip and jump from town and across the road from the park.

SOUTHERN SASKATCHEWAN

Along the Trans-Canada Hwy (Hwy 1) is iconic Saskatchewan, the sort of wide open prairie that country songs are written about. As you explore the rabbit warren of unpaved, lonely back roads, it's easy to feel divorced from modern life. It's not hard to imagine thousands of bison charging over a nearby hill, aboriginal villages in the valley or the North West Mounted Police (NWMP) patrolling the prairie on horseback. There is diversity among this immensity, with rolling grasslands, short sharp hills and badlands befitting a classic Western.

Moose Jaw

POP 33,617

Moose Jaw is a welcome island in a prairie sea, a rough diamond with surprising charm. From grassroots beginnings as a Canadian Pacific Railway outpost, the town grew steadily in size and infamy, earning a reputation for rebellion, corruption, brushes with the KKK and even slavery. In the days of US Prohibition, it was a haven for Al Capone and his gang, who used it as a base for smuggling whiskey across the border.

Today's Moose Jaw bears little resemblance to its wild past, although it has done well to memorialize the fascinating stories of less respectable days. It's also known as 'Little Chicago' for its well preserved art-deco buildings and colorful murals.

◉ Sights & Activities

Main St and the historic downtown should be your focus. Expect to spend a couple of hours wandering about.

Tunnels of Moose Jaw   TUNNELS
(☎306-693-5261; www.tunnelsofmoosejaw.com; 18 Main St; tours adult/child $15/8.50) Buried deep under the town's streets is a series of passages that have a tragic and fascinating history. Take a tour and learn about the hardship and discrimination heaped upon Chinese workers on their 'Passage to Fortune.' Fast-forward a few decades to make the 'Chicago Connection.' Al Capone is rumored to have visited Moose Jaw in the 1920s to oversee his bootlegging operation, masterminded in these very tunnels.

Western Development Museum   MUSEUM
(WDM; ☎306-693-5989; www.wdm.ca; 50 Diefenbaker Dr; adult/child $9/2.50; ⊗9am-5pm) If you can drive it, fly it, pedal it or paddle it, odds are you'll find an example of it at this branch of the WDM. Dedicated to transport within Saskatchewan, it has planes, trains, automobiles and even the odd wagon.

Yvette Moore Gallery   GALLERY
(☎306-693-7600; www.yvettemoore.com; 76 Fairford St W; ⊗10am-5pm) FREE Just west of Main St in a proud heritage building, this renowned local artist displays her evocative and hyper-realistic works portraying Saskatchewan and its people.

Temple Gardens Mineral Spa   SPA
(☎306-694-5055; www.templegardens.sk.ca; 24 Fairford St E; adult/child $8/7; ⊗10am-late) This modern complex houses the locally famous indoor-outdoor pool filled with steaming mineral water from deep below the prairie. A long list of treatments are available. Admission doubles Friday to Sunday. The annexed resort accommodations don't justify the hole they'll burn in your wallet.

☞ Tours

Over three dozen **murals** capturing tamer moments in Moose Jaw's history adorn walls around town. Download walking maps from www.tourismmoosejaw.ca. The **Moose Jaw Trolley Company** (☎306-693-8537; adult/child $12/10; ⊗May-Aug) runs tours from the visitors center.

🛏 Sleeping & Eating

Travelodge   MOTEL $$
(☎306-692-1884; www.travelodge.com; 45 Athabasca St E; d from $79; ✸🛜) Drive-up rooms in this compact downtown motel are spotlessly clean and feature widescreen TVs and free wi-fi.

Wakamow Heights   B&B $$
(☎306-693-9963; www.wakamowheights.com; 690 Aldersgate St; r incl breakfast $99-119; 🛜) In an elevated spot on the outskirts of town, this historical B&B has wonderful gardens and a variety of deliciously furnished rooms of differing color schemes.

Bobby's Place   PUB $
(☎306-692-3058; 63 High St E; mains from $9; ⊗11am-late Mon-Sat) Bobby's place is always busy and has been for years. Come for a beer on the patio or, as everyone else does, for the fabulous home-cooked meals that have

DON'T MISS

OGEMA

We almost want to keep this one to ourselves, but the locals insist we tell you about their fascinating hamlet and its two extraordinary attractions.

Ogema's **Southern Prairie Railway** (☑306-459-1200; www.southernprairierailway. com; Railway Ave; tours adult/child from $45/30; ☺ Jun-Sep) has been turning heads since its maiden voyage for the town's centenary in 2012. The station you see today was acquired from a farmer who'd been using it to store grain. In 2002, the townsfolk relocated it 280km to the site of the original Ogema station and then spent a decade painstakingly restoring it. The informative two-hour round-trip **Heritage Tour** chugs its merry way across the prairie to explore the abandoned Horizon grain elevator. Special tours are held throughout the year including the occasional stargazing expedition.

Formed as early as 1977 from a desire to preserve the memories, stories and possessions of Ogema's forefathers, the unexpected **Deep South Pioneer Museum** (☑306-459-2904; www.deepsouthpioneermuseum.com; ☺10am-5pm Sat & Sun) is an astounding collection of over 30 preserved buildings, along with farming equipment, scores of vehicles and a huge volume of historic artifacts. Townsfolk young and old have contributed to the creation and maintenance of this unique memorial site. The authenticity of its lovingly preserved buildings and the openness with which they are presented is extra ordinary. From **Smiths Store** to the **Edgeworth School**, you'll visit a place lost in time, but far from forgotten: you'll almost feel the spirits of Ogema's ancestors as you tread from room to room.

been perfected over two decades. The home-breaded chicken fingers are tender, juicy and finger lickin' good.

Veroba's Family Restaurant DINER $
(☑306-693-5943; 28 Fairford St W; meals from $7; ☺7am-8pm) This family business understands what eggs *over medium* means. The best breakfast in town includes amazing hash browns and brilliant crispy bacon. Veroba's had been in business for years and were forced out of early retirement into a new location because their customers complained so much over the fact that they'd closed.

ℹ Information

Visitors Centre (☑866-693-8097; www.tourismmoosejaw.ca; Thatcher Dr E at Hwy 1; ☺9am-4.30pm) Look for the huge anatomically correct moose statue.

ℹ Getting There & Away

STC (www.stcbus.com) runs buses to Regina ($17, one hour, two to three daily) from the downtown **bus station** (☑306-692-2345; 63 High St E).

Gravelbourg

About 190km southwest of Regina, delightful Fransaskois Gravelbourg is one of the last places you'd expect to find a little taste of Europe, adrift on a vast sea of prairie. The best way to explore this surprising destination is to do the **Heritage Walking Tour** found at www.gravelbourg.ca.

The undisputed centerpiece of this *très jolie* little town is the disproportionately large and beautiful **Our Lady of the Assumption Co-Cathedral** (☑306-648-3322; www.gravelbourgcocathedral.com), built in 1919 in a Romanesque and Italianate style. It was designated a national historic site in 1995. Enter if it's open and crane your neck to marvel at the Sistine Chapel–esque frescoes. Monsignor Maillard, who not only designed the chapel's interior and presided over the parish, painted the frescoes himself, from 1921 to 1931: an astonishing feat.

Catholics and history buffs will want to spend a night in the neighboring **Bishop's Residence** (☑888-648-2321; www.bishopsresidencebandb.com; 112 1st Ave W; r incl breakfast from $60). The handsome yellow-brick residence has been turned into a unique B&B with nine rooms, some with en suites and balconies.

The palatial building further down 1st Ave is the tiny community's elementary school, **École Élémentaire de Gravelbourg**: presently the headquarters of learning for 140 lucky kids.

Find out why all of these rich cultural properties are here in a visit to the **Gravelbourg and District Museum** (☑306-

2332; 300 Main St; admission $5; ☺9am-6pm Mon-Sat, noon-6pm Sun Jun-Sep, by appointment Oct-May), then pop in to see the friendly folks at the **Café Paris** (☑306-648-2223; 306 Main St; light lunches $6-12; ☺9am-6pm Mon-Sat) for a light lunch and a delicious milkshake.

If the Bishop's former digs aren't quite your style, the **Gravelbourg Inn** (☑306-648-3182; cnr Hwys 43 & 58; d from $70; ❋🛜) has neat and tidy motel rooms on the eastern approach to town.

Swift Current

Celebrating its centenary in 2014, Swift Current's main claim to fame is as a travelers' oasis on Hwy 1. The downtown area is about 3km south of the highway strip – follow the signs.

◉ Sights

Mennonite Heritage Village　　　MUSEUM
(☑306-773-7685; www.mennoniteheritagevillage.ca; 17th Ave SE; ☺2-7pm Fri-Sun Jul-Sep) This 1900s heritage village depicts a way of life unfamiliar to most. Many Mennonite and Hutterite communities still exist in the area. There's an annual watermelon festival in August.

Swift Current Museum and Visitors Centre　　　MUSEUM
(☑306-778-9174; www.tourismswiftcurrent.ca; 44 Robert St W; ☺9am-4pm Mon-Fri) **FREE** You'll want to make a stop to check out the massive woolly bison in this great little museum at the Swift Current visitors center.

Sleeping & Eating

A sensible place to stop before dipping down to Grasslands and Cypress Hills National Parks: there's a glut of highway motels here.

Home Inn & Suites　　　MOTEL **$$**
(☑306-778-7788; www.homeinnswiftcurrent.ca; 1411 Battleford Trail E; d incl breakfast from $159) Modern, tastefully decorated suites have kitchenettes, comfortable beds and room to move. There's an indoor pool with waterslide and a little day spa so you can relieve those tired driving muscles.

★**Russell Up Some Grub**　　　DINER **$$**
(☑306-778-4782; 12A 1081 Central Ave N; breakfast from $8, burgers from $13.50; ☺7am-3pm Mon-Wed & Sat, 6am-9pm Thu-Fri) Homestyle Mennonite meals like cheddar pierogies in sausage gravy, cranberry chicken, and a great selection of sandwiches, burgers and salads are reason enough to pull off the highway. A gluten-free menu, friendly staff and a spotlessly clean, bright dining room complete the picture.

Akropol Family Restaurant　　　GREEK **$**
(☑306-773-5454; 133 Central Ave N; mains $9-17; ☺11am-late Mon-Sat) This friendly Greek restaurant serves up traditional favorites like *gyros*, calamari and spanakopita. There's a lovely outdoor patio for when it's warm outside.

Miso House　　　ASIAN **$**
(☑306-778-4411; 285 N Service Rd W; mains $6-18; ☺11am-10pm Tue-Sun) Miso House has done

---

OFF THE BEATEN TRACK

VAL MARIE & GRASSLANDS NATIONAL PARK

Due south of Swift Current, you'll find the endearing hamlet of Val Marie, gateway to **Grasslands National Park** (www.parkscanada.ca/grasslands; admission free, primitive campsites $16). The park is a place of isolation and beauty, where treeless hills meet the endless sky. Heading south on Hwy 4 will bring you straight here. The road is in good condition until the junction of Hwy 13 at Cadillac, but deteriorates rapidly from this point: don't come without a 4WD.

The **visitors center** (☑306-298-2257; Hwy 4 & Centre St, Val Marie; ☺8am-4pm) is an essential port of call for advice on where to camp and how best to experience the full majesty of the park. Prepare well for expeditions and BYO shade – Grasslands is wild, isolated, treeless terrain and there's the potential for rattlesnake encounters. If you're lucky, you might catch a glimpse of the herd of resident bison.

If hardcore camping isn't your scene, how about a holy night in the **Convent** (☑306-298-4515; www.convent.ca; Hwy 4; r incl breakfast from $69)? Built in 1935, this former residential school has beautifully restored rooms with comfy beds, classic brickwork and lots of hardwood. Bathrooms are shared. There's even a confessional in case you break any vows.

a great job of bringing tasty sushi, Korean delights and Japanese bento boxes to this far-flung corner of the prairies.

🍷 Drinking & Entertainment

Living Sky Casino
CASINO

(📞306-778-5759; www.livingskycasino.ca; 1401 N Service Rd E; ⊙9am-2am) What better way to blow your travel budget than at this teeny casino? On the plus side, there's a nice little eatery inside and most hotels will give you a free play voucher to get you through the doors...just remember not to lose your shirt!

Lyric Theatre
THEATER

(📞306-773-6292; www.lyrictheatre.ca; 227 Central Ave N) Saskatchewan's oldest running theater celebrated its centenary in 2012: it's older than the city itself! Ongoing renovations to restore it to its former glory don't hamper the little joint's ability to showcase quality live music, theater and literary events year-round.

❶ Getting There & Away

Hwy 1 passes directly through Swift Current, about 170km east of the Alberta border. STC (www.stcbus.com) buses run a daily service to Saskatoon ($46, four hours).

Eastend

Isolated in southwest Saskatchewan, Eastend is tumbleweed quiet but not without charm. Nestled into a small valley, the town's few streets are lined with older buildings.

Eastend's claim to fame was for the 1994 discovery of one of the most complete *Tyrannosaurus rex* skeletons ever found. The **T-Rex Discovery Centre** (📞306-295-4009; www.trexcentre.ca; T-Rex Dr; admission by donation; ⊙10am-6pm) is a glitzy working lab carved into the hillside. There are a variety of tours available, along with dinosaur dig options if you feel the need to, er, bone up.

The **Eastend Historical Museum and Visitor Information** (📞306-295-4144; www. dinocountry.com; Red Coat Dr; ⊙9am-5pm Mon-Fri May-Oct) has more fossils and bones on display.

Cypress Hills Interprovincial Park

The contrasts within this isolated **interprovincial park** (📞306-662-4411; www.cypresshills. com) straddling the Alberta–Saskatchewan border, are arresting: endless prairies turn to undulating hills forested with cypress, harboring inland lakes. Elk, deer, moose and birdlife flourish in this fertile sanctuary. Each section has a distinctly different feel. We recommend exploring both to get the full perspective. The easiest way is to cross over on Hwy 1; the road traversing the park from the inside is often impassable. Roads leading to the Saskatchewan side of the park can be rough going.

Centre Block

Approaching from the east, the park entrance is 37km south of Hwy 1 on Hwy 21. The popular **Cypress Hills Campgrounds** (📞info 403-893-3833, reservations 877-537-2757; www.cypresshills.com; campsites $17-26) fill up over weekends and on holidays: 10 campgrounds accommodate over 400 campsites throughout the park. Surrounded by a dense thicket of cypress, the **Resort at Cypress Hills** (📞306-662-4477; www.resortatcypresshills. ca; Maple Creek; d/cabins from $97/115) has a bunch of comfortable motel rooms and great-value cabins. There's an on-site restaurant and a plethora of fun activities within the park.

The friendly outdoorsy folks at **Cypress Hills Eco-Adventures** (📞306-662-4466; www. zipcypresshills.ca; Ben Nevis Dr, Maple Creek; tours from $75; ⊙10am-6pm) will have you whizzing above the forest floor on Saskatchewan's only zipline canopy tour in next to no time. A bunch of other adrenaline-fueled activities including slacklining, rock-wall climbing and our fave, the treetop freefall, are available. Reservations are recommended.

Be sure to follow Bald Butte Rd to **Lookout Point** and **Bald Butte**. These are some of the highest elevations between the Rockies and Labrador and offer literally breathtaking views (if you run excitedly to the top) over the sea of prairies.

Western Block & Cypress Hills

Even more remote, the Western Block spills over into Alberta's Cypress Hills. Here amid the rolling landscape you'll find **Fort Walsh National Historic Site** (📞306-662-3590; www.parkscanada.ca/fortwalsh; adult/child $10/5; ⊙9:30am-5:30pm Jun-Sep). Established in 1875 and operational for eight years, this outpost had a small yet significant role in the history of the west. After the battle of Custer's Last Stand, Chief Sitting Bull and 5000 of his followers arrived in the area. The local Mounties moved their headquarters to Fort Walsh and maintained peaceful relations with the Sioux while they remained in Canada.

Camping in the Western Block is serene and backcountry. Be sure to check in with the **Centre Block Visitors Centre** (✉306-662-5411; ⊙9am-4pm Mon-Fri) when you arrive. Gap Rd, which connects to the Centre Block often deteriorates into a dodgy 4WD track. Otherwise, the gateway to the backcountry is 50km south of Hwy 1 on Hwy 271.

For a taste of the Hills' beauty and serenity with a few more creature comforts, cross the border to the **Elkwater Lake Lodge and Resort** (✉403-893-3811; www.elkwaterlakelodge.com; 401 4th St, Elkwater; d from $125; ❋ 🛜 ☀) in Alberta. In a dreamy lakeside spot, this secluded resort offers a variety of modern rooms and suites, some with jacuzzis and fireplaces. All are decorated in a style befitting the woodsy location. For delicious, original cuisine in this isolated location, sample the 'fresh air, fresh ideas, fresh ingredients' premise at **Bugler's Dining Room** (✉403-893-3033; www.elkwaterlakelodge.com; Elkwater Lake Lodge, 401 4th St Elkwater; mains $12-32; ⊙11am-2pm & 5-9pm): think tempura mushrooms sprinkled with bacon dust and white chocolate sauce (amazing!) and herb-roasted chicken with caramelized white wine sauce. Friendlier service you will not find.

Take a leisurely stroll around the lake and surrounding park – you might encounter elk as they feed at dusk. Outside of summer high season, the silence will only be interrupted by light birdsong and the sound of your thoughts.

SASKATOON

POP 222,200

Saskatchewan's pride, coined the 'Paris of the Prairies' by Canada's favorite homegrown rockers, the Tragically Hip, Saskatoon is full of hidden treasures. Don't be misled by first appearances – head into the downtown core and inner neighborhoods to get a sense of this surprisingly cosmopolitan city. The majestic South Saskatchewan River winds through the spacious downtown, enhancing the city's genteel air.

A rich tradition of farm-to-table cuisine is evident in Saskatoon's many restaurants and is complemented by some fantastic accommodations, including one of Canada's best boutique hotels. Leafy parks and rambling

riverside walks help you make the most out of long sunny, summer days: there are plenty of great spots to stop for a refreshing lager and a chinwag with some of the friendliest folks for miles.

Despite the town's legacy as an 1883 settlement by Ontario's bunch of anti-funsters the 'Temperance Colonization Society,' Saskatoon knows how to heat up cold winter days and short summer nights, with a proud heritage of local rock and country music and a vibrant live-music scene.

⊙ Sights

The river is crossed by a gaggle of attractive bridges including the rickety 1907 **Victoria Bridge** and the soaring 1908 **Canadian Pacific Railway Bridge**. The banks are lined with walking and cycling paths that link serene parks throughout the center including **Kiwanis Memorial Park** and the **Riverfront at River Landing**.

★**Western Development Museum**   MUSEUM
(WDM; ✉306-931-1910; www.wdm.ca; 2610 Lorne Ave S; adult/child $9/2.50; ⊙9am-5pm) About 4km from downtown, the flagship Saskatoon branch of the province's Western Development Museum is a faithful re-creation of Saskatoon the boomtown, c 1910. Inside Canada's longest indoor street, you can roam through the town's many buildings, from a dentist's office straight out of a horror film to the pharmacy whose walls are lined with hundreds of vintage concoctions. There are trains, tractors, buggies, sleighs and even a jail.

★**Meewasin Valley**   NATURE RESERVE
The Meewasin Valley, formed by the South Saskatchewan's wide swath through the center of town, is named for the Cree word for beautiful. Mature trees populate the riverbanks, while sections of the 60km **Meewasin Trail** extend from downtown paths, winding through forests and along the riverbank. Popular with walkers, cyclists and wandering travelers, picnic areas line the trails. Further north, **Mendel Island** is home to abundant wildlife.

Stop in at the informative **Meewasin Valley Centre** (✉306-665-6887; www.meewasin.com; 402 3rd Ave S; ⊙9am-5pm) FREE to learn about the river and the city it feeds. Guided and self-guided **walking tours** are available.

Saskatoon

Saskatoon

Ukrainian Museum of Canada MUSEUM

(☑306-244-3800; www.umc.sk.ca; 910 Spadina Cres E; adult/child $5/3; ☺10am-5pm Tue-Sat, 1-5pm Sun) This museum tells the story of Ukrainian immigration to Canada. With an emphasis on traditional clothing and contemporary artwork, it provides a good insight into the world of Ukrainian Canadians. Check out the gift shop for *pysanka* (decorated wooden eggs).

Mendel Art Gallery GALLERY

(☑306-975-7610; www.mendel.ca; 950 Spadina Cres E; ☺9am-9pm) FREE A short walk northeast along the river from the downtown area brings you to this vibrant gallery. With a focus on local artists and frequently changing exhibits, it's a pleasant addition to a stroll by the river. The conservatory has a Zen garden to quiet the soul.

Saskatchewan Railway Museum MUSEUM

(☑306-382-9855; www.saskrailmuseum.org; 202 Ave M S; adult/child $5/3; ☺10am-5pm May-Sep) The railroad opened up Saskatchewan to settlers and was a vital lifeline for getting grain to market. This museum shows how things were when rails, not roads, were the most important links in the province. It's west of the center on Hwy 7, then 2km south on Hwy 60.

Saskatchewan Forest Park & Zoo ZOO

(☑306-975-3395; www.saskatoonzoosociety.ca; 1903 Forestry Farm Dr; adult/child Apr-Oct $10/6, Nov-Mar free; ☺8am-5pm) About 9km from downtown, this pleasant little zoo, nestled among shaded picnic grounds, is great for kids. Animals are predominantly rescues or no longer able to survive in the wild, and residents include grizzly bears, alpacas, wolves, cougars and prairie dogs.

Wanuskewin Heritage Park PARK

(☑306-931-6767; www.wanuskewin.com; Penner Rd, off Hwy 11; adult/child $5.50/3.50; ☺9am-4:30pm) Devoted to the history of the province's first inhabitants, this riverside heritage park 17km north of Saskatoon, interprets a 7000-year history. At Wanuskewin (wah-nus-*kay*-win; Cree for 'seeking peace of mind') you can wander interpretive trails through the 116 hectares of grassy hills and valley meadows, discovering some of the 19 pre-contact sites. Invisible from the surrounding prairie, the untouched Opamihaw Valley is a spiritual and sacred place. Cultural dance performances take place on summer afternoons.

⛵ Tours

Shearwater Boat Cruises BOAT TOUR

(☑888-747-7572; www.shearwatertours.com; Spadina Cres E; adult/child from $18/12; ☺May-Sep) Open-top boats cruise the river all summer long. Ponder the bridges while enjoying a cool drink from the bar. The dock is behind the Mendel Art Gallery.

★☆ Festivals & Events

Sasktel Saskatchewan Jazz Festival MUSIC

(☑800-638-1211; www.saskjazz.com; ☺late Jun) Come show your soul patch at this jazzy festival, Saskatchewan's largest, at venues throughout town.

Taste of Saskatchewan FOOD

(☑306-975-3175; www.tasteofsaskatchewan.ca; Kiwanis Memorial Park; ☺mid-Jul) More than 30 local restaurants sell various high-caloric treats over the course of a week; performers help you work up an appetite.

PotashCorp Fringe Theatre Festival THEATER

(☑306-664-2239; www.25thstreettheatre.org; tickets from $10; ☺early-Jul) Rough-edged acts, music and avant-garde theater quirk up the streets and performance halls.

Shakespeare on the Saskatchewan THEATER

(☑306-652-9100; www.shakespeareonthesaskatchewan.com; tickets from $25; ☺Jul & Aug) Enjoy the best of the Bard in the great outdoors by the riverbank.

Saskatoon Ex CARNIVAL

(☑306-931-7149; www.saskatoonexhibition.ca; adult/child $15/11; ☺mid-Aug) Saskatoon comes alive for the Ex, with live music, racing pigs, chuck-wagon races and rides to reacquaint you with your fairy floss. Kids under 10 free.

🛏 Sleeping

Saskatoon has some great accommodation options downtown, although rates are higher than other parts of the country and there aren't many budget alternatives. Motels near the airport and Hwy 16 have cheaper rates.

Gordon Howe Campground CAMPGROUND $

(☑306-975-3328; www.saskatoon.ca; 1640 Ave P S; campsites/RV sites $20/31; ☺Apr-Oct; ＠) How cool to have a campground just 2km southwest of downtown! There are enough trees amid the 135 sites to give you a bit of privacy and sites are fairly large.

Inn on College
HOSTEL $

(☏ 306-665-9111; www.innoncollege.com; 1020 College Dr; ⊙ s/d from $60/70) Saskatoon's best value digs, this hostel-style property has clean, compact rooms that feel a little bit as if you're visiting relatives. It's a satisfying 15-minute walk across the bridge towards town.

★ Delta Bessborough
HOTEL $$

(☏ 800-268-1133, 306-244-5521; www.deltahotels.com; 601 Spadina Cres E; r from $169; ❄ @ ☎ ⊛) In the grand tradition of the famed Canadian railway hotels, the Bessborough lives up to the castle standard; it is the architectural exclamation point on the Saskatoon skyline. The refurbished interior blends modern pastel styling with grand post-deco architecture. Rooms and suites come in many shapes and sizes.

Hotel Senator
HOTEL $$

(☏ 306-244-6141; www.hotelsenator.ca; 243 21st St E; s/d $115/136; ❄ @ ☎) Dating from 1908, this well-maintained and updated hotel is creaky but cool. You can get a sense of the ornate past in the compact lobby. The pub downstairs is a good place to while away the night.

Park Town Hotel
HOTEL $$

(☏ 306-244-5564; www.parktownhotel.com; 924 Spadina Cres E; r from $149; ❄ @ ☎ ⊛) This recently refurbished hotel occupies prime real estate with park and river frontage. Ask for a river-view room, or splurge on a suite. There's a jolly ol' pub and liquor store on-site.

Holiday Inn
HOTEL $$

(☏ 306-986-5000; www.holidayinn.com; 101 Pacific Ave; d from $179) One of Saskatoon's better looking hotels outside and in, this flagship new Holiday Inn is right in the center. Original rooms are bright, airy and stylish. There's a fantastic penthouse suite with a grand piano and pool table.

Radisson
HOTEL $$

(☏ 306-665-3322; www.radisson.com; 405 20th St E; d from $179) Refurbished guest rooms in this fresh and funky hotel near the river wait to brighten your day. All have extra-comfy beds and large flatscreen TVs.

★ James
BOUTIQUE HOTEL $$$

(☏ 306-244-6446; www.thejameshotel.ca; 620 Spadina Cres E; d from $259) In the James, you've found one of Canada's finest boutique hotels. Exceptional, attentive service begins with your welcome to the property. From the deliciously minimalist yet sumptuous rooms featuring marble bathrooms, balconies and I've-never-slept-this-well-in-my-life bedding to the stylish cocktail bar, the James gets it right. Rates include parking and a gourmet breakfast daily.

✖ Eating

Across the handsome art-deco Broadway Bridge, the Nutana and Broadway neighborhoods boast the best selection of bars, pubs and restaurants.

Saskatoon Farmers Market
MARKET $

(☏ 306-384-6262; www.saskatoonfarmersmarket.com; cnr Ave B S & 19th St W; ⊙ 8am-2pm Sat) In the nascent River Landing area, this market has a small indoor area with stalls open daily throughout the year, but the main action is outside on summer Saturdays.

Yip Hong's Dim Sum
CHINESE $

(☏ 306-956-3375; 1501 8th St E; dim sum from $4; ⊙ 11:30am-10pm Wed-Mon) Although a little out of the way, Yip Hong's is one of the best joints for a good cheap feed of Hong Kong dim sum and spicy Szechuan cuisine. It's nothing fancy, but you're not here for the decor. Best enjoyed with friends.

Jake's on 21st
CAFE $

(☏ 306-373-8383; www.jakeson21st.ca; 307 21st St E; light meals from $9; ⊙ 8am-5pm Mon-Fri; ☎) Great coffee, a hipster vibe, lots of sandwiches, soups (think rosemary mushroom or beef and broccoli cheddar) and baked goods; deservedly popular for a weekday lunch.

Park Cafe
CAFE $

(☏ 306-652-6781; www.parkcafe.ca; 515 20th St W; mains $8-14; ⊙ 8am-4pm) For breakfasts to fuel your adventures, this unassuming joint serves up legendary morning platters: the hash browns are works of art.

Red Pepper
ASIAN FUSION $

(☏ 306-477-1977; 145 3rd Ave S; mains from $9; ⊙ 11am-9pm Mon-Sat) The hiss of hot woks competes with the chatter of patrons. Excellent pan-Asian food pours forth on plates older than you are.

Taverna Italian
ITALIAN $$

(☏ 306-652-6366; 291 21st St E; mains from $12; ⊙ 11am-10pm Mon-Fri, 5-10pm Sat & Sun) If it's good enough for Oprah, it's good enough for me: well, that's what the owners of this

MEACHAM

Almost 70km due east of Saskatoon you'll find the village of Meacham, where free-thinking, multidisciplinary artists and salt-of-the-earth farmers find themselves in quiet, harmonious coexistence. It's a great spot to get a sense of the silent golden prairies. There are two delightful one-woman galleries, **Harvest Moon** (⛯306-376-4700; www.harvestmoonantiques.ca; 401 3rd Ave) and **Hand Wave** (⛯306-376-2221; www.handwave.ca; 409 3rd Ave), a tiny by-appointment **museum**, and the professional **Dancing Sky Theatre** (⛯306-376-4445; www.dancingskytheatre.com; 201 Queen St), which has been producing rural Canadian plays since 1997. There's also an original Pool Saskatchewan **grain elevator**. Meacham is a relaxing half-day trip from Saskatoon or an easy detour en route to Manitou Springs.

downtown Italian joint, established in 1969 are hoping you'll decide. And if hearty, old-fashioned Italian favorites are what you fancy, you probably will.

2nd Ave Grill
CANADIAN $$

(⛯306-244-9899; www.2ndavegrill.com; 123 2nd Ave S; mains $12-36; ⏰11:30am-10pm Mon-Sat) This dark and somewhat club-like restaurant has a broad menu featuring steaks, burgers, pasta, salads and more: no surprises, but that's a compliment. The bar is a popular after-work spot.

Christie's Il Secondo
BAKERY $$

(⛯306-384-0509; 802C Broadway Ave; pizza from $15; ⏰8am-5pm Tue-Thu, to 9pm Fri & Sat) Fresh pizzas, daily-baked bread specials and delicious Italian-style filled sandwiches go like hotcakes in the new Broadway branch of this local institution, founded in 1932.

★ Calories
MODERN CANADIAN $$$

(⛯306-665-7991; www.caloriesrestaurants.com; 721 Broadway Ave; dinner mains $24-32; ⏰11am-10pm Mon-Thu, 10am-11pm Fri & Sat, to 4pm Sun) Menus change every six weeks or so at this classy yet casual affair, proud of its commitment to using local, organic ingredients in its creative cuisine. With an extensive wine list, a brunch menu to look forward to and a dessert counter that will make you drool, you're on a winner whatever time of day.

★ Truffles Bistro
FRENCH $$$

(⛯306-373-7779; www.trufflesbistro.ca; 230 21st St E; dinner mains $24-29; ⏰11:30am-2:30pm & 5pm-late Mon-Sat, 10am-2pm Sun) Smooth jazz sets up the classic ambience of this progressive French bistro. Fine wines accompany beautifully presented, delightfully simple preparations of *steak frites*, pork tenderloin and local Lake Diefenbaker trout.

🍷 Drinking & Nightlife

Broadway Ave in Nutana is the go-to place for nocturnal entertainment.

Yard & Flagon Pub
PUB

(⛯306-653-8883; ⏰11:30am-11pm) Hop on up to the rooftop deck and enjoy views of the historic Nutana neighborhood. Inside, the vintage feel continues with a well-worn 'ye olde tyme' shtick.

Spadina Freehouse
PUB

(⛯306-668-1000; www.thefreehouse.com/spadina; 608 Spadina Cres E; ⏰11am-midnight Mon-Sat) In summer the terrace out front will make you forget the architecture behind so you can focus on the swell selection of brews and live music that runs from soul to rock.

Hudsons Canadian Tap House
PUB

(⛯306-974-0944; www.hudsonstaphouse.com; 401 21st St E; ⏰11am-2am) This new branch of an increasingly popular Western Canadian franchise boasts a killer downtown location, atmospheric dark wood and a streetside patio made for people-watching or being seen.

Hose and Hydrant
PUB

(⛯306-477-3473; www.hoseandhydrant.com; 612 11th St E; ⏰11:30am-11pm) If you've never been to a pub in a converted fire station, now is the time. There are two great patios with a nice side-street outlook. The atmosphere is smokin'.

Diva's Nightclub
GAY

(⛯306-665-0100; www.divasclub.ca; 220 3rd Ave S; ⏰8pm-late Wed-Sun) Gay or straight, you don't have to be a diva to get your groove on at this straight-friendly gay bar...but it helps.

Tequila
CLUB

(⛯306-668-2582; www.tequilanightclub.ca; 1201 Alberta Ave; ⏰9pm-late Wed-Sat)

Twentysomethings come to Tequila to drink the eponymous tipple and d-d-d-dance the night away.

☆ Entertainment

Live Music

Amigo's Cantina   LIVE MUSIC
(☑306-652-4912; www.amigoscantina.com; 632 10th St E; ☺11.30am-late) Live music, Mexican munchies and a bunch of cold beers keeps Saskatoon powering through the weekend and beyond.

Lydia's Pub   LIVE MUSIC
(☑306-652-8595; 650 Broadway Ave; ☺11:30am-late) Broadway Ave's grungy watering hole packs 'em in when the joint is rocking. With 15 beers on tap and another 40 by the bottle, you'll find one you like eventually.

Bud's   LIVE MUSIC
(☑306-244-4155; 817 Broadway Ave; ☺11:30am-late) Classic blues and old-time rock and roll are the standards in this cowboy joint.

Credit Union Centre   CONCERT VENUE
(☑306-975-3155; www.creditunioncentre.com; 3535 Thatcher Ave) This is the local place for big-name concerts; it's 12.5km north of downtown.

Theater & Cinemas

Persephone Theatre   THEATER
(☑306-384-7727; www.persephonetheatre.org; 100 Spadina Cres E; ticket prices vary) This perennial theatrical standout has proud new quarters in the Remai Arts Centre at River Landing. Comedy, drama and musicals are all regulars.

Broadway Theatre   CINEMA
(☑306-652-6556; www.broadwaytheatre.ca; 715 Broadway Ave; adult/child $10/5) This historic Nutana cinema shows cult classics, arthouse films and occasional local live performances.

Saskatchewan Native Theatre Co   THEATER
(☑306-933-2262; www.sntc.ca; 914 20th St W; ☺Feb-Jun) Contemporary stage productions by Canadian Aboriginal artists highlight cultural issues through comedy and drama.

TCU Place   THEATER
(☑306-975-7777; www.tcuplace.com; 35 22nd St E) There's a variety of concerts, lectures, dance performances and plays held here through the year. The **Saskatoon Symphony** (☑306-665-6414; www.saskatoonsymphony.org; tickets $15-55) plays regularly.

Sports

Saskatoon Blades   HOCKEY
(☑306-975-8844; www.saskatoonblades.com; Credit Union Centre; ☺Sep-Mar) This WHL team plays a fast, rough and sharp style of hockey.

❶ Information

Frances Morrison Library (☑306-975-7558; www.saskatoonlibrary.ca; 311 23rd St E; ☺10am-9pm Mon-Thu, to 6pm Fri & Sat; ☏) Free internet access.

Main Post Office (☑800-267-1177; www.canadapost.ca; 215 Ontario Ave; ☺8am-5pm Mon-Fri)

Planet S (www.planetsmag.com) Irreverent and free biweekly newspaper with good entertainment listings.

Saskatoon City Hospital (☑306-655-8000; 701 Queen St; ☺24hr)

Tourism Saskatoon (☑306-242-1206, 800-567-2444; www.tourismsaskatoon.com; 202 4th Ave N; ☺8:30am-5pm Mon-Fri) The proudest and friendliest visitors center in the prairies.

❶ Getting There & Away

John G Diefenbaker International Airport (☑306-975-8900; www.yxe.ca; 2625 Airport Dr) is 5km northeast of the city, off Idylwyld Dr and Hwy 16. WestJet and Air Canada have services to major Canadian and a small selection of US cities. The friendly staff at **Enterprise** (www.enterpriserentacar.ca) can hook you up with hot wheels.

STC (www.stcbus.com) covers the province extensively from the **bus station** (☑306-933-8000; 50 23rd St E); buses head south to Regina ($44, three hours, three daily) and north to Prince Albert ($27, two hours, three daily). **Greyhound Canada** (www.greyhound.ca) runs buses to Winnipeg ($134, 12 hours, two daily), Calgary ($79, eight hours, one daily) and Edmonton ($79, seven hours, three daily).

Unlike in days past, Saskatoon's **train station** (Chappell Dr) sees little passenger traffic since the provincial railways wound down. It's 8km from downtown; the thrice-weekly VIA Rail *Canadian* leaves about midnight westbound and in the morning eastbound.

❶ Getting Around

A taxi to the airport costs between $15 to $20. A direct line to **Blueline Taxi** (☑306-653-3333; www.unitedgroup.ca) is available at the train station, with a trip downtown costing $20.

City buses (☑360-975-7500; www.saskatoon.ca; adult/child $2.75/1.65) converge on the transit hub of 23rd St E (between 2nd and 3rd Aves N).

LITTLE BEACHES ON THE PRAIRIE

Regina Beach

Kids play by Last Mountain Lake and picnickers enjoy the shady waterfront park at this idyllic summer spot. The **Blue Bird Cafe** (☑306-729-2385; 108 Centre St; mains from $7; ☉10am-8pm May-Sep) is an old-time classic with wooden floors and creaky screen doors. The fish and chips are legendary: lighter-than-air crispy batter on tender white fish. Follow that with an ice cream and you're set.

Manitou Beach

Near the town of Watrous, **Manitou Lake** (www.watrousmanitou.com) has Dead Sea–style waters full of minerals and salt. Soak in these reputedly healing waters at the **Manitou Springs Resort & Mineral Spa** (☑800-667-7672, 306-946-2233; www.manitousprings.ca; cnr Lake Ave & Watrous St; baths $11, r from $120). A stop at nearby **Danceland** (☑306-946-2743; www.danceland.ca; 511 Lake Ave; ☉May-Oct), an amazing dance hall caught in a vortex immune to the passing of time, is a must. Locals have been treading the boards here for over 80 years and they tell us Elvis, Buddy Holly, Glen Miller and Duke Ellington all played in its heyday.

SASKATCHEWAN YORKTON

Bike Doctor (☑306-664-8555; www.bikedoctor.ca; 623 Main St; rentals per day from $25) and **Saskatoon Bicycle Rentals** (☑306-270-9985; www.saskatoonbicyclerentals.com; cnr Ave A & Sonnenschein Way; rentals per hour from $10) do exactly that.

EASTERN SASKATCHEWAN

Yorkton

Yorkton (www.tourismyorkton.com) honors its strong Eastern European and Ukrainian roots at its large branch of the **Western Development Museum** (WDM; ☑306-783-8361; www.wdm.ca; Hwy 16 W; adult/child $6.50/2.50; ☉9am-5pm Mon-Fri, noon-5pm Sat & Sun). Indoor and outdoor displays tell the stories of settlers from over 50 countries who carved an existence out of the rough landscape.

The 16m-high dome at **St Mary's Ukrainian Catholic Church** (☑306-783-4549; 155 Catherine St) is a breathtaking work of art, painted from 1939 to 1941 by Stephen Meuhsh.

Canadian filmmakers and producers compete for Canada's Golden Sheaf Awards at the acclaimed **Yorkton Film Festival** (☑306-782-7077; www.goldensheafawards.com; ☉late May).

Veregin

A century ago in mother Russia lived a group of people called the Doukhobors. Oppressed because of their pacifist leanings and opposition to the Orthodox church, 7500 Doukhobors immigrated to Canada in 1899. Their benefactor? Leo 'War and Peace' Tolstoy.

Learn the whole story at the **National Doukhobor Heritage Village** (☑306-542-4441; www.ndhv.ca; Hwy 5; adult/child $5/1; ☉10am-6pm May-Sep), a living artifact of provincial life in the early 1900s. Against a backdrop of historic grain elevators, a compound of buildings furnished in period style are open to the public. If you're lucky, they'll be baking bread.

Veregin is about 70km northeast of Yorkton.

NORTHERN SASKATCHEWAN

North of Saskatoon, driving options funnel into one northern route as the scenery changes around you. Gone are the vast wheat fields of the south, replaced by rugged boreal forests and myriad lakes. There is a cultural shift up here, too: an independent spirit that carved a life out of the rugged landscape is still bubbling just below the surface.

The Battlefords

Linked by bridge across the North Saskatchewan River, Battleford and North Battleford (www.battlefordstourism.com) seem only slightly removed from a century ago when they embodied the hard-scrabble existence of early prairie settlers.

The re-created town at North Battleford's branch of the **Western Development Museum** (WDM; ☎306-445-8083; www.wdm.ca; Hwy 16, at Hwy 40; adult/child $9/2.50; ⏲9am-5pm daily, outdoor village closed Oct-May) is an insight into the immense amount of labor required by the pioneers to convert prairie to farmland. Walking along the boardwalk-covered streets and through the preserved houses, it's easy to imagine how hard life would have been. At the **Fort Battleford National Historic Site** (☎306-937-2621; www.parkscanada.ca/battleford; adult/child $4/2; ⏲May-Sep), costumed guides and **cannon firings** give life to the NWMP fort, built in 1876.

Art lovers will be enthralled by the **Allen Sapp Gallery** (☎306-445-1760; www.allensapp.com; 1 Railway Ave; admission by donation; ⏲11am-5pm). Sapp's work, depicting his Cree heritage, is a breathtaking mix of landscapes and portraits.

Motels and campgrounds abound in the Battlefords, which are 140km northwest of Saskatoon on the Yellowhead Hwy (Hwy 16).

Prince Albert National Park

The rough-edged but evocative riverside redbrick downtown of **Prince Albert** is the gear-up spot for trips further north. Stop in at the **Tourism and Convention Bureau** (☎306-953-4385; www.princealberttourism.com; 3700 2nd Ave W; ⏲9am-5pm) for the lowdown on exploring this former fur-trading post, settled as early as 1776.

About 90km further north, **Prince Albert National Park** (☎306-663-4522; www.parkscanada.ca/princealbert; adult/child $8/4) is a jewel in the wild. Just when you thought the vast prairie would never end, the trees begin, signaling the beginning of the vast boreal forest. This park puts the 'wild' back into 'wilderness', with expanses of untracked land, lakes and rivers to be explored. Do so on foot or by canoe, or just chill on a beach. The trek to **Grey Owl's cabin** (a 20km hike) is unforgettable.

The quaint outpost of **Waskesiu** is your base for exploration within the park. The **Chamber of Commerce** (☎306-663-5410; www.waskesiulake.ca; 35 Montreal Dr; ⏲9am-5pm May-Sep) and park **visitors center** (☎306-663-4522; 969 Lakeview Dr; ⏲8am-8pm May-Sep) can help with accommodations. There are many campgrounds, including the wooded **Beaver Glen**. Outside the western border of the park, **Sturgeon River Ranch** (☎306-469-2356; www.sturgeonriverranch.com; Big River; camping expeditions per person from $500) is regarded for its nature focus and horseback rides (from $100 per person) into the wilderness.

For a little bit of luxury, consider the sprawling **Elk Ridge Resort** (☎306-663-4653; www.elkridgeresort.com; Hwy 264; d from $139), Saskatchewan's newest, or yurt it up in the delightful **Flora Bora Forest Lodging** (☎877-763-5672; www.florabora.ca;

DON'T MISS

BATOCHE NATIONAL HISTORIC SITE

A virtual civil war was fought here in 1885 when Louis Riel led the Métis in defending their land. The children of French fur traders and aboriginal mothers, the Métis were forced from Manitoba in the mid-1800s and many made their home in Batoche. Frustrated by the government's continual betrayal of treaties, the Métis and a number of Cree declared their independence from Canada: an announcement met by military force, led by Major General Frederick Middleton. Although outnumbered by 800 to 200, the Métis fought for four days and almost won, but Riel was captured (and later hung for treason).

Once-prosperous Batoche was devastated and within a few years almost nothing was left except for the church you see today. The **historic site** (☎306-423-6227; www.parkscanada.ca/batoche; Rte 225; adult/child $8/4; ⏲9am-5pm May-Sep) is an auspicious place to contemplate the events of 1885, as silent waves of prairie grass bend in the wind.

Batoche is 70km north of Saskatoon, east of Hwy 11.

Hwy 263; yurts from $164), between Emma and Christopher Lakes.

Waskesiu Marina (☑306-663-1999; www.waskesiumarina.com; kayaks per hr from $17) rents canoes, kayaks and motor boats. **Canoeski Discovery** (☑306-653-5693; www.canoeski.com) offers multiday paddling trips: check the website for details.

La Ronge & the Far North

La Ronge is the southern hub of the far north – your last chance for supplies before heading off the grid. It's a rough, basic town, popular with anglers, hunters and dudes on the run.

Robertson's Trading Post (☑306-425-2080; 308 La Ronge Ave; ☺8am-5pm Mon-Sat) is the place to go if you're in the market for a bear trap, wolf hide or case of baked beans. You can buy pretty much anything you'd ever need here and some stuff that you never would. **Lac La Ronge Provincial Park** (☑800-772-4064, 306-425-4234; Hwy 2; ☺May-Sep) surrounds huge, island-filled Lac La Ronge, great for fishing, canoeing and hikes

among stubby pines. The park has six year-round campgrounds and endless backcountry camping. Check in with the **Visitors Information Centre** (☑306-425-3055; www.townoflaronge.ca; 207 La Ronge Ave; ☺8am-8pm) if you're contemplating further explorations.

Transwest Air (www.transwestair.com) offers charter flights in floatplanes to points north of La Ronge. **STC** (www.stcbus.com) has a daily bus to Prince Albert ($50, three hours) and onward to Saskatoon ($71, 6½ hours).

It's hard to believe that almost half of Saskatchewan still lies further north of remote La Ronge. This is frontier territory – the end of the paved road. If you're not skittish about extreme isolation and outfitted appropriately, then this is it! You'll discover tiny burgs such as **Southend** and pass the vast **Reindeer Lake** before arriving at the winter-only section at **Stony Rapids**, some 12 hours north of La Ronge. Self sufficiency is key: make sure you maintain your vehicle, have plenty of fuel, gear and supplies, and keep your head together.

Alberta

Best Places to Eat

➡ Da-De-O (p566)

➡ Model Milk (p581)

➡ Bison Restaurant &
Terrace (p598)

➡ Other Paw (p610)

Best Places to Stay

➡ Fairmont Banff Springs
(p597)

➡ Metterra Hotel on Whyte
(p562)

➡ Park Place Inn (p609)

➡ Hotel Alma (p577)

Why Go?

Alberta does lakes and mountains like Rome does churches and cathedrals, but without the penance. For proof head west to Jasper and Banff, two of the world's oldest national parks which, despite their wild and rugged terrain, remain well-trammeled and easily accessible. No one should leave this mortal coil without first laying eyes on Lake Louise and the Columbia Icefield. And think twice about dying before you've traveled east to the dinosaur-encrusted badlands around Drumheller, south to the Crypt Lake trail in Waterton Lakes National Park, and north to spot bison in the vast, empty northern parklands. Alberta's cities are of patchier interest. There are people still alive older than Calgary and Edmonton's downtowns. But, what these metropolises lack in history they make up for with their festivals. Edmonton's fringe theater festival is the world's second largest, while Calgary's July 'Stampede' is as unapologetically ostentatious as the city that hosts it.

When to Go
Edmonton

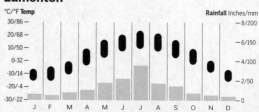

Jul Prime time for festivals, with Edmonton's Street Performers and the Calgary Stampede.

Jul–Sep Banff and Jasper trails are snow free, making a full range of hikes available.

Dec–Feb Winter-sports season in the Rocky Mountains.

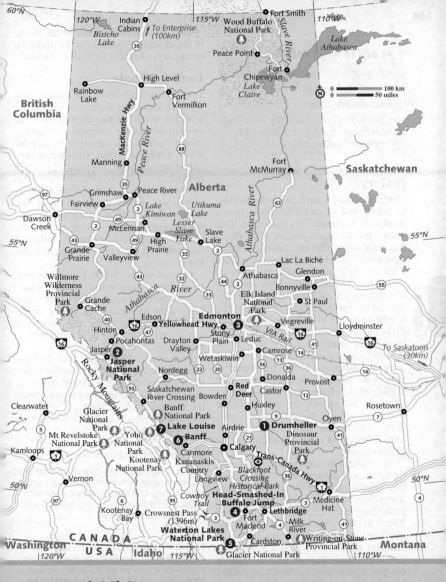

Alberta Highlights

1 Explore the Jurassic remnants of **Drumheller** (p612) and call into the Royal Tyrrell Museum of Palaeontology.

2 Make fresh tracks on a cross-country skiing trail in **Jasper National Park** (p584).

3 Attend the **Edmonton International Fringe Festival**

(p562) and unlock the more bohemian side of the Albertan capital.

4 Decipher the foggy history of First Nations culture at **Head-Smashed-In Buffalo Jump** (p622).

5 Get above the tree line on the Carthew-Alderson Trail

in **Waterton Lakes National Park** (p625).

6 Take afternoon tea after a morning hike in the **Fairmont Banff Springs** (p597) hotel.

7 Enjoy a brew in the **Lake Agnes Teahouse** (p603) high above bluer-than-blue Lake Louise.

ALBERTA FAST FACTS

→ Population: 3,768,284

→ Area: 642,317 sq km

→ Capital: Edmonton

→ Quirky fact: A relative of the T-rex, the Albertosaurus, was first discovered in the Horseshoe Canyon in 1884.

History

Things may have started off slowly in Alberta, but it's making up for lost time. Human habitation in the province dates back 7500 years – the Aboriginal peoples of the Blackfoot, Kainaiwa (Blood), Siksika, Peigan, Atsina (also called Gros Ventre), Cree, Tsuu T'ina (Sarcee) and Assiniboine tribes all settled here in prehistoric times, and their descendants still do. These nomadic peoples roamed the southern plains of the province in relative peace and harmony until the middle of the 17th century, when the first Europeans began to arrive.

With the arrival of the Europeans, Alberta began to change and evolve: the impact of these new arrivals was felt immediately. Trading cheap whiskey for buffalo skins set off the decline of both the buffalo and the traditional ways of the indigenous people. Within a generation, the Aboriginal peoples were restricted to reserves and the buffalo all but extinct.

In the 1820s the Hudson's Bay Company set up shop in the area, and European settlers continued to trickle in. By 1870 the North West Mounted Police (NWMP) – the predecessor of the Royal Canadian Mounted Police (RCMP) – had built forts within the province to control the whiskey trade and maintain order. And it was a good thing they did, because 10 years later the railway reached Alberta and the trickle of settlers turned into a gush.

These new residents were mostly farmers, and farming became the basis of the economy for the next century. Vast riches of oil and gas were discovered in the early 20th century, but it took time to develop them. At the conclusion of WWII there were 500 oil wells; by 1960, there were 10,000, by which time the petroleum business was the biggest in town.

From humble pastoral beginnings to one of the strongest economies in the world, Alberta has done alright for itself financially.

Land & Climate

The prairies that cover the eastern and southern parts of Alberta give way to the towering Rocky Mountains that form the western edge of the province. That mountainous spine forms the iconic scenery for which Alberta is known. The eastern foothills eventually peter out, melding into the flatland.

Alberta is a sunny sort of place; any time of year you can expect the sun to be out. Winters can be cold, when the temperature can plummet to a bone-chilling -20°C (-4°F). Climate change has started to influence snowfall, with the cities receiving less and less every year.

Chinook winds often kick up in the winter months. These warm westerly winds blow in from the coast, deposit their moisture on the mountains and give Albertans a reprieve from the winter chill, sometimes increasing temperatures by as much as 20°C in one day!

Summers tend to be hot and dry; the warmest months are July and August, when the temperature sits at a comfortable 25°C. The 'June Monsoon' is, as you'd expect from the nickname, often rain-filled, while the cooler temperatures and fall colors of September are spectacular.

ⓘ Getting There & Around

Alberta is easily accessible by bus, car, train and air. The province shares an international border with Montana, USA and provincial borders with the Northwest Territories (NWT), British Columbia (BC) and Saskatchewan.

AIR

The two major airports are in Edmonton and Calgary, and there are daily flights to both from major hubs across the world. Carriers serving the province include Air Canada, American Airlines, British Airways, Delta, Horizon Air, KLM, United Airlines and WestJet.

BUS

Greyhound Canada (www.greyhound.ca) has bus services to Alberta from neighboring provinces, and Greyhound has services from the USA. Times can vary greatly, based upon connections, and fares can be reduced by booking in advance.

Useful destinations, with one-way fares, from Edmonton:

Prince George ($100, 10 hours, daily)
Vancouver ($150, 17 hours, five daily)
Whitehorse ($214, 29 hours, one daily)
Winnipeg ($167, 18 hours, three daily)

Destinations from Calgary:

Kamloops ($99, 10 hours, four daily)
Regina ($82, 10 hours, two daily)
Saskatoon ($81, nine hours, four daily)
Vancouver ($104, 15 hours, five daily)
Winnipeg ($171, 20 hours, two daily)

Moose Travel Network (www.moosenetwork. com) runs a variety of trips in western Canada. Most start and finish in Vancouver, but along the way hit the highlights of the mountain parks and other Alberta must-sees. In winter it operates ski-focused tours that are a great option for carless ski bums. Trips depart daily during the summer months and a few times per week in the winter season.

CAR

Alberta was designed with the automobile and an unlimited supply of oil in mind. There are high-quality, well-maintained highways and a network of back roads to explore. Towns for the most part will have services, regardless of the population. Be aware that in more remote areas, especially in the north, those services could be a large distance apart. Fill up the gas tank where possible and be prepared.

TRAIN

Despite years of hard labor, countless work-related deaths, and a reputation for being one of the great feats of 19th-century engineering, Alberta's contemporary rail network has been whittled down to just two regular passenger train services. **VIA Rail** (www.via.ca) runs the thrice-weekly *Canadian* from Vancouver to Toronto, passing through Jasper and Edmonton in both directions. Edmonton to Vancouver costs $225 and takes 27 hours; Edmonton to Toronto costs $405 and takes 55 hours. The Toronto-bound train stops in Saskatoon, Winnipeg and Sudbury Junction. VIA Rail also operates the train from Jasper to Prince Rupert, BC ($117, 32 hours, three weekly).

EDMONTON

POP 730,000

Modern, spread out and frigidly cold for much of the year, Alberta's second-largest city and capital is a demure government town that you're more likely to read about in the business pages than the travel

---

ALBERTA ITINERARIES

One Week

Spend the day in **Calgary** exploring the sites from the 1988 Winter Olympics and grab a meal on trendy 17th Ave. The next day, get into dino mode by taking a day trip to **Drumheller** and visiting the Royal Tyrrell Museum of Palaeontology (p621). Back in Calgary, go for a wander through the neighborhoods of Kensington and Inglewood and fight for a table at world-class Rouge (p581).

Wake early and head west. Stop first in **Canmore** before continuing into Banff National Park and arriving in **Banff Town**. Hike up Sulphur Mountain, ride back down on the Banff Gondola (p591) and finish off at the bottom with a soak in Banff Upper Hot Springs (p593).

After a stay in Banff, continue north to **Lake Louise**, stopping for the view outside the Chateau (p603). Find time for the short, steep hike to the Lake Agnes Teahouse (p603), then continue the drive to the Columbia Icefield (p588). Get ready to stop every five minutes to take yet another amazing photograph.

Roll into **Jasper** and splash out on the Park Place Inn (p609). After some much-needed sleep, stop off at Maligne Canyon (p605) on the way to Maligne Lake (p607), where a short hike might bag you a bear or a moose. Escape the mountains and head to **Edmonton**. Once there dive into the Old Strathcona neighborhood, finishing your Alberta adventure with a plate of smoking hot jambalaya at Da-De-O (p566).

The Complete Rockies

Follow the One Week itinerary, but include side trips into **Kananaskis Country**, the **Icefields Parkway** and north to **Grande Cache** to see the start of the mountains. Also tack on some time down south heading to **Waterton Lakes National Park**, experiencing this less-visited mountain paradise.

supplements. Maybe that's why the city's surprises, when (or if) you find them, are so delightful. Edmonton's annual fringe theater festival is the second largest in the world after Edinburgh, while the yawning fissure of a river valley that splits the city in half is less a park than its own self-contained ecosystem.

Despite all this, Edmonton acts more as a staging post than a destination in itself. Most non-Albertans pass through on their way to somewhere else – usually Jasper National Park, which lies four hours to the west, or, for a handful of visitors, the overhyped West Edmonton Mall, the largest mall in North America. Edmonton is also a frontier town: north of here the landscape is vast and empty, with practically no civilization to speak of until Yellowknife. If you're searching for the soul of the city, head south of the river to the university district and happy-go-lucky Whyte Avenue, home to small theaters, dive diners and a spirited Friday-night mood.

History

The Cree and Blackfoot tribes can trace their ancestry to the Edmonton area for 5000 years. It wasn't until the late 18th century that Europeans first arrived in the area. A trade outpost was built by the Hudson's Bay Company in 1795, which was dubbed Fort Edmonton.

Trappers, traders and adventurers frequented the fort, but it wasn't until 1870, when the government purchased Fort Ed and opened up the area to pioneers, that Edmonton saw its first real growth in population. When the railway arrived in Calgary in 1891, growth really started to speed up.

Meanwhile, the Aboriginal tribes had been severely weakened by disease and the near extinction of their primary food source, the bison. Increasingly vulnerable, they signed away most of their land rights to the Canadian government in a series of treaties

Edmonton

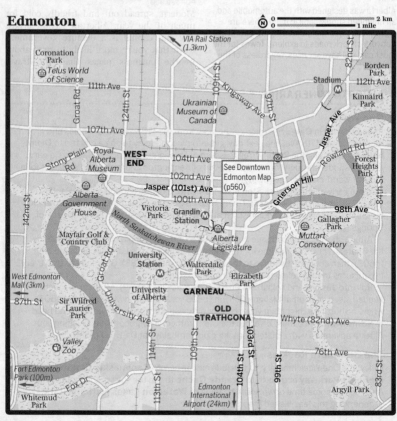

between 1871 and 1921 in return for money, reservation lands and hunting rights.

Gold was the first big boom for the area – not gold found in Alberta, but gold in the Yukon. Edmonton was the last stop in civilization before dreamers headed north to the Klondike. Some made their fortunes, most did not; some settled in Edmonton, and the town grew.

In the 1940s, WWII precipitated the construction of the Alaska Hwy, and the influx of workers further increased the population. Ukrainians and other Eastern European immigrants came to Edmonton in search of work and enriched the city.

Edmonton is again the hub for those looking to earn their fortune in the north. But it isn't gold or roads this time – it's oil.

⊙ Sights & Activities

★ Royal Alberta Museum   MUSEUM
(Map p558; ☎780-453-9100; www.royalalberta-museum.ca; 12845 102nd Ave; adult/child $11/5; ⊙9am-5pm) Since getting its 'royal' prefix in 2005 when Queen Liz II dropped by, Edmonton's leading museum has successfully received funding – a cool $340 million – for a new downtown home which should be complete by 2015. For the time being, you can call in to these long-standing digs, on a bluff overlooking the river valley 2km west of downtown.

The museum is known for its enormous collection of insects (the world's largest) and a lauded display of Alberta's aboriginal culture. The highlight, however, is the 'Wild Alberta' gallery, which splits the province into different geographical zones and displays plants and animals from each.

★ Art Gallery of Alberta   GALLERY
(Map p560; ☎780-422-6223; www.youraga.ca; 2 Sir Winston Churchill Sq; adult/child $12.50/8.50; ⊙11am-5pm Tue-Sun, to 9pm Wed) With the opening of this maverick art gallery in 2010, Edmonton at last gained a modern signature building to counter the ubiquitous boxy skyscrapers. Looking like a giant glass-and-metal space helmet, the futuristic structure in Churchill Sq is an exhibit in its own right. Its collection comprises 6000 pieces of historical and contemporary art, many of which have a strong Canadian bias, including a couple of works by BC's master of green, Emily Carr.

However, this is Alberta not Paris. The gallery is relatively small and can't emulate its arty rivals in Toronto or Vancouver, although some decent temporary shows pass through. Additional facilities include a 150-seat theater, shop and restaurant.

Alberta Government House   HISTORIC BUILDING
(Map p558; ☎780-427-2281; 12845 102nd Ave; ⊙11am-4:30pm Sun & holidays) **FREE** This opulent mansion was the former residence of the lieutenant governor. It's steeped in history and immaculately preserved – you'd never guess it's over 100 years old. The artwork alone is worth visiting: the walls are lined with stunning works by Alberta artists.

Alberta Legislature   NOTABLE BUILDING
(Map p558; ☎780-427-7362; www.assembly.ab.ca; cnr 97th Ave & 107th St; ⊙8:30am-5pm) **FREE** Home to politicians, debate and some surprisingly good art is the Alberta Legislature. Where Fort Edmonton once stood, the Leg is a grand old building that, with its iconic dome and marble interiors, has grown to become a local landmark.

Free 45-minute tours (every hour) take you behind the scenes, and the grounds themselves are a splendid place to vegetate on a warm day. If you've less time, view the shop and **interpretive center** (pedway, 10820 98th Ave), which displays details of the building's architectural and political history.

Fort Edmonton Park   HISTORIC SITE
(Map p558; ☎780-496-8787; www.fortedmontonpark.ca; cnr Fox & Whitemud Drs; adult/child $17.25/12.90; ⊙10am-6pm May-Sep; ⊙) Originally built by the Hudson's Bay Company in 1795, Fort Edmonton was moved several times before being finally dismantled in 1915. This newer riverside reconstruction began life in the 1960s and captures the fort at its 1846 apex. On site are very authentic mock-ups of Edmonton's city streets at three points of their historical trajectory: 1885, 1905 and 1920.

Come on a day devoid of school groups and you can almost imagine mildly inebriated emigrant Victorians prowling the unpaved streets on horseback. A vintage

REGIONAL DRIVING DISTANCES
....
Calgary to Banff: 130km
Banff to Jasper: 290km
Edmonton to Calgary: 300km

ALBERTA EDMONTON

Downtown Edmonton

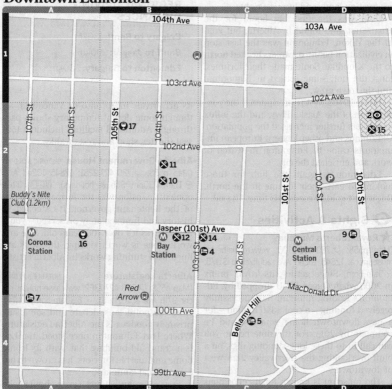

---

steam train links all the exhibits, and non-theatrical-costumed guides answer questions and add some flavor.

Muttart Conservatory
GARDEN

(Map p558; ☑780-496-8755; www.muttartconservatory.ca; 9626 96A St; adult/child $12/6.50; ⊙10am-5pm Fri-Wed, to 9pm Thu) Looking like some sort of pyramid-shaped, glass bomb shelter, the Muttart Conservatory is actually a botanical garden that sits south of the river off James MacDonald Bridge. Each of the four pyramids holds a different climate region and corresponding foliage. It's an interesting place to wander about, especially for gardeners, plant fans and those in the mood for something low-key.

Sir Winston Churchill Square
SQUARE

(Map p560) The subject of a controversial 2005 face-lift, this pubic space, named a little bizarrely after a British prime minister, is a rather brutal treeless plaza where people

meet and hang out (assuming it's not -20°C degrees outside) and various festivals and public events kick off.

The square's former green areas have been replaced with a small amphitheater, a fountain and a cafe. Around the perimeter is a quadrangle of important buildings, including the City Hall, the Provincial Court and the impressive new Art Gallery of Alberta.

Alberta Railway Museum
MUSEUM

(☑780-472-6229; www.albertarailwaymuseum.ca; 24215 34th St; adult/child $5/2; ⊙10am-5pm May-Aug) This museum, on the northeast edge of the city, has a collection of more than 75 railcars, including steam and diesel locomotives and rolling stock, built and used between 1877 and 1950. It also has a collection of railway equipment, old train stations and related buildings.

On weekends, volunteers fire up some of the old engines, and you can ride along for $4 (the diesel locomotives run every Sunday

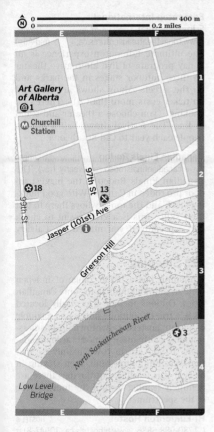

Downtown Edmonton

ALBERTA EDMONTON

in season; the 1913 steam locomotive gets going only on holiday weekends). To get there, drive north on 97th St (Hwy 28) to Hwy 37, turn right and go east for 7km to 34th St, then turn right and go south about 2km.

Ukrainian Museum of Canada   MUSEUM
(Map p558; www.umcalberta.org; 10611 110th Ave; ⊙10am-4pm May-Aug) **FREE** With a huge Ukrainian population and a long history of immigration, there are a few places around town to learn about the culture of the old country and its transplantation in Canada. This museum has its main branch in Saskatoon, but it retains a small collection of exhibits in Edmonton and has been in operation sine 1941.

In the pipeline is a new and more comprehensive Ukrainian museum on Jasper Ave. Plans are currently being launched by the Ukrainian Canadian Archives.

North Saskatchewan River Valley   PARK
Edmonton has more designated urban parkland than any other city in North America, most of it contained within an interconnected riverside green belt that effectively cuts the metropolis in half. The green zone is flecked with lakes, bridges, wild areas, golf courses, ravines and approximately 160km worth of cycling and walking trails. It is easily accessed from downtown.

A fine way to get a glimpse of the downtown core from the river is to take a ride on the **Edmonton Queen** (Map p560; ⌨780-424-2628; www.edmontonqueen.com; 9734 98th Ave; 1hr cruises from $19.95, dinner cruises $54.95; ⊙May-Sep). This modern sternwheeler will take you for an hour-long cruise up- or downriver, depending on the mood of the captain. There is often onboard live entertainment to keep the mood festive.

West Edmonton Mall
SHOPPING MALL

(Map p558; www.westedmontonmall.com; 170th St; ☉10am-9pm Mon-Fri, to 6pm Sat, noon-6pm Sun; ⛲) Kitsch lovers who can't afford the trip to Vegas will have a field day in West Edmonton Mall, while those less enamored by plastic plants and phony re-creations of 15th-century galleons will hate it.

Not content to simply be a shopping mall, Edmonton's urban behemoth has the world's largest waterslides, an equipped indoor wave pool, a full-size amusement park, a skating rink, two minigolf courses, a fake reef with real seals swimming around, a petting zoo, a hotel and 800 stores thrown in as a bonus. Stroll through Chinatown, grab a meal at an imitation Bourbon St or go for a skate or bungee jump. Then dive into the sea of retail shops – all of them chains.

☞ Tours

Quirky free **walking tours** of downtown are offered in the summer months by students on vacation employed by the Downtown Business Association. They leave weekdays at 1pm from the corner of 104th St and 101st Ave.

Edmonton Ghost Tours
WALKING TOUR

(www.edmontonghosttours.com; tours per person $10; ☉9.30pm Mon-Thu Jul & Aug) Spooky walking tours start from 10322 83rd Ave in Old Strathcona. No booking is required – just turn up 15 minutes early.

✦✦ Festivals & Events

Festivals are where Edmonton comes into its own. The city's identity is closely attached to its many annual festivals.

International Street Performers Festival
THEATER

(www.edmontonstreetfest.com) Sometimes the best theater is outside. International performers perform alfresco in this busker bonanza in the second week of July.

K-Days
CARNIVAL

(www.k-days.com; ☉late Jul) For years, Capital Ex (Klondike Days) was the big summer festival in Edmonton. Since 2012, it has been known as K-Days, with less focus on gold-rush history and more on contemporary fun. Live music, rides and a nugget's worth of olden-days fun are the highlights of this evolving event.

Edmonton International Fringe Festival
THEATER

(www.fringetheatreadventures.ca; ☉mid-Aug) The ultimate Edmonton experience is an 11-day program of live alternative theater on three outdoor stages in the parks and on the streets. Many shows are free and no ticket costs more than $15. There's no booking – you choose a theater and stand in line. The festival draws half a million people each year to Old Strathcona.

Canadian Finals Rodeo
RODEO

(www.canadianfinalsrodeo.ca; ☉early Nov) The Canadian Finals Rodeo is the biggest indoor pro rodeo in Canada. With good bucking stock and the top cowboys there to test their skills, this is a great event to check out, especially if you missed the Calgary Stampede.

⌂ Sleeping

Edmonton has a better range of independent accommodations than some Canadian cities. Options include a centrally located B&B, a trio of boutique hotels and a couple of cheap hostels. Downtown is business-oriented, with more generic accommodations. If you are in town mainly to visit the West Edmonton Mall, then staying in or near it is feasible, but the digs there are definitely leaning toward the touristy side of the spectrum.

HI-Edmonton Hostel
HOSTEL $

(☑780-988-6836; www.hihostels.ca; 10647 81st Ave; dm/d $30/67; @🖙) Right in the heart of Old Strathcona, this busy hostel is a safe bet. The rooms are a bit jam-packed with bunks and it feels somewhat like a converted old people's home (it used to be a convent), but the location and price are hard to beat.

Rainbow Valley Campground & RV Park
CAMPGROUND $

(☑780-434-5531, 888-434-3991; www.rainbow-valley.com; 13204 45th Ave; campsites/RV sites $32/36; ☉Apr-Oct) For an inner-city camping spot, this one is pretty good. It's in a good location to get to 'The Mall' and keep some distance from it at the same time.

★ Metterra Hotel on Whyte
BOUTIQUE HOTEL $$

(☑780-465-8150; www.metterra.com; 10454 Whyte Ave; r from $150; @🖙) If you can wade through the uncreative hotel-brochure blurb ('urban oasis,' 'contemporary decor,' 'traditional hospitality'), you'll find that the Met is actually a decent place to stay and a fitting reflection of the happening entertainment district (Old Strathcona) in which it sits. The modern, luxurious interior is accented with Indonesian artifacts hinting at the owner's secret love for all things Eastern.

Matrix BOUTIQUE HOTEL **$$**
(Map p560; ☑780-429-2861; www.matrixedmonton.com; 10001 107th St; r from $150; @🛜) One of a triumvirate of Edmonton boutique hotels, the Matrix claims to serve the 'sophisticated traveler,' and largely succeeds, with cool minimalist architecture punctuated with woody color accents and plenty of handy modern gadgets. In keeping with its boutique image, there's free wine and cheese every evening at 5:30pm.

Varscona BOUTIQUE HOTEL **$$**
(☑780-434-6111; www.varscona.com; 8208 106th St, cnr Whyte Ave; r incl breakfast from $140; @🛜) Right in the heart of Old Strathcona, this charming hotel is elegant but not too hoity-toity, suggesting you can roll up either in a tracksuit or a business suit – or some kind of combination of the two. With the coolest neighborhood in town right on the doorstep, it's all the easier to stick your finger on the collective pulse of Edmonton. Breakfast, parking and evening wine and cheese are thrown in to sweeten the deal.

Chateau Lacombe HOTEL **$$**
(Map p560; ☑780-428-6611; www.chateaulacombe.com; 10111 Bellamy Hill; r from $120; ✳@🛜) Going defiantly against the grain, the spectacular Chateau was a chain hotel that, in 2013, was bought out by local private investors. There's some superficial work to do on this riverside behemoth, which has 24 floors, wonderful views and a revolving restaurant, but with an opulent lobby, fitness center and club-ish bar, it remains regally plush – and now at a bargain price!

Sutton Place Hotel HOTEL **$$**
(Map p560; ☑780-428-7111; www.suttonplace.com; 10235 101st St; r from $104; @🛜❄) Part of a chain (albeit a small one) the upmarket Sutton Place lacks the intimacy of smaller hotels. Aside from classy rooms, replete with glitz and glamour, there are numerous additional facilities here. The indoor water park is fantastic, and there are res-

taurants, cocktail lounges and a casino on the grounds. Look out for cheap specials.

Hotel Selkirk HOTEL **$$**
(☑780-496-7227; www.hotelselkirk.com; 1920 St, Fort Edmonton Park; r from $124; ✳🛜) If you're into the idea of visiting the past at Fort Edmonton Park, why not take it to the next level and spend the night? This historic hotel has period-decorated rooms from the roaring 1920s, and staying here gives you free entry into the fort and its surrounds.

There's an on-site restaurant and English high tea ($19.50) on offer during the summer. The downside: it's isolated.

Glenora Inn B&B B&B **$$**
(☑780-488-6766; www.glenorabnb.com; 12327 102nd Ave; r with shared/private bathroom $100/130; @🛜) A B&B of the frilly Victorian variety, Glenora inhabits the burgeoning West End strip of 124th St. The building is of 1912 vintage, meaning it's 'historic' by Edmonton standards, though not technically 'Victorian.' It also houses a shop and a downstairs bistro where inn dwellers can procure breakfast.

There's a communal parlor and an outdoor patio for when the weather's less arctic.

Alberta Place Suite Hotel HOTEL **$$**
(Map p560; ☑780-423-1565; www.albertaplace.com; 10049 103rd St; studios/ste $144/174; @🛜❄) What was once an apartment building is now a suite hotel with a range of room configurations from studios to one-bedroom suites to family suites. It's well located and refreshingly midpriced, and all rooms have private kitchen facilities, work desks and well-designed if austere furnishings. On the communal level, there's a pool and fitness center.

Fairmont Hotel Macdonald HOTEL **$$$**
(Map p560; ☑780-424-5181; www.fairmont.com; 10065 100th St; r from $210; @🛜❄) Stealing the best nook in town (as Fairmont always does), Edmonton's historic Fairmont Hotel exhibits the usual array of intricate stucco, Italian marble, ornate chandeliers and lush carpets. In the early 20th century it was one in a luxurious chain of railway hotels that dotted the cross-continental line from east to west.

Preserved in all its regal glory, it's still fit for monarchs. The regularly renovated rooms with all the expected amenities are almost worth the premium price.

Canterra Suites Hotel
HOTEL $$$

(☑780-421-1212; www.canterrasuites.com; 11010 Jasper Ave; suites from $199; ❋☎) Catering to traveling businesspeople, the Canterra has large, efficient suites equipped with modern kitchenettes – and is close to downtown and right next to a supermarket. Ideal for long- or short-term stays.

Union Bank Inn
BOUTIQUE HOTEL $$$

(Map p560; ☑780-423-3600; www.unionbankinn. com; 10053 Jasper Ave; r from $199; ❋@☎) This posh boutique hotel on Jasper Ave, in a former bank building dating from 1910, is an upmarket masterpiece. With just 34 rooms, the staff will be at your beck and call, and the in-room fireplaces make even Edmonton's frigid winters almost bearable. There's an equally fancy restaurant – Madison's – on the ground floor.

Fantasyland Hotel
HOTEL $$$

(☑780-444-3000; www.fantasylandhotel.com; 17700 87th Ave; r from $278, themed rooms $448; ❋@☎☲) As if West Ed wasn't surreal enough, this adjoining hotel is something to behold. There are standard rooms, but the real draw is the themed rooms. With 13 themes to choose from – Africa, igloo, Roman, Polynesian – it's hard to pick one. Barely staying on the cool side of kitsch, it's a big hit with families.

It also has a wide variety of bedding options to suit any imaginable situation, plus plenty of giant Jacuzzis, thick carpets, ceiling mirrors and, above all, space.

✖ Eating

Edmonton's food scene reflects its multiculturalism, though you're never far from the default dinner, Alberta beef. If you're willing to hunt around, you can get a quality meal at any price. The most varied and economical place to eat is in Old Strathcona on or around its arterial road, Whyte Ave. Here, you can traverse the globe gastronomically as well as choose from plenty of good vegetarian options. The best downtown nexus is Jasper Ave, the main road that slices through downtown. The up-and-coming option is the rejuvenated warehouse district centered north of Jasper Ave on 104th St.

✖ Downtown & West End

★ Duchess Bake Shop
BAKERY, CAFE $

(☑780-488-4999; www.duchessbakeshop.com; 10720 124th St; baked goods from $1.50; ⊙9am-

8pm Tue-Fri, 10am-6pm Sat, to 5pm Sun) Duchess is what you call a destination cafe/bakery. You'd cross town to eat here – on foot in the snow if necessary. It possesses a detectable French flavour in both taste and decor: the croissants and cakes are buttery, and the furniture is all marble tables and Louis XV–style chairs. Arrive early, before the queuing locals have stripped the cases bare.

There's an affiliated provisions shop next door.

Remedy Cafe
INDIAN $

(Map p560; ☑780-433-3096; www.remedycafe.ca; 10279 Jasper Ave; mains $8-10; ⊙8am-midnight; ☎) The 'remedy' here is cheap, authentic Indian food served in an ultracasual cafe setting – meaning you can wi-fi with one hand and dip your naan in curry sauce with the other. Everyone raves about the chai tea and the butter chicken, but you can also get good cakes (vegans are catered for) and excellent *masala dosas* (curried vegetables inside a crisp pancake).

There's another **branch** (8631 109 St) – the original – in Garneau on the south side of the river.

Three Bananas
CAFE $

(Map p560; www.threebananas.ca; Sir Winston Churchill Sq, 9918 102nd Ave; ⊙7am-7pm Mon-Fri, 10am-5pm Sat, 11am-5pm Sun) ✎ This bookish coffee bar in Churchill Sq, with its mosaic walls and Warhol-esque banana prints, is a good place to grab a caffeine hit on the way to the new art museum.

Cavern
CAFE, DELI $

(Map p560; ☑780-455-1336; www.thecavern.ca; 10169 104th St NW; plates $6-16; ⊙7am-8pm Mon-Thu, to 11pm Fri, 8am-11pm Sat, 10am-5pm Sun) ✎ Edmonton doesn't often resemble a liberal Pacific Northwest city – except at this small cafe, an underground bastion of good taste in vogue 104th St, and particularly in the deli department. The clipboard menu suggests cheese plates (for two). Browse the glass cabinet before you choose and wash it down with a glass of wine.

If you're into good coffee, Cavern serves Coava, the small gourmet roasters from Portland, Oregon.

Tiramisu Bistro
ITALIAN $$

(☑780-452-3393; www.cafetiramisu.ca; 10750 124th St; pastas $12-15; ⊙9am-8pm Mon, to 9pm Tue-Thu, to 10pm Fri & Sat; 🖈) If you just walked satiated out of Duchess Bake Shop, you'll be crushed or ecstatic (depending on your ap-

GO WEST

While Edmonton's downtown struggles to forge a collective personality, a small neighborhood 3km to the west centered on 124th St and sometimes referred to as the original 'West End' exhibits more charisma. Acting as a kind of quirky antidote to West Edmonton Mall, 124th St between Jasper Ave and 111th Ave is home to an abundance of small art galleries linked by occasional art walks, along with some interesting locally owned restaurants, the cutting-edge Roxy Theatre and two of the best European bakery/cafes this side of Winnipeg – Duchess Bake Shop and Tiramisu Bistro. More recently, a small street market has taken root: **124 Grand Market** (www.124grandmarket. com; 108th Ave btwn 123rd St & 124th St; 4-8pm Thu) plies organic wares sold by local producers. It's a classic case of local businesses and businesspeople claiming back their community.

petite) to discover another vision of sweet deliciousness a few doors down. Tiramisu complements its cakes with simple Italian plates and panini. The setting's more cafe than bistro, with a special kids' room.

Blue Plate Diner VEGETARIAN $$

(Map p560; 780-429-0740; www.blueplatediner.ca; 10145 104th St; mains $12-18; 11am-10pm, 9am-10pm Sat & Sun;) In one of the redbrick buildings in Edmonton's warehouse district, this vegetarian-biased diner serves healthy food in hearty portions. And there's style too. Cool colored lighting and exposed brickwork embellish the atmospheric interior, meaning you can eat your tofu and lentils without feeling as if you've joined a hippy commune.

Try the tofu stir-fry or steak sandwich and enjoy larger-than-average plates of crisp, locally grown vegetables.

Madison's Grill FUSION $$$

(Map p560; 780-401-2222; www.unionbankinn. com; 10053 Jasper Ave; mains $26-42; 8am-10pm Mon-Thu, to 11pm Fri & Sat, to 8pm Sun) Located in the Union Bank Inn and practicing the same high standards of service and quality, Madison's Grill prepares delicate meats and seafood with flair. The dining

room is elegant, the service is top-notch and the wine-pairing menu goes for a wallet-stretching $50.

Corso 32 ITALIAN $$$

(Map p560; 780-421-4622; www.corso32. com; 10345 Jasper Ave; mains $21-32; 5-11pm Tue-Sun) This new-wave Italian restaurant seems as if it was plucked from a far larger, trendier city (it wasn't). The quirks? Narrow minimalist decor, with at least one communal table, homemade pasta, an ultrasimple, ultraeffective menu and the best wine list in Edmonton (if you're Italian).

Hardware Grill STEAKHOUSE $$$

(Map p560; 780-423-0969; www.hardwaregrill. com; 9698 Jasper Ave; mains $36-48; 5pm-late Mon-Sat) When you really want to impress even yourself, head to this plush oasis high on a bluff above the river in what is traditionally thought of as the seedier part of town. The Hardware occupies an old (for Edmonton) redbrick building that has retained its more elegant features and had the rest spruced up.

Try the expertly prepared duck breast, rack of lamb or Alberta beef.

Old Strathcona & Garneau

★ **Transcend Coffee** COFFEE $

(www.transcendcoffee.ca/garneau; 8708 109th St; 7:30am-9pm Mon-Sat, to 5pm Sun;) In a city where cafes that produce their own microroasted coffee beans are lacking, Transcend should be treated like the gold dust that it is. Expert baristas on first-name terms with their Guatemalan farmer-producers concoct cups of their own roasted coffee with enough precision to satisfy a severely decaffeinated Seattleite. This spot in Garneau is hip but not remotely pretentious.

High Level Diner DINER $

(780-433-1317; www.highleveldiner.com; 10912 88th Ave; mains $6-15; 8am-10pm Mon-Thu, to 11pm Fri & Sat, 9am-9pm Sun;) When you head south of the river crossing the High Level Bridge from downtown you start to enter a noticeably cooler universe, starting with this cheap and cheerful diner popular with students, neighborhood types and the odd hipster. The menu challenges the normal Albertan meat obsession with some decent vegetarian options and staff make their own ketchup in house.

Block 1912
CAFE $

(www.block1912.com; 10361 Whyte Ave; snacks $3-12; ⊙9am-midnight Mon-Sat, 10am-11pm Sun) A regal attempt at a genuine Torinese coffee bar on Whyte Ave, this inviting place allows you to recline on European-style sofas and armchairs and enjoy your coffee with a range of snacks – or even a gelato. There's a small bar open evenings.

Café Mosaics
VEGETARIAN $

(☑780-433-9702; www.cafemosaics.com; 10844 Whyte Ave; mains $6-12; ⊙9am-9pm Mon-Sat, 11am-2:30pm Sun; ☑🖐) 🍴 A Strathcona institution, this artsy, activist-frequented vegetarian-vegan haunt is a meat-free zone that has taken a page out of San Francisco's book: it makes vegetable dishes both interesting and tasty. As a litmus test, check the number of carnivores who take a day off meat to come here.

Try the tofu curry, cowgirl breakfast or Moroccan chickpea soup. There's even a special meat-free kids' menu.

Tokyo Noodle Shop
JAPANESE $

(☑780-430-0838; 10736 Whyte Ave; mains $7-12; ⊙11:30am-9:30pm Mon-Thu, to 10:30pm Fri & Sat, noon-9pm Sun) Good sushi and noodles by the gallon. Nothing fancy, but that's the point.

★Da-De-O
CAJUN $$

(☑780-433-0930; www.dadeo.ca; 10548A Whyte Ave; mains $10-16; ⊙11:30am-11pm Mon, Tue & Thu-Sat, noon-10pm Sun) Wave goodbye to cloth serviettes and serious waitstaff and say hello to retro jukeboxes, art-deco lighting and jazz etchings on the wall. This dive diner serving Cajun food could well be Edmonton's best eating establishment. The key lies in the food – an unexpected summoning up of the Big Easy in the frozen north.

The oysters, gumbo and jambalaya are all done well, but plucked straight out of Louisiana legend are the spice-dusted sweet-potato fries and the ginormous po'boys (especially the blackened catfish). Save your New Orleans airfare and eat here.

Three Boars Eatery
TAPAS $$

(☑780-757-2600; www.threeboars.ca; 8424 109th St; small plates $13-21; ⊙4pm-late) 🍴 Three Boars is part of the burgeoning farm-to-table food movement, in which the owners retain cordial relations with most of their suppliers (who are all local). It specializes in small plates, cool local ambience and fine Edmonton microbrews on draught.

If you have an appetite for a large Alberta steak, this isn't your bag. If you're up for tasting pork terrine and smoked quail, it definitely is.

Origin India
INDIAN $$

(☑780-436-0556; www.theoriginindia.com; 10511 Whyte Ave; mains $13-16; ⊙11:30am-10:30pm Sun-Thu, to 3am Fri & Sat) Jumping on the burgeoning Indian fusion bandwagon, Origin India embraces a chic modern look while staying true to its origins – *dal makhani,* butter chicken and spicy *paneer.*

🍷 Drinking & Nightlife

The best nightlife scene has traditionally centered on or around Whyte Ave in Old Strathcona. Recently, things have gotten more interesting on Jasper Ave, particularly on its western section between 108th and 118th Sts. Clubs open and close in a blink; bars tend to stay longer. Some host music and/or DJs.

Yellowhead Brewery
BREWERY

(Map p560; www.yellowheadbrewery.com; 10229 105th St NW; ⊙11am-6pm Mon-Fri) Last things first. This isn't a pub. It's just a tasting room next door to a brewery where you can sup on Yellowhead's one and only offering: Yellowhead amber ale – a light, not unpleasant lager, brewed in the big vats visible through a glass partition. It also serves small snacks and offers brewery tours if you book in advance.

Black Dog Freehouse
PUB

(☑780-439-1089; www.blackdog.ca; 10425 Whyte Ave; ⊙2pm-2am) Insanely popular with all types, the Black Dog is essentially a pub with a couple of hidden extras: a rooftop patio, known as the 'wooftop patio,' with heaters (naturally: this is Alberta), a traditional ground-floor bar (normally packed cheek to jowl on weekday nights), and a basement that features live music, DJs and occasional parties. The sum of the three parts has become a rollicking Edmonton institution.

Public House
BAR

(www.yourpublichouse.com; 10765 Jasper Ave; ⊙11am-2am Wed-Fri, 2pm-2am Sat, noon-10pm Sun) In the era of Amazon and ebooks, it appears to have become fashionable to furnish your bar/coffee shop with plush floor-to-ceiling bookshelves – especially in the parts of town that consider themselves hip. Thus, new-bar-on-the-block Public House on Jasper Avenue offers a pleasing perch for bibliophiles, beer-drinkers and casual diners as well.

Beers on tap include a couple of local microbrews. Food is American pub grub.

Elephant & Castle   PUB
(www.elephantcastle.com; 10314 Whyte Ave; ☺11:30am-midnight Mon-Fri, 9am-2am Sat & Sun) What passes for damn ordinary in London (where the Elephant & Castle is a rather grotesque shopping center) is strangely exotic in Edmonton. A red phone box, velvety bar stools and the smell of beer emanating from the thick, carpeted floor add British authenticity to this sporty drinking nook where you're more likely to see Manchester United than the Oilers.

Fluid Lounge   CLUB
(www.thefluidlounge.com; 10888 Jasper Ave; ☺8pm-2am Thu-Sat) An upscale club on Jasper Ave's burgeoning nightlife strip west of 108th St. Join the line and compete with the beautiful people for dancing space, cocktails and how well you know the DJ.

O'Byrne's   PUB
(☑780-414-6766; www.obyrnes.com; 10616 Whyte Ave; ☺11:30am-2am) Get lost in the labyrinth of rooms in this popular Irish pub – Edmonton's oldest. There's a variety on tap, including the obligatory stout. Live music (from 8:30pm) keeps the place interesting in the evenings.

Pub 1905   PUB
(Map p560; ☑780-428-4711; 10525 Jasper Ave; ☺11am-midnight) A popular local watering hole with a happening happy hour, billiards

and a plethora of TVs usually tuned in to the latest Oilers game.

Next Act   PUB
(www.nextactpub.com; 8224 104th St NW; ☺11am-1am Sun-Thu, to 2am Fri & Sat) Theater district pub just off Whyte Avenue with a good quotient of arty types. There are well-selected ales, including local stalwarts Yellowhead and Alley Kat, plus decent burgers, and mac-and-cheese.

Buddy's Nite Club   GAY
(www.buddysedmonton.com; 11725B Jasper Ave; ☺9pm-3am) The font of wet T-shirt comps, drag shows and ominous-sounding 'dance-your-pants-off' nights, Buddy's is ever popular with gay men.

☆ Entertainment

Theater! Don't leave Edmonton without trying some. *See* and *Vue* are free local alternative weekly papers with extensive arts and entertainment listings. For daily listings, see the entertainment section of the *Edmonton Journal* newspaper.

★ New Varscona Theatre   THEATER
(www.varsconatheatre.com; 10329 83rd Ave; tickets from $14) There are only 176 precious seats at the Varscona, a cornerstone of the Old Strathcona theater district that puts on edgy plays, late-night comedy and morning kids' shows. A $6-million renovation may or may not be underway by the time you read this.

Garneau Theatre   CINEMA
(www.metrocinema.org; 8712 109th St NW) Edmonton's only surviving art-deco-era

---

EDMONTON FOR CHILDREN

With its wallet-lightening mall, Edmonton likes to think of itself as kid friendly, but if you can pry your offspring away from the fake plastic trees, there are plenty more family-oriented things to do. **Telus World of Science** (Map p558; www.edmontonscience.com; 11211 142nd St; adult/child $13.95/11.95; ☺10am-7pm; ☺) is an obvious starting point. With an emphasis on interactive displays, it has a million things to do, all under one roof. Fight crime with the latest technology, see what living on a spacecraft is all about, go on a dinosaur dig and explore what makes the human body tick. The center also includes an IMAX theater (extra cost) and an observatory with telescopes (no extra cost).

The **Valley Zoo** (Map p558; ☑780-496-8787; www.valleyzoo.ca; 13315 Buena Vista Rd; adult/child $10.50/5.25; ☺9:30am-6pm; ☺), with more than 100 exotic, endangered and native animals, is another option. Kids will enjoy the petting zoo, camel and pony rides, miniature train, carousel and paddleboats. If you want to brave the zoo in the frigid winter, admission costs are reduced.

Fort Edmonton Park (p559) has a small amusement park for kids, while West Edmonton Mall (p562) could keep even the most hyperactive seven-year-old distracted for days.

cinema has operated under various guises since 1940, changing hands most recently in 2011. It's affectionately described as 'vintage,' meaning the seats could be more comfortable, but who cares when you roll in for a *Trainspotting* matinee and the concession stand is open for beer?

Citadel Theatre
THEATER

(Map p560; www.citadeltheatre.com; 9828 101A Ave; tickets from $45; ☺ Sep-May) Edmonton's foremost company is based right in downtown's Winston Churchill Sq. Expect glowing performances of Shakespeare and Stoppard, Dickens adaptations, and the odd Sondheim musical.

Princess Theatre
CINEMA

(☑ 780-433-0728; www.rainbowcinemas.ca; 10337 Whyte Ave; tickets adult/child $8/6) The Princess is another grand old theater that defiantly sticks her finger up at the multiplexes that are dominant elsewhere. Dating from the pretalkie days (1915), it screens first-run, art-house and cult classics. Tickets for Mondays and weekend matinees are $5.

Roxy Theatre
THEATER

(☑ 780-453-2440; www.theatrenetwork.ca; 10708 124th St NW) Another unexpected thespian surprise, this one hidden in the trendy 'West End,' the Roxy is intimate (198 seats), historic (since 1938) and eclectic, showing burlesque, live bands and comedy.

Blues on Whyte
LIVE MUSIC

(☑ 780-439-981; www.bluesonwhyte.ca; 10329 Whyte Ave) This is the sort of place your mother warned you about: dirty, rough, but still somehow cool. It's a great place to check out some live music; blues and rock are the standards. The small dance floor is a good place to shake a leg.

Jubilee Auditorium
THEATER

(www.jubileeauditorium.com; 11455 87th Ave) The place to check out the **Edmonton Opera** (☑ 780-424-4040; www.edmontonopera.com; tickets from $24; ☺ Oct-Apr). Otherwise, this is a great venue for live performances of every kind.

Edmonton Oilers
SPECTATOR SPORT

(www.edmontonoilers.com; tickets from $38.50) To avoid any embarrassing situations, wise up on the Oilers before you arrive in Edmonton. The local National Hockey League (NHL) team dominated the game in the 1980s thanks to a certain player named Wayne Gretsky – aka 'The Great One' – but hasn't won much since. Games are played at oft-renamed **Rexall Place** (7424 118th Ave NW) in the northeast of town. The season runs from October to April.

Edmonton Eskimos
SPECTATOR SPORT

(www.esks.com; adult/child from $43/21.50) The Eskimos take part in the Canadian Football League (CFL) from July to October at **Commonwealth Stadium** (11000 Stadium Rd).

 Shopping

Old Strathcona is the best area for unique independent stores – vintage magazines, old vinyl, retro furnishings and the like. If you're in search of the opposite – ie big chains selling familiar brands – sift through the 800-plus stores in West Edmonton Mall.

FRINGE BENEFITS

Edmonton becomes a different city in August, when thespians, buskers, food vendors and unorthodox local performers – with names like Three Dead Trolls in a Baggie, and Mump and Smoot – rev up the crowds at the annual Edmonton International Fringe Festival (p562). Using Edinburgh's famous festival as its inspiration, the fringe was launched in 1982 in the Old Strathcona district, where small theater venues provided performance space for self-produced indie artists to showcase their alternative, low-budget, uncensored shows. The idea was a hit, and the fringe evolved in the ensuing years to become the world's second largest, with 600 artists entertaining up to half a million visitors. As well as being uniquely Edmontonian in its humor and atmosphere, it has gone on to inspire countless other fringe festivals across Canada.

The Fringe usually kicks off in mid-August, with tickets going on sale around 10 days beforehand. True to its DIY ethos, prices are kept low (around $10 to $15 per performance), or you can buy one of a limited number of Frequent Fringer festival passes. Most of the best small venues are in and around Whyte Avenue, including the Waterdale Theatre and the New Varscona Theatre. Creating a buzz in the surrounding neighborhood are myriad street performers and buskers, as well as an outlandish street carnival.

Avenue Guitars
MUSIC

(www.avenue-guitars.com; 10550 Whyte Ave; ⊙10am-6pm Mon-Sat) You can warm your fingers plucking opening stanzas to 'Stairway to Heaven' in Old Strathcona's premier music store. It sells custom-made and collectors' guitars and all the usual suspects.

Decadence
VINTAGE

(www.divineplanet.com; 10760 Whyte Ave NW; ⊙11am-8pm Mon-Fri, to 7pm Sat, noon-6pm Sun) Come here to see what you won't find in 800 stores in West Edmonton Mall.

Old Strathcona Farmers Market
FOOD

(☑780-439-1844; 10310 83rd Ave, at 103rd St; ⊙noon-5pm Tue, 8am-3pm Sat Jul & Aug) *✐* This not-to-be-missed indoor market offers everything from organic food to arts and crafts, and hosts some 130 vendors. Everyone comes here on Saturday morning – it's quite the scene.

Junque Cellar
ACCESSORIES

(10442 Whyte Ave; ⊙10am-9pm Mon-Sat, to 6pm Sun) What is plain old junk to some is retro-cool to others. Sift through the typewriters, lava lamps, old phones, comics, clothes and other flashbacks of erstwhile pop culture.

ℹ Information

Custom House Global Foreign Exchange (10104 103rd Ave) Foreign currency exchange.

Edmonton Tourism (Map p560; 9797 Jasper Ave; ⊙8am-5pm) Friendly place with tons of flyers and brochures.

Main Post Office (9808 103A Ave; ⊙8am-5:45pm Mon-Fri)

Royal Alexandra Hospital (☑780-477-4111; 10240 Kingsway Ave) Has a 24-hour trauma center. Located 1km north of the downtown core.

ℹ Getting There & Away

AIR

Edmonton International Airport (YEG; www.flyeia.com) is about 30km south of the city along the Calgary Trail, about a 45-minute drive from downtown.

BUS

The large **bus station** (Map p560; 10324 103rd St) has Greyhound Canada services to numerous destinations, including Jasper ($67, 4½ hours, four daily) and Calgary ($49, from 3½ hours, from 10 daily).

Red Arrow (Map p560; www.redarrow.ca) buses stop downtown at the Holiday Inn Express and serve Calgary ($70, 3½ hours, six daily) and

Fort McMurray ($86, 5½ hours, three daily). The buses are a step up, with wi-fi, sockets for your laptop, single or double seats, a free minibar and hot coffee.

CAR

All the major car-rental firms have offices at the airport and around town. **Driving Force** (www.thedrivingforce.com; 11025 184 St) will rent, lease or sell you a car. Check the website; it often has some good deals.

TRAIN

The small **VIA Rail station** (www.viarail.ca, 12360 121st St) is rather inconveniently situated 5km northwest of the city center near Edmonton City Centre Airport. The *Canadian* travels three times a week east to Saskatoon ($85, eight hours), Winnipeg ($181, 20 hours) and Toronto ($405, 55 hours) and west to Jasper ($117, 5½ hours), Kamloops ($172, 16½ hours) and Vancouver ($225, 27 hours). At Jasper, you can connect to Prince George and Prince Rupert.

ℹ Getting Around

TO/FROM THE AIRPORT

Bus 747 leaves from outside the arrivals hall every 30 to 60 minutes and goes to Century Park ($5), the southernmost stop on Edmonton's Light Rail. From here regular trains connect to Strathcona and downtown.

Sky Shuttle Airport Service (www.edmontonskyshuttle.com; adult/child $18/10) runs three different routes that service hotels in most areas of town, including downtown and the Strathcona area. The office is by carousel 12. Journey time is approximately 45 minutes.

Cab fare from the airport to downtown is about $50.

CAR & MOTORCYCLE

There is metered parking throughout the city. Most hotels in Old Strathcona offer complimentary parking to guests. Visitors can park their car for the day and explore the neighborhood easily on foot. Edmonton also has public parking lots, which cost about $12 per day or $1.50 per half hour; after 6pm you can park for a flat fee of about $2.

PUBLIC TRANSPORTATION

City buses and a 16-stop Light Rail Transit (LRT) system cover most of the city. There are plans for four more LRT lines. The fare is $3.20. Buses operate at 30-minute intervals between 5:30am and 1:30am. Check out the excellent transit planning resources at www.edmonton.ca. Daytime travel between Churchill and Grandin stations on the LRT is free.

Between mid-May and early September you can cross the High Level Bridge on a streetcar

ALBERTA EDMONTON

($5 round-trip, every 30 minutes between 11am and 10pm). The vintage streetcars are a great way to travel to the Old Strathcona Market (103rd St at 94th Ave), where the line stops. Or go from Old Strathcona to the downtown stop, next to the Grandin LRT Station (109th St between 98th and 99th Aves).

TAXI

Two of the many taxi companies are **Yellow Cab** (☑ 780-462-3456) and **Alberta Co-Op Taxi** (☑ 780-425-2525). The fare from downtown to the West Edmonton Mall is about $25. Flag fall is $3.60, then it's $0.20 for every 150m.

AROUND EDMONTON

East of Edmonton

When Edmontonians want to get away from it all and retreat back to nature, **Elk Island National Park** (www.pc.gc.ca/eng/pn-np/ab/elkisland/index.aspx; adult/child/senior $7.80/3.90/6.80, campsites & RV sites $25.50, campfire permits $8.80; ☉ dawn-dusk) is often their first port of call. Just 45km east of Edmonton on the Yellowhead Hwy (Hwy 16), it's convenient for weekend getaways, meaning the campgrounds are quite popular. Some of the park's campgrounds close from early October to May.

The **Ukrainian Cultural Heritage Village** (☑ 780-662-3640; www.history.alberta.ca/ ukrainianvillage; adult/child $9/4; ☉ 10am-5pm May-Aug), 50km east of Edmonton on Hwy 16 (3km east of Elk Island National Park), is an exact replica of a turn-of-the-century Ukrainian town, paying homage to the 250,000 Ukrainian immigrants who came to Canada in the late 19th and early 20th centuries. Many settled in central Alberta, where the landscape reminded them of the snowy steppes of home. Among the exhibits are a dozen or so structures, including a restored pioneer home and an impressive Ukrainian Greek Orthodox church. The staff are dressed in period garb and are in character, too, adding a slice of realism and fun to the day.

South of Edmonton

Halfway between Edmonton and Calgary on Hwy 2 is Alberta's third-largest city, **Red Deer** (population 97,000), a growing community fueled by agricultural production and, more recently, oil. Beyond being a rest stop and an all-else-fails place to stay during the tourist season, there is very little for the traveler here. Red Deer is about 1½ hours away from either Calgary or Edmonton, and accommodations will not be as tight or as expensive. For more information, contact the **Red Deer Visitor & Convention Bureau** (www.tourismreddeer.net; 30 Riverview Park), or just drive through the city, where you'll have your pick of chain establishments.

WORTH A TRIP

ELK ISLAND NATIONAL PARK

In case you hadn't noticed, there are five national parks in Alberta, and three of them *aren't* Jasper or Banff. Overshadowed by the gothic Rockies, tiny **Elk Island National Park** (adult/child $7.70/3.90) attracts just 5% of Banff's annual visitor count despite its location only 50km east of Edmonton. Not that this detracts from its attractions. The park – the only one in Canada that is entirely fenced – contains the highest density of wild hoofed animals in the world after the Serengeti. If you come here, plan on seeing the 'big six' – plains bison, wood bison, mule deer, white-tailed deer, elk and the more elusive moose. The wood bison live entirely in the quieter southern portion of the park (which is cut in two by Hwy 16), while the plains bison inhabit the north. Most of the infrastructure lies in the north, too, around **Astotin Lake**. Here you'll find a campground, a nine-hole golf course (with a clubhouse containing a restaurant), a beach and a boat launch. Four of the park's 11 trails lead out from the lakeshore through trademark northern Albertan aspen parkland – a kind of natural intermingling of the prairies and the boreal forests.

Public transport to the park is nonexistent. Either hire a car or join a guided tour from Edmonton with **Watchable Wildlife Tours Group** (☑ 780-405-4880; www.birdsand-backcountry.com), led by wildlife expert Wayne Millar. It's a lovely way to watch the sunset surrounded by animals on a long summer evening.

West of Edmonton

Heading west from Edmonton toward Jasper, Hwy 16 is a gorgeous drive through rolling wooded hills that are especially beautiful in fall. Accommodations are available along the way. Greyhound buses ply the route.

Hinton is a small, rough-around-the-edges town carved from the bush. The pervasive logging industry keeps the majority of the town's population gainfully employed. There is some good mountain biking to be found here; the info center has information on trails.

If there is snow on the ground, the **Athabasca Lookout Nordic Centre** offers winter visitors beautiful groomed ski trails up to 25km long. It also has illuminated night skiing on a 1.5km trail, plus a 1km luge run. There's a user fee of $5. For more information, contact the **Hinton Tourist Information Centre** (☑780-865-2777; 309 Gregg Ave), off Hwy 16.

Just northwest of Hinton lies the tiny settlement of **Grande Cache**. There is little of interest in this small industry town – only a few overpriced hotels aimed at expense-account-wielding natural-resources workers. However, the drive along Hwy 40 between Hinton and Grande Cache is spectacular, with rolling forested foothills, lakes and abundant wildlife.

CALGARY

POP 1,065,000

Calgary, to most non-Calagarians, is Canada in a Stetson with a self-confident American swagger and a seemingly insatiable thirst for business, especially if it involves oil. But like most stereotypes, the truth is more complex. Shrugging off its image as the city other Canadians love to hate, and standing strong despite serious flooding that caused havoc in June 2013, Alberta's largest metropolis continues to stride cool-headed toward the future with a thick skin and clear sense of its own destiny. Lest we forget, this is a city that hosted the highly successful 1988 Winter Olympics, produced Canada's current prime minister (Stephen Harper), elected North America's first Muslim mayor, and throws one of Canada's biggest parties. The famous July Stampede is subtitled, with typical Calgarian immodesty, 'the greatest outdoor show on earth.'

Overtaken sometimes by the pace of its own development, Calgary has often forsaken quality for quantity in the past, following a path more in tune with Dubai or Dallas than Austin or Portland, but there are signs that the trend may be changing. Community activists in emerging Calgary neighborhoods such as Inglewood and Kensington are finally waking up and smelling the single-origin home-roasted coffee, with new bars, boutiques, restaurants and entertainment venues exhibiting more color and experimentation. Before you know it, the city that to unaffiliated non-Calgarians has long served as an unloved and somewhat bland business center or a functional springboard for the wonders of Banff and the Rockies might actually become – ahem – interesting.

History

From humble and relatively recent beginnings, Calgary has been transformed into a cosmopolitan modern city that has hosted an Olympics and continues to wield huge economic clout. Before the growth explosion, the Blackfoot people called the area home for centuries. Eventually they were joined by the Sarcee and Stoney tribes on the banks of the Bow and Elbow Rivers.

By the time the 1870s rolled around, the NWMP built a fort and called it Fort Calgary after Calgary Bay on Scotland's Isle of Mull. The railroad followed a few years later, and, buoyed by the promise of free land, settlers started the trek west to make Calgary their home. The Blackfoot, Sarcee and Stoney Aboriginals signed Treaty 7 with the British Crown in 1877 that ushered them into designated tribal reservations and took away their wider land rights.

Long a center for ranching, the cowboy culture was set to become forever intertwined with the city. In the early 20th century, Calgary simmered along, growing slowly. Then, in the 1960s, everything changed. Overnight, ranching was seen as a thing of the past, and oil was the new favorite child. With the 'black gold' seeming to bubble up from the ground nearly everywhere in Alberta, Calgary became the natural choice of place to set up headquarters.

The population exploded, and the city began to grow at an alarming rate. As the price of oil continued to skyrocket, it was good times for the people of Cowtown. The '70s boom stopped dead at the '80s bust. Things slowed and the city diversified.

Calgary

KENSINGTON

11th St NW

10A St NW

10th St NW

C-Train

Memorial Dr

Bow River

Prince's
Island Park

6

7

18

16

38

4

Eau Claire
Ave SW

1st Ave SW

2nd Ave SW

3rd Ave SW

21

13

DOWNTOWN

35

33

14

49

25

Louise
Bridge

6th Ave SW

7th Ave SW

C-Train

Stephen Ave Walk

8th Ave SW

48

39

2

20

Greyhound Bus Station
(400m)

34

8

9th Ave SW

10th Ave SW

51

45

37

40

**DESIGN
DISTRICT**

28

11th Ave SW

12th Ave SW

46

BELTLINE

15

41

10

12th St SW

11th St SW

10th St SW

9th St SW

8th St SW

6th St SW

5th St SW

4th St SW

3rd St SW

2nd St SW

1st St SW

27

13th Ave SW

14th Ave SW

24

11

15th Ave SW

19

29

42

44

43

16th Ave SW

23

32

31

17th Ave SW

**UPTOWN
17TH AVE**

18th Ave SW

18th Ave SW

7th St SW

19th Ave SW

19th Ave SW

20th Ave
SW

21st Ave
SW

**4TH ST -
MISSION
DISTRICT**

23rd Ave SW

30

24th Ave SW

25th Ave SW

Prospect Ave

Hillcrest Ave

17

The 21st century began with an even bigger boom. House prices have gone through the roof, there is almost zero unemployment and the economy is growing 40% faster than the rest of Canada. Not bad for a bunch of cowboys.

⊙ Sights

Calgary's downtown isn't particularly interesting unless you've got your finger in an oil well. More alluring are a handful of still-evolving city neighborhoods. **Uptown 17th Ave** is a rainbow of obnoxious hockey crowds, beer-hall-style bars, and emerging locavore restaurants. **Inglewood**, just east of downtown, is the city's hippest neighborhood, with antique shops, indie boutiques and some esoteric eating options. **Kensington**, north of the Bow River, is a little more upscale but has some decent coffee bars and a tangible community spirit. **4th St – Mission District** is an extension of 17th Ave that's a little more mellow and worth visiting for its Italian restaurants.

★**Glenbow Museum**　　　　　MUSEUM
(☑403-777-5506; www.glenbow.org; 130 9th Ave SE; adult/child $14/9; ⊙9am-5pm Fri-Wed, to 9pm Thu) For a town with such a short history, Calgary does a fine job telling it at the commendable Glenbow Museum, which traces the legacy of Calgary and Alberta from pre- to post-oil. Contemporary art exhibitions and story-worthy artifacts dating back centuries fill its halls and galleries.

With an extensive permanent collection and an ever-changing array of traveling exhibitions, there is plenty for the history buff, art lover and pop-culture fiend to ponder.

Fort Calgary Historic Park　　HISTORIC SITE
(☑403-290-1875; www.fortcalgary.com; 750 9th Ave SE; adult/child $12/7; ⊙9am-5pm) In 1875 Calgary was born at Fort Calgary. The site today is occupied by a replica of a military barracks that stood here in the 1880s (the original fort has long since disappeared). The barracks acts as a museum of Calgary history from 1875 to the 1920s, with more than a passing nod to the NUMP.

Granted, it's not particularly old, but this is fast-moving Calgary, where last week is considered ancient history.

Calgary Zoo　　　　　　　ZOO
(☑403-232-9300; www.calgaryzoo.ab.ca; 1300 Zoo Rd NE; adult/child $22.50/14.50; ⊙9am-6pm; 🖼) More than 1000 animals from around the

ALBERTA CALGARY

Calgary

◎ Top Sights
1 Glenbow Museum E4

◎ Sights
2 Art Gallery of Calgary D3
3 Bow E3
4 Calgary Chinese Cultural Centre D2
5 Calgary Tower..E4
6 Prince's Island Park D1

◎ Activities, Courses & Tours
7 Rapid Rent D2

◎ Sleeping
8 Fairmont Palliser....................................D4
9 HI-Calgary F3
10 Hotel Arts D4
11 Hotel Elan A5
12 Hotel Le Germain E4
13 International Hotel D3
14 Kensington Riverside Inn.......................A2
15 Nuvo Hotel Suites B4
16 Sheraton Suites Calgary Eau
   Claire D2
17 Twin Gables B&B C7

◎ Eating
18 1886 Buffalo Cafe D2
19 Analog Coffee C5
20 Blink D3
21 Caesar's Steak House C2
22 Catch...E3
23 Farm B5
24 Galaxie Diner A5

25 Higher Ground A2
26 Home Tasting Room E3
27 Jelly Modern Doughnuts B5
28 King and I..B4
29 Melrose Café & Bar C5
30 Mercato D6
31 Model Milk C5
32 Ox and Angela C5
33 Pulcinella A2
34 Rush D4
35 Sushi Club A2
36 Teatro..E3

◎ Drinking & Nightlife
37 Back Lot..D4
38 Barley Mill D2
39 Flames Central...D3
40 HiFi Club D4
41 Hop In Brew..D4
42 National C5
43 Rose & Crown C5
44 Ship & Anchor C5
45 Twisted Element......................................B4

◎ Entertainment
46 Broken City C4
47 Epcor Centre for the
   Performing Arts E4
48 Globe Cinema C3
49 Plaza Theatre A2
50 Saddledome F5

◎ Shopping
51 Mountain Equipment Co-op..................B4

world, many in enclosures simulating their natural habitats, make Calgary's zoo one of the top rated in North America and almost on a par with Toronto's.

Besides the animals, the zoo has a **Botanical Garden**, with changing garden displays, a **tropical rain forest**, a good **butterfly enclosure** and the 6½-hectare **Prehistoric Park**, featuring fossil displays and life-size dinosaur replicas in natural settings. Picnic areas dot the zoo, and a cafe is on-site. During winter, when neither you nor the animals will care to linger outdoors, the admission price is reduced. To get here, take the C train east to the Zoo stop.

Heritage Park Historical Village HISTORIC SITE (☑403-259-1900; www.heritagepark.ab.ca; 1900 Heritage Dr SW, at 14th St SW; adult/child $21/15; ◎9.30am-5pm daily May-Aug, Sat & Sun Sep & Oct) Want to see what Calgary used to look like? Head down to this historical park and step right into the past. With a policy that all buildings within the village are from

1915 or earlier, it really is the opposite of modern Calgary. There are 10 hectares of re-created town to explore, with a fort, grain mill, church, school and lots more.

You can ride on the steam train, catch a trolley and even go for a spin on the SS *Moyie*, the resident stern-wheeler, as it churns around the Glenmore Reservoir. Heritage Park has always been a big hit with the kiddies and is a great place to soak up Western culture. To get there, take the C train to Heritage station, then bus 20. The park is located 10km south of Calgary's downtown.

Bow NOTABLE BUILDING (500 Centre St) In the competition to be the tallest building in Calgary, the 58-storey, 236m-high Bow stole top honours in 2012, though its reign looks like it will be fleeting.

The shiny, curvaceous headquarters of the EnCana Corporation is certainly more aesthetically pleasing than some of the city's brutalist architecture. It's finished off nicely at its (main) southwest entrance by a huge mesh sculpture of a human head, called *Wonderland*, by Spanish artist Jaume Plensa.

Inglewood Bird Sanctuary   NATURE RESERVE
(☑403-268-2489; 2425 9th Ave SE; sanctuary & interpretive center donations appreciated; ☺dawn-dusk, interpretive center 10am-4pm) FREE Get the flock over here and look out for some foul play at this nature reserve. With more than 260 bird species calling the sanctuary home, you're assured of meeting some feathered friends. It's a peaceful place, with walking paths and benches to observe the residents.

There is a small **interpretive center** to give you some more information about the birds, complete with displays that are popular with the young ones.

Calgary Chinese Cultural Centre   CULTURAL BUILDING
(☑403-262-5071; 197 1st St SW; center admission free, museum adult/child $2/1; ☺9am-9pm, museum 11am-5pm) Inside this impressive landmark building, built by skilled Chinese artisans in 1993, you'll find a magnificent 21m-high dome ornately painted with 561 dragons and other imagery. Its design was inspired by Beijing's Temple of Heaven. The 2nd and 3rd floors frequently house changing art and cultural exhibitions. Downstairs, the **museum** holds Chinese art and artifacts, including a collection of replica terracotta soldiers.

Prince's Island Park   PARK
For a little slice of Central Park in the heart of Cowtown, take the bridge over to this island, with grassy fields made for tossing Frisbees, bike paths and ample space to stretch out. During the summer months, you can catch a Shakespeare production in the park's natural grass amphitheater.

Watch yourself around the river. The water is cold and the current is strong and not suitable for swimming; the island was badly flooded during the summer 2013 floods. The bridge to the island from downtown is at the north end of 3rd St SW, near the Eau Claire Market shopping area.

Fish Creek Provincial Park   PARK
(☑403-297-5293; ☺8am-dusk) Cradling the southwest edge of Calgary, this huge park is a sanctuary of wilderness hidden within the city limits. Countless trails intertwine to form a labyrinth, to the delight of walkers, mountain bikers and the many animals who call the park home.

Severe flooding in the park in the mid-2000s washed away many bridges and, in many cases, severely impacted the landscape. The park is slowly returning to normal with the assistance of the city and Mother Nature. There are numerous access points to the park, which stretches for 20km between 37th St in the west and Bow River in the east. From downtown, take bus 3 via Elbow Dr.

Calgary Tower   NOTABLE BUILDING
(☑403-266-7171; www.calgarytower.com; 101 9th Ave SW; adult/youth $15/7; ☺observation gallery 9am-9pm) This 1968 landmark tower is an iconic feature of the Calgary skyline, though it has now been usurped by numerous taller buildings and is in danger of being lost in a forest of skyscrapers. There is little doubt that the aesthetics of this once-proud concrete structure have passed into the realm of kitsch, but, love it or hate it, the slightly phallic 191m structure is a fixture of the downtown area.

The views from the top are fantastic, and, copying Seattle's Space Needle, there's a revolving restaurant.

Art Gallery of Calgary   GALLERY
(☑403-770-1350; www.artgallerycalgary.org; 117 8th Ave SW; adult/child $5/2.50; ☺10am-5pm Tue-Sat) Calgary isn't really an art city (yet), and this aspiring gallery is more an exhibition space than a weighty portfolio of art. Indeed, the Art Gallery of Calgary has no permanent collection like Vancouver or Edmonton, meaning you'll have to rely on getting lucky with a decent temporary expo of contemporary Canadian paintings.

Military Museums   MUSEUM
(☑403-974-2850; www.themilitarymuseums.ca; 4520 Crowchild Trail SW; adult/child $10/4; ☺9am-5pm Mon-Fri, 9:30am-4pm Sat & Sun) Those with an interest in the military will enjoy the Military Museums (essentially one museum), providing a very thorough overview of Calgary's military background – air force, army and navy – and its role in Canadian conflicts over the years, from British colonial escapades in the 1880s to Afghanistan. Follow Crowchild Trail to Flanders Ave about 3km south of Downtown.

ALBERTA CALGARY

🏃 Activities

Canada Olympic Park
SPORTS

(☑403-247-5452; www.canadaolympicpark.ca; 88 Canada Olympic Rd SW; mountain biking hill tickets/lessons $22/99; ⏰9am-9pm Mon-Fri, 10am-5pm Sat & Sun) In 1988 the Winter Olympics came to Canada for the first time. Calgary played host, and many of the events were contested at Canada Olympic Park. It's near the western edge of town along Hwy 1 – you won't miss the distinctive 70m and 90m ski jumps crowning the skyline.

Check out the **Sports Hall of Fame** (admission $12) and learn about some great Canadian athletes and the story of the Calgary games. If you're feeling more daring, go for a 60-second bobsled ride ($135) with a professional driver on a 120kmh Olympic course. It could be the most exhilarating and expensive minute of your life. Alternatively, you can take a trip along a zip line ($65) from the top of the ski jump. In winter you can go for a ski, or strap on a snowboard and hit the superpipe. Summer is for mountain biking, when you can ride the lift-serviced trails till your brakes wear out.

Olympic Oval
ICE SKATING

(☑403-220-7954; www.ucalgary.ca/oval; adult/child $6/4) Get the Olympic spirit at the University of Calgary, where you can go for a skate on Olympic Oval. Used for the speed-skating events at the Olympics, it offers public skating on the long track and has skates available to rent.

👉 Tours

Free two-hour **walking tours** led by local retirees leave from the Glenbow Museum every Wednesday at 10am between May and September. See www.walkaroundcalgary.com for bookings and more details.

Hammerhead Tours
CULTURAL TOUR

(☑403-590-6930; www.hammerheadtours.com; tours $45-135) Has a variety of tour options to choose from, including city tours and trips to the Columbia Icefield, Drumheller, Banff and more.

Legendary Tours
CULTURAL TOUR

(☑403-285-8376; www.legendarytravels.net; tours from $115) Gets you out to some of Alberta's lesser-known sites, including the new Blackfoot Crossing Historical Park.

⚜ Festivals & Events

For a year-round list of the city's events, go to www.visitcalgary.com/things-to-do/events-calendar. The big festival in Calgary is the annual Calgary Stampede.

Calgary International Children's Festival
CHILDREN'S

(www.calgarychildfest.org; Epcor Centre for the Performing Arts, 205 8th Ave SE; tickets $14-21; ⏰late May) Kids have all the fun at this annual event, with music, performers and all sorts of kidding around.

Carifest
CARNIVAL

(www.carifestcalgary.com; Stephen Ave & Prince's Island Park; ⏰early Jun) The Caribbean comes alive right here in Calgary. Concerts, food stalls, street parties and stuff for kids.

Calgary Stampede
RODEO

(www.calgarystampede.com; ⏰2nd week Jul) Billed as the greatest outdoor show on earth and now over 100 years old, Calgary's Stampede is world-famous. Rodeos don't come much bigger than this, with daily shows featuring bucking broncos, steer wrestling, barrel racing and, of course, bull riding. At night there's a grandstand show and the ever-popular chuckwagon races. It's a great time to visit Calgary: civic spirits are on a yearly high, and there's live music, free stampede breakfasts and seemingly a cowboy hat on every head in the city. Book ahead for accommodations.

Calgary Folk Music Festival
MUSIC

(www.calgaryfolkfest.com; ⏰late Jul) Grassroots folk is celebrated at this annual four-day event featuring great live music on Prince's Island. Top-quality acts from around the globe make the trek to Cowtown. It's a mellow scene hanging out on the grass listening to the sounds of summer with what seems like 12,000 close friends.

🛏 Sleeping

Calgary has found its independent spirit in the last few years and established a pleasant assortment of boutique hotels across different price ranges that promote individual quirks and design features.

Downtown hotels are notoriously expensive, although many run frequent specials. Business-oriented hotels are often cheaper over weekends. Hotels near the western edge of town are concentrated into an area called, appropriately, Motel Village (next to

LOCAL KNOWLEDGE

CARLESS IN CALGARY

As the main operations center for Canada's oil industry, Calgary has a reputation for big, unsubtle automobiles plying endless low-rise suburbs on a network of busy highways. But, hidden from the ubiquitous petrol-heads is a parallel universe of urban parkways (712 kilometers of 'em!) dedicated to walkers, cyclists and skaters, and many of them hug the banks of the city's two mighty rivers, the Bow and the Elbow. Even better, this non-car-traffic network is propped up by a cheap, efficient light-rail system: the C-Train was significantly expanded in 2012 and carries a number of daily riders comparable to the Amsterdam metro. Yes, dear reader, Calgary without a car is not an impossible – or even unpleasant – experience.

Not surprisingly, the best trails hug the riverbanks. The Bow River through downtown and over into Prince's Island is eternally popular, with the new pedestrian-only Peace Bridge providing a vital link. If you're feeling strong, you can follow the river path 20km south to Fish Creek Provincial Park and plenty more roadless action. Nose Creek Parkway is the main pedestrian artery to and from the north of the city, while the leafy Elbow River Pathway runs from Inglewood to Mission in the south.

Bike Bike (www.bikebike.ca; 1501A 17th Ave SW; bicycles per day from $35; ⊘10am-5pm Tue, Wed & Sat, to 7pm Thu & Fri, noon-5pm Sun) rents nonsporty city bikes April to September. Abutting the downtown Bow River Pathway is **Rapid Rent** (www.outlawsports.ca; Barclay Parade; bikes/in-line skates per day from $30/15; ⊘10am-7pm Mon-Fri, to 6pm Sat, to 5pm Sun), an outlet of Outlaw Sports located next to the Eau Claire shopping center.

The city publishes an official Calgary Bikeways and Pathways map available from any local leisure center or downloadable from the City of Calgary website (www.calgary.ca). There's also a mobile app at www.calgary.ca/mobileapps.

the Banff Trail C-Train station). Every chain hotel you can think of has a property here, from shabby to chic. If you are looking for a deal, investigate this area.

During the Stampede (early July), demand causes rates to rise and availability to plummet. Be sure to book ahead.

HI-Calgary
HOSTEL **$**

(☏403-269-8239; www.hostellingintl.ca/Alberta; 520 7th Ave SE; dm/r from $30/75; @ 🖙) For the budget-minded, this pleasant hostel is one of your only options for the price in Calgary. Fairly standard bunk rooms and a few doubles are available. It has a kitchen, laundry, games room and internet facilities; it's a popular crossroads for travelers and a good place to make friends, organize rides and share recommendations.

Be careful at night in this area – you are only a couple of blocks from the roughest bar in town.

Calaway RV Park
CAMPGROUND **$**

(☏403-240-3822; www.calawaypark.com; Hwy 1; campsites/RV sites $27/33; 🖙) The youngsters will love camping at the amusement park, 25km west of downtown. During the Stampede it runs a shuttle into town.

Calgary West Campground
CAMPGROUND **$**

(☏403-288-0411; www.calgarycampground.com; Hwy 1; campsites/RV sites $36/44; @ 🖙 🏊) West of downtown Calgary on the Trans-Canada Hwy (Hwy 1), this campground is close to the city and has good facilities.

★Hotel Alma
BOUTIQUE HOTEL **$$**

(☏403-220-3203; www.hotelalma.ca; 169 University Gate NW; r from $129, apt $180; 🖙) Some cruel critics claim Calgary lacks *alma* (soul), and although this fashionable boutique establishment in – of all places – Calgary's university campus can't really be described as soulful, it *is* funky and arty. Supermodern rooms are either one- or two-bedroom apartments or 'Euro-style' rooms, which in Alberta means 'small,' although small by Alberta standards isn't that small.

Guests also get access to all on-campus facilities, including a proper fitness center, a pool and a fine lobby bistro. The university is 6km northeast of downtown, but easily accessible on the C-train.

Centro Motel
MOTEL **$$**

(☏403-288-6658; www.centromotel.com; 4540 16th Ave NW; r incl breakfast from $114; 🕸 @ 🖙) A 'boutique motel' sounds like an oxymoron until you descend on the misleadingly named Centro 7km northwest of Calgary's real 'centro' on the Trans-Canada Hwy (Hwy 1). Taking an old motel building in March 2010 and making it over with modern boutique features, the indie owners have left no detail missing, from light fittings to bathrobes to the flower baskets hanging from the walkways. Calls to anywhere in Canada and the US are free.

Nuvo Hotel Suites
HOTEL $$

(☑ 403-452-6789; www.nuvohotelsuites.com; 827 12th Ave SW; ste from $150; ❄🤖) Now this is more like it.... Large, comfortable studio apartments with full kitchens including washing machines, all for a decent price in the Beltline neighborhood. Handy for downtown and Uptown 17th action.

Twin Gables B&B
B&B $$

(☑ 403-271-7754; www.twingables.ca; 611 25th Ave SW; ste $99-175; ❄) In a lovely old home, this B&B features hardwood floors, stained-glass windows, Tiffany lamps and antique furnishings. The three rooms are tastefully decorated, and the location across from the Elbow River provides opportunities for serene walks.

International Hotel
HOTEL $$

(☑ 403-265-9600; www.internationalhotel.ca; 220 4th Ave SW; d from $135; @❄🤖) All 35 floors of this property were renovated a few years ago and the results are uplifting. Large living spaces with great city views are standard, while the sweet suites may have the comfiest beds you'll ever pay to sleep on.

Carriage House Inn
INN $$

(☑ 403-253-1101; www.carriagehouse.net; 9030 Macleod Trail S; r from $159; ❄@🤖) When you arrive here, the boxlike exterior is less than inspiring, but things perk up inside. Recent renovations have done wonders in bringing the Carriage House back up to speed. The rooms are tidy and it's close to lots of eating and shopping options. The inn is 8km south of downtown Calgary on the arterial MacLeod Trail.

★ Hotel Le Germain
BOUTIQUE HOTEL $$$

(☑ 403-264-8990; www.germaincalgary.com; 899 Centre St SW; d from $329; ❄@🤖) 🍴 At last, a posh boutique hotel to counteract the bland assortment of franchise inns that service downtown Calgary. Germain is actually a member of a franchise, albeit a small French-Canadian one, but the style (check out the huge glass wall in reception) verges on opulent, while the 24-hour gym, in-room massage, complimentary newspapers and funky lounge add luxury touches.

Even better, the hotel is efficiently built and has a long list of conservation policies.

Hotel Arts
BOUTIQUE HOTEL $$$

(☑ 403-266-4611; www.hotelarts.ca; 119 12th Ave SW; ste from $269; ❄@🤖) Setting a new standard in Calgary, this boutique hotel plays hard on the fact that it's not part of an international chain. Aimed at the modern discerning traveler with an aesthetic eye, there are hardwood floors, thread counts Egyptians would be envious of and art on the walls that should be in a gallery.

Fairmont Palliser
HOTEL $$$

(☑ 403-262-1234; www.fairmont.com/palliser; 133 9th Ave SW; r from $319; @🤖) Cut from the same elegant cloth as other Fairmont hotels, the Palliser is easily the most stunning place to bed down in Calgary. With crystal chandeliers, marble columns, wood-inlaid arched ceiling domes and antique furniture, the interior has a deep regal feel to it, unlike anything else within the city limits. Classic, beautiful and worth every penny.

Hotel Elan
BOUTIQUE HOTEL $$$

(☑ 403-229-2040; www.hotelelan.ca; 1122 16th Ave SW; r/ste $419/629; ❄🤖) Elan is a luxury boutique hotel that opened in 2013 in a fancily refurbished Uptown condo building. For a slightly inflated price, you get rooms with personal internet routers, rainfall showerheads, heated toilet seats and heat-controlled floors. There's also a small gym. Parking costs $18 extra. If you're not the sultan of Brunei, come off-season, when prices fall to a more reasonable $200-ish a night.

Kensington Riverside Inn
BOUTIQUE HOTEL $$$

(☑ 403-228-4442; www.kensingtonriversideinn.com; 1126 Memorial Dr NW; r from $269; 🤖) This impressive hotel in Kensington is a delight; a refined attitude permeates the smart-looking, beautifully finished property. The rooms are elegant and have river views. Highly recommended.

Sheraton Suites Calgary Eau Claire
HOTEL $$$

(☑ 403-266-7200, 800-325-3535; www.sheraton.com; 255 Barclay Pde SW; ste from $379; ❄@🤖) With a great location and overflowing with amenities, this business-oriented all-suite hotel should satisfy even the fussiest of travelers. The staff love to go the extra mile. Valet parking, a pool and a beautiful interior top it all off.

✗ Eating

If Calgary is a fast-moving city, then its burgeoning restaurant scene is supersonic. Eating establishments come and go here like thieves in the night, making gastronomic Top 10s out of date before critics can even tweet them. The overall culinary trend is one of constant improvement in terms of both quality and eclecticism. Where solitary cows once roamed, vegetables and herbs now prosper, meaning that the trusty old stalwart, Alberta beef, is no longer the only thing propping up the menu.

You will find good eat streets in the neighborhoods of Kensington, Inglewood, 4th St – Mission District and Uptown 17th Ave, and downtown on Stephen St.

✗ Downtown

1886 Buffalo Cafe   BREAKFAST $

(187 Barclay Pde SW; ⊘ 6am-3pm Mon-Fri, from 7am Sat & Sun) A salt-of-the-earth diner in the high-rise-dominated city center that the realty lords forgot to knock down, this wooden shack construction is famous for its brunches fortified by huevos rancheros.

Peter's Drive-In   BURGERS $

(🖉 403-277-2747; www.petersdrivein.com; 219 16th Ave NE; mains $2.50-5; ⊘ 9am-midnight) In 1962 Peter's opened its doors and locals have been flocking here ever since to a largely unchanged menu of superthick shakes, burgers off the grill and fries that make no pretense of being healthy. It's a true drive-in, so either bring the car along or be happy to eat on the lawn out front. Peter's is handily located on 16 Ave NE, aka the Trans-Canada Hwy, 3km north of downtown.

Catch   SEAFOOD $$

(🖉 403-206-0000; www.catchrestaurant.ca; 100 8th Ave SW; mains $17-27; ⊘ 11:30am-2pm Mon-Fri & 5-10pm Mon-Sat) The problem for any saltwater fish restaurant in landlocked Calgary is that, if you're calling it fresh, it can't be local. Overcoming the conundrum, Catch, situated in an old bank building on Stephen Ave Walk, flies its 'fresh catch' in daily from both coasts (BC and the Maritimes).

You can work out the carbon offsets for your lobster, crab and oysters on one of three different floors: an oyster bar, a dining room or an upstairs atrium.

Blink   FUSION $$

(🖉 403-263-5330; www.blinkcalgary.com; 111 8th Ave SW; mains from $20; ⊘ 11am-2pm Mon-Fri & 5-10pm Mon-Sat) 🏶 Blink multiple times but you still won't miss this trendy city-center gastro haven where an acclaimed British chef oversees an ever-evolving menu of fine dishes that yell out that well-practised modern restaurant mantra of 'fresh, seasonal and local.'

The decor is all open-plan kitchens and exposed brick, and you can delve even deeper into the culinary process through regular cooking classes (last Sunday of the month; $125).

Home Tasting Room   CANADIAN, FUSION $$

(🖉 403-262-8100; www.hometastingroom.ca; 110 8th Ave SW; tasting plates $14-23; ⊘ 11am-10pm Mon-Fri, 5-11pm Sat, noon-10pm Sun) Sure, there's no accounting for taste, but if you can whip up food as good and as varied as Home Tasting Room, then you've got most bases covered. Wine pairing and shared plates of experimental Euro-influenced food are the order of the day at this new downtown perch where quality reigns over quantity.

Drop by and take the sting out of your midmorning appetite.

King and I   THAI $$

(🖉 403-264-7241; www.kingandi.ca; 822 11th Ave SW; mains from $12; ⊘ 11:30am-10:30pm Mon-Thu, to 11:30pm Fri, 4:30-11:30pm Sat, to 9:30pm Sun) Not just a movie with Yul Brynner, but Bangkok-good Thai food too. This downtown classic with an exotic atmosphere is popular with groups. Try the curries or the pad thai – both are fantastic.

Rush   FUSION $$$

(🖉 403-271-7874; www.rushrestaurant.com; 207 9th Av SW; mains from $25; ⊘ 11:30am-2pm Mon-Fri & 5-10pm Mon-Sat) Not to be confused with the so-bad-they're-almost-good Canadian rock band of the same name, Rush the restaurant is a decidedly cooler affair, with glass walls, gold millwork and not a head banger in sight. Foodwise, this is gastronomy from the top drawer, with intelligent wine pairings and a chef's tasting menu winning almost universal plaudits.

Opt for the foie gras or the halibut and enjoy the complimentary canapés and petit fours.

Teatro   ITALIAN, FUSION $$$

(🖉 403-290-1012; www.teatro.ca; 200 8th Ave SE; mains $32-45, 8-course tasting menus $135;

CALGARY FOR CHILDREN

Calgary is a very kid-friendly destination, with most attractions having a portion aimed at the younger set.

Encased in new digs east of downtown, **Telus Spark** (☑817 6800; www.sparkscience. ca; 220 St George's Drive NE; adult/child $19.95/12.95; ☉9am-5pm; 🚇) is the obligatory science center for kids. There is a dome theater, a kids' museum and exhibits on space, energy and science. On the same side of town is the highly rated Calgary Zoo (p573), which has a kids club, kids' camp and various youth programs.

The Heritage Park Historical Village (p574) is one of the best ways to teach a child about history, with costumed actors roaming wonderful re-creations of Calgary's early-20th-century streets.

Children of all ages enjoy **Calaway Park** (☑403-240-3822; www.calawaypark.com; admission/family $35.95/89; ☉10am-7pm Jul-early Sep, 11am-6pm Sat & Sun early Sep-early Oct, 5-9pm Fri, 10am-7pm Sat & Sun late May–Jul), western Canada's largest outdoor family amusement park. It has 30 rides from wild to mild, live entertainment, food vendors, different carnival games, a trout-fishing pond and an interactive maze. To get there, head 10km west of the city on Hwy 1.

☉noon-4pm Mon-Fri & 5-10pm daily) With performing waitstaff and Tony Award–worthy food, the aptly-named Teatro, in a regal bank building next to the Epcor Centre of Performing Arts, could quite easily be mistaken for a theater at first glance. This has long been one of Calgary's most discussed restaurants, and the dishes fuse Italian influences, French nouvelle cuisine and a bit of traditional Alberta.

The chef's eight-course tasting menu is an epic journey through the best parts of the fancy menu.

Caesar's Steak House   STEAKHOUSE $$$
(☑403-264-1222; www.caesarssteakhouse.com; 512 4th Ave SW; steaks from $35; ☉11am-10:30pm) In Naples, you eat pizza. In Vancouver, you eat salmon. In Calgary, you eat prime Alberta AAA steak – right here.

🍴 Uptown 17th Ave & 4th St – Mission District

Jelly Modern Doughnuts   BAKERY $
(☑403-453-2053; www.jellymoderndoughnuts. com; 1414 8th St SW; doughnuts from $2; ☉7am-6pm Mon-Fri, 9am-6pm Sat, to 5pm Sun) A Calgary tradition in the making, Jelly Modern has grabbed the initiative on weird doughnut flavors. The maple and bacon, and carrot cake (with dried carrots) varietals won't help ward off any impending heart attacks, but they'll make every other doughnut you've ever tasted seem positively bland by comaprison.

Everything's baked on-site, meaning once you've taken one sniff inside the glass door, you're putty in their hands.

Analog Coffee   COFFEE $
(www.fratellocoffee.com; 740 17th Ave SW; coffees $2-5; ☉7am-10pm) The third-wave coffee scene is stirring in Calgary (at last!) led by companies like Fratello, which runs this new hipster-ish cafe on 17th Ave that displays the beans of the day on a clipboard and has rows of retro vinyl spread along the back wall.

Galaxie Diner   BREAKFAST $
(☑403-228-0001; www.galaxiediner.com; 1413 11th St SW; mains $5-9; ☉7am-3pm Mon-Fri, to 4pm Sat & Sun) Classic no-nonsense 1950s-style diner that serves all-day breakfasts. Squeeze into one of the half-dozen tables, grab a pew at the bar or (more likely) join the queue at the door.

Mercato   ITALIAN $$
(☑403-263-5535; www.mercatogourmet.com; 2224 4th St SW; mains $16-22; ☉11:30am-11pm) Attached to an open-plan Italian market/ deli that sells everything from coffee to salami, Mercato is one of those local restaurants that gets everything right. Decor, service, atmosphere, food and price all hit the spot in a modern but authentic take on la dolce vita in the endearing Mission neighborhood.

Ox and Angela   TAPAS $$
(☑403-457-1432; www.oxandangela.com; 528 17th Ave; tapas $4-14; ☉11:30am-late) Re-creating Spain in modern Calgary isn't an obvious business project – there's the lack of palm

trees, qualified matadors and Latin lovers, for starters – but the new Ox and Angela has a good shot at it, at least in the gastronomic sphere. Inside a gorgeous modern-meets-Euro-rustic interior, tapas are served with a strong Iberian bias. Order piecemeal from a menu of Manchego cheese, tortilla (Spanish omelette) and cured *jamón serrano*.

Farm FUSION $$
(☑ 403-245-2276; www.farm-restaurant.com; 1006 17th Ave SW; tasting plates $12-19; ☉ 11.30am-10pm Sun Fri, 10.30am 11pm Sat) ✐ Raising the ox citement bar on 17th Ave, Farm is a 'tasting kitchen' for fine meats, beer, wine and particularly cheese. The menu is about attention to detail, back-to-the-land purity and a genuine love of good food.

Melrose Café & Bar CANADIAN $$
(☑ 403-228-3566; www.melrosecalgary.com; 730 17th Ave SW; mains $9-15; ☉ 11am-midnight Mon-Fri, 10am-1am Sat & Sun) Right in the epicenter of what passes for cool in Calgary on 17th Ave, Melrose is split into three sections: obligatory patio, casual sit-down restaurant and a sports bar with enough TV screens to make you feel like Winston Smith in *Nineteen Eighty-Four*. The scene alternates between boisterous post-hockey-game euphoria and unironic pre-Stampede cowboy antics. Count the 'yee-haws.'

★ Model Milk CANADIAN $$$
(☑ 403-265-7343; www.modelmilk.ca; 108 17th Ave SW; mains $19-32; ☉ 5pm-1am) Model Milk has a revolving menu that changes before the ink's even dry, so it's impossible to predict what you'll get to eat at the former dairy turned hip restaurant. Grits and prawns with a fried egg on top was heading the 'starter' lineup at last visit.

More certain is the service (knowledgeable waitstaff), the decor (mezzanine floor, communal seating and open kitchen) and the ambience (cool without trying too hard).

✕ Kensington

Higher Ground CAFE $
(☑ 403-270-3780; www.highergroundcafe.ca; 1126 Kensington Rd; snacks $5-8; ☉ 7am-11pm Mon-Thu, 8am-midnight Fri-Sun) ✐ Giving Calgary's as-yet-uncrowded indie coffee-bar scene the shot of home-roasted caffeine it needs, Higher Ground is a delicious mix of art gallery, gossip shop, public theater and community resource. It is also where you come for

lunch-size panini and a damned fine cup of coffee.

Pulcinella ITALIAN $$
(☑ 403-283-1166; www.pulcinella.ca; 1147 Kensington Crescent NW; pizzas $15-20; ☉ 11:30am-11pm) So Italian that the pizza oven was – apparently – made with rocks quarried from Mt Vesuvius near Naples, Pulcinella specializes in thin crispy Neapolitan pies with purposefully simple toppings. The decor is silvery metallic, and a casual bar area out front offers sanctuary for lone diners or those stood up on a first date.

Sushi Club JAPANESE $$
(☑ 403-283-4100; 1240 Kensington Rd NW; mains from $10; ☉ 11:30am-2pm & 5-9pm Mon & Wed-Fri) This could well be the best sushi in town. It's perhaps a bit on the pricey side, but you get what you pay for. It has a great lunch special, where a massive spread costs less than $10.

✕ Inglewood

★ Gravity Espresso & Wine Bar CAFE $
(www.cafegravity.com; 909 10th St SE; light lunches $6-12; ☉ 8am-6pm Sun & Mon, to 10pm Tue-Thu, to midnight Fri & Sat) ✐ More evidence that Calgary might be abandoning its bland race to modernity for more thoughtful community-led business is this hybrid cafe-bar, which alters its personality depending on the clientele and the time of day. The crux of the operation is the locally roasted Phil & Sebastian coffee beans, but that's just an overture for loads of other stuff, including live acoustic music, curry nights, home-baked snacks and fund-raisers.

★ Rouge FUSION $$$
(☑ 403-531-2767; www.rougecalgary.com; 1240 8th Ave SE; mains $36-80; ☉ 11:30am-1:30pm Mon-Fri & 5-10pm Mon-Sat) Rouge is becoming the city's – and one of Canada's – most celebrated restaurants. Located in a historic 1891 mansion in Inglewood, it's expensive and hard to get into, but once inside you're on hallowed ground. Enjoy the inspired, creative and sustainable food choices and exceptional fit-for-a-king service.

● Drinking & Nightlife

For bars hit 17th Ave NW, which has a slew of martini lounges and crowded pubs, and 4th St SW, which has a lively after-work scene. Other notable areas include Kensington Rd NW and Stephen Ave Walk (a six-block downtown stretch of 8th Ave). You can see the money walking Calgary's streets after dark in the form of beautiful, well-dressed 20-somethings in stretch limos and noisy stag nights in corporate bars.

For more on gay and lesbian nightlife, pick up a copy of *Outlooks* (www.outlooks.ca), a monthly newspaper distributed throughout the province. The website has an extensive gay resource guide to Calgary and beyond.

Hop In Brew
PUB

(☑ 403-266-2595; 213 12th Ave SW; ☉ 4pm-late) An old Craftsman-style house clinging on for dear life amid the spanking-new condos of the Victoria Park district, the Hop still gets hopping on a good night, with good tunes, a grungy atmosphere and plenty of beers on tap.

National
BAR

(www.ntnl.ca; 550 17th Ave SW; ☉ 11am-midnight) A new bar with old-school Calgary pretensions, the National blends seamlessly into the 17th Ave action. On its outdoor patio, office bods in Stetsons cluster loudly around communal tables and you'll hear the odd unashamed cry of 'yee-haw' (especially during Stampede). There's loads of beer choice, including some microbews on tap, plus typical pub grub.

Barley Mill
PUB

(☑ 403-290-1500; www.barleymill.net; 201 Barclay Pde SW; ☉ 11am-late) This freestanding structure next to Eau Claire Market is a favorite after-work stop for the downtown working stiffs who hug the outdoor patio when the temperature pulls itself out of its deathly winter chill.

Ship & Anchor
PUB

(☑ 403-245-3333; www.shipandanchor.com; 534 17th Ave SW; ☉ 11am-2am) The frankly ugly Ship is a classic Calgary institution – an all-time favorite of university students, people who think they're hip, and indie music fans. With an abundance of beers on tap, the shadowy interior is a cozy winter hideaway, while the picnic-table-filled patio is Posing Central come summertime.

Flames Central
BAR

(☑ 403-935-2637; www.flamescentral.com; 219 8th Ave SW; ☉ 9am-5pm Mon, 11am-5pm Tue-Thu, 11am-2am Fri, 4pm-2am Sat) The huge interior of what used to be a cinema has been transformed into the sports bar to end all sports bars. With more TVs than an electronics shop, it'll definitely give you a good view of the beloved Calgary Flames hockey team, even when they're playing avowed rival the Oilers. There is an on-site restaurant, and concerts are held from time to time.

Rose & Crown
PUB

(☑ 403-244-7757; www.roseandcrowncalgary.ca; 1503 4th St SW; ☉ 11am-late) A popular, multilevel British-style pub in the Beltline neighborhood.

HiFi Club
CLUB

(www.hificlub.ca; 219 10th Ave SW; ☉ 9pm-2:30am Wed-Sun) The HiFi is a hybrid. Rap, soul, house, electro, funk – the dance floor swells nightly to the sounds of live DJs who specialize in making you sweat. Check out Sunday Skool, the weekly soul and jazz session, or Saturday night's showcase for touring bands and DJs.

Twisted Element
GAY, LESBIAN

(www.twistedelement.ca; 1006 11th Ave SW) Consistently voted the best gay dance venue by the local community, this club has weekly drag shows, karaoke nights and DJs spinning nightly.

Back Lot
GAY

(209 10th Ave SW; ☉ 9pm-2:30am) This one's for boys mainly. There's a patio and drink specials while you take in the view.

☆ Entertainment

For complete entertainment guides, pick up a copy of *ffwd* (www.ffwdweekly.com), the city's largest entertainment weekly. The paper is free and found in numerous coffee bars, restaurants and street boxes in Calgary, Banff and Canmore.

Plaza Theatre
CINEMA

(☑ 403-283-3636; 1113 Kensington Rd NW) Right in the heart of Kensington, the Plaza shows art-house flicks and cult classics – it's where you'll end up doing the 'Time Warp' (again!).

Globe Cinema
CINEMA

(www.globecinema.ca; 617 8th Ave SW) Specializing in foreign films and Canadian cinema – both often hard to find in mainstream movie houses.

Epcor Centre for the Performing Arts
THEATER

(www.epcorcentre.org; 205 8th Ave SE) This is the hub for live theater in Calgary, with four theaters and one of the best concert halls in North America.

Loose Moose Theatre Company
THEATER

(www.loosemoose.com; 1235 26th Ave SE) Guaranteed to be a fun night out, Loose Moose has recently transferred to new digs near the Inglewood neighborhood. It specializes in improv comedy and audience participation.

Pumphouse Theatres
THEATER

(www.pumphousetheatres.ca; 2140 Pumphouse Ave SW) Set in what used to be, you guessed it, the pumphouse, this theater company puts on avant-garde, edgy productions.

Ironwood Stage & Grill
LIVE MUSIC

(www.ironwoodstage.ca; 1229 9th Ave SE; ⊘ shows 8pm Sun-Thu, 9pm Fri & Sat) Cross over into the hipper universe of Inglewood to find the grassroots of Calgary's not-exactly-legendary music scene. Local bands alternate with bigger touring acts for nightly music in the woody confines of Ironwood. Country and folk are the staples.

Broken City
LIVE MUSIC

(✒403-262-9976; www.brokencity.ca; 613 11th Ave SW; ⊘11am-2am) There's music here most nights – everything from jazz jams to hip-hop. There's also food and a patio.

Jubilee Auditorium
CONCERT VENUE

(www.jubileeauditorium.com/southern; 1415 14th Ave NW) You can hang with the upper crust at the ballet or rock out to a good concert, all under the one roof.

Calgary Flames
SPECTATOR SPORT

(✒403-777-0000; www.flames.nhl.com) Archrival of the Edmonton Oilers, the Calgary Flames play ice hockey from October to April at the **Saddledome** (Stampede Park). Make sure you wear red to the game and head down to 17th Ave or the 'Red Mile' afterwards as they call it during play-offs.

Calgary Stampeders
SPECTATOR SPORT

(✒403-289-0258; www.stampeders.com; ⊘Jul-Sep) The Calgary Stampeders, part of the CFL, play at **McMahon Stadium** (1817 Crowchild Trail NW) in the University District, 6km northwest of downtown.

🔒 Shopping

Calgary is shopping heaven or hell depending on your taste for modern mall ubiquity. There are several hot spots, but these districts are reasonably far apart. The Kensington area and 17th Ave SW have a good selection of interesting, fashionable clothing shops and funky trinket outlets. Stephen Ave Walk is a pedestrian mall with shops, bookstores and atmosphere. Inglewood is good for antiques, junk, apothocaries and secondhand books and vinyl.

Alberta Boot Co
SHOES

(✒403-263-4605; www.albertaboot.com; 50 50th Ave SE; boots $235-1700; ⊘9am-6pm Mon-Sat) Visit the factory and store run by the province's only Western boot manufacturer and pick up a pair of your choice made from kangaroo, ostrich, python, rattlesnake, lizard, alligator or boring old cowhide.

Chinook Centre
MALL

(✒403-259-2022; www.chinookcentre.com; 6455 Macleod Trail SW; ⊘9:30am-9pm Mon-Sat, 11am-7pm Sun) If you're in need of some retail therapy, Chinook, 6km south of downtown, is a good place to get your treatment. Chain retail shops, department stores, a movie theater and lots of greasy food are all present and accounted for.

Mountain Equipment Co-op
OUTDOOR EQUIPMENT

(✒403-269-2420; www.mec.ca; 830 10th Ave SW; ⊘10am-9pm Mon-Fri, 9am-6pm Sat, 11am-5pm Sun) MEC is the place to get your outdoor kit sorted before heading into the hills. It has a huge selection of outdoor equipment, travel gear, active clothing and books.

Smithbilt Hats
CLOTHING

(✒403-244-9131; www.smithbilthats.com; 1103 12th St SE; ⊘9am-5pm Mon-Thu, 8am-4:30pm Fri) Ever wondered how a cowboy hat is made? Well, here is your chance to find out. Smithbilt has been shaping hats in the traditional way since you parked your horse out front.

ℹ️ Information

Banks seem to live at every corner downtown; look to 17th Ave or Stephen Ave Walk if one isn't within sight. Many branches are open on Saturday and bank machines are open 24/7.

Alberta Children's Hospital (✒403-955-7211; 2888 Shaganappi Trail NW) Emergency room open 24 hours.

Calforex (228 8th Ave SW; ⊘8:30am-7pm Mon-Fri, 10am-5pm Sat & Sun) Currency exchange facilities.

Main Post Office (207 9th Ave SW; ⊘8am-5:45pm Mon-Fri)

Rockyview General Hospital (✒403-943-3000; 7007 14th St SW) Emergency room open 24 hours.

Tourism Calgary (www.tourismcalgary.com; 101 9th Ave SW; ⊙8am-5pm) Operates a visitors center in the base of the Calgary Tower. The staff will help you find accommodations. Information booths are also available at both the arrivals and departures levels of the airport.

ⓘ Getting There & Away

AIR

Calgary International Airport (YYC; www.calgaryairport.com) is about 15km northeast of the center off Barlow Trail, a 25-minute drive away.

BUS

The Greyhound Canada **bus station** (877 Greyhound Way SW) has services to Banff ($29, 1¾ hours), Edmonton ($49, 3½ hours), Drumheller ($38, 1¾ hours) and Lethbridge ($48, 2½ hours). Note that discounts are available online.

For a more comfortable experience, go with the superluxurious **Red Arrow** (www.redarrow.pwt.ca; 205 9th Ave SE) buses to Edmonton ($70, 3½ hours, six daily) and Lethbridge ($49, 2½ hours, one daily).

Canmore and Banff ($54, 2¼ hours, eight daily) are served by the legendary **Brewster** (www.brewster.ca).

Red Arrow picks up downtown on the corner of 9th Ave SE and 1st Ave SE. Brewster buses pick up at various downtown hotels. Inquire when booking.

CAR

All the major car-rental firms are represented at the airport and downtown.

TRAIN

Inexplicably, Calgary welcomes no passenger trains (which bypass the city in favor of Edmonton and Jasper). Instead, you get **Rocky Mountaineer Railtours** (www.rockymountaineer.com), which runs expensive cruise-ship-like rail excursions (two-day tours per person from $1000).

ⓘ Getting Around

TO/FROM THE AIRPORT

Sundog Tours (☑403-291-9617; www.sundogtours.com; 1 way adult/child $15/8) runs every half hour from around 8:30am to 9:45pm between all the major downtown hotels and the airport.

You can also go between the airport and downtown on public transportation. From the airport, take bus 57 to the Whitehorn stop (northeast of the city center) and transfer to the C-Train; reverse that process coming from downtown. This costs only $3, and takes between 45 minutes and an hour.

A taxi to the airport costs about $35 from downtown.

CAR & MOTORCYCLE

Parking in downtown Calgary is an expensive nightmare – a policy designed to push people to use public transportation. Luckily, downtown hotels generally have garages. Private lots charge about $20 per day. There is also some metered parking. Outside the downtown core, parking is free and easy to find.

PUBLIC TRANSPORTATION

Calgary Transit (www.calgarytransit.com) is efficient and clean. You can choose from the Light Rapid Transit (LRT) rail system, aka the C-Train, and ordinary buses. One fare ($3) entitles you to transfer to other buses or C-Trains. The C-Train is free in the downtown area along 7th Ave between 10th St SW and 3rd St SE. If you're going further or need a transfer, buy your ticket from a machine on the C-Train platform. Most buses run at 15- to 30-minute intervals daily. There is no late-night service. The C-Train was recently expanded, and there are plans for more lines in the future.

TAXI

For a cab, call **Checker Cabs** (☑403-299-9999) or **Yellow Cab** (☑403-974-1111). Fares are $3 for the first 150m, then $0.20 for each additional 150m.

BANFF & JASPER NATIONAL PARKS

While Italy has Venice and Florence, Canada has Banff (Map p46) and Jasper (Map p50), legendary natural marvels that are as spectacular and vital as anything the ancient Romans ever built. But don't think these protected areas have no history. Of the thousands of national parks scattered around the world today, Banff, created in 1885, is the third oldest, while adjacent Jasper was only 22 years behind. Situated on the eastern side of the Canadian Rockies, the two bordering parks were designated Unesco World Heritage sites in 1984, along with BC's Yoho and Kootenay, for their exceptional natural beauty coupled with their manifestation of important glacial and alluvial geological processes. In contrast to some of North America's wilder parks, they both support small towns that lure between 2 to 5 million visitors each year. Despite all this, the precious balance between humans and nature continues to be delicately maintained – just.

Visiting the Parks

Visitors come here for all sorts of reasons: to ski, climb and hike on the mountains, to raft and kayak the rivers, to camp among the trees, or explore on their mountain bikes. But most come simply to look, and to stand in awe of the sheer beauty of this amazing place.

As you pass through this special area, you are under the ever-watchful eye of the animals that call it home. This is the place to see the Canadian Rockies' Big Five: deer, elk, moose, wolf and bear. (But only if you're lucky: they don't pose for everyone's photos.)

The one-day park entry fee (for entry to both parks) is $9.80/4.90 per adult/child; the passes are good until 4pm the following day.

History

Banff National Park, Canada's first park, became the template for conservation. When Jasper joined the park system just over a century ago, this corridor of conservation was complete. Within that protected zone, the small towns of Banff and Jasper have emerged. These two towns, where development is frozen and the idea of ecotourism has been around since the 1880s, have lived in harmony with the surrounding wilderness for decades.

Banff is far from a secret these days: crowds are inevitable and you will have to share those scenic lookouts. But most will agree that that's a small price to pay for a part of this country that will remain in your thoughts long after you leave the mountains behind.

Kananaskis Country

Kananaskis, or K-Country as the locals call it, is a mountainous Shangri-la, with all the natural highlights of Banff National Park, but with almost no clamor. It abuts Banff National Park in the southeast, acting as both a buffer zone and a first-class wilderness area in its own right. At an impressive 4000 sq km, it's a hefty tract of landscape to try and take in. Luckily, there is a network of hiking trails to get you into the backcountry and away from the roads. Hikers, cross-country skiers, bikers and climbers – mainly in-the-know Albertans – all lust over these hills, which are the perfect combination of wild, accessible, unspoiled and inviting. If

you recognize anything, it's probably because you've seen it in one of a score of films made here, including *Brokeback Mountain*.

On the eastern edge of the mountains you can drive the scenic and sparsely trafficked Hwy 40 (south off Hwy 1, 20km east of Canmore) to the Kananaskis lakes, before turning down onto the unsealed Smith-Dorian Rd to complete the drive back to Canmore by a circuitous picturesque route. Or if you can, continue along Hwy 40 – which will treat you to blankets of pine forest interspersed with craggy peaks and the odd moose in the verge – all the way to Highwood House. This scenic drive is definitely the road less traveled and well worth exploring; be aware that this portion of the road is closed over winter.

🏃 Activities

K-Country is also C-Country. Cowboy-up and go for a ride with **Boundary Ranch** (☑403-591-7171; www.boundaryranch.com; Hwy 40; rides from $43.50; ☺May-Oct), which will take you for a trail ride that could last anywhere from an hour to days.

Purpose-built to host the alpine skiing events in the 1988 Olympics, **Nakiska** (www.skinakiska.com; Hwy 40), five minutes' drive south of the region's main service center, Kananaskis Village, is a racer's dream. Top Canadian skiers still train here. K-Country's other ski resort, Fortress Mountain, has been closed on and off (mainly off) since 2004.

The Kananaskis River has grade II and III rapids and is popular with white-water rafting companies operating out of Banff.

🛏 Sleeping & Eating

Proof of Kananaskis' get-away-from-it-all ethos came when it was selected to host the 2002 G8 summit, with leaders hidden away at the **Delta Lodge at Kananaskis** (☑403-591-7711; www.deltahotels.com; 1 Centennial Dr, Kananaskis Village; r from $189). The amazing scenery, tip-top facilities and isolation were a big hit. Delta's pricey **Fireweed Grill** (Delta Lodge; mains $20-30) does baked river fish and AAA Alberta steak.

Alternatively, sleep under the stars at the **Boulton Creek Campground** (☑403-591-7226; Kananaskis Lakes Rd; campsites/RV sites $23/35; ☺May-Oct).

ℹ Information

About 8km from Hwy 1 along Hwy 40 is the **Barrier Lake Information Centre** (☑403-

Banff National Park

Banff National Park

◎ Sights
1. Athabasca Glacier A1
2. Peyto Lake B2
3. Weeping Wall A1

⊕ Activities, Courses & Tours
Athabasca Glacier Icewalks .... (see 8)
Brewster .... (see 8)
4. Lake Louise Ski Area C3
5. Ski Banff@Norquay C3
6. Sunshine Village C4

⬤ Sleeping
7. Fairmont Chateau Lake Louise B3
8. Glacier View Inn A1
9. Mosquito Creek International
      Hostel B2
10. Num-Ti-Jah Lodge B2
11. Rampart Creek International
      Hostel A1
12. Waterfowl Lakes Campground B2
13. Wilcox Creek Campground A1

673-3985; www.tpr.alberta.ca/parks; Hwy 40;
☺9am-5pm), which has loads of info and sells
backcountry camping permits ($12).

Canmore

A former coal-mining town, Canmore was
once the quiet alternative to the mass tourism of Banff. Then, after one too many 'best-
kept secret' travel articles, everybody started
coming here for a little peace and quiet. Despite the commotion, the soul of the town
has remained intact, and Canmore, although
not national-park protected, has been developed sensibly and sustainably – so far. At
just 26km from Banff and on the cusp of
Kananaskis Country, it's at the crossroads of
some of the most magnificent scenery you
will ever see. For those seeking a mountain
holiday with slightly less glitz, more of a rugged feel and less pretension, Canmore can
still cut it.

Sights & Activities

Canmore excels in three mountain activities: cross-country skiing, mountain biking and rock climbing.

Cross-Country Skiing

Both winter and summer are prime times at the **Canmore Nordic Centre** (☑403-678-2400; www.canmorenordic.com; 1988 Olympic Way; day ski pass $10). Used for the cross-country skiing events at the 1988 Olympics, the Nordic Centre is arguably the best facility of its kind in Canada and the training ground for many national champions. It offers ski rentals and lessons for the uninitiated and a network of trails that would keep an Olympian busy for days.

Mountain Biking

Once the snow melts, the Nordic Centre's trails transform into some of the best mountain biking around, with over 80km of off-road to test your skills. On-site rentals cost $45 per day. Close to here, the Rundle Riverside and Spray River/Goat Creek trails both head north to Banff Town.

Rock Climbing

Canmore is one of the premier rock-climbing destinations in the Rockies. Not surprisingly, national mountaineering organization the Alpine Club of Canada has its HQ here. In the summer there are numerous climbing crags, such as Cougar Creek, Grassi Lakes and Grotto Canyon, all within a relatively short distance of each other. For those looking for multipitch rock, the limestone walls of Mt Rundle and Mt Yamnuska are local classics, with routes of all grades. In the colder months Canmore is the place to be for frozen waterfall climbing: learn at the Junkyards, practise on Grotto Falls or take the final exam on The Terminator.

If you're keen to give climbing in any of its forms a try, talk to **Yamnuska Mountain Adventures** (☑403-678-4164; www.yamnuska.com; Suite 200, Summit Centre, 50 Lincoln Park), which will provide expert instruction, qualified guides and all the gear you might need (two-day beginners' courses start from $325). Yamnuska also offers longer courses for those wanting to gain the skills necessary to spend some serious time in the hills.

Sleeping

Canmore Clubhouse
HOSTEL $

(☑403-678-3200; www.alpineclubofcanada.ca; Indian Flats Rd; dm from $36) Steeped in climbing history and mountain mystique, the Alpine Club of Canada's beautiful hostel sits on a rise overlooking the valley. You'll find all of the usual hostel amenities here, along with a sauna. The Alpine Club offers classes in mountaineering and maintains several backcountry huts.

The Clubhouse is a great place to find climbing partners or just soak up the spirit of adventure. Located 5km south of town, it's an inconvenient 45-minute walk or pleasant five-minute drive away.

Windtower Lodge & Suites
HOTEL $$

(☑403-609-6600; www.windtower.ca; 160 Kananaskis Way; d/ste $139/239; @☏) Named for the stunning rock feature only a few kilometers to the east, this modern and well-appointed hotel is a good option. The rooms are a bit small, so spending more on a suite is a good idea. Some rooms have fine views of the Three Sisters, and all have access to the hot tub and fitness center.

Falcon Crest Lodge
HOTEL $$$

(☑403-678-6150; www.falconcrestlodge.ca; 190 Kananaskis Way; r from $209; ✱☏) Of all the salubrious woody lodges in Canmore, Falcon Crest is perhaps the best. Ample deluxe rooms have balconies with views of Canmore's famous peaks, incuding Three Sisters, and there are various suite options. An exercise room and outdoor hot tub complement the Rocky Mountain experience.

Eating

Bagels for breakfast, beer and burgers for lunch, and steak for dinner. Look no further than the following trio.

Rocky Mountain Bagel Co
CAFE $

(☑403-678-9978; www.thebagel.ca; 829 8th St; bagels $6-8; ☉6am-6pm; ☏) 🍴 Is there anything better in life than sitting under the flower baskets at Rocky Mountain Bagel Co, studying the morning shadows on the Three Sisters while enjoying a toasted maple bagel and a latte? Possibly not.

Grizzly Paw
PUB $$

(☑403-678-9983; www.thegrizzlypaw.com; 622 Main St; mains $13-20; ☉11am-midnight) Shock horror exclusive. Alberta's best microbrewery (offering six year-round beers) is hiding in the mountains of Canmore. The veterans of raspberry ale and Grumpy Bear beer have just built a new brewery to support their legendary brewpub (tours and tasters are promised). There's also a micro-distillery on the way. And, yes, the pub serves grub.

Wood
STEAKHOUSE $$

(☑403-678-3404; www.thewood.ca; 838 8th St; mains $12-29; ☺7:30am-11pm) Plenty of wood and a big fireplace create a relaxed, sophisticated vibe in this log building in Canmore's town center. If you're having a day off from AAA Alberta steak (not easy here), plump for the excellent salmon burger with a Dijon tartar relish.

ⓘ Information

Canmore Visitors Information Centre (www.tourismcanmore.com; 907A 7th Ave; ☺9am-5pm) Just off the main drag.

ⓘ Getting There & Away

Canmore is easily accessible from Banff Town and Calgary from Hwy 1. The **Banff Airporter** (www.banffairporter.com) runs up to 10 buses a day to/from Calgary Airport ($55). **Brewster** (Map p592; ☑1-800-760-6934; www.explore-rockies.com) has connections with the airport and downtown Calgary for roughly the same price. **Roam** (www.roamtransit.com) buses connect every hour to Banff ($6, 20 minutes) .

Icefields Parkway

Paralleling the Continental Divide for 230km between Lake Louise and Jasper Town, plain old Hwy 93 has been wisely rebranded as the Icefields Parkway (or the slightly more romantic 'Promenade des Glaciers' in French) as a means to somehow prepare people for the majesty of its surroundings. And what majesty! The highlight is undoubtedly the humungous Columbia Icefield and its numerous fanning glaciers, and this dynamic lesson in erosive geography is complemented by weeping waterfalls, aquamarine lakes, dramatic mountains and the sudden dart of a bear, an elk, or was it a moose?

The parkway was completed in 1940, and most people ply the asphalt by car, meaning it can get busy in July and August. For a clearer vision consider taking a bus or, even better, tackling it on a bike – the road is wide, never prohibitively steep, and sprinkled with plenty of strategically spaced campgrounds, hostels and hotels.

◉ Sights

There are two types of sights: static (lakes, glaciers and mountains) and moving (elk, bears, moose etc). If you don't see at least one wild animal (look out for the inevitable 'bear jams') you'll be very unlucky. Static sights are arranged here geographically from south to north.

Peyto Lake
LAKE

(Map p586) You'll have already seen the indescribable blue of Peyto Lake in a thousand publicity shots, but there's nothing like gazing at the real thing; especially since the viewing point for this lake is from a lofty vantage point roughly 100m above the water. The lake is best visited in early morning, between the time the sun first illuminates the water and the first tour bus arrives.

From the bottom of the lake parking lot, follow a paved trail for 15 minutes up a steady gradual incline to the wooden platform overlooking the lake. From here you can continue up the paved trail, keeping right along the edge of the ridge. At the junction of three trails, follow the middle trail until you reach an unmarked dirt road; if you continue down it for about 2.5km you'll find yourself in a serene rocky bowl with a stream running through the center.

Weeping Wall
WATERFALL

(Map p586) This towering rock wall sits just above the east side of the highway. In the summer months it is a sea of waterfalls, with tears of liquid pouring from the top creating a veil of moisture. Come winter, it's a whole different story. The water freezes up solid to form an enormous sheet of ice.

The vertical ice field is a popular playground for ice climbers, who travel from around the globe to test their mettle here. Scaling the wall is a feather in the cap for the alpinists lucky enough to clamber to the top. Be sure to observe the ice from the safety of the roadside lookout; falling chunks of ice the size of refrigerators are not uncommon.

★ Columbia Icefield
OUTDOORS

About halfway between Lake Louise Village and Jasper Town is the only accessible section of the vast Columbia Icefield, which covers an area the size of the city of Vancouver and feeds eight glaciers. This remnant of the last ice age, which is up to 350m thick in places, stretches across the plateau between Mt Columbia (3747m) and Mt Athabasca (3491m).

It's the largest ice field in the Rockies and feeds the North Saskatchewan, Columbia, Athabasca, Mackenzie and Fraser River systems with its meltwaters. The mountainous sides of this vast bowl of ice are some of the highest in the Rockies, with nine peaks higher than 3000m.

Be sure to stop at the **Icefield Centre** (Map p586; ☑780-852-6288; ☺9am-6pm May-Oct) FREE, where you can chat with the rangers from Parks Canada about camping options and climbing conditions; they can answer any questions you might have regarding the park. There's a fairly insipid cafeteria here, along with some equally bland hotel rooms at the Glacier View Inn (p590).

Athabasca Glacier   OUTDOORS
(Map p586) The tongue of the Athabasca Glacier runs from the Columbia Icefield almost down to the road opposite the Icefield Centre and can be visited on foot or in specially designed buses. The glacier has retreated about 1.6km in the last 150 years. To reach its toe (bottom edge), walk or drive 1km to a small parking lot and the start of the 0.6km **Forefield Trail**.

While it is permitted to stand on a small roped section of the ice, do not attempt to cross the warning tape. Many do, but the glacier is riddled with crevasses and there are fatalities nearly every year.

The best way to experience the Columbia Icefield is to walk on it. For that you will need the help of **Athabasca Glacier Icewalks** (Map p586; ☑780-852-5595; www.icewalks.com; Icefield Centre; 3hr tours adult/child $70/35, 6hr tours $85/45), which supplies all the gear you'll need and a guide to show you the ropes. It offers a three-hour tour (departing 10:40am daily June to September), and a six-hour option (Sunday and Thursday) for those wanting to venture further out on the glacier.

The other far easier (and more popular) way to get on the glacier is via a 'Snocoach' ice tour offered by **Brewster** (Map p586; ☑877-423-7433; www.brewster.ca; adult/child $49.95/24.95; ☺tours 9am-5pm May-Oct). For many people this is the defining experience of their Columbia Icefield visit. The large hybrid bus-truck grinds a track onto the ice where it stops to allow you to go for a short walk in a controlled area on the glacier. Dress warmly and wear good shoes. Tickets can be bought at the Icefield Centre or online; tours depart every 15 to 30 minutes.

CYCLING THE ICEFIELDS PARKWAY

With its ancient geology, landscape-altering glaciers, and lakes bluer than Picasso paintings from the blue period, the 230km-long Icefields Parkway is one of the world's most spectacular roads, and, by definition, one of the world's most spectacular bicycle rides – if your legs and lungs are up to it. Aside from the distance, there are several long uphill drags, occasional stiff headwinds and two major passes to contend with: namely Bow Summit (2088m) and Sunwapta Pass (2035m). Notwithstanding, the route is highly popular in July and August (don't even think about doing it in the winter), with aspiring cyclists lapping up its bicycle-friendly features. No commercial trucks are allowed on the parkway, there's a generous shoulder throughout, two-wheeled company is virtually guaranteed, and accommodations along the route (both campgrounds and hostels/hotels) are plentiful and strategically placed. Some ply the parkway as part of an organized tour (with back-up vehicles), others do it solo over two to five days. There's a choice of six HI hostels and four lodge/motel accommodations en route. Book ahead. Basic provisions can be procured at Saskatchewan River Crossing, 83km north of Lake Louise.

It's considered slightly easier to cycle from north to south, starting in Jasper and finishing in Lake Louise, but the differences aren't great. Some people tack on the extra 60km between Banff and Lake Louise at the start or finish proceeding along the quiet Bow Valley Parkway and avoiding the busy Trans-Canada (Hwy 1).

Sturdy road bikes can be rented from **Wilson Mountain Sports** (www.wmsll.com; Samson Mall; ☺9am-7pm) in Lake Louise village. Brewster buses can sometimes transport bicycles, but always check ahead. **Backroads** (☑510-527-1555; www.backroads.com) runs a Canadian Rockies Bike Tour, a six-day organized trip that incorporates cycling along the parkway.

Athabasca Glacier to Jasper Town
SCENIC HIGHWAY

As you snake your way through the mountains on your way to Jasper, there are a few places worth stopping at. **Sunwapta Falls** (Map p604) and **Athabasca Falls** (Map p604), closer to Jasper, are both worth a stop. The latter is the more voluminous and is at its most ferocious in the summer when it's stoked with glacial meltwater.

A less-visited spot is idyllic blue-green **Horseshoe Lake** (Map p604), revered by ill-advised cliff-divers. Don't be tempted to join them.

At Athabasca Falls, Hwy 93A quietly sneaks off to the left. Take it. Literally the road less traveled, this old route into Jasper offers a blissfully traffic-free experience as it slips serenely through deep, dark woods and past small placid lakes and meadows.

🛏 Sleeping & Eating

The Icefields Parkway is punctuated by several well-camouflaged hostels. Most are close to the highway in scenic locations. More substantial hotels/lodges are available at Bow Lake, Saskatchewan Crossing, Columbia Icefield and Sunwapta Falls. There are also numerous primitive **campgrounds** (per night $16) in the area. Good options are **Honeymoon Lake** (Map p604), **Jonas Creek** (Map p604), **Mt Kerkeslin** (Map p604), **Waterfowl Lakes** (Map p586) and **Wilcox Creek** (Map p586) campgrounds.

Mosquito Creek International Hostel
HOSTEL $

(Map p586; ☎ 403-670-7589; www.hihostels.ca; dm member/nonmember $24/26) Don't let the name put you off. Mosquito Creek, 26km north of Lake Louise, is a perfect launching pad for backcountry adventures, the sauna is an ideal flop-down-and-do-nothing end to the day, and the adjacent river just adds to the atmosphere. The hostel sometimes closes in winter, so call ahead.

Rampart Creek International Hostel
HOSTEL $

(Map p586; ☎ 403-670-7589; www.hihostels.ca; dm member/nonmember $24/26) Rampart, 11km north of the Saskatchewan River Crossing, has long been a popular place with climbers, cyclists and other troublemakers. The tiny crag at the back is good fun for a bouldering session, and the 12 bunks and facilities are clean and cozy. Then there's the sauna –

for lethargy. Call ahead in winter in case it's closed.

Beauty Creek International Hostel
HOSTEL $

(Map p604; ☎ 780-852-3215; www.hihostels.ca; Icefields Parkway; dm member/nonmember $24/26; ⏰ check-in 5-10pm) 🚭 Forget the lack of electricity, propane-powered lights, outdoor loos and well-drawn water, and home in on the all-you-can-eat pancake breakfast and poetry-inspiring scenery.

Sunwapta Falls Resort
HOTEL $$$

(Map p604; ☎ 888-828-5777; www.sunwapta.com; r from $209; @) A handy Icefields pit stop 53km south of Jasper Town, Sunwapta offers a comfortable mix of suites and lodge rooms cocooned in pleasant natural surroundings. The home-style restaurant and gift shop on-site are popular with the tour-bus crowd.

Glacier View Inn
HOTEL $$$

(Map p586; ☎ 877-423-7433; Icefield Centre, Icefields Parkway; r from $249; ⏰ May-Oct) Panoramic views of the glacier are unbelievable at this chalet – if only the windows were a bit bigger. You are in the same complex as the madness of the Icefield Centre, so it can feel like you are staying in a shopping mall at times. But after all the buses go away for the night, you are left in one of the most spectacular places around. A nothing-to-write-home-about cafeteria shares the complex.

Num-Ti-Jah Lodge
INN $$$

(Map p586; ☎ 403-522-2167; www.sntj.ca; d from $233, mains from $14, 3-course dinners $45) Standing like a guardian of Bow Lake, the historic Num-Ti-Jah Lodge is full to the brim with character and backcountry nostalgia. Carved-wood interior decor, animal heads and photos from the golden age adorn the walls. The rooms are tidy, if a little small. The lodge restaurant has an extensive wine list.

Banff Town

Like the province in which it resides, Banff is something of an enigma. A resort town with souvenir shops, nightclubs and fancy restaurants is not something any national-park purist would want to claim credit for. But, looks can be misleading. First, Banff is no ordinary town. It developed not as a residential district, but as a service center for the park that surrounds it. Second, the commercialism of Banff Ave is delusory. Wander five minutes in either direction and (though you may not initially realize it) you're in wild country, a primeval food chain of bears, elk, wolves and bighorn sheep. Banff civilized? It's just a rumor.

History

While most mountain towns have their roots in the natural-resource industry, Banff was created in the late 1800s with tourism in mind. The railway arrived first, then the Cave and Basin hot springs were discovered, and the potential to make some money became evident. First came the hordes of wealthy Victorians, staying at the Banff Springs Hotel and soaking in the soothing waters. Everything changed in 1911 when the road finally reached the town and the doors were flung open to the masses.

Banff continued to grow as more tourists arrived and services aimed at not just the upper class began to take root. Town developers have long been frustrated by the inclusion of the town within the national park. This has meant that building restrictions are tight, new development has ceased and the future of building in Banff is both a political and ecological hot potato. Actually living in Banff is a challenge: the federal government owns all the land, only those employed can take up residence and businesses are obligated to provide accommodations for their employees.

Though the infrastructure and size of the town remains fixed, the number of tourists has continued to spiral skywards. For as long as the town has been incorporated, locals have bickered about tourism. While they may pay everyone's wages, the visitors overrun the town and move it away from the quiet mountain town it once was.

◎ Sights

Banff supports a healthy four museums, virtually unprecedented for a 'natural' national park.

★ Whyte Museum of the Canadian Rockies
MUSEUM

(Map p592; www.whyte.org; 111 Bear St; suggested donation $5; ⊙10am-5pm) The century-old Whyte Museum is more than just a rainy-day option. There is a beautiful gallery displaying some great pieces on an ever-changing basis. The permanent collection tells the story of Banff and the hardy men and women who forged a home among the mountains.

Attached to the museum is an archive with thousands of photographs spanning the history of the town and park; these are available for reprint. The museum also gives out leaflets for a self-guided **Banff Culture Walk**.

Banff Gondola
CABLE CAR

(⊋403-762-2523; Mountain Ave; adult/child $34.95/16.95; ⊙8am-9pm) In summer or winter you can summit a peak near Banff thanks to the Banff Gondola; its four-person enclosed cars glide up to the top of Sulphur Mountain in less than 10 minutes. Named for the thermal springs that emanate from its base, this peak is a perfect viewing point and a tick-box Banff attraction.

There are a couple of restaurants on top plus an extended hike on boardwalks to Sanson Peak, an old weather station. Some people hike all the way up on a zigzagging 5.6km trail. You can travel back down on the gondola for half price and recover in the hot springs.

The gondola is 4km south of central Banff.

Cave & Basin National Historic Site
HISTORIC SITE

(⊋403-762-1557; Cave Ave; adult/child $3.90/1.90; ⊙10am-5pm daily May-Oct, noon-4pm Wed-Sun Oct-May) Attention. National Historic Site ahead. The Canadian National Park system was effectively born at these hot springs, discovered accidently by three Canadian Pacific Railway employees on their day off in 1883, but known to Aboriginals for 10,000 years. Uncovering a thermal gold mine, the springs quickly became a bun fight for private businesses who offered facilities for bathers to enjoy the then trendy thermal treatments.

To avert an environmental catastrophe, the government stepped in, deciding to declare Banff Canada's first national park in order to preserve the springs. You can't swim here any more, but the site reopened as an impressive museum in May 2013 after a two-year restoration. Viewable is the original cave, the old outdoor springs and bathhouse (closed in 1971) and a lovingly curated cinematic display of Parks Canada's cache of 42 national parks. Leading out from the complex are two trails: an interpretive walk along boardwalks to the cave vent, and the 2.5km **Marsh Loop Trail** across the park's only natural river marsh.

ALBERTA BANFF TOWN

Banff Town

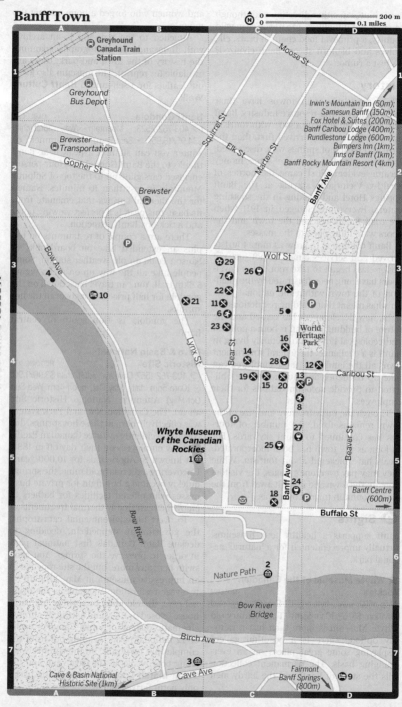

Greyhound
Canada Train
Station

Greyhound
Bus Depot

Brewster
Transportation

Gopher St

Brewster

Moose St

Irwin's Mountain Inn (50m);
Samesun Banff (150m);
Fox Hotel & Suites (200m);
Banff Caribou Lodge (400m);
Rundlestone Lodge (600m);
Bumpers Inn (1km);
Inns of Banff (1km);
Banff Rocky Mountain Resort (4km)

Squirrel St

Elk St

Marten St

Banff Ave

Bow Ave

4

10

21

29

7

22

26

11

6

23

17

5

Wolf St

Bear St

Lynx St

16

14

28

19

15

20

13

12

8

Caribou St

World
Heritage
Park

Beaver St

Whyte Museum
of the Canadian
Rockies

1

27

25

18

24

Banff Ave

Buffalo St

Banff Centre
(600m)

Bow River

2

Nature Path

Bow River
Bridge

Birch Ave

3

Cave Ave

Cave & Basin National
Historic Site (1km)

9

Fairmont
Banff Springs
(800m)

Banff Town

◎ Top Sights
1 Whyte Museum of the Canadian
Rockies... B5

◉ Sights
2 Banff Park Museum.............................. C6
3 Buffalo Nations Luxton Museum.......... B7

✪ Activities, Courses & Tours
4 Blue Canoe.. A3
Canadian Rockies Rafting
Company...(see 5)
Discover Banff Tours......................(see 5)
5 GyPSy Guide... C3
6 Hydra River Guides.............................. C3
7 Snowtips/Bactrax................................. C3
8 Warner Guiding & Outfitting................. C4

🛏 Sleeping
9 Banff Y Mountain Lodge........................ D7
10 Bow View Lodge.................................... A3

✖ Eating
11 Bison Restaurant & Terrace................. C3

12 Bruno's Cafe & Grill.............................. D4
13 Cows... C4
14 Coyote's Deli & Grill............................ C4
15 Eddie Burger & Bar.............................. C4
16 Evelyn's Coffee Bar............................. C4
17 Giorgio's Trattoria............................... C3
18 Le Beaujolais....................................... C5
19 Magpie & Stump................................... C4
20 Maple Leaf Grille.................................. C4
21 Melissa's Restaurant........................... B3
22 Saltlik... C3
23 Wild Flour... C4

🍷 Drinking & Nightlife
24 Banff Ave Brewing Co........................... C5
25 Elk & Oarsman...................................... C5
Hoodoo Club..................................(see 20)
26 St James's Gate Olde Irish Pub.......... C3
27 Tommy's Neighbourhood Pub.............. C5
28 Wild Bill's Legendary Saloon................ C4

🎭 Entertainment
29 Lux Cinema Centre............................... C3

Banff Upper Hot Springs
SPA

(☎403-762-1515; Mountain Ave; adult/child $7.30/6.30; ☺9am-11pm) Modern tourists use these soothing (if often crowded) hot pools, steam room and spa furnished with excellent mountain views near the Banff Gondola, 4km south of town. The water emerges from the spring at 47°C; in winter it has to be cooled to 39°C before entering the pool, but in spring the snowmelt does that job.

In addition to the pool, you can indulge in a massage or an aromatherapy wrap. Bathing suits, towels and lockers can be rented.

Lake Minnewanka
LAKE

Lake Minnewanka, pronounced miniwonka, as in Willy Wonka (not miniwanker, as Australian visitors enjoy saying), sits 13km east of Banff Town, making it a popular escape from downtown. The scenic recreational area has plenty of hiking, swimming, sailing, boating and fishing opportunities.

The nonchallenging trail around the lake is a good option for a walk; the path is easy to follow and popular. **Minnewanka Lake Cruises** (www.explorerockies.com/minnewanka; adult/child $44.95/19.95; ☺departures 10am-6pm May-Sep) offers a 60-minute interpretive cruise on the lake, giving plenty of insight into the region's history and geol-

ogy. You can also fish here or hike to the Alymer Lookout trail for spectacular lake and mountain views. A Brewster bus can transport you to the lake for an extra fee.

Banff Park Museum
MUSEUM

(Map p592; ☎403-762-1558; 93 Banff Ave; adult/child $3.95/1.95; ☺10am-6pm) Occupying an old wooden Canadian Pacific Railway building dating from 1903, this museum is a national historic site. Its exhibits – a taxidermic collection of animals found in the park, including grizzly and black bears, plus a tree carved with graffiti dating from 1841 – have changed little since the museum opened a century ago.

Buffalo Nations Luxton Museum
MUSEUM

(Map p592; ☎403-762-2388; 1 Birch Ave; adult/child $10/6; ☺11am-6pm) The Luxton Museum is essentially the story of the Alberta Aboriginal people, with a strong emphasis on the Cree, Blackfoot, Blood and Stony people. The displays, though a bit dusty, are pretty informative and contain some impressive eagle-feather headdresses and a life-size replica of a rather macabre sundance ceremony.

You'll probably learn an interesting fact or two here, but the museum won't delay you more than 30 minutes, making the $10 entrance fee a little steep.

🏃 Activities

Canoeing & Kayaking

Despite a modern penchant for big cars, canoe travel is still very much a quintessential Canadian method of transportation. The best options near Banff Town are Lake Minnewanka and nearby **Two Jack Lake**, both to the northeast, or – closer to the town itself – the **Vermilion Lakes**. Unless you have your own canoe, you'll need to rent one; try **Blue Canoe** (Map p592; ☑ 403-760-5007; www.bluecanoeing.com; cnr Wolf St & Bow Ave; canoes per hour/additional hours $36/20).

Cycling

There are lots of riding options around Banff, both on road and on selected trails. Popular routes around Banff Town include **Sundance** (7.4km round-trip) and **Spray River Loop** (12.5km); either is good for families. **Spray River & Goat Creek** (19km one way) and **Rundle Riverside** (14km one way) are both A to Bs with start/finish points near Canmore. The former is pretty straightforward; the latter is more challenging, with ups and downs and potential for thrills and spills.

Serious road cyclists should check out Hwy 1A between Banff and Lake Louise; the rolling hills and quiet road here are a roadie's dream. Parks Canada publishes the brochure *Mountain Biking & Cycling Guide – Banff National Park,* which describes trails and regulations. Pick it up at the Banff Information Centre.

Snowtips/Bactrax (Map p592; www.snowtips-bactrax.com; 225 Bear St; bicycles per hour/day from $12/42) has a barn full of bikes to rent and will also take you on a tour to one of the many bike trails in the Banff area ($20 per hour). Ask about shuttles to trailheads.

Hiking

Hiking is Banff's tour de force and the main focus of many travelers' visit to the area. The trails are easy to find, well signposted, and maintained enough to be comfortable to walk on, yet rugged enough to still get a wilderness experience.

In general, the closer to Banff Town you are, the more people you can expect to see and the more developed the trail will be. But regardless of where in the park you go walking, you are assured to be rewarded for your efforts.

Before you head out, check at the Banff Information Centre for trail conditions and possible closures. Keep in mind that trails are often snow-covered much later into the summer season than you might realize, and trail closures due to bears are a possibility, especially in berry season (June to September).

One of the best hikes from the town center is the **Bow River Falls and the Hoodoos Trail**, which starts by the Bow River Bridge and tracks past the falls to the Hoodoos, weird rock spires caused by wind and water erosion. The trail plies its way around the back of Tunnel Mountain through forest and some river meadows and is 10.2km return.

You can track the north shore of Lake Minnewanka for kilometers on a multi-use trail that is sometimes closed due to bear activity. The classic hike is to walk as far as the **Alymer Lookout** just shy of 10km one way. Less taxing is the 5.6km-return hike to **Stewart Canyon**, where you can clamber down rocks and boulders to the Cascade River.

Some of the best multiday hikes start at the Sunshine parking lot where skiers grab the gondola in winter. From here you can plan two- to four-day sorties up over Healy

ALBERTA BANFF TOWN

LOCAL KNOWLEDGE

LEGACY TRAIL

After years of planning, Parks Canada opened the long-awaited **Legacy Trail** in 2010, a paved multiuse path for cyclists, skaters and pedestrians that runs between Canmore and Banff. The 19km trail extends from Banff National Park's eastern gate 6km west of Canmore all the way to Banff town closely shadowing Hwy 1. From the park gate you can then pick up the **Canmore Trail**, which crosses the highway to reach Canmore. For those not up to cycling/walking in both directions, **Bike 'n' Hike Shuttle** (☑ 403-762-4453; www.bikeandhikeshuttle.com; one-way from $10) offer a handy bus service between the trailheads to get you back to your starting point.

Banff and Canmore are linked by two additional trails, the rugged **Rundle Riverside Trail** (for experienced off-road cyclists) and the easier **Goat Creek Trail**. All of the trails were washed out in the June 2013 floods. Check with **Parks Canada** (www.pc.gc.ca) for current status.

Pass and down to **Egypt Lake**, or get a bus up to Sunshine Village where you can cross the border into BC and head out across Sunshine Meadows and **Mount Assiniboine Provincial Park**.

The best backcountry experience is arguably the **Sawback Trail** that travels from Banff up to Lake Louise the back way over 74km, six primitive campsites and three spectacular mountain passes.

Check out Lonely Planet's *Banff, Jasper & Glacier National Parks* guide for more details about single-day and multiday hikes.

Horseback Riding

Banff's first European explorers – fur traders and railway engineers – penetrated the region primarily on horseback. You can re-create their pioneering spirit on guided rides with **Warner Guiding & Outfitting** (Map p592; ✆403-762-4551; www.horseback.com; 132 Banff Ave; 1hr rides from $45), which will fit you out with a trusty steed and lead you along narrow trails for part of the day. Instruction and guiding are included; a sore backside is more or less mandatory for beginners. Grin and bear it. If you're really into it, opt for Warner's six-day Wildlife Monitoring Adventure Expeditions out to limited-access areas accompanied by a Parks Canada researcher.

Skiing & Snowboarding

Strange though it may seem, there are three ski areas in the national park, two of them in the vicinity of Banff Town. Large, snowy Sunshine Village is considered world-class. Tiny Norquay, a mere 5km from the center, is your half-day, family-friendly option.

Sunshine Village (Map p586; www.skibanff. com; day ski passes $75) straddles the Alberta-BC border. Though slightly smaller than Lake Louise in terms of skiable terrain it gets much bigger dumpings of snow, or 'Champagne powder' as Albertans like to call it (up to 9m annually). Aficionados laud Sunshine's advanced runs and lengthy ski season, which lingers until Victoria Day weekend in late May. A high-speed gondola whisks skiers up in 17 minutes to the village, which sports Banff's only ski-in hotel, the Sunshine Mountain Lodge.

Ski Banff@Norquay (Map p586; ✆522 3555; www.banffnorquay.com; Mt Norquay Rd; lift tickets $46), just 6km north of downtown Banff, has a long history of entertaining Banff visitors. The smallest and least visited of the three local hills, this is a good place to

body-swerve the major show-offs and hit the slopes for a succinct half day.

Local buses shuttle riders from Banff hotels to both resorts (and Lake Louise) every half hour during the season.

White-Water Rafting

The best rafting is outside the park (and province) on the Kicking Horse River in Yoho National Park, BC. There are grade IV rapids here, meaning big waves, swirling holes and a guaranteed soaking. Lesser rapids are found on the Kananaskis River and the Horseshoe Canyon section of the Bow River. The Bow River around Banff is better suited to mellower float trips.

The following companies all have representation in the park. They offer tours starting at around $79. Factor in $15 more for a Banff pickup.

Canadian Rockies Rafting Company RAFTING
(Map p592; ✆403-763-2007; www.chinookraft. com; Sundance Mall, 215 Banff Ave)

Hydra River Guides RAFTING
(Map p592; ✆403-762-4554; www.raftbanff.com; 211 Bear St)

Wild Water Adventures RAFTING
(✆403-522-2211; www.wildwater.com; Lake Louise Dr) Has a desk at the Chateau Lake Louise, but will pick up from Banff for a fee.

👉 Tours

GyPSy Guide DRIVING TOUR
(Map p592; ✆403-760-8200; www.gpstourscan-ada.com; Sundance Mall, 215 Banff Ave; per day $39) The GyPSy is a hand-held GPS device that you take in your car and guides you around the area. There is a lively running commentary that broadcasts through your stereo, pointing out highlights as you travel. All you have to do is follow the directions and you get a great self-guided tour of the area – Banff, Lake Louise, Columbia Icefield, Jasper and Calgary are all included on the tour. Best of all, if you get tired of the tour guide you can always turn it off.

Discover Banff Tours GUIDED TOUR
(Map p592; ✆403-760-5007; www.banfftours.com; Sundance Mall, 215 Banff Ave; tours from $54) Discover Banff has a great selection of tours to choose from: three-hour Banff Town tours, sunrise and evening wildlife tours, Columbia Icefield day trips and even a 10-hour

grizzly bear tour, where if you don't see a bear you get your money back.

✷ Festivals & Events

The town's biggest annual event is the **Banff Mountain Film and Book Festival** (www.banffcentre.ca/mountainfestival) in late October and early November. Attracting the cream of the mountain-culture aficionados, this event is a must-do for the armchair adventurer and mountain guru alike with film screenings and book readings.

🛏 Sleeping

Compared with elsewhere in the province, accommodations in Banff Town are fairly costly and, in summer, often hard to find. The old adage of the early bird catching the worm really holds true here, and booking ahead is strongly recommended.

The Banff/Lake Louise Tourism Bureau tracks vacancies on a daily basis; check the listings at the Banff Information Centre. You might also try **Enjoy Banff** (☑1-888-313-6161; www.enjoybanff.com), which books rooms for more than 75 different lodgings.

Camping in Banff National Park is popular and easily accessible. There are 13 campgrounds to choose from, most along the Bow Valley Parkway or near Banff Town.

HI-Banff Alpine Centre   HOSTEL $
(☑403-762-4122; www.hihostels.ca; 801 Hidden Ridge Way; dm/d from $45/143; @ 🛜) Banff's best hostel is near the top of Tunnel Mountain and well away from the madness of Banff Ave. Walkers will find the commute a good workout, and their efforts will not go unrewarded. The buildings are finished in classic mountain-lodge style but without classic mountain-lodge prices.

There are clean, comfortable accommodations in bunk rooms and a few doubles, fireplaces in the common areas, and good views top it all off. The public bus runs right by the front door, so don't let the location deter you. The hostel is located off Tunnel Mountain Rd, an extension of Banff's Otter St.

Samesun Banff   HOSTEL $
(☑403-762-5521; www.banffhostel.com; 449 Banff Ave; dm/d incl breakfast $31.50/85; @ 🛜) 🛶 One of a half a dozen Canadian hostels, the Samesun is zanier, edgier and a little cheaper than the other local budget digs. Features include a large central courtyard with barbecue, compact four- or eight-person dorms,

an on-site bar, plus a selection of hotel-style rooms in an adjacent 'chalet' (they're billed as four-star standard though they're not quite there). The clientele is international, backpacker and young (or young at heart).

Banff Y Mountain Lodge   HOSTEL $
(Map p592; ☑403-762-3560; www.ymountainlodge.com; 102 Spray Ave; dm $33, d with shared/private bathroom $115/135; @ 🛜) The YWCA is Banff's swankiest hostel option, offering dorm rooms along with private family-oriented accommodations down by the river.

Tunnel Mountain Village   CAMPGROUND $
(☑877-737-3783; www.pccamping.ca; Tunnel Mountain Rd; campsites/RV sites $27/38) It's hard to imagine this campground filling its nearly 1000 sites, but come summer it's bursting at the seams with holidaymakers from around the globe. Located at the top of Tunnel Mountain with sites among the trees, it's not nearly as grim as it sounds.

Part of it is open during winter too, so if you want to sleep under canvas at -20°C, you can do it here.

★ Banff Rocky Mountain Resort   HOTEL $$
(☑403-762-5531; www.bestofbanff.com; 1029 Banff Ave; r from $159; 🛜🛏) Being 4km out of town at the far, far end of Banff Ave is a small price to pay for the preferential prices and excellent all-round facilities here (including a hot tub, pool, tennis courts and cafe-restaurant).

Added to this is the greater sense of detachment, quiet tree-filled grounds (it never feels like a 'resort') and generously sized bedrooms with sofas, desks and extra beds. There's a free shuttle into town (hourly) or you can walk or cycle 4km along the Legacy Trail.

Banff Caribou Lodge   HOTEL $$
(☑403-762-5887; www.bestofbanff.com; 521 Banff Ave; d from $179; @ 🛜🛏) One of the posher places in the locally run Banff Lodging Co empire (who don it three-and-a-half stars), the Caribou fits the classic stereotype of a mountain lodge, with its log and stone exterior, giant lobby fireplace and general alpine coziness.

Aside from 189 comfy rooms, you get free local bus passes here, a heated underground car park, an on-site Keg Steakhouse, and a hard-to-avoid spa with various pools and treatment rooms.

Irwin's Mountain Inn
HOTEL **$$**

(☎403-762-4566; www.irwinsmountaininn.com; 429 Banff Ave; d inc breakfast from $174; @🐾🅿️❄️) A marginal drop in price and quality on the upper echelons of Banff Ave lands you in Irwin's, where the rooms are verging on motel-like and the decor is more 'plastic' than granite. Not surprisingly, the place is popular with families who take advantage of the hot tub, steam room, fitness center and continental breakfast.

Bow View Lodge
HOTEL **$$**

(Map p592; ☎403-762-2261; www.bowview.com; 228 Bow Ave; r from $144; ✴️🐾🅿️❄️) The Bow View is a journeyman Banff option – older than most of the attractive log inns that line Banff Avenue, but neat and tidy all the same. Without any surcharge you can use the fitness facilities and pool in the huge Banff Park Lodge next door.

Inns of Banff
HOTEL **$$**

(☎403-762-4581; www.bestofbanff.com; 600 Banff Ave; r from $149; @🐾🅿️❄️) Slightly out of the hustle and bustle, there are some good deals to be found here. Though the architecture is a little passé, there are loads of facilities, including both indoor and outdoor pools, ski and bike rentals, and a Japanese restaurant.

Bumpers Inn
MOTEL **$$**

(☎403-762-3386; www.bumpersinn.com; 603 Banff Ave; r from $125; 🐾) Banff provides a rare no-frills motel in bog-standard Bumpers, which offers zero pretension, but plenty of financial savings.

★Fairmont Banff Springs
HOTEL **$$$**

(☎403-762-2211; www.fairmont.com/banffsprings; 405 Spray Ave; r from $412; @🐾🅿️❄️) Sitting at the top end of the 'lost-for-words' category comes this exquisite beauty. Imagine crossing a Scottish castle with a French chateau and then plonking it in the middle of one of the world's most spectacular (and accessible) wilderness areas.

Rising like a Gaelic Balmoral above the trees at the base of Sulphur Mountain and visible from miles away, the Banff Springs is a wonder of early 1920s revivalist architecture and one of Canada's most iconic buildings. Wandering around its museumlike interior, it's easy to forget that it's also a hotel.

Rimrock Resort Hotel
HOTEL **$$$**

(☎403-762-3356; www.rimrockresort.com; 300 Mountain Ave; r $298-313; @🐾🅿️❄️) Next door to the hot springs, the Rimrock is plush and spectacularly located, although it often gets overshadowed by Banff's crème de la crème hotel, the Fairmont. Controversially located in a wildlife corridor on the slopes of Sulphur Mountain, the views here are nonetheless inspiring.

Mountain decadence coats the chaletlike interior, the restaurant (Eden) is considered fine dining, and the rooms almost match the stunning outdoor vistas. Worth every penny.

Fox Hotel & Suites
HOTEL **$$$**

(☎800-760-8500; www.bestofbanff.com; 461 Banff Ave; d from $229; @🐾🅿️❄️) A relative newcomer opening in 2007, the Fox justifies its four-star billing with an eye for the aesthetic and great attention to detail. Bright, modern rooms have retro-patterned wallpaper and unique, interesting artworks, while the reception has enough trickling water to invoke flashbacks of Rome.

The highlight is the inspired re-creation of the Cave & Basin springs in the hot-tub area, with an open hole in the roof that gives out to the sky. The bar-restaurant is called Chilis and serves, among other things, excellent margaritas. The town is a 10-minute walk away.

Rundlestone Lodge
HOTEL **$$$**

(☎403-762-2201; www.rundlestone.com; 537 Banff Ave; d/ste from $209/274; 🐾❄️) This place is filled with pseudo old-English charm, complete with Masterpiece Theater chairs in the lobby. The standard rooms are fairly, well... standard, but family and honeymoon suites come with a kitchen, fireplace and loft.

The centrally located indoor pool is a nice feature, and the obligatory Banff hotel restaurant – this one's called Toloulous – makes a game attempt at food with a Creole twist.

✖️ Eating

Banff dining is more than just hiker food. Sushi and foie gras have long embellished the restaurants of Banff Ave, and some of the more elegant places will inspire dirty hikers to return to their hotel rooms and take a shower before pulling up a chair. Aside from the following establishments, many of Banff's hotels have their own excellent on-site restaurants that welcome nonguests. AAA Alberta beef makes an appearance on even the most exotic à la carte menu.

Evelyn's Coffee Bar
CAFE **$**

(Map p592; ☎403-762-0352; www.evelynscoffeebar.com; 201 Banff Ave; mains $6-10;

⊙6.30am-11pm; 🛜) Pushing Starbucks onto the periphery, Evelyn's parades four downtown locations all on or within spitting distance of Banff Ave. Dive in to any one of them for wraps, pies and – best of all – its own selection of giant homemade cookies.

Wild Flour
CAFE **$**

(Map p592; 📞 403-760-5074; www.wildflourbakery.ca; 211 Bear St; mains $5-10; ⊙7am-7pm; 🛜📶) 🌿 Banff's antidote to Tim Hortons is heavy on organic, vegan and frankly strange-looking cakes, pastries and cinnamon buns backed up with free-trade, organic coffee. They also bake their own bread.

Cows
ICE CREAM **$**

(Map p592; 📞 403-760-3493; www.cows.ca; 134 Banff Ave; ice cream $3.50-5; ⊙11am-9pm) A Prince Edward Island import, Cow's ice cream is legendary out east, but this is one of only two branches in western Canada. Bypass the tacky T-shirts and choose from 32 extracreamy flavors.

Bruno's Cafe & Grill
BREAKFAST, BURGERS **$**

(Map p592; 📞 403-762-8115; 304 Caribou St; mains $10-16; ⊙8am-10pm) While other joints stop serving breakfasts at 11am, Bruno's keeps going all day, replenishing the appetites of mountain men and women as it once replenished its one-time Swiss guide owner, Bruno Engler. It's a kind of greasy spoon meets pub. The walls are decorated with antique ski gear, and the crowd at the next table could well be last night's live band refueling for tonight's gig.

The formidable Mountain Breakfast ($17) is served in a basket and requires a Mt Rundle-size appetite.

Coyote's Deli & Grill
FUSION **$$**

(Map p592; 📞 403-762-3963; www.coyotesbanff.com; 206 Caribou St; lunch mains $8-14, dinner mains $20; ⊙7:30am-10:30pm) Coyote's is best at lunchtime, when you can bunk off hiking and choose a treat from the deli and grill menu, which is inflected with a strong southwestern slant. Perch on a stool and listen to the behind-the-bar banter as you order up flatbreads, seafood cakes, quesadillas or some interesting soups (try the sweet potato and corn chowder).

Eddie Burger & Bar
BURGERS **$$**

(Map p592; 📞 403-762-2230; www.theeddieburgerbar.ca; Caribou St; burgers $13) Avoid the stereotypes. The Eddie might appear pretentious (black leather seats and mood lighting), and

its name may contain the word 'burger,' but it welcomes all types (including exhausted hikers and kids) and its gourmet meals-in-a-bun are subtler and far less greasy than your standard Albertan patty.

Try the Spicy Italian or the Mexican and wash it down with a Kokanee beer.

Melissa's Restaurant
STEAKHOUSE **$$**

(Map p592; 📞 403-762-5511; www.melissasrestaurant.com; 218 Lynx St; mains $17-27; ⊙7am-10pm; 👪) Melissa's is a casual ketchup-on-the-table type of place in a 1928 heritage building. It's huge in the local community and has an equally huge selection of food and price ranges. Nonetheless, its brunch, dinnertime steaks and deep-dish pizzas are probably its most defining dishes.

Giorgio's Trattoria
ITALIAN **$$**

(Map p592; 📞 403-762-5114; www.giorgiosbanff.com; 219 Banff Ave; mains $16-30; ⊙5-10pm) Slightly fancier than your average salt-of-the-earth trattoria, Giorgio's nonetheless serves up authentic Italian classics like osso buco risotto and a fine pear-and-Gorgonzola pizza mixed with the odd Alberta inflection (buffalo pappardelle!). The interior is elegant and there are prices to go with it (especially the wines).

Saltlik
STEAKHOUSE **$$**

(Map p592; 📞 403-762-2467; www.saltliksteakhouse.com; 221 Bear St; mains $16-27; ⊙11am-2am) With rib eye in citrus-rosemary butter and peppercorn New York striploin on the menu, Saltlik is clearly no 'plain Jane' steakhouse knocking out flavorless T-bones. No, this polished dining room abounds with rustic elegance and a list of steaks the length of many establishments' entire menu. In a town not short on steak-providers, this could be No 1.

Magpie & Stump
MEXICAN **$$**

(Map p592; 📞 403-762-4067; 203 Caribou St; mains $9-14; ⊙noon-2am) A classic musty cantina full of dreadlocked Sol-swigging snowboarders. You'll feel it's almost your dinnertime duty to demolish an overloaded plate of oven-finished chicken enchiladas with a tangy side relish.

★Bison Restaurant & Terrace
CANADIAN, FUSION **$$$**

(Map p592; 📞 403-762-5550; www.thebison.ca; 211 Bear St; mains $29-45; ⊙5pm-late) The Bison might look like it's full of trendy, well-off Calgarians dressed in expensive hiking gear, but its a two-level affair, with a rustically elegant restaurant upstairs sporting a menu saturated with meat, and a cheaper, more casual terrace below, which serves big salads and weird starch-heavy pizzas with butternut squash and rosemary-potato toppings.

Maple Leaf Grille   CANADIAN $$$
(Map p592; ☑ 403-762-7680; www.banffmapleleaf. com; 137 Banff Ave; mains $20-40; ☺11am-10pm) With plenty of local and foreign plaudits, the Maple Leaf eschews all other pretensions in favor of one defining word: 'Canadian.' Hence, the menu is anchored by BC salmon, east coast cod, Albertan beef and Okanagan Wine Country salad...you get the drift. All very patriotic – and tasty.

Le Beaujolais   FRENCH $$$
(Map p592; ☑ 403-762-2712; www.lebeaujolais-banff.com; Banff Ave, at Buffalo St; 3-/6-course meals $68/95; ☺6-10pm) Stick the word 'French' in the marketing lingo and out come the ironed napkins, waiters in ties, snails (billed as 'escargot' because it makes them sound so much more palatable) and elevated prices.

Beaujolais might not be everybody's post-hiking cup of tea, but if you just came here to gaze romantically at the mountains, why not do it over wild boar, bison and foie gras.

🍷 Drinking & Nightlife

Throw a stone in Banff Ave and you're more likely to hit a gap-year Australian than a local. For drinking and entertainment, follow the Sydney accents to local watering holes or look through the listings in the 'Summit Up' section of the weekly *Banff Crag & Canyon* newspaper.

★ Banff Ave Brewing Co   PUB
(Map p592; www.banffavebrewingco.ca; 110 Banff Ave; ☺11:30am-2am) An offshoot of the excellent Jasper Brewing Co, this brewpub opened in Banff in 2010. It's best for a drink of craft beer, brewed on the premises and infused with Saskatoon berries and the like.

St James's Gate Olde Irish Pub   PUB
(Map p592; www.stjamesgatebanff.com; 205 Wolf St; mains from $10; ☺11am-1am Sun-Thu, to 2am Fri & Sat) As Celts pretty much opened up western Canada and gave their name to the town of Banff, it's hardly surprising to find an Irish pub in the park, and a rather good one at that. Aside from stout on tap and a healthy selection of malts, St James's offers classic pub grub such as burgers and stew.

Tommy's Neighbourhood Pub   PUB
(Map p592; www.tommysneighbourhoodpub.com; 120 Banff Ave; ☺11am-11pm) Tommy's pub-grub menu stretches to crab cakes and spinach-artichoke dip. More importantly for traditionalists there's good draft beer, a darts board, and plenty of opportunity to meet the kind of globe-trotting mavericks who have made Banff their temporary home.

Wild Bill's Legendary Saloon   BAR
(Map p592; www.wbsaloon.com; 201 Banff Ave; ☺11am-late) Cowboys – where would Alberta be without them? Check this bar out if you're into line dancing, calf-roping, karaoke and live music of the twangy Willy Nelson variety. The saloon is named after Wild Bill Peyto, a colorful 'local' character who was actually born and raised in that not-so-famous cowboy county of Kent in England.

Elk & Oarsman   PUB
(Map p592; www.elkandoarsman.com; 119 Banff Ave; ☺11am-1am) Upstairs with a crow's-nest view of Banff Ave, this is the town's most refined pub. The rooftop patio is prime real estate in the summer, and the kitchen will fix you up with some good food if you so desire.

Hoodoo Club   CLUB
(Map p592; 137 Banff Ave) If you came to Banff to go nightclubbing (silly you!) look no further than this joint, where you can drink, pose and dance in your sexy fleece not a mile from where wild animals roam.

☆ Entertainment

Banff Centre   THEATER
(www.banffcentre.ca; 107 Tunnel Mountain Dr) A cultural center in a national park? Banff never ceases to surprise. This is the cultural hub of the Bow Valley – concerts, art exhibitions and the popular Banff Mountain Film Festival are all held here.

Lux Cinema Centre   CINEMA
(Map p592; 229 Bear St) The local movie house screens first-run films.

ℹ Information

Banff Information Centre (Map p592; www. parkscanada.gc.ca/banff; 224 Banff Ave; ☺8am-8pm) Offices for Parks Canada.
Banff Warden Office Dispatch Line (☑403-762-1470) Open 24 hours for nonemergency backcountry problems.
Custom House Currency Exchange (211 Banff Ave; ☺9am-10pm) In the Park Ave Mall.

Main Post Office (Map p592; 204 Buffalo St; ⊘8:30am-5:30pm Mon-Sat)

Mineral Springs Hospital (☑403-762-2222; 301 Lynx St; ⊘24hr) Emergency medical treatment.

ⓘ Getting There & Away

The nearest airport is in Calgary.

Greyhound Canada (Map p592; ☑1-800-661-8747; 327 Railway Ave) operates buses to Calgary ($29, two hours, six daily), Vancouver ($130, 14 hours, five daily) and points in between.

Brewster Transportation (Map p592; www.brewster.ca) will pick you up from your hotel. It services Jasper ($69, 4¾ hours, daily) and Lake Louise ($20, one hour, several daily).

SunDog Tour Co (www.sundogtours.com) also runs transport between Banff and Jasper (adult/child $69/39, four hours, daily).

All of the major car-rental companies have branches in Banff Town. During summer all the cars might be reserved in advance, so call ahead. If you're flying into Calgary, reserving a car at the airport (where the fleets are huge) may yield a better deal than waiting to pick up a car when you reach Banff Town.

ⓘ Getting Around

Over 20 shuttle buses a day operate year-round between Calgary International Airport and Banff. Buses are less frequent in the spring and fall. Companies include Brewster Transportation and **Banff Airporter** (www.banffairporter.com). The adult fare for both is around $54 one way.

Banff Transit (☑403-762-1215) runs four hybrid 'Roam' buses on two main routes. Stops include Tunnel Mountain, the Rimrock Resort Hotel, Banff Upper Hot Springs, Fairmont Banff Springs and all the hotels along Banff Ave. Route maps are printed on all bus stops. Buses start running at 6:30am and finish at 11pm; the fare is $2.

Taxis can easily be hailed on the street, especially on Banff Ave. Otherwise call **Banff Taxi** (☑403-762-4444). Taxis are metered.

Lake Louise

Famous for its teahouses, grizzly bears, grand hotel, skiing, Victoria Glacier, hiking and lakes (yes, plural), Lake Louise is what makes Banff National Park the phenomenon it is, an awe-inspiring natural feature that is impossible to describe without resorting to shameless clichés. Yes, there is a placid turquoise-tinted lake here; yes, the natural world feels (and is) tantalizingly close; and yes, the water is surrounded by an amphitheater of finely chiseled mountains that Michelangelo couldn't have made more aesthetically pleasing. Then there are the much commented-on 'crowds', plus a strangely congruous (or incongruous – depending on your viewpoint) lump of towering concrete known as Chateau Lake Louise. But, frankly, who cares about the waterside claustrophobia? Lake Louise isn't about dodging other tourists. It's about viewing what should be everyone's god-given right to see.

When you're done with gawping, romancing or pledging undying love to your partner on the shimmering lakeshore, try hiking up into the mountainous amphitheater behind. Lake Louise also has a widely lauded ski resort and some equally enticing cross-country options. Thirteen kilometers to the southeast along a winding seasonal road is another spectacularly located body of water, Moraine Lake, which some heretics claim is even more beguiling than its famous sibling.

The village of Lake Louise, just off Hwy 1, is little more than an outdoor shopping mall, a gas station and a handful of hotels. The object of all your yearnings is 5km away by car or an equitable distance on foot along the pleasantly wooded Louise Creek trail, if the bears aren't out on patrol (check at the visitors center).

The Bow Valley Parkway between Banff Town and Lake Louise is slightly slower, but much more scenic, than Hwy 1.

⊙ Sights

★Lake Louise   LAKE
Named for Queen Victoria's otherwise anonymous fourth daughter (who also lent her name to the province), Lake Louise is a place that requires multiple viewings. Aside from the standard picture-postcard shot (blue sky, even bluer lake), try visiting at six in the morning, at dusk in August, in the October rain or after a heavy winter storm.

You can rent a canoe from the **Lake Louise Boathouse** (per hour $45; ⊘9am-4pm Jun-Oct) and go for a paddle around the lake. Don't fall overboard – the water is freezing.

Moraine Lake   LAKE
The scenery will dazzle you long before you reach the spectacular deep-teal colored waters of Moraine Lake. The lake is set in the Valley of the Ten Peaks, and the narrow winding road leading to it offers views of these distant imposing summits. As there is little hustle or bustle and lots of beauty,

Lake Louise Area

0 —— 4 km
0 —— 2 miles

To Golden
(75km)

Trans-Canada Hwy

Icefields
Pkwy

Bow River

Gondola
Base
Terminal

To Lake Louise
Ski Area (4km)

Hl-Lake
Louise

Whitehorn
Rd

Lake Louise
Station
Restaurant

Lake Louise
Inn

Lake Louise
Village

Mt St Piran
(2649m)

Little
Beehive

Fairmount
Chateau
Lake Louise

Deer
Lodge

Laggan's
Bakery

Bow Valley Pkwy

Lake Louise
Trailer
Campground

Lake Agnes
Teahouse

Mirror
Lake

Lake
Agnes

Mt Niblock
(2976m)

Big
Beehive

Lake
Louise
Boathouse

Louise
Creek Trail

Fairview
Rd

To Banff
(54km)

Mt Whyte
(2983m)

Lake
Louise

Lake
Louise Dr

Trans-Canada Hwy

To Banff
(52km)

Mt Fairview
(2744m)

Saddle
Mountain
(2433m)

Plain of Six Glaciers

Paradise Creek

Moraine Lake Rd
(closed Oct–Jun)

Mt Sheol
(2779m)

Mt Aberdeen
(3152m)

Paradise Valley

Banff
National
Park

The Mitre
(2886m)

Lake
Annette

Trail

Mt Lefroy
(3423m)

Moraine Creek

Ringrose
Peak
(3278m)

Mt Temple
(3453m)

Pinicle
Mountain
(3067m)

Sentinel
Pass

Larch
Valley
(2360m)

Moraine
Lake
Lodge

Mt Hungabee
(3490m)

Eiffel Peak
(3084m)

Wenkchemna
Peaks (3170m)

Trail

Moraine
Lake
Boathouse

Mt Bell
(2910m)

Wenkchemna
Pass

Eiffel
Lake

Moraine
Lake

Consolation
Lakes

Yoho
National
Park

Mt Neptuak
(3233m)

Valley of the Ten Peaks

Alberta

Mt Babel
(3101m)

Mt Tuzo
(3245m)

Mt Bowlen
(3072m)

Mt Fay
(3235m)

Mt Deltaform
(3424m)

Mt Tonsa
(3054m)

Kootenay
National
Park

British
Columbia

Mt Allen
(3301m)

Mt Perren
(3051m)

Mt Little
(3088m)

many people prefer the more rugged and remote setting of Moraine Lake to Lake Louise.

There are some excellent day hikes from the lake, or rent a boat at the **Moraine Lake Boathouse** (per hour $40; ⊘9am-4pm Jun-Oct) and paddle through the glacier-fed waters.

Moraine Lake Rd and its facilities are open from June to early October.

Lake Louise Sightseeing Gondola CABLE CAR (www.lakelouisegondola.com; 1 Whitehorn Rd; round-trip adult/child $28.75/14.25, guided hikes per person $5; ⊘9am-5pm, guided hikes 11am, 1pm & 3pm) To the east of Hwy 1, this sightseeing gondola will lever you to the top of Mt Whitehorn, where the views of the lake and Victoria Glacier are phenomenal. At the top, there's a restaurant and a Wildlife Interpretive Centre where you can partake in 45-minute guided hikes.

🏃 Activities

Hiking

In Lake Louise beauty isn't skin-deep. The hikes behind the stunning views are just as impressive. Most of the classic walks start from Lake Louise and Moraine Lake. Some are straightforward, while others will give even the most seasoned alpinist reason to huff and puff.

From Chateau Lake Louise, two popular day walks head out to alpine-style teahouses perched above the lake. The shorter but slightly harder hike is the 3.4km grunt past **Mirror Lake** up to the Lake Agnes Teahouse on its eponymous body of water. After tea and scones you can trek 1.6km further and higher to the view-embellished **Big Beehive** lookout and Canada's most unexpectedly sited gazebo. Continue on this path down to the Highline Trail to link up with the **Plain of Six Glaciers**, or approach it independently from Chateau Lake Louise along the lakeshore (5.6km one way). Either way, be sure to get close enough for ice-crunching views of the Victoria Glacier. There's another teahouse on this route that supplements its brews with thick-cut sandwiches and spirit-lifting mugs of hot chocolate with marshmallows.

From Moraine Lake, the walk to **Sentinel Pass**, via the stunning **Larch Valley**, is best in the fall when the leaves are beginning to turn. A strenuous day walk with outstanding views of Mt Temple and the surrounding peaks, the hike involves a steep scree-covered last push to the pass. If you're lucky you might spy some rock climbers scaling The Grand Sentinel – a 200m-tall rock spire nearby.

Shorter and easier, the 6km out-and-back **Consolation Lakes Trail** offers that typical Banff juxtaposition of crowded parking lot disappearing almost instantly into raw, untamed wilderness.

In recent years there has been a lot of bear activity in the Moraine Lake area. Because of this, a minimum group size of four has been imposed by the park on some hikes during berry-gathering season (June to September). If you're arriving solo, check on the noticeboard in the information center in Lake Louise for other hikers looking to make up groups.

Skiing & Snowboarding

Lake Louise Ski Area (Map p586; www.skilouise.com; lift tickets from $75), 3km east of Lake Louise Village and 60km northwest of Banff, is marginally larger than Sunshine Village but gets less natural snow. The ample runs, containing plenty of beginner and intermediate terrain, are on four separate mountains, so it's closer to a European ski experience than anything else on offer in Canada. The front side is a good place to get your ski legs back with a good selection of simpler stuff and fantastic views. On the far side there are some great challenges, from the knee-pulverizing moguls of Paradise Bowl to the high-speed cruising of the Larch area. Make sure you grab a deck burger at the Temple Lodge – it's part of the whole experience.

🛏 Sleeping

Lake Louise has a campground, a hostel, a couple of midpriced inns, and a handful of places that fall into the 'special night' category for many travelers.

HI-Lake Louise HOSTEL $ (☎403-522-2200; www.hihostels.ca; Village Rd; dm/d from $44/123) This is what a hostel should be – clean, friendly, affordable and full of interesting travelers. The building itself is a stunning example of Rockies architecture, with raw timber and stone melding to a rustic aesthetic masterpiece. The dorm rooms are fairly standard, but beware of the private rooms: they are on the small side and a bit overpriced.

Lake Louise Trailer
Campground   CAMPGROUND $
(☑ 403-522-3833; off Lake Louise Dr; RV sites $32; ⊗ May-Oct) This is the closest campground to the village and your best option if you plan to sleep in a million-star hotel. It's a vast place that has great views of Mt Temple. Steer clear of the sites near the railroad tracks as the thundering trains do wonders for keeping you up all night. This campground is for RVs only.

Deer Lodge   HOTEL $$
(☑ 403-410-7417; www.crmr.com; 109 Lake Louise Dr; r from $175) Tucked demurely behind the Chateau Lake Louise, the Deer Lodge is another historic throwback dating from the 1920s. But, although the rustic exterior and creaky corridors can't have changed much since the days of bobbed hair and F Scott Fitzgerald, the refurbished rooms are another matter, replete with new comfy beds and smart boutiquelike furnishings.

TV addicts, beware – there aren't any.

Lake Louise Inn   HOTEL $$
(☑ 403-522-3791; www.lakelouiseinn.com; 210 Village Rd; d from $119; @ 🛜 🏊) A large, sprawling resort close to the village that has its merits, including a pool, restaurant and a tiny historic ice-cream chalet. Room quality is variable, with some of the older wings more downbeat and motel-like.

★ Fairmont Chateau
Lake Louise   HOTEL $$$
(Map p586; ☑ 403-522-3511; www.fairmont. com/lake-louise; Lake Louise Dr; d from $450; @ 🛜 🏊) This opulent Fairmont enjoys one of the world's most enviable locations on the shores of Lake Louise. Originally built by the Canadian Pacific Railway in the 1890s, the hotel was added to in 1925 and 2004.

While opinions differ on its architectural merits, few deny the luxury and romance of its facilities, which include a spa, fine dining, a mini-museum, fine views and unforgettably grandiose decor. Rooms are comfortable, if a little generic.

Moraine Lake Lodge   HOTEL $$$
(☑ 800-522-2777; www.morainelakelodge.com; d $345-599; ⊗ Jun-Sep) Few people would shirk at an opportunity to hang around Moraine Lake for a day or three – and here's your chance. The experience here is intimate, personal and private, and the service is famously good.

While the lodge is billed as rustic (ie no TVs), the rooms and cabins offer mountain-inspired luxury with real fireplaces and balconies overlooking *that* view. There's a fine-dining restaurant on-site which wins equal plaudits.

✖ Eating

If you can't scrape together the $43 necessary for afternoon tea in the Lakeview Lounge at the Chateau Lake Louise, reconvene to one of the following.

★ Lake Agnes Teahouse   CAFE $
(Lake Agnes Trail; snacks $3-6; ⊗ Jun-Oct) You thought the view from Lake Louise was good? Wait till you get up to this precariously perched alpine-style teahouse that seems to hang in the clouds beside ethereal Lake Agnes and its adjacent waterfall. The small log cabin runs on gas power and is hike-in only (3.4km uphill from the Chateau).

Perhaps it's the thinner air or the seductiveness of the surrounding scenery, but the rustic $6 tea and scones here taste just as good as the $43 spread at the Chateau Lake Louise.

Laggan's Bakery   BAKERY $
(☑ 403-522-2017; Samson Mall; mains $5-10; ⊗ 6am-8pm) Laggan's (named after Lake Louise's original settlement) is a cafeteria/ bakery with limited seating that's famously busy in the summer. The pastries and savories aren't legendary, but they're handy hiking snacks and tend to taste better the hungrier you get. The pizza bagels are worth a special mention.

Lake Louise Station Restaurant CANADIAN $$
(mains $15-25; ⊗ 11:30am-9:30pm) Restaurants with a theme have to be handled so carefully – thankfully this railway-inspired eatery, at the end of Sentinel Rd, does it just right. You can either dine in the station among the discarded luggage or in one of the dining cars, which are nothing short of elegant. The food is simple yet effective. A must-stop for train-spotters.

❶ Information

Lake Louise Visitors Centre (Samson Mall, Lake Louise village; ⊗ 9am-8pm) Has some good geological displays, a Parks Canada desk and a small film theater.

Jasper National Park

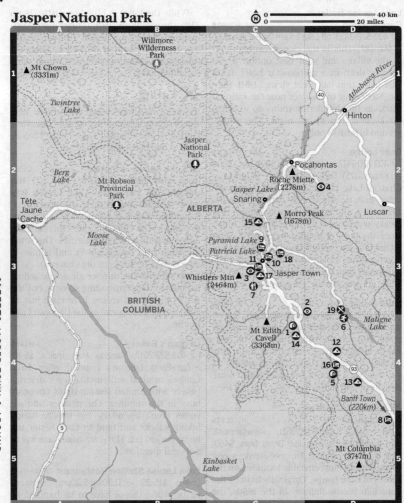

ℹ️ Getting There & Around

The bus terminal is basically a marked stop at Samson Mall. The easiest way to get here from Banff is by car or Brewster bus.

Jasper Town & Around

Take Banff, half the annual visitor count, increase the total land area by 40%, and multiply the number of bears, elk, moose and caribou by three. The result: Jasper, a larger, less-trammeled, more wildlife-rich version of the other Rocky Mountains parks. Its rugged backcountry wins admiring plaudits for its vertiginous river canyons, adrenalin-charged mountain-bike trails, rampartlike mountain ranges and delicate ecosystems.

Most people enter Jasper Town from the south via the magnificently Gothic Icefields Parkway that meanders up from Lake Louise amid foaming waterfalls and glacier-sculpted mountains, including iconic Mt Edith Cavell, easily visible from the town. Another option is to take a legendary VIA train from either Edmonton or BC through foothills imbued with fur-trading and aboriginal history.

Jasper National Park

Stacked up against Canada's other national parks, Jasper scores high marks for its hiking, pioneering history (it's the country's eighth-oldest park), easy-to-view wildlife and hut-to-hut backcountry skiing possibilities. Similarly, bike enthusiasts consistently laud it as having one of the best single-track cycling networks in North America.

◎ Sights

Jasper Tramway　　　　　　　CABLE CAR
(Map p604; ☎780-852-3093; www.jaspertramway.com; Whistlers Mountain Rd; adult/child $32/16; ◎9am-8pm Apr-Oct) If the average, boring views from Jasper just aren't blowing your hair back, go for a ride up this sightseeing tramway. The vista is sure to take your breath away, with views, on a clear day, of the Columbia Icefield 75km to the south.

From the top of the tram you can take the steep 1.5km hike to the summit of Whistlers Mountain, where the outlook is even better. The tramway is about 7km south of Jasper Town along Whistlers Mountain Rd, off the Icefields Parkway.

Miette Hot Springs　　　　　　　SPA
(Map p604; www.parkscanada.gc.ca/hotsprings; Miette Rd; adult/child/family $6/5/18.50;

◎8:30am-10:30pm) More remote than Banff's historic springs, Miette Hot Springs, 'discovered' in 1909, are 61km northeast of Jasper off Hwy 16, near the park boundary. The soothing waters are kept at a pleasant 39°C and are especially enjoyable when the fall snow is falling on your head and steam envelops the crowd.

There are a couple of hot pools and a cold one too – just to get the heart going – so it's best to stick a toe in before doing your cannonball.

You can hike 1km from the parking lot to the **source** of the springs, which is overlooked by the original aquacenter built in the 1930s.

Patricia & Pyramid Lakes　　　LAKE
There's nothing like seeing the mountains reflected in a small deserted alpine lake. These two lakes, a convenient 7km from town, fit that order nicely. Abundant activities are available on the water, with canoes, kayaks and windsurfers available for rent. For those wanting to stay dry, there are hiking and horseback-riding trails too.

Keep your eyes peeled for animals – these are prime spotting locations.

Lakes Annette & Edith　　　　LAKE
On the opposite side of the highway to the town, Lakes Annette and Edith are popular for water activities in the summer and skating in the winter. If you're brave and it's very hot, Annette is good for a quick summer dip – just remember the water was in a glacier not too long ago! Edith is more frequented by kayakers and boaters.

Both are ringed by cycling/hiking trails and picnic areas. The trail that circumnavigates Lake Annette is wheelchair-accessible.

Jasper Town to Maligne Lake　SCENIC DRIVE
The inspiring 46km drive between Jasper and Maligne Lake is almost obligatory for anyone with a day to spare in Jasper. The road twists and turns and it would seem that at every corner there is an opportunity to see some wildlife. This is one of the best places in Jasper to look for deer, elk, moose and, if you're lucky, bear.

The ideal time to see wildlife is early in the morning.

Maligne Canyon　　　　　　　CANYON
A steep, narrow gorge shaped by a river flowing at its base, this canyon at its narrowest is only a few meters wide and drops a stomach-turning 50m beneath your feet.

ALBERTA JASPER TOWN & AROUND

Jasper Town

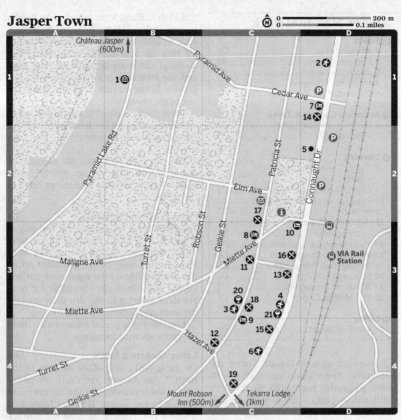

Jasper Town

Sights

1	Jasper-Yellowhead Museum & Archives	B1

Activities, Courses & Tours

2	Jasper Adventure Centre	D1
	Jasper Walks & Talks	(see 4)
3	Maligne Rafting Adventures	C3
	Maligne Tours	(see 3)
4	Rocky Mountain River Guides	C3
5	SunDog Tour Company	D2
6	Vicious Cycle	C4

Sleeping

7	Astoria Hotel	D1
8	Athabasca Hotel	C3
9	Park Place Inn	C4
10	Whistlers Inn	C3

Eating

11	Coco's Café	C3
12	Evil Dave's Grill	C4
13	Fiddle River Seafood Co	C3
14	Jasper Pizza Place	D1
15	Karouzo's	C4
16	Other Paw	C3
17	Raven Bistro	C2
18	Something Else	C3
19	Villa Caruso	C4

Drinking & Nightlife

	Atha-B Nightclub	(see 8)
20	Horseshoe Club	C3
21	Jasper Brewing Co	C3

Crossed by six bridges, various trails lead out from the parking area on Maligne Lake Rd. In the winter waterfalls freeze solid into sheets of white ice and are popular with ice climbers.

Maligne Lake
LAKE

Almost 50km from Jasper at the end of the road that bears its name, 22km-long Maligne Lake is the recipient of a lot of hype. It is billed as one of the most beautiful lakes within the park and there's no denying its aesthetics: the baby blue water and a craning circle of rocky, photogenic peaks are feasts for the eyes.

Although the north end of the lake is heavy with the summer tour-bus brigade, most of the rest of the shoreline is accessible only by foot or boat – hence it's quieter. Numerous campgrounds are available lakeside and are ideal for adventurous kayakers and backcountry hikers. Moose and grizzly bears are also sometimes seen here.

The **Maligne Lake Boathouse** (Map p604; ☑ 780-852-3370; boats per hour/day $30/90) rents canoes for a paddle around the lake. Not many people paddle all the way to Spirit Island – the lake's most classic view; it would take you all day. If you are really keen to see it, **Maligne Tours** (Map p606; ☑ 780-852-3370; www.malignelake.com; 616 Patricia St; adult/child $59/35; ⊙ 10am-5pm May-Oct) will zip you out there on its 1½-hour boat tours to the island.

Jasper-Yellowhead Museum & Archives
MUSEUM

(Map p606; ☑ 780-852-3013; www.jaspermuseum.org; 400 Pyramid Lake Rd; admission $6; ⊙ 10am-5pm) Poke your head into this museum if it's raining, snowing or too hot. Even if the weather is nice, it does an ample job of telling the Jasper story and the stories of those who arrived here to make it into the town it is today.

🏃 Activities

Cycling

Jasper is way better than Banff for single-track mountain biking; in fact, it's one of the best places in Canada for the sport. Many routes are within striking distance of the town. Flatter, on-road options include the long-distance grunt along the Icefields Parkway. The holy grail for experienced off-road bikers is the **Valley of the Five Lakes**, varied and scenic with plenty of places where you can let rip. For more information, get a copy of *Mountain Biking Guide, Jasper National Park* from the Jasper Information Centre.

Vicious Cycle (Map p606; ☑ 780-852-1111; www.viciouscyclecanada.com; 630 Connaught Dr; per day from $32; ⊙ 9am-6pm) can sort out bike rentals and offer additional trail tips.

Hiking

Even when judged against other Canadian national parks, Jasper's trail network is mighty, and with comparatively fewer people than its sister park to the south, you've a better chance of seeing more wildlife and fewer humans.

Initiate yourself on the interpretative **Discovery Trail**, an 8km easy hike that encircles the town and highlights its natural, historical and railway heritage.

Other short trails include the 3.2km **Mary Schäffer Loop** by Maligne Lake, named for one of the earliest European visitors to the area; the **Old Fort Loop** (3.5km) to the site of an old fur-trading post; and the 9km **Mina and Riley Lakes Loop** that leads out directly from the town.

Further away and slightly harder is the famous 9.1km **Path of the Glacier Trail** below the impressive face of Mt Edith Cavell, which takes you to the foot of the Angel Glacier through the wildflowers of the Cavell meadows.

The blue-ribbon multiday hike is the **Skyline Trail**, unusual in that almost all of its 46km are on or above the tree line, affording amazing cross-park views. The hike is usually split over two days, starting at Maligne Lake and emerging near Maligne Canyon on Maligne Lake Rd. You can pitch your tent in a campground or stay in the historic Shovel Pass Lodge.

The leaflet *Day-Hikers' Guide to Jasper National Park* has descriptions of most of the park's easy walks, while the backcountry visitors guide *Jasper National Park* details longer trails and backcountry campsites and suggests itineraries for hikes of two to 10 days. If you're hiking overnight, you must obtain a backcountry permit (per person per night $10, or buy a season pass for $69) from Parks Canada in the Jasper Information Centre.

Horseback Riding

Incredible fully guided summer pack trips head into the roadless Tonquin Valley where you are bivouacked in the backcountry (but comfortable) Tonquin Amethyst Lake Lodge. The trips are run by **Tonquin Valley Adventures** (☑ 780-852-1188; www.tonquinadventures.com; 3-/4-/5-day trips $795/1050/1295) and include accommodations, meals and complimentary fishing trips on Amethyst Lake.

JASPER IN WINTER

Half of Jasper shuts down in the winter; the other half just adapts and metamorphoses into something just as good (if not better) than its summertime self. Lakes become skating rinks; hiking and biking routes (and some roads) become cross-country skiing trails; waterfalls become ice climbs; and – last but by no means least – prices become far more reasonable.

The best natural outdoor skating rink is on Lac Beauvert in front of the Fairmont Jasper Park Lodge, an area that is floodlit after dark. More skating can be found 6km northeast of the town on Pyramid Lake.

The park has an incredible 200km of cross-country skiing trails. Routes less prone to an early snow melt are the **Pyramid Lake Fire Road**, the **Meeting of the Waters** (along a closed section of Hwy 93A), the **Moab Lake Trail** and the **Mt Edith Cavell Road**. Relatively safe, but dramatic, backcountry skiing can be found in the Tonquin Valley, where you can overnight in a couple of lodges. See www.tonquinvalley.com for more details.

Slightly less athletic is the iconic three-hour **Maligne Canyon Ice Walk** offered by **Jasper Adventure Centre** (Map p606; ☑780-852-5595; www.jasperadventurecentre.com; 618 Connaught Dr; adult/child $55/25), a walk through a series of frozen waterfalls viewable from December to April. Extremists tackle these slippery behemoths with rappels and ice axes.

Skiing & Snowboarding

Jasper National Park's only downhill ski area is **Marmot Basin** (Map p604; www.skimarmot.com; Marmot Basin Rd; day pass adult/child $72/58), which lies 19km southwest of town off Hwy 93A. Though not legendary, the presence of 86 runs and the longest high-speed quad chairlift in the Rockies, mean Marmot is no pushover, and its relative isolation compared to the trio of ski areas in Banff means shorter lift lines.

On-site are some cross-country trails and a predictably expensive day lodge, but no overnight accommodations. Regular shuttles link to Jasper Town in season. Seriously cold weather can drift in suddenly off the mountains, so be sure to dress appropriately.

White-Water Rafting

There's nothing like glacial waters to fight the summer heat. The Jasper area has lots of good rafting opportunities, from raging to relaxed, on the **Maligne**, **Sunwapta** and **Athabasca Rivers**. The season runs from May to September.

Maligne Rafting Adventures RAFTING
(Map p606; ☑780-852-3370; www.raftjasper.com; 616 Patricia St; trips from $59) Everything from float trips to grade II and III adventures, plus overnight trips.

Rocky Mountain River Guides RAFTING
(Map p606; ☑780-852-3777; www.rmriverguides.com; 626 Connaught Dr; trips from $64) Fun for beginners and also for more experienced river-runners.

☞ Tours

There is a variety of tour companies and booking centers in Jasper. They run a plethora of tours, including horseback riding, boat trips, wildlife-watching, hiking, and other outdoor activities.

Jasper Walks & Talks HIKING
(Map p606; ☑780-852-4994; www.walksntalks.com; 626 Connaught Dr) Walks & Talks Jasper leads small groups of people on personalized tours that include two-hour wildlife tours ($60) at 6.45am from June to October, and Mount Edith Cavell Meadows picnics ($85) departing at 9.30am from June to October.

SunDog Tour Company GUIDED TOUR
(Map p606; ☑780-852-4056, 888-786-3641; www.sundogtours.com; Connaught Dr) SunDog Tour Company is one of many tour companies and booking centers in Jasper. It runs a whole host of tours, including trips to the icefields, train rides, boat rides, wildlife-viewing, rafting, horseback riding and more.

📛 Sleeping

Despite its reputation as a quiet antidote to Banff, Jasper Town still gets busy in the summer. Book ahead or consider visiting in the less-crowded late winter/early spring shoulder season when the deserted mountainscapes (best accessed on cross-country skis) take on a whole new dimension.

Accommodations in Jasper are generally cheaper than Banff, but that's not really saying much. Jasper's 10 park campgrounds are open from mid-May to September/October. One (Wapiti) is partly open year-round. Four of them take reservations. For information, contact **Parks Canada** (☑780-852-6176; 500 Connaught Dr) at the Jasper Information Centre.

Several places outside the town proper offer bungalows (usually wooden cabins) that are only open in summer. There are considerable winter discounts.

YHA Maligne Canyon　　　　HOSTEL $
(Map p604; ☑1-877-852-0781; www.hihostels.ca; Maligne Lake Rd; dm $24.20) 🏃 Well positioned for winter cross-country skiing and summer sorties along the Skyline Trail, this very basic hostel is poised a little too close to the road to merit a proper 'rustic' tag. Die-hards can get back to nature with six-bed dorms, outhouse toilets and regular visits to the water pump.

Whistlers Campground　　CAMPGROUND $
(Map p604; ☑780-852-6177; Whistlers Rd; campsites/RV sites $22.50/38; ☺May-Oct) Ever spent the night with 780 other campers? Well, here is your chance. This mini camping city isn't particularly private, but it is the closest option to Jasper Town. Unbelievably, it regularly fills up in the high season. There are interpretive programs, flush toilets and fire pits.

HI-Jasper　　　　　　　　HOSTEL $
(Map p604; ☑780-852-3215; www.hihostels.ca; Whistlers Mountain Rd; dm/d $30.80/78.10; @☎) It would be easy not to like this hostel. With dorm rooms that sleep upward of 40 people, giving it that distinctive refugee-camp feel, and a location just far enough from town that the walk is a killer, it's already two strikes down. Despite all of this, though, it's a great place to stay.

The proximity of roommates and relative isolation foster a real community feel, and the nice interior, friendly staff and pristine surroundings make it that much better.

Snaring River Campground　CAMPGROUND $
(Map p604; Hwy 16; campsites $15.70; ☺May-Sep) Situated 17km north of Jasper Town, this basic campground – the park's most primitive and isolated – is the perfect antidote to the busy campgrounds found elsewhere in the park.

Athabasca Hotel　　　　　HOTEL $$
(Map p606; ☑780-852-3386; www.athabasca-hotel.com; 510 Patricia St; r with shared/pirvate bathroom $99/175; @☎) If you can take the stuffed moose heads, noisy downstairs barnightclub and service that is sometimes as fickle as the mountain weather, you'll have no problems at the Athabasca (or Atha-B, as it's known). Centrally located with an attached restaurant and small, but comfortable, rooms (many with shared bathroom) it's been around since 1929 and is the best bargain in town.

★**Park Place Inn**　　BOUTIQUE HOTEL $$$
(Map p606; ☑780-852-9970; www.parkplaceinn.com; 623 Patricia St; r from $229; @) Giving nothing away behind its rather ordinary exterior among a parade of downtown shops, the Park Place is a head-turner as soon as you ascend the stairs to its plush open lobby. The 14 self-proclaimed heritage rooms are well deserving of their superior status, with marble surfaces, fine local art, claw-foot baths and a general air of refinement and luxury. The service is equally professional.

Tekarra Lodge　　　　　HOTEL $$$
(☑780-852-3058; www.tekarralodge.com; Hwy 93A; d from $219; ☺May-Oct) The most atmospheric cabins in the park are set next to the Athabasca River amid tall trees and splendid tranquility. Hardwood floors, wood-paneled walls plus fireplaces and kitchenettes inspire coziness. It's only 1km from the town, but has a distinct backcountry feel.

Fairmont Jasper Park Lodge　HOTEL $$$
(Map p604; ☑780-852-3301; www.fairmont.com/jasper; 1 Old Lodge Rd; r from $600; @☎) Sitting on the shore of Lake Beauvert and surrounded by manicured grounds and mountain peaks, this classic old lodge is deservedly popular. With a country-club-meets-1950s-holiday-camp air, the amenity-filled cabins and chalets are a throwback to a more opulent era.

The lodge's gem is its main lounge, open to the public, with stupendous lake views. It's filled with log furniture, chandeliers and fireplaces and is the best place in town to write a postcard over a quiet cocktail. There are often off-season discounts.

Whistlers Inn
HOTEL $$$

(Map p606; ☑780-852-9919; www.whistlersinn. com; cnr Connaught Dr & Miette Ave; r $195; @🛜🛁) A central location and above-standard rooms give Whistlers an edge over many of its rivals. The rooftop hot tub alone is worth spending the night for – watch the sun dip behind the hills as the recuperative waters soak away the stress of the day. What more could you ask for?

Astoria Hotel
HOTEL $$$

(Map p606; ☑780-852-3351; www.astoriahotel. com; 404 Connaught Dr; d from $188; 🛜) With its gabled Bavarian roof, the Astoria is one of the town's most distinctive pieces of architecture and one of an original trio of Jasper hotels that has been owned by the same family since the 1920s. Journeyman rooms are functional and comfortable, and are bolstered by the presence of a downstairs bar (De'd Dog) and restaurant (Papa George's).

Coast Pyramid Lake Resort
HOTEL $$$

(Map p604; ☑780-852-4900; www.coasthotels. com; Pyramid Lake Rd; d from $249; ⊙May-Sep) This large property has fantastic views of the lake and great access to it. The design is a bit strange, with a huge swath of concrete driveway bisecting the hotel. The chalet-style buildings fan up the hill, giving most rooms an unencumbered view of the lake.

Ample opportunities for lake fun abound, with canoes for rent and a small beach to hang out on. The prices are a bit on the high side and it would do well to improve some of the finishing touches.

Mount Robson Inn
MOTEL $$$

(☑780-852-3327; www.mountrobsoninn.com; 902 Connaught Dr; r incl breakfast from $255; ❄@🛜) A clean, plush place laid out motel-style on the edge of Jasper Town which offers hot tubs, on-site restaurant and a substantial breakfast.

Château Jasper
HOTEL $$$

(☑780-852-5644; www.mpljasper.com; 96 Geikie St; r from $242; ❄@🛜🛁) The Château Jas-per is more conference hotel than castle, though with the right expectations, it shouldn't disappoint. It's a 700m stroll into the town center.

✖ Eating

Jasper's cuisine is mainly hearty post-hiking fare. Inexplicably, there's an abundance of Greek-themed places. Most of the restaurants are located in the town around Connaught Dr and Patricia St. Outlying nexuses such as Maligne Lake and the Whistlers have cafeteria-style restaurants that close in the winter.

★ Other Paw
CAFE, BAKERY $

(Map p606; ☑780-852-2253; 610 Connaught Dr; snacks $2-6; ⊙7am-6pm) An offshoot of The Bear's Paw, a larger cafe around the corner, the Other Paw offers the same insanely addictive mix of breads, pastries, muffins and coffee, but it stays open longer, plus it's right opposite the train station. The aromatic memory of its white chocolate and raspberry scones is enough to jerk your senses into action during the last few kilometers of a lengthy hike/bike/ski.

Coco's Café
CAFE $

(Map p606; ☑780-852-4550; 608 Patricia St; mains $5-10; ⊙8am-4pm) 🍃 Rating Jasper's best overall cafe is a toss-up for some punters, but few disagree that Coco's usually comes out on top on the breakfast front. There's not much room inside, but plenty of bodies are content to cram in to plan hikes, trade bear sightings or compare rucksack burns. Ethical eaters are well catered for, with tofu scrambles and fair-trade coffee.

View Restaurant
FAST FOOD $

(Map p604; Maligne Lake Lodge; snacks $4-10; ⊙9am-7pm) On first impressions this aptly named restaurant (behold the view!) at the head of Maligne Lake is just another overpriced cafeteria for tourists. But, beyond the sandwiches, soups and summer jobbers, this place serves up some of the best pastries, muffins and cinnamon buns in the park.

Jasper Pizza Place
PIZZA $$

(Map p606; ☑780-852-3225; 402 Connaught Dr; pizzas $13-16; ⊙11am-11pm) Ask a local (if you can find one) where to grab a cheap meal and they'll mention this place. There's a method to the queuing madness, if you're prepared to stick around long enough to fight for a table. Not surprisingly, the much-sought-after pizzas are rather good.

Karouzo's
STEAKHOUSE $$

(Map p606; ☑780-852-4640; www.karouzojasper.com; 626 Connaught Dr; mains $15-30; ☺11am-11pm Mar-Oct; ☻) Flying the flag for simple, family-friendly restaurants serving big portions from internationally themed menus (with an inevitable Greek subsection), Karouzo's suceeds in numerous fields – especially steak.

Something Else
MEDITERRANEAN, STEAKHOUSE $$

(Map p606; 621 Patricia St; mains $13-24; ☺11am-11pm; ☻) Essentially a Greek restaurant, Something Else wears many hats (American, Italian, Cajun) and doesn't always succeed. What it *is* good for is space (even on a Saturday night), decent beer, menu variety, copious kids' options and the good old homemade Greek stuff. Try the lamb or chicken souvlaki.

Raven Bistro
MEDITERRANEAN $$

(Map p606; ☑780-852-5151; 504 Patricia St; mains $10-28; ☺5-10pm; ☻) It's not every day that Jasper sprouts a new restaurant, so make the most of this small, tastefully designed bistro that pushes vegetarian dishes, encourages shared plates and wouldn't be out of place in a small Spanish city.

Villa Caruso
STEAKHOUSE $$$

(Map p606; ☑780-852-3920; 640 Connaught Dr; mains $22-36; ☺11am-11:30pm) Carnivore, pescatarian and vegetarian needs are all catered for here. Plush wood trimmings and great views are the perfect appetizer for a fine meal out.

Evil Dave's Grill
CANADIAN, FUSION $$$

(Map p606; ☑780-852-3323; www.evildaves.com; 622 Patricia St; mains $22-29; ☺4-11pm) There's nothing evil about Dave's, one of a handful of local attempts to bury Jasper's dodgy image as a bastion of family-friendly, posthiking grub that fills stomachs rather than excites taste buds. The excellent fusion food's all over the map, with Caribbean, Middle Eastern and Japanese influences lighting up the fish and beef.

Fiddle River Seafood Co
SEAFOOD $$$

(Map p606; ☑780-852-3032; 620 Connaught Dr; mains $22-32; ☺5-10pm) Being almost 1600km from the sea makes some customers understandably leery, but Jasper's premier seafood joint is no slouch. Pull up a seat near the window and tuck into one of the innovative creations, such as pumpkin-seed-crusted trout.

🍷 Drinking & Nightlife

Jasper Brewing Co
BREWERY, PUB

(Map p606; ☑780-852-4111; www.jasperbrewingco.ca; 624 Connaught Dr; ☺11:30am-1am) 🌿 Open since 2005, this brewpub, the first of its type in a Canadian national park, uses glacial water to make its fine ales, including the signature Rockhopper IPA or – slightly more adventurous – the Rocket Ridge Raspberry Ale. It's a sit-down affair, with TVs and a good food menu.

Atha-B Nightclub
BAR, CLUB

(Map p606; ☑780-852-3386; Athabasca Hotel, 510 Patricia St; ☺4pm-2am) Nightclubbing in a national park is about as congruous as wildlife-viewing in downtown Toronto. Bear this in mind before you hit the Atha-B, a pub-slash-nightclub off the lobby of the Athabasca Hotel where mullets are still high fashion and the carpet's probably radioactive.

Horseshoe Club
CLUB

(Map p606; ☑780-852-6262; www.thehorseshoeclub.ca; 610 Patricia St; ☺9pm-3am) Local hive of scary Led Zeppelin tribute bands.

ℹ Information

Jasper Information Centre (Map p606; ☑780-852-6176; www.parkscanada.gc.ca/jasper; 500 Connaught Dr; ☺8am-7pm) Informative office in historic 'parkitecture' building.

Post office (Map p606; 502 Patricia St; ☺9am-5pm Mon-Fri)

Seton General Hospital (☑780-852-3344; 518 Robson St)

ℹ Getting There & Around

BUS

The **bus station** (Map p606; www.greyhound.ca; 607 Connaught Dr) is at the train station. Greyhound buses serve Edmonton ($67, from 4½ hours, four daily), Prince George ($64, five hours, one daily), Kamloops ($70, six hours, two daily) and Vancouver ($115, from 11½ hours, two daily).

Brewster Transportation (www.brewster.ca), departing from the same station, operates express buses to Lake Louise village ($74, 4½ hours, at least one daily) and Banff Town ($84, 5½ hours, at least one daily).

The **Maligne Valley Shuttle** (www.malignelake.com) runs a May to October bus from Jasper Town to Maligne Lake via Maligne Canyon. Fares are one way/return $25/50.

CAR

International car-rental agencies have offices in Jasper Town.

If you're in need of a taxi, call **Jasper Taxi** (☑780-852-3600), which has metered cabs.

TRAIN

VIA Rail (www.viarail.ca) offers triweekly train services west to Vancouver ($125, 20 hours) and east to Toronto ($340, 62 hours). In addition, there is a triweekly service to Prince Rupert, BC ($102, 32 hours). Call or check at the **train station** (607 Connaught Dr) for exact schedule and fare details.

SOUTHERN ALBERTA

The national parks of Banff and Jasper and the cities of Calgary and Edmonton grab most of the headlines in Alberta, leaving the expansive south largely forgotten. Here, flat farmland is interrupted by deep coulees or canyons that were caused by flooding at the end of the last ice age. Another symbolic feature of the landscape is the towering hoodoos, funky arid sculptures that look like sand-colored Seussian realizations dominating the horizon. History abounds in both the recent Head-Smashed-In Buffalo Jump and the not so recent Dinosaur Provincial Park, two areas preserving the past that have attained Unesco World Heritage status.

Natural wonders are plentiful in this sleepy corner of the province. The dusty dry badlands around Drumheller open up into wide open prairies to the east that stretch all the way to the Cyprus Hills of western Saskatchewan. To the west there is Waterton Lakes National Park, with some of the most spectacular scenery in the Rockies – yet still under the radar of most visitors.

Drumheller

Founded on coal but now committed to another subterranean resource – dinosaur bones – Drumheller is a small (some would say 'waning') town set amid Alberta's enigmatic badlands. It acts as the nexus of the so-called Dinosaur Trail. While paleontology is a serious business here (the nearby Royal Tyrrell Museum is as much research center as tourist site), Drumheller has cashed in on its Jurassic heritage – sometimes shamelessly. Aside from mocked-up stegosauruses on almost every street corner and dino-related prefixes to more than a few business names, there's the large matter of a 26m-high fiberglass T rex that haunts a large tract of downtown.

But don't let the paleontological civic pride deter you: once you get beyond the kitsch, the town itself is has a certain je ne sais quoi. The summers are hot and the deep-cut river valley in which Drumheller sits provides a much-needed break to the monotony of the prairies. Hoodoos dominate this badland landscape which has featured in many a movie, Westerns mainly.

◉ Sights & Activities

Horseshoe Canyon   CANYON
The baddest of the badlands can be seen at Hosreshoe Canyon, a spectacular chasm cut into the otherwise flat prairie located 17km west of Drumheller on Hwy 9. A large sign in the parking lot explains the geology of the area, while trails lead down into the canyon. There, stripey coloured rock reveals millions of years of geological history (beware: it's very slippery when wet). There are helicopter rides if you're flush ($50/100 for 5/10 minutes).

Dinosaur Trail & Hoodoo Drive   SCENIC DRIVE
Drumheller is on the Dinosaur Trail, a 48km loop that runs northwest from town and includes Hwys 837 and 838; the scenery is quite worth the drive. Badlands and river views await you at every turn.

The loop takes you past **Midland Provincial Park** (no camping), where you can take a self-guided hike; across the Red Deer River on the free, cable-operated **Bleriot Ferry**, which has been running since 1913; and to vista points – including the eagle's-eye **Orkney Viewpoint** – overlooking the area's impressive canyons.

The 25km Hoodoo Drive starts about 18km southeast of Drumheller on Hwy 10; the route is usually done as an out-and-back with Wayne as the turnaround point. Along this drive you'll find the best examples of **hoodoos**: weird, eroded, mushroomlike columns of sandstone rock. This area was the site of a once-prosperous coal-mining community, and the **Atlas Mine** is now preserved as a provincial historic site. Take the side trip on Hwy 10X (which includes 11 bridges in 6km)

(Continued on page 621)

National Parks

If there's one thing that Canada excels at in the global pecking order (other than hockey), it's national parks. An early pioneer in ecological management in the late 1800s, the nation now flaunts 44 national parks from groundbreaking, user-friendly Banff, to the vast, empty wildernesses of the Arctic.

Contents

Above Peyto Lake, Banff National Park, Alberta

DAVID KIENE / GETTY IMAGES ©

1. Mt Edith Cavell, Jasper National Park, Alberta **2.** Canoeing, Yoho National Park, British Columbia **3.** Armchair Glacier & Mt Weart, British Columbia **4.** Elk, Banff National Park, Alberta

The Early Western Parks

The Canadian National Parks system has its roots in the imposing gothic spires of the Rocky Mountains. Galvanized by the formation of Banff in 1885, the early parks were directly linked to the development of the cross-continental railway, which toted rich and curious tourists into previously unexplored wilderness areas.

Banff

Predated only by Yellowstone in the USA and Royal National Park in Australia, Banff's history is entwined with the history of the national park movement and the pioneering Canadian Pacific Railway that helped pave its way.

Yoho

Named for the ancient Cree word for wonder and awe, Yoho is one of the geological highlights of the Rocky Mountain Parks, with its Burgess Shale fossil deposits exhibiting 120 marine species over a 500-million-year trajectory.

Waterton Lakes

The Canadian Rockies' forgotten corner is a continuation of the Glacier National Park (USA) to the south and is notable for its easily accessible high alpine day hikes. Its trademark Prince of Wales hotel is linked by historic red buses to Amtrak's Seattle–Chicago *Empire Builder* train.

Jasper

Once a nexus for fur traders, Jasper welcomed two railroads in the 1910s. They are both still in operation, running passenger services to Prince Rupert and Vancouver and allowing easy access to this larger, quieter, more fauna-packed northern neighbor of Banff.

Glacier

Established just one year after Banff in 1886, Glacier was another 'railroad park,' these days better known for its legendary dumpings of powdery snow ideal for heli-skiing and backcountry excursions.

Expanding East

With the formation of the world's first coherent national parks service – Parks Canada – in 1911, the park network spread east as the age of the motorcar brought Canada's spectacular natural beauty to the masses. While environmental protective measures were always important, the early national parks were tailored more to a first-class 'visitor experience.'

Prince Edward Island

PEI, a park since 1937, enhances its diminutive stature with dune-backed beaches, narrow wetlands and a gigantic literary legacy enshrined in the old farm 'Green Gables,' the inspiration for the 1908 novel *Anne of Green Gables* by Lucy Maud Montgomery.

Riding Mountain

A huge array of trails – more than 400km worth – pepper this forested Unesco Biosphere Reserve that sits like a wooded island amid fertile agricultural land in southern Manitoba. In winter many trails are groomed for cross-country skiing.

Point Pelee

Geographically tiny but vital to birds (and birdwatchers), Point Pelee in Ontario on Canada's most southerly tip overlooking Lake Erie, is an important fly-through for over 360 feathered species.

Cape Breton Highlands

The font of Nova Scotia's once distinct French-Acadian culture, Cape Breton – made a park in 1936 – is best accessed via 25 moderate day hikes that contour the coast near the Cabot Trail scenic highway.

Gros Morne

A spectacular jumble of fjords, headlands, sheer cliffs and waterfalls on the Newfoundland coast, Gros Morne came late to the Parks Canada fold in 1973. It has since been listed by Unesco for its importance in understanding the processes of continental drift.

1. Point Pelee National Park, Ontario **2.** Canoeing, Riding Mountain National Park, Manitoba **3.** Green Gables, Cavendish, Prince Edward Island **4.** Cape Breton Highlands National Park, Nova Scotia

MICHELLE VALBERG / GETTY IMAGES ©

1. Auyuittuq National Park, Nunavut **2.** Aulavik National Park, Northwest Territories **3.** Polar bear, Wapusk National Park, Manitoba **4.** Rafting, Firth River, Ivvavik National Park, Yukon Territory

WAYNE LYNCH / GETTY IMAGES ©

Northern Exposure

By the 1980s, the national parks service had shifted its philosophy from a purely visitor-centric view of park management to a position that prioritized ecological integrity. Vast wildernesses in the north of Canada were gradually taken under the parks umbrella, often with the cooperation of local Aboriginal peoples.

Aulavik

More people have visited the moon than drop by Aulavik annually (official annual tourist numbers rarely exceed a dozen). Situated on arctic Banks Island, this land of musk oxen and 24-hour summer sunlight is the true 'back of beyond'.

Wapusk

Polar bears are Wapusk's *raison d'être* (the name means 'white bear' in Cree) and the best place in the world to see these animals in the wild. Book a guided tour and head for Churchill, Manitoba.

Auyuittuq

A name few Canadians will recognize (or be able to pronounce), Auyuittuq (the land that never melts) is another leave-your-car-at-home kind of park. Situated on Baffin Island it is ideal for ski touring, climbing or backcountry camping.

Ivvavik

No services, no facilities, just miles of untamed tundra. Save some money, hone your backcountry survival skills, and live out your expedition fantasies.

A TICKET TO FREEDOM

The Park Canada Discovery Pass (adult/child/family $67.60/33.30/136.40) includes 26 of Canada's national parks and offers unlimited entry and access for a full year. The pass also includes 63 national historic sites. For more details see the Parks Canada website (www.pc.gc.ca).

Wild horses, Sable Island, Nova Sco

New Parks

Parks Canada has always been an open-ended project with a long-term roll-out plan, and parks continue to be formed. Eight have gained federal approval since 2000 and the network now covers an impressive 3% of Canada's total land mass – roughly the size of Italy.

Nahanni

Nahanni in the Northwest Territories became a national park in the 1970s and had the honour of being made Unesco's first natural World Heritage site in 1978. After years of negotiations, it was significantly expanded in 2011. It is now Canada's third-largest national park covering an area the size of Belgium.

Torngat Mountains

A stark mélange of glaciated mountains and roaming caribou on the wild coast of Labrador; created in 2005 as Canada's 42nd national park.

Nááts'ihch'oh

This park, inaugurated in 2012, abuts the newly expanded Nahanni National Park and has a strong spiritual significance to the Métis and Dene First Nations who played a role in the legal negotiations. It is also a northern roaming ground for grizzly bears, caribou and Dall sheep.

Sable Island

A sinuous sand spit 300km off Nova Scotia, grassy Sable Island is home to hundreds of feral horses thought to be left over from the Great Acadian Expulsion in the 1750s. More than 350 ships have met their watery end on this hard-to-reach outpost. It became Canada's newest national park in 2013.

(Continued from page 612)

from Rosedale to the small community of **Wayne**, population 27 and fast approaching ghost-town status.

★ Royal Tyrrell Museum of Palaeontology
MUSEUM

(☑403-823-7707; www.tyrrellmuseum.com; adult/child $11/6; ☺ 9am-9pm; ⑭) This fantastic museum is one of the preeminent dinosaur museums on the planet. It's not an overstatement to say that no trip to Alberta is complete without a visit to this amazing facility. Children will love the interactive displays and everyone will be in awe of the numerous complete dino-skeletons.

There are opportunities to get among the badlands on a guided tour and to discover your own dino treasures either on a guided hike or a dinosaur dig. You'll feel like you're behind the scenes of *Jurassic Park* – and in many ways this is the real Jurassic Park.

World's Largest Dinosaur
LANDMARK

(60 1st Ave W; admission $3; ☺10am-6pm; ⑭) Warning – cheesy tourist attraction ahead! In a town filled to the brim with dinosaurs, this T rex is the king of them all and features in the *Guinness Book of Records*. Standing 26m above a parking lot, it dominates the Drumheller skyline.

It's big, not at all scary and cost more than a million bucks to build, which explains the admission price to go up the 106 steps for the view from its mouth. Kids love it and, truth be told, the view *is* pretty good. Ironically, the dinosaur isn't even Jurassically accurate; at 46m long, it's about 4.5 times bigger than its extinct counterpart.

Dinosaur Discovery Museum
MUSEUM

(☑403-823-6666; www.fossilworld.com; 1381 North Dinosaur Trail; admission $6; ☺9:30am-7pm; ⑭) If the Tyrrell didn't satisfy your kids completely, this place ought to, while lightening your wallet in the process. On top of the admission fee, you'll pay extra for your kids to do a fossil dig ($12) or scale a climbing wall ($6). There *is* some real dino-related stuff here, but most of it isn't local.

🛏 Sleeping

The quality of accommodations is limited in Drumheller, so book ahead to ensure you're not stuck with something you don't like, or worse, nothing at all.

River Grove Campground & Cabins
CAMPGROUND $

(☑403-823-6655; www.camprivergrove.com; 25 Poplar St; campsites/RV sites/tepees/cabins from $32/38/64/119; ☺May-Sep; ⑳) Right in town and close to the big dinosaur, this is a pleasant campground with lots of amenities. The tent facilities are alright, with a few shady trees to keep you cool in the hot summer sun. You can even rent a tepee for the night, although the Stoney people likely didn't have concrete floors in theirs.

Heartwood Inn & Spa
INN $$

(☑403-823-6495; www.innsatheartwood.com; 320 N Railway Ave E; d $149-275; ⑲) Standing head and shoulders above most of the accommodations in town, this lovely country inn is awesome. The small rooms are luxurious, comfortable and tastefully done. It has an onsite spa facility that will welcome you like a queen or king.

All the rooms have Jacuzzis, and there are romance packages available: the staff decorate your room with candles and rose petals, draw you a bath made for two and let you handle the rest.

Taste the Past B&B
B&B $$

(☑403-823-5889; 281 2nd St W; s/d $100/125) This converted turn-of-the-century house has evolved into a cozy downtown B&B. All rooms have a private bathroom, and there is a shared facility downstairs. With only three rooms, this feels more like staying with friends – and by the end of your stay, that's often what it is.

✖ Eating & Drinking

Whif's Flapjack House
CANADIAN $

(☑403-823-7595; 801 N Dinosaur Trail; mains $6-10; ☺6am-2pm) The name is the menu: waffles, hamburgers, ice cream, flapjacks and salad. Big portions, a miniature train track suspended from the ceiling, and good value are all found at this local greasy spoon.

Bernie and the Boys Bistro
DINER $

(☑403-823-3318; www.bernieandtheboys.com; 305 4th St W; burgers $6-8; ☺11am-8:30pm Tue-Sat) Bistro it isn't. On the contrary, Bernie's is one of those small-town family-run diners that have replenished appetites on many a lengthy road trip. Join the queue (the place is small *and* popular!) for big, fresh Albertan burgers and legendary milkshakes.

Vietnamese Noodle House VIETNAMESE $
(☑403-823-2000; 202 2nd St W; mains $9-12; ⊙noon-11pm) If you're looking for something quick that isn't a burger the Noodle House might cut it. It's a long ways from Saigon in both geography and authenticity, but it's economical and cheerful and offers a couple of well-stacked Western food options.

★ **Last Chance Saloon** BAR
(☑403-823-9189; Hwy 10X, Wayne; ⊙11:30am-midnight) In a land partial to fast-food franchises, the words 'there's nowhere else remotely like it' are a backhanded compliment. For a taste of something completely different, take the 15-minute drive from Drumheller to the tiny town of Wayne to find this former hell-raising bar-hotel turned Harley Davidson hangout.

Last Chance is a classic Western saloon, but without a hint of tourist kitsch. Check out the mining relics, Brownie cameras, old cigarette tins, fully functioning band-box, and the brick that somebody tossed through the window circa 1913. The food (mains from $4.50) is almost an afterthought – bog-standard burgers with optional beans or fries – but it'll fill you up and give you a little longer to ponder the unique offbeat atmosphere.

ℹ Information

Tourist information center (☑403-823-1331; www.traveldrumheller.com; 60 1 Ave W; ⊙9am-9pm) At the foot of the T rex. The entrance to the beast's entrails is in the same building.

ℹ Getting There & Away

Greyhound Canada runs buses from the **bus station** (308 Centre St) to Calgary ($38, 1¾ hours, two daily) and Edmonton ($68, seven hours, two daily).

Hammerhead Tours runs a full-day tour ($90) from Calgary to the Drumheller badlands and Royal Tyrrell Museum.

Dinosaur Provincial Park

Where *The Lost World* meets *Little House on the Prairie*, **Dinosaur Provincial Park** (☑403-378-4344; www.dinosaurpark.ca; off Hwy 544; ⊙8:30am-5pm Sun-Thu, to 7pm Fri & Sat) **FREE** isn't just the Grand Canyon in miniature – it's also a Unesco World Heritage site. The final resting place of thousands of dinosaurs, it's a stellar spot to check out some fossils. It's halfway between Calgary and Medicine Hat, and some 48km northeast of Brooks. From Hwy 1, take Secondary Hwy 873 to Hwy 544.

The park comes at you by surprise as the chasm in which it lives opens before your feet from the grassy plain. A dehydrated fantasy landscape, there are hoodoos and colorful rock formations aplenty. Where 75 million years ago dinosaurs cruised around a tropical landscape, it's now a hot and barren place to be. Make sure you dress for the weather with sunscreen and water at the ready.

The 81-sq-km park begs to be explored, with wildflowers, the odd rattler in the rocks and, if you're lucky, maybe even a T rex. This isn't just a tourist attraction, but a hotbed for science; paleontologists have uncovered countless skeletons, which now reside in many of the finest museums around the globe.

There are five short interpretive **hiking trails** to choose from and a **driving loop** runs through part of the park, but to preserve the fossils, access to 70% of the park is restricted. The off-limits areas may be seen only on **guided hikes** (adult/child $14/8) or **bus tours** (adult/child $12/8), which operate from late May to October. The hikes and tours are popular, and you should reserve a place.

The park's **visitors center** (☑403-378-4342; adult/child $3/2; ⊙8:30am-5pm) has a small yet effective series of dino displays. Some complete skeletons and exhibits on the practicalities of paleontology are worthy of a look.

The park's **campground** (☑403-378-3700; campsites/RV sites $23/29, reservations $10) sits in a hollow by a small creek. The ample tree cover is a welcome reprieve from the volcanic sun. Laundry facilities and hot showers are available, as is a small shop for last-minute supplies. This is a popular place, especially with the RV set, so phone ahead.

Head-Smashed-In Buffalo Jump

The story behind the place with the strangest name of any attraction in Alberta is one of ingenuity and resourcefulness and is key to the First Nations' (and Canada's) cultural heritage. For thousands of years, the Blackfoot people used the cliffs near the town of Fort Macleod to hunt buffalo. **Head-Smashed-In Buffalo Jump** (☑403-

BAR U RANCH & THE COWBOY TRAIL

Cowboy culture is woven into the cultural fabric of southern Alberta, but to experience it in its rustic purity you have to exit Calgary and its Stetson-wearing oil entrepreneurs and head south through the province's verdant rolling foothills on Hwy 22, aka the Cowboy Trail. What is today a smooth asphalt road frequented by shiny SUVs was once a dirt track used by dust-encrusted cow herders who drove their cattle north to the Canadian Pacific Railway in Calgary. Unperturbed by the modern oil rush, these rolling foothills are still punctuated by giant ranches, one of which, **Bar U Ranch** (www.friendsofthebaru. ca; adult/child $7.80/3.90; ⊙9am-5pm May-Sep), has been converted into a historic site by Parks Canada for posterity.

Founded in 1882, Bar U was once one of the largest commercial ranches in the world, covering 160,000 acres. John Ware, a freed African-American slave and, allegedly, Alberta's first cowboy, was an early visitor. A decade later, the ranch's horses were trained by Harry Longabaugh (known to history and Hollywood as the Sundance Kid) a dapper bank robber who worked at the ranch in 1891 before taking up a more lucrative career holding up banks with the Wild Bunch. The next visitor was more regal but no less notorious. The Prince of Wales, later Edward VIII, passed through in 1919 and was so taken with the place that he bought the EP Ranch next door. Edward visited the region five times, including twice after his abdication, and the EP was managed in his name until 1962.

Bar U Ranch is just off Hwy 22, 13km south of the town of Longview. Two dozen buildings, including a cookhouse, post office, corral, blacksmith's, and slaughterhouse, have been preserved in their Sundance Kid–era glory. Visitors can also partake in wagon rides, saddle up horses or even try to rope a steer.

553-2731; www.head-smashed-in.com; Secondary Hwy 785; adult/child $10/5; ⊙10am-5pm) was a marvel of simple ingenuity. When the buffalo massed in the open prairie, braves from the tribe would gather and herd them toward the towering cliffs. As the animals got closer, they would be funneled to the edge and made to stampede over it to their doom, thus ensuring the survival of the tribe. For the Blackfoot, the buffalo was sacred; to honor the fallen prey, every part of the animal was used.

The well-presented displays at the interpretive centre built cleverly into the hillside are befitting of a Unesco World Heritage site, and it's well worth the excursion from Calgary or Lethbridge. The site, about 18km northwest of Fort Macleod and 16km west of Hwy 2, also has a cafe, a shop staffed by Blackfoot First Nations and a couple of short walking trails.

Lethbridge

Right in the heart of southern Alberta farming country sits the former coal-mining city of Lethbridge, divided by the distinctive coulees of the Oldman River. Though there isn't a lot to bring you to the city, copious park-

land, a couple of good historical sites and an admirable level of civic pride might keep you longer than you first intended. There are ample hiking opportunities in the Oldman River Valley, a 100m-deep coulee bisected by the proverbial Eiffel Tower of steel railway bridges, and the largest of its kind in the world. The downtown area, like many North American downtowns, has made a good stab at preserving its not-so-ancient history. To the east, less-inspiring Mayor McGrath Dr (Hwy 5) is a chain-store-infested drag that could be Anywhere, North America.

◎ Sights & Activities

Nikka Yuko Japanese Garden GARDENS
(www.nikkayuko.com; cnr Mayor Mcgrath Dr & 9th Ave S; adult/child $8/5.50; ⊙9am-5pm) The Nikka Yuko Japanese Garden is the perfect antidote to the stresses of the road. The immaculate grounds, interspersed with ponds, flowing water, bridges, bonsai trees and rock gardens, form an oasis of calm amid the bustle of everyday life, and authentic Japanese structures sit among the grassy mounds.

Indian Battle Park PARK
(3rd Ave S) In the coulee between the east and west sides of the city, Indian Battle Park, west of Scenic Dr and named after a famous

1870 battle between the Blackfoot and the Cree, is no ordinary manicured green space. Instead, this is an expansive, surprisingly wild place astride the Oldman River that is strafed with trails, wildlife and some unsung mining history.

Impossible to miss in the middle of it all is 96m-high, 1623m-long **High Level Bridge**, the largest trestle bridge in the world, built in 1909 to carry the railway across the deep coulee to the prairies on the other side.

Almost directly under the bridge, the **Helen Schuler Coulee Centre & Lethbridge Nature Reserve** (⊙10am-6pm) contains a small interpretive center and is the starting point for various nature trails on the reserve's 80 wooded hectares along the river. It runs special nature programs in the summer. At the other end of the car park is the Coalbanks Interpretive kiosk, an open-air shelter containing an impressive stash of information on Lethbridge's early mining history. Trails nearby lead to gazebos, picnic areas and viewpoints.

Fort Whoop-Up   FORT, MUSEUM
(☑403-329-0444; www.fortwhoopup.ca; 200 Indian Battle Park Rd; adult/child $7/5; ⊙10am-5pm) Inside expansive Indian Battle Park, bizarrely named Fort Whoop-Up is a replica of Alberta's first and most notorious illegal-whiskey trading post. Around 25 of these outposts were set up in the province between 1869 and 1874 to trade whiskey, guns, ammunition and blankets for buffalo hides and furs from the Blackfoot tribes.

Their existence led directly to the formation of the NWMP, who arrived in 1874 at Fort Macleod to bring law and order to the Canadian west. The fort has exhibits on the Blackfoot tribe, the mounties and, most notably, one of the largest firearms collections in Canada. It was open but undergoing renovations at last visit.

Galt Museum & Archives   MUSEUM
(www.galtmuseum.com; 320 Galt St; adult/child $6/3; ⊙10am-5pm Mon-Sat, 1-5pm Sun) The story of Lethbridge is continued at the Sir Alexander Galt Museum, encased in an old hospital building (1910) on the bluff high above the river. Interactive kid-oriented displays sit beside a small gallery with contemporary and historical art that will interest the bigger kids. The view from the lobby out onto the coulee is great and free.

🛏 Sleeping

A huge selection of chain hotels from fancy to thrifty can be found on Hwy 5. Take your pick.

Lethbridge Lodge   HOTEL $$
(☑403-328-1123; www.lethbridgelodge.com; 320 Scenic Dr S; r from $104; @ 🛜) Like most Canadian hotels, the rooms here are clean if a little unmemorable; the atrium, on the other hand, is something else. All the rooms look down into the fake-foliage-filled interior, complete with winding brick pathways, a kidney-shaped pool and water features.

The Cotton Blossom Lounge sits among the jungle and is good fun – the piano player is stranded on a small island – and the pseudo Italian facade of the rooms completes the bizarre picture.

Holiday Inn   HOTEL $$
(☑403-380-5050; www.ihg.com; 2375 Hwy 5 S; r from $141; @ 🛜 🏊) This slightly out-of-the-box Holiday Inn (formerly a Ramada hotel) has an indoor water park complete with dueling waterslides, wave pool and special kids' area. All the standard stuff is here too, and despite the wacky selling features, the hotel retains a sense of class. It was completely refurbished in 2011.

🍴 Eating

Round Street Café   CAFE $
(☑403-381-8605; 427 5th St S; sandwiches $7; ⊙7am-6pm Mon-Sat; 🛜) A simple but effective indie coffee bar near the Greyhound depot with a fine line in cinnamon buns and thick-cut sandwiches, plus free internet browsing rights.

Mocha Cabana Café   CAFE $$
(☑403-329-6243; www.mochacabana.ca; 317 4th St; lunches from $12; ⊙7am-9pm Sun-Thu, to 11pm Fri & Sat; 🛜) Austere from the outside, the multifunctional Mocha is anything but within. Billing itself as a coffee lounge, wine bar, patio and music venue, it grabs 'best in Lethbridge' prize in each genre. The bright interior has an appealing European ambience, and the substantial lunchtime salads are fantastic.

Ric's Grill   STREAKHOUSE $$$
(☑403-317-7427; www.ricsgrill.com; 103 Mayor McgrathDr; mains $19-40; ⊙11am-10pm) Ever eaten in a water tower – or an ex–water tower, to be more precise? Well, here is your chance. Ric's sits 40m high above the prairie in the

old Lethbridge water tower (decommissioned in 1999). Turned into a restaurant in 2004, the curved interior affords great views of the city.

There is a lounge on one level and a classy dining room upstairs. The steaks are thick and the wine list long; best to reserve a good spot as it's deservedly popular.

ℹ Information

Chinook Country Tourist Association (www.chinookcountry.com; 2805 Scenic Dr S; ⊙9am 5pm)

Main Post Office (✆403-382-4604; 704 4th Ave S)

ℹ Getting There & Around

AIR

The **Lethbridge airport** (✆403-329-4474; 417 Stubb Ross Rd), a short drive south on Hwy 5, is served by commuter affiliates of Air Canada. Six or seven flights per day go to Calgary.

BUS

Greyhound Canada (✆403-327-1551; 411 5th St S) goes to Calgary ($48, 2½ hours, five daily) and Regina ($103, from 14½ hours, two daily).

Luxurious **Red Arrow** (✆1-800-232-1958; www.redarrow.ca; 449 Mayor Magrath Dr S) buses connect once daily with Calgary ($49, 2½ hours) and Fort MacLeod ($34, 45 minutes).

For detailed information about local bus services, call the **Lethbridge Transit Infoline** (✆403-320-4978, 403-320-3885). The downtown bus terminal is on 4th Ave at 6th St. Local bus fares are $2.

Writing-on-Stone Provincial Park

Perhaps the best thing about this **park** (✆403-647-2364; ⊙9am-6pm) **FREE** is that it really isn't on the way to *anywhere*. For those willing to get off the main thoroughfare and discover this hidden gem, all efforts will be rewarded. It's named for the extensive carvings and paintings made by the Plains Indians more than 3000 years ago on the sandstone cliffs along the banks of Milk River. There is an excellent self-guided interpretive trail that takes you to some of the more spectacular viewpoints and accessible pictographs.

The best art is found in a restricted area (to protect it from vandalism), which you can only visit on a guided tour with the park ranger. Other activities possible here include canoeing and swimming in the river in summer and cross-country skiing in winter. Park wildlife is ample, and a new **visitors center** (⊙9am-7pm), built in the shape of a traditional tepee, blends perfectly with the region's natural and cultural heritage. Pick up tickets for tours at the park entrance, from the naturalist's office. Tours generally run Saturday and Sunday at 2pm from May to October (adult/child $12/8), but check ahead. Beware: it can get exceedingly hot in the summer.

The park's riverside **campground** (✆403-647-2877; campsites/RV sites from $20/26) has 64 sites, running water, showers and flush toilets and is popular on weekends.

The park is southeast of Lethbridge and close to the US border; the Sweetgrass Hills of northern Montana are visible to the south. To get to the park, take Hwy 501 42km east of Hwy 4 from the town of Milk River.

Waterton Lakes National Park

Who? What? Where? The name **Waterton Lakes National Park** (adult/child per day $7.80/3.90) is usually prefixed with a question rather than a sigh of recognition. While its siblings to the north – Canmore, Banff and Jasper – hemorrhage with tourists and weekend warriors, Waterton is a pocket of tranquility. Sublime. Established in 1895 and now part of a Unesco World Heritage site, Unesco Biosphere Reserve and International Peace Park (with Glacier National Park in the US), 525-sq-km Waterton Lakes lies in Alberta's southwestern corner. Here the prairies meet the mountains, and the relief from the flat land is nothing short of uplifting. The park is a sanctuary for numerous iconic animals – grizzlies, elk, deer and cougars – along with 800-odd wildflower species.

The town of **Waterton**, a charming alpine village with a winter population of about 40, provides a marked contrast to larger, tackier Banff and, to a lesser extent, Jasper. There is a lifetime's worth of outdoor adventure to discover here. Highlights include serene Waterton Lake, the regal 1920s-era Prince of Wales Hotel, and the immediacy of the high-alpine hiking terrain; you can be up above the tree line in less than one hour from leaving the town.

Sitting right on the US border and next to the immense **Glacier National Park**, this

BLACKFOOT CROSSING HISTORICAL PARK

A First Nations reservation with a historical centre rather than a casino, the **Blackfoot Crossing Historical Park** (☑ 403-734-5171; www.blackfootcrossing.ca; adult/child $12/8; ☺ 9am-5pm Tue-Sat) goes proudly against the grain, choosing to celebrate and embrace authentic Siksika (Blackfoot) culture with something that is both educational and inspiring.

The history of southern Alberta pre-1880 belongs to the Blackfoot confederacy, an amalgamation of the Peigan, Blood and Montana-based Blackfeet tribes. Blackfoot Crossing, long an important tribal nexus, was unique in that it was the only place where nomadic First Nations tribes built a semipermanent settlement (out of grassy earth-lodge). It was here that notorious Treaty 7 was signed by Chief Crowfoot in 1877, ceding land to the British crown and establishing the Siksika reservation. After a visit from Prince Charles in 1977, the idea for a historical site was hatched and, after 30 years of planning, the park finally opened in 2007.

It is anchored by a magnificent ecofriendly main building that incorporates elements of tepees and feathered headdresses into its creative design. Within its walls lie a 100-seat theater showcasing cultural dances, a set of exhibits chronicling Blackfoot history and guided tours with local Siksika interpreters and storytellers. Outside, you can enjoy various trails, prairie viewpoints, and a tepee village where traditional crafts are practiced and taught.

To get to the centre, head 100km east of Calgary on Hwy 1 and then 7km south on Hwy 842. Still in its infancy, the historical park remains curiously light on visitors who have yet to discover its latent glories.

is a good spot to forge neighborly relations with the people to the south. You can even flash your passport and do a poly-country backcountry adventure. Together the two parks comprise Waterton-Glacier International Peace Park. Although the name evokes images of binational harmony, in reality each park is operated separately, and entry to one does not entitle you to entry to the other.

For more information on Glacier National Park, see the excellent US National Park Service website at www.nps.gov/glac.

⊙ Sights & Activities

A highlight for many visitors is a boat ride with **Waterton Shoreline Cruises** (☑ 403-859-2362; www.watertoncruise.com; 1 way adult/child $25/14; ☺ May-Oct) across the lake's shimmering waters to the far shore of Goat Haunt, Montana, USA. The 45-minute trip is scenic, and there is a lively commentary as you go. Grab your passport before you jump on the often rather full boats, as they dock in the USA for about half an hour.

Those looking to stretch their legs are in luck – Waterton is a hiker's haven. With over 225km of walking tracks, you'll run out of time before you run out of trails. The trails are shared with bikes and horses (where

permitted), and once the snow flies, cross-country skis will get you to the same places. The 17km walk to **Crypt Lake** is a standout: there's a 20m tunnel, a stream that materializes out of the ground and a ladder to negotiate. The only way to get to the trailhead is by boat. Waterton Shoreline Cruises leaves the town's marina in the morning and picks up the weary at the Crypt Lake trailhead in the afternoon (adult/child $18/9).

Another example of Waterton's 'small is beautiful' persona is the 19km **Carthew-Alderson Trail**, often listed as one of the best high alpine day hikes in North America. The **Tamarack Shuttle** (☑ 403-859-2378; 214 Mount View Rd) runs every morning in the summer to the trailhead by Cameron Lake (reservations recommended). From here you hike back over the mountains to the town.

🛏 Sleeping

The park has three Parks Canada vehicle-accessible campgrounds, none of which takes reservations. Backcountry campsites are limited and should be reserved through the visitors center.

Waterton Townsite Campground
CAMPGROUND $
(☑ 877-737-3783; Hwy 5; campsites/RV sites $22.50/38.20; ☺ May-Oct) Dominating the

southern end of Waterton village, the town campground isn't ideal, but it's a means to an end. Consisting mainly of an enormous gopher-hole-covered field aimed at RV campers, it has all the charm of a camping area at a music festival. There are some treed sites near the edges, but by midsummer you'll be lucky to get anything.

Book ahead for this one.

Crandell Mountain Campground
CAMPGROUND $

(☑ 403-859-5133; Red Rock Pkwy, campsites & RV sites $21.50; ☺ May-Sep) For a more rustic alternative to the town, head out to this secluded camping spot a few minutes' drive from the park gates.

Aspen Village Inn
HOTEL $$

(☑ 403-859-2255; www.aspenvillageinn.com; 111 Windflower Ave; r $159-199; ☎) Aspen is a more economical, family-friendly version of the Bayshore. Rooms are in two main buildings and several cottage units. Bonuses include a kids' play area, a barbecue and picnic area, and the sight of wild deer grazing the grass outside your room.

Bear Mountain Motel
MOTEL $$

(☑ 403-859-2366; www.bearmountainmotel.com; 208 Mount View Rd; s/d from $105/130) Small, bog-standard motel rooms in a central location. Throw in friendly, knowledgeable owners, and you're laughing all the way to the ATM.

★ Prince of Wales Hotel
HISTORIC HOTEL $$$

(☑ 403-859-2231; www.princeofwaleswaterton.com; Prince of Wales Rd; r from $239; ☺ May-Sep; ☎) You can't come to Waterton and not check out this iconic alpine landmark. Situated to take full advantage of the best view in town, this hotel is nothing short of spectacular. When seen from a distance, the serene scene is perhaps the most photogenic in all the Canadian Rockies.

Up close, the old girl is starting to show her age, but she's aging like a fine wine. The grand lobby is illuminated with a chandelier worthy of a Scottish castle, and the elevator is the oldest working example in North America. The rooms are small but retain the classic feel of this historical hotel. There's antique porcelain in the bathrooms and views that justify the price.

Bayshore Inn
HOTEL $$$

(☑ 403-859-2211; www.bayshoreinn.com; 111 Waterton Ave; r $174-225; ☺ Apr-Oct; @ ☎) Taking the prize as the biggest hotel in the downtown area, the Bayshore is nothing if not centrally located. With rooms that back right onto the lake and a location only a couple of steps away from the shops, this is a popular option. The lake views are great, but be sure to book early if you want to see them.

Waterton Glacier Suites
HOTEL $$$

(☑ 403-859-2004; www.watertonsuites.com; 107 Windflower Ave; ste from $239; @ ☎ ☎) With amenities aplenty, these suites have two fireplaces, Jacuzzis, microwaves and fridges. The rooms are spotless, and the rock-and-log exterior looks the part too. It's open all year round – come winter you'll appreciate those dual fireplaces.

✗ Eating & Drinking

Waterton specializes in unsophisticated but filling cuisine, ideal for topping up your energy both pre- and posthike. Everything is contained within the town.

Waterton Bagel & Coffee Co
CAFE $

(☑ 403-859-2466; 309 Windflower Ave; bagels from $5; ☺ 10am-10pm) A godsend if you've just staggered out of the wilderness, this tiny caffeine stop has a handful of window stools, life-saving peanut-butter-and-jam bagels and refreshing frappuccinos.

Zum's Eatery
CANADIAN $$

(☑ 403-858-2388; 116B Waterton Ave; mains $13-18; ☺ 11am-10pm) Good home-style cooking of the burger, pizza, and fish-and-chips variety is brought to you by hard-up students working their summer breaks. The lack of sophisticated flavors is made up for by the character of the decor: several hundred North American license plates embellish almost every centimeter of wall.

Bel Lago Ristorante
ITALIAN $$$

(☑ 403-859-2213; www.bellagoristorante.com; 110 Waterton Ave; mains $19-32; ☺ noon-10pm) ✐ Homemade-pasta-in-North-American-national-park shock! The decor's relatively simple, but this is probably Waterton's most ambitious eatery: the chef studied in Italy and creates tasty (but not gigantic) mains that embody that old Italian ethos of eating local where possible. The wine list's international with an Italian bias (Amarone anyone?).

Thirsty Bear Saloon
PUB

(☑ 403-859-2111; www.thirstybearsaloon.com; Main St; ☺ 4pm-2am Mon-Sat) Wild nights in the wilderness happen in this large pub/performance space aided by live music, karaoke and good beer.

❶ Information

Waterton Visitors Centre (☑403-859-5133; www.parkscanada.gc.ca/waterton; ☺8am-7pm May-Sep) Across the road from the Prince of Wales Hotel. It's the central stop for information.

❶ Getting There & Around

Waterton lies in Alberta's southwestern corner, 130km from Lethbridge and 156km from Calgary. The one road entrance into the park is in its northeastern corner along Hwy 5. Most visitors coming from Glacier and the USA reach the junction with Hwy 5 via Hwy 6 (Chief Mountain International Hwy) from the southeast. From Calgary, to the north, Hwy 2 shoots south toward Hwy 5 into the park. From the east, Hwy 5, through Cardston, heads west and then south into the park.

There is no public transportation from Canadian cities outside the park. However, a shuttle service (adult/child US$50/25) operated by **Glacier Park Inc** (www.glacierparkinc.com) offers daily transport from Prince of Wales Hotel to Glacier Park Lodge in Montana, USA from May to September. Here you can link up with the Amtrak train network.

A hikers' shuttle ($13.50) operates around the park in the summer, linking Cameron Lake with the town and the US border at Chief Mountain. It leaves from Tamarack Outdoor Outfitters (p626) in town.

Crowsnest Pass

West of Fort Macleod the Crowsnest Hwy (Hwy 3) heads through the prairies and into the Rocky Mountains to Crowsnest Pass (1396m) and the BC border. The Pass, as it's known, is a string of small communities just to the east of the BC border. Of note is the story of the town of **Frank**. In 1903, Frank was almost completely buried when 30 million cu meters (some 82 million tonnes' worth) of nearby Turtle Mountain collapsed and killed around 70 people. The coal mine dug into the base of the mountain was to blame, some say. But the mining didn't stop; this black gold was the ticket to fortune for the entire region some hundred years ago. Eventually the demand for coal decreased, and after yet more tragedy below the earth, the mines shut down for good.

Frank Slide Interpretive Centre (adult/child $10/5; ☺9am-6pm), 1.5km off Hwy 3 and 27km east of the BC border, overlooks the Crowsnest Valley. It's an excellent interpretive center that helps put a human face on the tragedy of the Frank landslide, with many interesting displays about mining, the railroad and the early days of this area. There's also a fantastic film dramatizing the tragic events of 1903. Most of the staff can trace their roots to the area and thus the slide.

NORTHERN ALBERTA

Despite the presence of the increasingly infamous oil sands, the top half of Alberta is little visited and even less known. Once you travel north of Edmonton, the population drops off to Siberian levels, and the sense of remoteness is almost eerie.

If it's solitude you seek, then this is paradise found. Endless stretches of pine forests seem to go on forever, nighttime brings aurora borealis displays that are better than any chemical hallucinogens, and it is here you can still see herds of buffalo.

This is also where the engine room of the Alberta economy lives. The oil sands near Fort McMurray are one of the largest oil reserves in the world. This helps to bring in workers from every corner of Canada, and the oil exported earns the province millions of dollars – per hour.

The Cree, Slavey and Dene were the first peoples to inhabit the region, and many of them still depend on fishing, hunting and trapping for survival. The northeast has virtually no roads and is dominated by Wood Buffalo National Park, the Athabasca River and Lake Athabasca. The northwest is more accessible, with a network of highways connecting Alberta with northern BC and the NWT.

Peace River & Around

Alaska, here we come! Heading northwest along Hwy 43 leads to the town of Dawson Creek, BC, and mile zero of the Alaska Hwy. Dawson is a whopping 590km from Edmonton, so it's a long way to go to check out this isolated section of northern Alberta. Along the way you'll pass through **Grande Prairie**, the base of operations for the local agricultural industry and home to chuckwagon legend Kelly Sutherland. If you decide to spend the night, most of the accommodations are centered on 100th St and 100th Ave.

Peace River is so named because the warring Cree and Beaver Indians made peace along its banks. The town of **Peace River** sits at the confluence of the Heart, Peace and Smoky Rivers. It has several motels and two campgrounds. Greyhound Canada buses leave daily for the Yukon and NWT. West out of town, Hwy 2 leads to the Mackenzie Hwy.

Mackenzie Highway

The small town of **Grimshaw** is the official starting point of the Mackenzie Hwy (Hwy 35) north to the NWT. There's not much here except for the mile-zero sign and a few shops. The relatively flat and straight road is paved for the most part, though there are stretches of loose gravel or earth where the road is being reconstructed.

The mainly agricultural landscape between Grimshaw and Manning gives way to endless stretches of spruce and pine forest. Come prepared as this is frontier territory and services become fewer (and more expensive) as the road cuts northward through the wilderness. A good basic rule is to fill your tank any time you see a gas station from here north.

High Level, the last settlement of any size before the NWT border, is a center for the timber industry. Workers often stay in the motels in town during the week. The only service station between High Level and Enterprise (in the NWT) is at Indian Cabins.

Lake District

From St Paul, more than 200km northeast of Edmonton, to the NWT border lies Alberta's immense lake district. Fishing is popular (even in winter, when there is ice fishing), but many of the lakes, especially further north, have no road access and you have to fly in.

St Paul is the place to go if you are looking for little green people. The **flying-saucer landing pad**, which is still awaiting its first customer, is open for business. Residents built the 12m-high circular landing pad in 1967 as part of a centennial project and as a stunt to try to generate tourism (it's billed as the world's largest, and only, UFO landing pad) to the remote region. It worked: UFO enthusiasts have been visiting ever since.

Hwy 63 is the main route into the province's northeastern wilderness interior. The highway, with a few small settlements and campgrounds on the way, leads to **Fort McMurray**, which is 439km northeast of Edmonton. Originally a fur-trading outpost, it is now home to one of the world's largest oilfields. The town isn't particularly interesting. Non-oil workers generally come here to see the aurora borealis (northern lights). The story of how crude oil is extracted from the vast tracts of sand is told at the **Oil Sands Discovery Centre** (515 MacKenzie Blvd; adult/child $7/4; ☺ 9am-5pm May-Sep).

Wood Buffalo National Park

This huge park (p810) is best accessed from Fort Smith in the NWT. Covering an area the size of Switzerland, the park is known for its free-roaming herds of Wood buffalo (bison) and rare whooping cranes.

In Alberta, the only access is via air to Fort Chipewyan. In winter an ice road leads north to Peace Point (which connects to Fort Smith), and another road links the park to Fort McMurray.

British Columbia

Best Places to Eat

➡ Hawksworth (p654)

➡ Araxi Restaurant (p681)

➡ Flying Pig (p655)

➡ Red Fish Blue Fish (p693)

Best Places to Stay

➡ Wickaninnish Inn (p711)

➡ Rockwater Secret Cove Resort (p685)

➡ Free Spirit Spheres (p706)

➡ Nita Lake Lodge (p680)

Why Go?

British Columbia visitors need a long list of superlatives when describing their trips – the words spectacular, breath-taking and jaw-dropping only go so far. But it's hard not to be moved by towering mountains, wildlife-packed forests and dramatic coastlines that slow your heart like sigh-triggering spa treatments. Canada's westernmost province is more than just nature-hugging dioramas, though.

Cosmopolitan Vancouver fuses cuisines and cultures from Asia and beyond, while vibrant smaller cities like Victoria and Kelowna are increasingly creating their own intriguing scenes. For sheer character, it's hard to beat the kaleidoscope of quirky little communities from rustic north-ern BC to the ever laid-back Southern Gulf Islands.

Wherever you head, the great outdoors will always call. Don't just point your camera at it. BC is unbeatable for the kind of life-enhancing skiing, kayaking and hiking that can easily make this the trip of a lifetime.

When to Go
Vancouver

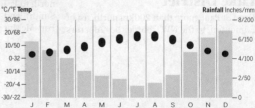

Dec–Mar Best powder action on the slopes of Whistler and Blackcomb mountains	**Jul & Aug** Beaches, patios and a plethora of outdoor festivals in sun-dappled Vancouver	**Sep & Oct** Dramatic surfing and the start of storm-watching season in beach-hugging Tofino

Getting There & Around

The sheer size of BC can overwhelm some visitors: it's a scary-sounding 1508km drive from Vancouver to Prince Rupert, for example. While it's tempting to simply stick around Vancouver – the main point of entry for most BC-bound visitors – you won't really have experienced the province unless you head out of town.

Despite the distances, driving remains the most popular method of movement in BC. Plan your routes via the handy DriveBC website (www.drivebc.ca) and check out the dozens of services offered by the extensive **BC Ferries** (www.bcferries. com) system.

VIA Rail (www.viarail.com) operates two BC train services. One trundles across the north from the coastline to Jasper. Pick up the second in Jasper for a ride back to Vancouver. A third line on Vancouver Island may also reopen in the coming years.

PARKS & WILDLIFE

BC's national parks include snow-capped **Glacier** and the Unesco World Heritage sites of **Kootenay** and **Yoho**. The newer **Gulf Islands National Park Reserve** protects a fragile coastal region. Visit the website of **Parks Canada** (www.pc.gc.ca) for information.

The region's almost 1000 provincial parks offer 3000km of hiking trails. Notables include **Strathcona** and remote **Cape Scott**, as well as the Cariboo's canoe-friendly **Bowron Lake** and the Kootenays' Matterhorn-like **Mt Assiniboine**. Check the **BC Parks** (www.bcparks.ca) website for information.

Expect to spot some amazing wildlife. Ocean visitors should keep an eye out for orcas, while land mammals – including elk, moose, wolves, grizzlies and black bears – will have most scrambling for their cameras. And there are around 500 bird varieties, including blue herons and bald eagles galore.

Raise a Glass: BC's Top Five Beers

➡ Back Hand of God Stout by Crannóg Ales: a rich, java-colored brew with a cult following.

➡ Red Racer ESB by Central City Brewing: a smooth, malty ale with nicely balanced hops.

➡ Fat Tug IPA by Driftwood Brewery: BC's best and most hoptastic Pacific Northwest IPA.

➡ Old Jalopy Pale Ale by Powell Street Craft Brewery: Canadian Brewery Awards' Beer of the Year winner, made by a tiny Vancouver nanobrewery.

➡ Zunga by Townsite Brewing: the Sunshine Coast's favorite quaff is a beautifully balanced blonde ale.

GUILT-FREE FISH & CHIPS

Seafood is BC's main dining choice. Support the sustainability of the region's aquatic larder by frequenting restaurants operating under the Ocean Wise banner; see www. oceanwise.ca.

BC Fast Facts

➡ Population: 4.6 million

➡ Area: 944,735 sq km

➡ Capital: Victoria

➡ Fact: BC is North America's third-largest film and TV production center.

It's Official

BC's provincial bird is the Steller's jay and its official mammal is the Kermode bear, a black bear with white fur.

Resources

➡ Destination British Columbia (www.hellobc.com)

➡ Cycling BC (www.cyclingbc. net)

➡ British Columbia Beer Guide (www.bcbeer.ca)

➡ BC Government (www2. gov.bc.ca)

➡ BC Wine Institute (www. winebc.com)

➡ Van Dop Arts & Cultural Guide (www.art-bc.com)

➡ Discover Camping (www. discovercamping.ca)

➡ Surfing Vancouver Island (www.surfing vancouverisland.com)

BRITISH COLUMBIA

British Columbia Highlights

1 Stretch your legs on a seawall stroll around Vancouver's spectacular **Stanley Park** (p637).

2 Surf up a storm (or just watch a storm) in **Tofino** (p709) on Vancouver Island's wild west coast.

3 Slurp some celebrated tipples on an ever-winding **Okanagan Valley** winery tour (p730).

4 Ski the Olympian slopes at **Whistler** (p675), then enjoy a warming après-ski beverage in the village.

5 Explore the ancient and ethereal rainforest of **Gwaii Haanas National Park Reserve** (p764) and kayak the coastline for a fish-eye view of the region.

6 Putter around the lively Saturday Market on **Salt Spring Island** (p719) and scoff more than a few treats.

7 Indulge in some lip-smacking Asian hawker food at the two night markets in **Richmond, Vancouver** (p672).

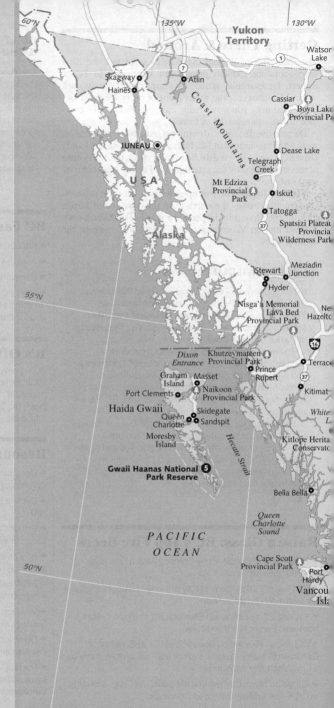

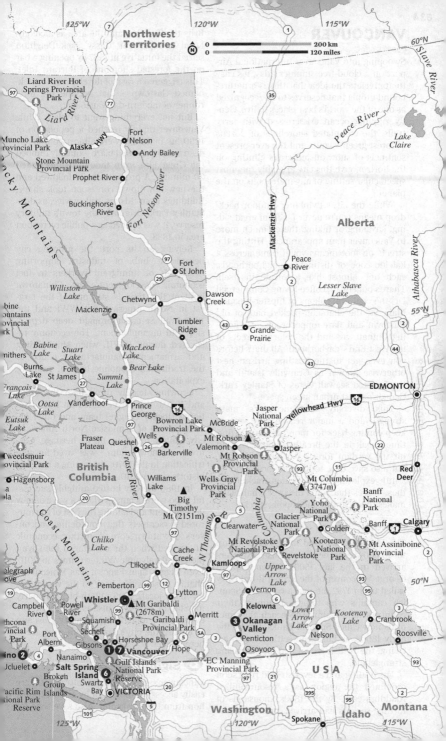

VANCOUVER

POP 666,500

Swooping into Vancouver International Airport on a cloud-free summer's day, it's easy to appreciate the idea that this is a nature-bound utopia that deserves to be recognized as one of the world's best places to live. Gently rippling ocean crisscrossed with ferry trails, the crenulated shorelines of dozens of forest-green islands and the ever-present sentinels of snow-dusted crags glinting on the horizon give this city arguably the most spectacular setting of any metropolis on the planet.

While the city's twinkling outdoor backdrop means you're never far from great skiing, kayaking or hiking, there's much more to Vancouver than appearances. Hitting the streets on foot means you'll come across a kaleidoscope of distinctive neighborhoods, each one almost like a village in itself. There's bohemian, coffee-loving Commercial Dr; the cool indie shops of hipster-hugging Main St; the character-packed bars of old Gastown and flare-topped roofs of adjoining Chinatown; and the colorful streets of the West End's 'gayborhood.' All that's before you even get to the bustling artisan nest otherwise known as Granville Island and the forested seawall vistas of Stanley Park, Canada's finest urban green space.

This diversity is Vancouver's main strength and a major reason why visitors keep coming back for more. If you're a first timer, soak in the breathtaking views and hit the verdant forests whenever you can, but also save time to join the locals and do a little exploring off the beaten track; it's in these places that you'll discover what really makes this beautiful metropolis special.

History

The First Nations lived in this area for up to 16,000 years before Spanish explorers arrived in the late 1500s. When Captain George Vancouver of the British Royal Navy sailed up in 1792, he met a couple of Spanish captains who informed him of their country's land claim. The beach they met on is now called Spanish Banks. But by the early 1800s, as European settlers began arriving, the British crown had an increasing stranglehold.

Fur trading and a feverish gold rush soon redefined the region as a resource-filled Aladdin's cave. By the 1850s, thousands of fortune seekers had arrived, prompting the Brits to officially claim the area as a colony. Local entrepreneur 'Gassy' Jack Deighton seized the initiative in 1867 by opening a bar on the forested shoreline of Burrard Inlet. This triggered a rash of development – nicknamed Gastown – that became the forerunner of modern-day Vancouver.

But not everything went to plan. While Vancouver rapidly reached a population of 1000, its buildings were almost completely destroyed in an 1886 blaze – quickly dubbed the Great Fire, even though it only lasted 20 minutes. A prompt rebuild followed and the new downtown core soon took shape. Buildings from this era still survive, as does Stanley Park. Originally the town's military reserve, it was opened as a public recreation area in 1888.

Relying on its port, the growing city became a hub of industry, importing thousands of immigrant workers to fuel economic development. The Chinatown built at this time is still one of the largest in North America. But WWI and the 1929 Wall St crash brought deep depression and unemployment. The economy recovered during WWII, when shipbuilding and armaments manufacturing added to the traditional economic base of resource exploitation.

Growing steadily throughout the 1950s and 1960s, Vancouver added an NHL (National Hockey League) team and other accoutrements of a midsize North American city. Finally reflecting on its heritage, Gastown – by now a slum – was saved for gentrification in the 1970s, becoming a national historic site in 2010.

In 1986 the city hosted a highly successful Expo world's fair, sparking a wave of new development and adding the first of the mirrored skyscrapers that now define Vancouver's downtown core. A further economic lift arrived when the city staged the Olympic and Paralympic Winter Games in 2010. Even bigger than Expo, it was Vancouver's chance to showcase itself to the world. But for many locals, 2013's 125th birthday party for Stanley Park was just as important: big events come and go, but Vancouverites aim to ensure the city's greatest green space is here forever.

⊙ Sights

Vancouver's most popular attractions are easily accessible on foot or by a short transit hop from the city center. Also save time for

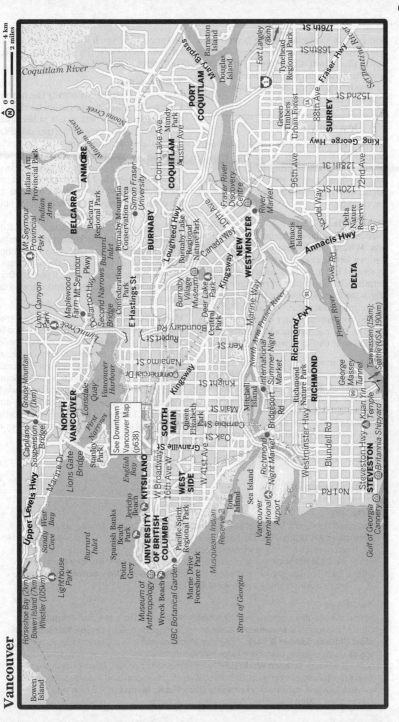

BRITISH COLUMBIA VANCOUVER

Vancouver

some urban exploring off the beaten path: the neighborhoods here – especially Gastown, Chinatown, Commercial Dr, Main St and Kitsilano – are well worth an afternoon of wandering and all have great places to eat when it's time for a break.

◉ Downtown

Lapped by ocean on two sides and with Stanley Park on its tip, downtown Vancouver combines shimmering glass apartment and business towers with the shop-lined attractions of Robson St, the city's central promenade.

Canada Place
LANDMARK

(Map p638; www.canadaplace.ca; 999 Canada Place Way; Ⓜ Waterfront) Vancouver's version of the Sydney Opera House, this iconic landmark is shaped like a series of sails. A cruise-ship terminal, it's also a pier where you can stroll the waterfront for camera-triggering North Shore mountain vistas. The adjoining grass-roofed convention center expansion opened in 2010. The nearby plaza houses the tripod-like Olympic Cauldron from the 2010 Games.

Fly Over Canada
AMUSEMENT RIDE

(Map p638; www.flyovercanada.com; 999 Canada Pl; adult/child $20/15; ⊙10am-9pm; Ⓜ Waterfront) The newest attraction in Canada Pl, this breathtaking movie-screen simulator ride makes you feel like you're swooping across the entire country, waggling your legs over landmark scenery from coast to coast. En route, your seat will lurch, your face will be sprayed and you'll likely have a big smile on your face. Once the short ride is over, you'll want to do it all again.

Jack Poole Plaza
PLAZA

(Map p638; Canada Pl; Ⓜ Waterfront) The heart of Vancouver's 2010 Olympic Games hosting duties, this handsome waterfront public space is the permanent home of the tripod-like Olympic Cauldron. The flame is lit for special occasions or you can pay $5000 to have it switched on. The plaza offers great views of the mountain-backed Burrard Inlet and you can follow the shoreline walking trail around the convention center West Building for public artworks and historic plaques.

If you fancy a further taste of the 2010 Games, nip along the subterranean pedestrian tunnel between the two convention buildings. You'll find a small display of medals, Olympic torches and even a podium from the event where you can pretend you won the skeleton.

Marine Building
HISTORIC BUILDING

(Map p638; 355 Burrard St; ⊙9am-5pm Mon-Fri; Ⓜ Burrard) Vancouver's best art-deco building, this graceful, 22-story beauty celebrates the city's maritime past with an elaborate exterior of sea horses, lobsters and streamlined ships. Nip into the lobby where a walk-through artwork of stained-glass panels and a polished floor inlaid with signs of the zodiac await – peruse the inlaid wood interiors of the brass-doored elevators as well.

VANCOUVER IN...

One Day

Begin with a heaping breakfast at the **Templeton** (p653) before strolling south to the **Vancouver Art Gallery** (p637). Next, take a window-shopping wander along **Robson St**, then cut down to the waterfront for panoramic sea and mountain vistas. Walk west along the **Coal Harbour** seawall and make for the dense trees of **Stanley Park** (p637). Spend the afternoon exploring the beaches, totem poles and **Vancouver Aquarium** (p637) here before ambling to the **West End** for dinner.

Two Days

Follow the one-day itinerary, then, the next morning, head to clamorous **Chinatown**. Stop at the towering **Millennium Gate** and duck into the nearby **Dr Sun Yat-Sen Classical Chinese Garden & Park** (p642) for a taste of tranquility. Check out the colorful stores (and tempting pork buns) around the neighborhood before strolling south along Main St towards **Science World** (p642) for some hands-on fun. Afterwards hop on the SkyTrain at the nearby station, trundle to Waterfront Station, and then take the scenic SeaBus to North Vancouver's **Lonsdale Quay Public Market** (p669). On your return, hit Gastown's **Alibi Room** (p659) for some craft beers.

Vancouver Art Gallery
GALLERY

(Map p638; ☎604-662-4700; www.vanartgallery. bc.ca; 750 Hornby St; adult/child $20/6; ⊙10am-5pm Wed-Mon, to 9pm Tue; 🚇5) The VAG has dramatically transformed in recent years, becoming a vital part of the city's cultural scene. Contemporary exhibitions – often showcasing Vancouver's renowned photo-conceptualists – are now combined with blockbuster international traveling shows. Check out kid-friendly activities and **Fuse**, a late-night party every few months where you can hang with the city's young arties over wine and live music.

Bill Reid Gallery of Northwest Coast Art
GALLERY

(Map p638; www.billreidgallery.ca; 639 Hornby St; adult/child $10/5; ⊙11am-5pm Wed-Sun; Ⓜ Burrard) Showcasing carvings, paintings and jewelry from Canada's most revered Haida artist, this gallery is lined with exquisite works, plus handy touch screens to tell you all about them. Check out the Great Hall, where there's often a carver at work; then hit the mezzanine level, where you'll be face-to-face with an 8.5m-long bronze of intertwined magical creatures with impressively long tongues.

Vancouver Lookout
LOOKOUT

(Map p638; www.vancouverlookout.com; 555 W Hastings St; adult/child $15.75/7.75; ⊙8:30am-10:30pm; Ⓜ Waterfront) Expect your stomach to make a bid for freedom as the glass elevator whisks you 169m to the apex of this needle-like viewing tower. Up top, there's not much to do but admire the awesome 360-degree vistas of city, sea and mountains unfurling around you. Tickets are pricey but are valid all day – return for a soaring sunset view.

BC Place Stadium
STADIUM

(Map p638; www.bcplacestadium.com; 777 Pacific Blvd; Ⓜ Stadium-Chinatown) With its fancy new roof, BC Place is now an even bigger downtown landmark. But it's not all about size: the city's main stadium is home to the BC Lions Canadian Football League team and the Vancouver Whitecaps soccer team. Also check out the stadium's family-friendly BC Sports Hall of Fame & Museum for a glimpse at the region's sporty history.

Rogers Arena
STADIUM

(Map p638; www.rogersarena.ca; 800 Griffiths Way; tours adult/child $12/6; ⊙tours 10:30am, noon & 1:30pm Wed, Fri & Sat; Ⓜ Stadium-Chinatown)

TOP FIVE MUSEUMS

➡ Museum of Anthropology (p645)

➡ Museum of Vancouver (p645)

➡ Beaty Biodiversity Museum (p646)

➡ Vancouver Police Museum (p642)

➡ Roedde House Museum (p641)

Vancouver's other stadium hosts the National Hockey League's Vancouver Canucks. On game nights, when the 20,000-capacity venue heaves with fervent fans, you'll enjoy the atmosphere even if the rules are a mystery. Behind-the-scenes tours last 75 minutes and take you into the hospitality suites and the nosebleed press box up in the rafters and are popular with visiting sports fans.

◉ Stanley Park

The magnificent 404-hectare **Stanley Park** (Map p638; www.vancouver.ca/parks; ♿; 🚇19) combines attractions with a mystical natural aura. Don't miss a stroll or cycle around the 8.8km seawall: a kind of visual spa treatment fringed by a 150,000-tree temperate rainforest. The path takes you right alongside the park's camera-luring totem poles. There are bike rentals near the W Georgia St entrance.

★Vancouver Aquarium
AQUARIUM

(☎604-659-3474; www.vanaqua.org; 845 Avison Way; Jul & Aug adult/child $27/17; ⊙9:30am-6pm; ♿; 🚇19) Stanley Park's biggest draw houses 9000 water-loving critters, including sharks, beluga whales and a rather shy octopus. There's also a small rainforest of birds, turtles and a statue-still sloth. Peruse the mesmerizing iridescent jellyfish and consider an Animal Encounter tour, where you'll learn about being a trainer. Expansion was underway on our visit, so look out for changes.

Miniature Railway
MINIATURE RAILWAY

(adult/child from $5; ⊙hours vary; 🚇19) A short walk from the aquarium, this beloved family-friendly attraction – a replica of the first passenger train that trundled in from Montréal in 1887 – takes on several incarnations throughout the year. In summer, it's a First Nations–themed ride; in winter, it becomes a Christmas train; and, at Halloween, it takes on a spooky, haunted ghost-loving allure.

Downtown Vancouver

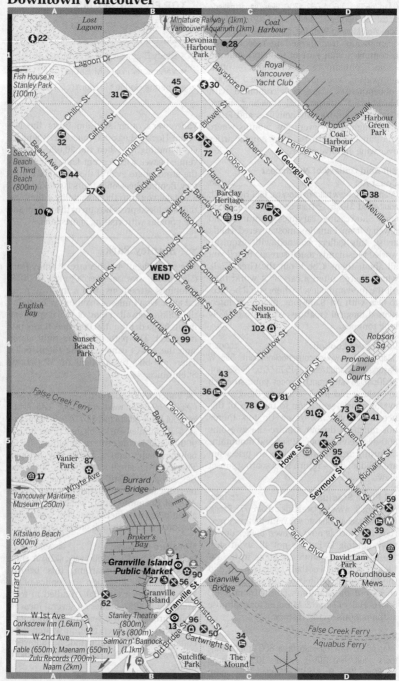

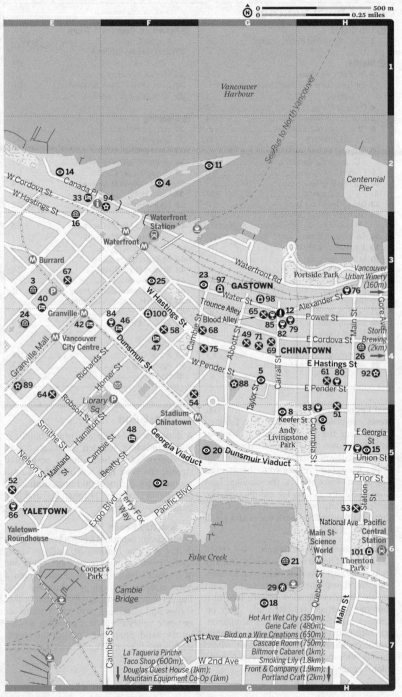

BRITISH COLUMBIA VANCOUVER

Downtown Vancouver

Lost Lagoon
LAKE

(www.stanleyparkecology.ca; 🚍19) This forested lagoon near the park entrance is Vancouver's downtown nature sanctuary. Its perimeter pathway makes for a wonderful stroll – keep your eyes peeled for beady-eyed blue herons and duck into the excellent Lost Lagoon Nature House for exhibits on the park's multitudinous flora and fauna. Check ahead for their guided park walks and you'll spot even more.

Second Beach & Third Beach
BEACH

(🚍19) Second Beach is a busy, family-friendly area on the park's western side, with a grassy playground, waterfront swimming pool and nearby Ceperley Meadow, where free outdoor movie screenings often take place on summer nights (see www.freshaircinema.ca). Alternatively, Third Beach is possibly Vancouver's best sunset-viewing spot, where the sky often comes alive with pyrotechnic color – hence the picnicking locals.

⊙ West End

A dense nest of older apartment buildings and handsome wooden heritage homes on dozens of well-maintained residential streets, the West End has beaches, seawall promenades, plenty of midrange dining (especially on Davie and Denman Sts) and BC's largest gay community.

English Bay Beach
BEACH

(Map p638; cnr Denman St & Beach Ave; 🚍5) Wandering south on Denman St, you'll suddenly spot a rustle of palm trees announcing one of Canada's best urban beaches. There's a party atmosphere here in summer as West Enders catch the rays, crowd the busker shows and check out artwork vendors...or just ogle volleyball players prancing around on the sand. Snap some pics of the laughing bronze figures – Vancouver's fave public artwork.

Roedde House Museum   MUSEUM
(Map p638; www.roeddehouse.org; 1415 Barclay St; admission $5; ⊙ 1-4pm Tue-Fri & Sun; 🚌 5) For a glimpse of what the West End used to look like, drop by this handsome 1893 mansion, now a lovingly preserved museum. The house is packed with antiques and the surrounding gardens are planted in period style. The abode is the showpiece of **Barclay Heritage Sq**, a one-block site containing nine historic West End houses dating from 1890 to 1908.

◉ Yaletown

An evocative, brick-lined former warehouse district transformed into swanky bars, restaurants and boutiques, pedestrian-friendly Yaletown is where the city's chichi socialites come to see and be seen. Roughly bordered by Nelson, Homer and Drake Sts and Pacific Blvd, the area's gritty past is recalled by the old rail tracks still embedded in many of its roads.

Engine 374 Pavilion   MUSEUM
(Map p638; www.roundhouse.ca; Roundhouse Community Arts & Recreation Centre, 181 Roundhouse Mews; Ⓜ Yaletown-Roundhouse) **FREE** May 23, 1887 is an auspicious date in Vancouver's history. It was the day when Engine 374 pulled the first transcontinental passenger train into the fledgling city, symbolically linking the country and kick-starting the eventual metropolis. Retired in 1945, the engine was (after many years of neglect) finally restored and placed in this lovely free-entry pavilion. Drop by for a chat with the friendly volunteers.

David Lam Park   PARK
(Map p638; www.vancouverparks.ca; cnr Drake St & Pacific Blvd; Ⓜ Yaletown-Roundhouse) A crooked elbow of landscaped waterfront at the neck of False Creek, this is Yaletown's main green space. A popular spot for free shows at the Vancouver International Jazz Festival (p649), it's also sometimes used for alfresco summer movie screenings and is the perfect launch

point for a 2km seawall stroll along the north bank of False Creek to Science World (p642).

On your walk, you'll pass intriguing public artworks, glass condo towers foresting the old Expo '86 site and the stadium where the Vancouver Canucks NHL team plays. Look out for beady-eyed birdlife along the route.

◎ Gastown

Now a national historic site, Vancouver's brick-paved old town area is where the city began. Many heritage buildings remain, most now housing cool bars, restaurants or trendy shops.

Steam Clock   LANDMARK

(Map p638; cnr Water & Cambie Sts; M Waterfront) Halfway along Water St, this oddly popular tourist magnet lures the cameras with its tooting steam whistle. Built in 1977, the clock's mechanism is actually driven by electricity while only the pipes on top are fueled by steam, although this information might cause a riot if you reveal it to the patiently waiting tourists. Sounding every 15 minutes, it marks each hour with little whistling symphonies.

Once you have the required photo, spend time exploring the rest of cobbled Water St, one of Vancouver's most historic thoroughfares.

Gassy Jack Statue   MONUMENT

(Map p638; Maple Tree Sq; ☐4) It's amusing to think that Vancouver's favorite statue is a testament to the virtues of drink. At least that's one interpretation of the jaunty 'Gassy' Jack Deighton bronze, perched atop a whiskey barrel in Maple Tree Sq. Erected in 1970, it recalls Deighton's 1867 arrival, after which he built a bar, triggering development that soon became Vancouver.

Vancouver Police Museum   MUSEUM

(Map p638; ☑604-665-3346; www.vancouver-policemuseum.ca; 240 E Cordova St; adult/child $12/8; ◎9am-5pm Tue-Sat; ☐4) Contextualizing the city's crime-colored history, this quirky little museum is lined with confiscated weapons, counterfeit currency and a grizzly former mortuary room where the walls are studded with preserved slivers of human tissue – spot the bullet-damaged brain slices. If your interest in crime is triggered, take their excellent Sins of the City walking tour around the area.

◎ Chinatown

Adjoining Gastown, North America's third-largest Chinatown is a highly wanderable explosion of sight, sound and aromas. Start your exploration at the **Chinatown Millennium Gate** (Map p638; cnr W Pender & Taylor Sts; M Stadium-Chinatown) and don't miss the bustling newly reinvigorated summertime night market.

Dr Sun Yat-Sen Classical
Chinese Garden & Park   GARDENS

(Map p638; www.vancouverchinesegarden.com; 578 Carrall St; adult/child $12/9; ◎9:30am-7pm; M Stadium-Chinatown) A tranquil break from clamorous Chinatown, this intimate 'garden of ease' illustrates Taoist symbolism through the placing of gnarled pine trees, winding covered pathways and limestone formations. Entry includes a 45-minute guided tour, where you'll learn that everything in the garden reflects balance and harmony. Look out for the lazy turtles bobbing in the jade-colored water.

If you're on a budget, check out the free park next door: not quite as elaborate as its sister, it's still a pleasant oasis of whispering grasses, a large fishpond and a small pagoda.

Chinatown Night Market   MARKET

(Map p638; www.vancouverchinatownnightmarket. com; Keefer St, btwn Columbia & Main Sts; ◎6-11pm Fri-Sun mid-May–early Sep; M Stadium-Chinatown) Recently reinvented to compete with the success of larger night markets in Richmond, Chinatown's version is well worth a summer evening visit. Cheap and cheerful trinkets still feature, but the highlight is the food – it's like a walk-through buffet of fish balls, bubble tea and tornado potatoes. Check ahead: there's an eclectic roster of entertainment, including alfresco movie screenings.

Jimi Hendrix Shrine   NOTABLE BUILDING

(Map p638; 207 Union St; ◎1-6pm Mon-Sat Jun-Sep; ☐3) **FREE** Said to occupy the building that formerly housed Vie's Chicken and Steak House – the 1960s restaurant where Hendrix' grandmother cooked and the young guitarist frequently strummed – this is worth a quick look. A quirky, homemade attraction, the red-painted shack is lined with old photos and album covers and is staffed by a chatty volunteer or two.

Science World   MUSEUM

(Map p638; www.scienceworld.ca; 1455 Quebec St; adult/child $22.50/15.25; ◎10am-5pm Mon-Fri, to 6pm Sat & Sun; ☑; M Main St-Science World) Nes-

VANCOUVER FOR CHILDREN

Family-friendly Vancouver is stuffed with things for vacationing kids. Pick up a copy of the free *Kids' Guide Vancouver* flyer from racks around town and visit www.kids-vancouver.com for tips, resources and family-focused events. Car-hire companies rent car seats – legally required for young children here – for a few dollars per day, but you'll need to reserve in advance. If you're traveling around the city without a car, make sure you hop on the SkyTrain or SeaBus transit services or the miniferry to Granville Island: kids love 'em, especially the newer SkyTrain cars, where they can sit up front and pretend they're driving. Children under five travel free on all transit.

Stanley Park (p637) can keep most families occupied for a full day. If it's hot, make sure you hit the water park at Lumberman's Arch or try the swimming pool at Second Beach; also consider the **Miniature Railway** (p637) for a fun trundle. The park is a great place to bring a picnic, and its beaches especially are highly kid-friendly. Save time for the **Vancouver Aquarium** (p637) and, if your kids have been good, consider a behind-the-scenes trainer tour. Kids who are into nature and critters will also enjoy the Nature House at **Lost Lagoon** (p640) and the **Capilano Suspension Bridge** (p668) with its forest walks – take them to nearby **Grouse Mountain** (p668) and they can also spot grizzly bears close-up.

The city's other educational family-friendly attractions – the kind where your moppets get educated without even noticing – include **Science World** (p642) and the **HR MacMillan Space Centre** (p645). If it's raining, you can also duck inside **Bloedel Conservatory** (p647) and hang with exotic birds.

If you time your visit right, the city has an array of family-friendly festivals, including the **Pacific National Exhibition** (p649), the **Vancouver International Children's Festival** (p649) and the fireworks fiesta known as the **Celebration of Light** (p649).

tled under the city's favorite geodesic dome (OK, its only one), this recently revamped hands-on science and nature showcase brings out the kid in almost everyone. Expect to spend a half-day here as your squirts run themselves ragged learning scientific principles, especially in the new outdoor park area.

Also consider checking out a movie in the on-site Omnimax Theatre or hanging out without the kids at one of the regular After Dark social events – there's also a teen-only version if you're looking for ways to entertain a sullen adolescent or two.

◉ Main Street & Commercial Drive

Vancouver's indie crowd has colonized an area of town that used to be a byword for down-at-the-heels. Radiating south from the Main St-Science World SkyTrain Station (and easily accessed by the number 3 bus that runs along its length), Main St is the city's hippest hood: think skinny jeans and cool-ass coffeehouses, plus great independent shops (especially past the intersection with 18th Ave).

But Main isn't the city's first alternative district. Further east, Commercial Dr – just called 'the Drive' by locals – has a long counterculture history and was also settled by generations of Italian immigrants. It has great indie shops, patio-fronted restaurants and arguably the city's best family-run coffeehouses.

The 99 B-Line express bus along Broadway links both areas in 10 minutes.

Hot Art Wet City   GALLERY
(www.hotartwetcity.com; 2206 Main St; ⊙noon-5pm Wed-Sat; 🚌3) **FREE** Possibly the most fun you can have at a private gallery in Vancouver, trip up the stairs at this funky little space and you're guaranteed some eye-popping art to look at. Mostly local artists are showcased and there's a new exhibition every month. Past themes have ranged from bizarre paintings of doll heads to art on beer bottles.

Check the retail space in the corner for quirky souvenir ideas and peruse the calendar before you arrive: there's a lively roster of artist talks, workshops and show openings.

Portobello West   MARKET
(Map p638; www.portobellowest.com; 1 Athletes Way, Creekside Community Recreation Centre; adult/child $2/free; ⊙11am-5pm Sat & Sun, 4 times per year; 👶; Ⓜ Main St-Science World) This weekend-long arts, crafts and fashion market runs four times a year – once each season – in the cavernous Creekside Community Recreation

Centre in the Olympic Village. Expect to find an eclectic blend of handmade, one-of-a-kind goodies and locally designed togs to take back home, or just enjoy the live music and fresh-made bakery and lunch treats.

Punjabi Market
NEIGHBORHOOD

(🚇3) Located on Main St, past 48th Ave, and also known as 'Little India,' this enclave of sari stores, bhangra music shops and some of the region's best-value curry buffet restaurants is a good spot for a spicy all-you-can-eat lunch followed by a restorative walkabout. Plans are afoot to possibly add a gate, like the one in Chinatown.

Grandview Park
PARK

(Commercial Dr, btwn Charles & William Sts; 🚇20) The Drive's alfresco neighborhood hub is named after the smashing views peeking between its trees: to the north are the North Shore mountains, while to the west is a city-scape vista of twinkling towers. Teeming with buskers, dreadlocked drummers, impromptu

sidewalk sales and a waft or two of naughty cigarette smoke, the park is a big summertime lure for nearby locals.

◉ Granville Island

Fanning out under the giant iron arches of Granville Bridge, this gentrified former industrial peninsula – it's not actually an island – is one of the best spots to spend a lazy afternoon. Studded with restaurants, bars, theaters and artisan businesses, it's often crowded in summer, as visitors chill out with the buskers and wrestle the seagulls for their fish and chips.

★ Granville Island Public Market
MARKET

(Map p638; www.granvilleisland.com/public-market; Johnston St; ⊙9am-7pm; 🚇50, 🚢miniferries) Granville Island's highlight is the covered Public Market, a multisensory smorgasbord of fish, cheese, fruit and bakery treats. Pick up some fixings for a picnic at nearby Vanier Park (a 10-minute walk west along the seawall) or hit the little international food court (dine off-

---

FERRY HOPPING

If you don't arrive or depart from Granville Island via one of the tiny miniferries operated by Aquabus Ferries (p666) or False Creek Ferries (p666), you haven't really conducted your visit correctly. But these signature little boats – the Aquabus vessels tend to be rainbow hued while the False Creek Ferries are blue – don't only transport passengers from the north side of False Creek to the market on the south side. Both have several additional ports of call around the shoreline and, if you have time, a 'cruise' of the area is a great way to see the city from the water. An all-day pass on each service costs $10 to $15 (tickets are not interchangeable between the operators, who remain cutthroat rivals) and there are several highlight stop-offs to consider along the way.

Aquabus can get you to Yaletown's David Lam Park (p641), a waterfront green space that's ideal for watching the gently lapping waters of False Creek from a grassy promontory, preferably with a picnic. On the opposite shoreline, you can step off at **Stamps Landing**, one of Vancouver's first urban waterfront housing developments: there's a pub here in the delightfully medieval-sounding **Leg-in-Boot Sq**. Back on the northern shoreline, there's a stop at the bottom of Davie St, which is a short stroll from the heart of Yaletown. You'll find the fascinating Engine 374 Pavilion (p641) here, home of the locomotive that pulled the first passenger train into Vancouver in 1887.

You can see how things have transformed around False Creek in recent years at one final stop. The shoreline here used to be crammed with grungy industry, but in 2010 the **Olympic Village** opened. Providing housing for the athletes at the 2010 Winter Games, this swanky development is now a slick new city neighborhood. It's also just a short stroll to Science World (p642), one of Vancouver's most popular family-friendly attractions.

False Creek Ferries covers many of the same locations but also includes a unique stop at another popular – and appropriate – Vancouver attraction. From Granville Island and via a stop at the Aquatic Centre in the West End, it takes 25 minutes to voyage to the Vancouver Maritime Museum (p645). On the shoreline of verdant Vanier Park, it's a great spot to dive into the region's seafaring past, from historic vessels to scale models. And since you're now a veteran sea dog, you'll fit right in.

peak and you're more likely to snag a table). In summer, there's also a farmers market outside.

This is a great spot to pick up unusual souvenirs for home and – if you're a true foodie – market tours are available, with samples included.

Granville Island Brewing   BREWERY
(Map p638; ☑604-687-2739; www.gib.ca; 1441 Cartwright St; tours $9.75; ☉tours noon, 1:30pm, 3pm, 4:30pm & 5:30pm; ☑50) Canada's oldest microbrewery offers half hour tours where smiling guides walk you through the tiny brewing nook, before depositing you in the Taproom for some tasty samples, often including the summer-favorite *Hefeweizen*. You can also buy takeout in the adjoining store – look for special-batch seasonals, like smooth Irish Red and hoppy Imperial IPA. Production has mostly shifted to larger premises.

⊙ Kitsilano

A former hippie haven where the counterculture flower children grew up to reap professional jobs, 'Kits' is a pleasant neighborhood of wooden heritage homes, cozy coffee bars and highly browsable shops. Store-lined W 4th Ave is especially recommended for a lazy afternoon stroll. A short seawall amble from Granville Island, Vanier Park houses three museums and is ideal for picnicking.

Museum of Vancouver   MUSEUM
(Map p638; www.museumofvancouver.ca; 1100 Chestnut St; adult/child $12/8; ☉10am-5pm Fri-Wed, to 8pm Thu; ☀; ☑22) One of Vanier Park's three well-established educational attractions, the MOV has been upping its game in recent years with cool temporary exhibitions and regular late-opening parties for adults. It hasn't changed everything, though. There are still colorful displays on local 1950s pop culture and 1960s hippie counterculture, plus plenty of hands-on stuff for kids, including scavenger hunts and fun workshops.

HR MacMillan Space Centre   MUSEUM
(Map p638; www.spacecentre.ca; 1100 Chestnut St; adult/child $15/11; ☉10am-5pm; ☀; ☑22) Popular with packs of marauding schoolkids – expect to have to elbow them out of the way to push the flashing buttons – this high-tech science center illuminates the eye-opening world of space. There's plenty of fun to be had battling aliens and designing a spacecraft. There's also an observatory and planetarium; check ahead for the schedule of openings and events.

Vancouver Maritime Museum   MUSEUM
(www.vancouvermaritimemuseum.com; 1905 Ogden Ave; adult/child $11/8.50; ☉10am-5pm Tue-Sat, noon-5pm Sun; ☑22) The final member of Vanier Park's museum triumvirate combines intricate model ships with detailed re-created boat sections and some historic vessels. The main draw is the *St Roch*, a 1928 Royal Canadian Mounted Police Arctic patrol sailing ship that was the first vessel to navigate the legendary Northwest Passage in both directions. Evocative free tours of the vessel are offered.

Kitsilano Beach   BEACH
(cnr Cornwall Ave & Arbutus St; ☑22) Facing English Bay, Kits Beach is one of Vancouver's fave summertime hangouts. The wide, sandy expanse attracts buff Frisbee tossers and giggling volleyball players, as well as those who just like to preen while catching the rays. The water is fine for a dip, though serious swimmers should dive into the heated 137m Kitsilano Pool, a giant outdoor saltwater pool.

Old Hastings Mill Store Museum   MUSEUM
(☑604-734-1212; www.hastings-mill-museum.ca; 1575 Alma St; admission by donation; ☉1-4pm Tue-Sun; ☑4) Built near Gastown in 1865, this historic wooden structure is Vancouver's oldest surviving building. Originally a store for sawmill workers, it survived the Great Fire of 1886 and was used as a makeshift morgue on the fateful day. Saved from demolition by locals, it was relocated here by barge in the 1930s and now houses an eclectic array of pioneer-era and First Nations exhibits.

⊙ University of British Columbia

West from Kits on a 400-hectare forested peninsula, the **University of British Columbia** (UBC; ☑604-822-2211; www.ubc.ca) is the province's largest university. Its concrete campus is surrounded by the University Endowment Lands, complete with accessible beach and forest areas and a smattering of visitor attractions.

★ Museum of Anthropology   MUSEUM
(Map p635; ☑604-822-3825; www.moa.ubc.ca; 6393 NW Marine Dr; adult/child $14/12; ☉10am-5pm Wed-Mon, to 9pm Tue; ☑99 B-Line) Newly renovated and expanded, Vancouver's best

museum houses northwest coast aboriginal artifacts, including Haida houses and totem poles, plus non–First Nations exhibits, such as European ceramics and Cantonese opera costumes. The free guided tours are highly recommended, as is the excellent artsy gift shop. Give yourself a couple of hours at this museum.

Morris & Helen Belkin Gallery   GALLERY
(www.belkin.ubc.ca; 1825 Main Mall; ⊙10am-5pm Tue-Fri, noon-5pm Sat & Sun; 🚌99 B-Line) FREE This excellent little gallery specializes in contemporary and often quite challenging pieces. This explains the billboard-style depiction of an Iraqi city outside, complete with the caption 'Because there was and there wasn't a city of Baghdad.' Inside, you can expect a revolving roster of traveling shows, plus chin-stroking exhibits from a permanent collection of Canadian avant-garde works.

Beaty Biodiversity Museum   MUSEUM
(www.beatymuseum.ubc.ca; 2212 Main Mall; adult/child $12/8; ⊙10am-5pm; 🚌99B-Line) UBC's newest museum is also its most family friendly. Start with the giant blue whale skeleton in the entrance lobby, then descend to the main exhibition hall showcasing more than two million natural-history exhibits. Check ahead for kid-friendly storytelling, puppet shows and hands-on events. Hit the

on-site cafe if you need a rest from all that knowledge.

UBC Botanical Garden   GARDENS
(Map p635; www.ubcbotanicalgarden.org; 6804 SW Marine Dr; adult/child $8/4; ⊙9:30am-5pm; 🚌99 B-Line, then C20) You'll find a giant collection of rhododendrons, a fascinating apothecary plot and a winter green space of off-season bloomers in this 28-hectare complex of themed gardens. The recently added Greenheart Canopy Walkway lifts visitors 17m above the forest floor on a 308m guided ecotour. Walkway tickets include garden entry. If here in October, hit the annual Apple Festival.

Nitobe Memorial Garden   GARDENS
(www.nitobe.org; 1895 Lower Mall; adult/child $6/3; ⊙9:30am-5pm; 🚌99 B-Line, then C20) Exemplifying Japanese horticultural philosophies, this verdant, tranquil oasis includes the Tea Garden – complete with ceremonial teahouse – and the Stroll Garden, which reflects a symbolic journey through life, with its little waterfalls and languid koi carp. The gardens are named after Dr Inazo Nitobe, a scholar whose mug appears on Japan's ¥5000 bill. Consider a springtime visit for the florid cherry-blossom displays.

Pacific Spirit Regional Park   PARK
(Map p635; www.pacificspiritparksociety.org; cnr Blanca St & W 16th Ave; 🚌99 B-Line) This stunning 763-hectare park stretches from Burrard Inlet to the North Arm of the Fraser River. A smashing spot to hug some trees and explore, you'll also find Camosun Bog wetland – accessed by a boardwalk at 19th Ave and Camosun St – a haven for native bird and plant species. There are 54km of walking, jogging and cycling trails.

⊙ West Side
A large, catch-all area covering City Hall, the heritage homes of Fairview, the neighborhood eateries of Cambie Village and the strollable stores and restaurants of South Granville, there are several good reasons to visit this part of the city. And it's just a few minutes away from downtown by Canada Line SkyTrain (along the Cambie corridor) or number 10 bus (along South Granville).

Queen Elizabeth Park   PARK
(Map p635; www.vancouverparks.ca; entrance cnr W 33rd Ave & Cambie St; 🚌15) This 52-hectare park claims to house specimens of every tree

native to Canada. It's also the city's highest point, at 167m above sea level, and has panoramic views of the mountain-framed downtown skyscrapers. Sports fields, manicured lawns and two formal gardens keep locals happy, and you'll likely also see wide-eyed couples posing for wedding photos.

If you want to be taken out to the ball game, the recently restored Nat Bailey Stadium is a popular summer-afternoon haven for baseball fans.

Bloedel Conservatory GARDENS
(604-257-8584; www.vancouverparks.ca; Queen Elizabeth Park; adult/child $6.50/3.25; 9am-8pm Mon-Fri, 10am-8pm Sat & Sun; 15) Cresting the hill in Queen Elizabeth Park, this Triodetic domed conservatory is an ideal indoor warm-up spot on a rainy day. It has three climate-controlled zones with 400 plant species, dozens of koi carp and many free-flying tropical birds, including noisy parrots and macaws: ask for a free brochure to help you identify the flora and fauna.

VanDusen Botanical Garden GARDENS
(www.vandusengarden.org; 5251 Oak St; adult/child $10.75/5.75; 9am-9pm; 17) Vancou-

ver's favorite ornamental green space, this 22-hectare idyll is a web of paths weaving through small, specialized gardens: the Rhododendron Walk blazes with color in spring, while the Korean Pavilion is a focal point for a fascinating Asian plant collection. There's also a fun Elizabethan maze. A popular Christmastime destination, expect twinkling fairy lights illuminating the dormant plant life in December.

🏃 Activities

With a reputation for steely calved locals who like nothing better than an early morning 20km jog and a lip-smacking rice cake for breakfast, Vancouver is all about being active. Popular pastimes include running, biking and kayaking, while you're also just a short hop from some serious winter-sport action on the North Shore.

Walking & Running
For arm-swinging strolls or heart-pounding runs, the 8.8km **Stanley Park seawall** is mostly flat – apart from a couple of hills, where you could hang onto a passing bike. UBC's Pacific Spirit Regional Park is also a popular running spot, with tree-lined trails

STROLLING VANCOUVER'S PAST

Just a few weeks after renaming itself Vancouver (no one liked the original name 'Granville' or the insalubrious 'Gastown' slang name that preceded it), the fledgling city of around 1000 homes burnt almost to the ground in minutes in what was accurately termed the Great Fire. But locals weren't about to jump on the next boat out of town. Within days, plans were drawn up for a new city. This time, brick and stone would be favored over wood. The first buildings to be erected radiated from Maple Tree Sq – in particular along Carral St. This thoroughfare, one of the shortest streets in Vancouver, still exists today and links the historic center of Gastown to Chinatown. Take a stroll south on this street from Maple Tree Sq and you'll spot some grand buildings from the early days of the city. Perhaps due to an abundance of caution, they are also some of the sturdiest structures around and will likely survive for many years to come, whether or not there's a fire.

If you'd visited 30 years ago, however, you would have seen many of these buildings seemingly on their last legs. This part of Vancouver hadn't attracted any new development or investment for years and Carrall St's old, paint-peeled taverns, hotels and storefronts were spiraling into skid-row degradation. Two things changed the inevitable: historians and heritage fans banded together to draw attention to the area's important role in the founding years of the city, a campaign that finally culminated in a National Historic Site designation in 2010. Secondly, gentrification took hold. Developers had all but abandoned this part of the city for much of the last century. But with few neighborhoods left to enhance, they finally came back. While gentrification has many detractors here – worried that new development will change the area's old-school character – an undeniable positive is that it has preserved and protected Gastown's historic old buildings for decades to come. The brick and stone landmarks that once lined Carrall have, for the most part, been sympathetically restored and renovated, giving the entire area a new lease on life beyond its heritage designation.

marked throughout the area. If you really want a workout, try North Vancouver's Grouse Grind, a steep, sweat-triggering slog up the side of Grouse Mountain that's been nicknamed 'Mother Nature's StairMaster.' You can reward yourself at the top with free access to the resort's facilities – although you'll have to pay $10 to get down on the Skyride gondola.

South False Creek Seawall WALKING
(Map p638; end of Terminal Ave; ⓂMain St-Science World) Starting a few steps from Science World, this popular waterfront trail can take you all the way along the shoreline to Granville Island (about 3km). Or you can just take it easy and view a few sights along the way: look out for the giant bird sculptures in Olympic Village and Habitat Island, where visiting birdlife frequently perches.

Cycling
Joggers share the busy Stanley Park seawall with cyclists (and in-line skaters), necessitating a one-way traffic system to prevent bloody pileups. The sea-to-sky vistas are breathtaking, but the exposed route can be hit with crashing waves and icy winds in winter. Since slow-moving, camera-wielding tourists also crowd the route in summer, it's best to come early in the morning or late in the afternoon.

After circling the park to English Bay, energetic cyclists can continue along the north side of False Creek towards Science World, where the route heads up the south side of False Creek towards Granville Island, Vanier Park, Kitsilano Beach and, finally, UBC. This extended route, including Stanley Park, is around 25km. If you still have some energy, UBC's Pacific Spirit Regional Park has great forested bike trails, some with challenging uphill stretches.

There's a plethora of bike- and blade-rental stores near Stanley Park's W Georgia St entrance, especially around the inter section with Denman St. One of these, **Spokes Bicycle Rentals** (Map p638; www.vancouverbikerental.com; 1798 W Georgia St; adult per hr/7hr from $8.60/34.30; ◷8am-9pm; ⛟5), can also arrange guided tours. At time of writing, the city was planning to introduce a public bike-share scheme in addition to its expanding network of urban bike trails – check the City of Vancouver website for the latest info and resources (www.vancouver.ca/cycling).

Watersports
It's hard to beat the joy of an early evening paddle around the coastline here, with the sun sliding languidly down the mirrored glass towers that forest the city like modern-day totem poles. With its calm waters, Vancouver is a popular spot for both veteran and novice kayakers.

Ecomarine Paddlesport Centres KAYAKING
(Map p638; ☎604-689-7575, 888-425-2925; www.ecomarine.com; 1668 Duranleau St; single kayak rental per 2/24hr $39/94; ◷9am-6pm Sun, Mon, Wed & Thu, to 9pm Tue, Fri & Sat; ⛟50) With headquarters on Granville Island, the friendly folk at Ecomarine Paddlesport Centres offer equipment rentals and guided tours.

Windsure Adventure Watersports WATER SPORTS
(☎604-224-0615; www.windsure.com; 1300 Discovery St; ◷9am-8:30pm Apr-Sep; ⛟4) For those who want to be at one with the sea breeze, Windsure Adventure Watersports specializes in kiteboarding, windsurfing and skimboarding and offers lessons and equipment rentals from its Jericho Beach base.

☞ Tours

★Forbidden Vancouver WALKING TOUR
(www.forbiddenvancouver.ca; adult/concession $22/19; ◷Apr-Nov) This quirky company offers two core, highly entertaining, tours: a delve into Prohibition-era Vancouver and a poke around the seedy underbelly of historic Gastown. Not recommended for kids. Book ahead: they fill up quickly. At the time of research, a third tour covering Granville St's colorful nightlife history was being introduced.

★Vancouver Foodie Tours GUIDED TOUR
(☎877-804-9220; www.foodietours.ca; tours $49-69; ◷year-round) The perfect way to dive into the city's food scene, the two belt-busting guided tours include a street-food crawl ($49) and a gourmet drink-and-dine tour ($69).

Architectural Institute of British Columbia WALKING TOUR
(☎604-683-8588; www.aibc.ca; tours $10; ◷Tue-Sun Jul & Aug) Local architecture students conduct these excellent one- to two-hour wanders, focusing on the buildings, history and heritage of several key Vancouver neighborhoods. There are six tours in all and areas covered include Gastown, Strathcona,

Yaletown, Chinatown, downtown and the West End.

Accent Cruises
BOAT TOUR

(Map p638; ✆604-688-6625; www.accentcruises. ca; 1698 Duranleau St, Granville Island; dinner cruise $89; ⊙May-Oct; ▣50) Popular salmon buffet cruise along the coastlines of English Bay, Stanley Park and Ambleside Beach in West Vancouver. Departures are from Granville Island and it's a relaxing way to spend your evening after a long day spent trawling the sights.

Vancouver Trolley Company
BUS TOUR

(✆604-801-5515, 888-451-5581; www.vancouvertrolley.com; adult/child from $40/22; ⊙year-round) This company operates jolly replicas of San Francisco trolley cars (without the tracks), providing a hop-on, hop-off service to attractions around the city. The circuit takes 80 minutes and you buy your tickets from the driver – attraction tickets are also sold on board.

Harbour Cruises
BOAT TOUR

(Map p638; ✆800-663-1500, 604-688-7246; www.boatcruises.com; Denman St; adult/child $30/10; ⊙May-Oct) View the city – and some unexpected wildlife – from the water on a 75-minute narrated harbor tour. Tours weave past Stanley Park, Lions Gate Bridge and the North Shore mountains. There's also a 2½-hour sunset dinner cruise ($79/69 per adult/child), with West Coast cuisine (ie salmon) and live music.

☆ Festivals & Events

Dine Out Vancouver
FOOD

(www.tourismvancouver.com; 3-course menus $18, $28 or $38; ⊙mid-Jan) Two weeks of three-course tasting menus at area restaurants.

Chinese New Year
CULTURE

(www.vancouver-chinatown.com; ⊙Jan or Feb) Festive kaleidoscope of dancing, parades and great food held in January or February.

Winterruption
PERFORMING ARTS

(www.winterruption.com; ⊙mid-Feb) Granville Island brushes off the winter blues with a music and performance festival.

Vancouver International Wine Festival
WINE

(www.vanwinefest.ca; ⊙late Mar) The city's oldest and best annual wine celebration takes place in late March.

Vancouver Craft Beer Week
BEER

(www.vancouvercraftbeerweek.com; ⊙late May) A boozy roster of tastings, pairing dinners and tipple-fueled shenanigans.

Vancouver International Children's Festival
CHILDREN'S

(www.childrensfestival.ca; ⊙late May) Storytelling, performance and activities on Granville Island.

Bard on the Beach
THEATER

(✆604-739-0559; www.bardonthebeach.org; ⊙Jun-Sep) A season of four Shakespeare and Bard-related plays in Vanier Park tents.

Vancouver International Jazz Festival
MUSIC

(www.coastaljazz.ca; ⊙Jun & Jul) FREE City-wide cornucopia of superstar shows and free outdoor events.

Car Free Day Vancouver
STREET CARNIVAL

(www.carfreevancouver.org; ⊙mid-Jun) Neighborhoods across the city turn over their streets for food, music and market stalls. Main St's is usually the biggest.

Dragon Boat Festival
CULTURE

(www.dragonboatbc.ca; ⊙3rd week Jun) A two-day splashathon of boat-racing fun in False Creek.

Vancouver Folk Music Festival
MUSIC

(www.thefestival.bc.ca; ⊙mid-Jul) Folk and world-music shows at Jericho Beach.

Celebration of Light
FIREWORKS

(www.hondacelebrationoflight.com; ⊙late Jul) Free international fireworks extravaganza in English Bay.

Pride Week
CARNIVAL, PARADE

(www.vancouverpride.ca; ⊙late Jul) Parties, concerts and fashion shows culminating in a giant pride parade.

Pacific National Exhibition
CULTURE, CHILDREN'S

(www.pne.bc.ca; Hastings Park, East Vancouver; ⊙mid-Aug–Sep) Family-friendly shows, music concerts and a fairground.

Vancouver International Fringe Festival
PERFORMING ARTS

(www.vancouverfringe.com; ⊙mid-Sep) Wild and wacky theatricals at mainstream and unconventional Granville Island venues.

Vancouver International Film Festival
FILM

(www.viff.org; ⊙late Sep–Oct) Popular two-week showcase of Canadian and international movies.

Vancouver Writers Fest
LITERATURE

(www.writersfest.bc.ca; ☉ Oct) Local and international scribblers populate literary seminars, galas and public forums.

Eastside Culture Crawl
CULTURE

(www.eastsideculturecrawl.com; ☉ late Nov) East Vancouver artists open their studios for three days of wandering visitors.

Santa Claus Parade
CHRISTMAS

(www.rogerssantaclausparade.com; ☉ early Dec) Christmas procession, complete with the great man himself.

🛏 Sleeping

With more than 25,000 metro Vancouver hotel, hostel and B&B rooms, this region has options for all tastes and budgets. While rates peak in July and August, there are good deals available in fall and spring, when the weather is often amenable and the tourist crowds reduced. The **Tourism Vancouver** (www.tourismvancouver.com) website lists options and packages, while the province's **Hello BC** (☎ 800-435-5622; www.hellobc.com) service provides further information and bookings. Be aware that hotels charge up to $40 for overnight parking, while parking at B&Bs is typically free.

🛏 Downtown

Samesun Backpackers Lodge
HOSTEL $

(Map p638; ☎ 604-682-8226, 877-972-6378; www.samesun.com; 1018 Granville St; dm/r incl breakfast $35/95; ☻@☎; 🖵10) Vancouver's party hostel, the brightly painted Samesun is on the city's nightlife strip – ask for a back room if you fancy a few hours of sleep – or just head down to the on-site bar (naughtily called the Beaver) to join the beery throng. Dorms are comfortably small and there's a large kitchen for your mystery-meat pasta dishes.

★ St Regis Hotel
BOUTIQUE HOTEL $$

(Map p638; ☎ 604-681-1135, 800-770-7929; www.stregishotel.com; 602 Dunsmuir St; d incl breakfast $220; ☻✳@☎; Ⓜ Granville) Transformed in recent years, the St Regis is now an art-lined boutique sleepover in a 1913 heritage shell. The rooms – which, befitting its age, almost all seem to be a different size – exhibit a loungey élan, complete with leather-look wallpaper, earth-tone bedspreads, flatscreen TVs and multimedia hubs. Rates include cooked breakfast, nearby gym access and free international phone calling.

HI Vancouver Central
HOSTEL $$

(Map p638; ☎ 866-762-4122, 604-685-5335; www.hihostels.ca/vancouver; 1025 Granville St; dm/r incl breakfast $40/113; ☻✳@☎; 🖵10) This warren-like sleepover is more of a party joint than its HI Downtown sibling. Enjoying some of the benefits of its past hotel incarnation – air-conditioning and small dorms – there are dozens of two-bed rooms for privacy fans (some en suite). There are Granville St noise issues, so snag a back room.

Victorian Hotel
HOTEL $$

(Map p638; ☎ 877-681-6369, 604-681-6369; www.victorianhotel.ca; 514 Homer St; r incl breakfast with shared/private bathroom $99/159; ☻@☎; Ⓜ Granville) The high-ceilinged rooms at this popular heritage-building Euro-style hotel combine glossy hardwood floors, a sprinkling of antiques, an occasional bay window and plenty of historical charm. The best rooms are in the renovated extension, where raindrop showers, marble bathroom floors and flatscreen TVs add a slice of luxe. Rooms are provided with fans in summer.

Urban Hideaway Guesthouse
GUESTHOUSE $$

(Map p638; ☎ 604-694-0600; www.urban-hideaway.com; 581 Richards St; d with shared bathroom/ste $109/159; ☻@; Ⓜ Granville) This cozy but fiendishly well-hidden home away from home is a budget word-of-mouth favorite in the heart of the city. Tuck yourself into one of the comfy rooms – the loft is recommended – or spend your time in the lounge areas downstairs. There are laundry facilities, a free-use computer and loaner bikes are also gratis. Bathrooms are mostly shared, although the loft's is private.

Rosewood Hotel Georgia
HOTEL $$$

(Map p638; ☎ 604-682-5566; www.rosewoodhotels.com; 801 W Georgia St; d $410; ☻✳@☎✖✖; Ⓜ Vancouver City Centre) Vancouver's current 'it' hotel underwent a recent spectacular renovation that brought the 1927-built landmark back to its golden-age glory. Despite the abstract modern art lining its public areas, the rooms take a classic, elegant approach with warming earth and coffee tones alongside pampering treats, such as deep soaker tubs and sparkling downtown cityscape views (in some rooms).

Save time for the lobby-level restaurant. Alongside the hotel's successful resurrection, Hawksworth (p654) has become the place to be seen for the city's movers and shakers – and you, if you look the part.

Loden Hotel BOUTIQUE HOTEL $$$
(Map p638; ☎877-225-6336, 604-669-5060; www.theloden.com; 1177 Melville St; r $300; ❄@📶🐾; Ⓜ Burrard) The stylish Loden is the real designer deal – and one of the first boutique properties in years to give Yaletown's Opus a run for its money. The chic, chocolate-hued rooms combine a knowing contemporary élan with luxe accoutrements, like marble-lined bathrooms and those oh-so-civilized heated floors. Service is top-notch – make sure you try the complimentary London taxicab limo service.

Fairmont Pacific Rim HOTEL $$$
(Map p638; ☎877-900-5350, 604-695-5300; www.fairmont.com/pacificrim; 1038 Canada Pl; d $249; ⊖❄📶🏊🐾; Ⓜ Waterfront) Near the convention center, this chic 377-room property is Vancouver's newest Fairmont. While many rooms have city views, the ones with waterfront vistas will blow you away, especially as you sit in your jetted tub or cube-shaped Japanese bath with a glass of bubbly. Flourishes include iPod docks and Nespresso machines, but the rooftop swimming pool should monopolize your time.

West End

HI Vancouver Downtown HOSTEL $
(Map p638; ☎866-762-4122, 604-684-4565; www.hihostels.ca/vancouver; 1114 Burnaby St; dm/r incl breakfast $42/108; ⊖@📶; 🚌6) It says 'downtown' but this purpose-built hostel is on a quiet residential West End side street. Popular with older hostelers and families, the dorms are all mercifully small – private rooms are also available. There's also bike storage, a full kitchen, and TV and games rooms, plus twice-weekly April to November tours with legendary local guide Erik.

Buchan Hotel HOTEL $$
(Map p638; ☎800-668-6654, 604-685-5354; www.buchanhotel.com; 1906 Haro St; d with private/shared bathroom $139/99; ⊖@📶; 🚌5) The cheap and cheerful, 1926-built Buchan has bags of charm and is steps from Stanley Park. Along corridors lined with old prints of yesteryear Vancouver, its budget rooms – most with shared bathrooms – are clean, cozy and well maintained, although some furnishings have seen better days. The pricier rooms are correspondingly prettier, while the east-side rooms are brighter. Friendly front desk staff.

Sunset Inn & Suites HOTEL $$
(Map p638; ☎800-786-1997, 604-688-2474; www.sunsetinn.com; 1111 Burnaby St; ste incl breakfast $175; ⊖❄@📶; 🚌6) A generous cut above most of the West End's self-catering suite hotels, the popular Sunset Inn offers larger-then-average rooms with full kitchenettes. Each has a balcony, while some rooms – particularly those on south-facing higher floors – have partial views of English Bay. Rates include rare-for-Vancouver free parking and the attentive staff are among the best in the city.

Times Square Suites Hotel APARTMENT $$$
(Map p638; ☎877-684-2223, 604-684-2223; www.timessquaresuites.com; 1821 Robson St; ste $225; ⊖❄📶🐾; 🚌5) Superbly located just steps from Stanley Park, this excellent West End hidden gem (even the entrance can be hard to spot) is the perfect apartment-style Vancouver sleepover. Rooms – mostly one-bedroom suites – are spacious, with tubs, laundry facilities, full kitchens and superbly well-maintained, if slightly 1980s, decor. Rates include nearby gym access and there's a supermarket just across the street.

Sylvia Hotel HOTEL $$
(Map p638; ☎604-681-9321; www.sylviahotel.com; 1154 Gilford St; r $189; ⊖🐾; 🚌5) Built in 1912, the ivy-covered Sylvia enjoys a prime location overlooking English Bay. Generations of guests keep coming back – many request the same room every year – for a dollop of old-world charm plus a side order of first-name service. There's a wide array of comfortable room configurations, but the best are the bed-sitting suites, with kitchens and waterfront views.

English Bay Inn B&B $$
(Map p638; ☎866-683-8002, 604-683-8002; www.englishbayinn.com; 1968 Comox St; r incl breakfast $175; ⊖📶; 🚌6) Each of the six, antique-lined rooms in this Tudoresque B&B near Stanley Park has a private bathroom and two have sumptuous four-poster beds: you'll think you've arrived in Victoria, BC's determinedly traditional-English capital, by mistake. There's complimentary port in the parlor, a secluded garden for hanging out and a three-course breakfast – arrive early for the dining room alcove table.

Listel Hotel BOUTIQUE HOTEL $$
(Map p638; ☎800-663-5491, 604-684-8461; www.thelistelhotel.com; 1300 Robson St; d $180; ⊖❄@📶; 🚌5) A sophisticated, art hotel, the

Listel attracts grown-ups with its on-site installations and package deals with local art galleries. There's original artwork – including contemporary installations and First Nations creations – in many rooms, which all have a relaxing, mood-lit West Coast feel. Artsy types should also check out the adjoining private gallery, plus Forage (p655), the hotel's new farm-to-table on-site restaurant.

Yaletown

★YWCA Hotel
HOSTEL $

(Map p638; 604-895-5830, 800-663-1424; www.ywcahotel.com; 733 Beatty St; s/d/tr with shared bath $73/90/117; Stadium-Chinatown) This good value, well-located option offers well-maintained, if spartan, rooms of the student accommodation variety. There's a wide range of configurations, from singles to five-bed rooms that are ideal for groups. Some rooms have shared bathrooms while all have access to communal kitchens – each room also has a minifridge. Rates include access to the **YWCA Health & Fitness Centre**, a 10-minute walk away.

Opus Hotel
BOUTIQUE HOTEL $$$

(Map p638; 604-642-6787, 866-642-6780; www.opushotel.com; 322 Davie St; r $299; Yaletown-Roundhouse) The Opus kick-started Vancouver's boutique-hotel scene and, with its recent full-on revamp, it's still high up on the city's most-stylish-sleepovers list. The spruced-up rooms have contemporary-chic interiors – think bold colors, mod furnishings and feng-shui bed placements – while the luxe bathrooms have clear windows overlooking the streets (visiting exhibitionists take note).

Granville Island & Kitsilano

HI Vancouver Jericho Beach
HOSTEL $

(866-762-4122, 604-224-3208; www.hihostels.ca/vancouver; 1515 Discovery St, Kitsilano; dm/r with shared bathroom $36/88; May-Sep; 4) One of Canada's largest hostels looks like a Victorian hospital from the outside but has a great location if you're here for the sun-kissed Jericho Beach vibe (downtown is a 40-minute bus ride away). Basic rooms make this the least palatial Vancouver HI, but there's a large kitchen, bike rentals and a recently revamped cafe. Dorms are also larger here: book ahead for private rooms.

Granville Island Hotel
BOUTIQUE HOTEL $$

(Map p638; 800-663-1840, 604-683-7373; www.granvilleislandhotel.com; 1253 Johnston St; r $220; 50) This gracious boutique property hugs Granville Island's quiet eastern tip, enjoying tranquil views across False Creek to Yaletown's mirrored towers. You'll be a five-minute walk from the Public Market (p644), with shopping and theater options on your doorstep. Rooms have an elegant, West Coast feel with some exposed wood flourishes. There's also a cool rooftop Jacuzzi, while the on-site brewpub-restaurant has a great patio.

Corkscrew Inn
B&B $$

(877-737-7276, 604-733-7276; www.corkscrewinn.com; 2735 W 2nd Ave, Kitsilano; d incl breakfast $180; 84) This immaculate, gable-roofed property appears to have a drinking problem: it houses a little museum, available only to guests, that's lined with quirky corkscrews and antique vineyard tools. Aside from the boozy paraphernalia, this lovely century-old Craftsman home has five artsy rooms – we like the art deco room – and is just a short walk from the beach. Sumptuous breakfast included.

University of British Columbia & West Side

University of British Columbia Accommodation
ACCOMMODATION SERVICES $$

(888-822-1030, 604-822-1000; www.ubc-conferences.com; 5961 Student Union Blvd, UBC; r $35-199; May-Aug; 99 B-Line) Pretend you're still a student with a UBC campus sleepover. Well-maintained accommodation options include good-value college-dorm units at Pacific Spirit Hostel; private rooms, most with great views, in shared apartments at Gage Towers; and impressive, hotel-style West Coast Suites with flatscreen TVs and slick interiors, which are the only accommodations available year-round and also include breakfast and wi-fi.

Douglas Guest House
GUESTHOUSE $$

(888-872-3060, 604-872-3060; www.dougwin.com; 456 W 13th Ave; r incl breakfast $125-195; 15) A tangerine-hued Edwardian B&B in a quiet characterful neighborhood near City Hall, the Douglas offers good rates, especially in winter, and the kind of laid-back feel where you don't have to worry about creaky floors and knickknacks being knocked over. Its six rooms – comfortable and old-school rather than antique lined – include flowery singles with shared bathrooms, larger doubles with en-suite bathrooms and two family-friendly suites. Free off-street parking is included.

✖ Eating

Vancouver is one of Canada's top dine-out cities, with a huge menu of authentic ethnic dining, a recent renaissance in locally sourced West Coast cuisine and a miniwave of new vegetarian restaurants. You can have the best sushi outside Japan for lunch, then follow up with lip-smacking Fraser Valley duck and foraged morels for dinner. Whatever you go for, don't miss the city's flourishing food truck scene and consider a craft beer or two to go with your dinner: BC is arguably Canada's microbrewery capital.

✖ Downtown

Finch's
CAFE $
(Map p638; www.finchteahouse.com; 353 W Pender St; mains $5-10; ⊙9am-5pm Mon-Fri, 11am-4pm Sat; ▣4) For a coveted seat at one of the dinged old tables, arrive off-peak at this sunny corner cafe that has a 'granny chic' look combining creaky wooden floors and junk-shop bric-a-brac. You'll be joining in-the-know hipsters and creative types who've been calling this their local for years. They come for the well-priced breakfasts (eg egg and soldiers for $2.95), plus freshly prepared gourmet baguette sandwiches and house-made soups.

★ Mario's Coffee Express
COFFEE $
(Map p638; 595 Howe St; mains $4-8; ⊙7am-4pm Mon-Fri; Ⓜ Burrard) A java-lover's favorite that only downtown office workers seem to know about, you'll wake up and smell the coffee long before you make it through the door here. The rich aromatic beverages served up by the man himself are the kind of ambrosia brews that should make Starbucks drinkers weep – you might even forgive the 1980s Italian pop percolating through the shop.

Hidden in plain view, this is arguably downtown's best cup of coffee.

Japadog
JAPANESE $
(Map p638; www.japadog.com; 530 Robson St; mains $5-8; ⊙11am-10pm Mon-Thu, to 11pm Fri & Sat, to 9pm Sun; ▣10) You'll have spotted the lunchtime lineups at the Japadog hotdog stands around town, but these celebrated, ever-*genki* Japanese expats opened a storefront here in 2010. The menu is almost the same – think turkey smokies with miso sauce and

bratwursts with onion, daikon and soy – but there are also naughtily seasoned fries; try the wasabi version.

Templeton
DINER $$
(Map p638; www.thetempleton.ca; 1087 Granville St; mains $10-14; ⊙9am-11pm Mon-Wed, to 1am Thu-Sun; ▣; ▣10) A chrome-and-vinyl '50s-look diner with a twist, Templeton cooks up giant organic burgers, addictive fries, vegetarian quesadillas and perhaps the best hangover cure in town, the 'Big Ass Breakfast'. Sadly, the mini jukeboxes on the tables don't work but you can console yourself with a waistline-busting chocolate ice-cream float. Avoid weekend peak times or you'll be queuing for ages.

La Bodega
SPANISH $$
(Map p638; www.labodegavancouver.com; 1277 Howe St; tapas $3-13; ⊙5pm-midnight; ▣10) It's all about the tasting plates at this rustic, checked-tablecloth tapas bar, arguably Vancouver's most authentic Spanish restaurant. Pull up a chair, order a jug of sangria and decide on a few shareable treats from the extensive menu. If you're feeling spicy, the chorizo sausage hits the spot and the Spanish meatballs are justifiably popular.

Twisted Fork Bistro
FRENCH $$
(Map p638; www.twistedforkbistro.ca; 1147 Granville St; mains $20-22; ⊙10am-2pm Fri-Sun & 5:30-11pm daily; ▣10) The best place to park your appetite among Granville St's greasy pub-grub options, this narrow, art-lined bistro feels like it should be somewhere else. But even clubbers need to eat well sometimes. The menu of rustic French classics includes mussels, lamb shank and an excellent beef bourguignon, but there are also smaller tasting plates if you want to share.

Coast
SEAFOOD $$
(Map p638; ☎604-685-5010; www.coastrestaurant.ca; 1054 Alberni St; mains $18-42; ⊙11:30am-1am Mon-Thu, to 2am Fri, 4pm-2am Sat, 4pm-1am Sun; ▣5) A buzzing seafood joint where Vancouver movers and shakers like to be seen scoffing a wide array of aquatic treats. Knowing reinventions of the classics include prawn or salmon flatbread pizzas, but it's the mighty seafood platter of salmon, cod, scallops and tiger prawns that sates true fish nuts. Lunchtime fish and chips to go is $14 and there's an excellent raw bar with oysters aplenty.

★ Hawksworth
WEST COAST $$$
(Map p638; ☎604-673-7000; www.hawksworth-restaurant.com; 801 W Georgia St; mains $29-39;

⊙7am-11pm) A top spot for the city's movers and shakers, this is the fine-dining anchor of the top-end Rosewood Hotel Georgia (p650). But unlike most hotel restaurants, this one has a starry-eyed local following. Created by and named after one of the city's top local chefs, the menu fuses contemporary West Coast approaches with clever international influences, hence dishes such as soy-roasted sturgeon. The seasonal tasting menu is also heartily recommended.

Chambar   EUROPEAN $$$

(Map p638; ☎604-879-7119; www.chambar.com; 562 Beatty St; mains $23-33; ⊙5pm-midnight; ⓜStadium-Chinatown) This candlelit, brick-lined cave is a great place for a romantic night out. The sophisticated Belgian-influenced menu includes delectable *moules-frites* (mussels and fries) and a braised lamb shank with figs that's a local dining legend. An impressive wine and cocktail list – try a Blue Fig Martini – is coupled with a great Belgian beer menu dripping with *tripel* and *lambic* varieties to tempt drinkers.

West End & Stanley Park

Sushi Mart   JAPANESE $

(Map p638; www.sushimart.com; 1686 Robson St; sushi combos $7-18; ⊙11:30am-3pm & 5-9pm Mon-Sat; Ⓡ5) You'll be rubbing shoulders with chatty young ESL students at the large communal dining table, one of the best spots in town for an extra-fresh sushi feast in a casual setting. Check the ever-changing blackboard showing what's available and then tuck into expertly prepared and well-priced shareable platters of all your fave *nigiri, maki* and sashimi treats. Udon dishes are also available.

★Guu with Garlic   JAPANESE $$

(Map p638; www.guu-izakaya.com; 1689 Robson St; small plates $4-9, mains $8-16; ⊙11:30am-2:30pm Tue-Sun & 5:30pm-midnight daily; Ⓡ5) Arguably the best of Vancouver's many authentic *izakayas,* this welcoming, wood-lined joint is a cultural immersion. Hot pots and noodle bowls are available but it's best to experiment with some Japanese-bar tapas, such as black cod with miso mayo, deep-fried egg pumpkin balls or finger-lickin' *tori-karaage* fried chicken. Garlic is liberally used in most dishes, and it's best to arrive before opening time for a seat.

★Forage   WEST COAST $$

(Map p638; ☎604-661-1400; www.foragevancouver. com; 1300 Robson St; mains $17-21; ⊙6:30-10am & 5pm-midnight Mon-Fri, 7am-2pm & 5pm-midnight Sat & Sun; Ⓡ5) 🖉 A champion of the local farm-to-table scene, this sustainability-loving restaurant is the perfect way to sample the

FOOD-TRUCK FRENZY

Keen to emulate the legendary street-food scenes of Portland and Austin, Vancouver jumped on the kitchen-equipped bandwagon in 2010, launching a pilot scheme with 17 carts. Things took off quickly and by mid-2013, there were 114 tasty trucks dotted around the city, serving everything from halibut tacos to Korean sliders and from pulled pork sandwiches to French stews. The downtown core is home to many of the four-wheeled takeouts and, while there are lots of experimental fusion trucks, several have quickly risen to the top table: look out for local favorites **TacoFino**, **Re-Up BBQ**, **Roaming Dragon**, **Feastro**, **Fresh Local Wild**, **Yolk's Breakfast**, **Pig on the Street** and **Vij's Railway Express**. And don't miss one of the **JapaDog** locations: the nori-and-miso-flavored hotdog vendors arguably kicked off the scene by nudging the original rules that limited street food in the city to hotdogs and hot chestnuts – those were *not* the days.

There are usually a few vendors around the Vancouver Art Gallery complex (p637), but downtown arteries like Howe St, Burrard St, Georgia St and Seymour St are also good bets. The city has recently moved to address one concern: since they are so spread out, the carts can sometimes be hard to find, unlike those in Austin and Portland, which are typically grouped together into multicart pods. A proposed grouping of carts on Hamilton St aims to provide several dining options in one strollable spot.

For up-to-the-minute listings, opening hours and locations for street food carts, go to www.streetfoodapp.com/vancouver. And keep your eyes peeled for special appearances by the carts at events around the city. If you want some extra help, Vancouver Foodie Tours (p649) offers the tasty Street Eats Tour.

flavors of the region. Brunch has become a firm local favorite – the turkey sausage hash is recommended – but for dinner the idea is to sample an array of tasting plates. Though the menu is innovative and highly seasonal, look out for the delectable pork tongue ravioli and roast bison bone marrow.

Espana
SPANISH $$

(Map p638; www.espanarestaurant.ca; 1118 Denman St; tapas plates $5-12; ☺5pm-1am Sun-Thu, to 2am Fri & Sat; 🚇5) Reservations are not allowed but it's worth the line-up to get into Vancouver's best new Spanish tapas joint. The tables are crammed close and the atmosphere is warm and welcoming, triggering a hubbub of chat that's mostly centered on the great grub. The crispy squid and cod and potato croqettes are delish, while the crispy chickpeas dish is a bit of a revelation.

Fish House in Stanley Park
SEAFOOD $$$

(☎877-681-7275, 604-681-7275; www.fishhousestanleypark.com; 8901 Stanley Park Dr; mains $22-42; ☺11:30am-10pm; 🚇19) 🍽 The park's fanciest dine out, this double-patioed joint serves some of the city's best seafood. The menu changes based on seasonality but typical favorites include salmon Wellington and smoked-cod linguine, while fresh oysters are ever popular with visiting shuckers. Weekend brunch is a highlight – the smoked-salmon Benedict is recommended. The restaurant is committed to serving sustainable seafood and locally sourced beef, duck and chicken dishes are also available.

If you haven't eaten enough already come back for a rich treat-focused afternoon tea, served 2pm to 4pm, then run around the park four times to work it off.

Yaletown

★ Flying Pig
WEST COAST $$

(Map p638; www.theflyingpigvan.com; 1168 Hamilton St; mains $18-24; ☺11:30am-midnight Mon-Fri, 10:30am-midnight Sat & Sun; Ⓜ Yaletown-Roundhouse) Yaletown's best midrange restaurant has mastered the art of friendly service and excellent, savor-worthy dining. But since everyone else knows that, too, it's a good idea to dine off peak to avoid the crowds. A warm, woodsy bistro, the dishes focus on seasonal local ingredients and are virtually guaranteed to make you smile: scallops and halibut are perfect, and the roasted chicken is the city's best.

Reservations are not accepted for dinner. At the time of writing, a new, much bigger Flying Pig had just opened in Gastown.

Rodney's Oyster House
SEAFOOD $$

(Map p638; ☎604-609-0080; www.rohvan.com; 1228 Hamilton St; mains $16-32; ☺11:30am-11pm; Ⓜ Yaletown-Roundhouse) Vancouver's favorite oyster eatery for many years, Rodney's always has a buzz about it. And it's not just because of the convivial room with its nautical flourishes: these guys really know how to do seafood. While the fresh-shucked oysters with a huge array of sauces – try the spicy vodka – never fail to impress, there's everything from sweet mussels to superb Atlantic lobster available.

Blue Water Café + Raw Bar
SEAFOOD $$$

(Map p638; ☎604-688-8078; www.bluewatercafe.net; 1095 Hamilton St; mains $25-44; ☺5pm-midnight; Ⓜ Yaletown-Roundhouse) Under expert chef Frank Pabst, this has become one of Vancouver's best high-concept seafood restaurants and is a highlight of Yaletown fine dining. Music gently percolates through the brick-lined, blue-hued interior, while seafood towers, Arctic char and BC sablefish grace the tables inside and on the patio. Consider the semicircular raw bar and watch the whirling blades prepare delectable sushi and sashimi.

Gastown

★ Rainier Provisions
WEST COAST $

(Map p638; www.rainierprovisions.com; 2 W Cordova St; mains $8-12; ☺11am-8pm Mon-Fri, 9am-8pm Sat & Sun; 🚇4) Revitalizing a former Gastown hotel building, this great-value cafe-bistro is a perfect fuel-up spot. Drop in for Stumptown coffee or dive into a hearty menu, ranging from hot-sandwich specials served with soup or salad to a heaping roast with all the extras. The locally made sausages with roast potatoes is the winner though.

Meat & Bread
SANDWICHES $

(Map p638; www.meatandbread.ca; 370 Cambie St; mains $7-9; ☺11am-5pm Mon-Sat; 🚇14) Arrive early to avoid the lunchtime queue at Vancouver's favorite gourmet sandwich shop and you might even snag one of the four tiny window perches. If not, you can hang with the hip locals at the chatter-filled long table, tucking into the daily changing special, usually featuring slices of perfectly roasted local lamb, pork or chicken. The grilled cheese sandwich is ace, too.

Wash it down with a $6 craft beer and expect to come back: this place has a cult-like following and it's hard not to return when your next sandwich craving rears its savory head.

Save On Meats
DINER $

(Map p638; www.saveonmeats.ca; 43 W Hastings St; mains $4-14; ⊗7am-10pm Mon-Wed, 7am-midnight Thu-Sat, 8am-10pm Sun; ⊛; ⊠14) A former old-school butcher shop, Save On Meats has been transformed into the Downtown Eastside's fave hipster diner, though it's not just about looking cool. Slide into a booth or take a perch at the long counter and tuck into comfort dishes, including great-value all-day breakfasts and a menu of basic faves such as macaroni and cheese, and chicken pot pie.

Acme Cafe
DINER $$

(Map p638; www.acmecafe.ca; 51 W Hastings St; mains $9-13; ⊗8am-9pm Mon-Fri, 9am-9pm Sat & Sun; ⊠14) The black-and-white, deco-style interior here is enough to warm up anyone on a rainy day – or maybe it's the comfy booths and retro-cool U-shaped counter. The hipsters have been flocking here since day one for hearty breakfasts and heaping comfort-food lunches flavored with a gourmet flourish: the meatloaf, chicken club and shrimp guacamole sandwiches are worth the trip.

Judas Goat Taberna
TAPAS $$

(Map p638; www.judasgoat.ca; 27 Blood Alley; tapas $4-12; ⊗5pm-midnight Mon-Sat; ⊠4) Named after the goats used to lead sheep off slaughterhouse trucks, this tiny backstreet tapas nook has nailed the art of simply prepared small plates, such as duck confit, beef brisket meatballs, and beet and goat-cheese terrine. Like its Salt Tasting Room brother next door, you'll also find a good, although shorter, wine and Spanish sherry drinks list.

Wildebeest
WEST COAST $$$

(Map p638; www.wildebeest.ca; 120 W Hastings St; mains $13-42; ⊗5pm-midnight Tue-Sun; ⊠14) This mood-lit, bi-level joint is a carnivore's dream dinner destination. In fact, they eat vegetarians here – just kidding, there are choices for vegetarians, too. Find a table among the chattering classes – or better still at the communal long table downstairs – and tuck into short ribs, pork jowl or the juiciest roast chicken you'll ever eat.

✗ Chinatown

★ Bao Bei
CHINESE $$

(Map p638; ☑604-688-0876; www.bao-bei.ca; 163 Keefer St; small plates $9-18; ⊗5:30pm-

---

TOP FIVE ASIAN RESTAURANTS

➡ Bao Bei (p656)

➡ Guu With Garlic (p654)

➡ Maenam (p659)

➡ Gam Gok Yuen (p656)

➡ Sushi Mart (p654)

midnight Mon-Sat; ✐; ⊠3) Reinventing a Chinatown heritage building interior with funky flourishes, this hidden-gem Chinese brasserie is the area's most seductive dinner destination. Enjoying a local cult following, it brings a contemporary edge to Asian-style, tapas-sized dishes such as *shao bing,* octopus salad and crispy pork belly. There's also a tasty commitment to inventive cocktails, so don't despair if you have to wait at the bar for your table.

Campagnolo
ITALIAN $$

(Map p638; www.campagnolorestaurant.ca; 1020 Main St; mains $12-25; ⊗11:30am-2:30pm & 5-10pm; ⊠3) Eyebrows were raised when this contemporary Italian restaurant opened in a hitherto sketchy part of town, but intimate, minimalist Campagnolo has lured locals into making the effort to get here. They've been rewarded with some of the city's best Italian cuisine: share some dishes but don't miss the truffle sausage rigatoni or the citrusy local octopus salad.

Gam Gok Yuen
CHINESE $$

(Map p638; 142 E Pender St; mains $7-14; ⊗10:30am-8pm; ⊠3) Try to block out the faded, 1980s decor in this unassuming Chinatown dining room: the carnivorous, Hong Kong–style food is what keeps this place humming, especially the barbecued pork and duck dishes – the clammy front window of roasted meats probably gives the game away. Order at will, but make sure you include a hearty bowl of noodle soup.

✗ Main Street & Commercial Drive

Gene Cafe
COFFEE $

(2404 Main St; baked goods $3-6; ⊗7:30am-7pm Mon-Fri, 8:30am-7pm Sat & Sun; ☎; ⊠3) Colonizing a flatiron wedge of concrete floors and expansive windows, slide onto a chunky cedar bench with your well-thumbed copy of *L'Étranger* and you might catch the eye of an available local. If not, console yourself with a perfectly made cappuccino and a chunky home-baked cookie. The fruit pies are recommended for additional consolation.

Café Calabria
COFFEE $

(1745 Commercial Dr; sandwiches $4-9; ⏰6am-10pm Mon-Thu to midnight Fri & Sat; 🚌20) When Vancouverites tell you the Drive is the city's best coffee street, this is one of the places they're thinking about. It tops a healthy cupful of cafes founded here by Italian immigrants. Don't be put off by the chandeliers-and-statues decor – not everyone likes a side order of statuesque genitalia with their drink. Just order an espresso, sit outside and watch the Drive slide by.

★Cannibal Café
BURGERS $$

(www.cannibalcafe.ca; 1818 Commercial Dr; main $12-15; ⏰11:30am-midnight; 🍴; 🚌20) A punkish diner for fans of seriously real burgers, the jaw-dislocating treats are the real deal here. Expect to drown in a pool of your own drool as you wait for your aromatic meal to arrive, then enter burger heaven. Made with real love, the service here is ever friendly and you'll find an inventive array from classics to the highly recommended Korean-BBQ burger.

Acorn
VEGETARIAN $$

(www.theacornrestaurant.ca; 3995 Main St; mains $17-19; ⏰5:30pm-1am Tue-Thu, to 2am Fri & Sat, to midnight Sun; 🍴; 🚌3) Quickly becoming one of Vancouver's hottest vegetarian restaurants soon after its 2012 opening – hence the sometimes long wait for a table – the Acorn has since settled into being a dependable, diner-inspired joint for vegetarians looking for something more upscale than a mung-bean soup kitchen. Consider artfully presented dishes such as beet ravioli and the excellent, crunch-tastic kale caesar salad.

Sun Sui Wah Seafood Restaurant
CHINESE $$

(www.sunsuiwah.com; 3888 Main St; mains $8-22; ⏰10:30am-3pm & 5-10:30pm; 🚌3) One of the best places in the city for dim sum, this large, chatty Hong Kong–style joint has been a deserved local favorite for years. Order an array of treats, then sit back for the feast, although you should expect to be fighting over the lazy Susan to see who gets the last mouthful. Seafood is a huge specialty here, hence the live tanks.

Via Tevere
PIZZERIA $$

(www.viateverepizzeria.com; 1190 Victoria Dr; mains $12-19; ⏰5-10pm Tue-Thu, to 11pm Fri & Sat, to 9pm Sun; 🚌20) Just two blocks east from the Drive, it's worth the five-minute walk for what may well be East Van's best pizza. Which is saying something, since the Drive is studded like an over-packed pepperoni pie with good pizza joints. Run by a family with true Neapolitan roots, check out the mosaic-tiled wood-fired oven, then launch yourself into a feast. The *capricciosa* is highly recommended.

✖ Granville Island

★Go Fish
SEAFOOD $

(Map p638; 1505 W 1st Ave; mains $8-14; ⏰11:30am-6:30pm Tue-Sun; 🚌50) A short stroll westwards along the seawall from the Granville Island entrance, this almost too-popular seafood stand is one of the city's fave fish-and-chips joints, offering halibut, salmon or cod encased in crispy golden batter. The smashing, lighter fish tacos are also recommended, while ever-changing daily specials, brought in by the nearby fishing boats, often include scallop burgers or ahi tuna sandwiches.

Agro Café
CAFE $

(Map p638; www.agrocafe.org; 1363 Railspur Alley; mains $5-8; ⏰8am-7pm Mon-Fri, 9am-7pm Sat & Sun; 📶; 🚌50) This slightly hidden cafe on Railspur Alley is a smashing coffee stop. It also serves the best value breakfast on Granville Island – go for the $7 eggs, hash browns and turkey sausage. Lunch delivers soups, salads, sandwiches and wraps and there's always a BC craft beer or two if you need to crank it up from coffee.

★Edible Canada at the Market
WEST COAST $$

(Map p638; 📞604-682-6681; www.ediblecanada.com/bistro; 1596 Johnston St; mains $18-29; ⏰11am-9pm Mon-Thu, to 10pm Fri-Sun; 🚌50) Granville Island's most popular bistro delivers a short but tempting menu of seasonal dishes from across Canada, often including perfectly prepared Alberta beef, Newfoundland fish and several BC treats – look out for slow-roasted pork belly. Consider sharing some small plates if you're feeling adventurous, perhaps topped with a naughty maple-sugar pie and a glass of ice wine. Book ahead.

✕ Kitsilano & West Side

★ La Taqueria Pinche Taco Shop MEXICAN $

(www.lataqueria.ca; 2549 Cambie St; 4 tacos $7-9.50; ⊙11am-8:30pm Mon-Sat; 🖋; Ⓜ Broadway-City Hall) Vancouver's fave taco spot expanded from its tiny Hastings St location (which is still there) with this much larger storefront. It's just as crowded but, luckily, many of the visitors are going the takeout route. Snag a brightly painted table perch, then order at the counter from a dozen or so meat or veggie soft tacos (take your pick or ask for a selection), washed down with a cheap-ass beer.

Service is warm and friendly here and the prices and quality ingredients are enough to keep you coming back: the tacos are $2.50 each or four for $9.50 (or just $7 if you take the vegetarian option).

★ Fable WEST COAST $$

(🖋604-732-1322; www.fablekitchen.ca; 1944 W 4th Ave; mains $18-28; ⊙11:30am-2pm Mon-Fri, 5:30-10pm Mon-Sat, brunch 10:30am-2pm Sat & Sun; 🖵4) One of Vancouver's favorite farm-to-table restaurants is a lovely rustic-chic room of exposed brick, wood beams and prominently displayed red-rooster logos, but looks are just part of the appeal. Expect perfectly prepared bistro dishes showcasing local seasonal ingredients, often including duck, chicken or halibut. It's great gourmet comfort food with little pretension, hence

the packed room most nights. Reservations recommended.

Salmon n' Bannock WEST COAST $$

(www.salmonandbannock.net; 1128 W Broadway; mains $14-24; ⊙11am-3pm Mon-Fri, 5-9pm Mon-Thu, 5-11pm Fri & Sat; 🖵9) Vancouver's only First Nations restaurant is a delightful little art-lined bistro among an unassuming strip of Broadway shops. It's worth the bus trip, though, for freshly-made aboriginal-influenced dishes made with local ingredients. If lunching, tuck into the juicy signature salmon-and-bannock burger, made with their popular aboriginal flatbread. If you're planning dinner, go for the velvet-soft braised deer shank.

Naam VEGETARIAN $$

(www.thenaam.com; 2724 W 4th Ave; mains $9-16; ⊙24hr; 🖋; 🖵4) An evocative relic of Kitsilano's hippie past, this vegetarian restaurant has the feel of a comfy, highly chatty farmhouse. It's not unusual to have to wait for a table here at peak times, but it's worth it for the hearty stir-fries, Mexican platters and sesame-fried potatoes with miso gravy. This is the kind of veggie spot where carnivores are happy to dine.

Maenam THAI $$

(🖋604-730-5579; www.maenam.ca; 1938 W 4th Ave; mains $15-19; ⊙noon-2:30pm Tue-Sat & 5-10pm Mon-Sat; 🖋; 🖵4) At this contemporary reinvention of the Thai-restaurant model, subtle and complex traditional and

---

FARMERS MARKETS
....

A tasty cornucopia of BC farm produce hits the stalls around Vancouver from June to October. Seasonal highlights include crunchy apples, lush peaches and juicy blueberries, while home-baked cakes and treats are frequent accompaniments. Don't be surprised to see zesty local cheese and a few arts and crafts added to the mix. To check out what's on offer, visit www.eatlocal.org.

➡ **East Vancouver Farmers Market** (Commercial Dr, north parking lot of Trout Lake Park; ⊙9am-2pm Sat mid-May–mid-Oct; 🖵20)

➡ **Kitsilano Farmers Market** (Kitsilano Community Centre, 2690 Larch St; ⊙10am-2pm Sun mid-May–mid-Oct; 🖵4)

➡ **Main Street Station Farmers Market** (Map p638; Thornton Park, 1100 Station St; ⊙3-7pm Wed Jun-Sep; Ⓜ Main St-Science World)

➡ **UBC Farmers Market** (6182 South Campus Rd, UBC; ⊙9am-1pm Sat mid-Jun–Sep; 🖵99B-Line)

➡ **West End Farmers Market** (Map p638; Nelson Park, btwn Bute & Thurlow Sts; ⊙9am-2pm Sat Jun–mid-Oct; 🖵6)

➡ **Winter Farmers Market** (Wise Hall, 1882 Adanac St, off Commercial Dr; ⊙10am-2pm 2nd & 4th Sat of month Nov-Apr; 🖵20)

international influences flavor the menu in a room with a modern lounge feel. Inviting exploration, you can start with the familiar – although even the pad thai here is eye-poppingly different – but save room for something new: the *geng pa neua* beef curry is a sweet, salty and nutty treat.

Vij's   INDIAN $$$
(www.vijsrestaurant.ca; 1480 W 11th Ave; mains $24-30; ◎5:30-10pm; ▢10) Just off southern Granville St, this Vancouver favorite is the high-water mark of contemporary East Indian cuisine, fusing regional ingredients, subtle global flourishes and classic Indian flavors to produce an array of innovative dishes. The unique results range from signature wine-marinated 'lamb popsicles' to savorworthy meals, such as halibut, mussels and crab in a tomato-ginger curry. Reservations are not accepted, which sometimes means a very long wait.

🍷 Drinking & Nightlife

Distinctive new lounges and pubs are springing up in Vancouver like persistent drunks at an open bar. Wherever you end up imbibing, sip some of the region's excellent craft brews, including tasty tipples from Driftwood Brewing, Howe Sound Brewing and Central City Brewing. Granville St, from Robson to Davie Sts, is a party district of mainstream haunts, but Gastown, Main St and Commercial Dr offer superior options loved by the savvy locals.

★**Alibi Room**   PUB
(Map p638; www.alibi.ca; 157 Alexander St; ◎5-11:30pm Mon-Fri, 10am-11:30pm Sat & Sun; ▢4) Vancouver's best craft-beer tavern, this exposed brick bar stocks an ever-changing roster of around 50 drafts from celebrated BC breweries, such as Phillips, Driftwood and Crannóg. Adventurous taste trippers – hipsters and old-lag beer fans alike – enjoy the $9.50 'frat bat' of four sample tipples: choose your own or ask to be surprised. And always check the board for ever-changing guest casks.

★**Railway Club**   PUB
(Map p638; www.therailwayclub.com; 579 Dunsmuir St; ◎4pm-2am Mon-Thu, noon-3am Fri, 3pm-3am Sat, 5pm-midnight Sun; Ⓜ Granville) A local-legend, pub-style music venue, the upstairs 'Rail' is accessed via an unobtrusive wooden door next to a 7-Eleven. Don't be put off: this is one of the city's friendliest bars and you'll

fit right in as soon as you roll up to the bar – unusually for Vancouver, you have to order at the counter, since there's no table service. Live music nightly.

★**Shameful Tiki Room**   BAR
(www.shamefultikiroom.com; 4362 Main St; ◎5pm-midnight Wed-Mon; ▢3) Slip through the curtains into this windowless snug and you'll be instantly transported to a Polynesian beach. The lighting – including glowing puffer-fish lamp shades – is permanently set to dusk and the walls are lined with Tiki masks and rattan coverings under a straw-shrouded ceiling, but it's the drinks that rock: seriously well-crafted classics from zombies to scorpion bowls.

★**Brickhouse**   PUB
(Map p638; 730 Main St; ◎8pm-2am Mon-Sat, to midnight Sun; ▢3) Possibly Vancouver's most original pub, this old-school hidden gem is a welcoming, windowless tavern lined with Christmas lights, fish tanks and junk-shop couches. Popular with artsy locals and in-the-know young hipsters, it's like hanging out in someone's den. Grab a Storm Scottish Ale at the bar, slide onto a perch and start chatting: you're bound to meet someone interesting.

★**Storm Crow Tavern**   PUB
(www.stormcrowtavern.com; 1305 Commercial Dr; ◎4pm-1am Mon-Thu, 11am-1am Fri & Sat; ▢20) Knowing the difference between Narnia and *Neverwhere* is not a prerequisite for enjoying this smashing Commercial Dr nerd pub but, if you do, you'll certainly make new friends. It has displays of *Dr Who* figures and steampunk ray guns, plus a TV that seems to be always screening *Game of Thrones*. Dive into the craft beer and settle in for a fun evening.

Portland Craft   BAR
(www.portlandcraft.com; 3835 Main St; ◎4pm-1am Mon-Thu, 11:30am-2am Fri & Sat, 10am-midnight Sun; ▢3) With its unique-for-Vancouver 20-strong draft list of mostly Western US beers, this convivial new restaurant-bar is tapping into the popularity of craft brews from Portland and beyond. You'll find Rogue, Hopworks, Elysian and Deschutes well represented, so if you're a fan of super-hoppy IPAs, you'll soon be puckering your lips with pleasure. Arrive early on weekend evenings to snag a table.

VANCOUVER'S OTHER BREWS

If you're a true beer nut, consider checking out a round of little, off-the-beaten-path East Vancouver microbreweries that even some locals don't know about. Start on Commercial Drive and walk north from the intersection with Venables St for about 10 minutes. You'll soon be in a light industrial part of town – don't worry, it's perfectly safe. You'll come to **Storm Brewing** (☑604-255-9119; www.stormbrewing.org; 310 Commercial Dr; ⬚20), a legendary local brewery that's been crafting great ales since 1995. Call ahead for an impromptu tour – Wednesday is brewing day, so that's the best time to come. With any luck, you'll be able to sample their excellent **Black Plague Stout**. Continue north for two blocks and turn right onto Powell St. A few minutes along, you'll find the lovely **Powell Street Craft Brewery** (www.powellbeer.com; 1830 Powell St; ◷1-7pm Wed-Sat; ⬚4). This art-lined, gable-roofed nanobrewery is one of the city's smallest beer producers. Consider a sample of the lip-smacking **Dive Bomb Porter**, and pick up a growler to go. Despite its diminutive stature, this producer stunned beer fans across the country in 2013 when its **Old Jalopy Pale Ale** was named the nation's Beer of the Year at the annual Canadian Brewing Awards. Continue east on Powell, turn right onto Victoria Dr and then left on Triumph St. Within a couple of minutes, you'll hit the storefront of **Parallel 49 Brewing Company** (www.parallel49brewing.com; 1950 Triumph St; ◷noon-9pm; ⬚14). Nip into the tasting room here and sample their array of quirky tipples, including **Hoparazzi India Pale Lager** and **Gypsy Tears Ruby Red Ale**.

Diamond
COCKTAIL BAR

(Map p638; www.di6mond.com; 6 Powell St; ◷5:30pm-1am Wed & Thu, to 2am Fri & Sat, to midnight Sun; ⬚4) Head upstairs via the unassuming entrance and you'll find yourself in one of Vancouver's warmest little cocktail bars. A renovated heritage room studded with sash windows – try for a view seat – it's popular with local coolsters but is rarely pretentious. A list of perfectly nailed, though not cheap, cocktails helps, coupled with a tasty tapas menu.

Six Acres
BAR

(Map p638; www.sixacres.ca; 203 Carrall St; 5pm-1am Mon-Sat; ⬚4) Gastown's coziest tavern, you can cover all the necessary food groups via the extensive, mostly bottled, beer menu. There's a small, animated summer patio out front, but inside is great for hiding in a candlelit corner and working your way through the brews, plus a shared small plate or three – the sausage platter is recommended.

Keefer Bar
COCKTAIL BAR

(Map p638; www.thekeeferbar.com; 135 Keefer St; ◷5pm-midnight Mon, to 1am Tue-Thu & Sun, to 2am Fri & Sat; Ⓜ Stadium-Chinatown) A dark, narrow and atmospheric Chinatown bar, it's been claimed by local cocktail-loving coolsters from day one. Drop in for a full evening of liquid taste-tripping and you'll have a blast. From perfectly prepared rosemary gimlets and Siamese slippers to an excellent whis-

key menu and a side dish of tasty tapas – go for the late-night Keefer dog – this is a great night out.

Irish Heather
PUB

(Map p638; www.irishheather.com; 210 Carrall St, Gastown; ◷11:30am-midnight Mon-Thu & Sun, to 2am Fri & Sat; ⬚4) Belying the clichés about expat Irish bars, with the exception of its reclaimed-Guinness-barrel floor, the Heather is one of Vancouver's best gastropubs. Alongside lovingly prepared sausage and mash, and steak-and-ale pie, you'll find top craft beers and some well-poured Guinness. Best time to come? The seasonal Sunday to Wednesday long-table nights: dinner and a pint is around $18.

Cascade Room
BAR

(www.thecascade.ca; 2616 Main St; ◷5pm-1am Mon-Thu, to 2am Fri & Sat, to midnight Sun; ⬚3) The perfect contemporary reinvention of a trad neighborhood bar, this is arguably Mount Pleasant's merriest watering hole. The top-drawer craft beer list runs from Fullers to Phillips and includes own-brand Main Street Pilsner, soon to be produced in a nearby new brewery building. Indulge in Main St's best Sunday roast or hang with the locals at Monday's funtastic quiz or 'name that tune' night.

Vancouver Urban Winery
WINE BAR

(www.vancouverurbanwinery.com; 55 Dunlevy Ave; ◷11am-6pm Mon-Wed, to 11pm Thu & Fri, noon-

5pm Sun; 🖵4) Vancouver's only winery is actually a barrel-lined warehousing business storing tipples from BC and beyond, but there's also a large public tasting bar that's one of the city's hidden gems. Roll up for an afternoon tasting during the week (a five-glass tasting flight is $12) or, better still, drop by on Friday night when the place is a hopping nightlife spot for those in the know.

St Augustine's   PUB
(www.staugustinesvancouver.com; 2360 Commercial Dr; ⊙ 11am-1am Sun-Thu, to 2am Fri & Sat; Ⓜ Commercial-Broadway) It looks like a regular neighborhood sports bar from the outside, but step inside St Aug's and you'll find more than 40 on-tap microbrews – one of the largest selections in the city. Most are from BC – look out for beer from Russell Brewing, Howe Sound Brewing and Storm Brewing – but there's also an intriguing selection from south of the border.

Yaletown Brewing Company   BREWERY
(Map p638; www.drinkfreshbeer.com; 1111 Mainland St; ⊙ 11:30am-midnight Sun-Wed, to 1am Thu, to 3am Fri & Sat; Ⓜ Yaletown-Roundhouse) There's a brick-lined brewpub on one side and a giant dining room on the other. Both serve pints of beer made on site, and the restaurant adds a long menu of comfort foods. Check to see if there's an unusual small-batch beer on offer, otherwise hit one of the mainstays: Brick & Beam IPA is recommended. Beer nuts should drop by 4pm Thursdays for cask night.

Fortune Sound Club   CLUB
(Map p638; www.fortunesoundclub.com; 147 E Pender St; ⊙ Wed-Sat; 🖵3) The city's best club has transformed a tired Chinatown spot into a slick space with the kind of genuine staff and younger, hipster-cool crowd rarely seen in Vancouver venues. Slide inside and you'll find a giant dance floor bristling with party-loving locals out for a good time. Expect weekend queues and check-out Happy Ending Fridays, when you'll possibly dance your ass off.

☆ Entertainment

Pick up the free *Georgia Straight* or check www.straight.com for local happenings. Event tickets are available from **Ticketmaster** (✆ 604-280-4444; www.ticketmaster.ca) but **Tickets Tonight** (Map p638; ✆ 604-684-2787; www.ticketstonight.ca) also sells half-price day-of-entry tickets. Live music shows are listed at www.livevan.com; cinema listings, at www.cinemaclock.com.

Live Music

★**Commodore**   LIVE MUSIC
(Map p638; www.commodoreballroom.ca; 868 Granville St; 🖵10) Local bands know they've made it when they play Vancouver's best mid-sized venue, a restored art-deco ballroom that still has the city's bounciest dance floor, courtesy of tires placed under its floorboards. If you need a break from your moshing, collapse at one of the tables lining the perimeter, catch your breath with a bottled Stella and then plunge back in.

BRITISH COLUMBIA VANCOUVER

GAY & LESBIAN VANCOUVER

Vancouver's gay and lesbian scene is part of the city's culture rather than a subsection of it. The legalization of same-sex marriages has resulted in a huge number of couples using Vancouver as a kind of gay Vegas for their destination nuptials. For more information on tying the knot, visit www.vs.gov.bc.ca/marriage/howto.html.

Vancouver's West End district – complete with its pink-painted bus shelters, fluttering rainbow flags and hand-holding locals – houses western Canada's largest 'gayborhood,' while the city's lesbian contingent is centered more on Commercial Dr.

Pick up a free copy of *Xtra!* for a crash course on the local scene, and check www. gayvancouver.net, www.gayvan.com and www.superdyke.com for pertinent listings and resources. In the evening, start your night off at the **Fountainhead Pub** (Map p638; www.thefountainheadpub.com; 1025 Davie St; ⊙ 11am-midnight Sun-Tue, to 1am Wed-Sat; 🖵6), the West End's loudest and proudest gay bar, with its sometimes-raucous patio. Later, move on to the scene's biggest club, **Celebrities** (Map p638; www.celebritiesnightclub. com; 1022 Davie St; ⊙ 8pm-3am Wed, 10pm-3am Thu, 9pm-3am Tue, Fri & Sat; 🖵6). For an even bigger party, don't miss the giant annual Pride Week (p649) in late July, which includes Vancouver's biggest street parade. You can also drop in and tap the local community at the popular **Little Sister's Book & Art Emporium** (Map p638; www.littlesisters.ca; 1238 Davie St; ⊙ 10am-11pm; 🖵6).

★ **Biltmore Cabaret** LIVE MUSIC
(www.biltmorecabaret.com; 2755 Prince Edward St; 🖳9) One of Vancouver's best alternative venues, the Biltmore is a firm favorite on the local indie scene. A low-ceilinged, vibe-tastic spot to mosh to local and touring musicians, there are also regular event nights: check their online calendar for upcoming happenings or hit the eclectic monthly Talent Time, Wednesday's rave-like dance night or Sunday's ever-popular Kitty Nights burlesque show.

Rickshaw Theatre LIVE MUSIC
(Map p638; www.liveatrickshaw.com; 254 E Hastings St; 🖳14) Revamped from its grungy 1970s incarnation, the funky Rickshaw shows that Eastside gentrification can be positive. The stage of choice for many punk and indie acts, it's an excellent place to see a band, with a huge mosh area near the stage, and rows of theater-style seats at the back. Head to the front for a mega moshpit experience with plenty of sweat-triggering action.

Cinemas

Scotiabank Theatre CINEMA
(Map p638; www.cineplex.com; 900 Burrard St; tickets $12.50; 🖳2) Downtown's shiny multiplex was big enough to attract its own corporate sponsor when it opened in 2005 and it's the most likely theater to be screening the latest must-see *Avengers* sequel. In contrast, it also shows occasional live broadcast performances from major cultural institutions, like London's National Theatre and New York's Metropolitan Opera. Note that there are no matinee or Tuesday discounts.

Pacific Cinémathèque CINEMA
(Map p638; www.cinematheque.bc.ca; 1131 Howe St; tickets $11, double bills $14; 🖳10) This beloved repertory cinema operates like an ongoing film festival with a daily changing program of movies. A $3 annual membership is required – pick it up at the door – before you can skulk in the dark with the chin-stroking movie buffs.

Vancity Theatre CINEMA
(Map p638; www.viff.org; 1181 Seymour St; tickets $11, double bills $14; 🖳10) The state-of-the-art headquarters of the Vancouver International Film Festival (p649) screens a wide array of movies throughout the year in the kind of auditorium that cinephiles dream of: generous legroom, wide arm rests and great sight lines from each of its 175 seats. It's a place where you can watch a four-hour sub-titled epic about a dripping tap and still feel comfortable.

Rio Theatre THEATER, CINEMA
(www.riotheatre.ca; 1660 E Broadway; Ⓜ Commercial-Broadway) A recently restored 1980s movie house with very comfy seats, the Rio is like a community repertory theater staging everything from blockbuster and art-house movie screenings to live music, spoken word and saucy burlesque nights. Check the highly eclectic calendar to see what's on: Friday's midnight cult movies (from *Donny Darko* to *The Rocky Horror Picture Show*) are always popular.

Cineplex Odean International Village CINEMA
(Map p638; www.cineplex.com; 88 W Pender St; Ⓜ Stadium-Chinatown) Incongruously located on the 3rd floor of a usually half-empty Chinatown shopping mall, this popular Vancouver theater combines blockbuster and art-house offerings. Comfy stadium seating is the norm here and it's ideal for sheltering on a rainy Vancouver day with a bottomless cup of coffee. Often used as a venue for the city's many film festivals, there's free mall parking for patrons.

Theater & Classical Music

★ **Cultch** THEATER
(Vancouver East Cultural Centre; www.thecultch.com; 1895 Venables St; 🖳20) This once-abandoned 1909 church has been a gathering place for performers and audiences since being officially designated a cultural space in 1973. Following a comprehensive recent renovation, the beloved Cultch, as everyone calls it, is now one of Vancouver's entertainment jewels with a busy roster of local, fringe and visiting theatrical shows, from spoken word to touring Chekhov productions.

★ **Bard on the Beach** PERFORMING ARTS
(Map p638; ☎604-739-0559; www.bardonthebeach.org; Vanier Park, Kitsilano; ⏱ Jun-Sep; 🖳22) Watching Shakespeare performed while the sun sets against the mountains through the open back of a tented stage is a Vancouver summertime highlight. There are usually three Bard plays, plus one Bard-related work (*Rosencrantz and Guildenstern are Dead,* for example) to choose from during the run. Question-and-answer talks are staged after Tuesday-night performances, along with regular opera, fireworks and wine-tasting nights throughout the season.

Arts Club Theatre Company THEATER

(www.artsclub.com) Musicals, international classics and works by contemporary Canadian playwrights are part of the mix at Vancouver's leading theater company. If you're curious about West Coast theatrics, look out for plays by Morris Panych, BC's favorite playwright son. The company's three performance spaces are the **Granville Island Stage** (Map p638; 1585 Johnston St; 🚌50), the nearby and more intimate **Revue Stage** (Map p638; 1601 Johnston St; 🚌50) and the refurbished 1930s **Stanley Theatre** (2750 Granville St; 🚌10).

Vancouver Symphony
Orchestra PERFORMING ARTS

(🎫604-876-3434; www.vancouversymphony.ca) Led by popular maestro Bramwell Tovey, the city's stirring symphony orchestra serves up accessible classics and 'pops.' Shows to look out for include Symphony Sundays and film nights (when live scores are performed to classic movies), plus visits from revered soloists. Concerts often take place at the Orpheum Theatre, but the orchestra frequently unpacks its kettledrums at auditoriums across the Lower Mainland.

Sports
Vancouver Canucks HOCKEY

(Map p638; www.canucks.com; Rogers Arena, 800 Griffiths Way; Ⓜ️Stadium-Chinatown) The city's National Hockey League (NHL) team toyed with fans in 2011's Stanley Cup finals before losing Game 7 to the Boston Bruins, triggering riots and looting across Vancouver. But love runs deep and 'go Canucks, go!' is still boomed out from a packed Rogers Arena at every game. Book your seat early or just head to a local bar for some raucous game-night atmosphere.

Vancouver Whitecaps SOCCER

(Map p638; www.whitecapsfc.com; BC Place Stadium, 777 Pacific Blvd; tickets $25-150; ⊙Mar-Oct; Ⓜ️Stadium-Chinatown) Now using BC Place Stadium as its home, Vancouver's leading soccer team plays in North America's top-tier Major League Soccer (MLS) arena. They've struggled a little since being promoted to the league in 2011, but have been finding their feet (useful for soccer players) in recent seasons. A fun couple of hours; save time for a souvenir soccer shirt purchase to impress everyone back home.

BC Lions FOOTBALL

(Map p638; www.bclions.com; BC Place Stadium, 777 Pacific Blvd; tickets $32-112; ⊙Jun-Nov; Ⓜ️Stadium-Chinatown) The Lions are Vancouver's Canadian Football League (CFL) team, a game that's arguably more exciting than its US NFL counterpart. They've had some decent showings over the past few years, winning the all-important Grey Cup championship most recently in 2011. Tickets are easy to come by – unless the boys are laying into their arch enemies, the Calgary Stampeders.

🛍 Shopping

Robson St is ideal for wanton chain-store browsing, but if you're aiming your credit cards at independent retailers, you'll have to do a little sleuthing. If you prefer an edgier look, it's hard to beat Gastown and the quirky Main St boutiques south of 18th Ave. For window shopping, try Granville Island, South Granville (especially from Broadway southwards) and Kitsilano's W 4th Ave.

★Regional Assembly of Text ARTS & CRAFTS

(www.assemblyoftext.com; 3934 Main St; ⊙11am-6pm Mon-Sat, noon-5pm Sun; 🚌3) This ironic antidote to the digital age lures ink-stained locals with its journals, handmade pencil boxes and T-shirts printed with typewriter motifs. Check out the tiny under-the-stairs gallery showcasing zines from around the world, and don't miss the monthly letter-writing club (7pm, first Thursday of every month), where you can sip tea, scoff cookies and hammer away on vintage typewriters.

One of Vancouver most original stores, check out the array of handmade self-published minibooks near the front window – where else can you read *One Shrew Too Few* and *Secret Thoughts of a Plain Yellow House*?

★Smoking Lily CLOTHING

(www.smokinglily.com; 3634 Main St; ⊙11am-6pm Mon-Sat, noon-5pm Sun; 🚌3) Art-school cool rules here, with skirts, belts and halter tops whimsically accented with prints of ants, bicycles and the periodic table. Men's clothing is a smaller part of the mix, with fish, skull and tractor T-shirts. It's hard to imagine a better souvenir than the silk tea cozy printed with a Pierre Trudeau likeness – ask the friendly staff for more recommendations.

★Mountain Equipment
Co-Op OUTDOOR EQUIPMENT

(www.mec.ca; 130 W Broadway; ⊙10am-7pm Mon-Wed, to 9pm Thu & Fri, 9am-6pm Sat, 11am-5pm Sun; 🚌9) Grown hikers weep at the amazing selection of clothing, kayaks, sleeping bags and clever camping gadgets at this cavernous outdoors store: MEC has been encouraging fully fledged outdoor enthusiasts for years. You'll have to be a member to buy, but that's easy to arrange for just $5. Equipment – canoes, kayaks, camping gear etc – can also be rented here.

★ **Gallery of BC Ceramics**   ARTS & CRAFTS
(Map p638; www.bcpotters.com; 1359 Cartwright St; ⊙ 10:30am-5:30pm; 🚌 50) The star of Granville Island's arts-and-crafts shops, the public face of the Potters Guild of BC exhibits and sells the striking works of its member artists. You can pick up one-of-a-kind ceramic tankards or swirly-painted soup bowls – the hot items are the cool ramen noodle cups, complete with holes for chopsticks. Well-priced art for everyone.

Macleod's Books   BOOKS
(Map p638; 455 W Pender St; ⊙ 11am-6pm Mon-Sat, noon-5pm Sun; 🚇 Granville) From its creaky floorboards to those scuzzy carpets and ever-teetering piles of books, this legendary locals' fave is the best place in town to peruse a cornucopia of used tomes. From dance to the occult, it's the ideal spot for a rainy-day browse. Check the windows for posters of local readings and artsy happenings around the city.

John Fluevog Shoes   SHOES
(Map p638; www.fluevog.com; 65 Water St; ⊙ 10am-7pm Mon-Wed, to 8pm Thu & Fri, to 7pm Sat, noon-6pm Sun; 🚇 Waterfront) Like an art gallery for shoes, this alluringly cavernous store showcases the famed footwear of local designer Fluevog, whose men's and women's boots and brogues are what Doc Martens would have become if they'd stayed interesting and cutting edge. Pick up that pair of thigh-hugging dominatrix boots you've always wanted or settle on some designer-twisted loafers that would make anyone walk tall.

Zulu Records   MUSIC
(www.zulurecords.com; 1972 W 4th Ave; ⊙ 10:30am-7pm Mon-Wed, to 9pm Thu & Fri, 9:30am-6:30pm Sat, noon-6pm Sun; 🚌 4) It's easy to spend a rainy afternoon in Kitsilano's fave indie music store sifting the racks of new and used vinyl and hard-to-find imports, including some of those newfangled CDs. There's an old-school *High Fidelity* ambience here – the scuffed blue carpet and Death Race vintage video game help. Ask the music nerd

staff for tips on the local live scene: they know their stuff.

Bird on a Wire Creations   ARTS & CRAFTS
(www.birdonawirecreations.com; 2535 Main St; ⊙ 10am-6pm Mon-Sat, noon-5pm Sun; 🚌 3) Eminently browsable and highly tempting, there's a surprisingly diverse array of tasteful handmade goodies at this cute and ever-friendly store. Your credit cards will start to sweat as you move among the printed purses, flower-petal soaps, artsy T-shirts and grinning monster kids' toys that adults always want, too. It's not just for show: there are regular craft classes here too.

Hill's Native Art   ARTS & CRAFTS
(Map p638; www.hills.ca; 165 Water St; ⊙ 9am-9pm; 🚇 Waterfront) Launched in 1946 as a small trading post on Vancouver Island, Hill's flagship store has many First Nations carvings, prints, ceremonial masks and cozy Cowichan sweaters, plus traditional music and books of historical interest. Artists are often found at work in the 3rd-floor gallery and it's a great spot to pick up some authentic aboriginal artworks for savoring at home.

Front & Company   CLOTHING, ACCESSORIES
(www.frontandcompany.ca; 3772 Main St; ⊙ 11am-6:30pm; 🚌 3) A triple-fronted store where you could easily spend a couple of hours, its largest section contains trendy consignment clothing – where else can you find that vintage velvet smoking jacket? Next door houses new, knowingly cool house wares, while the third area includes must-have gifts and accessories, such as manga figures, peace-sign ice trays and nihilist chewing gum (flavorless, of course).

Barefoot Contessa   CLOTHING
(www.thebarefootcontessa.com; 1928 Commercial Dr; ⊙ 11am-6pm; 🚌 20) Vintage-look dresses and sparkling costume jewelry , plus a 1920s-style flapper hat or two , are the mainstays of this popular women's clothing boutique aimed at those who never want to be a clone of a chain-store mannequin. You'll find cute tops and accessories from Canadian and international designers, plus artsy-craftsy purses and laptop bags trimmed with lace.

Attic Treasures   VINTAGE
(www.attictreasuresvancouver.com; 944 Commercial Dr; ⊙ 11am-6pm Tue & Thu-Sat, noon-5pm Sun; 🚌 20) One of Vancouver's favorite antiques stores, this retro-cool double-room

shop specializes in mid-century furniture and treasures, which means you'll likely spot items that recall something you remember from an elderly relative's house. Peruse the candy-colored coffee pots and cocktail glasses and save time for the clutter room at the back, where bargains sometimes live.

Information

INTERNET ACCESS

Vancouver Public Library (☎604-331-3603; 350 W Georgia St; ⊙10am-9pm Mon Thu, to 6pm Fri & Sat, noon-5pm Sun; Ⓜ Stadium-Chinatown) Free internet access on library computers, as well as free wi-fi access with guest card from the information desk.

MEDIA & INTERNET RESOURCES

CBC Radio One 88.1 FM (www.cbc.ca/bc) Canadian Broadcasting Corporation's commercial-free news, talk and music station.

CKNW 980AM (www.cknw.com) News, traffic and talk radio station.

City of Vancouver (www.vancouver.ca) Resource-packed official city site with downloadable maps.

Georgia Straight (www.straight.com) Alternative weekly providing Vancouver's best entertainment listings. Free every Thursday.

Inside Vancouver (www.insidevancouver.ca) Stories on what to do in and around the city.

Miss 604 (www.miss604.com) Vancouver's favorite blogger.

Tyee (www.thetyee.ca) Award-winning online local news source.

Vancouver Magazine (www.vanmag.com) Upscale lifestyle, dining and entertainment monthly.

Vancouver Sun (www.vancouversun.com) Main city daily, with Thursday listings pullout.

MEDICAL SERVICES

St Paul's Hospital (☎604-682-2344; 1081 Burrard St; ⬜22) Downtown accident and emergency hospital.

Shoppers Drug Mart (☎604-669-2424; 1125 Davie St; ⊙24hr; ⬜6) Pharmacy chain.

Ultima Medicentre (☎604-683-8138; www.ultimamedicentre.ca; Bentall Centre Plaza Level, 1055 Dunsmuir St; ⊙8am-5pm Mon-Fri; Ⓜ Burrard) Appointments not necessary.

MONEY

RBC Royal Bank (www.rbc.com; 1025 W Georgia St; ⊙9am-5pm Mon-Fri) Main bank branch with money-exchange services.

Vancouver Bullion & Currency Exchange (☎604-685-1008; www.vbce.ca; 800 W Pender St; ⊙9am-5pm Mon-Fri; Ⓜ Granville) Currency exchange with competitive rates.

POST

Canada Post Main Outlet (Map p638; ☎604-662-5723; 349 W Georgia St; ⊙8:30am-5:30pm Mon-Fri; Ⓜ Stadium-Chinatown) There is no separate poste-restante counter, so you must join the queue, show some identification and the person behind the counter will look for your mail. The post office will keep poste-restante mail marked 'c/o General Delivery' for two weeks and then return it to sender.

Howe St Postal Outlet (Map p638; ☎604-688-2068; 732 Davie St; ⊙9am-7pm Mon-Fri, 10am-5pm Sat; ⬜6)

TOURIST INFORMATION

Tourism Vancouver Visitors Centre (Map p638; ☎877-826-1717, 604-683-2000; www.tourismvancouver.com; 200 Burrard St; ⊙8:30am-6pm; Ⓜ Waterfront) The Tourism Vancouver Visitors Centre is a large repository of resources for visitors, with a staff of helpful advisors ready to assist in planning your trip. Services include free maps, visitor guides, half-price theater tickets, accommodation and tour bookings.

ⓘ Getting There & Away

AIR

Vancouver International Airport (YVR; Map p635; www.yvr.ca) is the main West Coast hub for airlines from Canada, the US and international locales. It's in Richmond, a 13km (30 minute) drive south of downtown.

Domestic flights arriving here include regular **Westjet** (☎888-937-8538; www.westjet.com) and **Air Canada** (www.aircanada.com) services. Linked to the main airport by free shuttle bus, the tiny South Terminal receives BC-only flights from smaller airlines and floatplane operators.

Several handy floatplane services can also deliver you directly to the Vancouver waterfront's **Seaplane Terminal** (☎604-647-7570; www.vhfc.ca; 1055 Canada Place; Ⓜ Waterfront). These include frequent Harbour Air Seaplanes (p683) services from downtown Victoria and beyond.

BOAT

BC Ferries (www.bcferries.com) services arrive at **Tsawwassen** – an hour's drive south of downtown – from Vancouver Island's Swartz Bay (passenger/vehicle $15.50/51.25, 1½ hours) and Nanaimo's Duke Point (passenger/vehicle $15.50/51.25, two hours). Services also arrive here from the Southern Gulf Islands.

Ferries arrive at West Vancouver's **Horseshoe Bay** – 30 minutes from downtown – from Nanaimo's Departure Bay (passenger/vehicle $15.50/51.25, 1½ hours), Bowen Island (passenger/vehicle $11.10/31.65, 20 minutes) and

Langdale (passenger/vehicle $14.55/49.05, 40 minutes) on the Sunshine Coast.

BUS

Most out-of-town buses grind to a halt at Vancouver's **Pacific Central Station** (1150 Station St). **Greyhound Canada** (www.greyhound.ca) services arrive from Whistler (from $18, 2¾ hours), Kelowna (from $29, five hours) and Calgary (from $57, 14 to 17 hours), among others.

Traveling via the BC Ferries Swartz Bay–Tsawwassen route, frequent **Pacific Coach Lines** (PCL; www.pacificcoach.com) services also trundle in from downtown Victoria (from $44, 3½ hours). PCL also operates services between Whistler, Vancouver and Vancouver International Airport. **Snowbus** (☑ 888-794-5511; www.snowbus.com) also offers a winter-only ski bus service to and from Whistler ($38, 3 hours).

Quick Coach Lines (www.quickcoach.com; ☎) runs an express shuttle between Seattle and Vancouver, departing from downtown Seattle (US$43.85, four hours) and the city's Sea-Tac International Airport (US$58.50, 3½ hours).

CAR & MOTORCYCLE

If you're coming from Washington State in the US, you'll be on the I-5 until you hit the border town of Blaine, then on Hwy 99 in Canada. It's about an hour's drive from here to downtown Vancouver. Hwy 99 continues through downtown, across the Lions Gate Bridge to Horseshoe Bay, Squamish and Whistler.

If you're coming from the east, you'll probably be on the Trans-Canada Hwy (Hwy 1), which snakes through the city's eastern end, eventually meeting with Hastings St. If you want to go downtown, turn left onto Hastings and follow it into the city center, or continue on along the North Shore toward Whistler.

If you're coming from Horseshoe Bay, Hwy 1 heads through West Vancouver and North Vancouver before going over the Second Narrows Bridge into Burnaby. If you're heading downtown, leave the highway at the Taylor Way exit in West Vancouver and follow it over the Lions Gate Bridge toward the city center.

All the recognized car rental chains have Vancouver branches. **Avis** (☑ 604-606-2847, 800-230-4898; www.avis.ca), **Budget** (☑ 604-668-7000, 800-219-3199; www.budgetbc.com), **Hertz** (☑ 604-606-4711, 800-654-3131; www.hertz.ca) and **Thrifty** (☑ 604-606-1655, 800-847-4389; www.thrifty.com) also have airport branches.

TRAIN

Trains trundle in from across Canada and the US at Pacific Central Station (p666). The Main Street-Science World SkyTrain station is just across the street for connections to downtown and the suburbs.

VIA Rail (www.viarail.ca) services arrive from Kamloops North (from $77.70, 10 hours), Jasper (from $162.75, 20 hours) and Edmonton (from $219.45, 27 hours), among others.

Amtrak (www.amtrak.com; ☎) US services arrive from Eugene (from US$64, 11 hours), Portland (from US$47, eight hours) and Seattle (from US$30, three hours).

ℹ Getting Around

TO/FROM THE AIRPORT

SkyTrain's 16-station Canada Line (adult one-way fare to downtown $7.50 to $9) operates a rapid-transit train service from the airport to downtown. Trains run every few minutes and take around 25 minutes to reach downtown's Waterfront Station.

If you prefer to cab it, budget $30 to $40 for the 30-minute taxi ride from the airport to your downtown hotel.

BICYCLE

With 300km of dedicated routes, Vancouver is a good cycling city. Pick up a *Metro Vancouver Cycling Map* ($3.95) at convenience stores; it's also free to download from www.translink.bc.ca. Cyclists can take their bikes for free on SkyTrain and SeaBus services and rack-fitted transit buses. Additional maps and resources are available at the **City of Vancouver** (www.vancouver.ca/cycling) website.

BOAT

Aquabus Ferries (www.theaquabus.com; adult/child from $3/1.50) runs mini-vessels (some big enough to carry bikes) between the end of Hornby St and Granville Island, and services spots along False Creek as far as Science World. Its rival is **False Creek Ferries** (Map p638; www.granvilleislandferries.bc.ca; adult/child from $3/1.50), which operates a similar Granville Island service from the Vancouver Aquatic Centre near the end of Thurlow St, plus additional ports of call around False Creek.

CAR & MOTORCYCLE

The rush-hour vehicle lineup to cross the Lions Gate Bridge to the North Shore frequently snakes far up W Georgia St. Try the alternative Second Narrows Bridge. Other peak-time hot spots to avoid are the George Massey Tunnel and Hwy 1 to Surrey.

Parking is at a premium downtown: there are few free spots available on residential side streets and traffic wardens are predictably predatory. Some streets have metered parking, but pay-parking lots (from $4 per hour) are a better proposition – arrive before 9am at some for early-bird discounts. Underground parking at either the Pacific Centre (entrance at Robson and Howe St intersection) or the Vancouver

Public Library (entrance at Hamilton and Robson intersection) will have you in the heart of the city.

PUBLIC TRANSPORTATION

The website for **TransLink** (www.translink.bc.ca) bus, SkyTrain and SeaBus services has a trip-planning tool. A ticket bought on any of its three services is valid for 1½ hours of travel on the entire network, depending on the zone you intend traveling in. The three zones become progressively more expensive the further you journey.

One-zone tickets are adult/child $2.75/1.75, two-zone tickets $4/2.75 and three-zone tickets $5.50/3.75. An all-day, all-zone pass costs $9.75/7.50. If you're traveling after 6:30pm or on weekends or holidays, all trips are classed as one-zone fares and cost $2.75/1.75. Children under five travel free on all transit services. At the time of writing, a new swipeable fare card system called Compass was being introduced: check the TransLink website for the latest information.

Bus

The bus network is extensive in central areas and many vehicles have bike racks. All are wheelchair accessible. Exact change is required since all buses use fare machines and change is not given.

The 99 B-Line express buses operate between the Commercial-Broadway SkyTrain station and UBC. These buses have their own limited arrival and departure points and do not use the regular bus stops.

There is also a handy night-bus system that runs every 30 minutes between 1:30am and 4am across the Lower Mainland. The last bus leaves downtown Vancouver at 3:10am. Look for the night-bus signs at designated stops.

SeaBus

The aquatic shuttle **SeaBus** (Map p638) operates every 15 to 30 minutes throughout the day, taking 12 minutes to cross the Burrard Inlet between Waterfront Station and Lonsdale Quay. At Lonsdale there's a bus terminal servicing routes throughout North Vancouver and West Vancouver (take bus 236 to Grouse Mountain and Capilano Suspension Bridge). Vessels are wheelchair accessible and bike friendly.

SkyTrain

The SkyTrain rapid-transit network consists of three routes and is a great way to move around the region: consider taking a spin on it, even if you don't have anywhere to go. A fourth route, the Evergreen Line, is scheduled for 2016 completion.

The original 35-minute Expo Line goes to and from downtown Vancouver and Surrey, via stops throughout Burnaby and New Westminster. The Millennium Line alights near shopping malls and suburban residential districts in Coquitlam and Burnaby. Opened in late 2009, the new Canada Line links the city to the airport and Richmond.

While SkyTrain ticket prices mirror the zones used across the TransLink network, there is one notable exception: passengers departing on Canada Line trains from the airport are charged an extra $5 AddFare when purchasing their ticket from station vending machines. You do not have to pay this extra charge when traveling to the airport from downtown.

TAXI

Flagging a downtown cab shouldn't take long, but it's easier to get your hotel to call one. Operators include **Vancouver Taxi** (☑ 604-871-1111) and **Yellow Cab** (☑ 604-681-1111). Many taxis take credit cards.

LOWER MAINLAND

Stretching from coastal Horseshoe Bay as far inland as the Fraser Valley, this region encompasses the towns and suburbs within an hour or so by car from downtown Vancouver, including the communities immediately adjoining the city that are also known as Metro Vancouver. Ideal for day-tripping from the city, the area is chock-full of looming mountains, crenulated coastal parks, wildlife sanctuaries and historic attractions.

North Vancouver
POP 52,000

A commuter burb for downtown professionals, the city of 'North Van' rises from the waterfront at the Lonsdale Quay SeaBus dock, where you'll also find a popular public market. The area is home to two of the region's most popular attractions. For more visitor information on North Vancouver and adjoining West Vancouver, see www.vancouversnorthshore.com.

◉ Sights & Activities

Capilano Suspension Bridge   PARK
(Map p635; www.capbridge.com; 3735 Capilano Rd; adult/child $34.95/12; ⊙8:30am-8pm; ⛟; ☐236 from Lonsdale Quay) As you walk gingerly onto one of the world's longest (140m) and highest (70m) suspension bridges, swaying gently over the roiling Capilano Canyon, remember that its thick steel cables are embedded in concrete. That should steady your feet – unless there are teenagers stamping

across. Added park attractions include a glass-bottomed cliffside walkway and an elevated canopy trail through the trees.

A hugely popular attraction (hence the summer tour buses), try to arrive early during peak months and you'll be able to check out the historic exhibits, totem poles and tree-shaded nature trails on the other side of the bridge in relative calm. From May to September, Capilano makes it very easy to get here from downtown by running a **free shuttle** from Canada Pl and area hotels. Check their website for details.

Grouse Mountain
OUTDOORS

(off Map p635; www.grousemountain.com; 6400 Nancy Greene Way; Skyride adult/child $39.95/13.95; ⊘9am-10pm; ; ☐236 from Lonsdale Quay) Calling itself the 'Peak of Vancouver,' this mountaintop playground offers smashing views of downtown, shimmering in the water below. In summer, **Skyride** gondola tickets include access to lumberjack shows, alpine hiking, movie presentations and a grizzly-bear refuge. Pay extra for zip lining and Eye of the Wind, a 20-story, elevator-accessed turbine tower with a panoramic viewing pod that will have your camera itching for action.

There are also restaurants up here if you fancy dining: it's an ideal sunset-viewing spot. You can reduce the gondola fee by hiking the ultra-steep Grouse Grind (p668) up the side of the mountain – you have to pay $10 to get back down on the Skyride, though. Like Capilano, Grouse lures visitors from downtown in summer by offering a **free shuttle** from Canada Pl. In winter, it's all about skiing and snowboarding as Grouse become the locals' fave powder playground.

Lynn Canyon Park
PARK

(Map p635; www.lynncanyon.ca; Park Rd; ⊘7am-9pm; ; ☐229 from Lonsdale Quay) Amid a dense bristling of ancient trees, the main feature of this provincial park is its **suspension bridge**, a free alternative to Capilano. Not quite as big as its tourist-magnet rival, it provokes the same jelly-legged reaction as you sway over the river 50m below, and is always far less crowded. Hiking trails, swimming areas and picnic spots will keep you busy.

The **Ecology Centre** (www.dnv.org/ecology; 3663 Park Rd; entry by $2 donation; ⊘10am-5pm) houses interesting displays on the area's rich biodiversity, including dioramas and video presentations. It stages regular talks and events for kids, especially in summer.

Lonsdale Quay Public Market
MARKET

(www.lonsdalequay.com; 123 Carrie Cates Ct; ⊘9am-7pm) As well as being a transportation hub, this waterfront facility houses a colorful public market. Look for fresh fruit and glassy-eyed whole fish on the main floor, plus trinkets and clothing on the 2nd floor. There's also a lively food court; **Montgomery's Fish & Chips** is recommended. The SeaBus from downtown docks here and you can pick up transit buses to Capilano, Grouse and beyond.

Mt Seymour Provincial Park
OUTDOORS

(Map p635; www.bcparks.ca; 1700 Mt Seymour Rd; ⊘dawn-dusk) A popular, rustic retreat from the clamor of downtown, this giant, tree-lined park is suffused with more than

---

MOTHER NATURE'S STAIRMASTER

If you're finding your vacation a little too relaxing, head over to North Vancouver and join the perspiring throng snaking almost vertically up the **Grouse Grind** trail. The entrance is near the parking lot, across the street from where slightly more sane visitors to Grouse Mountain (p668) pile into the Skyride gondola and trundle up to the summit without breaking a sweat. Around 3km in total, the steep, rock-studded forest trek will likely have your joints screaming for mercy within 15 minutes as you focus on the feet of the person in front of you. Most people take around an hour to reach the top, where they collapse like gasping fish on the rocks. If you're feeling energetic, you might want to try and beat the record of Vancouverite Sebastian Albrecht who nailed the trail 14 times in one day in 2010. Things to keep in mind if you're planning to join the 110,000 who hike the Grind every year: take a bottle of water, dress in thin layers so you can strip down, and bring $10 with you: the trail is one way, so when you reach the summit you have to pay a special rate to take the Skyride back down – your consolation is that you get to enjoy the summit's many attractions for free in exchange for your exploding calf muscles.

a dozen summertime hiking trails that suit walkers of most abilities; the easiest path is the 2km Goldie Lake Trail. Many trails wind past lakes and centuries-old Douglas firs and offer a true break from the city. This is also one of the city's three main winter playgrounds. Drivers can take Hwy 1 to the Mt Seymour Pkwy (near the Second Narrows Bridge) and follow it east to Mt Seymour Rd.

Maplewood Farm FARM
(Map p635; www.maplewoodfarm.bc.ca; 405 Seymour River Pl; adult/child $7.50/4.50; ⊙10am-4pm; ⋒; ⬚239 from Lonsdale Quay, then C15) A popular family-friendly site, this farmyard attraction includes plenty of hands-on displays plus a collection of over 200 domestic animals. Your wide-eyed kids can pet some critters, watch the daily milking demonstration and feed some squawking, ever-hungry ducks and chickens. The highlight is the daily 'running of the goats' at around 3:30pm, when the starving hair balls streak from the paddock to their barn for dinner.

🛏 Sleeping & Eating

Pinnacle Hotel at the Pier HOTEL $$
(⬚877-986-7437, 604-986-7437; www.pinnaclehotelatthepier.com; 138 Victory Ship Way; d $169; ⊜❉@☎☎☎; ⬚230) North Van's new Pinnacle is an excellent option if you want to stay on this side of the water and hop to the city center on the nearby SeaBus. The hotel balances itself between business and leisure travelers, and rooms are furnished with contemporary elegance, with calming hues favored over bold colors. Harbor views are recommended but typically cost $10 to $20 extra.

★ Tomahawk Restaurant DINER $$
(www.tomahawkrestaurant.com; 1550 Philip Ave; mains $8-16; ⊙8am-9pm Sun-Thu, to 10pm Fri & Sat; ⬚240) A colorful blast from North Van's pioneering past, the family-run Tomahawk has been heaping its plates with comfort food since 1926. A bustling weekend brunch spot – if the massive Yukon bacon and eggs grease fest or the frightening Skookum Chief burger don't kill your hangover, nothing will – it's also fun for lunch or dinner, when bulging burgers and chicken potpies hit the menu.

Grab a spot at the counter, with its swivel stools, and check out the surfeit of First Nations artifacts lining the walls: it's like stuffing your face in a museum.

Burgoo Bistro WEST COAST $$
(www.burgoo.ca; 3 Lonsdale Ave; mains $10-18; ⊙11am-10pm Sun-Wed, to 11pm Thu-Sat; ⬚230) With the feel of a cozy, rustic cabin, complete with a large stone fireplace, Burgoo's menu of comfort foods with a twist aims to warm up North Van's winter nights: the spicy apricot lamb tagine or smile-triggering butter chicken would thaw a glacier from 50 paces. There's also a wide array of house-made soups and heaping salads. As for drinks, try the tasty craft beers.

Observatory WEST COAST $$$
(⬚604-980-9311; www.grousemountain.com; Grouse Mountain; mains $39; ⊙5-10pm; ⬚236 from Lonsdale Quay) Crowning Grouse Mountain, the fine-dining Observatory serves its chorizo scallops and lamb medallions alongside breathtaking views over Stanley Park and Vancouver's twinkling towers far below. A perfect venue for a romantic dinner – you wouldn't be the first to propose here – there's an excellent wine list if you suddenly need to console yourself. Reserve in advance and you'll get free Sky-ride passes.

The atmosphere is more laid-back at the adjacent, pub-like **Altitudes Bistro**, which offers comfort grub of the burgers and fish-and-chips variety in a casual ski-lodge ambience.

❶ Getting There & Around

SeaBus vessels arrive at Lonsdale Quay from Vancouver's Waterfront Station ($4, 12 minutes) every 15 to 30 minutes throughout the day. From the bus terminal at the quay, bus 236 runs to Capilano Suspension Bridge then on to the base of Grouse Mountain.

Rocky Mountaineer Vacations runs its popular Whistler Sea to Sky Climb (p683) train into North Vancouver from Whistler (from $169, three hours, daily May to mid-October).

West Vancouver

POP 44,000
Adjoining North Vancouver, the considerably wealthier 'West Van' is studded with multilevel mansions that cling to the cliff tops and look down – in more ways than one – across the region. It's a stop-off point on the drive from downtown to the Horseshoe Bay ferry terminal and other points north on the way to Whistler.

BRITISH COLUMBIA WEST VANCOUVER

◉ Sights

Cypress Provincial Park
OUTDOORS

(www.bcparks.ca; Cypress Bowl Rd; ⊙ dawn-dusk) Around 8km north of West Van via Hwy 99, Cypress offers great summertime hikes, including the Baden-Powell, Yew Lake and Howe Sound Crest trails, which plunge through forests of cedar, yellow cypress and Douglas fir and wind past little lakes and alpine meadows. Also a popular area for mountain bikers, Cypress becomes a snowy playground in winter.

If you're driving from downtown Vancouver, cross the Lions Gate Bridge to the Upper Levels Hwy via Taylor Way in West Vancouver. Then, follow the signs to the park entrance.

Lighthouse Park
PARK

(Map p635; www.lighthousepark.ca; cnr Beacon Lane & Marine Dr; ⊙ dawn-dusk; ◻ 250) Some of the region's oldest trees live within this accessible 75-hectare park, including a rare stand of original coastal forest and plenty of those gnarly, copper-trunked arbutus trees. About 13km of hiking trails crisscross the area, including a recommended trek that leads to the rocky perch of **Point Atkinson Lighthouse**, ideal for shimmering, camera-worthy views over Burrard Inlet.

If you're driving from downtown, turn left on Marine Dr after crossing the Lions Gate Bridge to reach the park.

⊙ Tours

Sewell's Sea Safari
BOAT TOUR

(☑ 604-921-3474; www.sewellsmarina.com; 6409 Bay St, Horseshoe Bay; adult/child $83/53; ⊙ Apr-Oct; ◻ 250) West Vancouver's Horseshoe Bay is the departure point for this two-hour marine-wildlife-watching boat tour. Orcas are always a highlight but, even if they're not around, you'll almost certainly spot harbor seals lolling on the rocks pretending to ignore you. Seabirds are also a common sight, while bald eagles are frequent contributors to the show as well.

⌂ Sleeping & Eating

Lighthouse Park B&B
B&B $$

(☑ 604-926-5959, 800-926-0262; www.lighthousepark.com; 4875 Water Lane; ste from $175) This elegant two-suite sleepover, complete with private entrances and a flower-decked courtyard, will have you feeling like a West Van aristo in no time. Each suite has a fridge and DVD player, as well as a decanter of sherry for that essential alfresco evening tipple. You can sober up with a stroll to nearby Point Atkinson Lighthouse.

Savary Island Pie Company
BAKERY, CAFE $$

(www.savaryislandpiecompany.com; 1533 Marine Dr; mains $8-14; ⊙ 6am-9pm; ◻ 250) Ask North Shore locals where to get a great slice of pie and they'll point you to this popular bakery cafe, opened in 1989. The bulging, fresh-baked pies are the mainstay of the business – don't miss the raspberry rhubarb – though the extended menu, with breakfasts, soup and sandwiches, suggests dessert is not the only meal.

Fraîche
WEST COAST $$

(☑ 604-925-7595; www.fraicherestaurant.ca; 2240 Chippendale Rd; mains $18-42; ⊙ 11am-3pm & 5-10pm Tue-Sun; ◻ 256) It's worth tearing your gaze from the mesmerizing shoreline vistas here to focus on your plate. Perfect Canadian gourmet is the approach, with typical highlights on the seasonal menu including charred octopus and juicy roast duck. If you fancy a taste of the high life without the price, drop in for lunch or weekend brunch when many dishes hover around $20.

Salmon House on the Hill
SEAFOOD $$$

(☑ 604-926-3212; www.salmonhouse.com; 2229 Folkestone Way; mains $30-40; ⊙ 5-9:30pm Sun-Thu, 6-10pm Fri & Sat, brunch 10:30am-2:30pm Sat & Sun; ◻ 256) West Vancouver's old-school destination restaurant, this landmark has been luring locals for special-occasion dinners for years. But Salmon House doesn't rest on its laurels – if laurels can be defined as a gable-roofed wooden interior and floor-to-ceiling windows with sunset cliff-top city views. Instead, you'll find a menu of delectable seasonal BC seafood with serious gourmet credentials.

Burnaby

POP 232,000

Immediately east of Vancouver and accessible via SkyTrain from the city, Burnaby is a residential suburb with a half-day's worth of attractions.

The pathways of tranquil **Deer Lake Park** (Map p635) crisscross meadows and woodlands, circling a lake where fowl and other wildlife hang out. In summer, it's the home of the annual **Burnaby Blues + Roots Festival** (www.burnabybluesfestival.com). The adjoining **Burnaby Village Museum** (Map

IDYLLIC ISLAND JAUNT

Just because you've found yourself running out of road in shoreline West Vancouver, doesn't mean you have to end your adventures. You can hit the Horseshoe Bay ferry terminal – with or without your car (transit bus 257 will also get you here from downtown Vancouver) – for a quick hop to **Bowen Island** (off Map p635). Once a favored summertime retreat for colonials looking for a seaside escape, it's now populated by a friendly clutch of writers and artists.

Once you alight in Snug Cove – the breathtaking crossing over the glassy, tree-lined water takes around 20 minutes – you'll find yourself in a rustically charming little community that suddenly feels a million miles from big-city life. Drop into the **visitors center** (www.bowenchamber.com; 432 Cardena Rd; ☺10am-3pm) for a crash course on what to do...then set about doing it.

Scenic paddle tours are offered by **Bowen Island Sea Kayaking** (☑800-605-2925, 604-947-9266; www.bowenislandkayaking.com; Snug Cove; rentals 3hr/day $45/70, tours from $65), but just strolling the forest trails – and stopping for a picnic overlooking the waterfront – is always a good idea. You'll likely also spend a lot of time clattering along the boardwalk area near the ferry dock. This is where you'll find **Doc Morgan's Restaurant & Pub** (www.docmorgans.com; 439 Bowen Island Trunk Rd; mains $10-12; ☺11am-midnight Sun-Thu, to 1am Fri & Sat), where the chatty patios overlook the park and harbor. Pub grub is the main focus here and the fish and chips are popular – along with BC craft beer. On summer weekends, local artisans gather beside the marina to showcase their wares at the **Summer Market**. If you miss it, climb the hill to **Artisan Square** for little shops of the gallery and jewelery-store variety.

p635; www.burnabyvillagemuseum.ca; 6501 Deer Lake Ave; ☺11am-4:30pm May-Aug) **FREE** colorfully re-creates a BC pioneer town, complete with replica homes, businesses and a handsome 1912 carousel. To get directly there by car, take the Sperling Ave exit off Hwy 1 and follow the museum signs.

Topping Burnaby Mountain, **Simon Fraser University** (Map p635; www.sfu.ca; 8888 University Dr) is the Lower Mainland's second-biggest campus community. Small visitor attractions here include the free-admission **SFU Gallery** and the **Museum of Archaeology & Ethnology**.

For information on the area, visit **Tourism Burnaby** (www.tourismburnaby.com) website.

New Westminster

A 30-minute SkyTrain ride from downtown Vancouver, New West is one of BC's most historic communities – it was briefly designated the capital of the new Colony of British Columbia in 1859. Its star faded during much of the last century but recent years have seen attempts at revival. It's easily worth a couple of hours of your time if you're looking for an easy excursion from Vancouver.

Hop off at the New Westminster SkyTrain station and stroll downhill to the Fraser River waterfront. The newly revitalized covered **River Market** (Map p635; www.rivermarket.ca; 810 Quayside Dr; ☺10am-6pm) is a good place for lunch – **Re-Up BBQ** is recommended – and you'll also spot what claims to be the **world's largest tin soldier** looming over the boardwalk. If you have time, nip into the **Fraser River Discovery Centre** (Map p635; www.fraserdiscovery.org; 788 Quayside Dr; entry by $6 donation; ☺10am-4pm) to uncover the story of the mighty river flowing alongside. Hit nearby **Front St** for shops and historic buildings and then hop back on the SkyTrain at Columbia Station for your return to Vancouver.

For more information on the area, visit the **Tourism New Westminster** (www.tourismnewwestminster.com) website.

Fort Langley

Little Fort Langley's tree-lined streets and 19th-century storefronts make it one of BC's most picturesque historic villages, ideal for an afternoon jaunt from Vancouver. Its highlight is the colorful **Fort Langley National Historic Site** (☑604-513-4777; www.pc.gc.ca/fortlangley; 23433 Mavis Ave; adult/child

$7.80/3.90; ⊘10am-4pm; 🚌501, then C62), the region's most important old-school landmark.

A fortified trading post since 1827, it's where James Douglas announced the creation of BC in 1858, giving the site a legitimate claim to being the province's birthplace. With costumed reenactors, re-created artisan workshops and a gold-panning area that's a kid-friendly must-do (they also enjoy charging around the wooden battlements), this is an ideal destination for families aiming to add a little education to their trips.

If you need an introduction before you start wading into the buildings, there's a surprisingly entertaining time-travel-themed movie presentation on offer. Make sure you check the website before you arrive: there's a wide array of events that evocatively bring the past back to life, including a summertime evening campfire program that will take you right back to the 1800s pioneer days.

If you're driving from Vancouver, take Hwy 1 east for 40km, then take the 232nd St exit north. Follow the signs along 232nd St until you reach the stop sign at Glover Rd. Turn right here, and continue into the village. Turn right again on Mavis Ave, just before the railway tracks. The fort's parking lot is at the end of the street.

Richmond & Steveston

POP 200,000

Hop aboard the Canada Line and head down to the region's Chinatown for a half-day of Asian shopping malls – centered on the Golden Village area – followed by a taste-trip through Chinese, Japanese and Vietnamese restaurants.

Don't miss the city's charming historic waterfront Steveston village, a popular destination for sunset-viewing locals with a penchant for great fish and chips. For more information on both areas, check www.tourismrichond.com.

◉ Sights & Activities

Richmond Night Market   MARKET
(Map p635; www.richmondnightmarket.com; 8351 River Rd, Richmond; admission $2; ⊘7pm-midnight Fri & Sat, 6pm-11pm Sun mid-May–mid-Oct; Ⓜ Bridgeport) One of two Asian-style night markets in Richmond – the other is called the International Summer Night Market – this seasonal bonanza is alive with steaming food stalls serving everything from sizzling fish balls to dragon's beard candy. Come hungry and don't forget to take a break from filling your face via the shiny trinket vendors and live entertainment.

Of the two markets, this one is easiest to reach on transit.

International Summer Night Market   MARKET
(Map p635; www.summernightmarket.com; 12631 Vulcan Way, Richmond; ⊘7pm-1am Fri & Sat, to midnight Sun mid-May–early Oct; 🚌407) Much larger than downtown Chinatown's version, thousands of hungry locals are lured here every weekend to check out the tacky vendor stands and, more importantly, the dozens of hawker food stalls. Don't eat before arriving and you can taste-trip through steaming Malaysian, Korean, Japanese and Chinese treats.

Gulf of Georgia Cannery   MUSEUM
(Map p635; www.gulfofgeorgiacannery.com; 12138 4th Ave, Steveston; adult/child $7.80/3.90; ⊘10am-5pm Feb-Oct; Ⓜ Richmond-Brighouse, then 🚌401) Once you've perused the boats hawking the day's fresh catch, check out Steveston's excellent cannery museum, illuminating the sights and sounds of the region's bygone era of labor-intensive fish processing. Most of the machinery remains and there's an evocative focus on the people who used to work here. Take one of the free tours, sometimes run by former cannery workers.

Britannia Shipyard   MUSEUM
(Map p635; www.britannia-hss.ca; 5180 Westwater Dr, Steveston; ⊘10am-6pm Tue-Sun; Ⓜ Richmond-Brighouse, then 🚌410) FREE After you've done the cannery, hit Steveston's lovely waterfront boardwalk – complete with art installations evoking the area's bustling fishing sector – and within 15 minutes you'll stroll into the area's other national historic site. Not as slick as the cannery, it's nevertheless a fascinating complex of creaky old sheds housing dusty tools, boats and reminders of the region's maritime past.

🛏 Sleeping & Eating

Fairmont Vancouver Airport   HOTEL $$$
(📞866-540-4441, 604-207-5200; www.fairmont.com/vancouverairport; Vancouver International Airport, Richmond; d from $250; ❋@🛜❄; Ⓜ YVR Airport) You can wave from the overhead walkway to the harried economy-class plebs below as you stroll toward the lobby of this

luxe airport hotel in the US departure hall. This is a great option for boarding long-haul flights in a Zen-like state of calm. The rooms are elegantly furnished with high-end flourishes including remote-controlled curtains and marble-lined bathrooms.

★ Pajo's
SEAFOOD $

(www.pajos.com; The Wharf, Steveston; mains $6-9; ⊙11am-dusk; ⋈Richmond-Brighouse, then ⛴402) It's hard to find a better spot to enjoy fish and chips than the boat-bobbing wharf at Steveston. Luckily, this floating, family-run local legend fully delivers. After perusing the fresh catches on the backs of the nearby fishing boats, descend the ramp to Pajo's little ordering hatch. Go the fresh-fried salmon or halibut route or mix things up with a yellowfin tuna burger.

Parker Place
FOOD COURT $

(www.parkerplace.com; 4380 No 3 Rd, Richmond; mains $5-10; ⊙11am-7pm Sun-Thu, to 9pm Fri & Sat; ⋈Aberdeen) There are several popular Asian shopping malls in Richmond but, while Aberdeen Centre and Lansdowne Centre are bigger, Parker Place's highly authentic food court feels like a Singaporean hawker market. Beloved of Asian-Canadian locals, dive in for good-value noodle, fishball and dragon's-beard-candy dishes: buy a few plates and share 'em at your table.

Once you're full, peruse the labyrinth of surrounding international-flavored retailers or nip outside to the food court's adjoining parking lot for a surprise: a shimmering shrine.

Cattle Cafe
ASIAN $

(www.cattlecafe.ca; 8580 Alexandra Rd, Richmond; mains $6-14; ⊙11am-1am; ⋈Lansdowne) Richmond's lip-smacking Asian dining scene is it's main lure and, if you want to get to the heart of the matter, head straight to Alexandra Rd, also called 'Eat Street', where dozens of restaurants await. Among the funkiest, this Hong Kong–style joint is great for trying barbecued-eel sandwiches, washed down with some delectable bubble tea.

Shanghai River Restaurant
CHINESE $$

(7381 Westminster Hwy, Richmond; mains $6-18; ⊙11am-2:30pm & 5:30-11pm; ⋈Richmond-Brighouse) Grab a seat overlooking the kitchen window at this cavernous northern-Chinese eatery and you'll be mesmerized by the handiwork that goes into preparing the area's best dim sum. Order plates to share – one dish per person is the usual ratio – and

be careful not to squirt everyone with the delicate but juicy pork or shrimp dumplings.

Jang Mo Jib
ASIAN $$

(www.jangmojib.com; 8230 Alexandra Rd, Richmond; mains $12-24; ⊙10am-1am Mon-Thu, to 2am Fri & Sat; ⋈Lansdowne) If you're in the mood for a spot of Korean hot pot and barbecue, this friendly, large restaurant is the one for you. Just look for the wacky carved poles outside, then nip into this gable-roofed restaurant for a host of immersive, mostly meaty dishes. The must-have specialty is the pork-blood sausage, which divides the table between real and pretend carnivores.

ⓘ Getting There & Away

The Canada Line SkyTrain link has made the region's modern-day Chinatown much easier to reach from downtown Vancouver.

SEA TO SKY HIGHWAY

Otherwise known as Hwy 99, this picturesque cliffside roadway links a string of communities between West Vancouver and Lillooet and is the main route to Whistler from Vancouver. Recently upgraded, the winding road has several worthwhile stops – especially if you're an outdoor-activity fan, history buff or lover of BC's variegated mountain landscape. **Mountain FM radio** (107.1) provides handy traffic and road-condition updates en route.

Squamish & Around
POP 18,500

An hour north of Vancouver and another hour to Whistler, Squamish sits at the meeting point of ocean, river and alpine forest. Originally just a grungy logging town, it's now a popular base for outdoor activities, especially in summer.

⊙ Sights & Activities

The dozens of tree-fringed trails around Squamish draw plenty of mountain-bike enthusiasts. The **Cheekeye Fan trail** near Brackendale has some easy rides, while downhill thrill seekers prefer the **Diamond Head/Power Smart area**. Check the website of the **Squamish Off Road Cycling Association** (www.sorca.ca) for an intro to the area's two-wheeled scene.

If you prefer to hit the water, **Squamish Spit** is a kiteboarding (and windsurfing) hot spot. The season runs May to October and the website of the **Squamish Windsports Society** (www.squamishwindsports.com) is your first point of contact for weather, water conditions and information on access to the spit.

At time of research a new sightseeing gondola attraction was also being built in the area; check http://seatoskygondola.com for the latest details.

Britannia Mine Museum MUSEUM
(www.britanniaminemuseum.ca; adult/child $21.50/13.50; ⊙ 9am-5pm) Around 10 minutes before Squamish on Hwy 99, the Britannia Mine Museum is a recommended stop. Once the British Empire's largest copper mine, it's been restored as an impressive industrial museum. The underground mine-tunnel train tour is a highlight and there are plenty of additional kid-friendly exhibits, including gold panning, plus a large artsy gift shop.

Shannon Falls Provincial Park WATERFALL
(www.bcparks.ca) About 4km before you reach Squamish, you'll also hear the rushing waters of Shannon Falls Provincial Park. Pull into the parking lot and stroll the short trail to BC's third-highest waterfall, where water cascades down a 335m drop. A few picnic tables make this a handy spot for an alfresco lunch.

West Coast Railway Heritage Park MUSEUM
(www.wcra.org; 39645 Government Rd; adult/child $15/10; ⊙ 10am-5pm) Historic-train nuts should continue just past town to the smashing West Coast Railway Heritage Park. This large, mostly alfresco museum is the final resting place of BC's legendary Royal Hudson steam engine and has around 90 other historic railcars, including 10 working engines and the original prototype SkyTrain car. Check out the slick new Roundhouse building, housing the park's most precious trains and artifacts.

Stawamus Chief Provincial Park PARK
(www.bcparks.ca) On the way into Squamish from Vancouver, you'll see a sheer, 652m-high granite rock face looming ahead. Attracting hardy climbers, it's called the 'Chief' and it's the highlight of Stawamus Chief Provincial Park. You don't have to gear up to experience the summit's breathtaking vistas: there are hiking routes up the back for anyone who wants to have a go. Consider

Squamish Rock Guides (☎ 604-892-7816; www.squamishrockguides.com; guided rock climbs half-day/day from $75/115) for climbing assistance or lessons.

★ Festivals & Events

Squamish Valley Music Festival MUSIC
(www.squamishfestival.com; ⊙ Aug) If you're here in August, consider the giant Squamish Valley Music Festival, the region's biggest outdoor music event.

🛏 Sleeping & Eating

Alice Lake Provincial Park CAMPGROUND $
(☎ 800-689-9025; www.discovercamping.ca; Hwy 99; campsites from $30) This large, family-friendly campground, 13km north of Squamish, has more than 100 sites. There are two shower buildings with flush toilets, and campers often indulge in activities like swimming, hiking and biking (rentals available). Consider an interpretive ranger tour through the woods (July and August only). Reserve far ahead – this is one of BC's most popular campgrounds.

Howe Sound Inn & Brewing Company INN $$
(☎ 604-892-2603; www.howesound.com; 37801 Cleveland Ave; d from $99; ☎ ☎) Quality rustic is the approach at this comfortable sleepover: rooms are warm and inviting with plenty of woodsy touches. There's an outdoor climbing wall where you can train for your attempt on the nearby Stawamus Chief and a sauna for recovering afterwards. The downstairs brewpub serves some of BC's best house-made beers – guests can request free brewery tours.

Even if you're not staying, it's worth stopping at the restaurant here for great pub grub with a gourmet twist.

Sunflower Bakery Cafe CAFE $
(www.sunflowerbakerycafe.com; 38086 Cleveland Ave; mains $5-9; ⊙ 7:30am-5:30pm Mon-Sat) Just look for the bright yellow exterior and then nip inside for hearty, handmade lunches, often of the organic or vegetarian variety. Soups and sandwiches abound but the quiches are recommended if you fancy a change. On the way out, fill your car with chunky cakes and bulging fruit pies to keep you going until Whistler.

Galileo Coffee COFFEE $
(www.galileocoffee.com; 173 Hwy 99; baked goods $3-5; ⊙ 7am-3pm) Across from the entrance

to Britannia Mine Museum, Galileo Coffee is everyone's fave fuel-up spot en route to Whistler.

❶ Information

Head to the slick visitors center, **Squamish Adventure Centre** (☑ 604-815-4994, 866-333-2010; www.tourismsquamish.com; 38551 Loggers Lane; ⊗ 8am-8pm), to see what's on offer. It has lots of good info on area hiking and biking trails.

❶ Getting There & Away

Greyhound Canada (www.greyhound.ca) buses arrive in Squamish from Vancouver (from $10, 80 minutes, six daily) and Whistler (from $7, 55 minutes, five daily). Slightly more salubrious **Pacific Coach Lines** (www.pacificcoach.com) buses also arrive here from downtown Vancouver ($49, 70 minutes, five daily).

Garibaldi Provincial Park

Visiting outdoors types should make a bee-line for the 1950-sq-km **Garibaldi Provincial Park** (www.bcparks.ca), justly renowned for hiking trails colored by diverse flora, abundant wildlife and panoramic wilderness vistas. Summer hikers seem magnetically drawn here but the trails also double as cross-country ski routes in winter. There are five main trail areas – directions to each are marked by the blue-and-white signs you'll see off Hwy 99.

Among the park's most popular trails, the **Cheakamus Lake hike** (3km) is relatively easy with minimal elevation. The **Elfin Lakes trail** (11km) is a lovely, relatively easy day hike. The **Garibaldi Lake hike** (9km) is an outstanding introduction to 'Beautiful BC' wilderness, fusing scenic alpine meadows and breathtaking mountain vistas.

Brandywine Falls Provincial Park

A few kilometers north of Squamish and adjacent to Hwy 99, this tree-lined 143-hectare **park** (www.bcparks.ca) is centered on a spectacular 70m waterfall. A short stroll through the forest leads to a leg-jellying platform overlooking the top of the falls, where water drops suddenly out of the trees like from a giant faucet. There are also great vistas over Daisy Lake and the mountains of Garibaldi Provincial Park. A 7km looped trail leads further through the dense forest and ancient lava beds to Cal-Cheak Suspension Bridge.

WHISTLER

POP 10,600

Named for the furry marmots that populate the area and whistle like deflating balloons, this gabled alpine village – and 2010 Olympic and Paralympic Winter Games venue – is one of the world's most popular ski resorts. Nestled in the shade of the formidable Whistler and Blackcomb Mountains, the wintertime village has a frosted, Christmas-card look. But summer is now even more popular, with Vancouverites and visitors lured to the region's natural charms by everything from mountain biking to scream-triggering zip-line runs.

There are several neighborhoods and smaller enclaves, including Function Junction, but Whistler Village is the key hub for hotels, restaurants and shops. You'll find humbler B&B-type accommodations in the quieter Village North, while the Upper Village is home to some swanky hotels, clustered around the Blackcomb base. Don't be surprised if you get lost when you're wandering around on foot: Whistler is a bit of labyrinth until you get used to it.

⦿ Sights

Squamish Lil'wat Cultural Centre MUSEUM
(www.slcc.ca; 4584 Blackcomb Way; adult/child $18/8; ⊗ 9:30am-5pm) ⊘ This handsome, wood-beamed facility showcases two quite different First Nations groups – one coastal and one interior based. Take a tour for the vital context behind the museum-like exhibits, including four newly carved totem poles and a new upstairs gallery that includes a 1200-year-old ceremonial bowl. Ask about the summer barbecue dinners ($58) or nip into the downstairs cafe for delicious venison chili with traditional bannock.

Whistler Museum MUSEUM
(www.whistlermuseum.org; 4333 Main St; adult/child $7.50/4; ⊗ 11am-5pm) Tracing Whistler's development from wilderness outpost to Olympic resort, quirky exhibits include a stuffed hoary marmot, a toilet-seat sailing trophy and a 2010 Olympic torch you can hold. A new permanent exhibit on skiing history was also being developed on our visit. Check ahead for events – October's adult Lego party is a must – and consider their

Whistler

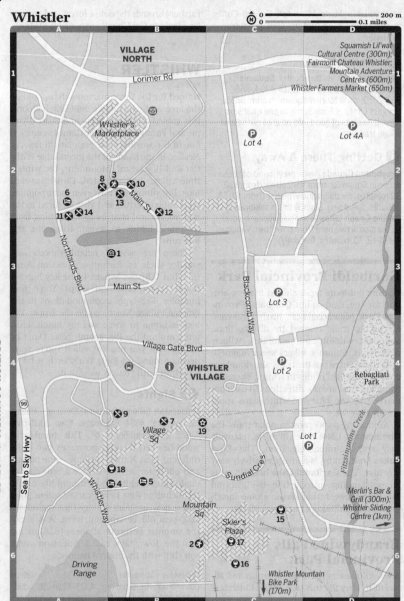

excellent by-donation village tours (held 1pm daily, from June to August).

Whistler Farmers Market   MARKET
(www.whistlerfarmersmarket.org; Upper Village; ⊙11am-4pm Sun Jun-Oct) If you're here in summer, head to the Upper Village and the plaza in front of the Fairmont Chateau Whistler for the lively Whistler Farmers Market, where you can peruse more than 50 tent-topped stands hawking everything from arts and crafts to stuff-your-face sea-

Whistler

sonal fruits and bakery treats. A Whistler summer highlight, arrive early for the best selection of goodies.

Whistler Sliding Centre   ADVENTURE SPORTS
(www.whistlerslidingcentre.com; 4910 Glacier Lane; ⊙10am-5pm Dec-Mar) Perched just above the village on Blackcomb, Whistler Sliding Centre hosted 2010's Olympic bobsled, luge and skeleton events and is now open to the public. You can wander exhibits, check out video footage from the track and take a self-guided tour. True sports fans should also consider trying bobsled and skeleton: gear, training and runs costs $159.

🏃 Activities

Skiing & Snowboarding
Comprising 37 lifts and crisscrossed with over 200 runs, the **Whistler-Blackcomb** (www.whistlerblackcomb.com; 1-day winter lift ticket adult/child $98/52) sister mountains were physically linked for the first time when the resort's mammoth 4.4km Peak 2 Peak gondola opened in 2009. It takes 11 minutes to shuttle wide-eyed powder hogs between the two high alpine areas, so you can hit the slopes on both mountains on the same day. More than half the runs are aimed at intermediate-level skiers.

The winter season kicks off here in late November and typically runs to April on Whistler and June on Blackcomb; December to February is the peak. If you want to emulate your fave Olympic ski heroes, Whistler Creekside was the setting for the downhill skiing events at the 2010 Games.

You can beat the crowds with an early morning Fresh Tracks ticket ($18) which must be bought in advance at Whistler Vil-

lage Gondola Guest Relations. With your regular lift ticket, it gets you an extra hour on the slopes and the ticket includes breakfast at the Roundhouse Lodge up top. Night owls might prefer the evening Night Moves program, operated via Blackcomb's Magic Chair lift after 5pm.

Snowboard fans should also check out the freestyle terrain parks, mostly located on Blackcomb, including the Snow Cross and the Big Easy Terrain Garden. There's also the popular Habitat Terrain Park on Whistler.

If you didn't bring your own gear, **Mountain Adventure Centres** (☎800-766-0449, 604-967-8950; www.whistlerblackcomb.com/rentals; 4599 Chateau Blvd) has several equipment rental outlets around town. It offers online reservations – choose your favorite gear before you arrive – as well as lessons for ski and snowboard first timers.

Cross-Country Skiing & Snowshoeing
A pleasant stroll or free shuttle bus away from the village, Lost Lake is a hub of wooded cross-country ski trails, suitable for novices and experts alike. Around 4km of the trail is lit for nighttime skiing until 10pm and there's a handy 'warming hut' providing lessons and equipment rentals. Snowshoers are also well served in this area: you can stomp off on your own on 10km of trails or rent equipment and guides.

The **Whistler Olympic Park** (www.whistlerolympicpark.com; 5 Callaghan Valley Rd, Callaghan Valley) is 16km southwest of the village via Hwy 99. It hosted several 2010 Olympic events and is now a prime wilderness area for cross-country skiing and snowshoeing, plus summertime bike tours.

BRITISH COLUMBIA WHISTLER

FUNCTION JUNCTION

Take bus number 1 southbound from the village and within 20 minutes you'll be in the heart of the locals' fave neighborhood. **Function Junction** started life as a hidden-among-the-trees area where industrial businesses carried on without affecting the Christmas card visuals of the village. But things have changed in recent years and this area now resembles the early days of Vancouver's Granville Island, its industrial units now slowly colonized by galleries and cafes. It's ideal for an afternoon of leisurely browsing, especially if you plan to dine. The are a couple of streets to explore, but the best is **Millar Creek Rd**.

Start with a late breakfast at **Wild Wood Cafe** (www.wildwoodrestaurants.ca; 1085 Millar Creek Rd; mains $6-12; ⊙6:30am-2pm Mon-Thu, to 3pm Fri & Sat, 9am-3pm Sun; 🐾), a folkie, ever-friendly neighborhood haunt where the eggs Benedict is recommend; they also chef up great burgers if it's lunchtime. Then wander past the yarn-bombed trees en route to **White Dog Whistler Studio Gallery** (www.whitedogwhistler.com; 1074 Millar Creek Rd; ⊙11am-6pm). Luna, the white dog in question, will be waiting to welcome you at the door of this smashing gallery where artist Penny Eder works. As well as her own work, the snob-free spot showcases the eclectic creations of dozens of local artists: look out for pottery, paintings and a glass kaleidoscope or two and ask Eder about her guided village art tours – also check to see whether one of her regular workshops is running if you fancy being creative.

If you need inspiration first, nip across the street to **Whistler Brewing Company** (www.whistlerbeer.com; 1045 Millar Creek Rd; tours $13.95; ⊙1-8pm Mon-Thu, to 10pm Fri, noon-7pm Sat & Sun). The area's very own beer maker is responsible for challenging the choke hold of factory-made suds at bars in the village. You can take a tour of the facilities and try a few brews in the taproom – with any luck, the sought-after winter-only Chestnut Ale will be available. Finally, sober up with a coffee and some of Whistler's best bakery treats at nearby **Purebread** (www.purebread.ca; 1040 Millar Creek Rd; baked goods $3-5; ⊙9am-5pm), where pudgie pies and and lemon sugar buns are essential. There are lots of nearby hiking routes if you suddenly need to work off 1000 calories.

Mountain Biking

Taking over the melted ski slopes in summer and accessed via the lift at the village's south end, **Whistler Mountain Bike Park** (http://bike.whistlerblackcomb.com; 1-day pass adult/child $53/31; ⊙May-Oct) offers barreling downhill runs and an orgy of jumps, beams and bridges twisting through 200km of well-maintained forested trails. You don't have to be a bike courier to stand the knee-buckling pace: easier routes are marked in green, while blue intermediate trails and black-diamond advanced paths are offered if you want to **Crank It Up** – the name of one of the park's most popular routes. Those with calves of steel should also hit the spectacular **Top of the World Trail**.

Outside the park area, winding trails around the region include the gentle **Valley Trail**, an easy 14km loop that encircles the village and its lake, meadow and mountain-château surroundings – recommended for first timers.

Hiking

With more than 40km of flower-and-forest alpine trails, most accessed via the Whistler Village Gondola, the region is ideal for those who like nature of the strollable variety. Favorite routes include the **High Note Trail** (8km), which traverses pristine meadows and has stunning views of the blue-green waters of Cheakamus Lake. Route maps are available at the visitors center. Guided hikes are also offered by the friendly folk at **Whistler Alpine Guides Bureau** (📞604-938-9242; www.whistlerguides.com; 207B, 4368 Main St; adult/child from $79/59), who can also help with rock-climbing and rap-jumping excursions.

Rafting

Tumbling waterfalls, dense forest and a menagerie of wildlife are some of what you might see as you lurch along the Elaho or Squamish Rivers on an adrenalin-charged half- or full-day rafting trip. **Wedge Rafting** (📞604-932-7171, 888-932-5899; www.wedge-rafting.com; 4293 Mountain Sq; tours adult/child

$99/69) offers paddle-like-crazy-or-you'll-never-make-it excursions, plus more gentle jaunts for the less energetic.

✦ Festivals & Events

Winterpride
COMMUNITY
(www.gaywhistler.com; ☉ early Feb) A week of gay-friendly snow action and late-night partying.

World Ski & Snowboard Festival
SKIING
(www.wssf.com; ☉ mid-Apr) A nine-day showcase of pro ski and snowboard competitions, plus partying.

Crankworx
MOUNTAIN BIKING
(www.crankworx.com; ☉ mid-Aug) An adrenalin-filled celebration of bike stunts, speed contests and mud-splattered shenanigans.

Cornucopia
FOOD & WINE
(www.whistlercornucopia.com; ☉ Nov) Bacchanalian food and wine fest crammed with parties.

Whistler Film Festival
FILM
(www.whistlerfilmfestival.com; ☉ Dec) Four days of Canadian and independent movie screenings, plus industry schmoozing.

🛏 Sleeping

Winter, especially December and January, is the peak for prices, but last-minute deals can still be had if you're planning an impromptu overnight from Vancouver – check the website of **Tourism Whistler** (www.whistler.com) for room sales and packages. Most hotels extort parking fees of up to $40 daily and some also slap on resort fees of up to $25 daily, so confirm these before you book.

★ HI Whistler Hostel
HOSTEL $
(☑ 866-762-4122, 604-962-0025; www.hihostels. ca; 1035 Legacy Way; dm/r $36/95; @ 🖱) Built as athlete accommodation for the 2010 Winter Olympics, this sparkling hostel is 7km south of the village near Function Junction. Transit buses to/from town stop right outside. Book ahead for private rooms (with en-suite bathrooms and TVs) or save by staying in a small dorm. Eschewing the sometimes institutionalized HI hostel feel, this one has IKEA-style furnishings, art-lined walls and a licensed cafe. There's also a great TV room for rainy-day hunkering.
If it's fine, hit the nearby biking and hiking trails or barbecue on one of the two mountain-view decks. When it's time to hit the

village, the bus will have you there in around 15 minutes.

Riverside Resort
CAMPGROUND, CABINS $$
(☑ 604-905-5533; www.riversidewhistler.com; 8018 Mons Rd; campsites/yurts/cabins $35/89/157; 🖱) Beloved of in-the-know BC residents and just a few minutes past Whistler on Hwy 99, this facility-packed, family-friendly campground has elevated itself in recent years by adding cozy cabin and yurt options. The yurts, with basic furnishings and electricity, and bedding provided, are especially recommended. The resort's on-site Junction Café serves great breakfasts.

Adara Hotel
HOTEL $$
(☑ 604-905-4009, 866-502-3272; www.adarahotel. com; 4122 Village Green; r from $149; ❄ 🖱 🖱) Unlike all those lodges now claiming to be boutique hotels, the sophisticated and centrally located Adara is the real deal. Lined with designer details, including fake antler horns in the lobby, accommodations have spa-like bathrooms and fireplaces that look like TVs. Despite the ultra-cool aesthetics, service is warm and relaxed. Check ahead for the popular summertime bike packages.

Crystal Lodge & Suites
HOTEL $$
(☑ 800-667-3363, 604-932-2221; www.crystal-lodge.com; 4154 Village Green; d/ste from $130/175; ❄ 🖱 🖱) Not all rooms are created equal at the Crystal, forged from the fusion of two quite different hotel towers. Cheaper rooms in the South Tower are standard style – baths and fridges are the highlight – but those in the Lodge Wing match the handsome rock-and-beam lobby, complete with small balconies. Both share excellent proximity to restaurants and ski lifts.

Chalet Luise B&B Inn
B&B $$
(☑ 800-665-1998, 604-932-4187; www.chaletluise. com; 7461 Ambassador Cres; d from $125; 🖱) A five-minute trail walk from the village, this Bavarian-look pension has eight bright and sunny rooms – think pine furnishings and crisp white duvets – and a flower garden that's ideal for a spot of evening wine quaffing. Or you can just hop in the hot tub and dream about the large buffet breakfast coming your way in the morning. Free parking.

Edgewater Lodge
HOTEL $$$
(☑ 604-932-0688, 888-870-9065; www.edgewater-lodge.com; 8020 Alpine Way; d incl breakfast from $189; 🖱 🖱) A few minutes' drive past Whistler on Hwy 99, this 12-room waterside lodge

is a nature lover's idyll and has a celebrated on-site restaurant. Each room overlooks the glassy waters of Green Lake through a large picture window – sit in your window alcove and watch the ospreys or hit the surface with a kayak rental. Rates include parking.

Pinnacle Hotel Whistler   HOTEL $$

(✆888-999-8986, 604-938-3218; www.whistler-pinnacle.com; 4319 Main St; d from $159; 🛜☀🐕) Just across the street from the museum, this friendly, well-established, adult-oriented lodge has the perfect extra in almost every room: a large jetted soaker tub that dominates proceedings. Balconies and full kitchens are also de rigueur and there's an on-site restaurant if it's too cold to stray far from your room.

Nita Lake Lodge   HOTEL $$$

(✆604-966-5700, 888-755-6482; www.nita-lakelodge.com; 2135 Lake Placid Rd; d from $199; 🛜🐕) Adjoining Creekside railway station – very handy if you're coming up on the **Rocky Mountaineer train** (www.rockymountaineer.com; tickets from $129; ⊙May to mid-Oct) – this swanky timber-framed lodge is perfect for a pampering retreat. Hugging the lakeside, the chic but cozy rooms feature individual patios, rock fireplaces and bathrooms with heated floors and large tubs; some also have handy kitchens. Creekside lifts are a walkable few minutes away.

There's an excellent on-site West Coast restaurant but a free shuttle can whisk you to the village if you want to dine further afield. Summer rates also include free-use bikes and fishing rods.

Fairmont Chateau Whistler   HOTEL $$$

(✆800-606-8244, 604-938-8000; www.fairmont.com/whistler; 4599 Chateau Blvd; d from $289; ❄🛜🐕) Combining dramatic baronial lodge lobbies and comfortably palatial rooms, many with mountain views, the Fairmont is a handsome reproduction of the high-end chain's Canadian 'castle hotels.' Close enough to enjoy ski-in, ski-out privileges on Blackcomb, it's tempting just to stay indoors trawling the lower-level shops and hopping from restaurant to bar. The heated outdoor pool is a highlight.

✕ Eating

★ Purebread   BAKERY $

(www.purebread.ca; 4338 Main St; baked goods $3-5; ⊙8:30am-7pm) When this Function Junction legend finally opened a village branch,

the locals came running, and they've been queuing ever since. They're here for the cornucopia of eye-roll-worthy bakery treats, including salted caramel bars, sour-cherry choc-chip cookies and the amazing Crack, a naughtily gooey shortbread cookie bar. There's savory here, too; go for the hearty homity pie.

Service is ever friendly and, if you arrive just after the early morning bakeathon, you can expect the aromas to lure you into at least tripling your purchase. Wash it all down with a large coffee from Portland-based Stumptown.

Gone Village Eatery   CAFE $

(www.gonevillageeatery.com; 4205 Village Sq; mains $6-12; ⊙6:30am-9pm; 🛜) Aim for the only booth at this well-hidden locals' fave and tuck into a wide range of hearty, good-value comfort grub of the chili, chicken-curry and steak-and-potatoes variety. This is where many fuel up for a calorie-burning day on the slopes and have a Mars-bar coffee when they return. There are also internet terminals ($1 per 10 minutes).

Mount Currie Coffee Co   CAFE $

(www.mountcurriecoffee.com; 4369 Main St; ⊙6:30am-5:30pm) A Pemberton fave recently opened this toe-hold in the village. Though off the beaten path, this coffee nook is worth searching out for its perfectly prepped Intelligentsia java. Extras include hearty Pemberton beef wraps and, when you've reached your Americano limit, 'green machine smoothies.' Consider a mason-jar travel mug as a cool souvenir. Follow Main St and you'll soon find it.

Splitz Grill   BURGERS $

(www.splitzgrill.com; 4369 Main St; mains $9-13; ⊙11am-8pm Mon-Thu & Sun, to 9pm Fri & Sat) Whistler's best burgers are served up at this unassuming storefront, which opens onto a surprisingly large seating area inside, plus a hidden tree-framed patio. The hand-rolled cannonballs of meat make for tasty burgers, served with perfect crunchy fries, that are far from regular fast food. Buffalo, salmon and turkey join the classic beef patties, but the juicy Salt Spring lamb burger is recommended.

★ Rimrock Cafe   WEST COAST $$

(✆604-932-5565; http://rimrockcafe.com; 2117 Whistler Rd; mains $16-28; ⊙5:45-9:30pm) On the edge of Creekside and accessible just off Hwy 99, the menu at this locals' favorite includes highlights such as seared scallops, venison tenderloin and a recommended seafood trio of grilled prawns, ahi tuna and nut-crusted sablefish. All are served in an intimate room with two fireplaces and a large, flower-lined patio where you can laugh at the harried highway drivers zipping past.

Mexican Corner
MEXICAN $$

(http://themexicancorner.ca; 4340 Lorimer Rd; mains $14-22; ⊙11am-9:30pm) Bringing authentic Mexican dishes to Whistler for the first time, this chatty little corner spot is the real deal for fans of perfect, fresh-made taco, enchilada and quesadilla dishes. Go for the four-taco *pastor* plate (roasted pork tacos topped with a pineapple sliver), coupled with a pleasingly sour tamarind margarita. An additional larger location was being eyed during our visit.

Crêpe Montagne
FRENCH $$

(http://crepemontagne.com; 4368 Main St; mains $8-24; ⊙8am-10:30pm) This small, authentic and highly cozy *crêperie* – hence the French accents percolating among the staff – offers a bewildering array of sweet and savory buckwheat crepes with fillings including ham, brie, asparagus, banana, strawberries and more. Fondues are also available. A good breakfast spot, go the waffle route and you'll be perfectly set up for a calorie-burning day on the slopes.

Christine's Mountain Top Dining
WEST COAST $$

(☏604-938-7437; Rendezvous Lodge, Blackcomb Mountain; mains $12-22) The best of the handful of places to eat while you're enjoying a summertime summit stroll or winter ski day on the slopes at Blackcomb Mountain. Socked into the Rendezvous Lodge, try for a patio table with a view and tuck into a seasonal seafood grill or a lovely applewood-smoked-cheddar grilled-cheese sandwich. Reservations recommended.

Sachi Sushi
JAPANESE $$

(www.sachisushi.com; 106-4359 Main St; mains $8-22; ⊙5:30-10pm) Whistler's best sushi spot doesn't stop at California rolls. It serves everything from crispy popcorn shrimp to seafood salads and stomach-warming udon noodles – the tempura noodle bowl is best. This bright and breezy eatery is a relaxing après-ski hangout and is good for a glass of hot sake on a cold winter day.

Araxi Restaurant & Bar
WEST COAST $$$

(☏604-932-4540; www.araxi.com; 4222 Village Sq; mains $24-41; ⊙5-11pm daily, plus brunch 10am-2pm Sat & Sun) Whistler's best splurge restaurant, Araxi cooks up an inventive and exquisite Pacific Northwest menu and has charming and courteous service. Try the BC halibut and drain the 15,000-bottle wine selection but save room for a dessert: a regional cheese plate or the amazing Okanagan apple cheesecake...or both.

Drinking & Entertainment

Merlin's Bar & Grill
PUB

(4553 Blackcomb Way; ⊙11am-1am) The best of Whistler's cavernous ski pubs, this Upper Village local also looks the part: log-lined walls, ceiling-mounted lift cars, bra-draped moose head and a large slope-facing patio. Menus, mounted on snowboard tips, cover the pub-grub classics and, although the beer is mostly of the generic Kokanee-like variety, there are usually some tasty Whistler Brewing ales available. There is regular live music during peak season.

Dubh Linn Gate
PUB

(☏604-905-4047; www.dubhlinngate.com; 4320 Sundial Cres; ⊙8am-1am) Whistler's archetypal pub, this dark, wood-lined joint would feel just like an authentic Ireland watering hole if not for the obligatory heated patio. Tuck yourself into a shady corner table and revive your inner leprechaun with a stout – there's Guinness as well as Murphy's. Even better is the slightly pricey BC-craft-brew menu and regular live music, often of the trad Irish variety.

Garibaldi Lift Company
PUB

(4165 Springs Lane, Whistler Village Gondola; ⊙11am-1am) The closest bar to the slopes, you can smell the sweat of the skiers or mountain bikers as they hurtle past the patio at this cavernous bar that everyone calls the GLC. The furnishings have the scuffs and dings of a well-worn pub, but the best time to come is when DJs or bands turn the place into a clubbish mosh pit.

Longhorn Saloon & Grill
PUB

(www.longhornsaloon.ca; 4284 Mountain Sq; ⊙9am-1am) Across from lifts at the base of Whistler Mountain, the sprawling patio at this raucous joint sometimes threatens to take over the village. Popular with twenty-somethings, it's all about downing jugs of fizzy lager and eyeing up potential partners

WORTH A TRIP

DETOUR TO COWBOY COUNTRY

The next town north of Whistler on Hwy 99, **Pemberton** has a welcoming vibe and a distinctive provenance as a farming and cowboy region, which explains why its kitsch-cool mascot is a potato in a neckerchief called Potato Jack. But there's more to the region's top tubers than great fries.

Pemberton Distillery (www.pembertondistillery.ca; 1954 Venture Pl; ⊙ noon-6pm Wed-Sat) started making great artisan vodka from local potatoes several years back. The smooth, organic liquor was such a success that more booze was added to the roster and the company now also makes gin, apple brandy and one of BC's only absinthe concoctions. In total, they use up to 100,000lb of local spuds every year.

On our visit, the owners were close to bottling their first whiskey and were also planning to add beer to the lineup, made from their own-grown hops. A visit to the friendly little distillery, located on an unassuming industrial strip on the edge of town, includes a generous free sample or two at the **tasting bar**. The best time to visit is on Saturdays at 4pm (year-round) when $5 buys you a **guided tour** followed by some well-informed tastings. If you're suddenly inspired to take a bottle home, prices range from $24 to $58.

If you end up indulging a little too much and suddenly need something more substantial to ingest, don't leave town without visiting the locals' other fave hangout. The ever-animated **Pony** (☑ 604-894-5700; www.thepony.ca; 1392 Portage Rd; mains $10-22; ⊙ 8am-10pm)is the kind of bistro-style restaurant that effortlessly combines smiley service with excellent gourmet comfort nosh, from triple-decker shrimp clubs to perfect pizzas and heaping salads, plus a carefully curated craft-beer list. Aim for a patio table and, even better, drop by on Thursday evening for beer and pizza night: you'll likely meet every Pembertonian in the vicinity.

For more information on visiting Pemberton, head to www.tourismpembertonbc.com.

from your plastic lawn chair. The food is nothing special, but it's hard to beat the atmosphere on a hopping winter evening.

Moejoe's
CLUB

(www.moejoes.com; 4155 Golfer's Approach; ⊙ 9pm-2am Tue-Sun) Popular with the kind of under-30s that work in Whistler shops and coffeehouses, this is the best place in town if you like dancing yourself into a drooling heap. It's always crowded on Friday and Saturday nights but, if you want to mix it up with those locals, drop by on twice-a-month Wednesdays when Whistler workers roll in for free.

Village 8 Cinema
CINEMA

(www.village8cinema.com; 4295 Blackcomb Way) Shows first-run flicks in the heart of the village. Discounts on Tuesdays.

❶ Information

Pick up the weekly *Pique* or *Whistler Question* newspapers for local happenings.

Northlands Medical Clinic (☑ 604-932-8362; www.northlandsclinic.com; 4359 Main St; ⊙ 9am-5:30pm) Walk-in medical center.

Post Office (www.canadapost.ca; 4360 Lorimer Rd; ⊙ 8am-5pm Mon-Fri, to noon Sat)

Public Library (☑ 604-935-8433; www.whistlerlibrary.ca; 4329 Main St; ⊙ 11am-7pm Mon-Thu, to 5pm Fri-Sun; 🛜) Free 24-hour wi-fi, including around the building, outside opening hours. Also has internet-access computers (free for up to one hour per person per day).

Whistler Visitors Centre (☑ 800-944-7853, 604-935-3357; www.whistler.com; 4230 Gateway Dr; ⊙ 8am-10pm) Flyer-lined visitors center with friendly staff.

Whistler Inside Blog (www.whistler.com/blog)

Whistler is Awesome (www.whistlerisawesome.com)

❶ Getting There & Around

While most visitors arrive by car from Vancouver via Hwy 99, **Greyhound Canada** (www.greyhound.ca) buses also service the route, arriving at Creekside and Whistler Village from the city (from $14, two to 2½ hours, six daily). Most buses are equipped with free wi-fi.

Pacific Coach Lines (www.pacificcoach.com) services also arrive from Vancouver (from $49, two hours, five daily) and Vancouver International Airport and drop off at Whistler hotels. **Snowbus** (www.snowbus.com) operates a winter-only service from Vancouver (adult/child $38/22, two to three hours, two to three daily).

Train spotters can trundle into town on Rocky Mountaineer Vacations' **Whistler Sea to Sky**

Climb (www.rockymountaineer.com), which winds along a picturesque coastal route from North Vancouver (from $169, three hours, one daily May to mid-October).

Whistler's **WAVE** (www.busonline.ca) public buses (adult/child/one-day pass $2.50/2/7) are equipped with ski and bike racks. In summer, there's a free service from the village to Lost Lake.

SUNSHINE COAST

Stretching 139km along the water from Langdale to Lund, the Sunshine Coast – separated from the Lower Mainland by the Coast Mountains and the Strait of Georgia – has an independent, island-like mentality that belies the fact it's only a 40-minute ferry ride from Horseshoe Bay. Hwy 101 links key communities Gibsons, Sechelt and Powell River, plus tiny Roberts Creek, and it's an easy and convivial region to explore. There are also plenty of activities to keep things lively: think ocean kayaking and spectacular wilderness hiking with a side order of artists' studios. Peruse the website of **Sunshine Coast Tourism** (www.sunshinecoastcanada. com) for information and get a copy of the *Recreation Map & Activity Guide* ($3) – available in upper- and lower-region versions – for outdoorsy suggestions throughout the area.

ℹ Getting There & Around

BC Ferries (www.bcferries.com) Services arrive at Langdale, 6km northeast of Gibsons, from West Vancouver's Horseshoe Bay (passenger/vehicle $14.55/49.05, 40 minutes, eight daily).

Sunshine Coast Transit System (www.busonline.ca; adult/child $2.25/1.75) Runs buses from the ferry terminal into Gibsons, Roberts Creek and Sechelt.

Malaspina Coach Lines (www.malaspina-coach.com) Buses arrive daily from Vancouver, via the ferry, in Gibsons ($35, two hours), Sechelt ($45, three hours) and Powell River ($66, five to six hours). Rates include ferry fares.

Harbour Air Seaplanes (www.harbour-air.com) Flies floatplanes from downtown Vancouver to Sechelt three times a day (from $78, 20 minutes).

Pacific Coastal Airlines (www.pacific-coastal. com) Flies into Powell River from the South Terminal of Vancouver International Airport up to five times daily (from $117, 35 minutes).

Gibsons

POP 4400

Your first port of call after docking in Langdale and driving or busing into town, the pretty waterfront strip here is called Gibsons Landing. A rainbow of painted wooden buildings overlooking the marina, it's famous across Canada as the setting for *The Beachcombers,* a TV show from the 1970s that fictionalized a town full of eccentrics. You can soak up the TV nostalgia with breakfast at the landmark **Molly's Reach** (www.mollysreach.ca; 647 School Rd; mains $8-19; ☺8am-9pm) restaurant.

Once you're fully fueled, putter around the rows of galleries and artisan stores, especially along Marine Dr and Molly's Lane. Be sure to drop into the **Gibsons Public Art Gallery** (www.gibsonspublicartgallery.ca; 431 Marine Dr; ☺11am-4pm Thu-Mon), where monthly exhibitions showcase local artists; check the website for show openings. As for activities, hit the water with a rental or guided tour via the friendly folks at **Sunshine Kayaking** (☑604-886-9790; www.sunshinekayaking.com; Molly's Lane; rentals 2/24hr $29/75; ☺hours vary, book ahead), whose guided sunset tours ($85) are recommended.

Your best bet for a sleepover is the lovely **Bonniebrook Lodge** (☑604-886-2887; www. bonniebrook.com; 1532 Ocean Beach Esplanade; d from $200; ☎✿), a historic wood-built inn overlooking a quiet waterfront stretch. The area also abounds with B&Bs, including the homely, family-friendly **Arcturus Retreat Bed & Breakfast** (☑877-856-1940, 604-886-1940; www.arcturusretreat.ca; 160 Pike Rd; d from $160; @☎), handily located just up the hill

---

SUNSHINE COAST GALLERY CRAWL

Pick up the free *Sunshine Coast Purple Banner* flyer from area visitors centers for the location of dozens of studios and galleries throughout the region. Many are open for drop-in visitors – look out for the purple flags along the road on your travels – and they're a great way to meet the locals and find unique souvenirs. For further information, see www.suncoastarts.com. And, if you're here in October, check out the weekend-long **Sunshine Coast Art Crawl** (www.sunshinecoastartcrawl.com).

from the ferry dock. They can also point you to the nearby **Sprockids Mountain Bike Park**. For other B&Bs in the vicinity, see www.gibsonsgetaways.com.

Gourmet seafood fans shouldn't miss **Smitty's Oyster House** (www.smittysoysterhouse.com; 643 School Rd; mains $9-23; ⊗noon-late Tue-Sat, to 8pm Sun), which faces the boat-bobbling marina, for perfect fresh-catch treats. Alternatively, amble along the pier at the nearby Government Dock and you'll find a local fave: the friendly, shack-like **Shed** (mains $6-12; ⊗11am-4pm & 6-8pm) serves tasty tacos and burritos, with ingredients of the fish variety sourced from nearby boats. Snag a seat alongside for a side order of mesmerizing waterfront views.

Drop by the **visitors center** (☑604-886-2374, 866-222-3806; www.gibsonschamber.com; 417 Marine Dr; ⊗9am-5pm Sat-Thu, to 7pm Fri) for more information and resources.

Roberts Creek

POP 3100

Just off Hwy 101 via Roberts Creek Rd, the funky 'downtown' here looks like a little hobbit community, if hobbits had gone through a hippie phase. Poke around the wood-built, shack-like stores and eateries and then tootle downhill onto **Roberts Creek Pier**, overlooking the Strait of Georgia. Backed by a large waterfront park, with a beach at low tide, it's an idyllic spot to watch the natural world float by.

The Sunshine Coast's best hostel, the effortlessly welcoming **Up the Creek Backpacker's B&B** (☑877-885-8100, 604-837-5943; www.upthecreek.ca; 1261 Roberts Creek Rd; dm/r $28/80; @⊙) has small dorms, one family-friendly private room and a recommended cozy cabin in the fruit-tree-lined garden. Organic breakfast costs $6 extra and there are free loaner bikes for exploring the many area trails. Transit buses from the Langdale ferry terminal stop nearby.

On hot days, pick up an icy treat at cute **Batchworks Sorbet** (www.batchworkssorbet.com; Gumboot Gardens; ⊗noon-5pm Thu & Fri, 11am-5pm Sat & Sun) or join the locals for coffee and baked goodies at the wood-floored **Gumboot Cafe** (1057 Roberts Creek Rd; mains $4-8; ⊗7am-5pm Mon-Fri, 8am-5pm Sat, 10am-4pm Sun), where the pizza slices are recommended. For heartier fare, the recently revamped **Gumboot Restaurant** (1041 Roberts Creek Rd; mains $11-18) is a great spot

to slide onto a veranda table, catch a live band most Wednesdays and indulge in locally sourced, West Coast dishes from lamb to seafood; check the chalkboard for daily specials.

Sechelt

POP 9900

The second-largest Sunshine Coast town, Sechelt isn't as funky as Gibsons or Powell River, but there are lots of outdoor activity options, plus some good spots to fuel up.

With a good kayak launch site and a sandy, stroll-worthy beach, the fir-and-cedar-forested **Porpoise Bay Provincial Park** (www.bcparks.ca) is 4km north of Sechelt along East Porpoise Bay Rd. There are trails throughout the park and a large **campground** (www.discovercamping.ca; campsites $25) with handy hot showers.

For visiting paddlers (and pedalers), **Pedals & Paddles** (☑604-885-6440; www.pedalspaddles.com; 7425 Sechelt Inlet Rd; rentals 2/24hr $32/80) organizes kayak rentals and can take you on tours of the inlet's wonderfully tranquil waters.

Alternatively, chat with local artists and growers at the summertime **Sechelt Farmers & Artisans Market** (www.secheltmarket.org; ⊗9am-2:30pm Sat Apr-Sep) on Cowrie St. There's also a night market nearby on Thursdays from June to August. If you have an artsy itch to scratch, check out mid-August's **Sunshine Coast Festival of the Written Arts** (www.writersfestival.ca).

If you like the idea of a secluded waterfront retreat, check out the two spacious suites and the cottage at **Beachside by the Bay** (☑604-741-0771; www.beachsidebythebay.com; 5005 Sunshine Coast Hwy; d $199-$239; ⊙). You'll be waking up to spectacular Davis Bay panoramas, while facilities include full kitchens, covered outdoor hot tub and a huge private beach deck where you can spend the evening barbecuing and watching passing eagles. Alternatively, drive along Hwy 101 past Sechelt to swanky **Rockwater Secret Cove Resort** (☑877-296-4593, 604-885-7038; www.rockwatersecretcoveresort.com; 5356 Ole's Cove Rd; r/cabin/ste/tent $209/209/249/419; ⊙⊠), where the highlight accommodations include luxury tent suites perched like nests on a steep cliff. For a wealth of area B&B options, visit www.bbsunshinecoast.com.

If it's time to eat, join the locals and dive into a fresh-baked maple cinnamon bun at ever-buzzing **Wheatberries Bakery** (www.wheatberriesbakery.com; 5500 Wharf St; baked goods from $2; ☉7am-5pm; 📶). Alternatively, go for a curry or pizza – yes, they've mastered both – at **Saffron** (www.saffronrestaurant.ca; 5755 Cowrie St; mains $11-18; ☉11:30am-9pm), a friendly but fiendishly well-hidden restaurant behind the Trail Bay Centre mall. Save time for the **Lighthouse Pub** (www.lighthousepub.ca; 5764 Wharf Rd; mains $12-22), a quality neighborhood haunt where you can eavesdrop on Sunshine Coast gossip while feasting on boat-bobbling waterfront views and hearty pub grub; fish and chips plus the incredible banana cheesecake churro are recommended.

For information, drop by the **Sechelt Visitors Centre** (📞877-885-1036, 604-885-1036; www.secheltvisitorcentre.com; 5790 Teredo St; ☉9am-5pm).

Powell River

POP 13,600

Founded as a paper-mill town more than a century ago, the largest Sunshine Coast community has been busily reinventing itself in recent years, luring many from Vancouver and beyond to move in and set up cool businesses. The result is an increasingly funky town – especially in the historic Townsite area – that's also a gateway to splendid outdoor activities.

Pick up a free flyer from the **visitors center** (📞877-817-8669, 604-485-4701; www.discoverpowellriver.com; 4670 Joyce Ave; ☉9am-6pm) and explore the Townsite's heritage buildings, many of them century-old Arts and Crafts constructions, on a self-guided stroll. Highlights include the **Henderson House**, now open to the public after a five-year renovation, and the lovely **Patricia Theatre** (www.patriciatheatre.com; 5848 Ash Ave), Canada's oldest continually operating cinema. Step inside for a chat with Ann the owner and she'll tell you some stories and let you snap shots of the art-painted interior. The **Townsite Heritage Society** (www.powellrivertownsite.com; 6211 Walnut Ave, Henderson House; $5; ☉tours 2pm Wed & 10am Sat Jul & Aug) runs summer guided tours of the neighborhood, starting at Henderson House.

End your exploration with a free tour at **Townsite Brewing** (www.townsitebrewing.com; 5824 Ash Ave; ☉11am-7pm daily, tours 3pm Thu & Sat), plus a $5 sampling of all the top tipples and seasonal specials. Zunga Golden Blonde

THE 'OTHER WEST COAST TRAIL'

Vancouver Island's West Coast Trail is so popular it's hard not to run into other hikers en route – that's if you can get one of the coveted daily access spots in the first place. But the Sunshine Coast offers its own under-the-radar version that many BC locals have only just started discovering. Running from Sarah Point to Saltery Bay, the 180km-long **Sunshine Coast Trail** is a wilderness paradise of ancient forests, stirring waterfronts and snow-capped vistas. Unlike the West Coast Trail, this one is free and reservations are not required – there are free-use sleeping huts dotted along the route. For more information, visit www.sunshinecoast-trail.com.

Ale is the top seller, but fans of the dark side will savor Pow Town Porter. If you're here on the third Friday of the month, look out for the ever-changing 'experimental cask.' If you need to blow away a few cobwebs the next morning, hit the water for a paddle with **Powell River Sea Kayak** (www.bcseakayak.com; 10676 Crowther Rd; 3/12hr rental $35/44).

When it's time to rest your weary noggin, it's hard to beat the highly welcoming **Old Courthouse Inn** (📞604-483-4000, 877-483-4777; www.oldcourthouseinn.ca; 6243 Walnut St; d from $89; 📶), a transformed, immaculately preserved historic court building where recent new owners have lined the rooms with period knickknacks and spruced things up with mod flourishes like a jazzy new restaurant, serving cooked breakfasts (included with rates), lunches and dinnertime tapas – aim for a summertime patio table.

Alternatively, drop in for tacos at the tiny, bright-painted **Costa del Sol** (www.costadelsolcuisine.com; 4578 Marine Ave; mains $9.50-14; ☉11:30am-9pm Sun, Mon, Wed & Thu, to 10pm Fri & Sat); the 'meaty maverick' is recommended. Or hang with the locals over fish and chips and a Townsite Brewing beer or three at the chatty **Hub** (www.thehub101.ca; 6275 Marine Ave; mains $11-15). For something fancier, try the **Alchemist Restaurant** (www.alchemistrestaurant.com; 4680 Marine Ave; mains $21-28; ☉from 5pm Tue-Sat), where local seasonal ingredients are fused with Mediterranean approaches to produce mouthwatering dishes.

Vancouver Island

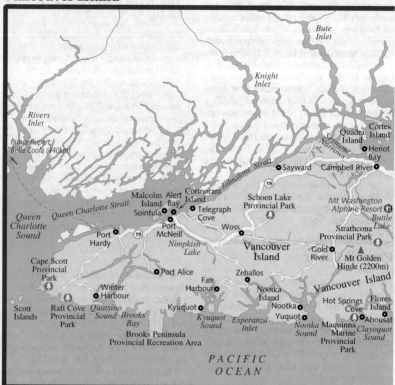

VANCOUVER ISLAND

The largest populated landmass between western North America and New Zealand – it's around 500km long and 100km wide – Vancouver Island is laced with colorful, often quirky communities, many founded on logging or fishing and featuring the word 'Port' in their name.

The locals are generally a friendly bunch, proud of their region and its distinct differences. Traveling around, you'll find a wide range of attractions, experiences and activities that feel many miles away from the bustle of mainland Vancouver. Which reminds us: if you want to make a good impression, don't mistakenly refer to the place as 'Victoria Island.'

While the history-wrapped BC capital Victoria is the first port of call for many, it should not be the only place you visit. Food and wine fans will enjoy weaving through the verdant Cowichan Valley farm region; those craving a laid-back, family-friendly enclave should hit the twin seaside towns of Parksville and Qualicum; outdoor-activity enthusiasts shouldn't miss the surf-loving west-coast area of Tofino and beyond; and those who fancy remote backcountry far from the madding crowds should make for the north, an undiscovered gem that's among BC's most rewarding wilderness areas.

ℹ Information

For an introduction to the island, contact **Tourism Vancouver Island** (☑250-754-3500; www.vancouverisland.travel) for listings and resources.

Victoria
POP 84,000

With a wider metro population approaching 360,000, this picture-postcard provincial capital was long-touted as North America's most English city. Thankfully, the tired theme-park

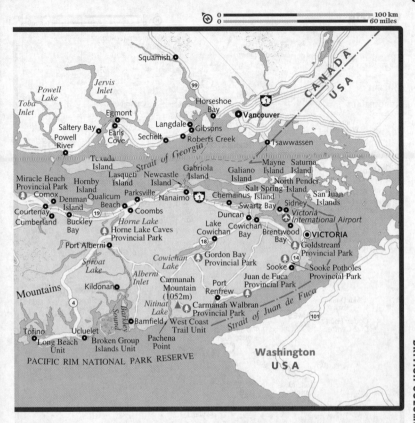

version of old-fashioned England has faded in recent years. Fueled by an increasingly younger demographic, a quiet revolution has seen lame tourist pubs, eateries and stores transformed into the kind of brightly painted bohemian shops, coffee bars and innovative restaurants that would make any city proud. It's worth seeking out these enclaves on foot, but activity fans should also hop on their bikes: Victoria has more cycle routes than any other Canadian city. Once you've finished pedaling, there's BC's best museum, a park fringed by a windswept seafront and outdoor activities from kayaking to whale watching.

◉ Sights

Royal BC Museum
MUSEUM

(Map p690; www.royalbcmuseum.bc.ca; 675 Belleville St; adult/child from $16/10; ⊙10am-5pm Sun-Wed, to 10pm Thu-Sat) Start in the natural-history gallery on your visit to the province's best museum. Fronted by a beady-eyed woolly

mammoth, it's lined with evocative dioramas – the elk peeking through trees is a favorite. Next, head up to the First Peoples exhibit with its fascinating mask gallery – look out for a ferret-faced white man. The highlight is the walk-through colonial street with its chatty Chinatown and detailed storefronts.

The museum hosts regular special exhibitions and also has a popular IMAX theater screening documentaries and Hollywood blockbusters.

Robert Bateman Centre
GALLERY

(Map p690; www.batemancentre.org; 470 Belleville St; adult/child $12.50/8.50; ⊙10am-6pm Sun-Wed, to 9pm Thu-Sat) Victoria's newest cultural attraction isn't just a gallery showcasing the photo-realistic works of Canada's most popular nature painter, it's also a testament to Bateman's commitment to environmental issues. Start with the five-minute intro movie, then move through a series of small exhibit areas with 160 achingly beautiful paintings and

Victoria

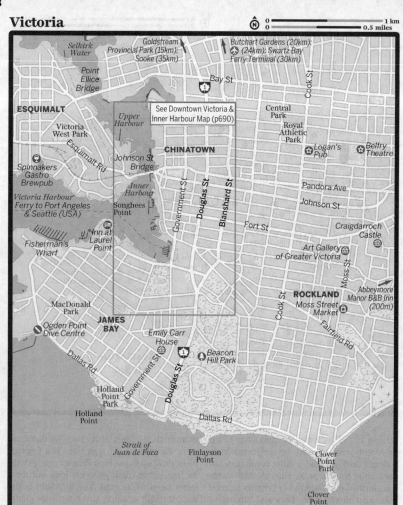

prints showing animals in nature from BC and beyond.

Use your smart phone or a loaner available at the front desk to scan QR codes near many works and you'll get the story behind them from the man himself. Better still, check the website ahead of your visit: Bateman lives on Salt Spring Island and gives talks and presentations here whenever possible; book ahead.

Parliament Buildings
HISTORIC BUILDING

(Map p690; www.leg.bc.ca; 501 Belleville St; ☺tours 9am-5pm) **FREE** Across from the museum,

this handsome confection of turrets, domes and stained glass is the province's working legislature and is open to history-loving visitors. Peek behind the facade on a colorful (and free) 30-minute tour led by costumed Victorians, then stop for lunch at the 'secret' politicians' restaurant. Return in the evening when the elegant exterior is illuminated like a Christmas tree.

Art Gallery of Greater Victoria
GALLERY

(Map p688; www.aggv.bc.ca; 1040 Moss St; adult/child $13/2.50; ☺10am-5pm Mon-Wed, Fri & Sat, to 9pm Thu, noon-5pm Sun) Head east of downtown on Fort St and follow the gallery street signs to one of Canada's best Emily Carr collections. Aside from Carr's swirling nature canvases, you'll find an ever-changing array of temporary exhibitions. Check online for events, including lectures, presentations and monthly late-night Urbanite socials, when artsy coolsters roll in to mingle. Admission is by donation on the first Tuesday of every month.

Craigdarroch Castle
MUSEUM

(Map p688; www.thecastle.ca; 1050 Joan Cres; adult/child $13.75/5; ⊙9am-7pm) If you're in this part of town checking out the gallery, don't miss this elegant turreted mansion a few minutes' walk away. A handsome, 39-room landmark built by a 19th-century coal baron with money to burn, it's dripping with period architecture and antique-packed rooms. Climb the tower's 87 steps, checking out the stained-glass en route, for views of the snowcapped Olympic Mountains.

Victoria Bug Zoo
ZOO

(Map p690; www.bugzoo.com; 631 Courtney St; adult/child $10/7; ⊙10:30am-5:30pm Mon-Sat, 11am-5pm Sun) The most fun any kid can have in Victoria without realizing it's educational, step inside the brightly painted main room for a cornucopia of show-and-tell insect encounters. The excellent young guides talk about critters such as frog beetles, dragon-headed crickets and the disturbingly large three-horned scarab beetles. There are plenty of chances to snap shots of your kids handling the goods (under supervision).

Beacon Hill Park
PARK

(Map p688; www.beaconhillpark.ca; Douglas St) Fringed by crashing ocean, this waterfront park is ideal for feeling the wind in your hair – check out the windswept trees along the cliff top. You'll also find a gigantic totem pole, Victorian cricket pitch and a marker for Mile 0 of Hwy 1, alongside a statue of Canadian legend Terry Fox. If you're here with kids, consider the popular **children's farm** as well; see www.beaconhillchildrensfarm.ca.

Emily Carr House
MUSEUM

(Map p688; www.emilycarr.com; 207 Government St; adult/child $6.75/4.50; ⊙11am-4pm Tue-Sat May-Sep) The birthplace of BC's best-known painter, this bright-yellow gingerbread-style house has plenty of period rooms, plus displays on the artist's life and work. There's an ever-changing array of local contemporary works on display, but head to the Art Gallery of Greater Victoria if you want to see more of

Carr's paintings. On your visit here, look out for the friendly house cats.

🏃 Activities

Whale-watching

Raincoat-clad tourists head out by the boatload throughout the May-to-October viewing season. The whales don't always show, so most excursions also visit the local haunts of lolling sea lions and portly elephant seals.

Prince of Whales
BOAT TOUR

(Map p690; ☎888-383-4884, 250-383-4884; www.princeofwhales.com; 812 Wharf St; adult/child from $110/85) Long-established local operator.

Springtide Charters
BOAT TOUR

(Map p690; ☎800-470-3474, 250-384-4444; www.springtidecharters.com; 1119 Wharf St; adult/child from $105/75) Popular local operator.

Water Sports

Paddling around the coastline is the perfect way to see this region, especially if you spot soaring eagles and starfish-studded beaches. If you like what you see on the surface, consider a dive below.

Ocean River Adventures
KAYAKING

(Map p690; ☎800-909-4233, 250-381-4233; www.oceanriver.com; 1824 Store St; rental per 2hr $40, tours from $75; ⊙9:30am-6pm Mon-Wed & Sat, to 8pm Thu & Fri, 10am-5pm Sun) Rentals and popular three-hour harbor tours.

Ogden Point Dive Centre
DIVING

(Map p688; ☎250-380-9119; www.divevictoria.com; 199 Dallas Rd; ⊙9am-6pm) Dive courses

Downtown Victoria & Inner Harbour

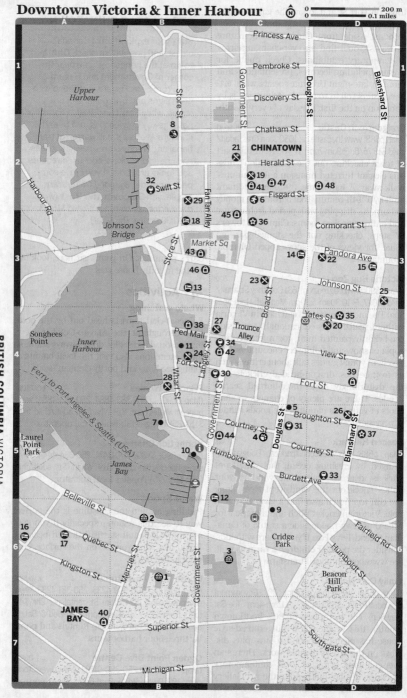

Downtown Victoria & Inner Harbour

and rentals a few minutes from the Inner Harbour.

🚶 Tours

Architectural Institute of BC   WALKING TOUR
(Map p690; ☑800-667-0753, ext 333, 604-683-8588; www.aibc.ca; 1001 Douglas St; tours $10; ◔10am & 1pm Tue-Sun Jul & Aug) Six great-value, building-themed walking tours, covering angles from art deco to ecclesiastical.

Harbour Air   SCENIC FLIGHTS
(Map p690; ☑800-665-0212, 250-385-9131; www.harbour-air.com; tours from adult/child $104/52) For a bird's-eye Victoria view, these breathtaking floatplane tours from the Inner Harbour are fab, especially when they dive-bomb the water on landing.

Pedaler   BICYCLE TOUR
(Map p690; ☑778-265-7433; www.thepedaler.ca; 719 Douglas St; tours from $59; ◔9am-6pm) Guided bike tours weave around local breweries, plus there are history-themed and coffee-and-cake tour alternatives.

CVS Cruise Victoria   BUS TOUR
(Map p690; ☑877-578-5552, 250-386-8652; www.cvscruisevictoria.com; 721 Government St; tours from adult/child $30/16) With its fleet of bio-diesel coaches, CVS offers a hop-on, hop-off city tour, plus shuttles to Butchart Gardens.

🎉 Festivals & Events

Victoria Tea Festival   FOOD
(www.victoriateafestival.com; ◔Feb) Huge show case of tea and tea-making paraphenalia in North America's cuppa-loving capital.

Victoria Day Parade   PARADE
(◔mid-May) Street fiesta, with dancers, marching bands and 50,000-plus spectators.

Victoria International Buskers Festival   PERFORMING ARTS
(www.victoriabuskers.com; ◔mid-Jul) Ten days of street performing action from local and international artists.

Victoria Ska Fest   MUSIC

(www.victoriaskafest.ca; ☉mid-Jul) Canada's largest skank-filled music festival.

Victoria International JazzFest   JAZZ

(www.jazzvictoria.ca; ☉late Jun) Toe-tapping jazz shows over 10 days.

Victoria Fringe Theater Festival   THEATER

(www.victoriafringe.com; ☉late Aug) Two weeks of quirky short plays and stand-up performances throughout the city.

Rifflandia   MUSIC

(www.rifflandia.com; ☉Sep) Victoria's coolest music festival sees indie bands playing around the city.

🛏 Sleeping

From heritage B&Bs to cool boutiques and swanky high-end sleepovers, Victoria is stuffed with accommodation for all budgets. Off-season sees great deals. Tourism Victoria's **room reservation service** (☎800-663-3883, 250-953-2033; www.tourismvictoria.com/hotels) can show you what's available.

HI Victoria Hostel   HOSTEL $

(Map p690; ☎888-883-0099, 250-385-4511; www.hihostels.ca; 516 Yates St; dm/d $30.80/88; @🛜) A quiet downtown hostel with two large single-sex dorms, three small coeds and a couple of private rooms. There are also movie nights, a large games room and a book-lined reading area to keep you occupied. Free city tours are also scheduled.

Ocean Island Inn   HOSTEL $

(Map p690; ☎888-888-4180, 250-385-1788; www.oceanisland.com; 791 Pandora Ave; dm/s/d from $28/40/46; @🛜) This funky, multicolored sleepover is a labyrinth of small dorms and private rooms, some without windows. There's a large communal kitchen on the ground floor and a licensed lounge for breakfast, quiz nights and live music. They also have private, self-catering suites across town in a James Bay character house from $121; see www.oisuites.com for information.

Hotel Rialto   HOTEL $$

(Map p690; ☎250-383-4157; www.hotelrialto.ca; 653 Pandora Ave; d from $179; 🛜) Completely refurbished from the faded former budget hotel it once was, the Rialto is a well-located downtown option in an attractive century-old heritage building. Each of the mod-decorated rooms has a fridge, microwave and flatscreen TV and some have tubs as well as showers. The lobby's tapas lounge is popular, whether or not you're staying here. Highly solicitous staff.

Oswego Hotel   HOTEL $$$

(Map p690; ☎250-294-7500, 877-767-9346; www.oswegovictoria.com; 500 Oswego St; d $205; 🛜🐾) Well hidden on a residential side street a short stroll from the Inner Harbour, this contemporary boutique sleepover is an in-the-know favorite. Rooms come with granite floors, cedar beams and, in most units, small balconies. All have kitchens – think stainless steel – and deep baths, making them more like apartments than hotel rooms. Cleverly, the smaller studio rooms have space-saving high-end Murphy beds.

Inn at Laurel Point   HOTEL $$

(Map p688; ☎800-663-7667, 250-386-8721; www.laurelpoint.com; 680 Montreal St; d from $169; ❄@🛜🏊🐾) Tucked along the Inner Harbour a short seaside stroll from the downtown action, this friendly, art-lined and ever-comfortable sleepover is all about the views across the waterfront. Spacious rooms come with private balconies for drinking in the mesmerizing sunsets. Still owned by a local family, there's a resort-like level of calm relaxation.

Abbeymoore Manor B&B Inn   B&B $$$

(Off Map p688; ☎888-801-1811, 250-370-1470; www.abbeymoore.com; 1470 Rockland Ave; d from $199; 🛜) A romantic 1912 Arts and Crafts mansion, Abbeymoore's handsome colonial exterior hides seven antique-lined rooms furnished with Victorian knickknacks. Some units have kitchens and jetted tubs and the hearty breakfast will fuel you up for a day of exploring: Craigdarroch Castle and the Art Gallery of Greater Victoria are nearby.

Royal Scot Hotel & Suites   HOTEL

(Map p690; ☎250-388-5463, 800-663-7515; www.royalscot.com; 425 Quebec St; d from $175; 🛜🏊🐾) The best of several midrange options crowding the banks of the Inner Harbour near the Parliament Buildings, rooms at the Royal Scot are spotlessly maintained. Expect a friendly welcome and lots of cruise-ship seniors in the lobby. Rooms come in a variety of configurations, some with full kitchens. A free local shuttle service is available.

Fairmont Empress Hotel   HOTEL $$$

(Map p690; ☎866-540-4429, 250-384-8111; www.fairmont.com/empress; 721 Government St; d $250; ❄@🛜🏊) Rooms at this ivy-covered, century-old Inner Harbour landmark are elegant but conservative and some are quite small, but the overall effect is grand and classy, from the raj-style curry and cocktail restaurant to the sumptuous high tea sipped while overlooking the waterfront. Even if you don't stay, make sure you stroll through and soak up the Old World charm.

Swans Suite Hotel
HOTEL $$$

(Map p690; ☑ 800-668-7926, 250-361-3310; www. swanshotel.com; 506 Pandora Ave; d incl breakfast $185; ☎ ⊛) This former brick-built warehouse has been transformed into an art-lined boutique sleepover. Most rooms are spacious loft suites where you climb upstairs to bed in a gabled nook, and each is decorated with a comfy combination of wood beams, rustic chic furniture and deep leather sofas. The full kitchens are handy but continental breakfast is included. There's a brewpub downstairs.

Eating

Victoria's dining scene has been radically upgraded in recent years. Pick up the free *Eat Magazine* to check out the latest foodie happenings.

★ Red Fish Blue Fish
SEAFOOD $

(Map p690; www.redfish-bluefish.com; 1006 Wharf St; mains $6-20; ⊛ 11:30am-7pm Mon-Thu, to 8pm Fri-Sun) On the waterfront boardwalk at the foot of Broughton St, this freight-container takeout shack serves a loyal clientele who just can't get enough of its fresh-made sustainable seafood. Highlights like scallop *tacones,* wild-salmon sandwiches, tempura-battered fish and chips and chunky Pacific Rim chowder all hit the spot. Find a waterfront perch to enjoy your nosh, but watch for hovering seagull mobsters.

Picnic
CAFE $

(Map p690; www.picniccoffee.com; 506 Fort St; mains $8-10; ⊛ 7:30am-4pm Mon-Fri) Downtown's funkiest little cafe is easy to miss, but it's worth the hunt. There's a Canadiana feel to the interior, hence the artwork moose head, but there's nothing kitsch about the menu: fresh-made sandwiches, salad and soup as daily specials, plus beverages from great coffee to tasty lavender lemonade. Ask about their new place: plans were afoot on our visit for a larger additional venue.

Hernandéz
MEXICAN $

(Map p690; www.hernandezcocina.com; 735 Yates St; mains $5-8; ⊛ noon-8pm; ☑) Fiendishly well-hidden in an office building lobby between Yates and View Sts, this Mexican hole-in-the-wall is a local favorite. Vegetarian options abound but the *huarache de pollo* (thick tortilla with chicken) is legendary. Despite a recent expansion, there are never enough peak-time tables, so consider packing your butcher-paper parcel to Beacon Hill Park for a picnic. Cash only.

Pig BBQ Joint
BARBECUE $

(Map p690; www.pigbbqjoint.com; 1325 Blanshard St; mains $7.50-15; ⊛ 11am-10pm) Started as a hole-in-the wall but now in larger new digs, this joint is all about the meat, starting with bulging, Texas-style pulled-pork sandwiches (beef-brisket and smoked-chicken variations are also offered). Go for the 'pig size' serving if you're starving and make sure you add a side of crispy-fried mac 'n' cheese plus a draft of local Phillips Brewing beer.

★ Jam Cafe
BREAKFAST $$

(Map p690; www.jamcafevictoria.com; 542 Herald St; mains $8-16; ⊛ 8am-3pm) The locals won't tell you anything about this slightly off-the-beaten-path place. But that's not because they don't know about it; it's because they don't want you to add to the lineups for the best breakfast in town. The delectable eggs Benedict varieties are ever popular, but we also recommend the amazing, and very naughty, chicken French toast.

Their main social occasion, Victorians are passionate about their brunches and this place is always humming. Arrive off-peak as there are no reservations and waiting for a table is common.

Legislative Dining Room
WEST COAST $$

(Map p690; ☑ 250-387-3959; www.leg.bc.ca; room 606, Parliament Bldgs, 501 Belleville St; mains $9-15; ⊛ hours vary) One of Victoria's best-kept dining secrets, the Parliament Buildings have their own subsidized, old-school restaurant where both MLAs and the public can drop by for a silver-service menu of regional dishes, ranging from salmon salads to velvety steaks and a BC-only wine list. Entry is via the security desk just inside the building's main entrance; photo ID is required.

John's Place
DINER $$

(Map p690; www.johnsplace.ca; 723 Pandora Ave; mains $7-16; ⊛ 7am-9pm Mon-Fri, 8am-4pm & 5-9pm Sat & Sun) This ever-friendly, wood-floored local hangout is lined with quirky memorabilia, while its menu is a cut above standard diner fare. They'll start you off with a basket of addictive house-made bread, but save room for heaping pasta dishes or an eggs Benedict brunch. Don't leave without trying a thick slab of pie from the case at the front. Perfect breakfast spot.

Lotus Pond Vegetarian
Restaurant
CHINESE $$

(Map p690; www.lotuspond.webs.com; 617 Johnson St; mains $9-16; ⊙11am-3pm & 5-9pm Mon-Sat, noon-3pm & 5-8:30pm Sun; ⓕ) This unassuming downtown spot was satisfying local vegetarians long before meat-free diets became fashionable. Far superior to most Chinese eateries and with a menu that easily pleases carnivores as well as veggie types, the best time to come is lunch, when the busy buffet lures everyone in the vicinity. Don't miss the turnip cakes, a house specialty.

Pink Bicycle
BURGERS $$

(Map p690; www.pinkbicycleburger.com; 1008 Blanshard St; mains $12-15; ⊙11:30am-9pm Mon-Sat) Look for the bubble-gum-pink bike hanging in the window, then nip inside to the city's best gourmet burger joint. You'll be joining chatty locals, who'll never go back to regular fast food again. Spend time perusing the menu of more than a dozen made-with-love varieties, then dive into a blue-cheese lamb burger or Pacific halibut burger. Feeling naughty? Go for a side of truffle fries.

ReBar
VEGETARIAN, FUSION $$

(Map p690; www.rebarmodernfood.com; 50 Bastion Sq; mains $8-16; ⊙11am-9pm Mon-Thu, to 10pm Fri, 8:30am-10pm Sat, to 8pm Sun; ⓕ) A laidback downtown fixture, ReBar mixes colorful interiors with a mostly vegetarian menu. Carnivores will be just as happy to eat here, though, with hearty savory dishes such as shrimp quesadilla, mushroom-based curries and heaping weekend brunches – the salmon-topped bagel melt is great. There's also a wholesome specialty juice selection – try the orange, pear and cranberry.

Ulla
WEST COAST $$$

(Map p690; ☑250-590-8795; www.ulla.ca; 509 Fisgard St; mains $24-30; ⊙5:30-10pm Tue-Sat; ⓕ) Hidden at the quiet end of Chinatown's Fisgard St, this is the best restaurant in the city to dive into perfectly prepared West Coast dining. In a wood-floored but contemporary room studded with local artworks and cookbooks, you'll find a seasonal menu often including BC halibut or lamb plus a bounty of organic veggies. If you're a vegetarian, the options for you are top-notch.

Brasserie L'École
FRENCH $$$

(Map p690; ☑250-475-6260; www.lecole.ca; 1715 Government St; mains $18-26; ⊙5:30-11pm Tue-Sat) Preparing West Coast ingredients with French bistro flare, this warm and ever-popular spot is perfect for an intimate night out. The dishes constantly change to reflect seasonal highlights, like figs, salmonberries and heirloom tomatoes, but we recommend any seafood you find on the menu, or the ever-available *steak frites* with a red wine and shallot sauce. Great cocktail spot, too.

🍷 Drinking & Nightlife

One of BC's best beer towns, look out for local-made craft brews at pubs around the city. Repeated first-hand research was undertaken for this section.

★ Garrick's Head
PUB

(Map p690; www.bedfordregency.com; 1140 Government St; ⊙11am-11pm Mon-Thu, to midnight Fri & Sat, to 10pm Sun) A huge overhaul has transformed this once humdrum downtown pub into Victoria's best spot for trying local-made brews. Pull up a perch at the long bar and you'll be faced with 40-plus taps serving a comprehensive menu of beers from Driftwood, Phillips, Hoyne and beyond. Once or twice a month, there are guest casks to keep things lively.

A good spot to fill up on pub grub before hitting the beer list, the fish and chips are recommended. You can also find the remnants of the old pub in the back room if you're feeling nostalgic.

★ Spinnakers Gastro Brewpub
PUB

(Map p688; www.spinnakers.com; 308 Catherine St; ⊙11am-10:30pm) One of Canada's first craft brewers, this wood-floored smasher is a short hop from downtown via Harbour Ferry. Sail in for copper-colored Nut Brown Ale and hoppy Blue Bridge Double IPA and check out the daily casks to see what's on special. Save room to eat: the menu here is true gourmet gastropub grub.

Clive's Classic Lounge
LOUNGE

(Map p690; www.clivesclassiclounge.com; 740 Burdett Ave; ⊙11am-midnight Mon-Wed, to 1am Thu & Fri, 5pm-1am Sat, to midnight Sun) Tucked into the lobby level of the Chateau Victoria Hotel, this has been the best spot in town for perfectly prepared cocktails as long as anyone can remember. Completely lacking the snobbishness of big-city cocktail haunts, this ever-cozy spot is totally dedicated to its mixed drinks menu, which means timeless classic cocktails, as well as cool-ass fusion tipples that are a revelation.

Canoe Brewpub
PUB

(Map p690; www.canoebrewpub.com; 450 Swift St; ⏱11:30am-11pm Sun-Wed, to midnight Thu, to 1am Fri & Sat) The cavernous brick-lined interior is great on rainy days, but the patio is also the best in the city with its usually sunny views over the harbor. Indulge in on-site-brewed treats, like the hoppy Red Canoe Lager and the summer-friendly Siren's Song Pale Ale. Grub is also high on the menu, with roasted halibut recommended.

Big Bad John's
PUB

(Map p690; www.strathconahotel.com; 919 Douglas St; ⏱noon-2am) Easily missed from the outside, this grungy little hillbilly-themed bar feels like you've stepped into the backwoods. But rather than some dodgy banjo players with mismatched ears, you'll find good-time locals enjoying the cave-like ambience of peanut-shell-covered floors and a ceiling dotted with dusty bras. A good spot to say you've been to, at least once.

Bard & Banker
PUB

(Map p690; www.bardandbanker.com; 1022 Government St; ⏱11am-1am) This cavernous Victorian reproduction pub is handsomely lined with cut-glass lamps, open fireplaces and a long granite bar topped with brass beer taps. Pull up a stool and taste test Phillips Blue Buck, Nova Scotia's Alexander Keith's and the house-brand Robert Service Ale. There's nightly live music, plus a nosh menu ranging from pub standards to fancier fare.

☆ Entertainment

Check the weekly freebie *Monday Magazine* for the lowdown on local happenings. Entertainment resources online include Live Victoria (www.livevictoria.com) and Play in Victoria (www.playinvictoria.net).

Logan's Pub
LIVE MUSIC

(Map p688; www.loganspub.com; 1821 Cook St; ⏱3pm-1am Mon-Fri, 10am-1am Sat, 10am-midnight Sun) A 10-minute walk from downtown, this no-nonsense pub looks like nothing special from the outside, but its roster of shows is a fixture of the local indie scene. Fridays and Saturdays are your best bet for performances but other nights are frequently also scheduled; check the online calendar to see what's coming up.

McPherson Playhouse
THEATER

(Map p690; ☑250-386-6121; www.rmts.bc.ca; 3 Centennial Sq) One of Victoria's main stages, McPherson Playhouse offers mainstream visiting shows and performances.

Royal Theatre
THEATER

(Map p690; www.rmts.bc.ca; 805 Broughton St) With a rococo interior, the Royal Theatre hosts mainstream theater productions, and is home to the Victoria Symphony and Pacific Opera Victoria.

Belfry Theatre
THEATER

(Map p688; www.belfry.bc.ca; 1291 Gladstone Ave) A 20-minute stroll from downtown, the celebrated Belfry Theatre showcases contemporary plays in its lovely former-church-building venue.

Cineplex Odeon
CINEMA

(Map p690; www.cineplex.com; 780 Yates St) The city's main first-run cinema.

IMAX Theatre
CINEMA

(Map p690; www.imaxvictoria.com) The IMAX Theatre at the Royal BC Museum (p687) shows larger-than-life documentaries and Hollywood blockbusters.

🛍 Shopping

While Government St is a souvenir shopping magnet, those looking for more original purchases should head to the Johnson St stretch between Store and Government, which is lined with cool independent stores.

Regional Assembly of Text
STATIONERY

(Map p690; www.assemblyoftext.com; 560 Johnson St; ⏱11am-6pm Mon-Sat, noon-5pm Sun) Vancouver's hipster stationery store has finally opened its much-anticipated Victoria branch, socked into a quirky space that resembles a hotel lobby from 1968. You'll find the same array of clever greeting cards and cool-ass journals, plus the best Victoria postcards you'll ever find; postage is available. Add the button-making table and typewriter stations ($2 for 20 minutes) and you'll be as happy as a shiny new paper clip.

Smoking Lily
CLOTHING

(Map p690; www.smokinglily.com; 569 Johnson St; ⏱11am-5:30pm Tue-Sat, noon-5pm Sun & Mon) LoJo's smallest shop is an almost-too-tiny boutique stuffed with eclectic garments and accessories that define art-school chic. Tops and skirts with insect prints are hot items, but there are also lots of cute handbags, socks and brooches to tempt your credit card. Two's a crowd here, though – it really is *that* small.

Silk Road
TEA

(Map p690; www.silkroadtea.com; 1624 Government St; ⊗10am-6pm Mon-Thu, to 8pm Fri & Sat, 11am-5pm Sun) A pilgrimage spot for regular and exotic tea fans, you can pick up all manner of leafy paraphernalia here. Alternatively, sidle up to the tasting bar to quaff some adventurous brews. There's also a small on-site spa, where you can indulge in oil treatments and aromatherapy.

Munro's Books
BOOKS

(Map p690; www.munrobooks.com; 1108 Government St; ⊗9am-9pm Mon-Sat, 9:30am-6pm Sun) Like a cathedral to reading, this high-ceilinged local legend lures browsers who just like to hang out among the shelves. There's a good array of local-interest tomes, as well as a fairly extensive travel section at the back on the left. Check out the piles of bargain books, too – they're not all copies of *How to Eat String* from 1972.

Ditch Records
MUSIC

(Map p690; www.ditchrecords.com; 784 Fort St; ⊗10am-6pm Mon-Sat, 11am-5pm Sun) In its larger new location for a couple of years now, Ditch is the locals' fave record store. Lined with tempting vinyl and furtive musos perusing releases by bands like the Meatmen and Nightmares on Wax, it's an ideal rainy-day hangout. If it suddenly feels like time to socialize, you can book gig tickets here, too.

Milkman's Daughter
CLOTHING, ARTS & CRAFTS

(Map p690; www.smokinglily.com; 1713 Government St; ⊗11am-6pm Tue-Sat, noon-5pm Sun & Mon) The larger offshoot of Johnson St's tiny Smoking Lily, this enticing shop carries the full range of men's and women's togs and mixes in must-have arts and crafts from both local artisans and those from further afield, mostly from the West Coast. It's an eclectic mix, from jewelry to pottery and from buttons to notebooks, but it's easy to find something to fall in love with.

Rogers' Chocolates
FOOD

(Map p690; www.rogerschocolates.com; 913 Government St; ⊗10am-10pm Mon-Sat, to 7pm Sun) This charming, museum-like confectioner has the best ice-cream bars in town, but repeat offenders usually spend their time hitting the menu of rich Victoria Creams, one of which is usually enough to substitute for lunch. Varieties range from peppermint to seasonal specialties and they're good souvenirs, so long as you don't scoff them all before you get home.

ⓘ Information

Downtown Medical Centre (☑250-380-2210; 622 Courtney St; ⊗8:30am-5pm) Handy walk-in clinic.

Main Post Office (Map p690; 709 Yates St; ⊗9am-5pm Mon-Fri) Near the corner of Yates and Douglas Sts.

Victoria Visitors Centre (Map p690; www.tourismvictoria.com; 812 Wharf St; ⊗8:30am-8:30pm) Busy, flyer-lined visitors center overlooking the Inner Harbour.

ⓘ Getting There & Away

AIR

Victoria International Airport (www.victoria-airport.com) is 26km north of the city via Hwy 17. **Air Canada** (www.aircanada.com) services arrive from Vancouver (from $87, 25 minutes, up to 16 daily), while **Westjet** (www.westjet.com) flights arrive from Calgary (from $161, 1½

TO MARKET, TO MARKET

The much-anticipated **Victoria Public Market** (Map p690; www.victoriapublicmarket.com; 1701 Douglas St; ⊗9:30am-6:30pm Tue-Sat, to 5pm Sun; ◻4) opened in 2013 with various food-focused vendors – from Silk Road Tea to Salt Spring Island Cheese – in this refurbished spot in downtown's heritage Hudson Building.

Outside the building, the **Victoria Downtown Farmers Market** (Map p690; www.victoriapublicmarket.com; 1701 Douglas St, back carriageway; ⊗11am-3pm Wed; ◻4), which runs all year, sells locally made and farmed food.

If you want more alfresco shopping, downtown's **Bastion Square Public Market** (Map p690; www.bastionsquare.ca; Bastion Sq; ⊗from 11am Thu-Sun May-Sep) houses art-and-craft stalls all summer, while **James Bay Market** (Map p690; www.jamesbaymarket.com; 494 Superior St; ⊗9am-3pm May-Oct; ◻27) and the large **Moss Street Market** (Map p688; www.mossstreetmarket.com; cnr Moss St & Fairfield Rd; ⊗10am-2pm May-Oct; ◻7) offer a community-focused combo of both arts and food.

HIT THE TRAILS

Easily accessed along the Island Hwy just 16km from Victoria, **Goldstream Provincial Park** (off Map p688; www.goldstreampark.com), at the base of Malahat Mountain, makes for a restorative nature-themed day trip from the city. Dripping with ancient, moss-covered cedar trees and a moist carpet of plant life, it's known for its chum-salmon spawning season from late October to December. Hungry bald eagles are attracted to the fish and bird-watchers come ready with their cameras. Head to the park's **Freeman King Visitors Centre** (☑ 250-478-9414; 2390 Trans-Canada Hwy; ☺ 9am-4:30pm) for area info and natural history exhibits.

Aside from nature watching, you'll also find great hiking: marked trails range from tough to easy and some are wheelchair accessible. Recommended treks include the hike to 47.5m-high Niagara Falls (not *that* one) and the steep, strenuous route to the top of Mt Finlayson, one of the region's highest promontories. The visitors center can advise on trails and will also tell you how to find the park's forested **campground** (☑ 800-689-9025, 604-689-9025; www.discovercamping.ca; campsites $30) if you feel like staying over.

hours, four daily). Both offer cross-Canada connections.

Harbour Air (www.harbour-air.com) flies into the Inner Harbour from downtown Vancouver ($185, 35 minutes) throughout the day. Similar **Helijet** (www.helijet.com) helicopter services arrive from Vancouver (from $199, 35 minutes).

BOAT

BC Ferries (www.bcferries.com) arrive from mainland Tsawwassen (adult/vehicle $15.50/51.25, 1½ hours) at Swartz Bay, 27km north of Victoria via Hwy 17. Services arrive frequently throughout the day in summer, less often off-season.

Victoria Clipper (www.clippervacations.com) services arrive in the Inner Harbour from Seattle (adult/child US$88/44, three hours, up to three a day). **Black Ball Transport** (www.ferrytovictoria.com) boats also arrive here from Port Angeles (adult/child/vehicle US$17/8.50/$60.50, 1½ hours, up to four daily).

BUS

Buses rolling into the city's main **bus depot** (Map p690; 700 Douglas St) include **Greyhound Canada** (www.greyhound.ca) services from Nanaimo (from $13.50, 2½ hours, three daily) and across the island, along with frequent **Pacific Coach Lines** (www.pacificcoach.com) services, via the ferry, from Vancouver (from $38, 3½ hours) and Vancouver International Airport ($44, four hours).

ℹ Getting Around

TO/FROM THE AIRPORT

AKAL Airporter (www.victoriaairporter.com) minibuses run between the airport and area hotels ($21, 30 minutes). In contrast, a taxi to downtown costs around $50, while airport-serving transit buses 83, 86 and 88 take around

35 minutes, run throughout the day and cost $2.50 – you may need to change buses at McTavish Exchange.

BICYCLE

Victoria is a great cycling capital, with routes crisscrossing the city and beyond. Check the website of the **Greater Victoria Cycling Coalition** (Map p690; www.gvcc.bc.ca) for local resources. Bike rentals are offered by **Cycle BC Rentals** (☑ 866-380-2453, 250-380-2453; www.cyclebc.ca; 685 Humboldt St; ☺ 9am-5pm; ➊).

BOAT

Victoria Harbour Ferry (Map p690; www.victoriaharbourferry.com; fares from $5) covers the Inner Harbour and beyond with its colorful armada of little boats.

PUBLIC TRANSPORTATION & TAXI

Victoria Regional Transit (www.busonline.ca) buses (fare/day pass $2.50/5) cover a wide area from Sidney to Sooke, with some routes served by modern-day double-deckers. Children under five travel free.

Established taxi providers:

BlueBird Cabs (☑ 800-665-7055, 250-382-2222; www.taxicab.com)

Yellow Cab (☑ 800-808-6881, 250-381-2222; www.yellowcabofvictoria.ca)

Southern Vancouver Island

Not far from Victoria's madding crowds, southern Vancouver Island is a laid-back region of quirky little towns that are never far from tree-lined cycle routes, waterfront hiking trails and rocky outcrops bristling

ON YER BIKE

Bring your bike across on the ferry from the mainland and, when you arrive in Swartz Bay, you can hop onto the easily accessible and well-marked **Lochside Regional Trail** to downtown Victoria. The 29km, mostly flat route is not challenging – there are only a couple of overpasses – and it's an idyllic, predominantly paved ride through small urban areas, waterfront stretches, rolling farmland and forested countryside. There are several spots to pick up lunch en route and, if you adopt a leisurely pace, you'll be in town within four hours or so.

with gnarly Garry oaks. The wildlife here is abundant and you'll likely spot bald eagles swooping overhead, sea otters cavorting on the beaches and perhaps the occasional orca sliding silently by just off the coast.

Saanich Peninsula & Around

Home to Vancouver Island's main airport and busiest ferry terminal, this north-of-Victoria peninsula has plenty to offer day-trippers from the city.

SIDNEY

At the peninsula's northern end, seafront Sidney is studded with 10 or so bookshops, enabling it to call itself BC's only 'Booktown.'

It takes an hour to get here by transit bus from Victoria ($2.50, number 70 or 72) and the heart of the town is Beacon Ave. Drop into the friendly **chamber of commerce** (☏ 250-665-7362; www.sidney.ca; 2281 Beacon Ave; ⊙ 9am-5pm) when you arrive for tips.

You can spend a leisurely afternoon ducking into the likes of **Tanner's Books** (www.tannersbooks.com; 2436 Beacon Ave; ⊙ 8am-9pm), with its massive magazine and large travel-book sections; and **Beacon Books** (2372 Beacon Ave; ⊙ 10am-5:30pm Mon-Sat, noon-4pm Sun), where the used tomes are guarded by store cat Rosabelle. See www.sidneybooktown.ca for additional page-turning options.

The popular **Shaw Ocean Discovery Centre** (www.oceandiscovery.ca; 9811 Seaport Pl; adult/child $15/5; ⊙ 10am-5pm) is Sidney's kid-luring highlight. Enter through a dramatic Disney-style entrance – it makes you think you're descending below the waves –

then step into a gallery of aquatic exhibits, including alien-like jellyfish, a large touch tank with purple starfish and an octopus that likes to unscrew a glass jar to snag its fresh crab dinner. Continue your marine education aboard a whale-watching boat trek with **Sidney Whale Watching** (www.sidneywhalewatching.com; 2537 Beacon Ave; adult/child $109/89), located a few steps away.

If you decide to stick around, the swish **Sidney Pier Hotel & Spa** (☏ 866-659-9445, 250-655-9445; www.sidneypier.com; 9805 Seaport Pl; d from $175; @ ☎) on the waterfront fuses West Coast lounge cool with beach pastel colors. Many rooms have shoreline views, some side on, and each has local artworks lining the walls. If you're missing your pooch back home, there's a resident dog available for walkies.

If it's time to eat, duck into **Carlos Cantina & Grill** (www.carloscantina.ca; 9816 4th St; mains $10-14; ⊙ 11:30am-8:30pm) for authentic Mexican grub in a colorful, friendly setting; the fish tacos and $7.95 lunch special are recommended. Crank it up a notch with dinner at local fave **Sabhai Thai** (www.sabhai.ca; 2493 Beacon Ave; mains $12-18; ⊙ 11:30am-2pm & 5-10pm), a cozy, wood-floored room with a bonus patio and a good line in authentic curry and *phad* dishes. The lunch combos are good value.

When you just need to fuel up on java, join the gossiping locals at the art-lined **Red Brick Café** (2423 Beacon Ave; mains $4-9; ⊙ 6:30am-5pm), where coffee and a large ginger snap make for an ideal pit stop. Light lunches are also available.

BRENTWOOD BAY

A 30-minute drive from Victoria via West Saanich Rd, the rolling farmlands of waterfront Brentwood Bay are chiefly known for **Butchart Gardens** (off Map p688; www.butchartgardens.com; 800 Benvenuto Ave; adult/child $30.20/10.30; ⊙ 9am-10pm; ☐ 75), Vancouver Island's leading visitor attraction. The immaculate grounds are divided into separate gardens where there's always something in bloom. Summer is crowded, with tour buses rolling in relentlessly, but evening music performances and Saturday night fireworks in July and August make it all worthwhile. Tea fans take note: the **Dining Room Restaurant** serves a smashing afternoon tea, complete with quiches and Grand Marnier truffles; leave your diet at the door.

If you have time, also consider nearby **Victoria Butterfly Gardens** (www.butterfly-gardens.com; 1461 Benvenuto Ave; adult/child $15/5; ⊙9am-7pm), which offers a kaleidoscope of thousands of fluttering critters, from around 75 species, in a free-flying environment. As well as watching them flit about and land on your head, you can learn about ecosystem life cycles, and eyeball exotic fish, plants and birds. Look out for Spike, the long-beaked puna ibis, who struts around the trails as if he owns the place.

Sooke & Around

Rounding Vancouver Island's rustic southern tip towards Sooke, a 45-minute drive from Victoria, Hwy 14 is lined with twisted Garry oaks and unkempt hedgerows, while the houses – often artisan workshops or homely B&Bs – seem spookily hidden in the forest shadows.

Sharing the same building and hours as the visitors center, the fascinating **Sooke Region Museum** (www.sookeregionmuseum.com; 2070 Phillips Rd; ⊙9am-5pm) FREE illuminates the area's rugged pioneer days. Check out Moss Cottage in the museum grounds: built in 1869, it's the oldest residence west of Victoria.

If you're craving some thrills, find your inner screamer on the forested zip-line tours operated by **Adrena LINE** (www.adrenalinezip.com; 5128 Sooke Rd; adult/child from $80/70; ⊙8am-5pm). Its full-moon zips are the most fun and, if you don't have your own transport, they'll collect you from Victoria.

A more relaxed way to encounter the natural world is the **Sooke Potholes Provin-** cial Park (www.bcparks.ca), a 5km drive from Hwy 14 (the turnoff is east of Sooke). With rock pools and potholes carved into the river base during the last ice age, it's ideal for swimming and tube floating. Camping is available through the website of the **Land Conservancy** (www.conservancy.bc.ca; campsites $25; ⊙May-Sep).

You'll find B&Bs dotted along the route here but, for one of the province's most delightful and splurge-worthy sleepovers, head to Whiffen Spit's **Sooke Harbour House** (☑250-642-3421, www.sookeharbourhouse.com; 1528 Whiffen Spit Rd; d from $299; 🕿🐾). Paintings, sculptures and carved wood line its interiors. Some of the 28 rooms have fireplaces and steam showers and all have views across the wildlife-strewn waterfront – look for gamboling sea otters and swooping cranes. The restaurant is also a great place for fine West Coast dining, whether or not you're staying here.

Port Renfrew

Conveniently nestled between the Juan de Fuca and West Coast Trails, Port Renfrew is a great access point for either route.

If you've had enough of your sleeping bag, try **Port Renfrew Resorts** (☑250-647-5541; www.portrenfrewresorts.com; 17310 Parkinson Rd; r from $190), a waterfront miniresort with motel-style rooms and some luxurious, wood-lined cabins.

For respite from campground pasta, the **Coastal Kitchen Café** (17245 Parkinson Rd; mains $8-16; ⊙8am-9pm Fri-Wed) serves fresh

---

JUAN DE FUCA PROVINCIAL PARK

The 47km **Juan de Fuca Marine Trail** (www.juandefucamarinetrail.com) in **Juan de Fuca Provincial Park** (www.bcparks.ca) rivals the West Coast Trail as a must-do trek. From east to west, its trailhead access points are China Beach, Sombrio Beach, Parkinson Creek and Botanical Beach.

It takes around four days to complete the route, but you don't have to go the whole hog if you want to take things easier. Be aware that some sections are often muddy and difficult to hike, while bear sightings and swift weather changes are not uncommon. The most difficult stretch is between Bear Beach and China Beach.

The route has several basic backcountry campsites and you can pay your camping fee ($10 per adult) at any of the trailheads. The most popular spot to pitch your tent is the more salubrious, family-friendly **China Beach Campground** (☑800-689-9025, 604-689-9025; www.discovercamping.ca; campsites $30; ⊙May-Sep), which has pit toilets and cold-water taps but no showers. There's a waterfall at the western end of the beach and booking ahead in summer is essential.

Booking ahead is also required on the **West Coast Trail Express** (☑888-999-2288, 250-477-8700; www.trailbus.com; fares from $30; ⊙May-Sep) minibus that runs between Victoria, the trailheads and Port Renfrew.

salads and sandwiches, plus burgers and pizzas. The seafood is the star attraction, especially Dungeness crab and chips.

Cowichan Valley

A swift Hwy 1 drive northwest of Victoria, the farm-filled Cowichan Valley region is ripe for discovery, especially if you're a traveling foodie or an outdoor activity nut. Contact **Tourism Cowichan** (☑ 888-303-3337, 250-746-4636; www.tourismcowichan.com) for more information.

Duncan

POP 5000

Developed as a logging-industry railroad stop – the gabled little station now houses a museum – Duncan is the valley's main community. A useful base for regional exploration, it's known for its dozens of totem poles, which dot downtown like sentinels.

If your First Nations curiosity is piqued, head to the **Quw'utsun' Cultural & Conference Centre** (www.quwutsun.ca; 200 Cowichan Way; adult/child $13/6; ⊘ 10am-4pm Mon-Sat Jun-Sep) to learn about carving and traditional salmon runs. Its on-site **Riverwalk Café** serves First Nations–inspired cuisine.

Alternatively, drive 3km north of town to the **BC Forest Discovery Centre** (www.bcforestdiscoverycentre.com; 2892 Drinkwater Rd; adult/child $16/11; ⊘ 10am-4:30pm), complete with its pioneer-era buildings, logging machinery and a working steam train.

The area's chatty hub, **Duncan Garage Cafe** (www.communityfarmstore.ca; 3330 Duncan St; mains $4-9; ⊘ 7:30am-6pm Mon-Sat, 9am-5pm Sun) is in a refurbished heritage building that also houses a bookshop and an organic grocery store. Libations of the boozy variety are on the menu at **Craig Street Brew Pub** (www. craigstreet.ca; 25 Craig St; mains $11-16; ⊘ 11am-11pm Mon-Thu, to midnight Fri & Sat, to 10pm Sun), where comfort grub and own-brewed beer lure the locals; the pizzas are recommended.

But the town's newest restaurant has really cranked Duncan dining up a notch. Housed in an immaculately restored former music-school building, the delightful **Hudson's on First** (www.hudsonsonfirst.ca; 163 First St; mains $16-26; ⊘ 11am-2.30pm & 5-8.30pm Tue-Sun) would be a top table option in far bigger cities. Farm-to-table local produce is the approach on an ever-changing seasonal menu that fuses West Coast ingredients

CANADA'S ONLY TEA FARM

Hidden in bucolic farmland 8km north of Duncan, you'll find one of Canada's rarest agricultural operations. Tucked into the hillside, the oasis-like **Teafarm** (www.teafarm.ca; 8530 Richards Trail, North Cowichan; ⊘ 10am-5pm Wed-Sun) has been growing its own tea plants for several years. The main harvest is coming soon, but until that time its contemporary, winery-like tasting room – or, better still, its flower-framed outdoor seating area – is the perfect spot to indulge in one of dozens of excellent tea blends – Sweet Morocco recommended – along with some decadent sweet treats. The tea is served in lovely pottery teapots made by owner Margit, while husband and tea guru Victor will be on hand to tell you about the operation. One of the most relaxing and surprisingly good-value ways to spend an hour or two in the region. It's not well signposted, so deploy your GPS.

with subtle European influences. For lunch, the red-snapper fish and chips is a regular, while weekend brunch lures locals with the region's best eggs Benedict. If you come for dinner, start with a cocktail in the tin-ceilinged bar.

Cowichan Bay

'Cow Bay' to the locals, the region's most attractive pit stop is a colorful string of wooden buildings perched over a mountain-framed ocean inlet. It's well worth an afternoon of your time, although it might take that long to find parking on a busy summer day. Arrive hungry and drop into **Hilary's Artisan Cheese** (www.hilaryscheese.com; 1737 Cowichan Bay Rd; ⊘ 9am-6pm) and **True Grain Bread** (www.truegrain.ca; 1725 Cowichan Bay Rd; ⊘ 8am-7pm Mon-Sat, to 5pm Sun) for the makings of a great picnic.

Alternatively, let someone else do all the work with fish and chips from **Rock Cod Café** (www.rockcodcafe.com; 1759 Cowichan Bay Rd; mains $10-14; ⊘ 11am-9pm). Or push out the boat – not literally – on the patio deck of the charming **Masthead Restaurant** (☑ 250-748-3714; www.themastheadrestaurant.com; 1705 Cowichan Bay Rd; mains $24-37; ⊘ 5-10pm), where the three-course BC-sourced tasting menu is good value.

Before you leave, duck into Cow Bay's **Maritime Centre** (www.classicboats.org; 1761 Cowichan Bay Rd; admission by donation; ☺ dawn-dusk) to peruse some salty boat-building exhibits and intricate models.

Carmanah Walbran Provincial Park

Home to some of BC's eldest residents, the old growth spruce and cedar trees in this magnificent but remote **park** (www.bcparks.ca) frequently exceed 1000 years of age. With an ancient and mythical ambience, it's a half-hour walk down the valley to commune with the tallest trees. Be aware that the trails are primitive and not suitable for the unprepared.

For those without a map looking for the main Carmanah Valley trailhead, follow South Shore Rd from Lake Cowichan to Nitinat Main Rd and bear left. Then follow Nitinat Main to Nitinat Junction and turn left onto South Main. Continue to the Caycus River Bridge and, just south of the bridge, turn right and follow Rosander Main (blue-and-white BC Parks signs reassuringly point the way) for 29km to the trailhead. These are active logging roads, which means bumpy, often narrow tracks and the promise of a rumbling approach from a scary log truck – they have the right of way, so don't give them a hard time.

Chemainus

POP 4500

After the last sawmill shut down in 1983, tiny Chemainus became the model for BC communities dealing with declining resource jobs. Instead of submitting to a slow death, town officials commissioned a giant wall mural depicting local history. More than three dozen artworks were later added and a tourism industry was born.

Stroll the Chemainus streets on a mural hunt and you'll pass artsy boutiques and tempting ice-cream shops. In the evening, the surprisingly large **Chemainus Theatre** (www.chemainustheatrefestival.ca; 9737 Chemainus Rd) stages professional productions, mostly popular plays and musicals, to keep you occupied.

Nearby, the town's **Chemainus Inn** (☎877-246-4181, 250-246-4181; www.chemainushotel.com; 9573 Chemainus Rd; d from $169; ❋ ❋ ❋) is like a midrange business hotel from a much larger community. Rooms are slick and comfortable and many include kitchens. Rates include breakfast.

Drop by the charming, heritage building housing **Willow Street Café** (www.willowstreetcafe.com; 9749 Willow St; mains $5-12; ☺8:30am-5pm) for a chat with the locals and a side order of hearty, house-made wraps, pizzas and sandwiches. In summer aim for a patio perch.

Check in at the **visitors center** (☎250-246-3944; www.chemainus.bc.ca; 9796 Willow St;

VANCOUVER ISLAND BOOZE TRAIL

Vancouver Island's burgeoning local food movement has spread to booze in recent years, with wineries, cideries and distilleries popping up across the island and giving regional craft-beer producers a run for their tipsy money. But unless you know where to go, many of these artisan operators can be hard to find. Here are some thirst-slaking recommendations for visitors.

In the Cowichan region, check out **Cherry Point Vineyards** (www.cherrypointvineyards.com; 840 Cherry Point Rd, Cobble Hill; ☺10am-5pm), with its lip-smacking blackberry port; **Averill Creek** (www.averillcreek.ca; 6552 North Rd, Duncan; ☺11am-5pm), with its patio views and lovely pinot noirs; and the smashing **Merridale Estate Cidery** (www.merridalecider.com; 1230 Merridale Rd, Cobble Hill; ☺10:30am-7pm), an inviting apple-cider producer that also makes brandy and has a great patio bistro.

But it's not all about the Cowichan. Further south in Saanich – and just a short drive from Victoria – organic apples are also on the taste-tripping menu at **Sea Cider** (www.seacider.ca; 2487 Mt St Michael Rd, Saanichton; ☺11am-4pm). While booze of a stronger hue is the approach at nearby **Victoria Spirits** (www.victoriaspirits.com; 6170 Old West Saanich Rd, Victoria; ☺10am-5pm Sat & Sun Apr-Sep), where the lovely Oaken Gin is recommended). Both offer tours and tastings.

For more information on wineries, cideries and distilleries throughout Vancouver Island, check www.wineislands.ca.

⊙9am-5pm) for mural maps and further information.

Nanaimo

POP 87,000

Vancouver Island's 'second metropolis,' Nanaimo will never have the allure of tourist-magnet Victoria, but the Harbour City has undergone a quiet upgrade since the 1990s, with the emergence, especially on Commercial St and in the Old City Quarter, of some good shops and eateries, plus a slick new museum. With dedicated ferry services from the mainland, the city is also a handy hub for exploring the rest of the island.

◉ Sights

Nanaimo Museum   MUSEUM

(www.nanaimomuseum.ca; 100 Museum Way; adult/child $2/75¢; ⊙10am-5pm) Just off the Commercial St main drag, this excellent museum showcases the region's heritage, from First Nations to colonial, maritime, sporting and beyond. Highlights include a strong Coast Salish focus and a walk-through evocation of a coal mine that's popular with kids. Ask at the front desk about summer-only city walking tours and entry to the nearby Bastion, an 1853 wooden tower fortification.

Newcastle Island Marine
Provincial Park   PARK

(www.newcastleisland.ca) 🌿 Nanaimo's rustic outdoor gem offers 22km of hiking and biking trails, plus beaches and wildlife spotting. Traditional Coast Salish land, it was the site of shipyards and coal mines before becoming a popular summer excursion for locals in the 1930s when a tea pavilion was added. Accessed by a 10-minute ferry hop from the harbor (adult/child return $9/5), there's a seasonal eatery and regular First Nations dancing displays.

Old City Quarter   NEIGHBORHOOD

(www.oldcityquarter.com; cnr Fitzwilliam & Wesley Sts) A steep hike uphill from the waterfront on Bastion and Fitzwilliam Sts delivers you to a strollable heritage hood of independent stores, galleries and eateries in brightly painted old buildings. Highlights include McLeans Specialty Foods; A Wee Cupcakery; and Fibber Magees, a handsome large pub that has taken over the town's old train station. Look out for the heritage plaques on buildings in this area.

Wild Play Element Parks   AMUSEMENT PARK

(☑250-716-7874, 888-716-7374; www.wildplay.com; 35 Nanaimo River Rd; adult/child from $43/23; ⊙10am-6pm) The perfect spot to tire your kids out, this tree-lined adventure playground is packed with adrenalin-pumping fun, from bungee jumping to scream-triggering zip-lining. Along with its fun obstacle courses, there's plenty of additional action to keep the family occupied, from woodsy walking trails to busy volleyball courts. Bring a picnic and come for at least half a day.

🛏 Sleeping

Painted Turtle Guesthouse   HOSTEL $

(☑250-753-4432, 866-309-4432; www.painted-turtle.ca; 121 Bastion St; dm/r $27/80; @ 🛜) This beautifully maintained heart-of-downtown budget property combines small dorms with very popular private rooms (book ahead). An HI affiliate, its hardwood floors and IKEA-style furnishings line a large and welcoming kitchen-lounge combo. You can book tours from the front desk if you've had enough of strumming the hostel's loaner guitar.

Buccaneer Inn   MOTEL $$

(☑250-753-1246, 877-282-6337; www.buccaneer-inn.com; 1577 Stewart Ave; d/ste from $80/140; 🛜) Handy for the Departure Bay ferry terminal, this friendly, family-run motel has a gleaming white exterior that makes it hard to pass by. It's worth stopping though, as the neat-and-tidy approach is carried over into the maritime-themed rooms, many of which have kitchenettes. Splurge on a spacious suite and you'll have a fireplace, full kitchen and flatscreen TV.

Coast Bastion Hotel   HOTEL $$

(☑250-753-6601, 800-716-6199; www.coast-hotels.com; 11 Bastion St; d from $157; ✳ @ 🛜 🐾) Downtown's best hotel has an unbeatable location overlooking the harbor, with most guests enjoying sparkling waterfront views, when it's not foggy. Rooms have been well refurbished with a modern élan in recent years, adding flatscreen TVs and, in most rooms, small fridges. The lobby restaurant-bar is a popular hangout and there's a spa if you want to chillax. The front desk staff are excellent.

Dorchester Hotel   HOTEL $$

(☑800-661-2449, 250-754-6835; www.dorchester-nanaimo.com; 70 Church St; d from $119; 🛜) The cheaper of downtown's two waterfront ho-

Nanaimo

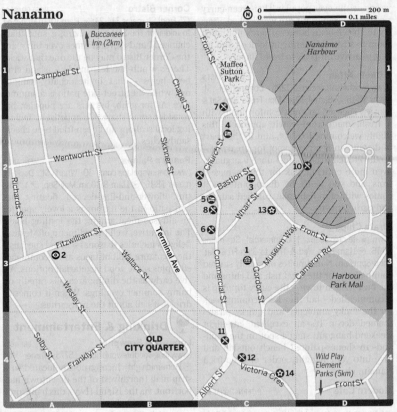

Nanaimo

⊚ Sights
1 Nanaimo Museum C3
2 Old City Quarter A3

🛏 Sleeping
3 Coast Bastion Hotel C2
4 Dorchester Hotel C2
5 Painted Turtle Guesthouse C2

✕ Eating
6 2 Chefs Affair C3
7 Corner Bistro C1

8 Gabriel's Café C2
9 Modern Cafe C2
10 Penny's Palapa D2
11 Pirate Chips C4
12 Thirsty Camel Café C4

✪ Entertainment
13 Port Theatre C2
14 Queen's Hotel C4

tels, the Best Western–affiliated Dorchester is not as slick as its neighbor and has an unusual labyrinthine layout. Rooms, some with refrigerators, have a standard business-hotel look. Give yourself plenty of time to get here: the clunky elevator may be the slowest in Nanaimo. There are often good last-minute and off-season rate deals.

✕ Eating

★ Gabriel's Café
INTERNATIONAL $

(183 Commercial St; mains $6-9; ⊙ 8am-7pm Mon-Fri, 9am-5pm Sat & Sun; 🖉) This perfectly located downtown hole-in-the-wall is like a static food truck. Chat with the man himself behind the counter, then tuck into made-from-scratch treats, such as pulled-pork breakfast

wraps or the ever-popular Thai-green-curry rice bowl. Vegetarians are well looked after; try the black-bean burger. There's not much room to sit in this sunny little nook and it's best to arrive off-peak to avoid lineups.

2 Chefs Affair
WEST COAST **$**

(www.twochefsaffair.com; 123b Commercial St; mains $8-15; ⊘ 8am-4:30pm Mon-Fri, to 3pm Sat & Sun; 🗟) Focused on great comfort food, with a fresh, made-from-scatch approach, this highly welcoming locals' haunt in the heart of downtown is a great spot for breakfast – go the French toast route. Lunch is arguably even more enticing: ask for the 'ménage à trois' and you won't be disappointed – it comes with crab fish cake, candied salmon and garlic prawns.

Pirate Chips
FAST FOOD **$**

(www.pirate-chips.com; 1 Commercial St; mains $5-16; ⊘ 11am-8pm Wed & Thu, to 3am Fri & Sat, noon-8pm Sun) Nanaimoites originally started coming here for the great fish and chips and the best fries in town – the curry topping is recommended – but they keep coming back for the funky ambience and quirky pirate-themed decor. It's an excellent late-night weekend hangout: snag a spot on the skull-and-crossbones-painted bench outside and dive into your naughty order of deep-fried Nanaimo bars.

Modern Cafe
INTERNATIONAL **$$**

(www.themoderncafe.ca; 221 Commercial St; mains $15-23; ⊘ 11am-11pm Mon-Wed, to midnight Thu-Sat, 10am-11pm Sun) This reinvented old coffee shop has cool, loungy interiors combining exposed brick and comfy booths and, for when it's sunny, a ray-warmed street-side patio. The menu has risen up a notch or two in recent years and now includes gourmet comfort food with international influences – go for the Caribbean-jerk-chicken dish. Excellent burgers are also served up.

Thirsty Camel Café
MIDDLE EASTERN **$$**

(www.thirstycamelcafe.ca; 14 Victoria Cres; mains $8-14; ⊘ 11am-3pm Mon-Wed, to 7pm Thu & Fri, noon-4pm Sat; 🖉) Partake of a lip-smacking Middle Eastern feast at this sunny little family-owned joint, tucked into an elbow of Victoria Cres. Everything's prepared from scratch, which makes for addictive hummus, spicy soups and the region's best falafel. The shareable platters, especially the spice-encrusted Persian chicken, are recommended and there are several excellent vegetarian options that even meat eaters will love.

Corner Bistro
WEST COAST **$$**

(75 Front St; mains $14-24; ⊘ 11am-10pm Mon-Wed, to midnight Thu-Sat) Colonizing a spot that's changed hands several times over the years, the Corner Bistro may be the one that sticks. There's a pub-like feel inside – island craft beer helps – that invites chatty hanging out, while the street-side patio is a summer fave. As for grub, burgers are popular, but consider some shareable appetizers, including local scallops and deep-fried blue-cheese sandwiches.

Penny's Palapa
MEXICAN **$$**

(www.pennyspalapa.com; 10 Wharf St, Dock H; mains $8-16; ⊘ 11am-8:30pm May-Sep; 🖉) This tiny, flower-and-flag-decked floating hut and patio in the harbor is a lovely spot for an alfresco meal among the jostling boats. The inventive, well-priced menu of Mexican delights includes seasonal seafood specials – the signature halibut tacos are recommended – plus some good vegetarian options. Arrive early, as the dining area fills rapidly on balmy summer evenings. When it comes to drinks, it's all about the margaritas.

🍷 Drinking & Entertainment

Longwood Brewpub
BREWERY

(www.longwoodbrewpub.com; 5775 Turner Rd; ⊘ 11am-midnight) Incongruously located in a strip mall (northwest of the downtown harborfront, via the Island Hwy), this handsome stone and gabled restaurant-pub combines a surprisingly good menu with lip-smacking self-brewed beers. Try for a deck table and decide between recommended mains, like Cajun chicken quesadilla or halibut and prawn wraps; vegetarians should hit the roasted-vegetable lasagna. For drinks, try the four-glass tasting flight of beer.

Dinghy Dock Pub
PUB

(www.dinghydockpub.com; 8 Pirates Lane; mains $12-17; ⊘ 11:30am-11pm) Accessed via a mini-ferry hop, this lively but old-school pub and restaurant combo floating offshore from Protection Island is a salty local legend and a unique place to knock back a few malty brews on the deck. The menu doesn't stretch too far beyond fish and chips, but there's live music on weekends to keep your toes tapping. To get to the pub, take the 10-minute ferry (return $9) from the harbor.

Queen's Hotel
LIVE MUSIC

(📞 250-754-6751; www.thequeens.ca; 34 Victoria Cres) The city's best live music and dance spot, hosting an eclectic roster of performances and club nights, ranging from indie to jazz and country.

Port Theatre   THEATER
(☑250-754-8550; www.porttheatre.com; 125 Front St) Presenting local and touring live-theater shows.

ⓘ Information

Nanaimo Visitors Centre (☑800-663-7337, 250-751-1556; www.tourismnanaimo.com; 2450 Northfield Rd; ⊗9am-6pm) For tourist information, drop into the main visitors center or the summer-only satellite behind downtown's Nanaimo Museum (p702).

ⓘ Getting There & Away

AIR

Nanaimo Airport (www.nanaimoairport.com) is 18km south of town via Hwy 1. **Air Canada** (www.aircanada.com) flights arrive here from Vancouver (from $77, 25 minutes) throughout the day.

Frequent and convenient **Harbour Air** (www.harbour-air.com) floatplane services arrive in the inner harbor from downtown Vancouver ($105, 25 minutes).

BOAT

BC Ferries (www.bcferries.com) from Tsawwassen (passenger/vehicle $14.55/49.05, two hours) arrive at Duke Point, 14km south of Nanaimo. Services from West Vancouver's Horseshoe Bay (passenger/vehicle $15.50/51.25, 95 minutes) arrive at Departure Bay, 3km north of the city center via Hwy 1.

BUS

Greyhound Canada (www.greyhound.ca) buses arrive from Victoria (from $13.50, two hours, three daily), Campbell River (from $18.50, three hours, three daily), Tofino ($46, four hours, two daily) and beyond.

ⓘ Getting Around

Downtown Nanaimo, around the harbor, is highly walkable, but after that the city spreads out and a car or strong bike legs are required. Be aware that taxis are expensive here.

Nanaimo Regional Transit (www.busonline.ca; single trip/day pass $2.50/6.25) Buses stop along Gordon St, west of Harbour Park Mall. Bus 2 goes to the Departure Bay ferry terminal. No city buses run to Duke Point.

Nanaimo Airporter (www.nanaimoairporter. com; from $26) Provides door-to-door service to downtown from both ferry terminals, as well as handy airport drop-off and pick-up.

Parksville, Coombs & Qualicum Beach

This popular mid-island seaside region, which also includes rustic Coombs, has been a traditional destination for vacationing families for decades – hence the water parks and miniature golf attractions. It's a great spot to take a breather on your trip up or down island. For more information on the area, visit www.parksvillequalicumbeach.com.

◉ Sights

Coombs Old Country Market   MARKET
(www.oldcountrymarket.com; 2326 Alberni Hwy, Coombs; ⊗9am-7pm) The mother of all pit stops, this sprawling food and crafts menagerie is stuffed with bakery and produce delectables. It attracts huge numbers of visitors on balmy summer days, when cameras are pointed at the grassy roof where a herd of goats spends the season. Nip inside for giant ice-cream cones, heaping pizzas and the deli makings of a great picnic.

Save some time to explore the attendant store and attractions clustered around the site.

World Parrot Refuge   WILDLIFE RESERVE
(www.worldparrotrefuge.org; 2116 Alberni Hwy, Coombs; adult/child $14/10; ⊗10am-4pm) Rescuing exotic birds from captivity and nursing them back to health, this excellent educational facility preaches the mantra that parrots are not pets. Pick up your earplugs at reception and stroll among the enclosures, each alive with recovering, and very noisy, birds. Don't be surprised when some screech a chirpy 'hello' as you stroll past.

Milner Gardens & Woodland   GARDENS
(www.milnergardens.org; 2179 W Island Hwy, Qualicum Beach; adult/child $11/free; ⊗10am-4:30pm) This idyllic summertime attraction combines rambling forest trails shaded by centuries-old trees with flower-packed gardens planted with magnificent rhododendrons. Meander down to the 1930s **tearoom** on a stunning bluff overlooking the water. Then tuck into a full afternoon tea ($17.95) on the porch and drink in views of the bird-lined shore and snowcapped peaks shimmering on the horizon.

Morningstar Farm   FARM
(www.morningstarfarm.ca; 403 Lowry's Rd, Parksville; ⊗9am-5pm) **FREE** Check out the

region's 'locavore' credentials at this little working farmstead, which is a family-friendly visitor attraction. Let your kids run wild – most will quickly fall in love with the roaming pigs and goats – then hunt down some samples from the on-site Little Qualicum Cheeseworks and Mooberry Winery: blueberry, cranberry and gooseberry fruit wines are recommended.

Horne Lake Caves   PARK
(☑250-248-7829; www.hornelake.com; tours adult/child from $24/20; ☺10am-5pm) Horne Lake Caves Provincial Park is a 45-minute drive from Parksville, but it's worth it for BC's best spelunking. Some caves are open to the public for self-exploration, though the excellent guided tours are recommended, from family friendly to 'extreme' – book ahead for these. To get there, take Hwy 19 towards Courtenay, then exit 75 and proceed for 12km on the gravel road.

🛏 Sleeping & Eating

⭐ Free Spirit Spheres   CABINS $$
(☑250-757-9445; www.freespiritspheres.com; 420 Horne Lake Rd, Qualicum Beach; cabins from $145) These unique spherical tree houses enable guests to cocoon themselves in the forest canopy. Compact inside, 'Eve' is small and basic, while 'Eryn' and 'Melody' are lined with built-in cabinets. It's all about communing with nature, with TVs replaced by books, and guests receive a basket of tasty snacks on arrival. There's also a ground-level facilities block with sauna, BBQ and hotel-quality showers. Book early for summer.

Blue Willow Guest House   B&B $$
(☑250-752-9052; www.bluewillowguesthouse.com; 524 Quatna Rd, Qualicum Beach; d from $140) A surprisingly spacious Victorian-style cottage, this lovely B&B has a book-lined lounge, exposed beams and a fragrant country garden. The two rooms and one self-contained suite are lined with antiques and each is extremely homely. The attention to detail carries over to the gourmet breakfast: served in the conservatory, it's accompanied by finger-licking home-baked treats.

Crown Mansion   BOUTIQUE HOTEL $$
(☑250-752-5776, 800-378-6811; www.crown-mansion.com; 292 E Crescent Rd, Qualicum Beach; d from $160; ☎) A sumptuous family home built in 1912, this handsome white-painted mansion was restored to its former glory

and opened as a unique hotel in 2009. Recall past guests Bing Crosby and John Wayne as you check out the family crest in the library fireplace, then retire to your elegant room. Rates include continental breakfast; arrive early to snag the window table.

Fish Tales Café   SEAFOOD $$
(336 W Island Hwy, Qualicum Beach; mains $8-24) This Qualicum fixture has the look of an old-school English tea shop, but it's been reeling in visitors with its perfect fish and chips for years. It's worth exploring the non-deep-fried dishes; the two-person platter of scallops, shrimp, smoked salmon and mussels is recommended. If you arrive early enough, you can grab a table in the lovely garden.

ℹ Getting There & Away

Greyhound Canada (www.greyhound.ca) services arrive in Parksville from Victoria (from $18.50, from three hours, five daily) and Nanaimo (from $6.50, 40 minutes, five daily) among others. The same buses, with similar times and rates, serve Qualicum Beach.

Port Alberni

POP 17,500

With its fishing and forestry sectors declining, Alberni – located on Hwy 4 between the island's east and west coasts – has been ramping up its visitor appeal in recent years. A good location for outdoor exploration, there are also some intriguing historic attractions. For more on what to do in the region, visit www.albernivalleytourism.com.

◉ Sights

Cathedral Grove   PARK
(www.bcparks.ca) Between Parksville and Port Alberni, this spiritual home of tree huggers is the mystical highlight of MacMillan Provincial Park. It's often overrun with summer visitors – try not to knock them down as they scamper across the highway in front of you. The accessible forest trails wind through a dense, breathtaking canopy of vegetation, offering glimpses of some of BC's oldest trees, including centuries-old Douglas firs more than 3m in diameter. Try hugging that.

Alberni Valley Museum   MUSEUM
(www.alberniheritage.com; 4255 Wallace St; admission by donation; ☺10am-5pm Tue, Wed, Fri, & Sat, to 8pm Thu) Studded with fascinating aboriginal and pioneer-era exhibits, the museum's intriguing section on the West Coast

Trail shows how the route was once a life-saving trail for shipwreck victims. History buffs should extend their visit by boarding the town's Alberni Pacific Railway heritage steam train (July and August) for a trundle to McLean Mill – a national historic site, it's Canada's only working steam-powered sawmill.

☞ Tours

MV Frances Barkley   BOAT TOUR
(www.ladyrosemarine.com; 5425 Argyle St; return trip $52-74; ☺May-Sep) This historic boat is a vital link for the region's remote communities, ferrying freight, supplies and passengers between Alberni and Bamfield thrice weekly. In summer, with its route extended to Ucluelet and the lovely Broken Group Islands, it lures kayakers and mountain bikers, but it's also open for those who just fancy an idyllic cruise up Barkley Sound.

Batstar Adventure Tours   ADVENTURE TOUR
(www.batstar.com; 4785 Beaver Creek Rd) If you're unsure about exploring the jaw-droppingly beautiful but undeniably remote Broken Group Islands by kayak on your own, these guys can sort you out. From long-weekend jaunts to multiday odysseys of the life-changing variety, all the details, including food and accommodations, are taken care of on these guided adventures.

🛏 Sleeping & Eating

Fat Salmon Backpackers   HOSTEL $
(☎250-723-6924;   www.fatsalmonbackpackers.com; 3250 3rd Ave; dm $25; ☺May-Sep; @ 🛜) Driven by its highly sociable owners, this funky, eclectic backpacker joint offers four-to eight-bed dorms (that means no private rooms) with names like 'Knickerbocker' and 'Mullet Room.' There are lots of books, free tea and coffee and a kitchen bristling with utensils. Say 'hi' to Lily, the world-famous house dog and she'll almost certainly let you take her for a walk.

Hummingbird Guesthouse   B&B $$
(☎888-720-2114,   250-720-2111;   www.hummingbirdguesthouse.com; 5769 River Rd; ste $125-180; 🛜) With four large suites and a huge deck with its own hot tub, this modern B&B has a home-away-from-home feel – just ask Jasper, the laid-back house cat. There's a shared kitchen on each of the two floors and each suite has satellite TV; one has its own sauna. For families, there's a teen-friendly games room out back.

All Mex'd Up   MEXICAN $
(5440 Argyle St; mains $4-10) A funky and highly colorful little Mexican comfort food shack near the waterfront – it's decorated with chili-shaped fairy lights – this spot makes everything from scratch and focuses on local ingredients as much as possible. Pull up a stool and tuck into a classic array of made-with-love tacos, quesadillas and big-ass burritos and you'll be full for your day of exploring.

ℹ Getting There & Away

Greyhound Canada (www.greyhound.ca) buses arrive here from Victoria (from $46, four to five hours, three daily) and Tofino (from $28.40, two hours, two daily), among others.

Pacific Rim National Park Reserve

Dramatic, wave-whipped beaches and brooding, mist-licked forests make the **Pacific Rim National Park Reserve** (www.pc.gc.ca/pacificrim; park pass adult/child C$7.80/6.80) a must-see for anyone interested in experiencing BC's raw West Coast wilderness. The 500-sq-km park comprises the northern Long Beach Unit, between Tofino and Ucluelet; the Broken Group Islands Unit in Barkley Sound; and, to the south, the ever-popular West Coast Trail Unit. First timers should drop by the **Pacific Rim Visitors Centre** (☎250-726-4600; www.pacificrimvisitor.ca; 2791 Pacific Rim Hwy; ☺10am-4:30pm) for maps and advice on exploring the region. If you're stopping in the park, you'll need to pay and display a pass, available from the visitors center or from the yellow dispensers dotted along the highway.

Long Beach Unit

Attracting the lion's share of visitors, Long Beach Unit is easily accessible by car along the Pacific Rim Hwy. Wide sandy beaches, untamed surf, lots of beachcombing nooks, plus a living museum of old-growth rainforest, are the main reasons for the summer tourist clamor. Cox Bay Beach alone is an ideal hangout for surfers and families. Seabirds, sand dollars, and purple and orange starfish abound.

For an introduction to the area's natural history and First Nations heritage, visit the **Kwisitis Centre** (Wick Rd; free with park pass admission; ☺10am-4:30pm Mar-Aug) overlooking

Wickaninnish Beach. If you're suddenly inspired to plunge in for a stroll, try one of the following trails, keeping your eyes peeled for swooping bald eagles and giant banana slugs. Safety precautions apply: tread carefully over slippery surfaces and never turn your back on the mischievous surf.

Long Beach Great scenery along the sandy shore (1.2km; easy).

Rainforest Trail Two interpretive loops through old-growth forest (1km; moderate).

Schooner Trail Through old- and second-growth forests with beach access (1km; moderate).

Shorepine Bog Loops around a moss-layered bog (800m; easy and wheelchair accessible).

Broken Group Islands Unit

Comprising some 300 islands and rocks scattered across 80 sq km around the entrance to Barkley Sound, this serene natural wilderness is beloved of visiting kayakers – especially those who enjoy close-up views of whales, porpoises and multitudinous birdlife. Compasses are required for navigating here, unless you fancy paddling to Hawaii.

If you're up for a trek, **Lady Rose Marine Services** (www.ladyrosemarine.com) will ship you and your kayak from Port Alberni to its Sechart Whaling Station Lodge three hours away in Barkley Sound on the MV *Frances Barkley*. The lodge rents kayaks ($40 to $60 per day) if you'd rather travel light and offers accommodations (single/double $150/235, including meals).

From there, popular paddle destinations include Gibraltar Island, one hour away, with its sheltered campground and explorable beaches and tidal pools. Willis Island (1½ hours from Sechart) is also popular. It has a campground and, at low tide, you can walk to the surrounding islands. Remote Benson Island (four hours from Sechart) has a campground, grazing deer and a blowhole.

Camping fees are $9.80 per night, payable at Sechart or to the boat-based staff who patrol the region – they can collect additional fees from you if you decide to stay longer. The campgrounds are predictably basic and have solar composting toilets, but you must carry out all your garbage. Bring your own drinking water since island creeks are often dry in summer.

West Coast Trail Unit

The 75km West Coast Trail is BC's best-known hiking route. It's also one of the toughest. Not for the uninitiated, there are two things you'll need to know before tackling it: it will hurt and you'll want to do it again next year.

The trail winds along the wave-licked rainforest shoreline between trailhead information centers at Pachena Bay, 5km south of Bamfield on the north end, and Gordon River, 5km north of Port Renfrew on the southern tip. The entire stretch takes between six and seven days to complete. Open May to September, access to the route during the mid-June to mid-September peak season is limited to 60 overnight backpackers each day and **reservations** (☑877-737-3783, 250-726-4453; www.reservation.pc.gc.ca; nonrefundable reservation fee C$24.50) are required. All overnighters must pay a trail-user fee ($127.50), plus $30 to cover the two short ferry crossings on the route. All overnighters must attend a 1½-hour orientation session before departing. If you don't have a reservation, some permits are kept back for a daily waitlist system.

If you don't want to go the whole hog (you wimp), you can do a day hike or even hike half the trail from Pachena Bay, considered the easier end of the route. Overnight hikers who only hike this end of the trail can exit from Nitinat Lake. Day hikers are exempt from the large trail-user fee, but they need to get a free day-use permit at one of the trailheads.

West Coast Trail walkers must be able to manage rough, slippery terrain, stream crossings and adverse, suddenly changing weather. There are more than 100 little, and some not-so-little, bridges and 70 ladders. Be prepared to treat or boil all water and cook on a lightweight camping stove; you'll be bringing in all your own food. Hikers can rest their weary muscles at any of the basic campsites along the route, most of which have solar-composting outhouses. It's recommended that you set out from a trailhead at least five hours before sundown to ensure you reach a campsite before nightfall – stumbling around in the dark is the prime cause of accidents on this route.

West Coast Trail Express (www.trailbus.com) runs a daily shuttle (May to September) to the trailheads. Book ahead in summer.

Tofino

POP 1900

Transforming from resource outpost to hippie enclave and now eco-resort town, Tofino is Vancouver Island's favorite outdoorsy retreat. It's not surprising that surf fans, families and city-escaping Vancouverites keep coming: packed with activities and blessed with stunning regional beaches, the funky community sits on Clayoquot Sound, where forested mounds rise from roiling, ever-dramatic waves.

◉ Sights & Activities

Tofino Botanical Gardens   GARDENS
(www.tbgf.org; 1084 Pacific Rim Hwy; 3-day admission adult/child $10/free; ⊘9am-dusk) ✦ Explore what coastal temperate rainforests are all about by checking out the frog pond, forest boardwalk, native plants and educational workshops at this smashing, bird-packed rustic attraction. There's a seasonal cafe onsite for that essential glass of wine, while classical music is piped through the gardens most evenings. There's a $1 discount if you arrive car free.

Maquinna Marine Provincial Park   PARK
(www.bcparks.ca) ✦ One of the most popular day trips from Tofino, the highlight here is **Hot Spring Cove**. Tranquility-minded trekkers travel to the park by Zodiac boat or seaplane, watching for whales and other sea critters en route. From the boat landing, 2km of boardwalks lead to the natural hot pools.

Meares Island   PARK
Visible through the mist and accessible via kayak or tour boat from the Tofino waterfront, Meares Island is home to the Big Tree Trail, a 400m boardwalk through old-growth forest that includes a stunning 1500-year-old red cedar. The island was the site of the key 1984 Clayoquot Sound antilogging protest that kicked off the region's latter-day environmental movement.

Ahousat   PARK
(www.wildsidetrail.com) Situated on remote Flores Island and accessed by tour boat or kayak, Ahousat is the mystical location of the spectacular Wild Side Heritage Trail, a moderately difficult path that traverses 10km of forests, beaches and headlands between Ahousat and Cow Bay. There's a natural warm spring on the island and it's also home to a First Nations band. A popular destination for kayakers, camping of the no-facilities variety is allowed.

Tofino Brewing Company   BREWERY
(www.tofinobrewingco.com; 681 Industrial Way; ⊘noon-11pm) Hidden around the back of an unassuming industrial building, this smashing little brewery makes islanders very merry, which is why its brews are in restaurants around town and beyond. Roll up to the tasting bar and check out a few free samples. Always ask for the seasonal offering, but check out the excellent Tuff Session Ale, then consider a takeout growler.

Inkwis Arts & Culture   GALLERY
(www.inkwis-portal.com; 368 Main St; ⊘11am-5pm Wed-Sun) The newest of several First Nations–focused galleries around Tofino's downtown drag, this spartan but friendly little space has a lively roster of ever-changing exhibitions; check the website for exhibition opening events. While the focus is contemporary First Nations, artists from other communities are also part of the mix, as are workshops and a growing art-for-sale section.

Pacific Surf School   SURFING
(www.pacificsurfschool.com; 430 Campbell St; board rental 6/24hr $15/20) Offers rentals, camps and lessons for beginners.

STORMING TOFINO

Started as a clever marketing ploy to lure off-season visitors, storm-watching has become a popular pastime on the island's west coast. View spectacularly crashing winter waves, then scamper back inside for hot chocolate with a face freckled by sea salt. There are usually good off-peak deals to be had in area accommodations during storm-watching season (typically November to March) and most hotels can supply you with loaner 'Tofino tuxedos,' otherwise known as waterproof gear. The best spots to catch a few crashing spectacles are Cox Bay, Chesterman Beach, Long Beach, Second Bay and Wickaninnish Beach. Just remember not to get too close or turn your back on the waves: these gigantic swells will have you in the water within seconds if given half the chance.

Surf Sister
SURFING

(www.surfsister.com; 625 Campbell St; lessons $79) Introductory lessons for boys and girls, plus women-only multiday courses.

☞ Tours

Remote Passages
KAYAKING

(www.remotepassages.com; 51 Wharf St; tours from $64) Gives short guided kayaking tours around Clayoquot Sound and the islands.

Tofino Sea Kayaking
KAYAKING

(www.tofino-kayaking.com; 320 Main St; tours from $60) Evocative guided paddles; one-day tours to the Freedom Cove floating gardens are recommended.

Jamie's Whaling Station
BOAT TOUR

(www.jamies.com; 606 Campbell St; adult/child $99/69) Spot whales, bears and sea lions on Jamie's boat jaunts.

Ocean Outfitters
BOAT TOUR

(www.oceanoutfitters.bc.ca; 368 Main St; adult/child $89/69) Popular whale-watching tours, with bear and hot-springs treks also offered.

🛏 Sleeping

★ Tofino Inlet Cottages
CABIN $$

(☑ 250-725-3441; www.tofinoinletcottages.com; 350 Olsen Rd; ste from $130; 🖤) Located in a pocket of tranquility just off the highway, this hidden gem is perfect for waking up to glassy-calm waterfront views. It consists of a pairing of two 1960s-built A-frame cottages, divided into two suites each, and a spacious woodsy house, which has a lovely circular hearth and is ideal for families.

Whalers on the Point Guesthouse
HOSTEL $$

(☑ 250-725-3443, 855-725-3443; www.tofinohostel. com; 81 West St; dm/r from $37/93; @🖤) Close to the town center, but with a secluded waterfront location, this excellent HI hostel is a comfy wood-lined retreat. The dorms are mercifully small, and some double-bed private rooms are available. Facilities include a granite-countered kitchen, BBQ patio, games room and a wet sauna, plus you'll spend plenty of time on the shoreline deck. Reservations are essential in summer. Free parking.

Ecolodge
HOSTEL $$

(☑ 250-725-1220; www.tbgf.org; 1084 Pacific Rim Hwy; r from $149; @🖤) In the grounds of the botanical gardens, this immaculate and quiet wood-built education center has a se-lection of rooms, a large kitchen and an on-site laundry. It's popular with families and traveling groups – there's a bunk room that works out at $40 each per night in summer for groups of four. Rates include entry to the surrounding gardens. A great sleepover for nature lovers.

Ocean Village Beach Resort
CABINS $$$

(☑ 866-725-3755, 250-725-3755; www.ocean-villageresort.com; 555 Hellesen Dr; ste from $229; 🖤🖤🖤) Recently renovated, this immaculate beachside resort of 53 beehive-shaped cedar cabins – hence the woodsy aroma when you step in the door – is a family favorite with a Scandinavian look. Each unit faces a shore-line just a few steps away and all have handy kitchens. If your kids tire of the beach, there are surf lessons and a saltwater pool to keep them occupied. No in-room TVs.

Pacific Sands Beach Resort
RESORT $$$

(☑ 800-565-2322, 250-725-3322; www.pacific-sands.com; 1421 Pacific Rim Hwy; d from $275; 🖤🖤) Combining comfortable lodge rooms, all with full kitchens, plus spectacular three-level beach houses, this family-friendly resort hugs dramatic Cox Bay Beach. Wher-ever you stay, you'll be lulled to sleep by the sound of the nearby roiling surf. The spacious, contemporary-furnished beach houses are ideal for groups and have stone fireplaces and top-floor bathtubs with views. There are free summertime nature pro-grams for kids.

Chesterman Beach B&B
B&B $$$

(☑ 250-725-3726; www.chestermanbeach.net; 1345 Chesterman Beach Rd; d from $185; 🖤) Lo-cated among a string of B&Bs, this classy, adult-oriented spot has two main rooms, each with a private entrance, and amaz-ing access to the beach close at hand. The smaller Lookout suite is our favorite, with its cozy, wood-lined ambience and mesmer-izing beach vistas. There's a separate cottage at the back of the property that's great for small groups.

Wickaninnish Inn
HOTEL $$$

(☑ 800-333-4604, 250-725-3100; www.wickinn. com; Chesterman Beach; d from $399; 🖤🖤) Cor-nering the market in luxury winter storm-watching packages, 'the Wick' is worth a stay any time of year. Embodying nature with its recycled wood furnishings, natu-ral stone tiles and the ambience of a place grown rather than constructed, the sump-tuous guest rooms have push-button gas

PACIFIC RIM PIT STOP

Don't drive too fast in your rush to get to end-of-the-highway Tofino or you'll miss the locals' favorite stomping ground. Ostensibly known as the **Beaches Shopping Centre** area, 1180 Pacific Rim Hwy is home to dozens of funky little wood-built businesses where you could easily spend a happy half-day. Drop into the **Juicery** (⊗9am-6pm) for fresh-made fruit smoothies or grab a java at **Tofitian** (⊗7:30am-5pm; ⊚). While bike and surf rentals are available, forget the exercise and go straight for the treats.

TacoFino (www.tacofino.com; mains $4-12; ⊗11am-5pm Sun-Thu, to 6pm Fri & Sat) is one of BC's most legendary food trucks, serving the best fish tacos in the region. **Chocolate Tofino** (www.chocolatetofino.com; ⊗10am-9pm Mon-Sat) steps up to the plate for dessert, with heaping house-made ice cream and naughty chocolates to go, including amazing salted caramels. Go for the lavender-honey ice cream or ask them for the 'secret' flavors hidden in the back that only the locals know about.

fireplaces, two-person hot tubs and floor-to-ceiling windows. The region's most romantic sleepover.

 Eating

Shelter   WEST COAST **$$**
(www.shelterrestaurant.com; 601 Campbell St; mains $12-30; ⊗11am-midnight) This woodsy, low-ceilinged haunt has kept expanding over the years, but has never lost its welcoming locals' hangout feel. The perfect spot to grab lunch; salmon surf bowls and a patio seat are recommended. Shelter becomes an intimate dinner venue every evening when the menu ratchets up to showcase finger-licking BC-sourced treats from seafood to gourmet burgers.

Sobo   WEST COAST **$$**
(www.sobo.ca; 311 Neill St; mains $15-30; ⊗11am-9pm) This local favorite started out as a still-remembered purple food truck and is now a popular sit-down eatery. The focus at Sobo – meaning Sophisticated Bohemian – is seasonal West Coast ingredients prepared with international influences. A brilliant place to dive into fresh-catch seafood for dinner, there's a hearty lunch menu if you need an early fill-up; the gourmet pizzas are recommended.

Schooner   SEAFOOD **$$**
(www.schoonerrestaurant.ca; 331 Campbell St; mains $18-28) Family run for 50 years, this local legend has been reinvigorated recently by the return of the owner to cheffing duties. Start your evening with a cocktail, then launch your voyage into the region's seafood bounty; the giant, two-person Captain's Plate blowout of local salmon, scallops et al

is the way to go. Come back on the weekend for the excellent brunch.

ⓘ Information

Tofino Visitors Centre (☑250-725-3414; www.tourismtofino.com; 1426 Pacific Rim Hwy; ⊗9am-5pm) A short drive south of town, the visitors center has detailed information on area accommodations, hiking trails and hot surf spots. There's also a blue-painted Tourism Tofino VW van parked around the town center in summer that dispenses advice to out-of-towners.

ⓘ Getting There & Around

Orca Airways (www.flyorcaair.com) Flights arrive at Tofino Airport from Vancouver International Airport's South Terminal (from $174, one hour, up to five daily).

Greyhound Canada (www.greyhound.ca) Buses (operated by Tofino Bus) arrive from Port Alberni ($29, two hours), Nanaimo ($46, three to four hours), Victoria ($69, six to seven hours) and beyond.

Tofino Bus (www.tofinobus.com) 'Beach Bus' services roll in along Hwy 4 from Ucluelet ($17, 40 minutes).

Ucluelet

POP 1600

Threading along Hwy 4 through the mountains to the west coast, you'll arrive at a junction sign proclaiming that Tofino is 33km to your right, while just 8km to your left is Ucluelet. Sadly, most still take the right-hand turn, which is a shame, since sleepier 'Ukee' has more than a few charms of its own and is a good reminder of what Tofino was like before tourism arrived.

◉ Sights & Activities

Ucluelet Aquarium
AQUARIUM

(www.uclueletaquarium.org; Main Street Waterfront Promenade; adult/child $12.50/6.25; ☺10am-6pm) ✎ Replacing the tiny waterfront shack that stood nearby, the excellent Ucluelet Aquarium opened this much larger facility in 2012. Retaining key approaches from the old place, the kid-luring touch tanks are still here, and the marine critters are local, with most on a catch-and-release program. But it's the enthusiasm of the young staff that sets this place apart, along with the ability to educate on issues of conservation without browbeating. Take your time to peer at the astonishing array of local aquatic life and, if you're lucky, you'll be here when a Pacific octopus is enjoying a live-crab feeding session. In summer, look out for family-friendly lab workshops (free).

Wild Pacific Trail
HIKING

(www.wildpacifictrail.com) The 8.5km Wild Pacific Trail offers smashing views of Barkley Sound and the Broken Group Islands. Starting at the intersection of Peninsula and Coast Guard Rds, it winds around the wave-slapped cliffs past the lighthouse (get your camera out here) and along the craggy shoreline fringing the town. Seabirds are abundant and it's a good storm-watching spot – stick to the trail or the crashing waves might pluck you from the cliffs. Plans were in place on our visit to expand the route by another few kilometers; check the website for progress reports.

Majestic Ocean Kayaking
KAYAKING

(www.oceankayaking.com; 1167 Helen Rd; tours from $67) Majestic Ocean Kayaking leads day trips around the area, plus multiday tours of the Broken Group Islands.

Relic Surf Shop
SURFING

(www.relicsurfshop.com; 1998 Peninsula Rd; rentals from $30) If you want to practice the ways of surfing, check in with Relic Surf Shop.

Ukee Bikes
CYCLING

(www.ukeebikes.com; 1559 Imperial Lane; bike rental 2/24hr $10/25; ☺10am-6pm Tue-Fri, to 5pm Sat) Rent some wheels from the friendly folk at Ukee Bikes. They also sell kites.

🛏 Sleeping & Eating

C&N Backpackers
HOSTEL $

(☎888-434-6060, 250-726-7416; www.cnnbackpackers.com; 2081 Peninsula Rd; dm/r $25/65; ☺Apr-Oct; 🛜) They're very protective of their hardwood floors, so take off your shoes at the door of this calm and well-maintained hostel. The dorms are mostly small and predictably basic, but private rooms are available and there's a spacious downstairs kitchen. The highlight is the landscaped, nap-worthy garden overlooking the inlet, complete with hammocks and a rope swing.

Surfs Inn Guesthouse
CABINS, HOSTEL $

(☎250-726-4426; www.surfsinn.ca; 1874 Peninsula Rd; dm/cottages from $28/139; 🛜) It's hard to miss this blue-painted house near the center of town, with its small, woodsy dorm rooms. But the real find is hidden out back: two cute cabins that are ideal for groups and families. One is larger and self-contained while the other is divided into two suites with kitchenettes. Each has a BBQ. Ask about surf packages if you fancy hitting the waves.

Black Rock Oceanfront Resort
HOTEL $$$

(☎250-726-4800, 877-762-5011; www.blackrockresort.com; 596 Marine Dr; d from $269; 🛜🐾) Ucluelet's fanciest sleepover feels like a transplant from Tofino. This dramatic waterfront resort offers kitchen-equipped suites, all wrapped in a contemporary wood-and-stone West Coast look. Many rooms have great views of the often dramatically stormy surf. There's a vista-hugging restaurant specializing in regional nosh, plus a lobby-level bar shaped like a rolling wave.

Ukee Dogs
CAFE $

(1576 Imperial Lane; mains $4-12; ☺8:30am-3:30pm Mon-Fri, 10:30am-3:30pm Sat & Sun) Focused on own-baked treats and comfort foods, this bright and breezy, good-value eatery offers hot dogs of the gourmet variety (go for the Imperial), plus rustic pizzas, hearty breakfasts and great salmon sliders with fries or salad. Whatever you indulge in, aim for a sunny picnic table outside and pick up a sprinkle-topped coconut cookie to go.

★ Hank's
WEST COAST $$

(www.hanksucluelet.com; 1576 Imperial Lane; mains $18-22; ☺5-11pm Wed-Mon) Closed every Tuesday so they can forage island farms for ingredients, this smashing addition to Ukee's dining scene has quickly become a local fave. The fresh and local menu is divided between seafood and succulent barbecue; go for lamb. There's a brilliant array of BC craft beers, plus more than 50 bottles from further afield – look out for twice-monthly beer-cask nights.

Norwoods
WEST COAST $$$

(www.norwoods.ca; 1714 Peninsula Rd; mains $24-34; ⏱5-10pm) Showing how far Ucluelet's dining scene has elevated itself in recent years, this lovely candlelit room would easily be at home in Tofino. The ever-changing menu focuses on seasonal regional ingredients; think halibut and duck breast. All are prepared with a sophisticated international approach, plus there's a full menu of BC and beyond wines, many offered by the glass.

❶ Information

Ucluelet Visitors Centre (☎250-726-2485; www.ucluelet.travel; 1604 Peninsula Rd; ⏱9am-5pm) For a few good reasons to stick around in Ukee, including a dining scene that finally has some great options, make for the new visitors center.

❶ Getting There & Around

Greyhound Canada (www.greyhound.ca) Operated by Tofino Bus, services arrive from Port Alberni (from $26, 1½ hours, three daily), Nanaimo (from $46, three to four hours, three daily) and Victoria (from $34, six hours, four daily), among others.

Tofino Bus (www.tofinobus.com) The 'Beach Bus' comes into town along Hwy 4 from Tofino ($17, 40 minutes, up to three daily).

Denman & Hornby Islands

The main Northern Gulf Islands, **Denman** (www.denmanisland.com) and **Hornby** (www.hornbyisland.net) share laid-back attitudes, artistic flair and some tranquil outdoor activities. You'll arrive by ferry at Denman first from Buckley Bay on Vancouver Island, then hop from Denman across to Hornby. Stop at **Denman Village**, near the first ferry dock, and pick up a free map for both islands.

❍ Sights & Activities

Denman has three provincial parks: **Fillongley**, with easy hiking and beachcombing; **Boyle Point**, with a beautiful walk to the lighthouse; and **Sandy Island**, only accessible by water from north Denman.

Among Hornby's provincial parks, **Tribune Bay** features a long sandy beach with safe swimming, while **Helliwell** offers notable hiking. **Ford's Cove**, on Hornby's south coast, offers the chance for divers to swim with six-gilled sharks. The island's large **Mt Geoffrey Regional Park** is crisscrossed with hiking and mountain-biking trails.

Denman Hornby Canoes & Kayaks
KAYAKING

(www.denmanpaddling.ca; 4005 East Rd, Denman Island) For kayaking rentals in the area.

🛏 Sleeping & Eating

Blue Owl
B&B $$

(☎250-335-3440; www.blueowlondenman.ca; 8850 Owl Cres, Denman Island; s/d incl breakfast $115/125; ❄) An idyllically rustic retreat for those craving an escape from city life, this woodsy little cottage is a short walk from the ocean. Loaner bikes are freely available if you fancy exploring (there's a swimmable lake nearby), but you might want to just cozy up for a night in.

Sea Breeze Lodge
HOTEL $$

(☎888-516-2321, 250-335-2321; www.seabreezelodge.com; 5205 Fowler Rd, Hornby Island; adult/child $180/75) This 12-acre retreat, with 16 cottages overlooking the ocean, has the feel of a Spanish villa with a Pacific Rim twist. Rooms are comfortable rather than palatial and some have fireplaces and full kitchens. You can swim, kayak and fish or just flop lazily around in the cliffside hot tub. Rates are per person and include three daily meals.

Cardboard House Bakery
BAKERY $

(www.thecardboardhousebakery.com; 2205 Central Rd, Hornby Island; mains $4-10) It's easy to lose track of time at this old shingle-sided farmhouse that combines a hearty bakery, pizza shop and cozy cafe. It's impossible not to stock up on a bag full of oven-fresh muffins, cookies and croissants for the road. Stick around for an alfresco lunch in the adjoining orchard, which also stages live music Wednesday and Sunday evenings in summer.

Island Time Café
CAFE $

(3464 Denman Rd, Denman Island; mains $7-11) This village hangout specializes in fresh-from-the-oven bakery treats, such as muffins and scones, plus organic coffee, bulging breakfast wraps and hearty house-made soups. The pizza is particularly recommended, and is served with a side order of gossip from the locals. If the sun is cooperating, sit outside and catch some rays.

❶ Getting There & Away

BC Ferries (www.bcferries.com) Services arrive throughout the day at Denman from Buckley Bay (passenger/vehicle $9.45/22.15, 10 minutes). Hornby Island is accessed by ferry from Denman (passenger/vehicle $9.45/22.15, 10 minutes).

Comox Valley

Comprising the towns of Comox and Courtenay and the village of Cumberland, this is a region of rolling mountains, alpine meadows and colorful communities. A good outdoor adventure base and mountain-biking hotbed, its activity-triggering highlight is Mt Washington.

◉ Sights & Activities

Save time for a poke around charming Cumberland, a town built on mining that's now luring artsy young residents from across BC to its clapboard shops and houses.

Courtenay & District Museum & Palaeontology Centre
MUSEUM

(www.courtenaymuseum.ca; 207 4th St, Courtenay; admission by donation; ⊙10am-5pm Mon-Sat, noon-4pm Sun) With its life-sized replica of an elasmosaur – a prehistoric marine reptile first discovered in the area – the excellent museum also houses pioneer and First Nations exhibits.

Cumberland Museum
MUSEUM

(www.cumberlandmuseum.ca; Dunsmuir Ave, Cumberland; ⊙10am-5pm) Get some historic context at the Cumberland Museum, with its little walk-through mine exhibit.

Mt Washington Alpine Resort
OUTDOORS

(www.mountwashington.ca; winter lift ticket adult/child $75/39) The main reason for winter visits, Mt Washington Alpine Resort is the island's skiing mecca, with its 81 runs, snowshoeing park and popular night skiing. There are also great summer activities, including some of the region's best hiking trails.

🛏 Sleeping & Eating

★ Riding Fool Hostel
HOSTEL $

(☎250-336-8250, 888-313-3665; www.ridingfool.com; 2705 Dunsmuir Ave, Cumberland; dm/r $25/60; @🛜) One of BC's top hostels colonizes a restored Cumberland heritage building with rustic wooden interiors, a large kitchen and lounge area and, along with its small dorms, the kind of neat and tidy private rooms often found in midrange hotels. Bicycle rentals are available downstairs: this is a great hostel to hang out with the mountain-bike crowd.

Cona Hostel
HOSTEL $

(☎877-490-2662, 250-331-0991; www.theconahostel.com; 440 Anderton Ave, Courtenay; dm/r $25/58; @🛜) It's hard to miss this orange-painted riverside hostel, a popular spot for families and young mountain-bike buddies gearing up for their next assault on the area's multitudinous trails. The friendly folks at the front desk have plenty of other suggestions for what to explore, but you might want to just stay indoors as there's a large kitchen, BBQ patio and board games to keep you busy.

Kingfisher Oceanside Resort
HOTEL $$

(☎250-338-1323, 800-663-7929; www.kingfisher-spa.com; 4330 Island Hwy, Courtenay; r/ste from $145/220; @🛜🛁🏊) At this boutique waterfront lodge, many of the rooms are oriented to focus on the waterfront, framed by islands and mountains. A good spot to take a break from your road trip, rooms are generally large and comfortable and many have full kitchens, so you can save on dining out – you'll likely blow it at the spa though. There are some good off-season deals.

Dark Side Chocolates
CHOCOLATE $

(www.darksidechocolates.com; 2722 Dunsmuir Ave, Cumberland; choc selections from $5; ⊙10am-4:30pm Tue-Sat) Drop into Dark Side Chocolates for treats; the mint melties are recommended.

Waverley Hotel Pub
BURGERS $$

(www.waverleyhotel.ca; 2692 Dunsmuir Ave, Cumberland; mains $9-15) If you're keen to meet the locals, hit this historic saloon for a pint of Blue Buck Ale. Food is of the hearty pub-grub variety – how many more reasons do you need to have a burger? There are often live bands on the kick-ass little stage.

Mad Chef Café
CANADIAN, FUSION $$

(www.madchefcafe.net; 492 Fitzgerald Ave, Courtenay; mains $8-20; ⊙11am-8pm Mon-Thu, to 9pm Fri & Sat) This bright and colorful neighborhood eatery serves a great selection of made-from-scratch meals, and is a good place for a salad, since they're heaping and crispy fresh. Sharers should go for the Mediterranean plate, piled high with olives, hummus, pita and lovely house-made bruschetta. Gourmet duck and salmon burgers are also popular.

Atlas Café
FUSION $$

(www.atlascafe.ca; 250 6th St, Courtenay; mains $12-24; ⊙8:30am-3:30pm Mon, to 9:30pm Tue-Sun) Courtenay's favorite dine-out has a pleasing modern bistro feel with a global menu, fusing Asian, Mexican and Mediterranean flourishes. Check out the gourmet fish tacos, plus ever-changing seasonal treats. Good vegetarian options, too.

ℹ Information

Vancouver Island Visitors Centre (☎885-400-2882; www.discovercomoxvalley.com; 3607 Small Rd, Cumberland; ☺9am-7pm) Drop by the slick visitors center for tips on exploring the area.

Campbell River

POP 29,500

Southerners will tell you this marks the end of civilization on Vancouver Island, but Campbell River is a handy drop off point for wilderness tourism in Strathcona Provincial Park and is large enough to have plenty of attractions and services of its own.

◉ Sights

Museum at Campbell River　　　MUSEUM
(www.crmuseum.ca; 470 Island Hwy; adult/child $8/5; ☺10am-5pm) This fascinating museum is worth an hour of anyone's time and showcases aboriginal masks, an 1890s pioneer cabin and video footage of the world's largest artificial, non-nuclear blast (an underwater mountain in Seymour Narrows that caused dozens of shipwrecks before it was blown apart in a controlled explosion in 1958). In summer, ask about their popular history-themed boat cruises around the area.

Discovery Pier　　　LANDMARK
(rod rentals per half-day $6) Since locals claim the town as the 'Salmon Capital of the World,' you should wet your line off the downtown Discovery Pier or just stroll along with the crowds and see what everyone else has caught. Much easier than catching your own lunch, you can buy fish and chips (and ice cream) here. The perfect sunset spot to hang with the locals.

🛏 Sleeping & Eating

Heron's Landing Hotel　　　HOTEL **$$**
(☎250-923-2848, 888-923-2849; www.heronslandinghotel.com; 492 S Island Hwy; d from $139; @☎) Superior motel-style accommodation with renovated rooms, including large loft suites ideal for families. Rates include breakfast.

Shot in the Dark Cafe　　　CAFE **$$**
(940 Island Hwy; mains $8-14; ☺8am-5pm Mon-Sat; ☎) Huge, freshly made sandwiches and soups are the way to go at this pastel-hued locals' fave. A good spot for cooked breakfast, especially if you haven't eaten for a couple of days.

ℹ Information

Campbell River Visitors Center (☎877-286-5705, 250-830-0411; www.campbellriver.travel; 1235 Shoppers Row; ☺9am-6pm) Will fill you in on what to do here and on nearby Quadra Island.

ℹ Getting There & Around

Pacific Coastal Airlines (www.pacific-coastal.com) Flights from Vancouver (from $88, 45 minutes, up to seven daily) arrive frequently.

Campbell River Transit (www.busonline.oa; adult/child $1.75/1.50) Operates buses throughout the area.

Strathcona Provincial Park

Driving inland via Hwy 28 from Campbell River, you'll find Vancouver Island's largest **park** (www.bcparks.ca) 🏊. Centered on Mt Golden Hinde (2200m), the island's highest point, Strathcona is a magnificent pristine wilderness crisscrossed with trail systems that deliver you to waterfalls, alpine meadows, glacial lakes and mountain crags.

On arrival at the main entrance, get your bearings at **Strathcona Park Lodge & Outdoor Education Centre** (www.strathcona.bc.ca). A one-stop shop for park activities, including kayaking, zip lining, guided treks and rock climbing, this is a great place to rub shoulders with outdoorsy types. All-in adventure packages are available, some aimed specifically at families. Head to the **Whale Room** or **Myrna's** eateries for a fuel up.

The lodge also offers good **accommodations** (☎250-286-3122; r/cabin from $139/175), ranging from rooms in the main building to secluded timber-framed cottages. If you are a true back-to-nature fan, there are several campsites available in the park. Alternatively, consider pitching your tent at **Buttle Lake Campground** (☎800-689-9025, 604-689-9025; www.discovercamping.ca; campsite $24); the swimming area and children's playground make it a good choice for families.

Notable park hiking trails include **Paradise Meadows Loop** (2.2km), an easy amble in a delicate wildflower and evergreen ecosystem; and **Mt Becher** (5km), with its great views over the Comox Valley and mountain-lined Strait of Georgia. Around Buttle Lake, easier walks include **Lady**

QUADRA ISLAND HOP

For a day out with a difference, take your bike on the 10-minute **BC Ferries** (www. bcferries.com; passenger/vehicle/bike $11.10/25.80/2) skip from Campbell River to rustic Quadra. There's an extensive network of trails across the island; maps are for sale in local stores. Many of the forested trails are former logging routes and the local community has spent a lot of time building and maintaining the trails for mountain bikers of all skill levels. If you didn't bring your wheels, you can rent on the island or in Campbell River. For more information on visiting the island, see www.quadraisland.ca.

Quadra's fascinating **Nuyumbalees Cultural Centre** (www.nuyumbalees.com; 34 Weway Rd; adult/child $10/5; ⏰10am-5pm May-Sep) illuminates the heritage and traditions of the local Kwakwaka'wakw First Nations people, showcasing carvings and artifacts and staging traditional dance performances. But if you just want to chill out with the locals, head to **Spirit Square** where performers entertain in summer.

If you decide to stick aroud for dinner, go for the waterfront pub or restaurant at the handsome **Heriot Bay Inn & Marina** (☎888-605-4545, 250-285-3322; www.heriotbayinn. com; Heriot Bay; d/cabins from $109/229) where, if you have a few too many drinks, you might want to stay the night. The hotel has motel-style rooms and charming rustic cabins.

Falls (900m) and the trail along **Karst Creek** (2km), which winds past sinkholes, percolating streams and tumbling waterfalls.

North Vancouver Island

Down islanders, meaning anyone south of Campbell River, will tell you, 'There's nothing up there worth seeing,' while locals here will respond, 'They would say that, wouldn't they?' Parochial rivalries aside, what this giant region, covering nearly half the island, lacks in towns, infrastructure and population, it more than makes up for in natural beauty. Despite the remoteness, some areas are remarkably accessible to hardy hikers, especially along the North Coast Trail. For further information on the region, check in with **Vancouver Island North** (www.vancouverislandnorth.ca).

Port McNeill

POP 2600

Barreling down the hill almost into Broughton Straight, Port McNeill is a useful supply stop for long-distance travelers heading to or from Port Hardy.

More a superior motel than a resort, the hilltop **Black Bear Resort** (☎866-956-4900, 250-956-4900; www.port-mcneill-accommodation. com; 1812 Campbell Way; d/cabin incl breakfast from $148/188; @🛜🐾) overlooks the town and is conveniently located across from shops and restaurants. The standard rooms are small but clean and include microwaves and fridges; full-kitchen units are also available and a string of new cabins was recently added.

If you're still hungry, head for lunch or dinner at **Northern Lights Restaurant** (1817 Campbell Way; mains $12-22; ⏰11am-9pm Mon-Sat). Alongside the usual burgers and pub-style grub, you'll find well-prepared seafood; the halibut is recommended.

Drop by the gabled **visitors center** (☎250-956-3131; www.portmcneill.net; 1594 Beach Dr; ⏰9am-5pm Mon-Fri, 10am-3pm Sat) for regional info, then stop in at the **museum** (351 Shelley Cres; ⏰10am-5pm) to learn about the area's logging-industry heritage.

Greyhound Canada (www.greyhound.ca) buses arrive from, among others, Port Hardy (from $6.50, 40 minutes, daily) and Nanaimo (from $36, six hours, daily).

Alert Bay

POP 500

Located on Cormorant Island, this visitor-friendly village has an ancient and mythical appeal, plus a lovely, walkable waterfront. Its First Nations community and traditions still dominate, but its blend with an old pioneer fishing settlement makes it an even more fascinating day trip from Port McNeill. Drop by the **visitors center** (☎250-974-5024; www.alertbay.ca; 116 Fir St; ⏰9am-4:30pm Mon-Fri) for an introduction and a chat with manager Norine, who will tell you all you need to know about checking the place out –

and especially how to ensure you don't miss any of the area's amazing totem poles.

The highly recommended **U'mista Cultural Centre** (☎250-974-5403; www.umista.ca; 1 Front St; adult/child $8/1; ⊙9am-5pm) showcases an impressive collection of Kwakwaka'wakw masks and other potlatch items originally confiscated by Canada's government. Singing, dancing and BBQs are often held here, while modern-day totem-pole carvers usually work their magic out front. One of the world's tallest totem poles was carved on site in the 1960s and is, appropriately, placed on the front lawn of the **Big House**, which hosts traditional dances in July and August. Also drop into the village's **Culture Shock Interactive Gallery** (www.cultureshockgallery.ca; 10 Front St; ⊙9:30am-6pm) for some exquisite artwork souvenirs.

If the ocean is calling you, **Seasmoke Whale Watching** (www.seaorca.com; adult/child $100/90) offers a five-hour whale-watching trek on its yacht, including afternoon tea.

Port Hardy

POP 3700

This small north-island settlement is best known as the departure point for BC Ferries spectacular Inside Passage trips. It's also a handy spot for gearing up for the rugged North Coast Trail.

🏃 Activities

Odyssey Kayaking   KAYAKING
(www.odysseykayaking.com; from $50) For those who prefer to paddle, Odyssey Kayaking can rent you some gear and point you to local highlights – Malei Island and Alder Bay are recommended.

Catala Charters   DIVING
(www.catalacharters.net; dive trips from $150) For dive fans, Catala Charters can have you hanging with local octopus and wolf eels.

☞ Tours

North Island Daytrippers   HIKING
(www.islanddaytrippers.com) A great access point for exploring the north-island wilderness, hikers can book customized guided tours with the friendly folk here.

🛏 Sleeping & Eating

North Coast Trail Backpackers Hostel   HOSTEL $
(☎250-949-9441, 866-448-6303; www.porthardy-hostel.webs.com; 8635 Granville St; dm/r from

$25/60; 🖘) Colonizing a former downtown storefront, this labyrinthine hostel is a warren of small and larger dorms, overseen by friendly owners with plenty of tips on how to encounter the region – they'll even pick you up from the ferry if you call ahead. The hostel's hub is a large rec room and, while the kitchen is small, the adjoining cafe can keep you well fueled.

Ecoscape Cabins   CABINS $$
(☎250-949-8524; www.ecoscapecabins.com; 6305 Jensen Cove Rd; cabins $130-175; 🖘) The clutch of immaculate cedar cabins are divided between compact units, with flatscreen TVs, microwaves and sunny porches, ideal for couples; and roomier hilltop units, with swankier furnishings, BBQs and expansive views. There's a tranquil retreat feel to staying here and you should expect to see eagles swooping around the nearby trees. Deer are not uncommon, too.

Café Guido   CAFE $
(7135 Market St; mains $5-8; ⊙7am-6pm Mon-Fri, 8am-6pm Sat, 8am-5pm Sun; 🖘) You'll easily end up sticking around for an hour or two at this friendly locals' hangout, especially if you hit the lounge sofas with a tome purchased from the bookstore downstairs. Grilled panini are the way to go for lunch – try the Nero – but there's always a good soup special. Afterwards, nip upstairs to the surprisingly large and diverse craft shop.

ⓘ Information

Port Hardy Visitors Centre (☎250-949-7622; www.porthardy.travel; 7250 Market St; ⊙9am-5pm) Lined with flyers and staffed by locals who can help you plan your visit in town and beyond, the visitors center should be your first port of call.

ⓘ Getting There & Around

Pacific Coastal Airlines (www.pacific-coastal.com) Services arrive from Vancouver (from $170, 1¼ hours, up to four daily).

Greyhound Canada (www.greyhound.ca) Buses roll in from Port McNeill (from $6.50, 45 minutes, daily) and beyond.

BC Ferries (www.bcferries.com) Ferries arrive from Prince Rupert (passenger/vehicle $195/444, 15 hours, schedules vary) via the scenically splendid Inside Passage.

North Island Transportation (☎250-949-6300; nit@island.net; shuttle $8) Operates a handy shuttle to/from the ferry and area hotels.

TELEGRAPH COVE

Built as a one-shack telegraph station, this charming destination has since expanded into one of the north's main visitor lures. Its pioneer-outpost feel is enhanced by the dozens of brightly painted wooden buildings perched around the marina on stilts. Be aware that it can get very crowded in summer.

Head first along the boardwalk to the smashing **Whale Interpretive Centre** (www.killerwhalecentre.org; suggested donation adult/child $3/1; ⊙9am-5pm), bristling with hands-on artifacts and artfully displayed skeletons of cougars, sea otters and a giant fin whale.

You can also see whales of the live variety just offshore: this is one of the island's top marine-life viewing regions and **Stubbs Island Whale Watching** (www.stubbs-island.com; adult/child $99/84) will get you up close with the orcas on a boat trek – you might also see humpbacks, dolphins and sea lions. For a bear alternative, **Tide Rip Grizzly Tours** (www.tiderip.com; tours $299; ⊙May-Sep) leads full-day trips to local beaches and inlets in search of the area's furry locals.

The well-established **Telegraph Cove Resorts** (☑250-928-3131, 800-200-4665; www.telegraphcoveresort.com; campsites/cabins from $28/120) provides accommodations in forested tent spaces and a string of rustic cabins on stilts overlooking the marina. The nearby and much newer **Dockside 29** (☑877-835-2683, 250-928-3163; www.telegraph-cove.ca; d from $140) is a good, motel-style alternative. Its rooms have kitchenettes with hardwood floors and waterfront views.

The **Killer Whale Café** (mains $14-18; ⊙May-Sep) is the cove's best eatery – the salmon, mussel and prawn linguine is recommended. The adjoining **Old Saltery Pub** is an atmospheric, wood-lined nook with a cozy central fireplace and tasty Killer Whale Pale Ale. It's a good spot to sit in a corner and pretend you're an old salty dog – eye patch optional.

Cape Scott Provincial Park

It's more than 550km from Victoria to the nature-hugging trailhead of this remote **park** (www.bcparks.ca) on the island's crenulated northern tip. This should be your number-one destination if you really want to experience the raw, ravishing beauty of BC, especially its unkempt shorelines, breeze-licked rainforests and stunning sandy bays animated with tumbling waves and beady-eyed seabirds.

Hike the well-maintained, relatively easy 2.5km San Josef Bay Trail and you'll stroll from the shady confines of the trees right onto one of the best beaches in BC, a breathtaking, windswept expanse of roiling water, forested crags and the kind of age-old caves that could easily harbor lost smugglers. You can camp right here on the beach or just admire the passing ospreys before plunging back into the trees.

One of the area's shortest trails (2km), in adjoining **Raft Cove Provincial Park** (www.bcparks.ca), brings you to the wide, crescent beach and beautiful lagoons of Raft Cove. You're likely to have the entire 1.3km expanse to yourself, although the locals also like to surf here – it's their secret, so don't tell anyone.

If you really like a challenge, consider the **North Coast Trail**, a 43km route opened in 2008. You can start on the western end at Nissen Bight, but you'll have to hike in 15km on the established and relatively easy Cape Scott Trail to get there. From Nissen Bight, the trail winds eastwards to Shushartie Bay. You'll be passing sandy coves, deserted beaches and dense, wind-whipped rainforest woodland, as well as a couple of river crossings on little cable cars. The trail is muddy and swampy in places, so there are boardwalks to make things easier. The area is home to elk, deer, cougars, wolves and black bears; make sure you know how to handle an encounter before you set off.

Like its west-coast sibling, the North Coast Trail is for experienced and well-equipped hikers only. There are backcountry campsites at Nissen Bight, Laura Creek and Shuttleworth Bight and the route should take five to eight days.

For more infortmation on visiting Cape Scott Provincial park and the North Coast Trail, visit www.capescottpark.com.

SOUTHERN GULF ISLANDS

Stressed Vancouverites often escape into the restorative arms of the rustic, ever-relaxed Southern Gulf Islands, strung like a necklace between the mainland and Vancouver Island. Formerly colonized by BC hippies and US draft dodgers, Salt Spring, Galiano, Mayne, Saturna, and North and South Pender Islands deliver on their promise of idyllic, sigh-triggering getaways.

ℹ Getting There & Around

BC Ferries (www.bcferries.com) Operates services, some direct, from Vancouver Island's Swartz Bay terminal to all the main Southern Gulf Islands. There are also services from the mainland's Tsawwassen terminal.

Gulf Islands Water Taxi (http://saltspring.com/watertaxi) Runs a myriad of handy walk-on boat services between some of the islands.

Salt Spring Air (www.saltspringair.com) Floatplanes service the area with camera-hugging short hops from the mainland.

Salt Spring Island

POP 10,500

The busiest and most developed of the islands, Salt Spring has a reputation for palatial vacation homes, but it's also lined with artist studios and artisan food and drink producers. Well worth a long weekend visit, the heart of the community is Ganges.

⦿ Sights & Activities

Saturday Market   MARKET
(www.saltspringmarket.com; Centennial Park, Ganges; ⊘ 8am-4pm Sat Apr-Oct) Locals tell you they avoid the gigantic Saturday Market that animates the heart of Ganges; they claim to do their shopping at the smaller Tuesday and Wednesday versions. But everyone on the island seems to be here on the big day, checking out the stalls topped with goodies made, baked or grown on the island.

Salt Spring Island Cheese   FARM
(www.saltspringcheese.com; 285 Reynolds Rd; ⊘ 10am-5pm) Drop by for a wander around the idyllic farmstead, and a tasting or two in the winery-style shop. Consider some Ruckles goat cheese to go.

Mistaken Identity Vineyards   WINERY
(www.mistakenidentityvineyards.com; 164 Noxton Rd; ⊘ 11am-6pm) If you're on a picnic-gathering push and need an accompanying libation, consider a tasting visit, with designated driver, to Mistaken Identity Vineyards, where the Bianco is the big seller.

Saltspring Island Ales   BREWERY
(www.gulfislandsbrewery.com; 270 Furness Rd; ⊘ hours vary) Hit Saltspring Island Ales, where the rustic upstairs tasting room serves little samples of great beers. Consider a takeout growler of Heatherdale Ale.

Ruckle Provincial Park   PARK
(www.bcparks.ca) Head to Ruckle Provincial Park, a southeast gem with ragged shorelines and gnarly arbutus forests. There are trails for all skill levels, with Yeo Point making an ideal pit stop.

Salt Spring Adventure Co   KAYAKING
(☑ 250-537-2764, 877-537-2764; www.saltspring-adventures.com; 124 Upper Ganges Rd, Ganges; tours from $50) When it's time to hit the water, touch base with Salt Spring Adventure Co. It can kit you out for a bobbling kayak tour around Ganges Harbour.

⛤ Tours

Salt Spring Studio Tour   TOUR
(www.saltspringstudiotour.com) Art fans should hit the trail on Salt Spring by checking out gallery and studio locations via the free downloadable *Studio Tour Map*. Highlights include **Blue Horse Folk Art Gallery** (www.bluehorse.ca; 175 North View Dr; ⊘ 10am-5pm Sun-Fri Mar-Dec) and **Duthie Gallery** (www.duthiegallery.com; 125 Churchill Rd, Ganges; ⊘ 10am-5pm & 9-11pm Thu-Mon Jul & Aug), which stages the popular summer Night Gallery in its art-lined woodland park.

🛏 Sleeping & Eating

Harbour House Hotel   HOTEL $$
(☑ 888-799-5571, 250-537-5571; www.saltspringharbourhouse.com; 121 Upper Ganges Rd, Ganges; d from $149; 🛜) This smashing rustic-chic hotel with 17 rooms is just up the hill from the main Ganges action, but it feels like staying in a country cottage estate in England. The immaculate grounds are strewn with locally made artworks and the waterfront views will have your camera itching to be used. The restaurant is high-end gourmet; breakfast is recommended.

Wisteria Guest House   B&B $$
(☑ 888-537-5899, 250-537-5899; www.wisteriaguesthouse.com; 268 Park Dr; d/cottage from $120/180; 🛜) This home-away-from-home

Southern Gulf Islands

10 km
6 miles

N

Patos Island

Point Roberts

Waldron Island

Washington

USA

CANADA

British Columbia

Ferry to Tsawwassen

Strait of Georgia

East Point

Tumbo Island

Cabbage Island Day Use Area

East Point Rd

Narvaez Bay

Narvaez Bay Rd

Saturna Island

Taylor Point Day Use Area

Winter Cove

Saturna

Bennett Bay

Samuel Island

Payne

Saturna Island

Mayne

Fernhill Rd

Village

Bay

Mayne Island

Nary Channel

Mt Norman (244m)

South Pender Island

Gowlland Point Rd

Otter Bay

North Pender Island

Medicine Beach

Canal Rd

Sturdies Bay

Gossip Island

Sturdies Bay

Dinner Bay Park

Swanson Channel

Moresby Island

Bay Rd

Arbutus Rd

Prevost Island

Ruckle Provincial Park

Bluffs Park

Georgeson Bay Rd

Portland Island

Swartz Bay (2km)

Montague Harbour Marine Provincial Park

Parker Island

Long Harbour

Captain Passage

Beddis Beach

Piers Island

Dionisio Point Provincial Park

Potlier Pass Rd

Galiano Island

Montague Harbour

Ganges Rd

Beddis Rd

Fulford Harbour

Bodega Ridge Provincial Park

Trincomali Channel

Upper Ganges Rd

Salt Harbour

Ganges

Mt Maxwell Provincial Park

Fulford Ganges Rd

Fulford Harbour

Satellite Channel

Wallace Island

North End Rd

Vesuvius Bay

Salt Spring Island

Secretary Islands

Southey Point

Sunset Dr

Booth Bay

Mt Maxwell Rd

Baynes Peak (588m)

Victoria (60km)

Reid Island

Hall Island

Norway Island

Tent Island

Sansum Narrows

Cowichan Bay

Thetis Island

Kuper Island

Willy Island

Maple Mountain Centennial Park

Maple Bay

Stuart Channel

Crofton

Vancouver Island

Quamichan Lake

Cowichan Bay

Island Hwy

B&B has brightly painted guest rooms in the main building, some with shared bathrooms. There are also a pair of private-entrance studios and a small cottage with a compact kitchen – the immaculate studio 1 is our favorite. Breakfast is served in the large communal lounge, surrounded by a rambling, flower-strewn garden. A two-night minimum stay sometimes applies; check ahead.

Salt Spring Inn   HOTEL $$
(☑ 250-537-9339; www.saltspringinn.com; 132 Lower Ganges Rd, Ganges; d from $90; ☎) In the heart of Ganges and located above a popular bar, the seven small but well-maintained rooms at this friendly inn are popular with midrange travelers. The pricier deluxe rooms have sea views, en-suite bathrooms and fireplaces, while the standard rooms share bathrooms. All are well maintained and well located if you're stumbling up from the bar below after a few too many.

Salt Spring Coffee   CAFE $
(www.saltspringcoffee.com; 109 McPhillips Ave, Ganges; baked goods $3-8; ⊙6:30am-6pm Mon-Sat, 7am-5pm Sun) The perfect place to catch up on local gossip over some java – if you want to partake of the conservation, ask your neighbor whether or not they support expanding the Saturday Market. Cakes and wraps are also part of the mix at this ever-animated local legend.

★ Tree House Café   CAFE $$
(www.treehousecafe.ca; 106 Purvis Lane, Ganges; mains $10-16) At this magical outdoor dining experience in the heart of Ganges, you'll be sitting in the shade of a large plum tree as you choose from a menu of comfort pastas, Mexican specialties and gourmet burgers and sandwiches. The tuna melt is a local fave, perhaps washed down with a Saltspring Island Ales porter. There's live music every night in summer.

Gathering   FUSION $$
(115 Fulford Ganges Rd, Ganges; mains $8-16; ⊙11am-midnight Tue-Sun) Lined with sci-fi artworks and crammed with loaner board games, this new hangout is the perfect spot to spend a few hours. As for food, there's tapas, plus larger dishes combining local ingredients with international influences; think Moroccan spiced duck. Don't miss the crab-stuffed donuts, a menu standout perfect for fueling a leisurely evening of role-play gaming.

Restaurant House Piccolo   WEST COAST $$
(www.housepiccolo.com; 108 Hereford Ave, Ganges; mains $14-24; ⊙5-10pm Wed-Sun) White-tablecloth dining in a beaUtifully intimate heritage-house setting, this is the locals' top spot for a romantic night out. Focused on local seasonal ingredients prepared with knowing international flourishes, you'll find memorable seafood and duck dishes, as well as velvet-soft venison. For wine fans, you'll find the best drinks menu on the island.

ℹ Information

Visitors Information Center (☑ 250-537-5252; www.saltspringtourism.com; 121 Lower Ganges Rd, Ganges; ⊙9am-5pm) The island has its own free app with a raft of resources for visitors; see www.hellosaltspring.com.

ℹ Getting Around

The island's three ferry docks are at Long Harbour, Fulford Harbour and Vesuvius Bay. Water taxis and floatplanes arrive in Ganges Harbour.

If you don't have your own car, **Salt Spring Island Transit** (www.busonline.ca; adult/under 5yr $2/free) runs a five-route service around the island, connecting all three ferry docks. Bus 4 runs from Long Harbour to Ganges. Alternatively, **Amber Taxi Co** (☑ 250-537-3277) provides a local cab service. If you're flying in on Salt Spring Air, they provide free loaner bikes to passengers.

North & South Pender Islands
POP 2200

Once joined by a sandy isthmus, North and South Pender attract those looking for a quieter retreat. With pioneer farms, old-time orchards and dozens of coves and beaches, the islands – now linked by a single-lane bridge – are a good spot for bikers and hikers. For visitor information, check www.penderislandchamber.com.

◎ Sights & Activities

Enjoy the sand at **Medicine Beach** and **Clam Bay** on North Pender, as well as **Gowlland Point** on the east coast of South Pender. Just over the bridge to South Pender is **Mt Norman**, complete with a couple of hikes that promise grand views of the surrounding islands.

Farmers Market   MARKET
(www.pifi.ca; Pender Islands Recreation & Agriculture Hall, North Pender; ⊙9:30am-1pm Sat

Apr-Nov) The island has a regular Saturday farmers market in the community hall.

Pender Island Kayak Adventures   KAYAKING
(www.kayakpenderisland.com; Otter Bay Marina; tours adult/child from $59/35) Hit the water with a paddle (and hopefully a boat) via the friendly folks here.

☞ Tours

Pender Creatives   WALKING TOUR
(www.pendercreatives.com) Many artists call Pender home and you can chat with them in their galleries and studios by downloading a pair of free maps from Pender Creatives that reveal exactly where they are. Most are on North Pender, where you can visit several within easy walking distance of each other.

🛏 Sleeping & Eating

Inn on Pender Island   INN $$
(☑ 800-550-0172, 250-629-3353; www.innon-pender.com; 4709 Canal Rd, North Pender; d/cabins from $79/159) A rustic lodge with motel-style rooms and a couple of cozy, wood-lined cabins, you're surrounded by verdant woodland, which explains the frequent appearance of wandering deer. The lodge rooms are neat and clean and share an outdoor hot tub; the waterfront cabins have barrel-vaulted ceilings, full kitchens and little porches out front.

Shangri-La Oceanfront B&B   B&B $$$
(☑ 250-629-3808, 877-629-2800; www.pender-islandshangrila.com; 5909 Pirate's Rd, North Pender; d from $199; 🐾) It's all about tranquility at this three-unit waterfront property, where each room has its own outdoor hot tub for drinking in the sunset through the trees. You'll have your own private entrance, plus pampering extrassuch as thick robes, large individual decks and a sumptuous breakfast. Our fave room is the Galaxy Suite, where the walls are painted with a glowing space theme.

Poet's Cove Resort & Spa   HOTEL $$$
(☑ 250-629-2100, 888-512-7638; www.poetscove. com; 9801 Spalding Rd, Bedwell Harbour, South Pender; d from $250; 🐾) This luxurious harbor-front lodge has Arts and Crafts–accented rooms, most with great views across the glassy water. Extras include an activity center that books ecotours and fishing excursions; and an elegant West Coast restaurant, Aurora, where you can dine in style. As well as this, the resort offers kayak treks plus a full-treatment spa, complete with that all-important steam cave.

Pender Island Bakery Café   CAFE $
(www.penderislandbakery.com; Driftwood Centre, 1105 Stanley Point Dr, North Pender; mains $6-16) At the locals' fave coffeehouse, the java is organic, as are many of the bakery treats, including some giant cinnamon buns, which will have you wrestling an islander for the last one. Gourmet pizzas are a highlight – the best is the Gulf Islander, with smoked oysters, anchovies, spinach and three cheeses. Heartier fare includes spinach and pine-nut pie and a bulging seafood lasagna.

Cafe at Hope Bay   WEST COAST $$
(www.thecafeathopebay.com; 4301 Bedwell Harbour Rd, North Pender; mains $14-23; ☺ 11am-8:30pm Tue-Sun) West Coast ingredients with international influences rule at this bistro-style spot, closely followed by the sterling views across Plumper Sound. Just a few minutes from the Otter Bay ferry dock, the fish and chips is predictably good, but dig deeper into the menu for less-expected treats, like the lip-smacking coconut curried mussels and prawns.

ⓘ Getting Around

Ferries stop at North Pender's Otter Bay. Pender also has a cool 'public transit' system, where car-driving locals pick up at designated stops across the islands. If you're driving, you can pick up a green card at the ferry dock to indicate you're also willing to pick up passengers.

Galiano Island
POP 1100

With the most ecological diversity of the Southern Gulf Islands, this skinny landmass – named after a 1790s Spanish explorer – offers activities for marine enthusiasts and landlubbers alike.

The Sturdies Bay ferry end is markedly busier than the rest of the island, which becomes ever more forested and tranquil as you continue your drive from the dock. Drop into the **visitors info booth** (www. galianoisland.com; 2590 Sturdies Bay Rd; ☺ Jul & Aug) before you leave the ferry area, though. There's also a garage, post office and bookstore nearby.

Once you've got your bearings – that is, driven off the ferry – head for **Montague Harbour Marine Provincial Park** for trails to beaches, meadows and a cliff carved by glaciers. In contrast, **Bodega Ridge Provincial Park** is renowned for its eagle and cormorant bird life and has spectacular drop-off viewpoints.

The protected waters of **Trincomali Channel** and the more chaotic waters of **Active Pass** satisfy paddlers of all skill levels. **Galiano Kayaks** (☑ 250-539-2442; www.seakayak.ca; 3451 Montague Rd; 2hr/day rental from $32/58, tours from $55) can help with rentals and guided tours. If you fancy exploring on land, rent a moped from **Galiano Adventures** (www.galianoadventures.com; Montague Harbour Marina; rental per hour from $20; ☺ May-Sep).

Among the places to sleep on the island, sophisticates will enjoy **Galiano Inn** (☑ 877-530-3939, 250-539-3388; www.galianoinn.com; 134 Madrona Dr; d from $249; ☎ ☕), a Tuscan-style villa with 10 elegant rooms, each with a fireplace and romantic oceanfront terrace. It's close to the Sturdies Bay ferry dock. Those craving a nature-hugging retreat will also enjoy **Bodega Ridge** (☑ 877-604-2677, 250-539-2677; www.bodegaridge.com; 120 Manastee Rd; cabin from $250; ☎ ☕), a tranquil woodland clutch of seven cedar cabins at the other end of the island.

Fuel up on breakfast, treats and local gossip at **Sturdies Bay Bakery Cafe** (2450 Sturdies Bay Rd; ☺ 7am-3pm Mon-Thu, to 5pm Fri-Sun; ☎). Once you're done exploring the island, drop in for beer and fish and chips at the venerable **Hummingbird Pub** (www.hummingbirdpub.com; 47 Sturdies Bay Rd; mains $8-12), where you'll likely spot some of the same people you saw at breakfast on the patio.

Ferries arrives at the Sturdies Bay dock.

Saturna Island

POP 325

Suffused with tranquility, tiny Saturna is a natural retreat remote enough to deter casual visitors. Almost half the island, laced with curving bays, stunning rock bluffs and towering arbutus trees, is part of the Gulf Islands National Park Reserve and the only crowds you'll see are feral goats that have called this munchable area home. If you've had enough of civilization, this is the place to be.

◉ Sights & Activities

On the north side of the island, **Winter Cove** has a white-sand beach that's popular for swimming, boating and fishing.

Great for a hike is **Mt Warburton Pike** (497m), where you'll spot wild goats, soaring eagles and restorative panoramic views of the surrounding islands: focus your binoculars and you might spy a whale or two sailing quietly along the coast.

Saturna Island Winery WINERY
(www.saturnavineyards.com; 8 Quarry Rd; ☺ 11:30am-5pm) Wine fans can partake of tastings and tours at Saturna Island Winery, which also has an on-site bistro. The winery is south of the ferry terminal, via East Point Rd and Harris Rd.

✦ Festivals & Events

Lamb Barbeque FOOD
(www.saturnalambbarbeque.com; adult/child $20/10; ☺ Jul 1) If you're here for Canada Day, you should also partake of the island's main annual event in the Hunter Field, adjoining Winter Cove. The communal event, complete with live music, sack races, beer garden and a carnivorous feast, is centered on a fire pit surrounded by staked-out, slow-roasting sheep.

🛏 Sleeping & Eating

Saturna Lodge HOTEL $$
(☑ 250-539-2254, 866-539-2254; www.saturna.ca; 130 Payne Rd; d from $129; ☎) A peaceful respite from the outside world, this friendly lodge property is surrounded by a tree-fringed garden and offers six country-inn-style rooms – go for the spacious honeymoon suite. You're not far from the waterfront and rates include a hearty breakfast to keep you going for a full day of exploring.

★ **Wild Thyme Coffee House** CAFE $
(www.wildthymecoffeehouse.com; 109 East Point Rd; mains $6-10; ☺ 6am-2pm Mon-Fri, 8am-4pm Sat & Sun; ☎) Located in and around a converted and immaculately preserved antique double-decker bus named Lucy, this charming local landmark is handily located not far from the ferry dock. Diners can snag seats inside the bus, where tables have been added, and tuck into wholesome breakfasts, soup and sandwich lunches, and baked treats all made with foodie love. There's a focus on local ingredients and fair trade coffee.

ℹ Information

Saturna Island Tourism Association (www.saturnatourism.com) Visit the Saturna Island Tourism Association website for more information.

ℹ Getting Around

The ferry docks at Lyall Harbour on the west of the island. A car is not essential here since some lodgings are near the ferry terminal. Only bring your bike if you like a challenge: Saturna is a little hilly for casual pedalers.

Mayne Island

POP 900

Once a stopover for gold-rush miners, who nicknamed it 'Little Hell,' Mayne is the region's most historic island. Long past its importance as a commercial hub, it now houses a colorful clutch of resident artists.

The heritage **Agricultural Hall** in Miners Bay hosts the lively **farmers market** (⊙10am-1pm Sat Jul-Sep) of local crafts and produce. Among the most visit-worthy galleries and artisan studios on the island is **Mayne Island Glass Foundry** (www.mayneislandglass.com; 563 Aya Reach Rd), where recycled glass is used to fashion new jewelry and ornaments – pick up a cool green-glass slug for the road.

The south shore's **Dinner Bay Park** has a lovely sandy beach, as well as an immaculate **Japanese Garden**, built by locals to commemorate early-20th-century Japanese residents.

For kayakers and stand-up paddleboarders, **Bennett Bay Kayaking** (www.bennettbaykayaking.com; kayak rentals/tours from $33/65; ⊙Apr-Oct) can get you out on the water via rentals and tours.

If you're just too tired to head back to the mainland, **Mayne Island Beach Resort** (☑866-539-5399; www.mayneislandresort.com; 494 Arbutus Dr; d from $139; 🔊🐾🐕) combines ocean-view rooms in a century-old inn with swanky luxe beach cottages. There's a spa and large restaurant-bar.

If it's time to eat, head for a patio seat at the ever-friendly **Green House Bar & Grill** (454 Village Bay Rd; mains $8-16; ⊙noon-8pm Wed-Sun) and dive into fresh-made fries and heaping burgers.

For further visitor information, see www.mayneislandchamber.ca.

If you didn't bring your own car via the ferry, just stick out your thumb: most locals are always ready to pick up a passenger or two.

FRASER & THOMPSON VALLEYS

Vancouverites looking for an inland escape shoot east on Hwy 1 through the fertile plains of places like Abbotsford. Most just whiz past this farmland and you should too, unless you have a hankering to see a turnip in the rough. The Fraser Canyon thrills with stunning river gorge beauty while the Thompson River looks little changed in decades.

ℹ Information

About 150km east of Vancouver, Hope has a good **visitors center** (☑604-869-2021; www.hope.ca; 919 Water Ave; ⊙9am-5pm) with plenty of information about the local provincial parks and the region.

EC Manning Provincial Park

After the farmlands of the Lower Mainland, this 708-sq-km **provincial park** (☑604-795-6169; www.bcparks.ca), 30km southeast of Hope, is a hint of bigger – much bigger – things to come in the east; think Rocky Mountains. It packs in a lot: dry valleys; dark, mountainous forests; roiling rivers; and alpine meadows. It makes a good pause along Hwy 3, but don't expect solitude as there are scores of folk from the burgs west seeking the same.

The following hiking choices are easily reached from Hwy 3:

Dry Ridge Trail Crosses from dry interior to alpine climate; excellent views and wildflowers (3km round trip, one hour).

Canyon Nature Trail Nice loop trail with a river crossing on a bridge (2km, 45 minutes).

Lightning Lake Loop The perfect intro: a level loop around this central lake. Look for critters in the evening (9km, two hours).

Manning is a four-seasons playground. **Manning Park Resort** (☑800-330-3321, 250-840-8822; www.manningpark.com; 7500 Hwy 3; dm $35, r $80-300) offers downhill skiing and snowboarding (adult/child day pass $50/30) and 100km of groomed trails for cross-country skiing and snowshoeing. It also has the only indoor accommodations throughout the park. The 73 rooms are housed in the lodge and cabins. All provide use of the

Fraser & Thompson Valleys

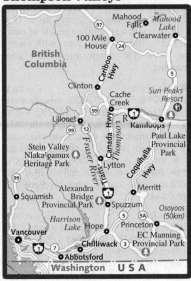

Just 2km north of Spuzzum, **Alexandra Bridge Provincial Park** (604-795-6169; www.bcparks.ca; off Hwy 1) makes for a scenic stop, where you can picnic while gazing up at the historic 1926 span. Further north, the ecologically diverse **Stein Valley Nlaka'pamux Heritage Park** (www.bcparks.ca; Stein Valley Rd, Lytton) is managed together with the Lytton First Nation. It offers some excellent long-distance hiking through dry valleys and snow-clad peaks amid one of the best-preserved watersheds in lower BC.

White-water rafting down the Fraser and its tributaries' fast-flowing rapids is popular and a number of companies near Lytton lead trips. One-day trips cost from $150 per adult. **Kumsheen Rafting Resort** (800-663-6667; www.kumsheen.com; Hwy 1, 5km east of Lytton; campsites/teepees from $35/130) offers a variety of trips and funky accommodations. **Fraser River Raft Expeditions** (604-863-2336; www.fraserraft.com; 30950 Hwy 1, Yale; trips from $150) covers all the main waterways.

Kamloops

POP 87,300

If you've opted to follow Hwy 1 from Vancouver east to the Rockies and Banff, Kamloops makes a useful break in the journey. Motels abound and there's a walkable heritage center. Historically, the Shuswap First Nation found the many rivers and lakes useful for transportation and salmon fishing. Traders set up camp for fur hunting in 1811.

The focus of the downtown area is tree-lined Victoria St, which is a lively place on sunny days; very busy train tracks separate the wide Thompson River from downtown. Franchises and malls line the highlands along Hwy 1.

◉ Sights

Using Victoria St as your anchor, stroll downtown, stopping at the art gallery and museum.

Kamloops Museum & Archives   MUSEUM
(250-828-3576; www.kamloops.ca/museum; cnr Seymour St & 2nd Ave; adult/child $3/1; ⊙9:30am-4:30pm Tue, Wed, Fri & Sat, to 7:30pm Thu Jun-Aug) Kamloops Museum is in a vintage building and has a suitably vintage collection of historic photographs. Come here for the scoop on river-namesake David Thompson and an entire floor dedicated to kids.

requisite hot tub. In summer enjoy the Alpine splendor on day hikes.

You can pitch your tent at **Coldspring**, **Hampton** or **Mule campgrounds** (campsites $21) or the more popular **Lightning Lake campground** (reservations 800-689-9025; www.discovercamping.ca; campsites $28), which takes reservations. There are 10 **backcountry campgrounds** (campsites per person $5) for overnight hikers that are normally not accessible before late June.

The park's **visitors center** (Hwy 3; ⊙9am-6pm) is 30km inside the western boundary and has detailed hiking descriptions and a relief model of the park and nearby beaver ponds.

Greyhound Canada (800-661-8747; www.greyhound.ca) has buses from Vancouver ($46, 2½ to four hours, two daily).

Fraser River Canyon

The name alone makes Spuzzum a fun stop along Hwy 1 on its way to Cache Creek, 85km west of Kamloops. The road shadows the swiftly flowing Fraser River and, as you'd expect, white-water rafting is huge here. The grand scenery and several good provincial parks make this a winning trip.

ⓘ WHICH ROAD?

Coming from Vancouver and the Lower Mainland, Hwy 1 does a three-way split at Hope. Your choices:

Hwy 1 Continue north on one of the world's great scenic drives, literally through the vertical walls of the beautiful Fraser Canyon. From Lytton, it follows the Thompson River and the terrain slowly smooths out and becomes drier, foreshadowing the ranchlands of the Cariboo region to the north beyond Cache Creek, where you can turn east for Kamloops. Note that this entire route can get choked with traffic.

Hwy 5 A multilane marvel that shoots 200km northeast to the commercial center of Kamloops through steep and pretty mountain scenery.

Hwy 3 The Crowsnest Hwy takes a circuitous and scenic course east through rugged EC Manning Provincial Park and on to Osoyoos and the southern Okanagan Valley.

Kamloops Heritage Railway   HISTORIC TRAIN
(☎250-374-2141; www.kamrail.com; 510 Lorne St) Across the train tracks from downtown, the Kamloops Heritage Railway runs steam-engine-powered excursions, although at the time of writing it was shut for maintenance.

Kamloops Art Gallery   GALLERY
(☎250-377-2400; www.kag.bc.ca; 465 Victoria St; adult/child $5/3; ☉10am-5pm Mon-Wed, Fri & Sat, to 9pm Thu) Suitably loft-like in feel, this gallery has an emphasis on contemporary Western and aboriginal works by regional artists.

BC Wildlife Park   ZOO
(☎250-573-3242; www.bczoo.org; Hwy 1; adult/child $15/11; ☉9:30am-5pm) This small zoo has examples of province natives such as bears and cougars.

Paul Lake Provincial Park   PARK
(☎250-819-7376; www.bcparks.ca; Pinantan Rd; campsites $16) On the often-hot summer days, the beach at Paul Lake Provincial Park beckons and you may spot falcons and coyotes. There is a 20km mountain-biking loop. It's 24km northeast of Kamloops via Hwy 5.

🛏 Sleeping

Older and shabbier motels can be found along a stretch of Hwy 1 east of downtown. Columbia St, from the center up to Hwy 1 above town, has another gaggle of chain and older indie motels, some with sweeping views. The nearby parks have good camping.

★ Plaza Hotel   HOTEL $$
(☎877-977-5292, 250-377-8075; www.plazaheritagehotel.com; 405 Victoria St; r $90-250; ☺❄🛜) In a town of bland modernity in the lodging department, the Plaza reeks character. This 67-room six-story classic has changed little on the outside since its opening in 1928. Rooms are newly redone in a chic heritage style and it does excellent free breakfasts.

Scott's Inn   MOTEL $$
(☎250-372-8221; www.scottsinn.com; 551 11th Ave; r $90-150; ❄@🛜🏊) Unlike many budget competitors, Scott's is close to the center and very well run. The 51 rooms are standard for a motel, but extras include an indoor pool, hot tub, cafe and rooftop sun deck.

South Thompson Inn Guest Ranch   LODGE $$
(☎800-797-7713, 250-573-3777; www.stigr.com; 3438 Shuswap Rd; r $130-260; ❄🛜🏊) Some 20km west of town via Hwy 1, this ranch-like waterfront lodge is perched on the banks of the South Thompson and set amid rolling grasslands. Its 57 rooms are spread between the wood-framed main building, a small manor house and some converted stables.

🍴 Eating & Drinking

Look for the free booklet *Farm Fresh,* which details the many local producers you can visit. Local farmers markets are held Wednesday (corner of 5th Ave and Victoria St) and Saturday (corner of 2nd Ave and St Paul St). Victoria St is the place for nightlife.

★ Art We Are   CAFE $
(www.theartweare.com; 246 Victoria St; mains from $8; ☉9am-9pm Mon-Fri, to 11pm Sat; 🛜🍴) Tea joint, local artist venue, hangout, bakery and more, this funky cafe is a great place to let some Kamloops hours slip by. The organic menu changes daily. Saturday night has live music.

Hello Toast
CAFE $

(📞250-372-9322; www.hellotoastkamloops.ca; 428 Victoria St; mains $5-9; ⏱7:30am-3pm; 🍴) 🍴 As opposed to Good Morning Croissant, this veggie-friendly, organic cafe offers whole grains for some, and fried combos of bacon and eggs or burgers for others. Nice open front and sidewalk tables.

Chapter's Viewpoint Restaurant
FUSION $$

(📞250-374-3224; www.chaptersviewpoint. com; 610 Columbia St; mains $12-26; ⏱7-10am, 11.30am-2pm & 5-9pm) The patio overlooking Kamloops is the best place to be on a balmy summer evening. The menu features steaks and salmon, but the New Mexican route is recommended.

Commodore
PUB

(📞250-851-3100; www.commodorekamloops. com; 369 Victoria St; ⏱11am-late Mon-Sat) An old-style pub with a long menu that highlights burgers and fondue (mains from $12), the Com is the place on Friday nights for live jazz and funk. Other nights, DJs spin pretty much anything.

ⓘ Information

The **visitors center** (📞800-662-1994, 250-374-3377; www.tourismkamloops.com; 1290 W Hwy 1, exit 368; ⏱8am-6pm; 🛜) is just off Hwy 1, overlooking town.

ⓘ Getting There & Around

Greyhound Canada (📞800-661-8747; www. greyhound.ca) is about 1km southwest of the center off Columbia St W.

TO	FARE	DURATION	FREQUENCY (PER DAY)
Calgary	$93	9hr	3
Jasper	$70	5½hr	1
Kelowna	$35	2½-5hr	3
Prince George	$93	7hr	2
Vancouver	$64	5hr	6

VIA Rail (📞888-842-7245; www.viarail.ca) serves Kamloops North Station, 11km from town, with the triweekly Canadian on its run from Vancouver (9½ hours) to Jasper (9½ hours) and beyond. Fares vary greatly by season and class of service.

Kamloops Transit System (📞250-376-1216; www.transitbc.com/regions/kam; adult/child $2.25/1.75) runs local buses.

Around Kamloops

The hills looming northeast of Kamloops are home to **Sun Peaks Resort** (📞800-807-3257; www.sunpeaksresort.com; 1280 Alpine Rd; lift tickets adult/child winter $79/40, summer $39/23). This ever-growing resort boasts 125 ski runs (including some 8km-long powder trails), 11 lifts and a pleasant base-area village. In summer, lifts provide access to more than two dozen mountain-bike trails.

Those saving their cash for the slopes and/or trails choose the **Sun Peaks Hostel** (📞250-578-0057; www.sunpeakshostel.com; 1140 Sun Peaks Rd; dm/d from $30/70; 🛜) over the many lodges, B&Bs and luxury condos.

Past the resort road, Hwy 5 continues north toward the Alberta border and Jasper National Park (440km from Kamloops). Along the way, it passes near Wells Gray Provincial Park (125km from Kamloops), one of BC's finest and a haven for those who really want to get away from civilization.

OKANAGAN VALLEY

It is hard to know which harvest is growing faster in this fertile and beautiful valley: tourists or fruit. Certainly, bounty abounds in this ever-more-popular lovely swath midway between Vancouver and Alberta. The moniker 'Canada's Napa Valley' is oft repeated and somewhat apt. The 180km-long Okanagan Valley is home to dozens of excellent wineries, whose vines spread across the terraced hills, soaking up some of Canada's sunniest weather.

This emphasis on highbrow refreshments contrasts with the valley's traditional role as a summertime escape for generations of Canadians, who frolic in the string of lakes linking the Okanagan's towns. And while retirees mature slowly in the sun, so do orchards of peaches, apricots and other fruits that may not have the cachet of grapes, but which give the air a perfumery redolence at the peak of summer.

Near the US border, Osoyoos is almost arid, but things soon become greener heading north. Near the center, Kelowna is one of the fastest-growing cities in Canada. It's a heady mix of culture, lakeside beauty and fun. In July and August, however, the entire valley can seem as overburdened as a grapevine right before the harvest. For many, the best time to visit is late spring and early fall, when the crowds are manageable.

Summer days are usually dry and hot, with the nights pleasantly cool. Winters are snowy but dry, making nearby Big White an attraction for skiers and snowboarders.

Osoyoos

POP 4900

Once-modest Osoyoos is embracing an upscale and developed future. The town takes its name from the First Nations word 'soyoos,' which means 'sand bar across' and, even if the translation is a bit rough, the definition is not: much of the town is indeed on a narrow spit of land that divides Osoyoos Lake. It is ringed with beaches and the waters irrigate the lush farms, orchards and vineyards that line Hwy 97 going north out of town.

Nature's bounty aside, this is the arid end of the valley and locals like to say that the town marks the northern end of Mexico's Sonoran Desert; much of the town is done up in a manner that loses something across two borders. From the cactus-speckled sands to the town's cheesy faux-tile-and-stucco architecture, it's a big change from the BC image of pine trees and mountains found in both directions on Hwy 3.

◉ Sights & Activities

Osoyoos Lake is one of the warmest in the country. That, together with the sandy beaches, means great swimming, a huge relief when the summer temp hits 42°C (108°F). Many lakeside motels and campgrounds hire out kayaks, canoes and small boats.

For sweeping valley views, go just 3km east of town up Hwy 3. About 8km west of town on Hwy 3, look for **Spotted Lake**, a weird natural phenomenon that once would have made a kitschy roadside attraction. In the hot summer sun, the lake's water begins to evaporate, causing its high mineral content to crystallize and leave white-rimmed circles of green on the water.

★ **Osoyoos Desert Centre**   PARK
(☏250-495-2470; www.desert.org; off Hwy 97; adult/child $7/6; ☺9:30am-4:30pm May-Sep, call other times) Hear the rattle of a snake and the songs of birds at the Osoyoos Desert Centre,

3km north of town, which has interpretive kiosks along raised boardwalks that meander through the dry land. The nonprofit center offers 90-minute guided tours. Special gardens focus on delights like delicate wildflowers.

Nk'Mip Desert & Heritage Centre   MUSEUM
(☏250-495-7901; www.nkmipdesert.com; 1000 Rancher Creek Rd; adult/child $14/10; ☺9:30am-6pm Jul & Aug, call other times) Part of a First Nations empire, the Nk'Mip Desert & Heritage Centre, off 45th St north of Hwy 3, features cultural demonstrations and tours of the arid ecology. It also has a desert golf course, the noted winery **Nk'Mip Cellars**, a resort and more.

3 Phase Adventures   WATER SPORTS
(☏250-498-9989; www.3phaseadventures.com; Cottonwood Beach; board rental per hour from $25; ☺Jun-Sep) Osoyoos Lake is mirror flat, perfect for paddleboard high jinks. From this pretty beach location, rent or take lessons.

Double O Bikes   BICYCLE RENTAL
(☏250-495-3312; www.doubleobikes.com; 8905 Main St; bicycle rental per day from adult/child $24/20; ☺9:30am-5pm) Trails wander through the vineyards and along the lakes, making the valley a prime biking locale. There's a second location in Oliver.

⊨ Sleeping & Eating

The eastern edge of the lake is lined with campgrounds. More than a dozen modest motels line the narrow strip of land that splits Osoyoos Lake, but beware of shabby older properties. Many cluster around Hwy 3 and there's another clump on the southwest shore near the border. Chains can be found at the junction.

Nk'Mip Campground &
RV Resort   CAMPGROUND $
(☏250-495-7279; www.campingosoyoos.com; 8000 45th St; campsites/RV sites from $30/35) Over 300 sites at this year-round lakeside resort off Hwy 3.

Sandy Beach Motel   MOTEL $$
(☏866-495-6931, 250-495-6931; www.sandybeachmotel.com; 6706 Ponderosa Dr; r $90-280; ❄@) Free canoes, kayaks and a volleyball court set the cheery tone at this 27-unit beachside place just north of Hwy 3. Bungalows and two-story blocks surround a shady lawn with BBQs.

Okanagan Valley

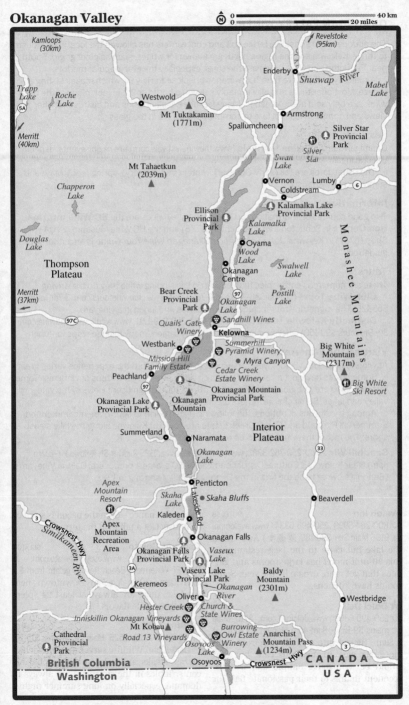

N

0   40 km

0   20 miles

Kamloops (30km)

Revelstoke (95km)

Enderby

Shuswap River

Mabel Lake

Trapp Lake

5A

Roche Lake

Westwold

97

Mt Tuktakamin (1771m)

Spallumcheen

Armstrong

Silver Star Provincial Park

Merritt (40km)

Silver Star

Mt Tahaetkun (2039m)

Swan Lake

Vernon

Coldstream

Lumby

6

Chapperon Lake

Kalamalka Lake Provincial Park

Douglas Lake

Ellison Provincial Park

Kalamalka Lake

Thompson Plateau

Oyama

Wood Lake

Swalwell Lake

Okanagan Centre

Merritt (37km)

Bear Creek Provincial Park

97

Okanagan Lake

Postill Lake

Monashee Mountains

97C

Quails' Gate Winery

Sandhill Wines

Kelowna

Westbank

Summerhill Pyramid Winery

Big White Mountain (2317m)

Mission Hill Family Estate

Myra Canyon

Peachland

Cedar Creek Estate Winery

Big White Ski Resort

97

Okanagan Mountain Provincial Park

Okanagan Lake Provincial Park

Okanagan Mountain

Summerland

Naramata

Interior Plateau

Okanagan Lake

33

Apex Mountain Resort

Penticton

Skaha Lake

Skaha Bluffs

Beaverdell

3

Crowsnest Hwy

Similkameen River

Apex Mountain Recreation Area

Kaleden

Okanagan Falls

Okanagan Falls Provincial Park

Vaseux Lake

3A

Keremeos

Vaseux Lake Provincial Park

Baldy Mountain (2301m)

Westbridge

Okanagan River

Oliver

Hester Creek

Church & State Wines

Cathedral Provincial Park

Inniskillin Okanagan Vineyards

Mt Kobau

Road 13 Vineyards

Burrowing Owl Estate Winery

Anarchist Mountain Pass (1234m)

3

Osoyoos Lake

CANADA

British Columbia

Osoyoos

Crowsnest Hwy

USA

Washington

OKANAGAN VALLEY WINERIES

The abundance of sunshine, fertile soil and cool winters has allowed the local wine industry to thrive. Kelowna and the region north are known for whites, such as pinot grigio. South, near Penticton and Oliver, reds are the stars, especially the ever-popular merlots.

A majority of the more than 100 wineries are close to Hwy 97, which makes tasting a breeze. Most offer tours and all will gladly sell you a bottle or 20; in fact, many of the best wines are only sold at the wineries. Many feature excellent cafes and bistros that offer fine views and complex regional fare to complement what's in the glass.

Festivals

Okanagan seasonal **wine festivals** (www.thewinefestivals.com) are major events, especially the one in fall.

The usual dates are fall (early October), winter (mid-January), spring (early May) and summer (early August).

Information

Two good sources of information on Okanagan Valley wines are the **BC Wine Information Centre** in Penticton's visitors center (p736) and the BC Wine Museum & VQA Wine Shop (p737) in Kelowna. *John Schreiner's Okanagan Wine Tour Guide* is an authoritative guidebook.

Tours

There are numerous companies that let you do the sipping while they do the driving.

Club Wine Tours (☑ 866-386-9463, 250-762-9951; www.clubwinetours.com; 3-7hr tours $65-125) The 'signature' tour includes four wineries and lunch in a vineyard.

Distinctly Kelowna Tours (☑ 866-979-1211, 250-979-1211; www.wildflowersandwine.com; 3½-9hr tours $90-150) Offers winery tours by valley region; many include stops for lunch.

Visiting the Wineries

At wineries open for visitors, you can expect to taste wine, but the experience varies greatly. Some places have just a couple of wines on offer; others offer dozens of vintages. Some tasting rooms are just glorified sales areas; others have magnificent views of the vineyards, valley and lakes. Some charge; others are free.

Among the dozens of options, the following (listed north to south) are recommended. Summerhill Pyramid and Cedar Creek Estate are south of Kelowna along the lake's east shore. The rest of the wineries can be reached via Hwy 97.

Sandhill Wines (☑ 250-762-3332; www.sandhillwines.ca; 1125 Richter St, Kelowna; ☻ 9am-6pm) Near Kelowna's Cultural District and one of BC's largest producers, Calona Vineyards (Sandhill's owner) was the first in the Okanagan Valley, starting in 1932.

Avalon Inn   MOTEL $$

(☑ 800-264-5999, 250-495-6334; www.avaloninn.ca; 9106 Main St; r $90-180; ❅ @ ❈) Away from the lake but close to the best restaurants, this 20-unit motel has large rooms and gardens that get more ornate by the year. Some rooms have kitchens.

★ Dolci Deli   CAFE $

(☑ 250-495-6807; www.dolcideli.com; 8710 Main St; mains $9-15; ☻ 8am-4pm Mon-Fri, to 2pm Sat & Sun) Tucked into a small storefront mid-block, it's easy to miss this cafe, but that would be a mistake. Simple fare is transcendent thanks to their passionate flair for food provenance – even the bacon is smoked in house. Get a table on the terrace.

Osoyoos Gelato   GELATO $

(☑ 250-495-5425; www.osoyoosgelato.com; 15 Park Pl, Watermark Beach Resort; gelato from $3; ☻ 11:30am-9:30pm Jun-Sep) Downtown near the lake, there are always at least 24 splendid house-made flavors.

Wildfire Grill   CANADIAN $$

(☑ 250-495-2215; 8526 Main St; mains $15-25; ☻ 11am-10pm) Wildfire serves up sandwiches, pizzas, steaks and salmon with global accents. Tables in the courtyard are always in demand, especially on long summer nights.

Summerhill Pyramid Winery (☎250-764-8000; www.summerhill.bc.ca; 4870 Chute Lake Rd, Kelowna; ☺9am-7pm) On Kelowna's eastern shore, wines are aged in a huge pyramid. Noted for ice wine, it has a cafe.

Cedar Creek Estate Winery (☎250-764-8866; www.cedarcreek.bc.ca; 5445 Lakeshore Rd, Kelowna; ☺10am-7pm) Known for excellent tours, as well as Rieslings and Ehrenfelser, a refreshing fruity white wine. The **Vineyard Terrace** (mains $12-20; ☺11am-4pm Jun-Sep) is good for lunch.

Quails' Gate Winery (☎250-769-4451; www.quailsgate.com; 3303 Boucherie Rd, Kelowna; ☺10am-8pm) A small winery with a huge reputation, it's known for its pinot noir, chardonnay and chenin blanc. The **Old Vines Restaurant** (mains $20-30; ☺11:30am-9pm) is among the best.

★**Mission Hill Family Estate** (☎250-768-7611; www.missionhillwinery.com; 1730 Mission Hill Rd, Westbank; ☺10am-6pm) Like a Tuscan hill town, this winery's architecture wows. Go for a taste of one of the blended reds (try the Bordeaux) or the excellent Syrah. **Terrace** (mains $25-33; ☺11am-9pm Jun-Oct) is one of the valley's finest restaurants and sources fine foods locally; book ahead.

Hester Creek (☎250-498-4435; www.hestercreek.com; 877 Road 8, Oliver; ☺10am-8pm Jul-Oct) Has a sweeping location and is known for its reds, especially is richly flavored cabernet franc. Terrafina (p732) has a Tuscan accent.

Inniskillin Okanagan Vineyards (☎250-498-6663; www.inniskillin.com; Road 11 W, Oliver; ☺10am-5pm) BC's first producer of zinfandel is also home to the elixirs known as ice wines; go for the golden-hued Riesling.

Road 13 Vineyards (☎250-498-8330; www.road13vineyards.com; 799 Ponderosa Rd, Road 13, Oliver; ☺10am-5:30pm) Its very drinkable reds (pinot noir) and whites (chenin blanc) win plaudits. The no-frills vibe extends to the picnic tables with gorgeous views and the motto 'It's all about dirt.'

Church & State Wines (☎250-498-2700; www.churchandstatewines.com; 31120 87th St, Osoyoos; ☺11am-6pm) This newcomer south of Oliver is making a big impression at its Coyote Bowl vineyards, especially with its full-bodied, luscious Syrahs.

Burrowing Owl Estate Winery (☎250-498-0620; www.bovwine.ca; 500 Burrowing Owl Pl, Oliver; ☺10am-5pm Mar-Dec) Wine with an eco-accent that includes organic farm techniques; try the Syrah. This Golden Mile landmark includes a hotel and the excellent Sonora Room (p732).

There's a stylish lounge area for enjoying the local wine bounty by the glass.

ⓘ Information

The large **visitors center** (☎888-676-9667, 250-495-5070; www.destinationosoyoos.com; cnr Hwys 3 & 97; ☺9am-6pm; 🖥) has internet access, maps and books, and it can book bus tickets and accommodation.

ⓘ Getting There & Away

Greyhound Canada (☎800-661-8747; www.greyhound.ca; cnr Hwys 3 & 97) runs to Vancouver ($80, 8½ hours, one daily) from outside the visitors center. There is no useful bus service north up the valley.

Around Osoyoos

West of Osoyoos, Hwy 3 follows the rugged Similkameen Valley for 47km to **Keremeos**, a cute town surrounded by orchards.

About 30km west of Keremeos is **Cathedral Provincial Park** (☎604-795-6169; www.bcparks.ca; Ashnola Rd; campsites $11), a 330-sq-km mountain wilderness that's a playground for the truly adventurous. The park offers excellent backcountry camping ($10) and hiking around wildflower-dappled alpine expanses and turquoise waters.

Oliver

POP 4900

Oliver is a center for organic produce and wine. Over the 20km drive between Oliver and Osoyoos, Hwy 97 plunges through orchard after orchard laden with lush fruits, earning it the moniker 'The Golden Mile.' Roadside stands display the ripe bounty and many places will let you pick your own.

◎ Sights & Activities

The small roads through the vineyards around Oliver are made for exploring on a bike. Local walking and biking routes include the excellent 10km **Golden Mile Trail**.

Pick up the heritage walking tour brochure from the tourist office to fully appreciate this traditional orchard town.

Double O Bikes BICYCLE RENTAL
(☑250-498-8348; www.doubleobikes.com; 35653 Main St; bicycle rental per day from adult/child $24/20; ☉9:30am-5pm) Has good route advice and another store in Osoyoos.

⊨ Sleeping & Eating

Oliver's vibrant **farmers market** (Lion's Park, Hwy 97; ☉8-11am & 4-7pm Thu) showcases local foodstuffs and is just off Hwy 97.

Mount View Motel MOTEL $$
(☑250-498-3446; www.mountviewmotel.net; 5856 Main St; r $80-120; ❄️🐾) Close to the center of town, seven units sunbathe around a flower-bedecked motor court. All have kitchens – and corkscrews. The decor is simple and cute.

★ Burrowing Owl Guest House BOUTIQUE HOTEL $$$
(☑877-498-0620, 250-498-0620; www.bovwine. ca; off Black Sage Rd; r $170-300; ❄️@🐾🏊) One of the Okanagan's best wineries has 10 rooms with patios facing southwest over the vineyards. There's a big pool, hot tub, king-size beds and corporate mission-style decor. The **Sonora Room** (mains $15-35; ☉11:30am-9pm) is noted for its fusion cuisine. It's 13km south of Oliver, off Hwy 97.

Hester Creek INN $$$
(☑250-498-4435; www.hestercreek.com; 877 Road 8; r $200-300; ❄️🐾) One of the valley's top wineries, Hester Creek has six rooms in a plush Mediterranean-style villa with a sweeping view over the vineyards. The trappings are plush, with fireplaces, soaking tubs

and more. **Terrafina** (☑250-495-3278; www. terrafinarestaurant.com; mains $18-34; ☉11:30am-9pm) has excellent Tuscan-accented fare, using foods from the region.

Medici's Gelateria GELATO $
(☑250-498-2228; www.medicisgelateria.ca; 522 Fairview Rd; gelato from $3; ☉10am-6pm) Frozen delights so good you'll want to worship – and you easily can, given this is an old church. There's also good coffee, plus soups, panini and more, all made with local produce.

Firehall Bistro BURGERS $$
(☑250-498-4867; www.thefirehallbistro.com; 34881 97th St; mains $12-25; ☉11am-9pm) You can't miss the fake hose tower of this family-friendly firehouse-themed restaurant. Eat inside or out on the patios, choosing from excellent burgers, pastas and other casual fare. Draft beers come from the on-site **Firehall Brewery** (www.firehallbrewery.com).

❶ Information

The **visitors center** (☑250-498-6321; www. winecapitalofcanada.com; 36250 93rd St; ☉9am-5pm), with its affable staff, is in the old train station near the center of town. It has excellent regional info, and walking and biking maps.

Oliver to Penticton

About 10km north of Oliver on Hwy 97, nature reasserts itself. **Vaseux Wildlife Centre** (Hwy 97; ☉dawn-dusk) has a 300m boardwalk for viewing oodles of birds (it's not just humans migrating here), bighorn sheep, mountain goats and some of the 14 species of bat. You can also hike to the **Bighorn National Wildlife Area** and the **Vaseux Lake National Migratory Bird Sanctuary**, with more than 160 bird species. The lake itself is an azure gem, well framed by sheer granite cliffs.

If you're not in a hurry, small roads on the east side of Skaha Lake between Okanagan Falls and Penticton are much more interesting for their wineries and views than Hwy 97.

Penticton

POP 33,200

Not as frenetic as Kelowna, Penticton combines the idle pleasures of a beach resort with its own edgy vibe. It's long been a final stop in life for Canadian retirees, which added a certain spin to its Salish-derived name Pen-Tak-Tin, meaning 'place to stay forever.' The town today is growing fast, along with the rest of the valley.

Penticton makes a good base for your valley pleasures. There are plenty of activities and diversions to fill your days, even when you don't travel further afield. Ditch Hwy 97, which runs west of the center, for Main St and the attractively walkable downtown area, which extends about 10 blocks southward from the picture-perfect lakefront; avert your eyes from the long stretch of strip malls and high-rise condos further south.

◉ Sights

Okanagan Beach boasts about 1300m of sand, with average summer water temperatures of about 22°C (72°F). If things are jammed, there are often quieter shores at 1.5km-long **Skaha Beach**, south of the center.

★ SS Sicamous Inland Marine Museum
HISTORIC SITE

(☑250-492-0405; www.sssicamous.ca; 1099 Lakeshore Dr W; adult/child $6/3.50; ☺9am-6pm) Back when the best way to get around inland BC was by boat, the *SS Sicamous* hauled passengers and freight on Okanagan Lake from 1914 to 1936. Now restored and beached, a tour of the boat is an evocative self-guided ramble.

Penticton Museum
MUSEUM

(☑250-490-2451; www.pentictonmuseum.com; 785 Main St; admission by donation; ☺10am-5pm Tue-Sat) Inside the library, the Penticton Museum has delightfully eclectic displays, including the de-rigueur natural-history exhibit with stuffed animals and birds, plus everything you'd want to know about the juicy fruits of the Peach Festival (p735).

Art Gallery of Southern Okanagan
GALLERY

(☑250-493-2928; www.pentictonartgallery.com; 199 Marina Way; adult/child $2/free; ☺10am-5pm Tue-Fri, noon-5pm Sat & Sun) The beachfront Art Gallery of Southern Okanagan displays a diverse collection of regional, provincial and national artists.

☆ Activities

Aquatic fun abounds. Otherwise, classic cheesy resort diversions like miniature golf await at the west end of Okanagan Beach.

ℹ IT'S TIME FOR FRUIT

Roadside stands and farms where you can pick your own fruit (or just buy it) line Hwy 97 between Osoyoos and Penticton. Major Okanagan Valley crops and their harvest times:

Cherries Mid-June to late July

Apricots Mid-July to mid-August

Peaches Mid-July to mid-September

Pears Mid-August to late September

Apples Early September to late October

Table Grapes Early September to late October

Water Sports

Both Okanagan and Skaha Lakes enjoy some of the best sailboarding, boating and paddling conditions in the Okanagan Valley.

There are several water-sports rental places on Okanagan Lake. If it floats, you can rent it, including kayaks for $16 an hour and ski boats for $300 for four hours. Outlets include **Castaways** (☑250-490-2033; www.castawayswatersports.com; Penticton Lakeside Resort, 21 Lakeshore Dr; ☺9am-7pm May-Sep) and **Pier Water Sports** (☑250-493-8864; www.pierwatersports.com; Rotary Park, Lakeshore Dr W; ☺9am-7pm May-Sep).

The paved **Okanagan River Channel Biking & Jogging Path** follows the rather arid channel that links Okanagan Lake to Skaha Lake. But why pound the pavement when you can float?

★ Coyote Cruises
WATER SPORTS

(☑250-492-2115; www.coyotecruises.ca; 215 Riverside Dr; rental & shuttle $10; ☺10am-5pm Jun-Aug) Coyote Cruises rents out inner tubes that you can float on to a midway point on the channel. It then buses you back to the start near Okanagan Lake. If you have your own floatable, it's $5 for the bus ride.

Mountain Biking & Cycling

Long dry days and rolling hills add up to perfect conditions for **mountain biking**. Get to popular rides by heading east out of town, toward Naramata. Follow signs to the city dump and Campbell's Mountain, where you'll find a single-track and dual-slalom course, both of which aren't too technical. Once you get there, the riding is mostly on the right-hand side, but once you pass the cattle guard, it opens up and you can ride anywhere.

For **cycling**, try the route through Naramata and onto the Kettle Valley Rail Trail (p741). Other good options are the small, winery-lined roads south of town and east of Skaha Lake.

Freedom – The Bike Shop BICYCLE RENTAL
(☏ 250-493-0686; www.freedombikeshop.com; 533 Main St; bicycle rental per day $40; ⊗ 9am-5:30pm Mon-Sat) Rents bikes and offers a wealth of information. Can arrange transport to/from the Kettle Valley Rail Trail.

Rock Climbing

Propelled by the dry weather and compact gneiss rock, climbers from all over the world come to **Skaha Bluffs Provincial Park** (www.bcparks.ca; Smythe Dr; ⊗ Mar-Nov) to enjoy climbing on more than 400 bolted routes. The local climbing group, **Skaha.org** (www.skaha.org), has comprehensive info on the bluffs, which are off Lakeside Rd on the east side of Skaha Lake.

★ **Skaha Rock Adventures** ROCK CLIMBING
(☏ 250-493-1765; www.skaharockclimbing.com; 437 Martin St; 1-day intros from $135; ⊗ by appointment) Skaha Rock Adventures offers advanced technical instruction, as well as introductory courses for anyone venturing into a harness for the first time.

Skiing & Snowboarding

Apex Mountain Resort (☏ 877-777-2739, conditions 250-487-4848; www.apexresort.com; lift tickets adult/child $60/37), 37km west of Penticton off Green Mountain Rd, is one of Canada's best small ski resorts. It has more than 68 downhill runs for all ability levels, but the mountain is known for its plethora of double-black-diamond and technical runs; the drop is over 600m. It is usually quieter than nearby Big White (p742).

⌖ Tours

Casabella Princess BOAT TOUR
(☏ 250-492-4090; www.casabellaprincess.com; Penticton Marina; adult/child $20/10; ⊗ May-Sep) If the Penticton's *SS Sicamous* stimulates your inner seaman, enjoy a one-hour, open-air lake tour on a faux stern-wheeler. There are multiple daily sailings at summer's peak.

✸ Festivals & Events

It seems like Penticton has nothing but crowd-drawing festivals all summer long.

DON'T MISS

SCENIC DRIVE TO NARAMATA

On all but the busiest summer weekends, you can escape many of Penticton's mobs by taking the road less traveled, 18km north from town along the east shore of Okanagan Lake. The route is lined with more than 20 wineries, as well as farms producing organic lavender and the like. This is a good route for cycling and at several points you can access the Kettle Valley Rail Trail (p741). There are lots of places to hike, picnic, bird-watch or do whatever else occurs to you in beautiful and often secluded surroundings. **Naramata** is a cute little village.

Elvis Festival MUSIC
(www.pentictonelvisfestival.com; ⊗ late Jun) Dozens of Elvis impersonators could be your idea of heaven or hound-dog hell, especially the afternoon of open-mike sing-alongs. Held in late June.

Peach Festival FOOD
(☏ 800-663-5052; www.peachfest.com; ⊗ mid-Aug) The city's premier event is basically a party that has taken place since 1948, loosely centered on the ripe succulent orbs and crowning a Peach Queen.

Pentastic Jazz Festival MUSIC
(☏ 250-770-3494; www.pentasticjazz.com; ⊗ early Sep) More than a dozen bands perform at five venues over three days.

⌂ Sleeping

Lakeshore Dr W and S Main St/Skaha Lake Rd are home to most of the local motels. The Okanagan Beach strip is the most popular area. The visitors center has a long list of B&Bs.

HI Penticton Hostel HOSTEL $
(☏ 250-492-3992; www.hihostels.ca; 464 Ellis St; dm/r from $28/64; ✱ @ 🛜) This 47-bed hostel is near the center in a heavily used 1908 house. It arranges activities, including wine tours.

Tiki Shores Beach Resort MOTEL $$
(☏ 866-492-8769, 250-492-8769; www.tikishores.com; 914 Lakeshore Dr W; condos $140-300; ✱ 🛜 ≋) This lively resort has 40 condo-style units with kitchens, most with separate bedrooms. Rooms have a light color scheme that seems ideal for a freshwater lakeside holiday.

Vancouver House Bed & Breakfast B&B $$
(☑250-276-3737; www.pentictonbedandbreakfast.
ca; 497 Vancouver Ave; r $100-170) This heritage-
listed home is only 500m from downtown
and is an easy walk to the beach. The
three rooms have their own HDTVs and
DVDs, plus other niceties. Breakfasts are
memorable.

Black Sea Motel MOTEL $$
(☑250-276-4040; www.blackseamotel.com; 988
Lakeshore Dr; r $100-275; ❀) As architecturally
challenged as its beachfront neighbors, the
Black Sea at least hints at a Soviet inspira
tion as you ponder its exterior. But it's what's
inside that counts and the hotel is a winner
for excellent service and large apartment-
style rooms.

Crooked Tree Bed & Breakfast B&B $$$
(☑250-490-8022; www.crooked-tree.com; 1278
Spiller Rd; ste $180-210; ☎) All of Okanagan
Lake glistens below you from this moun-
tainside retreat that's 9km east of downtown
Penticton. The three large apartments each
have multiple decks amid this woodsy aerie
and are well stocked with luxuries.

✖ Eating & Drinking

Penticton definitely has its share of good
eats. Stroll around Main and Front Sts in the
center and you will find numerous choices.
The **farmers market** (☑250-583-9933; 100
Main St; ⊙8:30am-noon Sat May-Oct) hosts large
numbers of local organic producers and
runs a few blocks south of the lake.

Look for local Cannery Brewing beers on
tap around town; the seasonal Blackberry
Porter is fresh and smooth.

★ **Burger 55** BURGERS $
(☑778-476-5529; www.burger55.com; 85 West-
minster Ave E; mains $7-12; ⊙11am-8pm) Best
burger in Canada? It's your own damn fault
if it isn't, as you have myriad ways to cus-
tomize at this tiny outlet by the creek and
downtown. Six kinds of buns, eight kinds of
cheese, and toppings that include roasted
garlic and *pico de gallo* are just some of the
options. Sides like fries are equally superb.

Il Vecchio Deli DELI $
(☑250-492-7610; 317 Robinson St; sandwiches $6;
⊙10am-6pm Mon-Sat) The smell that greets
you as you enter confirms your choice. The
best lunch sandwiches in town can be con-
sumed at a couple of tables in this atmos-
pheric deli, but will taste better on a picnic.

Choices are amazing; we like the garlic sa-
lami with marinated eggplant sandwich.

Fibonacci CAFE $
(☑250-770-1913; www.fibonacci.ca; 219 Main St;
mains $7-10; ⊙7am-8pm Mon-Sat, to 6pm Sun; ☎)
You see the large brass coffee roaster right
when you enter this downtown cafe that
serves up lots of healthy Mediterranean fare.
Thin-crust pizzas are made with local pro-
duce. Chillax on a sidewalk lounger; watch
for live events.

★ **Dream Cafe** FUSION $$
(☑250-490-9012; www.thedreamcafe.ca; 67 Front
St; mains $11-20; ⊙8am-late Tue-Sun) The heady
aroma of spices envelops your, well, head as
you enter this pillow-bedecked, upscale-yet-
funky bistro. Asian and Indian flavors mix
on the menu, which has many veggie options. On many nights there's live acoustic
music by touring pros; tables outside hum
all summer long.

Hillside Bistro BISTRO $$
(☑250-493-6274; www.hillsidewinery.ca; 1350
Naramata Rd; mains $16-27; ⊙11:30am-2pm &
5-9pm) Beautifully set among its namesake
vineyards, this casual eatery has great lake-
side views and upscale versions of burgers,
pasta and other dishes made from ingredi-
ents sourced locally. Enjoy a glass of Mosaic,
the house Bordeaux-style blended red.

Salty's Beach House SEAFOOD $$
(☑250-493-5001; www.saltysbeachhouse.com;
1000 Lakeshore Dr W; mains $12-25; ⊙noon-10pm
Apr-Oct) You expect deep-fried but what
you get is a nuanced menu of seafood with
global accents. Typical is Cayman Island
chowder, which is rich and multifaceted.
Dine under the stars on the patio or enjoy
the lake views from the upper level.

Theo's GREEK $$
(☑250-492-4019; www.eatsquid.com; 687 Main
St; mains $10-25; ⊙11am-10pm) The place for
locals on match.com second dates, serving
up authentic Greek island cuisine in the at-
mospheric firelit interior or out on the patio.
The *garithes uvetsi* is a symphony of start-
ers that will please two.

Hooded Merganser FUSION $$
(☑250-493-8221; www.hoodedmerganser.ca; Pen-
ticton Lakeside Resort, 21 Lakeshore Dr; mains $12-
30; ⊙7am-midnight) Named for a small breed
of duck noted for its vibrant plumage, this
huge lakeside pub attracts plenty of birds of
a similar feather. On a summer afternoon its

waterfront terrace literally heaves. Food is designed for sharing, with some steaks and burgers tossed in.

Shopping

★ Book Shop   BOOKSTORE

(☑ 250-492-6661; www.bookspenticton.com; 242 Main St; ⊘ 9:30am-8pm Mon-Fri, to 5:30pm Sat, 11am-5pm Sun) The perfect rainy day refuge, this used bookstore is one of Canada's largest and best.

ℹ Information

A whole room of the **visitors center** (☑ 250-493-4055, 800-663-5052; www.tourismpenticton.com; 553 Railway St, cnr Hwy 97 & Eckhardt Ave W; ⊘ 8am-7pm; ☎) is devoted to the BC Wine Information Centre, with regional wine information, tasting and sales of more than 600 varieties.

ℹ Getting There & Around

Greyhound Canada (☑ 800-661-8747; www.greyhound.ca; 307 Ellis St) Services Vancouver ($73, seven hours, one daily) and Kelowna ($20, 1¼ hours, two daily).

Penticton Transit (☑ 250-492-5602; www.bctransit.com; single trip/day pass $2/4) Runs between both waterfronts.

Penticton to Kelowna

A lakeside resort town 18km north of Penticton on Hwy 97, **Summerland** features some fine 19th-century heritage buildings on the hillside above the ever-widening and busy highway. The **Kettle Valley Steam Railway** (☑ 877-494-8424; www.kettlevalleyrail.org; 18404 Bathville Rd; adult/child $22/13; ⊘ May-Oct) is an operating 16km remnant of the famous tracks. Ride behind an old steam locomotive in open-air cars and enjoy orchard views.

Hugging the lake below Hwy 97, some 25km south of Kelowna, the little town of **Peachland** is good for a quick, breezy stroll. Smart stoppers will pause longer at the **Blind Angler Grill** (☑ 250-767-9264; 5899A Beach Ave; mains $8-25; ⊘ 7am-9pm), a shack-like place overlooking a small marina. What's lost in structural integrity is more than made up for in food quality: breakfasts shine, lobster wraps are a treat and nighttime ribs and halibut are tops.

Try not to lose your lunch on Canada's highest zip line at **Zipzone Peachland** (☑ 855-947-9663; www.zipzone.ca; Princeton Ave; adult/child from $100/80; ⊘ 9am-5pm May-Oct), where you can sail high over Deep Creek Canyon.

Between Peachland and Kelowna, urban sprawl becomes unavoidable, especially through the billboard-lined nightmare of **Westbank**.

Kelowna

POP 117,800

A kayaker paddles past scores of new tract houses on a hillside: it's an iconic image for fast-growing Kelowna, the unofficial 'capital' of the Okanagan and the sprawling center of all that's good and not-so-good with the region.

Entering from the north, the ever-lengthening urban sprawl of tree-lined Hwy 97/Harvey Ave seems to go on forever. Once past the ceaseless waves of chains and strip malls, the downtown is a welcome reward. Museums, culture, nightlife and the park-lined lakefront feature. About 2km south of the center, along Pandosy Ave, is **Pandosy Village**, a charming and upscale lakeside enclave.

Kelowna, an Interior Salish word meaning 'grizzly bear,' owes its settlement to a number of missionaries who arrived in 1858, hoping to 'convert the natives.' Settlers followed and, in 1892, the town was established. Industrial fruit production was the norm until the wine industry took off 20 years ago.

◉ Sights

The focal point of the city's shoreline, the immaculate downtown **City Park** is home to manicured gardens, water features and **Hot Sands Beach**, where the water is a respite from the summer air.

Restaurants and pubs take advantage of the uninterrupted views of the lake and forested shore opposite. North of the marina, **Waterfront Park** has a variegated shoreline and a popular open-air stage.

Be sure to pick up the **Cultural District** walking-tour brochures at the visitors center and visit www.kelownamuseums.ca.

Public Art   PUBLIC ART

Among the many outdoor statues near the lake, look for the one of the **Ogopogo**, the lake's mythical – and hokey – monster. More prosaic is **Bear** (Water St), a huge, lacy confection in metal. The visitors center has a good public-art guide.

BC Orchard Industry Museum
MUSEUM

(☑250-763-0433; 1304 Ellis St; admission by donation; ⊙10am-5pm Mon-Sat) Located in the old Laurel Packing House, the BC Orchard Industry Museum recounts the Okanagan Valley from its ranchland past, grazed by cows, to its present, grazed by tourists. The old fruit-packing-crate labels are works of art.

BC Wine Museum & VQA Wine Shop
MUSEUM

(☑250-868-0441; 1304 Ellis St; ⊙10am-6pm Mon-Fri, 11am-5pm Sat & Sun) **FREE** In the same building as the BC Orchard Industry Museum, the knowledgeable staff at the BC Wine Museum & VQA Wine Shop can recommend tours, steer you to the best wineries for tastings and help you fill your trunk from the selection of more than 600 wines on sale from 90 local wineries.

Kelowna Art Gallery
GALLERY

(☑250-979-0888; www.kelownaartgallery.com; 1315 Water St; adult/child $5/4; ⊙10am-5pm Tue, Wed, Fri & Sat, to 9pm Thu, 1-4pm Sun) The airy Kelowna Art Gallery features local works.

Turtle Island Gallery
GALLERY

(☑250-717-8235; www.turtleislandgallery.com; 115-1295 Cannery Lane; ⊙10am-5pm) Turtle Island Gallery sells and displays works by Aboriginal artists.

Okanagan Heritage Museum
MUSEUM

(☑250-763-2417; 470 Queensway Ave; admission by donation; ⊙10am-5pm Mon-Fri, to 4pm Sat) The Okanagan Heritage Museum looks at centuries of local culture in an engaging manner that includes a First Nations pit house, a Chinese grocery and a Pandosy-era trading post.

Kasugai Gardens
GARDENS

(Queensway Ave; ⊙9am-6pm) **FREE** Behind the Okanagan Heritage Museum, the exquisite grounds of Kasugai Gardens are good for a peaceful stroll.

🏃 Activities

The balmy weather makes Kelowna ideal for fresh-air fun, whether on the lake or in the surrounding hills.

You'll find great hiking and mountain-bike riding all around town. The 17km **Mission Creek Greenway** is a meandering, wooded path following the creek along the south edge of town. The western half is a wide and easy expanse, but to the east the route becomes sinuous as it climbs into the hills.

Knox Mountain, which sits at the northern end of the city, is another good place to hike or ride. Along with bobcats and snakes, the 235-hectare park has well-maintained trails and rewards visitors with excellent views from the top.

Cycling on the Kettle Valley Rail Trail and amid the vineyards is hugely popular.

★ Monashee Adventure Tours
BICYCLE RENTAL

(☑250-762-9253; www.monasheeadventuretours.com; bicycle rental per day from $40) Offers scores of biking and hiking tours of the valley, parks, Kettle Valley Rail Trail (from $80) and wineries. Many tours are accompanied by entertaining local guides. Prices usually include a bike, lunch and shuttle to the route. The same shuttle can also be used by independent riders looking for one-way transport. In winter, snowshoe tours are offered.

Okanagan Rent A Boat
BOATING

(☑250-862-2469; www.lakefrontsports.com; Grand Okanagan Lakefront Resort; kayak rental per 2hr $30; ⊙May-Sep) You can rent speedboats (starting at $110 per hour), canoes, kayaks, wakeboards, pedal boats and much more from this seasonal booth on the lakefront.

🛏 Sleeping

As in the rest of the Okanagan Valley, accommodations can be difficult to find on summer weekends. The visitors center lists dozens of area B&Bs. Chain motels dominate Harvey Ave/Hwy 97 going east. Rates fall as you head along the strip, but you pay the price by being in less-than-salubrious surroundings.

Kelowna International Hostel
HOSTEL $

(☑250-763-6024; www.kelowna-hostel.bc.ca; 2343 Pandosy St; dm/r from $25/60; 🖥) About 1km south of City Park, this small hostel is in a '50s home on a tree-lined residential street. Neighbors no doubt enjoy the regular keg parties and other social events that keep this cheery place hopping.

Kelowna Samesun International Hostel
HOSTEL $

(☑877-562-2783, 250-763-9814; www.samesun.com; 245 Harvey Ave; dm/r from $33/70; ❋@🖥) Near the center and the lake, this purpose-built hostel has 88 dorm beds plus private rooms. Activities include various group outings.

Kelowna

Willow Creek Family Campground
CAMPGROUND **$**

(☎ 250-762-6302; www.willowcreekcampground. ca; 3316 Lakeshore Rd; campsites/RV sites from $32/42; ☎) Close to Pandosy Village and a beach, this shady 82-site facility has a laundry. Tent sites are on a grassy verge.

Abbott Villa
MOTEL **$$**

(☎ 800-578-7878, 250-763-7771; www.abbottvilla. com; 1627 Abbott St; r $90-180; ❋@☎☒) Perfectly located downtown and across from City Park, this 52-room motel is as un-adorned as a grapevine in winter. There is

a decent outdoor pool and a hot tub. Self-cooked waffles are free for breakfast.

Royal Anne Hotel
HOTEL **$$**

(☎ 250-763-2277, 888-811-3400; www.royalanne-hotel.com; 348 Bernard Ave; r $90-200; ❋@☎) Location, location, location are the three amenities that count at this otherwise un-exciting, older five-story hotel in the heart of town. Rooms have standard modern decor, fridges and huge, openable windows.

Prestige Hotel
MOTEL **$$**

(☎ 877-737-8443, 250-860-7900; www.prestigeinn. com; 1675 Abbott St; r $130-250; ❋@☎☒) This

Kelowna

67-room place has a great location across from City Park and, once you're inside, you can't see the rather hideous exterior. The rooms have a modern, unfussy style, in an upscale-motel sort of way.

★ Hotel Eldorado   HOTEL $$$
(☑ 866-608-7500, 250-763-7500; www.hotel-eldoradokelowna.com; 500 Cook Rd; r $180-400; ✳@🖅🖳) This historic lakeshore retreat, south of Pandosy Village, has 19 heritage rooms where you can bask in antique-filled luxury. A modern low-key wing has 30 more rooms and six opulent waterfront suites. It's classy, artful and funky all at once. Definitely the choice spot for a luxurious getaway.

✗ Eating & Drinking

Many of Kelowna's restaurants take full advantage of the local bounty of foodstuffs. But don't let the feel of Vancouver East cause you to go all continental in your dining time: 8pm is late. The local microbrewer, **Tree Brewing**, has an excellent range of beers that are widely sold around town.

The **farmers market** (☑ 250-878-5029; cnr Springfield Rd & Dilworth Dr; ☉ 8am-1pm Wed & Sat Apr-Oct) has more than 150 vendors, including many with prepared foods. Local artisans also display their wares. It's off Hwy 97, east of the center.

★ BC Fruit Market   MARKET $
(☑ 250-763-8872; 816 Clement Ave; fruit from $1; ☉ 9am-5pm Mon-Sat) Like a county fair right inside the local fruit-packing cooperative, dozens upon dozens of the Okanagan's best fruits are on display and available for tasting. Prices are half that in supermarkets.

Pulp Fiction Coffee House   COFFEE $
(☑ 778-484-7444; www.pulpfictioncoffeehouse.com; 1598 Pandosy St; coffee $2; ☉ 7am-10pm) The blonde gave me the eye, her pneumatic... Ahem, the best of crime noir is sold here amid posters showing same. Buy a used book to go with your excellent coffee or tea at this sharp, category-busting cafe right downtown.

Bean Scene   CAFE $
(☑ 250-763-1814; www.beanscene.ca; 274 Bernard Ave; coffee $2; ☉ 6:30am-11pm; 🖅) Has a great bulletin board to check up on local happenings while you munch on a muffin. The coffee's the best locally.

★ RauDZ   FUSION $$
(☑ 250-868-8805; www.raudz.com; 1560 Water St; mains $12-25; ☉ 5-10pm) Noted chef Rod Butters has defined the farm-to-table movement with his casual bistro that's a temple to Okanagan produce and wine. The dining room is as airy and open as the kitchen and the seasonal menu takes global inspiration

BRITISH COLUMBIA KELOWNA

for Mediterranean-infused dishes good for sharing, as well as steaks and seafood. Suppliers include locally renowned Carmelis goat cheese.

★ Rotten Grape
TAPAS $$

(☑250-717-8466; www.rottengrape.com; 231 Bernard Ave; mains $10-20; ☺5pm-midnight Wed-Sat) Enjoy flights of local wines (over 200 by the glass) without the froufrou in the heart of town. If you utter 'tannin, the hobgoblin of pinot' at any point, be quiet and eat some of the tasty tapas inside or out.

Sturgeon Hall
PUB

(☑250-860-3055; 1481 Water St; ☺11am-late Mon-Sat) Fanatical fans of the Kelowna Rockets hockey team feast on excellent burgers and thin-crust pizza (mains $10 to $20) while quaffing brews at the bar or outside at sidewalk tables. In season, every TV shows hockey.

Micro
PUB

(www.microkelowna.com; 1500 Water St; ☺5pm-late) This great small bar from the RauDZ team is a 10, meaning there are 10 wines, 10 superb microbrews and 10 artisan bites from the valley on the changing menu (snacks from $10). Gather at the beautiful wood-block bar.

Old Train Station Public House
PUB

(☑778-484-5558; www.thetrainstationpub.com; 1177 Ellis St; ☺11am-late) The long-disused Canadian National train station has been reborn as an upscale pub with a fab selection of beers. The usual pub-food standards show color and flair (mains $11 to $20); enjoy the wide terrace on balmy days and live music Saturday nights.

Doc Willoughby's
PUB

(☑250-868-8288; 353 Bernard Ave; ☺11:30am-2am) Right downtown, this pub boasts a vaulted interior lined with wood, as well as tables on the street. Perfect for a drink or a meal; the fish and chips are good (mains $10 to $20). The beer selection is excellent, including brews from Tree Brewing and Penticton's Cannery Brewing.

Rose's Waterfront Pub
PUB

(☑250-860-1141; www.rosespub.com; Delta Grand Okanagan Hotel, 1352 Water St; ☺noon-late) Part of the upscale end of the waterfront, the vast lakeside terrace is the place for sunset drinks and snacks – from several hours before to several hours after. Rise above the masses at the rooftop cafe. Food is pub standard (mains $12 to $25).

☆ Entertainment

Downtown Kelowna's clubs are mostly at the west end of Leon and Lawrence Aves. Free summer nighttime concerts take place at various places along the waterfront.

Blue Gator
LIVE MUSIC

(☑250-860-1529; www.bluegator.net; 441 Lawrence Ave; ☺3pm-late Tue-Sun) There's blues, rock, acoustic jam and more at the valley's sweaty temple of live music and cold beer.

Kelowna Rockets
HOCKEY

(☑250-860-7825; www.kelownarockets.com; tickets from $24; ☺Sep-Mar) Kelowna Rockets is the much-beloved local WHL hockey team and a perennial contender, playing in the flashy 6000-seat **Prospera Place Arena** (☑250-979-0888; cnr Water St & Cawston Ave). Home games see the local pubs fill before and after the match.

Kelowna Actors Studio
THEATER

(☑250-862-2867; www.kelownaactorsstudio.com; 1379 Ellis St; tickets from $54) Enjoy works as diverse as *The Producers* and *Same Time Next Year* at this dinner theater with serious ambitions.

Rotary Centre for the Performing Arts
ARTS VENUE

(☑250-717-5304, tickets 250-763-1849; 421 Cawston Ave) There are galleries, a theater, cafe, craft workshops and live classical music.

Shopping

The many food purveyors offer locally produced items that make excellent gifts.

Mosaic Books
BOOKS

(☑250-763-4418; www.mosaicbooks.ca; 411 Bernard Ave; ☺9am-6pm Sat-Wed, to 9pm Thu & Fri) Mosaic Books is an excellent independent bookstore, selling maps (including topographic ones) and travel guides, plus books on aboriginal history and culture.

❶ Information

The **visitors center** (☑800-663-4345, 250-861-1515; www.tourismkelowna.com; 544 Harvey Ave; ☺8am-7pm) is near the corner of Ellis St.

❶ Getting There & Away

From **Kelowna airport** (YLW; ☑250-765-5125; www.kelownaairport.com), **Westjet** (www.westjet.com) serves Vancouver, Victoria, Edmonton, Calgary and Toronto. **Air Canada Jazz** (www.aircanada.com) serves Vancouver and Calgary.

KETTLE VALLEY RAIL TRAIL

The famous **Kettle Valley Rail Trail** vies with wine drinking and peach picking as the attraction of choice for visitors – smart ones do all three.

Once stretching 525km in curving, meandering length, the railway was built so that silver ore could be transported from the southern Kootenays to Vancouver. Finished in 1916, it remains one of the most expensive railways ever built on a per-kilometer basis. It was entirely shut by 1989, but it wasn't long before its easy grades (never over 2.2%) and dozens of bridges were incorporated into the Trans Canada Trail.

Of the entire Kettle Valley Rail Trail, the most spectacular stretch is close to Kelowna. The 24km section through the **Myra Canyon** has fantastic views of the sinuous canyon from **18 trestles** that span the gorge for the cliff-hugging path. That you can enjoy the route at all is something of a miracle as 12 of the wooden trestles were destroyed by fire in 2003. But all are rebuilt; much credit goes to the **Myra Canyon Trestle Restoration Society** (www.myratrestles.com). The broad views take in Kelowna and the lake. Although fire damage remains, you can see alpine meadows reclaiming the landscape.

To reach the area closest to the most spectacular trestles, follow Harvey Ave (Hwy 97) east to Gordon Dr. Turn south and then go east 2.6km on KLO Rd and then join McCulloch Rd for 7.4km after the junction. Look for the Myra Forest Service Rd, turn south and make a winding 8.7km climb on a car-friendly gravel road to the parking lot.

Myra Canyon is just part of an overall 174km network of trails in the Okanagan that follow the old railway through tunnels, past Naramata and as far south as Penticton and beyond. You can easily access the trail at many points or book hiking and cycling tours. **Myra Canyon Bike Rentals** (☑250-878-8763; www.myracanyonrental.com; Myra Canyon; bicycle rental per half-day from adult/child $40/30; ☉9am-5:30pm May-Oct) has bike rentals; confirm by calling in advance.

Horizon Air (www.alaskaair.com) serves Seattle. The airport is 20km north of the center on Hwy 97.

Greyhound Canada (☑800-661-8747; www.greyhound.ca; 2366 Leckie Rd) is inconveniently located east of the downtown area, off Hwy 97. City buses 9 and 10 make the run from Queensway station in downtown (every 30 minutes between 6:30am and 9:45pm). Bus routes include Calgary ($93, 10 hours, daily), Kamloops ($35, 2½ to five hours, three daily), Penticton ($20, 1¼ hours, two daily) and Vancouver ($73, five to six hours, six daily).

ℹ Getting Around

TO/FROM THE AIRPORT

Cabs cost about $36.

BUS

Kelowna Regional Transit System (☑250-860-8121; www.transitbc.com; adult/child $2.25/2) runs local bus services. A day pass costs $6. All the downtown buses pass through **Queensway station** (Queensway Ave, btwn Pandosy & Ellis Sts). Service is not especially convenient.

CAR & TAXI

All major car-rental companies are at Kelowna airport. Taxi companies include **Kelowna Cabs** (☑250-762-2222, 250-762-4444).

Big White Ski Resort

Perfect powder is the big deal at **Big White Ski Resort** (☑250-765-8888, 800-663-2772, snow report 250-765-7669; www.bigwhite.com; off Hwy 33; 1-day lift pass adult/child $79/43), located 55km east of Kelowna off Hwy 33. With a vertical drop of 777m, it features 16 lifts and 118 runs that offer excellent downhill and backcountry skiing, while deep gullies make for killer snowboarding. Because of Big White's isolation, most people stay up here. The resort includes numerous restaurants, bars, hotels, condos, rental homes and a hostel. The resort has lodging info and details of the ski-season shuttle to Kelowna.

Vernon

POP 38,400

The Okanagan glitz starts to fade before you reach Vernon. Maybe it's the weather. Winters have more of the traditional inland BC bite and wineries are few, but that doesn't mean the area is without its charms. The orchard-scented valley is surrounded by three lakes – Kalamalka, Okanagan and Swan – that attract fun seekers all summer long.

Most of the shops are found along 30th Ave, known as Main St. Confusingly, 30th Ave is intersected by 30th St in the middle of downtown, so mind your streets and avenues.

◉ Sights & Activities

Downtown Vernon is enlivened by more than 30 **wall murals**, ranging from schmaltzy to artistic.

The beautiful 9-sq-km **Kalamalka Lake Provincial Park** (☑250-545-1560; www.bcparks.ca; off Hwy 6) south of town lies on the eastern side of this warm, shallow lake. The park offers great swimming at Jade and Kalamalka Beaches, good fishing and a network of mountain-biking and hiking trails. **Innerspace Watersports** (☑250-549-2040; www.innerspacewatersports.com; 3103 32nd St; ☑10am-5:30pm Mon-Sat) operates a seasonal booth here, with canoe and stand-up paddleboard rentals; otherwise visit their store in town.

Two fun attractions make hay from local agriculture. **Davison Orchards** (☑250-549-3266; www.davisonorchards.ca; 3111 Davison Rd; ☑8am-6pm) FREE has tractor rides, homemade ice cream, fresh apple juice, winsome barnyard animals and more. Next door, **Planet Bee** (☑250-542-8088; www.planetbee.com; 5011 Bella Vista Rd; admission free; ☑8am-6pm) FREE is a working honey farm where you can learn all the sweet secrets of the golden nectar and see a working hive up close. Follow 25th Ave west, turn north briefly on 41st St, then go west on Bella Vista Rd and watch for signs.

🛏 Sleeping

Accommodations are available in all price ranges; chains are found at the north end of Hwy 97. Vacation rentals surround the lakes.

Ellison Provincial Park   CAMPGROUND $
(☑800-689-9025, info 250-494-6500; www.discovercamping.ca; Okanagan Landing Rd; campsites $30; ☑Apr-Oct) Some 16km southwest of Vernon, this is a great place near the lake. The 71 campsites fill up early, so reserve in advance.

Beaver Lake Mountain Resort   LODGE $$
(☑250-762-2225; www.beaverlakeresort.com; 6350 Beaver Lake Rd; campsites from $27, cabins $75-165; @) Set high in the hills east of Hwy 97, about midway between Vernon and Kelowna, this postcard-perfect lakeside resort has a range of rustic log and more luxurious cabins that sleep up to six people.

Tiki Village Motel   MOTEL $$
(☑800-661-8454, 250-503-5566; www.tikivillage-vernon.com; 2408 34th St; r $70-150; ❋ 🛜 🐾) Hide your brother's phone in the pool wall and he'll never find it again. An ode to the glory days of decorative concrete blocks, the Tiki has suitably expansive plantings and 30 rooms with a vaguely Asian-minimalist theme.

🍴 Eating

The evening **farmers market** (☑250-546-6267; cnr 48th Ave & 27th St; ☑3-7pm Fri) adds class to the Village Green Mall parking lot at the north end of town. There are also morning **markets** (Kal Tire Place, 3445 43rd Ave; ☑8am-1pm Mon & Thu), just west of Hwy 97.

Main St (30th Ave) east of Hwy 97 (32nd St) is prime territory for browsing eateries.

Talkin Donkey   CAFE $
(☑250-545-2286; www.talkindonkey.com; 5400 24th St; mains $7; ☑8am-10pm Mon-Thu, to 11pm Fri & Sat; 🛜) 🖉 When they talk about 'drinking responsibly' at this local institution, they mean ensuring that your coffee is fair trade. A good chunk of the proceeds at this funky coffeehouse with a spiritual edge goes to charity. Tap your Birkenstock-clad toes to regular live folk music.

★ Eclectic Med   MEDITERRANEAN $$
(☑250-558-4646; 2915 30th Ave; mains $12-25; ☑noon-9pm) The name sums up the menu, which brings a Mediterranean accent to local standards such as Alberta steaks, lake fish and lots of valley veggies. Plates are artfully presented. The local wine list is long, with many choices by the glass.

Bamboo Beach Fusion Grille   FUSION $$
(☑250-542-7701; 3313 30th Ave; mains $12-25; ☑noon-9pm; 🖉) Flavors from across Asia season popular local foods at this sprightly restaurant. Look for Japanese, Korean and Thai influences in the coconut halibut, the snapper fish and chips and much more. The curry soba noodles are good.

ℹ Information

The **visitors center** (☑800-665-0795, 250-545-3016; www.tourismvernon.com; 701 Hwy 97 S; ☑9am-6pm) is 2km south of the town center.

❶ Getting There & Around

Greyhound Canada (☏800-661-8747; www.greyhound.ca; 3102 30th St, cnr 31st Ave) Services from Vernon include Kelowna ($17, 45 minutes, four daily) and Revelstoke ($35, 2¾ hours, one daily).

Vernon Regional Transit System (☏250-545-7221; www.transitbc.com; fares from $2) Buses leave downtown from the bus stop at the corner of 31st St and 30th Ave. For Kalamalka Lake, catch bus 1; for Okanagan Lake, bus 7.

North of Vernon

Attractions are few in this area, which is more notable for its major highway connections. Just north of Vernon, beautiful Hwy 97 heads northwest to Kamloops via tree-clad valleys punctuated by lakes.

Home to the O'Keefe family from 1867 to 1977, the **O'Keefe Ranch** (www.okeeferanch.ca; Hwy 97; adult/child $14/9; ☺10am-5pm May-Sep) still has an original log cabin, plus lots of live displays of old ranching techniques. Before orchards – and later grapes – covered the valley, ranching as portrayed here was the way of life. It's 4km after Hwy 97 splits from Hwy 97A, which continues northeast to Sicamous and Hwy 1. **Armstrong**, 23km north of Vernon, is a cute little village.

Silver Star

Classic inland BC dry powder makes **Silver Star** (☏250-542-0224, snow report 250-542-1745; www.skisilverstar.com; 123 Shortt St; 1-day lift ticket adult/child $79/43) a very popular ski resort. The 115 runs have a vertical drop of 760m; snowboarders enjoy a half-pipe and a terrain park. In summer the lifts haul mountain bikers and hikers up to the lofty green vistas.

All manner of accommodations can be reserved through the resort. **Samesun Lodge** (☏877-562-2783, 250-545-8933; www.samesun.com; 9898 Pinnacles Rd; dm/r from $30/78; @🛜) runs a very popular and almost posh backpacker hotel.

To reach Silver Star, take 48th Ave off Hwy 97. The resort is 22km northeast of Vernon.

Shuswap Region

Rorschach-test-like **Shuswap Lake** anchors a somewhat bland but pleasing region of green, wooded hills, farms and two small towns, Sicamous and Salmon Arm. The latter has the area's main **visitors center**

(☏877-725-6667, 250-832-2230; www.shuswaptourism.ca; 20 Hudson Ave NE, Salmon Arm; ☺8am-6pm).

The area is home to several lake-based provincial parks and is a popular destination for families looking for outdoor fun. The main attraction, though, is the annual spawning of sockeye salmon at **Roderick Haig-Brown Provincial Park** (☏250-851-3000; www.bcparks.ca; Saquilax), just off Hwy 1. This 10.59-sq-km park protects both sides of the Adams River between Shuswap Lake and Adams Lake, a natural bottleneck for the bright-red sockeye when they run upriver every October. The fish population peaks every four years, when as many as four million salmon crowd the Adams' shallow riverbed – the next big spawn is due in 2014.

THE KOOTENAYS & THE ROCKIES

You just can't help sighing as you ponder the plethora of snow-covered peaks in the Kootenay Region of BC. Deep river valleys cleaved by white-water rivers, impossibly sheer rock faces, alpine meadows and a sawtooth of white-dappled mountains stretching across the horizon inspire awe, action and mere contemplation.

Coming from the west, the mountain majesty builds as if choreographed from above. The roughly parallel ranges of the Monashees and the Selkirks striate the West Kootenays with the Arrow Lakes adding texture. Appealing towns like Revelstoke and Nelson nestle against the mountains and are centers of year-round outdoor fun. The East Kootenays cover the Purcell Mountains region below Golden, taking in Radium Hot Springs and delightful Fernie. The Rockies climb high in the sky to the border with Alberta.

BC's Rocky Mountains parks (Mt Revelstoke, Glacier, Yoho and Kootenay) don't have the – no pun intended – high profile of Banff and Jasper National Parks over the border, but for many that's an advantage. Each has its own spectacular qualities, often relatively unexploited by the Banff-bound hordes.

Across this richly textured region, look for grizzly and black bear, elk, moose, deer, beaver, mountain goats and much more. Pause to make your own discoveries.

Revelstoke

POP 7300

Gateway to serious mountains, Revelstoke doesn't need to toot its own horn – the ceaseless procession of trains through the center does that. Built as an important point on the Canadian Pacific transcontinental railroad that first linked eastern and western Canada, Revelstoke echoes not just with whistles but with history. The compact center is lined with heritage buildings, yet it's not a museum piece. There's a vibrant local arts community and most locals take full advantage of the boundless opportunities for hiking, kayaking and, most of all, skiing.

It's more than worth a long pause as you pass on Hwy 1, which bypasses the town center to the northeast. The main streets include 1st St and Mackenzie Ave.

◉ Sights

Grizzly Plaza, between Mackenzie and Orton Aves, is a pedestrian precinct and the heart of downtown, where free live-music performances take place in the evenings throughout July and August.

While outdoor activities are Revelstoke's real drawcard, a stroll of the center and a

---

ⓘ AVALANCHE WARNING

The Kootenays are the heart of avalanche country, which kill more people in BC each year than any other natural phenomenon. The toll is stubbornly high every year.

Avalanches can occur at any time, even on terrain that seems relatively flat. Roughly half the people caught in them don't survive. It's vital that people venturing out onto the snow make inquiries about conditions first; if an area is closed, don't go there. Whether you're backcountry ski touring or simply hiking in the alpine region, you'll want to rent a homing beacon; most outdoor shops can supply one.

In Revelstoke, the Canadian Avalanche Centre is operated by the **Canadian Avalanche Association** (CAA; ☑ 250-837-2141, 24hr info 800-667-1105; www.avalanche.ca). It analyzes avalanche trends, weather patterns and issues forecasts for the Kootenays and beyond.

---

pause at the museums is a must. Pick up the *Public Art* and *Heritage* walking tour brochures at the tourist office.

★ Revelstoke Railway Museum   MUSEUM

(☑ 250-837-6060; www.railwaymuseum.com; 719 Track St W; adult/child $10/2; ☉ 9am-5pm) Revelstoke Railway Museum, in an attractive building across the tracks from the town center, contains restored steam locomotives, including one of the largest steam engines ever used on Canadian Pacific Railway (CPR) lines. Photographs and artifacts document the construction of the CPR, which was instrumental – actually essential – in linking eastern and western Canada.

Revelstoke Museum   MUSEUM

(☑ 250-837-3067; www.revelstokemuseum.ca; 315 1st St W; adult/child $5/free; ☉ 10am-5pm Mon-Fri, 11am-5pm Sat) Furniture and historical odds and ends, including mining, logging and railway artifacts that date back to the town's establishment in the 1880s, line the rooms. The local skiing history displays are good.

⊁ Activities

Sandwiched between the vast but relatively unknown Selkirk and Monashee mountain ranges, Revelstoke draws serious snow buffs looking for vast landscapes of crowd-free powder. It's where North America's first ski jump was built, in 1915.

For **cross-country skiing**, head to the 22km of groomed trails at Mt MacPherson Ski Area, 7km south of town on Hwy 23; see www.revelstokenordic.org.

All that white snow turns into white water come spring and rafting is big. **Mountain biking** is also huge, as it is across the region; pick up trail maps from the visitors center.

Revelstoke Mountain Resort   SKIING

(☑ 888-837-2188; www.revelstokemountain-resort.com; Camozzi Rd; 1-day lift ticket adult/child $80/28) Just 6km southeast of town, the Revelstoke Mountain Resort has ambitions to become the biggest ski resort this side of the Alps. But given its seemingly endless virgin slopes only opened in 2008, it has a way to go. In the meantime, you can, in one run (out of 59), ski both 700m of bowl and 700m of trees. At 1713m, the vertical drop is the greatest in North America.

Although the resort is making bowls accessible that were once helicopter or cat only, there are myriad more that are still remote. **Mica Heliskiing** (☑ 877-837-6191; www.

micaheli.com; 207 Mackenzie Ave; ⊙Dec-Apr) is one of several companies offering trips; costs begin at $1300 per day.

Free Spirit Sports
SNOW SPORTS

(✔250-837-9453; www.freespiritsports.com; 203 1st St W; ⊙10am-5pm Mon-Sat) Rents a wide variety of winter gear, including essential avalanche equipment.

Apex Rafting Co
RAFTING

(✔888-232-6666, 250-837-6376; www.apexrafting.com; 112 1st St E; adult/child $85/69; ⊙Jun-Aug) Runs kid friendly two hour guided trips on the Illecillewaet River in spring and summer.

Natural Escapes Kayaking
KAYAKING

(✔250-837-7883; www.naturalescapes.ca; 1115 Pineridge Cres; rental per 2hr from $35; ⊙Jun-Sep) Leads tours, offers lessons and rents kayaks and canoes.

Skookum Cycle & Ski
BICYCLE RENTAL

(✔250-814-0090; www.skookumcycle.com; 118 Mackenzie Ave; mountain-bike rental per day from $40; ⊙10am-5pm) Pick up trail maps and rent bikes.

Wandering Wheels
CYCLING

(✔250-814-7609; www.wanderingwheels.ca; lessons per 1hr from $30; ⊙Jun-Oct) Offers bike shuttle services, lessons and tours.

🛏 Sleeping

Revelstoke has a good selection of places to stay right in the center. Only truck spotters will gravitate to those out on Hwy 1.

Samesun Backpacker Lodge
HOSTEL $

(✔877-562-2783, 250-837-4050; www.samesun.ca; 400 2nd St W; dm/r from $25/60; @🛜) Ramble though the numerous rooms in this perennial backpacker favorite. The 80 beds are often full, so book ahead. It has bike and ski storage, plus summer barbecues.

Blanket Creek Provincial Park
CAMPGROUND $

(✔800-689-9025; www.discovercamping.ca; Hwy 23; campsites $21) This park, 25km south of Revelstoke, includes more than 60 campsites with flush toilets and running water. There's a playground, and a waterfall is nearby.

Courthouse Inn
B&B $$

(✔250-837-3369; www.courthouseinnrevelstoke.com; 312 Kootenay St; r $120-200; ✳🛜) A posh 10-room B&B close to the center, extras include a lavish breakfast, boot- and glove-driers in winter and lots of personal service.

ⓘ **WATCH YOUR GAS**

The closure of services at Rogers Pass means that there is no gas available along the 148km stretch between Revelstoke and Golden on Hwy 1.

You can't beat the quiet location; rooms have no TVs or phones.

Regent Inn
HOTEL $$

(✔888-245-5523, 250-837-2107; www.regentinn.com; 112 1st St E; r $100-190; ✳🛜♨) The poshest place in the center is not lavish, but is comfy. The 50 modern rooms (and exterior) bear no traces of the hotel's 1914 roots. The restaurant and lounge are justifiably popular. Many bob the night away in the outdoor hot tub.

Revelstoke Lodge
MOTEL $$

(✔250-837-2181, 888-559-1979; www.revelstokelodge.com; 601 1st St W; r $70-160; ✳@🛜♨) This 42-room, maroon-hued motel overcomes its inherent flaws – an all-encompassing parking area and stark cinder-block construction – thanks to its location. Check out a room or two, watch out for dark ones and take heed of their slogan: 'Your mom called and said to stay here.'

🍴 Eating & Drinking

The **farmers market** (⊙8:30am-1pm Sat May-Oct) sprawls across Grizzly Plaza. Mt Begbie Brewing makes good local microbrews that are available around town.

Modern Bakeshop & Café
CAFE $

(✔250-837-6886; 212 Mackenzie Ave; mains from $5; ⊙7am-5pm Mon-Sat; 🛜) Try a *croque monsieur* (grilled ham-and-cheese sandwich) or an elaborate pastry for a taste of Europe at this cute art-moderne cafe. Many items, such as the groovy muffins, are made with organic ingredients.

★ Woolsey Creek
FUSION $$

(✔250-837-5500; www.woolseycreekbistro.ca; 604 2nd St W; mains $20-30; ⊙5-10pm; 🍴) The food at this lively and fun place is both artistic and locally sourced. There are global influences across the menu, which features meat, fish and a fine wine list. Excellent starters encourage sharing and lingering on the large patio.

Benoît's Wine Bar
WINE BAR

(✔250-837-6606; www.benoitswinebar.com; 107 2nd St E; ⊙5pm-midnight Mon-Sat) Work on your French accent while munching on a

The Kootenays & The Rockies

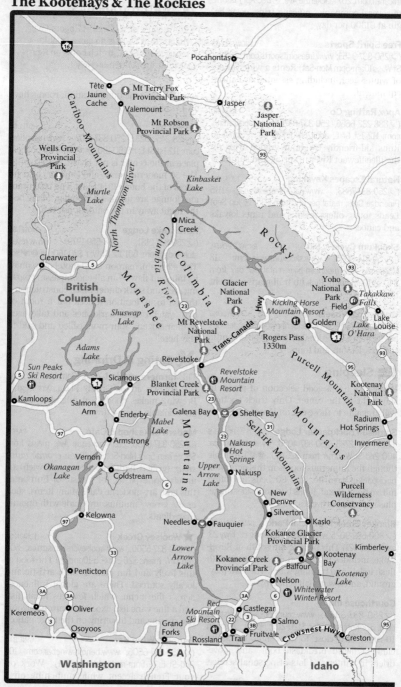

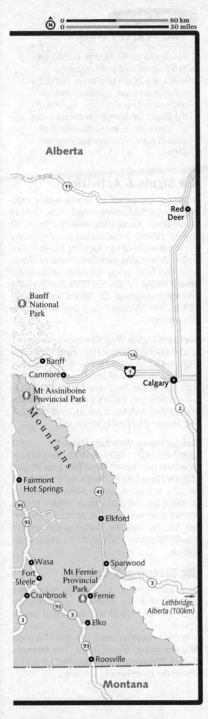

crepe or one of the many upscale sharing plates at this plush wine bar – or dig into some fondue (mains $8 to $20). Nightly specials include drinks; come for Scotch night.

Cabin BAR
(☎250-837-2144; www.cometothecabin.com; 200 1st St E; ⊕5pm-midnight Tue-Sat) Bowling alley, bar, outdoor-gear store and art gallery, it's a funky chill spot with a few snacks to go with the beers.

❶ Information

The **visitors center** (☎800-487-1493, 250-837-5345; www.seerevelstoke.com; cnr Victoria Rd & Campbell Ave; ⊕9am-6pm) is set to open in a new building right in the center in 2014.

❶ Getting There & Away

Greyhound Canada (☎800-661-8747; www.greyhound.ca; 1899 Fraser Dr) Located west of town, just off Hwy 1; it has storage lockers. Buses go east to Calgary ($63, six hours, four daily) via Banff, and west to Vancouver ($101, nine to 11 hours, two daily) via Kamloops or Kelowna.

Revelstoke Shuttle (☎888-569-1969; www.revelstokeconnection.com) Daily shuttle buses operate to/from Kelowna ($84, 2½ hours).

Mt Revelstoke National Park

Grand in beauty if not in size (only 260 sq km), this **national park** (www.pc.gc.ca/revelstoke), just northeast of its namesake town, is a vision of peaks and valleys – many all but untrodden.

From the 2223m summit of Mt Revelstoke, the views of the mountains and the Columbia River valley are excellent. To ascend here, take the 26km **Meadows in the Sky Parkway** (⊕8am-5pm May-Oct), 1.5km east of Revelstoke off the Trans-Canada Hwy (Hwy 1). Open after the thaw, this paved road winds through lush cedar forests and alpine meadows and ends at Balsam Lake, within 2km of the peak. From here, walk to the top or take the **shuttle** (free; ⊕10am-5pm).

There are several good hiking trails from the summit. You can camp only in designated backcountry campsites, and you must have a Wilderness Pass camping permit ($10; in addition to your park pass), which, along with lots of useful information, is available from **Parks Canada**

📝 250-837-7500; revglacier.reception@pc.gc.ca; 301 3rd St, Revelstoke; ☺8am-4:30pm Mon-Fri) or from the Rogers Pass Centre (p748) inside Glacier National Park. Admission to both Mt Revelstoke and Glacier National Parks (the two are administered jointly) is $8/4 per adult/child per day.

Glacier National Park

To be really accurate, this 1350-sq-km **park** (www.pc.gc.ca/glacier) should be called '430 Glaciers National Park'; the annual snowfall can be as much as 23m. Due to the sheer mountain slopes, this is one of the world's most active avalanche areas. For this reason, skiing, caving and mountaineering are regulated; you must register with park wardens before venturing into the backcountry. Call for a daily **weather and avalanche report** (📝250-837-6867) in season. Admission to this and Mt Revelstoke National Park (the two are administered jointly) is $8/4 per adult/child per day.

Whether you travel by car, bus, trail or bicycle (more power to you), Rogers Pass will likely rank as one of the most beautiful mountain passes you'll ever traverse. Be sure to pause at the **Hemlock Grove Trail**, 54km east of Revelstoke, where a 400m boardwalk winds through an ancient hemlock rainforest.

Spend some time with the Canadian Pacific Railway dioramas at the informative **Rogers Pass Centre** (📝250-814-5233; Hwy 1; ☺8am-7pm), 72km east of Revelstoke. The center shows films about the park and organizes guided walks in summer. As a bonus, there's an excellent bookstore run by the **Friends of Mt Revelstoke & Glacier** (www.friendsrevglacier.com).

Not far from here are the park's two campgrounds: **Illecillewaet** and **Loop Brook** (off Hwy 1; campsites $22; ☺Jul-Sep). Both have running water and flush toilets.

Golden

POP 3800

Golden is well situated for the national parks – there are six nearby. For excitement even closer, like white-water rafting, the Kicking Horse River converges with the Columbia.

Don't just breeze past the strip of franchised yuck on Hwy 1 or you'll miss the tidy little town center down by the tumbling river.

DON'T MISS

TWO PERFECT WALKS

Easily accessible, **Skunk Cabbage Trail**, 28km east of Revelstoke on Hwy 1, is a 1.2km boardwalk along the Illecillewaet River. It is lined with its huge namesakes. Another 4km east, the **Giant Cedars Boardwalk** winds a 500m course up and down and all around a grove of huge old-growth cedars.

◉ Sights & Activities

Golden is the center for **white-water rafting** trips on the turbulent and chilly Kicking Horse River. Along with powerful grade III and IV rapids, breathtaking scenery along the sheer walls of the Kicking Horse Valley makes this rafting experience one of North America's best. Local operators include **Alpine Rafting** (📝888-599-5299, 250-344-6778; www.alpinerafting.com; 101 Golden Donald Upper Rd; trips from $90; ☺Jun-Sep), next to the visitors center.

Northern Lights Wolf Centre　NATURE PARK
(📝250-344-6798; www.northernlightswildlife.com; 1745 Short Rd; adult/child $12/6; ☺9am-7pm) See wolves in nature and learn about bear conservation at the Northern Lights Wolf Centre. Visitors can expect to meet a resident wolf or two and learn about their complex and human-like family structure.

Kicking Horse Mountain Resort　SKIING
(📝866-754-5425, 250-439-5400; www.kickinghorseresort.com; Kicking Horse Trail; 1-day lift pass adult/child from $80/26) Some 60% of the 120 ski runs at Kicking Horse Mountain Resort are rated advanced or expert. With a 1260m vertical drop and a snowy position between the Rockies and the Purcells, the resort's popularity grows each year. It's 14km from Golden.

🍴 Sleeping & Eating

There are scores of chain motels along Hwy 1. Check with the chamber of commerce (p750) for B&Bs and the municipal campground.

In the walkable center, 9th Ave N is good for cafes, bakeries and shops. The **farmers market** (10th Ave N; ☺noon-5pm Wed Jun-Aug) is next to the chamber of commerce.

★ Dreamcatcher Hostel HOSTEL $

(☑ 250-439-1090; www.dreamcatcherhostel.com; 528 9th Ave N; dm/r from $35/90) Run by two veteran travelers, this centrally located hostel has everything a budget traveler could hope for. There are 33 beds across eight rooms, as well as a vast kitchen and a comfy common room with a stone fireplace.

Mary's Motel MOTEL $$

(☑ 866-234-6279, 250-344-7111; www.marysmotel.com; 603 8th Ave N; r $80-130; ❋ 🤶 ❄) In town, right on the roaring river, Mary's has 81 rooms spread across several buildings; get one with a patio. It's easy to get wet: there's a large outdoor pool, an indoor one and two hot tubs.

Chancellor Peak Chalets LODGE $$$

(☑ 250-344-7038, 800-644-8888; www.chancellorpeakchalets.com; 2924 Kicking Horse Rd; cabins from $200; 🤶) The 11 log chalets at this riverside retreat have two levels and sleep up to six. There are soaker tubs, full kitchens and all the nature you can breathe in. The chalets are 25km east of Golden.

★ Eleven22 FUSION $$

(☑ 250-344-2443; www.eleven22.ca; 1122 10th Ave S; mains $11-24; ⊙ 5-10pm; 🍴) A cross between a restaurant and a dinner party, this appealing restaurant has art on the walls of the small dining rooms and all the stars you can count out on the patio. Watch the kitchen action from the lounge area while sharing small plates. Foods are mostly sourced locally.

❶ Information

Visitors Center (☑ 250-344-7711; 111 Golden Donald Upper Rd; ⊙ 9am-6pm) The smiles are as shiny as the building, 1km east on Hwy 1 from the Hwy 95 turnoff into Golden.

Kicking Horse Country Chamber of Commerce (☑ 800-622-4653, 250-344-7125; www.goldenchamber.bc.ca; 500 10th Ave N; ⊙ 10am-5pm Mon-Fri) For lots of local info, visit the chamber of commerce down near the center.

❶ Getting There & Away

Delays may offset improvements on Hwy 1 east of Golden as the road is reconstructed from scratch; see www.kickinghorsecanyon.ca.

Greyhound Canada (☑ 800-661-8747; www.greyhound.ca; Husky Travel Centre, 1050 Hwy 1) serves Vancouver ($132, 10 to 13 hours, three daily) and Calgary ($48, 3½ hours, four daily) via Banff.

Yoho National Park

Fed by glaciers, the ice-blue Kicking Horse River plows through the valley of the same name. The surging waters are an apt image for this dramatic **national park** (Map p586; ☑ 250-343-6783; www.pc.gc.ca/yoho; adult/child $10/5), home to looming peaks, pounding waterfalls, glacial lakes and patches of pretty meadows.

Although the smallest (1310 sq km) of the four national parks in the Rockies, Yoho is a diamond in the (very) rough. This wilderness is the real deal; it's some of the continent's least tarnished.

East of Field on Hwy 1 is the **Takakkaw Falls road**, open late June to early October. At 254m, Takakkaw is one of the highest waterfalls in Canada. From here **Iceline**, a 20km hiking loop, passes many glaciers and spectacular scenery.

This World Heritage Site protects the amazing Cambrian-age **fossil beds** on Mt Stephen and Mt Field. These 515-million-year-old fossils preserve the remains of marine creatures that were some of the earliest forms of life on earth. You can only get to the fossil beds by guided hikes, which are led by naturalists from the **Yoho Shale Geoscience Foundation** (☑ 800-343-3006; www.burgess-shale.bc.ca; tours from adult/child $120/25; ⊙ Jul-Sep). Reservations are essential.

Near the south gate of the park, you can reach pretty **Wapta Falls** along a 2.4km trail. The easy walk takes about 45 minutes each way.

The four campgrounds within Yoho all close from mid-October to mid-May. Only the **Kicking Horse Campground** (off Hwy 1, Field; campsites $28; ⊙ May-Oct) has showers, making its 88 sites its most popular. Appealing **Takakkaw Falls Campground** (Yoho Valley Rd; campsites $18; ⊙ Jul-Oct), 13km along a gravel road, has 35 walk-in (200m) campsites for tents only.

BRITISH COLUMBIA YOHO NATIONAL PARK

---

❶ WINTER ROAD CONDITIONS

For up-to-date road conditions on the Hwy 1 and across the province, consult **DriveBC** (☑ 800-550-4997; www.drivebc.ca). This is essential in winter, when storms can close roads for extended periods.

The isolated **HI-Yoho National Park** (Whiskey Jack Hostel; ☑866-762-4122, 403-670-7580; www.hihostels.ca; Yoho Valley Rd; dm from $20; ☺Jul-Sep) offers 27 dorm-style beds. It's 13km off Hwy 1, just before the Takakkaw Falls Campground and close to the falls itself.

ℹ️ Information

At Yoho National Park Information Centre (☑250-343-6783; off Hwy 1, Field; ☺9am-7pm May-Oct), pick up maps and trail descriptions, however note that Parks Canada budget cuts mean that this vital resource is often closed. Rangers can advise on itineraries and conditions. Alberta Tourism staffs a desk here in summer.

Lake O'Hara

Perched high in the mountains east of Field, **Lake O'Hara** is worth the significant hassle involved in reaching the place, which is an encapsulation of the whole Rockies. Compact wooded hillsides, alpine meadows, snow-covered passes, mountain vistas and glaciers are all wrapped around the stunning lake. A basic day trip is worthwhile, but stay overnight in the backcountry and you'll be able to access many more trails, some quite difficult, all quite spectacular. The **Alpine Circuit** (12km) has a bit of everything.

To reach the lake, you can take the **shuttle bus** (Field; adult/child return $15/7.50; ☺mid-Jun–Sep) from the Lake O'Hara parking lot, 15km east of Field on Hwy 1. A quota system governs bus access to the lake and limits permits for the 30 backcountry campsites. You can freely walk the 11km from the parking area, but no bikes are allowed. The area around Lake O'Hara is usually covered with snow or very muddy until mid-July.

Make **reservations** (☑250-343-6433; reservation fee $12) for the bus trip or for **camping** (a permit costs $10 per night) three months in advance. Available spots often go the first hour lines are open, from 8am mountain time. Given the popularity of Lake O'Hara, reservations are basically mandatory, unless you want to walk. However, if you don't have advance reservations, six day-use seats on the bus and three to five campsites are set aside for 'standby' users. To try to snare these, call at 8am the day before.

Lake O'Hara Lodge (☑250-343-6418; www.lakeohara.com; r per person from $280) 🖊 has been leaving guests slack-jawed for over 80 years. The only place to stay at the lake

without a tent, the lodge is luxurious in a rustic way. Its environmental practices are lauded. There's a two night minimum stay.

Field

Don't go past Field without stopping. Right off Hwy 1, this historic railroad town has a dramatic overlook of the river and is a quaint yet unfussy place. Many of its buildings date from the early days of the railways, when it was the Canadian Pacific Railway's headquarters for exploration and, later, for strategic planning when engineers were trying to solve the problem of moving trains over Kicking Horse Pass. See the results from the Hwy 1 **Spiral Tunnel Lookout** 8km east of Field.

Field has more than 20 B&Bs. **Fireweed Hostel** (☑877-343-6999, 250-343-6999; www.fireweedhostel.com; 313 Stephen Ave; dm $30-40, r $80-170; 🕸) has four spotless rooms.

Truffle Pigs Bistro (☑250-343-6303; www.trufflepigs.com; 100 Centre St; r from $170, mains $14-32; ☺7:30am-9pm; 🕸) is a legendary cafe serving inventive, high-concept bistro fare that's locally sourced and usually organic. Their inn across the street has 14 rooms with the same cheeky style as the bistro.

Greyhound Canada buses stop at the park info center on Hwy 1 on their trips west to Golden and east to Banff.

Mt Assiniboine Provincial Park

Between Kootenay and Banff National Parks lies this lesser-known and smaller (39 sq km) **provincial park** (Map p586; www.bcparks.ca), part of the Rockies' Unesco World Heritage site. The pointed peak of Mt Assiniboine (3618m), often referred to as Canada's Matterhorn, and its near neighbors have become a magnet for experienced rock climbers and mountaineers. Backcountry hikers revel in its meadows and glaciers.

The park's main focus is crystal-clear **Lake Magog**, which is reachable on a 27km trek from Banff National Park or by helicopter. At the lake, there's the commercially operated **Mt Assiniboine Lodge** (☑403-678-2883; www.assiniboinelodge.com; r per person $230-340), a **campground** (campsites adult/child $10/5) and some **huts** (per person from $25), which may be reserved through the lodge. Helicopter transport is $150 to $165 each way.

Kootenay National Park

Shaped like a lightning bolt, **Kootenay National Park** (Map p586; ☑250-347-9505; www.pc.gc.ca/kootenay; Hwy 93; entrance fee adult/child $10/5, campsites $22-39; ☺camping May-Oct) is centered on a long, wide, tree-covered valley shadowed by cold, gray peaks. Encompassing 1406 sq km, Kootenay has a more moderate climate than the other Rocky Mountains parks and, in the southern regions especially, summers can be hot and dry, which is a factor in the frequent fires. It's the only national park in Canada to contain both glaciers and cacti. From BC you can create a fine driving loop via Kootenay and Yoho National Parks.

The interpretive **Fireweed Trail** (500m or 2km) loops through the surrounding forest at the north end of Hwy 93. Panels explain how nature is recovering from a 1968 fire. Some 7km further on, **Marble Canyon** has a pounding creek flowing through a nascent forest. Another 3km south on the main road is the easy 2km trail through forest to ochre pools known as the **Paint Pots**. Panels describe both the mining history of this rusty earth and its importance to Aboriginal people.

Learn how the park's appearance has changed over time at the **Kootenay Valley Viewpoint**, where informative panels vie with the view. Just 3km south, **Olive Lake** makes a perfect picnic or rest stop. A 500m lakeside interpretive trail describes some of the visitors who've come before you.

Radium Hot Springs

Lying just outside the southwest corner of Kootenay National Park, Radium Hot Springs is a major gateway to the whole Rocky Mountains national park area. The **Kootenay National Park & Radium Hot Springs Visitors Center** (☑250-347-9331; www.radiumhotsprings.com; 7556 Main St E, Hwy 93/95; ☺visitors center 9am-5pm year-round, Parks Canada May-Oct) has internet access, an excellent display on the park and is staffed with Parks Canada rangers.

Radium boasts a large resident population of **bighorn sheep**, which often wander through town, but the big attraction is the namesake **hot springs** (☑250-347-9485; www.pc.gc.ca/hotsprings; off Hwy 93; adult/child $7/6; ☺9am-11pm), 3km north of town. The hot springs' pools are quite modern and can

get very busy in summer. The water comes from the ground at 44°C, enters the first pool at 39°C and hits the final one at 29°C.

Radium glows with lodging, some 30 motels at last count. Directly outside the park gate, **Misty River Lodge** (☑250-347-9912; www.mistyriverlodge.bc.ca; 5036 Hwy 93; r $60-100; @) has six rooms and owners who are enthusiastic about the parks and ready to share their knowledge with guests; cyclists are welcomed.

Radium Hot Springs to Fernie

South from Radium Hot Springs, Hwy 93/95 follows the wide Columbia River valley between the Purcell and Rocky Mountains. It's not especially interesting, unless you're into the area's industry (building ski resorts), agriculture (golf courses) or wild game (condo buyers).

South of Skookumchuck, the road forks. Go left and after 31km you'll reach Hwy 3 for Fernie. Go left on Hwy 95A and you'll come to **Fort Steele Heritage Town** (☑250-426-7342; www.fortsteele.ca; 9851 Hwy 93/95; adult/child $12/5; ☺9:30am-6pm), a recreated 1880s town that's an order of magnitude less irritating than many of similar ilk.

From Fort Steele it's 95km to Fernie along Hwys 93 and 3.

Fernie

POP 4600

Surrounded by mountains on four sides – that's the sheer Lizard Range you see looking west – Fernie defines cool. Once devoted solely to lumber and coal, the town has used its sensational setting to branch out. Skiers love the 8m-plus of dry powder that annually blankets the runs seen from town. In summer, this same dramatic setting lures scores of hikers and mountain bikers.

Despite the town's discovery by pleasure seekers, it still retains a down-to-earth vibe, best felt in the cafes, bars, shops and galleries along Victoria (2nd) Ave in the historic center, three blocks south of Hwy 3 (7th Ave).

◉ Sights

One of many disasters, Fernie experienced a devastating fire in 1908, which resulted in a brick-and-stone building code. So today you'll see numerous fine **early-20th-century buildings**, many of which were built out of local yellow brick, giving the town an appearance unique in the East Kootenays. Get a copy of *Heritage Walking Tour* ($5), a superb booklet produced by the impressively expanded **Fernie Museum** (📞 250-423-7016; 491 2nd Ave; admission by donation; ☺ 10am-5:30pm).

🏃 Activities

Mountain biking is almost as big as skiing and Fernie has lots for riders. There are easy jaunts in **Mt Fernie Provincial Park** (www.bcparks.ca; Hwy 3), which is a mere 3km south of town; and legendary rides up and down the hills in and around the ski resort, which runs lifts in summer. Many come just to tackle the fabled **Al Matador**, which drops over 900m before finishing in the terrific Three Kings trail. Get a copy of the widely available *Fernie Mountain Bike Map* and check out the websites www.crankfernie.com and www.fernietrailsalliance.com.

Great hiking trails radiate in all directions from Fernie. The excellent and challenging **Three Sisters hike** (20km) winds through forests and wildflower-covered meadows, along limestone cliffs and scree slopes. Get directions at the visitors center.

★ Fernie Alpine Resort SKIING

(📞 250-423-4655, 877-333-2339, snow conditions 250-423-3555; www.skifernie.com; 5339 Ski Area Rd; 1-day pass adult/child $80/26) In fall, eyes turn to the mountains for more than their beauty: they're looking for snow. A five-minute drive from downtown, fast-growing Fernie Alpine Resort boasts 142 runs, five bowls and almost endless dumps of powder. Most hotels run shuttles here daily.

Ski & Bike Base SKIING, CYCLING

(📞 250-423-6464; www.skibase.com; 432 2nd Ave; bicycle rental per day from $45; ☺ 10am-6pm Mon-Sat) One of several excellent all-season gear sales and rental shops on 2nd Ave.

Mountain High River Adventures RAFTING

(📞 877-423-4555, 250-423-5008; www.raftfernie.com; 100 Riverside Way; trips adult/child from $125/100; ☺ May-Sep) The Elk River is a classic white-water river, with three grade IV rapids and 11 more grade III rapids. Besides rafting, Mountain High offers kayaking, floats and more on the surging waters.

Fernie Bike Guides CYCLING

(📞 250-423-3650; www.ferniebikeguides.ca; guiding/instruction per hour $30/60) Raise your cycling game with experts or let them show you the far reaches of the Elk Valley.

🛏 Sleeping

Being a big ski town, Fernie's high season is winter. You'll have most fun staying in the center, otherwise **Fernie Central Reservations** (📞 800-622-5007; www.ferniecentralreservations.com) can book you a room at the ski resort.

HI Raging Elk Hostel HOSTEL $

(📞 250-423-6811; www.ragingelk.com; 892 6th Ave; dm/r from $29/75; ☺ pub 4-11pm; @) Wide decks allow plenty of inspirational mountain gazing at this well-run central hostel that has good advice for those hoping to mix time on the slopes or trails with seasonal work. The pub is a hoot.

Mt Fernie Provincial Park CAMPGROUND $

(📞 800-689-9025; www.discovercamping.ca; off Hwy 3; campsites $21; ☺ May-Sep) Only 3km south from town, it has 40 sites, flush toilets, waterfalls and access to mountain-bike trails.

Park Place Lodge HOTEL $$

(📞 888-381-7275, 250-423-6871; www.parkplacelodge.com; 742 Hwy 3; r $100-220; ❄ @ ☀) The nicest lodging close to the center, its 64 comfortable rooms have high-speed internet, fridges, microwaves and access to an indoor pool. Some have balconies and views.

Snow Valley Motel & RV Park MOTEL $$

(📞 250-423-4421; www.snowvalleymotel.com; 1041 7th Ave, Hwy 3; campsites $20-30, r $70-130; ❄ @ ☀) Great value in the middle of town. The 20 motel units are large and come with microwaves and fridges, some with full kitchens. Nothing is fancy, but there is a barbecue deck with views.

🍴 Eating & Drinking

Get good produce year-round at **Cincott Farms Organic Market** (📞 250-423-5564; www.cincott.com; 851 7th Ave; ☺ 11:30am-6pm Mon-Sat) 🍏. Look for the excellent ales of Fernie Brewing Co, including 'What the Huck!' berry beer, at local pubs.

Blue Toque Diner CAFE $

(📞 250-423-4637; 500 Hwy 3; mains from $7; ☺ 9am-3pm Thu-Mon) Part of the Arts Station community gallery, this is *the* place for breakfast. The menu features lots of seasonal and organic vegetarian specials.

Mug Shots Bistro BAKERY $

(☑ 250-423-8018; 591 3rd Ave; mains $5; ⊙ 8am-5pm; 🐾) Always buzzing, it offers good coffee, baked goods, sandwiches and internet access.

★ Yamagoya JAPANESE $$

(☑ 250-430-0090; 741 7th Ave, Hwy 3 ; small dishes $4-8; ⊙ 5-10pm) As compact as a California roll, this gem of a sushi place does a wide range of classics, from hot to tempura. Even the miso soup is good, especially after a day skiing. Besides sake, there's a great beer selection.

Bridge Bistro CANADIAN $$

(☑ 250-423-3002; 301 Hwy 3; mains $10-20; ⊙ 11am-10pm) Enjoy the views of the Elk River and surrounding peaks from the deck, but save some attention for the long menu of good burgers, steaks and pizza.

 Shopping

Polar Peek Books BOOKS

(☑ 250-423-3736; 592 2nd Ave; ⊙ 10am-6pm) This eclectic mix of books has a good section of local interest. Great recommendations.

ℹ Information

The **visitors center** (☑ 250-423-6868; www.ferniechamber.com; 102 Commerce Rd; ⊙ 9am-5pm) is east of town off Hwy 3, just past the Elk River crossing. It includes the **Fernie Nature Centre**, which has displays on local critters. The **Fernie Museum** also has tourist info.

ℹ Getting There & Around

Shuttles operate between town and the ski resort.

Greyhound Canada (☑ 250-423-6811; www.greyhound.ca; Husky Petrol Station, 2001 Hwy 3) runs buses west to Kelowna ($113, 11 hours, one daily) and Nelson ($65, 5½ hours, one daily), and east to Calgary ($63, six hours, one daily). The stop is a 1.5km truck-buffeted walk west of the center.

Kimberley

POP 6700

When big-time mining left Kimberley in 1973, a plan was hatched to turn the little mountain village at 1113m altitude into a tourist destination with a Bavarian theme. The center was turned into a pedestrian zone named the **Platzl**, locals were encouraged to prance about in lederhosen and dirndl, and sausage was added to many a menu. Now, more than three decades later, the shtick is fading. There's still a bit of fake half-timbering about, but mostly it's a diverse place that makes a worthwhile detour off Hwy 95 between Cranbrook and Radium Hot Springs.

The **visitors center** (☑ 250-427-3666; www.kimberleychamber.com; 270 Kimberley Ave; ⊙ 10am-6pm) sits in the large parking area behind the Platzl.

Take a 15km ride on **Kimberley's Underground Mining Railway** (☑ 250-427-7365; www.kimberleysundergroundminingrailway.ca; Gerry Sorensen Way; adult/child $20/8; ⊙ tours 11am-3pm May-Sep, trains to resort 10am Sat & Sun), where the tiny train putters through the steep-walled Mark Creek Valley toward some sweeping mountain vistas. At the end of the line, you can take a chairlift up to the **Kimberley Alpine Resort** (☑ 877-754-5462, 250-427-4881; www.skikimberley.com; 1-day lift pass adult/child $68/22). In winter, the resort has over 700 hectares of skiable terrain, mild weather and 80 runs.

Cranbrook

POP 19,500

The area's main center, 31km southeast of Kimberley, **Cranbrook** is a dusty crossroads. Hwy 3/95 bisects the town, which is a charmless strip of motels.

However, it has one great reason for stopping: the **Canadian Museum of Rail Travel** (☑ 250-489-3918; www.trainsdeluxe.com; 57 Van Horne St S, Hwy 3/95; adult $14-22, child $1-6; ⊙ 10am-6pm). It has some fine examples of classic Canadian trains, including the luxurious 1929 edition of the Trans-Canada Limited, a legendary train that ran from Montréal to Vancouver.

Cranbrook to Rossland

Hwy 3 twists and turns its way 300km from Cranbrook to Osoyoos at the south end of the Okanagan Valley. Along the way it hugs the hills close to the US border and passes eight border crossings. As such, it's a road of great usefulness, even if the sights never quite live up to the promise.

Creston, 123km west of Cranbrook, is known for its many orchards and as the home of Columbia Brewing Co's Kokanee

ⓘ CHECK YOUR WATCH

It is a constant source of confusion that the East Kootenays lie in the mountain time zone along with Alberta, unlike the rest of BC, which falls within the Pacific time zone. West on Hwy 1 from Golden, the time changes at the east gate of Glacier National Park. Going west on Hwy 3, the time changes between Cranbrook and Creston. Mountain time is one hour ahead of Pacific time.

True Ale. But both of these products are mostly shipped out, so you should do the same. Hwy 3A heads north from here for a scenic 80km to the free **Kootenay Lake Ferry**, which connects to Nelson. This is a fun and scenic journey.

The **Creston Valley Wildlife Management Area** (☑ 250-402-6900; www.creston-wildlife.ca; Hwy 3; ⊙ dawn-dusk), 11km west of Creston, is a good place to spot oodles of birds, including blue herons, from the 1km boardwalk.

Some 85km west of Creston, **Salmo** is notable mostly as the junction with Hwy 6, which runs north for a bland 40km to Nelson. The Crowsnest Hwy splits 10km to the west. Hwy 3 bumps north through **Castlegar**, which is notable for having the closest large airport to Nelson and a very large pulp mill. Hwy 3B dips down through the cute little cafe-filled town of **Fruitvale** and industrial **Trail**.

Rossland

POP 3700

About 10km west of Trail, Rossland is a world apart. High in the Southern Monashee Mountains (1023m), this old mining village is one of Canada's best places for mountain biking. A long history of mining has left the hills crisscrossed with old trails and abandoned rail lines, all of which are perfect for riding.

The **visitors center** (☑ 888-448-7444, 250-362-7722; www.rossland.com; 1100 Hwy 3B; ⊙ 9am-5pm May-Sep) is located in the **Rossland Museum** building, at the junction of Hwy 22 (from the US border) and Hwy 3B.

Mountain biking is the reason many come to Rossland. Free riding is all the rage as the ridgelines are easily accessed and there are lots of rocky paths for plunging

downhill. The **Seven Summits & Dewdney Trail** is a 35.8km single track along the crest of the Rossland Range. The **Kootenay Columbia Trails Society** (www.kcts.ca) has tons of info, including downloadable maps.

Good in summer for riding, **Red Mountain Ski Resort** (☑ 250-362-7384, 800-663-0105, snow report 250-362-5500; www.redresort.com; Hwy 3B; 1-day lift pass adult/child $72/36) draws plenty of ski bums in winter. Red, as it's called, includes the 1590m-high Red Mountain and 2040m-high Granite Mountain, for a total of 1085 hectares of challenging, powdery terrain.

Hwy 3B curves through awesome alpine scenery before rejoining Hwy 3 28km northwest of Rossland. The road then wends its way 170km west to Osoyoos through increasingly arid terrain.

Nelson

POP 10,300

Nelson is reason enough to visit the Kootenays and should be on any itinerary in the region. Tidy brick buildings climb the side of a hill overlooking the west arm of deep-blue Kootenay Lake, and the waterfront is lined with parks and beaches. The thriving cafe, culture and nightlife scene is simply a bonus. However, what really propels Nelson over the top is its personality: a funky mix of hippies, characters, creative types and rugged individualists. You can find all these along Baker St, the pedestrian-friendly main drag where wafts of patchouli mingle with hints of fresh-roasted coffee.

Born as a mining town in the late 1800s, in 1977 a decades-long heritage-preservation project began. Today there are more than 350 carefully preserved and restored period buildings. Nelson is an excellent base for hiking, skiing and kayaking the nearby lakes and hills.

◉ Sights

Almost a third of Nelson's **historic buildings** have been restored to their high- and late-Victorian architectural splendor. Pick up the superb *Heritage Walking Tour* from the visitors center. It gives details of over two dozen buildings in the center and offers a good lesson in Victorian architecture.

Touchstones Nelson (☑ 250-352-9813; 502 Vernon St; adult/child $8/4; ⊙ 10am-5pm Mon-Wed, Fri & Sat, to 8pm Thu, noon-4pm Sun) combines engaging historical displays with art in Nelson's grand old city hall (1902).

By the iconic Nelson Bridge, **Lakeside Park** is both a flower-filled, shady park and a beach, with a great summer cafe. From the center, follow the **Waterfront Pathway**, which runs all along the shore – its western extremity passes the airport and has a remote river vantage. You could walk one way to the park and ride **Streetcar 23** (adult/child $3/2; ☺ 11am-4:30pm Sat & Sun Jun-Oct) the other way. It follows a 2km track from Lakeside Park to the wharf at Hall St.

🏃 Activities

Kayaking

The natural (meaning undammed) waters of Kootenay Lake are a major habitat for kayaks. **ROAM** (☑ 250-354-2056; www.roam-shop.com; 639 Baker St; ☺ 8am-7pm Mon-Sat, to 5pm Sun) sells gear, offers advice and works with the noted **Kootenay Kayak Company** (☑ 250-505-4549; www.kootenaykayak.com; kayak rentals per day $40-50, tours from $80). Kayaks can be picked up at ROAM or Lakeside Park.

Hiking

Great hikes starfish out from Nelson, especially in the Selkirk Mountains north of town.

★**Kokanee Glacier Provincial Park** HIKING
(☑ trail conditions 250-825-3500; www.bcparks.ca; Kokanee Glacier Rd) This park boasts 85km of some of the area's most superb hiking trails. The fantastic summer-only 2.5km (two hour) round-trip hike to **Kokanee Lake** on a well-marked trail can be continued to the treeless, boulder-strewn expanse around the glacier. Turn off Hwy 3A 20.5km northeast of Nelson, then it's another 16km on Kokanee Glacier Rd.

Along the way at the 11.4km mark, look for the **Old Growth Trail**, a 3km walk through 500-year-old trees.

Burlington Northern Rail Trail HIKING
Extending 42km from Nelson to Salmo along an old rail line, this trail has stunning views amid thick forest. Turn back when you want, but the first 6km has many highlights. The trailhead is at the corner of Cherry and Gore Streets.

Pulpit Rock HIKING
(www.pulpitrocknelson.com) The two-hour climb to Pulpit Rock, just across the lake, affords fine views of Nelson and Kootenay Lake. The trailhead starts at the parking lot on Johnstone Rd.

Mountain Biking

Mountain-bike trails wind up from Kootenay Lake along steep and challenging hills, followed by vertigo-inducing downhills. Pick up *Nelson Mountain Bike Guide* ($20), which details 105 trails, from **Sacred Ride** (☑ 250-362-5688; www.sacredride.ca; 213B Baker St; bicycle rentals per day $45-95; ☺ 9am-5:30pm Mon-Sat).

Skiing & Snowboarding

Known for its heavy powdery snowfall, **Whitewater Winter Resort** (☑ 250-354-4944, 800-666-9420, snow report 250-352-7669; www.skiwhitewater.com; off Hwy 6; 1-day lift ticket adult/child $68/34), 12km south of Nelson off Hwy 6, has the same small-town charm as Nelson. Lifts are few, but so are the crowds, who enjoy a drop of 623m on 78 runs.

🛏 Sleeping

By all means stay in the heart of Nelson so you can fully enjoy the city's beat. The visitors center has lists of B&Bs in heritage homes near the center.

★**WhiteHouse Backpacker Lodge** HOSTEL $
(☑ 250-352-0505; www.white-house.ca; 816 Vernon St; dm $25-30, r $50-65; @ 🛜) Relax on the broad porch overlooking the lake at this comfy heritage house, which has a cool book collection, a fireplace and more. You'll get all the pancakes you can cook yourself for breakfast.

HI Dancing Bear Inn HOSTEL $
(☑ 877-352-7573, 250-352-7573; www.dancing-bearinn.com; 171 Baker St; dm/r from $24/52; ☺ @ 🛜) 🏳 The brilliant management here offers advice and smooths the stay of guests in the 14 shared and private rooms, all of which share bathrooms. There's a gourmet kitchen and a library.

City Tourist Park CAMPGROUND $
(☑ 250-352-7618; campnels@telus.net; 90 High St; campsites from $20; ☺ May-Sep) Just a five-minute walk from Baker St, this small municipal campground has 43 shady sites.

★**Hume Hotel** HOTEL $$
(☑ 250-352-5331; www.humehotel.com; 422 Vernon St; r $100-200; @ 🛜) This 1898 classic hotel maintains its period grandeur. The 43 rooms vary in quality – beware of airless ones overlooking the kitchen on sultry

nights. Ask for the huge corner rooms with views of the hills and lake. Rates include a delicious breakfast. It has several appealing nightlife venues.

Cloudside Inn INN $$

(☎800-596-2337, 250-352-3226; www.cloudside. ca; 408 Victoria St; r $100-200; ❋@☎) Live like a silver baron at this vintage mansion, where the seven rooms are named after trees. Luxuries abound, and a fine patio looks over the terraced gardens and town.

Mountain Hound Inn GUESTHOUSE $$

(☎866-452-6490, 250-352-6490; www.mountainhound.com; 621 Baker St; r $70-120; ❋@☎) The 19 rooms are small, but have an industrial edge – to go with the cement-block walls. It's ideally located in the center and is a good, no-frills choice.

Victoria Falls Guest House INN $$

(☎250-505-3563; www.victoriafallsguesthouse. com; cnr Victoria & Falls Sts; r $105-135; ☎❋) The wide porch wraps right around this festive yellow renovated Victorian. The five suites have sitting areas and cooking facilities. Decor ranges from cozy antiques to family-friendly bunk beds.

✖ Eating & Drinking

Stroll the Baker St environs and you'll find a vibrant mix of eateries. Look for Nelson Brewing Co's organic beers on tap; we swoon for the intense Full Nelson IPA and the Hopgood Session Ale.

★ Cottonwood Community Market MARKET $

(Cottonwood Falls Park; ⊙9:30am-3pm Sat May-Oct) Close to downtown and next to the surging Cottonwood waterfall, this market encapsulates Nelson. There's great organic produce; fine baked goods, many with heretofore unheard of grains; and various craft items with artistic roots in tie-dyeing. A second event, the **Downtown Market** (400 block Josephine St; ⊙10am-4pm Wed Jun-Sep), also has live music.

★ Kootenay Bakery Cafe BAKERY $

(☎250-352-2274; www.kootenaybakerycafe.com; 377 Baker St; mains from $6; ⊙7:30am-6pm Mon-Sat; ✎) ✿ Organic ingredients and locally sourced foods come together in this bustling bakery with an excellent cafe. Sandwiches, soups, salads, breakfasts and more can be enjoyed while customers cart spelt loafs out the door by the bushel.

Oso Negro CAFE $

(☎250-532-7761; 604 Ward St; coffee from $2; ⊙7am-5pm) This local favorite corner cafe roasts its own coffee. Outside there are tables in a garden that burbles with water features amid statues.

Bibo FUSION $$

(☎250-352-2744; www.bibonelson.ca; 518 Hall St; mains $19-30; ⊙5pm-late) Bibo is all exposed brick inside, while outside a hillside terrace looks down to the lake. Small plates celebrate local produce: enjoy a meze or cheese and charcuterie plate with flights of wine. The short list of upscale mains includes burgers and seafood.

Cantina del Centro MEXICAN $$

(☎250-352-3737; 561 Baker St; small mains $6-10; ⊙11am-late) Bright and vibrant, it gets jammed with diners. The superfresh tacos and other small plates reflect the vivid colors of the Mexican tile floor. You can watch your meal grill up behind the counter while you chill with a margarita.

★ All Seasons Cafe FUSION $$$

(☎250-352-0101; www.allseasonscafe.com; 620 Herridge Lane; mains $20-32; ⊙5-10pm) Sitting on the patio under the little lights twinkling in the huge maple above is a Nelson highlight; in winter, candles provide the same romantic flair. The eclectic menu changes with the seasons but always celebrates BC foods. The wine list is iconic.

Library Lounge LOUNGE

(☎250-352-5331; Hume Hotel, 422 Vernon St; ⊙11am-late) This refined space in a classic hotel has some good sidewalk tables where you can ponder the passing parade. There's live jazz most nights. The adjoining **Mike's Place Pub** bustles and has a great beer selection plus fine chow (mains from $12).

🔒 Shopping

Otter Books BOOKS

(☎250-352-7525; 398 Baker St; ⊙9:30am-5:30pm Mon-Sat, 11am-4pm Sun) Books and maps.

Isis Essentials ACCESSORIES

(☎250-352-0666; www.isis.ca; 582 Ward St; ⊙11am-6pm Mon-Sat) The place to feel the local vibe: sex toys and oils in a feminist setting. Sniff out their line of Dungeon Sense scents.

ⓘ Information

The **visitors center** (☎877-663-5706, 250-352-3433; www.discovernelson.com; 225 Hall

St; ⊘ 8:30am-6pm daily May-Oct, 8:30am-5pm Mon-Fri Nov-Apr) contains good information about the region.

Listen to the Nelson beat on **Kootenay Co-Op Radio** (93.5FM).

ℹ Getting There & Around

Castlegar Airport (YCG; www.wkrairport.ca; Hwy 3A) The closest airport to Nelson is 42km southwest.

Greyhound Canada (☑ 250-352-3939; Chahko-Mika Mall, 1128 Lakeside Dr) Buses serve Fernie ($65, 5½ hours, one daily) and Kelowna ($65, 5½ hours, one daily).

Nelson Transit System (☑ 250-352-8201; www.bctransit.ca; fare $2) Buses 2 and 10 serve Chahko-Mika Mall and Lakeside Park. The main stop is at the corner of Ward and Baker Sts.

Queen City Shuttle (☑ 250-352-9829; www.kootenayshuttle.com; one-way adult/child $25/10) Links with Castlegar Airport (one hour); reserve in advance.

Nelson to Revelstoke

Heading north from Nelson, there are two options, both scenic, for reaching Revelstoke. Hwy 6 heads west for 16km before turning north at South Slocan. The road eventually runs alongside pretty Slocan Lake for about 30km before reaching New Denver. It's 97km between Nelson and New Denver.

Going north and east from Nelson on Hwy 3A is the most interesting route. After 34km there's the dock for the free **Kootenay Lake Ferry** at Balfour. This ride is worth it

even if you're not going anywhere, because of the long lake vistas of blue mountains rising sharply from the water.

At Balfour the road becomes Hwy 31 and follows the lake 34km north to Kaslo, passing cute little towns along the way.

Kaslo

A cute little lake town that's a good stop, Kaslo is a low-key gem. Don't miss the restored 1898 **SS Moyie** (324 Front St; adult/child $10/4; ⊘ 10am-5pm May-Oct) It has tourist info on the myriad ways to kayak and canoe the sparkling blue waters right outside.

There's a range of accommodations in and around town including the appealing downtown **Kaslo Hotel** (☑ 250-353-7714; www.kaslohotel.com; 430 Front St; r $120-200; @ ☎), which has lake views and a brewery.

New Denver

Wild mountain streams are just some of the natural highlights on Hwy 31A, which goes up and over some rugged hills. At the end of this twisting 47km road, you reach New Denver, which seems about five years away from ghost-town status. But that's not bad as this historic little gem slumbers away peacefully right on the clear waters of Slocan Lake.

The **Silvery Slocan Museum** (☑ 250-358-2201; www.newdenver.ca; 202 6th Ave; adult/child $4/free; ⊘ 9am-4pm Jun-Aug) is also home to the helpful visitors center. Housed in the 1897 Bank of Montreal building, it features well-done displays from the booming

---

INLAND FERRIES

The long Kootenay and Upper and Lower Arrow Lakes necessitate some scenic travel on **inland ferries** (www.th.gov.bc.ca/marine/ferry_schedules.htm; free). On busy summer weekends, you may have to wait in a long line for a sailing or two before you get passage.

Kootenay Lake Ferry (☑ 250-229-4215) sails between Balfour on the west arm of Kootenay Lake (34km northeast of Nelson) and Kootenay Bay, where you can follow Hwy 3A for the pretty 80km ride south to Creston. It is a 35-minute crossing. In summer the ferry leaves Balfour every 50 minutes between 6:30am and 9:40pm, and Kootenay Lake from 7:10am to 10:20pm.

Needles Ferry (☑ 250-837-8418) crosses Lower Arrow Lake between Fauquier (57km south of Nakusp) and Needles (135km east of Vernon) on Hwy 6. The trip takes five minutes and runs every 30 minutes in each direction. This is a good link between the Okanagan Valley and the Kootenays.

Upper Arrow Lake Ferry (☑ 250-837-8418) runs between Galena Bay (49km south of Revelstoke) and Shelter Bay (49km north of Nakusp) on Hwy 23. The trip takes 20 minutes and runs from 5am to midnight every hour from Shelter Bay and every hour between 5:30am and 12:30am from Galena Bay.

BOWRON LAKE PROVINCIAL PARK

The place heaven-bound canoeists go when they die, **Bowron Lake Provincial Park** (www.bcparks.ca; canoe circuit permit $30-60, campsite $16; ⊙ May-Sep) is a fantasyland of 10 lakes surrounded by snowcapped peaks. Forming a natural circle with sections of the Isaac, Cariboo and Bowron Rivers, its 116km canoe circuit is one of the world's finest. There are eight portages, with the longest (2km) over well-defined trails.

The whole circuit takes between six and 10 days, and you'll need to be completely self-sufficient. September is a good time to visit, both for the bold colors of changing leaves and lack of summertime crowds. The park website has maps and details everything you'll need to know for planning your trip, including mandatory reservations, which book up months in advance.

If you'd rather leave the details to others, **Whitegold Adventures** (☑ 250-994-2345; www.whitegold.ca; Hwy 26, Wells) offers four- to eight-day guided paddles of Bowron Lake. A full circuit costs $1800 per person.

To get to the park by car, turn off Hwy 26 just before Barkerville and follow the 28km gravel Bowron Lake Rd.

Sleeping

There are various options before you paddle out. Reserve park campsites in advance.

Bowron Lake Lodge (☑ 800-519-3399, 250-992-2733; www.bowronlakelodge.com; Bowron Lake; campsites $28, r $60-80; ⊙ May-Sep) is picture-perfect and right on the lake. It has cabins and motel rooms, and rents canoes and gear.

mining days, a tiny vault and an untouched tin ceiling.

Both New Denver and the equally sleepy old mining town of **Silverton**, just south, have fine cafes.

Making the loop from Nelson via Hwys 6 and 31 through New Denver is a great day trip. Otherwise, if you're headed to Revelstoke, continue north 47km on Hwy 6 from New Denver to Nakusp through somewhat bland rolling countryside.

Nakusp

Right on Upper Arrow Lake, both Nakusp and the chain of lakes were forever changed by BC's orgy of dam building in the 1950s and 1960s. The water level here was raised and the town had to be moved, which is why it now has a sort of 1960s-era look. It does have some attractive cafes and a tiny **museum**.

Nakusp Hot Springs (☑ 250-265-4528; www.nakusphotsprings.com; 8500 Hot Springs Rd; adult/child $9.50/8.50; ⊙ 9:30am-9:30pm), 12km northeast of Nakusp off Hwy 23, feel a bit artificial after a revamp. However, you'll forget this as you soak away your cares amid an amphitheater of trees.

From Nakusp you could head west on Hwy 6 to Vernon in the Okanagan Valley, a 245km drive that includes the Needles Ferry.

Or head north 55km on Hwy 23 to the Upper Arrow Lake Ferry and the final 48km to Revelstoke.

CARIBOO, CHILCOTIN & COAST

This vast and beautiful region covers a huge swath of BC north of the Whistler tourist hordes. It comprises three very distinct areas. The **Cariboo** region includes numerous ranches and terrain that's little changed from the 1850s when the 'Gold Rush Trail' passed through from Lillooet to Barkerville.

Populated with more moose than people, the **Chilcotin** lies to the west of Hwy 97, the region's north–south spine. Its mostly wild, rolling landscape has a few ranches and some aboriginal villages. Hwy 20 travels west from Williams Lake to the spectacular Bella Coola Valley, a bear-and-wildlife-filled inlet along the **coast**.

Much of the region can be reached via Hwy 97 and you can build a circle itinerary to other parts of BC via Prince George in the north. The Bella Coola Valley is served by ferry from Port Hardy on Vancouver Island, which makes for even more cool circle-route itineraries.

There is a twice-daily **Greyhound Canada** (☑800-661-8747; www.greyhound.ca) service along Hwy 97 (Cache Creek to Prince George takes six hours).

Williams Lake to Prince George

Cattle and lumber have shaped **Williams Lake**, the hub for the region. Some 206km north of the junction of Hwys 1 and 97, this small town has a pair of museums and numerous motels. The best reason to stop is the superb **Discovery Centre** (☑250-392-5025; www.williamslake.ca; 1660 Broadway S, off Hwy 97; ☺9am-5pm), a visitors center in a huge log building. It has full regional info and the lowdown for trips west to the coast on Hwy 20. Avoid the smear of fast fooderies along Hwy 97 and get a good sandwich and coffee from **Bean Counter Bistro** (180 3rd St; mains from $5; ☺7:30am-5:30pm Mon-Sat; ☏).

Quesnel, 124km north of Williams Lake on Hwy 97, is all about logging. There are some good motels and cafes in the tidy, flower-lined center. From Quesnel, Hwy 26 leads east to the area's main attractions, Barkerville Historic Park and Bowron Lake Provincial Park.

North of Quesnel it's 116km on Hwy 97 to Prince George.

Barkerville & Around

In 1862 Billy Barker, previously of Cornwall, struck gold deep in the Cariboo. Soon Barkerville sprung up, populated by the usual fly-by-night crowds of whores, dupes, tricksters and just plain prospectors. Today you can visit more than 125 restored heritage buildings in **Barkerville Historic Town** (☑888-994-3332; www.barkerville.ca; Hwy 26; adult/child $14/4.50; ☺8am-6pm May-Sep). In summer, people dressed in period garb roam through town and, if you can tune out the crowds, it feels more authentic than forced. It has shops, cafes and a couple of B&Bs. At other times of year, you can visit the town for free, but don't expect to find much open.

Near Barkerville, quirky **Wells** has accommodations, restaurants and a general store. The **visitors center** (☑877-451-9355, 250-994-2323; www.wellsbc.com; 11900 Hwy 26; ☺9am-6pm May-Sep) has details.

Barkerville is 82km east of Quesnel.

Wells Gray Provincial Park

Plunging 141m onto rocks below, **Helmcken Falls**, Canada's fourth highest, is but one of the undiscovered facets of **Wells Gray Provincial Park** (www.bcparks.ca; Wells Gray Rd), itself an under-appreciated gem.

BC's fourth-largest park is bounded by the Clearwater River and its tributaries, which define the park's boundaries. Highlights for visitors include five major lakes, two large river systems, scores of waterfalls and most every kind of BC land-based wildlife.

Most people enter the park via the town of **Clearwater** on Hwy 5, 123km north of Kamloops. From here, a 36km paved road runs to the park's south entrance. Part gravel, Wells Gray Rd then runs 29km into the heart of the park. Many hiking trails and sights, such as Helmcken Falls, are accessible off this road, which ends at Clearwater Lake.

You'll find opportunities for **hiking**, **cross-country skiing** and **horseback riding** along more than 20 trails of varying lengths. Rustic backcountry campgrounds dot the area around four of the lakes. **Clearwater Lake Tours** (☑250-674-2121; www.clearwaterlaketours.com; canoes per day from $50) rents canoes and leads treks.

Of the three vehicle-accessible yet simple **campgrounds** (☑250-674-2194; campsites $16) in the park, woodsy **Pyramid Campground** is just 5km north of the park's south entrance and is close to Helmcken Falls. There's plenty of **backcountry camping**, which costs $5 per person per night.

Clearwater has stores, restaurants and a slew of motels, including **Dutch Lake Resort** (☑888-884-4424, 250-674-3351; www.dutchlake.com; 361 Ridge Dr, Clearwater; campsites from $35, r $120-190), which has cabins, motel units and 65 campsites. Rent a canoe and practice for greater fun in the park.

Wells Gray Guest Ranch (☑866-467-4346, 250-674-2792; www.wellsgrayranch.com; Clearwater Valley Rd; campsites from $25, r $90-180) has cabins and cozy rooms in the main lodge building. It's inside the park, 27km north of Clearwater.

The Clearwater **visitors center** (☑250-674-2646; www.wellsgray.ca; 425 E Yellowhead Hwy, cnr Clearwater Valley Rd; ☺9am-6:30pm May-Oct; ☏) is a vital info stop for the park. It books rooms and fun-filled white-water-rafting trips.

BRITISH COLUMBIA WILLIAMS LAKE TO PRINCE GEORGE

Chilcotin & Highway 20

Meandering over the lonely hills west of the Chilcotin, Hwy 20 runs 450km from Williams Lake to the Bella Coola Valley. Long spoken about by drivers in the sort of hushed tones doctors use when describing a worrisome stool specimen, the road has been steadily improved and is now more than 90% paved. However, the section that's not is a doozy: the **Hill** is a 30km stretch of gravel that's 386km west of Williams Lake. It descends 1524m from Heckman's Pass to the valley, nearly at sea level, through a series of sharp switchbacks and 11% grades. But by taking your time and using low gear, you'll actually enjoy the stunning views. It's safe for all vehicles – tourists engorged with testosterone from their SUVs are humbled when a local in a Chevy beater zips past.

Driving the road in one go will take about six hours. You'll come across a few aboriginal villages, as well as gravel roads that lead off to the odd provincial park and deserted lake. Check with the visitors center at Williams Lake for details and available services.

Bella Coola Valley

Leaving the dry expanses of the Chilcotin, you're in for a surprise when you reach the bottom of the hill. The verdant Bella Coola Valley is at the heart of Great Bear Rainforest, a lush land of huge stands of trees, surging white water and lots of bears. It's a spiritual place: Nuxalk First Nation artists are active here and, for many creative types from elsewhere, this is literally the end of the road.

The valley stretches 53km to the shores of the North Bentinck Arm, a deep, glacier-fed fjord that runs 40km inland from the Pacific Ocean. The two main towns, **Bella Coola** on the water and **Hagensborg** 15km east, almost seem as one, with most places of interest in or between the two.

◉ Sights & Activities

Spanning the Chilcotin and the east end of the valley, the southern portion of **Tweedsmuir Provincial Park** (☑250-398-4414; www.bcparks.ca; off Hwy 20) is the second-largest provincial park in BC. It's a seemingly barely charted place, perfect for challenging backcountry adventures. **Day hikes** off Hwy 20 in the valley follow trails into lush and untouched coastal rainforest.

Walk amid 500-year-old cedars just west of Hagensborg at **Walker Island Park** on the edge of the wide and rocky Bella Coola River floodplain.

There's really no limit to your activities here. You can hike into the hills and valleys starting from roads (consider **Odegaard Falls**) or at points only reachable by boat along the craggy coast.

Kynoch Adventures (☑250-982-2298; www.bcmountainlodge.com; Hwy 20, Hagensborg; tours from adult/child $80/40) specializes in critter-spotting trips down local rivers and wilderness hikes. Highly recommended float trips to spot the valley's renowned grizzly bear population run from late August into October ($125 per person).

🛏 Sleeping & Eating

There are a dozen B&Bs and small inns along Hwy 20. Many offer evening meals; otherwise, there are a couple of cafes and restaurants.

Rip Rap Camp CAMPGROUND $
(☑250-982-2752; www.riprapcamp.com; 1854 Hwy 20, Hagensborg; campsites $17-25, cabins $60-125; ☺May-Oct; 🛜) A much-lauded campground, Rip Rap has plenty of services and a great viewing deck overlooking the river.

★ **Bella Coola Mountain Lodge** INN $$
(☑250-982-2298; www.bcmountainlodge.com; 1900 Hwy 20, Hagensborg; r $90-125; @🛜) The 14 rooms, many with kitchen facilities, are huge and there's an excellent **restaurant** (mains $20-30; ☺5:30-8:30pm Wed-Sun). The owners also run Kynoch Adventures, and guests can rent minivans and SUVs (from $65 per day).

Tallheo Cannery GUESTHOUSE $$
(☑604-992-1424; www.bellacoolacannery.com; campsite $15, r incl transport $125) One of BC's most unusual places to stay is 3km across the inlet from Bella Coola in an old cannery. On approach by boat, you may have misgivings, as large portions of the cannery are collapsing over the water. But fear not, for the rooms in an old 1920s bunkhouse are on solid ground. Transport for campers is $10; tours for day-trippers cost $50.

The adventurous will find that the views (stunning), explorations (it's an entire village with its own beach) and mystery (abandoned detritus of an old cannery) make this a fascinating stay.

ⓘ Information

Both the visitors center and your accommodations can point you to guides and gear for skiing, mountain biking, fishing, rafting and much more. Car repair, ATMs, laundry and groceries are available. Most tourist services are closed October to April.

Oodles of info and advice, including trail guides, is available at the volunteer-run **visitors center** (☑ 250-982-0092; www.bellacoola.ca; 1881 Hwy 20, Hagensborg; ☺10am-4pm Jun-Sep) in an atmospheric 1903 house.

ⓘ Getting There & Away

BC Ferries (☑ 888-223-3779; www.bcferries. com; adult/child $193/97, car from $386) runs the Discovery Coast route, which links Bella Coola and Port Hardy on Vancouver Island a couple of times per week in summer. The journey takes from 13 to 34 hours, depending on stops. Best are the weekly direct 13-hour trips as the usual boat, the *Queen of Chilliwack*, does not have cabins.

There are no buses along Hwy 20 to Williams Lake, although you can go by charter plane. **Pacific Coastal Airlines** (☑ 800-663-2872; www. pacificcoastal.com; one-way $175-340; ☺daily) has one-hour flights from Vancouver.

NORTHERN BRITISH COLUMBIA

Northern BC is where you will truly feel that you've crossed that ethereal border to some place different. Nowhere else are the rich cultures of Canada's Aboriginal people so keenly felt, from the Haida on Haida Gwaii to the Tsimshian on the mainland. Nowhere else does land so exude mystery, whether it's the storm-shrouded coast and islands or the silent majesty of glaciers carving passages through entire mountain ranges.

And nowhere else has this kind of promise. Highways like the fabled Alaska or the awe-inspiring Stewart-Cassiar encourage adventure, discovery or even a new life. Here, your place next to nature will never be in doubt; you'll revel in your own insignificance.

Prince Rupert

POP 12,600

People are always 'discovering' Prince Rupert, and what a find it is. This intriguing city, with a gorgeous harbor, is not just a transportation hub (ferries go south to Vancouver, west to Haida Gwaii and north to Alaska), but a destination in its own right. It has two excellent museums, fine restaurants and a culture that draws much from its aboriginal heritage. Yet the city struggles to attract the huge cruise ships plying the Inside Passage.

It may rain 220 days a year, but that doesn't stop the drip-dry locals enjoying activities in the misty mountains and waterways. Originally the dream of Charles Hays, who built the railroad here before going to a watery grave on the *Titanic*, Rupert always

BRITISH COLUMBIA PRINCE RUPERT

THE GREAT BEAR RAINFOREST

It's the last major tract of coastal temperate rainforest left on the planet. The Great Bear Rainforest is a wild region of islands, fjords and towering peaks. Covering 64,000 sq km (7% of BC), it stretches south from Alaska along the BC coast and Haida Gwaii to roughly Campbell River on Vancouver Island (which isn't part of the forest). The forests and waters are remarkably rich in life: whales, salmon, eagles, elk, otter and more thrive. Remote river valleys are lined with forests of old Sitka spruce, Pacific silver fir and various cedars that are often 100m tall and 1500 years old.

As vast as it is, however, the Great Bear is under great threat. Less than 50% is protected and industry and government keep missing deadlines for protection plans. Meanwhile mineral and logging companies are eyeing the forest, while others want to build the huge Northern Gateway Pipelines project that would bring supertankers to the coast. Among the many groups fighting to save this irreplaceable habitat is the Raincoast Conservation Foundation; see www.raincoast.org. The website www.savethegreatbear.org is a good source of info.

From Bella Coola, you can arrange boat trips and treks to magical places in the Great Bear, including hidden rivers where you might see a rare **Kermode bear**, a white-furred offshoot of the black bear known in tribal legend as the 'spirit bear' and the namesake of the rainforest.

seems one step behind a bright future. But its ship may finally have come in, or at least anchored offshore: the city's expanding container port speeds cheap tat from China to bargain-desperate Americans.

◉ Sights

A short walk from the center, **Cow Bay** is a delightful place for a stroll. The eponymous spotted decor is everywhere, but somehow avoids seeming clichéd. There are shops, cafes and a good view of the waterfront, especially from the cruise ship docks at the Atlin Terminal.

You'll see **totem poles** all around town; two flank the statue of Charlie Hays beside City Hall on 3rd Ave. Also watch around town for more than 30 huge **murals** adorning buildings. Noted artist Jeff King paints history and nature.

★ **Museum of Northern BC**   MUSEUM
(☑ 250-624-3207; www.museumofnorthernbc. com; 100 1st Ave W; adult/child $6/2; ⊙ 9am-5pm) Don't miss the Museum of Northern BC, which resides in a building styled after an aboriginal longhouse. The museum shows how local civilizations enjoyed sustainable cultures that lasted for thousands of years – you might say they were ahead of their time. The displays include a wealth of excellent Haida, Gitksan and Tsimshian art and plenty of info on totem poles. The bookshop is excellent.

🏃 Activities

Among the many local walks, a good place to start is the **Butze Rapids Trail**, a 4.5km loop starting 3km south of town. It has interpretive signs.

Further afield, **Khutzeymateen Grizzly Bear Sanctuary** is home to more than 50 of the giants.

Skeena Kayaking   KAYAKING
(☑ 250-624-5246; www.skeenakayaking.ca; kayak rentals per 4hr $50, tours from $80) Skeena Kayaking offers both rentals and custom tours of the area, which has a seemingly infinite variety of places to put in the water.

👉 Tours

★ **Prince Rupert Adventure Tours**   WILDLIFE
(☑ 250-627-9166; www.adventuretours.net; Atlin Terminal; bear tours adult/child $225/200, whale tours $115/100) Excellent boat tours include the Khutzeymateen grizzly-watching trips

(mid-May to early August) and whale tours (August to September). Voyages can last many hours as you track the region's rich wildlife.

🛏 Sleeping

Rupert has a range of accommodations, including more than a dozen B&Bs. When all three ferries have pulled in, competition gets fierce, so book ahead.

Pioneer Hostel   HOSTEL $
(☑ 888-794-9998, 250-624-2334; www.pioneerhostel.com; 167 3rd Ave E; dm $25-30, r $60-80; ☯@☎) Located in a residential neighborhood behind downtown, spotless compact rooms are accented with vibrant colors and there's a small kitchen and BBQ facilities out back. Ferry and train pickups are provided.

Black Rooster Guesthouse   GUESTHOUSE $
(☑ 250-627-5337; www.blackrooster.ca; 501 6th Ave W; dm $30, r $50-150; @☎) This renovated house just up the hill from the center has a patio and a bright common room. Rooms range from spartan singles to large apartments. Call for shuttle pickup.

Prince Rupert RV Campground   CAMPGROUND $
(☑ 250-624-5861; www.princeruperttrv.com; 1750 Park Ave; campsites/RV sites from $21/33; @☎) Located near the ferry terminal, this somewhat barren campground has 77 sites, hot showers, laundry facilities and a small playground.

Crest Hotel   HOTEL $$
(☑ 800-663-8150, 250-624-6771; www.cresthotel. bc.ca; 222 1st Ave W; r $120-300; ✳@☎) Prince Rupert's premier hotel has harbor-view rooms that are worth every penny, right down to the built-in bay-window seats with loaner binoculars. Avoid the smallish rooms overlooking the parking lot. Suites are opulent.

Inn on the Harbour   MOTEL $$
(☑ 250-624-9107, 800-663-8155; www.innontheharbour.com; 720 1st Ave W; r incl breakfast $120-260; ☎) Sunsets may dazzle you to the point that you don't notice the humdrum exterior at this modern, harbor-view motel. The 49 rooms have a plush, modern look.

Eagle Bluff B&B   B&B $$
(☑ 250-627-4955; www.eaglebluff.ca; 201 Cow Bay Rd; r $65-145; @) Ideally located on Cow Bay, this B&B on a pier is in a heritage building

NORTH PACIFIC CANNERY

The **North Pacific Cannery National Historic Site** (☏ 250-628-3538; www.northpacificcannery.ca; 1889 Skeena Dr; adult/child $12/6; ⊙ 10am-5pm), about 20km south of Prince Rupert, near the town of Port Edward, explores the early history of fishing and canning along the Skeena River. The fascinating all-wood complex was really a small town on stilts. It was used from 1889 to 1968. Exhibits document the miserable conditions of the workers; tours cover the industrial process and cannery life. Prince Rupert Transit (p764) has a bus service to the site.

that has a striking red and white paint job. Inside, however, the seven rooms have decor best described as homey; some share bathrooms.

Eating

Watch for halibut and salmon fresh from the fishing fleet.

Cowpuccino's   CAFE $
(☏ 250-627-1395; 25 Cow Bay Rd; coffee $2; ⊙ 7am-8pm; ☎) The coffee at this funky local cafe will make you forget the rain.

★Charley's Lounge   PUB $$
(☏ 250-624-6771; Crest Hotel, 222 1st Ave W; mains $8-20; ⊙ noon-late) Locals flock to trade gossip while gazing out over the harbor from the heated patio. The pub menu features some of Rupert's best seafood. The more formal **Waterfront Restaurant** (mains $12-35; ⊙ 6.30am-9pm Mon-Fri, 7am-9pm Sat & Sun) adjoins; it has a changing menu of dishes created in an open kitchen.

Opa Sushi   JAPANESE $$
(☏ 250-627-4560; www.opasushi.com; 34 Cow Bay Rd; mains $12-25; ⊙ 11:30am-2pm & 5-9pm Mon-Fri, noon-3pm & 5-9pm Sat, 1-8pm Sun) Super sushi is served in a renovated net loft, with easygoing style. Good wine selection.

Smiles Seafood   SEAFOOD $$
(☏ 250-624-3072; www.smilesseafoodcafe.ca; 113 Cow Bay Rd; mains $7-30; ⊙ 11am-9pm) Since 1934 Smiles has served classic, casual seafood meals. Slide into a vinyl booth or sit out on the deck. Enjoy a shrimp club sandwich or a fresh halibut steak.

Cow Bay Café   ITALIAN $$
(☏ 250-627-1212; 205 Cow Bay Rd; mains $10-20; ⊙ 11:30am-9pm) Now serving a heavy-on-the-red-sauce menu, this well-known bistro is right in Cow Bay and has wraparound water views.

🔒 Shopping

The smattering of boutiques at Cow Bay makes for the most interesting shopping.

Ice House Gallery   GALLERY
(☏ 250-624-4546; Atlin Terminal; ⊙ noon-5pm Tue-Sun) See the bounty of Rupert's vibrant creative community at this artist-run gallery.

Rainforest Books   BOOKS
(☏ 250-624-4195; www.rainforestbooks.net; 251 3rd Ave W; ⊙ 10am-6pm Mon-Sat) Good selection of new and used books.

ℹ Information

Javadotcup (☏ 250-622-2822; 516 3rd Ave W; internet access per hr $3; ⊙ 7:30am-9pm; ☎) This decent cafe has internet access and a couple of rooms upstairs for $60.

Visitors Center (☏ 250-624-5637, 800-667-1994; www.visitprincerupert.com; Museum of Northern BC, 100 1st Ave W; ⊙ 9am-5pm) Visitor services are limited to a rack of brochures and the front desk at the museum (p762).

ℹ Getting There & Away

The ferry and train terminals are 3km southwest of the center.

AIR

Prince Rupert Airport (YPR; ☏ 250-622-2222; www.ypr.ca) is on Digby Island, across the harbor from town. The trip involves a bus and ferry; pickup is at the Highliner Hotel (815 1st Ave) about two hours before flight time. Confirm all the details with your airline or the airport.

Air Canada Jazz (☏ 250-624-9633; www.aircanada.com) and **Hawkair** (☏ 250-624-4295; www.hawkair.ca) both serve Vancouver. Check in for the former is at the airport; for the latter, at Highliner Hotel.

BUS

Greyhound Canada (☏ 800-661-8747; www.greyhound.ca; 112 6th St) buses depart for Prince George ($160, 10½ hours) once a day in summer, possibly less often other times.

FERRY

Alaska Marine Highway System (☏ 250-627-1744, 800-642-0066; www.ferryalaska.com; passenger/car $160/356, cabins from $156) One or two ferries each week ply to the Yukon gateways of Haines and Skagway in Alaska via the spectacular Inside Passage.

BC Ferries (📞 250-386-3431; www.bcferries. com) The **Inside Passage** run to Port Hardy (adult $115 to $195, child fare 50%, car $250 to $445, cabin from $85, 15 to 25 hours) is hailed for its amazing scenery. There are three services per week in summer and one per week in winter on the *Northern Expedition*. The **Haida Gwaii** service goes to Skidegate Landing (adult $37 to $45, child fare 50%, car $132 to $160, six to seven hours) six times per week in summer and three times a week in winter on the *Northern Adventure*.

TRAIN

VIA Rail (www.viarail.ca; BC Ferries Terminal) operates triweekly services from Prince George (12½ hours) and, after an overnight stop, Jasper in the Rockies.

ⓘ Getting Around

Prince Rupert Transit (📞 250-624-3343; www.bctransit.com; adult/child $1.75/1.50) Infrequent services run to the ferry port and North Pacific Historic Fishing Village ($2.75). The main bus stop is at the ratty Rupert Square Mall on 2nd Ave.

Skeena Taxi (📞 250-624-2185) From the ferries to the center is about $15.

Haida Gwaii

Haida Gwaii, which means 'Islands of the People,' offers a magical trip for those who make the effort. Attention has long focused on the many unique species of flora and fauna to the extent that 'Canada's Galápagos' is a popular moniker. But each year it becomes more apparent that the real soul of the islands is the Haida culture itself. Long one of the most advanced and powerful First Nations, the Haida suffered terribly after Westerners arrived.

Now, however, their culture is resurgent and can be found across the islands in myriad ways beyond their iconic totem poles. Haida reverence for the environment is protecting the last stands of superb old-growth rainforests, where the spruce and cedars are some of the world's largest. Amid this sparsely populated, wild and rainy place are bald eagles, bears and much more wildlife. Offshore, sea lions, whales and orcas abound; in 2013 rare right whales and sea otters were spotted.

In 2010 the name used by Europeans since their arrival in the 18th century, Queen Charlotte Islands, was officially ditched; and the federal government moved forward with its plans to make the waters off Haida Gwaii a

marine preserve. In 2013 the magificent Gwaii Haanas Legacy Pole was raised at Windy Bay, the first new pole in the protected area in 130 years.

A visit to the islands rewards those who invest time to get caught up in their allure, their culture and their people – plan on a long stay. The number-one attraction here is remote **Gwaii Haanas National Park Reserve**, which makes up the bottom third of the archipelago. Named the top park in North America by *National Geographic Traveler* for being 'beautiful and intact,' it is a lost world of Haida culture and superb natural beauty.

Haida Gwaii forms a dagger-shaped archipelago of some 450 islands lying 80km west of the BC coast, and about 50km from the southern tip of Alaska. Mainland ferries dock at Skidegate Landing on Graham Island, which houses 80% of the 5000 residents. The principal town is Queen Charlotte (previously Queen Charlotte City and still known by its old QCC acronym), 7km west of Skidegate. The main road on Graham Island is Hwy 16, which is fully paved. It links Skidegate with Masset, 101km north, passing the small towns of Tlell and Port Clements.

Graham Island is linked to Moresby Island to the south by a ferry from Skidegate Landing. The airport is in Sandspit on Moresby Island, 12km east of the ferry landing at Aliford Bay. The only way to get to the park reserve, which covers the south part of Moresby Island, is by boat or floatplane.

◉ Sights & Activities

The Haida Gwaii portion of the **Yellowhead Hwy** (Hwy 16) heads 110km north from QCC past Skidegate, Tlell and Port Clements. The last was where the famous golden spruce tree on the banks of the Yakoun River was cut down by a demented forester in 1997. The incident is detailed in the best-selling *The Golden Spruce* by John Vaillant, an excellent book on the islands and Haida culture.

All along the road to **Masset**, look for little seaside pullouts, oddball boutiques and funky cafes that are typical of the islands' character.

★**Gwaii Haanas National Park Reserve, National Marine Conservation Area Reserve & Haida Heritage Site** PARK
(📞 250-559-8818; reservations 877-559-8818; www.parkscanada.ca/gwaiihaanas) This huge Unesco World Heritage site, with a name that's a mouthful, encompasses Moresby and 137 smaller islands at its southern end. It combines a time-capsule look at

abandoned Haida villages, hot springs, amazing natural beauty and some of the continent's best kayaking.

Archaeological finds have documented more than 500 ancient Haida sites, including villages and burial caves throughout the islands. The most famous village is **SGang Gwaay (Ninstints)** on Anthony Island, where rows of weathered **totem poles** stare eerily out to sea. Other major sights include the ancient village of **Skedans**, on Louise Island, and **Hotspring Island**, whose natural springs disappeared, possibly temporarily, as a result of the October 2012 earthquakes. The sites are protected by Haida Gwaii watchmen, who live on the islands in summer.

Access to the park is by boat or plane only. A visit demands a decent amount of advance planning and usually requires several days. From May to September, you must obtain a reservation, unless you're with a tour operator.

Contact **Parks Canada** (☑ 250-559-8818; www.parkscanada.ca/gwaiihaanas; Haida Heritage Centre at Kay Llnagaay, Skidegate; ☺ 8:30am-noon & 1-4:30pm Mon-Fri) with questions. The website has links to the **essential annual trip planner**. Any visitor not on a guided tour and who has not visited the park during the previous three years must attend a free orientation at the park office. All visitors must register.

The number of daily **reservations** is limited: plan well in advance. There are user fees (adult/child $20/10 per night). Nightly fees are waived if you have a Parks Canada Season Excursion Pass. A few much-coveted standby spaces are made available daily: call Parks Canada.

The easiest way to get into the park is with a tour company. Parks Canada can provide you with lists of operators; tours last from one day to two weeks. Many can also set you up with **rental kayaks** (average per day/week $60/300) and gear for independent travel.

Moresby Explorers (☑ 800-806-7633, 250-637-2215; www.moresbyexplorers.com; Sandspit) has one-day zodiac tours from $185, including the Louise Island trip that takes in Skedans and its totem poles, as well as much longer trips. It rents kayaks and gear.

Queen Charlotte Adventures (☑ 800-668-4288, 250-559-8990; www.queencharlotteadventures.com) offers lots of one- to 10-day trips using boats and kayaks, including a three-day kayak trip to the remote south for $550. It rents kayaks and gear.

Naikoon Provincial Park   PARK

(☑ 250-626-5115; www.bcparks.ca; off Hwy 16; campsites $16) Much of the island's northeastern side is devoted to the beautiful 726-sq-km Naikoon Provincial Park, which combines sand dunes and low sphagnum bogs, surrounded by stunted and gnarled lodgepole pine, and red and yellow cedar. The **beaches** on the north coast feature strong winds, pounding surf and flotsam from across the Pacific. They can be reached via the stunning 26km-long Tow Hill Rd, east of Masset. A 21km loop **trail** traverses a good bit of the park to/from Fife Beach at the end of the road.

New steps and a boardwalk make visiting the **Tow Hill Lookout** and **Blow Hole** near the end of Tow Hill Rd easy. Allow about one hour for a looping walk with many steps.

Yakoun Lake   HIKING

(☑ 250-557-6810) Hike 20 minutes through ancient stands of spruce and cedar to pristine **Yakoun Lake**, a large wilderness lake towards the west side of Graham Island. A small beach near the trail is shaded by gnarly Sitka alders. Dare to take a dip in the bracing waters or just enjoy the sweeping views.

The trailhead to the lake is at the end of a rough track off a branch from the main dirt and gravel logging road between QCC and Port Clements – watch for signs for the lake, about 20km north of QCC. It runs for 70km. On weekdays check in by phone for logging trucks.

BRITISH COLUMBIA HAIDA GWAII

🛏 Sleeping

Small inns and B&Bs are mostly found on Graham Island. There are numerous choices in QCC and Masset, with many in between and along the spectacular north coast. Naikoon Provincial Park has two **campgrounds**, including a dramatic windswept one on deserted Agate Beach, 23km east of Masset.

★ Premier Creek Lodging   INN $

(☎888-322-3388, 250-559-8415; www.qcislands. net/premier; 3101 3rd Ave, QCC; dm from $25, r $45-140; @☎) Dating from 1910, this friendly lodge has eight beds in a hostel building out back and 12 rooms in the main building, ranging from tiny but great-value singles to spacious rooms with views and porches.

North Beach Cabins   CABIN $$

(☎250-557-2415; www.northbeachcabins.com; 16km marker Tow Hill Rd; cabins $85-100) 🌿 Tucked into the dunes of beautiful North Beach are four cozy cabins. You're totally off the grid but, thanks to propane, you can cook, which will be about the only diversion from the fabulous views and endless sandy strolls.

Copper Beech House   B&B $$

(☎250-626-5441; www.copperbeechhouse.com; 1590 Delkatla Rd, Masset; r $100-160) This legendary B&B in a rambling old house on Masset Harbor is owned by poet Susan Musgrave. It has three unique rooms and there's always something amazing cooking in the kitchen.

✖ Eating

The best selection of restaurants is in QCC, although there are also a few in Skidegate and Masset. Ask at the visitors centers about local Haida feasts, where you'll enjoy the best salmon and blueberries you've ever had. Good supermarkets are found in QCC and Masset.

Queen B's   CAFE $

(☎250-559-4463; 3201 Wharf St, QCC; mains $3-10; ☺9am-5pm) This funky place excels at baked goods, which emerge from the oven all day long. There are tables with water views outside and lots of local art inside.

Moon Over Naikoon   BAKERY $

(☎250-626-5064; 17km marker Tow Hill Rd; snacks from $3; ☺8am-5pm Jun-Aug) Embodying the spirit of this road to the end of everything, this tiny community center–cum–bakery has a kaleidoscopic collection of artworks and stuff found on the beach.

Ocean View Restaurant   SEAFOOD $$

(☎250-559-8503; Sea Raven Motel, 3301 3rd Ave, QCC; mains $10-25; ☺11am-9pm) Good fresh seafood (try the halibut) is the specialty at this casual dining room, where some tables look out to the harbor.

Haida House   SEAFOOD $$

(☎855-557-4600; www.haidahouse.com; 2087 Beitush Rd, Tlell; mains $20-30) This seasonal restaurant has excellent and creative seafood and other dishes with island accents. Also rents plush rooms.

ℹ Information

Either download or pick up a free copy of the encyclopedic annual *Guide to Haida Gwaii* (www. guidetohaidagwaii.com). A good website for information is www.gohaidagwaii.ca. Parks Canada also has much information online.

The **QCC visitors center** (☎250-559-8316; www.qcinfo.ca; 3220 Wharf St, QCC; ☺8:30am-9pm) is handy and can make advance excursion bookings, although there's been a recent encroachment of gift items. Get a free copy of *Art Route*, a guide to more than 30 studios and galleries.

ℹ Getting There & Away

AIR

The main airport for Haida Gwaii is at **Sandspit** (YZP; ☎250-559-0052) on Moresby Island. Note that reaching the airport from Graham Island is time consuming: if your flight is at 3:30pm, you need to line up at the car ferry at Skidegate Landing at 12:30pm (earlier in summer). There's also a small airport at **Masset** (YMT; ☎250-626-3995).

Air Canada Jazz (☎888-247-2262; www. aircanada.com) Flies daily between Sandspit and Vancouver.

Pacific Coastal Airlines (☎800-663-2872; www.pacificcoastal.com) Flies Masset to Vancouver daily.

FERRY

The **BC Ferries** (☎250-386-3431; www.bcferries. com) service from Prince Rupert is the most popular way to reach the islands. Services ply from Prince Rupert to Skidegate Landing (adult $37 to $45, child fare 50%, car $132 to $160, six to seven hours) six times per week in summer and three times a week in winter on the *Northern Adventure*. Cabins are useful for overnight schedules (from $90).

ℹ Getting Around

Off Hwy 16, most roads are gravel or worse.

BC Ferries (adult/child $10/5, cars from $23, 20 minutes, almost hourly 7am to 10pm) links the two main islands at Skidegate Landing and Alliford Bay. Schedules seem designed to inconvenience air passengers.

Eagle Transit (☏877-747-4461; www.eagle-transit.net; adult/child $27/21) buses meet Sandspit flights and serve Skidegate and QCC.

Renting a car can be as expensive ($60 to $100 per day) as bringing one over on the ferry. **Budget** (☏250-637-5688; www.budget.com) is at the Sandspit airport, but may close permanently. **Rustic Car Rentals** (☏877-559-4641, 250-559-4641; citires@qcislands.net; 605 Hwy 33, QCC) is also in Masset.

Prince Rupert to Prince George

You can cover the 725km on Hwy 16 between BC's Princes in a day or a week. There's nothing that's an absolute must-see, but there's much to divert and cause you to pause if so inclined. Scenery along much of the road (with the notable exception of Skeena River) won't fill your memory card, but it is a pleasing mix of mountains and rivers.

Prince Rupert to Smithers

For the first 150km, Hwy 16 hugs the wide and wild **Skeena River**. This is four-star scenic driving and you'll see glaciers and jagged peaks across the waters. However, tatty **Terrace** is nobody's idea of a reward at the end of the stretch.

From Terrace, Hwy 16 continues 93km east to Kitwanga, where the **Stewart-Cassiar Hwy** (Hwy 37) strikes north towards the Yukon and Alaska.

Just east of Kitwanga is the Hazelton area (comprising New Hazelton, Hazelton and South Hazelton), the center of some interesting aboriginal sites, including **'Ksan Historical Village & Museum** (☏250-842-5544; www.ksan.org; off Hwy 16; admission $2; ☉9am-5pm). This re-created village of the Gitksan people features longhouses, a museum, various outbuildings and totem poles. The narrated tour ($10) is a must.

Smithers

Smithers, a largish town with a cute old downtown, is roughly halfway between the

---

ONE TALL TALE

Though most Aboriginal groups on the northwest coast lack formal written history as we know it, centuries of traditions manage to live on through artistic creations such as totem poles.

Carved from a single cedar trunk, totems identify a household's lineage in the same way a family crest might identify a group or clan in Britain, although the totem pole is more of a historical pictograph depicting the entire ancestry.

Two excellent places both to see totem poles and learn more are the Haida Heritage Centre at Kay Llnagaay (p765) at Skidegate and the Museum of Northern BC (p762) in Prince Rupert.

Unless you're an expert, it's not easy to decipher a totem. But you can start by looking for the creatures that are key to the narrative. Try to pick out the following:

Beaver Symbolizes industriousness, wisdom and determined independence.

Black bear Serves as a guardian and spiritual link between humans and animals.

Eagle Signifies intelligence and power.

Frog Represents adaptability, the ability to live in both natural and supernatural worlds.

Hummingbird Embodies love, beauty and unity with nature.

Killer whale Symbolizes dignity and strength; often depicted as a reincarnated spirit of a great chief.

Raven Signifies mischievousness and cunning.

Salmon Typifies dependable sustenance, longevity and perseverance.

Shark Exemplifies an ominous and fierce solitude.

Thunderbird Represents the wisdom of proud ancestors.

Watchmen The village watchmen, who warned of danger.

NORTH TO THE YUKON

From BC, there are three main ways to go north by vehicle. All are potentially good choices, so you have several ways of creating a circle itinerary to the Yukon and possibly Alaska.

Alaska Highway

Fabled and historic, the Alaska Hwy, from its start point in Dawson Creek (364km northeast of Prince George) through northeast BC to Watson Lake (944km), is being somewhat eclipsed by the Stewart-Cassiar Hwy. Still, it's an epic drive, even if the sections to Fort Nelson are bland. It's most convenient for those coming from Edmonton and the east.

Stewart-Cassiar

The Stewart-Cassiar (Hwy 37) runs 700km through wild scenery from the junction with Hwy 16, 240km east of Prince Rupert and 468km west of Prince George. A side trip to the incomparable glaciers around Stewart is essential and easy. This route is convenient for people from most of BC, Alberta and the western US. It ends at the Alaska Hwy, near Watson Lake, in the Yukon.

Alaska Marine Highway System

We love Alaska's car ferries (www.ferryalaska.com) that sail the **Inside Passage**. Free of frills, they let you simply relax and view one of the world's great shows of marine life while enjoying the same scenery cruise-ship passengers spend thousands more to see. You can take a three-day ride on boats from Bellingham (north of Seattle), Washington, to Haines and Skagway in southeast Alaska, on the Yukon border. Or catch the ferries in Prince Rupert for service to the same two towns; you could link this to the BC Ferries route from Port Hardy. The ferries, especially cabins, fill up fast in summer, so reserve.

Princes. The **visitors center** (☑800-542-6673, 250-847-5072; www.tourismsmithers.com; 1411 Court St; ⊘9am-6pm; 🛜) can steer you to excellent mountain biking, white-water rafting and climbing. Great hiking is found in nearby **Babine Mountains Provincial Park** (☑250-847-7329; www.bcparks.ca; Old Babine Lake Rd; backcountry cabins per person $5), a 324-sq-km park with trails to glacier-fed lakes and subalpine meadows.

Stork Nest Inn (☑250-847-3831; www.stork-nestinn.com; 1485 Main St; r $85-100; ❋🐾🛜) is a good choice among many. Main St has several good cafes including **Bugwood Bean** (www.bugwoodbean.com; 2nd & Main Sts; coffee $2; ⊘8am-5:30pm Mon-Sat; 🛜). **Mountain Eagle Books & Bistro** (☑250-847-5245; 3775 3rd St; ⊘9am-6pm Mon-Sat; 🛜) has books and info on the area's thriving folk-music scene; the tiny cafe has veggie soup and lunches.

Smithers to Prince George

South and east of Smithers, after 146km you pass through **Burns Lake**, the center of a popular fishing district. After another 128km, at **Vanderhoof**, Hwy 27 heads 66km north to **Fort St James National Historic**

Site (☑250-996-7191; www.pc.gc.ca; Kwah Rd; adult/child $8/4; ⊘9am-5pm May-Sep), a former Hudson's Bay Company trading post that's on the tranquil southeastern shore of Stuart Lake and has been restored to its 1896 glory.

From Vanderhoof, the 100km to Prince George passes through a region filled with the dead trees seen across the north. These dark grey specimens are victims of mountain pine beetles, whose explosive population growth is linked to comparatively mild winters due to climate change. Note the many sawmills processing the dead trees.

Prince George

POP 72,200

In First Nations times, before outsiders arrived, Prince George was called Lheidli T'Enneh, which means 'people of the confluence,' an appropriate name given that the Nechako and Fraser Rivers converged here. Today the name would be just as fitting, although it's the confluence of highways that matters most. A mill town since 1807, it is a vital BC crossroads and you're unlikely to visit the north without passing through at least once.

Hwy 97 from the south cuts through the center of town on its way north to Dawson Creek (360km) and the Alaska Hwy. Hwy 16 becomes Victoria St as it runs through town westward to Prince Rupert (724km), and east to Jasper (380km) and Edmonton. The downtown, no beauty-contest winner, is compact and has some good restaurants.

◉ Sights

Exploration Place   MUSEUM
(☑ 250-562-1612; www.theexplorationplace.com; Fort George Park, 333 Becott Pl; adult/child $10/7; ⊘ 9am-5pm) Exploration Place, southeast of downtown (follow 20th Ave east of Gorse St), has various kid-friendly galleries devoted to science, plus natural and cultural history.

Prince George Railway & Forestry Museum   MUSEUM
(☑ 250-563-7351; www.pgrfm.bc.ca; 850 River Rd; adult/child $6/3; ⊘ 10am-5pm) **Cottonwood Island Nature Park** has walks alongside the river and is home to the Prince George Railway & Forestry Museum, which honors choo-choos, the beaver and local lore.

⌫ Sleeping

Hwy 97 (Central St) makes an arc around the center, where you'll find legions of motels and big-box stores. The **Bed & Breakfast Hotline** (☑ 877-562-2626; www.princegeorgebnb.com) arranges bookings in your price range (from $70 to $135). Most provide transportation from the train or bus station.

Economy Inn   MOTEL $
(☑ 888-566-6333, 250-563-7106; www.economyinn.ca; 1915 3rd Ave; r $65-95; ✳ ⟐) Close to the center, this simple blue-and-white motel has 30 clean rooms and a whirlpool. Celebrate your savings with a Dairy Queen dip cone from across the street.

Bee Lazee Campground   CAMPGROUND $
(☑ 866-679-9699, 250-963-7263; www.beelazee.ca; 15910 Hwy 97 S; campsites $25-28; ⊘ May-Sep; ⟐ ⟐) About 15km south of town, this RV-centric place features full facilities, including free hot showers, fire pits and laundry.

Travelodge Prince George   MOTEL $$
(☑ 800-663-8239, 250-563-0666; www.travelodgeprincegeorge.com; 1458 7th Ave; r $80-130; ✳ @ ⟐) A real barker in the beauty department, the Travelodge is nicer on the inside – isn't everything? The 77 rooms are large and

have an easy-on-the-eyes motif. Better yet, it's steps from good restaurants and bars.

97 Motor Inn   MOTEL $$
(☑ 250-562-6010; www.97motorinn.ca; 2713 Spruce St; r $70-100; ✳ ⟐) Near the junction with Hwy 16, this modern motel is on – wait, you guessed it – Hwy 97. Some of the 19 basic rooms have balconies and kitchens. The noted Thanh Vu Vietnamese restaurant is out front.

✕ Eating

The **farmers market** (www.farmersmarketpg.ca; cnr George St & 3rd Ave; ⊘ 8:30am-2pm Sat May-Oct) is a good place to sample some of the array of local foods and produce.

★ Nancy O's   PUB $$
(☑ 250-562-8066; www.nancyos.ca; 1261 3rd Ave; mains $10-25; ⊘ 11am-late Mon-Fri, from 10am Sat & Sun) Nancy O's may make you want to spend two nights in Prince George. Locally sourced ingredients are combined for fabulous food: burgers, veggie specials, a great avocado salad and a truly amazing *steak frites*. The beer selection is fab and there's live music and DJs many nights. The vibe is hipster-comfy.

Cimo   MEDITERRANEAN $$
(☑ 250-564-7975; 601 Victoria St; mains $12-29; ⊘ 11:30am-2pm & 5-9:30pm Mon-Sat) The pesto and other excellent Mediterranean dishes never disappoint. Dine or just enjoy a glass of BC wine in the stylish interior or out on the patio. Much of the produce comes from the kitchen garden. Great BC wine list.

⌂ Shopping

Books & Company   BOOKS
(☑ 250-563-6637; 1685 3rd Ave; ⊘ 7am-7pm Mon-Wed, to 9pm Thu, to 10pm Fri, to 6pm Sat, 10am-5pm Sun; ⟐) The best bookstore in northern BC, it has a great cafe with a deck.

ℹ Information

The excellent **visitors center** (☑ 250-562-3700; www.tourismpg.com; VIA Rail Station, 1300 1st Ave; ⊘ 8am-8pm; ⟐) can make bookings, such as ferry tickets, and loans out free bikes and fishing rods.

ℹ Getting There & Away

Prince George Airport (YXS; ☑ 250-963-2400; www.pgairport.ca; 4141 Airport Rd) is off Hwy 97. **Air Canada Jazz** (www.aircanada.com) and **Westjet** (www.westjet.com) serve Vancouver.

Greyhound Canada (☎ 800-661-8747; www.greyhound.ca; 1566 12th Ave) service may be less than daily in winter. Routes include Dawson Creek ($80, six hours), Jasper ($70, five hours), Prince Rupert ($160, 10½ hours) and Vancouver ($95, 12 to 13 hours).

VIA Rail (www.viarail.ca; 1300 1st Ave) heads west three times a week to Prince Rupert (12½ hours) and east three times a week to Jasper (7½ hours) and beyond, through passengers must overnight in Prince George.

❶ Getting Around

Major car-rental agencies have offices at the airport.

Prince George Transit (☎ 250-563-0011; www.transitbc.com; fare $2.25) Operates local buses.

Emerald Taxi (☎ 250-563-3333)

Prince George to Alberta

Look for lots of wildlife along the 380km stretch of Hwy 16 that links Prince George with Jasper, just over the Alberta border. About 113km east of Prince George, the **Ancient Forest Trail** (www.ancientcedar.ca; Hwy 16) leads 1km to some real behemoths of the temperate inland rainforest: old-growth red cedars and hemlocks that reach heights of 60m and more.

The route's major attraction abuts Jasper National Park, but on the BC side of the border. **Mt Robson Provincial Park** (Map p604; ☎ 250-964-2243; www.bcparks.ca; off Hwy 16; campsites $16) has steep glaciers, prolific wildlife and backcountry hiking that is unfortunately overshadowed by its famous neighbor. **McBride** is good for a pause.

Stewart-Cassiar Highway

Much improved, the 700km Stewart-Cassiar Hwy (Hwy 37) is a viable and ever-more-popular route between BC and the Yukon and Alaska. But it's more than just a means to get from Hwy 16 (Meziadin Junction) in BC to the Alaska Hwy in the Yukon (7km west of Watson Lake), it's a window onto one of the largest remaining wild and woolly parts of the province. And it's the road to Stewart, the near-mandatory detour to glaciers, and more.

Except for areas of construction, the road is sealed throughout and is suitable for all vehicles. At any point, you should not be surprised to see bears, moose and other large mammals. Note that the region's untouched status is waning as projects like the invasive Northwest Transmission Line are carved across the wilderness.

There's never a distance greater than 150km between gas stations and you'll find the occasional lodge and campground. But note that many places keep erratic hours and are only open in summer. BC provides **road condition reports** (☎ 800-550-4997; www.drivebc.ca). When it's dry in summer, people drive from Stewart or even Smithers to Watson Lake in a single day, taking advantage of the long hours of daylight. But this a real haul, so prepare.

Gitanyow, a mere 15km north of Hwy 16, has an unparalleled collection of totem poles and you can often see carvers creating another.

Dease Lake, 488km north of Meziadin Junction, is the largest town and has year-round motels, stores and services.

Boya Lake Provincial Park (☎ 250-771-4591; www.bcparks.ca; Hwy 37; campsites $16) is less than 90km from the provincial border. This serene little park surrounds Boya Lake, which seems to glow turquoise. You can camp on the shore.

Alaska Highway

As you travel north from Prince George along Hwy 97, the mountains and forests give way to gentle rolling hills and farmland. Nearing Dawson Creek (360km), the landscape resembles the prairies of Alberta. There's no need to dawdle.

From **Chetwynd** you can take Hwy 29 along the wide vistas of the Peace River valley north via Hudson's Hope to join the Alaska Hwy north of Fort St John.

Dawson Creek is notable as the starting point (Mile 0) for the Alaska Hwy and it capitalizes on this at the **Alaska Highway House** (☎ 250-782-4714; 10201 10th St; admission by donation; ☉ 9am-5pm), an engaging museum in a vintage building overlooking the milepost. The nearby downtown blocks make a good stroll and have free wi-fi, and there's a walking tour of the old buildings. The **visitors center** (☎ 866-645-3022, 250-782-9595; www.tourismdawsoncreek.com; 900 Alaska Ave; ☉ 8am-5:30pm; ☎) has the usual listings of accommodations. Note that this corner of BC stays on Mountain Standard Time year-round. So in winter, the time is the same as Alberta, one hour later than

STEWART & HYDER

Awesome. Yes, it's almost an automatic cliché, but when you gaze upon the **Salmon Glacier**, you'll understand why it was coined in the first place. This horizon-spanning expanse of ice is more than enough reason to make the 67km detour off Hwy 37; the turnoff is 158km north of Meziadin Junction. In fact, your first confirmation comes when you encounter the iridescent blue expanse of the **Bear Glacier** looming over Hwy 37A.

The sibling border towns of Stewart and Hyder, Alaska, perch on the coast at the head of the Portland Canal. **Stewart**, the much more businesslike of the pair, has the **visitors center** (☑250-636-9224; www.stewart-hyder.com; 222 5th Ave; ◷9am-6pm) and excellent places to stay and eat.

Among several campgrounds and motels, the real star is **Ripley Creek Inn** (☑250-636-2344; www.ripleycreekinn.com; 306 5th Ave, Stewart; r $55-140; @ 🛜). The 40 rooms in various heritage buildings are stylishly decorated with new and old items and there's a huge collection of vintage toasters.

Hyder ekes out an existence as a 'ghost town.' Some 40,000 tourists come through every summer, avoiding any border hassle from US customs officers because there aren't any, although going back to Stewart you'll pass through beady-eyed Canadian customs. It has muddy streets and two businesses of note: the **Glacier Inn**, a bar you'll enjoy if you ignore the touristy 'get Hyderized' shot-swilling shtick; and **Seafood Express** (☑250-636-9011; mains $12-20; ◷noon-8pm Jun-Sep), which has the tastiest seafood ever cooked in a school bus. *This* is Hyder.

The enormous, horizon-filling Salmon Glacier is 33km beyond Hyder, up a winding dirt road that's OK for cars when it's dry. Some 3km into the drive, you'll pass the **Fish Creek viewpoint**, an area alive with bears and doomed salmon in late summer.

BC. In summer, the time is the same as Vancouver.

Now begins the big drive. Heading northwest from Dawson Creek, Fort St John is a stop best not started. In fact, the entire 430km to **Fort Nelson** gives little hint of the wonders to come.

Fort Nelson's **visitors center** (☑250-774-6400; www.tourismnorthernrockies.ca; 5500 Alaska Hwy; ◷7:30am-7:30pm) has good regional information for the drive ahead. The town itself is in the midst of the oil boom brought on by fracking. This is the last place of any size on the Alaska Hwy until Whitehorse in the Yukon – most 'towns' along the route are little more than a gas station and motel or two.

Around 140km west of Fort Nelson, **Stone Mountain Provincial Park** (☑250-427-5452; www.bcparks.ca; off Hwy 97; campsites $16) has hiking trails with backcountry

camping and a campground. The stretches of road often have dense concentrations of wildlife: moose, bears, bison, wolves, elk and much more. From here, the Alaska Hwy rewards whatever effort it took getting this far.

A further 75km brings you to **Muncho Lake Provincial Park** (www.bcparks.ca; off Hwy 97; campsites $16), centered on the emerald-green lake of the same name and boasting spruce forests, vast rolling mountains and some truly breathtaking scenery. There are two campgrounds by the lake, plus a few lodges scattered along the highway.

Finally, **Liard River Hot Springs Provincial Park** (☑250-427-5452; www.bcparks.ca; off Hwy 97; day use adult/child $5/3, campsite $16-21) has a steamy ecosystem that allows a whopping 250 species of plants to thrive. After a long day in the car, you'll thrive, too, in the soothing waters. From here it's 220km to Watson Lake and the Yukon.

Yukon Territory

Best Places to Eat

➡ Drunken Goat Taverna (p794)

➡ Klondike Kate's (p794)

➡ Klondike Rib & Salmon (p779)

➡ Burnt Toast (p779)

Best Places to Stay

➡ Coast High Country Inn (p778)

➡ Robert Service Campground (p778)

➡ Bombay Peggy's (p793)

➡ Klondike Kate's (p793)

Why Go?

This vast and thinly populated wilderness, where most four-legged species far outnumber humans, has a grandeur and beauty only appreciated by experience. Few places in the world today have been so unchanged over the course of time as has the Yukon. Aboriginal people, having eked out survival for thousands of years, hunt and trap as they always have. The Klondike gold rush of 1898 was the Yukon's high point of population, yet even its heritage is ephemeral, easily erased by time.

Any visit will mean much time outdoors. Canada's five tallest mountains and the world's largest ice fields below the Arctic are all within Kluane National Park. Canoe expeditions down the Yukon River are epic. You'll appreciate the people; join the offbeat vibe of Dawson City and the bustle of Whitehorse.

When to Go
Dawson City

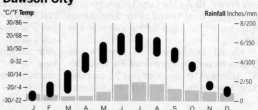

| | Nov–Apr Days of snowy winter solitude end when the river ice breaks up. | Jun–Aug Summers are short but warm, with long hours of daylight. | Sep You can feel the north winds coming. Trees erupt in color, crowds thin and places close. |

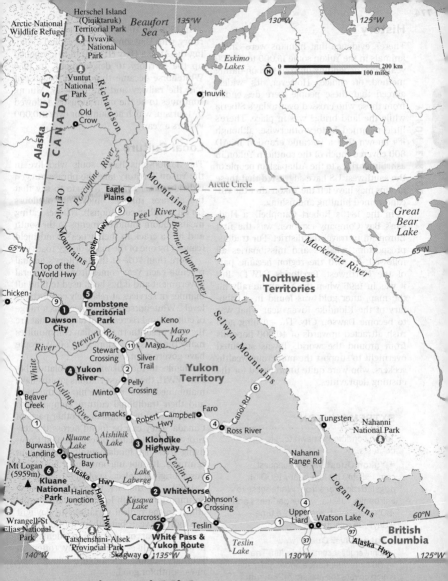

Yukon Territory Highlights

1 Get caught up in the modern vibe of **Dawson City** (p789), Canada's funkiest historic town.

2 Spend an extra day in surprising **Whitehorse** (p775), where culture abounds.

3 Count moose on the **Klondike Highway** (p786) – they may outnumber cars.

4 Live the dream of kayakers and canoeists by paddling the legendary **Yukon River** (p792).

5 Lose yourself – not literally! – in **Tombstone Territorial Park** (p796), where the grandeur of the north envelops you.

6 Find and name one of the 100 unnamed glaciers in **Kluane National Park** (p783).

7 Sit back and enjoy the ride on the fabled **White Pass & Yukon Route** (p780).

History

There's evidence that humans were eating animals in the Yukon some 15,000 to 30,000 years ago, depending on your carbon-dating method of choice. However, it's widely agreed that these people were descended from those who crossed over today's Siberia while the land bridge was in place. There's little recorded history otherwise, although it's known that a volcanic eruption in AD 800 covered much of the southern Yukon in ash. Similarities to the Athapaskan people of the southwest US have suggested that these groups may have left the Yukon after the volcano ruined hunting and fishing.

In the 1840s Robert Campbell, a Hudson's Bay Company explorer, was the first European to travel the district. Fur traders, prospectors, whalers and missionaries all followed. In 1870 the region became part of the Northwest Territories (NWT). But it was in 1896 when the Yukon literally hit the map, after gold was found in a tributary of the Klondike River, near what was to become Dawson City. The ensuing gold rush attracted upwards of 40,000 hopefuls from around the world. Towns sprouted overnight to support the numerous wealth-seekers, who were quite unprepared for the ensuing depravities.

EXTREME YUKON

Tough conditions spawn tough contests.

➡ **Yukon Quest** (www.yukonquest. com; ☺ Feb) This legendary 1600km dogsled race goes from Whitehorse to Fairbanks, Alaska, winter darkness and -50°C temperatures. Record time: 9 days, 26 minutes.

➡ **Yukon River Quest** (www. yukonriverquest.com; ☺ late Jun) The world's premier canoe and kayak race, which covers the classic 742km run of the Yukon River from Whitehorse to Dawson City in June. Record times include team canoe (39 hours, 32 minutes) and solo kayak (42 hours, 49 minutes).

➡ **Klondike Trail of '98 Road Relay** (www.klondikeroadrelay.com; ☺ early Sep) Some 100 running teams of 10 each complete the overnight course from Skagway to Whitehorse.

In 1898 the Yukon became a separate territory, with Dawson City as its capital. Building the Alaska Hwy (Hwy 1) in 1942 opened up the territory to development. In 1953 Whitehorse became the capital, because it had the railway and the highway. Mining continues to be the main industry, followed by tourism, which accounts for over 310,000 visitors a year.

Local Culture

The 33,000-plus hardy souls who live in the Yukon Territory take the phrase 'rugged individualist' to heart. It's safe to say that the average Yukoner enjoys the outdoors (in all weather conditions!), relishes eating meats seldom found on menus to the south and has a crack in their truck's windshield (caused by one of the many dodgy roads).

More than 70% of the territory's annual revenue each year comes from the federal government and it has been used to fund all manner of services at relatively comfortable levels. Whitehorse, for instance, has a range of cultural and recreational facilities that are the envy of southern Canadian communities many times its size. More than 5000 people have government jobs.

Thanks to the Yukon's long isolation before WWII, the 14 First Nations groups have maintained their relationship to the land and their traditional culture, compared to groups forced to assimilate in other parts of Canada. They can be found across the territory and in isolated places like Old Crow, living lives not fundamentally changed in centuries. It's not uncommon to hear various aboriginal dialects spoken by elders.

Light – or the lack thereof – does play an important role in local life. Many people adjust to the radical variations in daylight through the year, but others do not. Every year you hear of longtime residents and newcomers alike who one day (often in February) announce enough is enough and move south for good.

Parks

The Yukon has a major Unesco World Heritage site in raw and forbidding Kluane National Park which sits solidly within the Yukon abutting Tatshenshini-Alsek Provincial Park in British Columbia (BC). Glacier Bay and Wrangell-St Elias National Parks are found in adjoining Alaska.

The Yukon has a dozen parks and protected areas (www.yukonparks.ca), but much of the territory itself is parklike and government campgrounds can be found throughout. Tombstone Territorial Park is remote, yet accessible via the Dempster Hwy, so you can absorb the horizon-sweeping beauty of the tundra and majesty of vast mountain ranges.

ℹ Information

There are excellent visitor information centers (VICs) covering every entry point in the Yukon: Beaver Creek, Carcross, Dawson City, Haines Junction, Watson Lake and Whitehorse.

The Yukon government produces enough literature and information to supply a holiday's worth of reading. Among the highlights are *Camping on Yukon Time, Art Adventures on Yukon Time* and lavish walking guides to pretty much every town with a population greater than 50. Start your collection at the various visitors centers online (www.travelyukon.com). Another good internet resource is www.yukoninfo.com.

A great way to get a feel for the Yukon and its larger-than-life stories is to read some of the vast body of Yukon novels. Start with Jack London – *Call of the Wild* is free online at www.online-literature.com.

ℹ Getting There & Around

Whitehorse is linked by air to Vancouver, Calgary and Edmonton. There are even flights nonstop to Germany during summer. Dawson City has flights to Whitehorse, Inuvik in the NWT and to Fairbanks, Alaska.

There are three major ways to reach the Yukon by road: first by ferry to the entry points of Skagway and Haines, Alaska; by the Alaska Hwy from Dawson Creek, BC, and by the Stewart-Cassiar Hwy from northwest BC that joins the Alaska Hwy near Watson Lake.

You can reach Whitehorse from BC by bus. From there a patchwork of companies provides links to Alaska and Dawson. Rental cars and RVs are expensive and only available in Whitehorse. The Alaska and Klondike Hwys are paved and have services every 100km to 200km.

To check road conditions in the Yukon call 511 or visit www.511yukon.ca.

WHITEHORSE

POP 26,100

The leading city and capital of the Yukon, Whitehorse will likely have a prominent role in your journey. The territory's two great highways, the Alaska and the Klondike, cross here; it's a hub for transportation (it was a terminus for the White Pass &

Yukon Route railway from Skagway in the early 1900s, and during WWII was a major center for work on the Alaska Hwy). You'll find all manner of outfitters and services for explorations across the territory. Most of its residents have government-related jobs, but they escape for the outdoors no matter what the season.

Not immediately appealing, Whitehorse rewards the curious. It has a well-funded arts community (with an especially vibrant visual arts community), good restaurants and a range of motels. Exploring the sights within earshot of the rushing Yukon River can easily take a day or more. Look past the bland commercial buildings and you'll see a fair number of heritage ones awaiting discovery.

In 1953, Whitehorse was made the capital of the territory, to the continuing regret of much smaller and isolated Dawson City.

◉ Sights

You can explore Whitehorse's main sights in a day, mostly on foot.

★ SS Klondike   HISTORIC SITE
(867-667-4511; South Access Rd & 2nd Ave; 9:30am-5pm May-Aug) **FREE** Carefully restored, this was one of the largest sternwheelers used on the Yukon River. Built in 1937, it made its final run upriver to Dawson in 1955 and is now a national historic site. Try not to wish it was making the run now.

Waterfront   NEIGHBORHOOD
One look at the majestic Yukon River and you'll want to spend time strolling its bank. The beautiful **White Pass & Yukon Route Station** (1109 1st Ave) has been restored and anchors an area that's in the midst of a revitalization. **Rotary Peace Park** at the south end is a great picnic spot.

Whitehorse

The new **Kwanlin Dün Cultural Centre** (www.kwanlindunculturalcentre.com; 1171 1st Ave; ☺9:30am-4pm) has changing exhibits and plans a museum showing how local First Nations groups used the river.

At the north end of the waterfront, **Shipyards Park** has a growing collection of historic structures gathered territory-wide and a skateboard track and toboggan hill. Linking it all is a cute little **waterfront trolley** (www.yukonrails.com; one-way $2; ☺10am-6pm Jun-Aug) which runs all the way from the SS Klondike north to Quartz Rd north of Shipyards Park.

MacBride Museum MUSEUM
(☎867-667-2709; www.macbridemuseum.com; cnr 1st Ave & Wood St; adult/child $10/5; ☺9:30am-5pm) The Yukon's attic covers the gold rush, First Nations, intrepid Mounties and more. Old photos vie with old stuffed critters; daily special events like gold-panning are fun.

Old Log Church HISTORIC BUILDING
(☎867-668-2555; www.oldlogchurchmuseum.ca; 303 Elliott St; adult/child $6/5; ☺10am-6pm May-Aug) The only log-cabin-style cathedral in the world is a 1900 downtown gem. Displays include the compelling story of Rev Isaac Stringer, who boiled and ate his boots while

Whitehorse

◉ Top Sights
1 SS Klondike D5

◉ Sights
2 Arts Underground C4
3 Kwanlin Dün Cultural Centre C2
4 MacBride Museum C3
5 Old Log Church C4
6 White Pass & Yukon Route
   Station D3

◎ Activities, Courses & Tours
7 Cadence Cycle B3
8 Kanoe People C2
9 Up North Adventures C2
10 Yukon Conservation Society C4
11 Yukon Historical & Museums
   Association C3

◉ Sleeping
12 Beez Kneez Bakpakers C5
13 Coast High Country Inn C5

14 Edgewater Hotel D3
15 Historical House B&B B3
16 Midnight Sun Inn A2
17 River View Hotel C3

◎ Eating
18 Baked Café C3
19 Burnt Toast C3
   Deck ....(see 13)
20 Fireweed Community Market B1
21 Klondike Rib & Salmon ...., ...C3
22 Sanchez Cantina ..., ... C4
23 Yukon Meat & Sausage C4

◎ Drinking & Nightlife
24 Dirty Northern Public House C3

◎ Shopping
25 Mac's Fireweed Books C3
26 Midnight Sun Gallery & Gifts C3
27 North End Gallery C3

---

lost in the wilderness for 51 days. Fittingly, all that's left is his sole.

Yukon Beringia Interpretive Centre
MUSEUM

(☑ 867-667-8855; www.beringia.com; Km 1473 Alaska Hwy; adult/child $6/4; ☺ 9am-6pm) This place focuses on Beringia, a mostly ice-free area that encompassed the Yukon, Alaska and eastern Siberia during the last ice age. Engaging exhibits re-create the era, right down to the actual skeleton of a 3m-long giant ground sloth.

Yukon Transportation Museum
MUSEUM

(☑ 867-668-4792; www.goytm.ca; 30 Electra Circle; adult/child $10/5; ☺ 10am-6pm May-Aug) Find out what the Alaska Hwy was really like back in the day; let's just say mud was a dirty word. Exhibits cover planes, trains and dogsleds. The museum is near the Beringia Centre. Look for the iconic **DC-3 weather vane** (yes, it spins!) out front.

Whitehorse Fishway
LANDMARK

(☑ 867-633-5965; Nisutlin Dr; admission by donation; ☺ 9am-7pm Jun-Aug) Stare down a salmon at the Whitehorse Fishway, a 366m wooden fish ladder (the world's longest) past the hydro electric plant south of town. Large viewing windows let you see chinook salmon swim past starting in late July (before that it's grayling).

The fishway is easily reached on foot via the Millennium Trail.

Arts Underground
GALLERY

(☑ 867-667-4080; Hougen Centre lower level, 305 Main St; ☺ 10am-5pm Tue-Sat) Operated by the Yukon Arts Society. There are carefully selected and well-curated rotating exhibits.

Yukon Artists@Work
GALLERY

(☑ 867-393-4848; 120 Industrial Rd; ☺ noon-5pm) Operated by local artists, some of whom may be busily creating when you visit. It's situated just north of the big box shopping area.

🏃 Activities

The visitor information center can guide you to numerous local hikes and activities. Otherwise, Whitehorse is a major outfitting center for adventures on Yukon waterways.

Canoeing & Kayaking
Whitehorse is the starting place for popular canoeing and kayaking trips to Carmacks or on to Dawson City. It's an average of eight days to the former and 16 days to the latter. Outfitters offer gear of all kinds (canoes and kayaks are about $40 per day), guides, tours, lessons and planning services and can arrange transportation back to Whitehorse. Most paddlers use the map *The Yukon River: Marsh Lake to Dawson City* available at www.yukonbooks.com.

Kanoe People
CANOEING

(☑ 867-668-4899; www.kanoepeople.com; cnr 1st Ave & Strickland St) Can arrange any type of trip including paddles down Teslin and Big Salmon Rivers. Gear, maps and guides for sale; bikes for rent. Half-day paddles around Whitehorse are $60.

Up North Adventures
CANOEING

(☎867-667-7035; www.upnorthadventures.com; 103 Strickland St) Offers rentals and transport on the major rivers. Also paddling lessons, guided mountain-bike trips and winter sports.

Cycling

Whitehorse has scores of bike trails along the Yukon River and into the surrounding hills. The visitor information center has maps.

Cadence Cycle
CYCLING

(☎867-633-5600; 508 Wood St; rental per day from $35; ⊙10am-6pm Mon-Sat) Sells and rents good used mountain bikes and does repairs.

Icycle Sport
CYCLING

(www.icyclesport.com; 9002 Quartz Rd; rental per day from $45; ⊙10am-6pm Mon-Sat) Rents top-end mountain bikes and skis (in winter).

Walking & Hiking

You can walk a scenic 5km loop around Whitehorse's waters that includes a stop at the fishway. From the SS *Klondike* go south on the **Millennium Trail** until you reach the Robert Service Campground and the Rotary Centennial Footbridge over the river. The fishway is just south. Head north along the water and cross the Robert Campbell Bridge and you are back in the town center.

☞ Tours

★ Yukon Historical & Museums Association
WALKING TOUR

(☎867-667-4704; 3126 3rd Ave; admission $6; ⊙11am-6pm Mon-Sat Jun-Aug) Offers quirky and interesting downtown walking tours four times daily. Meet at its office in the 1904 Donneworth House. Ask your guide to show you the WWII-era American latrine that's still not winning any hearts and minds.

Boréale Mountain Biking
BIKE TOUR

(☎867-336-1722; www.borealebiking.ca; tours from $60) Highly regarded bike tours cover Whitehorse in a family-friendly half day. More-adventurous options include the 800km of trails in the region, which *Outside* magazine has named among the world's best.

Yukon Conservation Society
HIKING TOUR

(☎867-668-5678; www.yukonconservation.org; 302 Hawkins St; ⊙Tue-Sat Jun-Aug) FREE Discover the natural beauty all around Whitehorse with a free Yukon Conservation Society nature hike. There are various itineraries ranging from easy to hard.

🛏 Sleeping

Whitehorse can get almost full during the peak of summer, so book ahead. The visitor information center has lists of B&Bs. Whitehorse has a lot of midrange motels that earn the sobriquet 'veteran.' Check a room first before you commit.

★ Robert Service Campground
CAMPGROUND $

(☎867-668-3721; www.robertservicecampground. com; Robert Service Way; campsites $21; ⊙May-Sep; @🖙) It's a pretty 15-minute walk from town on the Millennium Trail to the 70 sites at this tents-only campground on the river 1km south of town. Excellent coffee, baked goods and ice cream in the cafe.

Beez Kneez Bakpakers
HOSTEL $

(☎867-456-2333; www.bzkneez.com; 408 Hoge St; dm/r $30/65; @🖙) Like the home you've left behind, this cheery hostel has a garden, deck, grill and bikes. Two cabins ($75) are much in demand.

Hi Country RV Park
CAMPGROUND $

(☎867-667-7445; www.hicountryrvyukon.com; 91374 Alaska Hwy; sites $27-40; @🖙) At the top of Robert Service Way, this woodsy campground offers hookups, showers, laundry and a playground.

Coast High Country Inn
HOTEL $$

(☎800-554-4471, 867-667-4471; www.highcountry inn.yk.ca; 4051 4th Ave; r $100-220; ❉@🖙) Towering over Whitehorse (four stories!), the High Country is popular with business travelers and high-end groups. The 84 rooms are large – some have huge whirlpools right in the room. The pub is popular.

Historical House B&B
B&B $$

(☎867-668-2526; www.yukongold.com; cnr 5th Ave & Wood St; r $95-120; ❉@) A classic wooden home from 1907 with three guestrooms. Top-floor ones have individual bathrooms down the hall and angled ceilings. A larger unit has a huge kitchen. Rooms have high-speed internet and a nice garden.

Midnight Sun Inn
B&B $$

(☑800-284-4448, 867-667-2255; www.midnightsunbb.com; 6188 6th Ave; r $110-145; ✳@🛜) A modern B&B in a sort of overgrown suburban-style house with five themed rooms. The Sun has a loyal following, is downtown and serves big breakfasts.

Edgewater Hotel
HOTEL $$

(☑877-484-3334, 867-667-2572; www.edgewaterhotelwhitehorse.com; 101 Main St; r $100-200; ✳@🛜) Much updated, the Edgewater has a dash of style. The 30 rooms are smallish (some lack air-con); better rooms have river views, some have kitchens.

River View Hotel
MOTEL $$

(Canada's Best Value Inn; ☑888-315-2378, 867-667-7801; www.riverviewhotel.ca; 102 Wood St; r $90-150; @🛜) The floors sound hollow here but many of the 53 rooms have the views implied by the name (ask for one) and all are very large. It's close to everything, yet on a quiet street.

✖ Eating & Drinking

Ignore the influx of chain eateries and enjoy one of Whitehorse's excellent downtown restaurants. There's a great range; look for fresh Yukon salmon in season and the tasty brews of the local Yukon Brewing Co year-round.

Fireweed Community Market
MARKET

(Shipyards Park; ⏲3-8pm Thu May-Sep) draws vendors from the region; the berries are fabulous.

Yukon Meat & Sausage
DELI $

(☑867-667-6077; 203 Hanson St; sandwiches $7; ⏲9am-5:30pm Mon-Sat) The smell of smoked meat wafts out to the street and you walk right in; there's a huge selection of prepared items and custom-made sandwiches. Great for picnics, or eat in.

Baked Café
CAFE $

(☑867-633-6291; 100 Main St; snacks $4; ⏲7am-7pm; 🛜) In summer, the outdoor tables at this buzzing cafe are packed. Smoothies, soups, daily lunch specials, baked goods and more. Don't miss the raspberry pecan scones.

★Klondike Rib & Salmon
CANADIAN $$

(☑867-667-7554; 2116 2nd Ave; mains $12-25; ⏲4-9pm May-Sep) It looks touristy and it seems touristy and it *is* touristy, but the food is excellent at this sprawling casual place

with two decks. Besides the namesakes (the salmon kebabs are tops), there are other local faves.

★Burnt Toast
BISTRO $$

(☑867-393-2605; 2112 2nd Ave; mains $10-25; ⏲9am-9pm) The food is far better than the coy name suggests! Brunch is excellent at this smart bistro (try the French toast) and lunch and dinner specials abound. Food is local and seasonal; just consult the blackboard. Good salads, sandwiches and Yukon meats.

Deck
PUB $$

(Coast High Country Inn; 4051 4th Ave, ; mains $10-20; ⏲noon-midnight) The eponymous covered deck here draws crowds of locals, tourists and guides ('and when you see the whites of his eyes...') through the season. Backed by a huge bar with a good draft beer selection, diners choose from huge burgers, salads and fresh Yukon fish (the Arctic char is sublime).

Sanchez Cantina
MEXICAN $$

(☑867-668-5858; 211 Hanson St; mains $14-24; ⏲11:30am-3pm & 5-9:30pm) You have to head south across two borders to find Mexican this authentic. Burritos are the thing – get them with the spicy mix of red and green sauces. Settle in for what may be a wait on the broad patio.

Dirty Northern Public House
PUB

(103 Main St; ⏲noon-late) There are hints of style at this upscale pub which has a great draft beer selection and makes excellent mixed drinks. Grab a booth and chase the booze with a wood-fired pizza.

🛍 Shopping

The galleries listed in Sights are excellent sources of local items.

★Mac's Fireweed Books
BOOKS

(☑867-668-2434; www.yukonbooks.com; 203 Main St; ⏲8am-midnight) Mac's stocks an unrivaled selection of Yukon titles. It also has topographical maps, road maps and periodicals.

Midnight Sun Gallery & Gifts
ARTS & CRAFTS

(☑867-668-4350; 205C Main St; ⏲9am-8pm) Has a good selection of Yukon arts, crafts and products.

North End Gallery
ARTS & CRAFTS

(☑867-393-3590; 1116 1st Ave; ⏲10am-6pm Mon-Sat) High-end Canadian art.

❶ Information

Yukon News Feisty local newspaper

What's Up Yukon (www.whatsupyuykon.com) Source for entertainment listings.

Visitor Information Center (☑867-667-3084; 100 Hanson St; ☺8am-8pm) Essential; has territory-wide information.

Whitehorse General Hospital (☑867-393-8700; 5 Hospital Rd; ☺24hr)

❶ Getting There & Away

Whitehorse is the transport hub of the Yukon.

AIR

Erik Nielsen Whitehorse International Airport (☑867-667-8440; www.gov.yk.ca/yxy/airports/yxy) Five minutes west of downtown off the Alaska Hwy.

Air Canada (☑888-247-2262; www.aircanada.com) Serves Vancouver.

Air North (☑800-661-0407; www.flyairnorth.com) Locally owned; serves Dawson City (with flights on to Inuvik, NWT and Fairbanks, Alaska) plus Vancouver, Kelowna, Edmonton and Calgary.

Condor (☑800-364-1667, in Germany 01805 707 202; www.condor.com) Weekly summer flights to/from Frankfurt.

Westjet (☑888-937-8538; www.westjet.com) Seasonal service to/from Vancouver.

BUS

Bus services, er, come and go; check the latest with the visitor information center.

Alaska/Yukon Trails (☑907-479-2277; www.alaskashuttle.com; ☺Jun–mid-Sep) Service (three times weekly) to Fairbanks (US$365) via a Dawson City overnight stop (stopovers only, trips must start/end in Alaska).

Greyhound Canada (☑800-661-8747, 867-667-2223; www.greyhound.ca; 2191 2nd Ave) Service south along the Alaska Hwy to Dawson Creek (from $250, 20 hours, three times per week); connects with buses for the rest of BC and Canada.

White Pass & Yukon Route (☑867-633-5710; www.wpyr.com; Whitehorse ticket office, 1109 1st Ave; ☺9am-5pm Mon-Sat mid-May–mid-Sep) Offers a jaw-dropping scenic 10-hour rail and bus connection to/from Skagway via Carcross, BC (one-way to Skagway adult/child $185/92.50). Service is not daily. Also offers one-day tours from Whitehorse that include a train ride.

❶ Getting Around

TO/FROM THE AIRPORT

Yellow Cab (☑867-668-4811) About $20 from the center for the 10-minute ride.

BUS

Whitehorse Transit System (☑867-668-7433; $2.50; ☺Mon-Sat) Main transfer point at the Qwanlin Mall. Route 3 serves the airport, Route 5 passes the Robert Service Campground.

CAR & RV

Check your rate very carefully as it's common for a mileage charge to be added after the first 100km, which will not get you far in the Yukon. Also understand your insurance coverage and whether damage from Yukon's rugged roads is covered.

Budget (☑867-667-6200; www.budget.com) At the airport.

Fraserway RV Rentals (☑867-668-3438; www.fraserwayrvrentals.com; 9039 Quartz Rd) Rents all shapes and sizes of RV from $100 per day depending on size (it matters) and season. Mileage extra; rates can quickly add up.

Whitehorse Subaru (☑867-393-6550; www.whitehorsesubaru.com; 17 Chilkoot Way) Good rates; most cars have manual transmissions.

ALASKA HIGHWAY

It may be called the Alaska Hwy but given that its longest stretch is in the Yukon (958km) perhaps another name is in order...

Roughly 2450km in length from Dawson Creek, BC, to Delta Junction, far inside Alaska, the Alaska Hwy has a meaning well beyond just a road; it's also a badge, an honor, an accomplishment. Even though today it's a modern road, the very name still evokes images of big adventure and getting away from it all.

As you drive the Alaska Hwy in the Yukon, you're on the most scenic and varied part of the road. From little villages to the city of Whitehorse, from meandering rivers to the upthrust drama of the St Elias Mountains, the scenery will overwhelm you.

British Columbia to Whitehorse

You'll never be far from an excuse to stop on this stretch of the highway. Towns, small parks and various roadside attractions appear at regular intervals. None are a massive draw, but overall it's a pretty drive made all the more compelling by the locale.

Watson Lake

Originally named after Frank Watson, a British trapper, Watson Lake is the first town in the Yukon on the Alaska Hwy and is just over the border from BC. It's a good rest stop with a superb **visitor information center**(☎867-536-7469; www.watsonlake. ca; Alaska Hwy; ⊗8am-8pm May-Sep), which has a good museum about the highway and a passel of territory-wide info. The town offers campgrounds, motels, services and a Greyhound Canada stop.

The town is famous for its **Sign Post Forest** just outside the visitor center. The first signpost, 'Danville, Illinois,' was nailed up in 1942. Others were added and now there are 72,000 signs, many purloined late at night from municipalities worldwide. The **Air Force Lodge** (☎867-536-2890; www. airforcelodge.com; Alaska Hwy; s/d $75/85) has spotless rooms with shared bathrooms in a historic 1942 barracks for pilots.

Twenty-six kilometers west of Watson Lake is the junction with the Stewart-Cassiar Hwy (Hwy 37), which heads south into BC.

Just west of the junction, family-run **Nugget City** (☎888-536-2307, 867-536-2307; www.nuggetcity.com; Alaska Hwy; campsites from $20, r from $65; ☎) has accommodations and food that's three cuts above the Alaska Hwy norm. Stop just for the baked goods, especially the berry pie.

Another 110km west, past the 1112km marker, look for the **Rancheria Falls**

HISTORY OF THE HIGHWAY

Nowadays the aura of the Alaska Hwy is psychological rather than physical. In every way it's a modern two-lane road, with smooth curves, broad sight lines and paving from one end to another, but that has not always been the case. A famous 1943 photo shows a jeep seemingly being sucked down to China through a morass of mud while soldiers look on helplessly.

With the outbreak of WWII, Canada and the US decided that years of debate should end and that a proper road was needed to link Alaska and the Yukon to the rest of Canada and the US.

That a road – any road – could be carved out of the raw tundra and wilderness of the north in a little over a year was a miracle, although unlimited money and manpower (US soldiers and Canadian civilians, including Aboriginal people) helped. The 2450km gravel highway ran between Dawson Creek in British Columbia and Fairbanks in Alaska. The route chosen for the highway followed a series of existing airfields – Fort St John, Fort Nelson, Watson Lake and Whitehorse – known as the Northwest Staging Route.

In April 1946 the Canadian section of the road (1965km) was officially handed over to Canada. In the meantime, private contractors were busy widening, graveling and straightening the highway, leveling its steep grades and replacing temporary bridges with permanent steel ones – a process that has continued since, creating the modern road you drive today.

Known variously as the Alaskan International Hwy, the Alaska Military Hwy and the Alcan (short for Alaska-Canada) Hwy, it's now called the Alaska Hwy. It has transformed both the Yukon and Alaska, opening up the north to year-round travel and forever changing the way of life of the aboriginal populations along the route.

The Alaska Hwy begins at 'Mile 0' in Dawson Creek in northeastern BC and goes to Fairbanks, Alaska, although the official end is at Delta Junction, about 155km southeast of Fairbanks.

Mileposts long served as reference points, but improvements shortening the road and Canada's adoption of the metric system have made mileage references archaic. Historic numbers persist in the names of some businesses and attractions.

For more on the Alaska Hwy and its harrowing past, check out the Watson Lake visitor information center, the Yukon Transportation Museum (p777) in Whitehorse, the Soldier's Summit Trail (p783) in Kluane National Park and the Alaska Highway House (p771) in Dawson Creek, BC.

For a detailed guide to every feature, including seemingly every pothole and moose turd, look for the *Milepost*, a legendary annual publication.

WORTH A TRIP

ROBERT CAMPBELL HIGHWAY

To get right off the beaten path, consider this lonely gravel road (Hwy 4) which runs 588km from Watson Lake north and west to Carmacks, where you can join the Klondike Hwy for Dawson City. Along its length, the highway parallels various rivers and lakes. Wilderness campers will be thrilled.

At 373km from Watson Lake at the junction with the Canol Rd (Hwy 6) is **Ross River**, home to the Kaska First Nation and a supply center for the local mining industry. There are campgrounds and motels in town.

Recreation Site. A boardwalk leads to powerful twin waterfalls. It's an excellent stop.

Teslin

Teslin, on the long, narrow lake of the same name, is 272km west of Watson Lake and has long been a home to the Tlingits (lin-*kits*). As elsewhere the Alaska Hwy brought both prosperity and rapid change to this aboriginal population. The engrossing **George Johnston Museum** (☏867-390-2550; www.gjmuseum.yk.net; Km 1294 Alaska Hwy; adult/child $5/2.50; ⊙9am-6pm May-Aug) details the life and culture of a 20th-century Tlingits leader through photographs, displays and artifacts.

Johnson's Crossing

Some 53km north of Teslin is Johnson's Crossing, at the junction of the Alaska Hwy and Canol Rd (Hwy 6). During WWII the US army built the Canol pipeline at tremendous human and financial expense to pump oil from Norman Wells in the NWT to Whitehorse. It was abandoned after countless hundreds of millions of dollars (in 1943 money, no less) were spent.

Whitehorse to Alaska

For long segments west of Whitehorse, the Alaska Hwy has been modernized to the point of blandness. Fortunately, this ends abruptly in Haines Junction. From here the road parallels legendary Kluane National Park and the St Elias Mountains. The 300km

to Beaver Creek is the most scenic part of the entire highway.

Haines Junction

It's goodbye flatlands when you reach Haines Junction and see the sweep of imposing peaks looming over town. You've reached the stunning Kluane National Park and this is the gateway. The town makes an excellent base for exploring the park or staging a serious four-star mountaineering, backcountry or river adventure.

The magnificent Haines Hwy heads south from here to Alaska.

🏃 Activities

Even the spectacular ridges surrounding Haines Junction don't begin to hint at the beauty of Kluane National Park. Although the park should be your focus, there are some good activities locally.

For a hike after hours of driving, there's a pretty 5.5km **nature walk** along Dezadeash River where Hwy 3 crosses it at the south end of town.

Tatshenshini Expediting (☏867-393-3661; www.tatshenshiniyukon.com; per person from $135) leads white-water rafting trips on the nearby Tatshenshini River, which has rapids from grade II to grade IV. Trips leave from Haines Junction and Whitehorse.

🛏 Sleeping & Eating

There's a cluster of motels and RV parks in Haines Junction. There's a beach and shade at **Pine Lake**, a territorial campground 6km east of town on the Alaska Hwy. Cerulean waters are a highlight at **Kathleen Lake** (campsites $16), a Parks Canada campground 24km south of Haines Junction off the Haines Hwy.

For most groceries, you'll need to stock up in Whitehorse.

Alcan Motor Inn   MOTEL $$
(☏888-265-1018, 867-634-2371; www.alcanmotorinn.com; Alaska Hwy; r $110-170; ❊🐾) The modern two-story Alcan has 23 large rooms with great views of the jagged Auriol Range. Some have full kitchens; the on-site cafe, **Northern Lights** (mains $13-20; ⊙7am-9pm), has hearty fare.

Raven Motel   INN $$
(☏867-634-2500; www.ravenhotelyukon.com; 181 Alaska Hwy; r $125-150; ⊙May-Sep; ❊🐾) There are 12 comfortable motel-style rooms here

and guests can partake of a German-style breakfast buffet.

★ **Village Bakery & Deli**   BAKERY **$**

(☑ 867-634-2867; cnr Kluane & Logan Sts; mains $6-11; ⊙ 7am-9pm May-Sep; 🛜) The bakery here turns out excellent goods all day, while the deli counter has tasty sandwiches you can enjoy on the huge deck. On Friday night there's a popular barbecue with live folk music. It has milk and other very basic groceries.

Frosty Freeze   BURGERS **$**

(☑ 867-634-7070; Alaska Hwy; mains $7-11; ⊙ 11am-9pm May-Sep) What looks like a hum-drum fast-food joint is several orders of magnitude better. The shakes are made with real ice cream, the sundaes feature fresh berries and the burgers (try the mushroom-Swiss number) are huge and juicy.

ℹ Information

The **visitor information center** (☑ 867-634-2345; www.hainesjunctionyukon.com; Alaska Hwy; ⊙ 8am-8pm Jun–mid-Sep) shares space with **Parks Canada** (☑ 867-634-7250; www.parkscanada.gc.ca/kluane; ⊙ 9am-5pm) in the new First Nations **Dä Ku Cultural Centre** (Alaska Hwy). There are excellent films about the park as well as engrossing exhibits on the park and aboriginal life. And that thing that looks like an acid-trip cupcake? It's a sculpture meant to be a winsome tableau of local characters and critters.

Kluane National Park & Reserve

Unesco-recognized as an 'empire of mountains and ice,' Kluane National Park and Reserve looms south of the Alaska Hwy much of the way to the Alaska border. This rugged and magnificent wilderness covers 22,015 sq km of the southwest corner of the territory. Kluane (kloo-wah-neee) gets its far-too-modest name from the Southern Tutchone word for 'lake with many fish.'

With British Columbia's Tatshenshini-Alsek Provincial Park to the south and Alaska's Wrangell-St Elias National Park to the west, this is one of the largest protected wilderness areas in the world. Deep beyond the mountains you see from the Alaska Hwy are over 100 named glaciers and as many unnamed ones.

Winters are long and harsh. Summers are short, making mid-June to early September the best time to visit. Note that winter conditions can occur at any time, especially in the backcountry. See Kathleen Lake (p782) for the park's campground.

◉ Sights

The park consists primarily of the **St Elias Mountains** and the world's largest non-polar **ice fields**. Two-thirds of the park is glacier interspersed with valleys, glacial lakes, alpine forest, meadows and tundra. The **Kluane Ranges** (averaging a height of 2500m) are seen along the western edge of the Alaska Hwy. A greenbelt wraps around the base where most of the animals and veg-etation live. Turquoise **Kluane Lake** is the Yukon's largest. Hidden are the immense ice fields and towering peaks, including **Mt Logan** (5959m), Canada's highest mountain, and **Mt St Elias** (5488m), the second high-est. Partial glimpses of the interior peaks can be found at the Km 1622 **viewpoint** on the Alaska Hwy and also around the Donjek River Bridge, but the best views are from the air.

In Haines Junction, **Kluane Glacier Air Tours** (☑ 867-634-2916; www.kluaneglacierair tours.com; Haines Junction Airport; tours from $250) offers flight-seeing of Kluane and its glaciers that will leave you limp with amaze-ment. Options begin with a one-hour tour.

🏃 Activities

There's excellent **hiking** in the forested lands at the base of the mountains, along either marked trails or less-defined routes. There are about a dozen in each category, some following old mining roads, others traditional aboriginal paths. Detailed trail guides and topographical maps are available at the information centers. Talk to the rang-ers before setting out. They will help select a hike and can provide updates on areas that may be closed due to bear activity. Overnight hikes require backcountry permits ($10 per person per night).

A good pause during your drive is the **Soldier's Summit Trail**, an easy 1km hike up from the Tachal Dhal information center. It has views across the park and plaques commemorating the inauguration of the Alaska Hwy at this point on November 20, 1942. You can listen to the original CBC broadcast of the opening.

The Tachal Dhal information center is also the starting point for **Slims West**, a popular 60km round-trip trek to **Kaskawulsh Gla-cier** – one of the few that can be reached on foot. This is a difficult route that takes from three to five days to complete and includes sweeping views from Observation Mountain (2114m). An easy overnight trip is the 15km **Auriol** loop, which goes from spruce forest to subalpine barrens and includes a wilderness campground. It's 7km south of Haines Junction.

Fishing is good and **wildlife-watching** plentiful. Most noteworthy are the thousands of Dall sheep that can be seen on Sheep Mountain in June and September. There's a large and diverse population of grizzly bear, as well as black bear, moose, caribou, goats and 150 varieties of birds, among them eagles and the rare peregrine falcon.

Many enjoy **skiing** or **snowshoeing**, beginning in February.

❶ Information

Parks Canada has two information centers. One is in Haines Junction, and the other at **Tachal Dhal** (Sheep Mountain; Alaska Hwy; ☺9am-4pm Jun-Aug), 130km west of Haines Junction. Get a copy of the park guide, which shows the scope of the park (and how little is actually easily accessible). The map shows hikes ranging from 10 minutes to 10 days.

Destruction Bay

This small village on the shore of huge Kluane Lake is 107km north of Haines Junction. It was given its evocative name after a storm tore through the area during construction of the highway. Most of the residents are First Nations, who live off the land through the year. **Congdon Creek** is 17km east of town on the Alaska Hwy and has an 81-site territorial campground and a fine lakeside setting.

Burwash Landing

Commune with an enormous, albeit stuffed, moose at the excellent **Kluane Museum** (☎867-841-5561; Alaska Hwy; adult/child $4/2; ☺9am-6:30pm May-Aug). Enjoy intriguing wildlife exhibits and displays on natural and aboriginal history.

Beaver Creek

Wide-spot-in-the-road Beaver Creek is a beacon for sleepy travelers or those who want to get gas – certainly its lackluster eateries will ensure the latter. The Canadian border checkpoint is just north of town;

the US border checkpoint is 27km further west. Both are open 24 hours.

The **visitor information center** (☎867-862-7321; Km 1202 Alaska Hwy; ☺8am-8pm May-Sep) has information on all of the Yukon. A strange **sculpture garden** just north tempts the silly (or intoxicated) into unnatural acts.

Of the four motels in town, the **1202 Motor Inn** (☎800-661-0540, 867-862-7600; www.1202motorinn.ca; 1202 Alaska Hwy; r from $80; ❄️❂) is the most appealing. The 30 rooms are basic and functional. Get one away from the idling trucks.

Alaska

The incredible scenery of the Alaska Hwy dims a bit once you cross into its namesake state. The Alaska Hwy department leaves the road much more despoiled than the pristine conditions in the Yukon.

From the US border, it's 63km (39 miles) to **Tetlin National Wildlife Refuge** (http://tetlin.fws.gov) on the Alaska Hwy. About 117km past Tetlin, you'll reach the junction with the Taylor Hwy (Hwy 5) which connects north with the Top of the World Hwy to Dawson City.

HAINES HIGHWAY

If you're doing only a short loop between Haines and Skagway via Whitehorse, this 259km road might be the highlight of your trip. In fact, no matter what length your Yukon adventure, the Haines Hwy (Hwy 3) might be the high point. In a relatively short distance you see glaciers, looming snow-clad peaks, lush and wild river valleys, windswept alpine meadows and a bald-eagle-laced river delta.

Heading south of Haines Junction, look west for a close-up of the St Elias Mountains, those glaciers glimpsed at the top stretch all the way to the Pacific Ocean. About 80km south, look for the **Tatshenshini River viewpoint**. This white-water river flows through protected bear country and a valley that seems timeless.

About 10km further, look for **Million Dollar Falls**. For once the sight lives up to the billing, as water thunders through a narrow chasm. Let the roar lull you to sleep at the nearby territorial **campground**.

The highway crosses into BC for a mere 70km but you'll hope for more as you traverse high and barren alpine wilderness,

---

SPRUCE BEETLES?

Even as beetles wreak havoc on forests across British Columbia and the Rockies, the forests of the Yukon are recovering. The millions upon millions of trees killed by the spruce beetle since 1994 have shed their brown needles and are now a ghostly gray. Meanwhile fast-growing opportunists are adding a bright green hue to the tableaux.

Many reasons for the tree deaths center on climate change, including warmer winters, allowing far more beetles than usual to survive from one year to the next.

In recent years, however, several factors have been working against the beetles: dead trees mean less food, a very cold winter killed many beetles and there is now a population explosion of beetle-eaters. Meanwhile, nature has opened the door to other trees, including birch and alder, which grow relatively quickly.

To get a sense of the devastation caused by beetles in the last two decades stop at the short **Spruce Beetle Loop**, 17km northwest of Haines Junction, just off the highway. It has interpretive signs.

---

where sudden snow squalls happen year-round. At the 1070m Chilkat Pass, an ancient aboriginal route into the Yukon, the road suddenly plunges down for a steep descent into Alaska. The US border is 72km north of Haines, along the wide **Chilkat River Delta**.

The delta is home to scores of **bald eagles** year-round; the handsome birds flock like pigeons each fall when they mass in the trees overlooking the rivers, drawn by the comparatively mild weather and steady supply of fish.

Pullouts line the Haines Hwy (Hwy 7 in Alaska), especially between mileposts 19 and 26. Take your time driving and find a place to park. Just a few feet from the road it's quiet, and when you see a small tree covered with 20 pensive – and sizable – bald eagles, you can enjoy your own raptor version of *The Birds*.

Haines (Alaska)

Unlike Skagway across the Lynn Canal, Haines has escaped the cruise-ship mobs and it's all the better for it. It's a real community with an appealing downtown close to the working waterfront. There are good shops, a couple of small museums and a historic fort. You can easily walk around much of the town in a few scenic hours.

Coming from the south on the Alaska Marine Highway ferries, Haines is definitely the port of choice for accessing the Yukon.

Prices are in US dollars. Haines is on Alaska time, one hour earlier than the Yukon. For more coverage of Haines and southeast Alaska, see Lonely Planet's *Alaska*.

☉ Sights & Activities

Walk the center and waterfront and then amble over to **Fort Seward**, an old army post dating back 100 years. Now a national historic site, the many mannered buildings have been given a range of new uses, from art galleries to funky stores and B&Bs.

Haines makes the most of its feathered residents and has an annual **eagle festival** (www.baldeagles.org/festival; ☉ mid-Nov) in their honor. Numerous local guides will take you to see the birds in ways you can't do from the side of the Haines Hwy.

🛏 Sleeping & Eating

The Haines Convention & Visitors Bureau has oodles of choices in all price ranges.

Portage Cove State
Recreation Site   CAMPGROUND **$**
(Beach Rd; campsites US$5; ☉ mid-May–Aug) It's worth losing your car so you can stay at this cyclist- and backpacker-friendly campground on the water 1.6km south of town. Light a campfire and let the mist roll in.

Captain's Choice Motel   MOTEL **$$**
(☏ 907-766-3111; www.capchoice.com; 108 2nd Ave N; s/d US$127/137; @ ☎) Haines' largest motel has the best view of the Chilkat Mountains and Lynn Canal and a huge sundeck to enjoy it.

Mountain Market & Spirits   MARKET **$**
(☏ 907-766-3340; 151 3rd Ave; meals US$4-10; ☉ 7am-7pm; ☎) Get your Haines Hwy or Alaska ferry picnic here. Treats include excellent coffee, baked goods, big sandwiches and lots of organic prepared foods.

★ **Fireweed Restaurant** BISTRO $$
(37 Blacksmith St; mains US$9-20; ⊙11:30am-3pm Wed-Sat & 4:30-9pm Tue-Sat; 🥄) In Fort Seward, Fireweed is an oasis of organic and creative cuisine. Enjoy the excellent pizzas, salads, chowders and seafood out on the deck overlooking the Lynn Canal. We swoon over the Haines Brewing Spruce Tip Ale.

❶ Information

Haines Convention & Visitors Bureau (☑907-766-2234; www.haines.ak.us; 122 2nd Ave; ⊙8am-5pm Mon-Fri, 9am-4pm Sat & Sun) Collect information here.

❶ Getting There & Away

There's no public transportation from Haines into the Yukon.

Alaska Marine Highway System (☑800-642-0066; www.ferryalaska.com) Superb service links Haines and the Yukon to BC and the US. Car ferries serve Skagway, the Inside Passage and, importantly, Prince Rupert in BC (p763); also Bellingham, Washington in the US. The ferry terminal is 6.5km south of town.

Haines–Skagway Fast Ferry (☑888-766-2103, 907-766-2100; www.hainesskagway-fastferry.com; one-way adult/child $35/18; ⊙Jun-Sep) Carries passengers only (45 minutes, one to seven per day) and docks near the center.

KLONDIKE HIGHWAY

Beginning seaside in Skagway, Alaska, the 716km Klondike Hwy climbs high to the forbidding Chilkoot Pass before crossing into stunning alpine scenery on the way to Carcross. For much of its length the road generally follows the **Gold Rush Trail**, the route of the Klondike prospectors. You'll have a much easier time of it than they did.

North of Whitehorse, the road passes through often-gentle terrain that has been scorched by wildfires through the years. Signs showing the dates let you chart nature's recovery.

Skagway (Alaska)

Skagway has been both delighting and horrifying travelers for over 100 years. In 1898 rogues of all kinds preyed upon arriving miners bound for Dawson. Today it's T-shirt vendors preying on tourists. When several huge cruise ships show up at once, the streets swarm with day-trippers.

However, behind the tat there's a real town that has many preserved attractions. At night, after the cruise ships have sailed, Skagway has its own quiet charm. Although it's in the US, it can only be reached by car on the Klondike Hwy from the Yukon (with a short stretch in BC). It's the starting point for the famed Chilkoot Trail and the White Pass & Yukon Route.

Skagway is the last stop on the Alaska Marine Highway System's inland passage service from the south and as such is an important entry point for the Yukon. Lonely Planet's *Alaska* has extensive coverage of Skagway and the rest of southeast Alaska.

Prices are in US dollars. Skagway is on Alaska time, one hour earlier than the Yukon. Most places close outside of summer.

◉ Sights & Activities

A seven-block corridor along Broadway, part of the **Klondike Gold Rush National Historical Park**, is home to restored buildings, false fronts and wooden sidewalks from Skagway's gold-rush era. The Park Service has tours, a museum and info.

★ **White Pass & Yukon Route Railroad** RAILROAD
(☑800-343-7373; www.wpyr.com; 231 2nd Ave; adult/child from US$115/57.50; ⊙May-Sep) The White Pass & Yukon Route is the stunning reason most people visit Skagway (other than T-shirts). The narrow-gauge line twists up the tortuous route to the namesake White Pass, tracing the notorious White Pass trail used during the Klondike gold rush. The three-hour Summit Excursion is the most popular ride, but longer trips are worth the time and money.

🛏 Sleeping & Eating

Reservations are strongly recommended during July and August. The Convention & Visitors Bureau has comprehensive accommodations lists.

Pullen Creek RV Park CAMPGROUND $
(☑907-983-2768, 800-936-3731; www.pullen-creekrv.com; 501 Congress St; campsites/RV sites US$22/36) This park is right next to the ferry terminal.

Sgt Preston's Lodge MOTEL $$
(☑866-983-2521, 907-983-2521; http://sgt-prestons.eskagway.com; 370 6th Ave; s US$97-115,

THE YUKON IS MELTING, MELTING...

The Yukon could serve as exhibit one in the case confirming climate change. Every corner of the territory is experiencing rapid changes in the environment because it's getting warmer a lot quicker than anybody ever imagined. In the far north, Herschel Island is literally dissolving as the permafrost thaws. One gruesome sign: long-buried coffins floating to the surface of the melting earth. Unesco has listed it as one of the world's most threatened historic sites.

In Dawson City locals have for decades bet on the day each spring when the Yukon River suddenly breaks up and begins flowing. Detailed records show that the mean date for this has moved one week earlier in the last century to May 5, with the pace accelerating.

Preparing the Yukon for a radically different and warmer future is now a major political topic, even if nobody has the answers.

d US$119-151; @ 🛜) This motel is the best bargain in Skagway and just far enough from Broadway St to escape most of the cruise-ship crush.

★**Stowaway Café** CAJUN **$$**
(☎907-983-3463; www.stowawaycafe.com; 205 Congress Way; mains US$11-24; ⊗10am-9pm May-Sep) Near the Harbor Master's office, this funky and fantastic cafe serves excellent fish and Cajun-style steak dinners. Make sure you try the wasabi salmon.

ℹ Information

Chilkoot Trail Centre (cnr Broadway & 2nd Ave; ⊗8am-5pm Jun-Aug; run by **Parks Canada** (☎800-661-0486; www.pc.gc.ca/chilkoot) and the **US National Park Service** (☎907-983-3655; www.nps.gov/klgo), provides advice, permits, maps and a list of transportation options to/from the Chilkoot Trail.

Skagway Convention & Visitors Bureau (☎907-983-2854; www.skagway.com; cnr Broadway St & 2nd Ave; ⊗8am-6pm Mon-Fri, to 5pm Sat & Sun) In the can't-miss Arctic Brotherhood Hall (think driftwood).

US National Park Service (☎907-983-2921; cnr Broadway & 2nd Ave; ⊗8am-6pm May-Sep) Pick up the *Skagway Trail Map* for area hikes; has full details on the Klondike Gold Rush National Historical Park and a small museum.

ℹ Getting There & Away

From Skagway to Whitehorse on the Klondike Hwy (Hwy 2) is 177km. Customs at the border usually moves fairly quickly.

BOAT
Alaska Marine Highway System (☎800-642-0066; www.ferryalaska.com) These great voyages link Skagway and the Yukon to BC and the US. The car ferries serve Haines, the Inside

Passage, and Prince Rupert in BC (p763); also Bellingham, Washington in the US. The ferry terminal is right in the center.

Haines–Skagway Fast Ferry (☎888-766-2103, 907-766-2100; www.hainesskagwayfastferry.com; one-way adult/child $35/18; ⊗Jun-Sep) Carries passengers only (45 minutes, one to seven per day) and docks near the center.

TRAIN & BUS
White Pass & Yukon Route Railroad (☎907-983-2217; www.wpyr.com; 231 2nd Ave; ⊗Jun-Aug) Offers a jaw-dropping scenic 10-hour rail and bus connection to/from Whitehorse via Carcross, BC (one-way to/from Whitehorse adult/child US$185/92.50). Service is not daily.

Chilkoot Trail

Arduous at best and deadly at worst in 1898, the Chilkoot Trail was the route most prospectors took to get over the 1110m Chilkoot Pass from Skagway and into the Yukon. Today, hikers reserve spots months in advance to travel the same route.

The well-marked 53km trail begins near **Dyea**, 14km northwest of Skagway, and heads northeast over the pass. It then follows the Taiya River to Lake Bennett in BC, and takes three to five days to hike. It's a hard route in good weather and often treacherous in bad. You must be in good physical condition and come fully equipped. Layers of warm clothes and rain gear are essential.

Hardware, tools and supplies dumped by the prospectors still litter the trail. At several places there are wooden shacks where you can put up for the night, but these are usually full, so a tent and sleeping bag are required.

There are 10 designated campgrounds along the route, each with bear caches.

At the Canadian end you can either take the White Pass & Yukon Route train from Bennett back to Skagway or further up the line to Fraser in BC, where you can connect with a bus for Whitehorse.

The Chilkoot Trail is a primary feature of the **Klondike Gold Rush International Historical Park**, a series of sites managed by both Parks Canada and the US National Park Service that stretches from Seattle, Washington, to Dawson City. Each Chilkoot hiker must obtain one of the 50 permits available for each day in summer; reserve well in advance. Parks Canada/US National Park Service charge $50 for a permit plus $12 for a reservation. Each day eight permits are issued on a first-come, first-served basis. For information, contact the **Chilkoot Trail Centre** in Skagway or go online. Necessary preplanning includes determining which campsites you'll use each night.

Carcross

Long a forgotten gold rush town, cute little Carcross, 74km southeast of Whitehorse, is on a roll. There are two to three trains in summer from Skagway on the **White Pass & Yukon Route** (www.wpyr.com; train/bus tour adult/child from $169/134.50; ☉Jun-Aug). Some old buildings are being restored and the site on Lake Bennett is superb. (Although Klondike prospectors who had to build boats here to cross the lake didn't think so.)

The **visitor information center** (☏867-821-4431; ☉8am-8pm May-Sep) is in a new complex with seasonal shops and cafes. Get the excellent walking tour brochure. The old **train station** has good displays on local history.

Carcross Desert, the world's smallest desert, is the exposed sandy bed of a glacial lake. It's 2km north of town.

Whitehorse to Carmacks

Leaving Whitehorse by the Klondike Hwy is none too exciting. There's land with low trees and a few cattle ranches. After about 40km, however, look for serene **Lake Laberge**, which has a beach, followed by **Fox Lake**, 24km further north, and **Twin Lakes**, 23km south of Carmacks. Each has a government campground with shelters and pump water.

Carmacks

This village of 400 sits right on the Yukon River and is named for one of the discoverers of gold in 1896, George Washington Carmacks. A rogue seaman wandering the Yukon, it was almost by luck that Carmacks (with Robert Henderson, Tagish Charlie and Keish – aka Skookum Jim Mason) made their claim on Bonanza Creek. Soon he was living the high life and it wasn't long before he abandoned his First Nations family and headed south to the US.

Given his record as a husband and father, it's fitting that Carmacks be honored by this uninspired collection of gas stations and places to stay. The main reason to stop is the excellent **Tagé Cho Hudän Interpretive Centre** (☏867-863-5830; admission by donation; ☉9am-4pm May-Sep). Volunteers explain aboriginal life past and present. Like elsewhere in the territory, residents here are keenly attuned to the land, which supplies them with game and fish throughout the year. A pretty 15-minute interpretive walk by the river provides a glimmer of insight into this life.

This is also the junction with the **Robert Campbell Hwy** (p782).

About 25km north of Carmacks, the **Five Finger Recreation Site** has excellent views of the treacherous stretch of the rapids that tested the wits of riverboat captains traveling between Whitehorse and Dawson. There's a steep 1.5km walk down to the rapids.

Minto

Easily missed – unless you're toting a canoe or kayak – Minto is where the Klondike Hwy leaves the route of the Gold Rush Trail. This is a popular place to put in for the four- to five-day trip down the Yukon River to Dawson City. It's about 72km north of Carmacks.

Stewart Crossing

Another popular place to get your canoe wet, Stewart Crossing is on the Stewart River, which affords a narrow and somewhat more rugged experience before it joins the Yukon to the west for the trip to Dawson.

Otherwise unexceptional, the village is the junction of the Klondike Hwy (Hwy 2) and the **Silver Trail** (Hwy 11).

North of Stewart Crossing the Klondike Hwy continues for 139 bland kilometers to the junction with the Dempster Hwy. From here it's only 40km to Dawson City.

DAWSON CITY

If you didn't know its history, Dawson would be an atmospheric place to pause for a while, plunging into its quirky culture and falling for its seductive, funky vibe. That it's one of the most historic and evocative towns in Canada is like gold dust on a cake: unnecessary but damn nice.

Set on a narrow shelf at the confluence of the Yukon and Klondike Rivers, a mere 240km south of the Arctic Circle, Dawson City was the center of the Klondike gold rush.

Today you can wander the dirt streets of Dawson, passing old buildings with dubious permafrost foundations leaning on each other for support. There's a rich cultural life, with many people finding Dawson the perfect place for free expression (that person downing a shot on the next bar stool may be a dancer, filmmaker, painter or miner).

Dawson can be busy in the summer, especially during its festivals. But by September the days are getting short, the seasonal workers have fled south and the 1300 year-round residents (professionals, miners, First Nations, dreamers, artists and those who aren't sure where they fit) are settling in for another long and quiet winter.

History

In 1890 more than 30,000 prospectors milled the streets of Dawson – a few newly rich, but most without prospects and at odds with themselves and the world. Shops, bars and prostitutes relieved these hordes of what money they had, but Dawson's fortunes were tied to the gold miners and, as the boom ended, the town began a decadeslong slow fade.

The territorial capital was moved to Whitehorse in 1952 and the town lingered on, surviving on the low-key but ongoing

---

KLONDIKE GOLD RUSH

The Klondike gold rush continues to be the defining moment for the Yukon. Certainly it was the population high point. Some 40,000 gold seekers washed ashore (some literally) in Skagway, hoping to strike it rich in the gold fields of Dawson City, some 700km north.

To say that most were ill-prepared for the adventure is an understatement. Although some were veterans of other gold rushes, a high percentage were American men looking for adventure. Clerks, lawyers and waiters were among those who thought they'd just pop up North and get rich. The reality was different. Landing in Skagway, they were set upon by all manner of flimflam artists, most working for the incorrigible Soapy Smith. Next came dozens of trips hefting their 1000lb of required supplies over the frozen Chilkoot Pass. Then they had to build boats from scratch and make their way across lakes and the Yukon River to Dawson. Scores died trying.

Besides more scamsters, there was another harsh reality awaiting in Dawson: by the summer of 1897 when the first ships reached the west coast of the US with news of the discoveries on Dawson's Bonanza Creek, the best sites had all been claimed. The Klondike gold rush mobs were mostly too late to the action by at least a year. Sick and broke, the survivors glumly made their way back to the US. Few found any gold and most sold their gear for pennies to merchants who in turn resold it to incoming gold seekers for top dollar. Several family fortunes in the Yukon today can be traced to this trade.

Today, even the hardiest folk seem like couch potatoes when compared to the protagonists of these harrowing stories. The deprivation, disease and heartbreak of these 'dudes' of the day make for fascinating reading. Among the many books about the Klondike gold rush, the following are recommended (and easily found in the Yukon):

➡ *The Klondike Fever* by Pierre Berton is the classic on the gold rush.

➡ *Sailor on Snowshoes* by Dick North traces Jack London's time in the Yukon and the hunt for his cabin. London's stories of the gold rush made his name as a writer.

➡ *Soapy Smith* by Stan Sauerwein is a delightful tale about the Skagway scalawag for whom the word incorrigible was invented.

Dawson City

gold-mining industry. By 1970 the population was under 900. But then a funny thing happened on the way to Dawson's demise: it was rediscovered. Improvements to the Klondike Hwy and links to Alaska allowed the first major influx of summertime tourists, who found a charmingly moldering time capsule from the gold rush. Parks Canada designated much of the town as historic and began restorations.

⊙ Sights

Dawson is small enough to walk around in a few hours, but you can easily fill three or more days with the many local things to see and do. If the summertime hordes get you down, head uphill for a few blocks where you'll find timeless old houses and streets.

Like a gold nugget on a tapped-out creek, street numbers are a rarity in Dawson. Unless noted otherwise, opening hours and times given here cover the summer. For the rest of the year, most sights, attractions and many businesses are closed.

Government budget cuts mean Parks Canada's sites and programs are currently in flux; it may require some dexterity to see

Dawson City

some of the world-class sites due to very limited opening hours.

★ Klondike National Historic Sites
HISTORIC SITE

(www.pc.gc.ca/dawson; passes adult $7-32) It's easy to relive the gold rush at myriad preserved and restored places. Parks Canada tries its best with limited resources. Various restored buildings such as the **Palace Grand Theatre** (King St) are open on a sporadic and rotating basis, usually from 10am to 1pm.

Robert Service Cabin
HISTORIC SITE

(cnr 8th Ave & Hanson St; admission $7; ⊙reading 1pm May-Aug) The 'Bard of the Yukon,' poet and writer Robert W Service, lived in this typical gold rush cabin from 1909 to 1912. Don't miss the dramatic readings.

Commissioner's Residence
HISTORIC SITE

(Front St; admission $7; ⊙2:30-4:30pm) Built in 1901 to house the territorial commissioner, this proud building was designed to give potential civic investors confidence in the city. The building was the longtime home of Martha Black, who came to the Yukon in 1898, owned a lumberyard and was elected to the Canadian Parliament at age 70. (*Martha Black* by Flo Whyard is a great book about this remarkable woman.)

SS Keno
HISTORIC SITE

(Front & Queen Sts; admission $7; ⊙9:30am-noon May-Aug) The SS *Keno* was one of a fleet of paddle wheelers that worked the Yukon's rivers for more than half a century. Grounded along the waterfront, the boat re-creates a time before any highways.

Harrington's Store
HISTORIC SITE

(cnr 3rd Ave & Princess St; ⊙9am-8:30pm) **FREE** This old shop has historic photos from Dawson's heyday.

★ Jack London Interpretive Centre
MUSEUM

(Firth St; adult/child $5/free; ⊙11am-6pm May-Aug) In 1898 Jack London lived in the Yukon, the setting for his most popular stories, including *Call of the Wild* and *White Fang*. At the writer's cabin there are daily interpretive talks. A labor of love by historian Dick North, Dawne Mitchell and others, this place is a treasure trove of stories – including the search for the original cabin.

Dawson City Museum
MUSEUM

(☎867-993-5291; 5th Ave; adult/child $9/free; ⊙10am-6pm May-Aug) Make your own discoveries among the 25,000 gold rush artifacts at this museum. Engaging exhibits walk you through the grim lives of the miners. The museum is housed in the landmark 1901 Old Territorial Administration building.

Dänojà Zho Cultural Centre   CULTURAL BUILDING
(☑867-993-6768; www.trondekheritage.com; Front St; adult $5; ☺10am-5pm Mon-Sat) Inside this impressive riverfront wood building there are displays and interpretative talks on the Tr'ondëk Hwëch'in (River People) First Nations. The collection includes traditional artifacts and a re-creation of a 19th-century fishing camp.

CIBC Building   HISTORIC BUILDING
(Front St) The city of Dawson has started a long-term restoration of this derelict, riverfront bank building that dates to the gold rush. Note how tin was molded to look like stone. Poet Robert Service was once a teller here.

Midnight Dome   LOOKOUT
The slide-scarred face of this hill overlooks the town to the north, but to reach the top you must travel south of town about 1km, turn left off the Klondike Hwy onto New Dome Rd, and continue for about 7km. The Midnight Dome, at 880m above sea level, offers great views of the Klondike Valley, Yukon River and Dawson City. There's also a steep **trail** that takes 90 minutes from Judge St in town; maps are available at the visitor center.

Cemeteries   CEMETERY
(Mary McLeod Rd) A 15-minute walk up King St and Mary McCloud Rd near town leads to 10 cemeteries that are literally filled with characters. Among them: Joe Vogler, who fought to have Alaska secede from the US. He was buried here in 1993, having vowed not to be buried in an Alaska that wasn't free. Todd Palin (husband of Sarah) is among his acolytes.

Crocus Bluff   LOOKOUT
(off Mary McLeod Rd) Near Dawson's cemeteries, a short path out to pretty Crocus Bluff has excellent views of Dawson and the Klondike and Yukon Rivers. If driving, take New Dome Rd and turn at Mary McLeod Rd (ignoring the 'No Exit' signs). It is a short walk up King St from town. You can also take the 400m **Crocus Bluff Connector** path off of the **Ninth Avenue Trail**, which intersects with numerous streets along its 2.5km.

Klondike Institute for Art & Culture   CULTURAL BUILDING
(KIAC; ☑867-993-5005; www.kiac.org; cnr 3rd Ave & Queen St) The Klondike Institute for

Art & Culture is part of Dawson's thriving arts community. It has an impressive studio building, galleries and educational programs.

ODD Gallery   GALLERY
(☑867-993-5005; cnr 2nd Ave & Princess St) The exhibition space of the Klondike Institute for Art & Culture, this gallery, has regular shows.

Fortymile Gold Workshop/Studio   GALLERY
(☑867-993-5690; 3rd Ave btwn York & King Sts; ☺9am-6pm May-Sep) Watch as jewelry is made from local refined gold, which is silky and has a rich yellow color, as opposed to the bling you see peddled on late-night TV. Examples of gold from various local claims and locations shows how old miners could tell where gold originated.

Mines
The deeply scarred valleys around Dawson speak of the vast amounts of toil that went into the gold hunt. Bike or drive Bonanza Rd to pass some of the earliest gold rush sites along Bonanza Creek.

★ Dredge No 4   HISTORIC SITE
(Bonanza Rd) Some 13km off the Klondike Hwy, this massive dredging machine tore up the Klondike Valley and left the tailings, which remain as a vast, rippled blight on the landscape. Budget cuts to Parks Canada have put its preservation in doubt.

Bonanza Creek Discovery Site   HISTORIC SITE
(Bonanza Rd) Some 1.5km up the valley from Dredge No 4, this national historic site is roughly where gold was first found in 1897. It's a quiet site today with a little water burbling through the rubble.

🏃 Activities
Besides arriving by **canoe** or **kayak**, many people also exit Dawson via the Yukon River. A popular trip good for novices goes from Dawson for three days and 168km downstream to Eagle, Alaska.

A three-hour **hike to Moosehead**, an old First Nations village, is popular. The trail follows hillsides above the river north of town. Be sure to get a map at the visitor center..

You can explore much of the Dawson area by bike, including the **Ridge Road Heritage Trail**, which winds through the gold fields south of town.

Dawson City River Hostel   CANOEING, CYCLING
(www.yukonhostels.com; bike rental per day from
$25; ⊙May-Sep) Arranges all manner of canoe
rentals, trips and transportation from Whitehorse and points further downstream to Dawson and from Dawson to the Alaskan towns of
Eagle and Circle.

Dawson Trading Post   CANOEING
(☑867-993-3618; Front St; canoe rental per day $35;
⊙9am-5pm Jun-Aug) Dawson Trading Post
rents out canoes and can arrange trips.

⟡ Tours

★**Parks Canada Walking Tours**   WALKING TOUR
(tours $7; ⊙May-Aug) Parks Canada docents,
often in period garb, lead excellent walking
tours. Learn about individual buildings and
the many characters that walked the streets
(many of whom could be called 'streetwalk-
ers'). There are also self-guided 90-minute
audio tours (adult $7, 9am to 5pm).

★**Goldbottom Tours**   GOLD RUSH TOUR
(☑867-993-5750; www.goldbottom.com; ticket office
Front St; tours with/without transportation from Dawson $55/45; ⊙May-Sep) Run by the legendary
Millar mining family. Tour their placer mine
15km up Hunker Creek Rd, which meets Hwy
2 just north of the airport. The three-hour
tours include a gold-panning lesson; you get
to keep what you find. You can also just pan
for gold on their site for $20 or spend the
night in a cabin for $100.

Husky Bus   BUS TOUR
(☑867-993-3821; www.huskybus.ca; Front St; tours
$25-60; ⊙May-Aug) Runs various tours that in-
clude Midnight Dome (two hours), the Gold-
fields (three hours) and Tombstone Park (six
hours). The latter is highly recommended.

Klondike Spirit Tickets   BOAT TOUR
(☑867-993-5323; www.klondikespirit.com; tickets
Triple J Hotel, cnr 5th Ave & Queen St; tours from $55;
⊙May-Sep) This faux old stern-wheeler cruises
the river on various tours.

✶ Festivals & Events

Dawson City Music Festival   MUSIC
(☑867-993-5384; www.dcmf.com; ⊙mid-Jul) Popular – tickets sell out months in advance and
the city fills up; reservations are essential.

Discovery Days   CULTURE
(⊙3rd Mon in Aug) Celebrates the you-know-
what of 1896 with parades and picnics. Events
begin days before, including an excellent art
show.

🛏 Sleeping

Reservations are a good idea in July and
August, although the visitor information
center can help. Many places will pick you
up at the airport; ask in advance. Unless
otherwise stated, the following are open
all year.

Dawson City River Hostel   HOTEL $
(☑867-993-6823; www.yukonhostels.com; dm
$20-22, r from $48; ⊙May-Sep) ✔ This delightfully eccentric hostel is across the river from town and five minutes up the hill
from the ferry landing. It has good views,
cabins, platforms for tents and a communal bathhouse. Tent sites are $14. Owner
Dieter Reinmuth is a noted Yukon author.

Yukon River Campground   CAMPGROUND $
(campsites $12; ⊙May-Sep) On the western
side of the river about 250m up the road to
the right after the ferry; has 98 shady sites.

**Gold Rush Campground
RV Park**   CAMPGROUND $
(☑866-330-5006,   867-993-5247;   www.
goldrushcampground.com; cnr 5th Ave & York St;
RV sites $24-44; ⊙May-Sep; ☏) Convenience
trumps atmosphere at this 83-site gravel
parking lot for RVs.

★**Bombay Peggy's**   INN $$
(☑867-993-6969; www.bombaypeggys.com; cnr
2nd Ave & Princess St; r $95-210; ⊙Mar-Nov;
❋☏) A renovated former brothel with
alluring period furnishings and spunky
attitude. Budget 'snug' rooms share bath-
rooms. Rooms are plush in a way that will
make you want to wear a garter. The bar is
a classy oasis.

Klondike Kate's   LODGE $$
(☑867-993-6527; www.klondikekates.ca; cnr King
St & 3rd Ave; cabins $140-200; ⊙Apr-Sep; @☏)
✔ The 15 cabins behind the excellent restaurant of the same name are rustic without the rusticisms. High-speed internet,
microwaves and fridges ensure comfort.
The porches are perfect for decompress-
ing. Green practices are many.

Aurora Inn   INN $$
(☑867-993-6860; www.aurorainn.ca; 5th Ave; r
$130-210; @) All 20 rooms in this Europe-
an-style inn are large and comfortable. And if
there's such a thing as old-world cleanli-
ness, it's here: the admonishments to re-
move your (invariably) muddy shoes start
at the entrance.

Triple J Hotel
HOTEL $$

(☑867-993-5323; www.triplejhotel.com; cnr 5th Ave & Queen St; r $100-180; ☎) The 47 rooms in this modern motel with a throw-back look are in a new wing, in the renovated main building or in a cabin. It's a good mainstream choice.

✗ Eating

Picnickers, hikers and backcountry campers will find two good grocery stores in town. A **farmers market** (Front St; ⏱11am-5pm Sat May-Sep) thrives by the iconic waterfront gazebo. The sweet-as-candy carrots are the product of very cold nights. Try some birch syrup.

Most of the motels have a restaurant serving burgers etc; few places stay open outside summer.

Cheechako's Bake Shop
BAKERY $

(☑867-993-6590; cnr Front & Princess Sts; mains $4-8; ⏱7am-4pm Mon-Sat) A real bakery and a good one, on the main strip. Muffins, cookies and treats vie for your attention with sandwiches made on homemade bread.

River West
CAFE $

(☑867-993-6339; near cnr Front & Queen Sts; meals $4-7; ⏱7am-7pm Mar-Oct) Busy throughout the day, this fine coffeehouse, bakery and cafe looks out on the Front St action. Grab an outside table.

★ Drunken Goat Taverna
GREEK $$

(☑867-993-5800; 2nd Ave; mains $14-25; ⏱noon-9pm) Follow your eyes to the flowers, your ears to the Aegean music and your nose to the excellent Greek food, run 12-months-a-year by the wonderful Tony Dovas.

★ Klondike Kate's
CANADIAN $$

(☑867-993-6527; cnr King St & 3rd Ave; mains $8-25; ⏱11am-9pm Mon-Sat, 8am-9pm Sun Apr-Sep) Two ways to know spring has arrived: the river cracks up and Kate's reopens. Locals in the know prefer the latter. The long and inventive menu has fine sandwiches, pastas and fresh Yukon fish. Look for great specials.

🍷 Drinking & Nightlife

The spirit(s) of the prospectors lives on in several saloons. On summer nights the action goes on until dawn, which would mean something if it weren't light all night.

★ Bombay Peggy's
PUB

(☑867-993-6969; cnr 2nd Ave & Princess St; ⏱11am-11pm Mar-Nov) There's always a hint of pleasures to come swirling around the tables of Dawson's most inviting bar. Enjoy good beers, wines and mixed drinks inside or out.

Billy Goat
PUB

(☑867-993-5800; 2nd Ave; ⏱5pm-1am) Not a branch of the famed Chicago original but a nice, friendly lounge from Tony of Drunken Goat fame. Serves food from the Drunken Goat menu until late. Note the murals on the walls.

Bars at Westminster Hotel
BAR

(3rd Ave; ⏱noon-late) These two legendary bars carry the mostly affectionate monikers 'Snakepit,' 'Armpit' or simply 'Pit.' The places for serious drinkers, with live music many nights.

Downtown Hotel
PUB

(☑867-993-5346; cnr Queen St & 2nd Ave; ⏱11am-late) This unremarkable bar comes to life at 9pm in summer for what can best be called the 'Sourtoe Schtick.' Tourists line up to drink a shot of booze ($10) that has a pickled human toe floating in it. It's a long-running gag that's delightfully chronicled in Dieter Reinmuth's *The Saga of the Sourtoe*. (That the toe – it *is* real – looks much like a bit of beef jerky should give pause to anyone used to late-night Slim Jim jonesing...)

☆ Entertainment

★ Diamond Tooth Gertie's Gambling Hall
CASINO

(☑867-993-5575; cnr Queen St & 4th Ave; admission $10; ⏱7pm-2am Mon-Fri, 2pm-2am Sat & Sun May-Sep) This popular re-creation of an 1898 saloon is complete with small-time gambling, a honky-tonk piano and dancing girls. The casino helps promote the town and fund culture. Each night there are three different floor shows with singing and dancing, which is often surprisingly contemporary.

🛍 Shopping

Maximilian's
BOOKS

(☑867-993-6537; Front St; ⏱8am-8pm) Has an excellent selection of regional books, periodicals, gifts and topographical and river maps.

Dawson Trading Post
GIFTS, OUTDOOR EQUIPMENT

(☑867-993-5316; Front St; ⏱9am-7pm) Sells interesting old mining gadgets, bear traps ($500) and old mammoth tusks so you can take up carving. It has a good bulletin board.

ℹ Information

Much of Dawson is closed October to May. The biweekly, volunteer-run *Klondike Sun* covers special events and activities.

CIBC ATM (2nd Ave) Near Queen St.

Northwest Territories Information Centre (☑867-993-6167; Front St; ☉9am-7pm May-Sep) Maps and information on the NWT and the Dempster Hwy.

Visitor Information Center (☑867-993-5566; cnr Front & King Sts; ☉8am-8pm May-Sep) Tourist and Parks Canada information.

ℹ Getting There & Away

Dawson City is 527km from Whitehorse. Public transport to/from Whitehorse is often in flux. Should you fly in, there are no rental cars.

Dawson City Airport (Klondike Hwy) About 19km east of Dawson.

Air North (☑800-661-0407; www.flyairnorth. com) Serves Whitehorse, Old Crow, Inuvik in the NWT and Fairbanks in Alaska.

Alaska/Yukon Trails (☑907-479-2277; www. alaskashuttle.com; ☉Jun–mid-Sep) Service (three times weekly) between Whitehorse and Fairbanks via a Dawson City overnight stop (stopovers only; trips must start/end in Alaska); to/from Fairbanks US$285.

Husky Bus (☑867-993-3821; www.huskybus. ca; Front St; ☉May-Sep) Much welcome regular bus service (two to three times weekly) to/from Whitehorse (fares from $90). Reserve in advance. Will do pickups of paddlers and canoes with advance arrangement along the Klondike Hwy.

DAWSON CITY TO ALASKA

From Dawson City, the free ferry crosses the Yukon River to the scenic **Top of the World Highway** (Hwy 9). Only open in summer, the mostly paved 106km-long ridge-top road to the US border has superb vistas across the region.

You'll continue to feel on top of the world as you cross the border. The land is barren alpine meadows with jutting rocks and often grazing caribou. The **border crossing** (☉ Yukon time 9am to 9pm, Alaska time 8am to 8pm, 15 May to 15 Sep) has strict hours – if you're late you'll have to wait until the next day.

On the US side, Alaska shows its xenophobic side, as the 19km connection to the Taylor Hwy (Hwy 5) is mostly dirt and often impassable after storms (expect to get dirt in parts of your vehicle and person you didn't think possible). The old gold-mining town of **Eagle** on the Yukon River is 105km north. Some 47km south over somewhat better roads, you encounter **Chicken**, a delightful place of free-thinkers happy to sell you a stupid T-shirt at one of the gas station-cafes or offer their views regarding government bureaucrats. Another 124km south and you reach the Alaska Hwy, where a turn east takes you to the Yukon. Just a tick west, **Tok** has services and motels. Alaska time is one hour earlier than the Yukon.

DEMPSTER HIGHWAY

Rather than name this road for an obscure Mountie (William Dempster), this road should be named the Michelin Hwy or the Goodyear Hwy for the number of tires it's sent to an explosive demise. This 736km thrill ride is one of North America's great adventure roads, winding through stark mountains and emerald valleys, across huge tracts of tundra and passing Tombstone Territorial Park.

The Dempster (Hwy 5 in the Yukon, Hwy 8 in the NWT) starts 40km southeast of Dawson City off the Klondike Hwy and heads north over the Ogilvie and Richardson mountains beyond the Arctic Circle and on to Inuvik in the NWT, near the shores of the Beaufort Sea.

Road Conditions

Built on a thick base of gravel to insulate the permafrost underneath (which would otherwise melt, causing the road to sink without a trace), the Dempster is open most of the year, but the best time to travel is between June and early September, when the ferries over the Peel and Mackenzie Rivers operate. In winter, ice forms a natural bridge over the rivers, which become ice roads. The Dempster is closed during the spring thaw and the winter freeze-up; the timing of these vary by the year and can occur from mid-April to June and mid-October to December, respectively.

Graveled almost its entire length, the highway has a well-deserved reputation for being rough on vehicles. Travel with extra gas and tires and expect to use them. Check road conditions in the **Yukon** (☑511; www.511yukon.ca) and the **NWT** (☑800-661-0750; www.dot.gov.nt.ca); the Northwest

WORTH A TRIP

TOMBSTONE TERRITORIAL PARK

Shades of green and charcoal color the wide valleys here and steep ridges are dotted with small glaciers and alpine lakes. Summer feels tentative but makes its statement with a burst of purple wildflowers in July. Clouds sweep across the tundra, bringing squalls punctuated by brilliant sun. Stand amid this and you'll know the meaning of the sound of silence.

Tombstone Territorial Park (www.yukonparks.ca) lies along Dempster Hwy for about 50km. The park's only formal **campground** (campsites $12) has a new and excellent **Interpretive Centre** (⊙9am-7pm Jun-Sep), which offers walks and talks. It's 71km from the start of the highway and is set in along the headwaters of the Yukon River just before **Tombstone Mountain**, the point where the trees run out and the truly wild northern scenery begins.

There are good **day hikes** near the campground, as well as longer, more rigorous **treks** for experienced wilderness hikers. Permits are required for backcountry camping, especially at several lakes popular in summer. (The park's backcountry camping guide shows refreshing honesty in its answer to this frequently asked question: 'Will you come looking for me if I don't return?' 'No.')

Tombstone is an easy day trip from Dawson City (112km each way). With preparations, however, a multiday park adventure could be the highlight of your trip.

Territories Information Centre (p795) in Dawson City is a good resource. It takes 10 to 12 hours to drive to Inuvik without stopping for a break. (Given that William Dempster regularly made 700km dogsled journeys in subzero weather, this rugged and challenging road is properly named after all.)

🛏 Sleeping & Eating

Accommodations and vehicle services along the route are few.

The first available services after the Klondike Hwy are 371km north in Eagle Plains. The **Eagle Plains Hotel** (☎867-993-2453; eagleplains@northwestel.net; KM 371 Dempster Hwy; r $100-150) is open year-round and offers 32 rooms. The next service station is 180km further at **Fort McPherson** in the NWT. From there it's 216km to Inuvik.

The Yukon government has three campgrounds – at **Tombstone Mountain** (72km from the start of the highway), **Engineer Creek** (194km) and **Rock River** (447km). There's also a NWT government campground at **Nitainlaii Territorial Park**, 9km south of Fort McPherson. Sites at these campgrounds are $12.

ARCTIC PARKS

North of the Arctic Circle, the Yukon's population numbers a few hundred. It's a lonely land with little evidence of humans and only the hardiest venture here during the short summers.

The 280-person village of **Old Crow** (www.oldcrow.ca) is home to the Vuntut Gwitch'in First Nations and is unreachable by vehicle. Residents subsist on caribou from the legendary 130,000-strong Porcupine herd, which migrates each year between the Arctic National Wildlife Refuge in Alaska and the Yukon.

On the Yukon side of this vast flat arctic tundra, a large swath of land is now protected in the adjoining **Vuntut** and **Ivvavik National Parks**. Information on both can be obtained from the Parks Canada office in Inuvik, NWT, where you can get information on the very limited options for organizing visits to the parks (think chartered planes, long treks over land and water, and total self-sufficiency). There are no facilities of any kind in the parks.

The aboriginal name of **Herschel Island (Qiqiktaruk) Territorial Park** means 'it is island' and indeed it is. Barely rising above the waters of Mackenzie Bay on the Beaufort Sea, **Herschel Island** (☎867-667-5648; www.yukonparks.ca) has a long tradition of human habitation. In the late 1800s American whalers set up shop at Pauline Cove. Abandoned in 1907, the whalers left behind several surviving wooden buildings. Today Inuvialuit families use the island for traditional hunting, although climate change is causing the island to dissolve into the sea.

Summer visits to Herschel Island are possible via tours from Inuvik.

Northwest Territories

Why Go?

On a planet containing seven billion people, it's difficult to imagine that there are still places as empty as the Northwest Territories (NWT). A vast swathe of boreal forest and arctic tundra five times the size of the United Kingdom, it has a population of a small provincial town. In the 19th century, gold prospectors passed it over as too remote; modern Canadians, if they head north at all, prefer to romanticize about iconic Nunavut or the grandiose Yukon. More people orbit the earth each year than visit lonely Aulavik, one of the territory's four national parks.

What they're missing is something unique: a potent combo of epic, accessible terrain and singular aboriginal culture. With one of the world's greatest waterfalls and North America's deepest lake, it has enough brutal wilderness to keep a modern-day David Livingstone happy for a couple of lifetimes.

Best Places to Eat

➡ Fuego (p805)

➡ Thornton's Wine & Tapas Room (p805)

➡ Frozen Grape (p809)

Best Places to Stay

➡ Embleton House B&B (p803)

➡ Yellowknife Bay Floating B&B (p803)

➡ Blachford Lake Lodge (p807)

➡ Mackenzie Rest Inn (p812)

➡ Whooping Crane Guest House (p810)

➡ Arctic Chalet (p816)

➡ Heritage Hotel (p815)

When to Go
Yellowknife

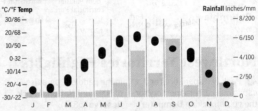

Jun See midnight sun before the horseflies hatch.

Jul & Aug Hyperactive summer season, good for fishing and canoeing in lakes and rivers.

Mar Best winter visits, with aurora viewing, husky mushing and Yellowknife's Snowking festival.

Northwest Territories Highlights

1 Pack two spare tires and a capacious camera memory for the gob-smacking **Dempster Highway** (p815).

2 Rent a kayak and float on **Great Slave Lake** (p801) amid technicolor houseboats and barnstorming floatplanes.

3 J-stroke past gorgeous hot springs and gorging bears

in the paddlers' paradise of **Nahanni National Park Reserve** (p813).

4 Be buffaloed by mating snakes, vanishing rivers and the eponymous ungulates of **Wood Buffalo National Park** (p810).

5 Go to the dogs during a husky-team ride near

Yellowknife (p800) beneath the aurora borealis.

6 Go where few have gone before and hike part or all of the **Canol Heritage Trail** (p815).

History

The first NWT residents, ancestors of today's Dene, tramped here from Asia about 14,000 years ago. The Inuvialuit, who migrated from Alaska, showed up more recently. Fur-hunting Europeans, followed by missionaries, penetrated the area in the 18th and 19th centuries. After oil turned up near Tulita in the 1920s, a territorial government was formed. In the '30s, gold near Yellowknife and radium near Great Bear Lake brought a population influx. In 1999 the territory was cut in half with the formation of Nunavut: NWT is now evenly divided between Aboriginals and non-Aboriginals. The latter group, and to a smaller extent the former, have benefited from oil, gas and diamond development.

Land & Climate

The NWT is a supersized wilderness reaching poleward from the 60th parallel. The south is evergreen flatlands, the east is the boulder-filled landscape of the Canadian Shield, and toothy mountains rear up from the west. Canada's jumbo river, the Mackenzie, bisects the territory, draining two gargantuan lakes, Great Slave and Great Bear.

Summers have been warm recently but can bring anything. One sure thing is daylight: from May through July there's no end of it. June's the driest summer month, but lake ice can linger until the month's end. Most visitors come in July, when much of the region is plagued with horseflies and mosquitoes, and August.

Winters are long and punishing. In January, lows in Yellowknife collapse to -40°C (-40°F) and daylight is feeble. If you're keen on a winter visit, try March or April, when the sun climbs and the mercury follows suit.

ⓘ Getting There & Away

AIR

Edmonton is the main gateway. **First Air** (☑ 867-669-6600; www.firstair.ca), **Canadian North** (☑ 867-669-4000; www.canadiannorth.com), **Air Canada** (☑ 888-247-2262; www.aircanada.com) and **WestJet** (☑ 888-937-8538; www.westjet.com) fly Edmonton–Yellowknife, starting around $330 return. Canadian North also flies from Edmonton direct to Inuvik ($1930 return) and Norman Wells ($1690). **Northwestern Air** (www.nwal.ca) serves Hay River and Fort Smith direct from Edmonton ($935 to $1100 return).

Air Canada also serves Yellowknife from Calgary ($580 return).

NWT FAST FACTS

➡ Population: 41,462

➡ Area: 1,346,106 sq km

➡ Capital: Yellowknife

➡ Quirky fact: The world's first 'grolar bear' (grizzly and polar bear hybrid) was discovered in the wild here in 2006.

From Whitehorse, Yukon, **Air North** (☑ 867-668-2228; www.flyairnorth.com) goes via Dawson City to Inuvik ($1090 return).

From Iqaluit, Nunavut, First Air and Canadian North depart for Yellowknife ($2900 return).

BUS

At time of research, there was no bus link into the NWT, though it was hoped that the Edmonton–Hay River service might resume.

CAR

There are two overland routes to the southern NWT. From Edmonton, a long day's drive up Hwy 35 brings you to the NWT border, 84km shy of Enterprise. From Fort Nelson, British Columbia (BC), the Liard Trail runs 137km to the border. Fort Liard is another 38km north.

If you're heading up to the Mackenzie Delta, you can set out from Dawson City, Yukon, on the shockingly scenic Dempster Hwy, which reaches the NWT border after 465km.

ⓘ Getting Around

AIR

Half of the NWT's 32 communities are fly-in only, accessed from Yellowknife with **Air Tindi** (www.airtindi.com), Norman Wells with **North-Wright Air** (☑ 867-587-2288; www.north-wrightairways.com), and Inuvik with **Aklak Air** (☑ 867-777-3555; www.aklakair.ca).

BUS

Frontier Coachlines (☑ 867-874-2566; frontier-coach@northwestel.net) runs between Hay River and Yellowknife (5½ hours, three times a week), and Fort Smith (three hours, twice a week).

CAR

To best appreciate the NWT, you need wheels. Automobiles can be rented in all major communities.

The territory has two highway networks: a southern system, linking most communities in the North Slave, South Slave and Deh Cho regions; and the Dempster Hwy, which winds through the Mackenzie Delta. Getting to the

NORTHWEST TERRITORIES IN...

One Week

Fly to **Yellowknife** and spend the first day at the **Prince of Wales Northern Heritage Centre**, ambling around the **Old Town**, and getting out on the lake among floatplanes and houseboats. In the evening, sip beer, eat lake fish and (in summer) watch the sun not set.

Then rent a car and head south. Car-camp along the **Waterfalls Route**, then drive to **Fort Smith** (p809) to snap the woolly behemoths that inhabit **Wood Buffalo National Park** (p810). Backtrack to **Fort Simpson** (p812) and join a flightseeing tour into **Nahanni National Park Reserve** (p813).

Two Weeks

Skip the road trip. Fly from Yellowknife to Fort Simpson, meet your outfitter and spend 10 days paddling the paradisiacal **South Nahanni River**.

Delta from southern NWT requires a two-day detour through BC and the Yukon.

In summer, free ferries cross several rivers; in winter, vehicles drive across on 4ft-thick ice. Travel is interrupted for several weeks during 'breakup' (April and May) and 'freeze-up' (November). Check www.dot.gov.nt.ca for current conditions.

YELLOWKNIFE

POP 19,234

Amid the droning bush planes and picturesque houseboats of Yellowknife's Old Town, it's still possible to detect a palpable frontier spirit. It's as if you're standing on the edge of a large, undiscovered and barely comprehensible wilderness – and you *are*. Draw a line north from Yellowknife to the Arctic Ocean and you won't cross a single road.

Friendly, Subarctic Yellowknife supports 50% of the NWT population and is a blend of Dene and Métis from across the territory; Inuit and Inuvialuit from further north; grizzled non-Aboriginal pioneers; get-rich-quick newcomers from southern Canada; and a sizable selection of more recent immigrants from different parts of the world.

Named Somba K'e (Place of Money) in the local Tlicho language, the city, a mining hub, has been territorial capital since 1967.

History

When the first Europeans reached Great Slave Lake in 1771, the north shore was home to the Tetsot'ine, who were dubbed the Yellowknives due to their penchant for copper blades. Wars and disease eradicated them, but the moniker remained.

Over a century later, Klondike-bound prospectors on Yellowknife Bay unearthed gold. By the mid-1930s, bush planes had made the area accessible to commercial mining. Yellowknife became a boomtown.

In 1967, when Ottawa devolved management of the NWT, Yellowknife became capital. When gold mining ceased in the early 21st century, diamond mines fueled a new boom, but locals are already wondering what's next when the stones run low in a few years' time.

◉ Sights

Uphill from the Old Town, Yellowknife's less-characterful downtown was built – quite literally – on gold in the 1940s and '50s.

★ Old Town   NEIGHBORHOOD

Plenty of living people are older than Yellowknife but, despite the fact the Old Town only dates from the mid-1930s, its ramshackle streets wedged between Back and Yellowknife Bays have a tangible gold-rush-era atmosphere. Funky cabins and eye-catching mansions share views with B&Bs, floating homes and legendary fish shacks. Beyond, picturesque Latham Island includes N'Dilo (meaning 'end of the road'), Yellowknife's aboriginal village.

★ Prince of Wales Northern Heritage Centre   MUSEUM

(☏867-873-7551; www.pwnhc.ca; ◷10:30am-5pm; ⊕) **FREE** Acting as NWT's historical and cultural archive, this well-laid-out museum is pleasantly situated overlooking Frame Lake. Expertly assembled displays address natural history, European exploration, northern aviation, mining and, especially, Dene and Inuit ways. There's a cafe with leafy perspectives and a good zone for younger kids.

Legislative Assembly   NOTABLE BUILDING
(☑867-669-2230;www.assembly.gov.nt.ca; ☺9am-6pm Mon-Fri year-round, tours 10:30am, 1:30pm & 3:30pm Mon-Fri Jun-Aug) FREE In the impressive, igloo-shaped Legislative Assembly, you can learn about the territory's aboriginal-style government by joining a free hour-long tour. There's excellent Northern art throughout.

Bush Pilot's Monument   MONUMENT
Perched atop 'The Rock,' a large outcrop in the middle of the Old Town, this simple needle pays homage to the gutsy bush pilots who opened up the NWT. Climb the stairs to the viewpoint to watch modern floatplane traffic and envy the people on polychromatic houseboats in the bay. Summer sunsets – if you can stay up that late – are stunning.

Ragged Ass Road   LANDMARK
Named by prospectors who had gone stone broke (ragged ass), this road was immortalized in a song and album by Tom Cochrane, himself the son of a bush pilot. The street sign went missing so often that the authorities starting selling souvenir copies. Mansions now outnumber sagging gold-rush-era cabins.

🏃 Activities

There are various hikes around town. Longest and best is the 9km **Frame Lake Trail**. Start downtown in Capital Area Park; spurs connect to the 1.2km **Range Lake Trail** and precipitous **Jackfish Lake Trail**.

In popular **Fred Henne Territorial Park**, opposite the airport off Hwy 3, there's chilly swimming at **Long Lake Beach** and hiking on the 3.2km **Prospector Trail**.

On hot, bug-infested days, the water is the best place to be.

Narwal Northern Adventures   KAYAKING
(☑867-873-6443; www.narwal.ca; 4702 Anderson-Thompson Blvd; kayak rental per day $50, bicycle rental per 1hr/day $5/20) Run out of a B&B on Back Bay (part of Great Slave Lake), it rents canoes, kayaks and bikes, and also offers tours and lessons. Call ahead.

Overlander Sports   KAYAKING, SKIING
(☑867-873-2474; www.overlandersports.com; 490 50th St; kayak rental per day/week $45/200, ski rental per day $18; ☺9:30am-6pm Mon-Fri, to 5pm Sat) Yellowknife's main outfitter store rents canoes and kayaks in summer and cross-country skis in winter.

Yellowknife Ski Club   SKIING
(☑867-669-9754; www.skiyellowknife.com; Ingraham Trail; day-pass individual/family $10/25) The nexus for ski activities is here on Hwy 4 near the Hwy 3 intersection. There are 14km of trails, some lit. Alternatively sally forth across the frozen Yellowknife Bay.

👉 Tours

Dogsledding, a Dene fish barbecue, overnighting in a trapper's tent, sightseeing from a bush plane: Yellowknife offers plenty of 'only in the NWT' experiences.

★ Air Tindi   SCENIC FLIGHTS
(☑867-669-8218; www.airtindi.com; 23 Mitchell Dr; ☺30min/1hr/4hr tour $659/1239/3719) Offers excellent 30-minute tours over the city, Ingraham Trail and Yellowknife Bay. There's also a dramatic four-hour tour to Great Slave Lake's cliff-flanked East Arm, with an hour-long stop for hiking. Prices are for up to seven people.

North Star Adventures   CULTURAL TOUR
(☑867-446-2900; www.northstaradventures.ca) This aboriginal-run company offers excellent Dene cultural trips, boat tours ($75), fishing trips ($175), aurora-viewing trips ($85), and snowmobiling on Great Slave Lake ($50 per hour).

Beck's Kennels   ADVENTURE TOUR
(☑867-873-5603; www.beckskennels.com; 124 Curry Dr) In winter, take an 8km guided dogsled tour ($65) or learn to drive your own team ($75). Multiday adventures cost $400 per day. In summer, the dogs pull ATVs: fun but not the same.

ℹ NORTHWEST TERRITORIES INFORMATION

Northwest Territories Tourism (www.spectacularnwt.com) has a detailed website and distributes excellent material via mail or download, including the annual *NWT Explorers' Guide*.

A great resource is the excellent *Up Here* (www.uphere.ca) magazine, with up-to-date info and interesting articles on all aspects of Northern life.

Yellowknife

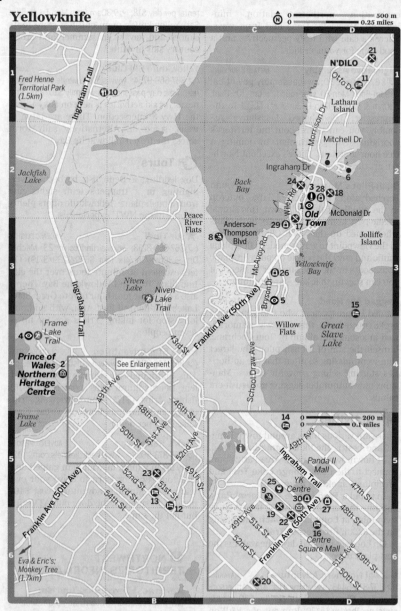

B Dene Adventures

CULTURAL TOUR

(☎ 867-444-0451; www.bdene.com) 🍃 These recommended summer and winter tours have a focus on Northern experiences and, particularly, Dene culture. The base for activities is a lakeside camp.

Bluefish Services

FISHING

(☎ 867-873-4818; www.bluefishservices.ca; Mitchell Dr) Bluefish takes you out on Great Slave Lake to battle grayling, pike and lake trout. Prices range from $125 for 4½ hours up to $275 for 10 hours. They also have simple

Yellowknife

one-hour boat tours ($45), and 3½-hour bird-watching excursions ($125).

Aurora Village   ADVENTURE TOUR
(☎867-669-0006; www.auroravillage.com) Specialists in aurora-viewing trips on special heated seats ($120 including transport, drinks and snacks), they also offer dogsledding ($95), snowmobiling ($95), and snowshoeing ($95).

★☆ Festivals & Events

★ Snowking Winter Festival   PERFORMING ARTS
(www.snowking.ca; ☺Mar) The Snowking, a grizzled houseboater, organizes this great winter event, hosting concerts, theatrical performances and hockey games right through March at a giant ice castle he builds on Yellowknife Bay.

Folk on the Rocks   MUSIC
(www.folkontherocks.com; day/weekend pass $90/120; ☺mid-Jul) This stellar two-day event on Long Lake features everything from hip-hop to Dene drumming. It draws musicians from throughout Canada.

⊨ Sleeping

Fred Henne Territorial Park   CAMPGROUND $
(☎867-920-2472; www.campingnwt.ca; Hwy 3; campsites $15, RV sites $22.50-32; ☺May-Sep; 🏊) This is the closest campground to town with full facilities. You can walk to downtown in 40 minutes via trails.

★ Embleton House B&B   B&B $$
(☎867-873-2892; www.bbcanada.com/embleton-house; 5203 52nd St; s/d with shared bathroom $91/120, with private bathroom $155/175; ☺@🛜) This well-kitted-out downtown B&B offers two options: compact, cozy rooms with shared bathroom and kitchen; or fabulous decorative themed suites with private whirlpool baths, robes and well-equipped kitchenettes. In both, ingredients are supplied for you to make your own breakfast. The owners are sociable and extremely congenial and both price and facilities outweigh any downtown hotel. Under-12s stay free.

★ Yellowknife Bay Floating B&B   B&B $$
(☎867-444-8464; www.ykbayfloatingbnb.com; s/d/apt $125/150/225; ☺🛜🏊) 🏊 Yellowknife's houseboats – really floating houses – are a picturesque and unusual feature, so where better to sleep? There's something really magical about this place: the floating feeling, the wraparound deck, the splendid bay views, the lapping water and the smooth ice. Accommodations are very stylish, including a cozy double decorated with furs and the host's inspiring Northern artwork and, by the time you read this, a separate apartment with en-suite bathroom and kitchenette.

As well as being beautiful and comfortable, this labor of love is logistically impressive. Ponder the challenges of offshore power, hot water and wi-fi as you relax into

Northern peace on the deck. You get a canoe to come and go and your welcoming hosts will also help with transportation. In winter, you can park alongside on the ice. Book ahead.

Eva & Eric's
B&B $$

(☎867-873-5779; www.ericeva.ca; 114 Knutsen Ave; s/d/q $90/100/130; ⊜🛜) On a quiet street in the western part of town, this highly satisfactory place offers a genuine welcome, very comfortable rooms (sharing good bathrooms) and a cracking breakfast including delicious home-baked goodies. Rooms share a kitchen area and a lounge with books and magazines about the North. It's run with kindness and good humor by a vigorous, well-traveled octogenarian couple who are gold mines of hospitality and Northern information.

Blue Raven B&B
B&B $$

(☎867-873-6328; tmacfoto@me.com; 37 Otto Dr Hill; s/d $85/100; ⊜@🛜) In an idyllic location on Latham Island, with quiet all around and great bay views from the lounge and deck, this welcoming spot feels like a rural retreat. There are three neat, compact rooms, two of which have a 'ladder loft' with an extra sleeping area. You can use the kitchen and you'll generally feel like you're staying at a friend's place.

Yellowknife Inn
HOTEL $$$

(☎867-873-2601; www.yellowknifeinn.com; 5010 49th St; r from $179; 🛜) Right in the center, this place has done a decent renovation job on its smallish rooms, which are now smartly decked out with commodious beds and neat gray fabrics. The airport shuttle stops here, and there's a restaurant and bar in the attached arcade. Rooms on the upper floors are quieter.

Coast Fraser Tower
HOTEL $$$

(☎867-766-8708; www.coasthotels.com; 5303 52nd St; r incl breakfast $199-244; 🛜▩) Yellowknife's original high-rise has very roomy, recently renovated one- and two-bedroom suites in two categories. All come with kitchens; some have balconies with lake and forest perspectives. Facilities include a restaurant, gym and steam room.

Explorer Hotel
HOTEL $$$

(☎867-873-3531; www.explorerhotel.ca; 4825 49th Ave; r $236, ste from $255; ⊜🛜▩) Looming over downtown, this generic high-rise has comfortable modern rooms, a restaurant

and a lounge, plus an imposing lobby polar bear. Odd-numbered rooms have a slightly nicer view. Standard suites are much larger for not a great deal extra. The airport shuttle stops here.

Eating

Prices are high.

Javaroma
CAFE $

(www.javaroma.ca; 5201 Franklin Ave; light meals $5-9; ⏰7am-10pm Mon-Fri, 8am-10pm Sat, 9am-10pm Sun; 🛜) This main-drag joint offers the best coffee in town, accompanied by sandwiches, soups, tasty muffins and bubble teas. There's outdoor seating, albeit on the busy road.

Smokehouse Café
BUFFET $$

(www.yksmokehouse.ca; 902 Sikyea Tili; buffet $15; ⏰11:30am-2pm Mon-Fri; ▨) They chose the only unattractive spot on Latham Island, a car park surrounded by garages, but this lunchtime venue offers great value for its tasty medley of buffet dishes. You can eye up the daily menu online; there's always a decent vegetarian option.

Dancing Moose Café
CAFE $$

(www.dancingmoosecafe.ca; 3505 McDonald Dr; mains $13-20; ⏰8am-10pm Tue-Sun; 🛜▨🖼) Watch floatplanes taking off as you kick back in the backyard of this pleasant licensed cafe. The interior gets busy at lunchtime, with soups, salads, and sandwich specials. It's also a good breakfast choice and bistro-style dinner venue. Art exhibitions and a cheery ambience make it a winner. There's a good attached B&B too.

Wildcat Café
CANADIAN $$

(☎867-873-8850; cnr Wiley Rd & Doornbos Lane; mains $15-30; ⏰11am-10pm Jun-Sep) A bit of local history, this refurbished Old Town log cabin has been churning out food since 1937. It operates under a different vendor each summer, meaning menu, prices and opening hours vary: those here refer to our last visit, when there was beer in enamel mugs, bison burgers and country music on the stereo. The summer deck is mighty nice for kicking back with a brew on a warm evening.

Sushi North
JAPANESE $$

(4910 Franklin Ave; mains $11-15; ⏰11:30am-7pm Mon-Sat) This excellent upstairs place does sushi with a polar spin: the raw fish is arctic char.

One of a Thai
THAI $$

(mains $13-14; ⊙11:30am-2pm Mon-Fri May-Oct) Look out for this mobile lunchtime van, which parks on Franklin Ave.

★ Fuego
FUSION $$$

(☑867-873-3750; www.diningon50th.com; 4915 50th St; mains $28-42; ⊙5-11pm Mon-Sat) This basement bistro stands in marked contrast to the Old Town fish shacks. Food covers a few bases: buffalo steaks take their place alongside Cajun, Asian, French and Italian dishes. Presentation is good, portions are hearty, and there's live music Thursdays to Saturdays.

Upstairs is Twist (11am to midnight Monday to Wednesday, to 2am Thursday to Saturday), with a '50s cocktail-bar theme, a pleasant summer deck, beer and sizeable, innovative burgers ($16 to $18, to 10pm). It has regular karaoke and open-mike sessions.

Thornton's Wine & Tapas Room
FRENCH $$$

(☑867-669-9463; 5125 52nd Ave; mains $20-40; ⊙5-9pm Tue-Thu, to 11pm Fri & Sat, 11am-3pm Sun) These guys weren't open when we were last in Yellowknife, but locals rave about the wine selection and innovative French-influenced dishes combining bistro classics such as oysters and charcuterie with Northern ingredients such as bison and char. Locals also flock here for Sunday brunch.

Bullock's Bistro
SEAFOOD $$$

(☑867-873-3474; 3534 Weaver Dr; mains $24-40; ⊙11:30am-9pm Mon-Sat, 4-9pm Sun) This legendary shack, brimful of bumper stickers, diners' graffiti and mix-and-match furniture, is a sassy, humorous place specializing in tourists and fish. The latter comes pan-fried, grilled or deep-fried with chips, salad and a very hefty price tag. It ain't gourmet, but it's fresh and tasty. Relax, go with the flow and you'll have a great time. Stews are the focus at lunchtime.

Expect serve-yourself drinks, expect to wait and wait some more for service, expect to sit at the counter, and expect smart, benevolent backchat from the staff.

♀ Drinking & Nightlife

Monkey Tree
PUB

(www.samsmonkeytree.com; 483 Range Lake Rd; mains $13-21; ⊙11am-1am Mon-Wed, to 2am Thu-Sat) Removed from downtown, this is less rough around the edges than other Yellowknife bars, offering a good selection of beers and pub grub until 10pm, including some of the biggest burgers you'll ever see. The large interior is furnished with sports-friendly screens and there's a small but desirable outside area.

Black Knight Pub
PUB

(www.blackknightpub.com; 4910 49th St; ⊙11am-2am Mon-Sat) Among the more straight-laced drinkeries, this local favorite is a sociable place with a Scottish theme. They pour a good pint and do decent pub food, with various special evenings – wings on Wednesdays are very popular – and a barrage of 'knight' puns.

⌂ Shopping

Yellowknife is the best place in Canada to buy Northern art, crafts and clothing.

★ Northern Images
ARTS & CRAFTS

(☑867-873-5944; www.northernimages.ca; 4801 Franklin Ave; ⊙10am-6pm Mon-Sat, noon-6pm Sun) ◢ Owned by aboriginal art-and-crafts cooperatives, this excellent place carries the famed Inuit prints from Cape Dorset, Pangnirtung and Ulukhaktok, along with Dene specialties such as birch-bark baskets. Prices are very fair and they can arrange delivery.

Weaver & Devore
OUTDOOR EQUIPMENT

(www.weaverdevore.ca; 3601 Weaver Dr; ⊙9am-6pm Mon-Sat) Poke your head into this historic trading post, once located in Bullock's opposite. It has a useful range of outdoorsy stuff and is still a place where grizzled wilderness veterans growl 'ten men, twelve days'; they'll prepare what's needed for the expedition.

Gallery of the Midnight Sun
SOUVENIRS

(☑867-873-8064; www.gallerymidnightsun.com; 5005 Bryson Dr; ⊙10am-6pm Mon-Sat, noon-5pm Sun) Has an ample supply of aboriginal art, including ornately decorated Dene moccasins and jackets. Also stocks souvenirs.

Old Town Glassworks
GLASS

(☑867-669-7654; www.oldtownglassworks.com; 3510 McDonald Dr; workshops $45; ⊙10am-6pm Mon-Fri, noon-5pm Sat & Sun) ◢ This Old Town shop makes exquisite glasses and vases from old bottles. Want to do it at home? Take a workshop class.

Yellowknife Book Cellar
BOOKS

(www.yellowknifebooks.com; 4923 49th St; ⊙9:30am-8pm Mon-Fri, to 6pm Sat, noon-5pm Sun) Contains a great selection of Northern and aboriginal titles and sells maps.

ℹ Information

You'll find the big banks downtown on Franklin Ave.

Ambulance & Fire (☑867-873-2222) Note that ☑911 is not the emergency number in the NWT.

Northern Frontier Visitors Centre (☑867-873-4262; www.visityellowknife.com; 4807 49th St; ☺9:30am-5:30pm Mon-Fri, noon-5pm Sat & Sun) This has reams of maps and brochures, plus the indispensable annual *Explorers' Guide*. Inside are good exhibits on the NWT environment, a decent souvenir selection and free internet. To explore town, grab a free bike.

Police (☑emergencies 867-669-1111, non-emergencies 867-669-5100; 5010 49th Ave)

Stanton Territorial Hospital (☑867-669-4111; www.stha.ca; 550 Byrne Rd; ☺24hr)

Yellowknife Public Library (2nd fl, Centre Square Mall; ☺9:30am-8:30pm Mon-Thu, 10am-6pm Fri, 10am-5pm Sat) Northern books, free internet, rowdy youths.

ℹ Getting There & Away

AIR

Yellowknife is the NWT's air hub. First Air (p799) serves Hay River ($350 one-way, 45 minutes), and Fort Simpson ($552 one-way, one hour), while both they and Canadian North (p799) fly to Inuvik ($752 one-way, 2½ hours) via Norman Wells ($591 one-way, one hour). Smaller airlines sometimes offer good specials. Northwestern Air (p799) hits Fort Smith ($392 one-way, one hour, Sunday to Friday); **Buffalo Airways** (☑867-873-6112; www.buffaloairways.com), Hay River ($200 one-way, 45 minutes, Sunday to Friday); and **Air Tindi** (☑867-669-8200; www.airtindi.com), Fort Simpson ($410 one-way, 80 minutes).

BUS

Frontier Coachlines depart 5pm Monday, Wednesday and Friday from the Shell gas station on Range Lake Rd, stopping in Fort Providence and Enterprise en route to Hay River ($106, 5½ hours).

CAR

Car rental is expensive. A small car typically costs about $80/500 per day/week, *plus* 35 cents per kilometer, with 250 free kilometers thrown in with weekly rentals only. If you're doing major miles, consider renting in Edmonton and driving up. Big-name agencies are at the airport.

The cheapest is **Rent-a-Relic** (Royal Rent-a-Car; ☑867-873-3400; xferrier@ssimicro.com; 356 Old Airport Rd; per day/week $50/325, 50km free per day then 30c per km). Expect a battered but serviceable vehicle and a laissez-faire attitude. They do airport pick-ups.

ℹ Getting Around

TO/FROM THE AIRPORT

Yellowknife's airport is a couple of kilometers west of downtown. Taxis charge about $15. A free shuttle bus runs to the Explorer Hotel and Yellowknife Inn, among other central hotels.

BICYCLE

From early June until early September, free bikes are available from the visitors center.

BUS

Yellowknife City Transit (☑867-920-5600; www.yellowknife.ca; single ticket adult/child $2.50/1.50) runs three bus routes. Route 1 serves Old Airport Rd and downtown Monday to Friday. Route 2 connects downtown and Old Town Monday to Friday. Route 3 runs Saturdays year-round plus Monday to Friday in summer and combines the two other routes. Buses run every half-hour, roughly 6:30am to 7:30pm Monday to Friday and hourly on Saturdays from 8am to 6pm.

TAXI

Cabs are plentiful. Try **City Cab** (☑867-873-4444).

AROUND YELLOWKNIFE

Ingraham Trail

The Ingraham Trail (Hwy 4), winding 69km east of Yellowknife, is where locals go to play. The partly sealed route reveals scenic, lake-dotted, pine-lined Canadian Shield topography, and offers good fishing, hiking, camping, paddling, picnicking and, in winter, skiing and snowmobiling. There's no gas or services.

Yellowknife's visitors center has an excellent series of leaflets on paddling routes along this stretch, available in pdf form from the website.

Prelude Lake, 28km from Yellowknife, is a busy, family-oriented weekend spot with a vast **campground** (www.campingnwt.ca; campsites/RV sites $15/22.50; ☺May-Sep; ❀), boat launch (rentals available) and nature trails.

At **Hidden Lake Territorial Park**, 46km from Yellowknife, a 1.2km trail leads to popular **Cameron Falls**. You can cross the footbridge and crawl to the brink of this marvelous cascade. Another 9km down the Trail, a 400m trail goes to Cameron River Ramparts, the falls' small but pretty cousin.

A FLYING VISIT

Excellent **Blachford Lake Lodge** (☑867-873-3303; www.blachfordlakelodge.com; 2 nights lodge/cabin per 2 adults incl transport, meals & tips $2310/3297; ☏) ✆ sits on a pristine lake a spectacular half-hour floatplane ride from Yellowknife. It's a stunning spot for relaxation in a remote location and offers a comprehensive range of summer and winter activities. Stay in either rustic wood cabins or in the lodge itself, where smart colorful rooms with shared bathrooms give you the chance to see the aurora from the warmest and comfiest viewing position: under the covers.

Attractive, sociable common areas include lounges, decks, the dining room serving impressively tasty meals, and an open-air Jacuzzi. Skis, skates, snowshoes, kayaks, canoes, hiking paths and more are available. Fishing, snowmobiling and husky sledding are enticing optional extras. Prince William and Kate made headlines when they came here in 2011.

It's a friendly, relaxed place and they're often looking for volunteer staff for the organic vegetable garden.

At **Reid Lake**, 61km from Yellowknife, you can swim, canoe or fish for pike, whitefish and trout. The friendly **campground** (www.campingnwt.ca; campsites $15, RV sites $11.50-22.50; ☺May-Sep; ☀) has a good beach, boat ramp and walking trail, plus campsites on the ridge with great lake views.

In summer, the trail ends at **Tibbitt Lake** where, fittingly, there's a stop sign. In winter, this is the beginning of the 570km ice road to the diamond mines. There are no services and non-industrial traffic is discouraged.

NORTH SLAVE

This region, between Great Slave and Great Bear Lakes, is rocky, lake-strewn and rich in minerals. Save for the people in Yellowknife, most people here are Tlicho, living traditional (and nontourist-oriented) lives.

Highway 3

From Yellowknife, Hwy 3 runs northwest, rounds the North Arm of Great Slave Lake, and dives to Fort Providence (314km).

The first stretch winds through bogs, taiga and pinkish outcrops of the Canadian Shield. Watch out for roller-coaster bumps, caused by the road's heat melting the permafrost in summer. **Behchokò** (population 1926), 10km north of Hwy 3 on an access road, is among the NWT's largest communities – and by far the biggest aboriginal settlement – but is insular and tourists may feel out of place.

Later, the land becomes flat boreal forest, ubiquitous in the southern NWT. **Mackenzie Bison Sanctuary**, with free-ranging wood bison, flanks the road. The animals outweigh your car and have tempers, so be observant. The sanctuary has no visitor facilities.

South of here, a 5km access road leads to Fort Providence. Beyond is a gas station with a cafe-bar and motel accommodations and, a few kilometers further, the recently opened **Deh Cho Bridge** over the Mackenzie River.

Fort Providence

POP 734

This low-key aboriginal community, near the head of the Mackenzie River, was settled in 1861 with the establishment of a Catholic mission. Off the access road is pretty **Fort Providence Territorial Park** (www.camping nwt.ca; campsites/RV sites $15/28; ☺May-Sep; ☀), with birch-shaded riverfront sites.

Fort Providence is a bucolic place – just ask the buffalo grazing in the grassy lots. Wander the lovely high riverside, admire the beautiful wooden church and shop for Dene handicrafts. The fishing's good: pike, walleye and sometimes grayling can be caught from the bank. Outfitters can take you out on the water; ask the folks at the Snowshoe Inn to put you in touch with an operator.

Warmly welcoming **Snowshoe Inn** (☑867-699-3511; www.snowshoeinn.ca; s/d $155/180; ☏☀) has decent, modern, waterfront rooms: some have a kitchen, while deluxe rooms boast big-screen TVs. Opposite, **Snowshoe Inn Restaurant** (www.snowshoeinn.ca; dishes $6-16; ⊘7am-8pm Mon-Fri, 8am-8pm Sat, 10am-7pm Sun; 🛜) whips up toothsome sandwiches and meals. Its fine craft shop features porcupine-quill items and the area's specialty: moose-hair tufting.

Frontier Coachlines buses between Yellowknife and Hay River stop in Fort Providence.

SOUTH SLAVE

The South Slave Region, encompassing the area south of Great Slave Lake, is mostly flat forestland, cut through by big rivers and numerous spectacular waterfalls.

Mackenzie Highway

From the Hwy 3 junction, 23km south of the Mackenzie River, the Mackenzie Hwy (Hwy 1) branches west into the Deh Cho region (p811) and southeast into the South Slave. This latter branch is well paved and runs 186km to Alberta (and then on to Edmonton) and is dubbed the **Waterfalls Route**, due to some stunning roadside cascades.

First up is **Lady Evelyn Falls Territorial Park** (www.campingnwt.ca; campsites/RV sites $15/28; ⊘May-Sep; 🐾), 7km down the access road to tiny **Kakisa**. There's a short path to the 17m falls, which pour over an ancient, crescent-shaped coral reef. The campground has showers, towering pines and lots of weekend anglers.

From the Kakisa access road, it's 83km to the crossroads settlement of **Enterprise** (population 87), which has gas and motel accommodations.

South of here, the Mackenzie Hwy parallels impressive **Twin Falls Gorge Territorial Park**. The eponymous pair of falls are linked by a lovely 2km forested trail. At one end is the tiered, 15m **Louise Falls** on the Hay River; there's **camping** (www.campingnwt.ca; campsites/RV sites $15/28; ⊘May-Sep; 🐾) in a boreal glade. The other end is impressive **Alexandra Falls** (33m).

At the Alberta border, 72km south, is the **60th Parallel Territorial Park. Visitors center** (⊘8:30am-8:30pm May-Sep) staff dispense pamphlets and coffee. There are also displays of aboriginal crafts, such as beaded moccasins, and a **campground** (www.campingnwt.ca; campsites/RV sites $15/22.50; ⊘May-Sep; 🐾) with toilets and showers.

Hay River

POP 3606

Blue-collar Hay River is the territory's second-largest town and an important rail terminus, lake harbor and freight distribution nexus. It's a useful service center rather than a drawcard in itself. The nicest part of town is the original settled area, Vale Island, with a picturesque beach on impossibly large Great Slave Lake. There's good fishing, boating and dogsledding available. Downtown is dominated by the highway and an out-of-place residential tower. Across the river is a Dene reserve.

◎ Sights & Activities

Kiwanis Nature Trail   ISLAND
The interpretive trail starts in Riverview Dr and runs along the banks of the Hay River and the West Channel of Great Slave Lake. The visitors center can provide additional information on hiking, flightseeing, fishing, golf and canoe rentals.

Vale Island   ISLAND
At the mouth of the Hay River on vast Great Slave Lake, this island, linked to the mainland by a bridge, is the oldest and nicest part of town. It's an ensemble of rickety wooden buildings, rusting boats, freight trains and the driftwood-strewn town beach, 7km by road from downtown.

Hay River Heritage Centre   MUSEUM
(☑867-874-3872; cnr Mackenzie Dr & 102nd Ave, Vale Island; ⊘1-5pm Jun-Oct) **FREE** In the town's old Hudson's Bay Company trading post on Vale Island, this is an enthusiastically run local history museum.

🛏 Sleeping

Paradise Gardens & Campground   CAMPGROUND $
(☑867-875-4430; 82 Paradise Rd; campsites/RV sites $21/31.50; 🐾) 🌿 Between Enterprise and Hay River, on a small organic farm, this friendly, idyllically located place has 15 campsites and offers berry picking.

Hay River Territorial Park   CAMPGROUND $
(☑867-874-3772; www.campingnwt.ca; 104th St, Vale Island; campsites/RV sites $15/28; ⊘May-Sep; 🐾) A Frisbee's throw from the beach, this densely wooded campground has hot showers, a barbecue area and a children's playground.

Ptarmigan Inn HOTEL $$
(☑867-874-6781; www.ptarmiganinn.com; 10J
Gagnier St; s/d $139/144; ❀❂❒) In the heart
of downtown, Hay River's only true hotel
has clean, spacious, well-appointed rooms,
a pub, a restaurant and a fitness center.
It's the community hub and is better value
than the motels lining the highway. Rooms
with kitchenette are available.

Harbour House B&B $$
(☑867-874-2233; www.greenwayaccommoda
tions.ca; 2 Lakeshore Dr, Vale Island; s/d $75/100;
❀❒) In a lovely, peaceful setting on Vale
Island right next to the beach, this sunny,
nautical-feeling B&B sits on flood-cheating
pilings. There's a kitchen, a great deck to
kick back on, and good continental breakfast. They'll pick you up from the airport
or bus stop.

✖ Eating

★Frozen Grape CAFE $
(www.frozengrape.ca; 2 Courtoreille St; light meals
$7-12; ◷9:30am-6pm Mon-Fri, 10am-5pm Sat; ❒)
During the long, long drive to Hay River,
we imagined a cafe like this but realized
it was way too much to ask. But here it is!
Excellent coffee, lip-smackingly good panini and lots of other tasty deli sandwiches,
soups and baked goods make this one of
the best of its kind in Northern Canada.

Fisherman's Wharf MARKET $
(cnr 101st St & 100th Ave, Vale Island; ◷10am-
2pm Sat Jun-Sep) ⚓ A weekly outdoor market with fresh fish and Northern-grown
produce.

Back Eddy SEAFOOD $$
(☑867-874-6680; 6 Courtoreille St; mains $15-25;
◷11am-2pm & 5pm-late Mon-Sat) This low-lit
bar and dining room (enter on Capital Dr)
is a reliable local favorite with varnished
tables that would look more at home in
a boardroom. Featured is fresh-caught
Great Slave Lake fish, including pan-fried
whitefish topped with scallops and shrimp.
There's a separate, unlicensed eating area
for families.

Boardroom CHINESE $$
(891 Mackenzie Hwy; mains $11-16; ◷11am-10pm)
By the Shell gas station on the main road,
this licensed place serves up westernized
Chinese, alongside pizza, fried chicken,
and burgers, with buffet specials. Quantity
trumps quality, but it's ok.

ℹ Information

Library (www.nwtpls.gov.nt.ca; 75 Woodland
Dr; ◷10am-5pm & 7-9pm Mon-Thu, 1-5pm Fri-
Sun) Free internet in the heart of town.
Visitors Information Centre (☑867-874-
3180; www.hayriver.com; cnr Mackenzie Hwy
& McBryan Dr; ◷9am-9pm May-Sep) On the
highway in the center. Off-season, stop by the
town hall, a block north on Commercial Dr.

ℹ Getting There & Away

AIR
Legendary Buffalo Airways (p806) ($200 one-
way, 45 minutes) and First Air (p799) ($350) fly
to Yellowknife. Northwestern Air (p799) serves
Edmonton ($455, 2¼ hours) and Fort Smith.

BUS
Frontier Coachlines goes from the downtown
Rooster convenience store to Yellowknife ($106,
six hours) via Fort Providence at 9am on Monday, Wednesday, and Friday; and to Fort Smith
($77, three hours) on Tuesday and Thursday.
Bus service to Edmonton has been discontinued,
though that may change.

CAR & MOTORCYCLE
By road, it's a paved 38km to Enterprise. About
5km out of town is the turnoff to partially paved
Hwy 5, leading 267km to Fort Smith.

TRAIN
Hay River is famously Canada's northernmost
rail terminus, but it's freight only.

Fort Smith
POP 2093

On a high bluff above the Slave River, Fort
Smith is friendly and idyllic. For years this
was the gateway to the North, situated at
the end of a portage route around the Slave
River rapids. The Hudson's Bay Company set
up shop here in 1874 and, until Yellowknife
became territorial capital in 1967, it was the
administrative center for most of Canada's
northern territories. Today it remains a
peaceful government hub and headquarters
of Wood Buffalo National Park. Two-thirds
of the residents are Cree, Chipewyan or
Métis.

◉ Sights

Northern Life Museum MUSEUM
(☑867-872-2859; cnr King St & McDougal Rd;
◷10am-5pm Mon-Sat) FREE The North's best
small-town museum has intriguing displays
on local history and culture, plus the corpse

of Canus, a whooping crane sire whose sexual efforts helped save his species from extinction. Outside is agricultural machinery, old buildings and a rusting riverboat that once transported radium.

Fort Smith Mission Historic Park PARK
(cnr Breynat St & Mercredi Ave; ☺May-Sep) FREE
This park commemorates the days when this was Catholicism's beachhead into the North. Self-guided tour maps are available from the visitors center.

🏃 Activities

The **rapids** in the area are famous for world-class **paddling**, and for being the northernmost nesting colony of white pelicans, which can be seen fishing from midriver islands. The Rapids of the Drowned, in front of town, are accessible off Wolf Ave. Upriver, the Mountain, Pelican and Cassette rapids can be viewed by **hiking** Fort Smith's 27km stretch of the Trans Canada Trail, or by shorter **walks** off the 24km road to Fort Fitzgerald. Trail guides are available at the visitors center.

🛏 Sleeping

**Queen Elizabeth
Territorial Park** CAMPGROUND $
(☑867-872-2607; www.campingnwt.ca; campsites/ RV sites $15/28; ☺May-Sep; 🐾) At the end of Tipi Trail, 4km west of the town center, this lovely underused campground with showers and firewood lies near the river bluff.

★Whooping Crane Guest House B&B $$
(☑867-872-3426; www.whoopingcraneguesthouse. ca; 13 Cassette Cres; s/d/apt $115/125/140; ☻@🛜) Luxurious, stylish and welcoming, this B&B occupies an intriguing octagonal wooden building down a very quiet street off Calder Ave. The many things to like include delicious breakfasts, the host's artistic quilting on the walls, and an abundance of books, bikes and hammocks. One spacious suite has kitchen and dining area, while two enchantingly decorated rooms boast magnificent private (exterior) bathrooms.

Stays of more than one night are preferred, and you'll prefer that, too.

Pelican Rapids Inn HOTEL $$
(☑867-872-2789; 152 McDougal Rd; r $155; 🕸🛜) In the center, this reliable standby has spacious, uninspired but comfortable rooms with much-appreciated summer air-con.

The on-site restaurant serves tolerable Chinese and decent steak dinners.

🍴 Eating

Anna's Kitchen CAFE $
(338 Calder Ave; lunch $7-9, mains $14-23; ☺8am-8pm Mon-Fri; ✐) ✿ Home cooking prepared with care is the key here, with a range of delicious salads, panini, burgers, tasty juice concoctions, and more substantial BBQ mains for dinner. It's a casual, cozy place with a yoga-healing vibe (massages and more available) and outdoor seating.

🛍 Shopping

North of 60 Books BOOKS, CAFE
(66 Portage Ave; ☺9:30am-5:30pm Mon-Sat, noon-5pm Sun) This sweet place sells handicrafts, as well as books. They also do decent coffee.

ℹ Information

Library (170 McDougal Rd; ☺2:30-5:30pm & 7-9pm Mon-Thu, 2:30-5:30pm Fri, 1-5pm Sat & Sun) Free internet. Closed Sundays July to September.

Wood Buffalo National Park Information Centre (☑867-872-7960; www.pc.gc.ca; 149 McDougal Rd; ☺9am-6pm Jun-Aug, reduced hours Sep-May; 🛜) Both national park information point and local visitors center, this excellent place has an interesting exhibition on local ecology, as well as inspiring audiovisual displays of the park. They run guided walks in the park in summer.

ℹ Getting There & Around

Northwestern Air (p811) serves Yellowknife ($381 one-way, one hour), Hay River ($208, 45 minutes) and Edmonton ($455 one-way, two hours), as well as Fort McMurray and Fort Chipewyan.

Frontier Coachlines has services to Hay River ($77, three hours, two weekly). In winter, an ice road runs to Fort McMurray, Alberta.

Partially paved Hwy 5 cuts through Wood Buffalo National Park 267km from Hay River.

Wood Buffalo National Park

Straddling the Alberta–NWT border, this is one of the world's largest national parks; its 44,000 sq km outrank countries like Denmark and the Netherlands. This vast expanse of taiga forest, karstic formations and enormous freshwater systems is an immense wilderness best experienced from the air or by taking some time to penetrate it by river.

The park was established in 1922 to protect wood buffalo, a large, dark, distinctly Northern subspecies of bison. Thousands inhabit the region and you'll likely see them grazing along roadsides or wallowing in the dust. Their interaction with wolves here was memorably filmed in the BBC's *Frozen Planet* and David Suzuki's *The Nature of Things*.

Also protected is the last wild migratory flock of whooping cranes on earth. These giant birds nearly disappeared, but are rebounding. They, along with millions of ducks and geese, avail themselves of the wetlands including the enormous Peace-Athabasca Delta, among the world's largest freshwater deltas. Moose, caribou, bears, and lynx are also residents, along with, in summer, countless mosquitoes and horseflies.

◉ Sights & Activities

Highway 5 OUTDOORS
Approaching from the west, roadside points of interest include the enormous **Angus Sinkhole** (signposted as Angus Fire Tower), disappearing **Nyarling River** and **Little Buffalo River Falls**, which has an unstaffed **campsite** (www.campingnwt.ca; campsites/RV sites $15/22.50; ⊙ May-Sep) and 2km nature trail. Further on, there's an 11km sideroad to **Salt Plains Lookout**, where a short trail leads down to a vast white field formed by saltwater burbling from an ancient seabed.

Peace Point Road OUTDOORS
Between Fort Smith and Peace Point is **Salt River Day-Use Area**, home to a snake hibernaculum (they only have group sex in late April), and the trailhead for excellent day hikes to salt flats and sinkholes. About 60km from Fort Smith, at popular **Pine Lake Campground** (www.pc.gc.ca; campsites $15.70; ⊙ May-Sep; ✸), you can bask on white-sand beaches and swim in the aquamarine water.

Parson's Lake Road OUTDOORS
Accessed at the same turnoff as the Salt Plains, this 54km sandy single-track forest drive is only accessible in summer when dry. It offers a great, lonely view of the region's forest and a good chance of seeing bison and other animals up close. It emerges between Fort Smith and Peace Point.

Hiking and Canoeing OUTDOORS
Various short hiking trails dot the park, particularly at Salt River. Ask park staff for advice on penetrating deeper. An adventurous option is to canoe from Peace Point, then hike 13km in to the Sweetgrass area, where there are vast grasslands, old bison corrals and camping and simple cabins available. Here you'll see herds of bison and possibly wolves.

For a real adventure continue down the Peace River to its junction with the Slave, then head back north to Fort Fitzgerald. Outfitters can arrange guided or self-guided trips of this nature.

☞ Tours

Check with the park office for licensed outfitters.

Northwestern Air SCENIC FLIGHTS
(☏ 867-872-2216; www.nwal.ca) Offers national park flightseeing excursions.

❶ Information

Park headquarters (p810) are in Fort Smith.

DEH CHO

Deh cho means 'big river' in the local tongue, and this southwestern region is awash in waterways, most notably the Mackenzie, Liard and Nahanni. The area is also blessed with mountains, warmer temperatures and rich aboriginal culture.

Mackenzie Highway

From the Hwy 3 junction, the Mackenzie Hwy (Hwy 1), gradually being sealed, cuts west through 288km of flat boreal forest to Fort Simpson. This is a lobotomizingly dull drive, with few views or points of interest. Note that the only fuel is at Fort Simpson and at Fort Liard.

The blessed exception is **Sambaa Deh Falls Territorial Park** (www.campingnwt.ca; campsites/RV sites $15/22.50; ⊙ May-Sep; ✸), halfway to Fort Simpson, featuring a marvelous roadside waterfall, fishing spots, the smaller Coral Falls, and a pleasant, clean campground with showers.

Another 90km along, at the junction of the Mackenzie Hwy and Hwy 7, is the **Checkpoint**, with accommodation but, frustratingly, no fuel.

A free car-ferry, the **MV Lafferty** (☏ 800-661-0750; www.dot.gov.nt.ca; ⊙ 8:30am-11:45pm mid-May–late Oct), crosses the Liard River

20km south of Fort Simpson. In winter there's an ice bridge. Traffic halts during freeze-up and thaw.

From Fort Simpson, the Mackenzie Hwy continues a rugged 222km north into rolling mountains, reaching beautifully situated **Wrigley** (population 113). Hunting, fishing and trapping remain the basis of this mainly log-cabin village. A winter ice road continues to Tulita, Norman Wells and beyond.

Fort Simpson

POP 1238

In the local tongue, Fort Simpson is *Liidlii Kue*, meaning 'where two rivers meet' – the voluminous Liard and Mackenzie Rivers converge here. With an easygoing blend of Dene, Métis and European cultures, it's the regional hub, has all services and is the gateway to nearby Nahanni National Park Reserve.

◉ Sights & Activities

Stroll along the Mackenzie riverfront with views of the driftwood-laden water and Papal Flats, where thousands gathered to welcome the Pope in 1987. Historic **McPherson House** and the **cabin** of eccentric trapper Albert Faille are nearby. There's a small golf course and a heritage center is gradually being built.

Flightseeing excursions or canoeing trips to the Nahanni are the reason most people are in town: air companies are located on Antoine Dr near the in-town airstrip.

Around Canada Day is the **Open Sky Festival** (www.openskyfestival.ca), a three-day music-and-arts event. The organizers have a **gallery** (100th St; ⊙9am-5pm) in the library building in town displaying contemporary and traditional Dehcho art.

☞ Tours

Simpson Air
SCENIC FLIGHTS

(☎867-695-2505; www.simpson-air.ca; Antoine Dr) Also runs a remote fly-in lodge on a lake in the Nahanni range.

Wolverine Air
SCENIC FLIGHTS

(☎867-695-2263; www.wolverineair.com; Antoine Dr) Friendly operator offering a range of trips.

🛌 Sleeping

Fort Simpson Territorial Campground
CAMPGROUND $

(☎867-695-2321; www.campingnwt.ca; campsites/RV sites $15/28; ⊙May-Sep; 🐾) Centrally located in woods near the river, the campground has showers, pit toilets and 32 pleasant campsites.

★ Mackenzie Rest Inn
B&B $$

(☎867-695-2357; www.mackenzierest.ca; 10518 99th St; s/d $150/180; ⊛@⊚) It's quite a surprise to come across such a sweet, charming, well-furnished B&B out in this land of float-planes and giant rivers. Faultless hospitality is matched with very cute, stylish rooms in a characterful, nobly furnished house with great river views, a grassy garden, and relaxing deck spaces. Rooms are all different – the top one is our favorite – and share spotless modern bathrooms. Breakfast is delicious.

Deh Cho Suites
GUESTHOUSE $$$

(☎867-695-2309; www.dehcho.net; 10509 Antoine Dr; s/d $195/225; ⊛❄⊚🐾) Spacious guest rooms are well furnished and come with modern kitchenettes and self-serve continental breakfast. It's a well-equipped place with the surprising bonus of some air-con rooms for the sometimes-sweltering summer heat.

🍴 Eating & Drinking

Pandaville
CHINESE $$

(9410 100th St; mains $11-18; ⊙11am-9pm; 🍴) One of only two places to eat in town, this has a straight-up Chinese menu with a lunchtime buffet and some Western dishes such as pizza and steak.

Ice Breaker Lounge
BAR

(9405 100th St; ⊙11am-2am; 🍴) The town bar is a good drink stop, with several bottled beers, wi-fi, a pool table and a back patio with comfortable stools.

ℹ Information

At the entrance to town, the **visitors center** (☎867-695-3182; www.fortsimpson.com; ⊙8am-8pm Mon-Fri, 10am-8pm Sat & Sun May-Sep) has helpful staff and brochures.

ℹ Getting There & Around

Air Tindi (p806) ($410 one-way, 80 minutes) and First Air (p799) ($552) serve Yellowknife. There's no bus service.

LOCAL KNOWLEDGE

BUSH PILOTING

Ted Duinker lives in Yellowknife and is a bush pilot, flying in the NWT, as well as Nunavut and northern Alberta.

Where's your favorite place to fly? The NWT has some amazing sights from the air. I see lots of wildlife from the plane – moose, caribou, muskox, bears, wolves. My favorite sight though is the tundra in the fall when colors change to a beautiful red. I'd recommend a flying trip up north to see it or a trip west to see the mountains in the Nahanni.

What challenges do you face? The main challenge up here would have to be the weather, especially in winter when temperatures drop to -40°C. Sometimes the most straightforward place to land can be very challenging if the wind is howling and visibility is reduced in rain. Runways have two take-off and landing directions, but on ice and water there could be hundreds of ways you could take off or land. That's why I love flying floatplanes in the north! It's never the same.

Nahanni National Park Reserve

To many, Nahanni *means* wilderness. Situated in the southwestern NWT near the Yukon border, this 30,000-sq-km park embraces its namesake, the epic **South Nahanni River**. This untamed river tumbles more than 500km through the jagged Mackenzie Mountains. It's a dream destination for canoeing and one of Canada's most spectacular places.

Appropriately, the Nahanni is a Canadian Heritage river, and the park is a Unesco World Heritage site. In 2009 the federal government and Dehcho First Nations signed an agreement increasing the park's size more than sixfold.

◎ Sights & Activities

Near its midpoint, the Nahanni River drops 30 stories over Canada's premier cascade, **Virginia Falls**. Elsewhere it's framed by canyons, flanked by caves and warmed by the **Rabbitkettle Hot Springs**. Moose, wolves, grizzly bears, Dall sheep and mountain goats patrol the landscape.

Paddling is what Nahanni is all about. If you plan to do this independently, you should be a capable white-water paddler (in grade IV rapids). This is no pleasure float; people have died here. Consult with the park office for advice and contact the tour companies for equipment rental.

☞ Tours

Flightseeing

The easiest way to see the park is from the air. There are several options, from flyovers to excursions in floatplanes that land. A typical trip follows the Nahanni upriver through steep-walled canyons and then lands just above Virginia Falls. Other trips take in further-flung Glacier Lake.

It's about $1850 for a four-passenger craft, and $2775 for six. Flyover tours are cheaper. To find fellow travelers to split the cost, phone the air companies in advance, or ask around town. Most flightseeing companies are based in Fort Simpson, but air companies based in places like Yellowknife can also bring you out here – at a price.

Paddling

Raft and canoe trips can be arranged with a licensed outfitter. Prices range from $4000 to $6500, depending on distance. Try to book months in advance. Canoes require some basic experience; rafts, steered by a guide, are relaxing and suitable for all.

Most trips begin at Moose Ponds, Rabbitkettle Lake or Virginia Falls, because those are where floatplanes can land. From Moose Ponds to Rabbitkettle is about 160km, much of it grade III white water. For the 118km from Rabbitkettle to the falls, the river meanders placidly through broad valleys. Once the falls are portaged, it's another 252km to Blackstone Territorial Park, first through steep-sided, turbulent canyons, and then along the broad Liard River. The lower-river trip requires seven to 10 days. From Rabbitkettle it's around 14 days, while from Moose Ponds it's 21.

Nahanni Wilderness Adventures
ADVENTURE TOUR
(☏ 403-678-3374; www.nahanniwild.com) Recommended operator, with trips ranging from eight ($4695) to 22 ($6150) days.

Black Feather ADVENTURE TOUR

(☎705-746-1372; www.blackfeather.com) This excellent operator's offerings include special family and women-only trips.

Nahanni River Adventures ADVENTURE TOUR

(☎867-668-3180; www.nahanni.com) Highly rated adventure travel company with top-notch guides.

🛏 Sleeping

Camping is allowed along riverbanks. There are eight designated campgrounds; the ones at Virginia Falls and Rabbitkettle Lake are staffed. Virginia Falls must be reserved ahead as admission quotas are strict.

ⓘ Information

You can obtain park information and permits in Fort Simpson at **Parks Canada** (☎867-695-7750; www.parkscanada.gc.ca/nahanni; cnr 100 St & 100 Ave; ⊙8:30am-noon & 1-5pm daily Jul & Aug, reduced hours Sep-Jun). The day-use fee is $24.50; longer-term visitors pay a flat fee of $147.20.

ⓘ Getting There & Away

If you are traveling independently, you'll need to charter an airplane into the park by contacting a flightseeing company.

Liard Trail

The dirt Liard Trail (Hwy 7) branches off the Mackenzie Hwy (Hwy 1) and heads south through the Liard Valley, with the Mackenzie Mountains appearing to the west. Black bear and bison abound. The only gas is at Fort Simpson and Fort Liard. Halfway between Checkpoint and Fort Liard is **Blackstone Territorial Park** (campsites/RV sites $15/22.50; ⊙May-Sep; 🐾), with a nature display, campground shaded by birch and spruce forest, short hiking trails and terrific views over mountains and the Liard-Nahanni confluence. Most South Nahanni canoeing trips end here.

Fort Liard

Fort Liard has lush forests, prim log homes and the balmiest weather in the NWT. This Dene village still values its traditions, such as weaving birch-bark baskets, which are ornately decorated with porcupine quills. These can be bought at one of the NWT's finest craft shops, **Acho Dene Native Crafts**

(☎867-770-4161; www.adnc.ca; cnr Main St & Poplar Rd; ⊙9am-7pm Mon-Sat, to 5pm Sun) ✈, in the middle of town. It doubles as the visitors center.

Before you reach the village of nearly 600 souls, the free, rudimentary **Hay Lake Community Campground** has drinking water and an outhouse. The **Liard Valley General Store & Motel** (☎867-770-4441; cnr Main St & Black Water Rd; s/d $125/150, r with kitchenette $155; ⊛❄), on the far side of town, has 12 huge rooms. It's often full, so make reservations.

A cafe and a service station are across the road from Acho Dene Native Crafts. The British Columbia border is 38km south.

SAHTU

Mountain-studded Sahtu is inaccessible by road except in winter. The Mackenzie, swollen by water draining from one-fifth of Canada, cuts its way through here, in places more than 3km wide. Either side, bald-headed peaks arise, guarding some of the wildest country – and best hiking and paddling – left in the world.

Norman Wells

POP 727

This historic oil town springs from the boreal frontier, halfway between Fort Simpson and Inuvik. It's a launch-pad for canoeists, hikers tackling the Canol Heritage Trail and fisherfolk heading for Great Bear Lake.

⊙ Sights & Activities

Norman Wells Historical Centre MUSEUM

(www.normanwellsmuseum.com; Mackenzie Dr; ⊙10am-5:30pm Mon-Fri, 10am-4pm Sat, noon-4pm Sun) FREE A labor of love, this small museum showcases regional history, geology, arts and crafts, and has information on the rivers and the Canol Heritage Trail. There's a cool gift shop, too.

Canoe North Adventures CANOEING, HIKING

(☎May-Sep 867-587-4440, Oct-Apr 519-941-6654; www.canoenorthadventures.com; Beaver Lane; ⊙Jun-Sep) This excellent setup has decades of experience organizing rugged canoeing trips. They also arrange hiking excursions on the Canol Heritage Trail. At their base at the North-Wright floatplane dock (open June to September), they hire out all necessary equipment for self-guided trips and offer accommodation in private and bunk rooms ($60 to $80 per person) with cooking facilities.

Sleeping & Eating

Annoyingly, the **campground** (campsites free) is a few kilometers upriver. Campers often pitch tents on the riverbanks by town. There are three hotels, all with restaurants.

★ Heritage Hotel   HOTEL $$$
(☎867-587-5000; www.heritagehotelnwt.com; 27 Mackenzie Dr; r incl breakfast $265; ❄@✆) This clean, minimalist, rather posh hotel seems out of place in working-class Wells. Many of the sparkling rooms have river views, plus there's a spa, an adjacent small golf course, and the Ventures dining room (mains $17 to $35), which, with mains such as Thai-marinated steak, is the best eatery in town – no contest.

❶ Getting There & Around

North-Wright Airways (☎867-587-2333; www.north-wrightairways.com), **Canadian North** (www.canadiannorth.com) and First Air (p799) serve Yellowknife and Inuvik.

In winter, an ice road runs 333km from Wrigley to Norman Wells and continues north as far as Colville Lake.

WESTERN ARCTIC

Comprising the Mackenzie Delta, the Richardson Mountains and several High Arctic islands, this is the NWT's most diverse region. Several national parks are here, plus aboriginal hamlets and prefabricated Inuvik, reached via the heart-wrenchingly beautiful Dempster Hwy.

Inuvik
POP 3463

Inuvik, a few dozen kilometers from the mouth of the Mackenzie River, was erected in 1955 as an administrative post. With its rainbow-colored rows of houses and warren of above-ground heated pipes, it still feels like a work in progress. During the summer's constant daylight, lots of visitors arrive via the rugged, awesome 747km Dempster Hwy from the Yukon.

◉ Sights & Activities

Our Lady of Victory Church   CHURCH
(☎867-777-2236; 174 Mackenzie Rd) The town landmark is Our Lady of Victory Church, also called the Igloo Church, with a resplendent white dome and a lovely interior. Contact the visitors center (p816) for opening times.

Dempster Highway   OUTDOORS
One of the best things you can do in Inuvik is get out of town to see the countryside. The easiest way is to drive the Dempster Hwy, a westward route into some of the most stunning alpine scenery available. Several operators rent vehicles.

☞ Tours

Most tours involve flights over the braided Mackenzie Delta and the weather-beaten Arctic coast, where trees peter out and the landscape becomes riddled with pingos (ice-cored hills that erupt from the tundra). Photographers should try for a seat at the rear of the plane.

Arctic Adventures   ADVENTURE TOUR
(White Huskies; ☎867-777-3535; www.whitehuskies.com; 25 Carn St) Year-round excursions include chauffeured runs on the Dempster Hwy and, in winter, daily dogsled tours ($158) with

---

CANOL HERITAGE TRAIL

The Canol Heritage Trail leads 358km southwest to the Yukon border, where a road leads to Ross River and the Yukon highway system. The trail was built at enormous monetary and human cost during WWII to transport oil to Whitehorse; 'Canol' is shorthand for 'Canadian Oil.' The huge project was abandoned in 1945, with the war nearly over and cheaper oil sources found.

The route traverses peaks, canyons and barrens. Wildlife is abundant and there are numerous deep river crossings. There are no facilities, although you can get a little shelter in old Quonset huts. Hiking the whole length takes three to four weeks and most people arrange food drops. Some visitors helicopter from Norman Wells to reach the most interesting sections. Contact Northwest Territories Tourism (p801) for outfitters.

beautiful snow-white huskies. They also rent vehicles and canoes.

Up North Tours ADVENTURE TOUR
(☑867-678-0510; www.upnorthtours.ca; 69 Mackenzie Rd) Offers numerous tours, including flights to Tuktoyaktuk on the Arctic coast ($440 per person) to view pingos and ice houses, summer boating in the Mackenzie Delta ($165 per person) and winter snowmobiling.

✦ Festivals & Events

Sunrise Festival FIREWORKS
(☑867-777-2607; ⊙early Jan) Fireworks on the ice greet the first sunrise after 30 days of darkness.

Great Northern Arts Festival ARTS
(☑867-777-8638; www.gnaf.org; ⊙mid-Jul) The North's top art festival draws carvers, painters and other creators from across the circumpolar world. It's great for buying Arctic art, watching it being made, and participating in cultural events.

🛏 Sleeping

Jàk Park Campground CAMPGROUND $
(☑867-777-3613; www.campingnwt.ca; campsites/RV sites $15/28; ⊙Jun-Aug; 🐾) This pretty government-operated campground, about 6km south of town on the Dempster Hwy, provides hot showers and firewood. There's a good view of the delta and the breeze keeps the mosquitoes at bay a bit. There's another campsite downtown.

★ Arctic Chalet GUESTHOUSE $$
(☑867-777-3535; www.arcticchalet.com; 25 Carn St; r $100-200; ⊙🐾🐾) With sunny cabins in a boreal glade 3km from town, this is Inuvik's best place to stay. Each building has simple kitchen facilities and there's one private cabin. Some rooms are en suite. The energetic owners rent canoes, kayaks and cars, run dogsledding tours and are objective sources of local info.

Nova Inn HOTEL $$
(☑867-777-6682; www.novainninuvik.ca; 300 Mackenzie Rd; s/d $135/175; 🐾🐾) There are three smart hotels in Inuvik now, and they're all pretty good for this latitude. The Nova wins plaudits for its helpful staff, decent prices and smart, spacious, well-equipped rooms with comfy beds and gas fireplaces.

Polar B&B B&B $$
(☑867-777-2554; www.polarbedandbreakfast.com; 75 Mackenzie Rd; s/d $105/115) This B&B has four large rooms with shared bathroom, common area and kitchen. It's very centrally located above the intriguing bookstore, which your hosts also run.

✕ Eating

Café Gallery CAFE $
(☑867-777-4829; 90 Mackenzie Rd; snacks $4-12; ⊙8am-5pm Mon-Sat) The town's best, make that only, coffee stop, this does decent espressos and is the locals' favorite spot for a latte and a gossip. They also do soup, muffins and other snacks.

★ Tonimoes CANADIAN $$
(☑867-777-2861; 185 Mackenzie Rd; lunch mains $10-13, dinner mains $12-36; ⊙7am-2pm & 5-9pm) With standard breakfasts, burgery lunches and a surf-and-turf dinner menu, this low-lit dining room in the Mackenzie Hotel is the town's sole respectable eatery.

ℹ Information

Parks Canada (☑867-777-8800; www.pc.gc. ca; 187 Mackenzie Rd; ⊙8:30am-5pm Jun-Aug, reduced hours Sep-May) Has info on Tuktut Nogait, Ivvavik and Aulavik National Parks. Park visitors must register and deregister here.

Western Arctic Regional Visitors Centre (☑867-777-4727, info off-season 867-777-7237; www.inuvik.ca; 284 Mackenzie Rd; ⊙9am-8pm May-Sep) Has tourism literature, eager staff, and a nature display.

ℹ Getting There & Away

AIR

The airport is 14km south of town. **Town Cab** (☑867-777-4777) charges $25 to downtown.

Air North (www.flyairnorth.com) flies to Dawson City, Old Crow and Whitehorse. **Aklak Air** (www.aklakair.ca) hits Tuktoyaktuk, Paulatuk and Sachs Harbour and provides charters to the national parks. Canadian North (p799) and First Air (p799) service Norman Wells and Yellowknife.

CAR

Arctic Chalet Car Rental (www.arcticchalet. com; 25 Carn St) and **NorCan** (☑867-777-2346; www.norcan.yk.ca) rent vehicles and have airport counters. If you are driving, it's vital that you check Dempster Hwy **road and ferry**

conditions (📱800-661-0750; www.dot.gov.
nt.ca and www.511yukon.ca).

Tuktoyaktuk

POP 854

About 140km northeast of Inuvik on the
storm-battered coast is Tuktoyaktuk, long
home of the whale-hunting Inuit and now
also a land base for Beaufort Sea oil and
gas explorations.

Pods of belugas may be seen in summer.
Visible year round are pingos, of which
the Tuk Peninsula has the world's highest
concentration. Some 1400 of these huge
mounds of earth and ice dot the land and
have been designated the **Pingo Canadian
Landmark**. The **hamlet office** (📱867-977-
2286; http://tuktoyaktuk.lgant.ca) can provide
more information on services.

There is a cold war **military base**, old
whaling buildings, and two charming
churches. A highway from Inuvik is gradually being built but, until its completion
in 2018, land access is limited to a winter
ice road. Most visitors arrive by air as part
of summer day trips from Inuvik.

Tuktut Nogait National Park

This wild place is a major calving ground
for bluenose caribou. It's an excellent place
to observe birds of prey and has spectacular pingos and beautiful walkable canyons.
There are no services or facilities: for information, contact Parks Canada (p816) in Inuvik. To get here, fly to Paulatuk, 45km west
of the park, where you can contract guides.

Banks Island

Adrift in the Arctic Ocean, Banks Island has
abundant wildlife by polar standards, and is
one of the world's best places to see musk
ox. The island has two bird sanctuaries with
summer flocks of snow geese and seabirds.
Sachs Harbour, a small Inuvialuit community, is the only settlement. On the north end
of the island, seldom-visited **Aulavik National Park** covers 12,275 sq km. It has the
world's largest concentration of musk ox, as
well as badlands, tundra and archaeological
sites. Contact Parks Canada (p816) in Inuvik
for details about visiting. **Aklak Air** (📱867-
777-3555; www.aklakair.ca) fly three times
weekly from Inuvik to Sachs Harbour.

Nunavut

Best Places to Eat

➡ Granite Room (p823)

➡ Dorset Suites (p827)

➡ Gallery (p824)

Best Places to Stay

➡ Dorset Suites (p827)

➡ Accommodations by the Sea (p822)

➡ Discovery Lodge Hotel (p822)

➡ Nanuq Lodge (p829)

➡ Nunattaq Suites (p822)

Why Go?

Picture a treeless, ice-encrusted wilderness lashed by unrelenting weather with a population density that makes Greenland seem claustrophobic. Add polar bears, narwhals, beluga whales and a scattered Aboriginal population who have successfully mastered a landscape so harsh that foreigners dared not colonize it.

Nunavut is Canada's largest and most lightly populated subdivision, a mythical assortment of uninhabited islands and frigid ocean that exists on the planet's climatic and geographic extremes. Visitors here face multiple obstacles, not least perennial blizzards, no roads and massive travel costs. But those that do get through have the benefit of welcoming communities and awe-inspiring natural wonders, as well as the privilege of joining a small band of intrepid trailblazers, safe in the knowledge that they are setting foot where few have trodden before.

When to Go
Iqaluit

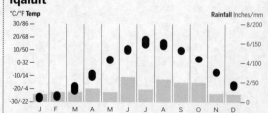

Jul & Aug Prime visiting time during the short hyperactive summer season.

Apr & May The ideal time for dog-sledding and other snow sports and activities.

Jun The midnight sun coincides with Iqaluit's Alianait Arts Festival.

Nunavut Highlights

1 Feel small beside the planet's most precipitous cliffs in **Auyuittuq National Park** (p826).

2 Encounter soapstone polar bears – but watch out for real ones – in the art mecca of **Cape Dorset** (p827).

3 Chomp char, chew caribou and munch musk ox at eateries in Canada's most curious capital, **Iqaluit** (p820).

4 Moonwalk across awesomely lunar **Resolute** (p828), where nothing grows despite four months of midnight sun.

5 Canoe amid cascades and caribou on the Edenic **Soper River** (p825).

6 Hit Pond Inlet for floe-edge wildlife-watching or the bird sanctuaries of **Sirmilik National Park** (p828).

7 Get seriously far north at **Quttinirpaaq National Park** (p828).

8 Boat in to see wildlife up close in **Ukkusiksalik National Park** (p830).

History

Nunavut has been populated for over 4000 years, though the Inuit (Thule) arrived from the west just a millennium ago. They lived nomadic lifestyles, pursuing game by season and devising an ingenious climate-proof material culture.

Vikings likely visited Baffin Island (Helluland in the sagas); later, in 1576, Martin Frobisher came seeking the Northwest Passage. Over the centuries came more explorers (including Sir John Franklin, who disappeared here in 1845), whalers, traders and missionaries. In a vast land, these visits had comparatively little effect on the Inuit.

After WWII, Canada finally recognized the Arctic's strategic importance. In the 1950s and '60s Inuit were settled into villages and, in some cases, relocated to the High Arctic to bolster national sovereignty.

In the 1960s and '70s rising political awareness inspired dreams of Inuit self-government. After years of negotiations, Nunavut split from the Northwest Territories in 1999 to become a separate territory.

Land & Climate

Gargantuan Nunavut sprawls across Canada's northeast. About half – the mainland – is the 'Barrenlands,' an expanse of undulating rock and tundra cut through by major rivers. Even more barren is the Arctic archipelago, scattering north to Ellesmere Island, just shy of the Pole, and east to enormous Baffin Island, home to sky-scraping mountains.

It's chilly. Snow holds sway from September to June; relentless winds create hard-to-fathom chill factors. July to mid-August is summer, when seas thaw beneath the perpetual sun.

The territory's 26 communities are incredibly isolated and rely on air transport and the July 'sealift,' when ships bring a year's worth of supplies to otherwise inaccessible harbors. Houses sit on stilts to negate ferocious winds. Water is rationed and delivered daily from a central village deposit by truck.

> ### ⓘ TOURIST INFORMATION
> **Nunavut Tourism** (☎ 866-686-2888; www.nunavuttourism.com) is the territory's visitor oracle, with a comprehensive website. They answer queries, and can send the swell *Explore Nunavut* magazine-guide (also downloadable).

> ### NUNAVUT FAST FACTS
> ➡ Population: 31,900
> ➡ Area: 2,038,722 sq km
> ➡ Capital: Iqaluit
> ➡ Quirky fact: There are more polar bears (17,000) than men (16,400) or women (15,500) in Nunavut

ⓘ Getting There & Around

Nunavut is essentially roadless; the only way to get here and around is via (impoverishingly pricey) flights. Iqaluit is served from Montréal, Ottawa and Yellowknife. Cambridge Bay is linked to Yellowknife, and Rankin Inlet to Yellowknife and Winnipeg. Smaller communities are reached from those three hubs. There are twice-weekly flights between Iqaluit and Nuuk, Greenland, from June to August.

Flying standby halves the price of normal flights. In winter it's not great, as fish get priority and there are lots of weather-induced cancellations, but in summer (if you're flexible) you've a chance of saving some money.

Cell-phone coverage is very patchy and limited to the Bell network.

IQALUIT

POP 6699

Nunavut's capital, Iqaluit (ee-*kal*-oo-eet), is a curious place. The dusty, debris-strewn townscape, with its spectacular natural setting and moon-base buildings, houses a fascinating mixture of Inuit professionals, politicians and drop-outs, Johnny-come-latelies from around Canada (and beyond) drawn by high salaries, enormous SUVs with elaborately courteous drivers limited by a few short kilometers of road, and barking dogs contesting territory with huge bossy ravens. It's a good introduction to the region, and has good places to stay and eat, as well as fine natural attractions nearby.

History

For centuries, nomadic Inuit trekked to the Sylvia Grinnell River to spear char in the roiling summer waters. They called the area Iqaluit: place of fish.

In 1576 English captain Martin Frobisher showed up seeking the Northwest Passage. He unearthed glittering yellow ore and sailed home with a million pounds of worthless fool's gold.

Local Inuit kept fishing, interrupted occasionally by whalers, explorers and missionaries. During WWII, an American airbase was established here. After the war, Canadian forces stayed on, and the outpost, named Frobisher Bay, became the administrative center of the eastern Arctic.

In 1995 voters picked Iqaluit – now officially named as such – as Nunavut's capital. Since then the population has more than doubled.

◉ Sights & Activities

Despite spongy, ankle-bending terrain, Iqaluit's wide-open landscapes make hiking a delight. Trails are few, but no trees means it's difficult to get lost.

★Nunatta Sunakkutaangit Museum
MUSEUM, GALLERY

(☑867-979-5537; Sinaa St; ⊙1-5pm) **FREE** As well as a permanent gallery of Inuit artifacts, this friendly little museum in an old Hudson's Bay Company building has high-quality exhibitions of contemporary artists. These, plus the interesting gift shop, make this a top place to pick up local art.

Sylvia Grinnell Territorial Park
PARK

(www.nunavutparks.ca; Iqaluit Rd) This park, 2km southwest of town and divided by the river of the same name, gives a good sense of the local landscapes via various short paths (25 to 45 minutes one way) leading to a waterfall, rapids and escarpments.

Legislative Assembly
NOTABLE BUILDING

(☑867-975-5000; www.assembly.nu.ca; Federal Rd; ⊙9am-5pm Mon-Fri, tours 1:30pm Jun-Aug or by appointment) **FREE** Nunavut's prefab parliament is no marble-columned forum, but has touches such as sealskin benches and a narwhal-tusk ceremonial mace. Local art is displayed in the foyer.

Apex
NEIGHBORHOOD

Five kilometers from downtown, Apex is now Iqaluit's beach suburb, but was where nomadic Inuit began to settle when modern Iqaluit was an airbase. On the shore is the photogenic **Hudson Bay Trading Post** complex. It's an interesting hike along the hilly waterfront from downtown. At low tide continue past Apex to explore **Tarr Inlet**.

Qaummaarviit Territorial Park
ISLAND

(www.nunavutparks.ca) This tiny bay island is a 12km boat ride from Iqaluit and preserves a 750-year-old Inuit (Thule) winter camp. You can see well-preserved sod houses and a grave site. It's a great half-day trip: to get there, contact Iqaluit outfitters.

☞ Tours

Consult the Nunavut Tourism website (www.nunavuttourism.com) or the visitors center for available tours and outfitters. Reserve early.

Arctic Kingdom
ADVENTURE TOUR

(☑867-979-1900, 867-222-3995; www.arctickingdom.com; Hotel Arctic, Bldg 923, Federal Rd) This professional set-up can organize everything from half-day hiking, boating or snowmobiling trips around Iqaluit to multiday wildlife-watching adventures throughout Nunavut. The best bet for something at short notice.

Inukpak Outfitting
ADVENTURE TOUR

(☑867-222-6489; www.inukpakoutfitting.ca) Inukpak rents inflatable canoes, camping equipment, satellite phones and polar clothing. Also run winter dog-sledding, snowmobiling, and igloo-building, and summer hiking, canoeing and sea-kayaking.

ARCTIC PACKAGES

Independent travel offers the chance for trailblazing, saving cash and seeing the reality. Except, perhaps, in Nunavut. Here you should consider a package tour: only groups can achieve the economies of scale that make the Arctic affordable.

Cruises, especially, let you visit several Nunavut communities and offer excellent wildlife-spotting. Sure, a $5000 cruise is costly, but you'll blow as much on a do-it-yourself trip of similar duration. The **Great Canadian Adventure Company** (☑780-414-1676; www.adventures.ca) offers good-value trips; Inuit-operated **Cruise North** (☑866-263-3220; www.cruisenorthexpeditions.com) also has lots of options.

Tours are numerous, ranging from guided national-park hiking to trips to middle-of-nowhere wilderness lodges used as bases for wildlife-watching. See **Nunavut Tourism** for details (☑866-686-2888, 867-979-6551; www.nunavuttourism.com).

Northwinds Arctic Adventures
ADVENTURE TOUR

(☎867-979-0551; www.northwinds-arctic.com) These seasoned pros lead arctic expeditions and dog-sledding programs and have worked with everyone from the BBC's *Top Gear* to *Canadian Geographic*.

★★ Festivals

Alianait Arts Festival
CULTURE

(www.alianait.ca; ☉late Jun–early Jul) A midsummer celebration of Inuit culture encompassing art, music, film, storytelling, food and a circus. Events such as seal thanksgiving and concerts around National Aboriginal Day (June 21) are sometimes tied in.

🛏 Sleeping

Camping is the only cheap option. For everything else, book ahead and hemorrhage cash. Hotels offer free airport pick-up.

Sylvia Grinnell Territorial Park
CAMPGROUND $

(Iqaluit Rd; campsites free; 🅿) There are no facilities here except pit toilets. Take the road to the right after entering, rather than continuing up to the hut on the hill.

★ Accommodations by the Sea
B&B $$

(☎867-979-0131; www.accommodationsbythe sea.ca; Bldg 2536, Paurngaq Cr; s/d with breakfast from $129/149; ⊛@🛜) A half-hour walk from downtown, this end-of-the-road spot has a lovely bay outlook. It's a comfortable, modern place decked out ski-chalet style in wood. Guests have use of a kitchen, with breakfast materials, and a great lounge with DVDs and views. Rooms are cozy – cheaper ones share a bathroom – with decent (for Nunavut) wi-fi. They'll pick you up from the airport.

★ Discovery Lodge Hotel
HOTEL $$$

(☎867-979-4433; www.discoverylodge.com; Bldg1056, Mivvik St; s/d/ste $225/245/320; ⊛🛜) Between airport and center, this well-run place sports a recent interior refit, and the fresh decor stands out from the town's samey other hotels. Big flatscreen TVs, cozy bathrooms, lots of hanging space and artistic touches make this an appealing stay. Little details such as free laundry and chaise longues in the business suites seal the deal.

Nunattaq Suites
B&B $$$

(☎867-975-2745; www.nunattaqsuites.com; Bldg 4141, Imiqtarviminiq Rd; r $189; ⊛🛜) This spotless, large, well-equipped grey-blue house in the higher part of town makes a fine base. Long views over a small lake can be enjoyed from handsome, comfortable rooms, which come with lofty sloping ceilings and excellent modern bathrooms. Guests also have the run of the kitchen, laundry facilities, and a lounge-balcony area with BBQ. The friendly host will make you very welcome and comes in daily to make up the rooms.

INUIT CULTURE & LANGUAGE

Most Nunavut residents are Inuit (singular: Inuk), whose transition from an isolated, nomadic culture to a settled population has been very swift: many living Inuit ('Eskimo' is considered insensitive and embarrassingly archaic) elders grew up moving between hunting grounds, living in sealskin tents and igloos.

The rapid change hasn't been without problems. Alcohol abuse, drugs, lack of opportunities, obesity, crime and suicide are all prevalent. Nevertheless, Nunavut still buzzes with optimism and can be the friendliest of places.

The population is concentrated almost wholly in settlements, which tend to be ramshackle. Inuit remain at heart rural hunter-gatherers: though the tools have changed, nature and its rhythms still hold sway. Harvesting animals remains a holy sacrament.

Inuktitut is the primary tongue of 70% of Nunavummiut, and, for some, the only language. It's not easy, and it's hard to read, as it's written in syllabics.

You'll generally get by fine with English, but a few local words will go down well:

How are you? *Qanuippit?*

Thank you *Nakurmiik*

Yes *Ii*

Good morning *Ullaakkut*

I am fine *Qanuinngitunga*

You're welcome *Ilaali*

No *Aakka*

Good afternoon *Unnusakkut*

EXTREME FACTS

➡ At over 2 million sq km, Nunavut is larger than many of the world's most populous nations including Mexico and Indonesia. If it were a country, it would rank 13th.

➡ Its total population is equivalent to that of Gibraltar (6.8 sq km).

➡ Nunavut has by far the highest birth rate of any Canadian province or territory.

➡ The territory has only 21km of public roads and almost no trees.

➡ It is home to nearly half of the world's polar bears.

➡ Alert (82.5°N) on Ellesmere Island is the planet's northernmost permanently inhabited settlement.

Capital Suites HOTEL $$$
(☑867-975-4000; www.capitalsuites.ca; Bldg 807, Aviq St; studio/ste $200/260; ⊜@⊛) Good facilities and commodious, spacious rooms, most of which are suites with kitchenette, belie the slightly plasticky feel of the lobby area here. Two- and three-bedroom suites are great for families or groups. It's very central, but off the main road.

Frobisher Inn HOTEL $$$
(☑867-979-2222; www.frobisherinn.com; Astro Hill Tce; r $260, ste $300-320; @⊛) On the hill, the 'Frobe' is a comfortable complex with good facilities including a convenience store, eateries, gym and business center. Modern rooms are warm and cheerfully colored, with flatscreen TVs and coffee makers. Try for the bay side for great views. Bathrooms are small.

Hotel Arctic HOTEL $$$
(☑867-979-6684; www.hotelarctic.ca; Bldg 923, Federal Rd; r $220-250, ste $300; ⊛) As central as it gets, this has dullish but commodious rooms including a good desk and office chair, snack-making facilities and small bathrooms. There's a gym and an on-site tour agency, and you can use computers in the nearby sister hotel.

🍴 Eating & Drinking

The best eateries are in the hotels. Expect big portions at hugely inflated prices (most stuff is flown in). Arctic specials such as char, caribou and musk ox are widely available.

In Iqaluit, most crimes and suicides are linked to drinking, so the town clamps down on alcohol. It's only served in hotels and there's no liquor store. In other Nunavut communities, alcohol isn't served at all.

Caribrew Café CAFE $
(www.frobisherinn.com; Astro Hill Tce; light meals $5-10; ⊙7am-6pm Mon-Fri, 9am-4pm Sat & Sun) This appealing place occupies a widened corridor in the Frobisher Inn, offering a warm refuge from the wind and reasonable value for coffee, banana bread, salads and sandwiches.

Grind & Brew CAFE $$
(☑867-979-0606; Sinaa St; mains $21-28, pizzas $17-31; ⊙6am-6pm, delivery later) Cappuccinos be damned: Iqaluit's friendly blue-collar beachfront coffee shop, just down the road from the museum, offers basic joe, deliciously greasy breakfast sandwiches, and pizza and Asian dishes (delivery available).

Yummy Shawarma & Pizza KEBAB $$
(☑867-979-1515; Bldg 1085E, Mivvik St; shawarma $10-15, pizza $24-32; ⊙11am-10pm Mon-Sat, to 7:30pm Sun) It's big news when a new cuisine comes to town, and Nunavut now has its first kebab joint, with a pleasant, Lebanese-themed dining area. You can diverge from the shawarma-pizza core of the menu to vine leaves, tabbouleh and baklava. Delivery available.

★ Granite Room FRENCH, FUSION $$$
(☑867-979-4433; www.discoverylodge.com; Bldg 1056, Mivvik St; mains $54-63; ⊙6:30-9am, noon-2pm, 6-9pm) Nunavut's top restaurant in the Discovery Lodge Hotel is consistently better and more imaginative than the competition. The fare is heavily French-influenced and offers a wide-ranging list of specials to complement an à la carte offering that includes northern meats such as arctic char and caribou. Homemade desserts are also excellent. On Sunday, 11am is brunchtime ($45): it's the best for miles...and miles.

Gallery
CANADIAN $$$

(☑867-979-2222; Astro Hill Tce; mains $34-50; ☺7-10:30am, 11:30am-1:30pm & 5-8:30pm Mon-Fri, from 8am Sat & Sun; ⚐) A popular, palatable dining room at the Frobisher Inn offering tasty pasta combinations and well-presented steak and Northern cuisine, including caribou, must ox and char flavors. There are pleasant bay views and the service is good.

Water's Edge & Kickin'
Caribou
STEAKHOUSE, BAR $$$

(☑867-979-4726; www.hotelarctic.ca; 923 Federal Rd; mains $24-55; ☺restaurant 7-10am, 11:30am-2pm & 5-8:30pm, pub noon-3pm & 4pm-midnight Mon-Sat, 11am-4pm Sun) With plenty of natural light (in summer anyway) flooding through the multiple windows, this makes a relaxed place for a meal of steak or seafood. Quality is average and portions are sizeable. The attached pub does cheaper bar meals ($12 to $22) until later. It gets rowdy at weekends, but it's usually friendly.

Storehouse Bar & Grill
BAR

(Astro Hill Tce; ☺5pm-12:30am Mon-Sat) As befits the main drinkery in town, this big, good-looking watering hole in the Frobisher Inn is a little bit of everything: pub, pool hall, sports bar and disco. The food (pizza, burgers, ribs; mains $10 to $22) is also good, but don't expect beer out of anything other than a can.

🛍 Shopping

Inuit prints, carvings and tapestries are world renowned and are widely available in Iqaluit – at a price. For much lower deals on less-refined pieces, you'll be approached on the street and in hotel restaurants by locals hawking wares.

Rannva
CLOTHING

(☑867-979-3183; www.rannva.com; Bldg 3102, Angel St; ☺4-6pm or by appointment) ✒ In Apex, Faroese designer Rannva Erlingsdóttir Simonsen sews together the ancient and the chic, generating beautiful fur and sealskin garments.

Carvings Nunavut
HANDICRAFTS

(www.carvingsnunavut.com; Bldg 626, Queen Elizabeth Way; ☺9am-5pm Mon-Fri, 11am-3pm Sat & Sun) ✒ Hidden away in Tumiit Plaza building, this has an excellent collection of Inuit sculpture for sale and not the worst prices in town.

ℹ TAG AWARE

Keep an eye out for the **Nuna Tag** while shopping for handicrafts. It's a guarantee that the item has been hand-produced by a Nunavut artist, so you know your dollars are staying up here where they should. See www.authentic-nunavut.com for more.

Arctic Ventures
BOOKS, SOUVENIRS

(Queen Elizabeth Way; ☺10am-10pm Mon-Sat, 1-10pm Sun) Upstairs in this multipurpose shop is a spectacular selection of arctic books and CDs, as well as souvenirs. They also run a shop at the airport.

ℹ Information

Note that 911 is not the emergency number in Nunavut. See below for ambulance, fire and police.

Ambulance & Fire (☑867-979-4422)

Iqaluit Centennial Library (www.public-libraries.nu.ca; Sinaa St; ☺1-6pm Mon, Wed & Fri, 3-8pm Tue & Thu, 1-4pm Sat & Sun) Free internet in the visitors center building.

Police (☑867-979-1111)

Qikiqtani Hospital (☑867-979-7300; Niaqunngusiaq Rd; ☺24hr)

Royal Bank of Canada (cnr Queen Elizabeth Way & Niaqunngusiaq Rd) At the Four Corners intersection.

Unikkaarvik Visitors Centre (☑867-979-4636; Sinaa St; ☺8:30am-6pm) Offers pamphlets, an informative museum and nature display and a reference collection of Nunavut books and videos that you can browse or watch in comfort. Often closed between noon and 1pm as staff meet flights.

ℹ Getting There & Around

Canadian North and First Air serves most Nunavut communities from here. Central Iqaluit is walkable; even the airport is a 10-minute stroll from downtown. Cabs charge $6 per person to anywhere. Hail them on the street – even if they have passengers – and expect to share. Try **Pai-Pa Taxi** (☑867-979-5222).

BAFFIN REGION

Comprising Nunavut's eastern and High Arctic islands, this region reaches from the swampy, forested isles of James Bay to the jagged peaks of Ellesmere Island, 3000km north. Half of Nunavut's population lives here, and visitors will find the best scenery, outdoor opportunities and tourism infrastructure.

Katannilik Territorial Park

One of Nunavut's finest parks is close to Iqaluit. *Katannilik* means 'place of waterfalls,' and comprises two main features.

A Canadian Heritage waterway, aquamarine **Soper River** splashes 50 navigable kilometers through a deep, fertile valley, past cascades, caribou, gemstone deposits and dwarf-willow forest to **Kimmirut** (population 455; www.kimmirut.ca). Most paddlers charter a plane from Iqaluit to the riverside airstrip at Mt Joy, float three to five days from the put-in to Kimmirut, and then fly back to Iqaluit. **Kenn Borek Air** (867-979-0040; www.borekair.com) do charters.

Hikers and skiers take the **Itijjagiaq Trail**, a traditional 120km route over the tablelands of the Meta Incognita Peninsula and through the Soper valley. From a trailhead on Frobisher Bay, about 10km west of Iqaluit, it will take you about a week to get to Kimmirut. Iqaluit outfitters can take you to the trailhead by boat.

For more details, contact **Nunavut Parks** (Mirnguiqsirviit; 867-975-7700; www.nunavutparks.com). Before entering, register either at the visitors center in Iqaluit (which stocks maps) or **Katannilik Visitors Centre** (867-939-2416; www.nunavutparks.com; 9am-5pm Mon-Fri, 1-4pm Sat & Sun Jun-Oct) in Kimmirut. There's a simple campground just outside Kimmirut, which is a scenic, friendly Inuit village worth a visit in itself. First Air links Kimmirut and Iqaluit four times weekly ($420 one-way).

Pangnirtung

POP 1425

Among Nunavut's outlying communities, Pangnirtung, or 'Pang,' is the best destination, with a thriving artistic scene and outdoor opportunities galore. Located 40km south of the Arctic Circle, Pang's natural beauty is stunning, set on a fjord and towered over by steep Mt Duval. It's the gateway to even more spectacular scenery at Auyuittuq National Park.

Sights & Activities

Stroll the picturesque waterfront admiring the handsome buildings of the old Hudson Bay Company blubber station. Hiking options include a trail up Mt Duval – a stiff climb rewarded by staggering views.

Uqqurmiut Centre for Arts & Crafts
GALLERY
(867-473-8669; www.uqqurmiut.com; 9am-noon & 1-5pm Mon-Fri) Pang is famous for weaving and prints, and this extraordinary place – a top-notch facility – brings it all together. There are few tapestry studios in the world, but one is here and you can watch the weavers at work. Artists create prints via a variety of techniques in the adjacent workshop, and there's a stunning archived collection available to browse and buy. Famous crocheted hats are another highlight, as are carvings and toasty-warm scarves.

Kekerten Historic Park
HISTORIC SITE
About 50km south of town is this old island whaling station. A heritage trail leads past the remains of 19th-century houses, tools and graves. Outfitters offer day-trips for $180 per person (minimum three people).

Alivaktuk Outfitting Services
OUTDOORS
(867-473-8721; www.alivaktukoutfitting.ca) Joavie, a recommended outfitter, can set you up with wildlife-spotting boat trips, fishing camps, igloo-building, day-trips to Kekerten Historic Park and excursions to Auyuittuq National Park.

PEO Services
OUTDOORS
(867-473-4060; www.kilabukoutfitting.com) From July to October, offers trips to Auyuittuq National Park and Kekerten Historic Park, wildlife-spotting boat trips on Cumberland Sound and fishing trips.

Sleeping & Eating

Territorial Campground
CAMPGROUND $
(867-473-8737; campsites $5;) Picturesquely situated atop town by the rushing Duval River, this has wooden shelter platforms to help with the howling wind, barbecues, pit toilets and great views; watch out for theft. Pay at the visitors center.

Hannah's Homestay
B&B $$$
(867-473-8834; jtautuajuk@hotmail.com; Bldg 765; per person incl breakfast $120;) Near the top of town, the spotless home of great-grandmother Hannah and three more generations is a great place to stay. Cozy rooms

share a spacious modern bathroom and meals are available. The collection of clocks has to be seen to be believed.

Auyuittuq Lodge HOTEL $$$

(☎ 867-473-8955; www.pangnirtunghotel.com; per person with/without bathroom $260/240; ☎) An enterprising, charismatic manager runs this as a one-man show and makes it a great place to stay (though the price is typically Nunavut-exorbitant) and eat. Renovated en-suite rooms outclass the older ones; some come with a marvelous view, also available from the lounge and balcony. Sharing is a possibility when busy. Dinner ($40) is a tasty, sociable affair, especially impressive given the logistical challenges.

ⓘ Information

Angmarlik Centre (☎ 867-473-8737; angmarlikcentre@qiniq.com; ⊗ 8:30am-8pm) This excellent, enthusiastically run place has great views as well as really interesting displays on Inuit and whaling history and information on local outfitters. Elders congregate here thrice weekly. Make sure staff explain the game of seal flipperbone Monopoly.

Parks Canada (☎ 867-473-2500; www.parks-canada.gc.ca; ⊗ 8:30am-noon & 1-5pm) Good information about Auyuittuq National Park next to the Angmarlik Centre. Register here and pay the park fee if you're going.

Qimiruvik Library (☎ 867-473-8678; www.publiclibraries.nu.ca; ⊗ 1-5pm Mon, Wed & Fri, 2-5pm Tue, Thu & Sat) In Angmarlik Centre. Free internet.

ⓘ Getting There & Away

There are daily flights with Canadian North and First Air from Iqaluit ($560 return).

Auyuittuq National Park

Among the globe's most flabbergasting places, Auyuittuq (ah-you-*ee*-tuk) means 'the land that never melts.' Appropriately, there are plenty of glaciers in this 19,500-sq-km park, plus jagged peaks, vertiginous cliffs and deep valleys. Hikers trek the 97km **Akshayuk Pass** (crossing the Arctic Circle) in summer, when it's snow-free. Nearby, experienced climbers and base jumpers scale **Mt Thor** (1500m), the earth's highest sheer cliff, and twin-peaked **Mt Asgard** (2015m), famed for the parachute scene from *The Spy Who Loved Me*. Camp in any safe, wind-proof, ecologically appropriate spot. Nine emergency shelters dot the pass.

Register at Parks Canada in Pangnirtung and pay the fee (day/overnight/maximum $12/24.50/147.20). They sell maps ($20), although the valley route is relatively intuitive.

Akshayuk's south end is 30km from Pangnirtung: a two-day hike or, more commonly, a boat-ride with an outfitter ($110 per person each way). It's worth doing this just for a daytrip – the boat ride is awe-inspiring, and the feeling of hiking this uninhabited wilderness, if only for a few hours, is memorable. Another multi-day hike heads 20km each way to **Summit Lake**. For about $200 per person,

ART IN PANGNIRTUNG

Eena Angmarlik is a local artist, print-maker and hat-maker at the Uqqurmiut Centre for Arts and Crafts.

How did you get started? As a little girl I liked people wearing crochet hats, so I started crocheting when I was 11. People liked the hat I was wearing. That encouraged me to make more: I started making hats for this baby or that baby. Then I went on to adult hats and started selling them. I've been drawing, too, since I was young and I started making prints in 2010. Here in the workshop we have many different techniques: stencils, etchings, lino-cut, stone-cut, linoleum, sugarlift, silk-screen, and more.

Can you describe the local art scene? Inuit art right now is a mixture. Some people focus on traditional drawings, some are more interested in new influences. My favorite symbols are shells, but I'm working on figures, too. People who come to Pangnirtung are happy when they see a lot of people doing carvings, making jewelry, prints, artwork. There are lots of artistic people here.

What is life like on Baffin Island? The only real dark days here are in December. It's not like further north where they have many totally dark days. Nowadays it doesn't get cold like it used to before. Climate change? I think so.

through-hikers can arrange to be picked up at the other end of the pass by an outfitter from Qikiqtarjuaq, served by First Air and Canadian North (one-way to Pangnirtung $280).

While wondrous, Auyuittuq is also brutal and isolated. To hike it you need to be an experienced wilderness operator, and fit. Think 10 days as an average for the route. Rivers must be crossed and polar bears are seen most seasons. A guide makes sense: speak to Pangnirtung outfitters or book a package from the south.

Cape Dorset

POP 1363

On a small rocky island just off Baffin Island's Foxe Peninsula, this is the epicenter of Inuit art. In the late 1950s residents pioneered modern arctic carving and print-making, marketing it to the world with remarkable success.

◎ Sights & Activities

West Baffin Eskimo Cooperative WORKSHOP (Kinngait Arts; ☑ 867-897-8965; www.dorsetfine-arts.com; ☺ 9am-5pm Mon-Fri) ✐ Though many Inuit communities now generate world-class artworks, Cape Dorset's remain the most revered. This cooperative has stonecutting and print workshops where you can watch artists work. The most activity occurs from September to May.

Mallikjuaq Historic Park ARCHAEOLOGICAL SITE (www.nunavutparks.ca) You can hike here in 45 minutes at low tide; otherwise, hire an outfitter to take you by boat. The park features ruins of 1000-year-old pre-Inuit stone houses, hiking trails, wildlife and tundra flowers.

⛟ Tours

Huit Huit Tours ADVENTURE TOUR (☑ 867-897-8806; www.capedorsettours.com) Based at Cape Dorset Suites, Huit Huit offers day trips, multiday dog-sled adventures and summertime excursions focusing on wildlife and culture.

⛺ Sleeping & Eating

Camp a 20-minute walk from the center at Aupaluktuk Park, beautifully set on a little bay overlooked by rugged hills.

POLAR BEARS

Polar bears aren't just on Nunavut's license plates. *Nanuq* (the Inuit name) is an inveterate wanderer and can turn up just about anywhere, any time of year. Worse, unlike grizzlies and black bears, they actively prey on people. Inquire about sightings before trudging out of town, or use a local guide.

★ Dorset Suites HOTEL $$$ (☑ 867-897-8806; www.dorsetsuites.com; r per person from $285; ⊜ ☎) This excellent place is Nunavut's most appealing hotel. In the main building, beautiful spacious rooms with balconies and views have warm wood furnishings, tiled floors, pleasing colors and ample space. Suites with kitchen and laundry are opposite; separate houses are also available. The restaurant (open to the public for lunch weekdays and for dinner Thursday and Friday; lunch mains $15 to $25, dinner mains $45 to $55) serves up delicious, generously proportioned meals that are a real treat.

Kingnait Inn HOTEL $$$ (☑ 867-897-8863; www.kingnaitinn.com; r per person $210; ⊜ ☎) With bay views and easy access to the town's points of interest, this friendly place gives visitors a free tour of town on arrival and offers solid meals (breakfast/lunch/dinner $20/30/40) and plain but comfortable rooms, with new mattresses, flatscreen TVs, iPod docks and ensuite bathrooms.

Nirivik Co-op FAST FOOD $$ (☑ 867-897-8548; Bldg 3603; meals $7-20; ☺ 11am-6pm Mon-Fri, noon-5pm Sat) ✐ Next to Dorset Suites, this friendly place serves burgers, fried chicken and similar at chipped green tables. They cook to order: you'll hear your chips being hand-cut. Delicious.

ⓘ Getting There & Away

First Air and Canadian North fly from Iqaluit ($770 return).

Pond Inlet

POP 1549

Inuit call it 'the place facing away from the sun,' but Pond Inlet faces majestic Bylot Island: national park, birdwatching paradise and glacier-draped arctic marvel. Make arrangements with outfitters beforehand for memorable nature-watching experiences.

Sights & Activities

Sirmilik National Park
NATIONAL PARK

(www.pc.gc.ca; overnight per night $24.50, max $147.20) Pond Inlet is the base for visits to this spectacular park, breeding ground for countless seabirds including the planet's largest flock of snow geese. The park has three main areas: Bylot Island, a glacier-draped bird sanctuary; Oliver Sound, a fjord with exciting canoeing; and Borden Peninsula with its striking hoodoos (eroded red sandstone towers).

Sirmilik's logistics are challenging, so most people choose to go on some kind of tour. Contact the park office in Pond Inlet.

Polar Sea Adventures and Black Feather
OUTDOORS

(☑ Ontario 705-746-1372, Pond Inlet 613-237-6401; www.polarseaadventures.com) Highly recommended for expeditions, particularly spring wildlife-viewing adventures to the floe edge, the biologically rich area where sea ice meets open water. A week at the floe edge is around $4200. They also run summer kayaking trips focused on narwhal-spotting.

Sleeping & Eating

Sauniq Inn
HOTEL $$$

(☑ 867-899-6500; www.pondinlethotel.com; r per person $260; 🖥) Operated by an aboriginal cooperative, this warehouse-like building offers the usual cozy, slightly austere facilities at typically weighty Nunavut rates. Rooms are spacious and comfortable enough, with decent bathrooms. Airport pick-up is included and staff can contact outfitters. The restaurant has generous comfort-food meals.

Information

Nattinnak Centre (☑ 867-899-8225; www. pondinlet.ca; ⊙ 10am-noon & 1-5pm Tue, Thu & Fri, 1-5pm & 7-9pm Wed, 2-4pm Sun) Has information on activities and outfitters, plus a fine minimuseum with displays on wildlife and local culture. Check out the life-size dioramas and the fish-skin baskets.

Sirmilik National Park Operations Centre (☑ 867-899-8092; www.pc.gc.ca; ⊙ 8:30am-noon & 1-5pm Mon-Fri) Brand new parks office with wildlife exhibition and great views. Register here and get information for Sirmilik.

Getting There & Away

First Air and Canadian North fly from Iqaluit ($1725 return).

Resolute

POP 214

The upside of living in Resolute, on Cornwallis Island, is you don't have to mow your lawn. The downside is everything else. A clutch of minuscule homes in a wind-lashed gravel desert, Canada's worst-climate community was founded when the feds lured the Inuit here to shore up national sovereignty. Visitors pass through heading for the North Pole, Quttinirpaaq National Park or scenic Grise Fiord.

Try local hiking or fly to the national historic site, **Beechey Island**, where the ill-fated Franklin expedition wintered in 1845–46 before vanishing forever.

Given the likelihood of being 'weathered in,' it's fortuitous there are good hotels. **Qausuittuq Inn** (☑ 867-252-3900; www.resolutebay.com; r $260; @🖥) has doting service, plus good home cooking. **South Camp Inn** (☑ 867-252-3737; www.southcampinn.com; s/d $275/375; @🖥), Resolute's nerve center, is friendly, labyrinthine and well appointed. Surprisingly good meals are $100 extra per day.

First Air flies from Iqaluit ($2800 return), while Kenn Borek Air does charters.

Quttinirpaaq National Park

If you like remote places and have a fortune to squander, visit Canada's second-biggest park, way up on Ellesmere Island. Fossil finds up here suggest that 4 million years ago, when camels roamed the forests, it was T-shirt territory. Now it boasts one of the world's most inhospitable climates.

Highlights include 24-hour daylight, 6ºC summers, **Mt Barbeau** (2616m), eastern North America's highest peak, and **Lake Hazen Basin**, a thermal oasis where animals, unfamiliar with humans, are strangely tame. Walking is not technical, but wilderness expertise is crucial. Begin at Tanquary Fiord, where a parks officer will give a compulsory orientation session. For information, contact **Parks Canada** (☑ 867-975-4673; www.pc.gc.ca).

A charter from Resolute costs from $15,000 to $25,000 (one-way) for up to 10 people. If you want a pick-up – you do – double that price.

KIVALLIQ REGION

This region takes in the Hudson Bay coast and the Barrenlands to the west. It's a flat, windswept area, thick with caribou and waterfowl, and cut through by wild rivers. Ukkusiksalik National Park (p830) is rife with a cornucopia of wildlife, including polar bears.

Rankin Inlet

POP 2266

Muddy, dusty, littered and busy, Rankin grew up around nickel mining in the late '50s and is now the Kivalliq's largest community. New goldmines and mineral exploration means it's still an important center. It's a base for accessing Kivalliq, and there's good char and grayling fishing close to town.

A highway between here and Manitoba, linking Nunavut with Canada's road network, is planned, but few are holding their breath.

◉ Sights & Activities

Matchbox Gallery   GALLERY
(☏ 867-645-2674;   www.matchboxgallery.com; ⊙hours vary) ◢ This small space is famed for having pioneered Inuit ceramic art. Watch artists at work and browse and buy a wide range of beautiful handicrafts.

Inukshuk   MONUMENT
Rankin's famed Inukshuk (humanoid stone cairn) lords over the community like a giant turned to stone.

Marble Island   HISTORIC SITE
(www.marbleisland.ca) In Hudson Bay, 50km east of town, this is a graveyard for James Knight and his crew, who sought the Northwest Passage in the 18th century. Some wrecks of 19th-century whalers are there, too. Ask at the visitors center for outfitters to take you there.

Iqalugaarjuup Nunanga Territorial Park   NATURE RESERVE
(www.nunavutparks.com) This tongue-twister of a park is located 10km from town and is popular for hiking and berry picking. Near the Meliadine River's mouth are archaeological sites where the Dorset people, who preceded the Inuit, dwelled.

⊨ Sleeping & Eating

★Nanuq Lodge   B&B $$$
(☏ 867-645-2650; www.nanuqlodge.com; 1 Atausiq St; s/tw $200/240; @🛜) This big, friendly, sunny B&B is the region's best place to stay. It rents kayaks, loans bicycles and arranges tours, especially dog-sledding. Enjoy comfortable en-suite rooms adorned with Inuit art, or trade polar-bear stories in the communal lounge. Its alternative accommodation, Nanuq Suites, has upmarket doubles with kitchenette and great modern facilities.

Sugar Rush Café   CAFE $$
(☏ 867-645-3373; www.thesugarrushcafe.com; 116 24 Inukshuk Ave; meals $10-25; ⊙7:30am-8pm Mon-Fri, 10am-8pm Sat, noon-6pm Sun) Rankin's best eatery is a welcoming place offering a staggering range of cuisines, from burgers, pizza and pasta to Chinese and sushi.

ⓘ Information

Visitors Centre (☏ 867-645-3838; kivalliqtourism@qiniq.com; ⊙8:30am-7pm Mon-Fri) Located in the airport.

NUNAVUT RANKIN INLET

WORTH A TRIP

THELON RIVER

Among the big Barrenland rivers, the most notable – and floatable – is the legendary Thelon. A Canadian Heritage river, it wends 1000km through utterly wild country, starting in the Northwest Territories and emptying near Nunavut's Baker Lake. Caribou, grizzly, wolf, musk ox and gyrfalcon abound, as do – weirdly – spruce trees, far north of the treeline. Ancient Inuit campsites flank the riverbanks.

Canoeing the river doesn't require remarkable paddling skills, but it does demand wilderness savvy. Most opt to paddle just a portion and charter a plane to drop-off and pick-up. A simpler option is to sign on with an outfitter, such as **Canoe Arctic** (☏ 867-872-2308; www.canoearctic.com).

LOCAL KNOWLEDGE

LIFE IN CAMBRIDGE BAY

Sarah Lynn Olayok Jancke is a 24-year-old Inuk woman from Ikaluktutiak. She works for Kitikmeot Inuit Association as programs coordinator for women and youth.

What is life like in Cambridge Bay? We have the perfect balance of isolation and access to the world. Winter gets cold! If you are bundled up, the -60°F does not seem as bad as the weather forecast makes it sound. In the darkness we spend a lot of time together with our families or playing sports, drum-dancing or just out visiting. Darkness is just how we live: kids still play out, and people are still out walking or driving snow-mobiles. It's amazing how the seasons differ and we definitely embrace them.

What issues face the community? Climate change is a very prominent issue; our surroundings are changing rapidly, forcing changes to our livelihood, the land and the animals, so to me it brings fear of the unknown. The opening of the Northwest Passage is a touchy subject that can be looked at from different viewpoints; the first thing that comes to mind is the increase in tourism, which brings a lot of potential business to our local people, giving the opportunity to share our beautiful community with the world.

ⓘ Getting There & Away

Canadian North and First Air fly from Yellowknife ($2020 return) and Iqaluit ($2020 return); First Air and Calm Air serve Winnipeg ($1830 return).

Ukkusiksalik National Park

Surrounding Wager Bay, a large inlet off Hudson Bay, **Ukkusiksalik National Park** (☏867-462-4500; www.pc.gc.ca) comprises 20,500 sq km of bleak uninhabited tundra and is one of the world's best places to observe polar bears as well as other arctic wildlife. To avoid adverse weather and bear danger it's best to visit in July and early August.

Charter flights from Baker Lake or motor-boats from Repulse Bay are the way in: both are accessible by air from Rankin Inlet. The boat trip is recommended for its wildlife-watching opportunities.

Highlights include abundant animals and birds, great hiking and boating, and a spectacular reversing waterfall. There are no services; an Inuit guide is highly recommended.

Contact the **park office** (☏867-462-4500; www.pc.gc.ca; Repulse Bay; ⊙8:30am-noon & 1-5pm Mon-Fri) in Repulse Bay for information.

KITIKMEOT REGION

Nunavut's least-populated region occupies the mainland's Arctic coast and the islands north of there. Between them runs the fabled Northwest Passage.

Cambridge Bay

POP 1608

Say 'Cambridge Bay' and even Inuit shiver. This wind-wracked settlement on Victoria Island is the regional center. A federal High Arctic Research Station is due to open here in 2017, potentially transforming the community. The Northwest Passage's gradual opening is also a crucial local issue. The Inuinnaqtun dialect is spoken here.

Explorers seeking the Northwest Passage often sheltered here; the remains of Roald Amundsen's schooner *Maud* lie in the harbor. **Ovayok Territorial Park**, accessible via a rough road or 15km hike, is a prime place to see musk ox and offers good views from **Mt Pelly** (200m). It has walking trails and camping spots. South across the passage is **Queen Maud Bird Sanctuary**, the world's largest migratory bird refuge.

Arctic Coast Visitors Centre (☏867-983-2224; Omingmak St; ⊙8:30am-5pm Mon-Fri, 10am-5pm Sat, 1-5pm Sun) has displays about exploration, supplies information and can help organize tours. **Green Row Executive Suites** (☏867-983-3456; www.greenrow.ca; apt per person $235; ⊖🛜🖥) is an excellent set-up with spacious, comfortable one- or two-bedroom suites. **Arctic Island Lodge** (☏867-983-2345; www.cambridgebayhotel.com; s/d $260/360; 🛜) is swanky by northern standards and has a restaurant.

Canadian North and First Air fly from Yellowknife ($1790 return).

Understand Canada

Canada Today

Oil and other natural resources have done much to maintain Canada's enviable economy, but questions linger over whether the environmental price is too high. As for politics, it's the belt-tightening Conservatives against the social-safety-net-championing New Democratic Party and the left-leaning Liberals. Meanwhile, Canada stays proud and progressive on issues of same-sex marriage, immigration and marijuana use.

Best on Film

Bon Cop, Bad Cop (directed by Eric Canuel; 2006) An Anglophone and Francophone join forces; one of Canada's top-grossing films.

Incendies (directed by Denis Villeneuve; 2010) Québec siblings travel to the Middle East and uncover their immigrant mother's tortured history.

Away from Her (directed by Sarah Polley; 2006) Alzheimer's breaks apart a rural Ontario couple.

C.R.A.Z.Y. (directed by Jean-Marc Vallée; 2005) A teen misfit in 1970s Montréal dreams of a brighter future.

Best in Print

Indian Horse (R Wagamese; 2012) A culturally displaced Ojibway boy grows up to become a hockey star.

The View from Castle Rock (Alice Munro; 2006) Short stories that merge fiction and family history by the 2013 Nobel Prize winner for Literature.

Beautiful Losers (Leonard Cohen; 1966) Experimental oddity involving love, sex and Aboriginals.

The Apprenticeship of Duddy Kravitz (Mordechai Richler; 1959) A Montréal Jew's quest to make money.

In the Skin of a Lion (Michael Ondaatje; 1987) Immigrants build Toronto circa 1920.

Economy

Compared to its international brethren, Canada has weathered the global financial crisis pretty well. Yes, the economy dropped into a recession, and Ottawa posted its first fiscal deficit in 2009 after 12 years of surplus, but Canadian banks bounced back, thanks to their tradition of conservative lending. The International Monetary Fund predicted Canada would be the only one of the seven major industrialized democracies to return to surplus by 2015, and the current federal government – led by the Conservatives – is focused on making this a reality, with federal job cuts impacting on departments such as Parks Canada and Aboriginal Affairs, among many others. While the Conservatives say they're removing inefficiencies, with most cuts coming from back-office jobs, the opposition says the cuts are affecting front-line services, and imperiling natural and historic sites.

Oil Between Neighbors

Voltaire may have written off Canada as 'a few acres of snow' back in the mid-18th century, but those 'few acres' have yielded vast amounts of oil, timber and other natural resources, and propelled Canada to an enviable standard of living.

Extracting and developing the resources has, however, come with an ecological price. Oil, in particular, is a conundrum. Northern Alberta's Athabasca Oil Sands (or Tar Sands, depending which side of the ecofence you're on) are the world's second-biggest oil reserves, and they've done an excellent job boosting the economy. They also produce 5% of Canada's greenhouse gas emissions, according to Environment Canada. The pro-industry camp says improvements are being made and, when compared to other oil producers such as Saudi Arabia and Venezuela, the oil sands measure up, especially when human-rights issues and decreased transportation distances are factored in (most of Canada's oil goes to the USA).

The controversial Keystone XL pipeline plays into these themes, and has caused discord between Canada and its southern neighbor. The pipeline will funnel Alberta's crude oil to refineries on the Texas and Louisiana coast. Much of it is already built, but the US State Department, which grants the final permits for building, has been hesitant to give approval for the pipeline's completion, saying Canada could be doing more to curb carbon emissions. The project is also contentious within Canada. Environmentalists and Aboriginal communities located near the pipe line have been vocal about their concerns regarding damage to sacred sites and water contamination that could cause health problems for residents.

Table Talk

The nation's much-cherished but ailing universal health-care system sparks serious table talk. Although no one will admit it, a two-tiered system is in place, and those with deep pockets can access additional, often quicker care in private facilities. Still, a free, portable health-care system that's available to everyone is quite a feat. To many citizens, it's at the very root of what makes Canada great. So are progressive views on same-sex marriage, immigration and marijuana use.

Climate change is another hot topic. A recent poll showed 53% of Canadians believed climate change caused the 2013 floods that put much of Calgary, Alberta underwater. It also revealed Albertans were least likely to believe the flooding came from climate change, while Atlantic Canadians were most likely to believe it.

Politics

In 2006 the Conservative Party took over from the Liberals for the first time in 12 years. Managing the economy (a Conservative tenet) and strengthening social services and health care (policies of the Liberals and left-leaning groups) were among the main issues. Stephen Harper became the new prime minister, but he led Canada's smallest minority government since Confederation. In 2008 he called an early election, hoping to boost the Conservatives' grip. It did, but only 22% of Canadians voted – the lowest in history.

The 2011 election held some surprises. The Conservatives won and picked up enough seats (166) to form a majority. But the big story was the surge of the New Democratic Party, a leftist group that had long been on the fringe, until it upped its seat count from 37 to 103 in 2011. It did so at the expense of the center-left Liberals. Canada's next federal election is scheduled for 2015, and it's pretty much up for grabs.

POPULATION: **34.6 MILLION**

AREA: **9,984,670 SQ KM**

GDP: **US$1.5 TRILLION**

GDP GROWTH: **1.8%**

INFLATION: **1.5%**

UNEMPLOYMENT: **7.3%**

if Canada were 100 people

28 would be of British Isles origin
23 would be of French origin
15 would be of other European origin
34 would be of other origin

belief systems
(% of population)

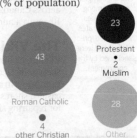

43 Roman Catholic
23 Protestant
2 Muslim
28 Other
4 other Christian

population per sq km

CANADA

USA

FRANCE

👤 ≈ 4 people

History

The human story of Canada begins around 15,000 years ago, when Aboriginal locals began carving thriving communities from the abundant wilderness. Everything changed, though, when the Europeans rolled in from the late 15th century onward, staking claims that triggered rumbling conflicts and eventually shaped a vast new nation. Much of this colorful heritage is accessible to visitors, with more than 950 national historic sites covering everything from forts to battlefields to famous homes.

The First Inhabitants

Canada's first inhabitants were most likely hunter-nomads who, in hungry pursuit of caribou, elk and bison, crossed over from Asia on the land bridge that once linked Siberia and Alaska. As the earth warmed and the glaciers retreated, these immigrants began to trickle all across the Americas.

About 4500 years ago, a second major wave of migration from Siberia brought the ancestors of the Inuit to Canada. The new arrivals took one look at the North, sized it up as a tasty icebox filled with fish-and-seal dinners, and decided to hang around. These early Inuit were members of the Dorset Culture, named after Cape Dorset on Baffin Island, where its remains were first unearthed. Around AD 1000 a separate Inuit culture, the whale-hunting Thule of northern Alaska, began making its way east through the Canadian Arctic. As these people spread, they overtook the Dorset Culture. The Thule are the direct ancestors of the modern Inuit.

By the late 15th century, when the first Europeans arrived, Aboriginal peoples had spread beyond the Arctic into four other major locations across Canada: the Pacific, the Plains, the southern Ontario/St Lawrence River area and the Northeast woodlands.

Atlantic Canada had a notorious history of pirates. Peter Easton was the first in 1602, plundering around Newfoundland. Black Bart, aka Bartholomew Roberts, was another, c 1720. He disliked booze and gambling and encouraged prayer among his employees. In Halifax pirates were called 'privateers' and were sanctioned by the government.

The Vikings & European Explorers

Viking celebrity Leif Eriksson was the first European to reach Canada's shores. In fact, he and his tribe of Scandinavian seafarers were the first Europeans in all of North America. Around AD 1000 they poked around the eastern shores of Canada, establishing winter settlements and way stations for repairing ships and restocking supplies, such as at L'Anse Aux Meadows

TIMELINE	c 70 million BC	c 25,000 BC	1000 BC
	Dinosaurs enjoy the warm coastal climate that exists in southern Alberta (the hefty creatures think of it like today's Victoria).	Hot on the hooves of juicy caribou and bison, the first humans arrive in Canada by crossing the land bridge that once connected Siberia to North America.	After hanging around for a few thousand years, the Maritime Archaic Indians, known for their ceremonial burials at sites like Port aux Choix, inexplicably disappear.

in Newfoundland. The local tribes didn't roll out the welcome mat for these intruders, who eventually tired of the hostilities and went home. There would be no more visits from the outside for another 300 to 400 years.

The action heated up again in the late 15th century. In 1492, backed by the Spanish crown, Christopher Columbus went searching for a western sea route to Asia and instead stumbled upon some small islands in the Bahamas. Other European monarchs, excited by his 'discovery,' quickly sponsored expeditions of their own. In 1497, Giovanni Caboto, better known as John Cabot, sailed under a British flag as far west as Newfoundland and Cape Breton.

Cabot didn't find a passage to China, but he did find cod, a much-coveted commodity in Europe at the time. In short order, hundreds of boats were shuttling between Europe and the fertile new fishing grounds. Basques whalers from northern Spain soon followed. Several were based at Red Bay in Labrador, which became the biggest whaling port in the world during the 16th century.

King François I of France looked over the fence at his neighbors, stroked his beard, then snapped his fingers and ordered Jacques Cartier to appear before him. By this time, the hunt was on not only for the Northwest Passage but also for gold, given the findings by Spanish conquistadors among the Aztec and Inca civilizations. François hoped for similar riches in the frosty North.

Upon arrival in Labrador, Cartier found only 'stones and horrible rugged rocks,' as he wrote in his journal in 1534. He dutifully kept exploring and soon went ashore on Québec's Gaspé Peninsula to claim the land for France. The local Iroquois thought Cartier a good neighbor, until he kidnapped two of the chief's sons and took them back to Europe. To his credit, Cartier returned them a year later when sailing up the St Lawrence River to Stadacona (present-day Québec City) and Hochelaga (today's Montréal). Here he got wind of a land called Saguenay that was full of gold and silver. The rumor prompted Cartier's third voyage, in 1541, but alas, the mythical riches remained elusive.

France retains a token of its early exploits in Canada: St-Pierre and Miquelon, two small islands off Newfoundland's coast, remain staunchly French to this day.

Explorer Jacques Cartier bestowed Canada with its name. Scholars say it comes from *kanata*, a Huron-Iroquois word for 'village' or 'settlement,' which was written in Cartier's journal and later transformed by mapmakers to 'Canada.'

THE MAPLE LEAF SYMBOL

It's on the penny, on Air Canada planes, on Toronto hockey-team jerseys – you can't escape the maple leaf. The leaf has been considered a national symbol for almost two centuries. In 1836, *Le Canadien* newspaper, published in Lower Canada, wrote about it as a suitable emblem for the nation. Ontario and Québec both were using it on their coat of arms by 1868. The Canadian Armed Forces used it during the world wars. And finally, after much wrangling over the design (one leaf? three leaves? 13 points?), the current 11-point leaf was granted national-symbol status and went on the flag in 1965.

AD 1000	1497	1528	1534
Viking Leif Eriksson and crew wash up at L'Anse aux Meadows, where they build sod houses. They're the first Europeans in North America, beating Columbus by 500 years.	John Cabot sails over from Britain and finds Newfoundland instead of China. It's not a bad trade-off because the waters are filled with fat, delicious codfish.	St John's, Newfoundland, bobs up as North America's first town. It belongs to no nation; rather it serves fishing fleets from all over Europe.	Jacques Cartier sails into what is now Québec. He searches for gold and precious metals, but finds only chilled rocks. He claims the land for France anyway.

Fur Trade Ignites

François I became bored with his distant colony, which wasn't producing the wealth he wanted. But his interest perked back up a few decades later when fur hats became all the rage. Everyone who was anyone was wearing one and, as the fashion mavens knew, there was no finer *chapeau* than one made from beaver pelts. With beavers pretty much extinct in the Old World, the demand for a fresh supply was strong.

In 1588 the French crown granted the first trading monopoly in Canada, only to have other merchants promptly challenge the claim. And so the race for control of the fur trade was officially on. The economic value of this enterprise and, by extension, its role in shaping Canadian history, cannot be underestimated. It was the main reason behind the country's European settlement, at the root of the struggle for dominance between the French and the British, and the source of strife and division between Aboriginal groups. All because of a silly hat!

In order to gain control of the distant lands, the first order of business was to put European bodies on the ground. In the summer of 1604, a group of French pioneers established a tentative foothold on Île Ste-Croix (a tiny islet in the river on the present US border with Maine). They moved to Port Royal (today's Annapolis Royal) in Nova Scotia the following spring. Exposed and difficult to defend, neither site made a good base for controlling the inland fur trade. As the would-be colonists moved up the St Lawrence River, they finally came upon a spot their leader, Samuel de Champlain, considered prime real estate – where today's Québec City stands. It was 1608 and 'New France' had become a reality.

> The Canadian Military History Gateway (www. cmhg.gc.ca) provides access to digitized resources on Canada's military history, including audio links to old war broadcasts from the CBC.

French vs English

The French enjoyed their plush fur monopoly for several decades, but in 1670 the British mounted a formidable challenge. They caught a lucky break when a pair of disillusioned French explorers, Radisson and Des Groseilliers, confided that the best fur country actually lay to the north and west of Lake Superior, which was easily accessible via Hudson Bay. King Charles II quickly formed the Hudson's Bay Company and granted it a trade monopoly over all the lands whose rivers and streams drained into the bay. This vast territory, called Rupert's Land, encompassed about 40% of present-day Canada, including Labrador, western Québec, northwestern Ontario, Manitoba, most of Saskatchewan and Alberta, and part of the Northwest Territories.

The English infuriated the French with such moves, and so the French kept right on galling the English by settling further inland. Both coun-

> **Top Historical Sites: West**
>
> *Klondike sites, Yukon*
>
> *Batoche, Saskatchewan*
>
> *Head-Smashed-In Buffalo Jump, Alberta*
>
> *Craigdarroch Castle, British Columbia*

1608

After four years of moving around, Samuel de Champlain finds his dream-home site, putting down stakes at Québec City and giving New France its first permanent settlement.

➤ Statue of Samuel de Champlain

1610

The British take their turn: merchant John Guy builds a plantation at Cupids, Newfoundland. It's England's first colony in Canada (and second in the New World after Jamestown).

1670

King Charles II creates the Hudson's Bay Company to shore up the local fur trade for the Brits. Years later, the company morphs into the Bay department store chain.

tries had claims to the land, but each wanted regional dominance. They skirmished back and forth in hostilities that mirrored those in Europe, where wars raged throughout the first half of the 18th century.

Things came to a head with the Treaty of Utrecht, which ended Queen Anne's War (1701–13) overseas. Under its provisions, the French had to officially recognize British claims to Hudson Bay and Newfoundland, and give up all of Nova Scotia (then called Acadia) except for Cape Breton Island.

The conflict simmered for a few decades, then ramped up to a new level in 1754 when the two countries battled each other in the French and Indian Wars (also known as the Seven Years' War). The tide soon turned in the Brits' favor with the capture of the Louisbourg fortress, giving them control of a strategically important entrance to the St Lawrence River.

In 1759 the British besieged Québec, scaling the cliffs in a surprise attack and quickly defeating the stunned French; it was one of Canada's bloodiest and most famous battles, and left both commanding generals dead. At the Treaty of Paris (1763), France handed Canada over to Britain.

Growing Pains

Managing the newly acquired territory presented quite a challenge for the British. First, they had to quell uprisings by the Aboriginal tribes, such as the attack on Detroit by Ottawa Chief Pontiac. The British government issued the Royal Proclamation of 1763, which prevented colonists from settling west of the Appalachian Mountains and regulated purchases of aboriginal land. Though well-intentioned, the proclamation was largely ignored.

The French Canadians caused the next headache. Tensions arose when the new rulers imposed British law that heavily restricted the rights of Roman Catholics (the religion of the French), including the rights to vote and hold office. The British hoped their discriminatory policy would launch a mass exodus and make it easier to anglicize the remaining settlers. The plan didn't work – the French just crossed their arms and further dug in their heels.

As if the tribes and French weren't problems enough, the American colonies started making revolutionary rumbles to the south. The British governor, Guy Carleton, wisely reasoned that winning the French settlers' political allegiance was more valuable than turning them into tea drinkers. This led to the passage of the Québec Act of 1774. The ct confirmed French Canadians' right to their religion, allowed them to assume political office and restored the use of French civil law. Indeed, during the American Revolution (1775–83) most French Canadians refused to

---

HISTORY GROWING PAINS

Top Historical Sites: East
....
L'Anse aux Meadows, New-foundland
....
Fortifications of Québec, Québec City
....
Louisbourg, Nova Scotia
....
Province House, Prince Edward Island

The USA has invaded Canada twice – in 1775 and 1812 – both times to no avail.

1755	1759	1763	1775
The English deport some 14,000 French Acadians from the Bay of Fundy region. They're forced onto ships during the Great Expulsion; many head to Louisiana in the USA.	Canada's most famous battle, a beauty between the French and English, happens on the Plains of Abraham at Québec City. It lasts less than an hour. France loses.	The Treaty of Paris boots France out of Canada after France loses the Seven Years' War. Thus, Canada ceases to ping-pong between power-mongering France and Britain.	American rebels invade Canada and try to entice Québec to join the revolt against the British in the American Revolution, but the locals refuse.

take up arms for the American cause, although not many willingly defended the British either.

After the Revolution, the English-speaking population exploded when some 50,000 settlers from the newly independent America migrated northward. Called United Empire Loyalists due to their presumed allegiance to Britain, many settlers were motivated more by cheap land than by love of king and crown. The majority ended up in Nova Scotia and New Brunswick, while a smaller group settled along the northern shore of Lake Ontario and in the Ottawa River Valley (forming the nucleus of what became Ontario). About 8000 people moved to Québec, creating the first sizeable anglophone community in the French-speaking bastion.

The Nation Splits: Upper & Lower Canada

Partly in order to accommodate the interests of Loyalist settlers, the British government passed the Constitutional Act of 1791, which divided the colony into Upper Canada (today's southern Ontario) and Lower Canada (now southern Québec). Lower Canada retained French civil laws, but both provinces were governed by the British criminal code.

The British crown installed a governor to direct each colony. The governor in turn appointed the members of his 'cabinet,' then called the Executive Council. The legislative branch consisted of an appointed Legislative Council and an elected Assembly, which ostensibly represented the interests of the colonists. In reality, though, the Assembly held very little power, since the governor could veto its decisions. Not surprisingly, this was a recipe for friction and resentment. This was especially the case in Lower Canada, where an English governor and an English-dominated Council held sway over a French-dominated Assembly.

Rampant cronyism made matters even worse. Members of the conservative British merchant elite dominated the Executive and Legislative Councils and showed little interest in French-Canadian matters. Called the Family Compact in Upper Canada and the Château Clique in Lower Canada, their ranks included brewer John Molson and university founder James McGill. The groups' influence grew especially strong after the War of 1812, an ultimately futile attempt by the USA to take over its northern neighbor.

In 1837 frustration over these entrenched elites reached boiling point. Parti Canadien leader Louis-Joseph Papineau and his Upper Canadian counterpart, Reform Party leader William Lyon Mackenzie, launched open rebellions against the government. Although both uprisings were quickly crushed, the incident signaled to the British that the status quo wasn't going to cut it any longer.

It was Newfoundland's Beothuk Aboriginals and their ceremonially ocher-coated faces who were dubbed 'red men' by arriving Europeans, a name soon applied to all of North America's indigenous groups. The Beothuk died out by 1829.

Best Historic Neighborhoods

Gastown, Vancouver

Québec City, Québec

Old Montréal, Montréal

Downtown Halifax, Nova Scotia

1793	1818	1858	1864
Explorer Alexander Mackenzie makes the first transcontinental journey across the land. He scrawls 'from Canada by land' on a rock near Bella Coola, British Columbia.	The USA and Britain hash out the Treaty of 1818. The upshot: Canada's border is defined as the 49th parallel from Lake of the Woods to the Rocky Mountains.	Yee-haw! Prospectors discover gold along the Fraser River in BC, spurring thousands of get-rich-quick dreamers to move north and start panning. Most remain poor.	The Fathers of the Confederation meet in Charlottetown, Prince Edward Island, and mold a new country called Canada from the group of loosely knit colonies that now comprise the land.

Cautious Reunion

The British dispatched John Lambton, the Earl of Durham, to investigate the causes of the rebellions. He correctly identified ethnic tensions as the root of the problem, calling the French and British 'two nations warring in the bosom of a single state.' He then earned the nickname 'Radical Jack' by asserting that French culture and society were inferior and obstacles to expansion and greatness – only assimilation of British laws, language and institutions would quash French nationalism and bring long-lasting peace to the colonies. These ideas were adopted into the Union Act of 1840.

Upper and Lower Canada soon merged into the Province of Canada and became governed by a single legislature, the new Parliament of Canada. Each ex-colony had the same number of representatives, which wasn't exactly fair to Lower Canada (ie Québec), where the population was much larger. On the plus side, the new system brought responsible government that restricted the governor's powers and eliminated nepotism.

While most British Canadians welcomed the new system, the French were less than thrilled. If anything, the union's underlying objective of destroying French culture, language and identity made Francophones cling together even more tenaciously. The provisions of the Act left deep wounds that still haven't fully healed.

Thus the united province was built on slippery ground. The decade or so following unification was marked by political instability as one government replaced another in fairly rapid succession. Meanwhile, the USA had grown into a self-confident economic powerhouse, while British North America was still a loose patchwork of independent colonies. The American Civil War (1861–65) and the USA's purchase of Alaska from Russia in 1867 raised fears of annexation. It became clear that only a less volatile political system would stave off these challenges, and the movement toward federal union gained momentum.

Confederation

In 1864, Charlottetown, Prince Edward Island (PEI), served as the birthing room for modern Canada. At the town's Province House, the 'Fathers of Confederation' – a group of representatives from Nova Scotia, New Brunswick, PEI, Ontario and Québec – got together and hammered out the framework for a new nation. It took two more meetings before Parliament passed the British North America Act in 1867. And so began the modern, self-governing state of Canada, originally known as the Dominion of Canada. The day the act became official, July 1, is celebrated as Canada's national holiday; it was called Dominion Day until it was renamed Canada Day in 1982.

Best History Museums

Maritime Museum of the Atlantic, Halifax

Canadian War Museum, Ottawa

Musée d'Archéologie et d'Histoire de Pointe-à-Callière, Montréal

Royal BC Museum, Victoria

Glenbow Museum, Calgary

Delegates to the Charlottetown Conference in 1864 had to sleep on their steam-ships because the circus was in town and all the inns were fully booked.

1867	1885	1893	1896
It's official: the British North America Act unites the colonies under the Dominion of Canada, a card-carrying member of the British Empire. Queen Victoria celebrates with Canadian bacon for breakfast.	Canada's first national park opens in Banff, Alberta; meanwhile, in Craigellachie, BC, workers drive in the spike that completes the Canadian Pacific Railway.	The Montréal AAA hockey team accepts the first Stanley Cup (donated by one Lord Stanley of Preston). It's now the oldest trophy North American pro sports teams compete for.	Prospectors find more of the shiny stuff, this time in the Yukon. The Klondike Gold Rush is on, with 40,000 hopefuls bringing their picks and pans to Dawson City.

How the West was Won

Manual laborers from China built much of the Canadian Pacific Railway's western stretch. They earned $0.75 to $1.25 per day, and often were given the most dangerous, explosive-laden jobs.

Task one on the infant dominion's to-do list was to bring the remaining land and colonies into the confederation. Under its first prime minister, John A Macdonald, the government acquired vast Rupert's Land in 1869 for the paltry sum of £300,000 (about $11.5 million in today's money) from the Hudson's Bay Company. Now called the Northwest Territories (NWT), the land was only sparsely populated, mostly by Plains First Nations and several thousand Métis (may-*tee*), a racial blend of Cree, Ojibwe or Saulteaux and French-Canadian or Scottish fur traders, who spoke French as their main language. Their biggest settlement was the Red River Colony around Fort Garry (today's Winnipeg).

The Canadian government immediately clashed with the Métis people over land-use rights, causing the latter to form a provisional government led by the charismatic Louis Riel. He sent the Ottawa-appointed governor packing and, in November 1869, seized control of Upper Fort Garry, thereby forcing Ottawa to the negotiating table. However, with his delegation already en route, Riel impulsively executed a Canadian prisoner he was holding at the fort. Although the murder caused widespread uproar in Canada, the government was so keen to bring the west into the fold it agreed to most of Riel's demands, including special language and religious protections for the Métis. As a result, the then-pint-sized province of Manitoba was carved out of the NWT and entered the dominion in July 1870. Macdonald sent troops after Riel but he narrowly managed to escape to the USA. He was formally exiled for five years in 1875.

Gold Diggers (2010), by Charlotte Gray, tells of the last great gold rush in history. Between 1896 and 1899 Dawson City, in the Yukon, boomed from 400 people to 30,000 people. The author uses letters and newspaper articles by resident journalists, bankers, prostitutes, priests and lawmen to depict the era.

British Columbia (BC), created in 1866 by merging the colonies of New Caledonia and Vancouver Island, was the next frontier. The discovery of gold along the Fraser River in 1858 and in the Cariboo region in 1862 had brought an enormous influx of settlers to such gold mine boom towns as Williams Lake and Barkerville. Once the gold mines petered out, though, BC was plunged into poverty. In 1871 it joined the dominion in exchange for the Canadian government assuming all its debt and promising to link it with the east within 10 years via a transcontinental railroad.

The construction of the Canadian Pacific Railway is one of the most impressive chapters in Canadian history. Macdonald rightly regarded the railroad as crucial in unifying the country, spurring immigration and stimulating business and manufacturing. It was a costly proposition, made even more challenging by the rough and rugged terrain the tracks had to traverse. To entice investors, the government offered major benefits, including vast land grants in western Canada. Workers drove the final spike into the track at Craigellachie, BC, on November 7, 1885.

1913	1917	1931	1933
Immigration to Canada crests, with more than 400,000 people embracing the maple leaf. Most are Americans and Eastern Europeans, who can't resist the call of the nation's fertile prairies.	Canada introduces the draft to replenish forces fighting for England in WWI. French Canadians, in particular, oppose the call-up, foreshadowing tensions to come.	The residential school system peaks. Aboriginal, Inuit and Métis children are removed from their communities and forced to attend schools (most operated by churches) far from home to 'assimilate.'	Three out of 10 people are out of work, as Canada feels the effects of the Great Depression. The prairies are especially hard hit by the drought-induced Dust Bowl.

EXTREME MAKEOVER: THE IMAGE OF LOUIS RIEL

Rebel, murderer, traitor – Métis leader Louis Riel was called many things, and not many of them were compliments, when he was hanged for treason in 1885. But today a growing number of Canadians see him as a hero who defended the rights of the oppressed against an unjust government. Statues of Riel stand on Parliament Hill in Ottawa and outside the Manitoba Legislature in Winnipeg, where his boyhood home and grave have become places of pilgrimage. The government's 1998 Statement of Reconciliation to Canada's Aboriginal peoples even included an apology for Riel's execution.

To bring law and order to the 'wild west,' the government created the North-West Mounted Police (NWMP) in 1873, which later became the Royal Canadian Mounted Police (RCMP). Nicknamed 'Mounties,' they still serve as Canada's national police force today. Although they were effective, the NWMP couldn't prevent trouble from brewing on the prairies, where the Plains First Nations had been forced to sign various treaties relegating them to reserves. It wasn't long before these groups began to challenge their status.

Meanwhile, many Métis had moved to Saskatchewan and settled around Batoche. As in Manitoba, they quickly clashed with government surveyors over land issues. In 1884, after their repeated appeals to Ottawa had been ignored, they coaxed Louis Riel out of exile to represent their cause. Rebuffed, Riel responded the only way he knew: by forming a provisional government and leading the Métis in revolt. Riel had the backing of the Cree, but times had changed: with the railroad nearly complete, government troops arrived within days. Riel surrendered in May and was hanged for treason later that year.

Cutting Ties to England

Canada rang in the 20th century on a high note. Industrialization was in full swing, prospectors had discovered gold in the Yukon, and Canadian resources – from wheat to lumber – were increasingly in demand. In addition, the new railroad opened the floodgates to immigration.

Between 1885 and 1914 about 4.5 million people arrived in Canada. This included large groups of Americans and Eastern Europeans, especially Ukrainians, who went to work cultivating the prairies. Optimism reigned: a buoyant Prime Minister Wilfrid Laurier said 'The 19th century was the century of the United States. I think we can claim that it is Canada that shall fill the 20th century.' It was only natural that this new-found self-confidence would put the country on track to autonomy from Britain. The issue took on even greater urgency when WWI broke out in 1914.

The Nova Scotia government maintains a website (http://titanic.gov.ns.ca) of all things *Titanic*, including a list of passengers buried in local graveyards and artifacts housed in local museums. The province played a vital role in the tragedy, as ships from Halifax were sent out to recover victims.

→ Abandoned barn, Saskatchewan

ANDREW PENNER / GETTY IMAGES ©

1942
Newfoundland becomes the only North American site directly attacked by German forces during WWII, when a U-boat launches a torpedo that strikes inland at Bell Island.

1962
Canada becomes the third nation in space, after the Soviet Union and the USA, when it launches the *Alouette* satellite into the stratosphere.

Canada – as a member of the British Empire – found itself automatically drawn into the conflict. In the war's first years, more than 300,000 volunteers went off to European battlefields. As the war dragged on and thousands of soldiers returned in coffins, recruitment ground to a halt. The government, intent on replenishing its depleted forces, introduced the draft in 1917. It proved to be a very unpopular move, to say the least, especially among French Canadians. Animosity toward Ottawa was already at an all-time high since the government had recently abolished bilingual schools in Manitoba and restricted the use of French in Ontario's schools. The conscription issue fanned the flames of nationalism even more. Thousands of Québecois took to the streets in protest, and the issue left Canada divided and Canadians distrustful of their government.

By the time the guns of WWI fell silent in 1918, most Canadians were fed up with sending their sons and husbands to fight in distant wars for Britain. Under the government of William Lyon Mackenzie King, an eccentric fellow who communicated with spirits and worshipped his dead mother, Canada began asserting its independence. Mackenzie King made it clear that Britain could no longer automatically draw upon the Canadian military, started signing treaties without British approval, and sent a Canadian ambassador to Washington. This forcefulness led to the Statute of Westminster, passed by the British Parliament in 1931. The statute formalized the independence of Canada and other Commonwealth nations, although Britain retained the right to pass amendments to those countries' constitutions.

Oddly, that right remained on the books for another half century. It was removed only with the 1982 Canada Act, which Queen Elizabeth II signed into law on Parliament Hill in Ottawa on April 17. Today, Canada is a constitutional monarchy with a parliament consisting of an appointed upper house, or Senate, and an elected lower house, the House of Commons. The British monarch remains Canada's head of state, although this is predominantly a ceremonial role and does not diminish the country's sovereignty. Within Canada, the appointed governor general is the monarch's representative.

Modern-Day Canada

The period after WWII brought another wave of economic expansion and immigration, especially from Europe.

Newfoundland finally joined Canada in 1949. Joey Smallwood, the politician who persuaded the island to sign up, claimed it would bring economic prosperity. Once he became Newfoundland's premier, he helped this prosperity along by forcing a resettlement program upon citizens. People living in small, isolated fishing communities (aka outports) were strongly encouraged to pack up and move inland where the government

More than one million Canadians served in the armed forces during WWII from a population of approximately 11.5 million; 42,000 died.

Searching for your Cajun roots? The Acadian Genealogy Homepage (www. acadian.org) has compiled census reports harking back to 1671, plus maps and histories of local Acadian communities.

1964	1967	1982	1990
Tim Hortons, started by the eponymous ice-hockey defenseman, serves its first doughnut and cup of coffee in Hamilton, Ontario. It's now Canada's largest restaurant franchise.	The Great Canadian Oil Sands plant opens at Fort McMurray, Alberta, and starts pumping out black gold. It's reputed to hold more oil than all of Saudi Arabia.	Queen Elizabeth II signs the Canada Act, giving Canada complete sovereignty. However, she retains the right to keep her face on the money and to appoint a governor general.	The Oka Crisis, a violent standoff between the government and a band of Mohawk activists near Montréal, is sparked by a land claim over a golf course. One person dies.

could deliver schools, health care and other services more economically. One method for 'encouraging' villagers was to cut ferry services to their communities, thus making them inaccessible since there were no roads.

The only province truly left behind during the 1950s boom years was Québec. For a quarter century, it remained in the grip of ultra-conservative Maurice Duplessis and his Union Nationale party, with support from the Catholic Church and various business interests. Only after Duplessis' death did the province finally start getting up to speed during the 'Quiet Revolution' of the 1960s. Advances included expanding the public sector, investing in public education and nationalizing the provincial

QUÉBEC'S SEPARATIST MOVEMENT

Québec's separatism movement began in earnest in 1968, when René Lévesque founded the sovereigntist Parti Québecois (PQ).

The issue intensified quickly. In October 1970 the most radical wing of the movement, the Front de Libération du Québec (FLQ; Québec Liberation Front), kidnapped Québec's labor minister Pierre Laporte and a British trade official in an attempt to force the independence issue. Prime Minister Pierre Trudeau declared a state of emergency and called in the army to protect government officials. Two weeks later, Laporte's body was found in the trunk of a car. The murder discredited the FLQ in the eyes of many erstwhile supporters and the movement quickly faded.

Still, Lévesque's PQ won the 1976 Québec provincial election and quickly pushed through a bill that made French the province's sole official language. His 1980 referendum on secession, however, was resoundingly defeated, with almost 60% voting *non*. The issue was put on the back burner for much of the 1980s.

Lévesque's successor, Robert Bourassa, agreed to a constitution-led solution – but only if Québec was recognized as a 'distinct society' with special rights. In 1987 Prime Minister Brian Mulroney unveiled an accord that met most of Québec's demands. To take effect, the so-called Meech Lake Accord needed to be ratified by all 10 provinces and both houses of parliament by 1990. Dissenting premiers in three provinces eventually pledged their support but, incredibly, the accord collapsed when a single member of Manitoba's legislature refused to sign. Mulroney and Bourassa drafted a new, expanded accord, but the separatists picked it apart and it too was trounced.

Relations between Anglos and Francophones hit new lows, and support for independence was rekindled. Only one year after returning to power in 1994, the PQ, under Premier Lucien Bouchard, launched a second referendum. This was a cliff-hanger: Québecois decided by 52,000 votes – a majority of less than 1% – to remain within Canada.

The issue lost some of its luster in the years that followed, though the PQ remained a viable force. In 2012, the PQ won 32% of the vote in Quebec's elections, enough to form a minority government. But by 2013, the party was losing ground again after its controversial proposal that public workers be banned from wearing religious headgear.

1992	1998	1999	2003
The government imposes the Atlantic cod moratorium, and thousands of fisherfolk lose their livelihoods. The ban was supposed to be lifted within a few years, but depleted stocks never rebounded.	The Canadian government apologizes to Aboriginal peoples, saying 'attitudes of racial and cultural superiority led to a suppression of Aboriginal culture and values.' It vows not to repeat past mistakes.	Nunavut, Canada's newest province, is chiseled from the icy eastern Arctic, giving about one-fifth of Canadian soil to the 28,000 Inuit who live there.	Canada becomes the world's third-largest diamond producer (after Botswana and Russia), thanks to riches discovered in the NWT. The baubles spark a modern-day boom similar to gold rush times.

hydroelectric companies. Still, progress wasn't swift enough for radical nationalists who claimed independence was the only way to ensure Francophone rights. Québec has spent the ensuing years flirting with separatism.

In 1960, Canada's Aboriginal peoples were finally granted Canadian citizenship. Issues involving land rights and discrimination played out in the decades that followed. In 1990, Aboriginal frustration reached boiling point with the Oka Crisis, a standoff between the government and a group of Mohawk activists near Montréal. The conflict was set off by a land claim: the town of Oka was planning to expand a golf course onto land that the Mohawk considered sacred. A 78-day clash ensued, and one policeman died of gunshot wounds. The event shook Canada.

In the aftermath of Oka, a Royal Commission on Aboriginal Peoples issued a report recommending a complete overhaul of relations between the government and indigenous peoples. In 1998 the Ministry of Indian and Northern Affairs issued an official Statement of Reconciliation that accepted responsibility for past injustices toward Aboriginal peoples. In 1999 the government resolved its biggest land claim, creating the new territory of Nunavut and handing it over to the Inuit people who have long lived in the northern region. Recent disputes have focused on renaming landmarks, such as Mt Douglas near Victoria, BC, which First Nations people want returned to its original name of Pkols.

In 1985, Canada became the first country in the world to pass a national multicultural act. Today, more than 20% of Canada's population is foreign-born. BC has a long history of welcoming Japanese, Chinese and south Asian immigrants. The prairie provinces have traditionally been the destination of large numbers of Ukrainians, and Ontario, which has sizable Caribbean and Russian populations, is also home to 60% of Canada's Muslims.

The new millennium has been kind to Canada. The Loonie took off around 2003 – thanks to the oil, diamonds and other natural resources fueling the economy – and tolerance marches onward, with medical marijuana and gay marriage both legalized. The country showed off its abundant assets to the world when it successfully hosted the 2010 Winter Olympics in Vancouver.

In *Canadian History for Dummies*, bestselling author Will Ferguson uses his irreverent, opinionated and energetic style to take you on an entertaining cruise through his country's wild and wacky past.

Canadian Inventions

Foghorn (1854)

Basketball (1892)

Insulin (1922)

Easy-Off Oven Cleaner (1932)

Plastic garbage bag (c 1950)

Blackberry smartphone (1999)

2005	2006	2010	2013
Canada legalizes gay marriage throughout the country. Most provinces and territories had permitted it, but now hold-outs Alberta, PEI, Nunavut and the NWT join the ranks.	The census shows almost 20% of the population is foreign-born – the highest proportion in 75 years. Immigrants from Asia (including the Middle East) make up the largest proportion of newcomers.	Vancouver and Whistler showcase the west coast's gorgeous mountains and cool urbanity when they host the 2010 Winter Olympics. Team Canada wins the gold medal for hockey.	Calgary is hit by epic floods; four people die and 100,000 others are forced from their homes. It's the costliest natural disaster in Canadian history.

Aboriginal Cultures

Canada's original inhabitants began living on the land more than 15,000 years ago. The term 'Aboriginal' refers to the descendants of these earliest residents, which now comprise three groups: First Nations (those of North American Indian descent), Métis (those with 'mixed blood' ancestry) and Inuit (those in the Arctic). Together they make up 4.3% of Canada's total population.

The People

First Nations

This broad term applies to all aboriginal groups except the Métis and Inuit. Almost 852,000 First Nations people live in Canada (about 2.5% of the total population), comprising more than 600 communities (sometimes called bands). British Columbia is home to the most First Nations (198 groups), while Ontario is second (126 groups).

Above Totem pole, Vancouver, British Columbia

Pacific

Historically, the people along the Pacific coast built cedar-plank houses and carved elaborate totem poles and canoes. The potlatch, a ritual feast where the host gives away lavish gifts and possessions, is a renowned facet of many local cultures. The Canadian government banned the practice from 1885 to 1951 for being 'uncivilized.'

The Haida of Haida Gwaii, a group of islands off BC's northern shore, are perhaps the region's best-known First Nations group. Their artistic traditions are extraordinary, and they're famed for their wood carvings, totem poles and stylized prints of animals.

The Tsimshians on the mainland and matrilineal Tlingit, who spread into Alaska, have similar art forms.

Plains

The Plains First Nations, which traditionally included the Sioux, Cree and Blackfoot, occupied the prairies from Lake Winnipeg to the Rocky Mountain foothills. Primarily buffalo hunters, they cunningly killed their prey by driving them over cliffs, such as at Head-Smashed-In Buffalo Jump in southern Alberta.

The Plains today still have a strong First Nations (and Métis) presence. Winnipeg has the largest number of First Nations people in Canada, with Edmonton not far behind. In Regina, **First Nations University of Canada** (www.fnuniv.ca) is the only First Nations–run institution of higher learning in the country.

Great Lakes & St Lawrence River Area

Present-day southern Ontario and the area along the St Lawrence River are the time-honored home of the Iroquoian-speaking peoples, who were once divided into the Five Nations (including the Mohawk, Oneida and Seneca), the Huron, the Erie and the Neutral confederacies. Although often at war with one another, they were relatively modern societies who lived in large farming communities, built sturdy longhouses and traded with other tribes.

Today Manitoulin Island, floating in Lake Huron, preserves Ojibwe culture through its several reserves, where visitors can attend powwows and follow the Great Spirit **Circle Trail** (www.circletrail.com).

Maritime Provinces

The Mi'kmaqs and Maliseets are the main First Nations in the Maritimes, accounting for just over 1% of the total population there. Traditionally they fished the shores in summer, and moved inland to hunt moose and caribou in winter.

In New Brunswick, the Maliseets (renowned basket-makers) live in the upper St John River valley in the west, while the Mi'kmaqs live to the east. In Nova Scotia, the Mi'kmaqs live in 14 communities, mostly around Bras d'Or Lake on Cape Breton and near Truro. A small group also lives on Prince Edward Island.

Urban Aboriginal Populations	
Winnipeg	68,380
Edmonton	52,100
Vancouver	40,310
Calgary	26,575
Toronto	26,575
Saskatoon	21,535
Ottawa	20,590
Montréal	17,865
Regina	17,105

Aboriginal Population Percentages	
Nunavut	86%
Northwest Territories	52%
Yukon Territory	23%
Manitoba	17%
Saskatchewan	16%
Alberta	6%
BC	5%
Ontario	2%

ABORIGINAL ARTISTS

There was little outside recognition of the art produced by aboriginal communities until the 20th century. But over the last 50 years or so, there's been a strong and growing appreciation of this body of work, led initially by the paintings, sculptures and carvings of revered Haida artist Bill Reid (1920–1998), whose work appears on the back of the $20 bill. Also look out for colorful paintings by Norval Morriseau; mixed-media works by Saskatchewan-born Edward Poitras; and challenging younger artists like Marianne Nicolson and Brian Jungen, who explore political and environmental themes in their art.

Salish canoes, West Vancouver, British Columbia

The Maritimes have experienced a revival of traditional song and dance, language programs, and healing and ritual ceremonies. Public powwows often take place, especially around Truro.

Northeastern Québec & Labrador

The Innu are the long-time inhabitants of the cold boreal forest stretching across the north of Québec and Labrador. The Innu are often confused with the Inuit, but they are not related. Rather, two First Nations – the Naskapi and the Montagnais – make up the Innu. In the past they were fairly nomadic, and survived by hunting caribou and moose for food and skins.

About 80% of Innu live in Québec, with 20% in Labrador.

Northern Ontario, Manitoba & Saskatchewan

The Cree dominate this chilly landscape. As one of Canada's largest First Nations, they also extend west into the Plains and east into Québec. There's a well-known reserve in Ontario at Moose Factory (a former Hudson Bay fur-trading post), which built the hemisphere's first aboriginal ecolodge. Many Cree also live in polar-bear-epicenter Churchill, Manitoba, where they make up about one-third of the local population; it's not uncommon to hear people speaking Cree in Churchill. The Cree have a reputation for being gifted healers.

Yukon & Northwest Territories

The Dene were the first people to settle in what is now the Northwest Territories. Today many live in Yellowknife, as well as villages throughout the Mackenzie Delta, west into the Yukon and Alaska, east toward Nunavut and south into the prairies. Traditionally they're hunters, fishers and trappers and known for their birch-bark basket weaving.

Aboriginal Peoples

Pacific: Haida, Tsimshians, Tlingit

Plains: Sioux, Cree, Blackfoot

Great Lakes/St Lawrence: Ojibwe, Huron

Maritimes: Mi'kmaq, Maliseet

Québec, Labrador: Innu

Northern Ontario, Manitoba, Saskatchewan: Cree

Yukon, NWT: Dene, Gwich'in

Arctic: Inuit

Inuit man with dogs, Nunavut

The Gwich'in First Nations people live further north and rely on caribou for a major part of their diet and lifestyle. They've actively protested drilling in the Arctic National Wildlife Refuge, saying it will deplete the caribou herd there that they depend on for food. The economy of their communities is based mostly on hunting and fishing.

Métis

Métis is the French word for 'mixed blood.' Historically, the term was applied to the children of French fur traders and Cree women in the prairies, and English and Scottish traders and Dene women in the north. Today the term is used broadly to describe people with mixed First Nations and European ancestry.

Métis account for about one-third of the overall aboriginal population. They are largely based in western Canada. Winnipeg and Edmonton are the cities with the highest number of Métis.

Louis Riel (1844–1885) is the culture's most famous individual. He battled for the rights of Métis, who were often trampled during Canada's westward expansion. Riel led two resistance movements against the government, the last at Batoche, Saskatchewan, in 1885. He was caught and convicted of treason, though today he's considered a hero by most Canadians.

Unlike First Nations, Métis never lived on reserves.

'Eskimo' was the term given to Inuit by European explorers. It's now rarely used in Canada. It derives from an Algonquian term meaning 'raw meat eaters,' and many find it offensive.

Inuit

The Inuit are native to Arctic Canada's. Today they number 59,000 (4% of the overall aboriginal population) and are spread throughout four Arctic regions: Nunavut, the Inuvialuit area in the Northwest Territories, Nunavik (northern Québec) and Nunatsiavut (Labrador). All in all, they cover one-third of Canada.

ABORIGINAL MEDIA
....

First Nations Drum (www.firstnationsdrum.com) National newspaper.

First Perspective (www.firstperspective.ca) Online news source.

CBC Aboriginal (www.cbc.ca/aboriginal) The broadcaster's online site devoted to aboriginal news and culture, with links to regional programming in native languages.

Aboriginal Peoples Television Network (APTN; www.aptn.ca) National cable/satellite network that produces and airs aboriginal programming.

Inuit have never lived on reserves, preferring small communities instead: 38% of their villages have a population of less than 500 people. About 29% have between 500 and 999 people, while 33% have 1000 or more residents.

Traditionally Inuit hunted whales and big game, traveled by kayak and dog sled, and spent winters in igloos. Snowmobiles and houses have replaced the sleds and igloos these days, but subsistence hunting is still a big part of the economy, as is traditional soapstone carving and printmaking.

The Inuit language is Inuktitut, a system of syllabics versus letters.

Recent History

Canada never experienced the all-out massacres that marred the clashes between Europeans and Native Americans in the USA. Nevertheless, Canada's aboriginal population still suffered discrimination, loss of territory and civil-rights violations throughout the country's history.

In 1993 Canada's biggest land claim was settled when Prime Minister Brian Mulroney signed into existence the new territory of Nunavut, which took effect in 1999, giving the Inuit self-government after more than 20 years of negotiations. The 28,000 people of the far north now had control over about one-fifth of Canadian soil.

It was big news in 2010 when the government said it was sorry for the relocation of Inuit families to the high Arctic during the 1950s. At the time, the government promised the families a better life by moving to the region, but it didn't follow through in providing them with necessary supports like adequate shelter and supplies. As a result, the families struggled greatly to survive. Many have argued the government moved the families not to help them, as stated, but to establish Canada's Arctic sovereignty during the Cold War. The apology was a follow-up to a 1996 settlement, in which the government agreed to pay $10 million into a trust fund to compensate the families.

Aboriginal Tourism

From learning to paddle a traditional canoe in Tofino, BC, to sampling bannock bread in a Mi'kmaq cafe on PEI's Lennox Island to perusing the Great Northern Arts Festival in Inuvik in the Northwest Territories, there are many opportunities to immerse yourself in aboriginal culture.

The further north in Canada you head, the more your travel dollars benefit aboriginal communities. First Air (p882) and Air Creebec (p882) are Aboriginal-owned, as are **Inns North hotels** (www.innsnorth.com), located in several communities throughout Nunavut and the Northwest Territories.

A good website with links to aboriginal tourism opportunities nationwide is http://canada.travelall.com/promos/Aboriginal.htm. BC has its own **Aboriginal Tourism Association** (www.aboriginalbc.com), with the lowdown on 60 Aboriginal-owned businesses in the province.

Top First Nations Cultural Centers

Museum of Northern BC, Prince Rupert

Haida Heritage Centre, Kay Llnagaay, BC

Dänojà Zho Cultural Centre, Dawson City, YK

Wanuskewin Heritage Park, Saskatoon, SK

Top Museums for Aboriginal Arts

Art Gallery of Ontario, Toronto

Museum of Civilization, Gatineau

National Gallery, Ottawa

UBC Museum of Anthropology, Vancouver

Above Shoshone-Cree woman wrapped in a Hudson's Bay blanket

Left Bill Reid's *The Raven and the First Men*, Museum of Anthropology, University of British Columbia, Vancouver

Outdoor Activities

While the great Canadian outdoors looks undeniably pretty on postcards, the wilderness here is not just about good looks. Locals have been jumping in head first – sometimes literally – for decades, with activities ranging from hiking and kayaking to biking and climbing. For visitors, there are countless operators across the country that can help you gear up and get out there.

Skiing & Snowboarding

It seems like almost everyone in Canada was born to ski. Visitors will find some of the world's most renowned resorts here – British Columbia, Alberta and Québec host the premier ones – but it's also worth asking the locals where they like to hit the slopes: for every big-time swanky resort, there are several smaller spots where the terrain and the welcome can be even better.

Above Snowboarding at Whistler, British Columbia

Québec boasts some big slopes – Le Massif, near Québec City, has a vertical drop of 770m (2526ft) – located handily close to the cities. Most of these non-alpine hills, such as Mont-Tremblant, are a day's drive from Toronto and less than an hour from Québec City and Montréal. Ski areas in Québec's Eastern Townships offer renowned gladed runs – courses that weave through a thinned forest.

Head west and you'll hit the big mountains and vast alpine terrains. Glide down gargantuan slopes at Whistler-Blackcomb, which has North America's highest vertical drop and most impressive terrain variation. You'll also slide through stunning postcard landscapes in the Canadian Rockies, especially at Sunshine in Banff National Park.

In BC's Okanagan Valley, resorts like Apex and Big White boast good snow year after year. Snowpack ranges from 2m to 6m-plus, depending on how close the resort is to the Pacific Ocean. The deepest, driest snow in the world piles up in BC's Kootenay Region. Ski it at Nelson's Whitewater, Rossland's Red Mountain or Fernie's Alpine Resort.

For cross-country skiing, Canmore, Alberta (www.canmorenordic.com) offers popular trails that were part of that other Canadian Winter Olympics, Calgary in 1988. For further information and resources covering the national scene, check the website of the **Canadian Ski Council** (www.skicanada.org).

Sweetest Slopes

Whistler-Blackcomb, Whistler, BC

Le Massif, Baie St-Paul, Québec

Sunshine Village, Banff, Alberta

Big White, Kelowna, BC

Fernie Resort, Fernie, BC

Hiking

You don't have to be a hiker to hike in Canada. While there are plenty of multiday jaunts for those who like tramping through the wilderness equipped only with a Swiss Army knife, there are also innumerable opportunities for those whose idea of a hike is a gentle stroll around a lake with a pub visit at the end.

The country's hiking capital is Banff National Park, crisscrossed with jaw-dropping vistas accessible to both hard and soft eco-adventurers. At Lake Louise, for example, you can march through dense spruce and pine forests, then ascend into alpine meadows carpeted with wildflowers and surrounded by crumbling glaciers and azure lakes. Also in the Rockies region, Wilcox Ridge and Parker Ridge offer breathtaking glacier views.

In BC's provincial parks system (www.bcparks.ca), you'll have a choice of more than 100 parks, each with distinct landscapes to hike through: check out Garibaldi Park's landscape of ancient volcanoes (not far from Whistler) and Mt Robson Park's popular Berg Lake alpine trail. And since you're in BC, head to Vancouver's North Shore for the Grouse Grind, a steep forest hike that's also known as 'mother nature's Stairmaster.' You'll understand why by the time you get to the top (if you get to the top).

Out east, awe-inspiring trails pattern the landscape. In southern Ontario, the **Bruce Trail** (www.brucetrail.org) tracks from Niagara Falls to Tobermory. It's the oldest and longest continuous footpath in Canada

Top Day Hikes

Lake Louise, Banff, Alberta

Skyline Trail, Cape Breton Highlands, Nova Scotia

Parker Ridge, Jasper, Alberta

Stanley Park, Vancouver, BC

Bruce Trail, Ontario

HOCKEY: THE NATIONAL PASTIME

Canadians aren't fooling around when it comes to hockey. They play hard and well.

Grassroots hockey, aka pond hockey, takes place in communities across the country every night on a frozen surface. All you need is a puck, a hockey stick and a few friends to live the dream.

If you'd rather watch than play, Vancouver, Edmonton, Calgary, Toronto, Ottawa, Winnipeg and Montréal all have **NHL** (www.nhl.com) teams who skate tough and lose the odd tooth. Minor pro teams and junior hockey clubs fill many more arenas with rabid fans; check the **Canadian Hockey League** (www.chl.ca) and **American Hockey League** (www.theahl.com) for local stick wielders.

Hikers at Yoho National Park, British Columbia

and spans more than 850km. Though portions are near cities like Hamilton and Toronto, it's surprisingly serene. Cape Breton Highlands National Park offers exquisite hiking over stark, dramatic coastline. Newfoundland's trails make for fantastic shoreline hiking and often provide whale views. The **East Coast Trail** (www.eastcoasttrail.ca) on the Avalon Peninsula is particularly renowned for its vistas.

And don't forget the cities. Canada's major metropolises offer some great urban hikes, an ideal way to get to know the communities you're visiting. Slip into your runners for a stroll (or a jog) with the locals in Montréal's Parc du Mont Royal or in Vancouver's gemlike Stanley Park, where the idyllic seawall winds alongside towering trees and lapping ocean.

Kayaking & Rafting

The Canadian Arctic, kayaking's motherland, still remains one of its special places: cruise the polar fjords of Ellesmere Island and watch narwhals and walruses during the fuse-short summer. Further south, slide silently past ancient forests and totem poles in BC's Gwaii Haanas National Park Reserve, or in the province's Johnstone Strait and watch orcas breaching. The east coast has sea kayaking galore. Paddlers in Witless Bay or Gros Morne, Newfoundland, often glide alongside whales.

If you're on a tight schedule and don't have time for multiday odysseys, there are plenty of more accessible ways to get your kayaking fix. Big cities like BC's Vancouver and Victoria offer tours and lessons near town, while the province's Sunshine Coast and Salt Spring Island offer crenulated coastlines combined with tranquil sea inlets.

As old as kayaking, and just as Canadian, is the canoe. Experienced paddlers can strike out on one of 33 **Canadian Heritage Rivers** (www.chrs.ca).

Top Places to Paddle

South Nahanni River, Northwest Territories

Witless Bay, Newfoundland

Johnstone Strait, BC

Gwaii Haanas National Park Reserve, BC

Surfing at Tofino, Vancouver Island, British Columbia

Some of the best include the Northwest Territories' South Nahanni River (near Fort Simpson) and Ontario's French River (near Sudbury).

Mountain Biking & Cycling

Mountain biking is a big deal in Canada. While cycling enthusiasts in other countries might be into trundling around town or along a gentle riverside trail, in Canada you're more likely to find them hurtling down a mountainside covered in mud. Given the landscape, of course, it was just a matter of time before the wheels went off-road here.

If you need to ease yourself in, start gently with BC's **Kettle Valley Rail Trail** (www.kettlevalleyrailway.ca), near Kelowna. This dramatic segment of converted railbed barrels across picturesque wooden trestle bridges and through canyon tunnels.

Looking for more of an adrenaline rush? In Vancouver's North Shore area, you'll be riding on much narrower and steeper 'trestles.' Birthplace of 'freeride' mountain biking (which combines downhill and dirt jumping), this area offers some unique innovations: elevated bridges, log rides and skinny planks that loft over the wet undergrowth. It's a similar story up at Whistler where the melted ski slopes are transformed into a summertime bike park that draws thousands every year – especially during the annual **Crankworx Mountain Bike Festival** (www.crankworx.com/whistler) in July.

For road touring, Canada's east coast, with more small towns and less emptiness, is a fantastic place to pedal, either as a single-day road ride or a multiday trip. Circle Québec's Lac St-Jean; try any part of the 4000km **Route Verte** (www.routeverte.com), the longest network of bicycle paths in the Americas; or follow Prince Edward Island's bucolic red roads and its **Confederation Trail** (www.tourismpei.com/pei-cycling).

Best Biking

Confederation Trail, PEI

Kettle Valley Rail Trail, Kelowna, BC

North Shore, Vancouver, BC

Route Verte, Québec

FISHING

Built on its aboriginal and pioneer past, Canada has a strong tradition of fishing and you can expect to come across plenty of opportunities to hook walleye, pike, rainbow or lake trout on your travels. Among the best fishing holes to head for are Lunenburg in Nova Scotia and the Miramichi River in New Brunswick. And while salmon are the usual draw on the Pacific coastline, hopping aboard a local vessel for some sea fishing off Haida Gwaii can deliver the kind of giant catches you'll be bragging about for years to come.

Climbing

All those inviting crags you've spotted on your trip are an indication that Canada is a major climbing capital, ideal for short scales or multiday crampon-picking jaunts.

British Columbia's Squamish region, located between Vancouver and Whistler, is a climbing center, with dozens of accessible (and not so accessible) peaks. Tap into the scene via **Squamish Rock Guides** (www. squamishrockguides.com). If mountaineering is more your thing, the Rockies are the recommended first stop. Canmore, near Banff, is an ideal destination for rock climbers, no matter what your skill level. **Yamnuska** (www.yamnuska.com) is one company that offers ice and other climbs in the region.

If you prefer the European approach, the Matterhorn of Canada is BC's Mt Assiniboine, located between the Kootenay and Banff National Parks. Other western classics include Alberta's Mt Edith Cavell, in Jasper; BC's Mt Robson and Sir Donald in the Rockies; and Garibaldi Peak, in Garibaldi Provincial Park, near Whistler. If you need a guide, check in with the excellent **Alpine Club of Canada** (www.alpineclubofcanada.ca).

If your trip takes you out east instead, Ontario's favorite climbing havens dot the Bruce Peninsula.

Top Climbs

The Chief,
Squamish, BC

Canmore, Alberta

Pont-Rouge,
Québec

Skaha Bluffs,
Okanagan
Valley, BC

Bugaboo Spire,
near Golden, BC

Surfing & Windsurfing

If you're aiming to become a temporary beach bum on your Canada trip, head to the wild west coast of BC's Vancouver Island and hang out on the beaches around Tofino. Surfing schools and gear-rental operations stud this region and you'll have an awesome time riding the swells (or just watching everyone else as you stretch out on the sand). Backed by verdant rainforest, it's an idyllic spot to spend some time.

June to September is the height of the season here, but serious surfers also like to drop by in winter to face down the lashing waves. Check **Surfing Vancouver Island** (www.surfingvancouverisland.com) for a taste of what to expect.

Some 6000km away, the east coast of Nova Scotia can also dish out some formidable swells. The US south coast's hurricane season (August to November) brings Canadians steep fast breaks, snappy right and left point breaks, and offshore reef and shoal breaks in areas like Lawrencetown, just outside Halifax, as well as across the entire South Shore region. There are also a couple of surf schools here. **Scotia Surfer** (www. scotiasurfer.com) has the lowdown.

Windsurfers set their sails for Howe Sound in Squamish, BC and for Québec's Magdalen Islands, a small chain in the Gulf of St Lawrence.

**Top Places
to Surf &
Windsurf**

Tofino, Vancouver
Island, BC

Lawrencetown,
Nova Scotia

Nitinat Lake, Vancouver Island, BC

Magdalen Islands,
Québec

Howe Sound, Squamish, BC

Wildlife

On land, in the water and in the air, Canada is teeming with the kind of camera-worthy critters that make visitors wonder if they haven't stepped into a safari park by mistake. And when we say 'critters,' we're not talking small fry: this is the home of grizzlies, polar bears, moose and bald eagles, and it offers perfect coastal viewing spots for a roll call of huge whales. Extra camera batteries are heartily recommended.

Grizzly Bears & Black Bears

Above Grizzly bear, British Columbia

Grizzly bears – *Ursus arctos horribilis* to all you Latin scholars out there – are most commonly found in the Rocky Mountain regions of British Columbia and Alberta. Standing up to 3m tall, you'll recognize them by their distinctive shoulder hump. Solitary animals with no natural enemies (except humans), they enjoy crunching on elk, moose or caribou, but they're usually content to fill their bellies with berries and, if available, fresh salmon. Keep in mind that you should never approach any bear. And in remote areas, be sure to travel in groups.

In 1994 coastal BC's Khutzeymateen Grizzly Bear Sanctuary (near the northern town of Prince Rupert) was officially designated with protected status. Over 50 grizzlies currently live on this 45,000-hectare refuge. A few ecotour operators have permits for viewing the animals.

Just to confuse you, grizzlies are almost black, while their smaller, more prevalent relative, the black bear, is sometimes brown. Canada is home to around half a million black bears and they're spread out across the country, except for Prince Edward Island, southern Alberta and southern Saskatchewan. In regions such as northern BC, as well as in Banff and Jasper National Parks, seeing black bears feasting on berries as you drive past on the highway is surprisingly common.

Polar Bears

Weighing less than a kilogram at birth, the fiercest member of the bear clan is not quite so cute when it grows up to be a hulking 600kg. But these mesmerizing animals still pack a huge visual punch for visitors. If your visit to Canada won't be complete until you've seen one, there's really only one place to go: Churchill, Manitoba, on the shores of Hudson Bay (late September to early November is the viewing season). About 900 of the planet's roughly 20,000 white-furred beasts prowl the tundra here.

Just remember: the carnivorous, ever-watchful predators are not cuddly cartoon critters. Unlike grizzlies and black bears, polar bears actively prey on people.

Moose

Canada's iconic shrub-nibbler, the moose is a massive member of the deer family that owes its popularity to its distinctively odd appearance: skinny legs supporting a humungous body and a cartoonish face that looks permanently inquisitive and clueless at the same time. And then there are the antlers: males grow a spectacular rack every summer, only to discard them come November.

Adding to their Bullwinkle appeal, moose can move at more than 50km/hr and easily outswim two adults paddling a canoe – all on a vegetarian diet comprised mostly of tasty leaves and twigs.

You'll spot moose foraging for food near lakes, muskegs and streams, as well as in the forests of the western mountain ranges in the Rockies and the Yukon. Newfoundland is perhaps the moosiest place of all. In 1904 the province imported and released four beasts into the wild. They enjoyed the good life of shrub-eating and hot sex, ultimately spawning the 120,000 inhabitants that now roam the woods.

During mating season (September), the males can become belligerent, so keep your distance.

Elk, Deer & Caribou

Moose are not the only animals that can exhibit a Mr Hyde personality change during rutting season. Usually placid, male elk have been known to charge vehicles in Jasper National Park, believing their reflection in the shiny paintwork to be a rival for their harem of eligible females. It's rare, though, and Jasper is generally one of the best places in Canada to see this large deer species wandering around attracting camera-toting travelers on the edge of town.

White-tailed deer can be found anywhere from Nova Scotia's Cape Breton to the Northwest Territories' Great Slave Lake. Its bigger relative, the caribou, is unusual in that both males and females sport enormous

Best Bear-Spotting

Churchill, Manitoba – polar bears

Khutzeymateen Grizzly Bear Sanctuary, Prince Rupert, BC – grizzlies

Rocky Mountain National Parks (Banff and Jasper, Alberta; Kootenay and Yoho, BC) – grizzlies and black bears

Best Moose-Viewing

Northern Peninsula, Newfoundland

Cape Breton Highlands National Park, Nova Scotia

Algonquin Provincial Park, Ontario

Maligne Lake, Jasper National Park, Alberta

WILDLIFE POLAR BEARS

Whale watching at the San Juan Islands, British Columbia

antlers. Barren-ground caribou feed on lichen and spend most of the year on the tundra from Baffin Island to Alaska. Woodland caribou roam further south, with some of the biggest herds trekking across northern Québec and Labrador. These beasts, which have a reputation for not being especially smart, also show up in the mountain parks of BC, Alberta and Newfoundland, which is where many visitors catch their glimpses.

Whales

Whale Hot Spots

Witless Bay, Newfoundland

Digby Neck, Nova Scotia

Victoria, BC

Tofino, BC

Tadoussac, Québec

Cabot Trail, Nova Scotia

More than 22 species of whale and porpoise lurk offshore in Atlantic Canada, including superstars like the humpback whale, which averages 15m and 36 tons; the North Atlantic right whale, the world's most endangered leviathan, with an estimated population of just 350; and the mighty blue whale, the largest animal on earth at 25m and around 100 tons. Then there's the little guy, the minke, which grows to 10m and often approaches boats, delighting passengers with acrobatics as it shows off. Whale-watching tours are very popular throughout the region.

You can also spot humpbacks and gray whales off the west coast. But it's the orca that dominates viewing here. Their aerodynamic bodies, signature black-and-white coloration and incredible speed (up to 40km/h) make them the Ferraris of the aquatic world, and their diet includes seals, belugas and other whales (hence the 'killer whale' nickname). The waters around Vancouver Island, particularly in the Johnstone Strait, teem with orcas every summer. Whale-watching tours depart from points throughout the region; Tofino and Victoria are particular hot spots for operators.

Belugas glide in Arctic waters to the north. These ghostly white whales are one of the smallest members of the whale family, typically measuring no more than 4m and weighing about 1 ton. They are chatty fellows

Atlantic puffin, Newfoundland

who squeak, groan and peep while traveling in closely knit family pods. Churchill, Manitoba, is a good place to view them, as is Tadoussac, Québec (the only population outside the Arctic resides here).

Birds

Canada's wide skies are home to 462 bird species, with BC and Ontario boasting the greatest diversity. The most famous feathered resident is the common loon, Canada's national bird – if you don't spot one in the wild, you'll see it on the back of the $1 coin. Rivaling it in the ubiquity stakes are Canada geese, a hardy fowl that can fly up to 1000km per day and seems to have successfully colonized parks throughout the world.

The most visually arresting of Canada's birds are its eagles, especially the bald variety, whose wingspan can reach up to 2m. Good viewing sites include Brackendale, between Vancouver and Whistler in BC, where up to 4000 eagles nest in winter. Also train your binoculars on Bras d'Or Lake in Cape Breton, Nova Scotia and on Vancouver Island's southern and western shorelines.

Seabirds flock to Atlantic Canada to breed. Think razorbills, kitti-wakes, Arctic terns, common murres and, yes, puffins. Everyone loves these cute little guys, a sort of waddling penguin-meets-parrot, with black-and-white feathers and an orange beak. They nest around New-foundland, in particular. The preeminent places to get feathered are New Brunswick's Grand Manan Island and Newfoundland's Witless Bay and Cape St Mary's (both on the Avalon Peninsula near St John's). The best time is May through August, before the birds fly away for the winter.

Best Bird watching

Cape St Mary's, Newfoundland

Point Pelee National Park, Ontario

Witless Bay, Newfoundland

Grand Manan Island, New Brunswick

Brackendale, BC

Cuisines of Canada

A couple of years back, when the *Globe and Mail* newspaper asked salivating Canadians to nominate the country's national dish, its website comments form heated up faster than a frying egg on a midsummer Toronto sidewalk. Poutine – golden fries drowned in gravy and cheese curds – dominated the exercise, while Montréal-style bagels, salmon jerky, pierogies and even ketchup-flavored potato chips jostled for taste-bud attention.

Aside from showing that Canadians love comfort food, the unscientific poll indicated that the national menu is as diverse as the locals, a casserole of food cultures blended together from centuries of immigration.

But before you start thinking that a sophisticated dinner here is a night out at a Tim Hortons doughnut outlet (go for the Canadian Maple), there's much more to scoffing in Canada than you might imagine. Big cities like Montréal, Toronto and Vancouver have internationally renowned fine-dining scenes, while regions across the country have rediscovered

Above Poutine: french fries topped with gravy and cheese curds

the unique ingredients grown, foraged and produced on their door-steps – bringing distinctive seafood, artisan cheeses and lip-smacking produce to the mouths of curious locavores...which explains why any Canadian area with a population of more than two has its own farmers market.

But don't take our word for it. Wherever you head on your travels here, sink your teeth into the wide array of available homegrown flavors and make dining like a Canadian a key focus of your trip.

Local Flavors

If you're starting from the east, the main dish of the Maritime provinces is lobster – boiled in the pot and served with a little butter – and the best place to get stuck in is a community hall 'kitchen party' on Prince Edward Island. Dip into some chunky potato salad and hearty seafood chowder while waiting for your crustacean to arrive, but don't eat too much; you'll need room for the mountainous fruit pie coming your way afterwards.

Next door, Nova Scotia visitors should save their appetites for butter-soft Digby scallops and rustic Lunenberg sausage, while the favored food of nearby Newfoundland and Labrador often combines rib-sticking dishes of cod cheeks and sweet snow crab. If you're feeling really raven-ous, gnaw on a slice of seal flipper pie – a dish you're unlikely to forget in a hurry.

Québec is the world's largest maple-syrup producer, processing around 6.5 million gallons of the sweet pancake accompaniment every year. In this French-influenced province, fine food seems to be a lifeblood for the locals, who will happily sit down for four-hour joie de vivre dinners where accompanying wine and conversation flow in equal measures.

The province's cosmopolitan Montréal has long claimed to be the na-tion's fine-dining capital, but there's an appreciation of food here at all levels that also includes hearty pea soups, exquisite cheeses and tasty pâtés sold at bustling markets. In addition, there's also that national dish, poutine, waiting to clog your arteries plus smoked-meat deli sandwiches so large you'll have to dislocate your jaw to fit them in your mouth.

Ontario – especially Toronto – is a microcosm of Canada's melting pot of cuisines. Like Québec, maple syrup is a supersweet flavoring of choice here, and it's found in decadent desserts such as beavertails (fried, sug-ared dough) and on breakfast pancakes the size of Frisbees. Head south to the Niagara Peninsula wine region and you'll also discover restaurants fusing contemporary approaches and traditional local ingredients, such as fish from the Great Lakes.

Far north from here, Nunavut in the Arctic Circle is Canada's newest territory, but it has a long history of Inuit food, offering a real culinary adventure for extreme-cuisine travelers. Served in some restaurants (but more often in family homes – make friends with locals and they may invite you in for a feast), regional specialties include boiled seal, raw frozen char and *maktaaq* – whale skin cut into small pieces and swallowed whole.

In contrast, the central provinces of Manitoba, Saskatchewan and Alberta have their own deep-seated culinary ways. The latter, Canada's cowboy country, is the nation's beef capital – you'll find top-notch Al-berta steak on menus at leading restaurants across the country. If you're offered 'prairie oysters' here, though, you might want to know (or maybe you'd prefer not to) that they're bull's testicles prepared in a variety of ways designed to take your mind off their origin.

There's an old Eastern European influence over the border in Manito-ba, where immigrant Ukrainians have added comfort-food staples such

Festivals

International Shellfish Festival, Prince Edward Island (www. peishellfish.com)

Shediac Lobster Festival, New Brunswick (www. shediaclobsterfes-tival.ca)

Feast Tofino, British Columbia (www.feasttofino. com)

Ribfest, Ontario (www.canad-aslargestribfest. com)

Festival des From-ages Fins, Québec (www.festivaldes-fromages.qc.ca)

Salmon drying in a smokehouse, British Columbia

as pierogies and thick, spicy sausages. Head next door to prairie-land Saskatchewan for dessert, though. The province's heaping fruit pies are its most striking culinary contribution, especially when prepared with tart Saskatoon berries.

In the far west, British Columbians have traditionally fed themselves from the sea and the fertile farmlands of the interior. Okanagan Valley peaches, cherries and blueberries – best purchased from seasonal road-side stands throughout the region – are the staple of many summer diets. In fact, you might find the occasional giddy local slumped against a tree with fruit-stained lips and a big smile. But it's the seafood that attracts the lion's share of culinary fans. Tuck into succulent wild salmon, juicy Fanny Bay oysters and velvet-soft scallops and you may decide you've stumbled on foodie nirvana.

Top Dining Neighborhoods

Ask anyone in Toronto, Montréal or Vancouver to name Canada's leading foodie city and they'll likely inform you that you've just found it. But while each of the big three claims to be at the top table when it comes to dining, their strengths are so diverse they're more accurately defined as complementary courses in one great meal.

First dish on the table is Montréal, which was Canada's sole dine-out capital long before the upstarts threw off their doughnut-based shackles. Renowned for bringing North America's finest French-influenced cuisine to local palates, it hasn't given up its crown lightly. Chefs here are often treated like rock stars as they challenge old-world conventions with daring, even artistic, approaches – expect clever, fusion gastronomy. You should also expect a great restaurant experience: Montréalers have a bacchanalian love for eating out, with lively rooms ranging from cozy

Foodie Books

Canada's Favourite Recipes (Rose Murray & Elizabeth Baird; 2012)

Sugar Shack Au Pied de Cochon (Martin Picard; 2012)

Modern Native Feasts: Healthy, Innovative, Sustainable Cuisine (Andrew George Jr; 2013)

The Salmon Recipes: Stories of Our Endangered North Coast Cuisine (Luanne Roth, Michael Ambach & Ken McCormich; 2013)

Apple orchard, Okanagan Valley, British Columbia

old-town restaurants to the animated patios of Rue Prince Arthur and the sophisticated, often funky eateries of the Plateau.

If Montréal serves as an ideal starter, that makes Toronto the main course – although that's a reflection of its recent elevation rather than its prominence. Fusion is also the default approach in Canada's largest city, although it's been taken even further here with a wave of contemporary immigration adding modern influences from Asia to a foundation of European cuisines. With a bewildering 7000 restaurants to choose from, though, it can be a tough choice figuring out where to unleash your top-end dining budget. The best approach is to hit the neighborhoods: both the Financial District and Old York areas are studded with classy, high-end joints.

And while that appears to make Vancouver the dessert, it could be argued this glass-towered west-coast metropolis is the best of the bunch. In recent years some of the country's most innovative chefs have set up shop here, inspired by the twin influences of an abundant local larder and Canada's most cosmopolitan population. Fusion is the starting point here in fine-dining districts like Yaletown and Kitsilano. But there's also a high level of authenticity in top-notch Asian dining: the best sushi bars and Japanese *izakayas* outside Tokyo jostle for attention with superb Vietnamese and Korean eateries.

Tasty Blogs

National Nosh (www.thenationalnosh.blogspot.com)

Dinner With Julie (www.dinnerwithjulie.com)

Seasonal Ontario Food (www.seasonalontariofood.blogspot.com)

Vancouver Foodster (www.vancouverfoodster.com)

Wine Regions

While many international visitors – especially those who think Canadians live under a permanent blanket of snow – are surprised to learn that wine is produced here, their suspicion is always tempered after a drink or two. Canada's wines have gained ever-greater kudos in recent years, and while smaller-scale production and the industry dominance of other wine regions means they'll never be a global market leader, there are some truly lip-smacking surprises waiting for thirsty grape lovers.

Above Harvesting pinot gris grapes, Okanagan Valley, British Columbia

As the best way to sample any wine is to head straight to the source – where you can taste the region in the glass – consider doing a little homework and locating the closest vineyards on your Canada visit. You won't want to miss the multitude of top wineries in Ontario's Niagara region or British Columbia's Okanagan Valley – the country's leading producers – but a visit to the smaller wineries of Québec and the charming boutique operations of Nova Scotia and Vancouver Island can be just as rewarding.

Regional Wine List

Depending on how thirsty you are, you're rarely too far from a wine region in Canada. Which means that most visitors can easily add a mini taste-tripping tour to their visit if they'd like to meet a few producers and sample some intriguing local flavors. Here's a rundown of the best areas, including the magnum-sized larger regions and the thimble-sized smaller locales – why not stay all summer and visit them all?

Okanagan Valley, British Columbia

The rolling hills of this lakeside region are well worth the five-hour drive from Vancouver. Studded among the vine-striped slopes are more than 100 wineries enjoying a diverse climate that fosters both crisp whites and bold reds. With varietals including pinot noir, pinot gris, pinot blanc, merlot and chardonnay, there's a wine here to suit almost every palate. Most visitors base themselves in Kelowna, the Okanagan's wine capital, before fanning out to well-known blockbuster wineries like Mission Hill, Quail's Gate, Cedar Creek and Summerhill Pyramid Winery (yes, it has a pyramid). Many of them also have excellent restaurants.

Find out more about BC's wine regions and annual festivals and download free touring maps at www.winebc.com.

Niagara Peninsula, Ontario

This picture-perfect region of country inns and charming old towns offers more than 60 wineries and grows more than three-quarters of Canada's grapes. Neatly divided between the low-lying Niagara-on-the-Lake area and the higher Niagara Escarpment, its complex mix of soils and climates – often likened to the Loire Valley – is ideal for chardonnay, riesling, pinot noir and cabernet-franc varietals. This is also the production center for Canadian ice wine (p132), that potently sweet dessert libation. While home to some of Canada's biggest and best wineries, including Inniskillin, Jackson-Triggs and Peller Estates, don't miss smaller pit stops such as Magnotta and Cave Spring Cellars.

Prince Edward County, Ontario

Proving that not all Ontario's wineries are clustered in Niagara, this comparatively new grape-growing region – located in the province's southeastern corner – is a charming alternative if you want to avoid the tour buses winding through the main wine area. A long-established fruit-growing district with generally lower temperatures than Niagara, cooler-climate wines are favored here including chardonnay and pinot noir. The most intriguing wineries include Closson Chase, Black Prince Winery and Grange of Prince Edward. If your taste buds are piqued, consider checking out other Ontario wine regions like Pelee Island and Lake Erie North Shore.

Eastern Townships, Québec

Starting around 80km southeast of Montréal, this idyllic farmland region is studded with quiet villages, leafy woodlands, crystal-clear lakes and winding country roads. A rising tide of wineries has joined the traditional farm operations here in recent years, with rieslings and chardonnays particularly suited to the area's cool climate and soil conditions. But it's the local ice wines, dessert wines and fruit wines that are the area's main specialties, so make sure you come with a sweet tooth. Wineries to perk up your taste buds here include Domaine Félibre, Vignoble de L'Orpailleur and Vignoble Le Cep d'Argent.

Wine Books

Okanagan Wine Tour Guide (John Schreiner; 2012)

Crush on Niagara: The Definitive Wine Tour Guide for Niagara, Lake Erie North Shore, Pelee Island and Prince Edward County (Andrew Brooks; 2010)

Wineries and Wine Country of Nova Scotia (Sean Wood; 2006)

Island Wineries of British Columbia (Gary Hynes; 2013)

Explore Ontario further by downloading a free map and wine country visitor guide from www.winesofontario.org.

Hundreds of Canadian wineries are sampled at the Wines of Canada website (www.winesofcanada.com).

Montérégie, Québec

The dominant player in Québec's wider Eastern Townships, this bumpy and bucolic area is packed with vineyards and orchards (not to mention a surfeit of maple groves). A major fruit-farming region – this is an ideal spot to try ciders and flavor-packed fruit wines – growers here are happy to try just about any red or white varietal, but it's their rosés that are particularly memorable. Recommended wineries include Domaine St-Jacques, Les Petits Cailloux and Vignoble des Pins; and keep in mind that Québecois restaurants often encourage diners to bring their own bottles, so fill your car as you explore the region.

Nova Scotia

Divided into six boutique wine-producing regions (from the warm shoreline of Northumberland Strait to the verdant Annapolis Valley), Nova Scotia's two-dozen wineries are mostly just a couple of hours' drive from Halifax. One of the world's coldest grape-growing areas, cool-climate whites are a staple here, including a unique varietal known as l'Acadie Blanc. Innovative sparkling wines are a Nova Scotia specialty and they tend to dominate the drops on offer at the popular stops such as the excellent Benjamin Bridge Vineyards. Other highly recommended destinations include Gaspereau Vineyards, Jost Vineyards and Domaine de Grand Pré.

Find out more about Nova Scotia's wine region, including information on courses and festivals, at www.winesofnova-scotia.ca.

Festivals

Canada is dripping with palate-pleasing wine events, which makes it especially important to check the dates of your trip: raising a few glasses with celebratory locals is one of the best ways to encounter the country.

If you're in BC, it's hard to miss one of the Okanagan's three main festivals – see www.thewinefestivals.com for dates. If you prefer not to leave the big city, check out March's **Vancouver International Wine Festival** (www.vanwinefest.ca).

Across the country in Ontario, Niagara also stages more than one annual event to celebrate its winey wealth, including June's New Vintage Festival and September's giant Niagara Wine Festival. For information, visit www.niagarawinefestival.com.

Québec-bound oenophiles should drop into the annual **Montréal Passion Vin** (www.montrealpassionvin.ca), a swish two-day charity fundraiser focused on unique and rare vintages. For regional food as well as wine, the Eastern Townships' Magog-Orford area hosts the multiday **Fête des Vendanges** (www.fetedesvendanges.com) in September.

Visitors to the east coast are not left out. Nova Scotia hosts a 50-event **Fall Wine Festival** (www.nsfallwinefestival.ca) in mid-September.

Wine Online

John Schreiner on Wine (www.johnschreiner.blogspot.com)

Dr Vino (www.drvino.com)

Girl on Wine (www.girlonwine.com)

Survival Guide

Directory A–Z

Accommodations

In Canada, you'll be choosing from a wide range of B&Bs, chain motels, hotels and hostels. Provincial tourist offices publish comprehensive directories of accommodations, and some take bookings online.

Seasons

➔ Peak season is summer, basically June through August, when prices are highest.

➔ It's best to book ahead during summer, as well as during ski season at winter resorts, and during holidays and major events, as rooms can be scarce.

➔ Some properties close down altogether in the off-season.

Amenities

➔ At many budget properties (campgrounds, hostels, simple B&Bs) bathrooms are shared.

➔ Midrange accommodation, such as most B&Bs, inns (auberges in French), motels and some hotels, generally offer the best value for money. Expect a private bathroom, cable TV and, in some cases, free breakfast.

➔ Top-end accommodations offer an international standard of amenities, with fitness and business centers and on-site dining.

➔ Most properties offer in-room wi-fi. It's typically free in budget and midrange lodgings, while top-end hotels often charge a fee.

➔ Many smaller properties, especially B&Bs, ban smoking. Marriott and Westin brand hotels are 100% smoke free. Other properties have rooms set aside for nonsmokers. We use the nonsmoking icon (⊝) to mean that *all* rooms within a property are nonsmoking rooms.

➔ Air-conditioning is not a standard amenity at most budget and midrange places. If you want it, be sure to ask about it when you book.

Discounts

➔ In winter prices can plummet by as much as 50%.

➔ Membership in the American Automobile Association (AAA) or an associated automobile association, American Association of Retired Persons (AARP) or other organizations also yields modest savings (usually 10%).

➔ Check hotel websites for special online rates. The usual suspects also offer discounted room prices throughout Canada:

Expedia (www.expedia.com)

Hotwire (www.hotwire.com)

Priceline (www.priceline.com)

Travelocity (www.travelocity.com)

B&Bs

➔ **Bed & Breakfast Online** (www.bbcanada.com) is the main booking agency for properties nationwide.

➔ In Canada, B&Bs (*gîtes* in French) are essentially converted private homes whose owners live on-site. People who like privacy may find B&Bs too intimate, as walls are rarely soundproof and it's usual to mingle with your hosts and other guests.

SLEEPING PRICE RANGES

The following price ranges refer to a double room with private bathroom in high season, unless stated otherwise. Tax (which can be up to 17%) is not included in prices listed.

$ less than $80 ($100 in major cities)

$$ $80–180 ($100–250 in major cities)

$$$ more than $180 ($250 in major cities)

→ Standards vary widely, sometimes even within a single B&B. The cheapest rooms tend to be small with few amenities and a shared bathroom. Nicer ones have added features such as a balcony, a fireplace and an en suite bathroom. Breakfast is always included in the rates (though it might be continental instead of a full cooked affair).

→ Not all B&Bs accept children.

→ Minimum stays (usually two nights) are common, and many B&Bs are only open seasonally.

Camping

→ Canada is filled with campgrounds – some federal or provincial, others privately owned.

→ The official season runs from May to September, but exact dates vary by location.

→ Facilities vary widely. Backcountry sites offer little more than pit toilets and fire rings, and have no potable water. Unserviced (tent) campgrounds come with access to drinking water and a washroom with toilets and sometimes showers. The best-equipped sites feature flush toilets and hot showers, and water, electrical

and sewer hookups for recreational vehicles (RVs).

→ Private campgrounds sometimes cater only to trailers (caravans) and RVs, and may feature convenience stores, playgrounds and swimming pools. It is a good idea to phone ahead to make sure the size of sites and the services provided at a particular campground are suitable for your vehicle.

→ Most government-run sites are available on a first-come, first-served basis and fill up quickly, especially in July and August. Several national parks participate in Parks Canada's **camping reservation program** (☎877-737-3783; www.pccamping.ca; reservation fee $11), which is a convenient way to make sure you get a spot.

→ Nightly camping fees in national and provincial parks range from $25 to $35 (a bit more for full hookup sites); fire permits often cost a few dollars extra. Backcountry camping costs about $10 per night. Private campgrounds tend to be a bit pricier. British Columbia's parks, in particular, have seen a hefty rate increase in recent years.

→ Some campgrounds remain open for maintenance year-round and may let you camp at a reduced rate in the off-season. This can be great in late autumn or early spring when there's hardly a soul about. Winter camping, though, is only for the hardy.

Homestays

How do you feel about staying on the couch of a perfect stranger? If it's not a problem, consider joining an organization that arranges homestays. The following groups charge no fees to become a member, and the stay itself is also free.

Couch Surfing (www.couch-surfing.org)

Hospitality Club (www.hospitalityclub.org)

CHAIN HOTELS

Budget

Econo Lodge (☎877-424-6423; www.econolodge.com)

Howard Johnson (☎800-446-4656; www.hojo.com)

Quality Inn & Suites (☎877-424-6423; www.qualityinn.com)

Super 8 (☎800-800-8000; www.super8.com)

Travelodge/Thriftlodge (☎800-578-7878; www.travelodge.ca)

Midrange

Best Western (☎800-780-7234; www.bestwestern.com)

Comfort Inn (☎877-424-6423; www.comfortinn.com)

Days Inn (☎800-329-7466; www.daysinn.com)

Fairfield Inn (☎800-228-2800; www.fairfieldinn.com)

Hampton Inn (☎800-426-7866; www.hamptoninn.com)

Holiday Inn (☎888-465-4329; www.holidayinn.com)

Top End

Delta (☎877-814-7706; www.deltahotels.com)

Fairmont (☎800-257-7544; www.fairmont.com)

Hilton (☎800-445-8667; www.hilton.com)

Hyatt (☎888-591-1234; www.hyatt.com)

Marriott (☎888-236-2427; www.marriott.com)

Radisson (☎888-201-1718; www.radisson.com)

Ramada (☎800-272-6232; www.ramada.com)

Sheraton (☎800-325-3535; www.sheraton.com)

Westin (☎800-937-8461; www.westin.com)

Hostels

Canada has independent hostels as well as those affiliated with Hostelling International (HI). All have dorms ($25 to $40 per person on average), which can sleep from two to 10 people, and many have private rooms (from $60) for couples and families. Rooms in HI hostels are gender segregated. Non-members pay a surcharge of about $4 per night.

Bathrooms are usually shared, and facilities include a kitchen, lockers, free wi-fi, internet access, laundry room and a shared TV room. Many also include a free continental breakfast. Some hostels allow alcohol, others don't; smoking is prohibited.

Most hostels, especially those in the big cities, are open 24 hours a day. If they are not, ask if you can make special arrangements if you are arriving late.

Backpackers Hostels Canada (www.backpackers. ca) Independent hostels.

Hostelling International Canada (www.hihostels.ca)

Hostels.com (www.hostels. com) Includes independent and HI hostels.

Hotels & Motels

Most hotels are part of international chains, and the newer ones are designed for either the luxury market or businesspeople. Rooms have cable TV and wi-fi; many also have swimming pools and fitness and business centers. Rooms with two double or queen-sized beds sleep up to four people, although there is usually a small surcharge for the third and fourth person. Many places advertise that 'kids stay free' but sometimes you have to pay extra for a crib or a rollaway (portable bed).

In Canada, like the USA (both lands of the automobile), motels are ubiquitous. They dot the highways and cluster in groups on the outskirts of towns and cities.

Although most motel rooms won't win any style awards, they're usually clean and comfortable and offer good value for travelers. Many regional motels remain your typical 'mom and pop' operations, but plenty of North American chains have also opened up around the region.

University Accommodations

In the lecture-free summer months, some universities and colleges rent beds in their student dormitories to travelers of all ages. Most rooms are quite basic, with rates ranging from $25 to $40 per night, and often including breakfast. Students can usually qualify for small discounts.

Activities

Snowboarding, sea kayaking, mountain biking – there's much to do. Resources:

Alpine Club of Canada (www.alpineclubofcanada.ca) Climbing and mountaineering.

Canada Trails (www.canadatrails.ca) Hiking, biking and cross-country skiing.

Canadian Ski Council (www.skicanada.org) Skiing and snowboarding.

Paddling Canada (www. paddlingcanada.com) Kayaking and canoeing.

Parks Canada (www.pc.gc. ca) National park action.

Customs Regulations

The **Canada Border Services Agency** (CBSA; www. cbsa.gc.ca) has the customs lowdown. A few regulations to note:

Alcohol You can bring in 1.5L of wine, 1.14L of liquor or 24 355mL beers duty free.

Gifts You can bring in gifts totaling up to $60.

Money You can bring in/take out up to $10,000; larger amounts must be reported to customs.

Personal effects Camping gear, sports equipment, cameras and laptop computers can be brought in without much trouble. Declaring these to customs as you cross the border might save you some hassle when you leave, especially if you'll be crossing the US–Canadian border multiple times.

Pets You must carry a signed and dated certificate from a veterinarian to prove your dog or cat has had a rabies shot in the past 36 months.

Prescription drugs You can bring in/take out a 90-day supply for personal use (though if you're taking it to the USA, know it's technically illegal, but overlooked for individuals).

Tobacco You can bring in 200 cigarettes, 50 cigars, 200g of tobacco and 200 tobacco sticks duty free.

Discount Cards

Discounts are commonly offered for seniors, children, families and people with disabilities, though no special cards are issued (you get the savings on-site when you pay). AAA and other automobile association members can also receive various travel-related discounts.

International Student Identity Card (ISIC; www.isic.org) Provides students with discounts on travel insurance and admission to museums and other sights. There are also cards for those who are under 26 but not students, and for full-time teachers.

Parks Canada Discovery Pass (www.pc.gc.ca/ar-sr/lpac-ppri/ced-ndp.aspx; adult/child/family $68/33/136) Provides access to more than 100 national parks and historic sites for a year. Can pay for itself in as few as seven visits over daily entry fees; also provides quicker entry into sites.

Many cities have discount cards for local attractions, such as the following:

Montréal Museum Pass (www.museesmontreal.org; $80)

Ottawa Museums Passport (www.museumspassport.ca; adult/family $45/99)

UBC Museums and Garden Pass Vancouver (p646)

Vanier Park Explore Pass (www.spacecentre.ca/explore-pass; adult/child $30/24) Vancouver

Embassies & Consulates

All countries have their embassies in Ottawa, including those listed here, and maintain consulates in such cities as Montréal, Vancouver, Calgary and Toronto. Contact the relevant embassy to find out which consulate is closest to you.

Australian High Commission (☑613-236-0841; www.canada.embassy.gov.au; Suite 710, 50 O'Connor St)

French Embassy (☑613-789-1795; www.ambafrance-ca.org; 42 Sussex Dr)

German Embassy (☑613-232-1101; www.ottawa.diplo.de; 1 Waverley St)

Irish Embassy (☑613-233-6281; www.embassyofireland.ca; 130 Albert St)

Italian Embassy (☑613-232-2401; www.ambottawa.esteri.it; 21st fl, 275 Slater St)

Japanese Embassy (☑613-241-8541; www.ca.emb-japan.go.jp; 255 Sussex Dr)

Mexican Embassy (☑613-233-8988; http://embamex.sre.gob.mx/canada_eng/; Suite 1000, 45 O'Connor St)

Netherlands Embassy (☑613-237-5030; http://ottawa.the-netherlands.org; Suite 2020, 350 Albert St)

New Zealand High Commission (☑613-238-5991; www.nzembassy.com/canada; Suite 727, 99 Bank St)

UK High Commission (☑613-237-2008; www.gov.uk/government/world/canada; 80 Elgin St)

US Embassy (☑613-238-5335; http://canada.usembassy.gov; 490 Sussex Dr)

Electricity

120V/60Hz

120V/60Hz

Food

For information on food, see the Cuisines of Canada chapter (p860). The following price ranges are for main dishes:

$ less than $12

$$ $12–25

$$$ more than $25

Gay & Lesbian Travelers

Canada is tolerant when it comes to gays and lesbians, though this outlook is more common in the big cities than in rural areas. Same-sex marriage is legal throughout the country (Canada is one of only 15 nations worldwide that permits this).

Montréal, Toronto and Vancouver are by far Canada's gayest cities, each with a humming nightlife scene, publications and lots of associations and support groups. All have sizable Pride celebrations too, which attract big crowds.

Attitudes remain more conservative in the northern regions. Throughout Nunavut, and to a lesser extent in the aboriginal communities of the Northwest Territories, there are some retrogressive attitudes toward homosexuality. The Yukon, in contrast, is more like British Columbia, with a live-and-let-live west-coast attitude.

The following are good resources for gay travel; they include Canadian information, though not all are exclusive to the region:

Damron (www.damron.com) Publishes several travel guides, including *Men's Travel Guide*, *Women's Traveller* and *Damron Accommodations;* gay-friendly tour operators are listed on the website too.

Gay Canada (www.gaycanada.com) Search by province or city for queer-friendly businesses and resources.

Out Traveler (www.outtraveler.com) Gay travel magazine.

Purple Roofs (www.purpleroofs.com) Website listing queer accommodations, travel agencies and tours worldwide.

Queer Canada (www.queercanada.ca) A general resource.

Xtra (www.xtra.ca) Source for gay and lesbian news nationwide.

Health

Before You Go
INSURANCE

Canada offers some of the finest health care in the world. However, unless you are a Canadian citizen, it can be prohibitively expensive. It's essential to purchase travel health insurance if your regular policy doesn't cover you when you're abroad. Check www.lonelyplanet.com/travel-insurance for supplemental insurance information.

Bring medications you may need clearly labeled in their original containers. A signed, dated letter from your physician that describes your medical conditions and medications, including generic names, is also a good idea.

MEDICAL CHECKLIST

➡ acetaminophen (eg Tylenol) or aspirin

➡ anti-inflammatory drugs (eg ibuprofen)

➡ antihistamines (for hay fever and allergic reactions)

➡ antibacterial ointment (eg Neosporin) for cuts and abrasions

➡ steroid cream or cortisone (for poison ivy and other allergic rashes)

➡ bandages, gauze, gauze rolls

➡ adhesive or paper tape

➡ safety pins, tweezers

➡ thermometer

➡ DEET-containing insect repellent for the skin

➡ permethrin-containing insect spray for clothing, tents and bed nets

➡ sunblock

➡ motion-sickness medication

RECOMMENDED VACCINATIONS

No special vaccines are required or recommended for travel to Canada. All travelers should be up to date on routine immunizations.

WEBSITES

Government travel-health websites are available for **Australia** (www.smarttraveller.gov.au), the **United Kingdom** (www.nhs.uk/healthcareabroad) and the **United States** (www.cdc.gov/travel/).

MD Travel Health (www.mdtravelhealth.com) General health resources.

Public Health Agency of Canada (www.phac-aspc.gc.ca) Canadian health resources.

World Health Organization (www.who.int) General health resources.

In Canada
AVAILABILITY & COST OF HEALTH CARE

Medical services are widely available. For emergencies, the best bet is to find the nearest hospital and go to its emergency room. If the problem isn't urgent, call a nearby hospital and ask for a referral to a local physician, which is usually cheaper than a trip to the emergency room (where costs can be $500 or so before any treatment).

Pharmacies are abundant, but prescriptions can be expensive without insurance. However, Americans may find Canadian prescription drugs to be cheaper than drugs at home. You're allowed to take out a 90-day supply for personal use (it's technically illegal to bring them into the USA, but overlooked for individuals).

INFECTIOUS DISEASES

Most are acquired by mosquito or tick bites, or environmental exposure. The **Public Health Agency of Canada** (www.phac-aspc.gc.ca) has details on all listed below.

Giardiasis Intestinal infection. Avoid drinking directly from lakes, ponds, streams and rivers.

Lyme Disease Occurs mostly in southern Canada. Transmitted by deer ticks in late spring and summer. Perform a tick check after you've been outdoors.

Severe Acute Respiratory Syndrome (SARS) At the time of writing, SARS had been brought under control in Canada.

West Nile Virus Mosquito-transmitted in late summer and early fall. Prevent by keeping covered (wear long sleeves, long pants, hats, and shoes rather than sandals) and apply a good insect repellent, preferably one containing DEET, to exposed skin and clothing.

ENVIRONMENTAL HAZARDS

Cold exposure This can be a significant problem, especially in the northern regions. Keep all body surfaces covered, including the head and neck. Watch out for the 'Umbles' – stumbles, mumbles, fumbles and grumbles – which are signs of impending hypothermia.

Heat exhaustion Dehydration is the main contributor. Symptoms include feeling weak, headache, nausea and sweaty skin. Lay the victim flat with their legs raised, apply cool, wet cloths to the skin, and rehydrate.

Insurance

Make sure you have adequate travel insurance, whatever the length of your trip. At a minimum, you need coverage for medical emergencies and treatment, including hospital stays and an emergency flight home. Medical treatment for non-Canadians is very expensive.

Also consider insurance for luggage theft or loss. If you already have a homeowners or renters policy, check what it will cover and only get supplemental insurance to protect against the rest. If you have prepaid a large portion of your vacation, trip-cancellation insurance is worthwhile.

Worldwide travel insurance is available at www.lonelyplanet.com/travel-insurance. You can buy, extend and claim online at anytime – even if you're already on the road. Also check the following providers:

Insure.com (www.insure.com)

Travel Guard (www.travelguard.com)

Travelex (www.travelex.com)

Internet Access

➜ It's easy to find internet access. Libraries and community agencies in practically every town provide free wi-fi and computers for public use. The only downsides are that usage time is limited (usually 30 minutes), and some facilities have erratic hours.

➜ Internet cafes are limited to the main tourist areas, and access generally starts around $2 per hour.

➜ Wi-fi is widely available. Most lodgings have it (in-room, with good speed), as do many restaurants, bars and Tim Hortons coffee shops. We've identified sleeping, eating, drinking and other listings that have wi-fi (whether free or fee-based) with a 🛜 symbol. We've denoted lodgings that offer internet terminals for guest use with a @ symbol.

➜ For a list of wi-fi hot spots around Canada, visit **Wi-Fi Free Spot** (www.wififreespot.com).

Legal Matters
Police

If you are arrested or charged with an offense, you have the right to keep your mouth shut and to hire any lawyer you wish (contact your embassy for a referral, if necessary). If you cannot afford one, ask to be represented by public counsel. There is a presumption of innocence.

Drugs & Alcohol

➜ The blood-alcohol limit is 0.08% and driving cars, motorcycles, boats and snowmobiles while drunk is a criminal offense. If you are caught, you may face stiff fines, license suspension and other nasty consequences.

➜ Consuming alcohol anywhere other than at a residence or licensed premises is also a no-no, which puts parks, beaches and the rest of the great outdoors off limits, at least officially.

➜ Avoid illegal drugs, as penalties may entail heavy fines, possible jail time and a criminal record. The only exception is the use of marijuana for medical purposes, which became legal in 2001. Meanwhile, the decriminalization of pot possession for personal use remains a subject of ongoing debate among the general public and in parliament.

Other

➜ Abortion is legal.

➜ Travelers should note that they can be prosecuted under the law of their home country regarding age of consent, even when abroad.

Maps

➜ Most tourist offices distribute free provincial road maps.

➜ For extended hikes or multiday backcountry treks, it's a good idea to carry a topographic map. The best are the series of 1:50,000 scale maps published by the government's Centre for Topographic Information. These are sold by bookstores and parks around the country.

➜ You can also download and print maps from **GeoBase** (www.geobase.ca).

Money

➜ All prices quoted are in Canadian dollars ($), unless stated otherwise.

➜ Canadian coins come in 5¢ (nickel), 10¢ (dime), 25¢ (quarter), $1 (Loonie) and $2 (toonie or twoonie) denominations. The gold-colored Loonie features the loon, a common Canadian waterbird, while the two-toned toonie is decorated with a polar bear. Canada started phasing out its 1¢ (penny) coin in 2012.

➜ Paper currency comes in $5 (blue), $10 (purple), $20 (green) and $50 (red) denominations. The $100 (brown) and larger bills are less common. The newest bills in circulation - which have enhanced security features - are actually a polymer-based material; they feel more like plastic than paper.

➜ The Canadian dollar has seen fluctuations over the last decade, though since

2007 it has tracked quite closely to the US dollar.

➡ For changing money in the larger cities, currency exchange offices may offer better conditions than banks.

➡ See Need to Know (p25) for exchange rates and costs.

ATMs

➡ Many grocery and convenience stores, airports, and bus, train and ferry stations have ATMs. Most are linked to international networks, the most common being Cirrus, Plus, Star and Maestro.

➡ Most ATMs also spit out cash if you use a major credit card. This method tends to be more expensive because, in addition to a service fee, you'll be charged interest immediately (in other words, there's no interest-free period as with purchases). For exact fees, check with your own bank or credit-card company.

➡ Visitors heading to Canada's more remote regions (such as in Newfoundland) won't find an abundance of ATMs, so it is wise to cash up beforehand.

➡ Scotiabank, common throughout Canada, is part of the Global ATM Alliance. If your home bank is a member, fees may be less if you withdraw from Scotiabank ATMs.

Cash

Most Canadians don't carry large amounts of cash for everyday use, relying instead on credit and debit cards. Still, carrying some cash, say $100 or less, comes in handy when making small purchases. In some cases, cash is necessary to pay for rural B&Bs and shuttle vans; inquire in advance to avoid surprises. Shops and businesses rarely accept personal checks.

Credit Cards

Major credit cards such as MasterCard, Visa and American Express are widely accepted in Canada, except in remote, rural communities where cash is king. You'll find it difficult or impossible to rent a car, book a room or order tickets over the phone without having a piece of plastic. Note that some credit-card companies charge a 'transaction fee' (around 3% of whatever you purchased); check with your provider to avoid surprises.

For lost or stolen cards, these numbers operate 24 hours:

American Express (☑866-296-5198; www.americanexpress.com)

MasterCard (☑800-307-7309; www.mastercard.com)

Visa (☑800-847-2911; www.visa.com)

Taxes & Refunds

Canada's federal goods and services tax (GST), variously known as the 'gouge and screw' or 'grab and steal' tax, adds 5% to just about every transaction. Most provinces also charge a provincial sales tax (PST) on top of it. Several provinces have combined the GST and PST into a harmonized sales tax (HST). Whatever the methodology, expect to pay 10% to 15% in most cases. Unless otherwise stated, taxes are not included in prices given.

You might be eligible for a rebate on some of the taxes. If you've booked your accommodations in conjunction with a rental car, plane ticket or other service (ie if it all appears on the same bill from a 'tour operator'), you should be eligible to get 50% of the tax refunded from your accommodations. Fill out the GST/HST Refund Application for Tour Packages form available from the **Canada Revenue Agency** (☑800-668-4748, 902-432-5608; www.cra-arc.gc.ca/E/pbg/gf/gst115).

TAX RATES BY PROVINCE

Percentages represent federal and provincial taxes combined:

PROVINCE	TAX RATE %
Alberta	5
British Columbia	12
Manitoba	13
New Brunswick	13
Newfoundland	13
Northwest Territories	5
Nova Scotia*	14
Nunavut	5
Ontario	13
Prince Edward Island	14
Québec	15
Saskatchewan	10
Yukon	5

* rate to increase 1% in 2015

Tipping

Tipping is a standard practice. Generally you can expect to tip as follows:

Bar staff $1 per drink

Hotel bellhop $1 to $2 per bag

Hotel room cleaners From $2 per day (depending on room size and messiness)

Restaurant waitstaff 15% to 20%

Taxis 10% to 15%

Traveler's Checks

Traveler's checks are becoming more and more obsolete. Traveler's checks issued in Canadian dollars are generally treated like cash by businesses. Traveler's checks in most other currencies must be exchanged for Canadian dollars at a bank or foreign-currency office. The most common issuers are American Express, MasterCard and Visa.

Opening Hours

The list below provides general opening hours for businesses. Reviews throughout the book show specific hours. Note that hours can vary by season. Our listings depict peak season operating times. Opening hours often decrease during off-peak months and a number of businesses close altogether.

Bars 5pm to 2am daily

Banks 10am to 5pm Monday to Friday; some open 9am to noon Saturday

Clubs 9pm to 2am Wednesday to Saturday

General office hours 9am to 5pm Monday to Friday

Museums 10am to 5pm daily, sometimes closed Monday

Restaurants breakfast 8am to 11am, lunch 11:30am to 2:30pm Monday to Friday, dinner 5pm to 9:30pm daily; some open 8am to 1pm Saturday and Sunday

Shops 10am to 6pm Monday to Saturday, noon to 5pm Sunday, some open to 8pm or 9pm Thursday and/or Friday

Supermarkets 9am to 8pm, some open 24 hours

Post

➡ Canada's national postal service, **Canada Post/ Postes Canada** (www. canadapost.ca), is neither quick nor cheap, but it is reliable. Stamps are available at post offices, drugstores, convenience stores and hotels.

➡ Postcards or standard letters cost 63¢ within Canada, $1.10 to the USA and $1.85 to all other countries.

➡ Travelers often find they have to pay high duties on items sent to them while in Canada, so beware.

Public Holidays

Canada observes 10 national public holidays and more at the provincial level. Banks, schools and government offices close on these days.

National Holidays

New Year's Day January 1

Good Friday March or April

Easter Monday March or April

Victoria Day Monday before May 25

Canada Day July 1; called Memorial Day in Newfoundland

Labour Day First Monday of September

Thanksgiving Second Monday of October

Remembrance Day November 11

Christmas Day December 25

Boxing Day December 26

Provincial Holidays

Some provinces also observe local holidays, with Newfoundland leading the pack.

Family Day Third Monday of February in Alberta, Ontario, Saskatchewan and Manitoba (second Monday in British Columbia); known as Louis Riel Day in Manitoba

St Patrick's Day Monday nearest March 17

St George's Day Monday nearest April 23

National Day Monday nearest June 24 in Newfoundland; June 24 in Québec (aka St-Jean-Baptiste Day)

Orangemen's Day Monday nearest July 12 in Newfoundland

Civic Holiday First Monday of August everywhere *except* Newfoundland, Québec and Yukon Territory

Discovery Day Third Monday of August in Yukon Territory

School Holidays

Kids break for summer holidays in late June and don't return to school until early September. University students get even more time off, usually from May to early or mid-September. Most people take their big annual vacation during these months.

Telephone

Canada's phone system is almost identical to the USA's system.

Domestic & International Dialing

➡ Canadian phone numbers consist of a three-digit area code followed by a seven-digit local number. In many

POSTAL ABBREVIATIONS

PROVINCES & TERRITORIES	ABBREVIATIONS
Alberta	AB
British Columbia	BC
Manitoba	MB
New Brunswick	NB
Newfoundland & Labrador	NL
Northwest Territories	NT
Nova Scotia	NS
Nunavut	NU
Ontario	ON
Prince Edward Island	PE
Québec	QC
Saskatchewan	SK
Yukon Territory	YT

parts of Canada, you must dial all 10 digits preceded by 1, even if you're calling across the street. In other parts of the country, when you're calling within the same area code, you can dial the seven-digit number only, but this is slowly changing.

➜ For direct international calls, dial ☑011 + country code + area code + local phone number. The country code for Canada is 1 (the same as for the USA, although international rates still apply for all calls made between the two countries).

➜ Toll-free numbers begin with 800, 877, 866 or 855 and must be preceded by 1. Some of these numbers are good throughout Canada and the USA, others only work within Canada, and some work in just one province.

Emergency Numbers

Dial ☑911. This is *not* the emergency number in the Yukon, Northwest Territories or Nunavut.

Cell Phones

➜ Local SIM cards can be used in European and Australian phones. Other phones must be set to roaming.

➜ If you have a European, Australian or other type of unlocked GSM phone, buy a SIM card from local providers such as **Telus** (www.telus. com), **Rogers** (www.rogers. com) or **Bell** (www.bell.ca).

➜ US residents can often upgrade their domestic cell-phone plan to extend to Canada. **Verizon** (www. verizonwireless.com) provides good results.

➜ Reception is poor in rural areas no matter who your service provider is.

Public Phones

Coin-operated public pay phones are fairly plentiful. Local calls cost 50¢; many phones also accept prepaid phonecards and credit cards. Dialing the operator (0) or directory assistance (411 for local calls, 1 + area code + 555-1212 for long-distance calls) is free of charge from public phones; it may incur a charge from private phones.

Phonecards

➜ Prepaid phonecards usually offer the best per-minute rates for long-distance and international calling. They come in denominations of $5, $10 or $20 and are widely sold in drugstores, supermarkets and convenience stores. Beware of cards with hidden charges such as 'activation fees' or a per-call connection fee.

➜ A surcharge ranging from 30¢ to 85¢ for calls made from public pay phones is common.

Time

➜ Canada spans six of the world's 24 time zones. The Eastern zone in Newfoundland is unusual in that it's only 30 minutes different from the adjacent zone. The time difference from coast to coast is 4½ hours.

➜ Canada observes daylight saving time, which comes into effect on the second Sunday in March, when clocks are put forward one hour, and ends on the first Sunday in November. Saskatchewan and small pockets of Québec, Ontario and BC are the only areas

---

UNIQUELY CANADIAN CELEBRATIONS

National Flag Day (February 15) Commemorates the first time the maple-leaf flag was raised above Parliament Hill in Ottawa, at the stroke of noon on February 15, 1965.

Victoria Day (late May) This day was established in 1845 to observe the birthday of Queen Victoria and now celebrates the birthday of the British sovereign who's still Canada's titular head of state. Victoria Day marks the official beginning of the summer season (which ends with Labour Day on the first Monday of September). Some communities hold fireworks.

National Aboriginal Day (June 21) Created in 1996, it celebrates the contributions of Aboriginal peoples to Canada. Coinciding with the summer solstice, festivities are organized locally and may include traditional dancing, singing and drumming; storytelling; arts and crafts shows; canoe races; and lots more.

Canada Day (July 1) Known as Dominion Day until 1982, Canada Day was created in 1869 to commemorate the creation of Canada two years earlier. All over the country, people celebrate with barbecues, parades, concerts and fireworks.

Thanksgiving Day (mid-October) First celebrated in 1578 in what is now Newfoundland by explorer Martin Frobisher to give thanks for surviving his Atlantic crossing, Thanksgiving became an official Canadian holiday in 1872 to celebrate the recovery of the Prince of Wales from a long illness. These days, it's essentially a harvest festival involving a special family dinner of roast turkey and pumpkin, very much as it is practiced in the US.

that do not switch to daylight saving time.

➜ In Québec especially, times for shop hours, train schedules, film screenings etc are usually indicated by the 24-hour clock.

Tourist Information

➜ The **Canadian Tourism Commission** (www.canada. travel) is loaded with general information, packages and links.

➜ All provincial tourist offices maintain comprehensive websites packed with information helpful in planning your trip. Staff also field telephone inquiries and, on request, will mail out free maps and directories about accommodations, attractions and events. Some offices can also help with making hotel, tour or other reservations.

➜ For detailed information about a specific area, contact the local tourist office, aka visitors center. Just about every city and town has at least a seasonal branch with helpful staff, racks of free pamphlets and books and maps for sale. Provincial tourist offices:

Newfoundland & Labrador Tourism (☎800-563-6353; www.newfoundlandlabrador. com)

Northwest Territories (NWT) Tourism (☎800-661-0788; www.spectacularnwt. com)

Nunavut Tourism (☎866-686-2888; www.nunavuttourism.com)

Ontario Tourism (☎800-668-2746; www.ontariotravel. net)

Prince Edward Island Tourism (☎800-463-4734; www.peiplay.com)

Tourism British Columbia (☎800-435-5622; www. hellobc.com)

Tourism New Brunswick (☎800-561-0123; www. tourismnewbrunswick.ca)

Tourism Nova Scotia (☎800-565-0000; www. novascotia.com)

Tourism Saskatchewan (☎877-237-2273; www.sask-tourism.com)

Tourisme Québec (☎877-266-5687; www.bonjourquebec. com)

Travel Alberta (☎800-252-3782; www.travelalberta.com)

Travel Manitoba (☎800-665-0040; www.travelmanitoba.com)

Yukon Department of Tourism (☎800-661-0494; www.travelyukon.com)

Travelers with Disabilities

Canada is making progress when it comes to easing the everyday challenges facing people with disabilities, especially the mobility impaired.

➜ Many public buildings, including museums, tourist offices, train stations, shopping malls and cinemas, have access ramps and/or lifts. Most public restrooms feature extrawide stalls equipped with hand rails. Many pedestrian crossings have sloping curbs.

➜ Newer and recently remodeled hotels, especially chain hotels, have rooms with extrawide doors and spacious bathrooms.

➜ Interpretive centers at national and provincial parks are usually accessible, and many parks have trails that can be navigated in wheelchairs.

➜ Car-rental agencies offer hand-controlled vehicles and vans with wheelchair lifts at no additional charge, but you must reserve them well in advance.

➜ For accessible air, bus, rail and ferry transportation check **Access to Travel** (www.accesstotravel.gc.ca), the federal government's website. In general, most transportation agencies can accommodate people with disabilities if you make your needs known when booking. Other organizations specializing in the needs of travelers with disabilities:

Access-Able Travel Source (www.access-able. com) Lists accessible lodging, transport, attractions and equipment rental by province.

Mobility International (www.miusa.org) Advises travelers with disabilities on mobility issues and runs an educational exchange program.

Society for Accessible Travel & Hospitality (www. sath.org) Travelers with disabilities share tips and blogs.

Visas

Citizens of dozens of countries – including the USA, most Western European nations, Australia, New Zealand, Japan and South Korea – do not need visas to enter Canada for stays of up to 180 days. US permanent residents are also exempt.

Citizenship & Immigration Canada (www.cic.gc.ca) has the details.

Nationals of other countries – including China, India and South Africa – must apply to the Canadian visa office in their home country for a temporary resident visa (aka visitor visa). A separate visa is required if you plan to study or work in Canada.

Single-entry visas ($75) are usually valid for a maximum stay of six months from the date of your arrival in Canada. Multiple-entry visas ($150) allow you to enter Canada from all other countries multiple times while the visa is valid (up to 10 years), provided no single stay exceeds six months. Note you don't need a multiple-entry visa for repeated entries into Canada from the USA, unless you have visited a third country.

Visa extensions ($75) need to be filed with the **CIC Visitor Case Processing Centre** (☎888-242-2100; ⊙8am-4pm Mon-Fri) in Alberta at least one month before your current visa expires.

For information about passport requirements, see p880.

Visiting the USA

Admission requirements are subject to rapid change. The **US State Department** (www.travel.state.gov) has the latest information, or check with a US consulate in your home country.

Under the US visa-waiver program, visas are not required for citizens of 36 countries – including most EU members, Australia and New Zealand – for visits of up to 90 days (no extensions allowed), as long as you can present a machine-readable passport and are approved under the **Electronic System for Travel Authorization** (ESTA; www.cbp.gov/esta). Note you must register at least 72 hours before arrival, and there's a $14 fee for processing and authorization.

Canadians do not need visas, though they do need a passport or document approved by the **Western Hemisphere Travel Initiative** (www.getyouhome.gov). Citizens of all other countries need to apply for a US visa in their home country before arriving in Canada.

All foreign visitors (except Canadians) must pay a US$6 'processing fee' when entering at land borders.

Volunteering

Volunteering provides the opportunity to interact with local folks and the land in ways you never would just passing through. Many organizations charge a fee, which varies depending on the program's length and the type of food and lodging it provides. The fees usually do not cover travel to Canada. Groups that use volunteers:

Churchill Northern Studies Centre (www.churchillscience.ca) Volunteer for six hours per day (anything from stringing wires to cleaning) and get free room and board at this center for polar-bear and other wildlife research.

Earthwatch (www.earthwatch.org) Help scientists track whales off the coast of British Columbia, track moose and deer in Nova Scotia, and monitor climate change in Churchill, Manitoba or the Mackenzie Mountains of the Northwest Territories. Trips last from seven to 14 days and cost from $2250 to $5050.

Volunteers for Peace (www.vfp.org) Offers tutoring stints in aboriginal communities in Canada's far north, as well as projects in Québec.

World-Wide Opportunities on Organic Farms (www.wwoof.ca; application fee $50) Work on an organic farm, usually in exchange for free room and board; check the website for locations throughout Canada.

Women Travelers

Canada is generally a safe place for women to travel, even alone and even in the cities. Simply use the same common sense as you would at home.

In bars and nightclubs, solo women are likely to attract a lot of attention, but if you don't want company, most men will respect a firm 'no thank you.' If you feel threatened, protesting loudly will often make the offender slink away – or will at least spur other people to come to your defense. Note that carrying mace or pepper spray is illegal in Canada.

Physical attack is unlikely, but if you are assaulted, call the police immediately (☎911 except in the Yukon, Northwest Territories and Nunavut) or contact a rape crisis center. A complete list is available from the **Canadian Association of Sexual Assault Centres**

PRACTICALITIES

➡ **Newspapers & Magazines** The most widely available newspaper is the Toronto-based *Globe and Mail*. Other principal dailies are the *Montréal Gazette*, *Ottawa Citizen*, *Toronto Star* and *Vancouver Sun*. *Maclean's* (www.macleans.ca) is Canada's weekly news magazine.

➡ **Radio & TV** The Canadian Broadcasting Corporation (CBC) is the dominant nationwide network for both radio and TV. The CTV Television Network (CTV) is the major competition.

➡ **Smoking** Banned in all restaurants, bars and other public venues nationwide.

➡ **Weights & Measures** Canada officially uses the metric system, but imperial measurements are used for many day-to-day purposes.

(☑604-876-2622; www.casac.ca). Hotlines in some of the major cities:

Calgary (☑403-237-5888)

Halifax (☑902-425-0122)

Montréal (☑514-934-4504)

Toronto (☑416-597-8808)

Vancouver (☑604-255-6344)

Resources for women travelers:

Her Own Way (www.travel.gc.ca/travelling/publications/her-own-way) Published by the Canadian government for Canadian travelers, but contains a great deal of general advice.

Journeywoman (www.journeywoman.com)

Work
Permits

In almost all cases, you need a valid work permit to work in Canada. Obtaining one may be difficult, as employment opportunities go to Canadians first. Before you can even apply, you need a specific job offer from an employer who in turn must have been granted permission from the government to give the position to a foreign national. Applications must be filed at a visa office of a Canadian embassy or consulate in your home country. Some jobs are exempt from the permit requirement. For full details, check with **Citizenship & Immigration Canada** (www.cic.gc.ca).

Employers hiring temporary service workers (hotel, bar, restaurant, resort) and construction, farm or forestry workers sometimes don't ask for a permit. If you get caught, however, you can kiss Canada goodbye.

Finding Work

Students aged 18 to 30 from more than a dozen countries, including the USA, UK, Australia, New Zealand, Ireland and South Africa, are eligible to apply for a spot in the **Student Work Abroad Program** (SWAP; www.swap.ca). If successful, you get a six-month to one-year, non-extendable visa that allows you to work anywhere in Canada in any job you can get. Most 'Swappers' find work in the service industry as waiters or bartenders.

Even if you're not a student, you may be able to spend up to a year in Canada on a 'working holiday program' with **International Experience Canada** (www.international.gc.ca/experience). The Canadian government has an arrangement with several countries for people aged 18 to 35 to come over and get a job; check the website for participants. The Canadian embassy in each country runs the program, but basically there are quotas and spaces are filled on a first-come, first-served basis.

Transportation

GETTING THERE & AWAY

Flights, tours and rail tickets can be booked online at www.lonelyplanet.com/bookings.

Entering the Country

Entering Canada is pretty straightforward. First, you will have to show your passport (and your visa if you need one). The border officer will ask you a few questions about the purpose and length of your visit. After that, you'll go through customs. See **Going to Canada** (www.goingtocanada.gc.ca) for details.

Note that questioning may be more intense at land border crossings and your car may be searched.

For updates (particularly regarding land border-crossing rules), check the websites for the **US State Department** (www.travel.state.gov) and **Citizenship & Immigration Canada** (www.cic.gc.ca).

Passport

Most international visitors require a passport to enter Canada. US citizens at land and sea borders have other options, such as an enhanced driver's license or passport card. See the **Western Hemisphere Travel Initiative** (www.getyouhome.

gov) for approved identification documents.

Visitors from certain countries also require a visa to enter Canada; see p877.

Air

Airports & Airlines

Toronto is far and away the busiest airport, followed by Vancouver. The international gateways you're most likely to use:

Calgary (YYC; www.calgary-airport.com)

Edmonton (YEG; www.flyeia.com)

Halifax (YHZ; www.hiaa.ca)

Montréal (Trudeau | YUL; www.admtl.com)

Ottawa (YOW; www.ottawa-airport.ca)

St John's (YYT; www.stjohns-airport.com)

Toronto (Pearson | YYZ; www.torontopearson.com)

Vancouver (YVR; www.yvr.ca)

Winnipeg (YWG; www.waa.ca)

Air Canada (www.aircanada.com), the national flagship carrier, is considered one of the world's safest airlines. All major global airlines fly to Canada. Other companies based in the country and serving international destinations:

Air Transat (www.airtransat.com) Charter airline from major Canadian cities to holiday destinations (ie southern USA

and Caribbean in winter, Europe in summer).

Porter Airlines (www.flyporter.com) Flies in eastern Canada and to US cities, including Boston, Chicago, Washington, DC, and New York.

WestJet (☑888-937-8538; www.westjet.com)

Land

Border Crossings

There are around 25 official border crossings along the US–Canadian border, from New Brunswick to British Columbia.

The website of the **Canadian Border Services Agency** (www.cbsa-asfc.gc.ca/bwt-taf/menu-eng.html) shows current wait times at each. You can also access it via Twitter (@CBSA_BWT).

In general, waits rarely exceed 30 minutes, except during the peak summer season, and on Friday and Sunday afternoons, especially on holiday weekends. Some entry points are especially busy:

➡ Detroit, Michigan to Windsor, Ontario

➡ Buffalo, New York to Fort Erie, Ontario

➡ Niagara Falls, New York to Niagara Falls, Ontario

➡ Rouse's Point/Champlain, New York to Québec

➡ Blaine, Washington to Surrey, British Columbia

When returning to the USA, check the website for the **US Department for Homeland Security** (http://apps.cbp.gov/bwt) for border wait times.

All foreign visitors (except Canadians) must pay a $6 'processing fee' when entering the USA by land; credit cards are not accepted.

Bus

Greyhound (www.greyhound.com) and its Canadian equivalent, **Greyhound Canada** (www.greyhound.ca), operate the largest bus network in North America. There are direct connections between main cities in the USA and Canada, but you usually have to transfer to a different bus at the border (where it takes a good hour for all passengers to clear customs/immigration). Most international buses have free wi-fi on board.

Other notable international bus companies (with free wi-fi):

Megabus (www.megabus.com) Runs between Toronto and US cities, including New York City, Philadelphia and Washington DC; usually cheaper than Greyhound. Tickets can only be purchased online.

Quick Coach (www.quickcoach.com) Runs between

Seattle and Vancouver; typically a bit quicker than Greyhound.

Car & Motorcycle

The highway system of the continental USA connects directly with the Canadian highway system at numerous points along the border. These Canadian highways then meet up with the east–west Trans-Canada Hwy further north. Between the Yukon Territory and Alaska, the main routes are the Alaska, Klondike and Haines Hwys.

If you're driving into Canada, you'll need the vehicle's registration papers, proof of liability insurance and your home driver's license. Cars rented in the USA can usually be driven into Canada and back, but make sure your rental agreement says so. If you're driving a car registered in someone else's name, bring a letter from the owner authorizing use of the vehicle in Canada.

Train

Amtrak (www.amtrak.com) and **VIA Rail Canada** (www.viarail.ca) run three routes between the USA and Canada: two in the east and one in the west. Customs inspections happen at the border, not upon boarding.

Sea

Various ferry services on the coasts connect the US and Canada.

➜ Bar Harbor, Maine to Yarmouth, Nova Scotia: Service halted in recent years but supposedly it will start again with a new operator.

➜ Eastport, Maine to Deer Island, New Brunswick: **East Coast Ferries** (www.eastcoastferries.nb.ca).

➜ Seattle to Victoria, BC: **Victoria Clipper** (www.clippervacations.com).

➜ Alaska to Port Hardy, BC: **Alaska Marine Highway System** (www.ferryalaska.com).

➜ Alaska to Prince Rupert, BC: **BC Ferries** (www.bcferries.com).

GETTING AROUND

Air

Airlines in Canada

Air Canada operates the largest domestic-flight network, serving some 150 destinations.

The Canadian aviation arena also includes many in-

GREYHOUND BUS ROUTES & FARES

ROUTE	DURATION (HR)	FREQUENCY (DAILY)	FARE (US$)
Boston-Montréal	7-8	4	85
Detroit-Toronto	5-6	5	73
New York-Montréal	8-9	6-10	84
Seattle-Vancouver	4	3-5	38

TRAIN ROUTES & FARES

ROUTE	DURATION (HR)	FREQUENCY (DAILY)	FARE (US$)
New York-Toronto (*Maple Leaf*)	13	1	125
New York-Montréal (*Adirondack*)	11	1	65
Seattle-Vancouver (*Cascades*)	4	2	52

dependent regional and local airlines, which tend to focus on small, remote regions, mostly in the North. Depending on the destination, fares in such noncompetitive markets can be high.

Air Canada (☏888-247-2262; www.aircanada.com) Nationwide flights.

Air Creebec (☏800-567-6567; www.aircreebec.ca) Serves northern Québec and Ontario, including Chisasibi and Chibougamau, from Montréal and other cities.

Air Inuit (☏888-247-2262; www.airinuit.com) Flies from Montréal to all 14 Inuit communities in Nunavik (northern Québec), including Kuujjuaq and Puvirnituq.

Air Labrador (☏800-563-3042; www.airlabrador.com) Flies mostly within Labrador.

Air North (☏in Canada 867-668-2228, in USA 800-661-0407; www.flyairnorth.com) Flies from the Yukon to British Columbia, Alberta, Northwest Territories and Alaska.

Air St-Pierre (☏877-277-7765, 902-873-3566; www.airsaintpierre.com) Flies from eastern Canada to the French territories off Newfoundland's coast.

Air Tindi (☏867-669-8260; www.airtindi.com) Serves the Northwest Territories' North Slave region.

Aklak Air (☏866-707-4977; www.aklakair.ca) Serves the Northwest Territories' Mackenzie Delta.

Bearskin Airlines (☏800-465-2327; www.bearskinairlines.com) Serves destinations throughout Ontario and eastern Manitoba.

Calm Air (☏800-839-2256, 204-778-6471; www.calmair.com) Flights throughout Manitoba and Nunavut.

Canadian North (☏800-661-1505; www.canadiannorth.com) Flights to, from and within the Northwest Territories and Nunavut.

Central Mountain Air (☏888-865-8585; www.flycma.com) Destinations throughout British Columbia and Alberta.

First Air (☏800-267-1247; www.firstair.ca) Flies from Ottawa, Montréal, Winnipeg and Edmonton to 24 Arctic destinations, including Iqaluit.

Harbour Air (☏800-665-0212; www.harbour-air.com) Seaplane service from the city of Vancouver to Vancouver Island, Gulf Islands and the Sunshine Coast.

Hawkair (☏866-429-5247; www.hawkair.ca) Serves northern British Columbia from Vancouver and Victoria.

Northwestern Air Lease (☏877-872-2216; www.nwal.ca) Flies in Alberta and the Northwest Territories.

North-Wright Air (☏867-587-2333; www.north-wrightairways.com) Serves the Northwest Territories' Mackenzie Valley.

Pacific Coastal Airlines (☏800-663-2872; www.pacific-coastal.com) Vancouver-based airline with service to many British Columbia locales.

Porter Airlines (☏888-619-8622; www.flyporter.com) Turboprop planes from eastern Canadian cities to Toronto's quicker, more convenient Billy Bishop Toronto City Airport downtown.

Provincial Airlines (☏800-563-2800; www.provincialairlines.ca) St John's–based airline with service throughout Newfoundland and to Labrador.

Seair Seaplanes (☏800-447-3247, 604-273-8900; www.seairseaplanes.com) Flies from Vancouver to Nanaimo and the Southern Gulf Islands in British Columbia.

Transwest Air (☏800-667-9356; www.transwestair.com) Service within Saskatchewan.

West Coast Air (☏800-347-2222; www.westcoastair.com) Seaplane service from Vancouver city to Vancouver Island and the Sunshine Coast.

WestJet (☏888-937-8538, 800-538-5696; www.westjet.com) Calgary-based low-cost carrier serving destinations throughout Canada.

Air Passes

Star Alliance (www.staralliance.com) members Air Canada, United Airlines and US Airways have teamed up to offer the North American Airpass, which is available to anyone not residing in the USA, Canada, Mexico, Bermuda or the Caribbean. It's sold only in conjunction with an international flight operated by any Star Alliance member airline. You can buy as few as three coupons

CLIMATE CHANGE & TRAVEL

Every form of transport that relies on carbon-based fuel generates CO_2, the main cause of human-induced climate change. Modern travel is dependent on aeroplanes, which might use less fuel per kilometer per person than most cars but travel much greater distances. The altitude at which aircraft emit gases (including CO_2) and particles also contributes to their climate change impact. Many websites offer 'carbon calculators' that allow people to estimate the carbon emissions generated by their journey and, for those who wish to do so, to offset the impact of the greenhouse gases emitted with contributions to portfolios of climate-friendly initiatives throughout the world. Lonely Planet offsets the carbon footprint of all staff and author travel.

(from US$399) or as many as 10.

Air North has an **Arctic Circle Air Pass** (www.flyairnorth.com/AirPasses/AirPasses.aspx) for those traveling around the Yukon and Northwest Territories.

Bicycle

Much of Canada is great for cycling. Long-distance trips can be done entirely on quiet back roads, and many cities (including Edmonton, Montréal, Ottawa, Toronto and Vancouver) have designated bike routes.

➡ Cyclists must follow the same rules of the road as vehicles, but don't expect drivers to always respect your right of way.

➡ Helmets are mandatory for all cyclists in British Columbia, New Brunswick, Prince Edward Island and Nova Scotia, as well as for anyone under 18 in Alberta and Ontario.

➡ The **Better World Club** (☎866-238-1137; www.betterworldclub.com) provides emergency roadside assistance. Membership costs $40 per year, plus a $12 enrollment fee, and entitles you to two free pickups, and transport to the nearest repair shop, or home, within a 50km radius of where you're picked up.

Transportation

➡ By air: most airlines will carry bikes as checked luggage without charge on international flights, as long as they're in a box. On domestic flights they usually charge between $30 and $65. Always check details before you buy the ticket.

➡ By bus: you must ship your bike as freight on Greyhound Canada. In addition to a bike box ($10), you'll be charged according to the weight of the bike, plus an oversize charge ($30) and GST. Bikes only travel on the same bus as the passenger if there's

enough space. To ensure that yours arrives at the same time as (or before) you do, ship it a day early.

➡ By train: VIA Rail will transport your bicycle for $25, but only on trains offering checked-baggage service (which includes all long-distance and many regional trains).

Rental

➡ Outfitters renting bicycles exist in most tourist towns.

➡ Rentals cost around $15 per day for touring bikes and $25 per day for mountain bikes. The price usually includes a helmet and lock.

➡ Most companies require a security deposit of $20 to $200.

Boat

Ferry services are extensive, especially throughout the Atlantic provinces and in British Columbia.

Walk-ons and cyclists should be able to get aboard at any time, but call ahead for vehicle reservations or if you require a cabin berth. This is especially important during summer peak season and holidays. Main operators:

Bay Ferries (☎888-249-7245; www.bayferries.com) Year-round service between Saint John, New Brunswick, and Digby, Nova Scotia.

BC Ferries (☎888-223-3779, 250-386-3431; www.bcferries.com) Huge passenger-ferry systems with 25 routes and 47 ports of call, including Vancouver Island, the Gulf Islands, the Sechelt Peninsula along the Sunshine Coast and the islands of Haida Gwaii – all in British Columbia.

Coastal Transport (☎506-662-3724; www.coastaltransport.ca) Ferry from Blacks Harbour to Grand Manan in the Fundy Isles, New Brunswick.

CTMA Ferries (☎888-986-3278, 418-986-3278; www.ctma.ca) Daily ferries to

Québec's Îles de la Madeleine from Souris, Prince Edward Island.

East Coast Ferries (☎877-747-2159, 506-747-2159; www.eastcoastferries.nb.ca) Connects Deer Island to Campobello Island, both in the Fundy Isles, New Brunswick.

Labrador Marine (☎866-535-2567, 709-535-0810; www.labradormarine.com) Connects Newfoundland to Labrador.

Marine Atlantic (☎800-341-7981; www.marine-atlantic.ca) Connects Port aux Basques and Argentia in Newfoundland with North Sydney, Nova Scotia.

Northumberland Ferries (☎888-249-7245, 902-566-3838; www.peiferry.com) Connects Wood Islands, Prince Edward Island and Caribou, Nova Scotia.

Provincial Ferry Services (www.gov.nl.ca/ferryservices) Operates coastal ferries throughout Newfoundland.

Bus

Greyhound Canada (www.greyhound.ca) is the king, plowing along an extensive network in central and western Canada, as well as to/from the USA. Regional carriers pick up the slack, especially in the east.

Buses are generally clean, comfortable and reliable. Amenities may include onboard toilets, air-conditioning (bring a sweater), reclining seats, free wi-fi and onboard movies. Smoking is not permitted. On long journeys, buses make meal stops every few hours, usually at highway service stations.

Autobus Maheux (☎888-797-0011; www.autobusmaheux.qc.ca) Service from Montréal to Québec's northwest regions.

Coach Canada (☎800-461-7661; www.coachcanada.com) Scheduled service within Ontario and from Toronto to Montréal.

DRL Coachlines (☎709-263-2171; www.drl-lr.com) Service throughout Newfoundland.

Intercar (📞888-861-4592; www.intercar.qc.ca) Connects Québec City, Montréal and Tadoussac, among other towns in Québec.

Limocar (📞866-700-8899; www.limocar.com) Regional service in Québec.

Malaspina Coach Lines (📞877-227-8287; www.malaspinacoach.com) Service between Vancouver and the Sunshine Coast communities of British Columbia.

Maritime Bus (📞902-429-2029; www.maritimebus.com) For New Brunswick, Prince Edward Island and Nova Scotia.

Megabus (www.megabus.com) Service between Toronto and Montréal via Kingston; tickets can only be purchased online.

Ontario Northland (📞800-461-8558; www.ontarionorthland.ca) Operates bus and train routes that service northern Ontario from Toronto.

Orléans Express (📞888-999-3977; www.orleansexpress.com) Service to eastern Québec.

Pacific Coach Lines (📞800-661-1725, 250-385-4411; www.pacificcoach.com) Service between Victoria, Vancouver and Whistler.

Parkbus (📞800-928-7101; www.parkbus.ca) Runs from Toronto to Algonquin, Killarney and other Ontario parks.

Red Arrow (www.redarrow.ca) Serves all the major cities in Alberta, with free wi-fi, snacks, drinks and plug-ins.

Saskatchewan Transportation Company (STC;📞800-663-7181; www.stcbus.com) Service within Saskatchewan.

Reservations

Tickets can be bought online or at bus terminals for Grey-

hound. Some companies, such as Megabus, take reservations online only. The earlier you buy a ticket online, the cheaper your fare.

Show up at least 30 to 45 minutes prior to departure.

Car & Motorcycle
Automobile Associations

Auto-club membership is a handy thing to have in Canada. The **Canadian Automobile Association** (CAA; 📞800-268-3750; www.caa.ca) offers services, including 24-hour emergency roadside assistance, to members of international affiliates such as AAA in the USA, AA in the UK and ADAC in Germany. The club also offers trip-planning advice, free maps, travel-agency services and a range of discounts on hotels, car rentals etc.

The **Better World Club** (📞866-238-1137; www.betterworldclub.com), which donates 1% of its annual revenue to environmental cleanup efforts, has emerged as an alternative. It offers service throughout the USA and Canada, and has a roadside-assistance program for bicycles.

Bringing Your Own Vehicle

There's minimal hassle driving into Canada from the USA as long as you have your vehicle's registration papers, proof of liability insurance and your home driver's license.

Driving Licenses

In most provinces visitors can legally drive for up to

three months with their home driver's license. In some, such as British Columbia, this is extended to six months.

If you're spending considerable time in Canada, think about getting an International Driving Permit (IDP), which is valid for one year. Your automobile association at home can issue one for a small fee. Always carry your home license together with the IDP.

Fuel

Gas is sold in liters. Prices are higher in remote areas, with Yellowknife usually setting the national record; drivers in Calgary typically pay the least for gas.

Fuel prices are usually lower in the USA, so fill up south of the border.

Insurance

Canadian law requires liability insurance for all vehicles, to cover you for damage caused to property and people.

➡ The minimum requirement is $200,000 in all provinces except Québec, where it is $50,000.

➡ Americans traveling to Canada in their own car should ask their insurance company for a Nonresident Interprovince Motor Vehicle Liability Insurance Card (commonly known as a 'yellow card'), which is accepted as evidence of financial responsibility anywhere in Canada. Although not mandatory, it may come in handy in an accident.

➡ Car-rental agencies offer liability insurance. Collision Damage Waivers

LONG-DISTANCE BUS FARES

ROUTE	STANDARD FARE	7-DAY FARE	DURATION (HR)
Vancouver-Calgary	$104	$80	14-17
Montréal-Toronto	$56	$32	8-10
Toronto-Vancouver	$229	$180	65-70

ROAD DISTANCES (KM)

	Banff	Calgary	Edmonton	Halifax	Inuvik	Jasper	Montreal	Ottawa	Quebec City	St John's	Toronto	Vancouver	Whitehorse	Winnipeg
Calgary	130													
Edmonton	410	290												
Halifax	4900	4810	4850											
Inuvik	3440	3515	3220	8110										
Jasper	280	415	370	5250	3150									
Montreal	3700	3550	3605	1240	6820	3950								
Ottawa	3450	3340	3410	1440	6620	3770	200							
Quebec City	3900	3800	3880	1020	7060	4210	250							
St John's	6200	6100	6150	1480	9350	6480	2530	2730	2310					
Toronto	3400	3400	3470	1790	6680	3820	550	450	800	3090				
Vancouver	850	970	1160	5880	3630	790	4580	4350	4830	7130	4360			
Whitehorse	2210	2290	2010	6830	1220	1930	5620	5390	5840	8150	5450	2400		
Winnipeg	1450	1325	1330	3520	4550	1670	2280	2140	2520	4820	2220	2290	3340	
Yellowknife	1800	1790	1510	6340	3770	1590	5050	4900	5350	7620	4950	2370	2540	2800

These distances are approximate only.

(CDW) reduce or eliminate the amount you'll have to reimburse the rental company if there's damage to the car itself. Some credit cards cover CDW for a certain rental period if you use the card to pay for the rental and decline the policy offered by the rental company. Always check with your card issuer to see what coverage it offers in Canada.

➡ Personal accident insurance (PAI) covers you and any passengers for medical costs incurred as a result of an accident. If your travel insurance or your health-insurance policy at home does this as well (and most do, but check), then this is one expense you can do without.

Rental

CAR

To rent a car in Canada you generally need to fulfill the following:

➡ be at least 25 years old (some companies will rent to drivers between the ages of 21 and 24 for an additional charge)

➡ hold a valid driver's license (an international one may be required if you're not from an English- or French-speaking country)

➡ have a major credit card

You should be able to get an economy-size vehicle for about $35 to $65 per day. Child safety seats are compulsory (reserve them when you book) and cost about $13 per day.

Major international car-rental companies usually have branches at airports, train stations and in city centers.

In Canada, on-the-spot rentals often are more expensive than prebooked packages (ie cars booked with a flight).

Avis (☎800-437-0358; www. avis.com)

Budget (☎800-268-8900; www.budget.com)

Dollar (☎800-800-4000; www.dollar.com)

Enterprise (☎800-261-7331; www.enterprise.ca)

Hertz (☎800-263-0600; www.hertz.com)

National (☎877-222-9058; www.nationalcar.ca)

Practicar (☎800-327-0116; www.practicar.ca) Formerly known as Rent a Wreck, Practicar often has lower rates. It's also affiliated with Backpackers Hotels Canada and Hostelling International.

Thrifty (☎800-847-4389; www.thrifty.com)

MOTORCYCLE

Several companies offer motorcycle rentals and tours. A Harley Heritage Softail Classic costs about $210 per day, including liability insurance and 200km mileage. Some companies have minimum rental periods, which can be as much as seven days. Riding a hog is especially popular in British Columbia.

Coastline Motorcycle
(☎866-338-0344, 250-335-1837; www.coastlinemc.com) Tours and rentals out of Victoria and Vancouver in British Columbia.

McScoots Motorcycle & Scooter Rentals (☎250-763-4668; www.mcscoots.com) Big selection of Harleys; also operates motorcycle tours. It's based in Kelowna, British Columbia.

Open Road Adventure
(☎250-494-5409; www.canada-motorcyclerentals.com) Rentals and tours out of Summerland, near Kelowna, British Columbia.

Harley-Davidson Laval
(☎877-459-2950; www.harleydavidsonlaval.com) Rentals by half-day, full day, weekend or longer out of suburban Montréal.

RECREATIONAL VEHICLES

The RV market is biggest in the west, with specialized agencies in Calgary, Edmonton, Whitehorse and Vancouver. For summer travel, book as early as possible. The base cost is roughly $160 to $265 per day in high season for midsize vehicles, although insurance, fees and taxes add a hefty chunk to that. Diesel-fueled RVs have considerably lower running costs.

Canadream Campers
(☎403-291-1000, 800-461-7368; www.canadream.com) Based in Calgary, with rentals (including one-way rentals) in eight cities, including Vancouver, Whitehorse, Toronto and Halifax.

Cruise Canada (☎800-671-8042; www.cruisecanada.com) Offers three sizes of RVs. Locations in Halifax, and in central and western Canada; offers one-way rentals.

Road Conditions & Hazards

Road conditions are generally good, but there are a few things to keep in mind:

➡ Fierce winters can leave potholes the size of landmine craters. Be prepared to swerve. Winter travel in general can be hazardous due to heavy snow and ice, which may cause roads and bridges to close periodically. **Transport Canada** (☎800-387-4999; www.tc.gc.ca/road) provides links to road conditions and construction zones for each province.

➡ If you're driving in winter or in remote areas, make sure your vehicle is equipped with four-season radial or snow tires, and emergency supplies in case you're stranded.

➡ Distances between services can be long in sparsely populated areas such as the Yukon, Newfoundland or northern Québec, so keep your gas topped up whenever possible.

➡ Moose, deer and elk are common on rural roadways, especially at night. There's no contest between a 534kg bull moose and a Subaru, so keep your eyes peeled.

Road Rules

➡ Canadians drive on the right-hand side of the road.

➡ Seat belt use is compulsory. Children under 18kg must be strapped in child-booster seats, except infants, who must be in a rear-facing safety seat.

➡ Motorcyclists must wear helmets and drive with their headlights on.

➡ Distances and speed limits are posted in kilometers. The speed limit is generally 40km/h to 50km/h in cities and 90km/h to 110km/h outside town.

➡ Slow down to 60km/h when passing emergency vehicles (such as police cars and ambulances) stopped on the roadside with their lights flashing.

➡ Turning right at red lights after coming to a full stop is permitted in all provinces (except where road signs prohibit it, and on the island of Montréal, where it's always a no-no). There's a national propensity for running red lights, however, so don't assume 'right of way' at intersections.

➡ Driving while using a hand-held cell phone is illegal in British Columbia, Newfoundland, Nova Scotia, Ontario, Prince Edward Island, Québec and Saskatchewan.

➡ Radar detectors are not allowed in most of Canada (Alberta, British Columbia and Saskatchewan are the exceptions). If you're caught driving with a radar detector, even one that isn't being operated, you could receive a fine of $1000 and your device may be confiscated.

➡ The blood-alcohol limit for drivers is 0.08%. Driving while drunk is a criminal offense.

Hitchhiking

Hitching is never entirely safe in any country and we don't recommend it. That said, in remote and rural areas in Canada it is not uncommon to see people thumbing for a ride.

➡ If you do decide to hitch, understand that you are taking a small but potentially serious risk. Remember that it's safer to travel in pairs and let someone know where you are planning to go.

➡ Hitchhiking is illegal on some highways (ie the 400-series roads in Ontario), as well as in the provinces of Nova Scotia and New Brunswick.

Ride-Sharing

Ride-share services link drivers and paying passengers headed in the same direction. **Kangaride** (☏855-526-4274; www.kangaride.com) is a Québec City–based service that is rapidly expanding across Canada. It costs $7.50 per year for membership and $5 per ride (on top of what the driver charges). **Allô Stop** (www.allostop.com) is a similar service operating in Québec; the website is in French.

Local Transportation

Bicycle

Cycling is a popular means of getting around during the warmer months, and many cities have hundreds of kilometers of dedicated bike paths. Bicycles typically can be taken on public transportation (although some cities have restrictions during peak travel times). All the major cities have shops renting bikes. Toronto and Montréal have bike-share programs; Vancouver will launch a bike share program in 2014.

Bus

Buses are the most common form of public transportation, and practically all towns have their own systems. Most are commuter oriented, and offer only limited or no services in the evenings and on weekends.

Train

Toronto and Montréal are the two Canadian cities with subway systems. Vancouver's version is mostly an aboveground monorail. Calgary, Edmonton and Ottawa have efficient light-rail systems. Route maps are posted in all stations.

Taxi

Most of the main cities have taxis. They are usually metered, with a flag-fall fee of roughly $2.70 and a per-kilometer charge around $1.75. Drivers expect a tip of between 10% and 15%. Taxis can be flagged down or ordered by phone.

Tours

Tour companies are another way to get around this great big country. Some reliable companies operating in multiple Canadian provinces:

Arctic Odysseys (☏206-325-1977, 800-574-3021; www.arcticodysseys.com) Experience Arctic Canada close up on tours chasing the northern lights in the Northwest Territories, heli-skiing on Baffin Island or polar-bear spotting on Hudson Bay.

Backroads (☏510-527-1555, 800-462-2848; www.backroads.com) Guided cycling, walking and/or paddling tours in the Rockies, Nova Scotia and Québec.

Moose Travel Network (☏in eastern Canada 888-816-6673, in western Canada 888-244-6673; www.moosenetwork.com) Operates backpacker-type tours in small buses throughout British Columbia, Alberta and beyond.

Nahanni River Adventures (☏800-297-6927; www.nahanni.com) Operates rafting and kayaking expeditions in the Yukon, British Columbia and Alaska, including trips on the Firth, Alsek and Babine Rivers, as well as down the Tatshenshini-Alsek watershed.

Road Scholar (☏800-454-5768; www.roadscholar.org) Formerly known as Elderhostel, this nonprofit organization offers study tours in nearly all provinces for active people over 55, including train trips, cruises, and bus and walking tours.

Routes to Learning (☏613-530-2222, 866-745-1690; www.routestolearning.ca) From walking in the steps of Newfoundland's Vikings to exploring New Brunswick's Acadians or Nova Scotia's lighthouses, this nonprofit group has dozens of educational tours throughout Canada.

Salty Bear Adventure Tours (☏902-202-3636; www.saltybear.ca) Backpacker-oriented van tours through the Maritimes with jump-on/jump-off flexibility. There's a three-day circuit around Cape Breton, Nova Scotia, and a five-day route that goes into Prince Edward Island.

Trek America (☏in UK 0870-444-8735, in USA 800-221-0596; www.trekamerica.com) Active camping, hiking and canoeing tours in small groups, geared primarily at people between 18 and 38, although some are open to all ages.

LONG-DISTANCE TRAIN ROUTES

ROUTE	DURATION (HR)	FREQUENCY	FARE
Toronto-Vancouver (Canadian)	83	3 weekly	from $590
Winnipeg-Churchill (Hudson Bay)	44	2 weekly	from $170
Halifax-Montréal (Ocean)	21	1 daily (Wed-Mon)	from $151
Prince Rupert-Jasper	33	3 weekly	from $163

Train

VIA Rail (📞888-842-7245; www.viarail.ca) operates most of Canada's intercity and transcontinental passenger trains, chugging over 14,000km of track. In some remote parts of the country, such as Churchill, Manitoba, trains provide the only overland access.

➡ Rail service is most efficient in the corridor between Québec City and Windsor, Ontario – particularly between Montréal and Toronto, the two major hubs.

➡ The rail network does not extend to Newfoundland, Prince Edward Island or the Northwest Territories.

➡ Free wi-fi is available on most trains.

➡ Smoking is prohibited on all trains.

Classes

There are four main classes:

➡ Economy class buys you a fairly basic, if indeed quite comfortable, reclining seat with a headrest. Blankets and pillows are provided for overnight travel.

➡ Business class operates in the southern Ontario/ Québec corridor. Seats are more spacious and have outlets for plugging in laptops. You also get a meal and priority boarding.

➡ Sleeper class is available on shorter overnight routes. You can choose from compartments with upper or lower pullout berths, and private single, double or triple roomettes, all with a bathroom.

➡ Touring class is available on long-distance routes and includes sleeper class accommodations plus meals, access to the sightseeing car and sometimes a tour guide.

Costs

Taking the train is more expensive than the bus, but most people find it a more comfortable way to travel. June to mid-October is peak season, when prices are about 40% higher. Buying tickets in advance (even just five days before) can yield significant savings.

Long-Distance Routes

VIA Rail has several classic trains:

➡ **Canadian** A 1950s stainless-steel beauty between Toronto and Vancouver, zipping through the northern Ontario lake country, the western plains via Winnipeg and Saskatoon, and Jasper in the Rockies over three days.

➡ **Hudson Bay** From the prairie (slowly) to the Subarctic: Winnipeg to polar-bear hangout Churchill.

➡ **Ocean** Chugs from Montréal along the St Lawrence River through New Brunswick and Nova Scotia.

➡ **Jasper to Prince Rupert** An all-daylight route from Jasper, Alberta, to coastal Prince Rupert, British Columbia; there's an overnight stop in Prince George (you make your own hotel reservations).

Privately run regional train companies offer additional rail-touring opportunities:

➡ **Algoma Central Railway** (www.agawacanyontourtrain. com) Access to northern Ontario wilderness areas.

➡ **Ontario Northland** (www. ontarionorthland.ca) Operates the seasonal *Polar Bear Express* from Cochrane to Moosonee on Hudson Bay (round-trip $112).

➡ **Rocky Mountaineer Railtours** (www. rockymountaineer.com; 2 days from $1000) Gape at Canadian Rockies scenery on swanky trains between Vancouver, Kamloops and Calgary.

➡ **Royal Canadian Pacific** (📞877-665-3044; www. royalcanadianpacific.com) Another cruise-ship-like luxury line between and around the Rockies via Calgary.

➡ **White Pass & Yukon Route** (www.wpyr.com; round-trip $160) Gorgeous route paralleling the original White Pass trail from Whitehorse, Yukon, to Fraser, British Columbia.

Reservations

Seat reservations are highly recommended, especially in summer, on weekends and around holidays. During peak season (June to mid-October), some of the most popular sleeping arrangements are sold out months in advance, especially on long-distance trains such as the *Canadian*. The *Hudson Bay* often books solid during polar-bear season (around late September to early November).

Train Passes

VIA Rail offers a couple of passes that provide good savings:

➡ The Canrailpass-System is good for seven trips on any train during a 21-day period. All seats are in economy class; upgrades are not permitted. You must book each leg at least three days in advance (doable online). Costs start at $1008/630 in high/low season.

➡ The Canrailpass-Corridor (from $360) is good for seven trips during a 10-day period on trains in the Québec City–Windsor corridor (which includes Montréal, Toronto and Niagara).

Language

English and French are the official languages of Canada. You'll see both on highway signs, maps, tourist brochures, packaging etc. In Québec the preservation of French is a major concern and fuels the separatist movement. Here, English can be hard to find, and road signs and visitor information is often in French only. Outside Montréal and Québec City, you'll need French at least some of the time.

New Brunswick is the only officially bilingual province. French is widely spoken, particularly in the north and east. It is somewhat different from the French of Québec. Nova Scotia and Manitoba also have significant French-speaking populations, and there are pockets in most other provinces. In the west of Canada, French isn't as prevalent.

The French spoken in Canada is essentially the same as in France. Although many English-speaking (and most French-speaking) students in Québec are still taught the French of France, the local tongue is known as 'Québecois' or *joual*. Announcers and broadcasters on Québec TV and radio tend to speak a more refined, European style of French, as does the upper class. Québecois people will have no problem understanding more formal French.

French sounds can almost all be found in English. The exceptions are nasal vowels (represented in our pronunciation guides by o or u followed by an almost inaudible nasal consonant sound m, n or ng), the 'funny' *u* (ew in our guides) and the deep-in-the-throat *r*. Bearing this in mind and reading the pronunciation guides in this chapter as if they were English, you'll be understood just fine.

WANT MORE?

For in-depth language information and handy phrases, check out Lonely Planet's *French Phrasebook*. You'll find it at **shop.lonelyplanet.com**, or you can buy Lonely Planet's iPhone phrasebooks at the Apple App Store.

BASICS

Hello.	*Bonjour.*	bon·zhoor
Goodbye.	*Au revoir.*	o·rer·vwa
Excuse me.	*Excusez-moi.*	ek·skew·zay·mwa
Sorry.	*Pardon.*	par·don
Yes./No.	*Oui./Non.*	wee/non
Please.	*S'il vous plaît.*	seel voo play
Thank you.	*Merci.*	mair·see
You're welcome.	*De rien.*	der ree·en

How are you?
Comment allez-vous?   ko·mon ta·lay·voo

Fine, and you?
Bien, merci. Et vous?   byun mair·see ay voo

My name is ...
Je m'appelle ...   zher ma·pel ...

What's your name?
Comment vous appelez-vous?   ko·mon voo·za·play voo

Do you speak English?
Parlez-vous anglais?   par·lay·voo ong·glay

I don't understand.
Je ne comprends pas.   zher ner kom·pron pa

ACCOMMODATIONS

Do you have any rooms available?
Est-ce que vous avez des chambres libres?   es·ker voo za·vay day shom·brer lee·brer

How much is it per night/person?
Quel est le prix par nuit/personne?   kel ay ler pree par nwee/per·son

Is breakfast included?
Est-ce que le petit déjeuner est inclus?   es·ker ler per·tee day·zher·nay ayt en·klew

a ... room	*une chambre ...*	ewn shom·brer ...
single	*à un lit*	a un lee
double	*avec un grand lit*	a·vek un gron lee

air-con	climatiseur	klee·ma·tee·zer
bathroom	salle de bains	sal der bun
campsite	camping	kom·peeng
dorm	dortoir	dor·twar
guesthouse	pension	pon·syon
hotel	hôtel	o·tel
window	fenêtre	fer·nay·trer
youth hostel	auberge de jeunesse	o·berzh der zher·nes

DIRECTIONS

Where's ...?
Où est ...?   oo ay ...

What's the address?
Quelle est l'adresse?   kel ay la·dres

Could you write the address, please?
Est-ce que vous pourriez   es·ker voo poo·ryay
écrire l'adresse,   ay·kreer la·dres
s'il vous plaît?   seel voo play

Can you show me (on the map)?
Pouvez-vous m'indiquer   poo·vay·voo mun·dee·kay
(sur la carte)?   (sewr la kart)

at the corner	au coin	o kwun
at the traffic lights	aux feux	o fer
behind	derrière	dair·ryair
in front of ...	devant ...	der·von ...
far (from ...)	loin (de ...)	lwun (der ...)
left	gauche	gosh
near (to ...)	près (de ...)	pray (der ...)
next to ...	à côté de ...	a ko·tay der...
opposite ...	en face de ...	on fas der ...
right	droite	drwat
straight ahead	tout droit	too drwa

EATING & DRINKING

A table for (two), please.
Une table pour (deux),   ewn ta·bler poor (der)
s'il vous plaît.   seel voo play

What would you recommend?
Qu'est-ce que vous   kes·ker voo
conseillez?   kon·say·yay

What's in that dish?
Quels sont les   kel son lay
ingrédients?   zun·gray·dyon

I'm a vegetarian.
Je suis   zher swee
végétarien/   vay·zhay·ta·ryun/
végétarienne.   vay·zhay·ta·ryen (m/f)

I don't eat ...
Je ne mange pas ...   zher ner monzh pa ...

KEY PATTERNS

To get by in French, mix and match these simple patterns with words of your choice:

Where's (the entry)?
Où est (l'entrée)?   oo ay (lon·tray)

Where can I (buy a ticket)?
Où est-ce que je   oo es·ker zher
peux (acheter   per (ash·tay
un billet)?   un bee·yay)

When's (the next train)?
Quand est   kon ay
(le prochain train)?   (ler pro·shun trun)

How much is (a room)?
C'est combien pour   say kom·buyn poor
(une chambre)?   (ewn shom·brer)

Do you have (a map)?
Avez-vous (une carte)?   a·vay voo (ewn kart)

Is there (a toilet)?
Y a-t-il (des toilettes)?   ee a teel (day twa·let)

I'd like (to book a room).
Je voudrais   zher voo·dray
(réserver   (ray·ser·vay
une chambre).   ewn shom·brer)

Can I (enter)?
Puis-je (entrer)?   pweezh (on·tray)

Could you please (help)?
Pouvez-vous   poo·vay voo
(m'aider),   (may·day)
s'il vous plaît?   seel voo play

Do I have to (book a seat)?
Faut-il (réserver   fo·teel (ray·ser·vay
une place)?   ewn plas)

Cheers!
Santé!   son·tay

That was delicious.
C'était délicieux!   say·tay day·lee·syer

Please bring the bill.
Apportez-moi   a·por·tay·mwa
l'addition,   la·dee·syon
s'il vous plaît.   seel voo play

Key Words

appetiser	entrée	on·tray
bottle	bouteille	boo·tay
breakfast	déjeuner	day·zher·nay
children's menu	menu pour enfants	mer·new poor on·fon
cold	froid	frwa
delicatessen	traiteur	tray·ter
dinner	souper	soo·pay
dish	plat	pla

food	nourriture	noo·ree·tewr
fork	fourchette	foor·shet
glass	verre	vair
grocery store	épicerie	ay·pees·ree
highchair	chaise haute	shay zot
hot	chaud	sho
knife	couteau	koo·to
local speciality	spécialité locale	spay·sya·lee·tay lo·kal
lunch	dîner	dee·nay
main course	plat principal	pla prun see pal
market	marché	mar·shay
menu (in English)	carte (en anglais)	kart (on ong·glay)
plate	assiette	a·syet
spoon	cuillère	kwee·yair
wine list	carte des vins	kart day vun
with	avec	a·vek
without	sans	son

Meat & Fish

beef	bœuf	berf
chicken	poulet	poo·lay
fish	poisson	pwa·son
lamb	agneau	a·nyo
pork	porc	por
turkey	dinde	dund
veal	veau	vo

Fruit & Vegetables

apple	pomme	pom
apricot	abricot	ab·ree·ko
asparagus	asperge	a·spairzh
beans	haricots	a·ree·ko
beetroot	betterave	be·trav
cabbage	chou	shoo
celery	céleri	sel·ree
cherry	cerise	ser·reez
corn	maïs	ma·ees
cucumber	concombre	kong·kom·brer
gherkin (pickle)	cornichon	kor·nee·shon
grape	raisin	ray·zun
leek	poireau	pwa·ro
lemon	citron	see·tron
lettuce	laitue	lay·tew
mushroom	champignon	shom·pee·nyon
peach	pêche	pesh
peas	petit pois	per·tee pwa

(red/green) pepper	poivron (rouge/vert)	pwa·vron (roozh/vair)
pineapple	ananas	a·na·nas
plum	prune	prewn
potato	pomme de terre	pom der tair
prune	pruneau	prew·no
pumpkin	citrouille	see·troo·yer
shallot	échalote	eh·sha·lot
spinach	épinards	eh·pee·nar
strawberry	fraise	frez
tomato	tomate	to mat
turnip	navet	na·vay
vegetable	légume	lay·gewm

Other

bread	pain	pun
butter	beurre	ber
cheese	fromage	fro·mazh
egg	œuf	erf
honey	miel	myel
jam	confiture	kon·fee·tewr
lentils	lentilles	lon·tee·yer
oil	huile	weel
pasta/noodles	pâtes	pat
pepper	poivre	pwa·vrer
rice	riz	ree
salt	sel	sel
sugar	sucre	sew·krer
vinegar	vinaigre	vee·nay·grer

Drinks

beer	bière	bee·yair
coffee	café	ka·fay
(orange) juice	jus (d'orange)	zhew (do·ronzh)
milk	lait	lay
red wine	vin rouge	vun roozh

Signs

Entrée	Entrance
Femmes	Women
Fermé	Closed
Hommes	Men
Interdit	Prohibited
Ouvert	Open
Renseignements	Information
Sortie	Exit
Toilettes/WC	Toilets

tea	*thé*	tay
(mineral) water	*eau (minérale)*	o (mee·nay·ral)
white wine	*vin blanc*	vun blong

EMERGENCIES

Help!
Au secours! — o skoor

I'm lost.
Je suis perdu/perdue. — zhe swee pair·dew (m/f)

Leave me alone!
Fichez-moi la paix! — fee·shay·mwa la pay

There's been an accident.
Il y a eu un accident. — eel ya ew un ak·see·don

Call a doctor.
Appelez un médecin. — a·play un mayd·sun

Call the police.
Appelez la police. — a·play la po·lees

I'm ill.
Je suis malade. — zher swee ma·lad

It hurts here.
J'ai une douleur ici. — zhay ewn doo·ler ee·see

I'm allergic to ...
Je suis allergique ... — zher swee za·lair·zheek ...

Where are the toilets?
Où sont les toilettes? — oo son lay twa·let

SHOPPING & SERVICES

I'd like to buy ...
Je voudrais acheter ... — zher voo·dray ash·tay ...

May I look at it?
Est-ce que je peux le voir? — es·ker zher per ler vwar

I'm just looking.
Je regarde. — zher rer·gard

I don't like it.
Cela ne me plaît pas. — ser·la ner mer play pa

How much is it?
C'est combien? — say kom·byun

It's too expensive.
C'est trop cher. — say tro shair

Can you lower the price?
Vous pouvez baisser le prix? — voo poo·vay bay·say ler pree

Question Words		
How?	*Comment?*	ko·mon
What?	*Quoi?*	kwa
When?	*Quand?*	kon
Where?	*Où?*	oo
Who?	*Qui?*	kee
Why?	*Pourquoi?*	poor·kwa

There's a mistake in the bill.
Il y a une erreur dans la note. — eel ya ewn ay·rer don la not

ATM	*guichet automatique de banque*	gee·shay o·to·ma·teek der bonk
credit card	*carte de crédit*	kart der kray·dee
internet cafe	*cybercafé*	see·bair·ka·fay
post office	*bureau de poste*	bew·ro der post
tourist office	*office de tourisme*	o·fees der too·rees·mer

TIME & DATES

What time is it?
Quelle heure est-il? — kel er ay til

It's (eight) o'clock.
Il est (huit) heures. — il ay (weet) er

It's half past (10).
Il est (dix) heures et demie. — il ay (deez) er ay day·mee

morning	*matin*	ma·tun
afternoon	*après-midi*	a·pray·mee·dee
evening	*soir*	swar

yesterday	*hier*	yair
today	*aujourd'hui*	o·zhoor·dwee
tomorrow	*demain*	der·mun

Monday	*lundi*	lun·dee
Tuesday	*mardi*	mar·dee
Wednesday	*mercredi*	mair·krer·dee
Thursday	*jeudi*	zher·dee
Friday	*vendredi*	von·drer·dee
Saturday	*samedi*	sam·dee
Sunday	*dimanche*	dee·monsh

January	*janvier*	zhon·vyay
February	*février*	fayv·ryay
March	*mars*	mars
April	*avril*	a·vreel
May	*mai*	may
June	*juin*	zhwun
July	*juillet*	zhwee·yay
August	*août*	oot
September	*septembre*	sep·tom·brer
October	*octobre*	ok·to·brer
November	*novembre*	no·vom·brer
December	*décembre*	day·som·brer

TRANSPORTATION

Public Transportation

boat	*bateau*	ba·to
bus	*bus*	bews
plane	*avion*	a·vyon
train	*train*	trun

I want to go to ...
Je voudrais aller à   zher voo·dray a·lay a ...

Does it stop at ...?
Est-ce qu'il s'arrête à ...?   es·kil sa·ret a ...

At what time does it leave/arrive?
À quelle heure est-ce   a kel er es
qu'il part/arrive?   kil par/a·reev

Can you tell me when we get to ...?
Pouvez-vous me   poo·vay·voo mer
dire quand   deer kon
nous arrivons à ...?   noo za·ree·von a ...

I want to get off here.
Je veux descendre   zher ver day·son·drer
ici.   ee·see

first	*premier*	prer·myay
last	*dernier*	dair·nyay
next	*prochain*	pro·shun

a ... ticket	*un billet ...*	un bee·yay ...
1st-class	*de première classe*	der prem·yair klas
2nd-class	*de deuxième classe*	der der·zyem las
one-way	*simple*	sum·pler
return	*aller et retour*	a·lay ay rer·toor

aisle seat	*côté couloir*	ko·tay kool·war
cancelled	*annulé*	a·new·lay
delayed	*en retard*	on rer·tar
platform	*quai*	kay
ticket office	*guichet*	gee·shay
timetable	*horaire*	o·rair
train station	*gare*	gar
window seat	*côté fenêtre*	ko·tay fe·ne·trer

Driving & Cycling

I'd like to hire a ...	*Je voudrais louer ...*	zher voo·dray loo·way ...
car	*une voiture*	ewn vwa·tewr
bicycle	*un vélo*	un vay·lo
motorcycle	*une moto*	ewn mo·to

Numbers

1	*un*	un
2	*deux*	der
3	*trois*	trwa
4	*quatre*	ka·trer
5	*cinq*	sungk
6	*six*	sees
7	*sept*	set
8	*huit*	weet
9	*neuf*	nerf
10	*dix*	dees
20	*vingt*	vung
30	*trente*	tront
40	*quarante*	ka·ront
50	*cinquante*	sung·kont
60	*soixante*	swa·sont
70	*soixante-dix*	swa·son·dees
80	*quatre-vingts*	ka·trer·vung
90	*quatre-vingt-dix*	ka·trer·vung·dees
100	*cent*	son
1000	*mille*	meel

child seat	*siège-enfant*	syezh·on·fon
diesel	*diesel*	dyay·zel
helmet	*casque*	kask
mechanic	*mécanicien*	may·ka·nee·syun
petrol/gas	*essence*	ay·sons
service station	*station-service*	sta·syon·ser·vees

Is this the road to ...?
C'est la route pour ...?   say la root poor ...

(How long) Can I park here?
(Combien de temps)   (kom·byun der tom)
Est-ce que je peux   es·ker zher per
stationner ici?   sta·syo·nay ee·see

The car/motorbike has broken down (at ...).
La voiture/moto est   la vwa·tewr/mo·to ay
tombée en panne (à ...).   tom·bay on pan (a ...)

I have a flat tyre.
Mon pneu est à plat.   mom pner ay ta pla

I've run out of petrol.
Je suis en panne   zher swee zon pan
d'essence.   day·sons

I've lost my car keys.
J'ai perdu les clés de   zhay per·dew lay klay der
ma voiture.   ma vwa·tewr

Where can I have my bicycle repaired?
Où est-ce que je peux   oo es·ker zher per
faire réparer mon vélo?   fair ray·pa·ray mon vay·lo

Behind the Scenes

SEND US YOUR FEEDBACK

We love to hear from travelers – your comments keep us on our toes and help make our books better. Our well-traveled team reads every word on what you loved or loathed about this book. Although we cannot reply individually to postal submissions, we always guarantee that your feedback goes straight to the appropriate authors, in time for the next edition. Each person who sends us information is thanked in the next edition – the most useful submissions are rewarded with a selection of digital PDF chapters.

Visit **lonelyplanet.com/contact** to submit your updates and suggestions or to ask for help. Our award-winning website also features inspirational travel stories, news and discussions.

Note: We may edit, reproduce and incorporate your comments in Lonely Planet products such as guidebooks, websites and digital products, so let us know if you don't want your comments reproduced or your name acknowledged. For a copy of our privacy policy visit lonelyplanet.com/privacy.

OUR READERS

Many thanks to the travelers who used the last edition and wrote to us with helpful hints, useful advice and interesting anecdotes:

Amanda Rutland, Ann Poole, Anna Spruce, Anthony Aarts, Anton Krist, Celine Castonguay, Christian De Win, Dolores Wongel, Duncan Spriggs, Erik Huber, Frank Smithson, Gemma Chapman, Giorgio Ferrante, Greg Hakonson, Hsuan Kai Kao, Joanna Emery, Katia Moretti, Katrin Sippel, Kim Dorin, Mario Prim Silva, Mathilde Foix-Cablé, Matthew Lombardi, Pat Stevenson, Paul Sampson, Sebastian Cool, Stefan Memminger, Steve Power, Susan Mitchell, William & Mary Lawrence

AUTHOR THANKS

Karla Zimmerman

Thanks to St John's gurus Bryan Curtis, Sarah Mathieson and their compadres. Huge gratitude to Lisa Beran for woman'ing the wheel once again. Kudos to fellow scribes Celeste, John, Ben, Andy, Sarah, Brendan, Caroline and RVB for awesome work. Thanks most to Eric Markowitz, the world's best partner-for-life.

Celeste Brash

Thanks to Andrea Young at Destination Halifax and Isabel MacDougall with PEI Tourism, to the good folks of Digby Backpackers, Bear on the River and Kiwi Kaboodle, John Tattrie, everyone at Authentic Seacoast in Guysburough, Coastal Adventures Sea Kayaking, Kate Prest and Doug in Pictou, Isaac in Mabou, Sandra in Creignish, Beartown Baskets. Juana in North Sydney and Brian and Al in Wolfville. I wish I could work with Karla Zimmerman on every book. Biggest thanks as always to my family.

John Lee

Thanks to the too-numerous-to-mention visitor center staff as well as the hundreds of locals I met en route for their friendly tips and advice for places to check out. I'd also especially like to thank my father – William Lee – for first bringing me to Vancouver for a visit from the UK during the Expo '86 world exposition all those years ago.

Sarah Richards

Special thanks to Marie and Jean-François in Percé, Bruno at Auberge St-Antoine, and all those friendly travellers who shared their Québec anecdotes, advice and impressions with me along the way.

Brendan Sainsbury

Thanks to all the untold bus drivers, tourist info volunteers, Parks Canada guides, restaurateurs, coffee baristas, theatrical performers and indie punk rockers who helped me during my research. Special thanks to my wife Liz and seven-year-old son Kieran for their company on the road, and to my sis-in-law Tina Varughese for putting me up in Calgary.

Caroline Sieg

Thanks to everyone who shared their tips with me and for the friendly conversations at all the local watering holes, where (thankfully) few things change.

Andy Symington

The kindness and hospitality shown to me in Nunavut and the NWT was extraordinary. Particular thanks go to Eena Angmarlik, Ted Duinker, Sarah Jancke, Aaron Spitzer, Ooleepeeka Arnaqaq, Louis Robillard, James Williams, James Paris, Mike Freeland and Bronwen Livingston, Richard Zaidan, Omar in Iqaluit and the guy with the spider wrench in Fort Smith. Thanks to Karla, Brendan and my fellow authors, my family for their support, José Eliseo Vázquez González for getting me to that flight when all was lost, and, with much love and gratitude, to Elena Vázquez Rodríguez for staying close while we're far apart.

Ryan Ver Berkmoes

The number of folks to thank outnumber Kermode bears, but here's a few: Russ Lester, my fearless co-pilot, the opinionated Susan Clarke, the organized Karla Zimmerman and the pinch-hitting Korina Miller. It's always good to share BC with John Lee. At LP, I am deeply indebted to the indefatigable Mark Griffiths, Martine Power and Saralinda Turner, who showed incredible understanding when I needed it. And while there may not be golden bears, there is the golden Alexis Averbuck, who discovered and shared my love for this beautiful part of the world.

Benedict Walker

This work is dedicated to Cheryl and Bruce Cowie, and Jessica and Casey Labelle, my Canadian family, for whom my love and gratitude knows no bounds. To Wendy and Heather in Toronto for keeping me sane and smiling. To the Delrues and Fauberts for your welcoming and encouragement, the folks at Stage and Screen Travel for keeping me busy between gigs, and to Trish Walker, the best Mum in the world: you are always in my heart!

ACKNOWLEDGMENTS

Climate map data adapted from Peel MC, Finlayson BL & McMahon TA (2007) 'Updated World Map of the Köppen-Geiger Climate Classification', *Hydrology and Earth System Sciences*, 11, 1633–44.

Transit map: Vancouver TransLink Map © TransLink 2013.

Cover photograph: Whiteshell River, Manitoba, Dave Reede/Alamy

THIS BOOK

This 12th edition of Lonely Planet's *Canada* guidebook was researched and written by Karla Zimmerman, John Lee, Ryan Ver Berkmoes, Sarah Richards, Celeste Brash, Benedict Walker, Andy Symington, Caroline Sieg and Brendan Sainsbury. This guidebook was commissioned in Lonely Planet's Oakland office, and produced by the following:

Commissioning Editors Jennye Garibaldi, Korina Miller

Coordinating Editors Saralinda Turner, Tracy Whitmey

Senior Cartographer Mark Griffiths

Book Designer Wendy Wright

Managing Editors Bruce Evans, Martine Power, Angela Tinson

Assisting Editors Amy Karafin, Kellie Langdon, Robyn Loughnane, Anne Mulvaney, Rosie Nicholson, Charlotte Orr, Gabrielle Stefanos

Assisting Cartographers Julie Dodkins, Mick Garett, Rachel Imerson, Eve Kelly

Cover Research Naomi Parker

Language Content Branislava Vladisavljevic

Thanks to Anita Banh, Ryan Evans, Samantha Forge, Larissa Frost, Genesys India, Jouve India, Trent Paton, Mazzy Prinsep, Luna Soo, Kerrianne Southway, Brian Turnbull

Index

NOTES

NOTES

Map Legend

Map Legend

Sights

- Beach
- Bird Sanctuary
- Buddhist
- Castle/Palace
- Christian
- Confucian
- Hindu
- Islamic
- Jain
- Jewish
- Monument
- Museum/Gallery/Historic Building
- Ruin
- Sento Hot Baths/Onsen
- Shinto
- Sikh
- Taoist
- Winery/Vineyard
- Zoo/Wildlife Sanctuary
- Other Sight

Activities, Courses & Tours

- Bodysurfing
- Diving
- Canoeing/Kayaking
- Course/Tour
- Skiing
- Snorkeling
- Surfing
- Swimming/Pool
- Walking
- Windsurfing
- Other Activity

Sleeping

- Sleeping
- Camping

Eating

- Eating

Drinking & Nightlife

- Drinking & Nightlife
- Cafe

Entertainment

- Entertainment

Shopping

- Shopping

Information

- Bank
- Embassy/Consulate
- Hospital/Medical
- Internet
- Police
- Post Office
- Telephone
- Toilet
- Tourist Information
- Other Information

Geographic

- Beach
- Hut/Shelter
- Lighthouse
- Lookout
- Mountain/Volcano
- Oasis
- Park
- Pass
- Picnic Area
- Waterfall

Population

- Capital (National)
- Capital (State/Province)
- City/Large Town
- Town/Village

Transport

- Airport
- BART station
- Border crossing
- Boston T station
- Bus
- Cable car/Funicular
- Cycling
- Ferry
- Metro/Muni station
- Monorail
- Parking
- Petrol station
- Subway/SkyTrain station
- Taxi
- Train station/Railway
- Tram
- Underground station
- Other Transport

Note: Not all symbols displayed above appear on the maps in this book

Routes

- Tollway
- Freeway
- Primary
- Secondary
- Tertiary
- Lane
- Unsealed road
- Road under construction
- Plaza/Mall
- Steps
- Tunnel
- Pedestrian overpass
- Walking Tour
- Walking Tour detour
- Path/Walking Trail

Boundaries

- International
- State/Province
- Disputed
- Regional/Suburb
- Marine Park
- Cliff
- Wall

Hydrography

- River, Creek
- Intermittent River
- Canal
- Water
- Dry/Salt/Intermittent Lake
- Reef

Areas

- Airport/Runway
- Beach/Desert
- Cemetery (Christian)
- Cemetery (Other)
- Glacier
- Mudflat
- Park/Forest
- Sight (Building)
- Sportsground
- Swamp/Mangrove

Brendan Sainsbury

Alberta An expat Brit from Hampshire, England, Brendan first came to Canada in 2004 in pursuit of a woman he had met in Spain (they married and are currently living happily ever after in White Rock, BC). He has covered Alberta numerous times for Lonely Planet both for this book and for a separate LP guide to Banff, Jasper & Glacier National Parks. He has a special affection for the province's national parks, particularly Lake Louise and the Lake Agnes Teahouse.

Read more about Brendan at:
lonelyplanet.com/members/brendansainsbury

Caroline Sieg

New Brunswick Caroline Sieg is a half-Swiss, half-American writer. Her relationship with New Brunswick began when she first lived in Boston and she began heading up to Canada to see the crazy high tides everyone told her about. She was delighted to return for Lonely Planet.

Read more about Caroline at:
lonelyplanet.com/members/carolinesieg

Andy Symington

Northwest Territories, Nunavut Though hailing from Australia, Andy has long been an aficionado of the far north, and it was years back, while watching whales plunge in icy seas, that he first fell in love with Canada's chilly extremities, whose harsh landscapes and endless wildernesses stir his soul. Andy has authored and co-authored many Lonely Planet and other guidebooks.

Read more about Andy at:
lonelyplanet.com/members/andy_symington

Ryan Ver Berkmoes

Manitoba, British Columbia, Yukon Territory Ryan's been bouncing around BC, the Yukon and Manitoba for more than two decades. As always he revelled in critter-spotting, whether from car, ferry, train or plane. It's fitting given Ryan's background with moose. At his first newspaper job he was tasked with placing random moose jokes in the classifieds to pique reader interest (What's a moose's favorite condiment? Moose-turd).

Read more about Ryan at:
lonelyplanet.com/members/ryanverberkmoes

Benedict Walker

Ontario, Saskatchewan Ben's mission is to continue travelling and living his dreams. Writing for LP takes the cake in the dream stakes: he received his first guidebook (*Japan*) when he was just 12. Born in Newcastle, Australia, Ben now calls Canada home but tries to get back to Japan to chat with the locals as much as possible. He thinks the best thing about travel writing isn't just visiting phenomenal places, but enjoying the kindness of strangers and living vicariously through their stories.

Read more about Ben at:
lonelyplanet.com/members/benedictwalker

OUR STORY

A beat-up old car, a few dollars in the pocket and a sense of adventure. In 1972 that's all Tony and Maureen Wheeler needed for the trip of a lifetime – across Europe and Asia overland to Australia. It took several months, and at the end – broke but inspired – they sat at their kitchen table writing and stapling together their first travel guide, *Across Asia on the Cheap*. Within a week they'd sold 1500 copies. Lonely Planet was born.

Today, Lonely Planet has offices in Melbourne, London and Oakland, with more than 600 staff and writers. We share Tony's belief that 'a great guidebook should do three things: inform, educate and amuse'.

OUR WRITERS

Karla Zimmerman

Coordinating Author, Newfoundland & Labrador Karla has covered Canada coast to coast for Lonely Planet. Newfoundland is her current beat, and over the years she has paddled by icebergs, come nose-to-beak with puffins, hiked in polar bear territory and driven by most of Newfoundland's 120,000 moose. She's visited Dildo, Come by Chance and Heart's Delight, and intends to get to Jerry's Nose one day soon. Karla writes travel features for books, magazines and online outlets. She has authored or co-authored several Lonely Planet guidebooks to the USA, Canada, Caribbean and Europe.

Read more about Karla at:
lonelyplanet.com/members/karlazimmerman

Celeste Brash

Nova Scotia, Prince Edward Island Trading Dungeness crab for lobster was no hardship on this, Celeste's fourth grand tour of the Maritimes. Over the years she's rafted the Fundy tidal bore, watched eagles nest, got stuck in a 'moose jam,' and climbed more lighthouses than she can count and yet, these provinces come up with new surprises on each visit. Celeste has written around 50 Lonely Planet guides. Celeste also wrote the Travel with Children chapter.

Read more about Celeste at:
lonelyplanet.com/members/celestebrash

John Lee

British Columbia Originally from the UK, John moved to British Columbia to study at the University of Victoria in the 1990s. Eventually staying and moving to Vancouver, he started a freelance travel-writing career in 1999. Since then, he's been covering the region and beyond for Lonely Planet plus magazines, newspapers and online outlets around the world. Winner of numerous writing awards, very active on Twitter and a weekly columnist for Canada's the *Globe and Mail* national newspaper, John also wrote the Cuisines of Canada and Wine Regions chapters.

Sarah Richards

Quebec Loyal to the mountains and forests of her native British Columbia, Sarah vowed to never love another Canadian province. But when she first set foot in Montréal, a torrid love affair with its enticing, exotic flavors threatened to break her ties with home forever. She blames the soft scent of freshly baked croissants in the wind and the city's vibrant nightlife for her betrayal.

Read more about Sarah at:
lonelyplanet.com/members/sarahrichards

OVER MORE
PAGE WRITERS

Published by Lonely Planet Publications Pty Ltd
ABN 36 005 607 983
12th edition – April 2014
ISBN 978 1 7422 0297 6
© Lonely Planet 2014   Photographs © as indicated 2014
10 9 8 7 6 5 4 3 2 1
Printed in Singapore